NEW NAME
NEW LOOK
STILL THE BEST

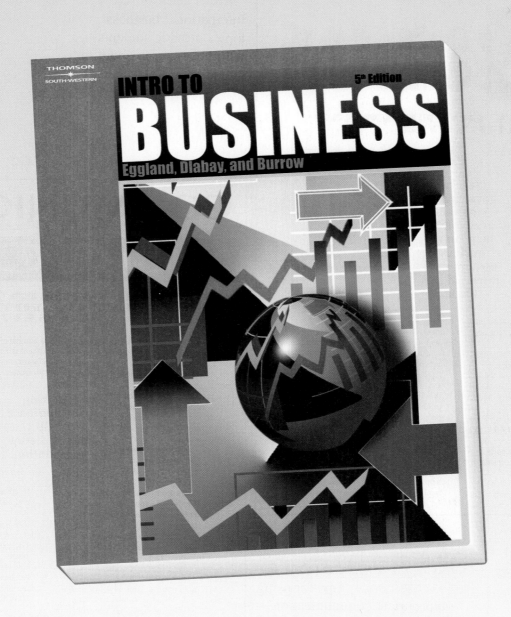

THE MOST UP-TO-DATE INTRO TO BUSINESS TEXT

Features provide coverage of international business, communications, technology, and Internet topics.

Global Navigator
International business topics provide students with information about the global marketplace.

FOREIGN GOVERNMENT AGENCIES

How can a small-business owner contact potential customers in other countries? Embassies, consulates, foreign trade offices, and foreign Chambers of Commerce are some of the foreign agencies available.

Embassies are official representatives of a foreign government. These offices usually have foreign trade specialists available to assist exporters with identifying potential markets. These trade specialists analyze current economic conditions and assist companies with various international trade activities.

Embassies also provide other services. As people travel to other countries, embassy staff members may assist them with various services and information. In an emergency, travelers commonly contact an embassy for assistance.

Similar to an embassy, a consulate is an office located in a foreign country that represents the home country, and serves the interests and businesses of the country it represents. Most countries have consulates in large cities throughout the world.

Countries and states establish trade offices in other nations to encourage inter-

> **Several government agencies are available to help small-business owners with international trade.**

national trade. For example, the European Union has a trade office in Washington, D.C. to contact potential buyers and sellers in the United States. Additionally, the state of Illinois has a foreign trade office in China in an attempt to expand exports to Asia.

Foreign Chambers of Commerce in the United States promote and encourage international trade for their countries. These organizations can assist importers and exporters with making contacts and providing information. Most of these Chambers of Commerce are located in New York City and Washington, D.C.; others, especially those representing Asian companies, are in San Francisco.

CRITICAL THINKING

1. Working in small groups, identify skills or abilities that would be useful for people who desire to work for an embassy, consulate, foreign trade office, or Chamber of Commerce.
2. Conduct a web search to locate information sources from embassies or Chambers of Commerce that would help a business when planning and implementing foreign trade activities.

Communicating for Success Tips for using appropriate communication— e-mail, letters, meetings, memos, and more.

COMMUNICATING for SUCCESS

GIVING PRESENTATIONS— WHAT DO YOU HAVE TO SAY?

Presentations are a common method for communicating information, ideas, and opinions to large groups of people. Although audience size may range from one or two colleagues to several hundred salespeople, there are certain methods and techniques that can help you make a better presentation.

First and foremost, know your audience. Know what kinds of information they need to hear and what they need to learn from you. Know what kinds of visual aids will appeal to them and hold their attention, and have an idea about their backgrounds, interests, and experiences. By having an understanding of how your audience will process information, you can more effectively decide on the use of visual aids to improve your presentation.

Typically, there are four types of presentations: oral, visual, computer-based, or discussion. Oral presentations generally consist of a speech or talk; a visual presentation adds some form of visual aid to this talk. Computer-based presentations are structured around a computer-generated or technology-aided presentation. Advancements in technology have increased the use

> **Knowing your audience will help you make a better presentation.**

of computer-based presentations. These technologies often include video clips, pictures, images, sounds, and cartoons. Discussions are also a form of presentation, where the presenter structures a talk or presentation of data around questions that are intended to prompt group discussion and feedback.

Overall, to guarantee a successful presentation, you should:

    —Prepare your materials in advance, including speaker notes and background research.
—Practice your presentation, especially difficult words or concepts that may require additional time to master.
—Use hand gestures to emphasize key points.
—Use visual aids and/or technology to enhance your audience's understanding of your comments.
—Have fun, and so will your audience.

CRITICAL THINKING

1. What are the four types of presentations?
2. What forms of technology could be used in a computer-based presentation?

Abundant practical applications help students learn about the business world and how to make business decisions in the global economy.

E-Commerce Explores the role of e-commerce in today's business world.

E-Commerce for Small Business Management

No longer does a company need to have a store, office, or factory. Instead, a book or clothing seller can serve customers online, and the shipping company representative is the only one who has to leave home.

Technology has reduced barriers to entry for new competitors in many industries. In the past, an entrepreneur would have to rent a facility, hire employees, obtain inventory, and advertise when starting a business. Now, a person can begin operations with a computer and a web site. Contacting suppliers, advertising, and filling orders are all executed online.

Online, big companies and small companies look alike. Customers do not see the big buildings, fancy offices, and well-dressed employees. A business is judged on the content and services it provides.

E-commerce also makes it easier for smaller organizations to expand internationally. Online exporting companies may be able to meet the needs of global customers without foreign sales offices. More and more, international buyers check the Internet for the best values in goods and services.

Critical Thinking
Most new businesses fail within five years. The failure rate for online companies is even higher. Research reasons why various cyber companies did not survive. Prepare a short oral presentation with visuals to illustrate the ingredients for online business success.

Global Business Project for each unit introduce students to real-world global business practices.

GLOBAL BUSINESS PROJECT

PLAN HUMAN RESOURCES IN THE GLOBAL WORKPLACE

Every worker for a business organization is involved in a service-producing or goods-producing industry. As countries move from a developing economy to an industrialized nation, the types of employment opportunities change.

This phase of the business plan project involves research related to needed training and skills for international business careers. Your ability to present yourself with a personal data sheet and a letter of application will be of value in every career field.

PROJECT GOALS
1. Compare employment trends in service-producing and goods-producing industries in a foreign country.
2. Research needed training and skills for working in a multinational company.
3. Create a personal data sheet and letter of application for an international business employment opportunity.

PROJECT ACTIVITIES
Using your textbook, library materials, web sites, interviews with people, and other resources, complete the following activities:
1. Using the country from your portfolio (or select a country), describe the major service-producing and goods-producing industries of the nation. In your opinion, which of these industries have the most potential for creating jobs in the future for this country?

2. A person's ability to understand and work with people in different cultures is a necessary skill for international business employment. List skills and training experience that would be of value to a person working for a multinational company.
3. Identify various skills and experiences you would need in order to work in an international business organization. Use this information to create a personal data sheet for yourself as it might look in the future. Also, write a letter of application that expresses your future interest and ability to work for an international company.

PROJECT WRAP-UP
1. Continue your portfolio (folder, file box, or other container) for storing and referring back to the information and materials you created in the activities above. Your portfolio provides the information needed for the various elements of a global business plan.
2. Create a video that shows strong interviewing skills and common job interview weaknesses when applying for a position with an international business organization.
3. In a small group create questions for a mock job interview. Conduct mock job interviews, exchanging the roles of candidate and interviewer.

TechnoTips Guides for using new technology such as the Internet, voice recognition in computers, and more.

Techno Tips
Small-Business Solutions

Today's computer applications make starting and running a small business easier than ever. Now you can set up your own home office, complete with computer, fax machine, and software to run your business.

Small-business software programs can help you conduct all of your business functions. These products enable you to print checks, bill customers, and issue purchase orders. You can

even keep payroll records for your employees.

You can also conduct all of your banking functions online from your home. You can see checks and deposits that have cleared, transfer money between accounts, and even communicate with your bank via e-mail. These features and many more give you all that you need to run your small business.

CREATE A LEARNING ENVIRONMENT WITH COMPLETE TEACHER RESOURCES

Instructor's Resource Box *includes*

Numerous resources provide students with more engaging activities

Activities and Projects provides chapter study guides and activities.

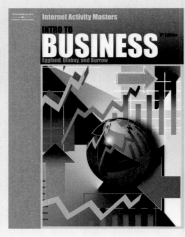

Spanish Resources provides key terms in both English and Spanish to help your Spanish-speaking students.

Chapter and Unit Tests with answers in place for grading convenience.

School-to-Work/SCANS Activity Masters provides activities to reinforce workplace competencies and to help students plan careers.

Internet Activity Masters help students develop Internet skills.

Teaching Tools provide support for the challenges you face with different learning styles, infusing technology, using media and the Internet, assessment, study skills, block scheduling, and encourage parent involvement.

MINIMIZE PREP TIME AND MAXIMIZE SUCCESS

INSTRUCTOR'S WRAPAROUND EDITION

Provides in-class discussion opportunities, teaching strategies, focus and motivate activities, answers to text questions, and more!

By completing the problems under Calculate Business Data, students will be able to strengthen and refine their abilities in mathematics. Technology Application allows students to demonstrate skill in using technology, primarily word processing, spreadsheet, and database software.

The end-of-chapter questions vary in level of difficulty. For a basic assignment, consider Review Your Reading and Develop Your Business Language at the end of the chapter. For an average assignment, consider the basic assignment plus Communicate Business Concepts and Calculate Business Data. For an enhanced assignment, consider the average assignment plus Technology Application and Decision-Making Strategies.

ASSESS

Review the goals at the beginning of the chapter and the corresponding Business Notes at the end of the chapter. Have students respond orally or in writing to each Note restated as a question. For students who may have difficulty providing answers, assign the reteaching activities that follow. Enrichment activities may also be assigned where appropriate.

1. What is the difference between needs and wants?
(Answer: Needs are necessary for survival; wants add pleasure to our lives.)
2. What is the difference between goods and services?
(Answer: Goods are things we can see and touch; services are the things that satisfy our wants

Name other highly skilled human resources, like this traffic control specialist.

The word **capital** is often used in place of capital resources, especially when referring to the factors of production. Capital includes money that is needed to run a business. A person may say she or he is trying to raise $40,000 in capital to expand a business or that she or he has a $10,000 capital investment in a store operated by friends.

All three economic resources—natural, human, and capital—are necessary to produce goods and services for our needs and wants. Unfortunately, we do not have an endless supply of these resources.

LIMITED RESOURCES

If Duke had a lot of money, do you think he could buy all of the things he would want? In reality, money is a limited resource.

Capital goods are important because they help us produce efficiently—that is, faster or cheaper. **FYI**

Therefore, Duke cannot buy everything he wants. Have you had the experience of wanting many things without having the money to pay for them?

Newscasts often report shortages of certain items. In recent years, newsprint, lumber, and orange juice have been reported as scarce. We do not have an endless supply of these economic resources. Because of pollution, we do not have an endless supply of clean air, water, and land. We also have shortages of certain kinds of human resources in some career areas. Since our natural and human resources are limited, we are limited in what we can build and produce.

Scarcity Affects Everyone

Just as meeting your unlimited wants with limited resources is a problem for you, so it is for everyone—your family, your neighbors, and your school club. People all over the world are affected by scarcity. For this reason, the conflict between unlimited wants and limited resources is called the **basic economic problem** (also called **scarcity**).

The members of your family may not be able to afford many of the things they want because the wages of your father or mother are needed for food, clothing, the house payment, the electric bill, or your school expenses. Your neighbors and the families of your friends face the same economic problem. Your school club might want to hire a band for its annual dance, but because its money is scarce, the club may have to use CDs instead.

Scarcity Affects Businesses and Governments

Just as individuals face the basic economic problem, so do businesses, governments, and all agencies that supply goods and services. A growing business might want to enlarge its plant and parking lot, but because the land it owns is limited and locating elsewhere would cost more than it can afford, it cannot do both.

All levels of government face the problem of supplying the almost unlimited wants of

their citizens with limited resources. For example, your town may wish to give a large wage increase to police officers and firefighters. However, because taxes may not provide enough money, the increase might have to be smaller in order to provide other services, such as a new school building or additional employees to collect the garbage. Cities, states, the United States, and all other nations must cope with the problem of providing the many services citizens want from limited resources—the taxes collected to pay for the services. Someone must decide which services will be provided. How do you, other individuals, businesses, and governments decide which of the unlimited wants to supply?

ECONOMIC CHOICES

Since you cannot have everything you want, you must choose which of the things you want most and can afford. Suppose you earn $25 a week. If you spend it on movies and

CAREER HIGHLIGHTS

An *economist's* job duties include:
- Studying ways in which society uses scarce resources
- Analyzing costs and benefits of distributing and consuming goods and services
- Conducting research, collecting and analyzing data, monitoring economic trends, and developing forecasts

An orderly approach to decision making can help you organize your thinking about problems and can result in effective decisions. **FYI**

pizza with your friends on Friday night, you will not have enough left to go to the hockey game on Saturday. So you must make a choice. You must decide which of your wants—the movie and pizza with friends or the hockey game—is more important to you. You must determine which alternative will satisfy you the most.

One of the purposes of this book is to help you learn how to make wise economic decisions. Learning and following a logical process will help you make better decisions.

What economic decisions have you recently made regarding wants versus needs?

NET FACTS

The Internet is a telecommunications system that connects many different networks of computers. The Internet is often called a "network of networks."

CAREER HIGHLIGHTS

The careers listed in Career Highlights come from the *Occupational Outlook Handbook*, an online publication (www.bls.gov/oco) of the federal government. The O*NET code for Economist is 19-3011.00. Tell your class about this resource and how to use it. This description of job duties can be used to demonstrate the relevancy of skills learned in this course.

through the efforts of other people or equipment.)
3. What are the economic resources used in the production of goods and services? (Answer: Natural, human, and capital; also called factors of production.)
4. Why does scarcity force individuals, businesses, and governments to make choices? (Answer: Since individuals, businesses, and governments cannot have everything they want, they must choose which of the things they want most and can afford.)
5. What is economic decision making? What are the six steps in

---

Workplace Competencies-Interpersonal Skills

Employers are looking for potential employees with good interpersonal skills. Participating as a member of a group or team is an example of one way to develop these interpersonal skills. As a successful team member, individuals share their part of the work load, learn to listen to each other, realize individual strengths, resolve conflicts, are responsible for accomplishing group goals, and challenge policies and procedures in a responsible manner. The Student Activity Worksheet, Workplace Competencies—Interpersonal Skills Checklist, in the School-To-Work/SCANS Activity Masters, may serve as a guideline for discussion of interpersonal skill development. The preceding activity, Teaching Strategies—Cooperative Learning, is a hands-on activity which develops these interpersonal skills.

Net Facts provides information and definitions of terms for the Internet. The more information that students have about the Internet, the better equipped they will be to use this resource. In the Internet Activity Masters, there is an Internet Activity Worksheet for each unit. You can use these activities to give students experience with finding information on-line. Options for assigning this activity are as follows:

1. Provide students with a list of addresses of resources for this activity;
2. Assign students to conduct their own searches; or
3. Use the addresses provided on the Internet Activity Worksheet.
You should complete the activity yourself before assigning it to resolve any discrepancies that may arise.

REACH YOUR STUDENTS WITH A VARIETY OF MEDIA AND TECHNOLOGY

Instructor's Resource CD
- PowerPoint Slides
- Lesson Plans
- Video Discussion Guide

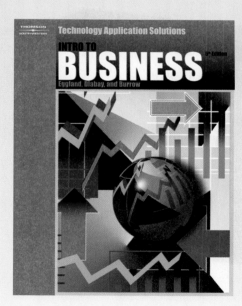

Technology Application Solutions provides solutions to all exercises.

CNBC and CNN Videos use actual news stories to teach business concepts. Use these video segments to introduce concepts and encourage classroom discussion.

Data CD provides templates for Application exercises.

ExamView CD provides assessment questions for every chapter. You can use this program to customize your testing program, edit questions, scramble questions and create different versions of the same test.

Business Connection CD provides an interactive study guide for every chapter.

Intro to Business, 5e

Student Edition	0-538-43612-3
Instructor's Wraparound Edition	0-538-43613-1
Activities and Projects Units 1–6	0-538-43614-X
Activities and Projects Units 7–12	0-538-43615-8
Activities and Projects Units 1–12	0-538-43636-0
Chapter and Unit Tests	0-538-43617-4
ExamView CD	0-538-43634-4
Data CD	0-538-43621-2
Business Connection CD	0-538-43633-6
Instructor's Resource CD	0-538-43635-2
CNBC Video	0-538-69212-X
CNN Looks at Accounting, Small Business, and Entrepreneurship Careers	0-538-68899-8

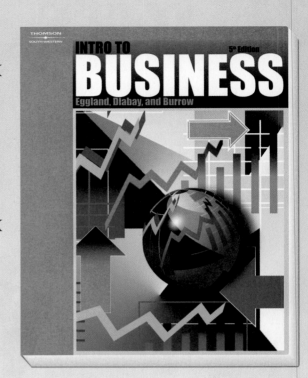

Instructor's Resource Box 0-538-43618-2

Activities and Projects Instructor's Edition Units 1–6
Activities and Projects Instructor's Edition Units 7–12
School-To-Work/SCANS Activity Masters
Business Math Activity Masters
Communications Activity Masters
International Business Activity Masters
Ethics Activity Masters
Chapter and Unit Tests Instructor's Edition
Alternative Assessment
Test Preparation and Study Skills
Spanish Resources
Technology Application Solutions
Distance Learning
Using Technology and the Internet
Internet Activity Masters
Diverse Populations and Learning Styles
Involving Parents and the Community
Strategies for Block Scheduling

Instructor's Wraparound Edition

INTRO TO
BUSINESS

5ᵗʰ Edition

Steven S. Eggland

Les R. Dlabay

James L. Burrow

THOMSON
™
SOUTH-WESTERN

Australia · Canada · Mexico · Singapore · Spain · United Kingdom · United States

THOMSON
SOUTH-WESTERN

Intro to Business, 5E
Instructor's Wraparound Edition
by Steven A. Eggland, Les R. Dlabay, James L. Burrow

Vice President/Executive Publisher
Dave Shaut

Team Leader
Karen Schmohe

Executive Editor
Eve Lewis

Project Manager
Enid Nagel

Production Manager
Patricia Matthews Boies

Production Editor
Alan Biondi

Director of Marketing
Carol Volz

Senior Marketing Manager
Nancy A. Long

Marketing Coordinator
Yvonne Patton-Beard

Manufacturing Coordinator
Kevin L. Kluck

Internal and Cover Design
Tippy McIntosh

Editorial Assistant
Linda Keith

Production Assistant
Nancy Stamper

Compositor
Better Graphics, Inc.

Printer
R.R. Donnelley & Sons
Willard, Ohio

About the Authors
Steven A. Eggland, Ph.D., is the Executive Director of the Accrediting Council for Independent Colleges and Schools (ACICS) in Washington, DC. ACICS is the largest accrediter in the world of business colleges and schools, accrediting over 600 institutions of higher education. Dr. Eggland is also Emeritus Professor of Vocational and Adult Education in Teachers College at the University of Nebraska. He has taught a wide variety of business courses and has a special interest in marketing education.

Les R. Dlabay, Ed.D., is Professor of Business at Lake Forest College, Lake Forest, Illinois, where he teaches courses in accounting, finance, international business, marketing, communications, and Latin American studies. He has taught more than 30 different courses in high school, community college, university, teacher preparation, and adult education programs.

James L. Burrow, Ph.D., is the coordinator of the graduate Training and Development Program at North Carolina State University in Raleigh, North Carolina. He has been a faculty member at the community college and university levels in marketing and human resource development as well as a consultant to business and public organizations.

Copyright © 2004 South-Western, a division of Thomson Learning, Inc. Thomson Learning™ is a trademark used herein under license.

ISBN: 0-538-43613-1

Printed in the United States of America

1 2 3 4 5 6 08 07 06 05 04 03

For permission to use material from this text or product, contact us by

Tel: 800-730-2214
Fax: 800-730-2215
Web: www.thomsonrights.com

For more information, contact South-Western, 5191 Natorp Boulevard, Mason, OH, 45040. Or you can visit our Internet site at www.swep.com.

CONTENTS

INSTRUCTOR'S WRAPAROUND EDITION

PROGRAM COMPONENTS

Activities and Projects (workbooks), Chapter and Unit Tests, Instructor's Resource CD, ExamView CD, CNBC Video, CNN Video, Technology Application Solutions, Data CD, Business Connection CD, School-To-Work/SCANS Activity Masters, Business Math Activity Masters, Communications Activity Masters, International Business Activity Masters, Ethics Activity Masters, Alternative Assessment, Test Preparation and Study Skills, Spanish Resources, Distance Learning Resources, Using Technology and the Internet, Internet Activity Masters, Teaching a Diverse Population, Family and Community Involvement, Strategies for Block Scheduling

TEACHING STRATEGIES

UNIT 2

BUSINESS OPERATIONS

This unit introduces the fundamentals of business organization, ownership, management and marketing. This unit serves as the foundation for the study of business activity in our economic environment.

Types of businesses and business activities are presented in Chapter 5. Chapter 6 focuses on the ways in which businesses organize. A detailed example of how a business grows from a sole proprietorship to a corporation is given. Other forms of business, including cooperatives, franchises, and nonprofit organizations, are discussed.

An entirely new chapter covers management and leadership. In Chapter 7, emphasis is given to various characteristics and styles of managers and leaders, and how managers become competent leaders. Chapter 8 covers issues related to the production and marketing of goods and services. Marketing topics are covered from product idea to distribution to promotion and final sale.

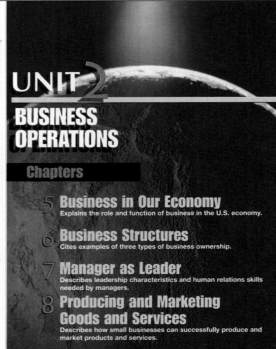

UNIT 2

BUSINESS OPERATIONS

Chapters

5 Business in Our Economy
Explains the role and function of business in the U.S. economy.

6 Business Structures
Cites examples of three types of business ownership.

7 Manager as Leader
Describes leadership characteristics and human relations skills needed by managers.

8 Producing and Marketing Goods and Services
Describes how small businesses can successfully produce and market products and services.

Kick-Off Activity

Investigating Business Media

To make the connection between today's business news and *Intro to Business,* an opening activity is provided for student research that pertains to Unit 2. The following exercise asks students to choose an article from *The Wall Street Journal,* 54

the financial section of a newspaper, or a business magazine and to inquire about a topic related to this unit.

In the past decade, the following business issues have had a dramatic impact on our economy: home-based businesses, the fluctuating stock market, and the increasing use of the Internet in business. Ask students to choose one of these issues and find two or three articles pertaining to the chosen issue. Then direct them to answer the following questions:

1 What is the impact (or the expected impact) of this issue on our economy? What groups of people are most likely to be affected?

2 How do you think this issue will affect the industry or job field that you hope to enter in the future?

BU$INESSBRIEF
TODAY'S CHANGING WORKFORCE

As the 21st century begins, we are seeing dramatic changes in employment and careers in the U.S. The end of the 20th century saw career opportunities in the dot.com world and the decline of some traditionally important jobs like manufacturing and agriculture.

From 1990 to 2000, total employment grew by 17 percent. In 2000, 145.5 million people held jobs. That number is projected to reach 157.8 million by 2010, an increase of over 15 percent.

Baby boomers, the large number of people born between 1946 and 1964, have dominated the labor market since they began working in the 1960s. They will continue to do so until they begin retiring in the 2010s. The average age of U.S. workers in 2010 will be over 40.

A mini-boom of younger workers will cause the 16-to-24-year-old age group to grow more rapidly than the overall labor force for the first time in 25 years. Other groups that will experience higher employment growth rates are Asian-, Hispanic-, and African-American workers. Currently, white workers make up 73 percent of the labor force, but that will drop to 69 percent by 2010.

Over the last 50 years, one of the most dramatic trends in employment has been the participation of women. In the early 1960s, 35 percent of women were working outside the home. That percentage doubled by 2000. By 2010, nearly one-half of all jobs (48 percent) in the U.S. will be held by women.

At one time it was thought that technology would allow people to work

fewer hours, but this has not occurred. Economic pressures have led to downsizing, production streamlining, and other attempts to reduce costs. Businesses ask employees to work additional hours and people may hold second jobs to meet their needs. A recent survey reported that seven of ten parents said they did not spend enough time with their children. At the same time, children see their parents changing jobs, taking on more responsibility, completing additional education to improve career opportunities, and making important decisions to balance work and family life. Those experiences will likely shape the career and family decisions of the next generation.

Economic pressures also resulted in the increased use of contingent workers. A contingent worker is one who has no explicit or implicit contract for long-term employment. About 5 percent of the U.S. workforce (nearly 6 million people) is composed of contingent workers. Some estimates project that number will double in ten years. Some people take contingent work because they cannot find the permanent employment they want. Others choose contingent work because they like the flexibility it offers.

CRITICAL THINKING

1 How do you think changes in the workforce in the 21st century will affect your career, education, and family decisions?

2 What do you think are some advantages and disadvantages of being a contingent worker?

55

BU$INESSBRIEF

A Business Brief sets the tone for a unit. To help students understand current and emerging trends, each unit will be introduced with a Business Brief. The Briefs were chosen for their importance to business, timeliness, and interest to students. The Briefs complement the many real-world examples woven into the text.

CRITICAL THINKING

Student answers will, of course, require thinking beyond what is presented in the Business Brief. The following are possible answers:

1 The workforce will be more diverse, so the ability to work as part of a diverse team will be important. It will be necessary to make choices about balancing career and family life, and to take part in lifelong education to improve career flexibility and opportunity.

2 Advantages:
- May offer individuals a way to enter the labor market that they otherwise may not have. Persons with special needs would either end up unemployed or be driven out of the workforce altogether.
- The flexibility could help them balance work with non-work obligations (childcare, care for elderly, etc.).
- More freedom to make own schedule.

Disadvantages:
- Some believe that contingent workers will be limited in their prospects for economic advancement, due to frequent job changes.
- Contingent workers may not be able to obtain or afford medical insurance, nor enjoy other benefits of working as a regular employee.
- Little opportunity to develop long-term relationships with co-workers.

BUILDING YOUR PORTFOLIO

The Building Your Portfolio work samples validate skill level and a student's ability to accomplish tasks frequently performed on the job. The most important reason for including samples in a portfolio is to demonstrate a student's abilities and skills. In selecting work samples for each unit, students should always have a choice of which activities to include. Students might be encouraged to include samples from the end-of-chapter activities, particularly Communicate Business Concepts, Calculate Business Data, Technology Application, and Decision-Making Strategies.

55

COMPLETE INSTRUCTOR'S WRAPAROUND EDITION!

What makes a good *Instructor's Wraparound Edition?* Having everything you need in one place and at your fingertips. *Intro to Business* is the only text to offer you a complete wraparound edition that contains ethics, school-to-work, SCANS, cooperative learning, and all the other tools you need to make your class a success! If the information you need is not in your wraparound text, chances are you won't use it. So we made it simple for you and put everything in one place—the *Instructor's Wraparound Edition.*

BUILDING YOUR PORTFOLIO activities at the beginning of the unit provide an alternative method for assessing student progress.

TEACHING STRATEGIES provide information on how to enhance your class through the use of the **SCANS Workplace Competencies** (information, interpersonal, resources, systems, technology), **Basic Skills** (listening, math, reading, speaking, writing), **Critical Thinking Skills** (creative thinking, decision making, knowing how to learn, problem solving, reasoning, visualizing),

and **Personal Qualities** (honesty, integrity, responsibility, self-esteem, self-management, sociability). School-to-work is emphasized along with **Cooperative and Team Learning**, **Alternate Modalities**, **Special Needs**, and **Safety/Health** suggestions.

RESOURCES present enrichment material available through South-Western Educational Publishing as well as other sources such as periodicals, books, and web sites. These resources will provide valuable enrichment and references.

KICK-OFF ACTIVITIES provide extension opportunities for students to connect subject matter with critical thinking activities and make the unit more meaningful.

UNIT OVERVIEW highlights the content of the unit and provides background information.

CHAPTER OVERVIEW gives you a quick preview of the chapter to help prepare lessons.

RESOURCES FOR TEACHERS lists resources which will enhance the course for both teacher and students.

TEACHING MATERIALS are listed with the Chapter Overview.

ASSESSMENT refers you to appropriate testing/assessment material for both formal and informal testing.

MEDIA/TECHNOLOGY serves as a reference to available media and technology that will make your *Intro to Business* course as dynamic and motivating as you and your students expect it to be.

ACTIVITY MASTERS and **WORKBOOKS** list the variety of content resources available which will make your course first-class. These ancillaries and workbooks provide in-depth coverage and stimulating activities that cover a full range of business-related topics.

LESSON PLANS

MOTIVATE and *FOCUS ON REAL LIFE* set the tone to get students interested in a lesson.

TEACH/APPLY provides suggestions for you to teach the lesson.

MAKE CONNECTIONS ties in new learning with previously covered material.

TRY THIS/GUIDED PRACTICE gives you suggestions on how to help students master content.

EXPLORE THIS/INDEPENDENT PRACTICE gives students an opportunity to apply what they have learned.

ASSESS suggests questions to insure student comprehension.

SUMMARIZE gives you activities to conclude the chapter.

EVALUATE makes suggestions for formal and informal testing.

Teaching suggestions and answers for Business Briefs, Perspectives, Global Navigator, Communicating for Success, and Focus On Careers give guidance for implementing each feature.

Chapter Review answers are where you need them for class discussion or checking homework.

---

where would you get the money to buy the equipment? Discuss the similarities between students' suggestions and what a business might do. Guide students through a discussion of how businesses benefit communities. Have volunteers explain what each benefit means to them and to their community in general. For example, businesses provide jobs for students now and/or in the future and help pay the cost of public facilities (such as schools or swimming pools) through taxes.

EXPLORE THIS/INDEPENDENT PRACTICE Ask students to investigate some new product ideas. What consumer needs do the new products or services fill? Are they technologically and financially reasonable? Have students prepare a report about their findings.

Have students examine a few companies with which they are familiar. How effectively do these companies conduct the seven key business activities? Do they innovate? Do they meet customer needs? How well do they market their products or services?

The Chapter Review questions at the end of the chapter vary in level of difficulty. For a basic assignment, consider Develop Your Business Language and Review Your Reading. For an average assignment, consider the basic assignment plus Communicate Business Concepts and Calculate Business Data. For an enhanced assignment, try the average assignment plus Technology Application and Decision-Making Strategies.

What are other raw materials, besides cotton, that need some processing before consumers can use them?

or prints the cloth, and a clothing manufacturer in New York buys the cloth and makes it into jeans. Together, extractors and manufacturers are industries that change the form of resources from their natural states into products for consumers.

Manufacturing businesses can be organized in several ways to produce products. Building

What form of manufacturing occurs in the production of your favorite products?

a specific and unique product to meet the needs of one customer is done with **custom manufacturing**. Products ranging from bicycles to dentures are specifically developed to meet particular design standards.

Mass production has been the standard of U.S. manufacturing for almost a century. With **mass production**, a large number of identical products are assembled using a continuous, efficient procedure. Mass production is seen in automobile assembly lines or beverage bottling plants.

Processing is a third type of manufacturing. **Processing** changes the form of materials so they can be consumed or used to manufacture other products. Crude oil is refined through processing to form gasoline and other petroleum products. Grain is processed into flour, cereal, and feed for animals. Film processors convert the film from your camera into pictures.

Marketers

Our skilled labor force and our advanced technology enable producers to make thousands of different products at a reasonable cost. However, if these products are not available where and when you and other consumers want to buy them, their value diminishes.

The scribes in the sixth century placed an inscription known as a colophon at the end of the closing paragraph of a manuscript. This colophon included the scribe's name, date, and location. Around the fifteenth century, some printers began including emblems on their works that they also called a colophon. Many publishers still use colophons on their books, usually on the title page or spine.

If all of the goods you use had to be bought directly from their producers, it would be a problem. You would have to fly to Central or South America to get a banana. You might have to drive to Minnesota or Michigan to buy your favorite cereal. Buying products in that way would be inefficient and expensive.

The services of many businesses are often needed before goods actually reach consumers. A business that is involved with moving goods from producers to consumers is called a **marketer**. The activities of marketers are called *marketing*.

Marketing includes more than just transporting and selling products. Marketers also help to identify, develop, and test new products to see whether consumers will like them and buy them. They package goods to protect products and to present them in attractive and convenient sizes. They also store the goods until they are needed by other marketers or consumers. They even design store windows and arrange displays in supermarkets to attract your attention. All of these marketing activities add value to products by bringing them to where the consumer is, at a time

they are wanted, in the assortment wanted, and at prices the consumer is willing to pay.

Service Businesses

A business firm that does things for you instead of making or marketing products is called a **service business**. Service businesses over the past several years are the fastest growing part of our business world. The number of people employed in service industries has reached over 100 million. By 2010, it is projected that 125 million, or three in every four U.S. workers, will hold jobs in the service industry.

Some service businesses serve individual consumers, some serve other businesses, and some serve both. Today you can find service businesses to move you from New Jersey to Arizona, fly you to Singapore, style your hair, wash your car, figure your income tax, board your pet, or provide almost any service you need or do not want to perform yourself. Businesses also need services. A service business might help a company export its product to the Czech Republic for the first time, install a new computer system, or train a group of employees on how to access and use databases.

What are some methods that marketers use to attract consumers' attention?

ASSESS

Review the goals at the beginning of the chapter and the Business Notes at the end of the chapter. Have students respond orally or in writing to each of the Business Notes restated as a question, provided below. For students who may have difficulty providing answers, assign the reteaching activities that follow. Enrichment activities may also be assigned where appropriate.

1. What are the four kinds of basic businesses? (Answer: Extractors, manufacturers, marketers, and service firms.)
2. Name the seven kinds of activities performed by businesses. (Answer: Developing or generating ideas, raising capital, buying goods and services, using human resources, marketing goods and services, producing goods and services, and keeping records.)
3. How are jobs created in our economy? (Answer: New jobs are frequently created when new businesses locate within a community.)

RETEACH

Place key terms and concepts such as extractors, manufacturers, marketers, service firms, channel of distribution, retailer, and wholesaler on cards that can be shuffled. Ask some students to draw a card and explain the meaning of the term or concept shown. Another activity may be to write the seven business activities on the board. Ask for seven volunteers or select seven students and ask each student randomly to describe a particular business

---

Basic Skills-**Reading**

Students may improve their reading skills by first developing pre-reading routines. Explore the goals at the beginning of the chapter with your students. Have a student read the goals out loud so that all will be aware of the various new learnings that will occur in the chapter. Explain to students that this is the first step to establishing the purpose of their reading assignments. By previewing goals, students will be able to recognize facts that are relevant when they begin reading the chapter. The Student Activity Worksheet, Basic Skills—Reading, in the School-To-Work/SCANS Activity Masters, may be used to serve as a guideline for discussion of each of these points. Ask students: Based on the chapter goals, what do you think you will learn?

Basic Skills-**Reading**

Direct students to the key terms that are listed in Develop Your Business Language at the end of the chapter. Have a student read these terms out loud so that all will be aware of the various new learning that will occur. This is the second step to establishing the purpose of reading assignments. By previewing terms, students will be able to decide facts that are relevant when they begin reading the chapter. Ask students to write what kind of information they are going to gain from this chapter. Then explore the various headings, illustrations, and captions in the chapter which will preview the actual material that will be covered. By previewing these chapter elements, students will be able to decide facts that are relevant when they begin reading the chapter. Ask students to write a summary of the points that will be covered in the chapter.

TEACHING STRATEGIES

STRATEGIES FOR INCORPORATING TECHNOLOGY

Technology is emphasized throughout the text. For teachers who would like the opportunity to use commercial software in their class, a template is available that includes the Technology Application problems that appear at the end of each chapter. Where applicable, the solutions in the *Technology Application*

Solutions ancillary include answers to the questions in each Technology Application problem.

The following grid identifies the type of problem that appears in each chapter and the software required to complete the problem.

CHAPTER	SPREADSHEET	DATABASE	WORD PROCESSING
1		Videotapes	
2		Census Data	
3	Supply and Demand		
4	GDP		
5	Business Income Statements		
6			Partnership Agreement
7			Leadership Characteristics
8		Clothing Store	
9			Ethics Checklist
10		Export and Imports	
11			Contract
12	Start-up Financing Analysis		
13		Employee Skill Bank	
14	Budget		
15		Computer Systems	
16	Survey of Software Preferences		
17			Purchase Orders
18	Employment Trends		
19		DOT Careers	
20			Résumé and Application
21		Small Businesses	
22		Consumer Agencies	
23	Comparison Shopping		
24			Complaint Letter
25		Federal Reserve	
26		Financial Institutions	
27	Check Register		

CHAPTER	SPREADSHEET	DATABASE	WORD PROCESSING
28	Bank Reconcilliation		
29	Credit Scoring		
30		Lenders	
31	Simple Interest		
32			Credit Applications and Installment Contract
33	Interest Earnings		
34			Signature Card and Certificate of Deposit
35		Stocks	
36			Rental Applications
37		Auto Insurance Rates	
38			Auto Insurance Applications
39		Home Inventory	
40	Cash Value		
41	Dental Insurance		
42	Personal Cash Flow		
43	Personal Budget		
44		Investments	

STRATEGIES FOR COLLABORATIVE LEARNING

The features and activities in *Intro to Business* allow you to make collaborative learning an integral part of your teaching. Collaborative learning involves small heterogeneous groups of students who work together in either a collaborative learning activity or a teams activity. In the collaborative learning activities, students work together on various projects to produce an end product as a group. In the teams learning activities, more individual responsibility is associated with the activities. Each team member is typically responsible for a particular task. If one team member fails to complete the responsibility for a task, the other team members cannot complete their tasks so the entire team suffers.

Collaborative learning activities should be designed with the following goals in mind:

1. Group size should be established.
2. Roles should be designated.
3. The process for the activity should be defined.
4. Time limits should be set.

Collaborative learning is more successful with heterogeneous rather than homogeneous groups. Research further supports collaborative learning as a teaching strategy to increase student motivation, achievement, and behavior.

Group composition should include a mixture of gender, ability level, cultural or ethnic background, and learning style. For example, placing a visual learner with an auditory learner enhances and strengthens the group's interaction. Group members should be rotated frequently.

Most teachers and school districts desire to expand their evaluation of student progress beyond traditional grading. While grades are likely to remain an important evaluation component, other assessment tools are being used to measure a student's ability to be successful in real-world situations. The resources and teaching suggestions for *Intro to Business* make it possible to go beyond traditional evaluation methods.

Portfolio Assessment

A portfolio is a collection of personal records, career-related documents, awards, achievements, and samples of skills performance. The records, documents, and samples should be neatly organized in a binder or folder for effective presentation. By requiring your students to prepare portfolios, you will be providing them with a useful tool for their career development.

Portfolio Components

The most effective portfolios are organized across the curriculum. Each discipline makes a contribution. A complete portfolio should include:

1. A résumé.
2. Copies of personal information such as a birth certificate, a Social Security card, and a driver's license.
3. Sample job applications to use as guides for completing actual job applications after graduation.
4. Copies of awards, achievements, and records of community service.
5. Samples of cover letters to attach with a résumé, and of thank-you letters for interviews.
6. Reference letters.
7. Samples of performance in skills, communications, and any other evaluations that would contribute to success in a job.
8. Background information for successful interviewing, including company profiles, answers to expected interview questions, and lists of potential career contacts.

The materials in a portfolio may be in a variety of forms including writing, visual presentations, and notes or tapes from oral presentations. The lesson plans in this teacher's edition provide suggestions for elements that may be included in a student's portfolio. However, students should also be given some responsibility for selecting the items to be included in their portfolio.

Portfolio Evaluation

A student's portfolio may be assessed on the basis of categories such as organization, accuracy and clarity of content, creativity of presentation, and relevance to the workplace. Suggestions for criteria may be obtained from local businesspeople or former students. A sample Portfolio Assessment sheet is in the *School-To-Work/SCANS Activity Masters*.

Each document added to the portfolio should be accompanied by an evaluation sheet. You may wish to use the Portfolio Work Sample (Cover Sheet) located in the *School-To-Work/SCANS Activity Masters*. The student might describe instructions that took less time or more time to complete than anticipated, accessibility to equipment, student time management and organization skills that enabled the project to flow smoothly, and how things could have been done differently. The Portfolio Work Sample sheet should be attached to each work sample submitted by a student. The teacher should then evaluate the student's effort and performance on the project.

A person's ability to objectively view her or his strengths and weaknesses is an indication of maturity and potential for career success. When selecting materials for a portfolio, students should decide what criteria to use for assessing their work. In addition, students should point out strengths, weaknesses, and improvements in the materials in their portfolio.

Working in small groups provides the opportunity for students to assess the contributions of others. By establishing criteria for evaluation, students should be able to assess the work of others. Commonly considered factors include cooperation, contributions to completion of task, and creativity.

You may also consider creating "accountability partners" in which students are teamed with another person. The pairs meet and talk on a regular basis to monitor the work of and accomplishment of goals by the other person.

On-the-job performance appraisals commonly involve conferences between workers and their supervisors. In a similar manner, a meeting between student and teacher can provide a time to set goals, evaluate performance, and suggest methods for an improved learning environment.

STRATEGIES FOR OPTIMUM INDIVIDUAL LEARNING

Our students reflect the cultural diversity in American society as well as different abilities and different styles of learning. Many of these individual student differences require an adjustment in teaching style or presentation. The following material describes teaching strategies for using *Intro to Business* with students possessing different learning abilities and for students with different learning styles.

Teaching Strategies for Students with Different Learning Abilities

The *Intro to Business* classroom typically has students with a wide variation of ability, intelligence, and motivation. Although the teacher must direct most instruction to the mass audience, optimal learning will occur only when the curriculum is modified to meet the needs of individual students.

The first and greatest challenge facing the teacher is identifying the special abilities of each student. While physical disabilities are usually easy to identify, learning disabilities can be very difficult to detect and classify. Classifying students solely on examination scores and prior classroom performance may be misleading and should be avoided. For example, poor subject examination scores and short attention spans may be the symptoms of either a student with a specific learning disability or a gifted student who is bored.

The correct assessment of students should be a combined effort of the teacher, the school counselor or special education teacher, the parent or guardian, and the student. Together, this team can design an individualized program that will challenge the student and provide adequate opportunity to achieve attainable goals.

Gifted Students
One objective of gifted student programs should be the development of leadership skills. Current literature suggests that four skill areas are involved in the development of effective leadership:

1. Cognition — The ability to identify, research, and learn factual knowledge.
2. Problem Solving — The ability to identify problems and develop creative solutions.
3. Interpersonal Communication — The ability to work with other people.
4. Decision Making — The ability to develop and implement realistic goals and evaluate performance of the goals.

Different hemispheres of the brain control these functions. Cognition and problem solving are typically associated with left-brain functions; interpersonal communication and decision making are associated with right-brain functions. Therefore, effective leadership training must target development of both hemispheres. Most students will enter the classroom with stronger development in some skill areas than others. Thus, for example, a student lacking interpersonal communication skills should undertake projects to develop those skills.

The Technology Application and Decision-Making Strategies activities in the student textbook provide opportunities for gifted students to develop these leadership skills. Encourage gifted students to extend these activities by developing related activities.

Gifted students may need to move through the course at an accelerated pace. These students may not need to work every problem provided. For example, after reviewing a chapter, gifted students may show mastery by answering selected questions and problems.

Limited-English-Proficiency (LEP) Students
Limited-English-Proficiency (LEP) students are individuals whose native or dominant language is a language other than English. Although these students

may be involved in special English-as-a-second-language (ESL) classes, the teacher can significantly improve learning *Intro to Business* by adopting some of these strategies:

1. Provide students with translations of key terms before presenting each chapter. Encourage students to use dictionaries.

2. Create visual instructional methods, such as posters and bulletin boards, that reinforce concepts in both English and the other dominant language(s).

3. Use simple words in oral presentations and testing materials. Avoid polysyllabic words. Simplify the nontechnical vocabulary.

4. At early levels, LEP students have limited comprehension of English and can respond with one or two word answers. Assess understanding by having students match, choose, move, draw, or point. Students at this level can respond to directions that require them to name, list, categorize, label, or reply with one or two words.

5. LEP students, like visual learners, require a variety of visual clues to support the lesson and help them understand abstract ideas. Use transparencies, textbook illustrations, and software demonstrations to provide these clues.

6. Allow for longer pauses when you ask questions. Nonnative speakers need more time to formulate their answers.

7. Stress key terms so that LEP students learn the language of business.

8. Speak directly. Avoid negative constructions and passive verbs, such as "Don't forget that outstanding checks are not added in the bank reconciliation process." Instead, say "Remember outstanding checks are subtracted in the bank reconciliation process."

9. Rather than asking students whether they understand what you have said, ask them to restate what you have said in their own words.

10. Adjust the length of time allotted to complete assignments and tests. Remember that the primary objective is to assess knowledge of business rather than the ability to translate and comprehend the question or problem.

11. Coordinate classroom activities with the school's ESL support staff.

12. Avoid misinterpreting a nod as understanding. The nod may instead mean that the listener did not understand.

13. Be cautious if there are no interruptions or questions. It may mean that very little has been understood.

14. In some cultures, "Yes" is the response to every question. It may mean "I heard your question" rather than "I understand."

15. In some cultures, giggling or inappropriate laughter may indicate embarrassment at poor comprehension rather than disrespect for the teacher.

Specific Learning Disability (SLD) Students

Adolescence is a period of turmoil and adjustment. What many teachers often view as adolescent behavior may, however, be caused by a student's specific learning disability (SLD). The correct assessment of SLD students is difficult because adolescent behavior is similar to the typical characteristics of SLD students.

Passive Learners

When faced with making a decision, SLD students avoid making a decision in favor of waiting for a teacher to provide specific direction.

Poor Self-Concept

Years of failure cause SLD students to have low self-esteem, thus reducing their confidence that they can achieve academic success.

Inept social skills

SLD students often have difficulty making and keeping friends.

Attention deficits

SLD students often lack the ability to concentrate on one topic for an extended period.

Lack of motivation

Years of failure have conditioned SLD students to doubt their abilities and, therefore, view their efforts as being futile.

Once an SLD student is correctly assessed, the

teacher should work with the student to develop an individualized program. The basic objective of the program should be the development of functional (life) skills. The student should be counseled to establish challenging yet attainable goals and provide frequent feedback about the attainment of these goals. The student's academic success should be measured on the demonstrated ability to learn as well as the mastery of a body of knowledge.

Several general instructional strategies may be effective with SLD students:

1. When asking questions during class, ask SLD students questions that they likely can answer successfully. Save more difficult or unstructured questions for other students.

2. Rotate instructional materials rather than trying to complete the entire text. Supplemental instructional materials may include additional books, business magazines, government publications, multimedia materials, and software.

3. Incorporate current readings from business magazines and newspapers to identify contemporary topics of interest to students.

4. Encourage students to maintain a daily log or journal that describes their academic progress. This journal may include questions, concerns, and personal impressions about course content and the learning process. Students may share this log, if they desire, with the teacher when updating their individual program.

5. When feasible, SLD students could be encouraged to become involved in work-study programs that are consistent with course content. When work-study opportunities are unavailable, simulations can be used to provide a simulated work environment. Field trips are an excellent method to expose students to the business world.

At-Risk Students

Many factors may negatively impact a student's ability and motivation for academic success. Any student who is a potential dropout may be classified as an at-risk student. At-risk students are commonly deficient in mathematics, reading, and language skills. These students provide a unique challenge to the *Intro to*

Business teacher since the teacher has little, if any, power to correct problems in the home environment.

Effective instructional strategies for at-risk students should be based on the premise that all individuals have a need for achievement and social acceptance. Within the classroom, these needs can be fulfilled by developing a curriculum that promotes academic success and acceptance by the teacher. Techniques for working with at-risk students include the following:

1. Develop a personal profile of the student. Avoid placing too much significance on past academic performance as this may represent a symptom rather than the underlying problem.

2. Together with the student, develop an individualized program that allows the student to attain both short-term and long-term goals. When identifying goals, consider the student's anticipated academic and career goals.

3. Modify presentation strategies to include more visual displays and supplement explanations with current, realistic examples.

4. Organize field trips and mentor programs to expose students to the business environment.

Visually Impaired Students

Students with mild visual impairments typically take a full program of courses and may elect to enroll in *Intro to Business*. The nature and degree of students' visual impairments will vary and may include a difficulty in reading print, an inability to distinguish colors, a sensitivity to light, and a limited field of vision. The teacher must identify each student's exact impairment and adapt teaching strategies appropriately.

Many sources exist for providing alternative teaching materials. Most states have schools for the blind and rehabilitation service agencies that can enlarge the textbook and working papers. Consult these organizations to identify the latest technologies available for helping the students.

The teacher and student should develop an individualized program that establishes a time frame for achieving specific learning objectives. The learning objectives should be consistent with the student's anticipated career goals. The time frame should consider the student's impairment and the availability of technical assistance, such as enlarged materials and closed-circuit television. The use of software should not be overlooked for visually impaired students, particularly if oversized monitors with larger displays are available.

Additional activities for visually impaired students might include the following:

1. Create confidence in the student's ability to participate fully within the business world. Encourage students to prepare an oral or written report that profiles a successful visually impaired business professional.

2. New technologies are continually being developed that assist visually impaired students to participate fully in both school and business. Students must be aware of these technologies and know how to learn about new technologies. Using government agencies as a resource, help students prepare a report about anticipated technologies.

3. The additional time required for visually impaired students to complete chapter materials will minimize the time available for future chapters. You may consider skipping selected chapters.

Hearing Impaired Students

Hearing impaired refers not only to those who are deaf but also to those who are hard of hearing. The sense of hearing for deaf students is nonfunctional for ordinary day-to-day life. However, those who are hard of hearing have a functional sense of hearing and sometimes use a hearing aid. In order to be an effective teacher, always be certain that you are facing the student when speaking so that lip reading will be possible. Keep instructions simple and clear and use as many printed materials as possible or videos to convey the lesson.

Students with Attention Deficit Disorder

Attention deficit disorder (ADD) is distinguished by critical and persistent difficulties with attention span, impulse control, and sometimes hyperactivity. The two types of ADD are Attention Deficit Hyperactivity Disorder (ADHD) and Undifferentiated ADD. Students with ADHD must display, for six months or more, at least eight of the following characteristics prior to age seven:

1. Fidgets, squirms or seems restless.
2. Has difficulty remaining seated.
3. Is easily distracted.
4. Has difficulty awaiting turn.
5. Blurts out answers.
6. Has difficulty following instructions.
7. Has difficulty sustaining attention.
8. Shifts from one uncompleted task to another.
9. Has difficulty playing quietly.
10. Talks excessively.
11. Interrupts or intrudes on others.
12. Does not seem to listen.
13. Often loses things necessary for tasks.
14. Frequently engages in dangerous actions.

Students with undifferentiated ADD primarily exhibit inattentiveness without hyperactivity. These students may have problems with organization and distractibility and may seem quiet or passive.

The following instructional strategies may be helpful with students with ADD:

1. Seat students with ADD near the teacher's desk, but include them as part of the regular class seating.

2. Surround students with ADD with good role models. Encourage peer tutoring and cooperative/collaborative learning.

3. Avoid distracting stimuli. Try not to place students with ADD near air conditioners, high traffic areas, heaters, or doors or windows.

4. Maintain eye contact during verbal instruction.

5. Make directions clear and concise. Be consistent with daily instructions.

6. Repeat instructions in a calm, positive manner, if needed.

7. Require a daily assignment notebook in which the student writes down all assignments. The student and parents or guardian should sign the notebook to indicate that assignments have been completed.

8. Modify assignments as needed. Consult with special-education personnel to determine specific strengths and weaknesses of each student. Develop an individualized education program.

9. Make sure you are testing knowledge and not attention span.

10. Keep in mind that children with ADD are easily frustrated. Stress, pressure, and fatigue can break down their self-control and lead to poor behavior.

11. Praise immediately any and all good behavior and performance.

12. Teach the child to reward himself or herself. Encourage positive self-talk (e.g., "You did very well in class discussion today. How do you feel about that?"). This encourages the child to think positively about himself or herself.

Students with Dyslexia

There is not a widely accepted definition for dyslexia. For most experts, dyslexia exists when normally intelligent children who are exposed to suitable educational opportunities in school and at home experience a great difficulty in learning to read and write. Be alert, however, to the fact that not all individuals who have problems with reading are dyslexic. Only a qualified reading professional should make the diagnosis of dyslexia.

The following instructional strategies may be helpful with dyslexic students:

1. Assign shorter reading assignments for a given time period. Instead of assigning an entire chapter for one class period, assign the goals at the beginning of the chapter and the Business Notes at the end of the chapter.

2. Pair a dyslexic student with a more capable reader who can help emphasize the major points of a reading assignment.

3. Emphasize the organization of a chapter before the student begins to read. Point out the relationship among the objectives, major headings, and Business Notes. A simple diagram or chart of the chapter's organization may help.

4. Encourage dyslexic students to create mental pictures of the words. The student can imagine actual business transactions. Before assigning reading, use videos, field trips, or photos to provide visual images of business activities.

5. Model a positive attitude. Self-esteem is critical to a dyslexic student's success.

Teaching Strategies for Students with Different Learning Styles

Students in your *Intro to Business* class will likely possess many different learning styles. Some people learn best from *reading* material. Others need to see a demonstration or learn by *feeling*. Still others may learn best from *auditory* cues. Remember, however, that a preferred learning style is not an indicator of intelligence. Two people of similar levels of intelligence may learn best with two different styles of learning. Learning style is also not necessarily a rigid behavior. Many people may have a dominant learning style; however, most also have the flexibility to adapt learning style to the demands of the material to be learned. Different learning styles include print, visual, auditory, tactile, and kinesthetic learning.

Print Learners

The print learner prefers to see the data in print—preferably printed in words.

1. When introducing course concepts or the steps of a process, a print learner would prefer to study an illustration or other visual presentation.

2. When covering key terms, the teacher should discuss the concepts using the textbook examples and referring to the textbook. The print learner can later go back and study the material.

3. When learning business calculations, the print learner would prefer to be able to study a formula as given in the textbook or as printed on a separate handout. The print material should show the formula as well as an example of performing the calculations.

Visual Learners

The visual learner needs to "see" the concept. One way for the learner to "see" the idea is mental visualization. Illustrations and visual aids are important to the visual learner.

1. Ask the student (with eyes closed) to picture a computer system. The student should be able to see a keyboard, screen, disk drive, printer, and other computer hardware. As this idea takes on a visual form, the student will be able to access it when needed.

2. When covering types of economic systems, the teacher should discuss the characteristics of each using a transparency or the board. In addition, the student should be asked to picture mentally each system before the teacher writes the description on the transparency or board.

3. To teach benefits and drawbacks of consumer credit, the teacher could use a transparency in the lecture. The transparency could be (a) a blank transparency that the teacher completes, or (b) a

prepared transparency that shows the advantages and disadvantages of consumer credit.

4. Formulas, such as calculating interest, should be illustrated on the board to help visual learners.

Auditory Learners

The auditory learner will best learn by hearing. Auditory learners who read a textbook chapter benefit from hearing reinforcement of key ideas spoken out loud.

1. When introducing the types of investments, have the student state out loud the definition for these items. Repeating the statement a few times will increase the chances of its being reinforced.

2. To reinforce the learning of the components of a computer system, the auditory learner should verbally repeat the four elements. The student should also verbally list examples of each component.

3. When learning how to write a check, the auditory learner would prefer to hear the steps involved. This can be done via a live lecture or a taped tutorial. To reinforce learning, the student could recite the check-writing steps to another student or group of students.

4. The auditory learner can reinforce the learning of formulas by verbally explaining the formula and calculations to other students in a small group. In a group of three, for example, each student should get the opportunity to "teach" the formula to the other two students. Through this process, each student in the group will "teach" the formula once and "learn" the formula two times.

Tactile Learners

The tactile learner learns best by touching or handling objects.

1. Using play money, have the student move funds from one pile to another to understand how funds are transferred among different financial institutions.

2. Tactile learners may benefit from using the computer to key data for various textbook problems. A ruler can be positioned on the input data as a guide when keying the entries. Encourage the student to place a finger on each item in the input report and trace it over to the amount on the

report to check it for accuracy. Tactile learners should also be given the opportunity to use a business simulation that contains source documents that need to be handled, analyzed, and recorded.

3. The tactile learner can use a group of index cards to represent types of business resources. Each card should represent a different item used in a business. Have the tactile learner use the cards to identify which are natural resources, which are human resources, and which are capital resources.

4. Suggest using a calculator with a printed tape to do mathematical calculations. Some calculators also print the operational signs of calculations $(+, -,$ etc.) for students to trace the steps in a calculation.

Kinesthetic Learners

The kinesthetic learner achieves best by taking an active part in the instruction. Motion is an important part of kinesthetic learning.

1. Have the student draw a flowchart showing the process used to move products from producers to consumers.

2. To teach check writing, the teacher should give the student sample checks and have the student prepare these documents as the teacher demonstrates on a transparency or board.

3. The kinesthetic learner would prefer to participate in the job interview process. Use a transparency of the common errors made during an interview and have each student demonstrate how this mistake might be avoided.

4. Provide the opportunity to do the calculations to solve formulas. One way to accomplish this is to develop an activity sheet with several examples listed or use appropriate drills from the working papers.

Strategies for Planning the Year's Work

A time schedule for a complete year should be planned before the year begins. Five steps for planning the year's work are suggested as follows:

1. Review previous experience with the pace of work that students have maintained in past *Intro to Business* classes.

2. Determine how many supplementary activities will be completed during the year such as simulations, etc.

3. Decide how much allowance should be made for interruptions in the school day that occur on short notice.

4. Determine if computers will be used in the class. Technology Application at the end of each chapter provides an opportunity for students to use word processing, database, or spreadsheet software. There are other opportunities to use computers with applied communication activities, etc.

5. Prepare a proposed work schedule that will meet your semester, quarter, or block schedule. Sample schedules are given that will help you in this process.

Semester Time Schedule
Two Semesters—180 Days Total (40–60 minute average classes)

Week	First Semester (Chapters 1-21)	Second Semester (Chapters 22-44)
1	Chapter 1	Chapters 22, 23
2	Chapter 2	Chapter 24
3	Chapters 3, 4	Chapter 25
4	Chapters 5, 6	Chapters 26, 27
5	Chapter 7	Chapter 28
6	Chapter 8	Chapter 29
7	Chapter 9	Chapters 30, 31
8	Chapter 10	Chapter 32
9	Chapter 11	Chapters 33, 34
10	Chapter 12	Chapter 35
11	Chapters 13, 14	Chapter 36
12	Chapter 15	Chapter 37
13	Chapters 16, 17	Chapters 38, 39
14	Chapter 18	Chapter 40
15	Chapter 19	Chapter 41
16	Chapter 20	Chapters 42, 43
17	Chapter 21	Chapter 44
18	Decision-Making Project, Portfolio Assessment	Decision-Making Project, Portfolio Assessment

Quarter Time Schedule
Three Quarters—180 Days Total (40–60 minute average classes)

Week	First Quarter (Chapters 1–15)	Second Quarter (Chapters 16–30)	Third Quarter (Chapters 31–44)
1	Chapter 1	Chapter 16	Chapters 31, 32
2	Chapter 2	Chapter 17, 18	Chapter 33
3	Chapters 3, 4	Chapters 19, 20	Chapter 34
4	Chapters 5, 6	Chapters 21, Decision-Making Project, Portfolio Assessment	Chapter 35
5	Chapter 7	Chapter 22	Chapter 36
6	Chapter 8	Chapter 23	Chapter 37
7	Chapter 9	Chapter 24	Chapter 38
8	Chapter 10	Chapter 25	Chapter 39
9	Chapter 11	Chapter 26	Chapters 40, 41
10	Chapter 12	Chapters 27, 28	Chapter 43
11	Chapters 13, 14	Chapter 29	Chapter 44, Decision-Making Project, Portfolio Assessment
12	Chapter 15	Chapter 30	

Block Schedule
(90 Days Total—90 minute average classes)

Day	Chapters 1-15	Day	Chapters 16-29	Day	Chapters 30-44
1	Chapter 1	31	Chapter 16	61	Chapter 30
2	Chapter 1	32	Chapter 16	62	Chapter 31
3	Chapter 2	33	Chapter 17	63	Chapter 31
4	Chapter 2	34	Chapter 17	64	Chapter 32
5	Chapter 3	35	Chapter 18	65	Chapter 32
6	Chapter 3	36	Chapter 18	66	Chapter 33
7	Chapter 4	37	Chapter 19	67	Chapter 33
8	Chapter 4	38	Chapter 19	68	Chapter 34
9	Chapter 5	39	Chapter 20	69	Chapter 34
10	Chapter 5	40	Chapter 20	70	Chapter 35
11	Chapter 6	41	Chapter 21	71	Chapter 35
12	Chapter 6	42	Chapter 21	72	Chapter 36
13	Chapter 7	43	Decision-Making Project, Portfolio Assessment	73	Chapter 36
14	Chapter 7			74	Chapter 37
15	Chapter 8	44	Chapter 22	75	Chapter 37
16	Chapter 8	45	Chapter 22	76	Chapter 38
17	Chapter 9	46	Chapter 23	77	Chapter 38
18	Chapter 9	47	Chapter 23	78	Chapter 39
19	Chapter 10	48	Chapter 24	79	Chapter 39
20	Chapter 10	49	Chapter 24	80	Chapter 40
21	Chapter 11	50	Chapter 25	81	Chapter 40
22	Chapter 11	51	Chapter 25	82	Chapter 41
23	Chapter 12	52	Chapter 26	83	Chapter 41
24	Chapter 12	53	Chapter 26	84	Chapter 42
25	Chapter 13	54	Chapter 27	85	Chapter 42
26	Chapter 13	55	Chapter 27	86	Chapter 43
27	Chapter 14	56	Chapter 28	87	Chapter 43
28	Chapter 14	57	Chapter 28	88	Chapter 44
29	Chapter 15	58	Chapter 29	89	Chapter 44
30	Chapter 15	59	Chapter 29	90	Decision-Making Project, Portfolio Assessment
		60	Chapter 30		

INTRO TO
BUSINESS

5ᵗʰ Edition

Steven S. Eggland

Les R. Dlabay

James L. Burrow

THOMSON
™
SOUTH-WESTERN

Australia · Canada · Mexico · Singapore · Spain · United Kingdom · United States

THOMSON
SOUTH-WESTERN

Intro to Business, 5E
by Steven A. Eggland, Les R. Dlabay, James L. Burrow

Vice President/Executive Publisher
Dave Shaut

Team Leader
Karen Schmohe

Executive Editor
Eve Lewis

Project Manager
Enid Nagel

Production Manager
Patricia Matthews Boies

Production Editor
Alan Biondi

Director of Marketing
Carol Volz

Senior Marketing Manager
Nancy A. Long

Marketing Coordinator
Yvonne Patton-Beard

Manufacturing Coordinator
Kevin L. Kluck

Internal and Cover Design
Tippy McIntosh

Editorial Assistant
Linda Keith

Production Assistant
Nancy Stamper

Compositor
Better Graphics

Printer
Von Hoffman Press
St. Louis, MO

About the Authors
Steven A. Eggland, Ph.D., is the Executive Director of the Accrediting Council for Independent Colleges and Schools (ACICS) in Washington, DC. ACICS is the largest accrediter in the world of business colleges and schools, accrediting over 600 institutions of higher education. Dr. Eggland is also Emeritus Professor of Vocational and Adult Education in Teachers College at the University of Nebraska. He has taught a wide variety of business courses and has a special interest in marketing education.

Les R. Dlabay, Ed.D., is Professor of Business at Lake Forest College, Lake Forest, Illinois, where he teaches courses in accounting, finance, international business, marketing, communications, and Latin American studies. He has taught more than 30 different courses in high school, community college, university, teacher preparation, and adult education programs.

James L. Burrow, Ph.D., is the coordinator of the graduate Training and Development Program at North Carolina State University in Raleigh, North Carolina. He has been a faculty member at the community college and university levels in marketing and human resource development as well as a consultant to business and public organizations.

For permission to use material from this text or product, contact us by

Tel: 800-730-2214
Fax: 800-730-2215
Web: www.thomsonrights.com

For more information, contact South-Western, 5191 Natorp Boulevard, Mason, OH, 45040. Or you can visit our Internet site at www.swep.com.

Expect More From South-Western...
...And Get It!

Law for Business and Personal Use
Give your students the most comprehensive coverage of contracts, ethics, employment law, banking, bankruptcy, and personal law available in one book. Maintain your fundamental emphasis on business law, while presenting topics such as criminal law, marriage law, and wills. Increase student interest with video segments that are linked to the chapter topics.

Text	0-538-43622-0
Student Activities and Study Guide	0-538-43624-7

Instructor Support and Other Materials Available

International Business 2E
Students develop the appreciation, knowledge, skills, and abilities needed to live and work in a global marketplace with this successful second edition of International Business. Every unit focuses on a different geographic region and the book includes features on historic international events, world climates, and graph and map analysis.

Text	0-538-69855-1
Student Activities Workbook	0-538-69857-8

Instructor Support and Other Materials Available

Mean Jeans Manufacturing Co. 3E
Mean Jeans is a unique simulation based on the operations of an imaginary, small business community. Students learn by doing as they become responsible for the daily operations and success of 15 businesses and agencies that interact with **Mean Jeans**, a maker of denim products. Great capstone simulation!

Student Reference Book (one per student)	0-538-43204-7
Operations Manual (see catalog for info)	0-538-43205-5
Supplies and Resources CD (one per class)	0-538-43206-3

Instructor Support and Other Materials Available

Banking and Financial Systems
This exciting new text gives an overview of banking and financial services, including career opportunities. It presents a survey of the principles and practices of banking and credit in the United States.

Text	0-538-43241-1
Module (includes ExamView CD, Instructor's Resource CD, Video, and Annotated Instructor's Edition	0-538-43242-X

Instructor Support and Other Materials Available

Fundamentals of Insurance
Explore health and property insurance, insurance rates, claims procedures, careers in insurance, and annuities. The extensive use of hands-on activities helps students understand the importance of insurance and how it affects people and businesses.

Text	0-538-43201-2
Module (includes ExamView CD, Instructor's Resource CD, Video, and Annotated Instructor's Edition	0-538-43248-9

Instructor Support and Other Materials Available

Marketing Yourself
Knowing how to sell yourself is critical to business success today. Marketing Yourself, a brand new title, utilizes a marketing framework to develop a self-marketing plan and portfolio. The self-marketing plan is based on the analysis of student marketable skills and abilities. Every student text includes a Portfolio CD.

Text/Portfolio CD Package	0-538-43640-9

Instructor Support and Other Materials Available

THOMSON

SOUTH-WESTERN

Join us on the Internet at www.swep.com

CONTENTS

INTRO TO BUSINESS

Consumers in the Economy 296

Financial Institutions and Banking Services 338

REVIEWERS

Dorothy Alexander
Teacher, Business
Arlington High School
Indianapolis, Indiana

Sara A. Baker
Teacher and Chairman, Career and Technology
Fabens High School
Fabens, Texas

Bruce J. (Ike) Bergeron
Business Teacher, Southeastern Vermont Career Education Center
Brattleboro Union High School
Brattleboro, Vermont

Cynthia Bertrand
Consultant, Vocational Education
Calcasieu Parish School Board
Lake Charles, Louisiana

Cinda M. Blythe
Teacher, Business Education Department
Indianola High School
Indianola, Iowa

Monica Caillouet
Teacher
East Ascension High School
Gonzales, Louisiana

Margaret L. Chester
Teacher, Business Technology Department
Biloxi High School
Biloxi, Mississippi

Maurice Ellington
Chairperson, Business Education Department
John Marshall Metropolitan High School
Chicago, Illinois

R. Edward Fielding
Teacher, Business Department
Brookville High School
Lynchburg, Virginia

Mary A. Gonzalez
C.A.T.E. Business Department Teacher
Weslaco High School
Weslaco, Texas

Tammy S. Guhl
Teacher, Business Education
Ben Davis High School
Indianapolis, Indiana

Alana Halsne-Baarda
Teacher, Business Department
Warren Township High School
Gurnee, Illinois

Mary Jane Hoag
Curriculum Consultant
Bryan, Texas

Ronda M. Matthews
Instructor
East Ascension High School
Gonzales, Louisiana

Kyle H. McDonald
Business Education Teacher
Evansville High School
Evansville, Wisconsin

Maria Medina
Assistant Principal
Miami Palmetto Senior High School
Miami, Florida

Kelvin M. Meeks
Teacher, Business and Technology
Raleigh Egypt High School
Memphis, Tennessee

Eric L. Skowronski
System Director, Continuing Education and Curriculum Development
Bryant & Stratton Business Institute
Buffalo, New York

Manny Stein
Chairman, Business Department
Ramapo High School
Spring Valley, New York

Rebecca Fulton Truluck
Chairperson, Business Department
South Effingham High School
Guyton, Georgia

Jamie C. Walker
Teacher, Marketing Education
Hunters Lane High School
Nashville, Tennessee

Jennifer Wegner
Business Education Teacher/Dept Head
Mishicot High School
Mishicot, Wisconsin

Vera Manigo White
Instructor, Vocational Business
Hallandale High School
Hallandale, Florida

Terry L. Wilson
Teacher, Economics Department
Mt. Carmel High School
San Diego, California

TO THE STUDENT

Intro to Business, 4th edition, will introduce you to the world of business and help prepare you for the economic roles of consumer, worker, and citizen. This course will serve as a background for other business courses you may take in high school and in college, assist you with consumer decision-making, prepare you for future employment, and help you effectively perform your responsibilities as a citizen.

HOW TO USE THIS TEXT

This text is carefully designed to help you learn. It is organized into 12 units with three or more chapters in each unit for a total of 44 chapters.
Each unit begins with a *Business Brief* that offers a contemporary view of various business topics and focuses your attention on issues and trends affecting businesses and consumers. *Critical Thinking* questions follow each *Business Brief* so that you may analyze the issues raised.

Each unit concludes with a *Focus on Careers* that will enrich your knowledge of career opportunities. This spotlight gives in-depth descriptions of various careers as they relate to the unit. This information will help broaden your understanding of different career paths.

Each chapter opens with a list of Chapter Goals. These goals will help you focus on the learning that will take place in the chapter.
Key Vocabulary Terms are highlighted within the text. These terms are also defined in the Glossary, which includes convenient page number references.

Chapter Headings Each chapter has headings that should be previewed to help you understand the chapter content. These headings can serve as a topical outline for a chapter if your studying method includes taking notes in outline format.

Business Notes at the end of each chapter summarize the major learning for that chapter.

SPECIAL FEATURES

Many special features have been included to enhance the content and broaden your knowledge of the world.

TechnoTips present technology tips related to each chapter's content. Many give tips on using the Internet and others include Internet activities that will enhance your learning.

Environmental Perspectives Ecology and environmental issues continue to be important topics of public concern. This feature highlights issues that businesses and consumers are facing in preserving our natural resources.

Ethical Perspectives News media are full of stories about unethical behavior in business and the effect of this behavior on businesses and individuals. This perspective presents ethical dilemmas that consumers encounter in real life.

Global Perspectives Global business topics provide information and activities to enhance preparation for working in the global economy. These topics provide practical, real-life information about trading across national boundaries.

Legal Perspectives Many laws affect business workers and customers. This feature introduces you to some of these important laws that guarantee your rights as a consumer.

Technological Perspectives Technology touches almost every part of our life, especially our work life. Computers, electronic cash, and the Internet create new opportunities and challenges for businesspeople. This feature provides information about technological advances that are influencing the way we do business.

Cultural Perspectives A variety of cultures have contributed to the business world as we know it today. Some of these features focus on historical contributions while others describe a present-day situation. This feature will help strengthen your awareness of the value of diversity in the work force and society.

Cultural Notes Bite-size pieces of cultural information are presented. These notes will enhance your knowledge of cultural diversity.

FYI ("For Your Information") These notes emphasize important points from the chapter and sometimes present additional interesting information about business. FYIs add interest and background to the concepts you are studying.

Net Facts These notations define Internet terminology and give useful background information about the Internet. You will be able to use this knowledge in your classes and career as the Internet becomes a bigger part of our lives.

Career Highlights Various jobs are highlighted using the *Dictionary of Occupational Titles* as the source. This feature will increase your knowledge about various career choices.

Business Notes This summary of the chapter highlights the key concepts that have just been presented, and it will help you understand the important points raised in the text material.

Communicating for Success This feature provides coverage of important workplace interpersonal communications issues and the proper uses of communications technology. *Critical Thinking* questions and activities give you the opportunity to apply the topics that are discussed.

Global Navigator Issues that are important to conducting business on a global level are thoroughly detailed in this feature. Key concepts and challenges faced by international corporations and small businesses alike are presented, followed by challenging *Critical Thinking* questions.

Global Business Project This end-of-unit project is packed with exciting activities that will increase your interest in the world of international business. You will feel like a real global participant as you complete activities using the Internet and other outside resources.

E-Commerce This new feature explores the role of e-commerce in today's business world.

CHAPTER REVIEW ACTIVITIES

Provide many opportunities to practice new skills and to demonstrate your understanding.

Review Your Reading allows you to review important concepts from the chapter.

Communicate Business Concepts enables you to apply concepts to real-world situations.

Develop Your Business Language gives you the opportunity to review key vocabulary terms.

Decision-Making Strategies gives you an opportunity to solve business and consumer problems using concepts learned in the chapter.

Calculate Business Data gives you an opportunity to demonstrate basic math skills.

Technology Application provides you with a problem to solve using commercial database, word processing, or spreadsheet software.

TEMPLATE

Intro to Business enables you to complete the end-of-chapter Technology Application problems using database, spreadsheet, or word processing software! A template file is provided on the *Intro to Business* Data CD for every Technology Application problem so that you may use real-world software and get hands-on experience using the computer.

REFERENCE MATERIAL

Reference material includes four appendices, a glossary of terms, and an index.

Appendix A, Using a Calculator and Computer Keypad, includes information for proper use of the calculator and computer keypad.

Appendix B, Math Review, provides a quick review of basic arithmetic for solving problems.

Appendix C, Determining Percentages and Interest in Business, gives practice calculating percentages.

Appendix D, Using Measurements in Business, provides information to help you become familiar with the metric system.

UNIT 1

BUILDING YOUR PORTFOLIO

CAREER DEVELOPMENT – CAREER PLANNING

The Building Your Portfolio career exercise will help your students establish a personal history—where they have been, where they are now, and where they are going. This career exercise will encourage students to think about their interests, skills, and achievements. Ask students to think about their goals, qualities, and achievements.

On a separate sheet of paper, direct students to write their thoughts about themselves: (1) personal goals, (2) career goals, (3) how to reach goals, (4) strengths and weaknesses, (5) important achievements.

As a supplemental activity, you may refer to the School–To–Work/SCANS Activity Masters.

TEACHING STRATEGIES

SCANS

Critical Thinking Skills

Workplace Competencies

Personal Qualities

Basic Skills

Cooperative Learning

Teaching Tips

Special Needs

Teams

Special Features

Media/Technology

Chapter	Spreadsheet Software	Database Software	Internet	Video
1		■		■
2		■		■
3	■		■	■
4	■			■

Resources

SOFTWARE

Excel, Word, WordPerfect, Works, and ClarisWorks for Mac and Windows

Word Pro, ASCII, QuattroPro, Lotus, and Access for Windows

SOUTH-WESTERN EDUCATIONAL PUBLISHING PRODUCTS

Wilson and Clark. *Introduction to Economics*. 1997. Cincinnati: South-Western Educational Publishing Company. Textbook. 0-538-65593-3.

Miller and Stafford. *Economic Education for Consumers* 2004. Cincinnati: South-Western Educational Publishing Company. Textbook. 0-538-43579-8.

BOOKS

The Economist Guide to Economic Indicators: Making Sense of Economics. John Wiley & Sons. 1998.

The Economist Desk Companion: How to Measure, Convert, Calculate and Define Practically Anything. John Wiley & Sons. 1998.

GOVERNMENT PUBLICATIONS

Occupational Outlook Handbook, U.S. Department of Labor, Washington, DC.

What Work Requires of Schools: A SCANS Report for America 2000, U.S. Department of Labor, Washington, DC

MEDIA/TECHNOLOGY

Publisher's web sites:
www.intro2business.swep.com
www.swep.com
www.thomson.com

UNIT 1

OUR ECONOMIC ENVIRONMENT

The content and activities of this unit provide students with an overview of the purposes and characteristics of our economic society. Use the resources listed on the previous page, especially those from South-Western Educational Publishing, as you prepare to teach the economic concepts. This unit introduces some basic essentials of economics that lay the foundation for the rest of the study of this book. Economics is presented in simplified terms, and definitions—while being accurate—are also simplified to cover just the fundamentals.

Economic decision making, including a six-step decision-making model, is presented in Chapter 1. Students are given an opportunity to apply the decision-making model in this chapter. Decision-making problems and scenarios are presented in subsequent chapters to reinforce the decision-making process. Economic systems, with a focus on market economies, are introduced in Chapter 2. Chapter 3 contains a discussion of the three economic roles each of us performs in our private enterprise, market-based economy. Chapter 4 concludes this unit with a look at ways in which the health and progress of our economy are measured.

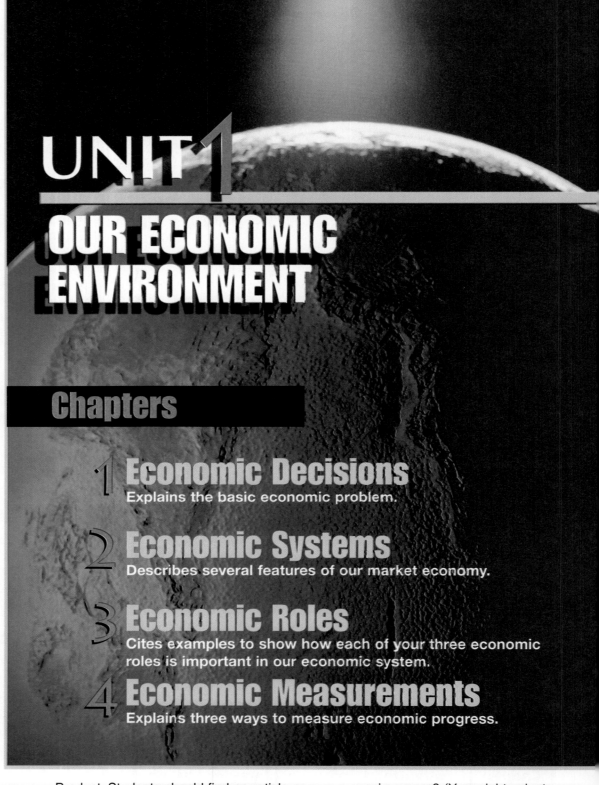

UNIT 1
OUR ECONOMIC ENVIRONMENT

Chapters

1 Economic Decisions
Explains the basic economic problem.

2 Economic Systems
Describes several features of our market economy.

3 Economic Roles
Cites examples to show how each of your three economic roles is important in our economic system.

4 Economic Measurements
Explains three ways to measure economic progress.

Kick-Off Activity

Investigating Business Media

To make the connection between today's business news and *Intro to Business*, an opening activity is provided for student research.

The most widely used estimate of national output is GDP—Gross Domestic Product. Students should find an article or series of articles in recent issues of financial newspapers or magazines about GDP. Students should follow articles about the GDP during the length of this course. Have students answer the following questions:

1 How often are GDP figures reported? What is the projected GDP for the current year? What was the GDP for the previous year? (You might ask students to create a graph using the computer to show the trend in GDP for the past five years.)

2 What does GDP indicate about general economic conditions?

BU$INESS BRIEF

YOU AND OUR ECONOMY

What do you think of when you hear the word "business"? Some of you may think of jobs, others may think of merchants who deal with consumers, and still others may think of the millions of firms that make up our global economy. Business provides the bulk of our employment as well as the products and services we enjoy. For the moment, let's focus on employment.

As a prospective employee, how might you be affected by "business" in the future? Employers will demand hard work from you. They will expect you to be flexible and responsive to change. Your key to successful employment will be life-long or continuous learning. A life-long passion for learning will provide you with the abilities and attributes you can transfer from one work environment to another.

Future workers must be creative thinkers and problem solvers. You will also need the foundation skills and attitudes on which employers can build. As an employee, you must be responsible, comfortable with technology, and able to work as a member of a team. The team approach to handling work is common in business today. Teams work on a particular project and then disband when the project is completed. Being able to work well with co-workers as a team member will determine your future success.

If you plan to seek employment in our economy, you probably have asked, "What kind of opportunities are available to me in business?" In reality, the size of many businesses will continue to decrease. Large companies will employ fewer people. Some leading companies will slow their growth in terms of the number of people employed. There will be many small businesses, including what has been described as a "world of networked one-person enterprises." Small businesses will have an increasingly important role in our economy. You may ask: "Who is affected by these changes in business?"

Three primary groups will be most affected by changes in "business":

- young adults without a high school diploma;
- semi-skilled workers in manufacturing;
- people over 40, often employed by large companies.

Many people in these groups do not have the basic skills and attributes that make them flexible and responsive to change.

What about you? There will be opportunities for you in both large and small businesses. A key to your job success will be your ability to transfer your skills from one work environment to another. Investing in your personal growth and self-development will help you remain responsive to change.

CRITICAL THINKING

1. Why do small businesses play such an important part in our economy?

2. What can you do now to help prepare yourself for a future in our economy?

3

BU$INESS BRIEF

A Business Brief sets the tone for a unit. To help students understand current and emerging trends, each unit will be introduced with a Business Brief. The Briefs were chosen for their importance to business, timeliness, and interest to students. The Briefs complement the many real-world examples woven into the text.

After reading the Business Brief, ask students what impressed them the most. Have they heard or read about this topic before? At the conclusion of the discussion, direct students to answer the Critical Thinking questions that follow the Brief.

CRITICAL THINKING

Student answers will, of course, require thinking beyond what is presented in the Business Brief. The following are possible answers:

1. Small businesses can be formed easily. They also can change more quickly than large corporations and, therefore, be more responsive to change. There is also a greater amount of control of the business by a small-business owner.

2. Students need to complete their high school programs, develop employability skills, and be prepared for many changes over their working lifetimes. They must be ready to take advantage of lifelong learning opportunities and to invest in education beyond high school.

BUILDING YOUR PORTFOLIO

The Building Your Portfolio work samples validate skill level and a student's ability to accomplish tasks frequently performed on the job. The most important reason for including samples in a portfolio is to demonstrate a student's abilities and skills. In selecting work samples for each unit, students should always have a choice of which activities to include. Students might be encouraged to include samples from the end-of-chapter activities, particularly Communicate Business Concepts, Calculate Business Data, Technology Application, and Decision-Making Strategies.

In Chapter 1, emphasis is placed on the economic fact that our wants are unlimited while at the same time the resources (natural, human, and capital) for satisfying these never ceasing wants are limited.

Resources for Teachers
- Lesson Plans
- School-To-Work/SCANS Activity Masters
- Spanish Resources
- Instructor's Resource CD

Assessment
- Chapter and Unit Tests, Ch. 1
- ExamView, Ch. 1

Media/Technology
- Applying Technology Data CD
- PowerPoint slides
- Business Connection CD
- Videotape

Activity Masters and Workbooks
- Activities and Projects, Ch. 1
- Internet Activity Masters
- Business Math Activity Masters
- Communications Activity Masters
- International Business Activity Masters
- Ethics Activity Masters

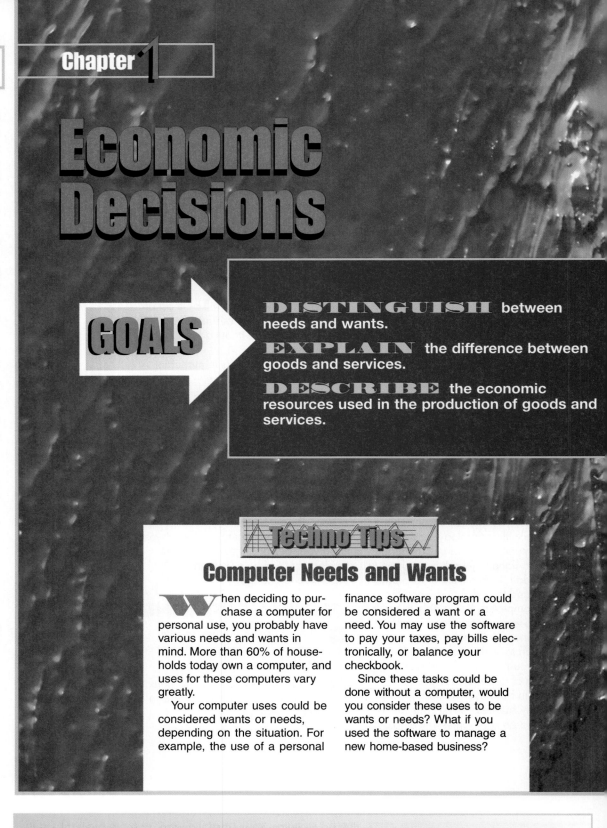

Chapter 1

Economic Decisions

GOALS

DISTINGUISH between needs and wants.

EXPLAIN the difference between goods and services.

DESCRIBE the economic resources used in the production of goods and services.

Techno Tips

Computer Needs and Wants

When deciding to purchase a computer for personal use, you probably have various needs and wants in mind. More than 60% of households today own a computer, and uses for these computers vary greatly.

Your computer uses could be considered wants or needs, depending on the situation. For example, the use of a personal finance software program could be considered a want or a need. You may use the software to pay your taxes, pay bills electronically, or balance your checkbook.

Since these tasks could be done without a computer, would you consider these uses to be wants or needs? What if you used the software to manage a new home-based business?

Students need to know the latest technologies and develop cutting edge Internet skills for use in current jobs, future careers, or in their homes. TechnoTips introduces students to today's cutting edge technologies and provides them with important Internet skills. Feature topics concentrate on Internet-specific technologies and computer or other hi-tech innovations for use by businesses and consumers.

FOCUS ON REAL LIFE

Sigdor and Duke were riding a bus to their jobs at a fast-food restaurant. Duke was looking at the businesses along the way. Duke nudged Sigdor and said, "Look at those ZXXY909s in that car dealer's window—I need one of them cars bad!"

"*Those* cars badly," corrected Sigdor. "But how can *you* afford to buy one?" he continued. "You don't even have enough money for the gas and insurance."

Duke went on. "Hey, look at that place.

They're having a sale on professional sports jackets. I need a new jacket; maybe I could get that Red Wings jacket I need, too." Sigdor just shook his head.

"And listen to this," Duke said excitedly, "I know about a great sale on CD players and a new ultra-focus sound system. There are just so many things I need. I can't wait until I get a credit card; then my troubles will be over."

"No," mused Sigdor, "then they'll just begin!"

NEEDS AND WANTS

Duke's desire to buy the things he sees and hears about is not unusual. You have many things that you want. The question is, "Do you *need* everything you see or hear about?"

Needs Are Basic to Survival

Things that are necessary for survival are called **needs**. Food, clothing, and housing are the basic needs that most people have. You often desire things beyond your basic needs. The car Duke wants is not necessary to his survival. He can get around without it, but he wants the car anyway.

Wants Add to the Quality of Life

Things not necessary for survival but which add comfort and pleasure to your life are called **wants**. You may want a new designer jacket, a stereo system, and a school ring. You could live without them, but having them would make life nicer and more fun for you. When we talk about needs and wants, you often lump them together and just call them wants.

Unlimited Wants

Wants never end. Your wants are limited only by your imagination. Your new jacket will satisfy you temporarily, but soon another

What are some items that fulfill your basic needs?

PURPOSE Have students skim the chapter, looking at photos, reading captions, and noting main headings. Read the chapter objectives aloud. Have students read through the vocabulary terms and note any entries that are familiar. Ask the students to try to define those terms or to recall the context in which they were used. Ask the students to state the purpose of studying this chapter.

TEACH/APPLY

MAKE CONNECTIONS On the board, note the names of a number of students and list for each the goods and services they name for satisfying their wants. The fundamental concept of the problem of scarcity or limited resources, along with unlimited wants, thus can be developed on a level that students can understand. This portrayal then should lead to the recognition of the need to make choices in the use of our resources. A discussion of this nature should enable the students to understand more readily and easily the basic economic ideas presented in Chapter 1 as well as in the chapters that follow.

At this point, use PowerPoint 1-7, *The Decision-Making Process*, to review the six steps in the decision-making process. Have students explain each one and give an example from their own lives or experiences with which they are familiar. Select a local community or school problem, such as urban renewal planning or planning for a car wash,

FOCUS ON REAL LIFE

One approach to launching Chapter 1 is to assume that each student has been given a certain amount of money, say $100, and then to ask the students how they would spend this money. Of course, answers will vary. Early in the discussion, it will become evident that the students' wants will probably far exceed what they can buy with the given amount. Recall with the students the wants listed by Duke in the opening scenario.

and have the class go through the steps in the decision-making process considering the many factors and decisions that must be taken into account. Review the steps in decision making throughout the course.

TRY THIS/GUIDED PRACTICE

Use PowerPoint 1-2, *Needs and Wants*, to review with students the definitions of needs and wants. Guide students in identifying the pictures of those things that are needs and those that are wants. Ask students what are some of the needs and wants they have right now; have them also do the same for their school and community. Then assign each student a letter of the alphabet. Let students choose any page beginning with their letter in the Yellow Pages of the phone book and classify the listings on the page as either a good for sale or a service offered.

Use PowerPoint 1-5, *Limited Resources*, to review the basic economic problem. Direct students to give examples of scarcity that affect their own lives. Then ask them to identify scarce resources in their school and community.

Demonstrate ways of dealing with scarcity. Direct students to line up in front of the room. Then remove one or two chairs so that there are fewer chairs than students. Now tell students to sit down. Give them time to solve the problem of the chair shortage on their own before you intervene and return the chairs to their customary positions. Then discuss how the class behaved under the conditions of scarcity.

"nicer" jacket appeals to you. One want fulfilled may lead to other wants. Sigdor bought a tennis racket that he wanted for a long time. That want was fulfilled: then he needed tennis balls. He also bought some tennis shorts and joined a tennis club. Your wants go on and on. For many reasons, your wants keep changing. You can never satisfy all of them. This is true for everyone—our wants are endless.

GOODS AND SERVICES

You satisfy most of your wants with goods and services. Goods and services are key words in the study of business, and you will use them often. **Goods** are things you can see and touch. Designer jackets, CD players, T-shirts, and soccer balls are examples of goods. All of the things that satisfy your

material wants are goods. Food, a television set, gasoline, cement, books, a bicycle, and clothes are examples. Goods are also called *products*.

Not all of your wants can be met with things you can see and touch. Some wants are satisfied through the efforts of other people or by equipment. These efforts are called services. When you go to a movie, make a deposit at the bank, get a haircut, take a swimming lesson, use your telephone, or ride a bus, you are using **services**. When you pay the hairstylist to cut your hair, you are buying a service performed by a person. When you deposit a coin to play a video arcade game, you are buying a service performed by a piece of equipment. You need both goods and services to satisfy your wants. Supplying goods and services is what business is all about.

ECONOMIC RESOURCES

Goods and services do not just appear as if by magic. You cannot create goods from nothing or supply a service without some effort. The means through which goods and services are produced are called **economic resources** (also called **factors of production**). There are three kinds of economic

What are some needs that are met by the services industry?

Basic Skills-Reading

SCANS

Direct students to the first main heading of the chapter. The first sentence of a paragraph is usually the main idea of the material being discussed. The last sentence of the paragraph usually summarizes or bridges to the paragraphs or subheadings that follow. Bold terms and italicized words draw attention to important facts or topics in the material. Direct students to pages in the chapter that illustrate bold terms or italicized terms. The Student Activity Worksheet, Basic Skills—Reading, in the School-To-Work/SCANS Activity Masters, may be used to serve as a guideline for discussion of each of these points. Ask students to write a summary of the points that will be covered in the chapter.

Name some natural resources found in the area where you live.

EXPLORE THIS/INDEPENDENT PRACTICE Before getting into a full and direct discussion of the content of any chapter, students should be expected to read the chapter material carefully. In view of the fact that all students vary widely in their ability to read effectively, it is advisable to have the students read the entire chapter, or sections thereof, silently in class if the material has not been previously read in connection with homework assignments. Ask individual students to read aloud to the class mainly to clarify, emphasize, or review certain points.

After students have read the chapter, ask them to complete the end-of-chapter questions. Review Your Reading questions can be used to check students' comprehension of what they have read. Develop Your Business Language is an excellent way to improve students' vocabulary. Only words used in the chapter are used in the vocabulary exercises. Communicate Business Concepts affords an opportunity for students to apply to practical life situations the information gained from reading the textbook. Decision-Making Strategies contains material to challenge students to utilize the decision-making model explained in Chapter 1 for problem solving. By completing the problems under Calculate Business Data, students will be able to strengthen and refine their abilities in mathematics. Technology Application allows students to demonstrate skill in using technology, primarily word processing, spreadsheet, and database software.

resources: natural, human, and capital resources. All three are needed to produce the goods and services that satisfy wants.

Natural Resources

The raw materials supplied by nature are called **natural resources**. All of the materials that come from the earth, the water, or the air are natural resources. We take iron ore, gold, oil, and copper from the earth to use in making many products. We also grow vegetables in the soil and take fish from the water for food. We use oxygen from the air to help sick people in hospitals breathe and to make such products as carbonated water for colas. All of the goods we use today began with one or more natural resources.

Human Resources

Natural resources do not satisfy wants by themselves. It takes people to turn them into goods and make the products and services available. **Human resources** are the people who work to produce goods and services. **Labor** is another name for this factor of production. Human resources include people who run farms and factories, manage banks, design machines, process food, announce the news on television, check out our purchases

at the supermarket, police the streets, or teach introduction to business courses. Human resources are very important in producing goods and services.

Capital Resources

The tools, equipment, and buildings that are used to produce goods and services are called **capital resources**. Office buildings, factories, tractors, carpenters' tools, computers, delivery trucks, and display cases are examples of capital resources. If you use a bicycle to deliver newspapers, your bicycle is a capital resource. It is the equipment you use to provide the newspaper delivery service. Likewise, a computer used by a bank to prepare a report of a customer's account is a capital resource. The grill used to cook the hamburger you buy for lunch as well as the restaurant building are capital resources.

Today more people work in jobs that provide services than in jobs that produce products.

TEACHING STRATEGIES
Cooperative Learning

Learning Together is a positive form of cooperative learning that encourages students to work together. Working in small groups helps students become at ease with participating in the learning process. When implementing cooperative learning, establishing guidelines will help students reach the desired goal. Plan the size of each group before you begin, decide specific roles for the groups, set a time limit, and give guidelines for the outcome. For this activity, students are assigned to groups with four or five members each. The groups should be mixed in performance level, gender, and culture. Students should remove the study guide for this chapter in Activities and Projects and work together as a group. Assign a time limit that is appropriate for the content matter. Only one study guide is turned into the teacher for the group. The teacher will evaluate each group's performance on the study guide and assign points or awards accordingly.

The end-of-chapter questions vary in level of difficulty. For a basic assignment, consider Review Your Reading and Develop Your Business Language at the end of the chapter. For an average assignment, consider the basic assignment plus Communicate Business Concepts and Calculate Business Data. For an enhanced assignment, consider the average assignment plus Technology Application and Decision-Making Strategies.

ASSESS

Review the goals at the beginning of the chapter and the corresponding Business Notes at the end of the chapter. Have students respond orally or in writing to each Note restated as a question. For students who may have difficulty providing answers, assign the reteaching activities that follow. Enrichment activities may also be assigned where appropriate.

1. What is the difference between needs and wants?
   (Answer: Needs are necessary for survival; wants add pleasure to our lives.)
2. What is the difference between goods and services?
   (Answer: Goods are things we can see and touch; services are the things that satisfy our wants through the efforts of other people or equipment.)

Name other highly skilled human resources, like this traffic control specialist.

The word **capital** is often used in place of capital resources, especially when referring to the factors of production. Capital includes money that is needed to run a business. A person may say she or he is trying to raise $40,000 in capital to expand a business or that she or he has a $10,000 capital investment in a store operated by friends.

All three economic resources—natural, human, and capital—are necessary to produce goods and services to satisfy our wants. Unfortunately, we do not have an endless supply of these resources.

LIMITED RESOURCES

If Duke had a lot of money, do you think he could buy all of the things he would want? In reality, money is a limited resource.

> **Capital goods are important because they help us produce efficiently—that is, faster or cheaper.**

Therefore, Duke cannot buy everything he wants. Have you had the experience of wanting many things without having the money to pay for them?

Newscasts often report shortages of certain items. In recent years, newsprint, lumber, and orange juice have been reported as scarce. We do not have an endless supply of these economic resources. Because of pollution, we do not have an endless supply of clean air, water, and land. We also have shortages of certain kinds of human resources in some career areas. Since our natural and human resources are limited, we are limited in what we can build and produce.

Scarcity Affects Everyone

Just as meeting your unlimited wants with limited resources is a problem for you, so it is for everyone—your family, your neighbors, and your school club. People all over the world are affected by scarcity. For this reason, the conflict between unlimited wants and limited resources is called the **basic economic problem** (also called **scarcity**).

The members of your family may not be able to afford many of the things they want because the wages of your father or mother are needed for food, clothing, the house payment, the electric bill, or your school expenses. Your neighbors and the families of your friends face the same economic problem. Your school club might want to hire a band for its annual dance, but because its money is scarce, the club may have to use CDs instead.

Scarcity Affects Businesses and Governments

Just as individuals face the basic economic problem, so do businesses, governments, and all agencies that supply goods and services. A growing business might want to enlarge its plant and parking lot, but because the land it owns is limited and locating elsewhere would cost more than it can afford, it cannot do both.

All levels of government face the problem of supplying the almost unlimited wants of

An *economist's* job duties include:

- **Studying ways in which society uses scarce resources**
- **Analyzing costs and benefits of distributing and consuming goods and services**
- **Conducting research, collecting and analyzing data, monitoring economic trends, and developing forecasts**

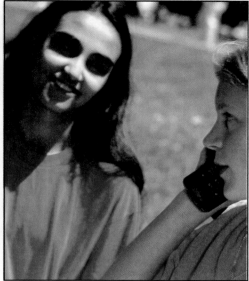

What economic decisions have you recently made regarding wants versus needs?

The careers listed in Career Highlights come from the *Occupational Outlook Handbook*, an online publication (www.bls.gov/oco) of the federal government. The O*NET code for Economist is 19-3011.00. Tell your class about this resource and how to use it. This description of job duties can be used to demonstrate the relevancy of skills learned in this course.

their citizens with limited resources. For example, your town may wish to give a large wage increase to police officers and firefighters. However, because taxes may not provide enough money, the increase might have to be smaller in order to provide other services, such as a new school building or additional employees to collect the garbage. Cities, states, the United States, and all other nations must cope with the problem of providing the many services citizens want from limited resources—the taxes collected to pay for the services. Someone must decide which services will be provided. How do you, other individuals, businesses, and governments decide which of the unlimited wants to supply?

ECONOMIC CHOICES

Since you cannot have everything you want, you must choose which of the things you want most and can afford. Suppose you earn $25 a week. If you spend it on movies and

An orderly approach to decision making can help you organize your thinking about problems and can result in effective decisions.

pizza with your friends on Friday night, you will not have enough left to go to the hockey game on Saturday. So you must make a choice. You must decide which of your wants—the movie and pizza with friends or the hockey game—is more important to you. You must determine which alternative will satisfy you the most.

One of the purposes of this book is to help you learn how to make wise economic decisions. Learning and following a logical process will help you make better decisions.

The Internet is a telecommunications system that connects many different networks of computers. The Internet is often called a "network of networks."

3. What are the economic resources used in the production of goods and services? (Answer: Natural, human, and capital; also called factors of production.)
4. Why does scarcity force individuals, businesses, and governments to make choices? (Answer: Since individuals, businesses, and governments cannot have everything they want, they must choose which of the things they want most and can afford.)
5. What is economic decision making? What are the six steps in the decision-making process? (Answer: Economic decision making is the process of choosing the wants, among those being considered, that will be satisfied. The steps in the

Net Facts provides information and definitions of terms for the Internet. The more information that students have about the Internet, the better equipped they will be to use this resource. In the Internet Activity Masters, there is an Internet Activity Worksheet for each unit. You can use these activities to give students experience with finding information online. Options for assigning this activity are as follows:

1. **Provide students with a list of addresses of resources for this activity;**
2. **Assign students to conduct their own searches; or**
3. **Use the addresses provided on the Internet Activity Worksheet.**

You should complete the activity yourself before assigning it to resolve any discrepancies that may arise.

process include: (1) define the problem; (2) identify the choices; (3) evaluate the advantages and disadvantages of each choice; (4) choose; (5) act on your choice; (6) review your decision.)

Ask students to prioritize their wants and share some of these with the class. Make the statement that one of the ways to "beat" scarcity is to have fewer wants. Ask students if they think this approach to scarcity is feasible. Which wants, if any, do they think they should eliminate?

Tell students to write down two goods that are in this classroom. Next, have them list the resources that went into producing the goods.

Students may also examine choices that they have recently made. For each choice, have students name the scarcity conditions that prompted the choice made. How are scarcity and choices linked? Call on students to share their ideas with the class. Have students list a series of decisions ranging from the simple to the complex. Ask students to rank order these decisions according to whether or not the six-step decision-making process should be applied.

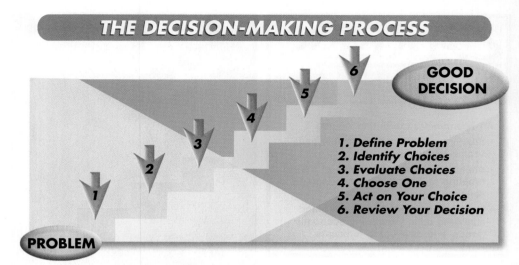

THE DECISION-MAKING PROCESS

GOOD DECISION

1. Define Problem
2. Identify Choices
3. Evaluate Choices
4. Choose One
5. Act on Your Choice
6. Review Your Decision

PROBLEM

FIGURE 1-1 How does the decision-making process lead to better choices?

Making Economic Decisions

There is a way that you can make almost any kind of decision. It is a proven way for good economic decision making. **Economic decision making** is the process of choosing which wants, among several wants being considered, will be satisfied. Once you learn the process, your decision making will be easier and your decisions may be better.

The Decision-Making Process

There are six steps in the decision-making process. You will use the model shown in Figure 1-1 as you proceed through this book. This process is used by many businesses and individuals to make important decisions.

1. *Define the problem.* If you have only $20 and want to buy several items, your problem is how to spend the money in a way that will give you the most satisfaction. In each situation, the problem must be defined in order to make a decision that will lead to its solution.

2. *Identify the choices.* There may be many choices or only two or three. In the movies, pizza, and hockey game decision, you had two wants or choices. There may be other choices, or alternatives, too. For example,

you might decide to save your money instead of going to either place. It is important to consider all of the alternatives in making a decision.

3. *Evaluate the advantages and disadvantages of each choice.* If you go to the movie, you will enjoy seeing the show. But you will miss the excitement of the hockey game. You also might miss being with your family on a Saturday outing. If you save the money and do neither, you will have the money for other things later. Some decision makers have found that it helps to write down the choices and to list the advantages and disadvantages of each. Being sure of your choices will help you with the next step.

4. *Choose.* This is really getting down to the "nitty gritty" of the problem. Even if you have done the first three steps as best you can, this is often a difficult step. You must learn to select from your choices the one that you believe will be the best for you and your interests at this particular time.

5. *Act on your choice.* This is the "take-action" step. If you have chosen to go to the movie, go and enjoy it. Try not to worry about the other choices that you

decided against. Some people agonize so much over making the choice, they fail to enjoy the activity they decided upon. Life is full of choices. Everyone probably regrets a decision from time to time. Using the six-step decision-making process each time you face an important decision will help you improve your ability to make choices.

6. *Review your decision.* Was your decision a good one? On a scale of one to ten, what score would you give your decision for the satisfaction it provided? What was right about it? What was wrong with it? Did you define the real problem? Did you evaluate your choices thoroughly enough? If you had it to do over, would you make the same choice? Did you miss a choice that might have been a better alternative? This step gives you the opportunity to think about your decision and learn from it so that you can make better decisions in the future.

Some decisions must be made quickly, and you will not have time to go through all of these steps. For example, if you are in a building when a fire alarm sounds, you will not have time to consider many choices before you decide to get out! For most decisions, however, following this six-step process will help you make better choices. The process has proven to be useful for businesses, governments, and individuals.

As you progress through this book, you will have an opportunity to practice the decision-making process with some situations presented at the end of each chapter—in "Making Decisions." You will apply the six-step decision-making model.

The word "decide" means to cut off or to cut the knot. Choosing one thing involves cutting yourself off from something else.

ENVIRONMENTAL PERSPECTIVES

Wetlands: A Quality of Life Factor

Marshes and bogs are commonly called "wetlands." Our land is spotted with marshes and bogs that filter water and purify it. Wetlands provide a habitat for many animals and birds. In some areas of the country, wetlands help prevent floods.

As we continue to build shopping centers, housing developments, condominiums, and other structures on vacant land, we sometimes destroy a critical natural resource—our wetlands. Wetlands are important for a healthy environment. Laws have been passed to help protect areas where wetlands are endangered. Business obviously is affected by these laws.

What have businesses done to expand and still protect wetlands? Some businesses,

after completing new facilities, have restored part of the property to wetland status. Many businesses realize that the need to expand and create new jobs does not necessarily have to conflict with preserving our natural resources. Business decisions are often made with the well-being of the environment in mind.

Critical Thinking

1. Why is it important to have wetlands where animals and birds can live and reproduce? What benefits do we as a society receive from the wetlands?
2. What are some things you can do to help preserve our environment, including wetlands?

ENVIRONMENTAL PERSPECTIVES

Have students relate experiences they have had with wetlands, if any. If there have been issues relating to wetlands that have appeared in the local newspapers, those issues should be brought to class for discussion. Students may also be assigned an extra-credit project in which they research this topic and make a presentation to the class.

CRITICAL THINKING

1. The birds and other animals are a vital part of our ecosystem and contribute to a healthy environment. The benefits to a society are indirect but nevertheless important in that all benefit from a balanced environment.
2. We can become conscious of the importance of our wetlands. We can support legislation and policies that protect the wetlands and our environment. We also can help spread the word and inform others about this economic concern.

REVIEW YOUR READING

1. Examples of needs are food, clothes, and housing. Wants include televisions, CDs, tennis shoes, and a trip to the beach. Explain here that needs and wants often overlap and that wants for some might be needs for others. Tennis shoes used in the performance of one's job as tennis coach would be a need, while tennis shoes for one who plays for recreation would be a want.

2. Answers will vary. People change in size and fashions in clothes change, so people want new clothes. Satisfying one want usually creates a new want; buy a stereo and you will want recordings to play on it.

3. In the American economy, businesses analyze demand and make efforts to supply goods and services to meet those demands. We depend on businesses to bring us the things we need and want. Some things, particularly services, are supplied by institutions such as hospitals and schools. Goods are provided by manufacturers, farmers, and other businesses.

4. Examples of services provided by people include house painting, swimming instruction, and financial advising. Services provided by machines include automatic change maker, automatic teller machine, and automatic car wash.

5. Our wants and needs are satisfied by goods and services; economic resources are the means through which goods and services are produced.

6. Natural resources: trees, minerals, water, and wildlife. Capital resources: tools, machinery, factories, buildings, power plants, tractors, and computers. Human resources: labor (men and women who run our farms, mines, and factories; who transport goods; who provide services for others; and who manage businesses).

7. It takes human resources to operate machines, run systems, and make decisions that are necessary in the process of producing goods and services. None of the goods we use today could be made without starting with one or more raw materials. These raw materials are classified as natural resources. Capital and human resources can be used only if there are raw materials to work with. As important as

BUSINESS NOTES

1. We all have needs that are basic to life and wants that improve the quality of life.
2. Goods are things we can see and touch. Services are tasks performed by people and equipment to satisfy needs and wants.
3. Economic resources vital to the production of goods and services are natural, capital, and human.
4. The basic economic problem of scarcity causes economic choices to be made by businesses, governments, and individuals.
5. Use of the decision-making model results in informed decisions benefiting the economy.

REVIEW YOUR READING

1. Give two examples each of needs and wants.
2. Explain why wants are unlimited.
3. Explain the ways in which businesses provide goods and services to satisfy our needs and wants.
4. Give one example of a service provided by a person and one by a machine.
5. How are economic resources involved in satisfying our needs and wants?
6. Name the three kinds of economic resources and give an example of each.
7. How important are human resources in producing goods and services? In what ways are natural resources and capital important?
8. Give two examples to show that economic resources are limited.
9. Explain what is meant by the basic economic problem.
10. Do businesses and governments also deal with scarcity? Give some examples to support your answer.
11. Name the six steps in the decision-making process.

COMMUNICATE BUSINESS CONCEPTS

12. Review the examples of limited resources given in the chapter. For each of the three economic resources, give two examples not listed in the text.
13. Sheila's father told her that with the family's limited resources, she will have to choose between a pair of hiking boots and season tickets to the ball games during the school year. This means that Sheila is on Step 3 of the decision-making process. List the advantages and disadvantages of Sheila's two choices.
14. Everyone must cope with the basic economic problem. Give one example to show how scarcity was dealt with for each of the following:
your family, one of your school's sport teams, your community, and the federal or state government.
15. Think about the clothes you own. Name one piece of clothing that you own but no longer wear. Give two reasons why you do not wear the item and tell how this situation contributes to unlimited wants.
16. List two businesses in your community that sell goods, two that sell services, and two that sell both.
17. Name some of the natural resources that were used in making each of the following: denim jeans, a pizza, jogging shoes, and this book.

natural resources are, they would be of little value without human resources. Products do not just happen, they are made by people or by machines that are operated by people.

8. Oil, which we use for many things from heating and cooling to making plastic for cars, dishes, and toys. Another limited resource is certain kinds of human resources in some career areas, such as doctors.

9. The problem of satisfying unlimited wants with limited resources that faces everyone—individuals, organizations, businesses, and governments—is called "the basic economic problem." The fact that it faces everyone is the reason it is called "basic." No person or group of people has all of the resources needed to satisfy all wants and needs.

10. Businesses might face a labor shortage in certain jobs. A decision must be made about whether or not to find another way to perform the service, to make the product, or to do the job for which the labor was needed. Governments

DEVELOP YOUR BUSINESS LANGUAGE

For each numbered item, find the term that has the same meaning.

18. The process of choosing which want, among several wants being considered, will be satisfied.

19. The means through which goods and services are produced.

20. The problem which faces individuals, businesses, and governments of satisfying unlimited wants with limited resources.

21. Raw materials supplied by nature.

22. Things you can see and touch.

23. Tools, equipment, and buildings used in producing goods and services.

24. Things that are necessary for survival, such as food, clothing, and shelter.

25. People who work to produce goods and services.

26. Things that are not necessary for survival but that add comfort and pleasure to our lives.

27. Things that satisfy our wants through the efforts of other people or equipment.

KEY TERMS
basic economic problem (scarcity)
capital resources (capital)
economic decision making
economic resources
(factors of production)
goods
human resources (labor)
natural resources
needs
services
wants

DECISION-MAKING STRATEGIES

Metrocity is a large, growing community. One of its problems has to do with land use. There is a big piece of land that borders a lake on the southeast side of the city. The land has been vacant for several years. Young people of the community occasionally use the area for unauthorized picnics and swimming.

The owners of the land have defaulted on their taxes. The city now has to decide what to do with the land. A group of citizens, who call themselves "Citizens for Better Living," want the city to develop the land as a recreational area complete with swimming and picnic areas. A local business group wants to buy the land for a luxury hotel and conference center—something the city does not have.

To develop the land for recreational purposes will cost $250,000. Funds also will be required to staff the area and to police and maintain it. The sale of the land for a hotel and conference center will provide $110,000 in revenue for the city. When the hotel and conference center are operational, there will be tax money coming into the city. But the community badly needs a recreational area, and the local citizens already pay high taxes for city services. The city manager has been asked to resolve this issue.

28. What are the advantages and disadvantages of the choices facing the city manager?

29. If you were the city manager, which choice would you favor? Why?

CALCULATE BUSINESS DATA

30. Amelia Descartes entered an open 10-K (kilometer) Run sponsored by her church to raise money needed by the local children's hospital which was short of funds. The 10-K Run drew 110 runners from the school and the community. Each runner paid a $5 entrance fee, $1.50 of which was used

to cover publicity, awards, and other expenses, with the remainder going to the hospital. (For help with problems involving metrics, see Appendix D.)

a. How long is the 10-K run, expressed in miles?

b. If all of the participants completed the run,

SUMMARIZE

Place all vocabulary words on slips of paper or cards and shuffle them. Select a panel of the three best students to sit in the center of the room to draw terms, verify answers, and keep score. Students should line up. One person on the panel draws a term for Student 1. The student must spell the word (worth 1 point) and give a correct definition (2 points). An appointed panel member must verify the answers. If a student cannot spell the term or give the definition, the student must sit down. The student with the most points wins. This activity could also be done using fill-in or short-answer questions reviewing the contents of this chapter.

might not materialize. Advantages for the tickets to the games might include enjoying watching the games, socializing with friends, and being "in" on the school sports events. A disadvantage would be not having the hiking boots when her friends plan a weekend hike.

14. A family might have to choose between taking a vacation and replacing a worn-out refrigerator. A sports team might have to choose between buying new uniforms and having the old ones cleaned. A town or city might have to choose between a large raise for members of the police force and a smaller raise in order to hire more police personnel. The federal government might have to decide whether to increase the number of military personnel or to buy more sophisticated equipment for more efficient use by the present personnel. Answers concerning the decisions as well as the choices will vary with each local situation.

15. Typical reasons are that the clothes no longer fit, they are out of style, or they have worn out. This contributes to the concept of unlimited wants in that people continue to buy new clothes as they grow in size, as styles change, as tastes in clothes change, or as clothes wear out. The need for clothes, therefore, is ongoing or unlimited.

16. Answers will differ according to the community. Types of businesses that sell goods are supermarkets, department stores, dairies, and various kinds of specialty stores such as gourmet food stores, hardware stores, drugstores, and stationery stores. Types of businesses that provide services include laundries, dry cleaning establishments, travel bureaus, telephone companies, telephone-answering services, and moving and storage companies. Types of businesses that supply both goods and services are hotels and motels, shoe repair shops, automobile dealers, radio and television repair services, plumbing contractors, and opticians.

17. Natural resources used for denim jeans would include cotton, vegetable dyes, and brass or copper for the snaps and buttons. A pizza would require wheat, tomatoes, dairy cows for cheese, plus other vegetables and spices, as desired. For jogging shoes, one would need animal skins for leather or oil and chemicals for synthetic materials, rubber, cotton for strings, metal or

how many kilometers did they cover in total?

c. How many miles did they cover?

31. The Jenkins family has a monthly take-home pay of $1,560. Each month they pay for the needs listed below.

a. What is the total monthly payment for the needs?

b. How much is left for other needs and wants?

Item	Amount
House payment	$410
Electric bill	105
Water bill	20
Food	375
Clothing	80

32. Forest fires take a heavy toll on land and timber resources, as shown recently in the Wildfire Report below for protected areas (those which are under the control of state and federal agencies, such as the Department of Agriculture or the Department of the Interior). Study the table and answer the questions that follow.

Acres of Protected Land		
	Federal	State and Private
Total land area	685,552,000	840,163,000
Area burned by wildfires	946,000	3,235,000
No. of fires reported	15,400	173,800

a. What is the total acreage of protected land?

b. What was the total number of fires reported in protected areas for the year?

c. How many acres were burned in the protected areas?

d. What was the average number of acres (show in round numbers) of federally protected land burned per fire?

33. To protect natural resources, businesses and various levels of government recently spent the amounts shown in this table in one year for water and air quality control activities.

a. How much did businesses spend on pollution control for air and water?

b. How much did each level of government spend during the year to protect the quality of air and water?

c. What was the total spent by all levels of government for air and water control?

d. What percent of the total amount was spent by all levels of government?

e. For which resource was the most money spent? What was the amount spent on the resource?

Quality Control Expenditures (in Millions of Dollars)		
Agency	Water	Air
Businesses	$18,857	$18,396
Federal government	110	639
State and local governments	10	403

TECHNOLOGY APPLICATION

Using the *Intro to Business* Data CD and your database program software, select problem CH01. After the problem appears on your screen, complete the following activities. Then, after you have completed each step, display or print a report for each activity. If you do not have a printer available, answer the questions before you leave the computer.

34. Sort the database in ascending order by title of videotape. Answer the following questions:

a. What is the eighth videotape listed?

b. What is the eleventh videotape listed?

35. Sort the videotapes in descending order by company name. Answer the following questions:

a. What is the first company listed?

b. What is the last company listed?

36. Select and list the videotapes that were released in the first six months of the year. How many videotapes are listed?

plastic for string tips, and vegetable or chemical dyes. For this textbook, one would need timber for pulp and paper, dyes for ink, cotton (or oil and chemicals for synthetic) thread, and resin for glue.

DECISION-MAKING STRATEGIES

28. An advantage of choosing the recreational area is that the community is in need of it. Also, it will

give young people a place to go and will add to the quality of life for the community. The disadvantage is that the city will lose some important tax revenues if the other choice is made. There are several advantages to the hotel and shopping center. Workers will be employed during the construction phase. Workers will be needed to operate the hotel and conference center after it is built. There will be tax revenues generated by the hotel and conference center. The disadvantage is

GLOBAL NAVIGATOR

BENEFITS OF INTERNATIONAL TRADE

Within the past 24 hours you have probably worn clothes, eaten food, traveled in a motor vehicle, and used electronic equipment made in part or entirely outside of the United States. Our global economy involves the exchange of goods and services among people in different countries. These international business transactions allow countries to buy and use items they might not otherwise be able to obtain.

International trade has several benefits for the consumers, workers, and society. For consumer, trade among countries gives you a wider selection of buying choices. For workers, the global economy creates new job opportunities. For society, international business activities can improve political and cultural relationships among nations, reducing the chance of war.

Some nations in the global economy are able to provide products more efficiently than other countries. An *absolute advantage* exists when a country can produce a good or service at a lower cost than other countries. This situation usually occurs as a result of the natural resources or raw materials of a country. For example, Canada has an absolute advantage for lumber, while certain South American countries have an

> **International business activities can improve political and cultural relationships.**

absolute advantage for coffee and countries in the Middle East are major oil producers.

A country may have an absolute advantage in more than one area. If so, a decision must be made on how to maximize economic wealth. For example, a country may be able to produce both computers and clothing more efficiently than other countries. If the world market for computers were stronger than for clothing, the country would benefit by manufacturing computers and buying clothing made in other countries. This is a *comparative advantage*, a situation in which a country specializes in the production of a good or service for which it is relatively more efficient.

CRITICAL THINKING

1. Select a country and find information about its natural resources and agricultural products. Explain how these items might result in an absolute or comparative advantage for the country.

2. As countries expand their global business activities, job opportunities change. Describe how expanded international trade might affect careers. What skills or abilities might be necessary for workers in a changing global economy?

Most students will either work with international clients or compete against businesses that do. Global Navigator introduces students to issues integral to working with international businesses. Key concepts and challenges faced by international businesses are presented, followed by two Critical Thinking questions that require students to analyze what they have learned.

state and local governments: $10,000,000 + $403,000,000 = $413,000,000; (c) $749,000,000 + $413,000,000 = $1,162,000,000; (d) $1,162,000.000 + $37,253,000,000 = $38,415,000,000 total; $1,162,000,000 ÷ $38,415,000,000 = 0.03; government spent 3% of total. (e) Most was spent on air quality control. The amount spent was: $18,396,000,000 + $639,000,000 + $403,000,000 = $19,438,000,000.

TECHNOLOGY APPLICATION

In this activity, students use a computer to solve a business problem using a file provided on the data CD that accompanies *Intro to Business*. Instructions for using the data CD are included in a **README** file on the disk. Solutions are provided on the Instructor's Resource CD.

that the community is in need of the recreational area and swimming beach.

29. Either is acceptable. Students should demonstrate logical thinking behind whichever choice is made.

CALCULATE BUSINESS DATA

30. (a) 10 × 0.6 = 6 miles; (b) 110 × 10 = 1100 kilometers; (c) 110 × 6 = 660 miles.

31. (a) $410.00 + $105.00 + $20.00 + $375.00 + $80.00 = $990.00; (b) $1,560.00 − $990.00 = $570.00.

32. (a) 685,552,000 + 840,163,000 = 1,525,715,000 acres; (b) 15,400 + 173,800 = 189,200 fires reported; (c) 946,000 + 3,235,000 = 4,181,000 acres; (d) 946,000 ÷ 15,400 = 61.43 or 61 acres.

33. (a) $18,857,000,000 + $18,396,000,000 = $37,253,000,000; (b) federal government: $110,000,000 + $639,000,000 = $749,000,000;

In Chapter 2, the basic economic questions of what to produce, how to produce, and for whom to produce are examined. These questions must be answered in any economic system.

Resources for Teachers
● Lesson Plans
● School-To-Work/SCANS Activity Masters
● Spanish Resources
● Instructor's Resource CD

Assessment
● Chapter and Unit Tests, Ch. 2
● ExamView, Ch. 2

Media/Technology
● Applying Technology Data CD
● PowerPoint slides
● Business Connection CD
● Videotape

Activity Masters and Workbooks
● Activities and Projects, Ch. 2
● Internet Activity Masters
● Business Math Activity Masters
● Communications Activity Masters
● International Business Activity Masters
● Ethics Activity Masters

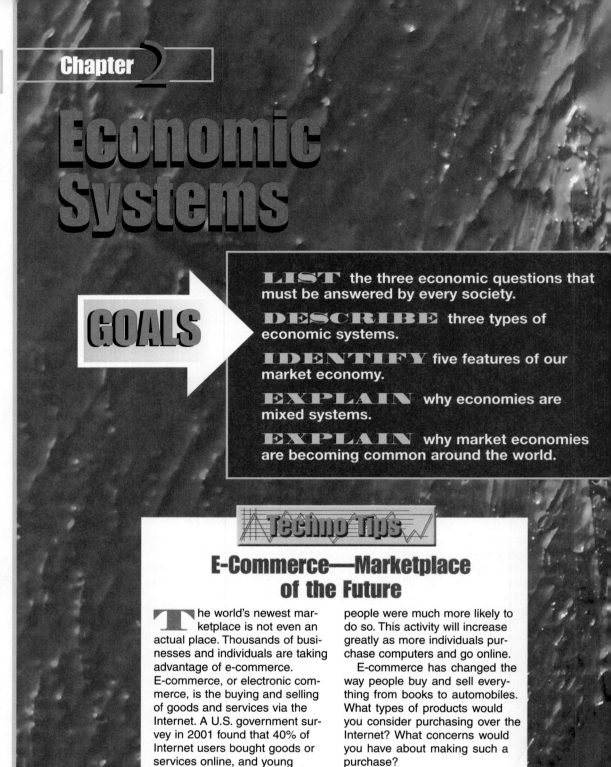

Chapter 2
Economic Systems

GOALS

LIST the three economic questions that must be answered by every society.

DESCRIBE three types of economic systems.

IDENTIFY five features of our market economy.

EXPLAIN why economies are mixed systems.

EXPLAIN why market economies are becoming common around the world.

Techno Tips

E-Commerce—Marketplace of the Future

The world's newest marketplace is not even an actual place. Thousands of businesses and individuals are taking advantage of e-commerce. E-commerce, or electronic commerce, is the buying and selling of goods and services via the Internet. A U.S. government survey in 2001 found that 40% of Internet users bought goods or services online, and young people were much more likely to do so. This activity will increase greatly as more individuals purchase computers and go online.

E-commerce has changed the way people buy and sell everything from books to automobiles. What types of products would you consider purchasing over the Internet? What concerns would you have about making such a purchase?

Students need to know the latest technologies and develop cutting edge Internet skills for use in current jobs, future careers, or in their homes. TechnoTips introduces students to today's cutting edge technologies and provides them with important Internet skills. Feature topics concentrate on Internet-specific technologies and computer or other hi-tech innovations for use by businesses and consumers.

FOCUS ON REAL LIFE

Laszlo was a shoemaker in a country in which the government made economic decisions. He was told how many shoes he could make and sell each year. Things are now different in Laszlo's country. His country no longer has a central committee that does all the planning. Today Laszlo does his own planning and determines the number and style of shoes he will sell. Department stores and shops in Laszlo's country display a variety of shoes available for sale to consumers. His country has a market economy. A market economy is one in which individuals are free to engage in business transactions. In such an economy, the questions of what, how, and for whom to produce are determined by the operation of markets. A market is an arrangement that allows buyers and sellers to come together to trade goods, services, and resources. Buyers and sellers participate freely in that market. It is open to all who want to participate and have the means to do so. The activity of buyers and sellers is not controlled—there is voluntary exchange.

Voluntary exchange allows buyers and sellers to come together in a market to trade goods, services, and resources. For example, consumers may exchange their resources (usually money) for what producers decide to make available to them (goods and services). Voluntary exchange occurs only when the trading parties believe that they will be better off after the exchange.

KEY ECONOMIC QUESTIONS

Even in market economies, governments have some influence on how the nation's resources are used. Regardless of how a country lets its market operate, there are key economic questions which must be answered because of scarce economic resources. The three economic questions are:

1. What goods and services are to be produced?

2. How should the goods and services be produced?

3. For whom should the goods and services be produced?

What to Produce?

Nations differ in their wants just as individuals do. In one country, resources may be used to produce spaceships and to explore other planets. Another might use its resources to build the biggest and best military force. Some might use most of their resources to provide such consumer goods as cars, television sets, dishwashers, and recreational parks. Still other countries might have such limited resources that they must concentrate on providing only the basic needs of food, clothing, and shelter.

Meeting some or all of its people's wants is a challenge. A country must learn how to best use its resources. A nation that concentrates too heavily on military goods may not have enough resources left for consumer goods and services. On the other hand, if all of its resources are used to supply consumer goods and services, it may not be able to protect its people from outside forces. Decisions must be made on which kinds of goods and services are valued the most and best serve the nation.

The word *market* derives from the Latin word *mercari* which means "to trade."

FOCUS ON REAL LIFE

Ask students to define *economic system*, basing their definitions on the information they learned in Chapter 1. Have volunteers read their definitions to the class. A possible definition might be "An economic system is an organized way of providing for the wants and needs of the people within a society."

MOTIVATE

PURPOSE Direct students to skim the chapter, looking at photos, reading captions, and noting main headings. The goals at the beginning of each chapter provide a valuable tool for having students pinpoint main ideas. The tasks required by the goals are signaled in the first word. Some emphasize information collection ("Identify," "List"), while others call for description ("Explain," "Describe"). Ask students to look through all the goals and note the first word of each. Then ask students to state the purpose of studying this chapter.

TEACH/APPLY

MAKE CONNECTIONS Have students review factors of production covered in Chapter 1. List on the board or overhead a number of economic activities; for example, teaching introduction to business, giving financial advice, producing CD players. Ask several students to identify the factors of production used in these activities.

Review with students the key economic questions: What to produce? How to produce? For whom to produce? These basic questions must be answered by businesses as well as economies. Ask students to assume the role of the manager of a local radio station. What must the manager of a radio station decide about the question, what to produce? Students should share answers to this question with classmates.

Write the following words on the board: custom, planned, market.

Students should then give examples of how these words are used in everyday life. For example, the term custom might be used to refer to the practice of family and friends gathering for a picnic to celebrate the Fourth of July. Then show PowerPoint 2-3, *Types of Economic Systems*, to review the definitions of these terms as they apply to economic systems. Ask students to identify some countries with these systems. Discuss the collapse of directed (communist) systems and the movement of former communistic countries to a market system. Provide some current examples of successes and struggles that are taking place within "new" market economies.

On the board or overhead, draw a circle with OUR ECONOMIC SYSTEM at the center and Voluntary Exchange, Private Property, Profit Motive, Competition, and Freedom of Choice around it. Ask students to explain the relationship of each satellite idea to the central idea—OUR ECONOMIC SYSTEM.

Review the meaning of profit. Ask students if they believe that businesses make too much profit, and why they feel that way. Stress that most businesses make a much smaller profit on sales than most people realize. (The average profit as a percentage of sales for manufacturing industries has been less than 5 percent.) Ask students to identify what the "profit motive" does. Have students project themselves as owners of a business and come up with things that they might do to increase profits. (All

How to Produce?

A country that has a great many people but limited capital resources might build roads by having many workers use equipment that requires much manual labor. In another country, road building may be accomplished with only a few workers using labor-saving equipment, such as bulldozers and power earthmovers. In the first case, the country uses its human resources to offset its lack of capital resources. In the second case, the country does the job with more capital resources and less labor. The second method is more efficient and enables the country to complete the road much sooner. Economic resources combine in different ways to produce the same goods and services. Each nation decides which combination of resources will best suit its circumstances.

For Whom to Produce?

A nation must decide which of its citizens should benefit from the production of goods and services. A country must also consider whose needs and wants are the most critical. Additional questions include: How will the goods and services be distributed? Should the goods and services be shared equally among the people? Should people who contribute more to producing the goods and services be able to get a larger share of them? If you have the money, shouldn't you be able to buy anything you want with your money?

In some economic systems, you can buy whatever you want and can afford. But in others, your ability to buy may be limited by the country's answer to the earlier question, "What to produce?" For example, a large share of a country's resources might be used to produce capital goods, such as tractors or

industrial robots. That country might limit its production of consumer goods, such as high-fashion clothes and CD players. Consumer goods then become scarce. In the United States, with our plentiful supply of goods and services, what you buy is largely determined by the amount of money you have and are willing to spend. In addition, the amount of money that you receive in wages will be affected by many things, including your abilities and how you use them. Figure 2-1 illustrates a variety of responses to the three basic economic questions.

TYPES OF ECONOMIC SYSTEMS

A nation's plan for answering the key economic questions is called its **economic system**. There are several kinds of economic systems operating in the world today.

Can you name various industries that use both human and capital resources?

Workplace Competencies-Technology

Employers are looking for potential employees with good technology skills. We may help students become proficient in selecting and using technology by teaching them how to make selections that will produce the desired results. The first step is to determine what the desired outcome should be, decide which form of technology is best suited for the task, and then evaluate the specifics for approaching the task. The Student Activity Worksheet, Workplace Competencies—Technology Checklist, in the School-To-Work/SCANS Activity Masters, may serve as a guideline for discussion. This textbook has a template that contains one computer problem per chapter. Students obtain experience using spreadsheets, word processing, and a database. These problems are found in Technology Application of the end-of-chapter activities.

SCANS

Governments which are democratic, socialistic, or communistic take differing approaches to how they allow their economic systems to operate. There are no systems that operate in a pure form.

Custom-Based Economy

In some countries, mainly those which are less developed and less responsive to the global economy, the answers to key economic questions are established by custom. In a **custom-based economy**, goods are produced the way they have always been produced. Children of each generation are taught to use the same method to make the same goods their parents and grandparents produced. The custom may be weaving cloth on a hand loom, making straw baskets, or planting rice by hand. Goods typically are produced by hand with simple tools using people or animals for energy. Change and growth occur slowly in countries whose economies follow customs and in which the people are poor in material goods.

Directed (Planned) Economy

In some countries, economic questions are answered by the owners of the resources. In a **directed** or **planned economy**, resources are owned and controlled by the government. The officials of the government, usually through centralized agencies and bureaucrats,

suggestions should be legal and ethical.)

Use PowerPoint 2-4, *Our Economic System*, to review the characteristics of our market economy. Ask the question: "Which of these characteristics do you think is the most important and why?" Students can draw on their own experiences or the experiences of family, relatives, or friends. There will be no one right answer, of course.

TRY THIS/GUIDED PRACTICE Call on students to identify how each of the three types of economic systems answers each of the key economic questions. Guide students in constructing a chart entitled "Comparing Economic Systems: Answering the Three Key Questions."

Direct students to suggest words that summarize some aspect of each of the three economic systems. (Sample: custom-based—static; planned—rigid; market—flexible.)

EXPLORE THIS/INDEPENDENT PRACTICE Have students write two or three paragraphs explaining how each of the three types of economic systems might respond to the introduction of new technology. For guidance, suggest that students consider how each system views new ideas. Select students to present their paragraphs to the class for discussion.

The end-of-chapter questions vary in level of difficulty. For a basic assignment, consider Develop Your Business Language and Review Your Reading at the

FIGURE 2-1 How are basic economic questions decided in the United States?

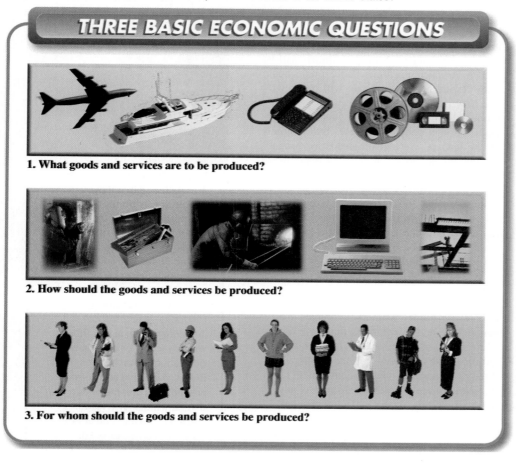

THREE BASIC ECONOMIC QUESTIONS

1. What goods and services are to be produced?

2. How should the goods and services be produced?

3. For whom should the goods and services be produced?

end of the chapter. For an average assignment, consider the basic assignment plus Communicate Business Concepts and Calculate Business Data. For an enhanced assignment, consider the average assignment plus Technology Application and Decision-Making Strategies.

ASSESS

Review the goals at the beginning of the chapter and the Business Notes at the end of the chapter. Have students respond orally or in writing to each of the Business Notes restated as a question, provided below. For students who may have difficulty providing answers, assign the reteaching activities that follow. Enrichment activities may also be assigned where appropriate.

1. What are the three economic questions that must be answered by every society? (Answer: What to produce? How to produce? For whom to produce?)

2. What are the three types of economic systems? (Answer: Custom-based economy; directed or planned economy; market economy.)

3. What are the five features of a market economy? (Answer: Private enterprise; private property; profit; competition; freedom of choice.)

4. Why can most economies in the world be classified as mixed systems? (Answer: Most decisions are left to individuals, but some are made by government.)

5. What are emerging market economies? (Answer: Formerly

What advantages or disadvantages do you think a custom-based economy has?

decide what and how goods will be produced and how they will be shared. They decide how much of the nation's resources will be spent on military uses and how much will be used to produce consumer and capital goods. They decide how much grain will be grown and how many pairs of shoes will be produced. In some countries, government leaders assign people to careers based largely on the leaders' view of the needs for producing the goods and services. They plan all phases of the economy and command that the plans be carried out, using the military or a police force to do so if necessary. In directed economies, the average citizen has little to say about how the three economic questions are answered. The freedom of the people is always limited in this system.

Market Economy

The third type of economic system is a **market economy**. Market economies are generally found in countries that have democratic forms of government. Here the three questions are answered by individuals through buying and selling activities in the marketplace. The **marketplace** is any place where buyers and sellers exchange goods, services, and some form of money. People who order goods from a mail-order catalog, go to a movie, buy food in a super-

market, subscribe to cable TV, buy shares of stock, or have a sweater cleaned are operating in the marketplace. When an airline orders a new jet, a business launches a satellite, or the government hires computer operators, each is operating in the marketplace. No one tells the consumers what to buy and no one tells businesses what to make and sell.

Consumers and businesses make economic decisions based on their own interests. For example, you may use your money to buy a leather jacket. One of your friends may spend his or her money to take tennis lessons and another may buy a compact disc player. When people in a market economy buy a product, they help to answer the question, "What to produce?" Resources are combined in such a way that the goods people want

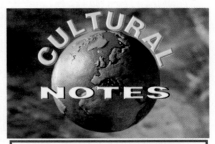

Diversity index is a measure of the likelihood that if two people are randomly selected in a particular area, they will be different from each other racially or ethnically. The United States has an average diversity index of approximately 40. In other words, if two persons are randomly selected, there is a 40 percent chance that they will be racially or ethnically different from each other. States like Maine and Vermont are the least diverse, with a diversity index of 4. New Mexico is the most diverse state, with an index of 60.

Basic Skills-Listening

Employers are looking for potential employees with good basic foundation skills. You can teach students to be good listeners by explaining to them the value of looking at the person speaking. If the listener doesn't pay attention to the speaker, important information may be missed. The Student Activity Worksheet, Basic Skills—Listening Checklist, in the School-To-Work/SCANS Activity

Worksheets, may be used as a guideline for discussion of listening skills. For a hands-on activity, invite a student to the front of the room to read the Global Perspectives in this chapter. Listeners should keep their books closed. When the speaker is finished, ask that person to leave the room. Now ask the listeners in the class to write down the details of what the reader was wearing. If listeners were paying attention to the speaker, they will note some details of the reader's appearance.

and buy will be produced. This answers the question, "How to produce?" Since people buy what they want and can afford in a market economy, they largely answer the question, "For whom to produce?"

OUR ECONOMIC SYSTEM

Were you able to identify our economy as you read the three types? If you selected "market economy," you were correct. The main differences among economic systems involve who owns the economic resources and who makes the decisions about production and distribution. Our system fits the definition of a market economy. But our economic system also has other names.

Another name for the economic system in the United States is capitalism. **Capitalism** means that economic resources are usually privately owned by individuals rather than by the government. Individual owners are free to decide what they will produce with the resources. This freedom of the individual to choose what to produce provides the rationale for another name: **free** or **private enterprise system**. The terms capitalism and free or private enterprise system mean the same thing. They refer to a system in which most economic resources are privately owned and decisions about production and distribution are largely made by **voluntary exchange** in the marketplace.

There are many aspects of our economic system that make it different from other systems of the world. You are aware that the words "freedom" and "individual choice" are frequently used in discussing our economy. The five major features, or rights, of our market economy are shown in Figure 2-2.

Private Enterprise

A **business** is an establishment or enterprise that supplies goods and services in exchange for payment in some form. The right of the individual to choose whether to own a business, what business to enter, and what to produce with only limited government direction is referred to as **private enterprise**. This private enterprise right ensures your freedom to decide how you will earn a living. In a private enterprise system, you may start or invest in any business you wish as long as you obey the law in doing so. You are free to choose to be a bricklayer, teacher, karate instructor, business owner, astronaut, dancer, or anything you strive for.

As a businessperson, you are generally free to offer goods and services at times, prices, and places of your choice. You are free to succeed or to fail in a business you select. Of course, there are some regulations that prevent you from performing activities that would harm others. For example, you may not dispose of chemical wastes in a way that would pollute the environment. Nor can you practice surgery unless you have been granted a medical license by the appropriate agency in the state in which you plan to practice surgery. These regulations are not designed to limit freedom but to protect people from harmful practices.

Private Property

If your family owns the home in which you live or the television set you watch, the family is enjoying the right of private property. The right of **private property** means you can own, use, or dispose of things of value. You may dispose of things you own by selling them, giving them away, or even by throwing them away. In our country, you can own any item and do what you want with it, as long as you do not violate a law in doing so. You also have the right to own, use, and sell whatever you invent or create.

One of the problems with the term "free enterprise" is that some think too much about "free" and too little about "enterprise"—the work required to succeed.

command-based systems that have changed or started to change to a market economy; e.g., China, Turkey, Russia, Argentina.)

RETEACH

People often debate issues that arise from the three basic economic questions, and newspapers often carry accounts of such debates. From reading the newspaper, have students choose an issue that illustrates one of the questions: What to produce? How to produce? For whom to produce?

As another reteaching activity, have students write a brief paragraph, using their own words and experiences, describing each type of economic system—custom, directed, and market. Whenever possible, students should use the computer for composing.

Students could also create a graphic organizer (such as a chart) to illustrate the five characteristics of our economic system.

ENRICH

Direct students to read the Global Perspectives in this chapter. Ask students to consider their part in our market economy. Ask them to identify the goods and services that they consume or the jobs they may hold. As another activity, students could conduct interviews with people in the community to establish how various groups of people view the term free enterprise and then report their findings. To compare our economic freedoms with those of other countries, have students ask friends and relatives who have lived in

Workplace Competencies-Resources

By acquiring competence at allocating resources, students learn to perform basic functions of management—planning, organizing, and controlling. Learning to allocate personal resources is a stepping stone for our students to learn how to allocate resources on the job. We can teach them how to allocate time by helping them understand that they must first iden-

tify the goals or tasks that must be completed and rank them in order of importance, estimate how much time it will take to complete each task, develop a schedule, and evaluate and adjust the schedule as appropriate. Assign students to read this chapter, complete the end-of-chapter activities, the assignments in the Activities and Projects, prepare for ExamView, and actually complete the exam.

SCANS

other countries about the freedoms they had and did not have. Perhaps it would be possible for several students to prepare a tape recording of an interview with an immigrant or international student. Students should prepare questions in advance that will bring out the similarities and differences in economic freedom and opportunity. Assurance should be made that the identity of the person interviewed would not be revealed without permission.

SUMMARIZE

To reinforce concepts learned, have students prepare an outline of the main ideas of this chapter. Discuss proper procedures for preparing an outline.

Much of the conceptual understanding of this chapter revolves around comprehension of the new vocabulary terms. Have your students make their own crossword puzzles using the Glossary as the basis for their definitions. After completing their crossword (with an answer key), have the creator exchange his or her paper with another student and complete the puzzle.

EVALUATE

- Assign Activities and Projects for Chapter 2.
- Administer the printed test or ExamView for Chapter 2.
- Assign School-To-Work/SCANS portfolio activities for Unit 1.

FEATURES OF THE U.S. MARKET ECONOMY

1. **Private Enterprise**

2. **Private Property**

3. **Profit**

4. **Competition**

5. **Freedom of Choice**

FIGURE 2-2 Why are freedom and private property critical to the success of the U.S. economy?

Businesses also have the right to own property. This property includes land, buildings, tools, and the goods the business produces. Businesses also have the right to use and dispose of their property in any lawful way.

Profit

Businesses supply goods and services to the marketplace for one main reason—to earn money. Unless business owners can expect to make a profit, they would not want to put time, energy, and money into an enterprise.

Critical Thinking Skills—Decision Making

Decision-making skills, which include specifying goals, generating alternatives, considering risks, and evaluating and choosing the best alternative, are applied throughout every chapter in this text. Each time a student participates in a Cooperative Learning Activity or Teams Activity, decision-making skills are applied in a group situation. For the end-of-chapter exercises, Communicate Business Concepts and Decision-Making Strategies, students must specify the goal of the activity, consider risks, and evaluate the best solution before completing the exercise.

Profit is the money left from sales after subtracting all the costs of operating the business. Business owners are entitled to make profits because they run the risk of losing the money they invested to start the business. They also face the extra hours of work and stress that are part of owning and running a business.

The desire to work hard and be creative to earn a higher profit is the **profit motive**. This profit motive also helps make our economy strong. Because of it, people are willing to invest money in a business and to develop new products to satisfy consumers' wants.

The profit motive is not the only reason for putting time, money, and effort into businesses. Some people enjoy bringing out new products or improving existing ones. Others get pleasure from knowing that the goods or services they produce make other people happier. Some individuals like the excitement of starting and running a new business. However, the profit motive is the heart of the private enterprise system.

Competition

You probably have seen television commercials that make you want to buy a "new" and "improved" product. A supermarket may claim in bold letters, "Ours are the lowest prices in town." An ad in a magazine urges you to buy the basketball shoes being modeled by a famous player. The rivalry among businesses to sell their goods and services to buyers is called **competition**.

This feature of a market economy gives you as a consumer the opportunity to make choices among countless goods and services that are available. You make these choices by comparing prices, quality, appearance, usefulness, and appeal of the goods and services you buy. And, if you are not satisfied with a purchase, you are free to buy from a competing business another time. Competition encourages business owners to improve products, offer better services, keep prices reasonable, and produce new things.

Freedom of Choice

The private enterprise system gives you the right to enter a business or career of your choice, to own property, to make a profit, and to compete. You also have other rights that contribute to your economic freedom of choice.

Sellers mark up the price of goods they purchase before selling them, but their profit is usually much less than the markup— sometimes only 1 percent on their sales.

Economic information web sites:
http://www.census.gov
http://www.econdata.net
http://www.your-nation.com
http://www.stls.frb.org/fred

E-Commerce for Economic Development

By many measures, the World Wide Web is not "world wide." In industrialized countries such as the United States, more than 50 percent of people have Internet access. In many developing economies, however, the Internet is available to fewer than 5 percent of the population.

As countries expand economic development, technology will help create more efficient production, faster distribution, and more effective information flow. These developing economies will encourage increased electronic connections among businesses and consumers. As the Internet growth rate increases around the globe, the U.S. is expected to have less than 50 percent of the worldwide Internet connections in the next few years.

Critical Thinking
Prepare a table summarizing the advantages and disadvantages of e-commerce for consumers and businesses.

Critical Thinking Skills-Problem Solving

Problem-solving skills, which include recognizing a problem and devising a plan of action, are applied throughout every chapter in this text. Each time a student participates in a Cooperative Learning Activity or Teams Assignment, problem-solving skills are applied in a group situation. When a student completes a math application in Calculate Business Data, decisions are made as to which mathematical approach must be taken. For each Technology Application problem, students must decide which template problem to use, which piece of software to load, and how to solve the problem.

Net Facts provides information and definitions of terms for the Internet. The more information that students have about the Internet, the better equipped they will be to use this resource. In the Internet Activity Masters, there is an Internet Activity Worksheet for each unit. You can use these activities to give students experience with finding information online. Options for assigning this activity are as follows:

1. **Provide students with a list of addresses of resources for this activity;**
2. **Assign students to conduct their own searches; or**
3. **Use the addresses provided on the Internet Activity Worksheet.**

You should complete the activity yourself before assigning it to resolve any discrepancies that may arise.

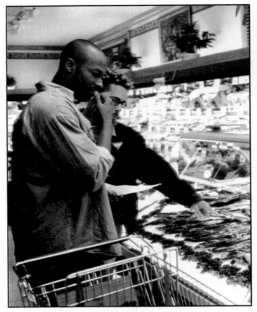

What advantages or disadvantages do you see with our market economy?

You have the right to buy where and what you please. The sale of some products and

An Internet address is a set of numbers or words that identifies a unique user or computer. Every user and computer on the Internet must have a different address so that the system knows where to send electronic mail and other data.

services that the government declares harmful to you, however, may be prohibited. Some products may have to carry a warning message.

There are a number of other rights that you have that you probably take for granted. You have the right as a worker to organize with other workers. Through such organization, you can strive to improve working

GLOBAL PERSPECTIVES

China "Frees" Enterprise

Would you expect to see Mercedes automobiles, mobile telephones, and DVDs in China? Would you expect thriving private shops alongside dreary state department stores? Well, that is happening today. There is an economic revolution under way—at least in certain parts of China. In cities such as Beijing, Shanghai, Guangzhou, and Shenzhen, some people earn many times the average Chinese income of $840 a year.

In Guangdong province on China's southern coast, thousands of businesses are run from neighboring Hong Kong. Hong Kong itself, which had the freest economy in the world under British rule until 1997, is now ruled by China. China has pledged to let it

remain capitalist. Meanwhile, Chinese organizations, many with ties to the government, have increased their ownership of Hong Kong enterprises.

Capitalism is still an exception in otherwise communist China. But the prosperity that private enterprise creates brings in foreign money and taxes to the central government, so it has been permitted.

Critical Thinking
1. What do you think will be the future of capitalism in Hong Kong?
2. What effect do you think this "experiment" will have on the rest of China? On countries that trade with China?

GLOBAL PERSPECTIVES

Display pictures of China. Use a map of China to show the location of Hong Kong and Guangdong Province.

CRITICAL THINKING

1. The future of capitalism in Hong Kong is very uncertain. While China very much wants to preserve the financial benefits of

Hong Kong's economy, eventually there are likely to be frictions caused by Chinese restrictions on individuals and businesses.
2. The Chinese government will probably continue to relinquish its role in central planning and will not be able to exercise the same degree of control over its citizens. Countries that trade with China will benefit if and when consumers throughout China have the resources necessary for purchasing goods and services not previously available to them.

conditions. You have the right to travel when and where you please in this country and to many other countries. You also have the right to express your opinions in newspapers, over radio and television, and in talking with others as long as you do not slander another person. The private enterprise system provides greater freedom of choice to the individual than any other economic system.

MIXED ECONOMIC SYSTEMS

An economic system usually gets its name from the way its economic resources are owned and controlled. But economies are complex and do not neatly fall under one category or another. In general, we think of most countries as having mixed economic systems.

Some countries combine government ownership and control of basic industries with some private ownership of consumer-goods businesses. In some countries, a limited amount of private enterprise is tolerated. For example, after farmers in some directed economies meet the government's quota for crop production, they are allowed to sell the rest of their crop in a free market and keep the profit.

In the United States there is some government regulation of business. There are also some government-operated enterprises, such as the post office, schools, and city water agencies. Our economic system is not pure capitalism, so it is often referred to as modified or mixed capitalism.

EMERGING MARKET ECONOMIES

The economic success of market economies has caused many countries to reexamine their economic systems. Many directed or controlled economies have not prospered in comparison to market economies. Directed economies are not designed to meet the wants and needs of individuals. In most controlled economies, workers with different skills and responsibilities receive similar wages. Therefore, there is little incentive for people to work hard.

The weaknesses of controlled economies have caused many nations throughout the world to change to market or mixed economies. The most notable example is the collapse of communism in the Soviet Union.

The Soviet Union was dominated by today's Russia. In the case of the Soviet Union, an entire generation was forced to do without many consumer goods such as cars, home appliances, and adequate housing. Emphasis was placed on industrial development. Today Russia is moving toward a market economy. Other countries once within the Soviet bloc, such as Poland, Hungary, and the Czech Republic, have made great strides toward establishing new economies. All of these economies now experience voluntary exchange and benefit from it.

One of the new "rights" that Laszlo now has is the "right to fail." There was a measure of security in his former economy. Laszlo knew how many shoes he would make and sell. Laszlo now does not know exactly how many of his shoes will sell. However, Laszlo has the potential to profit if his shoes are as good as or better than those of his competition. Free enterprise has given Laszlo an opportunity to succeed in the marketplace if he operates a dynamic business.

As in the old Soviet Union, what disadvantages exist with government ownership of industries?

Critical Thinking Skills-Visualizing

Visualizing, or being able to organize and process information, is a thinking skill we cannot ignore. Students need to learn how to visualize through the reading of information and observation of graphs, pictures, and other visuals. The feature Global Perspectives gives students an opportunity to visualize the various places around the globe that are described. This feature will also describe various business practices that are different around the world.

SCANS

REVIEW YOUR READING

1. (a) What goods and services are to be produced? (b) How should the goods and services be produced? (c) For whom should the goods and services be produced?
2. In a custom-based economy, things are produced in the same way they have always been produced. In a directed or planned economy, the government owns and controls the economic resources and makes all of the decisions regarding the production of goods and services. In a market economy, most economic resources are privately owned and decisions about production are largely made by free exchange in the marketplace.
3. The ownership and control of economic resources is in the hands of individuals, owners and managers of businesses, farmers, and citizens who own property.
4. Private enterprise, private property, profit, competition, and freedom of choice.
5. Profit is the difference between the selling price of a good or service and the cost of doing business. Business owners work harder and are more creative when they can keep the increased profits resulting from their extra efforts.
6. The right of private property gives the owner the right to own, use, and dispose of things of value.
7. Lower prices, higher quality, improved services, and new products.
8. People might want to operate their own businesses for their personal satisfaction and pride or because they get pleasure from producing goods and services that make other people's lives happier.
9. The right to buy where and what you please, the right as a worker to organize with other workers, the right to travel when and where you please, and the right to express your opinions.
10. A mixed economy is one that combines some of the features of two or more systems. Such a system is usually known by the name of the system whose features are dominant.
11. Market economies have prospered because of the success of these economies in satisfying the

BUSINESS NOTES

1. Every society must answer the questions: what to produce, how to produce, and for whom to produce.
2. There are three types of economic systems: custom-based, directed or controlled, and market.
3. The five important features of our market economy are private enterprise,
private property, profit, competition, and freedom of choice.
4. Economies are complex and do not fall easily and neatly into one category.
5. Market economies have replaced most controlled economies because of the successes of market economies around the world.

REVIEW YOUR READING

1. What are the three key economic questions that every society must answer to set up an economic system?
2. What are the major characteristics of the three types of economic systems?
3. Who owns and controls most economic resources in a system of capitalism?
4. What are the five features of a market economy?
5. What does the right to earn a profit influence a business owner to do?
6. What does the right of private property entitle the owner to do?
7. Give three ways in which consumers benefit from competition among businesses.
8. In addition to the profit motive, give two other reasons that might encourage people to invest their time, money, and energy in operating their own businesses.
9. In addition to private property and private enterprise, what are four other rights that are included in our economic freedom of choice?
10. Explain the nature of a mixed economy.
11. What are some reasons why market economies are becoming popular around the world?

COMMUNICATE BUSINESS CONCEPTS

12. How is the question of what goods and services will be produced determined under a custom-based system?
13. Who decides what will be produced in a directed, planned economic system?
14. Give examples showing how enterprises stay in business when they sell at higher prices the same goods and services sold by other businesses.
15. If you can choose any kind of work you wish under the right of free enterprise, why can't you
open a law office, practice dentistry, or pilot a plane when you feel you are ready to do so?
16. If the United States operated as pure capitalism, what changes might occur?
17. It has been said that the term "market" in our market economy refers to an idea and not to a place. What do you think this means?
18. Explain how the decisions of buyers and sellers in the marketplace largely answer the question of what to produce in our private enterprise system.

needs and wants of consumers. In controlled economies, workers often receive similar wages regardless of the contribution made to output or productivity. In a market economy, workers are paid according to their contribution to output (or for hard work).

COMMUNICATE BUSINESS CONCEPTS

12. The question of what to produce is usually not a problem; the people just keep producing what their parents and grandparents produced before them. Custom-based systems usually are found in less-developed countries.
13. Officials of the government decide what will be

19. Even though you have many freedoms under our economic system, there are many activities that you are not free to do. For example, you are not permitted to hunt and kill animals that are designated as endangered species. List several activities that you are not allowed to do in our society.

DEVELOP YOUR BUSINESS LANGUAGE

For each numbered item, find the term that has the same meaning.

20. A nation's plan for making decisions on what and how to produce and how to distribute goods and services.

21. An economic system in which goods are produced the way they have always been produced.

22. Buyers and sellers make their own economic decisions to determine what the price will be for goods and services produced and sold.

23. Any place where buyers and sellers exchange goods and services for some form of money.

24. The rivalry among businesses in selling to buyers.

25. The right of the individual to choose whether to own a business, what business to enter, and what to produce with only limited government direction.

26. The right to own, use, or dispose of things of value.

27. An economy in which individuals are free to engage in business transactions with buyers who are able and willing to buy and sellers who supply goods and services from which they earn a profit.

28. An economy in which resources are owned and controlled by the government.

29. The desire to work hard and be creative to earn a higher profit.

30. An economic system in which most economic resources are privately owned and decisions about production are largely made by free exchange in the marketplace.

31. Money left from sales after subtracting the cost of operating the business.

32. An establishment or enterprise that supplies goods and services in exchange for some form of payment.

KEY TERMS
business
capitalism (free or private enterprise system)
competition
custom-based economy
directed or planned economy
economic system
market economy
marketplace
private enterprise
private property
profit
profit motive
voluntary exchange

DECISION-MAKING STRATEGIES

Johakaim Jameson owns and operates a one-man deli. His regular and faithful customers love his "JJ Special." Recently he developed a new recipe and created his "Bountiful Muffin"—good tasting and nutritious. His new muffin is growing in popularity and is bringing in new customers. His problem: He can spend only four hours each day making "JJ Specials" and/or "Bountiful Muffins." He can make 50 specials in an hour and earns a 50-cent profit on each. He can make 60 muffins in an hour and can earn 60 cents on each.

33. How should Johakaim divide his production time between the "JJ Special" and the "Bountiful Muffin" to keep his profits up and to satisfy his customers?

34. If you were Johakaim, what are some things you could do to resolve this dilemma?

DEVELOP YOUR BUSINESS LANGUAGE

20. economic system
21. custom-based economy
22. voluntary exchange
23. marketplace
24. competition
25. private enterprise
26. private property
27. market economy
28. directed or planned economy
29. profit motive
30. capitalism (free or private enterprise system)
31. profit
32. business

deal with the public can be required to pass performance tests or health examinations or meet other standards.

16. If the United States operated as pure capitalism, many changes would be made. For example, we would not have government-operated post offices, schools, military, police, or road construction.

17. Some people refer to "market" as an idea rather than a place. The reason for this is that the word refers to both the concept of free exchange of goods as well as the actual transaction. We might speak of a supply of next year's wheat as the "market" even before the crop is planted. We might also speak of the "market" for a new product while the product is still on the drawing boards. Both uses of the term are correct.

18. Buyers in the marketplace largely answer the question of what to produce in the United States by giving their "dollar votes" to certain products and withholding them from others. The products that are bought will continue to be produced; the ones that are not bought will be forced out of the marketplace. Sellers produce those things that buyers want and buy.

19. Answers will vary. We are not permitted to do many things according to local, state, and federal laws. Among our limitations are the following examples: We are not permitted to fly an airplane without a license; park our cars in restricted places; burn rubbish in certain places; smoke in elevators, theaters, and public buildings; pollute our waterways or

produced. Communist governments typically determined what and how much would be produced through a central economic plan, which governed all of the country's industries.

14. Some firms stay in business by competing in ways other than lower prices. Examples will vary. Here are some acceptable ones: convenient location and 24-hour service (such as convenience stores), delivery service (such as gourmet and small food stores and caterers), and appeal to the ego (such as higher-priced cosmetics, which in their ads say "It costs more, but I'm worth it.").

15. To protect the public from unqualified individuals who might represent themselves as qualified specialists, licenses are required in certain professions or occupations. These licenses are granted to those who pass examinations or meet other requirements. This restriction applies to such workers as lawyers, doctors, dentists, nurses, teachers, hairstylists, etc. Bus drivers, airline pilots, and many others who

highways; build a store or factory where the law limits construction to residential housing; drive faster than the posted speed limit; or slander another person.

DECISION-MAKING STRATEGIES

33. There are several ways that Johakaim can approach this problem. He could divide his time equally and produce 100 specials and 120 muffins. His profit would be $110. If he makes only the specials, his profit would be $100; if he makes only the muffins, his profit would be $144. He would increase his profit by making only muffins, but his customers would be unhappy. It would seem that dividing his time equally would be one acceptable solution.

34. Other things that Johakaim could do include hiring some part-time workers to help him make more of both his special and his muffins. He might try to find a way to improve his production methods so that he can make more of each item. He might also try to find a way to spend less time on other business matters and more time on production of his specials and muffins.

CALCULATE BUSINESS DATA

35. (a) 34,350,000 − 4,380,000 = 29,970,000; (b) private enterprise system; (c) Each private enterprise worker supplied 42 more people than the worker in a planned system.

36. (a) Farm-to-You; price would be 97 cents (including 20-cents-off coupon). (b) Yes; without it she would pay 8 cents more at Kitchen Pride ($1.045 or $1.05). (c) Very likely; probably all prices were lower because of the three-store competition.

37. (a) 53.5 − 18.6 = 34.9 hours; (b) 24.7 − 18.6 = 6.1 hours; (c) Capital No. 1: 65 ÷ 8 = 8.125 days; Capital No. 2: 132 ÷ 8 = 16.5 days; Capital No. 3: 701 ÷ 8 = 87.625 days; (d) $650 ÷ 65 = $10 per hour.

TECHNOLOGY APPLICATION

In this activity, students use a computer to solve a business problem using a file provided on the data CD that

CALCULATE BUSINESS DATA

35. Countries that make efficient use of capital goods can produce more with fewer people in a shorter time than countries in which many workers perform the work by manual labor. Study the figures below for farm workers and their yearly output in two different kinds of economic systems; then answer the questions that follow.

    a. How many more people were working in agricultural jobs in the directed, planned economy than in the private enterprise system?

    b. In which system was each farm worker more productive?

    c. In terms of people supplied from the output of each farm worker, how much more productive was the worker cited in item (b)?

	Private Enterprise System	Directed, Planned System
Agricultural labor force	4,380,000	34,350,000
Number of people supplied with food from the output of each farm worker	49	7

36. Lani Oolan compares food prices in newspaper ads each week before doing her grocery shopping. One week she found these prices for Grade A eggs at three competing supermarkets: Food Mart, $1.09 per dozen; Farm-to-You, $1.17 per dozen and 20 cents off with a newspaper coupon; and Kitchen Pride, special, 2 dozen for $2.09.

    a. At which store would Lani pay the lowest price per dozen?

    b. Will the coupon be an advantage? Explain.

    c. Do you think the fact that there were three stores from which Lani could buy eggs benefited her in any way?

37. The table below shows the average number of working hours for a worker in three capital cities in different countries. Each worker lives under a different kind of economic system. The table shows how many hours an average plant worker would have to work to earn enough money to buy the items listed.

    a. How much longer than workers in Capital No. 1 must workers in Capital No. 3 work to earn enough to buy food for four for a week?

    b. How much longer than a worker in Capital No. 1 must a worker in Capital No. 2 work to earn enough to buy the weekly food needed?

    c. How many eight-hour days would a worker in each capital city have to work to earn enough to buy the color television?

    d. If the color television costs $650, what would workers' wages in Capital No. 1 be per hour?

	Capital No. 1	Capital No. 2	Capital No. 3
Hamburger meat, 1 lb.	17.0 min.	29.0 min.	56.0 min.
Color TV, large screen	65.0 hrs.	132.0 hrs.	701.0 hrs
Toothpaste	16.0 min.	13.0 min.	27.0 min.
Bus fare (2 mi.)	7.0 min.	11.0 min.	3.0 min.
Men's shoes (1 pair)	8.0 hrs.	7.0 hrs.	25.0 hrs.
Week's food for family of 4	18.6 hrs.	24.7 hrs.	53.5 hrs.

TECHNOLOGY APPLICATION

Using the *Intro to Business* Data CD and your database program software, select problem CH02. After the problem appears on your screen, complete the following activities. After you have completed each step, display or print a report for each activity. If you do not have a printer available, answer the questions before you leave the computer.

38. Select and list the ZIP Code areas in which the average household income was greater than or equal to $30,000. How many ZIP Codes are listed?

39. Sort the ZIP Code areas in descending order by population. Answer the following questions:

    a. What is the fourth ZIP Code area listed?

    b. What is the last ZIP Code area listed?

accompanies *Intro to Business*. Instructions for using the data CD are included in a **README** file on the disk. Solutions are provided on the Instructor's Resource CD.

40. Sort the database in ascending order by average monthly housing expenses. Answer the following questions:

    a. What is the first ZIP Code area listed?

    b. What is the fifth ZIP Code area listed?

COMMUNICATING for SUCCESS

INTRODUCTIONS—MORE THAN JUST A FIRST IMPRESSION

Introductions, whether presenting yourself or introducing others, set the tone and help determine the future of the relationship between those being introduced. In a business setting, the purpose of introductions is to lay the foundation for a working relationship between two or more people. Suggestions for an effective business introduction are:

- Offer a greeting, followed by the clear statement of your first and last name. ("Hello, my name is Amy Garcia.")
- If appropriate, tell how you prefer to be addressed. ("Please call me Amy.")
- Give your title and purpose for meeting. ("I'm the Director of Sales with Fashions Unlimited. I'd like to talk with you about carrying our line.")
- Present a firm handshake and make eye contact. Keep in mind that this step may be adapted for various cultures.
- Offer your business card.

Good methods for conducting introductions in a business meeting include:

- Ask everyone to introduce themselves, using names and titles. Begin with yourself.
- Introduce yourself as well as everyone else at the meeting.
- Ask one or more co-workers to introduce meeting participants.

Special attention to etiquette is necessary when making introductions with international or and cross-cultural individuals. Following are some techniques for effective international and cross-cultural introductions:

- Avoid using slang or jargon your listener may be offended by or not understand.
- Enunciate words carefully and speak a bit more slowly when addressing individuals whose first language is not English.
- Try to eliminate cultural stereotypes you may believe in. Focus on the individual.
- Avoid gestures—some could be offensive to the listener.
- If you have the opportunity, study the individual's cultural background to be aware of appropriate conventions for introductions.

It is important to be culturally sensitive when making introductions, as different groups of people have different rules of etiquette. If you are not prepared, you could lose their business.

CRITICAL THINKING

1. What is the purpose of a business introduction?
2. What are some suggestions for an effective business introduction?

COMMUNICATING for SUCCESS

Communications skills will help ensure students' success in the business world. Communicating for Success introduces workplace/interpersonal communications issues and proper uses of communications technology. Each feature discusses a key communications topic, and contains two Critical Thinking questions that require students to analyze what they have learned.

Since most students will very likely be applying for various jobs or positions in organizations in the near future, they need to learn the importance of person-to-person introductions. For many of them, their only prior experience with introductions has been in informal settings with family or friends. Communicating for Success details the components of good formal introductions and explains why introductions are critical building blocks for future business relationships. Critical Thinking questions require them to rethink and review the material they've just read.

CRITICAL THINKING

1. The purpose of business introductions is to lay the foundation for a working relationship between two or more people.
2. Some suggestions for an effective business introduction are:
   - Offer a greeting, followed by the clear statement of your first and last name.
   - If appropriate, tell how you prefer to be addressed.
   - Give your title and purpose for meeting.
   - Present a firm handshake and make eye contact. Keep in mind that this step may be adapted for various cultures.
   - Offer your business card.

As people go through their daily lives, they play many different roles. People assume the roles of consumers, workers, and citizens. Most people play more than one economic role at a time.

Resources for Teachers
- Lesson Plans
- School-To-Work/SCANS Activity Masters
- Spanish Resources
- Instructor's Resource CD

Assessment
- Chapter and Unit Tests, Ch. 3
- ExamView, Ch. 3

Media/Technology
- Applying Technology Data CD
- PowerPoint slides
- Business Connection CD
- Videotape

Activity Masters and Workbooks
- Activities and Projects, Ch. 3
- Internet Activity Masters
- Business Math Activity Masters
- Communications Activity Masters
- International Business Activity Masters
- Ethics Activity Masters

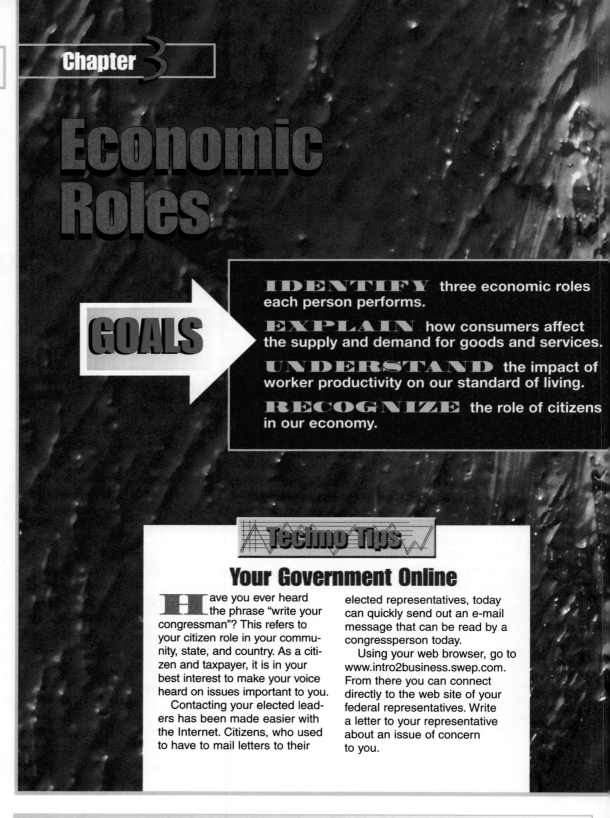

Chapter 3

Economic Roles

GOALS

IDENTIFY three economic roles each person performs.

EXPLAIN how consumers affect the supply and demand for goods and services.

UNDERSTAND the impact of worker productivity on our standard of living.

RECOGNIZE the role of citizens in our economy.

Techno Tips

Your Government Online

Have you ever heard the phrase "write your congressman"? This refers to your citizen role in your community, state, and country. As a citizen and taxpayer, it is in your best interest to make your voice heard on issues important to you.

Contacting your elected leaders has been made easier with the Internet. Citizens, who used to have to mail letters to their elected representatives, today can quickly send out an e-mail message that can be read by a congressperson today.

Using your web browser, go to www.intro2business.swep.com. From there you can connect directly to the web site of your federal representatives. Write a letter to your representative about an issue of concern to you.

Students need to know the latest technologies and develop cutting edge Internet skills for use in current jobs, future careers, or in their homes. TechnoTips introduces students to today's cutting edge technologies and provides them with important Internet skills. Feature topics concentrate on Internet-specific technologies and computer or other hi-tech innovations for use by businesses and consumers. At the www.intro2business.swep.com web site, students can complete the activity for this chapter.

FOCUS ON REAL LIFE

Gianfranco left his college campus right after his ten o'clock accounting class. He hurried to catch the bus so he would arrive at his part-time job on time. He works as a bank teller to earn money for college. He is also gaining work experience to go along with his accounting major. After work, he bought a new shirt that he needed. That evening, he reviewed in the newspaper issues to be decided in the next day's election. In the morning before class, he went to the polling place to cast his vote for a school levy. He also voted for a city council woman who showed support for environmental issues that Gianfranco believes are important. He may not be aware of it, but he performed three economic roles. Can you identify the three roles?

ECONOMIC ROLES YOU PERFORM

You also have three economic roles to play. A look at Gianfranco's activities will help you to identify those roles. As a consumer, he purchased a good (shirt) and a service (bus transportation). As a worker, he helped provide a service as a bank teller. As a citizen, Gianfranco voted on an economic issue (school levy) and supported a candidate.

You and everyone you know will play many different roles in life. You may become a famous recording star, a business executive, or even the president of the United States. A friend of yours may become a coach, an electrician, a minister, or a computer programmer. While you and your friend may follow different career paths, some of the roles you play will be the same.

The three roles that all people share are those of consumer, worker, and citizen. It is true that some people do not work outside the home for wages, and some people may not exercise their right to vote. However, we all are affected in some way by these three economic roles. As you perform these roles, you will make decisions that affect not only you, but the entire economy as well. Understanding how the private enterprise system works will help you understand the importance of your decisions—and may even help you make better ones—in each of your economic roles. It will also help you understand how your roles fit into the U.S. economy.

YOUR CONSUMER ROLE

We have a market economy in which buyers and sellers freely make economic decisions in the marketplace. These decisions basically answer the question of what will be produced. The buying decisions of all consumers—individuals, businesses, and governments—provide the answer to how we will use our scarce resources. The important role you and all other consumers play in making these decisions is one of the most interesting characteristics of our system.

Individual buying decisions have a great influence on our market economy. Individual consumers buy more than two-thirds of all goods and services produced. It is easy to see that consumers play a central role in our economic system.

It may seem to you that the United States economy is a big, unorganized system in which everyone does just about as he or she pleases. You may wonder how the system can work when each business makes its own decision about what to produce and each buyer makes a decision about what and where to buy. But the system does work and it works well. Let's explore how your consumer decisions affect the system.

Chapter 3 *Economic Roles* **31**

FOCUS ON REAL LIFE

To get students started, write the following question on the board or overhead: What experiences have you had as a consumer in our market economy? as a worker? as a citizen? Record students' responses to the question on the board or chart paper. You may wish to ask the same question at the end of the chapter and compare how students' responses may have changed.

MOTIVATE

PURPOSE Preview the key terms and have students write the ones with which they are unfamiliar on a sheet of paper. Then have them find each of those words, and briefly review the definition. Next, have students locate the major chapter headings that relate to each of the goals. Have students write a study question for each goal.

TEACH/APPLY

MAKE CONNECTIONS Before students read Chapter 3, ask them to define market economy, basing their definitions on information they learned in Chapter 2. Then have students consider their part in the market economy. Ask them to think about the goods and services they consume or the jobs they hold.

Show PowerPoint 3-2, *Economic Roles You Perform*. Discuss each of the three economic roles and how each is important in our economy. Ask students to come up with additional examples of how these roles are played.

Remind students that the term "dollar vote" really means "money vote." Students should make a list of five "dollar votes" that they cast within the past week. When demand is high, buyers sometimes have to go to two or more stores to cast dollar votes for the item desired. Was that the case for any item(s) students identified? If so, ask students the reason for short supply of the item(s) in demand. To help students understand how prices are determined in a market, ask them to find a store with merchandise on sale and investigate why the prices have been lowered. List on the board the reasons they discovered, which might include end-of-season clearance; manufacturer's close out; and over-stocked, overpriced, or damaged merchandise.

Ask students to give examples of different types of competition observed or experienced. Have students examine newspaper and TV ads and list different methods of competing. Discuss the effect of competition on keeping prices reasonable.

Select a student volunteer to define productivity (a measure of output per worker per unit of time) in a sentence. Discover if students are familiar with the term assembly line. Is dividing up the production tasks and then having each worker specialize in only a few operations an effective way to increase productivity?

Net Facts provides information and definitions of terms for the Internet. The more information that students have about the Internet, the better equipped they will be to use this resource. In the Internet Activity Masters, there is an Internet Activity Worksheet for each unit. You can use these activities to give students experience with finding information online. Options for assigning this activity are as follows:

1. **Provide students with a list of addresses of resources for this activity;**
2. **Assign students to conduct their own searches; or**
3. **Use the addresses provided on the Internet Activity Worksheet.**

You should complete the activity yourself before assigning it to resolve any discrepancies that may arise.

Dollar Votes Help Create Demand

As a consumer, you help businesses make their decisions. You do this by buying—or not buying—certain goods and services. When you buy something, you are casting a dollar vote for it. You are saying to a business, "I like this product or service, and I'm willing to pay for it." When a business receives your dollar votes and those of other consumers, it knows the demand for its products. **Demand** means the quantity of a product or service that consumers are willing and able to buy at a particular price.

Demand Helps Determine Supply

Knowing the demand tells a business what type and what quantity of products and services to supply. **Supply** means the quantity of a product or service that businesses are willing and able to provide at a particular price. Suppliers usually will produce a product or service as long as it can be sold at a price that covers the costs of operating the business to make and sell it, plus a reasonable profit. This is why you can buy a hamburger for about $1.50, but you will not find any for 35 cents. Suppliers of hamburgers could not cover their costs and make a profit at the 35-cent price.

Together, supply and demand play an important part in our market economy. The buyers and sellers in the marketplace help to determine not only what will be produced, but also what the price will be.

The Internet is not a single network but a super network made up of tens of thousands of smaller networks around the world.

Demand and Supply Affect Prices

Have you ever wondered how a business decides what price to charge for a product or service? Why does a sweater cost $60 and a new car $15,000? Why does the price of a swimsuit drop in the fall of the year or the cost of food go up after a long summer's drought? Shortages of a product affect supply and prices.

A business must decide what price to charge for a product or service. The price cannot be too high, or consumers won't buy. But if it's too low, there will be no profit. Generally speaking, prices are carefully determined after a good deal of study.

The demand for a product affects the price. If many people want (or demand) a particular product or service, its price will tend to go up. Holiday cards are priced higher in November and early December when many people want to buy them. Have you noticed, however, that the prices of the cards are often cut in half the day after a holiday? When demand is low, prices are usually lower.

Supply also affects the price of a product. Remember that a supplier needs to cover the costs of operating the business and make a reasonable profit. Prices are set to do these two things. If a supplier of jogging shoes, for example, sets a price too high, people will not buy the shoes. Therefore, the supplier will have to lower the price in order to sell the shoes. Of course, if the price is set too low, operating costs will not be covered. Then the supplier will lose money and soon go out of business. All this means that the supplier must produce a good product and operate in an efficient way. Prices can then be set at reasonable levels so that consumers will be willing and able to buy the products.

Personal Qualities-Self-Esteem

Self-esteem, or believing in one's own self-worth and maintaining a positive view of one's self, is a personal quality that we cannot ignore. It is important that students know who they are and believe in themselves in order to be productive in society. One important contributor to self-esteem is one's culture. It is important for students to understand not only their own cultures, but the cultures of those with whom they work. The Cultural Perspectives describe various cultures and their contributions to our current economic system. This feature offers an opportunity to encourage discussion of students and their cultural backgrounds. The discussion can be expanded by asking students to write down a description of themselves by asking, "Who am I?"

Of course, other factors may be involved in the pricing process. The prices of some products tend to stay high, for example, because the materials from which they are made are limited by nature. Diamonds have been found in only a few countries of the world and in relatively small quantities. Therefore, the price of diamonds is high.

Competition Keeps Prices Reasonable

Competition helps keep prices at a reasonable level. Businesses must set prices to cover operating costs and to earn a reasonable profit. But what is to prevent a seller from charging an unreasonably high price in order to earn larger profits? The answer is competition. Competition is one of the main characteristics of the private enterprise system. If one store offers CDs for $12.95 but another offers the same CDs for less, you probably would say to the merchant with the higher

price, "Forget it. I can buy that same CD at a store down the street for $10.95." If the owners of the store keep the price at $12.95, and do not compete in other ways—such as delivery or other services—they will soon go out of business because not many people will buy CDs at the higher price.

YOUR WORKER ROLE

Competition affects prices in another way, too. When a product has a very high demand and is making money for one supplier, other businesspeople will begin to offer the product also. With several businesses offering the

Discuss the different ways communities pay for public goods. Some communities charge small fees for the use of pools, skating rinks, and the like, while others charge nothing. Public goods must be paid for through fees or taxes. Fees, however, limit access to those who cannot afford to pay.

TRY THIS/GUIDED PRACTICE
Write the following statement on the board: "Dollar votes tell producers what consumers want." Tell students that this is to be the headline of a brief newspaper article on the role of the consumer in a market economy. Guide students through the process of writing a short article based on the headline.

Direct students to list on a sheet of paper three headings: National, State, Local. Guide students through the identification process and record goods and services provided by each level of government.

EXPLORE THIS/INDEPENDENT PRACTICE Students should find an article that illustrates how a change in demand or in supply changed the price of a particular good or service. Explain how that price change helps determine what is produced, how it is produced, and for whom it is produced.

ASSESS

Review the goals at the beginning of the chapter, and the Business Notes at the end. Restate each of the Business Notes as a question and have students respond orally. For students who may have difficulty providing answers, assign the reteaching activities that follow. Enrichment activities may also be assigned.

CULTURAL PERSPECTIVES

The Legacy of Arabic Numerals

Did you know that the numbers we use today are of Arabic origin? Arabic numerals are 0, 1, 2, 3, 4, 5, 6, 7, 8, 9 and are based on a value of 10. Combining these various numbers creates other numbers with different values. Because these Arabic numbers are based on 10, we are able to write numbers in columns and perform mathematical operations.

Early civilizations did not always use Arabic numbers. Other numbering systems, such as Roman numerals, were used instead. Roman numerals are based on letters such as I, V, X, L, C, D, and M. These letters represent various values, and when several letters are combined, a number is represented. Roman numerals are not based on 10 as are Arabic numerals.

Therefore, a column of Roman numerals is difficult to add.

Muslims added the symbol for zero to a system that they borrowed from Indian mathematicians. As the Muslims conquered other lands, they spread the idea of their new number system. The Arabic numbers we use today are based on that system. Thanks to the contributions of Muslims to the development of mathematics, we use a system of numbers that is easy to write and easy to use.

Critical Thinking
1. What is the importance of Arabic numerals in performing mathematical calculations?
2. Can you think of examples in our society where Roman numerals are still used?

CULTURAL PERSPECTIVES

This Cultural Perspectives feature will expose students to the concept that our society is composed of people from many different cultural backgrounds.

To further explore this cultural feature, "walk" students through a brief description of how to write Roman numerals (I=1, V=5, X=10, L=50, C=100, D=500, M=1,000).

Encourage students to investigate Islamic achievements in mathematics, astronomy, geography, and medicine that eventually benefited our society.

CRITICAL THINKING
1. We can write about any whole number, no matter how long, using only ten digits.
2. One example is their use in formal outlines.

The careers listed in Career Highlights come from the *Occupational Outlook Handbook*, online at www.bls.gov/oco. The O*NET code for Statistical Assistant is 43-9111.00.

1. What are your three roles in our free enterprise system? (Answer: Consumer, worker, and citizen.)
2. How do consumers affect the demand for and supply of goods and services? (Answer: The "dollar votes" of consumers guide businesses in their decisions about what to produce. When a business receives your dollar votes and those of all other consumers, it knows the demand for its product. Knowing the demand tells a business what type and what quantity of goods and services to supply.)
3. What is the importance of worker productivity on our standard of living? (Answer: Productivity indicates the quantity of a good that an average worker can produce in an hour. Productive workers help increase the overall standard of living of our nation.)
4. What is the role of citizens in our economy? (Answer: Citizens collectively decide how some of our scarce resources will be used and what will be provided for the common good.)

CAREER HIGHLIGHTS

A *statistical assistant* compiles and computes data according to statistical formulas used in statistical tests, performs mathematical computations, and compiles charts and graphs used by economists and marketing research analysts.

Name several ways that your worker role benefits you and others.

product, one of the suppliers could not afford to sell at extremely high prices. Consumers would go to the competitors to buy. This also tends to cause suppliers to produce goods and services efficiently. If a supplier cannot produce the product at a low cost so that it can be sold at competing prices, other suppliers who do so will get all of the business and the inefficient producer will be forced out of the market. In this way, competition tends to allow only efficient producers—those who can supply good products at competitive prices—to survive in the marketplace. Competition, then, aids the consumer by helping to keep prices and profits at reasonable levels.

No matter what price is set on products and services in the marketplace, you cannot enjoy the products and services unless you have the money to buy them. This is where your worker role comes into the picture.

Your Standard of Living
Your standard of living is affected by the money you earn as a worker. Most people work to earn money. You will earn money for a variety of reasons. The main reason will be

to buy the things you need and want. At this point in your life, most of your needs are provided by others: parents, guardians, or relatives. Before long, you will be meeting your own needs with the money you earn. Your success as a worker will be the most important factor in determining your standard of living. The term **standard of living** refers to the way you live as measured by the kinds and quality of goods and services you can afford. You use your earnings to buy the things you need to maintain and improve your standard of living. Your worker role, then, supports your consumer role.

Your Productivity as a Worker
The main way we improve our standard of living is to produce more as workers. One of the reasons this country has progressed so far in such a short time is that it has had a varied and skilled work force. We have provided this work force with technological advancements that have increased our productivity (see Figure 3-1). **Labor** (or **worker**) **productivity** refers to the quantity of a good that an average worker can produce in an hour. High productivity has enabled this country to achieve a standard of living that is among the highest in the world.

About two-thirds of the dollars teenagers spend is their own money earned from jobs or received as gifts and allowances.

As a worker, you will want to improve your productivity so that you can increase your earnings and your standard of living. Productive workers help increase the overall standard of living of our nation.

YOUR CITIZEN ROLE

So far, you have considered how you will satisfy your own wants and needs through your worker and consumer roles. But there are some needs and wants that you will not be able to satisfy for yourself.

As a citizen, you pay taxes. Your community uses the taxes collected to provide public goods, such as schools, parks, and civic centers where plays and concerts are performed. **Public goods** are something needed by a community and provided by its government. Public goods make a community a better place in which to live by improving the quality of life for everyone.

As a citizen, Gianfranco joined other citizens in making some economic decisions for the common good. He wanted to help assure quality schools for the children of his community. He wanted to help preserve the environment. His citizenship role allowed him to do that when he cast his vote.

Name several ways that public goods and services benefit you.

Your citizen role will allow you to make these kinds of decisions in your community as well. This process is known as *collective decision making*. As citizens, we decide collectively how some of our scarce resources will be used and what will be provided for our common use. As a citizen, you should remember that government cannot supply all that you and other people want. It, too, must make choices as to which services it can afford to provide. A great variety of services are provided by local, state, and national governments.

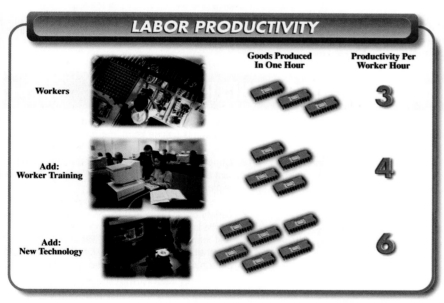

LABOR PRODUCTIVITY

		Goods Produced In One Hour	Productivity Per Worker Hour
Workers			3
Add: Worker Training			4
Add: New Technology			6

FIGURE 3-1
In what ways has your own productivity been improved by training or new technology?

Chapter 3 *Economic Roles* 35

Critical Thinking Skills-Problem Solving

Problem-solving skills, which include recognizing a problem and devising a plan of action, are applied throughout every chapter in this text. Each time a student participates in a Cooperative Activity or Teams Activity, problem-solving skills are applied in a group situation. Each time a student completes a math application in Calculate Business Data, decisions are made as to which mathematical approach must be taken. For each Technology Application problem, students must decide which template problem to use, which piece of software to load, and how to solve the problem. Emphasize to students how they use problem solving in their day-to-day tasks. Make them aware of the skills that they are developing.

REVIEW YOUR READING

1. The three economic roles are consumer, worker, and citizen.

2. When a person buys a product, or gives it a dollar vote, she or he is giving a message to the business that supplies it that she or he likes that product. All the dollar votes of all the purchasers added together tell the business the demand. From the demand, the business knows what and how much to produce.

3. A high demand for wheat generally will cause the price of wheat and all things made from wheat, such as bread, to rise. Conversely, a low demand will generally cause prices to be lower. Suppliers set their prices to cover their costs and make some profit. Consider "boom boxes," for example. If prices are set too high, people will not buy, the suppliers will be stuck with boom boxes, and they will have to lower the price to sell them. If suppliers set prices too low, even though sales might be high, costs and profit will not be covered. The suppliers will either have to raise prices or risk going out of business.

4. Suppliers usually set their prices to cover the costs of producing the good or service and to make a profit.

5. A business that has an oversupply of a product would likely lower the price to get more people to buy the product.

6. Prices of a product made with scarce natural resources, such as jewelry made of gold, tend to be high.

7. Answers will vary. Competition usually causes prices to be lowered. For example, if one store offers notebook paper for $2.19 for a 200-sheet pack and a nearby store offers the same pack for $1.79, the first store will probably lower the price. It should be noted, however, that the store that sells the paper for the higher price might compete in other ways, such as delivery service, and not lower the price.

8. The fast-food business is a good example of the way in which competition helps keep businesses operating efficiently. When products, such as buffalo wings and bacon-cheeseburgers, sell well at one fast-food restaurant, others will offer the same at better prices

Chapter REVIEW

BUSINESS NOTES

1. Everyone plays the economic roles of consumer, worker, and citizen.
2. Consumers vote with their dollars in favor of goods or services provided by businesses; thus, successful businesses must be responsive to the needs and wants of consumers.
3. Worker productivity is an important factor in advancing our nation's standard of living.
4. As a citizen, you join with other citizens in making some economic decisions for the common good.

REVIEW YOUR READING

1. State the three economic roles that most people in the United States perform.
2. Explain the way your dollar votes help to create demand.
3. Give one example each to show how demand and supply affect prices.
4. Suppliers usually set their prices to cover what two factors?
5. If a business has overstocked a product, would it be likely to raise or lower the price of the product?
6. Would the price of a product made with scarce natural resources tend to be high or low?
7. What effect does competition have on prices?
8. Give an example to show how competition tends to make businesses more efficient.
9. In what way does your worker role support your consumer role?
10. In what way might your selection of a career affect your future standard of living?
11. Give one example to show the importance of productivity in your worker role.
12. Give two examples of activities you perform in your citizenship role.

COMMUNICATE BUSINESS CONCEPTS

13. When the demand for small cars increases, what might the suppliers of large models do to sell their cars?
14. Name two products other than those cited in the text that are usually high-priced because they are scarce.
15. Discuss the importance of the consumer in a market economy.
16. If workers produce fewer goods and services than they are expected to produce, what effect will their lowered productivity have on the nation's standard of living?
17. Since Americans have the freedom to make individual choices in the marketplace, why would they make some decisions collectively?
18. Choosing your career is one of the most important economic decisions you will make. Can you explain why?
19. In your citizenship role, you will be performing a variety of activities in addition to voting on economic issues. After discussing this with friends and members of your family, list several activities that a good citizen does for either his or her personal satisfaction or for the common good.

or find a new product to compete with. To keep the business operating profitably, the original supplier must find ways to cut operating costs or offer other competitive features to continue to attract customers.

9. Because most people work to earn money to buy goods and services, their worker roles support their consumer roles and allow them to participate in the marketplace. This makes choosing a career very important.

10. The career one chooses, in setting level of income, will influence the standard of living a person is able to afford. Measured in terms of how many goods and services a person can buy, the standard of living is often equated with a career.

11. Productivity is important in the worker role because to a large extent it determines what income a person will have. If the standard of assembling calculators in your factory is 12 units per hour, and you assemble only an average of 5 units per hour, you are lowering

DEVELOP YOUR BUSINESS LANGUAGE

For each numbered item, find the term that has the same meaning.

20. The quantity of a good an average worker produces in one hour.

21. The quantity of a product or service that businesses are willing and able to provide at a particular price.

22. A measure of how well people in a country live—the quantity and quality of wants and needs that are satisfied.

23. The quantity of a product or service that consumers are willing and able to buy at a particular price.

24. Things that are needed and provided by a community and are equally accessible to everyone.

KEY TERMS
demand
labor (or worker) productivity
public goods
standard of living
supply

DECISION-MAKING STRATEGIES

Comparable worth means that people should receive equal pay for jobs that require similar levels of education, training, and skills. Comparable worth can be difficult to assess. Take the following situation as an example.

Amelia has worked on her job only three years. She turns out six more "gizmos" every hour than her co-worker, Jothan, who has been on the job for five years. Yet Jothan's salary is the same as Amelia's. Amelia feels cheated. Jothan has more education and training than Amelia and, therefore, has been assigned to troubleshoot the production process when problems occur. Jothan feels that he deserves to be paid a higher salary.

25. Should Amelia and Jothan receive the same salary? Why or why not?

26. Can you think of a measurement system other than the number of "gizmos" produced per hour for evaluating job performance?

CALCULATE BUSINESS DATA

27. The Video Rental Center purchased 24 dozen video tapes of a blockbuster new movie, at a cost of $20 per tape, to sell during the Christmas season.

    a. How many individual tapes did Video Rental Center buy?

    b. What was the total cost of the tapes?

    c. In January, the shop had one-fourth of the tapes left. How many tapes were unsold?

    d. If demand had dropped after the holidays, would the shop be more likely to increase or decrease the price to sell the tapes?

28. The following table shows information about the voting activity of young people in three national election years. Year Two was a presidential election year; Year One and Year Three were congressional election years. Study the data and answer the questions that follow.

    a. How many 18- to 20-year-olds voted in each year?

    b. How many 18- to 20-year-olds reported they registered but did not vote in Year Three?

    c. How many more 18- to 20-year-olds

Year	Number of People Age 18 to 20 Years Old (in Millions)	Percent Reporting They Are Registered to Vote	Percent Reporting They Voted
One	12.1	35.0%	19.8%
Two	11.2	47.0	36.7
Three	10.7	35.4	18.6

the productivity for the entire factory and increasing the cost per unit. If other workers in other factories also are less productive than expected, the whole economy will be affected. Workers will earn less and therefore can satisfy fewer needs and wants, thus lowering their standard of living.

12. Answers will vary. Examples of activities in the economic citizenship role are paying taxes through which public goods and services are purchased and voting on economic issues, such as a property tax increase to pay for a certain community project.

COMMUNICATE BUSINESS CONCEPTS

13. Answers will vary. Some typical answers will be: lower the price, offer premiums (gifts) to buyers, give a longer guarantee than standard, give a higher trade-in price.

DEVELOP YOUR BUSINESS LANGUAGE

20. labor or worker productivity
21. supply
22. standard of living
23. demand
24. public goods

14. Answers will vary. Examples of correct answers will be gold jewelry, silverware, and diamonds and other precious stones.

15. The consumer has a great deal of influence on what is to be produced in a market economy. Because consumers in the aggregate buy more than two-thirds of all the goods and services produced in the United States, consumer decisions in the marketplace have more influence than any other factor. Positive examples are television sets and McDonald's hamburgers. Negative examples are the Ford Edsel and the "new" Coke, both of which were rejected by consumers.

16. If workers produce fewer goods and services than their employers expect of the average worker, the cost of each unit produced will increase and prices to consumers will rise. When prices rise, consumers are less able to buy goods and services to satisfy their needs and wants, and their standard of living is lowered. When many workers produce less than expected, the standard of living of the entire nation is affected.

17. Even though Americans are free to make choices, it is to their advantage to make some group, or collective, decisions. For example, individuals cannot furnish their own police protection, fire protection, roads, schools, or other similar services. They therefore need to make collective decisions regarding situations that affect great numbers of people.

18. Choosing a career is one of the most important decisions a person makes because the choice will influence the remainder of one's life. Because a career usually determines level of income, and income often determines standard of living, choosing a career is important to one's economic future. In addition, choosing a career is important to the psychological well-being of the individual. A person is not usually happy in a job for which he or she is not suited by ability and interests.

19. Students might cite such activities as helping to prevent pollution, and cleaning around school grounds or public buildings.

DECISION-MAKING STRATEGIES

25. Students might have a variety of reasons for agreeing or disagreeing with Amelia and Jothan. Here are some possible answers: Amelia's productivity may suggest that she be paid more than her co-worker. However, many employers establish a pay rate and have increases based on longevity. If her employer gave merit increases, Amelia very likely would be paid more. Basically, she is not being cheated per se, but there is some basis for a feeling of wage inequality. Jothan is in a position similar to Amelia's. Jothan may have been hired at a higher wage rate because of his additional training and education; therefore, he has no strong basis now for wanting more pay.

26. Answers will vary. A common method today involves the employee and employer setting goals for the job, figuring out how to tell whether the goals have been met, determining how the employee will achieve the goals, and setting a time limit for them to be met.

CALCULATE BUSINESS DATA

27. (a) 24 × 12 = 288 tapes bought; (b) 288 × $20 = $5,760 total cost of the tapes; (c) 288 ÷ 4 = 72 tapes unsold; (d) decrease.

28. (a) 12,100,000 × 0.198 = 2,395,800 voted in Year One; 11,200,000 × 0.367 = 4,110,400 voted in Year Two; 10,700,000 × 0.186 = 1,990,200 voted in Year Three; (b) 10,700,000 × 0.354 = 3,787,800 registered; 3,787,800 − 1,990,200 = 1,797,600 registered but did not vote in Year Three; (c) 4,110,400 − 2,395,800 = 1,714,600; (d) Answers will vary. Typically, this applies to the whole population. Political activity, the national conventions, and campaigning stimulate more media coverage and interest in presidential election years. There is often a vigorous attempt to register voters.

29. (a) $3,007,000,000 − 2,275,000,000 = $732,000,000

---

reported they voted in the presidential election year than in Year One?

  d. Why do you think so many more voted in a presidential election year than in a congressional election year?

29. Diamonds are called precious gems because they are so scarce. Diamonds are used not only in jewelry but also in industrial production for cutting and grinding other materials. They are found in only a few places in the world. The leading producers are South Africa, Zaire, Botswana, and Russia. The table shows the diamonds imported by the United States in two recent years.

  a. What was the increase in value of the imported diamonds in Year Two over Year One?

  b. What was the percent of increase in the carat weight of the imported diamonds in Year Two over Year One?

Year	Volume (in Millions)	Value (in Millions)
One	6.3 carats	$2,275
Two	8.2 carats	$3,007

TECHNOLOGY APPLICATION

Using the *Intro to Business* Data CD and your spreadsheet program software, select problem CH03. After the problem appears on your screen, complete the following activities. Then, after you have completed each step, display or print the completed spreadsheet or graph for each activity. If you do not have a printer available, answer the questions before you leave the computer.

30. You are planning to attend a concert. The Demand Table in problem CH03 shows how many tickets you would be willing to buy for yourself and your friends at different possible prices per ticket. For example, you would be willing to buy 11 tickets at a price of $15 each. Using the Demand Table, create a graph with Quantity of Concert Tickets Demanded on the *x*-axis. Looking at your graph from left to right, does the line slope downward or upward?

31. Another student at your school is selling concert tickets as part of a fund-raising drive. The student who is selling must choose a price at which to sell the tickets. The Supply Table in problem CH03 shows how many tickets the seller would be willing to supply at different possible prices per ticket. For example, the seller would be willing to sell 11 tickets at a

price of $45 each. Using both the Demand Table and the Supply Table, make a graph with the Quantity of Concert Tickets on the x-axis, Price of Tickets Demanded in one range, and Price of Tickets Supplied in another range. Answer the following questions:

  a. What is the Quantity of Concert Tickets at the point at which the two graphs intersect?

  b. What is the Price of Tickets at the point at which the two graphs intersect?

32. Go to the part of problem CH03 in which the following four columns appear: Price of Tickets, Quantity of Concert Tickets Supplied, Quantity of Concert Tickets Demanded, and Supply–Demand. Enter formulas in the column Supply–Demand. For each row, the formula should subtract the Quantity of Concert Tickets Demanded from the Quantity of Concert Tickets Supplied. Answer the following questions:

  a. What is the value of Supply–Demand at a price of $30?

  b. How does this result compare to your answers to Question 31?

increase in value; (b) 8.2 − 6.3 = 1.9 amount of increase; 1.9 ÷ 6.3 = 0.3015 or 30% increase over Year One.

TECHNOLOGY APPLICATION

In this activity, students use a computer to solve a business problem using a file provided on the data CD that accompanies *Intro to Business*. Instructions for using the data CD are included in a **README** file on the disk. Solutions are provided on the Instructor's Resource CD.

LEVELS OF ECONOMIC DEVELOPMENT

Some people travel on a "bullet" train to manage a computer network in a high-rise building. Others go by oxcart to a grass hut to operate a hand loom to make cloth for family members and people in their village.

These differences in living and work environments reflect the level of economic development. Nations with extensive, modern business activity are commonly called *industrialized countries*. They have highly educated populations and use technology for production and distribution.

In contrast, *less-developed countries* (LDC) have very little economic wealth. These nations depend on agriculture or mining with few other industries. People have poor housing, food quality, and health care. This low level of economic development may result from poor weather, limited natural resources, low literacy, or uncertain political situations.

Nations moving from being an LDC to becoming industrialized are called *developing countries*. The U.S. Department of Commerce has identified some of these as "big emerging markets" since they offer great potential for U.S. exports. Examples of big emerging markets are Argentina, Brazil, China, India, Indonesia, Mexico,

> Some developing countries offer great potential for U.S. exports.

Poland, South Africa, South Korea, and Turkey.

What factors influence economic development? In addition to strong educational systems, technology, and industries beyond agriculture, a nation's economic success is affected by *infrastructure*. This refers to the transportation, communication, and utility systems of a country. Highways, airports, telephones, and electricity are needed for businesses to operate. Countries that desire to improve their economic well being usually start with improving their educational systems and infrastructure.

CRITICAL THINKING

1. You are planning to start an exporting business. Select a product that could be sold to nations with different levels of economic development. Describe why your product could be exported to countries with varied levels of economic development.

2. Go to the web site of the International Trade Administration (a division of the U.S. Department of Commerce). What skills or abilities would be useful for people who desire to work for this organization?

Most students will either work with international clients or compete against businesses that do. Global Navigator introduces students to issues integral to working with international businesses. Key concepts and challenges faced by international businesses are presented, followed by two Critical Thinking questions that require students to analyze what they have learned.

Although many countries' economies are in a state of flux, it is useful to group countries by the general levels of their economic development because those with similar levels tend to share many of the same characteristics. Global Navigator distinguishes the main categorizations—industrialized, emerging, developing and less-developed—currently in vogue. Note that the term "third world" is no longer used. It also explains to students how countries improve their levels of economic development. Critical Thinking questions encourage them to translate these concepts into practical applications.

CRITICAL THINKING

1. Answers will vary widely but should show recognition of the different needs and wants as well as financial resources that countries have at various levels of economic development. There must not only be a demand or desire for a product but also some reasonable expectation that the country can pay for it, given its resources and other needs.

2. Suggested answers include the ability to speak and write foreign languages, a knowledge of international accounting practices and/or international law, and training in import/export management.

This chapter examines the ways economic performance is measured in the free enterprise system. Gross Domestic Product (GDP), GDP per capita, labor productivity, the business cycle, inflation, deflation, and economic growth are discussed.

Resources for Teachers
- Lesson Plans
- School-To-Work/SCANS Activity Masters
- Spanish Resources
- Instructor's Resource CD

Assessment
- Chapter and Unit Tests, Ch. 4
- ExamView, Ch. 4

Media/Technology
- Applying Technology Data CD
- PowerPoint slides
- Business Connection CD
- Videotape

Activity Masters and Workbooks
- Activities and Projects, Ch. 4
- Internet Activity Masters
- Business Math Activity Masters
- Communications Activity Masters
- International Business Activity Masters
- Ethics Activity Masters

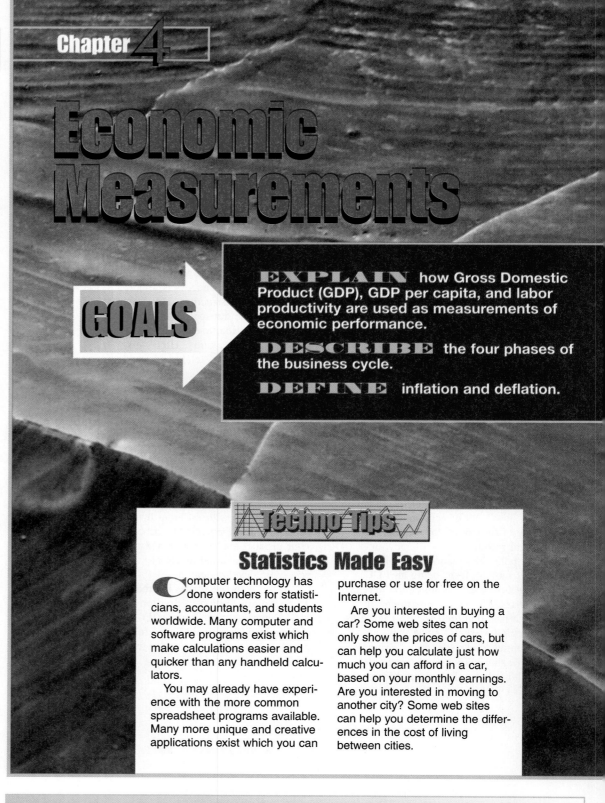

Chapter 4
Economic Measurements

GOALS

EXPLAIN how Gross Domestic Product (GDP), GDP per capita, and labor productivity are used as measurements of economic performance.

DESCRIBE the four phases of the business cycle.

DEFINE inflation and deflation.

Techno Tips

Statistics Made Easy

Computer technology has done wonders for statisticians, accountants, and students worldwide. Many computer and software programs exist which make calculations easier and quicker than any handheld calculators.

You may already have experience with the more common spreadsheet programs available. Many more unique and creative applications exist which you can purchase or use for free on the Internet.

Are you interested in buying a car? Some web sites can not only show the prices of cars, but can help you calculate just how much you can afford in a car, based on your monthly earnings. Are you interested in moving to another city? Some web sites can help you determine the differences in the cost of living between cities.

Students need to know the latest technologies and develop cutting edge Internet skills for use in current jobs, future careers, or in their homes. TechnoTips introduces students to today's cutting edge technologies and provides them with important Internet skills. Feature topics concentrate on Internet-specific technologies and computer or other hi-tech innovations for use by businesses and consumers.

An important part of life is measuring performance. In a recent basketball game, Rosa Rivera of Middletown High School scored 19 points, pulled down 8 rebounds, and had 7 assists. Later that day, Akira Eto, an aspiring amateur ice skater, scored 5.6 during his short program. By any standard, these were good performances.

How about you? How much have you grown in the past ten years? You can say, "I am ten years older." Or, "I am 50 pounds heavier." Or, "I now wear shoe size 10C." There are a lot of ways in which we can measure our own growth.

You grow in many other ways, too. As you mature, your abilities increase. You depend less on your parents and begin to plan for your future and look toward a career. You might be working part time and saving money for the future. Your grades may be improving so that you will have a better chance of getting into college.

You can measure your body growth by looking in a mirror, stepping on a scale, or trying on new shoes in a different size. Your interests, actions, and achievements measure your mental and psychological growth. Improvement in grades and the size of your savings account measure the extent to which you have goals and are meeting them.

These are just a few of the ways by which you can measure various growth factors in your life.

MEASURING ECONOMIC GROWTH

Economic growth refers to a steady increase in production of goods and services in an economic system. Just as you can use different ways to measure your own growth, we can use different methods to check on the growth of our economy. A high rate of employment and a low rate of business failures are two indications that our economy is doing well. However, the most important ways by which we can measure how well we are doing relate to how much we produce to help satisfy the needs and wants of our people.

Today more than 130 million Americans work in thousands of different jobs and produce thousands of different products and services. The total of all the goods and services that Americans produce is the output or production of our nation. We have only about 7 percent of the world's land and less than 5 percent of the world's population, yet our output accounts for more than 20 percent of all goods and services produced in the world.

Gross Domestic Product (GDP)

One way to find out how well our economy is doing is to compare output from year to year. The federal government collects information from producers and estimates our national output. The most widely used estimate is the gross domestic product (formerly gross national product). The **gross domestic product**, or **GDP**, is the total dollar value of all final goods and services produced in a country during one year. It is one measure of how the economy is performing.

GDP includes three major categories of expenditures:

1. What consumers spend for food, clothing, and housing.

2. What businesses spend for buildings, equipment, and supplies.

3. What government agencies spend to pay employees and to buy supplies.

There are some goods and services not included. For example, GDP does not include the value of the work you do for yourself, such as cutting your own lawn or building a

Write the following on the board: "Suppose you hear in the nightly news that the United States economy is experiencing growth. What do you think this means?" Also write inflation on the board. Then ask students: What do you think causes prices to go up? What causes inflation? Have students share their responses with the class.

MOTIVATE

PURPOSE Select individual students to read aloud the definitions of this chapter's Key Terms from the Glossary. Key Terms are listed under Develop Your Business Language in the Chapter Review. Ask other students to use each term in a sentence. Review each goal with the class and look through the chapter to identify the major topics that will be studied.

TEACH/APPLY

MAKE CONNECTIONS Review the three factors of production (natural, human, and capital resources) introduced in Chapter 1. Call on students to identify the factors and indicate how each factor might contribute to economic growth.

Discuss economic measurements with students. GDP is the value of all *final* goods and services produced in the economy in a calendar year. GDP per capita is a measure of each person's share of the GDP. Productivity is a measure of output per worker and is influenced by the introduction of new technologies, systems, and training programs. Ask how the United States compares on these measurements with other leading nations of the world, such as Japan and Germany.

Brainstorm with the class the importance of economic growth. Record reasons on the board as they are mentioned. Students should use the list to identify some of the signs of economic growth in their community. Then have them guess why such growth has taken place. Has the growth been good or bad for the community?

Review Figures 4-1 and 4-2 in the text. The difference between GDP and "real" GDP can be a difficult concept for many students to understand. Remind students that two variables are used to compute GDP—quantity and price. Emphasize that "real" GDP takes into account price changes in order to paint a more accurate portrait of any change in the quantity of final goods and services produced in an economy in one year. In other words, through the use of "real" GDP, economists can see if the number of final goods and services has grown or shrunk.

Show PowerPoint 4-4, *The Business Cycle*. Use this slide to help students understand the business cycle. Point out that over the entire cycle there is an overall increase in GDP even though there are periods with slowdowns or declines. Students should be encouraged to identify phases that have occurred during their lifetimes. Discuss the Great Depression of the 1930s and more recent recessions.

Ask the following questions: Is there anything you can do to protect yourself from the ups and downs of the business cycle? If so, what?

Then ask why it is important to find out if prices are changing from one month to the next or one year to the next. (Possible answer: In short, knowing what is happening to prices gives us information in terms of what is happening to our standard of living.) Students should list five items bought regularly that have increased in price in the last year. How much has the price increased? List items selected by students on the board. Has the price increase altered students' spending habits? How do consumer spending habits typically change during inflation?

picnic table for your yard. However, if you buy the lawn service or the picnic table from businesses, they would be included. Only final goods, such as cars, are counted when we measure GDP. Intermediate goods used in manufacturing, such as steel and fabrics, are not included in GDP. If intermediate goods were counted as well, the value of the intermediate goods would be counted twice.

If the GDP increases from year to year, this is a good sign that our economy is growing and is healthy. Even though we have had some bad years, our economy has enjoyed a steady climb over its history. GDP was more than $8.5 trillion by the end of the 1990s. There is one big difficulty in comparing a country's GDP from year to year, however. Prices of what we produce do not stay the same from year to year. Prices go up and down. In order to make comparisons that are fair and accurate, we need to take the current prices and adjust them each year so that they are equal in value over a period of years.

Suppose the fictitious nation of Robaland produces only megalamps. The output of Robaland is shown in Figure 4-1.

Note that under current prices the GDP for 2002 is $1,500. On this basis, you could say that the GDP (the total output) increased three times since 1992. However, this assumption is wrong. Actually, Robaland made no progress in producing megalamps. In each of the years, 1,000 units were produced. If prices were adjusted to account for price increases, the dollar value would have been $500 each year.

In this example, 1992 was the base year. **Base year** means the year chosen to compare an item, such as price, to any other year. We can choose any year as the base year.

Figure 4-2 shows a different picture. In 2002, Robaland produced three times as many megalamps as in 1992. If GDPs at current prices are compared, the GDP increase in 2002 was nine times that of 1992 ($4,500 ÷ $500 = 9). However, that figure can be misleading, too.

Why is the value of the work we do for ourselves not included as part of GDP?

TEACHING STRATEGIES
Teams

Assign students to teams with four members each. The teams should be mixed in performance level, gender, and culture. Each group will study and review the lesson making sure that all group members understand the objectives and content. Set a reasonable time limit. When the time has expired, send students back to their desks to take the ExamView (or printed test) on their own with no assistance from team members. Compare each student's score to the current average for that student's previous tests. Award two points to students who meet their average score. Give three points to students who beat their average score. The team that has the most points is the winner. This can be a continuing activity throughout the semester.

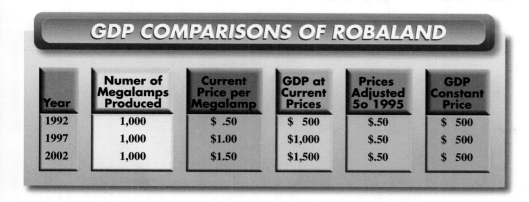

GDP COMPARISONS OF ROBALAND

Year	Numer of Megalamps Produced	Current Price per Megalamp	GDP at Current Prices	Prices Adjusted 5o 1995	GDP Constant Price
1992	1,000	$ .50	$ 500	$.50	$ 500
1997	1,000	$1.00	$1,000	$.50	$ 500
2002	1,000	$1.50	$1,500	$.50	$ 500

1992	1,000	$ .50	$ 500	$.50	$ 500
1997	1,500	$1.00	$1,500	$.50	$ 750
2002	3,000	$1.50	$4,500	$.50	$1,500

FIGURE 4-1 and FIGURE 4-2   Do higher prices create higher GDP?

Prices were higher in 2002. In constant prices, the GDP in 2002 was three times that of 1992—exactly the same as the actual increase in the total number of megalamps produced.

Constant dollar GDP is the value of gross domestic product after taking out the effect of price changes. When we convert any dollar measure to constant dollar terms, we take out the effect of price changes. Only actual, or real, changes remain. For this reason, we often use the term *real GDP* or GDP in real terms.

GDP Per Capita

The more goods and services we produce, the healthier our economy gets. Just referring to the dollar value of GDP as a measure of economic growth does not tell the whole story. Another way to measure economic growth is GDP per capita or output per person. **GDP per capita** is calculated by dividing GDP by the total population (see Figure 4-3). For example, suppose that there is no change in GDP this year over last year. Suppose, also,

that the population increases. The same output would have to be divided among more people. An increase in GDP per capita means that our economy is growing. A decrease may mean that our economy is having trouble.

Labor Productivity

Productivity is measured in terms of the number of items produced per worker. An important source of economic growth is an increase in output per worker. Improvements in the quality of capital resources (primarily equipment), worker training, and management techniques have resulted in more output from the same number of workers. This increase in goods and services from the same amounts of labor is called a *productivity increase*.

During the past 25 years, the rate of growth in labor productivity has had some ups and downs. While there has been an increase in productivity in many of those years, the amount of the increase has become smaller than in the past. In a few cases, productivity has actually decreased. At the same with it more pollution, a more hur-ried way of life, etc. Is the economic growth worth the costs? Do the benefits outweigh the costs?

Bring in a variety of magazines and newspapers. Ask students to locate a newspaper or magazine article that describes the current business cycle of our economy. Students should summarize the main points of the article and pres-ent their findings in either a written paper or an oral report to the class.

In order to get a firsthand view of inflation, ask students to select a business in the area and inter-view the owner to find out how inflation affects his or her busi-ness. Suggest that questions be asked not only about prices of products sold, but also on the cost of doing business. Have students discuss the impact of inflation on the business of their choice.

The Chapter Review questions at the end of the chapter vary in level of difficulty. For a basic assignment, consider Develop Your Business Language and Review Your Reading. For an average assign-ment, consider the basic assign-ment plus Communicate Business Concepts and Calculate Business Data. For an enhanced assignment, try the average assignment plus Technology Application and Decision-Making Strategies.

ASSESS

Review the goals at the beginning of the chapter and the Business Notes at the end of the chapter. Have students respond orally or in writing to each of the Business Notes restated as a question, pro-vided below. For students having dif-ficulty providing the answers, assign the reteaching activities that follow.

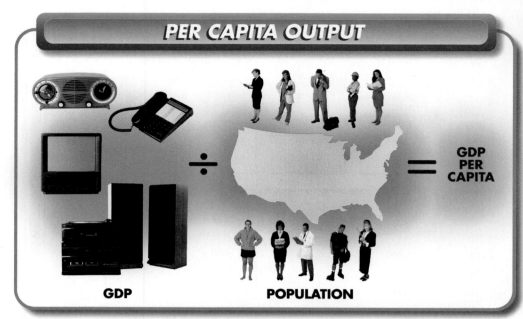

PER CAPITA OUTPUT

GDP ÷ POPULATION = GDP PER CAPITA

FIGURE 4-3   Can you see how per capita output is measured?

time, wages climbed steadily. In one recent ten-year period, wages increased five times more than did labor productivity.

If wages increase faster than gains in pro-ductivity, the cost of producing goods increases and prices rise accordingly. So even though workers earn more money, they are not able to improve their standard of living very much because of rising prices. For that reason, a great deal of attention has been given in recent years to ways of motivating workers to increase productivity. By doing so, the workers will be contributing to a higher standard of living in the nation as well as improving their own lifestyles.

Our ability to produce more and more goods and services as our country developed has made it possible to reduce the number of hours in a workweek. In the early 1890s, the average worker put in about 60 hours a week. Our average workweek has decreased to generally less than 40 hours. Even though we work fewer hours and have more leisure time, we produce more and earn more than ever before. We can produce more in less

time because we use modern technology and efficient work methods. We also have many highly skilled workers. Although pro-ductivity historically has increased nearly every year, increases have tended to become smaller.

THE BUSINESS CYCLE

We have learned over the decades that our economy has its ups and downs and that good times and bad times seem to run in cycles.

All nations experience good times and bad times—that is a fact of life. Fortunately, over a period of time bad conditions disappear and good conditions return. If we look at the eco-nomic changes that have occurred during our country's history, we can see that they form a pattern of good times to bad times and back to good times. This movement of the econ-omy from one condition to another and back again is called a **business cycle**.

Business cycles are the recurring ups and downs of GDP. Business cycles have

Basic Skills-Math

SCANS

Integrating math across the curriculum is an important ele-ment in contemporary education. As a part of end-of-chapter activities, Calculate Business Data enables students to apply their math skills. Appendix B: Math Review, Appendix C: Deter-mining Percentages and Interest in Business, and Appendix D:

Using Measurements in Business, also apply arithmetic and math skills.

four phases: prosperity, recession, depression, and recovery.

Prosperity

At the high point of the business cycle, we enjoy prosperity. **Prosperity** is a phase of the business cycle when most people who want to work are working and businesses produce goods and services in record numbers. In this phase, wages are good and the rate of GDP growth increases. The demand for goods and services is high. This period, such as the technology boom of the 1990s, is usually the peak of the business cycle. Prosperity, however, does not go on forever. The economy eventually cools off and activity slows down.

Recession

When the economy slows down, we enter a phase of the business cycle known as recession. **Recession** is a period where demand begins to decrease, businesses lower production of goods and services, unemployment begins to rise, and GDP growth slows for two or more quarters of the calendar year. As happened in 2001–02, this phase may not be too serious or last very long, but it often signals trouble for some groups of workers in related businesses. This drop in related businesses is called the *ripple effect*. Eventually, production weakens throughout the economy, and total output declines in the next quarter. Some recessions last for long periods of time as fewer factors of production are used, and total demand falls.

Depression

If a recession deepens and spreads throughout the entire economy, the nation may move into the third phase, depression. **Depression** is a phase marked by a prolonged period of high unemployment, weak sales of goods and services, and business failures. GDP falls rapidly during a depression. Fortunately, our economy has not had a depression for more than half a century. This period (1930-1940) is referred to as the Great Depression. Approximately 25 percent of the American labor force was then unemployed. Many people could not afford even the basic needs.

Recovery

Depressions also do not go on forever. A welcome phase of the business cycle, known as recovery, begins to appear. **Recovery** is the phase in which unemployment begins to decrease, demand for goods and services increases, and GDP begins to rise again. People gain employment. Consumers regain confidence about their futures and begin buying again. The U.S. economy staged a strong recovery in the 1980s following a deep recession. Recovery may be slow or fast. As it continues, the nation moves into prosperity again.

INFLATION AND DEFLATION

Another problem with which our nation has had to cope is inflation. **Inflation** is a sustained increase in the general level of prices. One type of inflation occurs when the demand for goods and services is greater than the supply. When a large supply of money, earned or borrowed, is spent for goods that are in short supply, prices increase. Even though wages (the price paid for labor) tend to increase during inflation, prices of goods and services usually rise so fast that the wage earner never seems to catch up.

Most people think inflation is harmful. Consumers have to pay higher prices for the things they buy. Therefore, as workers, they have to earn more money to maintain the same standard of living. Producers may receive higher prices for the goods and

---

Net Facts provides information and definitions of terms for the Internet. The more information that students have about the Internet, the better equipped they will be to use this resource. In the Internet Activity Masters, there is an Internet Activity Worksheet for each unit. You can use these activities to give students experience with finding information online. Options for assigning this activity are as follows:
1. **Provide students with a list of addresses of resources for this activity;**
2. **Assign students to conduct their own searches; or**
3. **Use the addresses provided on the Internet Activity Worksheet.**
   You should complete the activity yourself before assigning it to resolve any discrepancies that may arise.

Enrichment activities may also be assigned where appropriate.
1. What are three ways in which economic performance can be measured? (Answer: Economic performance is measured by calculating GDP, GDP per capita, and labor productivity.)
2. What are the four phases of the business cycle? (Answer: prosperity, recession, depression, recovery)
3. What is the difference between inflation and deflation? (Answer: Inflation is an overall

---

increase in the general level of prices; deflation is an overall decrease in the general level of prices.)

4. What developments might affect the future growth of our economy? (Answer: The future growth of our economy will hinge on our ability to solve certain economic problems and to achieve technological advances.)

Have students look through the community newspapers you or they bring to class and scan for articles related to the topics covered in this chapter: GDP, GDP per capita, labor productivity, the business cycle, inflation. Students should summarize their findings.

Call out, in random order, each phase of the business cycle. Have students provide the corresponding definition.

Direct students to read the Global Perspectives in this chapter. Have students create a graph for a bulletin board display that visually explains the trend in GDP for the last ten years. Make available a recent copy of the Statistical Abstract of the United States to find information about GDP. Display students' work on a classroom bulletin board. Or students might search for magazine or newspaper articles that discuss the economy in a recession or an expansion. Have students identify the main points of the articles and summarize their findings.

As a multicultural awareness activity, have students investigate economic growth in other countries. Might a country's particular customs

---

FYI

Japan in the past had a "lifetime employment principle," but it has been eroding in the face of global competition and economic strains. By the end of the 1990s, Japan's unemployment rate had risen to more than 4%, about the same as the U.S. rate.

services they sell. However, if wages go up faster than prices, businesses tend to hire fewer workers and so unemployment worsens.

Mild inflation (perhaps 2 or 3 percent a year) can actually stimulate economic growth. During a mildly inflationary period, wages often rise more slowly than the prices of products. The prices of the products sold are high in relation to the cost of labor. The producer makes higher profits and tends to expand production and hire more people. The newly employed workers increase spending, and the total demand in an economy increases.

In the United States, one of the most-watched measures of inflation is called the

Consumer Price Index (CPI). A price index is a number that compares prices in one year with some earlier base year. There are different kinds of price indexes.

There is an opposite to inflation called deflation. **Deflation** means a decrease in the general level of prices. It usually occurs in periods of recession and depression. Prices of products are lower, but people have less money to buy them. The most notable deflationary period in the United States was during the Great Depression of the 1930s. Between 1929 and 1933, prices declined about 25 percent.

OUR ECONOMIC FUTURE

The ability of an economy to produce output determines its growth. We have come a long way under our private enterprise system. We know it works well. We also know that it can be made to work even better as we strive to develop new technologies and find solutions to our economic problems.

Serious economic problems exist within

E-Commerce Transactions

E-commerce opens up opportunities to companies previously limited by geographic, financial, or political restrictions. These online economic activities involve four basic models with two selling and buying parties: businesses (B) and consumers (C).

The first and most familiar model is Business-to-Consumer, or B2C. Expanded sales of products in different geographic markets will create B2C growth. This area of e-commerce currently exceeds monthly revenue of several billion dollars. Examples are Amazon.com and Dell.com.

The second e-commerce model is Business-to-Business, or B2B. B2B online exchanges are the largest and fastest-growing segment of e-commerce, accounting for about 80 percent of Internet transactions. Examples are Ford or General Motors buying parts.

Consumer-to-Business (C2B) is the third e-commerce model. In C2B, consumers originate online transactions through price offers to businesses. Priceline.com, one of the first companies in this category, allows shoppers to make bids for products and services such as airline tickets and hotels, then companies decide whether to accept the offers. While small at this stage of online development, C2B could expand with new technologies and consumer initiatives.

Consumer-to-Consumer (C2C) is the fourth e-commerce model. In the long economic tradition of bartering and auctions, buying and selling among consumers is also expanding in the cyber marketplace. The ease and speed of transactions among online parties is encouraging more and more C2C exchanges. An example is eBay.com.

TEACHING STRATEGIES

Special Needs: Specific Learning Disability (SLD) Students

When asking students questions during class about economic measurements, ask SLD students questions that they can likely answer successfully. Save more difficult or unstructured questions for better students. Years of failure cause SLD students to have low self-esteem, thus reducing their confidence that they can achieve academic success.

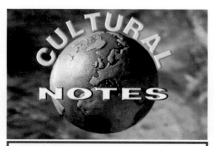
According to the United States Census Bureau, the population of the United States will exceed 392 million by 2050. At that time Hispanics will make up our nation's second-largest ethnic group behind white non-Hispanics. Proportionately, the fastest growing segment of our population is Asians and Pacific Islanders. The population of this group is rising at the rate of four percent a year. By 2050, Asians and Pacific Islanders will make up 10 percent of the population. The Arab-American population, composed of immigrants from Lebanon, Egypt, Jordan, Syria, and Iraq, is also starting to increase in numbers.

our economy that need to be solved. Many people do not have access to adequate health care. Some people do not have proper housing, especially in large cities. Our nation's traffic and crime problems are matters of concern to many citizens. Too many workers are unemployed or do not have appropriate employment. Having a "good" job is an important part of life for most people.

And what lies ahead on the technology front? Will computer-controlled robots perform most of the routine tasks in our factories? Will we see housekeeping chores done entirely by machines? Will we raise crops under water or on other planets? Will we work at home communicating with business associates using computers? These are some of the things occurring now or predicted for later in the 21st century.

No one knows for sure just how these changes will affect our future. We do know, however, that to maintain or increase our existing standard of living and to prevent unemployment from rising, we must increase our economic growth continuously. Economic growth is important because it provides jobs and enables people to better meet their needs and wants.

or traditions have an impact on economic growth? For example, suppose the custom in one country is to take every other day off to rest and relax. In such a country, economic growth would be less than in a country in which people worked five or six days a week. Have students prepare reports about the effect of a country's traditions on economic growth. Display the reports on a table and encourage students to read each other's work.

SUMMARIZE

A suggested vocabulary-building method is to play charades; that is, to have students "act out" selected words used in this unit. (Charades: a game in which the players alternately act out in pantomime a word or phrase, often syllable by syllable. While one student is acting, other members of the class must guess what is being represented.) Such expressions as the following are suitable for a charade activity: natural resources, capitalism, profit, competition, gross domestic product, standard of living, output per worker-hour. Add additional terms to the list if you wish.

EVALUATE

- Assign Activities and Projects for Chapter 4.
- Administer the printed test or ExamView for Chapter 4.
- Administer the printed test or ExamView for Unit 1.
- Assign School-To-Work/SCANS portfolio activities for Unit 1.

GLOBAL PERSPECTIVES

Hyperinflation

In the United States, we enjoy a moderate rate of inflation, about 3 percent in recent years. But moderate rates of inflation are not a reality throughout some parts of the world, especially Latin America. For instance, in some South American countries, the annual rate of inflation has been as high as 300 to 400 percent. This phenomenon is known as *hyperinflation*.

If left unchecked, it can run rampant, feed on itself, and create severe distortions in the economy. People learn to anticipate next month's price hikes, and everyone, from the largest companies to street vendors, includes the expected rate of inflation into prices asked.

So how do consumers survive? Many families buy all of their groceries for the month

as soon as the wage earner gets paid. If they do not buy right away, their money will buy fewer groceries later in the month. The challenge for workers is not so much making money but keeping what they have made. From week to week, the same amount of money buys less and less.

Critical Thinking

1. What effect would it have on your life, and that of your family and relatives, if the inflation rate in the United States were to increase to over 300 percent?
2. What wage increases would you expect to receive if our inflation rate more than doubled each year?

GLOBAL PERSPECTIVES

Get information about the rate of inflation in the United States for the current quarter and the projection for the year. Comment on what goods and services are currently showing the sharpest price increases. Acquire information about the rates of inflation in other countries.

CRITICAL THINKING

1. A United States inflation rate of 300 percent would cause the purchasing power of the dollar to erode rapidly. People might reduce savings since inflation erodes the value of money or put money into commodities which tend to increase in value with the inflation rate.
2. Workers would expect to get large wage increases so that they could keep up with inflation. Large wage increases would in turn fuel the rate of inflation to even higher levels.

REVIEW YOUR READING

1. The United States has about 7 percent of the world's land, about 5 percent of the world's population, and its output accounts for more than 20% of the goods and services produced in the world.
2. The statement means that by comparing GDP (total value of goods and services produced by a country) from year to year, it is possible to get an indication of how well our economic system is working. If GDP increases from year to year, this is a good sign that our economy is growing.
3. GDP includes the spending of consumers, business, and government for final goods and services.
4. If prices of goods and services remain exactly the same over a long period of time, it would be fair and accurate to compare a country's GDP from year to year at current prices. However, in reality this has not happened; therefore, the GDP must be adjusted to be compared.
5. A base year is used to compare items, such as price, to any other year. Changing current dollars to dollars of the base year means that the dollars will have the same value and can therefore be meaningfully compared. Using a base year helps to rule out other things that affect GDP figures, such as inflation, so that real values can be compared between two years.
6. Per capita output is determined by dividing GDP by the population. Output is compared from year to year as one indicator of growth in an economy.
7. Current prices are the prices actually paid for goods and services. Adjusted prices are prices held constant to their value on a certain date. Prices can be adjusted for purposes of computing comparisons of output over a period of time.

BUSINESS NOTES

1. We measure economic performance by calculating gross domestic product, per capita output, and labor productivity.
2. A business cycle has four important phases: prosperity, recession, depression, and recovery.
3. Inflation is a general rise in the level of prices; deflation is a decrease in the general price level.
4. There are some exciting possibilities for the future of our economy as we solve economic problems and use new technologies to increase output.

REVIEW YOUR READING

1. Compare the United States with the rest of the world in land size, population, and output of goods and services.
2. "One way to find out how our economy is doing is to compare output from year to year." What does this statement mean?
3. The spending of what three groups is included in GDP?
4. If prices of goods and services remain exactly the same over a long period of time, would it be fair and accurate to compare a country's GDP from year to year at current prices?
5. Explain the use of a base year in measuring output.
6. How is per capita output determined and used?
7. What is the difference between current prices and adjusted prices of goods and services?
8. Name three factors that have contributed to the high output of goods and services over the history of our economy. What changes have occurred in productivity in recent years?
9. Give an example to explain how productivity is related to the standard of living.
10. What is characteristic of each phase of the business cycle? Describe the present U.S. economy and identify the current phase of the business cycle.
11. Why is a high level of inflation generally considered harmful to our economy?
12. What are some economic problems that need solving in our economic system?

COMMUNICATE BUSINESS CONCEPTS

13. The GDP of a developing country in Africa increased 3.6 percent in one year from $5.6 billion to $5.8 billion. Does this mean the country had a 3.6 percent increase in the amount of goods and services produced?
14. If you and your classmates have jobs for which you are paid wages, you are contributing to the GDP. Survey your classmates who work and determine how much your class has contributed to the GDP in one week. (To protect confidentiality, report earnings on slips of paper without names.)
15. The GDP of Country A is $400,000. The GDP of Country B is $800,000. Does this mean that the per capita output of Country B is about twice that of Country A? Explain.
16. What difference does it make to you and to other people in your community whether the GDP is increasing or decreasing?
17. Explain how high wages and low productivity can increase the price you pay for goods and services.

Critical Thinking Skills-Decision Making

Decision-making skills, which include specifying goals, generating alternatives, considering risks, and evaluating and choosing the best alternative, are applied throughout every chapter in this text. Each time a student participates in a Cooperative Learning Activity or Teams Assignment, decision-making skills are applied in a group situation. For Communicate Business Concepts and Decision-Making Strategies, students must specify the goal of the activity, consider risks, and evaluate the best solution before the questions can be answered. Emphasize to students how they are using decision-making techniques in their day-to-day tasks and make them aware of the skills they are developing.

18. Explain how productivity has helped to increase a U.S. worker's leisure time.

19. Suppose that many auto and steel plants close throughout a country and that thousands of workers lose their jobs in a relatively short time period. If the country has been enjoying prosperous times, it may now be headed into what phase of the business cycle? Describe other conditions that might begin to occur.

DEVELOP YOUR BUSINESS LANGUAGE

For each numbered item, find the term that has the same meaning.

20. The total value of all final goods and services produced in a country in one year.

21. The year chosen to compare an item, such as price, to the same item in another year.

22. The GDP divided by the total population of a country.

23. The movement of an economy from one condition to another and back again.

24. A phase of the business cycle when most people who want to work are working and businesses produce goods and services in record numbers.

25. A period where demand begins to decrease, businesses lower production of goods and services, unemployment begins to rise, and GDP growth slows for several quarters.

26. A phase marked by high unemployment, weak sales of goods and services, and business failures.

27. A phase of the business cycle in which unemployment begins to decrease, demand for goods and services increases, and GDP begins to rise again.

28. An increase in the general price level.

29. A decrease in the general price level.

KEY TERMS
**base year
business cycle
deflation
depression
gross domestic product (GDP)
inflation
GDP per capita
prosperity
recession
recovery**

DECISION-MAKING STRATEGIES

In determining GDP, only *final goods* and *services* are included. This avoids having some items counted more than once. For example, a mining company sells iron ore to a steel-producing firm. That firm sells the steel to an auto manufacturer who uses it to produce a car. The iron ore, converted to steel, is counted once—in the price paid for the car, the final product. Read carefully the following list of goods and services produced in our economy and then answer the questions.

a. An electric toaster oven bought as a gift.

b. Telephone service installed in a government office.

c. Fiberglass sold to a company for use in making boats.

d. Grooming services for your pet.

e. Paper sold to a newspaper publishing company.

f. A computer paid for by the city government.

g. A computer bought for your family's use.

h. Broccoli bought by a food-processing firm.

30. Which of these items should be listed as a good and counted in GDP? Give reasons for your answer.

31. Which of these items should be listed as a service and counted in GDP? Give reasons for your answer.

20. gross domestic product (GDP)
21. base year
22. GDP per capita
23. business cycle
24. prosperity
25. recession
26. depression
27. recovery
28. inflation
29. deflation

11. Inflation makes it difficult for businesses and consumers to plan for the future. Inflation also slows economic growth.

12. Some people in our country—not to mention the millions throughout the world—still do not have enough food, proper housing, and medical care. We need to develop ways and means to satisfy the basic human needs of all our citizens. Other possible answers are up to the imagination of students.

COMMUNICATE BUSINESS CONCEPTS

13. An increase in the GDP does not necessarily indicate an increase in the amount of goods and services produced. The GDP must be adjusted to constant prices to serve as an accurate indicator of economic output in this nation.

14. Students' lists will vary. Any work performed for pay by any student contributes to the GDP. There are a few exceptions, e.g., any student who cuts the grass at home and is paid by the parents would not have this output included in GDP. However, if a student operates a lawn service company and operates with a license (which requires reporting sales and services), his or her output would be counted. The total of wages made by students in part-time jobs, especially in cities where many students work, will surprise the class.

15. No, not unless Country B had the same population as Country A, which would be unlikely. GDP per capita is determined by dividing GDP by the total population. If, in the example, Country B had twice the population of Country A, the per capita output would be about the same in both countries. In order

8. Some factors that have contributed to our high output are: modern technology, such as fax machines and personal computers; more efficient work methods and computer programs; and highly skilled and educated workers.

9. If workers produce less than is expected by their employers, the cost of producing each unit will rise. If costs rise, prices usually rise. When prices rise, people are able to buy fewer goods and services, thus lowering their standard of living. So, changes in productivity usually show up as changes in standard of living.

10. Prosperity: GDP growth increases, demand for goods and services is high (1990s). Recession: Demand begins to decrease, GDP growth slows, unemployment begins to rise (2001–2002). Depression: GDP is at its lowest point, unemployment is high, and sales of goods and services are low (1930–1940). Recovery: GDP begins to grow again, unemployment decreases, and demand for goods and services begins to rise (1980s).

49

for Country B to have twice the per capita output of country A, the population would have to be the same in both countries. (Ask a student to explain this question arithmetically on the board.)

16. A continual increase in the GDP is important to all of us. Our GDP should increase at least in a ratio proportionate with our increase in population. However, as people work more efficiently by using automated equipment and improved methods of production, the GDP should increase at a rate faster than our increase in population. An increase in our GDP means more and better goods and services for all of us, and it means jobs for more people. A substantial decrease in our GDP conversely means unemployment and a lower standard of living.

17. High wages and low productivity both increase the price you pay for goods and services because they both increase the cost of producing the goods and services. Because the supplier must cover the cost of doing business and at the same time make a profit, any increase in costs usually results in increased prices.

18. Over our history, our productivity has shown a substantial increase. This increase has resulted from better trained workers, better production methods, and better equipment. This means that we have been able to produce more in fewer hours, thus reducing the number of hours in a workweek and providing more leisure time.

19. The country might be headed into a recession. If so, the auto and steel workers who have lost their jobs will reduce their demand for other goods and services, causing other businesses to lose business and perhaps lay off more workers. This lowered demand, lowered production, and increasing unemployment might spread throughout the economy.

CALCULATE BUSINESS DATA

32. The 2002 production schedule of Robaland listed on page 43 shows its GDP at current prices of $4,500 and at constant 1992 prices of $1,500. If Robaland's population of 2002 was 500, what was its per capita output

   a. At current prices?

   b. At constant prices?

33. Seth Kisco, who works in a warehouse that imports many of its goods, can move from the loading pier to storage one 30-kilo box at a time by hand. Using a hand truck, he can move three 30-kilo boxes at once in the same amount of time.

   a. Seth can move six boxes in one hour without using a hand truck. What is his productivity?

   b. If he uses a hand truck, what is his productivity?

   c. How many workers without hand trucks would it take to do the same work Seth does with a hand truck?

   d. How many pounds can Seth move in an hour with a hand truck? (See Appendix D for information regarding metric conversions.)

34. A small Asian country produces teakwood carvings of water buffalo to sell to tourists. The country's production record is shown in the table.

Year	Number of Carvings Produced	Current Price per Carving
One	1,000	$ .50
Two	2,000	$1.00
Three	4,000	$2.00

   a. What is the country's GDP at current prices for each year?

   b. What is the amount of increase in the number of items produced in Year Two over Year One?

   c. What is the rate of increase in the number of items produced in Year Three over Year Two?

   d. If the country expects to maintain the same rate of increase for another year, how many carvings will it need to produce?

35. Productivity for Novaville was 25 units per worker hour in 1997. Productivity increased 20 percent between 1997 and 2002. What was the productivity figure for 2002? If the rate of increase is maintained, what will the figure be in 2007? in 2012? Workers are paid a rate of $.30 per unit. How much did workers earn per hour in 2002? If their rate increases to $0.35 in 2007 and $0.40 in 2012, how much would they earn per hour in those years?

TECHNOLOGY APPLICATION

Using the *Intro to Business* Data CD and your spreadsheet software, select problem CH04. After the problem appears on your screen, complete the following activities. Then, after you have completed each step, display or print the completed spreadsheet or graph for each activity. If you do not have a printer available, answer the questions before you leave the computer.

36. The first table in problem CH04 is similar to Figure 4-1 on page 43. Enter formulas to complete the columns for GDP at Current Prices, Prices Adjusted to 1997, and GDP at Constant Price. Answer the following:

   a. What is the GDP at Current Prices for 2006?

   b. What is the GDP at Constant Price for 2000?

37. The second table in problem CH04 is similar to Figure 4-2 on page 43. Enter formulas to

complete the columns for GDP at Current Prices, prices Adjusted to 1997, and GDP at Constant Price. Answer the following:

   a. What is the GDP at Current Prices for 1999?

   b. What is the GDP at Constant Price for 2005?

38. Create a single graph combining the results of both tables in problem CH04. Use the Year column as the x-axis. Use GDP at Constant Price from the first table for one range; use GDP at Constant Price from the second table for the other range. Answer the following:

   a. Looking at the graphs from left to right, how would you describe the directions of the graphs?

   b. Why does each graph look the way it does?

DECISION-MAKING STRATEGIES

30. (a) It is a good and is purchased at a store; (f) It is a good that is being purchased for use by the government; (g) Yes (same as f).

31. (b) The telephone service will be used by the government office employees; (d) The grooming service is being performed and paid for.

CALCULATE BUSINESS DATA

32. (a) $4,500 ÷ 500 = $9;
   (b) $1,500 ÷ 500 = $3

33. (a) 6 boxes;
   (b) 3 × 6 = 18 boxes;
   (c) 18 ÷ 6 = 3 workers.
   (d) 18 ÷ 30 = 540 kilos; 540 × 2.2 = 1,188 pounds.

34. (a)

Year	Number of Carvings Produced	Current Price Per Carving	GDP at Current Price
One	1,000	$0.50	$ 500
Two	2,000	$1.00	$2,000
Three	4,000	$2.00	$8,000

   (b) 2,000 − 1,000 = 1,000;
   (c) 4,000 ÷ 2,000 = 2 (double);
   (d) 4,000 × 2 = 8,000. The rate was doubled in Year Three over Year Two; therefore, twice the Year Three output must be produced for Year Four.

50

COMMUNICATING for SUCCESS

RESOLVING CONFLICT

Conflict can be defined quite simply as competing differences between two or more people. These differences are often caused by struggles over goals, motives, values, ideas, and resources. Believe it or not, conflict can be both good and bad, depending upon the results of the conflict. The consequences of negative, unresolved conflict are decreased productivity, low employee morale, and heightened workplace tensions. These all have the potential to damage the success of a business. However, conflict of the right nature can be beneficial to business. For example, friendly conflict can encourage competition, diverse thinking, creativity, and a wider variety of solutions to business problems.

Prevention is the solution to many problems, including workplace conflict. Some tips for preventing negative conflict in the workplace include the following:

* Be open to others' ideas; listen before making up your mind.
* Avoid stereotyping your co-workers and superiors.
* Do not use language or expressions that may be offensive or demeaning to others.
* Disagree constructively; offer alternative suggestions or solutions rather than simply rejecting others' ideas.
* Above all, treat your co-workers and superiors with the respect you want them to show you.

Unfortunately, conflict cannot always be avoided. All types of conflict can arise, from personality clashes to conflict over business ideas. The following strategies can be helpful in managing conflict with co-workers.

* Intervention: Ask a co-worker or supervisor to provide a setting for conflict resolution between you and those with whom you are in conflict. A supervisor also might speak on your behalf to the co-worker with whom you are in conflict.
* Confrontation: Approach the co-worker with whom you are having trouble. Both of you must recognize the problem, and then work together toward a solution.
* Compromise: If the conflict involves a disagreement over a particular business issue, you might work out a compromise solution. For example, you may agree to your co-worker's idea in exchange for similar treatment during the next conflict.
* Avoidance: The avoidance technique should be your last solution, but in some situations it may be best. If you simply cannot solve a personality conflict, deal with the individual when you need to, but otherwise steer clear.

Conflict between yourself and a superior is acceptable, and in some cases even beneficial, if it leads to increased mutual respect. However, conflict with superiors must be handled with care and should not be seen as a challenge to your superior's authority. Conflict with superiors should be kept professional and private.

CRITICAL THINKING
1. What is conflict?
2. What are the consequences of negative conflict?

---

35. 2002 productivity: 25 units ÷ worker hour × 0.20 = 5 units/worker hour; 25 + 5 = 30 units/worker hour; 2007 productivity: 30 × 0.20 = 6; 30 + 6 = 36 units/worker hour; 2012 productivity: 36 × 0.20 = 7.2 units/worker hour; 36 + 7.2 = 43.2 units/worker hour; 2002 earnings: 30 units ÷ worker hour × $0.30 per unit = $9.00 per hour; 2007 earnings: 36 units ÷ worker hour × $0.35 per unit = $12.60 per hour; 2012 earnings: 43.2 units ÷ worker hour × $0.40 per unit = $17.28 per hour

TEACHING Tip
Safety and Health

To promote a positive learning environment, students need comfortable chairs, good lighting, and adequate space in which to work.

COMMUNICATING for SUCCESS

Communications skills will help ensure students' success in the business world. Communicating for Success introduces workplace/interpersonal communications issues and proper uses of communications technology. Each feature discusses a key communications topic, and contains two Critical Thinking questions that require students to analyze what they have learned.

Students benefit from knowing how to resolve conflicts in just about every aspect of their lives, including personal and family relationships, school, and work. This feature points out that what is bad is not conflict itself, only unresolved, negative conflict that gets in the way of people's or organizations' goals. It points out various ways to avoid such conflicts, and it also provides strategies for managing conflicts that may not be avoidable.

CRITICAL THINKING
1. Conflict can be defined quite simply as competing differences between two or more people. These differences are often caused by struggles over goals, motives, values, ideas, and resources.
2. The consequences of negative, unresolved conflict are decreased productivity, low employee morale, and heightened workplace tensions.

TECHNOLOGY APPLICATION

In this activity, students use a computer to solve a business problem using a file provided on the data CD that accompanies *Intro to Business*. Instructions for using the data CD are included in a **README** file on the disk. Solutions are provided on the Instructor's Resource CD.

GLOBAL BUSINESS PROJECT

This end-of-unit project provides students with an opportunity to apply text learning in a business planning situation. Students are asked to develop a business idea and to select a country. These two decisions will be the basis for this continuing project throughout the course.

To complete each phase of this project, students are encouraged to use various resources—textbook content, library materials, World Wide Web sites, interviews, advertisements, product packages, in-store observations. The individual activities are planned for use as either (1) an on-going course project, or (2) individual assignments.

Whether used as a continuing project or for selected activities, consider having students work in teams. This small group experience provides a valuable skill for future learning and work situations.

In this first unit, the foundation for a business plan is developed. Students will research and identify a business opportunity that could be appropriate for a foreign market. If this project is used as a continuing activity, this business idea and the country selected will be used in other phases of the project.

In addition to search engines, these selected web sites can be helpful for this unit:

- International Trade Administration of the U.S. Dept. of Commerce (www.ita.doc.gov)
- World Factbook of the Central Intelligence Agency (www.odci.gov/cia/publications/factbook)
- World Trade Organization at (www.wto.org)
- Small Business Administration (www.sba.gov)
- Import-export information at (www.internationalist.com/)(www.exim.gov)
- Latin American country information (www.lanic.utexas.edu)

GLOBAL BUSINESS PROJECT

IDENTIFY BUSINESS OPPORTUNITIES

Economic systems, needs and wants, goods and services, supply and demand, and factors of production form the basis for business activities in the global economy. This project will give you the opportunity to create a company for doing business in other countries.

A business plan is a written description of a business idea. This document also includes information on planning, organizing, financing, marketing, and implementing the business idea. Throughout the book, this global business plan project will allow you to apply textbook learning while getting involved in business planning and decision making.

PROJECT GOALS

1. Research the economic environment of another country.
2. Analyze needs and wants of the people in a different culture.
3. Identify a business idea (product or service) for selling in another country.

PROJECT ACTIVITIES

Using your textbook, library materials, web sites, interviews with people, and other resources, complete the following:

1. Select a country. Conduct research on the economic situation of this country. Obtain information about the country's type of economic system, natural resources, agricultural products, imports, exports, standard of living, GDP, and inflation. Prepare a written summary to describe how this information could create a business opportunity for a company.
2. Locate information about foods, habits, customs, traditions, and beliefs of people in another country. If possible, talk to a person who has visited or lived in the country you are studying. List two or three ways in which the country is different from most others.
3. Using your knowledge of another country, prepare a description of a new business idea. This business opportunity could be based on climate, health care, food, transportation, natural resources, technology, or other aspects of the nation's economy.

PROJECT WRAP-UP

1. Prepare a portfolio (folder, file box, or other container) for storing and referring back to the information and materials you created in the activities above. This portfolio will be the foundation for your global business plan.
2. Create a poster (or other visual display) communicating the main ideas of a business idea (product or service) that could be sold in other countries. Be sure to highlight how the business opportunity was created and what needs or wants the company will satisfy.

- Asian country information (asnic.utexas.edu) (www.asia-inc.com)
- Eastern European country information (reenic.utexas.edu)
- Middle East country information (menic.utexas.edu)

FOCUS ON CAREERS

ECONOMICS

A career in the American free enterprise system could be anything you want it to be. If you have enough interest to acquire the training for it, you could be a corporate executive, an opera singer, or a professional clown. The choice is yours.

Each unit in this text will help you prepare to make your choice by outlining career opportunities in the area discussed in the unit. Since this unit introduces you to our market economy, this career section will focus on the people who work in the economics profession. Broadly defined, *economics* is the social science that deals with how society allocates its scarce resources among its unlimited wants and needs.

JOB TITLES

Job titles commonly found in this career area include:
- Economist
- Market Research Analyst
- Urban and Regional Planner
- Survey Researcher
- Statistician
- Statistical Assistant
- Budget Analyst
- Financial Analyst
- Operations Research Analyst

EMPLOYMENT OUTLOOK (THROUGH 2010)

- Job growth will be as fast or faster than average through 2010.
- Competition will be keen for most jobs.
- Many openings will arise from the need to replace people who transfer.
- Most new jobs will be in financial services, research, and consulting.

EDUCATION AND TRAINING

- Economists must have at least a bachelor's degree; most have master's degrees and many have doctorates.
- All jobs within this career area require at least a high school diploma for entry into the occupation.
- Special training in statistics, mathematics, and computer technology applications is common to all jobs.

SALARY LEVELS (IN RECENT YEARS)

Salaries will vary widely, depending upon the educational background, experience of the worker, and place of employment. Average (median) salaries:
- Economists: overall median, $65,000, but the top 10 percent earned more than $114,000.
- Statisticians: $52,000
- Urban planners: $46,500
- Budget analysts: $48,000

CRITICAL THINKING

1. Which job titles in this career area appeal to you most? Give some reasons for your choice.
2. What are some things you will have to do to achieve success in the career you selected?

FOCUS ON CAREERS

The careers listed in the Career Focus come from the *Occupational Outlook Handbook*, an online publication (www.bls.gov/oco) of the federal government. The O*NET codes for these job titles are Economist, 19-3011.00; Market Research Analyst, 19-3021.00; Urban and Regional Planner, 19-3051.00; Survey Researcher, 19-3022.00; Statistician, 15-2041-00; Statistical Assistant, 43-9111.00; Budget Analyst, 13-2031.00; Financial Analyst, 13-2051.00; Operations Research Analyst, 15-2031.00.

Students should study the job descriptions for occupations within economics. Additional job descriptions for careers in economics should be brought to class, and students should be encouraged to investigate other job titles in economics. If any students have had work experience in this career area, they should share their experiences with class members. If they know of persons who hold such jobs, these people could be contacted for additional job information. As an enrichment activity, use the Career Focus Activity worksheets which can be found in the School-To-Work/SCANS Activity Masters.

CRITICAL THINKING

Answers, of course, to the two critical thinking questions will vary widely. Students should be encouraged to select one job even if they are not really interested in a career area. Answering these questions gives certain career areas a sharper focus within students' minds.

UNIT 2

BUILDING YOUR PORTFOLIO

CAREER DEVELOPMENT – PROFILING YOUR QUALITIES

The Building Your Portfolio career exercise will help your students establish a personal history—where they have been, where they are now, and where they are going. This career exercise will encourage students to think about their interests, skills, and achievements.

Tell students that one of the most visible forms of advertising is a billboard. Ask students to assume the following situation: You have an opportunity to put a message of your choice on the most prominent billboard in your community. Direct students to create a message for the billboard highlighting the following information: career and education plans; paid and unpaid work experience; special interests, activities, and achievements; skills and abilities.

As a supplemental activity, you may refer to the School–To–Work/SCANS Activity Masters.

TEACHING STRATEGIES

SCANS

Special Features

Media/Technology

Chapter	Spreadsheet Software	Database Software	Word Processing Software	Internet	Video
5	■				■
6			■	■	■
7			■		■
8		■			■

Resources

SOFTWARE

Excel, Word, WordPerfect, Works, and ClarisWorks for Mac and Windows

Word Pro, ASCII, QuattroPro, Lotus, and Access for Windows

SOUTH-WESTERN EDUCATIONAL PUBLISHING PRODUCTS

Everard and Burrow. *Business Principles and Management*. 2001. Cincinnati: South-Western Educational Publishing Company. Textbook. 0-538-69793-8.

Goree. *Ethics In American Life*. 1996. Cincinnati: South-Western Educational Publishing Company. Text-Workbook. 0-538-63489-8.

BOOKS

Collins and Porras. *Built to Last : Successful Habits of Visionary Companies*. 1997. Harperbusiness.

Kotter. *Leading Change*. 1996. Harvard Business School Press.

GOVERNMENT PUBLICATIONS

Occupational Outlook Handbook, U.S. Department of Labor, Washington, DC.

What Work Requires of Schools: A SCANS Report for America 2000, U.S. Department of Labor, Washington, DC

MEDIA/TECHNOLOGY

Publisher's web sites:
www.intro2business.swep.com
www.swep.com
www.thomson.com

BUSINESS OPERATIONS

This unit introduces the fundamentals of business organization, ownership, management, and marketing. This unit serves as the foundation for the study of business activity in our economic environment.

Types of businesses and business activities are presented in Chapter 5. Chapter 6 focuses on the ways in which businesses organize. A detailed example of how a business grows from a sole proprietorship to a corporation is given. Other forms of business, including cooperatives, franchises, and nonprofit organizations, are discussed.

An entirely new chapter covers management and leadership. In Chapter 7, emphasis is given to various characteristics and styles of managers and leaders, and how managers become competent leaders. Chapter 8 covers issues related to the production and marketing of goods and services. Marketing topics are covered from product idea to distribution to promotion and final sale.

UNIT 2
BUSINESS OPERATIONS

Chapters

5 Business in Our Economy
Explains the role and function of business in the U.S. economy.

6 Business Structures
Cites examples of three types of business ownership.

7 Manager as Leader
Describes leadership characteristics and human relations skills needed by managers.

8 Producing and Marketing Goods and Services
Describes how small businesses can successfully produce and market products and services.

Kick-Off Activity

Investigating Business Media

To make the connection between today's business news and *Intro to Business*, an opening activity is provided for student research that pertains to Unit 2. The following exercise asks students to choose an article from *The Wall Street Journal*, the financial section of a newspaper, or a business magazine and to inquire about a topic related to this unit.

In the past decade, the following business issues have had a dramatic impact on our economy: home-based businesses, the fluctuating stock market, and the increasing use of the Internet in business. Ask students to choose one of these issues and find two or three articles pertaining to the chosen issue. Then direct them to answer the following questions:

1. What is the impact (or the expected impact) of this issue on our economy? What groups of people are most likely to be affected?

2. How do you think this issue will affect the industry or job field that you hope to enter in the future?

BU$INESSBRIEF
TODAY'S CHANGING WORKFORCE

As the 21st century begins, we are seeing dramatic changes in employment and careers in the U.S. The end of the 20th century saw career opportunities in the dot.com world and the decline of some traditionally important jobs like manufacturing and agriculture.

From 1990 to 2000, total employment grew by 17 percent. In 2000, 145.5 million people held jobs. That number is projected to reach 167.8 million by 2010, an increase of over 15 percent.

Baby boomers, the large number of people born between 1946 and 1964, have dominated the labor market since they began working in the 1960s. They will continue to do so until they begin retiring in the 2010s. The average age of U.S. workers in 2010 will be over 40.

A mini-boom of younger workers will cause the 16-to-24-year-old age group to grow more rapidly than the overall labor force for the first time in 25 years. Other groups that will experience higher employment growth rates are Asian-, Hispanic-, and African-American workers. Currently, white workers make up 73 percent of the labor force, but that will drop to 69 percent by 2010.

Over the last 50 years, one of the most dramatic trends in employment has been the participation of women. In the early 1960s, 35 percent of women were working outside the home. That percentage doubled by 2000. By 2010, nearly one-half of all jobs (48 percent) in the U.S. will be held by women.

At one time it was thought that technology would allow people to work fewer hours, but this has not occurred. Economic pressures have led to downsizing, production streamlining, and other attempts to reduce costs. Businesses ask employees to work additional hours and people may hold second jobs to meet their needs. A recent survey reported that seven of ten parents said they did not spend enough time with their children. At the same time, children see their parents changing jobs, taking on more responsibility, completing additional education to improve career opportunities, and making important decisions to balance work and family life. Those experiences will likely shape the career and family decisions of the next generation.

Economic pressures also resulted in the increased use of contingent workers. A contingent worker is one who has no explicit or implicit contract for long-term employment. About 5 percent of the U.S. workforce (nearly 6 million people) is composed of contingent workers. Some estimates project that number will double in ten years. Some people take contingent work because they cannot find the permanent employment they want. Others choose contingent work because they like the flexibility it offers.

CRITICAL THINKING

1 *How do you think changes in the workforce in the 21st century will affect your career, education, and family decisions?*

2 *What do you think are some advantages and disadvantages of being a contingent worker?*

55

BU$INESSBRIEF

A Business Brief sets the tone for a unit. To help students understand current and emerging trends, each unit will be introduced with a Business Brief. The Briefs were chosen for their importance to business, timeliness, and interest to students. The Briefs complement the many real-world examples woven into the text.

CRITICAL THINKING

Student answers will, of course, require thinking beyond what is presented in the Business Brief. The following are possible answers:

1 The workforce will be more diverse, so the ability to work as part of a diverse team will be important. It will be necessary to make choices about balancing career and family life, and to take part in lifelong education to improve career flexibility and opportunity.

2 Advantages:
- May offer individuals a way to enter the labor market that they otherwise may not have. Persons with special needs would either end up unemployed or be driven out of the workforce altogether.
- The flexibility could help them balance work with non-work obligations (childcare, care for elderly, etc.).
- More freedom to make own schedule.

Disadvantages:
- Some believe that contingent workers will be limited in their prospects for economic advancement, due to frequent job changes.
- Contingent workers may not be able to obtain or afford medical insurance, nor enjoy other benefits of working as a regular employee.
- Little opportunity to develop long-term relationships with coworkers.

BUILDING YOUR PORTFOLIO

The Building Your Portfolio work samples validate skill level and a student's ability to accomplish tasks frequently performed on the job. The most important reason for including samples in a portfolio is to demonstrate a student's abilities and skills. In selecting work samples for each unit, students should always have a choice of which activities to include. Students might be encouraged to include samples from the end-of-chapter activities, particularly Communicate Business Concepts, Calculate Business Data, Technology Application, and Decision-Making Strategies.

This chapter describes four kinds of businesses: extractors, manufacturers, marketers, and service firms. Emphasis is given to the functions performed by each type of business. The key activities of businesses are also described.

Resources for Teachers
- Lesson Plans
- School-To-Work/SCANS Activity Masters
- Spanish Resources
- Instructor's Resource CD

Assessment
- Chapter and Unit Tests, Ch. 5
- ExamView, Ch. 5

Media/Technology
- Applying Technology Data CD
- PowerPoint slides
- Business Connection CD
- Videotape

Activity Masters and Workbooks
- Activities and Projects, Ch. 5
- Internet Activity Masters
- Business Math Activity Masters
- Communications Activity Masters
- International Business Activity Masters
- Ethics Activity Masters

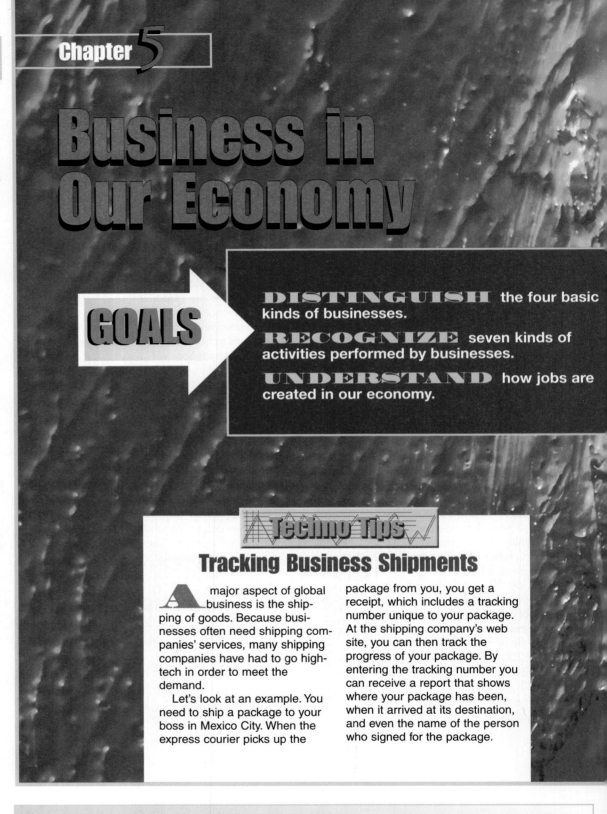

Chapter 5

Business in Our Economy

GOALS

DISTINGUISH the four basic kinds of businesses.

RECOGNIZE seven kinds of activities performed by businesses.

UNDERSTAND how jobs are created in our economy.

Techno Tips

Tracking Business Shipments

A major aspect of global business is the shipping of goods. Because businesses often need shipping companies' services, many shipping companies have had to go high-tech in order to meet the demand.

Let's look at an example. You need to ship a package to your boss in Mexico City. When the express courier picks up the package from you, you get a receipt, which includes a tracking number unique to your package. At the shipping company's web site, you can then track the progress of your package. By entering the tracking number you can receive a report that shows where your package has been, when it arrived at its destination, and even the name of the person who signed for the package.

Techno Tips

Students need to know the latest technologies and develop cutting edge Internet skills for use in current jobs, future careers, or in their homes. TechnoTips introduces students to today's cutting edge technologies and provides them with important Internet skills. Feature topics concentrate on Internet-specific technologies and computer or other hi-tech innovations for use by businesses and consumers.

FOCUS ON REAL LIFE

When you or your friends buy a pair of jeans, you very likely do not think much about the chain of businesses involved in making the jeans and getting them to the stores where you bought them. Most people don't. But there is an interesting sequence of events that occurs between the creation of your pair of jeans and your purchase of them.

First, the cotton is planted and harvested; then it is made into cloth and dyed different colors. The jeans are designed, made up in various sizes, labeled, boxed, and then stored until they are sold and transported to the store from which you and your friends buy them.

Several businesses are involved in this process. These businesses are different in many ways but are alike in that they help to put a product or service that you want on the market. That is what business is all about.

There are nearly 25 million business firms in the United States. While there are some differences among them, they all supply or help to supply goods and services to satisfy your wants and needs. Learning about them will help you understand what business does.

FOUR KINDS OF BUSINESSES

You and your family buy from many kinds of businesses. You buy food from a supermarket, shoes from a shoe store, furnace repairs from a plumbing and heating company, financial services from a bank, a car from an auto dealer, and electricity from a utilities company. In all of these cases, you are dealing with businesses that sell products and services to you and to other consumers.

Extractors

A business that grows products or takes raw materials from nature is called an **extractor**. The farmer who grows and sells cotton for your jeans is an extractor. Silver and coal miners are also extractors, as are those who dig copper in Montana, fish for salmon in Alaska, pump oil in Louisiana, grow fruit in California, and run lumber mills in Washington. Sometimes the extractor's products are ready to be sold just as they come from the earth or the sea, like the clams in New England, potatoes from Idaho, or pecans from Georgia. However, most food products and raw materials need some processing or change in form before the consumer can use them.

Manufacturers

A **manufacturer** takes the extractor's products or raw materials and changes them into a form that consumers can use. The manufacturer might make a product such as a snowmobile or process a product such as frozen and packaged vegetables. Other manufacturers may construct sections of a building that, when put together, become a house for people to live in. Some manufacturers are only a part of the total activity of producing goods from the extractor's products.

Think about those jeans again. The entire process might require several steps, which may be performed in several different locations, before the jeans are ready for you to purchase. For example, a textile mill in North Carolina takes cotton grown on an Alabama farm, spins it into yarn, and makes the yarn into cloth. A plant in New England then dyes

According to the U.S. Census Bureau, in 2000 there were 363,000 manufacturing businesses and 2.1 million farms in the United States.

Chapter 5 *Business in Our Economy* 57

FOCUS ON REAL LIFE

Where would you get the money to buy the equipment? Discuss the similarities between students' suggestions and what a business might do. Guide students through a discussion of how businesses benefit communities. Have volunteers explain what each benefit means to them and to their community in general. For example, businesses provide jobs for students now and/or in the future and help pay the cost of public facilities (such as schools or swimming pools) through taxes.

EXPLORE THIS/INDEPENDENT PRACTICE Ask students to investigate some new product ideas. What consumer needs do the new products or services fill? Are they technologically and financially reasonable? Have students prepare a report about their findings.

Have students examine a few companies with which they are familiar. How effectively do these companies conduct the seven key business activities? Do they innovate? Do they meet customer needs? How well do they market their products or services?

The Chapter Review questions at the end of the chapter vary in level of difficulty. For a basic assignment, consider Develop Your Business Language and Review Your Reading. For an average assignment, consider the basic assignment plus Communicate Business Concepts and Calculate Business Data. For an enhanced assignment, try the average assignment plus Technology Application and Decision-Making Strategies.

What are other raw materials, besides cotton, that need some processing before consumers can use them?

or prints the cloth, and a clothing manufacturer in New York buys the cloth and makes it into jeans. Together, extractors and manufacturers are industries that change the form of resources from their natural states into products for consumers.

Manufacturing businesses can be organized in several ways to produce products. Building

What form of manufacturing occurs in the production of your favorite products?

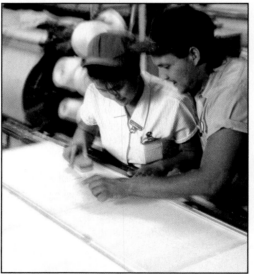

a specific and unique product to meet the needs of one customer is done with **custom manufacturing**. Products ranging from bicycles to dentures are specifically developed to meet particular design standards.

Mass production has been the standard of U.S. manufacturing for almost a century. With **mass production,** a large number of identical products are assembled using a continuous, efficient procedure. Mass production is seen in automobile assembly lines or beverage bottling plants.

Processing is a third type of manufacturing. **Processing** changes the form of materials so they can be consumed or used to manufacture other products. Crude oil is refined through processing to form gasoline and other petroleum products. Grain is processed into flour, cereal, and feed for animals. Film processors convert the film from your camera into pictures.

Marketers

Our skilled labor force and our advanced technology enable producers to make thousands of different products at a reasonable cost. However, if these products are not available where and when you and other consumers want to buy them, their value diminishes.

Basic Skills-Reading

Students may improve their reading skills by first developing pre-reading routines. Explore the goals at the beginning of the chapter with your students. Have a student read the goals out loud so that all will be aware of the various new learnings that will occur in the chapter. Explain to students that this is the first step to establishing the purpose of their reading assignments. By previewing goals, students will be able to recognize facts that are relevant when they begin reading the chapter. The Student Activity Worksheet, Basic Skills—Reading, in the School-To-Work/SCANS Activity Masters, may be used to serve as a guideline for discussion of each of these points. Ask students: Based on the chapter goals, what do you think you will learn?

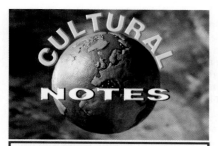
If all of the goods you use had to be bought directly from their producers, it would be a problem. You would have to fly to Central or South America to get a banana. You might have to drive to Minnnesota or Michigan to buy your favorite cereal. Buying products in that way would be inefficient and expensive.

The services of many businesses are often needed before goods actually reach consumers. A business that is involved with moving goods from producers to consumers is called a **marketer**. The activities of marketers are called *marketing.*

Marketing includes more than just transporting and selling products. Marketers also help to identify, develop, and test new products to see whether consumers will like them and buy them. They package goods to protect products and to present them in attractive and convenient sizes. They also store the goods until they are needed by other marketers or consumers. They even design store windows and arrange displays in supermarkets to attract your attention. All of these marketing activities add value to products by bringing them to where the consumer is, at a time

they are wanted, in the assortment wanted, and at prices the consumer is willing to pay.

Service Businesses

A business firm that does things for you instead of making or marketing products is called a **service business**. Service businesses over the past several years are the fastest growing part of our business world. The number of people employed in service industries has reached over 100 million. By 2010, it is projected that 125 million, or three in every four U.S. workers, will hold jobs in the service industry.

Some service businesses serve individual consumers, some serve other businesses, and some serve both. Today you can find service businesses to move you from New Jersey to Arizona, fly you to Singapore, style your hair, wash your car, figure your income tax, board your pet, or provide almost any service you need or do not want to perform yourself. Businesses also need services. A service business might help a company export its product to the Czech Republic for the first time, install a new computer system, or train a group of employees on how to access and use databases.

What are some methods that marketers use to attract consumers' attention?

acitvity. Also, using a computer if possible, have students write a brief paragraph describing the benefits to a community of a new business locating within the community or an existing business expanding its operations.

Direct students to read the Global Perspectives in this chapter. Have students interview the owner or manager of a retail store in your area to find if most of the products in the store come through direct or indirect marketing channels. Do any products come through more than one wholesaler? If so, give an example, identifying the types of wholesalers involved. Have students write a brief report entitled, "The Marketing Channels for (name of store), a Local Retail Store." Ask students to share their findings with the class.

Communities often advertise in newspapers and business magazines to encourage new businesses to locate in their towns. Find out what your community or your state is doing to attract new businesses. Consult such sources as your local newspaper, your Chamber of Commerce publications, and business magazines.

a. From the ads and other sources of information, list the advantages cited by your city or state to encourage businesses to locate in the area.
b. Which factors among those listed do you think are the most important?
c. Would some factors be more important to some kinds of businesses than others? Explain.

An increasing number of people who are retired, or who have leisure time and money to spend, look for businesses to provide opportunities for recreation, travel, and the like. Single parents and parents who both work have created a need for extensive child care services. Working parents tend to pay someone to perform many services that they once did for themselves. These are just two examples of service businesses that have increased greatly in size in recent years.

BUSINESS ACTIVITIES

Businesses may be large or small, simple or complex. A business might operate in just one community while another has worldwide operations. Although individual businesses differ in organization and operation, most perform seven basic activities.

What are common service businesses in your community?

Barbara Manzi started a heavy metal business in 1995. She doesn't make music. Instead she produces aluminum, titanium, and brass products for the military.

FYI

Generating Ideas
Someone must first think about a new product, a service, or an improved process or piece of equipment that can be put on the market. A business begins with someone's idea for a good or a service that will meet consumers' needs and wants. Examples include jogging shoes, lawn care businesses, and automatic load lifters for pickup trucks.

Once a business is established to sell a good or service, it must continue to develop ideas in order to survive. In our market economy, businesses compete with other firms that sell the same or similar products. To compete successfully, they must look for new or improved products and services. Many firms have research and development personnel who work full time creating, researching, and developing ideas that might result in new products and services.

Raising Capital
Businesses need capital resources to operate. Start-up money is critical and must be found to start the business. This may come from the owner's personal funds, from loans from banks or other financial institutions, or from others who wish to invest in the business.

Established businesses must continue to raise capital throughout the life of the firm. Companies may need to borrow money to buy equipment, to redesign a plant, build a new office building, or to buy another business. Most capital is obtained through loans from financial institutions, such as banks, or from people who wish to invest in the business.

Buying Goods and Services
Businesses buy goods and services both for resale and for their own use. The owner of a

FYI

men's clothing store, for instance, must buy slacks, jackets, suits, coats, and other items to sell. The store owner also needs sales tickets, a cash register, display cases, and other supplies. Services offered by other businesses, such as advertising space in a newspaper or a window cleaner to wash the display windows, will be needed.

In addition, businesses that manufacture products need to buy raw materials to produce their products. Buying raw materials, such as wheat, oil, plastic, steel, or chemicals, is an important activity in operating some businesses.

Using Human Resources

Businesses cannot operate without people. Except for the one-person business, all firms

What activities are involved in human resource management?

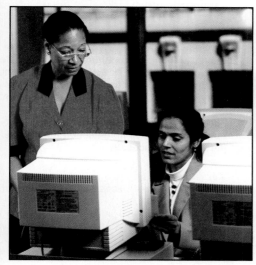

need to have a system for carrying out activities that attract, employ, and develop human resources. These include recruiting, or finding, workers; interviewing and testing applicants; selecting employees; training and developing both new and experienced employees; and appraising job performances.

Human resources management requires a knowledge of employment laws, health and safety regulations, and employee rights relating to issues such as promotions, transfers, layoffs, and firings. These activities are often carried out by a human resources department.

Marketing Goods and Services

Marketing involves a variety of activities, all directed toward providing the kind of product or service desired by consumers. Many marketing activities occur before a product is produced and ready for distribution and sale. Marketing today includes product and service planning. Marketers assist in the design and development of products and services that will meet the needs of prospective customers.

You might think of marketing and production as two sides of a coin. Businesses must produce and sell a needed product or service if they expect to succeed in the marketplace. Businesses use marketing to increase their effectiveness and the profits they make.

Producing Goods and Services

The heart of a successful business is the production of quality products and services. The

NET FACTS

A browser is a software program that gives access to most Internet services. A browser is required to connect to the multimedia documents on the World Wide Web.

good or service must be produced at the scheduled time, in the appropriate quantity and quality, and at competitive cost in order for the firm to stay in business. Assembling the people, raw materials, processes, and equipment to accomplish this task is essential to all businesses.

Keeping Records

All businesses must have some kind of a record keeping system. Most of these systems today utilize computer technology. Many records must be completed and compiled in the report to enable the owner or manager to know how the business is doing. Business managers need to know how much they have sold, how much of what they sold was returned by customers, and how much they owe to others. They need to know the amount they are spending for building repairs, rent, salaries, and other expenses. These records are important for

1. determining whether a business is making or losing money,

2. providing information for management decisions, and

3. supplying data for a variety of government reports, including tax forms.

THE IMPACT OF NEW BUSINESSES ON A COMMUNITY

When a new business opens, it begins paying wages to its employees. This is money that has not been in the community before. Workers spend this money for goods and services. The money is then spent again by the businesses from which those goods and services were bought. For example, part of each worker's income is spent for food. The grocery store manager uses part of this money for products to sell in his or her store. The

Contractors or builders replace $5 billion worth of equipment every year.

GLOBAL PERSPECTIVES

Joint Ventures

Sometimes a business firm wants to do business in an international market. One type of international partnership is the joint venture. This arrangement is especially popular when companies want to explore new markets while sharing the risk. Cooperation is the critical ingredient for success.

A *joint venture* is a special type of partnership. Two or more companies form an alliance to perform various business activities. Each business has a strength that is needed by the other. One company may provide most of the financing, another the channel of distribution, and another the production facilities.

Joint ventures can be created for just about any kind of business project. There are many examples of successful international joint ventures, especially in the automobile industry. The joint venture of Toyota and General Motors—called New United Motor Manufacturing, Inc.—is often cited as a success story. However, only about one-third of joint ventures meet their specific goals. A successful joint venture must be well managed, and good communication among the partners is a necessity.

Critical Thinking

1. What are some necessary ingredients of joint venture?
2. If a U.S. firm were interested in forming a joint venture, what advice would you give to help this firm succeed?

GLOBAL PERSPECTIVES

The Global Perspectives feature describes various international business practices. Complement this perspective with current articles dealing with joint ventures. These articles can be found in various business magazines and some management textbooks. Discuss with students successful joint ventures.

CRITICAL THINKING

1. The business must have a clearly defined goal or mission and know the formula for success in the international marketplace. Then a partner in another country must be selected in order to complete the business venture.
2. The firm should have a plan of action or business plan for operating in another country. Employees must be able to communicate effectively with individuals from another nation. An understanding of other cultures is very important.

manager also pays part of it to employees, who in turn spend their money somewhere else for other goods and services. If new people come to the community to work, more houses will probably be needed. Local builders will hire more workers and buy more materials. As each dollar is spent, each business is likely to buy more goods and hire more people to meet its customers' demands. This endless spending chain starts with businesses hiring employees and paying wages.

New businesses also buy products and services, such as electricity, office furniture and supplies, equipment, and tools. Some of these items will be bought from local busi-nesses. The additional sales provide local businesses with more income; in turn, these businesses may hire more employees to meet the demands of increased business.

Businesses also tend to attract other busi-nesses. When one business settles in a com-munity, other businesses often come to supply it. For example, small businesses may spring up to supply a large factory with such things as small parts, office supplies, cleaning services, and advertising services. Each of these smaller businesses hires people and buys goods and services. Thus, more jobs and more income are created in the community.

What impact does a new business have on a community?

TEACHING STRATEGIES

Alternate Modalities: Auditory Learner

The auditory learner will best learn by hearing. When intro-ducing new terms to an auditory learner, have the student repeat the term and its meaning out loud. Repeating this state-ment a few times will increase the chances of its being reinforced.

REVIEW YOUR READING

1. Answers will vary. Examples are extracting: mining, fishing, farming; manufacturing: T-shirts, shoes, cars; marketing: packaging, advertising, consumer surveys; service business: laundry, lawyers, banking.

2. Extracted products such as crabs from the sea or sunflower seeds from the earth are ready for the consumer in their natural state.

3. The three types of manufacturing are custom manufacturing, mass production, and processing.

4. Other marketing activities include designing store windows and displays, testing new products, advertising, packaging, and storing.

5. Most businesses (1) develop ideas to start a business and to keep it competitive; (2) carry out financing activities to start a new business, expand an ongoing business, and manage the firm's money both for operations and for growth; (3) buy goods, services, and raw materials; (4) carry out staffing and other personnel activities in managing the human resources of the firm; (5) produce goods or services for sale; (6) market goods or services; and (7) maintain accounting records.

6. Students might cite such contributions as (a) training unskilled workers; (b) helping people from minority groups set up or manage their businesses; (c) assisting schools; (d) contributing to charitable, civic, and cultural projects; and (e) donating land for parks and recreational areas.

COMMUNICATE BUSINESS CONCEPTS

7. Answers will vary. Extracting businesses include farming, fishing, mining, timber producers, and many others.

8. Answers will vary. Examples are:
   (a) Goods for resale such as flowers, ribbons, vases, and shells.
   (b) Goods for use in the store might include stationery, light bulbs, and display counters.
   (c) Services to customers such as free parking, delivery, personal shopper service, and free enclosure cards for gifts.
   (d) Services she might buy include custodial service, security guards, telephone service, and linen supply.

BUSINESS NOTES

1. Four basic kinds of businesses are extractors, manufacturers, marketers, and service businesses.

2. Businesses must perform the following activities: generating new ideas, raising capital, buying goods and services, using human resources, producing goods and services, marketing goods and services, and keeping records.

3. New jobs are created when new businesses locate within a community.

REVIEW YOUR READING

1. Give an example of each of the four basic types of businesses.

2. What is meant by the statement that some extractors' products are ready to be sold to the consumer in their natural states?

3. What are the three types of manufacturing used by businesses?

4. Name several marketing activities other than transporting and selling goods.

5. Cite seven activities that are performed by most businesses.

6. Explain ways in which new businesses benefit a community.

COMMUNICATE BUSINESS CONCEPTS

7. Identify three different types of products that are produced in your state by extractors.

8. Kim Sun operates the Sea Isle Treasures shop in the waterfront marketplace of her city. She sells fresh flower arrangements and leis as well as shell jewelry and ornaments. Give two examples of the following:
   a. Goods which she would buy for resale.
   b. Goods she would buy for use in her store.
   c. Services she might offer to her customers.
   d. Services she might buy from other businesses.

9. The Chamber of Commerce and the Economic Development Council of Central City have persuaded a fiberglass processing plant to open in the city's industrial park. The company expects to employ 200 people there. Name at least five ways in which the city would probably benefit from the new business.

9. Students might cite benefits such as (1) 200 new jobs in the new business; (2) other jobs created by the money spent by the 200 new workers and the new business; (3) new households created; (4) more tax money for city services; and (5) new leaders to help in civic, cultural, and charitable projects.

DEVELOP YOUR BUSINESS LANGUAGE

For each numbered item, find the term that has the same meaning.

10. A business involved with moving goods from producers to consumers.

11. A large number of identical products are assembled using a continuous, efficient procedure.

12. A business that takes an extractor's products or raw materials and changes them into a form that consumers can use.

13. Building a specific and unique product to meet the needs of one customer.

14. A business that grows products or takes raw materials from nature.

15. Changing the form of materials so they can be consumed or used to manufacture other products.

16. A business that does things for you instead of making or marketing products.

KEY TERMS
custom manufacturing
extractor
marketer
manufacturer
mass production
processing
service business

DECISION-MAKING STRATEGIES

Sonja Bartholomew started a lawn mowing service. However, she could not charge as much as she needed to make the profit she desired. Her competitors only charged $15 per lawn while she charged $20. But she did a superior job cutting lawns. Still, potential customers did not want to pay the extra $5.

A friend, Eduardo Guadalupe, suggested that they work together. He was good at trimming shrubs and had ideas for improving landscapes with flowers and lawn ornaments. They would offer a unique service when they combined their businesses. They could charge an amount that would result in a good profit for both of them. They would seek out homes in neighborhoods with above-average income levels.

17. What will be special about the services that Sonja and Eduardo can offer together? What additional services might they include?

18. Why would above-average income levels be targeted?

CALCULATE BUSINESS DATA

19. The Juan Iglesias Company is considering building a cannery in Santa Rosa. The company's accountants estimate the monthly income and expenses for the new plant as shown in this table.

    a. What is the total amount of the cannery's monthly expenses, including taxes?

    b. What will be the cannery's profit after taxes if the estimates are accurate? (Calculate after-tax profit by subtracting the total estimated expenses and taxes from estimated income.)

    c. What is the percent of after-tax profit based on income from sales?

Income from sales	$200,000
Expenses:	
Salaries	$100,000
Raw materials purchased	60,000
Rent on equipment	6,500
Miscellaneous expenses	5,000
Taxes	8,400

DEVELOP YOUR BUSINESS LANGUAGE

10. marketer
11. mass production
12. manufacturer
13. custom manufacturer
14. extractor
15. processing
16. service business

DECISION-MAKING STRATEGIES

17. Sonja and Eduardo will be able to mow lawns plus trim shrubs and offer ideas for improving landscapes with flowers and lawn ornaments. They will have a package of services that others do not offer.

18. People with above-average incomes very likely would have larger houses and larger yards; therefore, they might be the most interested in such services. People with average and below-average incomes should not be overlooked; however, there is greater profit potential in serving individuals with larger houses and yards.

CALCULATE BUSINESS DATA

19. (a) $100,000 + $60,000 + $6,500 + $5,000 + $8,400 = $179,900; (b) $200,000 − $179,900 = $20,100; (c) $20,100 ÷ $200,000 = 0.1005 or 10%.

20. (a) 788 + 244 + 718 + 473 = 2,223,000,000 pounds for Year One; 563 + 156 + 617 + 249 = 1,585,000,000 pounds for Year Two; (b) No; the catch decreased for all regions. (c) $327 + $97 + $130 + $148 = $702,000,000 for Year One; $449 + $114 + $131 + $155 = $849,000,000 for Year Two. (d) Yes; the dollar value increased in all regions.

21. (a) 15,825.5 × $0.78 = $12,343.89
$36,000 × 328 × 0.01 = $118,080
$12,343.89 + $118,080 = $130,423.89 total taxes collected
(b) The businesses and the employees will spend money at other businesses, resulting in taxes paid by those busineses; the employees will participate in community activities and organizations.

TECHNOLOGY APPLICATION

In this activity, students use a computer to solve a business problem using a file provided on the data CD that accompanies *Intro to Business*. Instructions for using the data CD are included in a **README** file on the disk. Solutions are provided on the Instructor's Resource CD.

---

20. The fish catch and the value of the catch along the Atlantic coast for two years are shown in this table.

a. What was the total weight of the catch for all the Atlantic areas, expressed in full (including the zeros) for Year One and Year Two?

b. Did the fish catch for any of the areas increase in Year Two?

c. What was the dollar value of the catch in Year One and Year Two?

d. Did the dollar value of the catch increase in any area in Year Two?

21. To provide additional employment and increase its tax base from businesses, Yorketowne's city council opened a business park on the edge of the city. After five years, they had attracted two new manufacturers and 4 supporting service businesses to the park. The total value of the property of all six businesses was $15,825,500. The companies paid $0.78 per $1,000 of property value each year as property tax. In addition, the businesses employed 328 people at an average salary of

Areas	Catch (in Millions of Pounds)		Value (in Millions of Dollars)	
	Year One	Year Two	Year One	Year Two
New England	788	563	$327	$449
Mid-Atlantic	244	156	97	114
Chesapeake Bay	718	617	130	131
South Atlantic	473	249	148	155

$36,000. Each person paid a 1% city income tax each year.

a. What is the total amount of taxes the city collected as a result of opening the business park?

b. In addition to the tax dollars, what other benefits might the city receive from opening the business park?

TECHNOLOGY APPLICATION

Using the *Intro to Business* Data CD and your spreadsheet program software, select problem CH05. After the problem appears on your screen, complete the following activities. Then, after you have completed each step, display or print the completed spreadsheet for each activity. If you do not have a printer available, answer the questions before you leave the computer.

22. Make two copies of the spreadsheet so that you have a total of three income statements. Do not copy the table entitled Net Income Comparisons. On the first income statement, enter a quantity of 1,000 and a price of $10. Answer the following questions:

a. What is the amount of gross profit on sales?

b. What is the amount of net income?

23. On the second income statement, enter a quantity of 2,000 and a price of $10. In the table entitled Net Income Comparisons, enter formulas to display the net income from the second income statement and to calculate the

percentage of increase in net income from the first income statement to the second. Answer the following questions:

a. What is the amount of net income on the second income statement?

b. What is the percentage of increase in net income from the first income statement to the second?

24. On the third income statement, enter a quantity of 1,000 and a price of $25. In the table entitled Net Income Comparisons, enter formulas to display the net income from the third income statement and to calculate the percentage of increase in net income from the first income statement to the third. Answer the following questions:

a. What is the amount of gross profit on sales on the third income statement?

b. What is the percentage of increase in net income from the first income statement to the third?

COMMUNICATING for SUCCESS

COMMUNICATING for SUCCESS

NONVERBAL COMMUNICATION—ACTIONS SPEAK LOUDER THAN WORDS!

Nonverbal forms of communication are always present and often play a deciding role in business success. Whether intentional or not, nonverbal messages influence how the receiver interprets what you are saying. You are constantly sending nonverbal messages to the world around you. These nonverbal messages contribute to creating a lasting impression on coworkers and clients. Negative nonverbal messages can destroy business opportunities and create conflict. The most common nonverbal messages are conveyed through:

- physical appearance
- body language
- emphasis on time
- use of space

Physical appearance is often the first impression you make on someone and is, therefore, quite important. Physical appearance doesn't just apply to how you look; it carries through to other aspects of your business communication. For instance, physical appearance can include how a letter looks—the color of the stationery, the neatness of the signature, and the organization and format of the letter.

Body language, or messages sent through the use of your body, can alter or influence the meaning of a verbal message.

For example, a person slumping in a chair may give the impression of being tired or depressed. Also, an individual who fails to make eye contact might be interpreted as dishonest or not listening.

The nonverbal factors of time and space provide indicators of the seriousness, formality, and importance of the communication process. A person who is always on time, for example, gives the impression of being well-organized, dependable, and valuing the importance of business commitments.

You should also be aware that different cultures have different nonverbal messages. For example, in the culture of corporate America, eye contact is typically expected among coworkers and superiors. Making eye contact shows respect and understanding. However, in some Asian cultures, direct eye contact would be considered disrespectful and a challenge to authority. It is important that you learn about nonverbal etiquette for a wide variety of cultures, and put your knowledge into practice.

CRITICAL THINKING

1. What role do nonverbal forms of communication play in the workplace?
2. How are the most common nonverbal messages conveyed?

Communications skills will help ensure students' success in the business world. Communicating for Success introduces workplace/interpersonal communications issues and proper uses of communications technology. Each feature discusses a key communications topic, and contains two Critical Thinking questions that require students to analyze what they have learned.

Nonverbal communication can sometimes be just as important to students' success as verbal communication, although students tend to think that only the latter matters in formal relationships such as school and work. This Communicating for Success feature discusses the importance of the nonverbal messages that we all send out constantly. It also details the ways in which we communicate nonverbally, even if we don't intend to or don't realize we are doing it.

CRITICAL THINKING

1. Nonverbal forms of communication play a critical role in the workplace.
2. The most common nonverbal messages are conveyed through physical appearance, body language, emphasis on time, and use of space.

Chapter 5 *Business in Our Economy* 67

Chapter 6

In Chapter 6, three popular forms of business ownership are examined: sole proprietorships, partnerships, and corporations. A few special types of business organizations are also described.

Resources for Teachers
- Lesson Plans
- School-To-Work/SCANS Activity Masters
- Spanish Resources
- Instructor's Resource CD

Assessment
- Chapter and Unit Tests, Ch. 6
- ExamView, Ch. 6

Media/Technology
- Applying Technology Data CD
- PowerPoint slides
- Business Connection CD
- Videotape

Activity Masters and Workbooks
- Activities and Projects, Ch. 6
- Internet Activity Masters
- Business Math Activity Masters
- Communications Activity Masters
- International Business Activity Masters
- Ethics Activity Masters

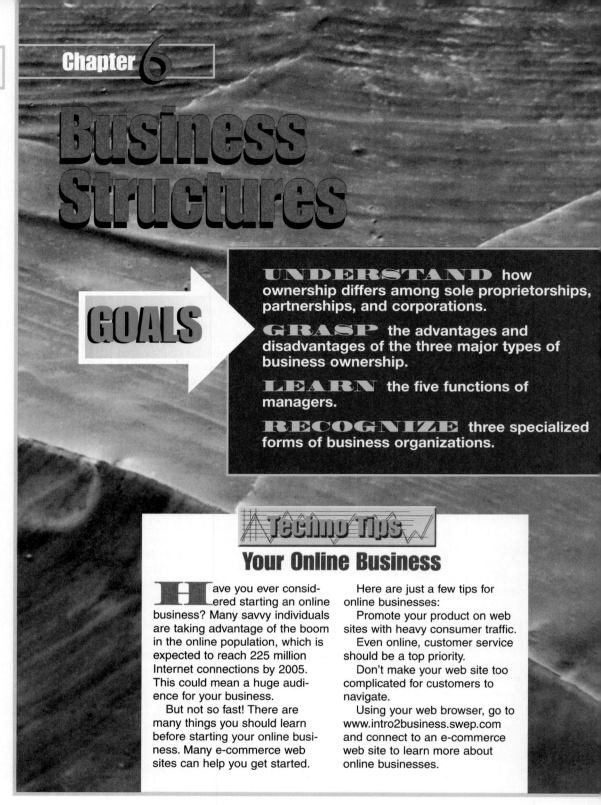

Chapter **6**

Business Structures

GOALS

UNDERSTAND how ownership differs among sole proprietorships, partnerships, and corporations.

GRASP the advantages and disadvantages of the three major types of business ownership.

LEARN the five functions of managers.

RECOGNIZE three specialized forms of business organizations.

Techno Tips
Your Online Business

Have you ever considered starting an online business? Many savvy individuals are taking advantage of the boom in the online population, which is expected to reach 225 million Internet connections by 2005. This could mean a huge audience for your business.

But not so fast! There are many things you should learn before starting your online business. Many e-commerce web sites can help you get started.

Here are just a few tips for online businesses:

Promote your product on web sites with heavy consumer traffic.

Even online, customer service should be a top priority.

Don't make your web site too complicated for customers to navigate.

Using your web browser, go to www.intro2business.swep.com and connect to an e-commerce web site to learn more about online businesses.

Students need to know the latest technologies and develop cutting edge Internet skills for use in current jobs, future careers, or in their homes. TechnoTips introduces students to today's cutting edge technologies and provides them with important Internet skills. Feature topics concentrate on Internet-specific technologies and computer or other hi-tech innovations for use by businesses and consumers. At the www.intro2business.swep.com web site, students can complete the activity for this chapter.

When your club decides to undertake a major project, such as sponsoring a big weekend car wash, what is the first thing that must be done? You must get organized! Questions must be answered: Where will the car wash be held? What are the best hours for a car wash? What supplies will be needed and who will get them? How much should be charged?

Committees may be formed, and someone may be appointed as the project chairperson. One committee might look into locations for the car wash, another might list and get supplies needed, and another might decide how much to charge and also keep the financial records. And, of course, people will be needed to do the car washing—club members (the human resources) must be willing to work. Organization is necessary if the car wash project is to be successful and earn a profit for the club.

In a similar way, a business also must organize to produce goods and services for the consumer. Many questions must be answered in the organizing process. Who will make the decisions? Who will buy the goods to sell? Who will keep the records of what is bought and sold? Who will get the profits? If there is a loss, who must bear it? How a business is structured determines these decisions.

TYPES OF BUSINESS OWNERSHIP

There are three major types of business ownership. They are the sole proprietorship, the partnership, and the corporation. Later in this chapter you will learn about other types of business ownership, including franchises, cooperatives, and non-profit corporations.

A **sole proprietorship** is a business owned by one person. Most are small firms such as jewelry stores, restaurants, gas stations, and hair-styling salons. As Figure 6-1 points out, more than two-thirds of U.S. businesses are operated as sole proprietorships. The sole proprietor has complete responsibility for all business decisions. In most cases, he or she also works in the firm.

A **partnership** is a business owned and managed by a small group, often not more than two or three people, who become partners. By written agreement, these partners share the profits or losses and have unlimited liability for the debts of their business.

A **corporation** is a business owned by a number of people and operated under written permission from the state in which it is located. The written permission is called a **certificate of incorporation**. The corporation acts as a single individual on behalf of its owners. By buying shares of stock, people become owners of corporations. They are then known as **shareholders**, also called stockholders. A corporation may have very few owners, but most corporations have many owners. Thus, the corporation is a *legal entity* with an existence and life separate from its owners. Large corporations, such as IBM, Texaco, and General Motors, may have millions of owners. Even if you own just one share of a company, you are still one of its owners. Most mining, manufacturing, and transporting of goods are performed by corporations. In addition, many of our consumer goods are supplied by supermarkets, department stores, and other businesses organized as corporations.

The size and the nature of a business are key factors in choosing the best type of ownership for it. To help you understand each type of ownership, the next few pages tell a story of how a young person started a business and worked to make it grow.

PURPOSE Have students review each of the chapter goals. Then have students skim the chapter to become familiar with its organization and the major topics to be covered. Ask them to write one question for each of the goals. Use some of the questions to guide discussion about the chapter.

TEACH/APPLY

MAKE CONNECTIONS Place the four business categories described in Chapter 5 on the board or overhead: extractors, manufacturers, marketers, and service firms. Then instruct students to write down one category of interest. Have them explain in writing why the category would be of interest.

Then ask students to select a business that they might one day wish to start or operate. Have each student

1. provide a name for the business;
2. write one or two sentences that describe the business;
3. indicate the location of the business;
4. list several questions that will need to be addressed before operating the business.

Allow students enough time to respond to each of the four points. Then write each student's name on the board, the name of the business, and the business category. Also list some of the questions raised. Lead the class in a discussion of how the businesses selected might be structured or organized. Most of the businesses probably would be organized initially as sole proprietorships.

Ask approximately ten students to name one or more local businesses with which they are familiar. Record the names of the businesses on the board or overhead. Ask students if they know what these businesses produce or sell and how they originally started. Write various forms of business ownership on the board or overhead—sole proprietorship, partnership, corporation, franchise, cooperative, or non-profit corporation. Ask students to identify the type of ownership for each business identified.

Show PowerPoint 6-2, *Types of Business Ownership.* Discuss each type of business organization with students in terms of its advantages and disadvantages. Ask if a sole proprietorship can be used to own any and all types of businesses. They should respond that any type of business could be owned as a sole proprietorship. Follow up with this question: "Why might it be necessary for more than one person to own a large business?" This question can be used to discuss the prevalence of corporations in capital-intensive industries—steel, autos, mining. Extractors and manufacturers require large amounts of capital resources.

TRY THIS/GUIDED PRACTICE
Ask students to review the description of a corporation and make a list of characteristics that make corporations different from sole proprietorships and partnerships. Call on students to read their responses. Ask the class if any of them own stock in a corporation. If any students respond that they do, inquire as to what rights they have as shareholders (i.e., what does the ownership get them?).

Show PowerPoint 6-5, *Expanding a Business.* Ask students why the owner of a small business might decide to reorganize as a partnership or corporation. Then discuss reasons it might be better to remain a sole proprietorship. Remind them that many more businesses are organized as sole proprietorships than the other two types, so many business owners see that form as preferable.

Discuss with students the parallels between a partnership and a marriage. Encourage students to

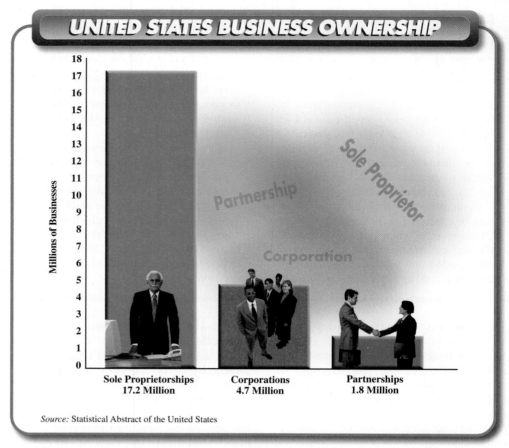

FIGURE 6-1 Do you know which type of business is the most complex?

GETTING STARTED IN BUSINESS

There are a number of ways of getting started in business. Let's consider the case of Julie Alcess. While in high school, Julie was a star player on her basketball team. She also worked part time at a number of different jobs after school and during summers. She thought about retailing as a career and took business courses in school. During her senior year, she became acquainted with the manager of the sporting goods store that supplied her school with equipment. The manager offered Julie a part-time sales job in his store.

After graduation, she accepted a full-time job in the store and continued to learn about small business operation. She took college night classes in business administration. Her selling techniques were excellent, and she quite often was put in charge of the store when the manager was gone for the day.

Julie earned a good salary and was able to save money as a sales clerk, but she dreamed about owning her own sporting goods store one day. She liked the idea of being her own boss.

The easiest way to become a business owner is to buy a share of stock in a corporation.

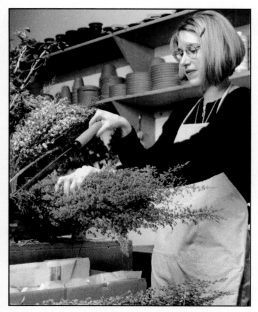

Why do you think that sole proprietorships make up over two-thirds of U.S. businesses?

Julie began planning for her own business. She located space that she liked in a new mall that was opening. A small store would get her started. She talked over her plans with her boss, and he encouraged her to pursue her dream.

She needed more money than she had in her savings account. Because she had a good work record and experience in the sporting goods business, the local bank gave her a start-up loan. She began by ordering merchandise, supplies, and equipment. Then she signed a one-year lease and paid the first month's rent. She resigned her job and opened Julie's Sports-4-All.

Julie was excited the day she greeted her first customers. She soon learned, though, that owning her own business required long hours and much decision making. She needed help. A good friend and schoolmate, Andy Davidson, was good in accounting and business law. In fact, he was studying to be an attorney. He agreed to help Julie keep the needed records and file the forms the government required.

Julie liked the feeling she got from running her own business. She was the sole owner of the business shown in Figure 6-2. All the

A recent survey revealed that 8 out of 10 people had a "secret desire" to start a business of their own.

FIGURE 6-2 Do you see why small businesses tend to be sole proprietorships?

provide qualities necessary for success in both.

Brainstorm to come up with a list of well-known franchises within your community. Then have students get the name and address of a franchise firm and write to secure information about how to buy a franchise. Information about franchises can be gained from library reference materials.

EXPLORE THIS/INDEPENDENT PRACTICE Have students prepare a one-page response to the question, "What are the most important skills of an effective manager?" Ask them to identify whether they would like to be a manager or business owner based on their study of management activities.

Have students analyze the various sections and provisions of a corporate charter. If you can get two corporate charters, have students compare the two.

If possible, secure a partnership agreement that is being used by a particular business. Make a transparency or duplicate parts or all of the agreement. Have students explain what is meant by various provisions in the agreement. (Some stationery and office supply firms have standard partnership agreement forms that can be used if you cannot get one that is actually being used.)

The Chapter Review questions at the end of the chapter vary in level of difficulty. For a basic assignment, consider Develop Your Business Language and Review Your Reading. For an average assignment, consider the basic assignment plus Communicate Business Concepts and Calculate Business Data. For an enhanced assignment, try the average

TEACHING STRATEGIES
Cooperative Learning

Group Investigation is a positive form of cooperative learning in which students learn to work together. Plan the size of each group before you begin, decide specific roles for the groups, set a time limit, and give guidelines for the outcome. For this activity, students form their own groups with two to six mem-

bers each. Groups will develop a list of items for the articles of partnership for a business of their choice. Some groups may present a list of items, whereas the more creative might actually draft a document that represents the articles of partnership. If you have access to computers, this textbook has a data CD that contains a word processing activity in which students can actually create a partnership agreement. This problem is found in Technology Application in the Chapter Review activities.

assignment plus Technology Application and Decision-Making Strategies.

ASSESS

Review the goals at the beginning of the chapter and the Business Notes at the end of the chapter. Have students respond orally or in writing to each of the Business Notes restated as a question, provided below. For students who may have difficulty providing answers, assign the reteaching activities that follow. Enrichment activities may also be assigned where appropriate.

1. How does ownership differ among sole proprietorships, partnerships, and corporations? (Answer: sole proprietorship—owned by one person; partnership—owned by two or more people; corporation—owned by many people.)

2. Name one advantage and one disadvantage of each type of common business organization. (Answer: Sole proprietorship: Advantage—easy to start; owner makes all the decisions and is own boss; owner receives all the profits. Disadvantage—capital is limited to what the owner can supply or borrow; owner is liable (responsible) for all debts, even losing personal property if business fails; long hours and hard work are often necessary. Partnership: Advantage—fairly easy to start the business; more sources of capital are available; more business skills are available. Disadvantage—each partner is liable for business debts made by all partners, even to

profits—or losses—were hers. And Julie's new business responsibilities gave special meaning to functions of management she had learned about in her business courses.

MANAGING A SUCCESSFUL BUSINESS

There are five management functions that must be completed by the people responsible for a business: planning, organizing, staffing, leading, and controlling. Corporations hire managers to complete the functions. The management functions are usually divided among the owners of a partnership. In a small business like Julie's, the owner usually performs all of the functions.

Planning

Julie remembered that this function included thinking, gathering and analyzing information, and then making decisions about all phases of the business. Goals must be set for the business and strategies devised for achieving them. Julie did a great deal of planning at the beginning. Later, however, she felt that she was spending too much time on day-to-day operations and did not have enough time for planning. She recalled that her instructor had warned about this pitfall in operating a small business.

Organizing

This function is the process of determining what work has to be done and who is to do each job. Jobs are assigned to workers and authority is given to certain people to see that the jobs are done. For example, Julie directs the work of two part-time sales clerks: Jason and Brianna. These workers report directly to her.

The organizing process usually results in a diagram, called an **organization chart**, that shows work relationships. The design of an organization chart shows the way the business is structured, the major work activities of the company, and the reporting relationships among the people who work for the business. Although Julie's business is too

small to require one, she sketched one out as shown in Figure 6-3. The chart shows that Julie has the authority to direct the work of her part-time employees. In turn, they are responsible to Julie to complete the work she assigns.

Staffing

Staffing includes all of the activities involved in finding, selecting, hiring, training, appraising, and rewarding the business's employees. Julie was able to perform these personnel activities for her two part-time workers.

Leading

The work of people must be directed so that their tasks will be performed correctly and on time. Influencing people to act according to company plans and procedures can be a difficult task. Effective leaders inspire workers to willingly perform their jobs and accept their share of responsibility for accomplishing the goals of the business. Leading requires good human relations and communications skills. Julie considers herself an effective leader.

Controlling

Owners must determine to what extent the business is accomplishing the goals it set out to reach in the planning stage. Controlling means comparing what actually happens with what was planned. If Julie had planned a

FIGURE 6-3 Can you tell who is the boss?

Simple Organization Chart

Julie Alcess
Owner/Manager
Julie's Sports-4-All

Brianna Donavon
Sales Clerk

Jason Smythe
Sales Clerk

Workplace Competencies-Interpersonal Skills

SCANS

Participating as a member of a team is an example of one way to develop interpersonal skills. As successful team members, individuals must learn to serve their customer, the teacher. This skill will then later transfer to the customer/client when the student enters the world of work. Team members must learn to listen in order to avoid misunderstandings, be positive in communication, and understand resources for meeting customer needs. The Student Activity Worksheet, Workplace Competencies—Interpersonal Skills Checklist, in the School-To-Work/SCANS Activity Masters, may serve as a guideline. The preceding activity, Teaching Strategies—Cooperative Learning, develops these interpersonal skills.

5 percent increase in sales for a three-month period, she would check the actual increase regularly to see whether she was moving toward her goal as planned. If, at the end of the second month she had already achieved a 4 percent increase, she could feel that her strategies were working well. If the increase were only 1 percent, she might consider a new strategy.

Controlling also means using the standards set up in the planning stage. For instance, if a business set a standard of production for workers to handle 12 customer inquiry calls per hour, the controlling activity would be to count the actual number of calls handled per hour for each employee. If the quality standard for each call was that the customer's questions would be answered and follow-up materials sent out, the controlling function would be to check each completed call and the follow-through. As you can see, controlling is directly related to planning.

EXPANDING A BUSINESS

Julie wondered how she could handle all the management activities as her business grew. She also needed the help of someone who knew more about finance and law than she did. Julie believed that Andy Davidson would fit in well. He was willing to invest in the business, and he could take over accounting, personnel administration, and preparation of records and reports. They would make a good team. Bringing in a partner, she thought, would be a solution.

Julie talked with Andy about her idea of opening a larger store, adding more merchandise, and doing more promotions. She offered a partnership deal to Andy, and he accepted.

A Partnership Is Formed

Andy drew up a written agreement that provided the details of how their partnership would operate. It was called the *articles of partnership*. Included in the articles of partnership were the essential things they agreed upon:

1. The name of the new business will be Sports Abundant.

2. Julie Alcess will invest $80,000 in cash and property. Andy Davidson will invest $40,000 in cash.

3. Each partner will draw a salary of $2,000 a month.

4. Profits and losses after salaries are paid will be shared in proportion to each partner's investment: two-thirds to Julie Alcess and one-third to Andy Davidson.

5. Julie Alcess will have the main responsibility for sales, selection and purchase of merchandise, and customer and community relations. Andy Davidson will handle financial records, payroll, store maintenance, government reports, and other details of operating the business.

6. In the event of the death or the necessary withdrawal of one partner, the remaining partner will have the right to purchase the departing partner's share of the business.

Users of the Internet include schools, government agencies, businesses, libraries, colleges and universities, military bases, and more.
   The fastest growing group of users, however, is individuals who access the Internet from their homes.

losing personal property if the business fails; each partner can make decisions (there is more than one boss); each partner shares the profit. Corporations: Advantage—more sources of capital are available; specialized managerial skills are available; owners are liable up to the amount of their investments; ownership can be easily transferred through sale of stock (the business is not affected by change of ownership). Disadvantage—difficult/complex process to start a corporation; owners do not have control of the decisions made each day, unless they are officers of the company; business activities of the corporation are limited to those stated in the certificate of incorporation.)

3. What are the five functions of managers? (Answer: Managers plan, organize, staff, lead, and control.)

4. What are three examples of specialized business organizations? (Answer: Franchises, cooperatives, and non-profit corporations.)

RETEACH

Develop a bulletin board showing the advantages and disadvantages of various forms of business ownership: sole proprietorship, partnership, corporation, cooperative, and franchise. Use this bulletin board to reteach the concepts of ownership.

Show PowerPoint 6-6, *Specialized Forms of Business Organizations*. Have students skim the text and identify key points about each type of business organization listed.

Net Facts provides information and definitions of terms for the Internet. The more information that students have about the Internet, the better equipped they will be to use this resource. In the Internet Activity Masters, there is an Internet Activity Worksheet for each unit. You can use these activities to give students experience with finding information online. Options for assigning this activity are as follows:

1. **Provide students with a list of addresses of resources for this activity;**
2. **Assign students to conduct their own searches; or**
3. **Use the addresses provided on the Internet Activity Worksheet.**

You should complete the activity yourself before assigning it to resolve any discrepancies that may arise.

Before they signed the articles of partnership, they discussed some of the legal responsibilities of becoming partners. For example, each partner could be held personally responsible for all of the debts of the business. This would even include debts incurred by the other partner without the first partner's consent. Each partner was also bound by the business agreements that the other partner made. To avoid problems, Julie and Andy agreed to discuss all important business matters, such as hiring people or signing a contract, before taking action.

The partnership, as shown in Figure 6-4, was very successful. At the end of the first year, there was a profit of $20,000 after the business expenses and the partners' salaries had been paid. Since they had agreed to share the profits in proportion to their investments in the business, Julie received two-thirds, or $13,333, and Andy received one-third, or $6,667.

A Corporation Is Created

Sports Abundant continued to grow. Julie and Andy were successful business partners. They saw a potential for a larger operation, one that would include large items such as boats and school gymnasium equipment. They

A corporation can sue or be sued; our courts consider a corporation to be a legal entity.

wanted to enlarge their operation and open a branch in a major shopping mall being built in one of the suburbs. They spent much time coming up with new ideas for improving their business. To do these things, they needed more money. They thought about adding more partners but decided against it. They reasoned that they did not need partners to help them manage the business since they could hire qualified assistants and managers. Also, there would be personal risks in being responsible for the actions of other partners.

Andy suggested that they form a corporation. They would then not be personally responsible for the debts of the business. In case of a business failure, each member of the corporation could lose only the amount he or she had invested. They dissolved the partnership and drew up a plan for a new corporation, J & A Sports and Recreation, Incorporated. The corporation was to represent a total investment of $240,000. Their financial

PARTNERSHIP

Sports Abundant

FIGURE 6-4 How can partners strengthen a business?

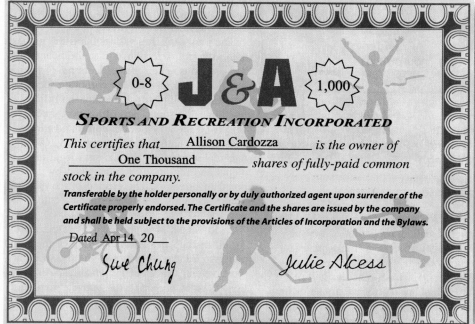

STOCK CERTIFICATE

0-8 **J &A** **1,000**

SPORTS AND RECREATION INCORPORATED

This certifies that ___Allison Cardozza___ is the owner of
___One Thousand___ shares of fully-paid common
stock in the company.

*Transferable by the holder personally or by duly authorized agent upon surrender of the
Certificate properly endorsed. The Certificate and the shares are issued by the company
and shall be held subject to the provisions of the Articles of Incorporation and the Bylaws.*

Dated _Apr 14_ 20___

Sue Chung   *Julie Alcess*

FIGURE 6-5 What does this stock certificate show?

records showed that the partnership was worth
$180,000; therefore, they needed to raise
another $60,000. Julie and Andy decided to
divide the $240,000 into 24,000 shares, each
with a value of $10. Based on the partnership
agreement and the corporation plans, they
divided the 24,000 shares this way:

1. Julie received 12,000 shares worth
   $120,000,

2. Andy received 6,000 shares worth $60,000,
   and

3. they offered for sale 6,000 shares valued at
   $60,000.

**Almost 50 percent
of all retail sales
are made at franchise
stores.**

FYI

Information about the division of shares of
stock and other information about the corporation was included in an application that was
submitted to the state government. The application requested permission to operate as a
corporation. After approving the application,
the state issued a certificate of incorporation
authorizing the formation of J & A Sports
and Recreation, Inc.

Julie and Andy now were part owners of a
corporation. They had received 18,000 shares
of stock in proportion to their original investment in the former partnership. The 6,000
shares offered for sale were bought by 30
people who had confidence in the new corporation. The corporation now had a total of 32
individual shareholders, or owners. The owners received stock certificates like the one
shown in Figure 6-5 as evidence of their part
ownership of the corporation.

ing types of structures: line organization, line-and-staff organization,
and project or matrix organization.
(Answer: In a line organization, all
work relationships develop in a
direct line from the top executive to
the lowest employee in the organization. In a line-and-staff organization, there are specialized units
like art and legal departments that
support the work of other units
and are not a part of the direct
reporting line. In a project or matrix
organization, the work relationships, and thus the organization
chart, will change based on specific projects and work assignments.)

SUMMARIZE

Secure a large sheet of paper to a
wall and label it BUSINESS
STRUCTURES. Invite students to
write, graffiti style, what they consider the most pertinent information explained in this chapter.

Students could also write about
their plans and ideas for future
ownership of a business. Ask students to share ways in which the
information they learned in this
chapter had an effect on these
plans and ideas.

EVALUATE

- Assign Activities and Projects for
  Chapter 6.
- Administer the printed test or
  ExamView for Chapter 6.
- Assign School-To-Work/SCANS
  portfolio activities for Unit 2.

TEACHING STRATEGIES

Alternate Modalities
Kinesthetic Learner

When learning how to distinguish the different types of ownership, the kinesthetic learner would prefer to actually
participate in the comparing process. Create a transparency

listing the three common types of ownership and have each
student complete one or more comparison features at the overhead projector. Other students can be completing the chart individually on plain paper at their desks.

Expanded Organization Chart

Board of Directors

President
Julie Alcess

Corporate Secretary
Sue Chung

Vice President
Jo Rabinski

Corporate Treasurer
Tom Lowe

FIGURE 6-6 Can you tell who is the boss now?

Julie and Andy, who were the controlling shareowners, called a meeting of the shareholders to elect officers, to make plans for operating a branch store, and to conduct other business. Each shareholder had one vote for each share of stock that she or he owned. Since Julie and Andy together owned 18,000 shares, they had enough votes to control the operation of the business.

At the meeting, seven people, including Julie and Andy, were elected as directors of the corporation. These seven people made up the board of directors. A *board of directors* is a group with responsibility to guide the operations of a corporation. The board's first act was to elect the executive officers of the corporation. The directors elected Julie Alcess as president, Jo Rabinski as vice president, Sue Chung as secretary, and Tom Lowe as treasurer. Andy decided to continue his law studies in pursuit of a career as a corporate attorney. He would eventually represent the new firm when legal matters arose. As full-time employees, Julie and the other officers receive regular salaries for managing the business. An organization chart for J & A Sports and Recreation, Inc., might look like Figure 6-6.

The chart shows that the board of directors oversees the operations of the corporation.

The directors are in the position of highest authority and will make policy decisions. When the board elected three of its members to hold corporate offices, it assigned authority and responsibility for the daily operation of the business to those officers.

The president, Julie Alcess, has the highest authority and is responsible to the board for her decisions. The other officers have specific functions. Sue Chung, the corporate secretary, has responsibility for managing the office function. She supervises office personnel employed to carry out the communication and clerical activities of the firm. As corporate secretary, she will also sign legal documents and reports of actions taken by the board of directors. The elected office of corporate secretary is an important executive position.

Jo Rabinski, vice president, is responsible for all of the sales and marketing of the company's products. Tom Lowe, the treasurer, is the financial officer of the business. His function includes preparing the budget, preparing financial reports, and managing the firm's investments.

The vice president, treasurer, and secretary have separate but equal authority over their assigned functions. Each one is responsible to the president. The president reports to the board of directors.

At the end of the year, after all taxes were paid, the corporation had a profit of $31,600. The board of directors voted to keep $10,000 of business profit for expansion and to divide the other $21,600 among the shareholders. Since the corporation had issued 24,000 shares, each of the 32 shareholders received 90 cents for each share of stock that he or she owned ($21,600.00 ÷ 24,000.00 = $0.90). The part of the profits that each shareholder receives is called a **dividend**. In addition to her salary, Julie received $10,800.00 ($0.90 × 12,000 shares). Andy received $5,400.00 ($0.90 × 6,000 shares) that helped to pay his college expenses. Figure 6-7 shows the prospering corporation.

Basic Skills-Listening

In order to prepare students for the school-to-work transition, we must teach these skills in our classroom. You can teach students to become good listeners by explaining to them the value of watching out for certain words that may distract the listener from effective listening. Good listeners overcome the tendency to wander when certain words are mentioned. Ask a student volunteer to write distracters on the board that cause students not to listen to what the speaker is saying. The Student Activity Worksheet, Basic Skills—Listening Checklist, in the School-To-Work/SCANS Activity Masters, may serve as a guide for discussion of listening skills.

CORPORATION

FIGURE 6-7 Why do businesses tend to incorporate as they become larger?

SPECIALIZED FORMS OF BUSINESS ORGANIZATIONS

As you now can see, choosing the right form of business ownership is central to a firm's success. And the first choice may not always be the right one. As shown in Figure 6-8, there are advantages and disadvantages to each of the major forms of business ownership.

In addition to the standard types of business ownership, there are some specialized forms of business organization with which you should be familiar. Each of these specialized types of business organizations plays an important role in our economy.

Franchises

If you have stayed in a national motel chain, eaten in a fast-food restaurant, or purchased a car from a dealership, you very likely bought services and goods from a franchised business. A **franchise** is a written contract granting permission to sell someone else's product or service in a prescribed manner, over a certain period of time, and in a specified territory. Franchises can be operated as a proprietorship, partnership, or corporation.

In a recent year, there were 499,000 franchised businesses. More than 81 percent were owned by one person or a group of people who received the franchise from a parent company to sell its products or services. This person or group is called the **franchisee**. Ownership of the remaining 19 percent was retained by the parent company granting the franchise, the **franchisor**.

The franchise agreement states the duties and rights of both parties. The franchisee agrees to run the business in a certain way.

What are some advantages of owning a franchise?

Personal Qualities-Responsibility

SCANS

Being responsible, or exerting a high level of effort and perseverance toward a goal, is a personal quality that employers seek in employees. We can help students learn responsibility by following the code of behavior established by many businesses for their employees.

FORMS OF BUSINESS OWNERSHIP

Types of Ownership	Advantages	Disadvantages
Sole Proprietorship	Easy to start business Owner makes all the decisions and is own boss Owner receives all profits	Capital is limited to what the owner can supply or borrow Owner is liable (responsible) for all debts, even losing personal property if business fails Long hours and hard work often necessary Life of the business depends upon owner; it ends if owner quits or dies
Partnership	Fairly easy to start the business More sources of capital available More business skills available	Each partner liable for business debts made by all partners, even to losing personal property if business fails Each partner can make decisions; more than one boss Partnership ends if a partner quits or dies Each partner shares the profit
Corporation	More sources of capital available Specialized managerial skills available Owners liable up to the amount of their investments Ownership can be easily transferred through sale of stock; business not affected by change of ownership	Difficult to start the corporation Owners do not have control of decisions made each day, unless they are officers of the company Business activities of the corporation limited to those stated in the certificate of incorporation

FIGURE 6-8 Which type would you choose if you were starting a business? Which would you prefer as an investor?

SCANS

Critical Thinking Skills-Problem Solving

Problem-solving skills, which include recognizing a problem and devising a plan of action, are applied throughout every chapter in this text. Each time a student participates in a Cooperative Learning or Teams activity, problem-solving skills are applied in a group situation. Each time a student completes a math application in Calculate Business Data, decisions are made as to which mathematical approach must be taken. For each Technology Application problem, students must decide which template problem to use, which piece of software to load, and how to solve the problem. Emphasize to students how they are using problem solving in their day-to-day tasks and make them aware of the skills they are developing.

CAREER HIGHLIGHTS

A *human resources manager* is responsible for attracting the most qualified employees available and matching them to the jobs for which they are best suited. She or he oversees several departments that are involved with training, evaluation, and salaries, and is also responsible for employee benefits programs.

The name of the business, the products or services offered, the design and color of the building, the price of the product or service, and the uniforms of employees are determined by the franchisor. This standardizing of the franchised business means that customers can recognize a business and know what to expect when they buy a product or service from any one of them. You know approximately what kind of hamburger you will get when you buy at the "golden arches," whether you are in Miami, Kansas City, or Tokyo.

A franchise is a relatively easy business to start. The franchisor agrees to help the franchisee get started. National advertising of the product or service by the parent company is one of the advantages of a franchise. For its service, the franchisor collects a percentage of sales or an agreed-upon fee from the franchisee each year. Franchises usually require a large investment of capital to start. Not all franchises succeed. Some fail because the

CAREER HIGHLIGHTS

The careers listed in Career Highlights come from the *Occupational Outlook Handbook*, an online publication (www.bls.gov/oco) of the federal government. The O*NET code for Human Resources Manager is 11-3040.00. Tell your class about this resource and how to use it. This description of job duties can be used to demonstrate the relevancy of skills learned in this course.

ENVIRONMENTAL PERSPECTIVES

Environmental Marketing Consultant

The public is concerned about our environment. So is corporate America. We are becoming increasingly aware that the earth's resources are not limitless. In fact, it is possible for us to run out of natural resources or to pollute our water and air so badly that it will affect the way we live.

Corporations spend billions of dollars every year on protecting and preserving our environment. *Ecology*—the study of the relationships between living things and their environment—is a legal as well as societal issue of concern among today's managers and business owners. Many businesses are finding creative ways to make a profit without damaging the environment.

Many corporations now use the services of environmental marketing consultants in response to society's concerns about the environment. Clients range from large manufacturers to retail chains. These consultants help corporations achieve goals for the protection of the environment. They also help business firms in marketing and producing goods and services that are ecologically sound.

The environmental marketing consultant will be a key player in the efforts of businesses to protect and preserve our environment for many years in the future. Many companies find that strategies developed by a special consultant to conserve the environment help sell their products.

Critical Thinking

1. What are some reasons why leading U.S. corporations are concerned about environmental problems?
2. Do you think that the role of the environmental marketing consultant will continue to be an important one?

ENVIRONMENTAL PERSPECTIVES

Environmental Perspectives discusses the responsibilities of businesses toward the environment.

CRITICAL THINKING

1. U.S. businesses that depend on natural resources, such as wood and minerals, are particularly aware of the need to protect and renew our environment. Most business firms want to be socially responsible. There is also the matter of government intervention when private industry does not comply with environmental laws and regulations.
2. Yes. Business firms need help in complying with environmental regulations and standards. An expert can give advice and work with employees in resolving environmental problems.

business is not competitive or because it is not in a good location. Nevertheless, franchises are a popular way of doing business.

Cooperatives

Sometimes people join together to operate a business known as a cooperative. A **cooperative** is owned by the members it serves and is managed in their interest. There are two main types of cooperatives. One type is a consumers' cooperative, an organization of consumers who buy goods and services more cheaply together than each person could individually. Another is a producers' cooperative, usually a farmers' organization that markets products such as fruit, vegetables, milk, and grains. A producers' cooperative lets farmers work together for greater bargaining power in selling their products. They are often created by large numbers of small producers that want to be more competitive in the marketplace.

A cooperative is much like a regular corporation. Its formation must be approved by the state. It may sell one or more shares of stock to each of its members. A board of directors may be chosen by the members to guide the cooperative. However, a cooperative differs from a corporation in the way that it is controlled. In a regular corporation, a person usually has one vote for each share she or he owns.

A cooperative may be controlled in two ways: each owner-member may have one vote, or each member's vote may be based on the amount of service he or she has bought from the cooperative. Most of the profits a cooperative earns may be refunded directly to members at the end of the business year. Part of the profit often is kept for expansion of the business.

Non-Profit Corporations

When driving into towns, you probably have seen signs like "Centreville–Incorporated." An incorporated town, called a **municipal corporation** or *municipality,* has its own officials, its own schools, its own police and

Why might farmers find it beneficial to be part of a producers' cooperative?

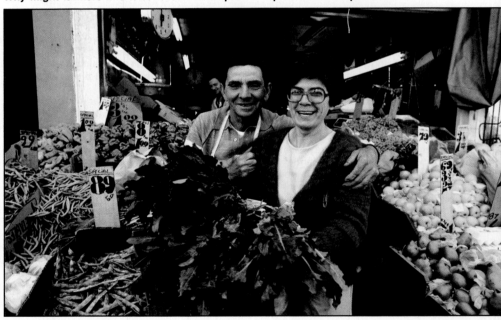

Unit 2 *Business Operations*

Basic Skills-Listening

Productivity increases as a result of effective listening. One activity to improve listening involves responding. Responding serves the primary purpose of reflecting what was heard. Clarification of what is heard encourages further communication. The response measures whether one has accurately interpreted the speaker's words and gives the speaker the opportunity to correct or clarify understanding. Among the clarifying responses are paraphrasing, summarizing, giving examples, and requesting additional information. An activity in responding is to have one student give directions for completing a particular work-related activity. The other students listen and then ask questions.

fire department, and provides street repairs, street lighting, and other services for its citizens. A municipality levies taxes and passes rules and regulations to operate effectively. To function, a municipal corporation buys supplies, equipment, and services just as any business does and pays for them under the corporate name of the city. Unlike a business corporation, services are provided for its citizens with money from taxes levied rather than from making a profit. Stock representing ownership is not issued.

Other groups also organize as non-profit corporations. Like the municipal corporation, these organizations operate to provide a service, but not for profit. Among these are private colleges and universities, American Red Cross, Boy Scouts of America, Future Business Leaders of America, and DECA. Both local governments and non-profit agencies find that the corporate form of organization provides the most effective way for them to deliver their services to the public.

E-Commerce for Business Operations

Marketing and distribution web sites:
www.adage.com
www.adweek.com
www.wilsonweb.com
www.ups.com
www.fedex.com

In a business environment with virtually no barriers to entry, a strong brand is needed to continue to attract customers and to defend against competition. Examples of successful online brands include Amazon.com, eBay, and CDNOW. Because of the importance of marketing to the success of e-commerce, investors in dot.com businesses insist that the management team of a start-up Internet company include a person with extensive marketing ability and experience.

When customers can be reached via the Internet, companies can use that tool to target goods and services to the most likely customers. For example, from information gathered from Internet users, a database can be created with information about gender, income, interests, and previous purchases. Based on these and other factors, targeted promotional e-mail messages can be sent to potential customers. Information requests and customer orders result in immediately updated information in the database. After a sale, artificial intelligence provides consumers with updates on order processing, total costs, and shipping information. Customer service representatives are available via e-mail, instant message systems, or telephone to help customers with questions and problems.

Not all products and services lend themselves to e-marketing, and the business world has seen many failures of companies that did not understand how to market products successfully. But both established and new businesses have found ways to use the Internet profitably. In addition, companies that provide product handling and distribution for e-commerce businesses have flourished.

With the online availability of items such as perishable foods, companies like FedEx and UPS are now offering free package design consultations to assist with developing appropriate shipping containers. Vibration testing simulates a truck on city streets to measure if the package provides adequate protection. Transportation companies provide access codes so customers can check on the status and delivery date of an order.

Critical Thinking

Research the steps involved in taking a product from raw materials to delivering the item to consumers. Create a flowchart or other visual presentation that shows how e-commerce might be used in each phase of the product development and distribution process.

Basic Skills-Reading

Study guides are most often used to review and reinforce the instructional material students learn in the classroom. Thus, a study guide is almost always used as a supplement in business courses. The extent to which study guides are used depends on student's capabilities. Unless students are grouped by ability when assigned to particular section of a text, some students may need the additional help a study guide offers. The Activities and Project for *Intro to Business* contain a study guide for each chapter.

REVIEW YOUR READING

1. Probably the greatest advantages to Julie Alcess were the opportunities to be her own boss and to earn profits for herself. In addition, she found that starting a proprietorship was relatively easy and inexpensive.

2. Julie's one-owner business caused her to work long hours, make decisions alone, and perform a variety of jobs in the business.

3. Julie Alcess performed the five functions of a manager: planning, organizing, staffing, leading, and controlling.

4. Julie added the additional capital and managerial skills of Andy Davidson. She also had Andy's help in filling out government forms.

5. Among the items the articles of partnership should include are (a) the name of the firm, (b) the amount of each partner's investment, (c) the salary of each partner, (d) a provision for sharing profits and losses, (e) the responsibility each partner will have in the business, and (f) a provision for dissolution of the business.

6. Some advantages of a corporation over a partnership are (a) limited liability of owners, (b) ease of increasing capital, (c) ease of employing specialized management, (d) ease of expansion, and (e) ownership can change without affecting the business.

7. The corporation is the most difficult and expensive to start. The business activities are limited to those stated in the certificate of incorporation. In addition, the owners do not have control of the decisions made each day, unless they are officers of the company. Also, there are many more government regulations imposed on a corporation than on other types of organizations. Furthermore, because management and ownership are often separated in a corporation, many people believe that this is an impersonal form of business ownership.

8. Julie and Andy each received shares of stock as evidence of ownership.

9. The executive officers manage a corporation.

10. Part of the profits is retained in the business for expansion.

BUSINESS NOTES

1. Sole proprietors and partners have unlimited liability for the debts of their businesses while the owners of corporations can only lose the amount they have invested.

2. Sole proprietorships and partnerships are easily formed while corporations must file applications with a state and obtain official approval.

3. Managers must plan, organize, staff, lead, and control to be effective.

4. Specialized forms of business organizations include franchises, cooperatives, and non-profit corporations.

REVIEW YOUR READING

1. What advantages did Julie Alcess find in starting her own business?

2. What disadvantages did Julie find as the operator of a sole proprietorship?

3. Name the five activities that Julie performed as a manager.

4. What advantages over her original organization resulted when Julie Alcess entered into a partnership with Andy Davidson?

5. Name six items that should be agreed upon and recorded in the articles of partnership.

6. State two advantages that a corporation has over a partnership.

7. Name two disadvantages of a corporation.

8. What evidence of ownership did Julie and Andy receive when they changed from a partnership to a corporation?

9. Who actually manages a corporation?

10. Why does a corporation's board of directors keep part of the profit before dividing the remainder among the stockholders?

11. What are the three conditions of a franchise agreement?

12. Name one advantage and one disadvantage of operating a business as a franchise.

13. How does a cooperative differ from a regular corporation?

14. What is the difference between a municipal corporation and a business corporation?

COMMUNICATE BUSINESS CONCEPTS

15. Features of the five types of business organizations you studied in this chapter are given in the following statements. Name the type of organization to which each statement applies. Some statements may apply to two types of organizations.

    a. The owner is his or her own boss.

    b. If one of the owners makes a large, unwise purchase and the business cannot pay the bill, another owner might have to do so.

    c. The business can sell stock to raise more money.

    d. If a profit is made, the owner receives all of it.

    e. Owners agree on how they will divide profits and share losses.

    f. Owners allow a board of directors to make decisions about the business.

    g. Owners/operators agree to operate the business in a prescribed manner set forth by the parent company.

11. A franchise agreement grants permission to (1) sell someone else's product in a prescribed manner, (2) over a certain period of time, and (3) in a specified territory.

12. Among the advantages of operating a franchise business are (a) a franchise is relatively easy to start, (b) the franchisor often helps the franchisee get started, and (c) the national advertising of the product or service by the franchisor helps in selling the product or service all over the country. Disadvantages include (a) franchises usually require large investments of capital to start and they often are competitive, and (b) franchises often fail because they were not competitive or they were not in good locations.

13. A cooperative differs from a corporation in the way it is controlled. In a corporation, each person has one vote for each share owned. A cooperative may be controlled in one of two ways. Each share owner-member has one vote, or each member's vote may be based on the amount of service bought from the cooperative.

14. A municipal corporation does not operate for a

h. Owners must get written permission from the state in which the business is located before it can operate.

i. An owner may be added to help make business decisions.

j. The amount of control a person has in the business may depend upon the value of the products and services bought from the business during the year.

k. A percentage of sales or a set fee must be paid annually to a parent company.

16. Explain how the planning activity is related to the controlling activity.

17. How does an organization chart change when a sole proprietorship becomes a corporation?

18. The community of Grandview has petitioned its state government for a certificate of incorporation so that it can become a town. When Grandview becomes a corporation, can it sell stock and issue dividends to shareholders? Explain.

19. Sarah Gray and her partner, John Tolkin, fail in their business venture. The debts are about $8,000.00 greater than the value of the business. Gray has personal property worth more than $10,000.00, but Tolkin owns nothing. Could Gray's personal property be taken to settle the debts of the business? Explain.

DEVELOP YOUR BUSINESS LANGUAGE

For each numbered item, find the term that has the same meaning.

20. A diagram that shows work relationships in a business.

21. A business owned by one person.

22. An organization that provides services for citizens with revenue from their taxes and that does not have earning a profit as a goal.

23. An association of two or more people operating a business as co-owners and sharing profits or losses according to a written agreement.

24. A business made up of a number of owners but authorized by law to act as a single person.

25. A document, generally issued by a state government, giving permission to start a corporation.

26. The part of the profits of a corporation that each shareholder receives.

27. A person who owns stock in a corporation.

28. A business that is owned by the members it serves and is managed in their interest.

29. A written contract granting permission to sell someone else's product or service in a prescribed manner, over a certain period of time, and in a specified area.

30. The person or group of people who have received permission from a parent company to sell its products or services.

31. The parent company that grants permission to a person or group to sell its products or services.

KEY TERMS

organization chart
certificate of incorporation
cooperative
corporation
dividend
franchise
franchisee
franchisor
municipal corporation
partnership
shareholder
sole proprietorship

DECISION-MAKING STRATEGIES

Jeremy Rindone is a successful furniture maker in a small shop that he built and designed. He earns a good living and gets great satisfaction from the high-quality furniture he builds. A large, reputable corporation has approached Jeremy with a proposal to take over his manufacturing facility and incorporate it into their nationwide furniture manufacturing operation. They offered Jeremy enough money so that his financial future would be secure. He would be appointed to the board of directors of the firm and could oversee production of his line of furniture. Jeremy would like to continue his own business, but he recognizes that the offer he has received is a great opportunity. He also is not sure how many more years he can continue to work for himself.

Right column (answers)

17. The board of directors replaces the sole proprietor at the top of the organization chart since it is in the highest position of authority. The corporate officers are added to the organization chart with responsibilities for the daily operation of the business.

18. A municipal corporation does not sell stock nor does it operate for a profit; therefore, dividends cannot be paid.

19. Sarah Gray probably will have to pay all of the debts in excess of the value of the business. When a partnership fails, each partner is personally responsible for the debts of the business. Of course, in this case each partner should bear $4,000 of the loss. However, because Tolkin has no property, Gray will no doubt have to pay the debts of the business.

DEVELOP YOUR BUSINESS LANGUAGE

20. organization chart
21. sole proprietorship
22. municipal corporation
23. partnership
24. corporation
25. certificate of incorporation
26. dividend
27. shareholder
28. cooperative
29. franchise
30. franchisee
31. franchisor

DECISION-MAKING STRATEGIES

32. Jeremy has the advantage of personal satisfaction from the business he started and developed; he also keeps all of the profits and can make changes whenever he wants to. Disadvantages include the long hours and hard work, the lack of capital to expand, and not having others to help with various business functions. Also, when he dies or quits, the business will end.

33. Jeremy would get a nice profit from the sale of his business. He would be given a directorship in the corporation and could influence business decisions. He still would have some control over the line of furniture he created. Disadvantages include not having

---

Bottom section

profit; it provides services to citizens paid for with their tax money. Business corporations operate for a profit.

COMMUNICATE BUSINESS CONCEPTS

15. The types of organizations represented in the statements are: (a) sole proprietorship, (b) partnership, (c) corporation, (d) sole proprietorship, (e) partnership and cooperative, (f) corporation and cooperative, (g) franchise, (h) corporation, (i) partnership (new articles of partnership would be needed), (j) cooperative (there would be one vote on business matters or a vote in proportion to one's use of the services), (k) franchise.

16. The standards used to measure the performance of the business are set up in the planning function. In the controlling function, the standards actually are used to compare what was planned to happen to what actually happened in the business.

personal control over the business (just being one of several directors), receiving only a share of the profits, and having limited decision-making authority.

CALCULATE BUSINESS DATA

34. $523,250 × 0.05 = $26,162.50

35. (a) $125 + $45 + $110 + $20 = $300; (b) $850 − $300 = $550;(c) $550 × 0.20 = $110.

36.

Company	Shares	Quarterly Dividend per Share (a)	Quarterly Dividend (Total)	Dividend for Year (c)
IBM	50	$1.10	$55.00	$220.00
Avon	20	.25	5.00	20.00
Wrigley	50	.18	9.00	36.00
PepsiCo	100	.21	21.00	84.00
Total Dividend Income:			(b) $90.00	(d) $360.00

37.

Member	Purchases	(a) Refund Received
Likens	$1,000	$20
J. Peery	650	13
S. Peery	750	15
Fonza	100	2
Reynolds	1,250	25
Total Refunds:		(b) $75

TECHNOLOGY APPLICATION

In this activity, students use a computer to solve a business problem using a file that is provided on the data CD that accompanies *Intro to Business*. Instructions for using the data CD are included in a **README** file on the disk. Solutions are provided on the Instructor's Resource CD.

---

32. What are the advantages and disadvantages of Jeremy continuing to operate his own business?

33. What are the advantages and disadvantages of Jeremy selling his business to the corporation?

CALCULATE BUSINESS DATA

34. Jake Simmons and Maury Gertz operate a small convenience store under a franchise agreement with a national company. The franchisor requires an annual payment of 5 percent of gross sales. At the close of the current year, the accountant who keeps the records for the Simmons–Gertz store reported gross sales of $523,250. How much will Simmons and Gertz pay to the franchisor for the year?

35. As an art major at a university, Lu-yin Chang specializes in creating inexpensive gemstone jewelry. To earn extra money, Lu-yin rents a stall and sells her art in the new festival marketplace in the revitalized downtown area. The table shows her income and expenses for the month of December.

   a. What was the total of Lu-yin's expenses for December?

   b. How much profit did Lu-yin make in December?

   c. If Lu-yin puts 20 percent of her profit into a savings account before spending on personal needs, how much will she save in December?

Income from sales:	$850.00
Expenses:	
Rent for stall and utilities	$125.00
Polishing/mounting tools	45.00
Gemstones and supplies	110.00
Ad in the university paper	20.00

36. Scott and Kristie de la Garza own stock in four corporations. Here is a record of the stock they own and the dividend they received for each share at the end of the first quarter.

   a. How much dividend income did the de la Garzas receive from each of their four stocks for the quarter?

   b. What was their total dividend income for the quarter?

   c. If each corporation paid the same amount per share for the remaining three quarters, how much dividend income would the de la Garzas receive from each corporation for the year?

   d. What total dividend income would the de la Garzas receive for the year?

Company	Number of Shares Owned	Quarterly Dividend per Share
IBM	50	$1.10
Avon Products	20	.25
William Wrigley, Jr.	50	.18
PepsiCo	100	.21

37. After all expenses were paid, Grant Valley Consumer Cooperative had $13,000.00 of profit left over. Of this amount, $3,000.00 was set aside for expansion of the business. According to its policy, Grant Valley would refund to each member an amount in proportion to the amount he or she bought during the year. Since total sales for the year were $500,000.00, the refund would be 2 percent, or 2 cents for every dollar each member had spent at the cooperative during the year. The persons in the table were among the members; their total purchases are shown in even dollars.

   a. How much refund did each of these members receive?

   b. What was the total amount refunded to these five members?

Randy Likins	$1,000.00
Jill Peery	650.00
Sam Peery	750.00
B. E. Fonza	100.00
H. E. Reynolds	1,250.00

TECHNOLOGY APPLICATION

Using the *Intro to Business* Data CD and your word processing software, select problem CH06. After the problem appears on your screen, complete the following activities. Then, print and sign your completed partnership agreement. If you do not have a printer available, save the partnership agreement on a data disk to give to your teacher.

38. You and your partner, Faith Ramirez, are starting a new business. Fill in the blanks with information about yourself. Where dates are required, use the last day of the current month.

39. Find all the words that appear in all capitals and change those words to boldface. Indent all the paragraphs.

MEASURING GLOBAL ECONOMIC PROGRESS

The World Cup, the World Series, and the Olympics are sports events that involve scorekeeping. In a similar way, international business also keeps score. These numbers are commonly called economic indicators.

A country's *gross national product* (GNP) has been one of the most popular measures of economic progress. GNP measures the total value of all goods and services produced by the resources of a country. This measurement includes production in other countries involving the resources of the country whose GNP is being measured. In recent years, as international business activities expanded, a slightly different economic measurement has evolved. *Gross domestic product* (GDP) measures the productive output of a country within its borders, including items produced with foreign resources. GDP would include, for example, motor vehicles manufactured in the United States by foreign-owned companies.

Comparing total GDP of different sized countries may not be meaningful. Instead,

> **Measures of economic progress include GDP, per capita GDP, and balance of trade.**

a per capita (per person) comparison may be used. The *per capita GDP* of a country is obtained by dividing the total GDP by the number of people in the country.

Another important measure of global economic progress is *balance of trade*. This figure is the difference between a nation's exports and imports. When a country exports (sells to other countries) more than it imports (buys from other countries), this is referred to as favorable balance of trade. This situation is also called a *trade surplus*. However, if a country imports more than it exports, the nation has an unfavorable balance of trade or a *trade deficit*.

CRITICAL THINKING

1. Using reference books in the library or a web search, obtain the most recent GDP figures for five countries, one in Africa, Europe, the Middle East, Asia, and Central or South America.

2. What actions might the government and businesses of a country take to improve the nation's economic situation?

Most students will either work with international clients or compete against businesses that do. Global Navigator introduces students to issues integral to working with international businesses. Key concepts and challenges faced by international businesses are presented, followed by two Critical Thinking questions that require students to analyze what they have learned.

Quantitative measures of countries' economic standing and progress help to put world events in perspective. Students can better assess the relative importance of various events and business developments by understanding the commonly used measures described in this Global Navigator feature. They include Gross Domestic Product (GDP), GDP per capita, and balance of trade. Critical Thinking exercises prompt students to research some current measures for countries around the world, and to examine their underlying causes.

CRITICAL THINKING

1. Answers will vary depending on which countries students choose.

2. Possible answers might be:
  - Remove legal restrictions on economic and financial activities.
  - Reduce taxes to promote spending and investment.
  - Invest in infrastructure and public works such as highways.
  - Promote education and training.
  - Maintain a stable currency.

In Chapter 7, emphasis is placed on leadership characteristics that students can develop and leadership styles used by managers. Students will also learn about various types of communication and influence incorporated by managers.

Resources for Teachers
- Lesson Plans
- School-To-Work/SCANS Activity Masters
- Spanish Resources
- Instructor's Resource CD

Assessment
- Chapter and Unit Tests, Ch. 7
- ExamView, Ch. 7

Media/Technology
- Applying Technology Data CD
- PowerPoint slides
- Business Connection CD
- Videotape

Activity Masters and Workbooks
- Activities and Projects, Ch. 7
- Internet Activity Masters
- Business Math Activity Masters
- Communications Activity Masters
- International Business Activity Masters
- Ethics Activity Masters

Chapter 7

Manager as Leader

GOALS

DISCUSS the common characteristics of effective leaders.

EXPLAIN the five human relations skills needed by managers.

IDENTIFY four types of influence that leaders use.

DESCRIBE the two main types of leadership styles.

Techno Tips

Computer Solutions for Disabilities

The computer industry has developed unique applications so that individuals with disabilities can use computers. For blind persons, software is available which gives audio signals for on-screen images like windows, menus, icons, and cursor location. Also, a computer can become a translator for the blind by converting printed pages to speech or Braille.

Special applications are also available for physically disabled persons. Touch-sensitive keyboards can make typing easier, and special seven-key keyboards are designed primarily for one-handed typists. Special keyboards can customize each key's size, position, and function. Switch-operated or on-screen keyboards allow typing with almost any part of your body. In addition, joysticks, writing pads and even remote-controlled mice can replace the standard mouse when the physical disability requires it.

Techno Tips Students need to know the latest technologies and develop cutting edge Internet skills for use in current jobs, future careers, or in their homes. TechnoTips introduces students to today's cutting edge technologies and provides them with important Internet skills. Feature topics concentrate on Internet-specific technologies and computer or other hi-tech innovations for use by businesses and consumers.

The Downtown Business Council's Leadership Award selection committee was meeting. The first item on the agenda was to identify possible nominees for the award. Janice Skelton spoke first.

Janice: I believe we should find out which businesses have been the most profitable during the past year. Each company's top manager should be nominated.

Franklin: I think there is more to leadership than having a profitable company. Probably the company should be successful, but I don't think we should nominate people just because they managed the most profitable companies.

Jacque: I'm not sure it should be the top manager. Often the managers who work with employees every day are as responsible for a company's success as the top manager. Don't you think it takes a real leader to manage the daily work of employees?

Felicia: Does the Leadership Award have to go to a manager? Many employees provide leadership in their organizations. If someone has successfully led a group of people who were responsible for a major project, does it matter that he or she was not a manager?

Janice: I know that management and leadership are not the same thing, but both are important to a successful organization.

THE IMPORTANCE OF LEADERSHIP

A business has many resources available that are used to accomplish its work and to make a profit. Those resources include such things as buildings, equipment, money, materials, supplies, and people. Managers are the people who are responsible for making sure that resources are used effectively, so that the business is successful. One of the most important responsibilities is managing people.

The management of people has changed a great deal in recent years. Managers must make sure that employees get the work of the business done. In the past, it was believed that if the manager wanted something done, he or she just had to tell the employees and they would do as they were told. Experience has shown, however, that when employees do not feel that they are involved in decisions they will not be as committed to the work.

It is often said that people are the most important resource of a business. The cost of hiring, training, and paying employees is usually one of a business' highest expenses. If employees are not satisfied they will not perform the work correctly, may not treat customers well, or may quit—requiring the company to hire and train new employees.

Today, managers are expected to do more than merely give orders. They must involve employees and find ways to meet employee needs as well as business needs. Managers must be effective leaders. **Leadership** is the ability to influence individuals and groups to accomplish important goals. Leaders must have effective human relations skills. **Human relations** is the way people get along with each other. When a manager can get individual employees and groups to work well together to get things accomplished, she or he is an effective leader.

Leadership Characteristics
Leadership is much more than just being friendly with employees. It takes skill to get people with different backgrounds and personalities to work well together and to do the

of tactical and strategic management, each leadership style should be used in certain situations. For example, ask students why a manager should use the tactical management approach when working with part-time or temporary employees.

Start a discussion with students about situations when managers may choose to use each of these leadership styles. You may also wish to have a discussion about the leadership styles that students find at their workplaces. Or, some students' parents may have experiences that they have shared about the leadership styles found at their workplaces.

TRY THIS/GUIDED PRACTICE
Show PowerPoint 7-3, *Human Relations*, and ask students to give their opinions regarding why each of these would be necessary skills for managers to have.

Pose this question to students: "How could the lack of these human relations skills in a manager or leader cause serious problems in a work environment?" Students could write a brief essay that answers this question for each of the five human relations skills listed in this chapter. Groups could be formed to break up this project, and each student's essay could discuss just one human relations skill from the list.

To add to this activity, students could also discuss and/or write about how they could develop these human relations skills to prepare for their own future roles as managers or leaders. Use the section of this chapter that covers these skills to guide the discussion.

work needed by the business. The characteristics of effective leaders are listed in Figure 7-1.

Developing Leadership Characteristics

You may have heard it said that "leaders are born and not made." Nothing could be further from the truth. Most leaders report that they did not always have the characteristics needed for success. Rather, they worked hard over many years to develop them.

It is more difficult for some people than for others to develop leadership skills. You may be shy and find it hard to work with others, or you may prefer to let others make decisions while you work to make those decisions successful. On the other hand, you may have friends who seem to have already mastered many leadership characteristics. They always seem to be willing to take control, take a risk, or make a hard decision. Others look to them for direction and ideas.

You do not have to be a manager to be a leader, and you don't have to wait until you become a manager to develop leadership skills. There are several ways you can develop them, including:

- Study leadership. Many books on the subject of leadership and leadership skills

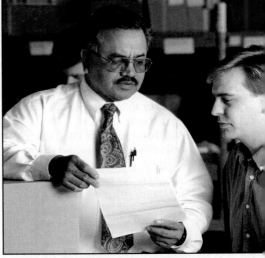

What are some leadership characteristics needed when training a new employee?

can help you understand what it takes to be a leader. You can also take courses to develop specific leadership skills.

- Participate in organizations and activities. Clubs, teams, and organizations offer opportunities to develop leadership skills.

- Practice leadership at work. If you have a part-time job, you can develop leadership

FIGURE 7-1   Can you identify people who have most of these leadership characteristics?

Leadership Characteristic	Description
Understanding	Respecting the feelings and needs of the people they work with.
Initiative	Having the ambition and motivation to get work done without being asked.
Dependability	Following through on commitments.
Judgment	Making decisions carefully.
Objectivity	Looking at all sides of an issue before making a decision.
Confidence	Being willing to make decisions and take responsibility for the results.
Stability	Avoiding being too emotional or unpredictable.
Cooperation	Working well with others, recognizing others' strengths, and helping to develop effective group relationships.
Honesty	Being ethical in their decisions and in their treatment of others.
Courage	Willing to take reasonable risks and to make unpopular decisions.
Communications	Able to listen, speak, and write effectively.
Intelligence	Having the knowledge and understanding needed to perform well.

TEACHING STRATEGIES
Special Needs: Gifted Students

Gifted students should master content quickly. Therefore, challenge them to identify a special research project that interests them. The students should be encouraged to identify a project that requires interaction with a businessperson and to share their work with the class. For example, a student could

contact a business manager or community leader to learn about management and leadership qualities. The student could invite the business manager or community leader to class and use role playing to demonstrate how management and leadership techniques are used in business situations.

skills as you help customers, complete work assignments, take initiative to solve problems, and demonstrate dependability and honesty.

- Observe leaders. Every day you can observe people in leadership positions. Some are effective, while others are not.

- Work with a mentor. An older brother or sister, a trusted adult, a teacher or coach, or your supervisor at work may be willing to help you learn about leadership skills.

- Do a self-analysis and ask for feedback. Find opportunities to demonstrate leadership characteristics, review the results to identify what you did well and what you can improve, then ask others for constructive feedback.

HUMAN RELATIONS

Managers and leaders must be able to work well with other people. Surveys show that, for many managers, more than half of their time is spent interacting with people. They work with employees, customers, people from other businesses, and other managers in their own organizations.

Human relations largely determines whether a manager is successful or not. Effective managers and leaders must be able to get along well with all of the people they work with. In addition, they must help their employees develop effective human relations skills. The important human relations skills of managers are 1) self understanding, 2) understanding others, 3) communications, 4) team building, and 5) developing job satisfaction.

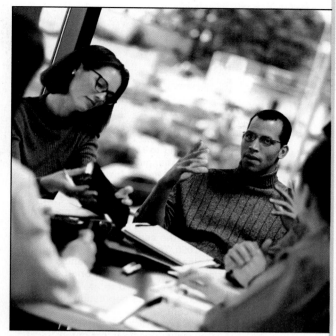

Which types of communication might be necessary in a business meeting?

Self Understanding

To be able to meet the expectations of others, leaders must first understand their own strengths and weaknesses. Although a manager cannot always do exactly what employees would prefer or make decisions that every employee agrees with, a manager cannot be viewed as either unpredictable or unfair.

To improve your human relations skills, study how you get along with others. Try to identify the ways you communicate and work with others individually and in groups. It is important to understand how you make decisions and to learn which were effective and which were not so you can improve your decision-making ability over time.

Understanding Others

Leaders recognize that people in a business often have more things alike than different. Recognizing those similarities will help develop a stronger team. Differences, however, can also improve a business. If everyone thought and acted the same, there would

EXPLORE THIS/INDEPENDENT PRACTICE Before assigning independent practice material for any chapter, students should be expected to read the textbook material carefully. In view of the fact that all students vary widely in their ability to read effectively, it is advisable to have the students read the entire chapter, or sections thereof, silently in class if the material has not been previously read in connection with homework assignments.

After students have read the chapter, ask them to complete the Chapter Review questions. Develop Your Business Language is an excellent way to improve students' vocabulary. Only words introduced in the chapter are used in the exercises. The Review Your Reading questions can be used to check students' ability to comprehend what they have read. The Communicate Business Concepts section affords an opportunity for students to apply to practical life situations the information gained from reading the chapter. By completing the problems under Calculate Business Data, students will be able to strengthen and refine their abilities in mathematics. Technology Application allows students to demonstrate skill in using word processing, spreadsheet, and database software. Decision-Making Strategies contains material to challenge students to utilize the model explained in Chapter 1 for problem solving.

The Chapter Review questions at the end of the chapter vary in level of difficulty. For a basic assignment, consider Develop Your Business Language and Review Your Reading. For an average assignment, consider the basic assignment plus Communicate Business Concepts and Calculate Business Data. For an enhanced assignment, try the average assignment plus Technology Application and Decision-Making Strategies.

ASSESS

Review the goals at the beginning of the chapter and the Business Notes at the end of the chapter. Have students respond orally or in writing to each of the Business Notes restated as a question, provided below. For students who may have difficulty providing answers, assign the reteaching activities that follow. Enrichment activities may also be assigned where appropriate.

1. How are a manager's responsibilities and a business's resources related? (Answer: A manager is responsible for making sure that resources are used effectively; one of managers' most important responsibilities is managing people.)

2. What are the characteristics of an effective leader? (Answer: Characteristics of an effective leader include understanding, initiative, dependability, judgment, objectivity, confidence, stability, cooperation, honesty, courage, communications, and intelligence.)

3. How are the various types of communication classified? (Answer: Various types of communication can be classified as formal or informal, internal or external, vertical or horizontal, and oral or written.)

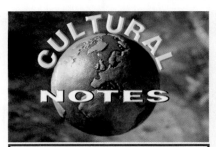

According to U.S. Census Bureau projections, people of Hispanic origin will be the fastest-growing population group in the United States in the first half of the 21st century, increasing from 11 percent of the U.S. population at the turn of the century to 25 percent by 2050. The next fastest-growing segment will be non-Hispanics descendant from Asian origins. They are projected to grow from 4 percent of the population to 8 percent.

The proportion of non-Hispanic Caucasian people is projected to fall to almost 50 percent by 2050. The proportion of African-Americans and Native-American groups are projected to remain relatively stable, with African-Americans increasing from 13 percent to 15 percent and Native-Americans from just under 1 percent to just over 1 percent.

seldom be new ideas or anyone to question a decision in order to improve it.

An effective leader gets to know each person, their skills, and their abilities, as well as their strengths and weaknesses. The leader will not treat everyone alike but will attempt to involve each person in the way that is most beneficial to the business and that employee.

Communication

Communication is very important in business, and managers must have effective communication skills. Various types of communication can be classified as:

- *Formal or informal.* Formal communications methods have been established and approved by the organization. Informal communications are common but unofficial ways that information moves in an organization.

- *Internal or external.* Internal communications occur between managers, employees, and work groups. External communications occur between those inside the organization and outsiders such as customers, suppliers, and other businesses.

- *Vertical or horizontal.* Vertical communications move up or down in an organization between management and employees. Horizontal communications move across the organization at the same level—employee to employee or manager to manager.

- *Oral or written.* Oral communications are word-of-mouth. Written communications include notes, letters, reports, and e-mail messages.

Managers need to recognize the many ways that communication occurs in the business and must be able to use all types of communication effectively. Communication must use words that are understandable and meaningful to the people receiving the communications, and they must be specific. An effective communicator must be a good listener as well as skilled at providing information. Listening helps managers understand employees and demonstrates that the manager respects their ideas.

Team Building

Businesses are made up of groups and teams, not individuals. The combined skills of the people in a team are greater than that of individuals working alone. However, if there are problems in the team and members cannot get along, the team will not be effective.

Managers need group-building skills to help people understand each other and their responsibilities. Managers should be able to identify any problems the group is having and help to solve the problems quickly.

Workplace Competencies-Resources

By acquiring competence at allocating resources, students learn to perform basic functions of management—planning, organizing, and controlling. We can guide our students and teach them how to allocate time by helping them understand that they must first identify the goals or tasks that must be completed and rank them in order of importance, estimate how much time it will take to complete each task, develop a schedule, and evaluate and adjust the schedule as appropriate. Assign students a project to complete that includes the activities of reading this chapter, completing the end of chapter activities, completing the assignments in the Activities and Projects, and preparing for the ExamView.

Members of effective groups take pride in the group and take responsibility for its work. A well-developed group requires much less attention from the manager, so the manager can concentrate on other responsibilities.

Developing Job Satisfaction

Do you believe most people enjoy going to work and like the work they do? Most people are more satisfied than dissatisfied because they have jobs that use their skills and interests, and they provide needed income and benefits.

Managers can influence how employees feel about their jobs on a daily basis. Many things can lead to dissatisfaction, such as regular assignments employees do not like or do not feel prepared for. Other sources of dissatisfaction include poor working conditions, ineffective communications, and lack of recognition. Daily difficulties can lead to long-term employee dissatisfaction. On the other hand, when a manager pays attention to the needs and concerns of individual employees and tries to support them and solve problems, employees appreciate that effort.

INFLUENCING PEOPLE

Have you been a part of a group that seldom agrees on what should be done and spends a long time making decisions? It is interesting to see what the leader of a group does when it is not working well. Some will complain and criticize group members. Others will give up on the group and attempt to do the work themselves. None of those improve the group's effectiveness.

Effective leaders must be able to influence members. There are several kinds of influence a leader can use:

- **Position Influence** is the ability to get others to accomplish tasks because of the position the leader holds. If the leader can influence an employee's job rating, wages, and chances for promotion, it is likely that people will respond to the leader's requests.

- **Reward Influence** results from the leader's ability to give or withhold rewards. Rewards may be in the form of money or job benefits, or they can be non-monetary such as recognition and praise. Leaders can use rewards in a negative way by requiring people to work overtime or by criticizing rather than praising employees.

- **Expert Influence** arises when group members recognize that the leader has special expertise in the area. If a group of inexperienced salespeople have a manager with years of successful selling experience, they will likely look to the manager for guidance.

- **Identity Influence** stems from personal trust and respect members have for the leader. If the leader is well liked and is thought to have the best interests of the group in mind, members are likely to support the leader.

The influence of leaders is not always positive and may not be effective for a long period of time. If a manager is not viewed as an expert and is not well liked, he or she will have to rely on position and reward influence. It is not easy to continue to get people to do things for you just because you are their manager. They will probably do just

4. What are the kinds of influence that a manager can use? (Answer: A manager can use position influence, reward influence, expert influence, and identity influence. Influence can also be of a formal or informal nature.)
5. What are the types of leadership styles that managers can use? (Answer: Managers can use one of the following leadership styles: tactical management, strategic management, or mixed management.)

Chapter 7 *Manager as Leader* **91**

Basic Skills-Speaking

Student Team Reading/Student Team Writing is an instructional method in which students use cooperative learning in peer groups. When using this instructional method, students are assigned to groups with four members each. The groups should be mixed in performance level, gender, and culture. Assign this chapter for the groups to read. The groups will then write a summary of the chapter in their own words. Each group should produce a written plan, draft, and then a final paper as a group. (Note: As a supplemental activity, you may wish to distribute the Student Activity Worksheet, Workplace Competencies—Interpersonal Skills Checklist, in the School-To-Work/SCANS Activity Masters to serve as a guideline for discussion.)

RETEACH

After reading the section entitled "Influencing People," guide students through a role-playing exercise. Divide the class into six groups. Assign each group to one of the six specific types of influence: position influence, reward influence, expert influence, identity influence, formal influence, and informal influence.

Have each group plan out, and then perform, a short role-playing skit that demonstrates the particular kind of influence. Some groups may need your guidance in acting out certain types of influence. You could even have the audience try to guess which type of influence is being played out.

ENRICH

Direct students to read the Ethical Perspectives feature. Have students conduct research on the International Olympics Committee scandal of early 1999, in which IOC officials were involved in very questionable activities. This scandal included many stories of bribery and/or gift giving. You may also want to have students investigate other well known stories of bribery and gift giving. These stories can be easily researched on the Internet or at any library.

What kinds of influence can a leader use?

enough to get by, get a reward, or avoid punishment. Most leaders try to develop expert and identity influence.

Formal Influence vs. Informal Influence

Is every manager a leader? Is every leader also a manager? How does a person influence a group to accomplish important goals? There are two types of leadership in an organization—formal influence and informal influence.

What happens when your teacher assigns a group project and the team members get together for the first time? Usually one or two people emerge as leaders to help get the group focused and organized. That is known as informal influence because the leadership role is not part of a formal structure.

Consider another situation where members of Student Council meet for the first time, and there are bylaws that call for the election of officers. The person elected president has formal influence, because the leadership position is part of the organization's structure.

Often in organizations there will be both formal and informal influence operating at the same time. One person will be the manager and have formal influence, yet there may be a well-liked and respected employee in the group whom other employees look to. That person will have informal influence.

If there is a conflict between the formal and informal influence, the group will probably not work effectively. Group members will have difficulty deciding which to follow. Effective managers recognize informal influence and work closely with the informal leaders to gain their support and to avoid conflicts.

PROS AND CONS OF DIFFERENT LEADERSHIP STYLES

Management is a very difficult job. It is not easy to get people with different backgrounds, personalities, and experience to work well together. Have you been a part of an athletic team or a musical group? If so, you can remember how difficult it was at the beginning to coordinate the talents of each of the group members so the team or group performed well.

Managers approach the task of leading a group in different ways based on their leadership style. **Leadership style** is the way a manager treats and directs employees. A manager's leadership style is often based on the urgency of the work to be done and the confidence the manager has in the employees. There are two very different leadership styles often used by managers.

Tactical Management

Sometimes managers are faced with a crisis and feel they don't have time to let the group decide how to complete the task. In other

Critical Thinking Skills-Creative Thinking

Developing creative thinking skills should be an important aspect of career preparation for every student. Encourage students to be creative in both their written work and collaborative learning situations. Whenever an opportunity poses itself for creativity, always respond in a positive manner to student suggestions no matter how extreme those suggestions might

be. If students are discouraged from brainstorming and coming up with original ideas, they will become discouraged and lose that creativity. Creative ideas sometimes come to light when using a board to list brainstorming ideas. By making these lists, the individual ideas can be revisited and refined to come to a final solution or suggestion.

situations, a manager may be working with a group of new employees or may have work for which the members have no previous experience. In those situations the manager should use tactical management. **Tactical management** is a leadership style where the manager is more directive and controlling. The manager will make the decisions and stay in close contact with employees while they work to make sure the work is done well.

Strategic Management

When a group of employees is experienced and work well together, a manager does not have to be as directive and controlling. Also, if there is adequate time to bring a team together to help plan a work assignment, team members will usually prefer being involved in the decision-making process. These are examples of strategic management. **Strategic management** is a leadership style where managers are less directive and involve employees in decision-making. A manager using a strategic leadership style will trust employees to work without direct supervision and will seek their advice on important decisions.

Mixed Management

Which of the two leadership styles would you prefer if you were an employee? If you were a manager, which of the styles would

you use? Do you believe everyone would answer those two questions the same way?

In the past many managers used the tactical leadership style. They believed they were responsible for getting work done and so needed to be very directive and controlling. That frequently led to employee dissatisfaction because they felt their manager did not trust them. On the other hand, some employees prefer that the manager makes day-to-day decisions, or other employees are not experienced enough to work without close supervision.

As a result, effective managers are prepared to use both leadership styles. The combined use of tactical and strategic management is known as **mixed management**. Sometimes a leadership style is selected based on the characteristics of the employees being managed. At other times the choice is based on the work assignment. Figure 7-2 describes situations where each leadership style will be more effective.

FIGURE 7-2   Managers should know when to use each of the leadership styles.

A manager should use tactical management when:	A manager should use strategic management when:
• Working with part-time or temporary employees • Working with employees who are not motivated • Working under tight time pressures • Assigning a new task for which employees are not experienced • Employees prefer not to be involved in decision-making	• Employees are skilled and experienced • The work is routine with few new challenges • Employees are doing work they enjoy • The manager wants to improve group relationships • Employees are willing to take responsibility for the results of their work

EMPLOYER/EMPLOYEE RELATIONS

Both managers and employees want their business to succeed. Unprofitable businesses have to reduce the number of employees they hire and limit salary and benefit increases. If everyone can work together to make the business successful, all should benefit.

Managers and employees do not always have the same immediate goals though. Managers must make sure that a company makes a profit, so they try to get more work done at a lower cost. Employees are most concerned about pay, working conditions, and job security.

Managing Labor Unions

Early in the 20th century, many U.S. businesses did not treat their employees well. Low wages and poor working conditions caused employees to band together and form labor unions. A labor union is an organized group of employees who negotiate with employers about issues such as wages and working conditions. Unions can be effective because they represent large numbers of employees.

The popularity of labor unions peaked in the 1940s and 1950s, when more than a third of the U.S. labor force was unionized. That percentage has been steadily declining since the 1960s and is now less than 15%.

ETHICAL PERSPECTIVES

Bribery and Gift Giving

In the United States, it is considered unethical for a business person to pay bribes to government officials or to other business persons in exchange for favorable treatment such as the award of lucrative contracts. In fact, it is against the law, whether the recipient is an American or someone in another country.

The Foreign Corrupt Business Practices Act of 1977 outlawed the payment of bribes by Americans to foreign officials, companies, or individuals, even though not doing so may at times put U.S. businesses at a competitive disadvantage. In some countries, paying and accepting bribes of various sorts is common, even expected. Fortunately, the trend is moving in our direction, as more countries recognize how harmful it is to economic progress.

While it is relatively easy to outlaw bribes, as such, it is much harder to define and identify what is a bribe and what is merely a gift given as a token of appreciation. Gift giving among business people is relatively limited and infrequent in the United States and Canada, but in other cultures it is very common and regarded as entirely appropriate.

The 1999 scandal over the conduct of International Olympics Committee officials highlighted the difficulty of policing such activities. Many organizations have policies that limit the monetary value and type of gifts that are acceptable. Policing intent, however, is much more difficult because it is highly subjective. After all, even a social dinner invitation is usually meant to influence the recipient's behavior, albeit in a subtle way and without obligation on the part of the recipient.

Critical Thinking
1. How can U.S. business people handle situations in foreign countries where officials expect bribes to be paid as a condition for doing business there?
2. If you worked for a manufacturing company and a plastics supplier who was trying to get more business sent you a case of golf balls—made with one of its high-tech composite materials—what would you do?

ETHICAL PERSPECTIVES

CRITICAL THINKING

Ethical Perspectives will give students a sense of individual diversity through the expression of their opinions.

1. One alternative is to simply forgo any attempts to do business in countries where such practices are common. Another is to partner with other companies not subject to U.S. restrictions. There are viable options that allow U.S. companies to do business in foreign countries without violating U.S. law.

2. The first step should be to see if there is a company policy that deals with gift giving and situations like this. If there is no established company policy, either written or unwritten, then it's probably best to check with your immediate supervisor to see what he or she suggests.

Occupations with strong union membership today include police and firefighters, government employees, communications workers, transportation workers, construction trades, manufacturing occupations, and utilities employees.

Unions and management resolve issues through collective bargaining between representatives of both groups. When agreement is reached, a written labor contract is signed by both groups. There are also federal and state laws that regulate relationships of businesses and unions.

Meeting Business and Employee Goals

Much has been made of the differences between management and employees, yet there may be more things that are alike than different between the two groups. Managers and employees have discovered that as they work together, they find ways to accomplish the goals of both the organization and the individuals who work for it. Managers who involve employees in decision-making find that better decisions are made and that employees are more likely to support those decisions. Employees discover that when they cooperate with management, managers have a better understanding of their needs and expectations. Both groups benefit through cooperation.

What are some occupations with strong union membership?

TEACHING STRATEGIES
Teams

Jigsaw is an instructional method in which students use cooperative learning in peer groups or teams. Each member of the team becomes an expert in one of the parts to which he or she is assigned. All students assigned section one meet as an expert group. All students assigned section two meet as an expert group, etc. These expert groups will discuss their section and decide how to go back and report this information to their respective groups. The students then go back to their original groups at which time they share the expert information that they have learned. Teammates are dependent upon that team member to thoroughly explain that part of the chapter. After each team member has presented expert information, everybody returns to their desk. Students then take the ExamView for this chapter.

REVIEW YOUR READING

1. It used to be that managers felt they could make the decisions and tell their employees what to do. Today, managers realize that employees will be more committed to their work if they are involved in making decisions.
2. Dissatisfied employees may not perform their work well, may mistreat customers causing the customer to stop purchasing from the business, or the employees may quit, requiring the business to hire and train new employees.
3. The characteristics that are common to most effective leaders are: understanding, initiative, dependability, judgment, objectivity, confidence, stability, cooperation, honesty, courage, communication, and intelligence.
4. Managers must be able to work well with other people. They spend more than half their time interacting with others including employees, customers, people from other businesses, and other managers. They must also be able to help their employees develop effective human relations skills.
5. If people have few differences they are likely to think and act alike. When there are differences among employees, there will be new ideas and questions asked to improve the way things are done.
6. Formal communications methods are established and approved by the organization. Informal communications are common but unofficial ways that information moves in an organization.
7. Businesses are made up of groups and teams, not individuals. If there are problems in a team and members cannot get along, the team will not be effective. A well-developed group will require less attention from the manager.
8. Informal influence.
9. Situations in which tactical management should be used are when there is a crisis without enough time to allow employees to decide how to complete a task and when the manager is working with a group of new employees or on work for which the employees have no experience.
10. Managers must make sure that a company makes a profit, so they try to get more work done at a lower cost. Employees are con-

BUSINESS NOTES

1. Managers are responsible for making sure that resources are used effectively. One of the most important responsibilities is managing people.
2. Characteristics of an effective leader include understanding, initiative, dependability, judgment, objectivity, confidence, stability, cooperation, honesty, courage, communications, and intelligence.
3. Various types of communication can be classified as formal or informal, internal or external, vertical or horizontal, and oral or written.
4. The kinds of influence that a manager can use are position influence, reward influence, expert influence, and identity influence. Influence can also be of a formal or informal nature.
5. Managers can use one of the following leadership styles: tactical management, strategic management, or mixed management.

REVIEW YOUR READING

1. How has the management of people changed in recent years?
2. In what ways do dissatisfied employees increase the costs of operating a business?
3. List at least five characteristics of effective leaders.
4. Why are human relations skills so important for managers?
5. How can differences among employees actually improve a business?
6. What is the difference between formal and informal communications?
7. Why would a manager want to have effective group-building skills?
8. What type of influence is being demonstrated when a well-respected employee is able to influence the decisions of coworkers?
9. Identify two situations in which a manager should use tactical management.
10. What are the differences between the goals of managers and the goals of employees?
11. What occurred in U.S. businesses in the early part of the 20th century that caused employees to band together and form labor unions?

COMMUNICATE BUSINESS CONCEPTS

12. Identify several things that managers can do to demonstrate that they are leaders rather than the old-style managers.
13. Using your school as an example of an organization, identify an example of each of the following types of communications that occurs in your school: Formal and Informal; Internal and External; Vertical and Horizontal; Oral and Written.
14. The types of influence that can be used are position, reward, expert, and identity influence. For each of the following situations, identify which type of influence is being used.
    a. A team has been asked to make recommendations on the purchase of new computers. The team members cannot agree. Jason has much more experience with computers than the other members. They ask Jason to

cerned about pay, working conditions, and job security.
11. Many businesses did not treat their employees well. There were low wages and poor working conditions.

COMMUNICATE BUSINESS CONCEPTS

12. Leaders should listen to employees and attempt to understand their needs. If an employee is having problems, the manager should try to find ways to help solve the problem. The leader should form teams and help the teams to work well together. Employees usually want to be involved in decisions on how work should be done.
13. Students should be able to identify several examples for each type of communication. Some common examples are:
Formal: school announcements; written assignments given to students by teachers.
Informal: student conversations before and after school and between classes; parents talking to

lead the discussion of the advantages and disadvantages of each.

b. A big order must be out today, but it isn't ready to go at 5 p.m. Although everyone wants to go home, their manager, Joice, says everyone must work one hour overtime to make sure the order is shipped.

c. A new training program is being implemented by the Cortez Company to improve communications skills. Most people don't want to take the time to go to training. Fredrique, the department manager, tells his employees that the people with effective communications skills will be more likely to earn the new position of team leader.

d. Sung-mi has been an employee of the Action Company for 25 years. She knows so much about the company that whenever a manager wants to know how the employees will react to a new decision, the manager seeks Sung-mi's advice.

15. A manager has learned that the number of products being manufactured by the production team is increasing but the number of finished products with defects is increasing also. The production team needs to reduce the number of defects. Describe a way the manager would attempt to solve the problem using tactical management and strategic management.

DEVELOP YOUR BUSINESS LANGUAGE

For each numbered item, find the term that has the same meaning.

16. When group members recognize that the leader has special expertise in the area.

17. The combined use of strategic and tactical management.

18. The ability to influence individual's and groups to accomplish important goals.

19. Results from the leader's ability to give or withhold rewards.

20. The way a manager treats and directs employees.

21. A leadership style where the manager is more directive and controlling.

22. The way people get along with each other.

23. Stems from personal trust and respect members have for the leader.

24. A leadership style where managers are less

directive and involve employees in decision-making.

25. The ability to get others to accomplish tasks because of the position the leader holds.

KEY TERMS

expert influence
human relations
identity influence
leadership
leadership style
mixed management
position influence
reward influence
strategic management
tactical management

DECISION-MAKING STRATEGIES

Alia Taylor has just become a supervisor in the Roxbury Manufacturing Company, where she has worked for eleven years. She had often heard employees complain that their supervisors were not interested in employees' ideas and did not involve them in decision-making. As a result, Alia felt it was important to avoid using power and reward influence and to try to adopt a strategic leadership style. From the first day of work as a supervisor, Alia asked employees to discuss how

the work could be improved. She knew that the other employees respected Manny, a long-time member of the work team. She would often ask Manny to lead the discussion when she wanted the team to make a decision so the employees would not think she was trying to influence them. After a month, Alia started to hear that employees believed she could not make a decision on her own and wasted too much time in meetings. Several even suggested that maybe Manny should

teachers during an extracurricular activity.
Internal: the Principal writing a memo to teachers; teachers talking to students.
External: a teacher talking to a business person to obtain a part-time job for a student; the Student Council from one school sending a letter to the Student Council from another school.
Vertical: the Superintendent speaking to teachers and students at an all-city meeting; the maintenance manager sending a work schedule to all building custodians.
Horizontal: teachers discussing salaries and

benefits at a Teachers Association meeting; students signing a petition to be sent to the School Board requesting after-school tutoring sessions to prepare for college admissions tests.
Oral: a coach describing to team members how to improve the defense during a time-out; a teacher complimenting students on their test performance when handing back the exams.
Written: the school newspaper; a memo sent to the parents of all new students describing course selection and registration procedures.

DEVELOP YOUR BUSINESS LANGUAGE

16. expert influence
17. mixed management
18. leadership
19. reward influence
20. leadership style
21. tactical management
22. human relations
23. identity influence
24. strategic management
25. position influence

14. a. Expert
    b. Position
    c. Reward
    d. Identity

15. Tactical Management: The manager would study how employees were performing the work, try to discover what people or what procedures were causing the defects, and then tell the employees what changes they should make in the way the work is being done.
Strategic Management: The manager would discuss the problem with employees, have them work together to identify the reasons for the increase in defects, then as a team develop improved procedures to reduce the defects.

DECISION-MAKING STRATEGIES

26. Alia was attempting to use effective communications and team building when she involved employees in decisions. She did understand identity and informal influence by selecting Manny to conduct meetings. She was trying to use strategic management by choosing not to be directive and controlling.

27. Employees may not have been used to a supervisor who involved them in all decisions. It was quite different from the styles of supervisors they had been used to. Even though they were not happy with the past management styles, they may believe from experience that managers should make the decisions and use power and reward influence.
Alia may need to use a mixed management style, making some of the decisions that employees view as less important or a waste of their time. She may want to work on some of the leadership characteristics so employees view

her as having judgment, confidence, courage, and intelligence. She may also want to talk with Manny informally and ask for his ideas but she may want to take responsibility for leading the meetings so employees begin to view her as the manager and leader. Alia does not want to overreact to what she is hearing and go back to the traditional management style because it is clear that employees don't like that style.

CALCULATE BUSINESS DATA

28. (a) 6($365 + 125 + 600) = $6,540
    (b) 6 × $300 = $1,800
    (c) $6,540 + $1,800 = $8,340
    (d) 2 employees work all three years, 2($365 + 125 + 600 + 600) = $3,380;
    2 employees work two years, 2($365 + 125 + 600 + 300) = $2,780;
    2 employees work one year, 2($365 + 125 + 600) = $2,180;
    2 replacement employees work one year, 2($365 + 125 + 600) = $2,180;
    2 replacement employees work two years, 2($365 + 125 + 600 + 300) = $2,780; Total hiring and training costs to the company, $3,380 + 2,780 + 2,180 + 2,180 + $2,780 = $13,300
30. (a) 43,995,543 − 4,721,056 = 39,274,487
    (b) (4,721,056 − 3,124,974) ÷ 4,721,056 = 33.8% are female
    (c) (4,721,056 − 4,041,205) ÷ 4,721,056 = 14.4% are not white

be the supervisor. They said that if Alia had to ask Manny to run her meeting, she must not have any confidence in her own supervisory skills.

26. What principles of effective leadership was Alia demonstrating as a supervisor?
27. Why were the employees not satisfied with the way Alia was leading? What would you recommend?

CALCULATE BUSINESS DATA

28. One company kept track of the average costs related to hiring one employee:

Recruiting	$365
Interviewing/testing	125
Initial training	600
Continuing training	300 per year after the first year

The company learned that it takes $1\frac{1}{2}$ years of work for each new employee before their work had covered the costs of hiring and training. Calculate:

a. The cost after one year of hiring and training 6 employees.
b. The additional costs to the company of training those employees for 3 more years.
c. The total hiring and training costs after three years if all 6 employees remained with the company.
d. The total hiring and training costs after three years if two employees quit at the beginning of the second year and two quit at the beginning of the third year and had to be replaced.

29. The percentage of the total number of people employed in the United States who are members of labor unions has changed dramatically from the early part of this century. The table shows that percentage for each ten-year period from 1930–2000. Construct a bar graph to illustrate the changes that have occurred in labor union membership for those years.

Year	Percentage
1930	12
1940	29
1950	32
1960	33
1970	27
1980	23
1990	16
2000	13

30. In 2000, the U.S. Department of Labor reported that the total number of people employed in the United States was 43,995,543. Of that number, 4,721,056 were officials and managers. Of all managers, 3,124,974 were male and 4,041,205 were Caucasian. Calculate:

a. The number of people in the workforce that are not employed as an official or manager.
b. The percentage of managers who are female.
c. The percentage of managers who are not white.

TECHNOLOGY APPLICATION

Using the *Intro to Business* Data CD and your word processing program software, select problem CH07. After the problem appears on your screen, complete the following activities. Then print your completed Leadership Self-Analysis and Outline. If you do not have a printer available, save the Self-Analysis and Outline on a data disk to give to your teacher.

31. The Descriptions relating to the Leadership Characteristics are in random order. Using the Table feature of your word processing software, create a table with three columns. Using the cut-and-paste or the move feature, match each Leadership Characteristic in the first column with its Description in the second column. In the third column, tell whether each particular Leadership Characteristic is a strength or weakness for you. If it is a strength, explain how. If it is a weakness, come up with a way to improve that Characteristic for you.

32. Using the outline feature of your word processing software and the headings provided from the chapter, create a detailed outline for a presentation on leadership. Use the material in Chapter 7 as the basis for your outline. Provide as much detail as possible, but be careful not to have too much information.

29.

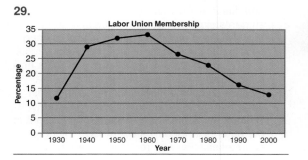

Labor Union Membership

TECHNOLOGY APPLICATION

In this activity, students use a computer to solve a business problem using a file that is provided on the data CD that accompanies *Intro to Business*. Instructions for using the data CD are included in a **README** file on the disk. Solutions are provided on the Instructor's Resource CD.

INTERNATIONAL TRADE INTERMEDIARIES

Getting a product to a rural area of China could involve an ocean freighter, a train, a bicycle, and eventually an ox cart. Movement of goods to desired locations is vital for international business. These distribution activities involve intermediaries, which are businesses that move goods from producers to consumers.

An *export management company* (EMC) provides complete distribution services for companies that desire to sell in foreign markets. EMCs make it easier for companies involved in foreign trade since they have immediate access to established buyers. Most EMCs are small firms that specialize in specific products or in a certain foreign market.

An *export trading company* (ETC) is a full-service global distribution intermediary. An ETC buys and sells products; conducts market research; and packages, ships, and distributes goods abroad. An ETC may also be involved in banking, financing, and production activities. Japanese trading companies, called sogo shoshas, handle the major portion of Japan's imports and exports.

A *freight forwarder* ships goods to customers in other countries. Like a travel agent for cargo, these companies move

> **The movement of goods from producers to consumers is critical for global business.**

merchandise to the required destination and help with proper documentation of shipments. Often a freight forwarder will accumulate several small export shipments and combine them into one larger shipment in order to get lower freight rates.

A *customs broker*, also called a custom house broker, is an intermediary that specializes in moving goods through the customs process. This process involves inspection of imported products and payment of duties (import taxes). Customs brokers are licensed in the countries where they work and must be aware of the import rules and fees.

CRITICAL THINKING

1. Working in small groups or on your own, prepare a description of skills or abilities that would be needed to work for an export management company, an export trading company, a freight forwarder, or a customs broker.
2. Conduct a web search for freight forwarders. Locate information about shipping products to other countries. Prepare a short written summary of your findings.

Most students will either work with international clients or compete against businesses that do. Global Navigator introduces students to issues integral to working with international businesses. Key concepts and challenges faced by international businesses are presented, followed by Critical Thinking questions that require students to analyze what they have learned.

This feature discusses the various types of international trade intermediaries, including EMCs (export management companies), ETCs (export trading companies), freight forwarders, and customs brokers. Because so many businesses now ship products or documents internationally, there is a good chance that many students will participate in the international shipment of goods, documents, etc. in their respective careers. Students can search the Internet for web sites of some of these international trade intermediaries.

CRITICAL THINKING

1. Answers may vary widely, but could include:
   - Learning a second language
   - Studying international business in college
   - Learning about various international trading practices, regulations, treaties, etc.
   - Customer service skills
2. Answers will vary. Students' written summaries may include:
   - Pricing information
   - Regulations and guidelines for shipping to various countries
   - Shipping methods for customers to select
   - Delivery schedules and tracking information

In Chapter 8, students will learn the 8 marketing functions needed for an exchange to occur. The steps of a marketing strategy are covered, as well as the 4 Ps of marketing. Students also learn about channels of distribution and effective selling techniques.

Resources For Teachers
- Lesson Plans
- School-To-Work/SCANS Activity Masters
- Spanish Resources
- Instructor's Resource CD

Assessment
- Chapter and Unit Tests, Ch. 8
- ExamView, Ch. 8

Media/Technology
- Applying Technology Data CD
- PowerPoint slides
- Business Connection CD
- Videotape

Activity Masters and Workbooks
- Activities and Projects, Ch. 8
- Internet Activity Masters
- Business Math Activity Masters
- Communications Activity Masters
- International Business Activity Masters
- Ethics Activity Masters

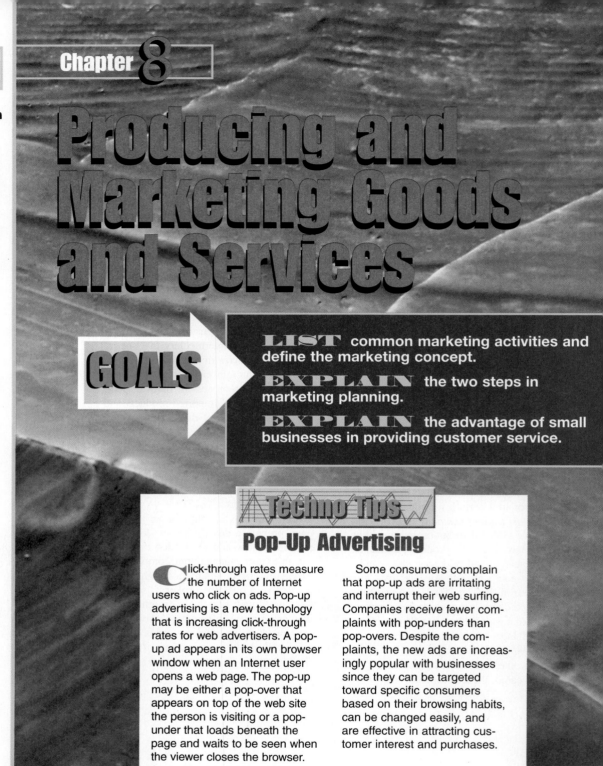

Chapter 8

Producing and Marketing Goods and Services

GOALS

LIST common marketing activities and define the marketing concept.

EXPLAIN the two steps in marketing planning.

EXPLAIN the advantage of small businesses in providing customer service.

Techno Tips

Pop-Up Advertising

Click-through rates measure the number of Internet users who click on ads. Pop-up advertising is a new technology that is increasing click-through rates for web advertisers. A pop-up ad appears in its own browser window when an Internet user opens a web page. The pop-up may be either a pop-over that appears on top of the web site the person is visiting or a pop-under that loads beneath the page and waits to be seen when the viewer closes the browser.

Some consumers complain that pop-up ads are irritating and interrupt their web surfing. Companies receive fewer complaints with pop-unders than pop-overs. Despite the complaints, the new ads are increasingly popular with businesses since they can be targeted toward specific consumers based on their browsing habits, can be changed easily, and are effective in attracting customer interest and purchases.

Techno Tips Students need to know the latest technologies and develop cutting edge Internet skills for use in current jobs, future careers, or in their homes. TechnoTips introduces students to today's cutting edge technologies and provides them with important Internet skills. Feature topics concentrate on Internet-specific technologies and computer or other hi-tech innovations for use by businesses and consumers.

FOCUS ON REAL LIFE

Jerome and Rochelle were eating lunch in the cafeteria after their Current Issues class. They had just watched a film on marketing that illustrated just how much it adds to the cost of many products.

Jerome: I've always felt that marketing is a waste of money. That film showed that marketing often doubles the cost of products. We pay for those advertisements, contests, and salespeople every time we buy something.

Rochelle: Yes, it does seem that marketing costs a lot, but I wonder what would happen if we didn't have marketing. Remember the examples that showed how marketing research resulted in products that customers preferred. Marketing research saved one company over $10 million dollars in one year because more of their products were successful. They were able to cut prices because of the savings.

Jerome: I don't usually think of research as a part of marketing. I always think of advertising and promotion.

Rochelle: It seems like businesses that want to be successful can use marketing to meet their customers' needs, but not all businesses think that way. I guess we should look at businesses carefully to see which ones understand how to use marketing.

THE ROLE OF MARKETING

Think of the thousands of products and services available for you and your family to purchase. It is not always easy when you go shopping to decide which product to buy and what price to pay. Now increase that number of products and services by the thousands and thousands that are sold all over the world, then multiply the number of your family members by millions, and you have the number of consumers that businesses are trying to sell their products and services to.

How can consumers be sure they have the products and services they need at the right time, right place, and right price? How can businesses insure that the products and services they offer are available to the customers who want them with the information needed to help them decide to buy? The answer is marketing. Marketing is all of the activities used to insure the effective exchange of goods and services between businesses and consumers.

Marketing activities begin with the very first idea for development of a new product or service. Marketers (the people and businesses who complete marketing activities) use research to determine the wants and needs of consumers and to test new ideas with consumers. As new products and services near completion, marketers select the product name, design packaging, and begin to develop advertising. The next decisions are where the products will be sold and how to get the products from the place they are produced to the selling location. Finally, marketers help set the price and decide what forms of payment customers can use (cash or credit). After products are sold, marketers provide customer service and work on product improvements.

When marketing works well, customers get the products and services they want at an

The top five most popular Internet activities, according to a recent survey from UCLA, were e-mail, instant messaging, web browsing, buying online, and reading news and other information.

FOCUS ON REAL LIFE

Find pictures of new product designs in advertisements or magazine and newspaper articles. Display the products on the bulletin board. Have students identify whether they like the designs and whether they believe the products will be successful. Ask if they can identify some examples of "off-the-wall" ideas that have resulted in successful products. Discuss why they believe such unique product ideas are successful, while others fail.

Research the steps involved in marketing a product from the producer or manufacturer to the consumer. Create a flowchart or other visual presentation that shows how e-commerce might be used in each step of the marketing process.

Have students agree on a definition of a target market and the elements of the marketing mix. List three or four products from each of the following categories on the board (automobiles, breakfast cereals, athletic equipment, electronic goods), and have students define as many target markets and marketing mixes as they can for each product.

Ask students if they have ever gone to a store only to find it out of the product they were looking for. How did they feel as a customer? Did they continue doing business with that store?

TRY THIS/GUIDED PRACTICE
Lead a discussion explaining the difference between production and manufacturing. Manufacturing always refers to tangible products. However, production can refer to tangible or intangible products—sometimes known as services. A product can be characterized as a tangible object, whereas a service is an intangible deed or performance. Ask: "Is a football game a product or a service?" The players are tangible and the broadcast can be videotaped and inventoried for later replay. Businesses keep products in inventory to meet future customer demand. However, does this make the game a product? No. The game itself is not tangible and cannot be inventoried. Compare this to a drapery

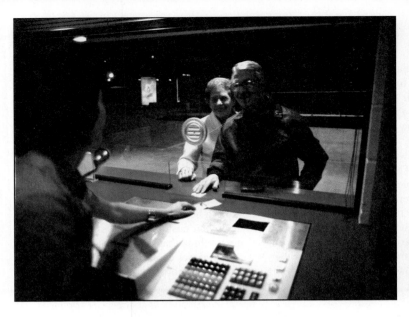

How do you think the eight marketing functions are completed in the motion picture industry?

affordable price, and businesses sell their products and services at a profit. Effective marketing leads to satisfying exchanges between businesses and customers. Marketing is not always successful, however. Sometimes businesses make things that cannot be sold profitably. Often consumers have needs for which they cannot find satisfactory products and services. Neither business people nor consumers are happy when marketing does not work.

Marketing is especially important in capitalistic or free enterprise economic systems. A capitalistic economy like that found in the United States is based on voluntary exchanges. Businesses are free to decide what they want to produce and sell. At the same time, consumers are free to choose what they want to buy and the prices they are willing to pay. Marketers serve as intermediaries, helping to match the production and consumption decisions among producers and consumers. Without marketers, it would be much more expensive and time-consuming for businesses to sell what they produced and for consumers to find what they needed.

Marketing Functions
Marketers perform hundreds of activities. Some work directly for a business that produces the goods and services (marketing researchers and sales people), while others operate their own service businesses (advertising agencies and transportation companies). Even consumers perform marketing activities, such as renting a trailer to move a new appliance rather than paying a delivery company.

Whatever specific activities are performed or whoever does them, the following eight **marketing functions** (groups of marketing activities) must be completed in order for an exchange to occur:

1. **Product/Service Planning** assists in design and development by gathering information and testing ideas.
2. **Purchasing** identifies and obtains the products (and services) needed for marketing activities.
3. **Financing** makes sure financing and credit are available to support both the purchase and sale of products.
4. **Distribution** involves getting products to customers.

TEACHING STRATEGIES

Special Needs
Hearing-Impaired Students

Hearing-impaired students may have difficulty comprehending new vocabulary and concepts. Present business vocabulary and new concepts in varied ways to ensure comprehension.

Other general strategies include using printed materials, facing the student when conversing to make lip reading possible, giving clear and simple instructions, and seating students preferentially to ensure the best visual position possible.

5. **Pricing** sets prices and payment methods.

6. **Risk Management** provides security and safety for products and people, and reduces business risks.

7. **Marketing Information Management** obtains and organizes information needed to make marketing decisions.

8. **Promotion** involves communicating with consumers to encourage purchases.

Each time a new product is planned, produced, and sold, all of the eight marketing functions are completed, though not always by the business that develops the new product. They are usually completed by a combination of that business, other specialized marketing businesses, and the customer. Let's look at an example of a company as it completes each of the marketing functions.

CarryEze, a company that makes briefcases for business executives, is always looking for new product ideas. Research indicates that people have trouble carrying and keeping track of all their cellular phones, pagers, personal digital assistants (PDAs), and other electronic devices.

Working with product designers, CarryEze develops a small leather case with pockets designed to hold the devices and accessories that executives regularly carry. They show models to prospective customers and, based on feedback, make changes and improvements.

While the product is being produced, marketers decide on a name, packaging, and how it will be distributed. They identify and purchase the supplies, materials, and services needed to complete marketing activities. They work with their financial people to develop budgets and line up cash to pay for marketing activities until products are sold.

The next marketing decision is how to get the products to the people most likely to buy them. Research indicates that business people will purchase them, as well as other people who regularly use portable telephones and pagers. Office supply stores, leather and luggage outlets, consumer electronics stores, and catalogs are identified as good sales outlets. CarryEze develops agreements with these

cleaning service. You can touch your clean draperies, but you cannot touch or inventory "clean."

Have the class suggest a new product (or products) that could be sold in the school store. Ask students how they might go about developing this product. Refer them to Figure 8-2 as you guide them through the steps necessary to develop a successful new product.

Write the following definition of marketing on the board or overhead: "Marketing is all of the activities used to ensure the effective exchange of goods and services between businesses and consumers." Lead a discussion of the activities that come to mind when students see that definition. Then have them compare their ideas with the list of marketing activities in Figure 8-1.

Lead students in a discussion of distribution decisions using PowerPoint 8-7, *Planning Distribution Channels*. Ask students why they believe a company may need to use more than one channel of distribution for the same product. Ask the following question, "How can the choice of a channel of distribution affect the characteristics of effective distribution?" Have students give examples of distribution channels they believe are effective or ineffective.

EXPLORE THIS/INDEPENDENT PRACTICE Pass out copies of the Yellow Pages. Have students review several pages of the directory and identify the businesses that are involved in producing or manufacturing products, those involved in marketing, and all others. After the businesses have been categorized, have students

FIGURE 8-1   How do you think marketing activities differ between large corporations and small businesses?

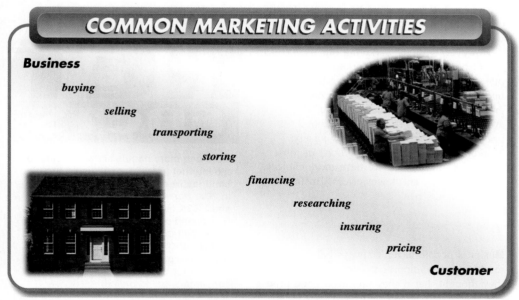

COMMON MARKETING ACTIVITIES

Business

buying

selling

transporting

storing

financing

researching

insuring

pricing

Customer

Workplace Competencies-Technology

In order for students to become contributing workers in our society, it is important that they understand technology and how to apply it appropriately. We may help students become proficient in technology by teaching them how to apply technology to tasks through understanding the basics of the appropriate equipment. Technology does not always mean just computers. Numerous other forms of technology are used by businesspeople. Continuous advancements in copier machines, telecommunications (pagers, cell phones, etc.), fax machines, and more, require most employees in businesses to keep up with the changes. Invite the computer resource person from your school to speak to your class about the various kinds of technology used at your school and that person's role in keeping the equipment in working order.

calculate the percentage of businesses in each group and compare and discuss the differences.

Have each student make a list of six items his or her family has recently purchased and identify the target market in each case. Each student should prepare a visual (preferably a chart or poster) that will identify the market for the items.

Have students select a product that is marketed successfully to more than one target market. Have them describe two different target markets for the product and then answer the following questions to compare the marketing mix for the two markets: (a) What differences in product characteristics exist? (b) What is the difference in the price paid for the product by the two groups? (c) What are the differences in the advertising media and messages? (d) Where does each market prefer to buy the product?

The Chapter Review questions at the end of the chapter vary in level of difficulty. For a basic assignment, consider Develop Your Business Language and Review Your Reading. For an average assignment, consider the basic assignment plus Communicate Business Concepts and Calculate Business Data. For an enhanced assignment, try the average assignment plus Technology Application and Decision-Making Strategies.

businesses to sell the cases. Then it makes plans to have the products shipped to each business. It also modfies the company's Internet web site to accommodate direct sales.

Product security is always a concern, so security procedures are developed and insurance policies are reviewed to minimize their risk.

CarryEze is relying on a great deal of information to make marketing decisions and manage marketing activities. That information is gathered, updated regularly, and maintained in its computer system, so it is available when needed.

Finally, since marketers know that consumers will need information about the product, they work with an advertising agency to develop ads, brochures, and product displays.

Can you go back through this description and match the activities with the various marketing functions?

Impact of Marketing on Your Life

Some people have a negative view of marketing, often caused by a misunderstanding of what marketing involves as well as the misuse of marketing by some businesses. People often think only of advertising and selling when they hear the term "marketing."

However, without marketing our lives would be very different. Marketing increases our standard of living by helping businesses understand our needs so they can produce the products and services we want. It makes us aware of the best products and the best prices, so we can use our money wisely. Marketing activities create millions of jobs. Because of marketing, we have more choices, better products, and lower prices. Businesses and consumers benefit.

EFFECTIVE MARKETING

Business people haven't always believed that marketing was important. For a long time they thought that if they produced good products, customers would find them, buy them,

and pay enough for the company to make a profit. But competition among many businesses offering similar products eventually taught business people that if they were going to be successful, they would have to do more. When consumers have choices, they buy the product that best meets their needs. They also expect that the product will be available when and where they want to buy it, at a reasonable price, and with adequate information and service to be able to use the product.

How do you feel if you see an ad, but when you go to the store you find that the product as described in the ad is not available? How do you feel when you are mistreated by a salesperson, or when you open a product and find it has been damaged because it was not packaged well? These are all examples of ineffective marketing.

Some business people try to take advantage of consumers. Others are unable to complete all of the needed marketing activities well, or they think that customers will not pay for effective service. But most businesses realize today that they will be more successful if they understand and use marketing well. To do that they have to adopt a marketing philosophy.

More and more homes are connected to the Internet at fast speeds using broadband (cable or DSL). The fastest modem in 2001 transmitted data at speeds of about 53K (kilobits per second). Broadband connections increase that speed by ten times or more. In 2001, 21 percent of U.S. home Internet connections were broadband. Broadband users account for over 50 percent of the time consumers spend online.

Net Facts provides information and definitions of terms for the Internet. The more information that students have about the Internet, the better equipped they will be to use this resource. In the Internet Activity Masters, there is an Internet Activity Worksheet for each unit. You can use these activities to give students experience with finding information online. Options for assigning this activity are as follows:

1. **Provide students with a list of addresses for this activity,**
2. **Assign students to conduct their own searches, or**
3. **Use the addresses on the Internet Activity Worksheet.**
   You should complete the activity yourself before assigning it to resolve any discrepancies that may arise.

A Marketing Philosophy

The most successful businesses think of the consumer as they produce and market products and services. That philosophy of business is known as the marketing concept. The **marketing concept** considers the needs of customers when planning, pricing, distributing, and promoting a product or service.

When you study the definition of the marketing concept, it seems obvious that businesses would want to use that philosophy. Why wouldn't a business want to satisfy customer needs? Well, it's not easy to use the marketing concept. To be successful, the business must be able to:

1. Identify the customers they want to serve and understand their needs.
2. Develop a product that will satisfy the customers and complete the necessary marketing activities effectively.
3. Complete all of those activities at a profit.

There are many examples of businesses that successfully implement the marketing concept. You probably have a favorite restaurant that you go to regularly because they serve food you want at fair prices with a friendly atmosphere. Do you have a favorite brand of clothing, a store where you do most of your shopping, or an entertainment spot? What do they offer that keeps you returning time after time? Probably they understand you and your needs and want to keep you and others like you as customers. If so, they are using the marketing concept.

A Marketing Strategy

Business people who believe in the marketing concept use a two-step process, called a **marketing strategy**, for successfully planning and marketing products and services. The first step is to identify a **target market**, a clearly identified group of consumers with needs that the business wants to satisfy. The second step is to develop a marketing mix. A **marketing mix** is a combination of marketing elements designed to meet the needs of a target market. There are four marketing mix

elements, sometimes referred to as the *4 Ps of marketing*. They are Product, Place (distribution), Price, and Promotion.

Product is anything offered to the target market to satisfy their needs, including both products and services. **Place** (distribution) includes the locations where products are sold and the ways they are made available to customers. **Price** is what customers pay and the method of payment. **Promotion** is the methods used to communicate information to customers in order to encourage purchases and to increase their satisfaction.

PRODUCT DEVELOPMENT

Producers and manufacturers develop new products for sale. Products are more than mere physical goods. A product also includes the brand name, packaging, accessories, and services that increase customer satisfaction.

Marketers help create new products through marketing research, which is used to gather information from consumers about

Name several target markets for snowboard manufacturers.

Review the goals at the beginning of the chapter and the Business Notes at the end of the chapter. Have students respond orally or in writing to each of the Business Notes restated as a question, provided below. For students who may have difficulty providing answers, assign the reteaching activities that follow. Enrichment activities may also be assigned where appropriate.

1. What are the eight marketing functions that must be completed in order for an exchange to occur? (Answer: The eight marketing functions are product/service planning, purchasing, financing, distribution, pricing, risk management, marketing information management, and promotion.)
2. Explain the two steps involved in a marketing strategy. (Answer: The first step is to identify a target market, and the second step is to develop a marketing mix.)
3. What are the four marketing mix elements, often referred to as the *4 Ps of Marketing*? (Answer: Product, place, price, and promotion.)
4. What are the four important differences that must be considered in developing an effective channel of distribution? (Answer: Differences in quantity, assortment, location, and time.)
5. What are the important steps to effective personal selling? (Answer: Preapproach, approach, demonstration, questioning, close, and follow-up.)

TEACHING STRATEGIES

Alternate Modalities
Kinesthetic Learner

Kinesthetic learners learn best by taking an active part in the instruction. When presenting the eight marketing functions to a kinesthetic learner, have the student make a list on the overhead of these eight functions of marketing, based on the material in this chapter.

Work with students to develop a crossword puzzle based on the vocabulary terms in the Chapter Review. Assemble the puzzle on the board or overhead, with different students adding blocks and providing definitions or clues. Have selected students provide the correct entries once the puzzle is completed.

Bring in samples of some common household products, such as pet food, toothpaste, soap, cereals, etc. Ask the students to identify the target market for each of the products.

Emphasize the four elements of the marketing mix by drawing a chart on the board. Have volunteers fill in the chart with definitions and examples. Remind students that the marketing mix is the combination of activities that encourage consumers to purchase a specific product or service.

ENRICH

Direct students to read the Cultural Perspectives in this chapter. Instruct students to bring in a picture from a magazine or newspaper that shows one of three types of manufacturing processes and create a bulletin board with these materials.

Have students think of a product that they could mass-produce and sell as a school fund-raising project. Suggestions might include baked goods or food baskets. Have them explain how they could make production as efficient as possible. Encourage students to make charts or floor plans to show how the item would be produced and distributed.

FIGURE 8-2 Why do you think it is important to follow these steps for developing a new product?

their wants and needs, their experience with related products, and any improvements they would prefer. Figure 8-2 shows the steps in developing a new product.

Planning, Developing, and Testing New Goods and Services

Marketers work with engineers and scientists to plan new products. If a new product idea is generated within a company, a model will be prepared. Market researchers will have a small group of consumers study the model to identify what they like and don't like and suggest how the product can be improved.

On average, companies spend much less than 50 percent of their total marketing budgets on advertising and selling. Even large companies that spend millions of dollars on advertising spend much more on other marketing activities.

Based on that, the company will decide if it can profitably produce and sell the new product.

A second way of developing new product ideas is for the marketing researchers to survey customers to determine what they like and dislike about products they currently use or what needs they have that are not well satisfied by available products. The researchers then take the information to product designers, who make improvements to existing products or attempt to create new products that respond to the customers' ideas. If new products are designed, they will probably be tested again before the decision is made to produce and market them.

After a new product is planned, the company develops procedures to produce it. Time and money are needed to set up the manufacturing process. A production facility is needed, materials must be obtained, equipment purchased, and employees hired and trained. Even after the products are produced, the company makes no money until they are

CAREER HIGHLIGHTS

A *public relations manager's* duties include:

- **Supervising public relations specialists and directing publicity programs and special events.**
- **Overseeing contacts with communication media to build and maintain support among consumers, stockholders, or the general public.**
- **Observing social, economic, and political trends that may have an effect upon the firm and making recommendations to enhance the firm's public image in light of those trends.**
- **Coordinating the production of internal company communications and shareholder reports.**
- **Assisting company executives in writing speeches or articles, arranging interviews, and other forms of public contact.**
- **Overseeing company archives and responding to information requests.**

sold. Because of the cost and time needed to produce something, companies want to be certain customers will want a new product and will buy it at a price that turns a profit.

Developing Products and Services That Consumers Want

Producing successful products is risky. Companies may spend years in planning a new product, and it is not unusual to invest millions of dollars before the first unit is sold. To reduce risk, companies use marketing research to understand consumers' wants, needs, and buying motives.

Needs are necessary for survival, while wants add to our comfort and pleasure. Everyone has needs and wants, sometimes quite similar, but the products we choose may be quite different from those selected by others. You may choose to stay at home and

watch a video, while someone else may prefer to go to a theater. Some people use e-mail; others insist on personalized stationery.

Marketers study consumer behavior to understand wants and needs. You may have received a questionnaire in the mail asking you about a recent purchase. People walking through a shopping center may be queried about new product ideas. Some retailers collect information through their checkout stations on customer preferences. Each of these methods and many others are procedures for understanding consumer wants and needs.

Buying motives are the reasons for making a purchase. Sometimes motives are very rational, based on facts or logic. For example, a person renting a car may select the company that is closest to the airport or that offers the best weekly rate. In other cases, motives may be emotional, based on feelings and attitudes. For example, a couple planning a vacation may choose a hotel that costs more but uses appealing advertisements showing people enjoying a hot tub.

THE FACTORS OF DISTRIBUTION

One of the greatest challenges that have faced businesses throughout history is how to get products to their customers. In the early history of the United States, people moved from the east to the west. To get products to them, companies used wagons, rivers, and trains. Today, products move by ocean, air, truck, and train as companies distribute to customers throughout the world.

Several *factors* need to be considered when planning product distribution. In what locations and in what businesses will the product be sold? What transportation methods will be used? How will the product be packaged and protected?

Getting Products and Services to Consumers

Few products are sold directly by the producer or manufacturer to the consumer. A

CAREER HIGHLIGHTS

The careers listed in Career Highlights come from the *Occupational Outlook Handbook*, an online publication (www.bls.gov/oco) of the federal government. The O*NET code for Public Relations Manager is 11-2031.00. Tell your class about this resource and how to use it. This description of job duties can be used to demonstrate the relevancy of skills learned in this course.

Ask students to look through business publications to see if they can find articles on the development of new products. Often the process used in development is discussed as well as the cost of development.

Even though most businesses are attempting to be customer-oriented (concerned about customer needs) today, some still are more production- or sales-oriented. In a production-oriented business, decisions about what and how to produce receive the most attention. In a sales-oriented business, promotion is emphasized in order to sell products. Have students identify businesses they believe fit each of the three categories and provide a justification for each of their decisions.

Chapter 8 *Producing and Marketing Goods and Services* **107**

TEACHING STRATEGIES

Special Needs
Attention Deficit Disorder

Provide students with activities that are short and focused. These students do better with basic assignments instead of

lengthy ones. (See lesson plan, Explore This/Independent Practice.)

CULTURAL PERSPECTIVES
Native American Enterprise

In Western European cultures, entrepreneurship is based on capitalism. Individual ownership of business and the accumulation of wealth are valued. Resources are used to expand the wealth of the owner.

Native Americans have held a very different view of enterprise. Historically, land for raising crops, hunting territories, and rivers for fishing were collectively owned and used by a village or an extended family. Economic production (hunting, fishing, and agriculture) was not aimed at personal gain.

In contrast to economic production leading to personal gain, the well-being of the village or community guided the work of Native Americans. Wealth was looked upon as a sign of individual greed. Prestige was not granted to the richest people in the community. Social status was gained by demonstrations of generosity.

Today's *consumer cooperatives* reflect the economic principles espoused by Native Americans. Consumer cooperatives are user-owned retail outlets for goods and services. They range from rural electric companies and credit unions to retail clothing and food stores. These nonprofit cooperatives are organized for the purpose of providing economic services to members who own and control them. Members of cooperatives are often concerned about the well-being of the family and community.

Critical Thinking
1. What types of today's business organizations reflect the economic roots of Native American culture?
2. Can you think of examples of cooperatives in your community?

A **channel of distribution** is the path that a product travels from producer to consumer. A **direct channel of distribution** is the process through which goods are bought by the consumer directly from the producer. An **indirect channel of distribution** is the process by which goods move through one or more middle firms between the producer and the consumer. This occurs through many other businesses, or intermediaries, to complete the process.

Some types of intermediaries are well known, and we expect them to be a part of the distribution channel. A **wholesaler** is a middle firm that assists with distribution activities between businesses. A **retailer,** which is a business firm that sells directly to the consumer, collects the products of many manufacturers, prices them, displays them, and makes it easy for you to buy. We go to a shopping center because we know we will find an assortment of products at a convenient location.

Other intermediaries are less well known. A company that owns underground pipelines, pumping facilities, and huge storage tanks, for example, may move gasoline across the country for our automobiles. Independent trucking companies fill tank trucks at the storage facility and transport the gasoline to local service stations. A number of specialized companies are often involved in the distribution of products. That is especially true as more and more products are exported to other countries.

Characteristics of Effective Distribution
Distribution adjusts for differences between production and consumption. There are four important *factors of distribution* that must be considered in developing an effective channel of distribution.

1. *Quantity:* Businesses usually produce enough for thousands of customers, but

---

CULTURAL PERSPECTIVES

This Cultural Perspective will expose students to the concept that our society is composed of people from many different cultural backgrounds. Teachers should have students read the feature; discuss the concepts explored; clarify any terms or questions; and direct students to answer the questions.

CRITICAL THINKING
1. Business oraganizations such as cooperatives reflect the economic roots of Native Americans. Unlike a corporation, a cooperative does not keep profits. Instead, it distributes profits to its members in proportion to their contributions. Since the cooperative keeps no profits it pays no taxes.
2. Examples might include seller cooperatives that are popular in agriculture. Another form is the buyer cooperative, which buys in volume for the best possible prices.

DIRECT AND INDIRECT DISTRIBUTION

EVALUATE

- Assign Activities and Projects for Chapter 8.
- Administer the printed test or ExamView for Chapter 8.
- Assign portfolio activities for Unit 2.

No Middle Firm

Direct

Producer   Consumer

One Middle Firm

Indirect

Producer   Retailer   Consumer

Two Middle Firms

Producer   Wholesaler   Retailer   Consumer

FIGURE 8-3   The last time you bought something, which channel was used?

a typical customer buys only a small quantity at a time. A channel of distribution adjusts the large quantity produced to the small quantity purchased.

2. *Assortment:* Manufacturers tend to specialize in a limited line of products, while consumers need an assortment of things, and they usually want to buy several things from a single source. Channels of distribution accumulate many varieties of products in one place.

3. *Location:* It's unlikely that many of the products you buy are made in your town, or even in your state. Distribution brings products from all over the world to locations convenient for consumers.

Chapter 8 *Producing and Marketing Goods and Services*   109

Critical Thinking Skills-Decision Making

Decision-making skills, which include specifying goals, generating alternatives, considering risks, and evaluating and choosing the best alternative, are applied throughout every chapter in this text. Each time a student participates in a Cooperative Learning or Teams activity, decision-making skills are applied in a group situation. For Communicate Business

Concepts and Decision-Making Strategies, students must specify the goal of the activity, consider risks, and evaluate the best solution before the questions can be answered. Emphasize to students how they are using decision-making techniques in their day-to-day tasks and make them aware of the skills they are developing.

SCANS

4. **Time:** At the time of the first snow storm, people rush to stores to purchase shovels and snow blowers. When it turns warm, they buy air conditioners and swimwear. Yet businesses cannot efficiently produce products only at the time they will be used. Effective distribution lets manufacturers maximize efficiency while delivering products to consumers when they want them.

THE ROLE OF PRICING

Price is what we pay for products and services. A price helps us to determine our level of satisfaction. People don't always pay the lowest price because a higher price may mean better quality. Consumers compare prices to the satisfaction they believe they will receive, and then they select the best value.

Goals and Objectives of Pricing

Businesses have several goals when setting a price. First, they hope to cover their costs and generate a profit. Second, they want a price that consumers will view as a good value. Third, they want a price that won't put them at a competitive disadvantage: too high a price attracts competitors who will undercut them; too low a price can't sustain adequate marketing support.

Based on their goals, a business will usually have one of three objectives:

1. Maximize Profits: If a company has a limited supply of a product or if there is an unusually high demand, it may increase its price in order to make a higher profit.

2. Increase Sales: If a company has a large quantity of a product for sale or if it is facing strong competition, it may lower its prices to increase sales.

3. Maintain an Image: Prices can support an image of quality, service, or value. They may be high, moderate, or low.

Factors That Will Influence a Product's Price

The free enterprise economy is based on supply and demand. Businesses supply products they want to sell, and customers demand products that they think will satisfy their needs. If supply is low and demand is high, prices will be high. On the other hand, if there is a large supply but limited demand, prices will drop.

There are also other factors that influence prices. For each factor listed, what effect do you think it has on price?

1. The quantity of a product purchased by a customer.

2. The level of customer service offered by the business.

3. Whether the product is fragile or requires special handling.

4. The number of businesses in the channel of distribution.

5. The amount of advertising and communications needed to inform customers.

PROMOTION FOR SUCCESSFUL MARKETING

Where do you get information about the products and services you buy? There are many information sources, including government and consumer publications, people who have purchased similar products, and materials prepared by businesses. Research indicates that, for most people, advertising is one of the primary sources.

Businesses have learned that it's not enough to have a good product. With so many products available, it is easy to become lost in the marketplace. Promotion is the marketing tool businesses use to communicate with consumers to persuade them to purchase its products. To be effective, promotion must be noticed, encourage consumers to pay attention to the message, and result in them taking some type of action.

TEACHING STRATEGIES

Special Needs
Dyslexia

One way to keep students with dyslexia interested in the class is to use teaching strategies that will make content clear through the use of visuals or graphics and reduce the reading load. Associate the visuals in the chapter with the content instead of assigning an overwhelming amount of text to read.

Steps in the Selling Process

Step	Purpose
Preapproach	Gather information about the customer, his or her needs, and appropriate products.
Approach	Contact the customer, confirm needs and buying motives, establish a positive relationship.
Demonstration	Present the product in an interesting way that demonstrates how it meets the customer's needs; involve customer in the use of the product.
Questioning	Help the customer get needed information and resolve any concerns.
Close	Encourage the customer to make a decision to purchase, or arrange for follow-up contact.
Follow-up	Continue contact with the customer after a purchase to ensure satisfaction, respond to any unsatisfied needs.

FIGURE 8-4 How many of these steps were evident the last time you dealt with a salesperson?

The Role of Promotion

Marketing is more than advertising and selling, yet promotion is an important part of marketing, one of the four elements of the marketing mix. To attract new customers, a business uses promotion to inform prospective customers and pursuade them that its product is a better choice. Once customers have bought the product, it uses promotion to reinforce their purchase decision and remind them of how it meets their needs.

Selecting Promotional Methods and Media

Today most promotion is done through media advertising—information that's paid for by a business to reach large numbers of prospective customers. Other types of promotion can also be effective. Sales promotions are intended to attract customers' interest or provide a direct incentive for customers to buy a product—things like coupons, contests, and free samples. Publicity is information about a business, product, or service that appears in the media but which is not paid for by the company. Personal selling is direct, personal communication between a salesperson and a customer to encourage the purchase of a product.

Businesses select promotional methods and media based on three factors:

1. Who are the prospective customers being targeted?
   How many?
   Where are they located?
   What information sources do they use?
2. What is the message?
   Does everyone need the same information?
   Is the message simple or complex?
   Should the information be repeated regularly?
3. What is the budget for promotion?

Personal Selling as a Promotional Activity

Salespeople do effective personalized promotion. They work with customers to learn their needs, understand their buying motives, and provide information to help the customer make a purchase decision. Effective personal selling follows the sequence of steps outlined in Figure 8-4.

Basic Skills-Math

SCANS

OIn order for students to become contributing workers in our society, it is important that they become proficient in the basic skills of reading, writing, arithmetic, and mathematics. In order to prepare students for the school-to-work transition, we must teach these skills in our classroom. Applying math across the curriculum is an important element in contemporary education. As a part of end-of-chapter activities, Calculate Business Data enables students to apply their math skills. Appendix B: Math Review, Appendix C: Determining Percentages and Interest in Business, and Appendix D: Using Measurements in Business, also apply arithmetic and math skills.

REVIEW YOUR READING

1. Marketers use research to determine the wants and needs of consumers and to test new ideas with consumers.
2. Effective marketing leads to satisfying exchanges between businesses and customers.
3. Because of marketing consumers have more choices of products and services, better products, and lower prices.
4. Consumers want products and services that meet their needs. They also expect that the products will be available when and where they want to buy them, at a reasonable price, and with adequate information and service to be able to use the product or service.
5. (a) Identify the customers they want to serve and understand their needs. (b) Develop a product that will satisfy the customers and complete the necessary marketing activities effectively. (c) Complete all of those activities at a profit.
6. The first step is to identify a target market. The second step is to develop a marketing mix.
7. Another name for the marketing mix is the 4 Ps of Marketing.
8. (a) Marketers work with engineers and scientists to plan new products. (b) Consumers are surveyed to determine what they like or dislike about current products or what needs they have that are not well satisfied. That information is then used by product designers to develop new product ideas.
9. The four differences are differences in quantity, differences in assortment, differences in location, and differences in time.
10. If the supply of a product is low and customer demand is high, the price will be high. If there is a large supply of a product but limited demand, prices will be low.
11. Businesses use advertising, sales promotion, publicity, and personal selling for promotion.

COMMUNICATE BUSINESS CONCEPTS

12. Student answers will vary. Possible answers for each of the marketing mix elements include:
Product: better features, higher quality, a preferred brand name, product gurarantee
Place: sold at a store I prefer,

Chapter REVIEW

BUSINESS NOTES

1. The 8 marketing functions that must be completed in order for an exchange to occur are the following: product/service planning, purchasing, financing, distribution, pricing, risk management, marketing information management, and promotion.
2. A marketing strategy is a two-step process used to plan and market products. The first step is to identify a target market, and the second step is to develop a marketing mix.
3. The four marketing mix elements, often referred to as the 4 Ps of Marketing, are product, place, price, and promotion.
4. There are four important factors of distribution that must be considered in developing an effective channel of distribution. These are quantity, assortment, location, and time.
5. Effective personal selling follows these important steps: preapproach, approach, demonstration, questioning, close, follow-up.

REVIEW YOUR READING

1. What is the purpose of marketing research?
2. What is the result of effective marketing?
3. Name three benefits consumers receive as a result of marketing activities.
4. What do consumers expect when they buy products and services?
5. Identify the three things a business must be able to do if it believes in the marketing concept.
6. Describe the two steps that are a part of a marketing strategy.
7. What is another name for the marketing mix?
8. There are two ways that a business can identify ideas for new products. What are those ways?
9. Describe the factors of distribution that need to be used to determine the channels of distribution for goods and services.
10. How does the economic concept of supply and demand affect the price of a product?
11. What are the four common methods of promotion used by businesses?

COMMUNICATE BUSINESS CONCEPTS

12. Often it is believed that people will purchase the lowest-priced product available, but often people will pay more for a product because they believe the higher-priced product is better than the lowest-priced products. Think of several products you purchase for which you know you pay more than you would have to. List the characteristics of the products that cause you to pay a higher price. After you have developed the list, classify the reasons according to the four elements of the marketing mix: product, price, place, promotion.
13. Use the Yellow Pages of your telephone directory or another business directory for your town or city. For each of the eight marketing functions, locate a business whose primary work

more convenient location, better customer service offered
Price: I can use credit rather than cash, I get special deals when I purchase the product
Promotion: effective advertising, helpful salespeople, advertisements appear in the magazines I read or the shows I watch, they seem to know my needs
13. Students can identify several types of businesses for each of the marketing functions. Examples of the types of businesses that fit into each category are:

Product/Service Planning: engineering firms, design businesses, architects
Purchasing: buyers, catalog companies, shopping services
Financing: banks, credit card companies
Distribution: trucking companies, airlines, mailbox rental companies
Pricing: property appraisers, pawn shops, auctioneers
Risk Management: insurance companies, private security firms

relates to that function. Identify the work of the business to show how it relates to the marketing function.

14. The price charged for a product is affected by a number of factors. For each of the following situations, identify whether you believe it will result in a higher or lower price. Write one or two sentences to justify each answer.

   a. One customer purchases a very large quantity of a product.

   b. A business builds an image of a high level of customer service.

   c. The product is very fragile and requires special handling.

d. The product moves through many businesses in the channel of distribution before it reaches the customers.

e. An effective advertising campaign results in a very large increase in the sales of the product.

15. Advertising is the most common form of promotion but many of the ways advertisements are delivered to consumers are uncommon and unusual. List as many different examples of advertising methods as you can think of. The common examples are newspapers, magazines, television, and radio.

Internet, clothing, sides of buses, flyers placed on automobile windows, sky writing with airplanes, product placements in movies, and many others.

DEVELOP YOUR BUSINESS LANGUAGE

For each numbered item, find the term that has the same meaning.

16. Groups of marketing activities.

17. Considering the needs of customers when planning, pricing, distributing, and promoting a product or service.

18. A two-step process for successfully planning and marketing products and services.

19. A clearly identified group of consumers with needs that the business wants to satisfy.

20. A combination of marketing elements designed to meet the needs of a target market.

21. The path that a product travels from producer to consumer.

22. Anything offered to the target market to satisfy its needs.

23. The process through which goods are bought by the consumer directly from the producer.

24. The locations where products are sold and the ways they are made available to customers.

25. What customers pay and the method of payment.

26. The process through which goods move through one or more middle firms between the producer and the consumer.

27. The methods used to communicate informa-

tion to customers in order to encourage purchases and to increase their satisfaction.

28. A business firm that sells directly to the consumer.

29. The reasons for making a purchase.

30. A middle firm that assists with distribution activities between businesses.

KEY TERMS
buying motives
channel of distribution
direct channel of distribution
indirect channel of distribution
marketing concept
marketing functions
marketing mix
marketing strategy
place
price
product
promotion
retailer
target market
wholesaler

DECISION-MAKING STRATEGIES

DeeLites is a popular bakery in a small Iowa town. The bakery produces a variety of fresh pastries, cakes, pies, and other specialty desserts that have reduced calories. Loyal customers say that the low-calorie baked goods are better tasting than similar higher-calorie products they can purchase

elsewhere. Customers have encouraged the owner of DeeLites to allow ordering over the Internet so their friends and relatives from other cities and states can purchase the products. The owner would like to increase sales, but is concerned whether the Internet is a good way to expand.

DEVELOP YOUR BUSINESS LANGUAGE

16. marketing functions
17. marketing concept
18. marketing strategy
19. target market
20. marketing mix
21. channel of distribution
22. product
23. direct channel of distribution
24. place
25. price
26. indirect channel of distribution
27. promotion
28. retailer
29. buying motives
30. wholesaler

DECISION-MAKING STRATEGIES

31. The Internet would allow the business to reach people who are unable to travel to the town in which it is located. The business would not have to open a new store in other cities but could sell products from the current location.

32. The products may have to be changed so that they will remain fresh while being shipped to people in other cities and states. The company will have to find a way to ship the products using companies such as FedEX or UPS. The company will have to develop effective Internet advertising, an effective web site, and a way to allow customers to securely pay for their orders. The company may have to increase prices or charge customers for packaging and shipping. The company will need customer service support for prople who have questions or problems.

Marketing Information Management: bookkeeping and accounting businesses, marketing research companies, data processing companies
Promotion: advertising agencies, sales agencies, promotional products companies

14. a. The price will decrease because the business saves money on advertising, storage, and transportation when one customer buys a large quantity of a product.

   b. The price will increase to pay for the higher level of service and to maintain the image of high service for the customer.

   c. The price will increase because it costs more to protect the product and for the special handling.

   d. The price will increase because each business that handles the product will have costs and will want a small profit.

   e. The price will decrease even though the advertising costs money. The much higher level of sales allows the company to decrease the price.

15. Encourage student creativity. Some examples of uncommon forms are advertising on: the

CALCULATE BUSINESS DATA

33. a. 3 manufacturers exchange with 1000 customers—3 × 1000 = 3000 exchanges
   b. 3 manufacturers exchange with 10 retailers (3 × 10 = 30); 10 retailers exchange with 100 customers (10 × 100 = 1000); 30 + 1000 = 1030 exchanges
   c. 3 manufacturers exchange with 1 wholesaler (3 × 1 = 3); 1 wholesaler exchanges with 10 retailers (1 × 10 = 10); 10 retailers exchange with 100 customers (10 × 100 = 1000); 3 + 10 + 1000 = 1013

34.

Product	Prod. cost	Markup %	Markup amount	Selling price	Total Cost	Net Profit
A				$42	$40	
B	$100			$150	$125	
C		40%	$24			$12

35. Student answers will vary and will be based on the advertisements they select. They should answer each question and develop one chart or graph.

TECHNOLOGY APPLICATION

In this activity, students use a computer to solve a business problem using a file that is provided on the data CD that accompanies *Intro to Business*. Instructions for using the data CD are included in a **README** file on the disk. Solutions are provided on the Instructor's Resource CD.

---

31. What would be the advantages of using the Internet to expand sales?
32. What changes in the marketing mix would have to be made to sell products using the Internet?

CALCULATE BUSINESS DATA

33. The use of intermediaries reduces the number of exchanges needed to distribute products from producers. Consider a situation where 3 manufacturers produce products that are purchased by 1000 customers. Use the following information to determine the number of exchanges needed for each customer to purchase one product from each manufacturer.
   a. How many exchanges will be needed if each manufacturer sells one product to each of the 1000 customers?
   b. How many exchanges will be needed if each manufacturer sells its products to 10 retailers and each of the retailers sells all three products to 100 customers?
   c. How many exchanges will be needed if each manufacturer sells its product to one wholesaler, the wholesaler sells the three products to each of the 10 retailers, and each retailer sells all three products to 100 customers?

34. When businesses determine the price they will charge customers for products, three factors are very important. The first is the price they pay for the product, known as cost. The second factor is the percentage they add to their cost, known as the markup. Markup added to the product cost determines the selling price. The selling price must cover their costs and leave an amount for net profit. The net profit is the amount remaining when all of the business' costs are subtracted from the selling price. Calculate the missing amounts in the table for each product.

35. Select 10 advertisements from a magazine or newspaper. Review each carefully and answer the following questions. Then prepare a bar graph or pie chart to illustrate your findings.
   a. How many of the advertisements specifically identify a target market to whom the product is being sold?
   b. How many of the advertisements specifically identify the customer needs that will be satisfied by the product?
   c. How many of the advertisements provide specific information about:
      Product features?
      The location where the product can be purchased?
      The price you will pay for the product?
   d. How many of the advertisements seem to be:
      Informing consumers about the product?
      Persuading consumers to purchase the product?
      Reminding people who have already purchased of the benefits they received?

Product	Prod. Cost	Markup %	Markup Amount	Selling Price	Total Cost	Net Profit
A	$30	40%	$12			$2
B		50%	$50			$25
C	$60			$84	$72	

TECHNOLOGY APPLICATION

Using the *Intro to Business* Data CD and your database program software, select problem CH08. After the problem appears on your screen, complete the following activities. Then, after you have completed each step, display or print a report for each activity. If you do not have a printer available, answer the questions before you leave the computer.

36. Sort the database in descending order by price. Answer the following questions:
   a. Which item of merchandise has the highest price?
   b. Which item of merchandise has the second to lowest price?

37. Select and list the items of merchandise that have a cost greater than $10. How many items are listed?

38. Sort the database in ascending order by stock number. Answer the following questions:
   a. What is the third item of merchandise listed?
   b. What is the last item of merchandise listed?

THE GLOBAL MARKETING ENVIRONMENT

Should a company sell a product in the same way in every foreign market? Or, is it necessary to adapt to various aspects of a country's business environment? For example, a food company may change the flavor of a product to adapt to the cultural tastes of a foreign market. Global marketing decisions are commonly influenced by geographic, economic, cultural, and political factors.

A country's climate, terrain, and other geographic factors influence marketing decisions. Cake mixes sold in the mountains of Peru have slightly different ingredients and instructions than those sold at lower elevations.

Economic factors include a country's infrastructure—transportation, communication, and utility systems. This can influence how a company distributes and advertises a product.

The social and cultural influences on marketing include family, customs, and religious beliefs. A company would not advertise showing a teenager talking back to a grandparent in a country in which the people show great respect for the elderly.

Trade barriers are examples of political and legal factors affecting global marketing. Tariffs and import restrictions can limit how and where a product is sold.

> **Various factors influence decisions in the global marketing environment.**

As international marketing managers look for potential customers in other countries, they need to identify a target market. This refers to the specific customers as defined by geography and demographic characteristics. For example, a target market for certain types of baby food may be defined as large families (five or more people), with children under age two, living in urban areas of countries with developing economies.

CRITICAL THINKING

1. Select a country. Using library materials and a web search, identify geographic, economic, cultural, and political factors that could influence the marketing decisions of an international company.

2. Based on a food item or other product, describe a target market for this item based on geographic and demographic factors. Be sure to clarify what types of countries would be appropriate for marketing this product.

Most students will either work with international clients or compete against businesses that do. Global Navigator introduces students to issues integral to working with international businesses. Key concepts and challenges faced by international businesses are presented, followed by Critical Thinking questions that require students to analyze what they have learned.

This feature introduces the various factors that can influence global marketing decisions. These factors can be of a geographic, economic, cultural, political, or legal nature. International trade concepts are also introduced, such as trade barriers, tariffs, and import restrictions. The marketing concept of target marketing is covered in this feature, and in more detail throughout the chapter. Students can learn more about the ideas presented in this feature by searching the Internet. Use keywords such as "international business," "global marketing," or "international trade." Various U.S. or foreign government web sites may also offer valuable information on this and related topics.

CRITICAL THINKING

1. Students' answers will vary widely, depending on the country selected. If students have trouble identifying factors that would influence an international company's marketing decisions, guide students to resources that show the geographic, economic, cultural, and political statistics of each country.

2. Answers will depend on the food item or other product chosen by each student. The instructor can assist students in narrowing their search for target markets by using library materials or by searching the Internet.

GLOBAL BUSINESS PROJECT

In this phase of the business plan project, students are asked to use a possible idea for international business to plan an organizational structure (sole proprietorship, partnership, or corporation). In addition, the four basic elements of marketing (product, price, promotion, and distribution) are considered for this business idea.

To complete each phase of this project, students are encouraged to use various resources—textbook content, library materials, World Wide Web sites, interviews, advertisements, product packages, in-store observations. The individual activities are planned for use as either (1) an on-going course project, or (2) individual assignments.

Whether used as a continuing project or for selected activities, consider having students work in teams. This small group experience provides a valuable skill for future learning and work situations.

In addition to search engines, these selected web sites can be helpful for this unit:

- International Trade Administration of the U.S. Dept. of Commerce (www.ita.doc.gov)
- World Trade Organization at (www.wto.org)
- International Chamber of Commerce (www.iccwbo.org/)
- Small Business Administration (www.sba.gov)
- Import-export information at (www.internationalist.com/) (www.ubs.com)
- Export assistance (www.unzco.com)

GLOBAL BUSINESS PROJECT

PLAN AN INTERNATIONAL BUSINESS ORGANIZATION

Business organizations are involved in extracting natural resources, manufacturing goods, selling goods, and providing services. While these business types are common from nation to nation, the specific companies will be affected by various factors. How a business organizes (sole proprietorship, partnership, or corporation) will also be influenced by various cultural and legal factors.

A business plan is designed to propose and execute a business idea. This phase of the business plan project involves decisions related to the type of enterprise and its structure. You also need to consider some aspects of marketing, such as pricing, promotion, and distribution channels.

PROJECT GOALS

1. Research types of businesses that would be most successful in a foreign market.
2. Analyze different business structures for the business idea.
3. Outline the marketing activities of a foreign business opportunity.

PROJECT ACTIVITIES

Using your textbook, library materials, web sites, interviews with people, and other resources, complete the following activities:
1. New business ideas can come from natural resources, agricultural products, major industries, and exports of a nation. From the country in your portfolio (or select a country), research and describe one or more businesses in each of these categories: (1) extracting, (2) manufacturing, and (3) service companies.
2. Companies commonly organize as a sole proprietorship, a partnership, or a corporation. Using the business idea that you developed in the previous unit (or another international business idea), analyze the positive and negative aspects of these three types of business structures. Describe in writing or on a visual chart the benefits and drawbacks of the three types of business organizations when doing business in a foreign country.
3. Marketing has four main elements: (1) the product, (2) pricing methods, (3) promotional activities, and (4) distribution channels. Using your business idea for this business plan project (or some other good or service), briefly describe each component of marketing for this item.

PROJECT WRAP-UP

1. Continue or start your portfolio (folder, file box, or other container) for storing and referring back to the information and materials you created in the activities above. Your portfolio provides the information needed for the various elements of a global business plan.
2. Develop a package design or advertisement that shows the main parts of your business idea for a foreign market.

FOCUS ON CAREERS

MANAGEMENT

The people who operate businesses are called managers. A manager's job typically involves a number of planned and unplanned activities. Many of these activities involve solving problems by making decisions. Managers must be able to make decisions that improve operations, handle disagreements among workers, and allocate resources efficiently. Some of these decisions are made after quick analysis of a situation; others involve more study and investigation.

JOB TITLES
- Property and Real Estate Manager
- Hotel/Motel Manager
- Education Administrator
- Purchasing Manager
- Industrial Production Manager
- Construction Manager
- Financial Manager
- Public Relations Manager
- Human Resources Manager
- Food Service Manager
- Medical and Health Services Manager
- Computer and Information Systems Manager
- Sales Worker Supervisor

EMPLOYMENT OUTLOOK
- Managers, administrators, and proprietors make up one of the largest career categories, with more than 15 million employed.
- Career opportunities will increase slowly in some areas as large businesses tend to reduce the size of their work forces and eliminate some management positions.
- Opportunities as proprietors of small businesses will continue to be excellent.
- Faster-than-average growth is expected in health services, information systems, and in the hotel/motel industry.

EDUCATION AND TRAINING
- Managerial positions generally require some education beyond high school plus a good work record in a responsible position.
- Courses in business administration with a degree from a two-year or four-year college are desirable.
- Training in the basic functions of management is desirable before moving into a manager's position. (Some firms offer management training programs.)

SALARY LEVELS
Salary levels vary widely depending upon a manager's education, training, work experience, and the business in which she/he is employed. Average (median) salaries include:
- Computer and Information Systems Managers: $75,000
- Medical and Health Services Managers: $56,000
- Hotel/Motel Managers: $31,000
- Production Managers: $62,000

CRITICAL THINKING
1. Which job titles in this career area appeal to you most? Give reasons for your choice.
2. What are some things you will have to do to achieve success in the career selected?

FOCUS ON CAREERS

The careers listed in the Career Focus come from the *Occupational Outlook Handbook*, an online publication (www.bls.gov/oco) of the federal government. The O*NET codes for these job titles are Property and Real Estate Manager 11-9141.00; Lodging Manager, 11-9081.00; Education Administrator, 11-9031.00, 11-9032.00, 11-9033.00; Purchasing Manager, 11-3061.00; Industrial Production Manager, 11-3051.00; Construction Manager, 11-9021.00; Financial Manager, 11-3031.00, 11-3031.02; Public Relations Manager, 11-2031.00; Human Resources Manager, 11-3040.00; Food Service Manager, 11-9051.00; Medical and Health Services Manager, 11-9111.00; Computer and Information Systems Manager, 11-3021.00; Sales Worker Supervisor, 41-1011.00, 41-1012.00.

Career Focus worksheets are available in the School-To-Work/SCANS Activity Masters.

CRITICAL THINKING
Answers, of course, to the two Critical Thinking questions will vary widely. Students should be encouraged to select one job even if they are not really interested in the career area. Thinking about why a certain job might possibly be appealing is a forced-thinking exercise that results in self-reflection and self-examination. Answering these questions also gives certain career areas a sharper focus within students' minds.

UNIT 3

BUILDING YOUR PORTFOLIO

CAREER DEVELOPMENT – NETWORKING FOR CAREER INFORMATION

The Building Your Portfolio career exercise will help your students establish a personal history—where they have been, where they are now, and where they are going. This Career Development Exercise will give students experience in making contacts with individuals who can help them find and secure employment.

Direct students to call on people who may be able to help them with career preparation. Students should do the following: (1) state their career goals with these contacts; (2) ask them for the names of at least two other people who could be contacted about career information; (3) contact the two recommended people and repeat the process. Students should then prepare a list of contacts for future job leads. Remind students to send a typewritten thank-you note on quality stationery to each person who has helped them.

As a supplemental activity, you may refer to the School-To-Work/SCANS Activity Masters.

TEACHING STRATEGIES

SCANS

Critical Thinking Skills

Workplace Competencies

Personal Qualities

Basic Skills

Cooperative Learning

Alternate Modalities

Teaching Tips

Special Needs

Teams

Special Features

Media/Technology

Chapter	Spreadsheet Software	Database Software	Word Processing Software	Internet	Video
9			■		■
10		■			■
11			■	■	■

Resources

SOFTWARE

Excel, Word, WordPerfect, Works, and ClarisWorks for Mac and Windows

Word Pro, ASCII, QuattroPro, Lotus, and Access for Windows

SOUTH-WESTERN EDUCATIONAL PUBLISHING PRODUCTS

Goree. *Ethics In American Life*. 1996. Cincinnati: South-Western Educational Publishing Company. Text-Workbook. 0-538-63489-8.

Dlabay and Scott. *International Business 2/e*. 2001. Cincinnati: South-Western Educational Publishing Company. Textbook. 0-538-69855-1.

BOOKS

Badaracco. *Defining Moments : When Managers Must Choose Between Right and Right*. 1997. Harvard Business School Press.

Morrison, Conaway, Douress, and Morrison. *Dun & Bradstreet's Guide to Doing Business Around the World*. 1997. Prentice Hall Trade.

PERIODICALS

Black Enterprise. E. G. Graves Publishing Co. New York, NY.

Entrepreneur. Entrepreneur, Inc. Irvine, CA.

Success. Success Magazine Co. New York, NY.

The Wall Street Journal. New York, NY.

GOVERNMENT PUBLICATIONS

Occupational Outlook Handbook, U.S. Department of Labor, Washington, DC.

What Work Requires of Schools: A SCANS Report for America 2000, U.S. Department of Labor, Washington, DC

MEDIA/TECHNOLOGY

Publisher's web sites:
www.intro2business.swep.com
www.swep.com
www.thomson.com

BUSINESS AND GOVERNMENT IN OUR GLOBAL ECONOMY

This unit covers the social responsibility of business, business ethics, international business, and the role of government.

Chapter 9 covers the social and ethical environment of business. Emphasis is given to the values that reflect appropriate and inappropriate business practices in our economy.

International business is the centerpiece of this unit. Chapter 10 covers the terminology associated with international business and the reasons for and benefits of international trade. In addition, this unit's Business Brief and several "perspectives" highlight international topics.

This unit concludes with a brief review of the role of government. Particular emphasis is given to how government protects, assists, and regulates. In Chapter 11, these functions will be studied along with the power of government to raise revenue through taxation and borrowing.

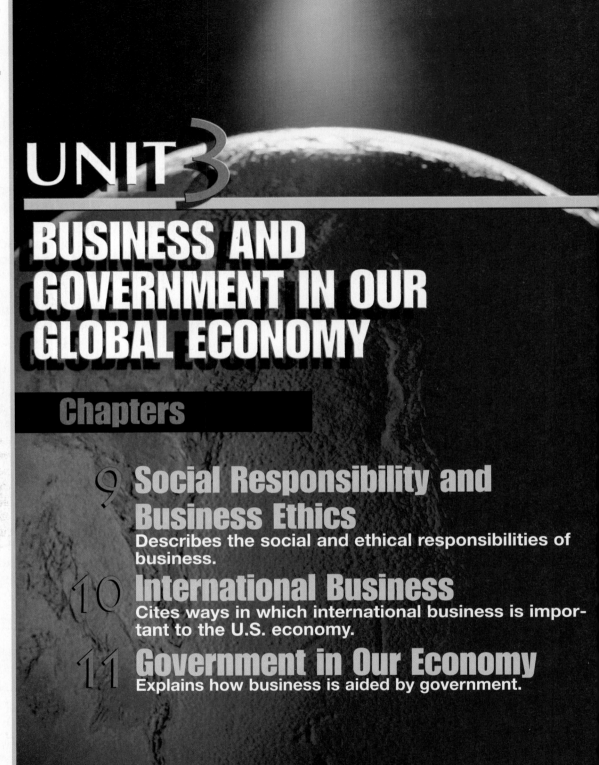

UNIT 3

BUSINESS AND GOVERNMENT IN OUR GLOBAL ECONOMY

Chapters

9 Social Responsibility and Business Ethics
Describes the social and ethical responsibilities of business.

10 International Business
Cites ways in which international business is important to the U.S. economy.

11 Government in Our Economy
Explains how business is aided by government.

Kick-off Activity

Investigating Business Media

To make the connection between today's business news and *Intro to Business*, an opening activity is provided for student research that pertains to Unit 3. The following exercise asks students to choose an article from *The Wall Street Journal*, the financial section of a newspaper, or a business magazine and to inquire about a topic related to this unit.

In recent years, important business issues have included workplace diversity, competition from foreign producers, and tax policies. Ask students to choose one of these issues and find two or three articles pertaining to the chosen issue. Then direct them to answer the following questions:

1 What is the impact (or the expected impact) of this issue on our economy? What groups of people are most likely to be affected?

2 How do you think this issue will affect the industry or job field that you hope to enter in the future?

BU$INESSBRIEF

CULTURAL DIFFERENCES AND BUSINESS OPPORTUNITIES

If you walked down the streets of Taipei, Barcelona, Cairo, and Buenos Aires, you would likely see some "signs of home." Perhaps you would notice a Burger King, the golden arches of McDonald's, or the red-and-white logo of KFC. As you crossed streets in these cities, you might have to watch out for speeding American-made cars. As you passed young people on the sidewalks, you would recognize jackets emblazoned with the emblems of U.S. sports teams and jeans with the labels of U.S. designers.

What is taking place here? Why are consumers in these cities buying American-made products? The answer relates to global dependency. *Global dependency* exists when many items consumers need and want are created in other countries. People frequently need and want products from other countries.

Companies sell to consumers in other countries to expand business opportunities. However, U.S. companies that sell their products in other countries often learn the hard way about doing business abroad. For instance, after establishing operations in an Asian country, a U.S. doughnut company learned that the people of this country did not like cinnamon. But cinnamon was the main ingredient in the company's traditional doughnuts. So, the company reduced greatly the amount of cinnamon in the doughnuts sold there. Gradually the company increased the amount of cinnamon. Today, people in this country like the traditional doughnut.

Another example of learning the hard way involved a toothpaste manufacturer. The manufacturer advertised its toothpaste as leaving a "fresh" taste. However, the people in this country preferred what they considered a clean, medicinal taste.

Why do these differences in consumer preferences exist? The answer lies in the word culture. *Culture* is the sum of a country's way of life, and it influences buying decisions. Culture sets the boundaries of what can and cannot be done.

Some parts of culture are taught in homes, in schools, in religious institutions, and at work. Still other parts are learned through experiences. Not all cultural groups, however, share their experiences willingly with outsiders.

Understanding cultural differences is a challenge for all U.S. businesses. The United States trades freely with Canada and the United Kingdom in part because the business cultures are somewhat similar. These similarities allow business to be conducted in similar ways.

To a large extent the future success of U.S. businesses will depend on their ability to sell products in the international marketplace. Becoming aware of and adjusting to various cultural differences is the first step toward success in the global economy.

CRITICAL THINKING

1 *What are some ways in which you are taught about our culture? How does our culture influence your buying decisions?*

119

BU$INESSBRIEF

A Business Brief sets the tone for a unit. To help students understand current and emerging trends, each unit will be introduced with a Business Brief. The Briefs were chosen for their importance to business, timeliness, and interest to students. The Briefs complement the many real-world examples woven into the text.

CRITICAL THINKING

Student answers will, of course, require thinking beyond what is presented in the Business Brief. Answers will be based on students' perceptions of the topic and experiences they have had with it. The following are possible answers:

1 We are taught about our culture through our schools, our religious institutions, and our families. As we discuss issues with friends, parents, or relatives, read newspapers and magazines, and watch television programs, elements of our culture are presented to us. Answers will vary as to the personal influence of our culture on buying decisions.

2 Goods frequently wanted that can only be supplied by other countries include bananas and coffee. These products are produced in Central and South America. Students will provide many other examples. Our U.S. domestic market has never been able to supply all the goods and services demanded by consumers.

BUILDING YOUR PORTFOLIO

The Building Your Portfolio work samples validate skill level and a student's ability to accomplish tasks frequently performed on the job. The most important reason for including samples in a portfolio is to demonstrate a student's abilities and skills. In selecting work samples for each unit, students should always have a choice of which activities to include. Students might be encouraged to include samples from the end-of-chapter activities, particularly Communicate Business Concepts, Calculate Business Data, Technology Application, and Decision-Making Strategies.

Chapter 9

Most of us would agree that businesses should be ethical and socially responsible. We define social responsibility as management's considerations of the social and economic effects of decision making.

Resources for Teachers
- Lesson Plans
- School-To-Work/SCANS Activity Masters
- Spanish Resources
- Instructor's Resource CD

Assessment
- Chapter and Unit Tests, Ch. 9
- ExamView, Ch. 9

Media/Technology
- Applying Technology Data CD
- PowerPoint slides
- Business Connection CD
- Videotape

Activity Masters and Workbooks
- Activities and Projects, Ch. 9
- Internet Activity Masters
- Business Math Activity Masters
- Communications Activity Masters
- International Business Activity Masters
- Ethics Activity Masters

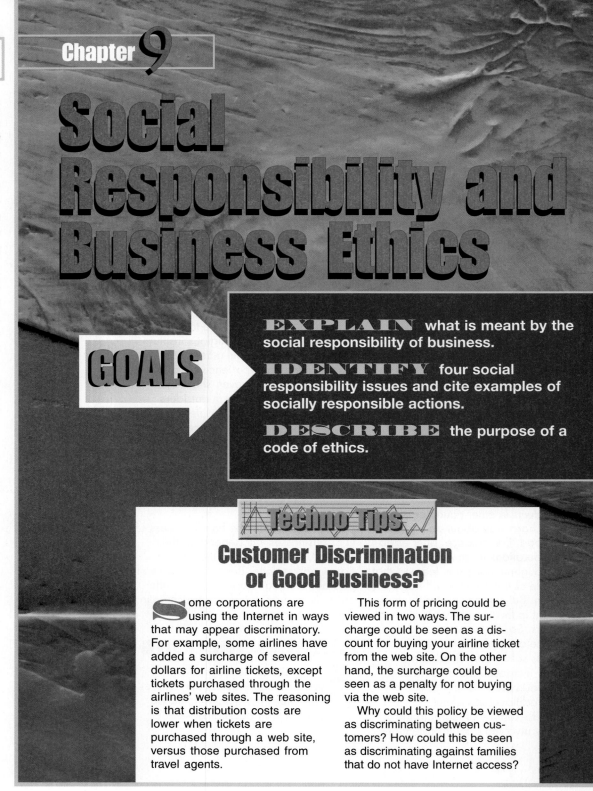

Social Responsibility and Business Ethics

GOALS

EXPLAIN what is meant by the social responsibility of business.

IDENTIFY four social responsibility issues and cite examples of socially responsible actions.

DESCRIBE the purpose of a code of ethics.

Techno Tips

Customer Discrimination or Good Business?

Some corporations are using the Internet in ways that may appear discriminatory. For example, some airlines have added a surcharge of several dollars for airline tickets, except tickets purchased through the airlines' web sites. The reasoning is that distribution costs are lower when tickets are purchased through a web site, versus those purchased from travel agents.

This form of pricing could be viewed in two ways. The surcharge could be seen as a discount for buying your airline ticket from the web site. On the other hand, the surcharge could be seen as a penalty for not buying via the web site.

Why could this policy be viewed as discriminating between customers? How could this be seen as discriminating against families that do not have Internet access?

 Students need to know the latest technologies and develop cutting edge Internet skills for use in current jobs, future careers, or in their homes. TechnoTips introduces students to today's cutting edge technologies and provides them with important Internet skills. Feature topics concentrate on Internet-specific technologies and computer or other hi-tech innovations for use by businesses and consumers.

Jo Ann Homer is the successful owner-manager of J A Kitchen Crafts. This business supplies kitchenware to retail stores. She has great pride in her ability to provide fair employment for her employees. She also considers herself a socially responsible employer.

Jo Ann Homer, for example, is on the board of directors of the local United Way. Her business contributes generously to several community groups, particularly groups in the performing arts. She serves on the job-training committee of the local Economic Development Board, and her company participates in a school-to-work program for underprivileged youngsters.

Jo Ann also encourages her employees to be active in community affairs. Employees get time off with pay to fulfill volunteer commitments during working hours. In addition, she believes in supporting her community to help make it a better place in which to live. Her philosophy is: "Workers are likely to be more satisfied on the job if they believe their company actively contributes to community life."

SOCIAL RESPONSIBILITY ISSUES

Social responsibility refers to the obligation of a business to contribute to the well-being of a community. In considering its responsibility to society, a business must weigh the interests and concerns of many groups. A broadened social responsibility of business requires greater attention to social concerns, such as protection of the environment, minorities and women in the workplace, employment of the physically challenged and older workers, and a healthy and safe work environment.

Environmental Protection

Conservation—preserving our scarce natural resources—is a goal of many companies. For example, lumber companies that consume trees have reforestation programs. Some natural resources, however, cannot be replaced. A **non-renewable resource** is a natural resource that cannot be replaced when used up. Examples are gas, oil, and mined minerals such as copper and iron ore.

When the environment is contaminated with the by-products of human activity, the result is *pollution*. Some production operations cause pollution of our lakes, rivers, and air. A socially responsible business takes action to reduce or completely eliminate operations that cause pollution. Engineers design new equipment and facilities for minimizing the effect of pollution on our environment.

The federal government has set measurable standards for water and air quality. Those standards are monitored and enforced by an organization known as the EPA, or the Environmental Protection Agency. The EPA and businesses work closely together to reduce pollution and to make our environment healthier.

Why do you think businesses would want to sponsor team sports and other community activities?

Ask students to identify as many of the social problems as possible within the United States. To get them started, provide several examples such as poverty and pollution. List the problems identified by students on the board. Point out that these are some of the social problems about which businesses must also be concerned. They impact on business organizations, managers, and workers.

PURPOSE Ask volunteers to read a single goal and another volunteer to say what he or she believes the goal to mean. Challenge other students to find the first heading in the chapter that shows the section in which the goal is first discussed. Allow time for students to look at all headings, figures, and illustrations to get the flavor of chapter contents.

MAKE CONNECTIONS Use the brainstorming technique to identify groups to which businesses must be responsible. Write the names of the groups identified on the board. What are each group's interests, and how can businesses serve them? What should businesses do when the interests conflict?

Discuss the benefits and costs of social actions. Is social responsibility good for business? Show PowerPoint 9-2 to summarize social responsibility issues. Ask students if they can describe ways in which they have been affected by social programs of local businesses.

Show PowerPoint 9-3, *Business Ethics.* Emphasize that a company must establish definite policies to encourage ethical behavior. A "visible, explicit code of ethics" should be pointed out as the primary way in which ethical behavior is communicated. The American Express "Blue Box Value" might also be used here as an example of such a code (see Figure 9-1 in the chapter).

Ask students to give examples of ethical and unethical behavior that they have witnessed in the workplace. Discuss ways management encourages ethical behavior. How important are managers' actions and attitudes in influencing ethical behavior by employees?

TRY THIS/GUIDED PRACTICE

Guide students in identifying the types of business—extractors, manufacturers, marketers, and service firms—that are affected by environmental issues. Then ask what their community is doing to reduce waste, recycle products, and dispose of trash.

Guide students in writing a brief response to the following question: What interests and concerns should a business consider in meeting its responsibility to society?

Walk students through an exercise in which the class develops a code of conduct for all students enrolled in *Intro to Business*. Refer students to the American Express code of conduct in Figure 9-1.

EXPLORE THIS/INDEPENDENT PRACTICE

Assign a work-related social issue, such as race or sex discrimination, the rights of older workers or the handicapped, or alcoholism or drug abuse. Require students to state how the social problem affects business and what business has done to deal with the issue. Findings should be reported to the class.

The Chapter Review questions at the end of the chapter vary in level of difficulty. For a basic assignment, consider Develop Your Business Language and Review Your Reading. For an average assignment, consider the basic assignment plus Communicate Business Concepts and Calculate Business Data. For an enhanced assignment, try the average assignment plus Technology Application and Decision-Making Strategies.

Workplace Diversity

Businesses are increasingly sensitive to the role of women, ethnic groups, the physically challenged, and older workers. The work force of a business should reflect the various groups that comprise the community. Members of these groups must have equal access to education, training, jobs, and career advancement. The major challenge facing businesses today involves learning how to manage a work force made up of the various cultures in our society.

Another issue involves the removal of employment barriers for women. Equal employment opportunity laws eliminated sex-based job descriptions and classified ads. Employers are not allowed to exclude women applicants from a physically demanding job unless the business can prove the job requires physical skills that women do not have.

Employers also have taken steps to accommodate individuals who are physically challenged. The Americans with Disabilities Act (ADA), along with other federal and state

NET FACTS

In certain browsers and other Internet programs, a bookmark or hotlist is a special file used to save addresses and locations. By saving and recalling addresses, it is easy for you to visit your favorite sites over and over.

legislation, has caused significant improvements to be made toward accommodating workers who are physically challenged. Buildings must have access for wheelchairs. People with sight or hearing limitations must be accommodated on the job.

Other laws have been passed to eliminate discrimination against older workers. The passage of the Age Discrimination in Employment Act prohibits employers from using age as a basis for employment decisions (hiring, promotions, or termination from a job). The law protects all persons 40 and older.

Safety on the Job

Having a safe place in which to work is important to all employees. They should be able to work in an office or factory free from the hazards that could cause accidents. The work environment should provide maximum protection from fire and other hazards.

In addition to protection from physical harm, workers need to know how to manage the unexpected. Therefore, safety also involves employee training in how to work safely, and what to do in the event of an emergency.

To ensure the right to safety, most employers have implemented a variety of programs

How has the Americans with Disabilities Act increased employment opportunities for those who are physically challenged?

 Net Facts provides information and definitions of terms for the Internet. The more information that students have about the Internet, the better equipped they will be to use this resource. In the Internet Activity Masters, there is an Internet Activity Worksheet for each unit. You can use these activities to give students experience with finding information online. Options for assigning this activity are as follows:

1. **Provide students with a list of addresses for this activity,**
2. **Assign students to conduct their own searches, or**
3. **Use the addresses on the Internet Activity Worksheet.**

You should complete the activity yourself before assigning it to resolve any discrepancies that may arise.

to protect workers. Our federal and state governments have also enacted legislation to make the workplace safer. Safety standards are regulated and enforced by agencies such as OSHA, the Occupational Safety and Health Administration.

Employee Wellness

A healthy work force is a productive work force. Workers who have good physical health are valuable assets. Businesses today do a number of things to improve the health of their work force. Among programs offered are stop-smoking seminars, counseling for employees with drug problems, and weight-loss sessions.

Your general well-being as an employee needs to be protected, too. Clauses that relate to employee well-being are commonly included in labor contracts and company policy manuals. These clauses are *conditions of work* that pertain to the health and safety of employees while on the job.

ETHICAL PERSPECTIVES
Doing Business in the International Marketplace

International business offers many U.S. companies an opportunity for growth and expansion. But doing business in some countries may require a company to compromise its ethical principles.

Different values and standards cause ethical dilemmas for many U.S. companies. Here are three examples of ethical dilemmas:

1. In a developing European nation, a company must give money to certain government officials to sell its products. A U.S. company would view this behavior as a bribe. Bribes are considered unethical behavior in the United States.
2. To enter a new market in an Asian country, a U.S. company would have to give gifts and lavishly entertain key business and political leaders. Gift giving and lavish entertainment are practices contrary to the written policies of some U.S. companies. Establishing business in this Asian country could represent a 25 percent increase in the company's sales.
3. In a South American country, government officials will not license the operation of a U.S. manufacturer unless the company promises to buy all raw materials from

certain South American manufacturers. The U.S. company considers this practice unfair and perhaps even unethical. The South American market presents tremendous potential for new customers. Company sales might increase by at least 10 percent.

Our society prefers that U.S. companies operate with high ethical and moral standards. Realistically it is very difficult—if not impossible—for businesses to operate in the international marketplace without experiencing some conflict in values. Each country has its own unique social and legal constraints. If a company in the international market observes both the spirit and letter of the laws of the other countries, then the activities of that company are usually considered to be socially responsible.

Critical Thinking

1. Why do you think that some countries engage in practices such as those just described?
2. Would you take the steps necessary to get into these new markets? Why or why not?

ETHICAL PERSPECTIVES
CRITICAL THINKING

1. Answers will vary. The countries do not have the same kinds of laws and customs as we do. Some foreign governments do not restrict or control many business practices we consider unethical.
2. Possible answers include: 1. In the United States, we consider bribes to be unethical, so the U.S. business would probably not offer a bribe. 2. The written policy against gifts and lavish entertainment might be overlooked if the company wishes to comply with a customary practice in an Asian country. 3. The company may want to look elsewhere for new business if buying South American goods and supplies at inflated prices makes business operations unprofitable.

Help students who are having difficulty grasping the concept of social responsibility complete with you an outline of the first three sections of the text.

Provide students with articles from newspapers or magazines that describe unethical business practices. Discuss this business behavior and why it is unethical.

Direct students to read the Ethical Perspectives in this chapter. Have students investigate laws passed by the federal government related to (a) a healthy and safe work environment, (b) equal opportunity, and (c) hazardous wastes.

Have students develop a code of ethics for a company in an industry of their choice. Before students develop the code, discuss possible topics for inclusion in the code of ethics. Codes of ethics generally address such topics as conflicts of interest, confidentiality of corporate information, misappropriation of corporate assets, bribes and kickbacks, and political contributions. Have students find examples online.

SUMMARIZE

Ask students to find one point in the chapter that they least understood. Have them identify the concept on an index card by stating "I least understood...." Read a card and ask a student who is comfortable with the topic to write an explanation on the card. After all cards have been distributed to students who are comfortable with the subject and have written a few

How do employees who are healthy and in good physical condition benefit their employers?

In-company seminars on eating a balanced diet, getting proper exercise, and maintaining a healthy life style are some initiatives taken by companies to promote good health. Some businesses sponsor sports teams and encourage employees to participate.

COSTS OF SOCIAL RESPONSIBILITY

In the long run, socially responsible actions by business may eliminate the need for government controls that regulate what a business can and cannot do. However, there are costs involved when a business takes socially responsible actions. Money must be spent for new non-polluting or safer equipment, for building renovations to remove hazards, for wellness and rehabilitation programs, and for social projects sponsored by a company.

A business must make a profit in order to stay in business. If a business does not earn a profit, the business will close and employees will be laid off. Spending on social programs

must be at an appropriate level so a business can still earn a reasonable profit.

BUSINESS ETHICS

A socially responsible business also engages in ethical business practices. **Ethics** are principles of morality or rules of conduct. **Business ethics** are rules about how businesses and their employees ought to behave. Ethical behavior involves conformity with these rules. Unethical behavior violates them. In dealing with business ethics, a code of ethics can help a business identify appropriate employee behavior.

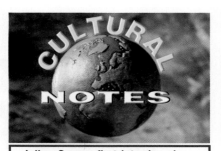

Julius Caesar first introduced "leap year" in 46 B.C. Caesar asked Egyptian astronomer Sosigenes to develop a calendar based on a $365\frac{1}{4}$ day year that was known as the Julian calendar. The Julian calendar allowed one extra day to be added every fourth year, giving us what we call leap year.

The solar year was calculated to be about 11 minutes longer than $365\frac{1}{4}$ days according to sixteenth-century astronomers. In 1582, the Gregorian calendar, which is what we use today, was adopted to correct this error. Therefore, we have a leap year every four years *except* century years that are not divisible by 400.

Workplace Competencies-Systems

In order for students to become contributing workers in our society, they must understand systems—technological, social, and organizational—that are important in the workplace. To operate effectively in an organization, the worker must know the goal of the organization, how to respond to the demands of the organization, and how to function in the organization. Students also need to be aware of the structure of systems and how they change. For example, your school may have policy changes, faculty changes, new facilities, etc., that students must adapt to in order to be successful in their studies. The Student Activity Worksheet, Workplace Competency—Systems, in the School-To-Work/SCANS Activity Masters, may serve as a guideline for discussion.

A **code of ethics** is a statement of rules for guiding the behavior of employees or members of an organization. Codes of ethics address topics such as confidentiality of business information. Figure 9-1 shows a statement of values, called "Blue Box Values," that guide the ethical behavior of employees at the American Express Company, a large U.S. corporation.

A **code** must be worded in terms of acceptable behavior rather than forbidden action. Even with a code of ethics, the choice of appropriate behavior can cause dilemmas for decision makers within a business. Here are some examples of ethical dilemmas:

- Should a company expand into a profitable market in another country where doing business requires giving expensive gifts to key government officials?

- Should a company continue to produce a popular product after it discovers a minor defect in it?

The ethical conduct of a business is greatly determined by its top management. Executives who exhibit strong moral character and make ethical business decisions set the ethical standards for a business. Companies concerned about ethical behavior in their employees have established educational programs on ethical conduct. These programs are designed to

Many professional groups, such as lawyers, doctors, and teachers, publish codes of ethics.

encourage employee honesty and integrity. Program topics range from making personal phone calls during work hours to taking supplies and materials for personal use (stealing). Employees are also instructed on how to make ethical decisions on the job.

FIGURE 9-1 Do you think a code of ethics can increase a business's profits? How?

CODE OF ETHICS

AMERICAN EXPRESS BLUE BOX VALUES

All our activities and decisions must be based on, and guided by, these values.

- **PLACING THE INTERESTS OF CLIENTS AND CUSTOMERS FIRST.**

- **A CONTINUOUS QUEST FOR QUALITY IN EVERYTHING WE DO.**

- **TREATING OUR PEOPLE WITH RESPECT AND DIGNITY.**

- **CONDUCT THAT REFLECTS THE HIGHEST STANDARDS OF INTEGRITY.**

- **TEAMWORK—FROM THE SMALLEST UNIT TO THE ENTERPRISE AS A WHOLE.**

- **BEING GOOD CITIZENS IN THE COMMUNITIES IN WHICH WE LIVE AND WORK.**

To the extent we act according to these values, we believe we will provide outstanding service to our clients and customers, earn a leadership position in our businesses and provide a superior return to our shareholders.

Source: Copyright © 1995 American Express Company

EVALUATE

- Assign Activities and Projects for Chapter 9.
- Administer the printed test or ExamView for Chapter 9.
- Assign School-To-Work/SCANS portfolio activities for Unit 3.

Personal Qualities-Integrity

SCANS

Employers are looking for potential employees with good values. Businesses are very aware of the severe implications of unethical behavior among employers. The Ethical Perspectives feature raises ethical questions but does not involve the teaching of right and wrong. Instead, it allows students to apply their own principles to business situations through the use of critical thinking skills.

Businesses often face the dilemmas described. Ethical issues related to foreign operations are commonly debated in the boardrooms of large corporations. You might have a corporate executive responsible for international operations explain some of the ethical dilemmas his/her company has faced while operating in foreign markets.

REVIEW YOUR READING

1. Jo Ann Homer serves on the board of directors for the United Way and on a training committee for the Economic Development Board. Her company also participates in a school-to-work program.
2. The physical environment, workplace diversity, safety on the job, and employee wellness.
3. When used up, non-renewable resources cannot be replaced. Many businesses use these resources in the production of goods.
4. Issues related to the role of women, ethnic groups, the physically challenged, and older workers.
5. Workers need to know how to avoid the unexpected. Employees need training about how to work safely and what to do in the event of an emergency.
6. Stop-smoking seminars, drug counseling, fitness and weight-loss programs.
7. A business may eliminate the need for government controls that regulate what a business can and cannot do.
8. An ethical business decision is based on a sense of morality and rules of conduct. A socially responsible decision is based on an understanding of what is good for the environment, the needs of a community, and fair treatment of employees.
9. A code of ethics encourages honesty and integrity on the job.

COMMUNICATE BUSINESS CONCEPTS

10. Answers will vary depending on the community. Examples could include taking a group of underprivileged children to a baseball game, setting up a relief center when a local disaster occurs, buying tickets for employees to attend a benefit concert at the civic center.
11. Examples of natural resources used every day can include water, natural gas, gasoline, tin, and copper. All of these resources need to be protected. Strategies to avoid depleting natural resources include avoiding the waste of water, recycling cans and bottles, driving only when necessary, and minimizing the use of electricity and natural gas.

Chapter REVIEW

BUSINESS NOTES

1. Socially responsible businesses care about their communities and help make them better places in which to live.
2. Social responsibility concerns relate to environmental protection, workplace diversity, safety on the job, and employee wellness.
3. Businesses spend money for installing non-polluting and safer equipment, for building renovations to remove hazards, for rehabilitation programs, and for community projects.
4. A code of business ethics is a standard or guide for employee behavior.

REVIEW YOUR READING

1. In what ways was Jo Ann Homer socially responsible?
2. What are four social responsibility issues?
3. Why are businesses concerned about non-renewable resources?
4. What are four diversity in the workplace issues?
5. What are some protections that workers need in addition to protection from physical harm?
6. What are some programs of businesses that deal with the issue of worker health?
7. What is the advantage of a company taking socially responsible actions?
8. How does an ethical business decision differ from a social responsibility decision?
9. Why should a company have a code of ethics?

COMMUNICATE BUSINESS CONCEPTS

10. Name some ways in which businesses in your community are socially responsible. Give examples different from those in this chapter.
11. What are some natural resources that you use every day? Which of those natural resources need to be protected? What can you as an individual do to avoid depleting our non-renewable resources?
12. Safety is often a matter of individuals being careful about where they place things and how they conduct their own business. Name several ways in which you and others can help make a workplace safe.
13. What does the term "discrimination" mean to you? What examples of discrimination in the workplace are you aware of?
14. Why do you think employers are willing to spend money to help employees improve their general health? Be specific about how a company might benefit.

12. Individuals can promote safety by picking up materials lying on the ground, learning where fire extinguishers are located, attending safety training programs, quitting smoking, and following the company's safety rules.
13. Answers will vary greatly. The term "discrimination" could mean an individual is denied a chance for employment or a promotion because of his/her sex, race, or age. The term could also mean not giving some people the same opportunities available to others. Examples of discrimination will vary depending on students' experiences.
14. Healthy employees are generally more productive employees. The cost of health care insurance is also a concern to employers. One estimate attributes 15 to 25 percent of corporate health care costs to the unhealthy life-styles of some employees.

DEVELOP YOUR BUSINESS LANGUAGE

For each numbered item, find the term that has the same meaning.

15. Principles of morality or rules of conduct.
16. The obligation of a business to contribute to the well-being of a community.
17. Rules about how businesses and their employees ought to behave.
18. A natural resource, such as gas, coal, copper, and iron ore, that cannot be replaced once it is used up.
19. A statement of values and rules that guides the behavior of employees or members of an organization.

KEY TERMS

business ethics
code of ethics
ethics
non-renewable resource
social responsibility

DECISION-MAKING STRATEGIES

Mr. Rolfson, a prosperous property developer, thinks a mall should be built on a large piece of land that he owns. Mr. Rolfson is a respected business person in his community, and he has eagerly supported community programs for many years. He has been asked by some prominent community members to donate the land to the community for a city park. He knows that a neighborhood park will help resolve the shortage of recreational areas in his community. Yet income from a mall located on his land could add to his profits each year. The extra income could then be used to support additional social programs within his community.

20. What is the dilemma that Mr. Rolfson faces?
21. What advice would you give Mr. Rolfson? Support your advice with sound reasoning.

CALCULATE BUSINESS DATA

22. Jo Ann Homer's business contributed $3\frac{1}{2}$ acres of company property to the city for a park. Land in that area sells for $8,250 per acre. What is the value of the land that was donated? At first Jo Ann wanted the city to buy the land at one-half the selling price. If the city had done that, how much would it have cost the city?

23. J A Kitchen Craft's current building measures 60 meters by 90 meters. What is the square footage of that building? A new building with a more effective waste disposal system is being considered that measures 75 meters by 105 meters. What is the square footage of that building? (Round off to the nearest whole number when computing square footage.) How many additional square feet are in the new building?

24. The Johnson Manufacturing Co. has an annual operating budget of $750,000. Each year it budgets for the following expenses: pollution control equipment, $37,500; contributions to community projects, $22,500; employee fitness and sports programs, $7,500.

a. What percentage of the annual budget is allocated to each socially responsible action (pollution control, community projects, fitness/sports)? What is the total spent?

b. What will be the amount budgeted for each expense category next year if there is a 15 percent increase? What will be the total spent?

DEVELOP YOUR BUSINESS LANGUAGE

15. ethics
16. social responsibility
17. business ethics
18. non-renewable resource
19. code of ethics

DECISION-MAKING STRATEGIES

20. Mr. Rolfson is a respected businessperson who supports community activities. A mall on his land will increase Mr. Rolfson's profits; however, the neighborhood park is badly needed by his community.
21. Answers will vary. If Mr. Rolfson goes ahead with the development of a mall, some revenue from the mall operations could be donated by him to support community projects or to obtain land elsewhere for a park. If he decides to donate the land, he will get a large tax deduction and help his community fill a need.

CALCULATE BUSINESS DATA

22. $3\frac{1}{2} \times \$8,250 = \$28,875$ (total value); $\$28,875 \times \frac{1}{2} = \$14,437.50$ (cost to buy the land).
23. 60 meters $\times$ 3.3 = 198 feet; 90 meters $\times$ 3.3 = 297 feet; 198 $\times$ 297 = 58,806 square feet; 75 $\times$ 3.3 = 247.5 feet; 105 $\times$ 3.3 = 346.5 feet; 247.5 $\times$ 346.5 = 85,758.75 square feet; 85,758.75 − 58,806 = 26,952.75 additional square feet.
24. (a) $37,500 ÷ 750,000 = 5% for pollution control equipment; $22,500 ÷ 750,000 = 3% for community projects; $7,500 ÷ 750,000 = 1% for fitness and sports programs; $37,500 + 22,500 + 7,500 = $67,500 total spent. (b) $37,500 × 1.15 = $43,125 for pollution control equipment; $22,500 × 1.15 = $25,875 for community projects; $7,500 × 1.15 = $8,625 for fitness and sports programs; $43,125 + 25,875 + 8,625 = $77,625 new total.
25. (a) $17,000 + 9,500 + 19,700 + 38,800 = $85,000 total cost; (b) $85,000 ÷ 950,000 = 8.9% of their operating budget.

25. The National Corporation is housed in a building that was built 25 years ago. This building lacks suitable access for persons who are physically challenged. Modifications must be made to the building to meet current government regulations. The following will be done to comply with the law:

    a. Ramps will be constructed leading up to the front and side doors of the building for $17,000.

    b. Six doorways will be widened on the top floor to accommodate wheelchairs for $9,500.

    c. Equipment will be purchased that can be operated by physically challenged persons for $19,700.

    d. A company van that can be operated by the physically challenged will be purchased for $38,800.

    What is the total cost incurred by the National Corporation? If the company's annual operating budget is $950,000, what percentage of that budget will be spent for these modifications?

TECHNOLOGY APPLICATION

Using the *Intro to Business* Data CD and your word processing program software, select problem CH09. After the problem appears on your screen, complete the following activities. Then, print your completed Ethics Checklists. If you do not have a printer available, save the Ethics Checklists on a data disk to give to your teacher.

26. The paragraphs of the Ethics Checklist are in random order. Using the cut-and-paste or the move feature of your software, rearrange the checklist steps into a logical order.

27. Copy the Ethics Checklist into the space below Ethics Case 1. Below each step in the checklist, enter the results of applying that step to the situation in Case 1.

28. Copy the Ethics Checklist into the space below Ethics Case 2. Below each step in the checklist, enter the results of applying that step to the situation in Case 2.

COMMUNICATING for SUCCESS

COMMUNICATING for SUCCESS

TEAMWORK—LET'S WORK TOGETHER

There is an old saying that says "Find a job you love and you'll never work another day in your life." It means that doing something you really like doesn't seem like drudgery or work. Instead, it will be pleasant, and challenging most of the time.

A very important part of enjoying a job is liking and successfully working with the other people at your workplace. Accomplishing this also implies that you are liked by those same people. Your ability to get along with coworkers who are members of your team depends to a great extent on how well you communicate with them.

Those who study reasons why people either leave or lose their jobs have found that there is one main reason. Usually it is not because a worker does not know how to do the job. Instead, the main reason is that many people have a difficult time getting along with and communicating with their coworkers.

The result of one study shown on the graph may surprise you. One of the most important skills you can learn is how to communicate with other employees. This skill will help you to become a good team member in any kind of job.

Getting along with coworkers on a team is a very high priority in most organizations. Below are some tips to help you get along:

- Accept praise gracefully—Thank your manager for praise.
- Share the credit—Be certain to tell your employer about the efforts of others.
- Flatter people sincerely—Say nice things to people because you want to.
- Don't flaunt special privileges—Accept privileges quietly.
- Let everyone be a winner—No one has to be a loser to make another person a winner.

Many teams fail to work well because one person will not tolerate another. The more tolerant you are, the better team member you will become. Tolerance of others' habits, mannerisms, styles and attitudes will serve you well at work.

Reasons why people leave their jobs

Inability to get along with others
Money
Lack of Skill
Working Conditions
Health Reasons
Retiring
0	10	20	30	40	50	60	70	80	90

People may give more than one reason for leaving a job, but, by far, the reason most often given is the inability to get along with others.

CRITICAL THINKING

1. What does the phrase "Find a job you love and you'll never work another day in your life" really mean?
2. On what does a good work team depend?

Communications skills will help ensure students' success in the business world. Communicating for Success introduces workplace/interpersonal communications issues and proper uses of communications technology. Each feature discusses a key communications topic, and contains two Critical Thinking questions that require students to analyze what they have learned.

Teamwork is critical to business success, but it may be a foreign concept to many students, at least in a non-sports environment. The Communicating for Success feature in this chapter emphasizes the importance of "getting along" for both the individual and for the organization. It also provides many practical tips for getting along, stressing the need for tolerance of others' differences.

CRITICAL THINKING

1. The phrase means that doing something you really like will never seem like work.
2. Good teamwork depends on, among other things, team members communicating well with one another.

Chapter 10 emphasizes how U.S. businesses benefit from world trade. The significance of international trade is discussed along with trade theories. Special emphasis is given to the exchange rate and multinational corporations.

Resources for Teachers
- Lesson Plans
- School-To-Work/SCANS Activity Masters
- Spanish Resources
- Instructor's Resource CD

Assessment
- Chapter and Unit Tests, Ch. 10
- ExamView, Ch. 10

Media/Technology
- Applying Technology Data CD
- PowerPoint slides
- Business Connection CD
- Videotape

Activity Masters and Workbooks
- Activities and Projects, Ch. 10
- Internet Activity Masters
- Business Math Activity Masters
- Communications Activity Masters
- International Business Activity Masters
- Ethics Activity Masters

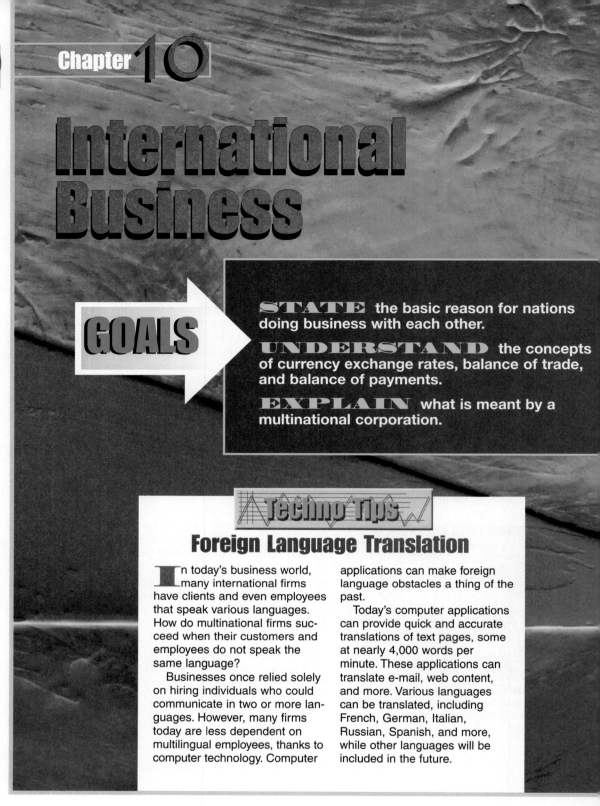

Chapter 10

International Business

GOALS

STATE the basic reason for nations doing business with each other.

UNDERSTAND the concepts of currency exchange rates, balance of trade, and balance of payments.

EXPLAIN what is meant by a multinational corporation.

Techno Tips

Foreign Language Translation

In today's business world, many international firms have clients and even employees that speak various languages. How do multinational firms succeed when their customers and employees do not speak the same language?

Businesses once relied solely on hiring individuals who could communicate in two or more languages. However, many firms today are less dependent on multilingual employees, thanks to computer technology. Computer applications can make foreign language obstacles a thing of the past.

Today's computer applications can provide quick and accurate translations of text pages, some at nearly 4,000 words per minute. These applications can translate e-mail, web content, and more. Various languages can be translated, including French, German, Italian, Russian, Spanish, and more, while other languages will be included in the future.

Students need to know the latest technologies and develop cutting edge Internet skills for use in current jobs, future careers, or in their homes. TechnoTips introduces students to today's cutting edge technologies and provides them with important Internet skills. Feature topics concentrate on Internet-specific technologies and computer or other hi-tech innovations for use by businesses and consumers.

Just as we specialize and trade among our states and communities, other countries also take advantage of special factors of production that they have. They produce goods according to these advantages and trade with other countries to help provide for the wants of their citizens. This trading affects your daily life more than you realize.

What did your family have for breakfast this morning? Coffee, cereal, and sliced bananas, perhaps? If it were not for trading with Brazil for coffee and with Honduras for the bananas, you might have had only cereal.

The sugar on your table may have come from the Philippines. Even your morning newspaper was printed on paper that may have come from Canada.

As you look around your house or apartment, you will find many products made in other countries. For instance, you may find a TV made in Japan or Korea; a stereo made in Taiwan or China; clothing made in Norway, Scotland, or Italy; kitchen appliances made in Hong Kong or Malaysia; and coffee from Brazil or Colombia. Also look around your classroom. Can you identify products made in other countries?

TRADING AMONG NATIONS

The majority of business activities still occur within a country's own borders. The making, buying, and selling of goods and services within a country is called *domestic business*. Your purchase of cereal produced in the United States is an example of domestic business. However, the United States today is part of a larger international business community.

International business includes all of the business activities necessary for creating, shipping, and selling goods and services across national borders. International business is frequently referred to as *foreign* or *world trade*. Evidence of foreign trade is everywhere.

While our country has many natural resources, a skilled labor force, and modern machines and methods of production, we cannot provide ourselves with all of the things we want. We go beyond our borders to get many things. We conduct trade with over 180 countries each year.

Most nations of the world have special advantages. Brazil, for example, has an advantage over the United States in producing coffee. Saudi Arabia has an advantage over

most other countries in crude oil. Australia has an advantage in wool. Korea and Taiwan have an advantage in the number of skilled laborers who can assemble electronic products. Compared with these and many other countries, the United States has advantages in the production of airplanes, tractors, computers, office equipment, and many varieties of food and other agricultural products. Because of trade and modern means of transportation, nations everywhere can specialize in the kinds of production they can do best.

Importing

The things we buy from other countries are called **imports**. Did you know that imports account for our total supply of bananas, coffee, cocoa, spices, tea, silk, and crude rubber? About half of the crude oil and fish we buy comes from other countries. Imports also account for 20 to 50 percent of our supply of

Exports of goods and services to foreign buyers account for one out of every $8 of U.S. GDP.

FYI

Chapter 10 *International Business* **131**

MOTIVATE

PURPOSE Have students preview the list of Key Terms in Chapter Review. Ask students in turn to describe what they believe is the meaning of each term. After this initial attempt, have them turn to the glossary and read the definitions to determine if their answers were correct. Then have them copy the major headings from the chapter onto a sheet of paper, allowing approximately one-half page between each heading. Ask them to compare the major headings to the chapter goals. Tell the students to use the headings as topics for recording notes as they read the chapter and discuss it in class.

TEACH/APPLY

MAKE CONNECTIONS Show PowerPoint 10-6, *Barriers to International Trade*. Ask students to provide the definitions for quotas, tariffs, and embargoes imposed against other nations.

Have students comment on this statement: "The foreign exchange market is indeed a market; only in this instance, the items bought and sold are various types of currencies."

List on the board the various ways in which government can encourage or discourage imports and exports. Then discuss the advantages and disadvantages of each. Have students name advantages and disadvantages of international trade. To emphasize the advantages derived from international trade, ask them to imagine how life would be without international business. Have students

FOCUS ON REAL LIFE

Ask students to list products they buy that are made in foreign countries. Write the names of these products on the board, and let students also venture the name of the country in which the product is made. Summarize the products and countries. Point out that international trade is an extremely important aspect of business.

name some products that people in the United States would live without if trade did not exist.

TRY THIS/GUIDED PRACTICE
Walk students through a discussion of free trade versus restricted trade. Write on the board two headings: For Restricted Trade (or Trade Barriers) and For Free Trade. Ask students to take a position either for or against restricted imports. List on the board points provided by students. The class can openly debate the topic and decide by vote which position the class favors.

Direct students to answer the following questions: Should an MNC (multinational corporation) always abide by the laws and ethical standards of the host country? What if the standards of the home country were stricter? For example, if bribes are acceptable in the host country but not in the home country, should an MNC use bribes or not? Lead students in a discussion of the legal and ethical implications of doing international business.

EXPLORE THIS/INDEPENDENT PRACTICE Have students check newspapers and news magazines for articles on foreign trade—particularly on U.S. companies and their overseas trade and manufacturing. Ask them to prepare one-page reports (using the computer if possible) on how many companies have expanded their operations worldwide, including locating plants in other countries.

How does the United States benefit from being able to produce such a large variety of products?

carpets, sugar, leather gloves, dishes, and sewing machines. In order to manufacture certain goods, we must import tin, chrome, manganese, nickel, copper, zinc, and several

Why do you think U.S. businesses would be interested in exporting?

other metals. Figure 10-1 shows how dependent the United States is on imported raw materials.

Without foreign trade, many of the things we buy would cost more or not be available to our consumers. Other countries can produce some goods at a lower cost because they have the needed raw materials or have lower labor costs. Some consumers purchase foreign goods, even at higher prices, if they perceive the quality to be better than domestic goods. Or, they may simply enjoy owning products made in other countries. French perfumes, Norwegian sweaters, and Swiss watches are examples.

Exporting
The goods and services we sell to other countries are called **exports**. Just as our imports benefit you, our exports benefit consumers in other countries. Workers in countries throughout the world use factory and farm machinery made in the United States. They eat food made from many of our agricultural products and use our chemicals, fertilizers, medicines, and plastics. People in

132   **Unit 3** *Business and Government in Our Global Economy*

IMPORTED RAW MATERIALS USED IN PRODUCTION IN THE U.S.

Silver 64%

Nickel 68%

Tin 72%

Chromium 73%

Cobalt 95%

Bauxite Aluminum Ore 97%

Mica 100%

Manganese 100%

Industrial Diamonds 100%

Import   U.S. Production

FIGURE 10-1 What effect would it have on U.S. production if access to these imports was cut off?

other countries like to view our movies; watch CNN and ESPN; and read many of our books, magazines, and newspapers. Producing the goods and services we export employs many of our workers. One of every six jobs in the United States depends on international business. Figure 10-2 shows our trade of goods with various nations.

INTERNATIONAL CURRENCY

One of the challenges facing businesses involved in trading with other countries is the variety of currency in the world. Each nation has its own banking system and its own kind of money. For instance, Russia uses the ruble; the European Union, the euro; Brazil, the real; India, the rupee; and Saudi Arabia, the riyal.

The process of exchanging one currency for another occurs in the foreign exchange market. The *foreign exchange market* consists of banks that buy and sell different currencies. Most large banks are part of the foreign exchange market and may provide currency services for businesses and consumers.

The value of a currency in one country compared with the value of a currency in another is called the **exchange rate**. The value of currency, like most things, is affected by supply and demand. The approximate values of various currencies on a recent date in relation to the U.S. dollar (USD) are given in Figure 10-3.

When a U.S. company sells products to a Canadian firm, for example, the U.S. firm must convert the Canadian dollars received in payment into U.S. dollars. On a given day in

Have students use the resource materials available to them in the school or local library to prepare a report that traces the U.S. balance of payments from World War II to the present. They should explain how the balance of payments situation became more serious from the 1970s on.

The Chapter Review questions at the end of the chapter vary in level of difficulty. For a basic assignment, consider Develop Your Business Language and Review Your Reading. For an average assignment, consider the basic assignment plus Communicate Business Concepts and Calculate Business Data. For an enhanced assignment, try the average assignment plus Technology Application and Decision-Making Strategies.

ASSESS

Review the goals at the beginning of the chapter and the Business Notes at the end of the chapter. Have students respond orally or in writing to each of the Business Notes restated as a question, provided on p. 134. For students who may have difficulty providing answers, assign the reteaching activities that follow. Enrichment activities may also be assigned where appropriate.

Basic Skills-Speaking

Employers are looking for potential employees with good basic foundation skills. Speaking does not always mean a presentation before a large group; it may simply be teaching or explaining procedures to a team member. Regardless of the situation, most of the basics still apply—students should know their audience, plan their presentation, rehearse (if possible), then make the presentation. Select two students from the class, one to be the presenter and one to be the learner. Have the presenter explain to the learner the advantages and disadvantages of international trade based on research and on what was presented in this chapter. The Student Activity Worksheet, Basic Skills—Speaking, in the School-To-Work/SCANS Activity Masters, may serve as a guideline to help the presenter organize thoughts.

SCANS

1. Why do nations engage in international trade? (Answer: To provide all the things needed and wanted by their citizens. Importing and exporting are the outcomes of trade among nations.)
2. What are currency exchange rates? (Answer: Exchange rates reflect the value of a currency in one country compared with the value of a currency in another country.)
3. What are three barriers to international trade? (Answer: Quotas, tariffs, and embargoes.)
4. What is the difference between balance of trade and balance of payments? (Answer: A balance of trade is the difference between a country's exports and imports. Balance of payments measures the total flow of money coming into a country minus the total flow going out.)
5. Describe a multinational company. (Answer: A multinational company or corporation (MNC) is an organization that conducts business in several countries.)
6. Name some advantages and disadvantages of international business. (Answer: More goods available, lower prices, and increased number of jobs; disadvantages include some loss of jobs and lowered demand for some U.S. products.)

U.S. TRADE, 2001

Goods Exported (In Billions) 984.7	All Countries	Goods Imported (In Billions) 1,282.9	U.S. Balance −238.2
164	Canada	217	− 53
101	Mexico	131	− 30
58	Japan	126	− 68
19	Netherlands	9	+ 10
10	Australia	6	+ 4
15	Brazil	14	+ 1
18	Taiwan	33	− 15
19	China	102	− 83
159	European Union	220	− 61

FIGURE 10-2 Which country has the largest trade imbalance with the U.S.?

a recent year, each Canadian dollar was worth 65 cents in the United States. What would the U.S. firm charge if goods worth approximately $10,000 in the United States were sold to a Canadian firm? The U.S. firm would have to charge about $15,000 in Canadian dollars (10,000 ÷ 0.65 = 15,385). That makes a U.S. dollar worth more than $1.50 in Canadian currency.

Travelers and business people must deal with currency exchanges as they go from one country to another. Exchanging currency is not as difficult as it may seem, however. Travelers in another country can simply go to a currency exchange window at the airport, train station, or local bank and buy whatever amount of local currency they want. How much of the local currency they will get depends on the value of the two currencies at that time. Rates are posted at exchange

One of every six U.S. manufacturing jobs produces something for export.

134 **Unit 3** *Business and Government in Our Global Economy*

TEACHING STRATEGIES
Cooperative Learning

For this cooperative learning activity, students form their own groups with two members each. A spokesperson should be selected by the members. The groups should list as many imported products as they can think of and the countries the products are from. Allow 15 minutes for this activity. Ask for a class recorder to go to the board and write one item from each group's list as the spokespersons take turns giving one item each round. Initiate discussion about each product and its country to make students aware of how many products are imported. As an additional activity, have students prepare a display of advertisements and/or labels of foreign-made goods.

Country	Currency	Units per USD*		Value in USD*
Britain	pound	0.68	pounds	1.46
Brazil	real	2.63	reals	0.38
Canada	dollar	1.54	Canadian dollars	0.65
European Union	euro	1.059	euro	0.94
Japan	yen	124.43	yen	0.008
Saudi Arabia	riyal	3.75	riyals	0.27
South Africa	rand	9.939	rands	0.1
South Korea	won	1219.57	won	0.0008
Venezuela	bolivar	1151.61	bolivars	0.00087

*United States Dollar

FIGURE 10-3 Which currency is worth the most in terms of U.S. dollars?

windows, and there is a charge made for exchanging currency.

BARRIERS TO INTERNATIONAL TRADE

Our government establishes international policies that guide our activities, including trade, with other countries. Several devices may be used to control the importing and exporting of goods and services. Among these controls are three barriers: quotas, tariffs, and embargoes.

Quotas

One of the devices used by governments to regulate international trade sets a limit on the quantity of a product that may be imported or exported within a given period of time. This limit is referred to as a **quota**.

Quotas may be set for many reasons. Countries that export oil may put quotas on crude oil so that the supply will remain low and prices will stay at a certain level. Quotas

The Internet reaches schools in more than 160 countries around the world. Through e-mail and other connections, you learn about students in other countries and foreign students can learn about you.

may also be imposed by one country on imports from another to express disapproval of the policies or social behavior of that country.

Quotas can also be set by one country to protect one of its industries from too much competition from abroad. This action often is done by a nation to shield its "infant industries," which need protection to get started.

NET FACTS

Net Facts provides information and definitions of terms for the Internet. The more information that students have about the Internet, the better equipped they will be to use this resource. In the Internet Activity Masters, there is an Internet Activity Worksheet for each unit. You can use these activities to give students experience with finding information online. Options for assigning this activity are as follows:
1. **Provide students with a list of addresses for this activity,**
2. **Assign students to conduct their own searches, or**
3. **Use the addresses on the Internet Activity Worksheet.**
   You should complete the activity yourself before assigning it to resolve any discrepancies that may arise.

RETEACH

On an overhead transparency, or on the board, draw a three-column chart and write across the top of it the barriers to trade: QUOTAS, TARIFFS, EMBARGOES. With student input, complete the chart with descriptions of each.

Next write the term INTERNATIONAL TRADE. Once again, with student input, list the advantages and disadvantages of international trade.

Workplace Competencies-Information

Effective communicators are able to acquire, evaluate, and convey information in an appropriate manner for various situations. One step a good communicator will initiate is to determine what information needs to be communicated, the media to be used (handouts, fliers), and the appropriate format (charts, graphs). Then the information needs to be compiled and the handout created. A method for conveying the information also needs to be identified (mail, personal presentation, etc.) The Student Activity Worksheet, Workplace Competencies—Information, in the School-To-Work/SCANS Activity Masters, may serve as a guideline for discussion. Students can get hands-on experience conveying information by creating a flyer describing the types of goods that the United States commonly trades with foreign nations.

Our government in the past has imposed quotas on sugar, cattle, dairy products, and textiles.

Tariffs

Another device that governments use to regulate international trade is the tariff. A **tariff** is a tax that a government places on certain imported products. Suppose you want to buy an English bicycle. The producer charges $140, but our government collects a 20 percent tariff ($28) on the bicycle when it is imported. This means that you will have to pay $168 plus shipping charges for the bike. The increased price may cause you to decide to buy a U.S. manufactured bike at a lower price.

Some tariffs are a set amount per pound, gallon, or other unit; others are figured on the value of the good as in the example of the bicycle. By increasing the price for an imported product, a high tariff tends to lower the demand for the product and reduce the quantity of that import. On many occasions, it has been argued that tariffs should be used to protect U.S. jobs from foreign competition.

Embargoes

If a government wishes to do so, it can stop the export or import of a product completely. This action is called an **embargo**. Governments may impose an embargo for many reasons. They may wish to protect their own industries from international competition to a greater degree than either the quota or the tariff will accomplish. The government may wish to prevent sensitive products, particularly those important to the nation's defense, from falling into the hands of unfriendly groups or nations. As with the quota, a government sometimes imposes an embargo to express its disapproval of the actions or policies of another country.

MEASURING TRADE BETWEEN NATIONS

A major reason people work is to earn money to buy the things they need and want. That is, they sell their labor for wages and then spend the major part of those wages for goods and services. People usually try to keep their income and spending in balance, knowing that if they spend more than they earn, they can experience financial problems. Nations are also concerned about balancing income with expenditures. When people buy more than their income allows, they go into debt. In the same way, when a country has an unfavorable balance of trade it owes money to others. *Foreign debt* is the amount a country owes to other countries.

Balance of Trade

Countries like to have a favorable balance of trade. That happens when they export more than they import.

The difference between a country's total exports and total imports is called the **balance of trade**. If a country exports (sells) more than it imports (buys), it has a *trade surplus* and its trade position is said to be favorable. But, if it imports more than it

LEGAL PERSPECTIVES
Eliminating Trade Barriers

Since World War II, there has been a trend toward multinational integration. Multinational economic integration is the removal of barriers to the movement of goods, capital, and people. The simplest approach to integration is to establish a *free trade zone* in which participating nations trade freely among themselves without tariffs or other trade restrictions.

The North American free trade agreement (NAFTA) is just one of more than 14 multinational *trade agreements* in the world. The combination of the United States, Canada, and Mexico united over 370 million consumers into a $6.5 trillion market. The agreement eliminates over a period of time tariffs and other trade barriers between Canada, Mexico, and the United States.

Opponents of NAFTA worry that the United States will lose too many jobs to Mexico's lower-paid workers. Environmentalists point to the pollution generated by Mexican plants which do not usually meet the same ecological standards required of U.S. companies. Proponents of the free trade pact argue that the United States has everything to gain from a more prosperous southern neighbor. With fewer trade restrictions, U.S. and Canadian companies will increase Mexico's economic growth. As Mexico becomes more prosperous, its standard of living will rise. This, in turn, will spur greater demand for U.S. and Canadian exports to Mexico.

Critical Thinking
1. In what ways do you feel you will benefit from NAFTA?
2. Can you name other multinational agreements affecting trade within a region of the world?

---

exports, it has a *trade deficit* and its trade position is unfavorable. Some countries continually buy more foreign goods than they sell.

A country can have a trade surplus with one country and a trade deficit with another. Overall, a country tries to keep its international trade in balance. Figure 10-4 shows the two possible international trade positions. After a long history of a favorable balance of trade, the United States has had a trade deficit every year for more than a decade. The trade deficit has been increasing. In a recent year, the U.S. trade deficit was over $175 billion.

Balance of Payments
In addition to exporting and importing of goods and services, other forms of exchange occur between nations that affect the economy. Money goes from one country to

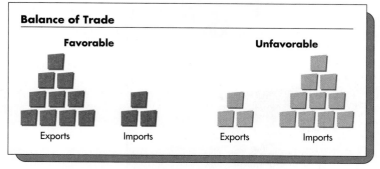

Balance of Trade

Favorable — Exports / Imports

Unfavorable — Exports / Imports

FIGURE 10-4 Why is it better to export more than we import?

LEGAL PERSPECTIVES

A wide variety of obstacles face countries desiring multinational agreements, including physical and cultural barriers, tariffs and trade restrictions, political and legal impediments.

CRITICAL THINKING
1. Answers will vary. Those who support it feel the agreement will bring more jobs and economic growth for Americans, Canadians, and Mexicans. Opponents of the agreement worry that the United States will lose many jobs to Mexican workers.
2. The best-known example is the European Union (EU). To achieve its goal of a "borderless Europe," the EU is erasing most barriers to free trade among its members.

another through investments and tourism. For example, a citizen of one country might invest in a corporation in another country. A business may invest in a factory or office complex in another country. Also, one government might give financial or military aid to another nation. Furthermore, banks may deposit funds in foreign banks.

When tourists travel, they contribute to the flow of money from their country to the country they are visiting. Some countries limit the amount of money their citizens can take out of the country when they travel.

The difference between the amount of money that comes into a country and the amount that goes out of it is called the **balance of payments**. A country's balance of payments can either be positive or negative. A *positive* or *favorable* balance of payments occurs when a nation receives more money in a year than it pays out. A *negative* balance of payments is *unfavorable*. It is the result of a country sending more money out than it brings in.

GLOBAL BUSINESS ORGANIZATIONS

Today, as a result of widespread international business activities, thousands of multinational corporations exist. A **multinational company** or **corporation (MNC)** is an organization that conducts business in several

countries and has management capable of doing business worldwide. MNCs usually consist of a parent company in a *home country* and divisions or separate companies in one or more host countries. The country in which the MNC locates is called the *host country*.

An MNC can become a major economic power in a host country. The workers of the host country may depend on the MNC for jobs. Consumers become dependent upon it for goods and services. The MNC may actually influence or control the political power of the country.

Multinational corporations can use either a global or multinational strategy. A *global strategy* uses a standardized product and marketing strategy worldwide. The same product is sold in essentially the same manner throughout the world. One example with which you are probably familiar is Coca-Cola. Under a *multinational strategy*, each national market is treated differently. Firms develop products and marketing strategies that appeal to the customs, tastes, and buying habits of particular national

What are some advantages of being a multinational corporation?

Basic Skills-Math

SCANS

In order for students to become contributing workers in our society, it is important that they become proficient in the basic skills of reading, writing, arithmetic, and mathematics. Employers are looking for potential employees with good basic foundation skills. In order to prepare students for the school-to-work transition, we must teach these skills in our classroom.

Applying math across the curriculum is an important element in contemporary education. As a part of end-of-chapter activities, Calculate Business Data enables students to apply their math skills. Appendix B: Math Review, Appendix C: Determining Percentages and Interest in Business, and Appendix D: Using Measurement Systems in Business, also apply arithmetic and math skills.

markets. Many restaurant chains employ a multinational strategy when they tailor their menus to local tastes.

ADVANTAGES AND DISADVANTAGES OF INTERNATIONAL BUSINESS

Many benefits are associated with international business. We have an abundance of goods available, often at lower prices than if we produced the goods domestically. With international business, consumer choices increase.

For workers, career opportunities expand because of international business. International business creates jobs. Many businesses, large and small, increase sales and profits with foreign trade.

Many people view international business as a way to promote mutual understanding, communication, and respect among people of different nations. An old saying tells us that "countries that trade with one another do not have wars with one another." Nations that are business partners usually try to maintain friendly relations for economic reasons.

International business also creates some problems. The competition from foreign producers can also lower the demand for our own products. Workers in some industries have lost jobs as the result of this competition. In recent years, our textile, automobile, and electronics industries have felt the negative impact of international competition. International competition, on the other hand, has caused some industries to be more productive and to improve product quality. U.S. industries have shown that they can compete in the international marketplace.

E-Commerce for Global Trade

"**I**n how many countries does your company do business?" While this is not a new question asked of global managers, the response today is slightly different than it was in the past. Instead of hearing a number of countries or a region of the world, today you are more likely to hear: "In *every* country that has Internet access!"

While e-commerce within the United States continues to grow, online exporting activities have even more potential. Federal and state governments help promote international trade by providing information and web sites for locating foreign customers.

In the past, many companies did not face international competition. Now these organizations must be concerned that customers with Internet access can easily locate and purchase products from around the world.

For example, at one time, publishers in Germany, France, and several other European nations could legally dictate retail book prices—both in stores and online. Today, however, online shoppers seek out more competitive prices elsewhere. A German consumer might buy a book online, but, instead of using Amazon.com's German web site, he may find a better deal through Amazon.com's United Kingdom site.

Critical Thinking
Research the availability of Internet service among the people in other countries. Analyze differences in design, content, and format for web sites based in foreign nations. Explain how culture and economic development might influence e-commerce activities in those countries.

Global Business Web Sites:
U.S. Government export assistance:
www.export.gov
More than 3,000 international business web links:
www.fita.org
Foreign trade data:
www.census.gov/foreign-trade
International business virtual library:
www.etown.edu/vl/intlbus.html

Critical Thinking Skills-Decision Making

Decision-making skills, which include specifying goals, generating alternatives, considering risks, and evaluating and choosing the best alternative, are applied throughout every chapter in this text. Each time a student participates in a Cooperative Learning or Teams activity, decision-making skills are applied in a group situation. For Communicate Business Concepts and Decision-Making Strategies, students must specify the goal of the activity, consider risks, and evaluate the best solution before the questions can be answered. Emphasize to students how they are using decision-making techniques in their day-to-day tasks and make them aware of the skills they are developing.

REVIEW YOUR READING

1. Televisions, stereos, clothing, and automobiles would be among products made in other countries.
2. Answers will vary. Food: bananas, coffee, cocoa; raw materials: tin, mica, industrial diamonds; manufactured goods: items made from tin, chrome, manganese.
3. Ninety-seven percent of our supply of aluminum ore (bauxite) is imported; sixty-four percent of silver; one hundred percent of industrial diamonds. See Figure 10-1.
4. You might prefer to buy imported goods even at a higher price because you believe that product to be of a higher quality than similar products made in the United States.
5. They use factory and farm machinery imported from the United States. They eat food made from many of our agricultural products and use chemicals, medicines, and fertilizers that are imported.
6. Exchange rates indicate the value of a nation's currency in relation to the currencies of other countries. A currency's exchange rate usually tells what a currency is worth in terms of other important currencies.
7. Tariffs are levied to protect defense industries, to protect new industries, and to protect domestic workers.
8. An import quota limits trade by allowing only a certain quantity of a product to be imported within a given period of time.
9. Balance of trade refers to the difference between a country's total exports and imports of goods. Balance of payments refers to the difference between the amount of money that flows into and out of a country from investments, tourism, and nontrade items.
10. MNCs use global and multinational strategies. A global strategy involves selling a product in the same manner throughout the world. Each market is treated differently when a multinational strategy is used.
11. Major advantages: enables a country to supply more of its citizens' wants and needs; creates jobs; tends to provide better products at lower prices; and helps to promote international understand-

BUSINESS NOTES

1. Nations do business with each other to increase the variety of goods and services available to their consumers.
2. An exchange rate is the amount of currency of one country that can be traded for one unit of the currency of another country.
3. Three barriers to international trade are quotas, tariffs, and embargoes.
4. Balance of trade is the difference between a country's exports and imports. The difference between a country's total payments to other countries and its total receipts from other countries is the balance of payments.
5. Multinational companies conduct business activities in several countries and have management capable of doing business worldwide.
6. Advantages of international business include more goods available, lower prices, and an increased number of jobs; disadvantages include some loss of jobs and lowered demand for some U.S. products.

REVIEW YOUR READING

1. Name several products that are typically found in U.S. households that are made in other countries.
2. Name a food, a raw material, and a manufactured good that we might not have without international trade.
3. What percentage of the following resources is imported: aluminum ore? silver? industrial diamonds?
4. State one reason why you might prefer to buy imported goods even at a higher price.
5. How might workers in other countries be affected by imports from the United States?
6. Why do we have exchange rates?
7. State three reasons for countries placing tariffs on imports.
8. How does a quota limit international trade?
9. What is the difference between balance of trade and balance of payments?
10. What strategies do multinational companies use to market products?
11. State two advantages and two disadvantages of international business.

COMMUNICATE BUSINESS CONCEPTS

12. It is said that no community or nation today can be completely independent. Do you agree or disagree? Explain.
13. How does international business contribute to a better standard of living for many people in various countries?
14. An American manufacturer of electric toasters wants to sell its products to the people of China. Can you think of some difficulties that this business might have in entering the Chinese market?

ing. Major disadvantages: competition from imports can lower demand for domestic goods; reduced demand can cause people working in certain industries to lose jobs; countries can become too dependent on trading partners for certain goods and services.

COMMUNICATE BUSINESS CONCEPTS

12. Students should agree. No community in the United States today produces all the things it needs. Nations also must trade with other nations to provide a variety of goods and services. All nations have limited resources. Trade is one solution to the problem of limited resources.
13. If international business did not exist among various countries, people would have to do without most of the things they use today. Diets and food selection would be altered drastically if imports were not available. Similarly, there

15. What is meant by "infant industries"? Give two examples of infant industries either in the United States or in other countries. Do you think that such industries should be protected by high tariffs? If so, how long should they be protected?

16. Some people believe that the United States should place stiff controls on imports of goods that compete with our businesses to prevent the "exporting of American jobs" to other countries. Give arguments for and against such a position.

DEVELOP YOUR BUSINESS LANGUAGE

For each numbered item, find the term that has the same meaning.

17. Goods and services sold to another country.

18. A limit on the quantity of a product that may be imported and exported within a given period of time.

19. An organization that conducts business in several countries.

20. The value of money of one country expressed in terms of the money of another country.

21. Goods and services bought from another country.

22. Stopping the importing or exporting of a certain product or service.

23. The difference between a country's total exports and total imports of goods.

24. A tax that a government places on certain imported products.

25. The difference between a country's total payments to other countries and its total receipts from other countries.

26. The business activities necessary for creating,

shipping, and selling goods and services across national borders.

KEY TERMS

balance of payments
balance of trade
exchange rate
embargo
exports
imports
international business
multinational company or corporation (MNC)
quota
tariff

DECISION-MAKING STRATEGIES

Assume you have started a business that manufactures ceramic products. These products are *new and exclusive* on the U.S. market. Your market research shows that consumers want them and will buy them for their homes. You already have invested in a small building, equipment, supplies, and materials. You have hired three people to work with you.

You soon discover that a trading partner of the United States has similar products to export. This country's labor costs are extremely low, and workers in this country receive few benefits. Your

business, without foreign competition, could grow to employ hundreds of workers. You consider this foreign producer of ceramic products *unfair competition*.

27. What can our government do to help you get started and have a chance for success in your business?

28. What might the other country do if the U.S. government does not allow it to trade ceramic products freely?

would be a great reduction in the selection and quality of almost all kinds of products we use. Without international trade, our standard of living would be adversely affected because it would be impossible to obtain or to make most of the things we use and enjoy today.

14. Some difficulties that an American manufacturer of toasters might have in selling the product to people in China would include (1) language barriers—very few Americans can communicate in Chinese; (2) trade barriers—special permission from the government would have to

be obtained before trading could take place; (3) competition—manufacturers in other countries also make toasters; (4) manufacturing problems—to work properly, American-made toasters would need modification to meet the wiring and electrical power standards of China; (5) distribution—appropriate channels of distribution would need to be set up in order to market the toaster; and (6) currency exchange rates—the Chinese yuan might not be readily convertible to American dollars.

DEVELOP YOUR BUSINESS LANGUAGE

17. exports
18. quota
19. multinational company or corporation (MNC)
20. exchange rate
21. imports
22. embargo
23. balance of trade
24. tariff
25. balance of payments
26. international business

15. Infant industries are new enterprises that are getting started in a country and which, during their early stages of development, might need protection from foreign competition. Examples of industries will vary. If a new industry shows an ability to produce desired goods as efficiently and at least as inexpensively as the same type of industry in other countries, then the government should encourage that industry to get established. High tariffs and quotas are often used by governments to help an infant industry develop. After an infant industry has reached the stage at which it can successfully compete with established industries of the same kind in other countries, continued protection by high tariffs and other barriers would be hard to justify.

16. Arguments in favor of stiff controls center on preventing the "exporting of American jobs" in certain industries overseas. Workers not only lose jobs, but workers in other fields that supply an industry experience declining employment. Competition from countries in which working conditions and wages are lower than ours will tend to diminish the standard of living enjoyed by U.S. workers. Arguments against stiff controls include (a) competition from abroad will force American businesses to be more responsive to the demand of the American public for products that are of high quality and less expensive; (b) competition will stimulate American businesses to design more innovative products; (c) American businesses, faced with import competition, will find ways to operate more efficiently; (d)

141

elimination of controls on foreign trade will improve international relations and will promote goodwill among nations.

DECISION-MAKING STRATEGIES

27. Our government could set a temporary quota on ceramic products imported from the other country. A tariff could also be levied that would cause ceramic products from the country to be very expensive in the United States.

28. The other country might retaliate and place quotas and/or tariffs on some products exported by the United States. The other country might look for other trading partners and reduce its general level of imports from the United States.

CALCULATE BUSINESS DATA

29.

Food	Year One	Year Two
Meat and meat products	$ 2,339	$ 2,367
Fruits and nuts	2,717	2,781
Coffee	3,130	4,293
Sugar	936	670
Fish	3,985	4,691
Cocoa	564	418
Totals	(a) $13,671	(b) $15,220

(c) increase—yes
(d) $15,220 − 13,671 = $1,549 million

30. (a) 120 yen × 0.008 = $0.96; (b) 5 Canadian dollars × 0.65 = $3.25 (c) 150 riyals × 0.27 = $40.50.

31. (a) 1 quart = 0.95 liter; 1 liter bottle; (b) 50 × 0.9 = 45 meters; (c) cubic centimeters (Many automobile engines are already measured in cubic centimeters.) (d) 12 × 2.5 = 30 centimeters; a 30-centimeter stick. (e) kilograms.

CALCULATE BUSINESS DATA

29. The table shows the approximate value of some imported foods for two years. The values are listed in millions of dollars.
   a. What is the total value in millions of dollars of the foods imported by the United States in Year One?
   b. What is the total value in millions of dollars of the foods imported in Year Two?
   c. Was there an increase from Year One to Year Two?
   d. What was the amount of increase or decrease?

Food	Year One	Year Two
Meat/meat products	$2,339	$2,367
Fruits and nuts	2,717	2,781
Coffee	3,130	4,293
Sugar	936	670
Fish	3,985	4,691
Cocoa	564	418

30. Using the information in Figure 10-3 on page 135, determine how many U.S. dollars someone could buy for these amounts of currencies from other countries:
   a. In Japan, 120 yen
   b. In Canada, 5 Canadian dollars
   c. In Saudi Arabia, 150 riyals

31. To make their exports suitable for use in other countries, U.S. manufacturers must produce goods that are measured in the metric system. For example, if a manufacturer wanted to export paint, which is sold in gallons in this country, it would probably export the paint in 4-liter (about 1¼ gallons) cans. To what sizes would the items listed be converted for export to countries using the metric system? (See Appendix D.)
   a. A quart bottle of liquid detergent
   b. A 50-yard bolt of polyester fabric
   c. An automobile engine measured in cubic inches
   d. A 12-inch ruler
   e. A bathroom scale that measures in pounds

32. The table shows approximate values of exports and imports going through nine ports in a recent year.
   a. What is the total value in millions of dollars of the exports for the year? the imports?
   b. Which port city reported the largest business in terms of value? What is the value?
   c. Which port imported and exported the least amount? What is the value for each?

City	Exports (In Millions)	Imports (In Millions)
Boston	$18,300	$40,300
New York	33,400	67,000
Baltimore	12,100	31,300
Miami	18,600	31,500
New Orleans	14,400	17,100
Houston	21,700	27,700
Los Angeles	22,200	53,100
San Francisco	32,100	44,100
Chicago	33,700	54,800

TECHNOLOGY APPLICATION

Using the *Intro to Business* Data CD and your database program software, select problem CH10. After the problem appears on your screen, complete the following activities. Then, after you have completed each step, display or print a report for each activity. If you do not have a printer available, answer the questions before you leave the computer.

33. Sort the database in descending order by amount of exports. Answer the following questions:
   a. What country purchased the highest amount of exports from the United States?
   b. What country purchased the second lowest amount of exports from the United States?

34. Select and list the countries that imported less than $10 million from the United States. How many countries are listed?

35. Sort the countries in ascending order by name of country. Answer the following questions:
   a. What is the amount of exports from the United States to the third country listed?
   b. What is the amount of imports into the United States from the last country listed?
   Optional: Create a pie chart showing the exports to each country.

32.

City	Exports in Millions	Imports in Millions	Totals
Boston	$18,300	$40,300	$58,600
New York	33,400	67,000	100,400 (b)
Baltimore	12,100	31,300	43,400
Miami	18,600	31,500	50,100
New Orleans	14,400	17,100	31,500 (c)
Houston	21,700	27,700	49,400
Los Angeles	22,200	53,100	75,300
San Francisco	32,100	44,100	76,200
Chicago	33,700	54,800	88,500
	(a) $206,500	(a) $366,900	

TECHNOLOGY APPLICATION

In this activity, students use a computer to solve a business problem using a file that is provided on the data CD that accompanies *Intro to Business*. Instructions for using the data CD are included in a **README** file on the disk. Solutions are provided on the Instructor's Resource CD.

COMMUNICATING for SUCCESS

MODES OF COMMUNICATION—GETTING THROUGH TO OTHERS

Communication is probably the most vital component of success in the business community. Simply defined, the communication process involves the exchange of information and meaning between individuals. Research shows that managers spend about 60% to 80% of their work time involved in communication.

The process of sending and receiving messages requires strong, effective communication skills. The communication process can be complicated because of the differences in how individuals receive and process information. In your communication encounters you must decide on the most effective and appropriate techniques for conveying your message.

As a businessperson, you can use many communication strategies. The most common form of business communication is the telephone. Telephone calls play an important role in conveying personal and immediate attention to issues of concern, and are an opportunity for timely feedback.

Similar to the telephone call, electronic mail (e-mail) has become increasingly popular in the business world because it is quick and inexpensive. The e-mail message is typically informal and can be used in the following situations:

- when a large amount of detail is required in a request,
- when requests are informal, and
- when work schedules are not conducive to telephone contact.

> **Many communication strategies are available to business people.**

Perhaps the most formal type of business communication is the letter, which requires a signature and is sent on company letterhead. Letters are used to communicate official or formal messages. Letters are often used to convey messages of gratitude or information, and are typically viewed as the least time-sensitive form of communication.

Letters and other documents may be sent to others through a facsimile transmission (fax). Faxes are used in a manner similar to letters, but are more time sensitive and viewed as slightly less formal. Although faxed messages are becoming more common, they usually are used only in instances where time pressures are extreme and formality not important.

CRITICAL THINKING

1. What does the communication process involve?
2. How much time do business managers spend in communication activities?

COMMUNICATING for SUCCESS

Communications skills will help ensure students' success in the business world. Communicating for Success introduces workplace/interpersonal communications issues and proper uses of communications technology. Each feature discusses a key communications topic, and contains two Critical Thinking questions that require students to analyze what they have learned.

Since students generally have limited exposure to many of the modes of communication used in business, it's important for them to learn how these modes are used in business for various purposes. The Communicating for Success feature in this chapter helps distinguish between formal and informal modes of communication and when they are most appropriate. It also discusses how immediacy, the level of required detail, and people's work schedules can affect the choice of the most effective mode of communication.

CRITICAL THINKING

1. The communication process involves the exchange of information and meaning between individuals.
2. Research shows that managers spend approximately 60% to 80% of their work time involved in communicating with others.

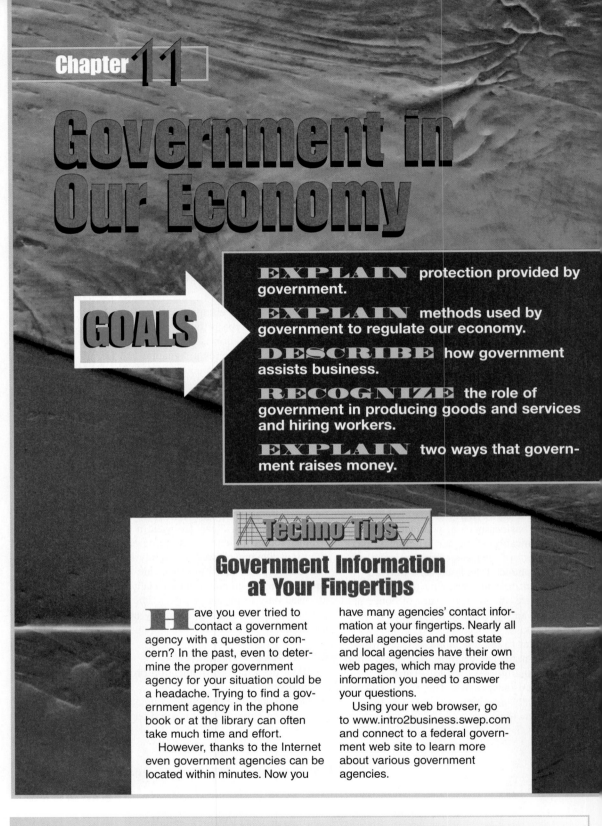

In Chapter 11, students explore the role of government in our society. Governments provide services at the federal, state, and local levels. To finance its operations, government at all levels has the power to tax and issue bonds.

Resources for Teachers
- Lesson Plans
- School-To-Work/SCANS Activity Masters
- Spanish Resources
- Instructor's Resource CD

Assessment
- Chapter and Unit Tests, Ch. 11
- ExamView, Ch. 11

Media/Technology
- Applying Technology Data CD
- PowerPoint slides
- Business Connection CD
- Videotape

Activity Masters and Workbooks
- Activities and Projects, Ch. 11
- Internet Activity Masters
- Business Math Activity Masters
- Communications Activity Masters
- International Business Activity Masters
- Ethics Activity Masters

Chapter 11
Government in Our Economy

GOALS

EXPLAIN protection provided by government.

EXPLAIN methods used by government to regulate our economy.

DESCRIBE how government assists business.

RECOGNIZE the role of government in producing goods and services and hiring workers.

EXPLAIN two ways that government raises money.

Techno Tips

Government Information at Your Fingertips

Have you ever tried to contact a government agency with a question or concern? In the past, even to determine the proper government agency for your situation could be a headache. Trying to find a government agency in the phone book or at the library can often take much time and effort.

However, thanks to the Internet even government agencies can be located within minutes. Now you have many agencies' contact information at your fingertips. Nearly all federal agencies and most state and local agencies have their own web pages, which may provide the information you need to answer your questions.

Using your web browser, go to www.intro2business.swep.com and connect to a federal government web site to learn more about various government agencies.

Students need to know the latest technologies and develop cutting edge Internet skills for use in current jobs, future careers, or in their homes. TechnoTips introduces students to today's cutting edge technologies and provides them with important Internet skills. Feature topics concentrate on Internet-specific technologies and computer or other hi-tech innovations for use by businesses and consumers. At the www.intro2business.swep.com web site, students can complete the activity for this chapter.

Government plays a role in every economic system. Your role as a citizen and voter affects decisions made and actions taken by government. In our private enterprise system, our government's role is much less extensive than in other economic systems but is nevertheless an important one.

The role of government in the economy changes as newly elected officials take office and as different political parties become dominant. As issues facing our society change, so must our government change. But there are some fundamental, basic roles of government.

Government is primarily concerned with these roles:

- Providing services for members of our society.
- Protecting citizens, consumers, businesses, and workers.
- Regulating utilities and promoting competition.
- Providing information and assistance to businesses.
- Purchasing goods and services.
- Hiring public employees.
- Raising revenue.

Each of these roles has either a direct or indirect impact on business expansion, consumer affairs, and economic growth in our economy.

OUR GOVERNMENT—FEDERAL, STATE, AND LOCAL

The main goal of the federal government is to oversee the activities that involve two or more states or other countries. In general, the Constitution gives the federal government the power to regulate foreign and interstate commerce. Business transactions involving companies in more than one state are called **interstate commerce**. For example, a trucking company that ships products to several states would be regulated by the federal government.

State governments regulate business activities within their own boundaries. **Intrastate commerce** refers to business transactions involving companies that do business only in one state. For instance, a trucking company that hauls products only within a state's boundaries would be regulated by that state and not the federal government.

All states have delegated some of their legislative authority to local governments.

Why do you think the federal government would regulate interstate commerce?

Chapter 11 Government in Our Economy

PURPOSE Ask students to copy each of the Key Terms onto a sheet of paper, then copy the definition from the glossary beside the term. Key Terms are listed under Develop Your Business Language in Chapter Review. They should also give an example that they believe illustrates each term and its definition. Also direct students to read the headings in the chapter, and then look at the illustrations and figures to get a sense for what the chapter contains.

TEACH/APPLY

MAKE CONNECTIONS Engage students in a discussion of why governments instead of businesses provide some goods and services. Ask them to identify goods and services provided by government at all levels—federal, state, and local. Why are these goods and services provided by government?

Have students discuss the following statement: "Some people say that one problem with government providing some goods and services is that there is little or no competition." Then have students name instances in your community in which private firms and government sometimes compete with one another for business. Examples include public and private schools, some forms of mail service, and recreation.

Have students list on the board various ways in which government has regulated items sold in a grocery store. Several examples of government regulations can be

FOCUS ON REAL LIFE

Ask students whether they agree or disagree with the following: (1) The education of children is a community's responsibility; (2) Much of citizens' tax money is wasted by government; (3) A constitutional amendment is needed to force Congress to balance the budget; (4) The federal government spends too much of its revenue on national defense. Have advocates of opposing points of view explain why they support their position.

named, including required ingredients labeling on canned goods, grading of meat, and truth in advertising promotions.

Show PowerPoint 11-5, *Intellectual Property Rights,* to emphasize the three types of intellectual property. Then review the ways patents, copyrights, and trademarks are alike (for example, all protect originality) and different (they cover different things). Ask if students know of patented products that have come on the market recently. Also ask them to name well-known trademarks. Have students create a display of logos for products with which they are familiar.

Give students an overview of the various taxes collected by local, state, and federal governments. Have students list the taxes they pay, those their parents pay, and taxes that a local business owner would pay.

TRY THIS/GUIDED PRACTICE
Lead students in a brief discussion of this topic: "Does government do more to protect the interests of businesses or consumers?" Guide students through a discussion of the many functions of government.

Walk students through a discussion of the government services that a typical student might benefit from directly or indirectly during the course of a normal school day. List the responses on the board. Then ask students to identify what kind of tax might be imposed by government to provide each service. Also list the tax next to the government service.

Local governments include county boards and city or town councils. Local governments provide services needed for an orderly society, such as police and fire protection.

GOVERNMENT PROTECTS

Government protects our rights in obvious ways. Citizens are protected through government-provided police and fire-fighting services. We also have armed forces to provide for our national defense. National security is a major concern of our federal government.

Laws have been established to help provide a safe work environment. As a worker, you have a basic right to safe working conditions. For example, safety standards for building, machines, and chemicals are set by government agencies. Government inspection and regulation of work areas helps to reduce the number of job-related accidents.

Additional government regulations stem from the need to protect the basic human rights of workers. For example, you cannot be denied work because of your race, religion, sex, or age. Selection of someone for a job must be based on job requirements, training, and experience and not on prejudices and personal biases.

Several laws exist to prevent air, water, noise, and chemical pollution. Other laws forbid the burning of substances that make our air unsafe to breathe. The Environmental Protection Agency (EPA) was established by the federal government to ensure that businesses would comply with the laws.

Another example of government protection is through contracts and special property rights. An enforceable contract is one that meets certain requirements. Patents, copy-

rights, and trademarks are important areas of federal law for many businesses. They protect the inventions and ideas that might generate profits for a company in the future.

Contracts
An agreement to exchange goods or services for something of value, usually money, is fundamental to doing business. That agreement is called a **contract**. A contract may be written or unwritten but certain elements must be included for the contract to be enforceable. Figure 11-1 highlights the main provisions of every enforceable contract. Examples of contracts include a lease to rent an apartment, a credit card agreement, and documents that state the terms of a purchase.

Both consumers and businesses benefit from government enforcement of contracts. If you agree to have repairs made on your car for $65, the business firm must perform the work as agreed upon and you must pay for the work when it is completed. If work is not done correctly or if you fail to make the payment, legal action through our court system can be taken to force the work to be corrected or force you to pay. Without enforcement, dishonest consumers or business owners could refuse to honor their agreements, and our daily business activities would be very unpleasant.

FIGURE 11-1 How often do you enter into contracts?

Contract Basics

Valid, enforceable contracts must contain:

Agreement	An offer must be made, and an acceptance must occur.
Competent Parties	Those entering into the contract must be of legal age and must be mentally competent.
Consideration	Something of measurable value must be exchanged by the parties involved.
Legality	The contract must be for a product or service that may be legally sold; also no fraud or deception exists in the agreement.

Critical Thinking Skills-Visualizing

SCANS

Visualizing, or being able to organize and process information, is a thinking skill we cannot ignore. Students need to learn how to visualize through the reading of information and observation of graphs, pictures, and other visuals. The Global Perspectives features give students an opportunity to visualize the various places around the globe that are described.

Intellectual Property Rights

Intellectual property is purely intangible; that is, a person cannot touch it. Intellectual property discussed in this section includes patents, copyrights, and trademarks.

When individuals or companies create new products, they may obtain a patent. A **patent** gives the inventor the exclusive right to make, use, or sell the item for 17 years. For example, a company that creates a new method to record programs from television could obtain a patent for this process to prevent other companies from making or selling recorders using this process.

In a similar manner, a **copyright** protects the creative work of authors, composers, and artists. Copyright protection continues for the life of the person receiving the copyright and for 50 years after the person's death. Examples of copyright statements can be found on the

How do businesses benefit from participating in trade shows and conventions?

GLOBAL PERSPECTIVES
Yoruba of Southwestern Africa

If you take a journey to the southwestern part of Africa, you might visit the area of Yoruba in Nigeria. The 20 million Yorubans trace their history back to A.D. 1200. Their land is divided into numerous city-states and villages. City-states are ruled by a king (oba). The king, a ritual leader, is believed to have divine powers. Villages are governed by chiefs.

Yoruba has rich farmlands. Maize (corn), yams, peanuts, and beans are among crops raised for local consumption. Cacao, used in making chocolate, is one of this area's specialties. Cacao is exported and is the main cash crop.

Most of the men are farmers; women do no farm work. Yurobans are skilled in many crafts. Handwoven cloth, reed baskets, metalwork, and pottery are among the crafts sold in the lively open markets. Women control much of the marketplace, and a woman's status is largely determined by her position in the market.

Critical Thinking
1. In what ways are the Yorubans different from or similar to us in the United States?
2. If you lived in Yoruba, what might be your role as a worker?

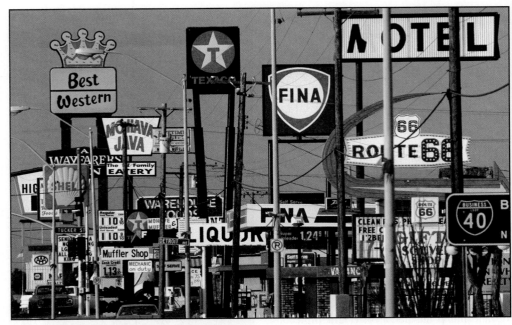

How can logos increase businesses' sales?

front pages of most books. Copyrights are identified with the symbol ©.

Another form of protection given to a business by government is a trademark. A **trademark** is a word, letter, or symbol associated with a specific company or product. Company names, team emblems, and label designs may be registered with the government. A trademark can be very valuable since many are famous throughout the world and often identified with a symbol, called a *logo*. Can you think of some well-known logos that you see frequently?

GOVERNMENT REGULATES

Business activity in the United States is organized as a private enterprise or free market system. Private organizations own the factors of production and choose efficient methods of production in order to earn a profit. Price and output decisions are made not by government decrees, but by the actions of thousands of

businesses operating under varying economic conditions. Our government does get involved, however, in our private enterprise system by regulating utilities and preventing unfair business practices.

Regulating Utilities

Most goods and services you use are obtained from private businesses that are relatively free of government regulation. However, a **public utility** is an organization that supplies a service or product vital to all people. These include companies that provide local telephone service, water, and electricity. A public utility is selected to serve a community. If your city had six different electric companies, each with its own utility poles, lines, and expensive equipment, the service you would get would be more expensive and less efficient. Also, the extra poles and wires would create an unsightly environment.

While many utility companies are privately owned, traditionally they have been closely

148

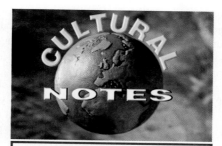

America is a nation of cultural diversity in which many languages are spoken. Some statistics show that one in seven people will grow up in the United States knowing a second language. Statistics also show that the most common first language, other than English, is Spanish.

regulated by government. The rates they can charge for things such as electricity, water, or natural gas generally have to be approved by government agencies, although in recent years there has been a trend toward deregulation of prices where competition can be introduced.

Preventing Unfair Business Practices

Most businesspeople are fair and honest, but a few may try to take advantage of their customers or competitors. Government attempts to promote fair competition. If a company charges different prices to different people for the same product, it is treating its customers unfairly. Likewise, if one business receives lower rates for the same quality and quantity of supplies than others, it has an advantage. Such action may result in unfair competition.

A **monopoly** exists when a business has control of the market for a product or service. While a public utility monopoly may be beneficial by making sure people receive a needed service at a fair price, other monopolies may not be good for the economy. For example, if all food stores in your city were owned by the same company, consumers might not be

treated fairly. This business could charge high prices and provide poor-quality products. When competition exists, consumers get the best values at the fairest prices.

One government action designed to promote competition and fairness and to prevent monopolies was the passage of **antitrust laws**. Antitrust laws also prevent other unfair business practices such as false advertising, deceptive pricing, and misleading labeling. Each of these unfair practices hurts competition and reduces consumer choice.

GOVERNMENT ASSISTS BUSINESSES

Government helps businesses by collecting and reporting valuable information. Data collected by the government can assist in planning for the future. Information about incomes, prices, worker availability, and business failures can help a businessperson make wiser decisions. For example, census information can help a business decide where the most potential customers live. The Bureau of Labor Statistics, the Department of Agriculture, and the Department of Commerce are a few of the government agencies that provide information.

Government loans can also be obtained to help new businesses get started. The federal government, through the Small Business Administration (SBA), is an important source of business loans. Farmers and others may receive financial help in times of extreme hardship such as during a drought, flooding, or other natural disasters. Destruction of home and property by a tornado may qualify a person for a low-interest government

The Sherman Act (1890), the first anti-trust law, declared illegal "every contract, combination . . . or conspiracy in restraint of trade or commerce."

NET FACTS

Net Facts provides information and definitions of terms for the Internet. The more information that students have about the Internet, the better equipped they will be to use this resource. In the Internet Activity Masters, there is an Internet Activity Worksheet for each unit. You can use these activities to give students experience with finding information online. Options for assigning this activity are as follows:

1. **Provide students with a list of addresses for this activity,**
2. **Assign students to conduct their own searches, or**
3. **Use the addresses on the Internet Activity Worksheet.**

You should complete the activity yourself before assigning it to resolve any discrepancies that may arise.

for the local, state, and federal governments. Students should also determine how businesses keep records for tax purposes.

NET FACTS

The Internet can be found on all seven continents, including Antarctica. A host at the South Pole sends out scientific and weather information.

loan. These programs are designed to promote the economic well-being of our society.

GOVERNMENT PURCHASES PRODUCTS AND SERVICES

All levels of government buy and use a wide range of items. Some services are provided more efficiently by government. Roads, schools, national defense, police and fire protection are some examples.

Government spends a great deal of money each day to buy a variety of products and services. Total federal, state, and local government purchases of goods and services account for about 20 percent of all the goods and services produced in the United States. Governments buy everything from file cabinets to buildings to fleets of automobiles to military jet aircraft. In this role, government is an important economic force. Many businesses depend on government contracts for their survival. For instance, government pays businesses to construct highways and build schools.

GOVERNMENT HIRES WORKERS

Government is the single largest employer in our economy. About one of every nine workers is a public employee. Most people think only of police officers, fire fighters, and sanitation workers as government workers; but government employs the same types of workers as private businesses. Administrative

assistants, lawyers, teachers, meat inspectors, and data analysts are examples. Although the number of government employees has grown slowly in recent years, good employment opportunities in government continue—in spite of efforts to eliminate or reduce the size of some agencies.

GOVERNMENT RAISES MONEY

Government must have a way to raise money to fund operations and pay wages to workers. Government income is called **revenue**. Governments can obtain revenue through taxes and borrowing. In addition, governments can raise revenue in other ways. Fines for traffic violations and other violations of the law provide revenue for government. Fees and licenses are also a source of income. Certain types of enterprises require a business license. For example, insurance and real estate agents pay a fee for the privilege of conducting business. Governments also charge fees for such things as driver's licenses and fishing privileges.

Taxes

A government establishes tax policies to pay for the services it provides. Taxes are levied on earnings, the value of property, and on the sale price of goods and services.

Your earnings as an individual are subject to an income tax. *Income taxes* are levied on the income of individuals. The individual income tax is the largest source of revenue for the federal government. Corporate income taxes also provide government revenue. The corporate income tax is based on business profits.

A major source of revenue for local governments is the real estate *property tax*. This tax is based on the value of the land and the

More than 15 million people in our country work full time for federal, state, and local governments.

TEACHING STRATEGIES   Special Needs
Specific Learning Disability (SLD) Students

When feasible, SLD students should become involved in work-study programs that are consistent with course content. When work-study opportunities are unavailable, simulations can be used to provide a simulated work environment. Field trips are an excellent method to expose students to the business world.

How do you think the management of our governments compares to the management of large corporations?

buildings attached to the land. Most property tax revenue is used to pay for schools and other local government services, such as police protection and community parks. Businesses also pay a property tax.

The cost of buying things can be increased by a sales tax. A *sales tax* is a state or local tax on goods and services that is collected by the seller. If you buy a can of paint for $15.00 and the state sales tax is 6 percent, the seller collects $15.90 from you. The seller then will pay 90 cents to the state, but you were the one who provided the money for the tax.

Paying taxes is a responsibility of citizens and businesses. You should pay your fair tax but not more than your share. Tax laws and policies are established to help make the paying of taxes fair and equitable. Whether a particular tax or tax policy is fair and equitable is always subject to debate. Businesses, in spite of public misconceptions, pay a lot of taxes to all levels of government.

Borrowing

Government income from taxes and other sources may not always be enough to cover the costs of providing services. Borrowing is another activity of government. When a government wants to build a building, such as a new court house or convention center, the revenue needed is often raised through borrowing.

Government borrows money by selling bonds. When you buy a government bond, you are helping to finance the services provided by government. Banks, insurance companies, and other financial institutions help finance our governments by purchasing bonds in large quantities. By borrowing money, the government becomes a debtor and must pay interest on its debt. Bonds issued by the U.S. government are backed by the "full faith and credit" of the federal government. Bonds issued by our federal government are considered the least risky of all debt.

Critical Thinking Skills-Problem Solving

SCANS

Problem-solving skills, which include recognizing a problem and devising a plan of action, are applied throughout every chapter in this text. Each time a student participates in a Cooperative Learning or Teams activity, problem-solving skills are applied in a group situation. Each time a student completes a math application in Calculate Business Data, decisions are made as to which mathematical approach must be taken. For each Technology Application problem, students must decide which template problem to use, which piece of software to load, and how to solve the problem. Emphasize to students how they are using problem solving in their day-to-day tasks and make them aware of the skills they are developing.

REVIEW YOUR READING

1. Government is organized in three levels: federal, state, and local.
2. Interstate commerce involves transactions between companies licensed to do business in different states. Intrastate commerce involves business transactions between parties licensed to do business in the same state.
3. Government protects our rights as consumers, business owners, and workers through police and fire-fighting services, regulations relating to the environment, enforcement of legal contracts, laws governing intellectual property (copyrights and patents), and laws affecting employment and safe workplaces.
4. The enforcement of contracts guarantees that consumers and businesses will receive what they are promised in a business transaction. Our economic system could not operate effectively without contract enforcement.
5. Copyrights and patents are granted to reward and protect the creative efforts of people.
6. Government creates laws to guarantee a safe work environment and establishes regulations that protect the basic human rights of workers.
7. One public utility can better serve a community than several because there is no duplication of costly equipment and services.
8. A monopoly is considered not to be in the best public interest when the lack of competition might cause consumers to receive poor quality merchandise at high prices with poor service.
9. Government collects and reports valuable information. The federal government has a loan program that helps individuals get started in business.
10. Governments buy file cabinets, buildings, fleets of automobiles, military jet aircraft, and many other products.
11. Government raises revenue through the levying of taxes and borrowing money.

BUSINESS NOTES

1. Government protects our rights as citizens through police and fire services; as consumers and business owners through the enforcement of contracts and intellectual property rights; and as workers through laws that require safe working conditions.
2. Government regulates utilities and prevents unfair business practices.
3. Government collects and reports valuable information, and provides loans to help businesses get started or overcome natural disasters.
4. Government buys a variety of goods and services and employs workers.
5. Government raises needed funds through taxes and borrowing.

REVIEW YOUR READING

1. What are the three levels of government?
2. How do interstate and intrastate commerce differ?
3. How does government protect society?
4. Explain how the enforcement of contracts helps consumers and businesses.
5. Why does the government grant special property rights such as copyrights and patents?
6. List ways in which government protects workers.
7. Why can one public utility serve a city better than several similar public utilities?
8. When is a monopoly not in the best public interest?
9. Name two ways in which government assists private businesses.
10. What types of products and services do governments buy?
11. What are two ways in which government raises revenue?

COMMUNICATE BUSINESS CONCEPTS

12. Below is a list of some of the public services provided by government. For each service, tell whether the federal, state, or local government would most likely have the responsibility for the service. (Some services may be provided by more than one level of government.)
    a. Fire protection
    b. Education
    c. Parks and recreation
    d. Water supply
    e. Highways between cities
    f. Assistance to low-income families
    g. Sewage and trash disposal
    h. Public buses
    i. Police protection
    j. Public libraries
    k. City street maintenance
    l. National defense
13. Make a list of public utilities that serve your community.
    a. What services do they provide?

COMMUNICATE BUSINESS CONCEPTS

12. (a) local; (b) local and state; (c) local, state, and federal; (d) local; (e) state and federal; (f) state and federal; (g) local; (h) local; (i) local and state; (j) local; (k) local; (l) federal
13. (a) Public utilities provide telephone, gas, water, electricity, and transportation services. (b) Responses will vary as to whether or not these services can be better performed by private businesses. Some services (electricity and water) are impractical when offered by several private companies. But some services (for example, garbage collection) might be appropriate for private enterprise.
14. (a) Contract examples include an agreement to borrow money, an agreement to purchase supplies or equipment by a business, and a labor agreement with a union or a contract for professional services. (b) Law enforcement agencies and the courts are government services provided to enforce contracts.

b. Do you think it would be better for these services to be offered by several competing businesses? Explain your answer.

14. Each day people enter into many contracts both written and unwritten.

   a. Give examples of contracts between a consumer and a business, between two businesses, and between a worker and a business.

   b. What services are provided by government to enforce contracts?

15. Two students are discussing the topic "Government is Our Biggest Business." Dan believes that some government activities are in direct competition with private businesses and that this is unfair. He believes that government should limit its activities to those that private businesses cannot or will not undertake. Brian thinks that government should undertake any business activities that it can perform better or less expensively than private business. What do you think? Give some examples of business activities undertaken by both private businesses and by government.

16. Why do you suppose government raises revenue through bonds which create debt and require interest payments when government could raise the revenue through an increase in taxes?

DEVELOP YOUR BUSINESS LANGUAGE

For each numbered item, find the term that has the same meaning.

17. A business that supplies a service or product vital to all people; the price charged for the service (or product) is determined by government regulation rather than by competition.

18. Business transactions involving companies that do business only in one state.

19. Government income.

20. Laws designed to promote competition and fairness and to prevent monopolies.

21. Protection of the work of authors, composers, and artists.

22. An agreement to exchange goods or services for something of value.

23. The exclusive right given to a person to make, use, or sell an invention for a period of 17 years.

24. Business transactions involving companies in more than one state.

25. A word, letter, or symbol associated with a specific product or company.

26. A business that has complete control of the market for a product or service.

KEY TERMS

antitrust laws
contract
copyright
interstate commerce
intrastate commerce
monopoly
patent
public utility
revenue
trademark

DEVELOP YOUR BUSINESS LANGUAGE

17. public utility
18. intrastate commerce
19. revenue
20. antitrust laws
21. copyright
22. contract
23. patent
24. interstate commerce
25. trademark
26. monopoly

DECISION-MAKING STRATEGIES

27. Proposal No. 1 will not cause property taxes to increase, and that will please property owners. Fees will be charged users, and some individuals and families may not be able to afford the fees. However, some of the fees would be paid by persons from outside of the community who use the complex. The building of the complex can be started immediately, and it will be available for use sooner than the other proposal.

   Proposal No. 2 will result in a slight increase in the sales tax. Visitors from other cities and states will pay the sales tax and help fund the complex. A user fee will not have to be charged. The sales tax may adversely affect lower-income families, since so much of their income goes toward the purchase of consumable goods. The delay in the construction of the complex will cause the cost of the complex to be higher than originally estimated.

DECISION-MAKING STRATEGIES

Centerville wants to build a new All-Sports Complex—the ASC. The ASC will be located near the center of town and will have facilities that will appeal to just about every kind of individual who wants to exercise or play sports.

The complex will cost $250,000. There are two financing proposals:

No. 1: Issue $250,000 worth of bonds at an interest rate of 4 percent. The town will pay $10,000 per year in interest for 15 years. The total interest would be $150,000. The amount borrowed ($250,000) would have to be paid off in 15 years. Fees charged to users of the complex would pay the interest each year and the amount due bondholders ($250,000). Construction of the complex could begin immediately.

No. 2: Establish a $\frac{1}{4}$ percent city sales tax on all purchases. The revenue needed could be raised in about 5 years. There would be no user fee charged to residents of Centerville. Construction of the complex would be delayed a few years.

27. What are the advantages and disadvantages of the two proposals?

28. Which proposal do you favor, and why?

15. Students should be able to identify the concept that government has certain responsibilities for the general welfare. If government attempted to undertake any business activity at will, the private enterprise system would no doubt be jeopardized. Some examples of business activities undertaken by both private business and by government include overnight mail service, health insurance, and retirement programs.

16. Governments sometimes prefer borrowing money. The continual increase in taxes can result in a taxpayer revolt. Higher taxes can discourage businesses from locating in a community and can cause some citizens to move to other communities or states. Borrowing is the most practical approach, especially when a large amount of money is needed right away for building construction or other large projects.

28. Answers will vary considerably. However, students will likely prefer No. 1 since construction can begin immediately. No. 1 also does not affect the tax burden of the community.

CALCULATE BUSINESS DATA

29. (a) 0.46 × $186,000 = $85,560; (b) $186,000 − $85,560 = $100,440; (c) $85,560 × 12 months = $1,026,720.

30. (a) 18,000 ÷ 90,000 = 0.20 or 20%; (b) 6,000 ÷ 18,000 = 0.30 or 30%; (c) 8,000 ÷ 90,000 = 0.088 or 9%.

31. 150 × 0.3 = 45 meters.

32. (a) $1,250 + $52,000 + $1,795 + $1,645 + $550 + $325 = $57,565; (b) $23,500 + $6,775 + $1,525 + $780 + $1,455 + $420 + $1,800 + $675 + $715 = $37,645; (c) $52,000 ÷ $57,565 = 0.903 or 90%; (d) $23,500 ÷ $37,645 = 0.624 or 62%.

TECHNOLOGY APPLICATION

In this activity, students use a computer to solve a business problem using a file that is provided on the data CD that accompanies *Intro to Business*. Instructions for using the data CD are included in a **README** file on the disk. Solutions are provided on the Instructor's Resource CD.

CALCULATE BUSINESS DATA

29. A city government spends $186,000 a month on public services. Of that amount, 46 percent is used for fire and police protection.
   a. How much is spent each month for fire and police protection?
   b. How much is spent each month for other services?
   c. How much is spent by the city in a year for fire and police protection?

30. In a city in which there are 90,000 employed workers, 18,000 are public employees. Of this number, 6,000 are employed by the federal government, 8,000 by the state, and 4,000 by the city.
   a. What percent of all workers are public employees?
   b. What percent of the public employees are employed by the federal government?
   c. What percent of all employees are employees of the state government?

31. The town of Clarksville wants to expand the main street from two to four lanes. To do so, 150 feet of land is needed. How many meters of land will be used for the road-widening project? (See Appendix D.)

32. Listed in the table is the cash income and expenditures record of the Midland Public Library for one year.

   a. What was the total of the cash on hand and cash received during the year?
   b. How much was paid out during the year?
   c. What percent of the total cash received was accounted for by town and state appropriations? (Round your answer to the nearest whole percent.)
   d. What percent of total expenditures was accounted for by salaries? (Round your answer to the nearest whole percent.)

Income	
Cash on hand, beginning of year	$ 1,250
Town and state appropriations	52,000
Income from investments	1,795
Gifts	1,645
Fines on overdue books	550
Miscellaneous income	325

Expenditures	
Salaries	$23,500
Books and periodicals	6,775
Utilities	1,525
Insurance	780
Equipment and supplies	1,455
Cleaning and repairs	420
Library binding	675
General administrative expenses	715

TECHNOLOGY APPLICATION

Using the *Intro to Business* Data CD and your word processing program software, select problem CH11. After the problem appears on your screen, complete the following activities. Then, print your completed contracts. Sign Contract 1 as the government official and Contract 2 as the building owner. If you do not have a printer available, save the contracts on a data disk to give to your teacher.

33. You are a county government official authorized to rent office buildings. You must complete a rental contract for an office building. Above Contract 1 is a list of items related to you and your county government office. Cut and paste the items into the appropriate blank spaces in the contract. When dates are required, use the first day of the current month.

34. You own an office building that your county government would like to rent. Above Contract 2 is a list of items related to you and your building. Cut and paste the items into the appropriate blank spaces in the contract. When dates are required, use the first day of the current month.

INTERNATIONAL TRADE AGREEMENTS

An economic community is an organization of countries that bond together to allow a free flow of goods and services. The group acts as a single country when conducting business with other regions of the world. An economic community is also called a common market.

The European Union (EU) is the largest and most extensive economic community. This economic community allows a free flow of goods, services, and workers among the member nations. As of 2002, the EU consisted of 15 countries with others (mainly in Eastern Europe) applying for future membership.

The North American Free Trade Agreement (NAFTA) consists of Canada, Mexico, and the United States. Trade within this economic community has created many new jobs in the region.

Other examples of regional economic cooperation include MERCOSUR (involving Argentina, Brazil, Paraguay, and Uruguay), the Economic Community of West African States (ECOOWAS), the Association of Southeast Asian Nations (ASEAN), and the Central American Common Market.

The exchange of goods and services between two parties with no money involved is *direct barter*. However, since trading

> **Economic communities include the European Union and the North American Free Trade Agreement.**

items of equal value is difficult, a different barter method is used. *Countertrade* is the exchange of goods and services among companies in different countries. With countertrade, however, some currency may be involved.

A *free-trade zone* is an area designated by a government for duty-free (no import taxes) entry of non-prohibited goods. Free-trade zones are commonly located at a point of entry into a nation, such as a harbor or airport. One example is the Colon Free Zone in Panama.

In a free-trade zone, merchandise may be stored, displayed, or used without duties (taxes) being paid. Duties are imposed on the goods only when the items pass from the free-trade zone into an area of the country subject to customs.

CRITICAL THINKING

1. Describe the benefits and potential disadvantages of an economic community such as the European Union, NAFTA, and MERCOSUR.
2. Go to the web site of the European Union. What information is available to assist companies that plan to do business in one or more of these countries?

Most students will either work with international clients or compete against businesses that do. Global Navigator introduces students to issues integral to working with international businesses. Key concepts and challenges faced by international businesses are presented, followed by Critical Thinking questions that require students to analyze what they have learned.

This feature describes the wide range of international trade associations, trade agreements, and free-trade zones. These have become increasingly important in the global economy as political leaders seek to embrace the popularity of free trade as an ideal— even as they simultaneously seek to extract concessions from foreign governments using trade policy as leverage and to maintain favor with domestic special interests who want protected markets.

CRITICAL THINKING

1. Answers may include benefits such as cheaper imports, expanded markets for exports, stronger economic growth throughout the community, and fairness. Disadvantages cited may include loss of some national sovereignty and control over trade policies, possible loss of jobs, and lost sales by domestic companies to cheaper foreign imports.
2. Answers might include demographic, trade, financial and economic data on member nations; links to web sites of member nation trade departments, and contact information for EU trade officials.

GLOBAL BUSINESS PROJECT

For this phase of the global business plan project, students are asked to become familiar with social and legal aspects of another country. In addition to the usual research methods, also encourage them to talk with people who are familiar with other countries and cultures. This process can be very helpful in gaining insight into unique aspects of other countries. For example, in some countries the work day goes from 10 a.m. until 2 p.m. with a two-hour break and then work resumes until 8 p.m. with dinner at 10 p.m.

Formal and informal trade barriers are also considered in this project. Formal trade barriers involve government actions to impede free trade, such as tariffs, import quotas, and currency control. An informal trade barrier usually relates to some cultural or economic aspect of a control. For example, in some countries family members work very closely in business situations. Not being aware of this cultural norm can result in a poor business relationship and unsuccessful international business operations.

To complete each phase of this project, students are encouraged to use various resources—textbook content, library materials, World Wide Web sites, interviews, advertisements, product packages, in-store observations. The individual activities are planned for use as either (1) an on-going course project, or (2) individual assignments.

Whether used as a continuing project or for selected activities, consider having students work in teams. This small group experience provides a valuable skill for future learning and work situations.

In addition to search engines, these selected web sites can be helpful for this unit:
- U.S. Dept. of Commerce (www.usatrade.gov and www.export.gov)

GLOBAL BUSINESS PROJECT

ANALYZE THE SOCIAL AND LEGAL ENVIRONMENT

The daily activities of people in a country reflect their beliefs, traditions, and customs. As a company expands into new global markets, managers must be sensitive to these social and cultural differences. In this phase of the business plan project, you will consider various social aspects of the global economy.

The international business activities of a company are also influenced by a nation's political and legal environment. Restrictions on imports and regulations affecting business activities will affect a company's business plan.

PROJECT GOALS
1. Research the social and cultural influences on a nation's business environment.
2. Identify political and legal factors affecting business activities in a foreign country.
3. Analyze potential trade barriers that could affect international business activities.

PROJECT ACTIVITIES
Using your textbook, library materials, web sites, interviews with people, and other resources, complete the following activities:
1. A nation's customs, traditions, family values, religious beliefs, and other cultural factors can affect business activities and consumer buying habits. Using the country from your portfolio (or select a country), identify specific aspects of the nation's culture that could influence a company's business activities.
2. Laws regulating business differ from country to country. Research the political and legal environment of your selected country. Explain some legal restrictions or consumer protection laws that are different from other countries.
3. Foreign governments commonly take actions to protect companies in their own country. These trade barriers might include tariffs, import quotas, taxes, and other restrictions. Using the country from your portfolio (or select a country), discuss an existing or potential trade barrier.
4. Present your findings on laws, barriers, and taxes in a chart, table, or other visual format.

PROJECT WRAP-UP
1. Continue or start your portfolio (folder, file box, or other container) for storing and referring back to the information and materials you created in the activities above. Your portfolio provides the information needed for the various elements of a global business plan.
2. Interview a person who has lived in or traveled to another country. Ask questions related to the culture, foods, leisure activities, customs, holidays, business environment, and other aspects unique to the nation. Ask the person for permission to tape (audio or video) the interview.

- Business, economic, political news for selected countries (www.globaledge.msu.edu/ibrd/ibrd.asp)
- *World Factbook* of the Central Intelligence Agency (www.cia.gov/cia/publications/factbook/)
- World Trade Organization at (www.wto.org)
- Current country information at (www.economist.com/countries/)
- Africa Business Guide at (www.newafrica.com/business/)
- Import-export information at (www.internationalist.com/business)
- Latin American country information (www.lanic.utexas.edu)
- Asian country information (asnic.utexas.edu) (www.asia-inc.com)
- Eastern European country information (reenic.utexas.edu)
- Middle East country information (menic.utexas.edu)

FOCUS ON CAREERS

IMPORT-EXPORT

The area of importing and exporting employs people in a wide variety of positions. In today's global economy there are people who direct foreign sales and service outlets, negotiate contracts with foreign sales and distribution centers, arrange shipping, and direct conversion of products from American to foreign standards and specifications. While the skills necessary to perform these tasks are increasingly important, job titles often will not reflect them directly, as the people will also have duties unrelated to importing and exporting. Transportation managers, for example, oversee both foreign and domestic shipping, including settlements between shippers. Customs inspectors examine, classify, and appraise imported merchandise according to federal laws in order to enforce regulations of the U.S. Customs Service. Customs special agents investigate persons, common carriers, and merchandise arriving in or departing from the United States, to prevent irregular or prohibited importing or exporting.

JOB TITLES
- Customs Inspector
- Transportation Manager
- Purchasing Manager
- Transportation Inspector
- Freight Inspectors
- Cargo and Freight Agent

EMPLOYMENT OUTLOOK
- Slower than average growth in employment of inspectors and compliance officers is expected.
- Employment of inspectors and compliance officers is seldom affected by general economic fluctuations. Federal, state, and local governments provide workers with considerable job security.
- Because of relatively attractive salaries and benefits, the number of qualified candidates exceeds the number of openings in many federal enforcement agencies; competition is expected to remain keen for the higher-paying jobs.

EDUCATION AND TRAINING
- Because of the diversity of the functions they perform, qualifications for inspector and compliance officer jobs differ greatly. Requirements include a combination of education, experience, and often a passing grade on a written examination. Employers may require college training, including courses related to the job.
- Special agents may be subjected to lie detector examinations, drug testing, or personality tests.

SALARY LEVELS
- In the federal government, the annual starting salaries for inspectors vary from $28,000 to $33,000. Average salaries include import specialists, $51,000, and customs inspectors, $43,000.
- Special agents can start at about $28,000 a year, with salaries progressing to over $60,000.

CRITICAL THINKING
1. Which job titles in this area appeal to you most? Give reasons for your choice.
2. What are some things you will have to do to achieve success in the career selected?

FOCUS ON CAREERS

The careers listed in Focus on Careers come from the *Occupational Outlook Handbook*, an online publication (www.bls.gov/oco) of the federal government. The O*NET codes for these job titles are: Customs Inspector, 33-3021.05; Transportation Manager, 11-3071.02; Purchasing Manager, 11-3061.00; Transportation Inspector, 53-6051.00; Freight Inspectors, 53-6051.06; Cargo and Freight Agent, 43-5011.00. Students can access O*NET Online (online.onetcenter.org) and use these codes to view the most important features of selected occupations, including characteristics of the worker and requirements of the work. They can also search for related occupations and for occupations that match selected skills.

As a supplemental activity, distribute the Career Focus worksheets found in the School-To-Work/SCANS Activity Masters.

CRITICAL THINKING
Answers, of course, to the two Critical Thinking questions will vary widely. Students should be encouraged to select one job even if they are not really interested in the career area. Thinking about why a certain job might possibly be appealing is a forced-thinking exercise that results in self-reflection and self-examination. Answering these questions also gives certain career areas a sharper focus within students' minds.

UNIT 4

BUILDING YOUR PORTFOLIO

CAREER DEVELOPMENT – SPECIFYING PERSONAL INFORMATION/ACCOMPLISHMENTS

The Building Your Portfolio career exercise will help your students establish a personal history–where they have been, where they are now, and where they are going. This career exercise will require students to focus on documents that verify their interests, skills, and achievements.

Emphasize that employers often ask students to supply personal information and evidence of achievements as part of the screening process for employment. Have students identify documents employers often use to assess a person's qualifications for a job. Examples include a driver's license, work permit, Social Security card, report cards, copies of awards, honors, or certificates. Ask students to list all special accomplishments, achievements, or recognition received in high school and through other activities. Also have them list any scholarships or honors earned. Students should write a report explaining why a person seeking employment should be thorough in documenting accomplishments and special achievements.

As a supplemental activity, you may refer to the School–To–Work/SCANS Activity Masters.

TEACHING STRATEGIES

SCANS

Special Features

Media/Technology

Chapter	Spreadsheet Software	Database Software	Word Processing Software	Internet	Video
12	■				■
13		■		■	■
14	■				■

Resources

SOFTWARE

Excel, Word, WordPerfect, Works, and ClarisWorks for Mac and Windows

Word Pro, ASCII, QuattroPro, Lotus, and Access for Windows

SOUTH-WESTERN EDUCATIONAL PUBLISHING PRODUCTS

Everard and Burrow. *Business Principles and Management*. 2001. Cincinnati: South-Western Educational Publishing Company. Textbook. 0-538-69793-8.

Greene. *Entrepreneurship: Ideas In Action*. 2004. Cincinnati: South-Western Educational Publishing Company. Textbook. 0-538-43600-X.

BOOKS

Sherman. *The Complete Guide to Running and Growing Your Business*. 1997. Times Books.

Bygrave and Bygrave. *The Portable MBA in Entrepreneurship*. 1997. John Wiley & Sons.

PERIODICALS

Black Enterprise. E. G. Graves Publishing Co. New York, NY.

Entrepreneur. Entrepreneur, Inc. Irvine, CA.

Success. Success Magazine Co. New York, NY.

The Wall Street Journal. New York, NY.

GOVERNMENT PUBLICATIONS

Occupational Outlook Handbook, U.S. Department of Labor, Washington, DC.

What Work Requires of Schools: A SCANS Report for America 2000, U.S. Department of Labor, Washington, DC

MEDIA/TECHNOLOGY

Publisher's web sites:

www.intro2business.swep.com

www.swep.com

www.thomson.com

UNIT 4

SMALL BUSINESS MANAGEMENT

This unit examines the cornerstone of our free enterprise system—small businesses. Small businesses are the largest employer in our economy, provide the primary opportunities for beginning employees, and illustrate the concept of equal opportunity. Almost anyone who has a business idea can develop that idea into a business if they have the desire.

The chapters in the unit develop an understanding of the requirements to be an entrepreneur, the importance of human resources to small businesses, the procedures for producing and marketing products and services, and the importance of financial decision making to small-business success. Together, the chapters provide an introduction to small-business management that should interest and challenge students who have dreams of owning their own business.

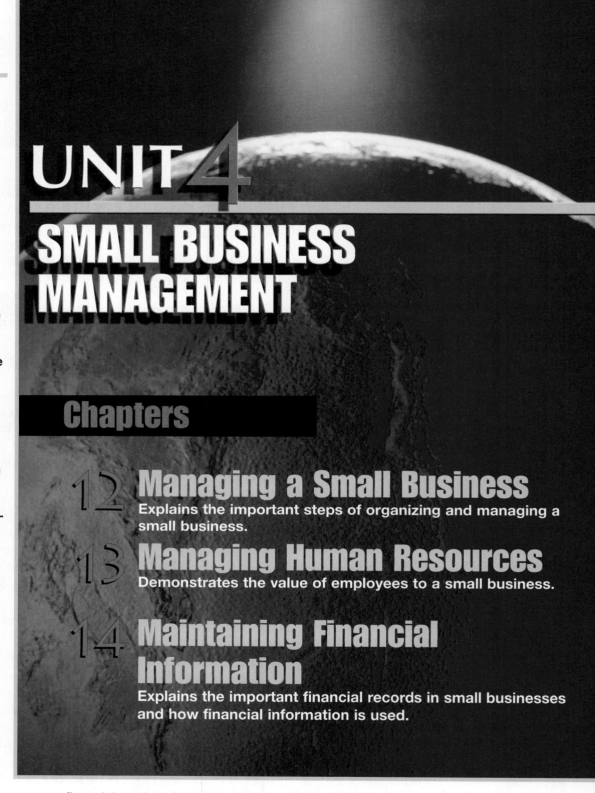

UNIT 4
SMALL BUSINESS MANAGEMENT

Chapters

12 Managing a Small Business
Explains the important steps of organizing and managing a small business.

13 Managing Human Resources
Demonstrates the value of employees to a small business.

14 Maintaining Financial Information
Explains the important financial records in small businesses and how financial information is used.

Kick-Off Activity

Investigating Business Media

To make the connection between today's business news and *Intro to Business*, an opening activity is provided for student investigation that pertains to Unit 4. The following exercise asks students to choose an article from *The Wall Street Journal*, the financial section of a newspaper, or a business magazine and to inquire about a topic related to this unit. The Critical Thinking questions are designed to help students conduct an organized and purposeful investigation of business media.

Have students find two articles from *The Wall Street Journal* or a financial magazine that profile two entrepreneurs and then answer the following questions:

1 What experience, skills, and business backgrounds do the two leaders have? Are there any striking differences in their backgrounds or leadership abilities?

2 What kinds of business challenges have these two leaders faced? What actions did they take to deal with these challenges?

BU$INESSBRIEF

BU$INESSBRIEF

BETTER THAN BIG

You need someone to mow your lawn, prepare a gourmet meal in your home for a few close friends, build a customized display case for a model train, or install some specialized hardware on your home computer. Where would you turn for help? It's not likely that you will find a large business for any of those services. Small businesses play an important role in our economy. They often serve customers where the number of products and services needed is small or the requirements are too specialized for large businesses to be profitable.

It is easier for a small business to meet the specific needs of customers than a large business. Even though a large business has more resources, to operate efficiently it must focus on products and services that meet the needs of a large group of customers. That makes it more difficult to satisfy the unique needs of individual customers.

While small businesses may not be able to match the lower operating costs of larger businesses, they can compete by paying attention to their customers. Small businesses serve fewer customers and usually have more frequent contact with those customers than large businesses. They are more likely to be located closer to the customer and depend less on other businesses to distribute or service their products. While large businesses may rely on consumer research to gather information, small businesses usually get direct information from their customers about what they like and dislike.

Small businesses are especially suited to provide unique services for customers ranging from wedding planning to designing a customized sound system for your home. Providing those types of services requires that the business representative take a special interest in the customer, spend time determining needs and discussing alternatives, and have the expertise to plan and deliver the services that satisfy the customer. Large businesses may not find it profitable to spend that much time with each customer, and each employee that works with customers may not have the expertise to design the needed service.

Big business has a decided advantage when a large number of customers is willing to buy standard products and prefer low cost and efficient delivery. Small businesses gain an advantage when customers have unique needs, want more individualized attention, and are willing to pay a bit more for the product or service to obtain what they really want. When asked, "What businesses do you believe are most concerned about you as a customer?" the majority of consumers identify small businesses.

CRITICAL THINKING

1 *Why would customers have greater confidence that small businesses could meet their needs even though they probably make more purchases from large businesses?*

2 *Identify two or three small businesses that have been successful for several years and describe what you think they do that allows them to compete successfully with large businesses.*

159

A Business Brief sets the tone for a unit. This particular Brief describes the advantages small businesses have over large corporations.

CRITICAL THINKING

1 Many routine purchases are common products that are not particularly unique so customers want to buy them at a convenient location for a low price. However, when customers have unique needs they may want to go to a local business that they believe will listen to their needs, sell them the best product or service, and be available to help if problems occur.

2 Students can provide many examples. Many of the examples will be businesses that emphasize unique products and services, have a reputation for quality and a high level of customer service, or are well-respected businesses in the community.

BUILDING YOUR PORTFOLIO

The Building Your Portfolio work samples validate skill level and a student's ability to accomplish tasks frequently performed on the job. The most important reason for including samples in a portfolio is to demonstrate a student's abilities and skills. In selecting work samples for each unit, students should always have a choice of which activities to include. Students might be encouraged to include samples from the end-of-chapter activities, particularly Communicate Business Concepts, Calculate Business Data, Technology Application, and Decision-Making Strategies.

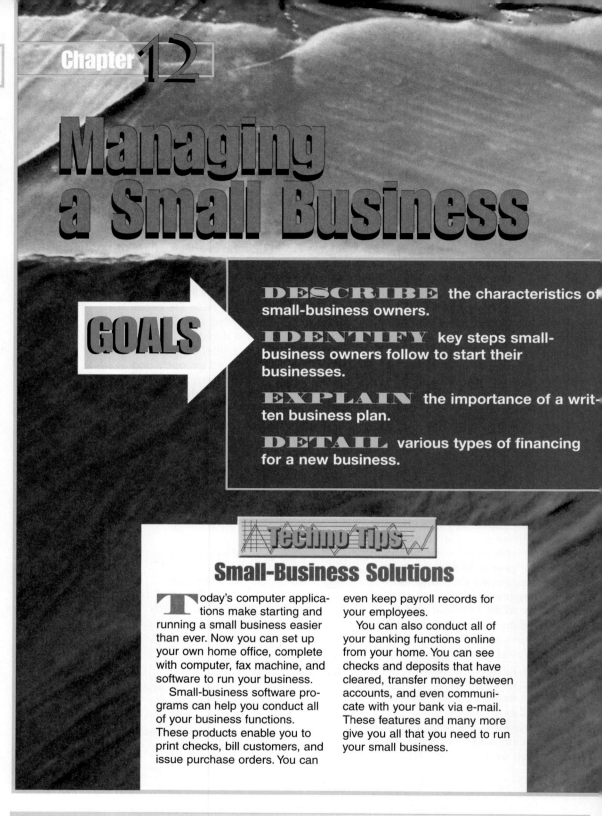

Small-business management involves a very complex set of tasks. This chapter explains the important steps of organizing and managing a small business. The outline of a business plan is presented.

Resources For Teachers
- Lesson Plans
- School-To-Work/SCANS Activity Masters
- Spanish Resources
- Instructor's Resource CD

Assessment
- Chapter and Unit Tests, Ch. 12
- ExamView, Ch. 12

Media/Technology
- Applying Technology Data CD
- PowerPoint slides
- Business Connection CD
- Videotape

Activity Masters and Workbooks
- Activities and Projects, Ch. 12
- Internet Activity Masters
- Business Math Activity Masters
- Communications Activity Masters
- International Business Activity Masters
- Ethics Activity Masters

Chapter 12

Managing a Small Business

GOALS

DESCRIBE the characteristics of small-business owners.

IDENTIFY key steps small-business owners follow to start their businesses.

EXPLAIN the importance of a written business plan.

DETAIL various types of financing for a new business.

Techno Tips

Small-Business Solutions

Today's computer applications make starting and running a small business easier than ever. Now you can set up your own home office, complete with computer, fax machine, and software to run your business.

Small-business software programs can help you conduct all of your business functions. These products enable you to print checks, bill customers, and issue purchase orders. You can even keep payroll records for your employees.

You can also conduct all of your banking functions online from your home. You can see checks and deposits that have cleared, transfer money between accounts, and even communicate with your bank via e-mail. These features and many more give you all that you need to run your small business.

Techno Tips

Students need to know the latest technologies and develop cutting edge Internet skills for use in current jobs, future careers, or in their homes. TechnoTips introduces students to today's cutting edge technologies and provides them with important Internet skills. Feature topics concentrate on Internet-specific technologies and computer or other hi-tech innovations for use by businesses and consumers.

During dinner, Jasmine excitedly told her family what happened in her Introduction to Business class that day. The class had spent the time considering opportunities for owning a small business and Jasmine knew that is what she wanted to do.

After the meal, Jasmine's grandfather sat down with her and said, "Did you know I ran a small business for almost 10 years when I was young? I was as excited as you are about starting a business when I graduated from high school. That was almost 50 years ago. I went to work for the owner of a small hardware store and hoped that I could save enough money to open my own store. Luckily, after eight years, he decided to retire. We worked out an arrangement where I could buy the store from him over a number of years."

"What happened to the business?" Jasmine asked.

"Being a small business owner is exciting, but it is a difficult life," explained her grandfather. "As the bigger stores moved in, I found it more and more difficult to attract customers. I decided to sell the business, but often wonder if I could have kept it going through all those years. I'm excited for you, but want you to know that your goals will be a challenge to achieve."

IDENTIFYING THE SMALL-BUSINESS OWNER

Independence, control, the chance to set your own schedule and make your own decisions—it sounds like everyone's dream. But long hours, customer complaints, meeting a payroll, taking responsibility for every problem—most people would want to avoid these job characteristics. As a small-business owner, you have to accept both the good and the bad. You own the business, so it is your responsibility to make it successful.

What It Takes

Small-business ownership is risky. Fewer than half of all new businesses will survive for five years. It takes a unique person to be a successful small-business owner. Some of the requirements are personality-based (such as self-motivation, risk-taking, and persistence). Other requirements are business-related (such as knowledge and skills). The small-business owner will be responsible for most, if not all, of the decisions needed to operate the business. Operating a business requires skill in management, finance, marketing, and other business activities.

One of the most important requirements for a successful small business is effort. Most small-business owners report working much harder than they did when they were employed by someone else. However, for people who want to own a business, the long hours of work provide a great deal of satisfaction.

Who Owns Small Businesses

No one set of characteristics describes small-business owners. Many years ago, the majority of small-business owners were middle-aged males with less than a college education. Today, small-business owners are more educated, younger, and are more likely to be female or minorities. New business owners who are women are increasing at a rate almost three times that of men. Women now make up over 40 percent of all small-business owners.

People of non-white ethnic and racial heritage are another fast growing segment of

Nearly 600,000 new businesses are started in the United States each year.

Find out which students have earned money by running their own businesses. Ask these questions: Did they start their businesses—out of the need for money? out of interest in the activity? out of a desire to do something independently? Then ask: How did they enjoy working for themselves? Would they do it again? What conclusions can they draw about the reasons why someone might start a business?

they will find them and what sort of investors they will be.

TRY THIS/GUIDED PRACTICE

Lead a discussion of the following question: Do you think it is absolutely necessary to start a business that involves something you know and like? Write on the board two headings: WHY? or WHY NOT? List on the board points provided by students. The class can openly debate the topic and decide by vote which position the class favors.

Before showing PowerPoint 12-2, *Identifying the Small Business Owner*, ask students to think about the typical characteristics of small business owners. Then use the slide to show how the characteristics are changing. Have students discuss why small business ownership provides opportunities for almost anyone.

Ask students to list on a sheet of paper various things a business owner will need to buy during the first three years of the business. Compile a complete list on the board based on student responses. Then show PowerPoint 12-6, *Financing the Small Business,* to explain the three types of financing. Walk the class through the list of items and classify them as fitting into the start-up, short-term, or long-term categories. Discuss why there are differences in the three categories.

Divide the class into four discussion groups. Using PowerPoint 12-3, *Starting the Small Business*, assign one of the bullet points to each group. Have the group discuss why the point they have been assigned is important to the success of the new small business.

NET FACTS

Instead of sending and reading written documents as e-mail, in the future you will use the Internet for video and voice mail. If the person you want to reach is not available, you will be able to leave a message for video playback later.

small-business owners. During the 1990s, the number of minority-owned small businesses grew to 3.2 million. That was an increase of over 30 percent during the decade. The three largest groups of minority business owners are Asian-Americans, Hispanic-Americans, and African-Americans. Some minority business owners often face serious limitations in starting a business. These limitations include lack of available financing, limited management experience, and prejudicial treatment by financial institutions, vendors, and other businesses.

Programs and services have been established by the federal government and by banks, universities, and some franchisors to assist minorities in their efforts to start and operate their own businesses. Minority-owned small businesses can be successful when adequate opportunities and resources are available.

STARTING THE SMALL BUSINESS

Many people think about starting a business but few do. The procedures followed to start a business often determine whether it will be successful. The process begins with an idea and concludes with a careful study of information to determine whether the idea can be successful.

An Idea Plus Experience

Every business begins with an idea. Business ideas come from many sources. Hobbies,

interests, and business experiences often give people ideas for new businesses. Books and magazines suggest new business opportunities, including available franchises.

Few people should consider starting a business without working for some time in a small business. Several years of training in various aspects of business operations will prepare you for the role of owner. Having opportunities to manage people and responsibility for decisions is an important part of that experience.

What challenges are faced by minority small-business owners?

Personal Qualities-Self-Management

Self-management is an important skill that students need to possess. The ability to assess oneself, set personal goals, monitor progress, and exhibit self-control can be reinforced in this chapter by having students examine successful entrepreneurs. Have students read an entrepreneurial success story. Biographies are available on many successful entrepreneurs including J. Paul Getty, Conrad Hilton, Henry Ford, etc. Students can write reports on what they conceive as the essential self-management characteristics of these entrepreneurs.

Right Place and Time

Putting your business idea into action means finding the right location to open the business. Most retail businesses require good customer traffic. If the business is difficult to find or requires a great deal of travel time, many potential customers will stay away. A wholesaler needs easy access to manufacturers where products are obtained for resale to other businesses. Manufacturers must be located in an area with access to the raw materials used in manufacturing. Transportation systems must also be accessible for distributing finished products. Timing is another important factor in starting a business. Most successful businesses start during a period when customer demand for certain products or services is high.

Team Approach

Many small-business owners are quite independent. Their businesses were started because they do not want to take direction from other people. A business is difficult to start, however, without the help of others. Even the smallest businesses need a few full- or part-time employees. The employees must be selected carefully for their ability to work as a team. Choosing the "team" becomes one of the most important initial business decisions.

In addition to employees, small-business owners will require assistance from bankers, lawyers, accountants, and other people with specialized business knowledge. If possible, business professionals who specialize in working with small businesses should be identified.

Preparation and Research

The most important step in starting a business is preparation. Preparation includes having adequate information to make good decisions about the business. Time spent gathering and studying information before the business is started will save time and avoid later problems.

Information is needed about customers, competitors, important operations and activities, government regulations, and many other topics. This information is available through libraries, colleges or universities, and small-business assistance centers. However, occasionally the new business owner will have to do additional research to gather more current data. Information will help to ensure that decisions are made objectively.

DEVELOPING A BUSINESS PLAN

When successful businesses are compared with those that failed, one factor stands out as the most important difference. The owners of successful businesses develop and follow a business plan. The owners of businesses that fail often do not have a business plan.

What Is a Business Plan?

A **business plan** is a written description of the business idea and how it will be carried out, including all major business activities. Key features of a business plan are a general description of the company, the qualifications of the owner(s), a description of the product or service, an analysis of the market (demand, customers, competition), and a financial plan. Most business plans are developed for one year and then updated for the next year. If the business owner needs assistance from others, especially for financing the new business, a business plan will usually be required.

Even if help is not needed, a business plan must be developed. By developing a plan, the owner is forced to think about important activities, the amount of time they will take, and their cost. That process may identify potential problems. The plan also serves as a guide to keep the business on track. Figure 12-1 is an outline of the sections of a business plan.

One purpose for which bankers use business plans is to see whether the prospective business owner is committed to the business.

Each group should summarize their discussion for the other groups.

EXPLORE THIS/INDEPENDENT PRACTICE Have students prepare a written one-page response to the question, "What are the most important skills of a small-business owner?" Ask if they would like to be an owner of a small business based on their study of this chapter and to provide reasons for their choices.

Have students consider two business plans—one for a retail store and another for a manufacturing firm. Other than in their operations sections, how would the two documents differ from each other? Students should refer to Figure 12-1 in preparing a written response to the question.

The Chapter Review questions at the end of the chapter vary in level of difficulty. For a basic assignment, consider Develop Your Business Language and Review Your Reading. For an average assignment, consider the basic assignment plus Communicate Business Concepts and Calculate Business Data. For an enhanced assignment, try the average assignment plus Technology Application and Decision-Making Strategies.

ASSESS

Review the goals at the beginning of the chapter and the Business Notes at the end of the chapter. Have students respond orally or in writing to each of the Business Notes restated as a question, provided on page 164. For those who may have difficulty providing

Basic Skills-Reading

SCANS

Employers are looking for potential employees with good basic foundation skills. Students may improve their reading skills by first developing pre-reading routines. Explore the goals at the beginning of the chapter with your students. Have a student read the goals out loud so that all will be aware of the various new learnings that will occur in the chapter. By previewing goals, students will be able to recognize facts that are relevant when they begin reading the chapter. The Student Activity Worksheet, Basic Skills—Reading, in the School-To-Work/SCANS Activity Masters, may be used to serve as a guideline for discussion of each of these points. After the students are comfortable with this pre-reading strategy, ask them this question: Based on the objectives, what do you think you will learn?

answers, assign the reteaching activities that follow. Enrichment activities may also be assigned where appropriate.

1. What are the characteristics of small-business owners? (Answer: Small-business owners are independent, self-motivated, risk-takers, persistent, hard workers, have technical knowledge and management ability.)

2. What are the steps a small-business owner takes to start a business? (Answer: Small-business ownership begins with an idea. Putting a business idea into action means finding the right location for a business and choosing the right team to help run the business. The most important step in starting a business is preparation—spending the necessary time gathering and studying information before the business is started.)

3. What is the importance of a business plan? (Answer: A written business plan serves as an objective guide to the development of a new business.)

4. Explain the types of financing needed to run a small business. (Answer: The three types of financing needed by many small businesses are start-up financing, short-term financing, and long-term financing.)

BUSINESS PLAN ELEMENTS

Description of the Business
- the business idea
- major products and services
- ownership structure
- strengths/weaknesses
- long- and short-term goals

Description of Competition
- characteristics of the industry
- condition of the economy
- strengths and weaknesses of major competitors

Customer Analysis
- description of customers
- location, number, and resources of customers
- sales forecasts

Operations Plan
- organization of the company
- description of major operations
- analysis of resources needed
- human resource plans

Marketing Plan
- description of major marketing activities
- description of resources needed
- schedule of marketing activities

Financial Plans
- start-up costs
- short- and long-term financial needs
- sources of financing
- budgets and financial statements

FIGURE 12-1 Do you see why each of these elements is needed?

Steps in Developing the Business Plan

The business owner is responsible for developing the business plan. The most popular use of business plans is to persuade lenders and investors to finance the venture. A well developed plan will lay out an idea, require an owner to analyze his or her concept, and make decisions about key business activities such as production, marketing, staffing, and financing.

Some owners hire someone to write the plan. Others get help from a bank or a local office of the Small Business Administration. Even if others are involved in developing the plan, the owner must be familiar with all of the information and make the major decisions for the plan.

The first step in developing the plan is to gather and review information. If possible, the owner should review other business plans and study information on the activities and financial performance of similar businesses, especially potential competitors. Next, the owner should develop the "game plan." Alternative plans for production, marketing, staffing, and financing should be studied and identified. The owner can select the best choices from the alternatives. Finally, each section of the business plan should be written. A plan devotes sections to a general description of the business, including the basic legal form of an organization and major products or services, the competition, potential customers, operations, marketing, and finances. Before the plan is completed, the owner should have other business professionals review the plan and offer their advice about its strengths and weaknesses.

FINANCING THE SMALL BUSINESS

A new business with a good product or service idea may run out of money before it can become profitable. Several years of operation usually are required before a new business earns a profit. Obtaining adequate financing is an important step in starting and operating a new business.

164 **Unit 4** *Small Business Management*

TECHNOLOGICAL PERSPECTIVES

Making Small Businesses Competitive

Small businesses sometimes have difficulty competing with large businesses. The resources of big businesses provide many advantages. Products are produced in greater quantities with attention to quality standards. Research departments provide access to information and new product ideas.

Today, technology has leveled the playing field. Inexpensive computer systems provide power to small businesses that once only large businesses could afford. The Internet has opened up data to every business at a low cost. Products are transported by express delivery services.

Low-cost technology makes all businesses competitive. Small businesses can compete if they have the technology and can use it.

Computer literacy is a requirement for small-business owners. A recent survey showed that small businesses using personal computers, facsimile machines, and cellular telephones were experiencing the highest rate of growth in their markets.

Critical Thinking

1. Should small businesses invest heavily in new technology as soon as it becomes available? Or, should a small business wait until the technology is more affordable? Provide reasons for your answer.

2. What are the important computer skills a small-business owner should have today? How do you believe those skills will change in the next ten years?

ENRICH

Direct students to read the Technological Perspectives in this chapter. Have students develop a new business idea. Then ask them to answer the following questions: Do I know enough about the business? How much will it cost to start the business? Will I have to borrow money? Do I need a partner? Does this business have a chance to grow? How much competition will I have? Will my interest be in this business in the future?

Ask students to investigate the advantages and disadvantages of working for someone else, particularly as a manager. How does the role of manager compare with the possible risks and rewards of owning a business?

SUMMARIZE

Complete this activity to help students fully understand the concepts in this chapter. Prepare questions pertaining to the chapter content ahead of time. Then, asking one question at a time, allow a student one minute, for example, to answer the question. After the time is up, go to the next student. Keep score of correct answers. The student with the most points wins the game.

EVALUATE

- Assign Activities and Projects for Chapter 12.
- Administer the printed test or ExamView for Chapter 12.
- Assign School-To-Work/SCANS portfolio activities for Unit 4.

Types of Financing

Three types of financing must be considered. **Start-up financing** is the amount of money needed to open the business. It includes the cost of buildings, equipment, *inventory* (goods or raw materials on hand), supplies, licenses, and the like.

Short-term financing is the money needed to pay for the current operating activities of a business. Short-term financing is obtained for a period of less than a year and often for one or two months.

Long-term financing is money needed for the important resources of a business (such as land, buildings, and equipment) that will last for many years. These resources usually require large amounts of money and will be paid for over a number of years.

Sources of Financing

Finding the necessary money may be the most difficult part of starting a business. The money needed to start and operate a new business usually comes from a combination of owner-supplied and borrowed funds. The source of owner-supplied money depends on the ownership structure.

In a proprietorship, one person will supply the money, while in a partnership, the partners will each be expected to contribute. A corporation is owned and financed by the shareholders. Borrowed funds are obtained through loans from banks and other financial institutions, or through financing provided by other companies.

TECHNOLOGICAL PERSPECTIVES

CRITICAL THINKING

1. A purchasing decision will hinge on the cost of the technology and whether competitors are using the technology. Small businesses have limited financial resources, so owners must be careful with money spent. Technology should probably be purchased if it will increase the amount of sales or allow the business to operate more efficiently.

2. A critical skill is the ability to operate the computer and use standard business software for word processing, spreadsheets, and databases. Computers are becoming easier to use, and computer usage among small-business owners will become more widespread.

REVIEW YOUR READING

1. Examples of positive aspects: in control, independent, set one's own schedule, and make decisions for the business. Examples of negative aspects: customer complaints, meeting payroll, and taking responsibility for every problem.
2. A successful business owner must be self-motivated, a risk-taker, persistent. Other requirements include knowledge of business operations, skill at operating a business, and willingness to work long hours.
3. Today small-business owners are more educated, younger, and more likely to be female or minorities.
4. Every business begins with an idea.
5. Preparation is important in starting a business because the person beginning it needs to plan ahead. In addition, money needs to be set aside, borrowed from the bank, and people need to decide how to start up the business.
6. Three important steps in developing a business plan are gathering and reviewing information; finding alternatives for operations, marketing, and financing; and each section of the business plan should be written.
7. A lack of adequate financing may cause a business to run out of money before becoming profitable.

COMMUNICATE BUSINESS CONCEPTS

8. Jasmine's grandfather stated that his small business took up a lot of his time. Because many small-business owners work long hours the first few years, they have time for little else. In addition, each small-business owner must take responsibility for every problem. Jasmine's grandfather may have wanted to work for someone else to make his life more stress-free.
9. Because Michael worked for a major clothing company for such an extended period of time, he learned the operations of that company. Michael was able to see how the business was set up, and he was able to learn how the company worked. Through the years, Michael probably learned how to handle problems and take responsibility for many aspects of business operations.

BUSINESS NOTES

1. Small-business owners are independent, self-motivated, risk takers, persistent, hard workers, and have technical knowledge and management ability.
2. Small-business ownership begins with an idea. Putting a business idea into action means finding the right location for a business and choosing the right team to help run the business. The most important step in starting a business is preparation—spending time gathering and studying information before the business is started.
3. A written business plan serves as an objective guide to the development of a new business.
4. The three primary types of financing needed by many small businesses are start-up financing, short-term financing, and long-term financing.

REVIEW YOUR READING

1. What are some of the positive and negative aspects of starting a small business?
2. What does it take to be a successful business owner?
3. How are the characteristics of small-business owners changing?
4. What is the first thing from which every business begins?
5. Why is preparation important when starting a business?
6. What are the three steps to follow when developing a business plan?
7. Why might a new business with a good product or service end up in failure?

COMMUNICATE BUSINESS CONCEPTS

8. Review the opening scenario about Jasmine and her grandfather. Why do you think Jasmine's grandfather decided to sell his small business instead of competing with larger companies?
9. Michael Andrews worked for a major clothing chain for 10 years, then decided to resign so he could open his own clothing store. What possible past experiences could enable Michael to start his own small business?
10. Timing and location are two key factors in starting a small business. Give an example of a particular small business from your community, and tell how either location or timing contributes to its success.
11. A business plan can be described as a "game plan." What features of such a plan justify that label?
12. Start-up financing, short-term financing, and long-term financing are all types of financing that must be considered when starting a new small business. Why should a new business owner be concerned about each of these types of financing?

10. Answers should specifically describe the location of the business or the time it was started or when products are sold.
11. A business plan is a written description that tells how the business is going to operate. A plan must be drawn up before a business can begin because lack of planning may cause the business to fail before it even gets started.
12. Each contributes to the growth and maintenance of the small business. Financing is essential at each stage of a company's development.

DEVELOP YOUR BUSINESS LANGUAGE

For each numbered item, find the term that has the same meaning.

13. The money needed to pay for the current operating activities of a business.

14. A written description of the business idea and how it will be carried out, including all major business operations.

15. The amount of money needed to open the business.

16. Money needed for the important resources of a business (such as land, buildings, and equipment) that will last for many years.

KEY TERMS
business plan
long-term financing
short-term financing
start-up financing

DECISION-MAKING STRATEGIES

David Obolski completed a community college program in Small Business Management. He now wanted to own his own florist business. He had worked for Flower-a-Bunda during high school and college. In addition to the work experience, he was able to save almost $20,000 toward starting his own business. However, he knew that he would need more than $20,000 to buy a florist shop. He would need almost double that amount to qualify for the necessary loans to start up the business.

David had studied three ways he might start his business.

    a. He could find a partner to provide the additional cash.

    b. He could work for the owner of Flower-a-Bunda until she retired in five years and buy the business with his accumulated savings.

    c. He could purchase a franchise available for an investment of $20,000. However, David would have to pay a franchise fee of 6 percent of total sales each year to the franchisor.

17. What are the advantages and disadvantages of each route to small-business ownership for David?

18. If you were David, which choice would you make? Why?

CALCULATE BUSINESS DATA

19. Jennifer Yukimura, a local high school student, started her own T-shirt business. The business had total sales for the year of $20,000. Jennifer's yearly expenses are shown in the table.

    a. What were the total expenses for the T-shirt business?

    b. What was the percentage of total expenses for each expense category?

    c. What percentage of total sales were the total expenses?

    d. How much profit, if any, did Jennifer earn?

20. According to a recent report of the Small Business Administration, the percentage of small businesses with access to the Internet increased from 21.5% to 41.2% in the last few years of the 1990s. In addition, small businesses that use the Internet have higher revenues than those that do not. They average $3.79 million compared to $2.72 million for non-Internet users. Small businesses report receiving 30% of their sales from the Internet.

Payroll	$5,000
Rent	7,000
Inventory	3,000
Equipment	2,500

Chapter 12 *Managing a Small Business*   **167**

DEVELOP YOUR BUSINESS LANGUAGE

13. start-up financing
14. business plan
15. short-term financing
16. long-term financing

DECISION-MAKING STRATEGIES

17. Sample answers are: (a) Advantages—lower investment by David; can go into business sooner; gets help with management. Disadvantages—has to share ownership, profits, and decision-making. (b) Advantages—gets to know the business well before taking over ownership; business is already successful. Disadvantages—takes a long time until ownership; business may change in five years. (c) Advantages—probably help with financing and management; buying a successful concept. Disadvantages—must follow the franchise business plan; the franchise fee could reduce profits.

18. Students should be able to justify any of the choices based on the perception of David's needs and resources.

CALCULATE BUSINESS DATA

19. (a) $5,000 + $7,000 + $3,000 + $2,500 = $17,500
(b) $5,000/$17,500 = 28.6%; $7,000 ÷ $17,500 = 40%; $3,000 ÷ $17,500 = 17.1%; $2,500 ÷ $17,500 = 14.3%
(c) $17,500 ÷ $20,000 = 87.5%
(d) $20,000 − $17,500 = $2,500

20. (a) 22.5 mil. × 41.2% = 9.27 mil. businesses; 41.2% − 21.5% × 22.5 mil. = 4.43 mil. businesses (b) (3.79 − 2.72) ÷ 2.72 = 39.3% (c) $3.79 × 0.30 = $1.14 mil.

21. (a) $80,000 + $6,700 + $4,300 + $4,950 + $2,050 + $750 = $98,750 total start-up costs
(b) $98,750 ÷ $110,000 = 89.8% spent on start-up costs
(c) $150,000 − $98,750 = $51,250 left over after short-term and long-term expenses

a. If there were approximately 22.5 million small businesses in the U.S. in the 1990s, how many had Internet access by the end of the 1990s? How many companies had added Internet access during the period reported?

b. By what percentage did the revenues of small businesses with Internet access exceed those of the other small businesses?

c. If the average small business with Internet access had sales of $3.79 million in one year, what amount was received from Internet sales?

21. Tahisha Bowers received a small-business loan for $110,000 to start a pet grooming business. She also invested $40,000 of her own savings. The amounts of her start-up expenses are shown in the table.

a. What were the total start-up costs for the business?

b. What percentage of the bank loan had to be spent for start-up costs?

c. How much money does Tahisha have available for short-term and long-term expenses?

Building	$80,000
Equipment:	
grooming	6,700
office	4,300
Inventory	4,950
Supplies	2,050
Licenses	750

TECHNOLOGY APPLICATION

Using the *Intro to Business* Data CD and your spreadsheet program software, select problem CH12. After the problem appears on your screen, complete the following activities. Then, after you have completed each step, display or print the completed spreadsheet. If you do not have a printer available, answer the questions before you leave the computer.

22. Enter formulas to calculate Total Start-up Expenses and Reserves (Total Funds Available − Total Start-up Expenses). Answer the following questions:
    a. What is the amount of Total Start-up Expenses?
    b. What is the amount of Reserves?

23. Copy all the data to an open part of the spreadsheet. Using absolute references, enter a formula to decrease the amount of the small-business loan by 10 percent. Answer the following questions:
    a. What is the new amount of Total Start-up Expenses?
    b. What is the new amount of Reserves?

24. Copy the second set of data to an open part of the spreadsheet. Enter formulas to increase each start-up expense by 12 percent. Answer the following questions:
    a. What is the new amount of Total Start-up Expenses?
    b. What is the new amount of Reserves?

Optional: For each set of data, create a pie chart showing the breakdown of the start-up expenses.

GLOBAL NAVIGATOR

FOREIGN GOVERNMENT AGENCIES

How can a small-business owner contact potential customers in other countries? Embassies, consulates, foreign trade offices, and foreign Chambers of Commerce are some of the foreign agencies available.

Embassies are official representatives of a foreign government. These offices usually have foreign trade specialists available to assist exporters with identifying potential markets. These trade specialists analyze current economic conditions and assist companies with various international trade activities.

Embassies also provide other services. As people travel to other countries, embassy staff members may assist them with various services and information. In an emergency, travelers commonly contact an embassy for assistance.

Similar to an embassy, a consulate is an office located in a foreign country that represents the home country, and serves the interests and businesses of the country it represents. Most countries have consulates in large cities throughout the world.

Countries and states establish trade offices in other nations to encourage inter-

> **Several government agencies are available to help small-business owners with international trade.**

national trade. For example, the European Union has a trade office in Washington, D.C. to contact potential buyers and sellers in the United States. Additionally, the state of Illinois has a foreign trade office in China in an attempt to expand exports to Asia.

Foreign Chambers of Commerce in the United States promote and encourage international trade for their countries. These organizations can assist importers and exporters with making contacts and providing information. Most of these Chambers of Commerce are located in New York City and Washington, D.C.; others, especially those representing Asian companies, are in San Francisco.

CRITICAL THINKING

1. Working in small groups, identify skills or abilities that would be useful for people who desire to work for an embassy, consulate, foreign trade office, or Chamber of Commerce.
2. Conduct a web search to locate information sources from embassies or Chambers of Commerce that would help a business when planning and implementing foreign trade activities.

Most students will either work with international clients or compete against businesses that do. Global Navigator introduces students to issues integral to working with international businesses. Key concepts and challenges faced by international businesses are presented, followed by two Critical Thinking questions that require students to analyze what they have learned.

This feature informs students about foreign government agencies and offices that can be of assistance to businesses seeking to expand into their markets. It differentiates and outlines the functions of embassies, consulates, trade offices, and foreign chambers of commerce in promoting trade and dispensing information to prospective trade partners . . . and students.

CRITICAL THINKING

1. Answers may include fluency in a relevant foreign language, experience in marketing, knowledge of international business law and accounting standards, experience working and traveling abroad.
2. Responses will vary widely, but most countries have numerous international trade offices that are accessible via the Internet.

Small-business owners must be able to determine when employees need to be hired. Other human resource responsibilities include developing compensation systems, determining employee benefits, and employee training.

Resources For Teachers
- Lesson Plans
- School-To-Work/SCANS Activity Masters
- Spanish Resources
- Instructor's Resource CD

Assessment
- Chapter and Unit Tests, Ch. 13
- ExamView, Ch. 13

Media/Technology
- Applying Technology Data CD
- PowerPoint slides
- Business Connection CD
- Videotape

Activity Masters and Workbooks
- Activities and Projects, Ch. 13
- Internet Activity Masters
- Business Math Activity Masters
- Communications Activity Masters
- International Business Activity Masters
- Ethics Activity Masters

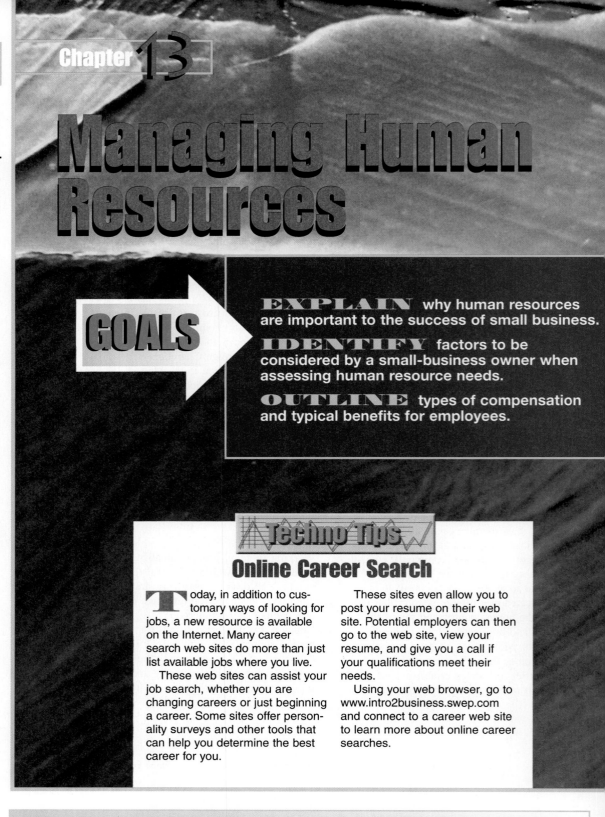

Managing Human Resources

GOALS

EXPLAIN why human resources are important to the success of small business.

IDENTIFY factors to be considered by a small-business owner when assessing human resource needs.

OUTLINE types of compensation and typical benefits for employees.

Techno Tips
Online Career Search

Today, in addition to customary ways of looking for jobs, a new resource is available on the Internet. Many career search web sites do more than just list available jobs where you live.

These web sites can assist your job search, whether you are changing careers or just beginning a career. Some sites offer personality surveys and other tools that can help you determine the best career for you.

These sites even allow you to post your resume on their web site. Potential employers can then go to the web site, view your resume, and give you a call if your qualifications meet their needs.

Using your web browser, go to www.intro2business.swep.com and connect to a career web site to learn more about online career searches.

Students need to know the latest technologies and develop cutting edge Internet skills for use in current jobs, future careers, or in their homes. TechnoTips introduces students to today's cutting edge technologies and provides them with important Internet skills. Feature topics concentrate on Internet-specific technologies and computer or other hi-tech innovations for use by businesses and consumers. At the www.intro2business.swep.com web site, students can complete the activity for this chapter.

Jaqueline Perez had come to the end of a busy week as she locked the door to her book-keeping service Friday evening. But she knew her work wasn't finished. For the third time this year, she was going to have to replace one of her best employees who had resigned to take a position with a larger competitor. She owned a small company employing 15 full-time and 12 part-time employees. The business had been more successful than she had hoped in its first three years, but the personnel problems were challenging.

Ms. Perez knew that her employees were important to the success of her business. They were responsible for completing the bookkeeping for customers accurately and on time. Because of their importance, Jaqueline had tried to support them with a good work environment. She encouraged them to develop their skills by giving them time off from work to attend training programs and to take college classes. Because of the training, all of her employees had become very skilled at using computer systems for maintaining business records. However, it seemed that just as an employee got to the point where he or she was really doing a good job, the employee would be hired by a larger business paying higher wages or offering better benefits.

Jaqueline knew that as a small-business owner she would not be able to compete with the wages and benefits offered by larger businesses. She had hoped that the small-business work environment and the emphasis on training would help her retain employees. Now it seemed that she was the one paying the training costs for the larger businesses.

IMPORTANCE OF HUMAN RESOURCES

Human resources, the people who work for a business, are important to every business. In small businesses with only a few employees, the impact of one person can be very noticeable. Employees of small businesses are usually responsible for a number of activities. A customer who has a problem with an employee may not have the opportunity to work with another employee of the business.

In a small business, the owner may be the only manager, or in the owner's absence, an experienced employee may be responsible for managing the business. In this case, employees of the small business may be called on to make key decisions and to solve problems as they occur. The employees may be responsible for many of the duties often considered management tasks.

HUMAN RESOURCE NEEDS

Since employees are so important to the success of a small business, the owner must be skilled in human resource management. **Human resource management** ensures that needed employees are available and that they are productive, paid, and satisfied with their work. Human resource management begins by an employer analyzing where the business currently is in terms of staffing and where it wants to be.

Categorizing Human Resources

Staffing is a vital part of human resource management. The decision to hire people must be made carefully. Once an employee is hired, the person's salary must be paid whether the company is profitable or not. An employee should be hired when the work of the employee will contribute more to the company's profitability

FOCUS ON REAL LIFE

Ask students to describe the ideal employee from a small-business owner's perspective. Use the characteristics that are suggested to compile a profile on the board. Then have students explain how a business owner might go about locating, hiring, and retaining such employees.

MOTIVATE

PURPOSE Have students review each of the chapter goals. Then have them skim the chapter to become familiar with its organization and the major topics to be covered. Ask them to write one question for each of the goals. Use some of the questions to guide discussion about the chapter.

TEACH/APPLY

MAKE CONNECTIONS Have students identify important needs of employees. What is more important to them—job interest, security, pay, prestige? Emphasize that motivation is influenced by needs.

Ask students to describe the best "boss" that they ever worked with—the "boss" could be an employer, coach, or teacher. Have them discuss that person's traits in terms of motivating others to perform to the best of their abilities.

Place the following definition of human resource management on the board: "The process of acquiring, training, developing, motivating, and using people properly to achieve the objectives of a business." Ask students to read the *Focus On Real Life.* Then ask them to discuss how they believe Jaqueline Perez can try to keep the employees of her business from leaving to work for larger businesses. For each suggestion, encourage students to consider what it might cost the business and why it might result in fewer employees leaving the business.

Lead a discussion of the following situation: Angela has been the owner of a health food store for the past year. Two part-time employees have children under the age of six. Another employee has a parent who is recovering from cancer surgery. All want additional time off. Ask students to explain how they would deal with this problem.

Walk students through a discussion of hiring new employees. Ask students who are employed if their businesses have increased or decreased the number of employees recently. If there have been changes, ask how they believe the owners/managers made decisions about the number of employees needed. Also review the outline of a business plan shown in Chapter 12 to identify parts of the plan that can give information about employment needs.

Ask students why they believe companies are relying more and more on temporary and part-time employees rather than permanent, full-time employees. What problems do they believe the company may encounter with this change?

Direct students to look up the word compensate in a dictionary. The equivalent definition is "counterbalance." Ask how this definition might apply to this chapter. (Possible answer: Compensation in the form of salary, wages, commissions, and fringe benefits acts to counterbalance a worker's expenditure of time and effort on the job.)

Why are good employees so vital to the success of a small business?

than it will cost. The owner must determine whether the person hired will be permanent or temporary.

A **permanent employee** is one to whom the company makes a long-term commitment. It is expected that the employee will continue to work for the business as long as the business is profitable and the employee's performance is satisfactory. A **temporary employee** is one hired for a specific time or to complete a specific assignment. Whether permanent or temporary, employees can be hired full-time or part-time. A **full-time employee** regularly works a schedule of 30 hours or more a week. A **part-time employee** works less than a full-time employee by working either fewer hours each day or fewer days each week.

Because permanent employees feel that they are a part of the business, they are often more motivated and productive than temporary employees. However, the owner has more

control over the company's resources when temporary employees are hired. The employee is paid only until the temporary assignment ends. Temporary employees are usually hired during a particularly busy time for the business or when a special task needs to be completed.

Determining Employee Qualifications

Before beginning the hiring process, the owner should study the work that must be completed in the business and compare the work requirements with the skills of the current employees. The goal is to hire people with skills that benefit the company but are not available from current employees.

There are two parts to the study of work requirements in preparation for hiring new employees. First, the current work of the business should be reviewed. Next, any new activities planned for the business should be considered. The business plan is a good source to identify those new activities. After completing the study, the owner will decide if a new employee is needed and the skills required of that person. At that time, it can be determined if the business's needs can be best met with temporary, permanent, part-time, or full-time employees.

Locating New Employees

Once the specific need and skill requirements are determined, prospective employees meeting the requirements must be located. If not done carefully, a great deal of time and expense may be required to complete the search and an appropriate employee may still not be found.

Young people and older people are frequently hired by small businesses. The first job

Small businesses are considered the best place to prepare for a career in business. Employees learn a greater variety of skills and are given more independence and responsibility sooner.

Personal Qualities-Sociability

Sociability skills are sometimes difficult for high school students to acquire. To demonstrate understanding, friendliness, adaptability, and politeness, group activities can be developed whenever cooperative learning or teams activities occur. Discuss sociability skills with students before beginning any collaborative learning situations.

many people hold in their working lives is in a small business. Also, people who have retired from full-time work and want to continue in part-time employment may be attracted to small businesses. The small business may provide a convenient work location, more flexibility in work schedules, and offer a pleasant place to work.

Another group of prospective employees are skilled people who want more decision-making responsibility, would like greater variety in their work, or prefer to work in a small organization. They are willing to work for less to obtain the benefits of a small company environment.

Several good sources of prospective employees exist that small-business owners should consider, as identified in Figure 13-1. Sources should be used that will provide an adequate number of candidates for the position who have the skills required for the job and the interest in working for the business.

Hiring a New Employee

The hiring procedure used by new small businesses is often much less formal than that used by larger companies. Even though less time may be spent in the hiring process and the business owner may not be an expert in hiring procedures, care should be taken to gather specific information to determine if the applicant is qualified for the job. Figure 13-2 lists sources of information about the qualifications of job applicants.

FIGURE 13-1 How would an employer find you if you were seeking a job?

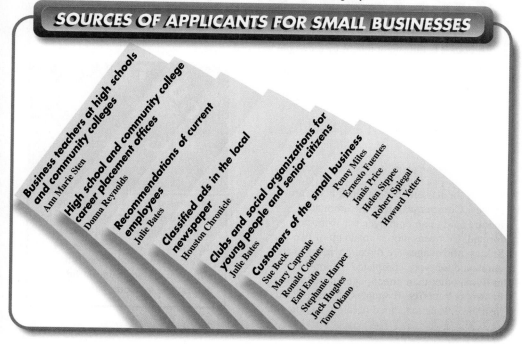

SOURCES OF APPLICANTS FOR SMALL BUSINESSES

Business teachers at high schools and community colleges
Ann Marie Sten

High school and community college career placement offices
Donna Reynolds

Recommendations of current employees
Julie Bates

Classified ads in the local newspaper
Houston Chronicle

Clubs and social organizations for young people and senior citizens
Julie Bates

Customers of the small business
Sue Beck
Mary Caporale
Ronald Costner
Emi Endo
Stephanie Harper
Jack Hughes
Tom Okano
Penny Miles
Ernesto Fuentes
Janis Price
Helen Sippee
Robert Spiegal
Howard Yetter

EXPLORE THIS/INDEPENDENT PRACTICE For each of the following situations, ask students to decide what might be done to correct the problem or improve the situation. Students should prepare written responses.

a. Lydia Aponte owns a small company. She is quite pleased with an employee's performance, David Mendez. However, because of the company's weak financial condition, she can only afford to give David a small raise. How can Lydia handle this situation? She wants to keep David highly motivated despite the small raise given.

b. A new worker, Mo Sun, is highly motivated and constantly looks for additional work to complete. He finishes all tasks accurately and more rapidly than most experienced employees. However, during the last month, he has begun to slow down and make some errors. What would you do to keep Mo motivated?

c. A newly hired employee, Dennis Murray, is being trained as a new sales representative. He is well qualified for the position and comes highly recommended from another company. However, he displays an attitude of seeming to "know it all." Other new employees find him obnoxious. How would you handle this person?

The Chapter Review questions at the end of the chapter vary in level of difficulty. For a basic assignment, consider Develop Your Business Language and Review Your Reading. For an average assignment, consider the basic

TEACHING STRATEGIES

Alternate Modalities
Auditory Learner

When learning how a small-business owner goes about determining human resource needs, the auditory learner would prefer to hear the steps involved. This can be done via a live lecture or a taped tutorial. To reinforce learning, the student could recite steps to another student or group of students.

assignment plus Communicate Business Concepts and Calculate Business Data. For an enhanced assignment, try the average assignment plus Technology Application and Decision-Making Strategies.

ASSESS

Review the goals at the beginning of the chapter and the Business Notes at the end of the chapter. Have students respond orally or in writing to each of the Business Notes restated as a question, provided below. For those who may have difficulty providing answers, assign the reteaching activities that follow. Enrichment activities may also be assigned where appropriate.

1. Why are employees important to the success of a small business? (Answer: Employees can make a difference to the success or failure of a business. The behavior of one person can be very noticeable in a small business with only a few employees.)
2. What factors should be considered by a business owner in determining the need for more employees? (Answer: Small-business owners should determine the category of employee needed, study work requirements in preparation for hiring a new employee, search for people who meet a specific need or skill requirement, and then hire the qualified applicant.
3. Name typical compensation and benefits for employees. (Answer: Compensation and

Applicant Qualifications	Information Sources
Business and technical knowledge and skills	• Transcripts • Grade reports • Teacher references • Employer references • Work samples
Communications and interpersonal skills	• Personal references • Interview • Role playing • Employer references
Attitude toward work and customers	• Interview • Employer references • Attendance records • Work history from résumé
Work experience	• Résumé • Employer references

FIGURE 13-2 Can you think of any other sources of information that might be helpful?

A *cookie* is information sent by a company's computer to the computer of a person who accesses the firm's web site. It may record a password, personal preferences, or other data that helps the company identify the consumer or make future electronic transactions easier.

COMPENSATION AND BENEFITS

One of the reasons people work is to earn money. **Compensation** is the amount of money paid to an employee for work performed. Compensation is made up of two parts. **Salary and wages** are direct payment to an employee for work completed. Compensation in forms other than direct payment for work is known as **benefits**. Examples of benefits are insurance, vacations, paid parking, and the like.

Salary and Wages

A **time wage** pays the employee a specific amount of money for each hour worked. A **straight salary** pays a specific amount of money for each week or month worked. Both of these types of compensation are not based on the amount or quality of work completed but are determined by the amount of time

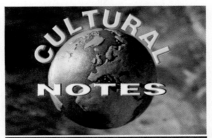

The United States is now recognized as a "tossed salad" instead of a "melting pot." This modern term has surfaced because the United States recognizes and affirms the many cultural heritages in our population.

Net Facts provides information and definitions of terms for the Internet. The more information that students have about the Internet, the better equipped they will be to use this resource. In the Internet Activity Masters, there is an Internet Activity Worksheet for each unit. You can use these activities to give students experience with finding information online. Options for assigning this activity are as follows:

1. **Provide students with a list of addresses of resources for this activity;**
2. **Assign students to conduct their own searches; or**
3. **Use the addresses provided on the Internet Activity Worksheet.**

You should complete the activity yourself before assigning it to resolve any discrepancies that may arise.

ETHICAL PERSPECTIVES

Dishonest Hiring Practices

"Three years of previous experience in the industry required." "Must be energetic and eager." "Requires heavy lifting." Each of these statements is from employment advertisements.

Do the statements reflect important qualifications for a job? Or, are the requirements designed to eliminate certain people as job applicants? Lack of related work experience excludes many high school students and recent graduates. A requirement of energy or stamina might discourage older workers from applying. Women might avoid applying for a position when heavy lifting is a job requirement.

Bias can be eliminated through a careful study of job requirements. Owners must focus on the job and *not* on the type of person best qualified to fill the position. If the owner believes a female is most appropriate for the job, the requirements stated to fill the position will reflect that belief. If the owner considers a person who is physically challenged unsuitable for a job, applicants with handicaps will seldom be hired.

Small-business owners need to hire employees who are both skilled and motivated. An owner should avoid any employment practice that discourages or eliminates applicants who may actually be effective employees.

Critical Thinking

1. Are you familiar with employment advertisements that unfairly restrict the people who will be considered for employment? Why do you believe those requirements were included in the advertisement?
2. Do you believe that small-business owners should develop requirements for new positions that would attract a variety of potential applicants? Why or why not?

---

spent on the job. For that reason, it is a simple system to manage because the business just has to keep records on the amount of time each employee works.

Financial Incentives

The compensation plans described above do not provide an incentive for employees to increase the quality or quantity of work produced. To reward performance, some businesses pay a **commission**. An employee is paid a percentage of sales for which he or she is responsible. Salespeople are often compensated with commissions. Another pay-for-performance plan is known as a **piece rate**. An employee receives a specific amount for each unit of work produced. Piece rates are most often used in factories and data processing centers.

Some companies use a base plus incentive compensation system. A **base plus incentive** system combines a wage or salary with an additional amount determined by the employee's performance. A type of base plus incentive plan is profit sharing. With **profit sharing**, employees receive their regular compensation plus a share of the profits earned by a company. This system encourages a commitment to the company, teamwork, and effective customer service so that profits will be high. Profit sharing provides a more direct work incentive in small companies than in large companies. The connection between individual performance and company success can be more easily understood.

Employee Benefits

Employee benefits can be an expensive addition to the cost of compensation. On average for all businesses, an additional 20 to

---

benefits include a salary or wages, financial incentives, and benefits such as medical insurance or paid vacations.)

4. What are some sources of training available to the employees of small businesses? (Answer: Sources of training within a small business include the owner or experienced employees. Other sources include trainers who conduct training sessions at the business site; training programs offered by schools and colleges; seminars, classes, and training materials available through the Small Business Administration; and vendors that sell products.)

RETEACH

List the following financial incentives on the board: commission, piece rate, base plus incentive, and profit sharing. Have students explain each method of compensation. Then ask students to identify which of the performance compensation plans they would prefer. Why?

Review the process of how small businesses determine human resource needs. Have students construct a chart listing the steps in the process of determining human resource needs.

Clarify the concept of locating/recruiting employees by asking students to bring in examples of job advertisements or job descriptions. Discuss what each ad tells about the prospective job.

On the board, a flip chart, or an overhead transparency, write the headings External Sources and

---

ETHICAL PERSPECTIVES

Ethical Perspectives will give students a sense of individual diversity through the expression of their opinions about the situations presented.

CRITICAL THINKING

1. Examples include experience, physical requirements, and educational degrees that are not directly related to the ability to perform a job. Bring in employment ads from the newspaper. Often managers have a preconceived idea of the type of person they want to hire for a job, so job requirements may be written to fit that type of person rather than the particular job.

2. Because small businesses may have difficulty competing for the best employees, a job announcement should clearly communicate requirements needed to be successful and encourage qualified people to apply.

Internal Sources. Have students brainstorm as many examples of training and development as possible. Review and correct misconceptions as necessary.

Direct students to read the Ethical Perspectives in this chapter. Ask students to interview their parents (or guardians) to find out how they got their jobs. What types of hiring process did their employers use? Students should be prepared to present their findings to the class.

Have students develop a compensation system for the class that will attract others to take Intro to Business, keep them satisfied, and inspire them to do their best in the class. Ask students to prepare a written report of their ideas and then share them with the class.

Have students identify various training programs used by small-business owners in their community. Parents, friends, neighbors, and relatives might be good sources of information.

On average, U.S. employees receive less than two days of training per year. Companies spend less than $100 per year on each employee.

40 percent of an employee's wages is spent on benefits. If an employee earns $7.00 an hour, 30 percent added for benefits increases the cost to $9.10 an hour. If the employee works 40 hours a week for 50 weeks, the additional cost to the company is $4,200.

Some benefits are required by state and federal law. Most new businesses must offer and pay costs of benefits including compensation for hours of overtime worked, Social Security, Medicare, and contributions to funds that pay for injuries to employees and for unemployed workers.

Full-time employees may expect companies to offer insurance plans including health, life, dental, and disability insurance. Many small businesses cannot afford the cost of all of those types of insurance. However, they may assist employees in purchasing insurance at lower rates through a group policy.

Time off for vacations is another popular benefit for employees. Paid vacations are an expensive benefit since employees are being paid for time when they will not be working. However, the time off may result in a more satisfied and productive employee. Many small businesses offer unpaid vacation time to most employees. Paid vacations are reserved as a benefit for those employees who have worked for the business for several years.

Small businesses seldom offer benefits to employees other than those required by law. Instead, small businesses attempt to attract and satisfy employees with non-financial benefits such as flexible schedules and work hours, a supportive work environment, and greater responsibility and involvement in decision making.

Why do you think that continuous employee training is important for a successful business?

Workplace Competencies-Resources

SCANS

By acquiring competence at allocating resources—time, money, people, and materials—students learn to perform basic functions of management—planning, organizing, and controlling. Allocating materials and space is an important resource that may present difficulty for many people. The materials to be allocated must first be identified, then a plan must be made on how to organize those materials, and then an inventory should be kept. To show students this skill in action, take a field trip to the front office of your school. Ask the person in charge of the supply room where photocopies are made, how the storage cabinets are organized, and how inventories are kept. Use the Student Activity Worksheet, Workplace Competencies—Resources, in the School-To-Work/SCANS Activity Masters, as a guideline for discussion.

TRAINING AND DEVELOPMENT

New employees often receive training within a small business. Training materials and manuals can be purchased or can be developed by experienced employees. Experienced employees can also be given the assignment to work with new employees to help them learn and practice procedures. Many employees enjoy the opportunity to provide training if they are given ample time to do it well. After the initial training is completed, the employee can become a coach for the new employee. Help is provided from time to time until the new employee is comfortable with the job.

When a new piece of equipment or a new procedure is added to a small business, many employees may need to receive training. The owner may hire a trainer and schedule training for a large number of employees at the same time. In this way, training is provided at a low cost for each employee.

Training is available from outside sources. High schools, community colleges, and universities offer short training programs, adult education classes, and advanced courses. The Small Business Administration sponsors seminars and classes and provides a variety of training materials through local offices. Equipment vendors and other businesses that sell products offer training to customers.

PLANNING FOR BUSINESS GROWTH

Of all small businesses in the U.S., nearly 3/4 have no employees other than the owners. Many are operated on a part-time basis with the owner holding another job. Others provide full-time employment to the owner and possibly members of his or her family but do not have enough revenue to afford other employees.

If a business is successful and profitable, most business owners want to expand. But one of the reasons for the high rate of small-business failures is that the owner is not prepared to manage a larger business and a number of employees. A second reason for that failure is a lack of money to pay the costs of expanding the business.

There are several ways to expand a business successfully. One way is to form a partnership. Partners can be brought into the business who have skills the original owner lacks. A partner may have successful human resource management skills to hire and manage new employees. Financial management skills of a partner may provide expertise in dealing with a larger budget.

When a small business expands, the owner may not want to offer ownership to a partner but may still need the expertise of others. In this case, the owner could hire one or more experienced managers to help operate the business. This gives the owner more time to devote to business growth while the managers concentrate on day-to-day operations.

The business owner may just need money to expand and so may arrange for a loan from a bank or other financial institution. The owner may decide to form a corporation and sell stock to raise money, but that would require sharing ownership with other stockholders.

Growth can be achieved by expanding the business at its original location or opening another business at a second location. For a manufacturer, it may be more efficient to expand at one location if there is adequate space. A retailer may need to open additional locations in order to more easily reach new customers.

SUMMARIZE

This activity is designed to help students develop an understanding of concepts related to human resource management. Ask them to find one point in the chapter that they least understood. Have them identify the concept on an index card by stating "I least understood...." Sort the index cards into four to six topical areas. Write the topics on the board, and ask all students to put themselves in a group where they feel most knowledgeable. If the groups are large, create several subgroups or assign the more capable students into groups with few students. Each student group may now attempt to develop explanations of their "least understood" concepts. Read the explanations to the class. Allow approximately 20 minutes for this activity.

EVALUATE

- Assign Activities and Projects for Chapter 13.
- Administer the printed test or ExamView for Chapter 13.
- Assign School-To-Work/SCANS portfolio activities for Unit 4.

Chapter 13 *Managing Human Resources*

SCANS

Personal Qualities-Integrity

Employers are looking for potential employees with solid ethics. Therefore, we must prepare students for the school-to-work transition and emphasize the value of ethical behavior. Businesses are very aware of the severe implications of unethical behavior in employees. The Ethical Perspectives feature raises ethical questions but does not involve the teaching of right and wrong. Instead, it allows students to apply their own principles to business situations through the use of critical thinking and decision-making skills.

REVIEW YOUR READING

1. The most important resource of a small business is its employees.
2. A permanent employee works for a business as long as the business is profitable and the employee's performance is satisfactory. Temporary employees are generally used to handle seasonal fluctuations in business or to complete specific tasks.
3. Temporary employees are usually hired during a particularly busy time for the business or when a special task needs to be completed.
4. The owner of the business must study the work that must be completed, and compare that to the skills of the current employees to see what type of employee would best benefit the business.
5. Because larger companies are usually able to offer a higher level of compensation, small businesses must develop a compensation program that attracts and satisfies employees with nonfinancial benefits.
6. Some examples of benefits are insurance, vacations, and paid parking.
7. Profit sharing encourages a commitment to the company, teamwork, and effective customer service so that profits will be high.
8. An owner may hire a trainer and schedule training for a large number of employees at one time to learn the new procedure or how to operate the new equipment.
9. The small business owner can hire one or more manages with expertise in areas that the owner does not have.

COMMUNICATE BUSINESS CONCEPTS

10. Employees in small businesses are often given greater responsibility and a wider range of tasks than those in large businesses. They may work with a smaller group of people who they know well and have a more flexible work environment.
11. Poor performance problems may be due to lack of skills needed for a task, working conditions, or employees who are not committed to the business. Mr. Chan should make sure employees know how to do the job and offer effective training. He should talk to them to

Chapter REVIEW

BUSINESS NOTES

1. Employees can make a difference in the success or failure of a business. The impact of one person can be very noticeable in a small business with only a few employees.

2. Small-business owners should carefully determine the category of employee needed, study work requirements in preparation for hiring a new employee, search for people who meet a specific need or skill requirement, and then hire the qualified applicant.

3. Compensation and benefits include a salary or wages, financial incentives, and other benefits.

4. Sources of training within a small business include the owner or experienced employees. Other sources include trainers who conduct training sessions at the business site; training programs offered by schools and colleges; seminars, classes, and training materials available through the Small Business Administration; and equipment vendors or other businesses that sell products.

REVIEW YOUR READING

1. Of all the resources available to small businesses, which is the most important?
2. How is a permanent employee different from a temporary employee?
3. When are temporary employees generally hired?
4. A small-business owner must be careful to hire the best possible employees. What are some steps that can be taken before a person is hired to be sure the person is right for the job?
5. Why is it important for a small business to develop the right compensation program for employees?
6. What are some examples of benefits?
7. Why do companies implement profit-sharing plans?
8. What is an effective way for small businesses to train employees when a new procedure or a piece of new equipment is added?
9. How can a small business expand without sharing ownership with other people?

COMMUNICATE BUSINESS CONCEPTS

10. Why might some people prefer to work for a small business at a lower wage or salary than to work for a large business?
11. Lee Chan owns a coffee shop and has problems with poor employee performance. Employees do not appear to be interested in their work. Mr. Chan is worried that if something is not done, his regular customers will begin to leave the business. What are some ways that Mr. Chan can motivate his employees and encourage them to improve their performance?

see if there are ways the work can be better organized. In addition, he needs to be careful in hiring decisions to try to find people who really want to do the work. The employees who are performing well or whose work improves should be recognized and rewarded.

12. Full-time employees generally work more hours, and expect to work specific shifts or time periods. Part-time employees are used to fill in when the workload is heavy or when extra help is needed. They are usually more flexible. Part-time employment provides a trial period to determine if a person might become a good full-time employee.

13. Because small businesses are unable to offer a lot of monetary compensation to their employees, many small businesses offer flexible schedules, time off for emergencies, the chance to shift work schedules or assignments, and opportunities to complete some management tasks.

12. Small-business owners may think they have to choose between hiring part-time and full-time employees. How can a business benefit by employing a combination of full-time and part-time employees?

13. Most small businesses cannot compete with large businesses on the level of salaries and wages paid to their employees. Suggest some types of inexpensive benefits that a small business could offer to attract and retain employees.

14. Training is important to businesses, but can be very expensive. What are some ways that small businesses can improve the performance of employees without spending a great deal of money on training?

DEVELOP YOUR BUSINESS LANGUAGE

For each numbered item, find the term that has the same meaning.

15. Ensuring that needed employees are available and that they are productive, paid, and satisfied with their work.

16. The people who work for the business.

17. A specific amount of money paid for each week or month worked.

18. An employee who works a schedule of at least 30 hours a week.

19. A system that pays the employee a percentage of the sales for which he or she is responsible.

20. An employee that has a long-term commitment to a company.

21. A system that combines a small wage or salary with an additional amount determined by performance.

22. A compensation plan that pays the employee a specific amount for each unit of work produced.

23. An employee hired for a specific time or to complete a specific assignment.

24. An employee who works less than full-time employees by working either fewer hours each day or fewer days each week.

25. Direct payment to an employee for work completed.

26. Compensation in forms other than direct payment for work.

27. An incentive plan in which employees receive their regular compensation plus a share of the profits earned.

28. The amount of money paid to an employee for work performed.

29. A wage that pays the employee a specific amount of money for each hour worked.

KEY TERMS

base plus incentive
benefits
commission
compensation
full-time employee
human resource management
human resources
part-time employee
permanent employee
piece rate
profit sharing
salary and wages
straight salary
temporary employee
time wage

DECISION-MAKING STRATEGIES

Arte Malik has operated a lawn care business for many years. The business offers landscaping services including seeding and sodding lawns, applying chemicals and fertilizer, and regular lawn mowing. Mr. Malik has 25 employees, many of whom have worked for him for 5–10 years. He usually hires 2 or 3 new employees each year. In the past, Arte has not been concerned about the skills of new employees, preferring to find people who are interested in the work and who want to learn about the business. However, the machinery he uses is getting more complex and employees must know a great deal about safe handling of chemicals, detecting plant diseases, and effective lawn care. The local community college has a two-year degree program in lawn care management. Arte is trying to decide whether to continue his present hiring procedure of allowing new employees to learn on the job, develop a

14. Small businesses may efficiently train new employees by having a more experienced employee train the new person. An owner/manager could take time out to work with new employees. The owner/manager may also get groups of people together to develop new ways to complete activities or to decide on how to improve performance.

DEVELOP YOUR BUSINESS LANGUAGE

15. human resource management
16. human resources
17. straight salary
18. full-time employee
19. commission
20. permanent employee
21. base plus incentive
22. piece rate
23. temporary employee
24. part-time employee
25. salary and wages
26. benefits
27. profit sharing
28. compensation
29. time wage

DECISION-MAKING STRATEGIES

30. Students should consider the problems the business may experience if new employees do not have the skills, what the cost of developing a training program would be, and how much more the company would have to pay employees who have a two-year college degree.

31. Students' answers will vary. They should support their decision with reasons related to the need to have well-trained employees and how the decision will affect the costs and profits of the business.

32. (a) ($80 × 35 employees) + ($130 × 6 employees) = $2,280
(b) $780 ÷ $2280 = 34%
(c) experienced employees = $88, new employees = $143, (41 employees × $88) + (4 employees × $143) = $3,180

33. (a) 68 ÷ 207 = 32.85%; 54 ÷ 207 = 26.09%; 37 ÷ 207 = 17.87%; 31 ÷ 207 = 14.98%; 19 ÷ 207 = 9.18% (b) 32.85% − 9.17% = 23.68% (c) 54 − 19 = 35

34. Monday: commission: $14.70; base: $25.50; total: $40.20; Tuesday: commission: $0; base: $17.00; total: $17.00; Wednesday: commission: $11.40; base: $21.25; total: $32.65; Thursday: commission: $0; base: $12.75; total: $12.75; Friday: commission: $0; base: $0; total: $0; Saturday: commission: $21.00; base: $34.00; total: $55.00 (b) $25.50 + $17.00 + $21.25 + $12.75 + $0 + $34.00 = $110.50 (c) $14.70 + $11.40 + $21.00 = $47.10 (d) $40.20 + $17.00 + $32.65 + $12.75 + $55.00 = $157.60

TECHNOLOGY APPLICATION

In this activity, students use a computer to solve a business problem using a file that is provided on the data CD that accompanies *Intro to Business*. Instructions for using the data CD are included in a **README** file on the disk. Solutions are provided on the Instructor's Resource CD.

---

training program to be offered to all new employees, or only hire people who have completed the community college program.

30. What are the advantages and disadvantages of each of the three choices Mr. Malik is considering?

31. What choice would you recommend? Why?

CALCULATE BUSINESS DATA

32. A small business budgets $80 per employee per year for training costs. The training cost for each new employee is $130 for their first year. Last year the firm had 35 employees and added 6 new employees. It is considering increasing both parts of the training budget by 10 percent for the next year.
   a. What was the total training budget for last year?
   b. What percentage of the budget is spent on new employee training?
   c. With the proposed increase, how much will be spent for training each experienced employee and each new employee? What will be the total new training budget for all employees if 4 new employees will be hired?

33. A local chamber of commerce research committee surveyed 207 business owners. They asked each of the owners to identify the greatest problem they faced with their employees. The table presents the responses given by the business owners.
   a. What is the percentage of the total responses represented by each of the categories of employee problems?
   b. What is the difference between the percentage of businesses reporting problems with employees working slowly and the percentage of businesses reporting no problems with employees?
   c. How many more businesses reported employee carelessness as a problem than those who reported they had no problems at all with employees?

Worked is performed slowly	68
Work is completed carelessly	54
Employee dishonesty	37
Poor service is provided to the customer	31
No problems with employees	19

34. Nicole Miller works for a store that uses an hourly wage plus commission compensation system. Her base rate is $5.15 an hour, and she earns a commission of 2 percent on all sales if sales are over $500 per day. She worked five days last week. Her hours worked and daily sales are shown in the table.
   a. How much did Nicole earn in base salary and commission for each of the days she worked?
   b. How much was the total of her base salary for the week?
   c. How much was the total of her commissions for the week?
   d. What were Nicole's total earnings for the week?

Monday	6 hrs	$ 735 total sales
Tuesday	4 hrs	$ 320 total sales
Wednesday	5 hrs	$ 570 total sales
Thursday	3 hrs	$ 450 total sales
Friday	0 hrs	
Saturday	8 hrs	$1,050 total sales

TECHNOLOGY APPLICATION

Using the *Intro to Business* Data CD and your database program software, select problem CH13. After the problem appears on your screen, complete the following activities. Then, after you have completed each step, display or print a report for each activity. If you do not have a printer available, answer the questions before you leave the computer.

35. Select and list the employees that have data-base skills. How many employees are listed?

36. Select and list the employees that have spreadsheet skills. How many employees are listed?

37. Select and list the employees that have word processing skills. How many employees are listed?

COMMUNICATING for SUCCESS

GIVING PRESENTATIONS— WHAT DO YOU HAVE TO SAY?

Presentations are a common method for communicating information, ideas, and opinions to large groups of people. Although audience size may range from one or two colleagues to several hundred salespeople, there are certain methods and techniques that can help you make a better presentation.

First and foremost, know your audience. Know what kinds of information they need to hear and what they need to learn from you. Know what kinds of visual aids will appeal to them and hold their attention, and have an idea about their backgrounds, interests, and experiences. By having an understanding of how your audience will process information, you can more effectively decide on the use of visual aids to improve your presentation.

Typically, there are four types of presentations: oral, visual, computer-based, or discussion. Oral presentations generally consist of a speech or talk; a visual presentation adds some form of visual aid to this talk. Computer-based presentations are structured around a computer-generated or technology-aided presentation. Advancements in technology have increased the use of computer-based presentations. These technologies often include video clips, pictures, images, sounds, and cartoons. Discussions are also a form of presentation, where the presenter structures a talk or presentation of data around questions that are intended to prompt group discussion and feedback.

> **Knowing your audience will help you make a better presentation.**

Overall, to guarantee a successful presentation, you should:

—Prepare your materials in advance, including speaker notes and background research.
—Practice your presentation, especially difficult words or concepts that may require additional time to master.
—Use hand gestures to emphasize key points.
—Use visual aids and/or technology to enhance your audience's understanding of your comments.
—Have fun, and so will your audience.

CRITICAL THINKING

1. What are the four types of presentations?
2. What forms of technology could be used in a computer-based presentation?

COMMUNICATING for SUCCESS

Communications skills will help ensure students' success in the business world. Communicating for Success introduces workplace/interpersonal communications issues and proper uses of communications technology. Each feature discusses a key communications topic, and contains two Critical Thinking questions that require students to analyze what they have learned.

Students should learn that leadership is critical to success in business, and a sure mark of leadership is the ability to make a lively and effective presentation. This feature provides students with detailed steps and other practical advice on the topic.

CRITICAL THINKING

1. Typically there are four types of presentations: oral, visual, computer-based, or discussion.
2. Technologies often include video clips, pictures, images, sounds, and cartoons.

A primary reason for business failure is the inability of the owner to manage the finances of the business. A small-business owner must be able to understand and use several financial tools, such as budgets and financial statements.

Resources for Teachers
- Lesson Plans
- School-To-Work/SCANS Activity Masters
- Spanish Resources
- Instructor's Resource CD

Assessment
- Chapter and Unit Tests, Ch. 14
- ExamView, Ch. 14

Media/Technology
- Applying Technology Data CD
- PowerPoint slides
- Business Connection CD
- Videotape

Activity Masters and Workbooks
- Activities and Projects, Ch. 14
- Internet Activity Masters
- Business Math Activity Masters
- Communications Activity Masters
- International Business Activity Masters
- Ethics Activity Masters

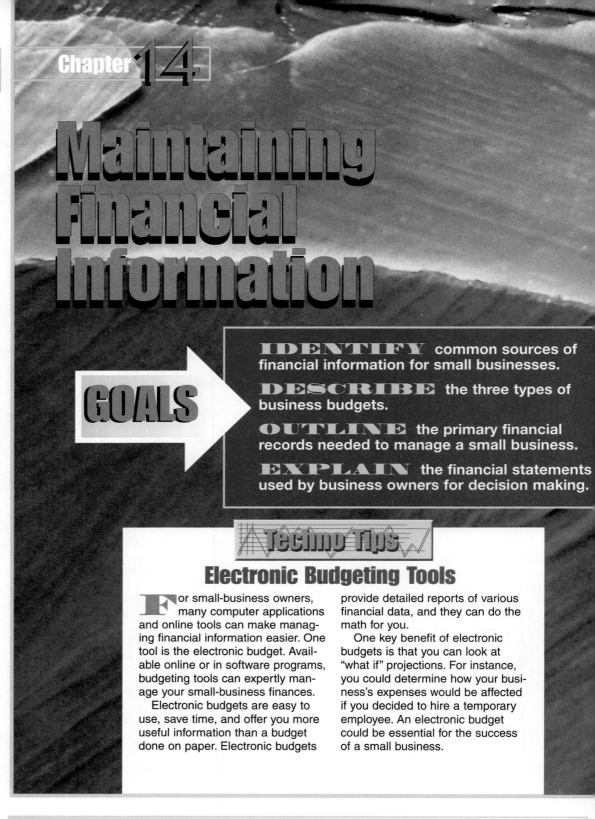

Chapter 14
Maintaining Financial Information

GOALS

IDENTIFY common sources of financial information for small businesses.

DESCRIBE the three types of business budgets.

OUTLINE the primary financial records needed to manage a small business.

EXPLAIN the financial statements used by business owners for decision making.

Techno Tips

Electronic Budgeting Tools

For small-business owners, many computer applications and online tools can make managing financial information easier. One tool is the electronic budget. Available online or in software programs, budgeting tools can expertly manage your small-business finances.

Electronic budgets are easy to use, save time, and offer you more useful information than a budget done on paper. Electronic budgets provide detailed reports of various financial data, and they can do the math for you.

One key benefit of electronic budgets is that you can look at "what if" projections. For instance, you could determine how your business's expenses would be affected if you decided to hire a temporary employee. An electronic budget could be essential for the success of a small business.

Students need to know the latest technologies and develop cutting edge Internet skills for use in current jobs, future careers, or in their homes. TechnoTips introduces students to today's cutting edge technologies and provides them with important Internet skills. Feature topics concentrate on Internet-specific technologies and computer or other hi-tech innovations for use by businesses and consumers.

FOCUS ON REAL LIFE

Envision yourself as a small-business owner. One of the constant problems you would face is financing. From the first day that you develop an idea for a business, financing questions must be addressed. The following questions are often asked when you initially plan a business: How much money will it take to start the business? Where will the money come from?

Once a business is open, financing becomes a more immediate concern for you. Few businesses are profitable in the first year. Therefore, you must determine how to obtain enough money to operate the business until it becomes profitable. Several important questions must be answered at this time: How will expenses be paid until the business becomes profitable? What can be done to increase income and reduce expenses?

Even successful small businesses must be concerned about finances. Bills must be paid. Worn out equipment must be replaced. A growing business may need larger facilities, and more employees may need to be hired. As an experienced small-business owner, you will regularly ask these questions: Is the business staying profitable? What expenses must be planned for in order to maintain operations? Will an expansion generate more sales? Will the business be more profitable after a planned expansion?

FINANCIAL PLANNING

Budgets provide detailed plans for the financial needs of individuals, families, and businesses. A **business budget** has two purposes:

1. to anticipate sources and amounts of income, and

2. to predict the types and amounts of expenses for a specific business activity or the entire business.

If you owned your own small business, the money that you would receive is called *income*. The word *revenue* is often used in place of the word income. The words mean the same. To operate your own business, you will also have expenses. *Expenses* are the costs of operating a business. The business owner must be able to identify and predict the amount of each source of income and each type of expense. In addition, the owner will need to determine when each expense must be paid and when income will be received. To determine financial needs, businesses use the basic financial equation shown in Figure 14-1. According to the equation,

adequate revenues must be available to pay all expenses. If revenues exceed expenses, the business makes a profit. If not, the business suffers a loss.

After several years of operation, the task of identifying sources of income and types of expenses will not be difficult. The primary source of that information is the financial records of the business. However, financial planning is difficult for a new business. No financial records exist to serve as a guidepost. Other sources of information must be used. The Small Business Administration (SBA) provides a number of planning tools for new small businesses. Among those tools are guides to developing a budget and financial information that will help the new business

New business owners seldom earn a salary during the first year or two. They must rely on savings or a second job until the business earns a profit.

FOCUS ON REAL LIFE

Ask students to write on a sheet of paper answers to these questions: (a) Who keeps track of how a business is doing financially? (b) What kind of records and reports are needed? (c) How does a business know if a profit has been earned? Place responses on the board, an overhead, or flip chart. Then discuss the need for careful record keeping in the operation of a small business.

Guide students through a discussion of the balance sheet. Have students classify the following as assets, liabilities, or equity: (a) delivery truck (asset); (b) owner's investment in the business (owner's equity); (c) money owed to a utility company (liability); (d) cash on hand (asset); (e) money owed on a bank loan (liability).

Walk students through the following math problem. A small service business has the following transactions in one month: Sales (revenue): credit sales, $15,000; cash sales, $7,000. Expenses

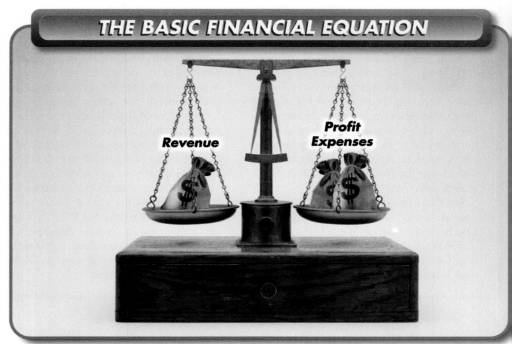

THE BASIC FINANCIAL EQUATION

Revenue

Profit Expenses

FIGURE 14-1 Do you know what happens to profit if expenses outweigh revenue?

owner anticipate the amount of revenue and the expenses.

Another source of information is private businesses that collect and publish financial information on similar businesses and industries. Examples of those companies are Dun and Bradstreet, Value Line, and Standard and Poor's. Some information is available from

NET FACTS

A Uniform Resource Locator (URL) is an address code for finding hypertext or hypermedia documents on World Wide Web (WWW) servers around the world. URLs can be accessed by WWW browsers.

business magazines and newspapers including *Fortune, Forbes, Entrepreneur, Black Enterprise,* and *The Wall Street Journal.* Professional associations, such as the National Federation of Independent Business and the National Retail Merchants Association, offer resources to assist with financial planning.

A new franchise will typically receive help with financial planning from the franchisor and may even have a complete beginning budget provided. New businesses working with a bank or other financial institution can obtain information and support there. Franchisors and financial institutions want to see businesses succeed, so they will encourage careful financial planning.

BUDGET PREPARATION

The most important step in financial planning is developing a budget. A budget can be compared to the use of a road map when you are traveling to an unfamiliar location. Without the map, you will have little idea of

How can a small business owner ensure that all expenses are included in a budget?

where you are and where you are going while you travel. If you take a wrong turn, you will have a difficult time knowing your mistake or how to get back to the correct road without the map. In the same way, a budget identifies where a business is going and allows the owner to determine whether the business is making progress toward its financial destination. By regularly comparing the business's financial performance to the budget, the owner can determine whether the budget goals are being met. If not, corrections can be made before serious financial problems occur.

Types of Budgets

A large business that has operated for several years may have many specialized budgets. Each manager will be responsible for one or more budgets in his or her area of operations. For a new small business, however, three budgets are essential. They are the start-up budget, the operating budget, and the cash budget.

The **start-up budget** plans income and expenses from the beginning of the business until it becomes profitable. Most new businesses require expenditures of thousands and even hundreds of thousands of dollars in order to open. Buildings and equipment must be purchased or leased. Inventory, supplies, and materials are needed. Employees will be hired who must be paid. Expenses for utilities, licenses, advertising, transportation, and the like will be incurred before the company begins to sell its products and services.

Money to pay for these expeditures must be contributed by the owner(s) or borrowed from banks or other sources. Financial institutions will want to see a detailed start-up budget before lending money to a new business.

The **operating budget** describes the financial plan for the ongoing operations of the business. The operating budget is usually planned for six months or a year. This budget follows the basic financial equation. All revenues and expenses are listed and the planned net income (or loss) for the time period is shown.

Every new business needs a cash budget. A **cash budget** is an estimate of the actual money received and paid out for a specific

(operating): rent, $3,000; wages, $6,000; utilities, $1,000; supplies, $2,000; insurance, $1,000. For that month, compute the firm's (a) revenue, (b) expenses, and (c) net income. (Answer: $22,000 (revenue) − $13,000 (expenses) = $9,000 (net income).

Ask students where they would get $25,000 to start a new sandwich shop in a large shopping mall. Lead students in a discussion of the need for *capital* (money for starting and running a business)— (a) Before a Business Can Be Opened? (b) During the First Year of a Business? (c) By Successful Small Businesses? If possible, ask a banker or accountant who works regularly with small businesses to talk to the class. Have the guest speaker address each of the three questions.

Lead students in a discussion of the different types of budgets. Ask each student to develop written definitions of each type of budget. Compare their definitions to those listed in the glossary of the textbook. Then discuss why each is important to the business and how the business owner should go about developing each of the budgets to make sure it is accurate.

Have students study the examples of the balance sheet and income statement in Figure 14-3. Then lead a discussion of the key features of these important financial statements. Ask students to consider how they would make comparisons if they had a similar financial statement from a previous period or from a competitor's business. Have them identify which of the items on each form they believe would be most important to

TEACHING STRATEGIES
Teams

Jigsaw is an instructional method in which students use cooperative learning in peer groups. Divide the chapter into six parts. Each team member becomes an expert in one of the parts to which they are assigned. All students assigned section one meet as an expert group. All students assigned section two meet as an expert group, etc. These expert groups will discuss their section and decide how to report this information to their respective groups. Students then go back to their original group, at which time they share the expert information they have learned. After all team members have presented expert information, everyone returns to his or her desk. Students then take the ExamView as individuals with no assistance from team members.

compare. (Various answers are appropriate for the question depending on what the student believes is important to the business owner.)

EXPLORE THIS/INDEPENDENT PRACTICE Have students find a copy at the library or by visiting a company web site of the latest balance sheet of a large corporation. Ask students to find the answers to the following: (a) What is the value of the corporation's assets? (b) What is the value of the corporation's liabilities? (c) What is the value of the owner's (stockholder's) equity? (d) Add the liabilities to the owner's equity. Does the sum equal the value of the assets?

The Chapter Review questions at the end of the chapter vary in level of difficulty. For a basic assignment, consider Develop Your Business Language and Review Your Reading. For an average assignment, consider the basic assignment plus Communicate Business Concepts and Calculate Business Data. For an enhanced assignment, try the average assignment plus Technology Application and Decision-Making Strategies.

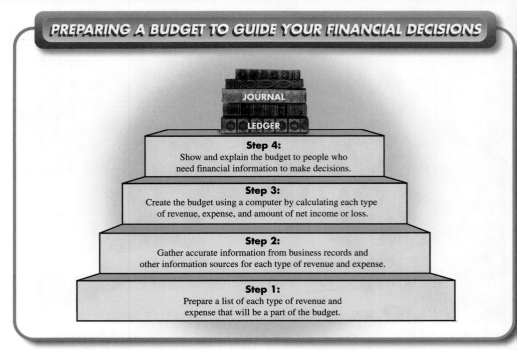

PREPARING A BUDGET TO GUIDE YOUR FINANCIAL DECISIONS

JOURNAL
LEDGER

Step 4:
Show and explain the budget to people who need financial information to make decisions.

Step 3:
Create the budget using a computer by calculating each type of revenue, expense, and amount of net income or loss.

Step 2:
Gather accurate information from business records and other information sources for each type of revenue and expense.

Step 1:
Prepare a list of each type of revenue and expense that will be a part of the budget.

FIGURE 14-2 Do you see why each step in the budget process is important?

time period. A cash budget anticipates that cash will come into a business and that cash will be paid out during each week or month of operation. Even if a new business is losing money, it must have adequate cash on hand to pay current expenses. Profitable businesses may have times when adequate cash is not available due to high expenses or a delay in receiving payments from customers.

Steps in Budgeting

In a small business, the budgeting goals are much the same as in a household—to determine what the sources of income are and how income will be distributed. The budgeting process involves four fundamental steps. Those steps are listed in Figure 14-2.

Several skills are needed by the person responsible for preparing business budgets. Budgeting requires an understanding of financial information, computer skills, basic mathematical abilities, and effective communications skills. New small-business owners often seek the help of an accountant or banker when preparing a budget for the first time.

FINANCIAL RECORDS

Budgets identify the financial plans of business. To determine if those plans have been achieved, financial records are needed. **Financial records** are used to record and analyze the financial performance of a business.

All successful businesses maintain accurate financial records. Several types of financial records are maintained by small businesses. Among the records commonly maintained to document the performance of a business are:

- *Cash records* that list all cash receipts and disbursements.
- *Records of accounts* that identify all credit purchases and sales. (An *accounts payable* record identifies the companies from which credit purchases were made; an *accounts receivable* record identifies customers that made credit purchases.)

Basic Skills-Writing

SCANS

Employers are looking for potential employees with good basic foundation skills. In order to prepare students for the school-to-work transition, we must teach these skills in our classroom. Language arts skills are an important component of good writing skills. Students should learn to paraphrase, write complete sentences, and identify objects of prepositional phrases. For additional practice in language arts skills, direct students to answer the Develop Your Business Language and Review Your Reading at the end of the chapter. Students should write the answers in their own words and in complete sentences. To further practice language arts skills, ask students to underline all the objects of prepositional phrases in their answers.

GLOBAL PERSPECTIVES
Franchising Around the World

Franchising has become a popular form of international business. An estimated 400 U.S. franchisors have international operations. The number of actual franchise locations worldwide is approaching 50,000. The most common international franchises are restaurants. Other successful franchises are automobile rentals, hotels, and retail stores.

The most popular international location for U.S. franchised companies is Canada. Nearly 30 percent of all international franchise outlets are located there. Twenty-six percent are in Japan, followed by the European continent with 14 percent; Australia and the United Kingdom, 9 percent each; and Asian locations, 6 percent. The remaining 7 percent of franchise outlets are located throughout the world.

One of the strengths of franchises in the United States has been a consistent product and image. Customers who shop one franchise location can expect to find the same products and services at any other location of the same franchise they visit. However, international franchisors have learned a valuable lesson. Some of the elements that work in the United States are successful in other countries. However, changes often need to be made to meet local tastes and expectations. For example, many 7-Elevens in Japan have a barrel from which fresh fish are sold.

Critical Thinking
1. Most small-business owners are reluctant to sell products in other countries. Why are franchisors much more interested in international business operations?
2. How can a franchisor interested in opening outlets in other countries determine whether changes need to be made in the operations of the franchise?

- *Inventory records* that identify the type and quantity of products available for sale. (Adequate records are essential to the control and security of inventory items.)
- *Payroll records* that contain information on all employees of the company and their earnings.
- *Asset records* that identify the buildings and equipment owned by the business, their original and current value, and the amount owed if money was borrowed to purchase the assets.

In the past, the preparation and maintenance of financial records was both an expensive and time-consuming process. Few new business owners were skilled in record keeping. Usually, a business would hire an accountant to set up a record keeping system and then employ a part-time bookkeeper to maintain the records.

The age of personal computers has made financial record keeping much more efficient and accurate. Complete computerized accounting systems can be purchased at a low cost for small businesses. The systems include all the financial records needed. The

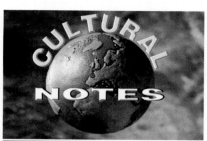

Cultural diversity in the United States has played an important role in business development. For example, the number of ethnic restaurants has increased because of the various immigrants that have come to the United States. These restaurants have provided success for the owners and employment for many workers.

Chapter 14 *Maintaining Financial Information* **187**

ASSESS

Review the goals at the beginning of the chapter and the Business Notes at the end of the chapter. Have students respond orally or in writing to each of the Business Notes restated as a question, provided below. For students who may have difficulty providing answers, assign the reteaching activities that follow. Enrichment activities may also be assigned where appropriate.

1. What are common sources of financial information for new and established businesses? (Answer: Common sources of financial information for established businesses are financial records. For businesses with limited or no previous financial information, the Small Business Administration provides planning tools. Private businesses also collect and publish financial information on similar businesses. A new franchise gets help from the franchiser.)
2. Name three types of business budgets. (Answer: Three types of budgets are the start-up budget, the operating budget, and the cash budget.)
3. What financial records are needed to manage a small business? (Answer: Common financial records are records of cash, accounts, inventory, payroll, and assets.)
4. Name two financial records used by business owners for comparing financial performance. (Answer: To compare financial performance, a balance sheet and income statement are used.)

GLOBAL PERSPECTIVES

Global Perspectives gives students an opportunity to visualize various places around the globe that are described.

CRITICAL THINKING
1. Franchisers are used to developing businesses and working with many different people and cultures. Successful franchisers usually expand into many markets and may look to international markets for additional opportunities.
2. Franchisers should gather information about the country, its economy, prospective customers, and its goods. Studies should be done to see if there are competing businesses. Methods of distribution and ways to complete other marketing activities should be studied.

Name some ways that computers have made financial record keeping more effective.

computer software will complete the necessary calculations and prepare financial reports. A business owner or employee with understanding of basic accounting concepts and computer skills can now maintain accurate records for the business.

FINANCIAL STATEMENTS

Financial statements are reports that summarize the financial performance of a business. When used in a business, the *balance sheet* lists the assets, liabilities, and owner's equity (or capital). The balance sheet is normally prepared every six months or once a year. The **income statement** reports the revenues, expenses, and net income or loss from business operations for a specific period of time. *Net income* is derived when income is greater than expenses. A *net loss* occurs when expenses are greater than income. Income statements are often prepared every month in a new business and at least every

six months in established businesses. Examples of the two financial statements for a small business are shown in Figure 14-3.

Business owners review financial statements carefully to determine how their businesses are performing. Since the statements summarize financial performance for a specific time, the owner can compare the performance of the current time period with the performance of last month or last year. If net income is increasing, the owner will want to maintain and improve performance if possible. On the other hand, if expenses are increasing but not revenues, the owner will want to determine the reasons for the problem and make changes to improve performance.

In addition to comparing financial performance from one time period to another, the owner will want to make comparisons with similar businesses. A business that is less profitable than similar businesses, or with lower sales or higher expenses, may have difficulty competing.

Basic Skills-Math

In order for students to become contributing workers in our society, it is important that they become proficient in the basic skills of reading, writing, arithmetic, and mathematics. Employers are looking for potential employees with good basic foundation skills. In order to prepare students for the school-to-work transition, we must teach these skills in our classroom.

Applying math across the curriculum is an important element in contemporary education. As a part of end-of-chapter activities, Calculate Business Data enables students to apply their math skills. Appendix B: Math Review, Appendix C: Determining Percentages and Interest in Business, and Appendix D: Using Measurements in Business, also apply arithmetic and math skills.

FINANCIAL STATEMENTS

Majestic Cleaners
Balance Sheet
December 31, 20--

Assets		Liabilities	
Cash	$22,500	Accounts Payable**	$22,800
Accounts Receivable*	19,050	Note Payable***	18,500
Supplies	12,800	Loan Payable****	16,250
Equipment	26,250	Total Liabilities	$57,550
		Owner's Equity	
		Andre Adams, Capital	$23,050
Total Assets	$80,600	Total Liabilities and Owner's Equity	$80,600

* Used for charge sales; shows the total amount due from customers.
** Other businesses owed money for supplies purchased.
*** Money borrowed from a bank to start the business.
****Money borrowed from a bank to purchase equipment.

Majestic Cleaners
Income Statement
For the Period Ended December 31, 20--

Operating Revenue		
Cash Sales	$ 9,854	
Charge Sales	14,781	
Total Operating Revenue		$24,635
Operating Expenses		
Salaries and Wages	$12,600	
Advertising	820	
Rent	4,600	
Utilities	1,640	
Supplies	1,055	
Other	410	
Total Operating Expenses		21,125
Net Income		$ 3,510

FIGURE 14-3 Can you tell from these statements if this business is successful?

Ask students to think of a small business that they could operate efficiently as a full-time high school student. Each should come up with a start-up budget. Select certain students to present their plans to the class. Have the rest of the class act as a bank and vote to accept or reject the loan application for the capital required to start up the business.

SUMMARIZE

Randomly select students and ask each to explain one of the key terms found in the chapter. Alternatively, place the terms on cards, ask students to draw a card, and to define the term in his/her own words. Also have students prepare an outline of the main ideas covered within the chapter.

EVALUATE

- Assign Activities and Projects for Chapter 14.
- Administer the printed test or ExamView for Chapter 14.
- Administer the printed test or ExamView for Unit 4.
- Assign School-To-Work/SCANS portfolio activities for Unit 4.

Critical Thinking Skills-Problem Solving

Problem-solving skills, which include recognizing a problem and devising a plan of action, are applied throughout every chapter in this text. Each time a student participates in a Cooperative Learning or Teams activity, problem-solving skills are applied in a group situation. Each time a student completes a math application in the Calculate Business Data, decisions are made as to which mathematical approach must be taken. For each Technology Application problem, students must decide which template problem to use, which piece of software to load, and how to solve the problem. Emphasize to students how they are using problem solving in their day-to-day tasks and make them aware of the skills they are developing.

SCANS

PREPARING A PAYROLL

One of the most important financial responsibilities of a small business owner is maintaining a payroll. Every employee will need to be paid on a weekly, bi-weekly, or monthly basis. Most employees in small businesses are paid an hourly wage but the wage rate may be different for each employee. Some employees work part-time while others work a full 40 hours or more a week.

To be competitive, small businesses may need to offer employees benefits such as health insurance, paid vacation days, or profit sharing, all of which are reflected in the payroll records. The small business is responsible for making required federal and state payments for each employee including income tax withholding, social security, Medicare, Medicaid, and workers' compensation. Payroll records must be maintained, paychecks must be processed, and required payments must be sent to the government on time.

Payroll Records

A payroll record keeping system is needed to manage a company's payroll. The software to manage a basic payroll system can be purchased at a relatively low cost, or the necessary forms can be prepared by the business owner using database or spreadsheet software. A sample payroll form is shown in Figure 14-4.

Payroll Record				Pay Period	from:	to:				
					_/__/20__	_/__/20__				
Employee Name	SS#	Pay Rate	Regular Hours	Overtime Hours	Gross Pay	Federal Tax	State Tax	Social Security	Medicare	Total Deductions	Net Pay
Company Payroll Summary		Pay Period		Year-to-Date						
Gross Pay										
Federal Tax Withheld										
State Tax Withheld										
Social Security										
Medicare										

FIGURE 14-4 Why is a record of each employee needed in addition to the company payroll summary?

Preparing Paychecks

After all employees' payroll amounts have been calculated, a paycheck is prepared for each person. Employees will want to know how the amount of pay they receive is determined so most businesses print an earnings report that is attached to or included with the employee's paycheck. The earnings report usually includes wages and deductions for the current pay period as well as the cumulative amounts for the year. An example employee paycheck and earnings report is shown in Figure 14-5.

Marquese Co.								
Anchora, IN				Pay Begin Date 11/22/20--				
				Pay End Date 12/29/20--				

Employee Jan Exraee   Employee ID 83-221   Check No. 18925
2346 Transport Dr.
Tollboard, IN

Description	Current	Year-to-Date	Taxes	Current	Year-to-Date	Deductions	Current	Year-to-Date
Regular Wage	$480.00	$22,560.00	Fed.	$91.20	$4,012.85	FICA	$31.99	$1,430.96
Overtime	$ 36.00	520.00	State	24.00	1,006.45	OASDI	7.48	334.66
						Net Pay		$361.33

- -

Marquese Co.   No. 18925
Anchora, IN   Date November 20, 20--

Pay to the
Order of _____ Jan Exraee _____ $ _361.33_

Amount _Three Hundred Sixty One and 33/100_____ dollars

BankCo, USA
Evincey, IN   _Paula Morris_
                                Paula Morris, Marquese Co.

FIGURE 14-5 How is the employee's net pay determined?

E-Commerce for Small Business Management

No longer does a company need to have a store, office, or factory. Instead, a book or clothing seller can serve customers online, and the shipping company representative is the only one who has to leave home.

Technology has reduced barriers to entry for new competitors in many industries. In the past, an entrepreneur would have to rent a facility, hire employees, obtain inventory, and advertise when starting a business. Now, a person can begin operations with a computer and a web site. Contacting suppliers, advertising, and filling orders are all executed online.

Online, big companies and small companies look alike. Customers do not see the big buildings, fancy offices, and well-dressed employees. A business is judged on the content and services it provides.

E-commerce also makes it easier for smaller organizations to expand internationally. Online exporting companies may be able to meet the needs of global customers without foreign sales offices. More and more, international buyers check the Internet for the best values in goods and services.

Critical Thinking

Most new businesses fail within five years. The failure rate for online companies is even higher. Research reasons why various cyber companies did not survive. Prepare a short oral presentation with visuals to illustrate the ingredients for online business success.

Small Business Management Web Sites
- U.S. Small Business Administration at www.sba.gov
- *Inc* magazine at www.inc.com
- *Entrepreneur* magazine at www.entrepreneur.com
- *Startup Journal for Entrepreneurs* at www.startupjournal.com

REVIEW YOUR READING

1. Student responses will vary. Possible questions include: (a) How much will it take to start a business, and where will the money come from? (b) How will expenses be paid until a new business becomes profitable? (c) What can be done to increase income and reduce expenses? (d) Will an expansion generate more sales?
2. (a) To anticipate sources and amounts of income. (b) To predict the types and amounts of expenses.
3. There is no financial information to serve as a guideline.
4. To develop a budget.
5. Start-up budget, operating budget, and cash budget.
6. Understanding of financial information sources, computer skills, basic mathematical abilities, and effective communication skills.
7. Financial records.
8. A balance sheet and an income statement.
9. So employees will know how the amount of pay they receive is determined.

COMMUNICATE BUSINESS CONCEPTS

10. If a business has a sound financial plan it should be possible to obtain money in the form of loans or investments in the business. Banks and other financial institutions, people looking to invest in a business to make money, family and friends are among the possible sources of money.
11. Without a budget, it will be very difficult to decide how to spend money or to anticipate the amount of money that will be available. Just as individuals or families without budgets often have difficulty managing their resources, so do businesses without a financial plan.
12. If inventory is not counted or recorded accurately, many businesses suffer because a true account of merchandise in the store cannot be kept. Merchandise may get lost or stolen and the owner will be unaware of the problem. The business may run out of products customers want or have too many of the products that will not sell. Ultimately sales

Chapter REVIEW

BUSINESS NOTES

1. Common sources of financial information for established businesses are financial records. For businesses with limited or no previous financial information, the SBA provides planning tools. Private businesses also collect and publish financial information on similar businesses. A new franchise gets help from the franchisor.

2. Three types of business budgets are the start-up budget, the operating budget, and the cash budget.

3. Common financial records maintained in small businesses are records of cash, credit accounts, inventory, payroll, and assets.

4. Balance sheets and income statements are used to compare financial performance.

REVIEW YOUR READING

1. What four key questions should be asked when deciding how to make effective financial planning decisions?
2. Why do business owners prepare budgets?
3. Why is it hard for new small businesses to do financial planning?
4. What is the most important step in financial planning?
5. Name the three essential budgets for a new business.
6. What skills are needed by the person preparing business budgets?
7. Budgets identify the financial plans of a business. What determines the financial performance of a business?
8. What are the two most-used financial statements?
9. Why do businesses include an earnings report with employee paychecks?

COMMUNICATE BUSINESS CONCEPTS

10. Few businesses are profitable in the first year, so financial planning is very important. How might an owner obtain enough money to operate the business until it becomes profitable?
11. Why is it essential for a business to have a budget, and how will that budget help the business in the years to come?
12. An inventory record is needed to determine the type and quantity of products available for sale.

If this type of record is not kept accurately, what can happen to a business?
13. Accurate financial records and budgets must be kept to make good financial decisions. How can a business owner ensure that the records and budgets are accurate?
14. Why are financial statements so important to business owners when they make decisions?

will be lost or the cost of maintaining inventory will be too high to make a profit.
13. Businesses may hire accountants to review the records once or twice a year. They often are able to determine if there have been problems with the accuracy of the financial records. Computers also are helpful for keeping accurate records. However, the people responsible for collecting and recording information have

the primary responsibility for record keeping.
14. The financial performance of a business determines whether it can succeed in the years to come. A business must use past financial information to plan budgets for the future. Reviewing financial information often identifies areas where the business is experiencing problems as well as where the business has been successful.

DEVELOP YOUR BUSINESS LANGUAGE

For each numbered item, find the term that has the same meaning.

15. An estimate of the actual money received and paid out for a specific time period.

16. A planning tool used to anticipate sources and amounts of income and to predict the types and amounts of expenses for a specific business activity or the entire business.

17. Reports that summarize the financial performance of a business.

18. Used to record and analyze the financial performance of a business.

19. Describes the financial plan for the day-to-day operations of a business.

20. Reports the revenue, expenses, and net income or loss of a business for a specific period of time.

21. Used to plan income and expenses from the beginning of a business until it becomes profitable.

KEY TERMS
business budget
cash budget
financial records
financial statements
income statement
operating budget
start-up budget

DECISION-MAKING STRATEGIES

Tyrone Anderson turned his hobby into a baseball card business. Tyrone began his business with a small loan from the bank and money saved from working while in college. The business grew steadily each year. By preparing a specific budget at the beginning of each year, Mr. Anderson was able to spend his money wisely on new inventory and improvements to his store.

This year he used the same budgeting process that he had implemented the past four years. He estimated that sales would increase 8 percent, so he planned to increase expenses accordingly. The budget projected another nice profit. The first two months of the year went well. Then the economy suddenly slipped into a recession that continued through the rest of the year. Customers cut back on their spending at his store. Tyrone's sales declined but his expenses continued to increase.

22. Why did Tyrone encounter problems in the fifth year when his planning had been so successful in the past?

23. What financial planning recommendations would you make that might have helped Mr. Anderson avoid the problem that he has experienced?

CALCULATE BUSINESS

24. Lee Chan has owned a video business for three years. The first year Mr. Chan barely earned a profit. The next year's profit was more substantial. As shown in the table, he has just received the financial results from the third year and wants to compare them to those of the second year of operations.

   a. How much money did Mr. Chan earn this year? last year?

	Last Year	This Year
Rent	$28,000	$28,000
Sales	78,250	80,725
Inventory (cost of videos)	15,000	13,750
Wages and salaries	17,850	18,210
Utilities	10,010	7,075
Supplies and materials	1,020	2,020

Chapter 14 *Maintaining Financial Information*   **193**

DEVELOP YOUR BUSINESS LANGUAGE

15. cash budget
16. business budget
17. financial statements
18. financial records
19. operating budget
20. income statement
21. start-up budget

DECISION-MAKING STRATEGIES

22. Tyrone did not plan for a recession, and that's why his financial planning was not accurate. Tyrone did well the first four years, and he assumed the fifth year would be just as prosperous. However, Tyrone did not figure for any problems; he just thought that his business would grow with the economy.

23. Mr. Anderson needs to use more types of information when developing his financial plans. Using past years' financial performance will not anticipate changes in the business cycle. Often economists predict when recessions will occur. To handle the current problem, Tyrone should have saved some of his profit from the first four years to use in the fifth year for expenses. He may need to reduce expenses. He could buy only necessities for his business as he waits for the economy to grow again and for the sales of his business to improve.

CALCULATE BUSINESS DATA

24. (a) $80,725 sales this year; $78,250 sales last year.
(b) $28,000 + $13,750 + $18,210 + $7,075 + $2,020 = $69,055 total expenses this year; $28,000 + $15,000 + $17,850 + $10,010 + $1,020 = $71,880 total expenses last year (c) $80,725 sales − $69,055 total expenses = $11,670 profit from this year. (d) This year's profit $11,670 − last year's profit $6,370 = $5,300 more profit this year.

25. Cash, asset; accounts payable, liability; accounts receivable, asset; loan payable, liability; inventory, asset; and equipment, asset. Cash $12,500 + accounts receivable $18,750 + inventory $31,270 + equipment $8,653 = $71,173 assets; accounts payable $27,140 + loan from the bank $7,438 = $34,578 liabilities; $71,173 assets − $34,578 liabilities = $36,595 capital

26. Company payroll summary:
Salary/wages: Current—$1,487.50 + 560.00 + 2,750.00 + 1,767.50 = $6,565.00
Year to date—$8,925.00 + 3,080.00 + 13,750.00 + 9,721.25 = $35,476.25
Taxes: Current—$193.38 + 0.00 + 577.50 + 247.45 = $1,018.33
Year to date—$1,160.25 + 0.00 + 3,465.00 + 1,263.76 = $5,889.01
Deducations: Current—$107.84 + 42.84 + 210.38 + 135.21 = $496.27
Year to date—$647.06 + 235.62 + 1,051.88 + 743.68 = $2,678.24
Net pay:
Toine $1,487.50 − 193.38 − 107.84 = $1,186.28
Rohne $560.00 − 42.84 = $517.16
Padrie $2,750.00 − 577.50 − 210.38 = $1,962.12
Schmidt $1,767.50 − 247.45 − 135.21 = $1,384.84

TECHNOLOGY APPLICATION

In this activity, students use a computer to solve a business problem using a file that is provided on the data CD that accompanies *Intro to Business*. Instructions for using the data CD are included in a **README** file on the disk. Solutions are provided on the Instructor's Resource CD.

b. What was his total cost of doing business this year? last year?
c. What profit or loss did Mr. Chan earn this year?
d. What is the difference in profit between this year and last year?

25. The list in the table identifies items found on a balance sheet. For each item, decide whether it is an asset or liability. Then figure the total for assets, liabilities, and owner's equity (or capital).

Cash	$12,500
Accounts payable (trade credit)	27,140
Accounts receivable	18,750
Loan payable (bank)	7,438
Inventory (goods on hand)	31,270
Equipment	8,653

26. The following table shows the payroll records of 4 employees. Calculate the company payroll summary for the current month and for the year to date. What was the net pay for each employee for the month?

Salary/Wages		
Employee	Current	Year to Date
Toine	$1,487.50	$ 8,925.00
Rohne	560.00	3,080.00
Padrie	2,750.00	13,750.00
Schmidt	1,767.50	9,721.25

Taxes		
Employee	Current	Year to Date
Toine	$193.98	$1,160.25
Rohne	0.00	0.00
Padrie	577.50	3,465.00
Schmidt	247.45	1,263.76

Deductions		
Employee	Current	Year to Date
Toine	$107.84	$ 647.06
Rohne	42.84	235.62
Padrie	210.38	1,051.88
Schmidt	135.21	743.68

TECHNOLOGY APPLICATION

Using the *Intro to Business* Data CD and your spreadsheet program software, select problem CH14. After the problem appears on your screen, complete the following activities. Then, after you have completed each step, display or print the completed spreadsheet for each activity. If you do not have a printer available, answer the questions before you leave the computer.

27. In the Percent column, enter formulas to show each item as a percentage of Total Estimated Sales. Format the results as percentages with one decimal place. Answer the following questions:
   a. What is the percentage of Total Estimated Sales budgeted for Salaries and Wages?
   b. What is the percentage of Total Estimated Sales budgeted for Utilities?

28. In the Difference column, enter formulas to calculate Actual minus Budget. Format the results as currency with two decimal places. Answer the following questions:
   a. How many expenditures had actual spending greater than budget?
   b. Which expenditure from Question (a) has the largest difference?

29. What if your actual Sales increased to $35,000? Copy the budget from Question 28 to another part of the spreadsheet. Enter the new amount of actual Sales. Answer the following questions:
   a. What is the new difference between actual Total Operating Expenses and budgeted Total Operating Expenses?
   b. What is the new amount of actual Net Income?

Optional: Using the spreadsheet from Question 28, create a bar chart comparing budgeted expenditures to actual expenditures. Repeat for Question 29.

PRICING FOR GLOBAL MARKETS

A new car that costs $16,000 in the United States could cost over $30,000 in South America. Production costs, consumer demand, and competition are the most common factors affecting prices in a country. However, in the global marketplace, prices are also affected by other economic and political influences.

Fluctuations of currency exchange rates can result in a company receiving less money than expected. This risk of fluctuating currency rates can be eliminated by setting prices based on the currency of the selling company's country. *Countertrade*, the process of directly exchanging products and services among companies in different countries, can also minimize pricing risks.

Sometimes a company may intentionally set extremely low prices for foreign trade. *Dumping* is the practice of selling exported products at lower prices than they are sold in the company's home country. While this can benefit consumers, others will suffer. The lower price drives out competition, causing workers to lose jobs.

Recently, Chilean salmon companies were accused of selling their fish for less

> **Prices in the global marketplace are influenced by political and economic issues.**

than the going market price. This put Norwegian and U.S. fisheries at a competitive disadvantage in the world market. However, the Chilean companies contended that the price they charged was based on their operating costs and the large supply of salmon during that harvest season.

Businesses often pressure governments into helping to prevent dumping. Countries may adopt antidumping laws or antidumping tariffs. These trade barriers prohibit importers from selling products at artificially low prices.

CRITICAL THINKING

1. Select a product that could be sold in other countries. Describe the factors you would consider when setting prices for that product. What economic and political factors affect global pricing strategies?

2. Conduct research on "dumping" using library materials and web sites. What are some examples of dumping? How were the disagreements between countries settled?

Most students will either work with international clients or compete against businesses that do. Global Navigator introduces students to issues integral to working with international businesses. Key concepts and challenges faced by international businesses are presented, followed by Critical Thinking questions that require students to analyze what they have learned.

In this feature, students will learn about some key pricing considerations that apply to foreign markets, including currency risks and dumping strategies. Since more and more businesses are selling products abroad and also buying products from foreign sources, it is important for students to understand how and why pricing decisions differ when they involve cross-border transactions.

CRITICAL THINKING

1. Students will likely select a variety of different products, but they should cite pricing factors such as the costs of direct and indirect trade barriers such as import duties, quotas, and restrictions imposed by the destination country; transportation expenses; currency risks; and the quality and intensity of competition in overseas markets. Economic and political factors include trade barriers, currency stability, political risks, availability and cost of financing; and the efficiency of distribution channels in foreign markets.

2. Some examples of dumping disagreements in recent years include charges by some U.S. businesses of dumping by Japanese and European steel producers, by Argentinean cattle ranchers, and South Korean car makers.

GLOBAL BUSINESS PROJECT

People and money are the focus of this phase of the global business plan project. Students are asked to think about what career skills would be necessary when working for a multinational company.

As students identify the start-up costs for their business idea, encourage them to find examples from other companies and to talk with people involved in business. Remind students that loans, money from investors, and personal assets are the most common sources of funding a new business. The web site of the Small Business Administration can provide information on this topic. When estimating income and expenses for their businesses, again encourage students to find examples of other companies and to talk with people in business.

To complete each phase of this project, students are encouraged to use various resources—textbook content, library materials, World Wide Web sites, interviews, advertisements, product packages, in-store observations. The individual activities are planned for use as either (1) an on-going course project, or (2) individual assignments.

Whether used as a continuing project or for selected activities, consider having students work in teams. This small group experience provides a valuable skill for future learning and work situations.

In addition to search engines, these selected web sites can be helpful for this unit:
- International Trade Administration of the U.S. Dept. of Commerce (www.ita.doc.gov)
- World Bank (www.worldbank.org)
- World Trade Organization at (www.wto.org)
- World Export-Import Bank of the United States (www.exim.gov)
- International Chamber of Commerce (www.iccwbo.org/)

GLOBAL BUSINESS PROJECT

ORGANIZE FOR GLOBAL BUSINESS ACTIVITIES

Two of the major resources of every business are people and money. Human resources involve the workers, their productive skills, and the salary and wages they earn. Financial resources are the necessary funds to start and operate a business.

In this phase of the business plan project, information will be obtained related to start-up costs, short-term and long-term financing, budgeting, and planning an income statement.

PROJECT GOALS

1. Analyze skills needed by managers and other workers when doing business with other countries.

2. Research start-up costs and financing sources for exporting companies.

3. Identify sources of income and operating expenses for a company involved in international business.

PROJECT ACTIVITIES

Using your textbook, library materials, web sites, interviews with people, and other resources, complete the following activities:
1. Some work skills can be used in every geographic setting. Other career competencies are unique to various regions and industries. Using a country from your portfolio (or select a country), describe two skills that would be unique to the area or business you have chosen.

2. When starting (or expanding) a business, several costs are involved. For the business idea used in previous units (or another international business idea), list items (with an estimated amount) that would be necessary to start your business. Also, describe sources of funding the business operations. These may include loans, money from investors, or personal assets.

3. Each business day, companies make sales and pay expenses. For your business idea, create a hypothetical income statement for your business. Estimate amounts for income and operating costs, including payroll.

PROJECT WRAP-UP

1. Continue your portfolio (folder, file box, or other container) for storing and referring back to the information and materials you created in the activities above. Your portfolio provides the information needed for the various elements of a global business plan.

2. Create a presentation listing start-up costs, projected monthly revenue, and monthly expenses for your international business idea. This may be done using spreadsheet software.

- Small Business Administration (www.sba.gov)
- Import-export information at (www.internationalist.com/)
- Global stock exchanges, foreign exchange (www.globalfindata.com) (www.ubs.com)
- Annual reports, company information (www.hoovers.com)

FOCUS ON CAREERS

HUMAN RESOURCE OCCUPATIONS

Human resources as a business function is responsible for identifying, selecting, assigning, training, compensating, and motivating personnel. Human resource specialists must also handle employment problems such as laws, reductions in the number of employees, and employee grievances and terminations.

JOB TITLES

Job titles in this career area include:
- Director of Human Resources
- Employment, Recruitment, and Placement Specialist
- Training and Development Manager
- Training Specialist
- Compensation Manager
- Employee Benefits Manager
- Recruiter
- Employer Relations Representative
- Job Analyst
- Mediator
- Labor Relations Manager
- Industrial Relations Director
- International Human Resources Manager

EMPLOYMENT OUTLOOK

- Job growth will be about as fast as the average for all occupations through 2010.
- Demand for specialists will be higher than demand for managers.
- Most jobs will be in the private rather than the public sector.
- Demand for consultants will be particularly high.
- Some companies will expect people to perform human resource tasks on a part-time basis while they do other jobs.

EDUCATION AND TRAINING

- Most entry level jobs are filled by college graduates.
- Many colleges offer undergraduate and graduate degrees in human resource management with specializations in areas such as law, finance, and training.
- Special skills are usually required in interpersonal communications, writing, and speaking. Computer skills are increasingly important.
- A master's degree is important for management-level positions; a doctorate is seldom required for most positions, but may be beneficial for consultants.

SALARY LEVELS

According to recent surveys, average (median) salaries include:
- Starting salaries in human resources with a bachelor's degree, $32,000; with a master's degree, $39,900.
- Employee relations specialists in the federal government, $58,000; personnel managers, $65,000.
- Top industrial/labor relations directors and divisional human resources directors, about $100,000.

CRITICAL THINKING

1. What job titles in this career area appeal to you most? Give some reasons for your choice.
2. What are some things you will have to do to achieve success in the career selected?

FOCUS ON CAREERS

The careers listed in this Focus on Careers come from the *Occupational Outlook Handbook*, an online publication (www.bls.gov/oco) of the federal government, under the heading Human Resources, Training, and Labor Relations Managers and Specialists. The O*NET codes for these job titles are: Director of Human Resources, 11-3040.00; Employment, Recruitment, and Placement Specialist, 13-1071.00; Training and Development Manager, 11-3042.00; Training Specialist, 13-1073.00; Compensation Manager, 11-3041.00; Employee Benefits Manager, 11-3041.00; Recruiter, 13-1071.02; Employee Relations Representative, 13-1079.99; Job Analyst 13-1072.00; Mediator, 23-1022.00; Labor Relations Manager, 11-3049.99; Industrial Relations Director, 11-3049.99; International Human Resources Manager, 11-3049.99. Students can access O*NET Online (online.onetcenter.org) to view important features of selected occupations. They can also search for related occupations and for occupations that match selected skills.

As a supplemental activity, distribute the Career Focus worksheets found in the School-To-Work/SCANS Activity Masters.

CRITICAL THINKING

Answers, of course, to the two critical thinking questions will vary widely. Students should be encouraged to select one job even if they are not really interested in a career area. Thinking about why a certain job might possibly be appealing is a forced-thinking exercise that results in self-reflections and self-examination. Answering these questions also gives certain career areas a sharper focus within students' minds.

UNIT 5

BUILDING YOUR PORTFOLIO

CAREER DEVELOPMENT – RESEARCHING CAREER OPPORTUNITIES

The Building Your Portfolio career exercise will help your students establish a personal history—where they have been, where they are now, and where they are going. This Career Development Exercise will compel students to investigate prospective employers.

Guide students to select a company that might hold future career interest for them. Through researching that company, students will be better able to relate their interests, skills, and achievements to the specific needs of an employer.

Direct students to research companies they may be targeting for future employment. Have students do the following: (1) visit companies to get a personal perspective; (2) ask for literature about each company, such as a brochure giving an overview of the company or an annual report to stockholders; (3) try out the company's product or service firsthand. Students should write a report about their visitations. The report should be keyed in an acceptable format and placed in the student's portfolio.

As a supplemental activity, you may refer to the School–To–Work/SCANS Activity Masters.

TEACHING STRATEGIES

SCANS

Critical Thinking Skills

PROBLEM SOLVING.................................221

Workplace Competencies

INTERPERSONAL SKILLS.......................214
TECHNOLOGY..204

Personal Qualities

INTEGRITY..231
SELF-ESTEEM..217

Basic Skills

LISTENING..232
MATH...218, 233
SPEAKING...203

Cooperative Learning
202,208

Alternate Modalities
Tactile Learner 219

Teaching Tips
Building Your Portfolio 199
Kick-Off Activity 198
Safety and Health 206

Special Needs
Hearing Impaired Students 216
Limited English Proficiency (LEP) Students 229

Special Features

Media/Technology

Chapter	Spreadsheet Software	Database Software	Word Processing Software	Internet	Video
15		■			■
16	■				■
17			■	■	■

Resources

SOFTWARE

Excel, Word, WordPerfect, Works, and ClarisWorks for Mac and Windows

Word Pro, ASCII, QuattroPro, Lotus, and Access for Windows

SOUTH-WESTERN EDUCATIONAL PUBLISHING PRODUCTS

Parsons and Oja. *Computer Concepts.* 2003. Course Technology. 0-619-10909-2.

Shelly, Cashman, and Vermaat. *Discovering Computers 2003: Concepts for a Digital World. Web and XP Enhanced.* Course Technology. 0-7895-6513-7.

BOOKS

Newton. *Newton's Telecom Dictionary: The Official Dictionary of Telecommunications & the Internet.* 1999. Miller Freeman Books.

Lynch and Horton. *Web Style Guide: Basic Design Principles for Creating Web Sites.* 1999. Yale University Press.

PERIODICALS

Computerworld Magazine. Framingham, MA.

PC Magazine. New York, NY.

The Wall Street Journal. New York, NY.

Wired Magazine. San Francisco, CA.

GOVERNMENT PUBLICATIONS

Occupational Outlook Handbook, U.S. Department of Labor, Washington, DC.

What Work Requires of Schools: A SCANS Report for America 2000, U.S. Department of Labor, Washington, DC

MEDIA/TECHNOLOGY

Publisher's web sites:

www.intro2business.swep.com

www.swep.com

www.thomson.com

UNIT 5

TECHNOLOGY FOR BUSINESS DECISIONS

The role of technology in business is the focus of this unit. In Chapter 15, students are introduced to the elements of computer systems and how businesses use computers. In Chapter 16, specific types of application programs are discussed. In Chapter 17, students will learn about the important present-day and future functions technology fulfills in our economy.

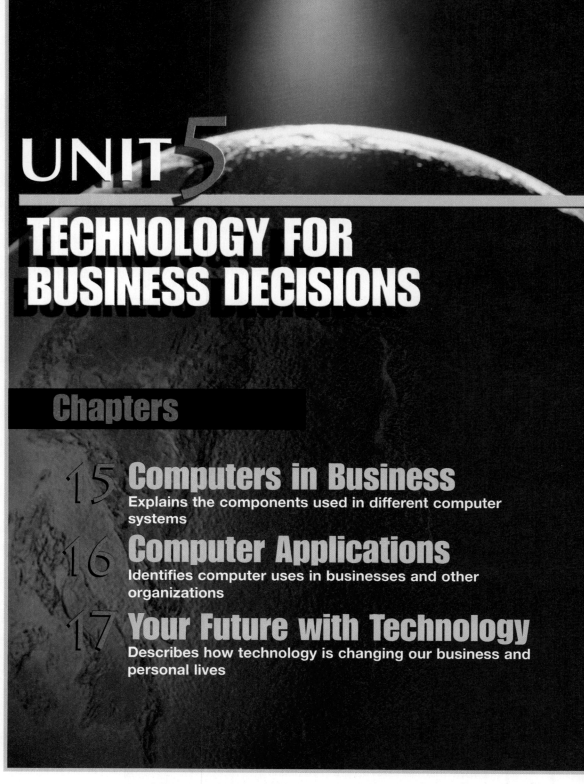

UNIT 5

TECHNOLOGY FOR BUSINESS DECISIONS

Chapters

15 Computers in Business
Explains the components used in different computer systems

16 Computer Applications
Identifies computer uses in businesses and other organizations

17 Your Future with Technology
Describes how technology is changing our business and personal lives

Kick-Off Activity

Investigating Business Media

The following exercise asks students to choose an article from *The Wall Street Journal*, the financial section of a newspaper, or a business magazine and to inquire about a topic related to this unit.

Direct students to select articles show- ing how computers or other technological advances have helped a company improve its competitive advantage or profitability. Have students find articles about a company of interest to them and answer the following questions:

1 What advantage did the new technology give the company you selected? Are other companies in the same industry using the same technology as effectively?

2 Did the article(s) mention any problems the company had implementing its new technology? What were they? Do you think the problems could have been avoided? How?

BU$INESSBRIEF

THE INTERNET: FOR WORK AND PLAY

"I received an e-mail today with the sales figures from our Asian office."

"Don't forget to check the Web for the latest exchange rates for foreign currencies."

A few years ago, these statements would not have made any sense. Today statements like these are a common part of our daily conversations.

Global information networks and online computer services make it possible to access more information from your home or office than is available in any library. The foundation of computer network communications is the Internet, which connects schools, government agencies, businesses, and homes.

The Internet includes *e-mail* service for sending messages from one computer to another anywhere in the world. An e-mail address has three parts. Reading from right to left, the first part is the domain, a three-letter code indicating the type of organization: *gov* is for government, *edu* is for an educational institution, *com* is for a commercial or business organization, and *mil* is for a military e-mail address. The second part — immediately following the "at" (@) sign — is the name of the computer receiving the message. The third part — immediately before the @ sign — is the name of the user receiving the message.

The World Wide Web, referred to as the *Web* is a major element of the Internet. This component allows you to browse through text, graphics, video clips, and sound bites from millions of information sources. For example, you can view current weather maps, or art from a museum along with an audio commentary.

Internet information providers offer a wide variety of services, including homework hotlines, current reference materials for doing reports, and discussion forums on a wide range of financial, economic, and political topics. Online users may also post their resumes and search for job opportunities on the computer network. A variety of business information can be accessed on the Internet, such as investment information.

Internet users may also obtain computer programs online. Software is available for video games, stories with graphics and sound, and learning activities. You can access software for budgeting, calculating net worth, determining loan payments, and graphing investment portfolios.

As businesses use the Internet for marketing products and services, shopping from home will increase. Today, you can order almost everything you need while sitting at your computer.

CRITICAL THINKING

1 *What types of technology make the Internet possible?*

2 *How can global computer networks benefit people throughout the world?*

199

BU$INESSBRIEF

After reading the Business Brief, ask students what impressed them the most. Have they heard or read about this topic before? Find out what students know about global computer networks. Have students create a chart or illustration of the Internet and other global computer networks.

CRITICAL THINKING

Student answers require thinking beyond what is presented in the Business Brief. Answers will be based on students' perceptions of the topic and experiences they have had with it. The following are possible answers:

1. The Internet is made possible with computers connected by telephone lines along with other telecommunications systems such as satellites and wireless technology.

2. Global computer networks can benefit people by allowing quicker and less expensive communications for correspondence and other business activities. These systems also make it possible for information to be easily available in areas difficult to reach by traditional transportation methods, such as rural areas or mountainous terrains.

BUILDING YOUR PORTFOLIO

The Building Your Portfolio work samples validate skill level and a student's ability to accomplish tasks frequently performed on the job. The most important reason for including samples in a portfolio is to demonstrate a student's abilities and skills. In selecting work samples for each unit, students should always have a choice of which activities to include. Students might be encouraged to include samples from the end-of-chapter activities, particularly Communicate Business Concepts, Calculate Business Data, Technology Application, and Decision-Making Strategies.

This chapter provides an overview of computers. Students are introduced to the four main elements of a computer system—input, processing, storage, and output—along with examples of these components.

Resources for Teachers
- Lesson Plans
- School-To-Work/SCANS Activity Masters
- Spanish Resources
- Instructor's Resource CD

Assessment
- Chapter and Unit Tests, Ch. 15
- ExamView, Ch. 15

Media/Technology
- Applying Technology Data CD
- PowerPoint slides
- Business Connection CD
- Videotape

Activity Masters and Workbooks
- Activities and Projects, Ch. 15
- Internet Activity Masters
- Business Math Activity Masters
- Communications Activity Masters
- International Business Activity Masters
- Ethics Activity Masters

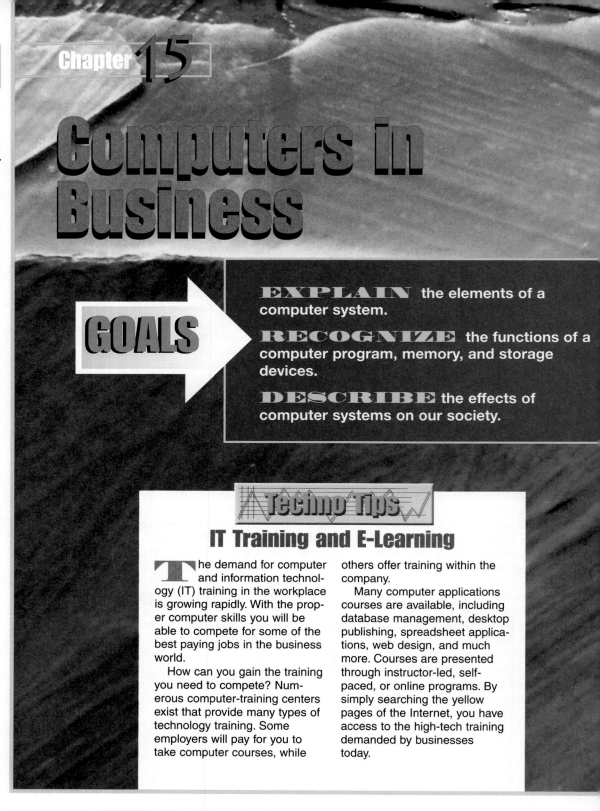

Chapter 15

Computers in Business

GOALS

EXPLAIN the elements of a computer system.

RECOGNIZE the functions of a computer program, memory, and storage devices.

DESCRIBE the effects of computer systems on our society.

Techno Tips

IT Training and E-Learning

The demand for computer and information technology (IT) training in the workplace is growing rapidly. With the proper computer skills you will be able to compete for some of the best paying jobs in the business world.

How can you gain the training you need to compete? Numerous computer-training centers exist that provide many types of technology training. Some employers will pay for you to take computer courses, while others offer training within the company.

Many computer applications courses are available, including database management, desktop publishing, spreadsheet applications, web design, and much more. Courses are presented through instructor-led, self-paced, or online programs. By simply searching the yellow pages of the Internet, you have access to the high-tech training demanded by businesses today.

Students need to know the latest technologies and develop cutting edge Internet skills for use in current jobs, future careers, or in their homes. TechnoTips introduces students to today's cutting edge technologies and provides them with important Internet skills. Feature topics concentrate on Internet-specific technologies and computer or other hi-tech innovations for use by businesses and consumers.

M s. Jenkins announced to her class, "The French Club will meet today during sixth period. The topic for discussion will be computers in international business."

Fran looked at her friend Brenda and said, "That doesn't make sense! What do computers have to do with the French Club?"

"Recently our club decided to use a database program to keep track of our membership records," said Brenda. "In addition," she went on, "the club is using e-mail to talk to students in France. Then, we are planning a video conference with other French clubs around the United States. And we will also use our computer network to..."

"Wait a minute!" Fran exclaimed. "Database! E-mail! Video conference! Computer network! I don't understand any of this!"

"Well it's really pretty easy," responded Brenda, "and you can start by coming to the meeting today after school."

COMPUTER SYSTEMS IN YOUR LIFE

A few years ago people would have thought it unusual to shop from home by computer or to pay an electric bill online. Today, however, these activities, and many others, have become common as a result of computers.

Nearly every business uses some type of computer. Quick, efficient processing is necessary for a company to control its operating costs, to manage its resources, and to stay competitive. Employment in today's workplace requires the use of computers for various business activities.

Uses of Computers

Computers are everywhere. These electronic devices process sales records, test scores, and sports statistics. Computers in business are used mainly to store, process, and report information. However, computers are also used to design factories, control traffic patterns, and measure the health of medical patients.

Computers enable people to handle data quickly and efficiently. **Data** consist of facts in the form of numbers, letters, words, or special symbols. Data with which you are probably familiar include addresses, school grades, and earnings from a part-time job. Data are usually combined into groups called *files* that are used to process and store information.

The amount of information used each day in our society is extensive. When you consider the billions of business transactions, checks, and school records that are processed each day, you can see that computers make life easier.

Elements of a Computer System

A home video game, a notebook computer, and an automated highway toll collection system all have four basic components:

1. an input device, such as a keyboard,
2. a processing unit that manages data,

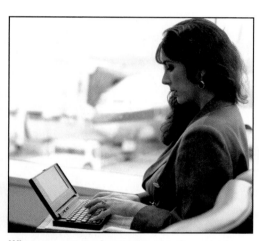

What are some advantages of using a laptop computer?

of a computer system. Instructions for processing come from computer programs. The third component is memory, the means of storing programs and data for later use. Memory can be internal storage or external storage. Output, the fourth component, allows computer users to see the results of processing. Output can appear on a screen or print out on paper. Also, emphasize the need to balance the costs of efficient data entry with the benefits of fast, accurate information.

TRY THIS/GUIDED PRACTICE
Ask students to name different types of data received by businesses (e.g., customer phone call, item with a price tag, printed purchase order, mailing list). Guide students through identifying which devices could be used to input and output the data. Explain that all data must be input and output, but that businesses use different devices depending on the nature of the data and the efficiency of the devices. Discuss the pros and cons of output on screens and paper.

EXPLORE THIS/INDEPENDENT PRACTICE Before assigning independent practice material for any chapter, students should be expected to read the textbook material carefully. In view of the fact that all students vary widely in their ability to read effectively, it is advisable to have students read the entire chapter, or sections thereof, silently in class if the material has not been previously read in connection with homework assignments.

After students have read the chapter, ask them to complete the

3. memory and storage facilities, and
4. an output device, most likely a printer.

These components combine to create what is called a **computer system**. The physical elements of a computer system are called the **hardware**. Examples of hardware include keyboards, monitors (or screens), chips, and printers.

New hardware for computer systems becomes available almost daily. For example, a **multimedia system** presents information using a combination of sound, graphics, animation, and video. In the past, this type of system was only available in large companies. Multimedia computer systems are now common in small businesses and homes.

In contrast to hardware, **software** refers to the instructions that run the computer system.

FIGURE 15-1 Why is it better to manage information with computers than without computers?

COMPUTER SYSTEM'S MAIN ELEMENTS

2. Processing

1. Input

3. Memory and Storage

4. Output

TEACHING STRATEGIES
Cooperative Learning

Assign students to groups of five or six. Appoint one student in each group to be the recorder/spokesperson and one student to be the systems analyst. Ask students to think of a task not currently performed using computers. Have students design a computer system to accomplish the task. The systems analyst should sketch on paper a simple drawing showing the components of the new computer system. The recorder/spokesperson should prepare an oral report to the rest of the class, describing the new computer system. During the oral report, the systems analyst should copy the sketch of the system onto the board or an overhead. (Note: As a supplemental activity, you may wish to distribute the Student Activity Worksheet, Workplace Competencies—Interpersonal Skills Checklist, in the School-To-Work/SCANS Activity Masters, to serve as guidelines for discussion.)

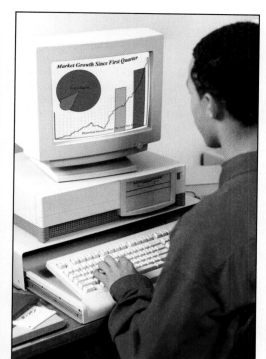

What are some of the many uses for computers?

Types of software commonly used in business organizations are word processing, spreadsheet, database, and communications programs.

You are probably most familiar with a *microcomputer*, also called a *personal computer (PC)*. These computers fall into two categories—desktop and portable models. Companies commonly link many desktop personal computers to create a **computer network**. Global computer networks also exist, such as the one the French Club will use to communicate with students in other countries.

Portable PCs may be called *notebooks*, *sub-notebooks*, *personal digital assistants (PDAs),* or *laptop* computers depending on their size. Small, handheld *personal digital assistants* process information with a pen stylus used to write on the pressure-sensitive screen.

Large computer systems used in business are called *mainframe* computers. These can handle many instructions and process data faster. Very large mainframe computers are referred to as *super computers*.

INPUT: GETTING STARTED

The first major component of a computer system is known as input. While people are mostly concerned with the end results of computer operations, there also has to be a starting point. Data are entered into a computer system with an **input device**. A commonly used input device is the keyboard, which allows you to input letters, words, numbers, and other symbols or commands.

A keyboard combined with a monitor may be referred to as a *computer terminal*. A terminal is usually part of a network connecting several computers. These communications networks may be created to handle banking transactions or to send information from one library to another.

Another input device is the *mouse*, which is a handheld device used to point to a certain command (or image) on the computer screen. For example, if you want to save a file, move the mouse pointer to the drawing of a disk on the screen. Then click the mouse on the symbol. The data will then be stored for future use.

Other types of input devices include:

- A controller for a video game system allows you to instruct the movement and actions of game characters.

- Touch-sensitive screens allow you to touch or point at the correct command to enter data.

Programmers use computer languages to write the instructions for telling a computer what functions to perform. The most common computer languages are C^{++}, Java, and Visual Basic.

end-of-chapter questions. Develop Your Business Language is an excellent way to improve students' vocabulary. Only words introduced in the chapter are used in the vocabulary exercises. The Review Your Reading questions can be used to check students' ability to comprehend what they have read. The Communicate Business Concepts section affords an opportunity for students to apply to practical life situations the information gained from reading the chapter. By completing the problems under Calculate Business Data, students will be able to strengthen and refine their abilities in mathematics. Technology Application allows students to demonstrate skill in using word processing, spreadsheet, and database software. Decision-Making Strategies contains material to challenge students to utilize the decision-making model explained in Chapter 1 for problem solving.

The Chapter Review questions at the end of the chapter vary in level of difficulty. For a basic assignment, consider Develop Your Business Language and Review Your Reading. For an average assignment, consider the basic assignment plus Communicate Business Concepts and Calculate Business Data. For an enhanced assignment, try the average assignment plus Technology Application and Decision-Making Strategies.

ASSESS

Review the goals at the beginning of the chapter and the Business Notes at the end of the chapter.

Basic Skills-Speaking

Before speaking to a group, students should know their audience, plan their presentation, rehearse, then make the presentation. Discuss characteristics of an audience and how that audience plays a role in the performance of the speaker. Developing a speech through an outline is an excellent planning tool, and every speech should have an introduction, body, and conclusion. Then discuss the rehearsal process and its purpose. As this unit of study is Technology for Business Decisions, assign several students the topic of "how technology can help me succeed in preparing and presenting a speech." Give students the Student Activity Worksheet, Basic Skills—Speaking, in the School-To-Work/SCANS Activity Masters, to serve as a guideline for preparation of a speech.

Restate each as a question and have students respond orally. For students who may have difficulty providing answers, assign the reteaching activities that follow. Enrichment activities may also be assigned where appropriate.

1. What are the elements of a computer system? (Answer: Data, hardware, software, input device, central processing unit, memory, output devices.)

2. With what devices are data entered into a computer system? (Answer: Keyboard, mouse, video game controller, touch-sensitive screen, scanner, voice-activated system.)

3. Why is a computer program important? (Answer: It provides step-by-step instructions to the computer about what functions to complete.)

4. What are examples of storage devices? (Answer: Tape, disk drive, floppy disk, hard disk, CD-ROM.)

5. How does a computer system report results? (Answer: Screen, disk storage, printer.)

6. What are the effects of computer systems on our society? (Answer: Faster and more efficient storing and retrieving of data.)

RETEACH

Collect advertisements, photos, and articles from newspapers and magazines that show different types of computer equipment, including input, storage, and output devices. Develop a bulletin board display or poster showing the elements of a computer system using these materials. Point out that all computer systems have the same components.

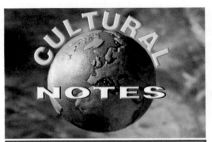

CULTURAL NOTES

The United States is a nation of cultural diversity in which many languages are spoken. From these languages, we have derived many words that reflect some of these cultures. For example, there are many names that Native Americans gave various places to describe accurately the features of the location. *Monongahela* is an example of a Native American word. Monongahela means "high banks breaking off and falling down in places."

- Scanning devices that read numbers, letters of the alphabet, symbols and photos to translate them into a format that can be recognized by the computer.

- Voice-activated systems allow you to enter

Why do you think that computer chips are as small as a thumbnail?

data or commands with a microphone. Instead of entering a complex series of computer instructions, you will be able to say, "Subtract the amount of this payment and determine how much money I have left in my account." The computer will be able to translate your words into instructions it can understand and will be able to perform the necessary processing.

PROCESSING: MAKING THINGS HAPPEN

The second major component of a computer system is known as processing. How do data become meaningful information to be used by organizations and individuals? This activity occurs in the **central processing unit (CPU)**, which is the control center of the computer. The CPU is the "brain" of a computer system. In a PC, the CPU consists of tiny wafers or chips, no bigger than your thumbnail. These chips are tiny pieces of silicon imprinted with circuits that carry instructions and data by electronic pulses.

Despite the automated process by which a computer operates, your efforts are still needed. Someone must tell the system what to do. The most common way to give instructions to a computer is with a program. A **program** is a series of detailed, step-by-step instructions that tell the computer what functions to complete.

The two main types of computer programs are application software and operating system software.

Application software refers to programs that perform specific tasks such as word processing, database management, or accounting.

Operating system software translates a computer user's commands and allows application programs to interact with the

Workplace Competencies-Technology

We may help students become proficient in technology by teaching them how to apply technology to tasks through understanding the basics of computers. A brief overview is always a good review before assigning problems to be completed. A brief discussion on the parts of the computer, how machines are installed, various systems that may be used to get different

results, interpretation of the output (perhaps printouts), and a discussion of error messages will be helpful to students. The user guides that accompany your hardware and software are a reliable resource for you to use. This way you can be sure that the material you are sharing with your students is relevant to the equipment they will use. The Student Activity Worksheet, Workplace Competencies—Technology Checklist, in the School-To-Work/SCANS Activity Masters, may aid class discussion.

computer's hardware. The most commonly used operating system is Windows®, a graphical user interface (GUI) system. With a GUI, commands are displayed with small graphics (called *icons*).

Most complex and powerful computer programs are in formats that are difficult to understand. The format of a computer program is a **computer language**, a system of letters, words, numbers, and symbols used to communicate with a computer. Since a wide variety of ready-to-use programs are available, most people do not have to create their own programs.

MEMORY AND STORAGE: SAVING THINGS FOR LATER

The third major component of a computer system is known as **memory**. When in use, a program is stored in a location called memory. This memory within the computer is also called *internal* (or *primary*) *storage*. During processing, both the program and any data entered with an input device are stored in memory.

Memory capacity is measured using terms such as *bit*, *nibble*, *byte*, and *kilobyte* (*K*). To give you an idea of a computer's internal

FIGURE 15-2 Why is it important to know the number of bytes of memory capacity on a computer?

MEMORY CAPACITY

BIT	KILOBYTE
SMALLEST UNIT	1,024 BYTES
NIBBLE	MEGABYTE
4 BITS; A 1/2 BYTE	A MILLION BYTES
BYTE	GIGABYTE
8 BITS	A BILLION BYTES

storage capacity, it would take at least a 1K computer to store the information on an average page in this book.

Primary storage cannot store all of the programs and all of the data needed by computer users. Therefore, *auxiliary* (or *external*) *storage* that is not part of memory is available for storing both programs and data. Disks and tapes are examples of auxiliary storage devices.

A **disk drive** is used to store information on a magnetic medium so that the information can be recalled and used again. Disks on which programs or data are stored come in two basic forms. A floppy disk is a small, pliable, oxide-coated plastic disk in protective hard plastic covers. A hard disk is built into the computer and is made from rigid material that does not bend. It allows storage of tens of millions of characters. Both types of disk systems use coded magnetic spots to represent information.

A **CD-ROM** (compact disk, read-only memory) is a data storage device that uses laser optics for reading data. One CD-ROM makes it possible to store over 250,000 pages of text.

OUTPUT: SEEING THE RESULTS

The fourth major component of a computer system is known as output, the phase of computer operations of greatest interest to most people. Your score on a video game, the results of a test, or the sales for a new product are important outcomes of data-processing activities. **Output devices** present data in a form that can be retrieved later or may be communicated immediately.

Most often output is displayed on a computer screen or monitor. For example, you can view sales reports sorted by salesperson, by geographic area, or by product. With a

What are some of the ways that CD-ROMs are used with computers?

video game, the screen shows scores for each player.

Viewing on a screen allows you to see quickly the results of your data processing efforts. However, the screen only allows you to see a limited number of lines at one time. Quite often, the computer may be instructed to produce a copy of the processed data on a printer, an output device that produces results on paper.

Two main types of printers are commonly used. First, an ink-jet printer uses a printhead with a series of little holes. These little holes, called *nozzles*, spray ink onto the paper to create the appropriate letters and images. Second, laser printers use an electrophotographic method of printing, similar to a photocopy machine. These printers produce

Electronic pens have been developed to link paper to your computer. The pen strokes are recorded in memory and viewed on the computer screen.

high-quality documents at rates of as high as several thousand lines per minute.

COMPUTER SYSTEMS IN ACTION

Each day in banks, stores, offices, factories, homes, and not-for-profit organizations, the use of computer systems is expanding. As managers plan and implement computerized activities, they must decide how best to use technology to serve the production and distribution needs of the organization. They must also balance the costs of efficient data entry with the benefits of fast, accurate information.

Can you think of different types of data output that would be used in the workplace?

TEACHING Tip
Safety and Health

Make sure that students position the keyboard and mouse in a manner so that their arms and hands are in a comfortable position at the keyboard.

NET FACTS

tions while increasing job growth in others. It will also continue to change the way our work is done. Remember, however, that computers do not make decisions. The information obtained from computer software is just a tool to help in the decision-making process.

Cyberspace is the electronic world of the Internet that exists only on computers. Cyberspace may also be called *virtual reality*.

New technology will continue to expand the potential uses of computers in business. New software will eliminate some occupa-

Computers make it possible for people who are disabled to work and run their own businesses.

For example, special scanners read documents and present them in an audio format so that workers with visual limitations can use printed materials.

NET FACTS

Net Facts provides information and definitions of terms for the Internet. The more information that students have about the Internet, the better equipped they will be to use this resource. In the Internet Activity Masters, there is an Internet Activity Worksheet for each unit. You can use these activities to give students experience with finding information online. Options for assigning this activity are as follows:
1. **Provide students with a list of addresses of resources for this activity;**
2. **Assign students to conduct their own searches; or**
3. **Use the addresses provided on the Internet Activity Worksheet.**
   You should complete the activity yourself before assigning it to resolve any discrepancies that may arise.

GLOBAL PERSPECTIVES
Computer Systems for Foreign Language

While on the job at an exporting company, you receive a phone call from a customer in Kenya. Unable to understand the caller's language, you switch on the language translator service. This software allows you to understand, in your language, the comments and questions of your customer.

Computerized translators recognize speech in one language and convert the spoken words into another language. In a language translation system three capabilities work together—speech recognition, machine translation, and speech synthesis. The computer recognizes words spoken in the first language and converts the words into a computer file. Then, the words are translated into the second language, also in a computer file. Finally, a voice synthesizer "speaks" the translated version. A typical one-page letter can be translated in less than one hour.

The earliest language translator programs

only had a vocabulary of about 500 words. However with advanced technology, today's systems can process all the words in typical dictionaries for commonly used international business languages, such as Arabic, Chinese, English, French, German, Italian, Japanese, Korean, Portuguese, Russian, Spanish, and Vietnamese.

In the future, an English-speaking businessperson might say, "I would like to register for the conference." Using a computerized translator, a German businessperson will hear, "Ich wuerde mich gerne zur Konferenz anmelden."

Critical Thinking
1. How does a language translation computer system work?
2. How do computerized language translators improve global business activities?

GLOBAL PERSPECTIVES

Global Perspectives gives students an opportunity to visualize various places around the globe. This feature also describes various business practices that are different around the world.

CRITICAL THINKING
1. Possible answers might include a computer system for language translation involves computer systems that (1) recognize speech patterns, (2) translate the speech patterns into a machine-understandable format, and (3) present the translated message in a voice-synthesized version.
2. Possible answers might include computerized language translators help make language translation faster and more efficient. Fast, accurate translation is necessary for effective international business activities.

REVIEW YOUR READING

1. Quick and efficient handling of data, collecting data, and solving business problems.
2. The input device, the processing unit, memory and storage, and the output device.
3. Keyboard and mouse are most common. Others include video game controllers, touch-sensitive screens, scanning devices, and voice-activated systems.
4. The central processing unit is the "brain" of a computer system. It reads instructions and performs needed operations to change data into useful information.
5. Storing data on a floppy disk uses coded, magnetic spots to represent information. On a CD-ROM, the data is read using laser optics.
6. Translates a computer user's commands and allows application programs to interact with the computer's hardware.
7. Screen and a printer.
8. Expand the potential uses of computers in business, eliminate some occupations, increase job growth in others.

COMMUNICATE BUSINESS CONCEPTS

9. (a) hardware, (b) software, (c) hardware, (d) hardware, (e) software, (f) hardware, (g) hardware, (h) hardware
10. A mouse allows the computer user to move quickly around the screen to access commands. The mouse frequently is used to complement the keyboard and as a pointing device to make selections from several options available.
11. A monitor can be thought of as both an input and output device. When entering data with a keyboard you can review your data as you key it in; and during the output phase, you can view processing results on your screen.
12. Storing and retrieving data is faster using a computer system, as is the preparation of letters, reports, documents, and financial statements. Many business tasks involving words and numbers can be accomplished more efficiently with a computer than if done manually. As technology expands, many other business activities are being computerized.

BUSINESS NOTES

1. Computer systems consist of data, hardware, and software. The four main components of a computer system are the input device, the processing unit, the memory and storage facilities, and an output device.
2. Commonly used input devices are the keyboard, mouse, video game controllers, touch-sensitive screens, scanners, and voice-activated mechanisms.
3. A computer program makes it possible to accept, process, and store data.
4. The main types of storage devices are the internal memory in a computer and disks (such as floppy disks, hard disks, and CD-ROMs).
5. Data processing results are most commonly reported on a computer screen or in a printed report.
6. Computer systems provide the information needed by managers to make business decisions.

REVIEW YOUR READING

1. What are the main uses of computers in businesses and other organizations?
2. What are the four components of a computer system?
3. What devices can be used to input data into a computer system?
4. What is the purpose of the central processing unit?
5. How does the process of storing data on a floppy disk differ from storing data on a CD-ROM?
6. What is the purpose of operating system software?
7. What are the common types of output of a computer system?
8. How will new technology affect the uses of computers in business?

COMMUNICATE BUSINESS CONCEPTS

9. Which of the following items are hardware and which are software?
   a. monitor (screen)
   b. a word processing program
   c. chips
   d. keyboard
   e. an operating system program
   f. disk drive
   g. mouse
   h. printer
10. What are the advantages of a mouse as an input device as compared to a keyboard?
11. Is a monitor an input device or an output device? Explain.
12. What types of business activities can be performed more efficiently by using a computer system than by doing the tasks manually?

DEVELOP YOUR BUSINESS LANGUAGE

For each numbered item, find the term that has the same meaning.

13. Computer programs that perform specific tasks such as word processing, database management, or accounting.

14. Mechanisms used to present data in a form that can be used or retrieved later or may be communicated immediately.

15. A data storage device that uses laser optics for reading data.

16. Several computers linked into a single system.

17. The control center of the computer.

18. The combination of an input device, a processing unit, memory and storage facilities, and an output device.

19. A series of detailed step-by-step instructions that tell the computer what functions to complete and when to complete them.

20. Software that translates a computer user's commands and allows application programs to interact with the computer's hardware.

21. A mechanism used to enter data into a computer system.

22 Facts in the form of numbers, alphabetic characters, words, or special symbols.

23. A computer system that presents information using a combination of sound, graphics, animation, and video.

24. A device that is used to store information on a magnetic disk so that the information can be recalled.

25. Storage locations for the instructions and data that the computer will use.

26. A system of letters, words, numbers, and symbols used to communicate with a computer.

27. The components or equipment of a computer system.

KEY TERMS
application software
CD-ROM
central processing unit (CPU)
computer language
computer network
computer system
data
disk drive
hardware
input device
memory
multimedia system
operating system software
output devices
program

DECISION-MAKING STRATEGIES

Before a computer system can facilitate business activities, the process or procedure that the hardware will execute must be defined. A flowchart is a visual presentation of the steps in a process or procedure. Computer programmers use this device to break down a process so that it can be understood by the computer.

28. What steps would need to be taken by a computer to total and compare the sales of three different products for the past three years?

29. What problems could occur when a programmer tries to write software to instruct a computer to perform this task?

DEVELOP YOUR BUSINESS LANGUAGE

13. application software
14. output devices
15. CD-ROM
16. computer network
17. central processing unit
18. computer system
19. program
20. operating system software
21. input device
22. data
23. multimedia system
24. disk drive
25. memory
26. computer language
27. hardware

DECISION-MAKING STRATEGIES

28. Answers will vary. This visual display will break down the steps of a process or procedure into simple phases. This can be done with words in boxes for each phase, or some photos or other visuals can be used to communicate the computer system application.

29. Programmer may misunderstand chart, violate the grammatical rules of the programming language, find processing steps that the maker of the flowchart did not anticipate, and so on.

30. 1,024 × 640K = 655,360 bytes

31. East: 4,200 allocated × 0.16 = 672 sold; 4,200 allocated − 672 sold = 3,528 current; Southern: 7,075 allocated × 0.29 = 2,051.75 or 2,052 sold; 7,075 allocated − 2,052 sold = 5,023 current; North Central: 9,500 allocated − 5,700 current = 3,800 sold; 3,800 sold ÷ 9,500 allocated = 0.40; Southwest: 600 sold ÷ 0.20 = 3,000 allocated; 3,000 allocated − 600 sold = 2,400 current; Northwest: 100 allocated − 86 current = 14 sold; 14 sold ÷ 100 allocated = 0.14

32. (a) $2,800.00 + $450.00 + $70.00 = $3,320.00 (b) $3,320.00 × 0.12 = $398.40; $3,320.00 + $398.40 = $3,718.40; $3,718.40 ÷ 12 = $309.87 (c) $2,800.00 + $450.00 = $3,250.00; $3,250.00 × 0.02 = $65.00

33. $19,000.00 + $2,500.00 = $21,500.00; $26,000.00 × 2.5 = $65,000.00; $65,000.00 − $21,500.00 = $43,500.00

In this activity, students use a computer to solve a business problem using a file that is provided on the data CD that accompanies *Intro to Business*. Instructions for using the data CD are included in a **README** file on the disk. Solutions are provided on the Instructor's Resource CD.

30. Using the measurements on page 205, how many bytes of information could be stored in a 640K computer?

31. Marvin Trotsky requested sales information from the computer about the Lightning pickup trucks from each of five sales districts in the United States. The computer-generated report is shown in the table below. Calculate the data that are missing in the report.

32. A notebook computer sells for $2,800. The printer costs $450 and the yearly maintenance fee is $70.
  a. How much will the buyer pay for all three items if it is a cash purchase?
  b. If all items are purchased, how much will the monthly payments be if there is a 10 percent interest charge and there will be 12 payments?
  c. How much will the buyer save if there is a 2 percent discount on the computer and printer for paying cash within ten days of purchase? *Hint:* Refer to Appendix C: Determining Percentage and Interest in Business.

33. The Bank of El Paso installed an automated teller machine (ATM). The ATM cost $19,000 plus $2,500 maintenance per year. If the machine replaced 2½ tellers whose salaries were $26,000 a year, how much was saved per year by installing the computer?

U.S. Region	Trucks Allocated	Percentage Sold	Number of Trucks Sold	Current Inventory*
East	4,200	16%	—	—
Southern	7,075	29%	—	—
North Central	9,500	—	—	5,700
Southwest	—	20%	600	—
Northwest	100	—	—	86

*Trucks Allocated − Trucks Sold = Current Inventory

Using the *Intro to Business* Data CD and your database program software, select problem CH15. After the problem appears on your screen, complete the following activities. Then, after you have completed each step, display or print a report for each activity. If you do not have a printer available, answer the questions before you leave the computer.

34. Select and list all computer systems costing less than $2,400. Answer the following questions:
  a. What is the second computer system listed?

  b. What is the last computer system listed?

35. Select and list the computer systems that can be purchased from companies with ZIP Codes of 09203 and 09204. How many computer systems are listed?

36. Select and list the computer systems that have at least 64 megabytes of RAM. Answer the following questions:
  a. What is the first computer system listed?
  b. What is the third computer system listed?

COMMUNICATING for SUCCESS

E-MAIL ETIQUETTE

Electronic mail is standard practice in business today. E-mail is preferred over regular mail and even fax machines as being quicker, yet less intrusive than a phone call. Simply type your message into the computer, and with one stroke your message is delivered instantly.

E-mail messages should be written with the same care as traditional letters, including proofreading and spell checking. However, many e-mail senders write their messages carelessly and without the proper etiquette.

There are three important guidelines that should be followed when sending e-mail.

1. **Your e-mail should cover only one topic.** If you have several topics to discuss, send them in separate e-mails.

2. **Your message should be brief,** using short sentences and paragraphs.

3. **Be courteous and professional in your message.** Remember, once the e-mail is sent, you cannot get it back.

> **Most people will work with e-mail in their careers.**

The most common e-mail mistake is "flaming," which is a nasty or offensive e-mail message. If you are tempted to send a flame, stop and consider "Is this something I would say to the person's face?" If not, don't send it.

Your e-mail etiquette could make or break your career success. The best habit is to use e-mail etiquette that will display your professionalism to others.

CRITICAL THINKING

1. How is e-mail like a letter? How is it like a phone call?
2. Why is it important to follow e-mail etiquette in the workplace?

COMMUNICATING for SUCCESS

Communications skills will help ensure students' success in the business world. Communicating for Success introduces workplace/interpersonal communications issues and proper uses of communications technology. Each feature discusses a key communications topic, and contains two Critical Thinking questions that require students to analyze what they have learned.

In business, communicating via e-mail has not only replaced other modes of communicating in many situations, but it has led to a substantial increase in the sheer quantity of business communications being exchanged. There are more messages than ever being sent and received, so students need to learn how to use e-mail effectively and efficiently. It's an important part of the "information revolution" that has transformed modern business practices. This feature provides detailed guidelines for students to follow.

CRITICAL THINKING

1. E-mail is like a letter in that it should be written with the same care as a traditional letter. It is like a phone call because it is quick and questions can be answered instantly.
2. E-mail etiquette will display your professionalism to others and it could make or break your career success.

The use of computers is the subject of this chapter. An explanation of management information systems (MIS) begins the discussion. Word processing, databases, and spreadsheets are also covered.

Resources for Teachers
- Lesson Plans
- School-To-Work/SCANS Activity Masters
- Spanish Resources
- Instructor's Resource CD

Assessment
- Chapter and Unit Tests, Ch. 16
- ExamView, Ch. 16

Media/Technology
- Applying Technology Data CD
- PowerPoint slides
- Business Connection CD
- Videotape

Activity Masters and Workbooks
- Activities and Projects, Ch. 16
- Internet Activity Masters
- Business Math Activity Masters
- Communications Activity Masters
- International Business Activity Masters
- Ethics Activity Masters

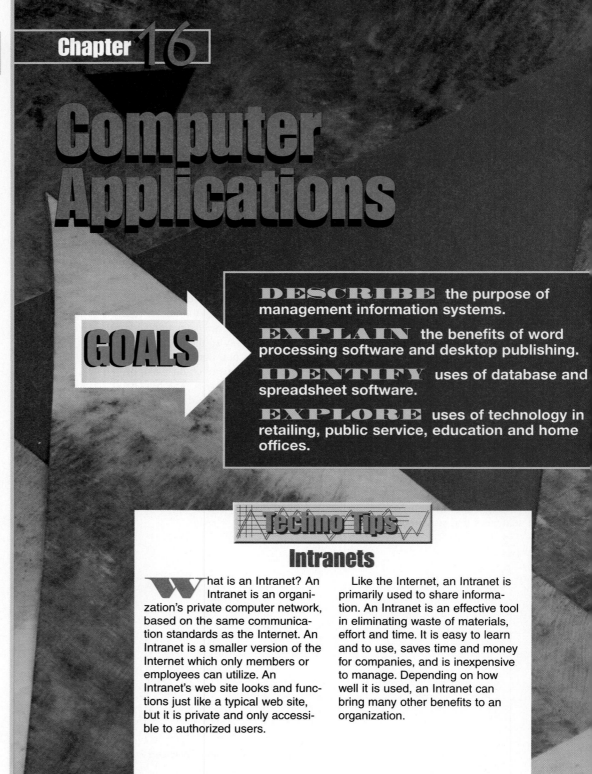

Chapter 16

Computer Applications

GOALS

DESCRIBE the purpose of management information systems.

EXPLAIN the benefits of word processing software and desktop publishing.

IDENTIFY uses of database and spreadsheet software.

EXPLORE uses of technology in retailing, public service, education and home offices.

Techno Tips

Intranets

What is an Intranet? An Intranet is an organization's private computer network, based on the same communication standards as the Internet. An Intranet is a smaller version of the Internet which only members or employees can utilize. An Intranet's web site looks and functions just like a typical web site, but it is private and only accessible to authorized users.

Like the Internet, an Intranet is primarily used to share information. An Intranet is an effective tool in eliminating waste of materials, effort and time. It is easy to learn and to use, saves time and money for companies, and is inexpensive to manage. Depending on how well it is used, an Intranet can bring many other benefits to an organization.

Students need to know the latest technologies and develop cutting edge Internet skills for use in current jobs, future careers, or in their homes. TechnoTips introduces students to today's cutting edge technologies and provides them with important Internet skills. Feature topics concentrate on Internet-specific technologies and computer or other hi-tech innovations for use by businesses and consumers.

Josh Aki arrived on the first day of his new part-time job at NBI Distributors. This retailing company sells a variety of products by mail, telephone orders, and via the Internet.

"Josh, please outline a report with the sales results of the new products we have introduced over the past six months," was the request of his supervisor. Based on comments from other employees, Josh knew that some of the products were doing well and others were just sitting in the warehouse. However, Josh wasn't sure how to approach this task.

Alicia saw that Josh looked confused, so she helped him by saying, "Check the database for sales results, summarize the data on the spreadsheet program, and prepare your report with our word processing software."

"Thanks for your help," Josh responded. "However, now I think I have even more questions to ask!"

MANAGEMENT INFORMATION SYSTEMS

Managers need information to make business decisions. A **management information system (MIS)** is an organized system of processing and reporting information in an organization. Computer systems and software are essential components of management information systems.

A company may need a departmental budget with expected income and expenses for the next three months. Using a special program, past company data and future projections can be combined to create this budget. The resulting document helps managers plan future business decisions.

Components of an MIS

As shown in Figure 16-1, the four main phases of an MIS are gathering data, analyzing data, storing data, and reporting results. These activities allow an organization to obtain needed information in four main categories:

1. financial information, including budgets, sales reports, and financial statements

2. production and inventory information, including production summaries, lists of tools and supplies, and finished goods reports

3. marketing information, including data on customer needs, current economic conditions, and actions of competitors

4. human resources information, including salaries, employee benefit data, and employee evaluations

Data Sources

The information for an MIS comes from several sources. *External* data sources are outside an organization. Financial institutions, government agencies, and customers are examples of external data sources.

In contrast, *internal* data sources provide input from within the organization. Internal data includes accounting records, inventory information, and company sales figures. While gathering raw data may be an easy task, changing these facts and figures into meaningful information is the major goal of an MIS.

The MIS in Action

What activities are involved in a management information system? How is needed

> **FYI**
> When searching the Internet, be as specific as possible with the nouns you use as keywords. Instead of "career planning," be more specific by using "resume preparation" or "preparing for an interview."

Chapter 16 *Computer Applications* **213**

software. Database software organizes and relates pieces of information about inventory, customers, and more. Spreadsheet software can be used to format data and perform calculations. As more organizations use management information systems, new services in retailing, government, and education become available. Technology also affects employment by making telecommuting possible through the use of modems and fax machines. Point out advantages of telecommuting such as fewer traffic and pollution problems, time saved not driving to and from work, space saved in offices and parking lots, and the ability of parents and others to work near dependent family members.

TRY THIS/GUIDED PRACTICE
Using photos or illustrations, walk through how a modem allows a computer user to access a database or to send messages to others. Ask students to describe situations in which businesses would use spreadsheet, word processing, database, and graphics software.

EXPLORE THIS/INDEPENDENT
PRACTICE Before assigning independent practice material for any chapter, students should be expected to read the textbook material carefully. In view of the fact that all students vary widely in their ability to read effectively, it is advisable to have students read the entire chapter, or sections thereof, silently in class if the material has not been previously read in connection with homework assignments.

MANAGEMENT INFORMATION SYSTEMS

Government · Finance · Customers · Gathering Data · Accounting · Sales · Inventory · Reporting Results · Analyzing Data · Storing Data

FIGURE 16-1 Do you see why these functions are important for decision-making and how they are interconnected?

information for business decisions communicated to managers? The operation of the MIS involves the following steps:

1. identify the information needs of the organization
2. obtain facts, figures, and other data
3. process, analyze, and organize data in a useful manner
4. distribute information reports to those who make decisions
5. update data files as needed

Computer networks are commonly used in an MIS to distribute information to managers, employees, and others. These networks connect computers, printers, and other equipment within a company or around the world. Worldwide networks are created through telephone lines, satellites, and other communication technology.

Also important for communicating information is **electronic mail**, also called *e-mail*.

E-mail gives users the ability to send data quickly through a computer system. After an employee prepares a letter or report, the document is sent electronically to another computer on the local or worldwide network. Electronic mail allows information to be exchanged without preparing a hard copy of the document, saving time and money.

WORD PROCESSING SOFTWARE

Every organization has a constant flow of reports, correspondence, and other information. **Word processing software** is used to create and revise written documents. Word processing allows the user to enter, store, revise, and print text for letters, memos, reports, or standard business forms.

Benefits of Word Processing
Using computerized word processing, you can create, store, retrieve, and print frequently used letters, memos, and reports.

On the Internet, you can visit libraries from around the world, take a class from a school on the other side of the country, order merchandise, and transfer money from your checking account to your savings account. More and more information and services appear on the Net every day.

FIGURE 16-2 Isn't it easier to use a menu than to type out every command?

Ease of editing, revising, and updating text allows you to quickly move a paragraph or add and delete words, sentences, or paragraphs. Word processing software allows you to check spelling and grammar by pushing one or two keys or pointing and clicking your mouse. Also possible is writing a letter or memo once and then personalizing copies

What are the benefits of having computers connected by a network?

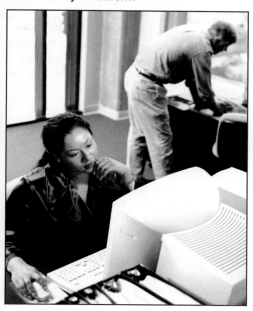

with the names and addresses of different people.

These activities are easy since most software allows you to select a task from a **menu**, which is a list of computer functions that appear on the screen (see Figure 16-2). For example, you may be asked if you want to save, edit, or create a new document. After making your menu selection, you are able to perform that task.

Desktop Publishing

Word processing activities are commonly expanded to produce newsletters, brochures, and other publications. **Desktop publishing** is the process of writing and designing high quality publications with the use of personal computers. A desktop publishing system includes the hardware and software needed to create professional formats with artistic designs. Many organizations use this method to publish high quality materials at a low cost.

In the chapter opening, Josh's supervisor wanted him to present data in a report format. However, instead of just listing numbers, Josh could have communicated the data clearly and quickly with the use of a graph or diagram. **Graphics software** is a computer program that prepares charts, graphs, and other visual elements. This software can create bar charts, line graphs, and pie charts as well as specialized graphics

After students have read the chapter, ask them to complete the end-of-chapter questions. Develop Your Business Language is an excellent way to improve students' vocabulary. Only words introduced in the chapter are used in the vocabulary exercises. The Review Your Reading questions can be used to check students' ability to comprehend what they have read. The Communicate Business Concepts section affords an opportunity for students to apply to practical life situations the information gained from reading the chapter. By completing the problems under Calculate Business Data, students will be able to strengthen and refine their abilities in mathematics. Technology Application allows students to demonstrate skill in using word processing, spreadsheet, and database software. Decision-Making Strategies contains material to challenge students to utilize the decision-making model explained in Chapter 1 for problem solving.

The Chapter Review questions at the end of the chapter vary in level of difficulty. For a basic assignment, consider Develop Your Business Language and Review Your Reading. For an average assignment, consider the basic assignment plus Communicate Business Concepts and Calculate Business Data. For an enhanced assignment, try the average assignment plus Technology Application and Decision-Making Strategies.

Chapter 16 *Computer Applications* 215

Net Facts provides information and definitions of terms for the Internet. The more information that students have about the Internet, the better equipped they will be to use this resource. In the Internet Activity Masters, there is an Internet Activity Worksheet for each unit. You can use these activities to give students experience with finding information online. Options for assigning this activity are as follows:

1. **Provide students with a list of addresses of resources for this activity;**
2. **Assign students to conduct their own searches; or**
3. **Use the addresses provided on the Internet Activity Worksheet.**

You should complete the activity yourself before assigning it to resolve any discrepancies that may arise.

ASSESS

Review the goals at the beginning of the chapter and the Business Notes at the end of the chapter. Restate each as a question and have students respond orally. For students who may have difficulty providing answers, assign the reteaching activities that follow. Enrichment activities also may be assigned where appropriate.

1. What is the purpose of a management information system? (Answer: Processing and reporting information in an organized way.)

2. Why are word processing software and desktop publishing beneficial? (Answer: An ability to create, store, and retrieve frequently used documents; ease of editing; an ability to check spelling and grammar; and creation of personalized letters and memos. Desktop

in the form of maps and other drawings. The use of graphics makes communication much clearer than the use of words alone. Computer graphics are commonly used in television commercials, movies, training materials for employees, and business documents.

MAINTAINING RECORDS WITH DATABASE SOFTWARE

"Create a list of employees who have perfect attendance on the job during the past six months." These types of requests are quite common in organizations. A **database** is an organized collection of information with the pieces of information related to one another in some way. For example, an inventory clerk may require a list of products sold, while the sales manager may need similar information sorted by the customers who purchased the products or the salespersons who sold the products. Each of these reports would come from the same database, but would require different sorting and rearranging.

Creating a Database

Database software processes a database. As shown in Figure 16-3, a database program can arrange and sort information in different ways. An organization might use database software to handle records for employee information, sales and inventory, and accounting. Business owners and managers depend upon different databases for making decisions about day-to-day operations and for meeting long-term organizational goals.

Database Use in Business

The data stored in a database are commonly used and shared in several ways. Data may be stored in one personal computer, and only the user of that computer can access the data. Or, data may be stored in a central location and may be accessed by several people on the computer network.

In recent years, *database marketing* has become popular. Software is used to maintain, analyze, and combine customer informa-

tion files. The information about customers is then used to increase sales by better serving customer needs. For example, a household with young children might receive advertising about educational software. Using a database increases the chance of reaching potential customers who are likely to buy the product.

BUSINESS DECISION MAKING WITH SPREADSHEET SOFTWARE

In the past, accountants used worksheets on paper with many rows and columns of information. Such a worksheet is an example of a manually prepared *spreadsheet*, which involves columns and rows of data. **Spreadsheet software** is a computer program that formats data in columns and rows in order to do calculations.

The Basics of Spreadsheets

Spreadsheet software makes data entry easier and more accurate. Also, spreadsheets make computations—such as totals, percentages, and averages—quickly and accurately with the use of built-in formulas.

The location where a column and row intersect is called a *cell*. As a spreadsheet is created with specific information, words, numbers, or formulas are entered into the cells. Other built-in features of spreadsheet software include formatting (for dollars or percentages), changing column widths, and copying of cells.

TEACHING STRATEGIES
Special Needs
Hearing Impaired

Hearing impaired students do well with instructions that are brief and allow for hands-on activities. Assess understanding by having students match, choose, move, draw, or point. GUI software and a mouse are ideal for these kinds of activities. Stu-

dents can respond to directions that require them to name, list, categorize, label, or reply with one or two words.

DATABASE SOFTWARE REPORTS

Sales Database

Date	Customer	Amount	Salesperson
Nov. 3	L. Collins	$ 58	Ellis
Nov. 9	V. Owen	$ 12	Ellis
Nov. 14	A. Browing	$178	Jones
Nov. 15	F. Brock	$ 45	Lowery
Nov. 16	L. Collins	$317	Ellis
Nov. 21	F. Brock	$216	Lowery
Nov. 24	L. Collins	$ 84	Ellis
Nov. 25	A. Browing	$193	Jones
Nov. 28	F. Brock	$ 61	Jones
Nov. 30	V. Owen	$111	Lowery

Database Selection—Sales Report

Salesperson	Total Sales
Ellis	$ 471
Jones	$ 432
Lowery	$ 372
Total Sales	$1,275

Database Selection—Customer Accounts

Customer	Amount Due
F. Brock	$ 322
A. Browing	$ 371
L. Collins	$ 459
V. Owen	$ 123
Total Amount Due	$1,275

FIGURE 16-3   Do you see how lots of different reports can be generated from the same database?

Computations with spreadsheets are more accurate because the computer will not make errors as a person might. As always, however, if the user instructs the computer to use the wrong formula, the results will be inaccurate.

3. How is database software used? (Answer: Records for employee information, sales and inventory, accounting; data for decisions about day-to-day operations and long-term organizational goals; database marketing.)
4. What are situations when spreadsheet software could be used? (Answer: Prepare payroll records, financial statements, budgets, and other financial documents; do a *what-if* analysis of a situation.)
5. How is technology used in retailing, public service, and education? (Answer: In retailing, entering sales information, updating inventory records, capturing accounting information, and preparing receipts or invoices. In public service, maintaining Social Security and military records, accessing medical and police records. In education, training and testing, computer-assisted instruction or CAI.)
6. How does technology allow people to work at home? (Answer: Through modems and faxes, workers at home can easily send reports, documents, and ideas to their offices.)

RETEACH

Using an LCD panel and an overhead projector, or visiting a computer lab, demonstrate various software applications. Use Technology Application problems from previous chapters for examples of word processing, database, and spreadsheet tasks. Talk about how the program used matches the task assigned.

Personal Qualities-Self-Esteem

SCANS

Self-esteem, or believing in one's own self worth and maintaining a positive view of one's self, is a personal quality that we cannot ignore. It is important that students know who they are and believe in themselves in order to be productive in society. One important contributor to self-esteem is one's own culture. It is important for students to understand not only who they are, but what is the culture of those with whom they work. Cultural Perspectives describes various cultures and their contributions to our current economic system. This feature offers an opportunity to encourage discussion of students and their cultural backgrounds. The discussion can be expanded by asking students to write down a description of themselves by asking "who am I?"

CULTURAL PERSPECTIVES
Calculators in Europe

"May I borrow your pebble?" This is a question one business math student might have asked another—in ancient Rome! The word calculator comes from a Latin term that means calculus or pebble.

An early Roman *calculator* used a system of tiny stones that were inserted in the grooves of a counting board. The board was divided into columns for ones, tens, hundreds, thousands, and so on. This system allowed merchants to keep track of their business transactions.

Over a thousand years later in 1642, Blaise Pascal, a French mathematician, developed the first adding calculating machine. This device was called the Pascaline and was the basis for adding machines invented in the 1800s and early 1900s.

Today, electronic calculators make it possible to perform mathematical operations that previously took several minutes or longer. Built-in functions on calculators allow you to quickly compute averages, square roots, and interest payments. This is quite different from ancient Roman times or the times of Pascal and his students in the 1600s. But without the contributions of calculating pioneers, we would not have the electronic calculators we have today.

Remember, the next time you have trouble with your calculator, at least you don't have to count stones!

Critical Thinking
1. How do the needs of a society influence the creation of new inventions?
2. What effect might the invention of the adding calculating machine have had on early business activities?

Using Spreadsheet Software

Spreadsheets are used to prepare payroll records, financial statements, budgets, and other financial documents (see Figure 16-4). This software may also be used to do a *what-if* analysis of a situation. For example, a manager may want to see the effect of different prices on profit. The spreadsheet automatically calculates each situation as the data are entered.

Integrated Software Packages

Word processing, database, and spreadsheet software are called single-function software packages. These programs each have one purpose. In contrast, **integrated software** is a computer program capable of doing more than one basic function. Common integrated software packages combine word processing, database, spreadsheet, and graphics applications along with a communications module for e-mail.

A major advantage of integrated software is the convenience of moving data from one portion of a program to another. For example, a spreadsheet or graph could be combined with text in a word processing document.

COMPUTER APPLICATIONS IN ORGANIZATIONS

Technology is changing the way we do business by allowing new services such as shopping at home or banking in supermarkets. The use of computers to access the Internet is increasing in every type of organization.

Sales and Retailing

In addition to the office, computers also have a great impact in stores. Salespeople enter sales information as a purchase takes place. A computer automatically updates the inventory record when an item is bought, sold, or returned. The amount of the sale and other transaction information is recorded in the company's database. In addition,

CULTURAL PERSPECTIVES

Cultural Perspectives features show both past contributions of many cultures and the benefits of a culturally diverse society.

CRITICAL THINKING
1. Satisfying the needs of a society motivates people to find solutions that will satisfy these needs. As business activities expanded in Rome and other areas of Europe, the number of business transactions also expanded. To keep from being overwhelmed by having to do calculations by hand, devices were created to calculate and keep financial records.
2. As calculating machines became available, the speed and efficiency of record keeping improved. This improved ability to keep records allowed businesses to maintain control of larger organizations, and allowed businesspeople more time for analysis and planning.

```
        A       B        C          D       E       F       G       H
 1                    20-- PROJECTED INCOME STATEMENT
 2
 3 ESTIMATED SALES      1000000
 4
 5 COST OF GOODS SOLD    722000
 6
 7 GROSS PROFIT          278000
 8
 9 LESS EXPENSES:
10   SALARIES            150000
11   ADVERTISING          50000
12   UTILITIES            30000
13   INSURANCE            30000
14
15 TOTAL EXPENSES        260000
16
17 PROFIT BEFORE TAX      18000
18
19
20 ESTIMATED SALES       950000
21
22 COST OF GOODS SOLD    685900
23
24 GROSS PROFIT          264100
25
26 LESS EXPENSES:
27   SALARIES            142500
28   ADVERTISING          47500
29   UTILITIES            30000
30   INSURANCE            29000
31
32 TOTAL EXPENSES        249000
33
34 PROFIT BEFORE TAX      15100
35
36
37      20-- PROJECTED INCOME STATEMENT WITH VARIABLE RESULTS
38
39                      PERCENT OVER/UNDER FORECAST
40                   %0      -5%     -10%     +5%     +10%
41
42 ESTIMATED SALES   1000000  950000  900000  1050000  1100000
43
44 COST OF GOODS SOLD 722000  685900  649800   759100   794200
45
46 GROSS PROFIT       278000  264100  250200   291900   305800
47
48 LESS EXPENSES:
49   SALARIES         150000  142500  135000   157500   165000
50   ADVERTISING       50000   47500   45000    52500    55000
51   UTILITIES         30000   30000   30000    30000    30000
52   INSURANCE         30000   29000   28000    31000    32000
53
54 TOTAL EXPENSES     260000  249000  238000   271000   282000
55
56 PROFIT BEFORE TAXES 18000   15100   12200    20900    23800
57
```

FIGURE 16-4 How can spreadsheet software improve accuracy?

a receipt or invoice is prepared for the customer.

Public Service

Government agencies use computers to maintain records. For example, the federal government keeps Social Security records for all past and present workers in the United States and military records for people who have served in a branch of the military. Agencies continually expand their use of computers. Medical information can be found within seconds to save lives. Police records can be sent from state to state minutes after a crime has occurred, helping to solve the crime. Schools and other agencies can transfer records easily when someone moves to another area of the country.

Education

Computers have become very important teaching devices. Computers make it possible to train and test workers in a variety of

What kind of uses would a retailer have for a computer?

professions. Office workers learn to use word processing software, while also receiving instruction on the proper use of grammar, spelling, punctuation, capitalization, and document forms. Airline pilots use computerized simulators to learn and improve skills needed for flying new types of aircraft.

Computer-assisted instruction (CAI) is the use of computers to help people learn or improve skills at their own pace. With CAI, students work at a speed that best serves their needs. The student does not have to go to a school building for instruction. The student can learn at home on a computer network system connected to a central training location.

TELECOMMUTING AND THE HOME OFFICE

Each morning, Brad Collins gets ready for work, eats breakfast, and travels to his office . . . in the next room! Brad is one of over 20 million Americans doing all or part of their work at home. **Telecommuting** is a term used to describe the activities of a worker using a computer at home to do a

job. Telecommuting saves travel time and costs and results in less traffic along with reduced noise and air pollution.

Each year more and more people become telecommuters. This working arrangement is especially attractive to people who have difficulty leaving their home to go to work, such as workers who are disabled or parents who desire to be near their children. A work-at-home arrangement is most common among workers such as

- writers and editors
- researchers
- accounting clerks
- sales representatives
- computer programmers
- Internet web site designers

They can easily send their reports, documents, and ideas to their employers' offices by computer.

Telecommuting is made possible with computers and other technology. A **modem** is a device that allows a person to communicate with other computer users through telephone lines. A modem allows an at-home computer

Basic Skills-Math

Integrating math across the curriculum is an important element in contemporary education. As a part of end-of-chapter activities, Calculate Business Data enables students to apply their math skills. Appendix B: Math Review, Appendix C: Determining Percentages and Interest in Business, and Appendix D:

Using Measurements in Business, also apply arithmetic and math skills.

SCANS

to communicate with the computer system at the company's main office.

Working at home is more practical since the development of a device that transmits a copy of a document from one location to another. A **fax**, or *facsimile,* machine allows the rapid sending or receiving of copies through telephone lines. Telecommuters can easily submit completed work and obtain new assignments with the use of a fax machine. In addition to fax machines, other devices used

to transfer documents are also increasingly common. Electronic scanners can copy documents directly to a computer file, which can then be sent via a modem to other computers anywhere in the world. Special software can translate scanned or faxed text documents into digital code that can be read by a word processing program. The converted text can then be edited or reformatted without anyone ever having to manually input the text with a keyboard.

What are some benefits of computer-assisted instruction?

Critical Thinking **Skills-Problem Solving**

SCANS

Problem-solving skills, which include recognizing a problem and devising a plan of action, are applied throughout every chapter in this text. Each time a student participates in a Cooperative Learning or Teams activity, problem-solving skills are applied in a group situation. Each time a student completes a math application in Calculate Business Data, decisions are made as to which mathematical approach must be taken. For each Technology Application problem, students must decide which template problem to use, which piece of software to load, and how to solve the problem. Emphasize to students how they are using problem solving in their day-to-day tasks and make them aware of the skills they are developing.

REVIEW YOUR READING

1. The four phases of a management information system are gathering data, analyzing data, storing data, and reporting results.
2. The four main categories of information used by most organizations are financial, production and inventory, marketing, and human resources.
3. External data are obtained from outside of an organization. Internal data are obtained from within an organization.
4. An ability easily to create, store, and retrieve frequently used documents; ease of editing; an ability to check spelling and grammar; and ease of creation of personalized letters and memos.
5. A database program is designed to sort and arrange information in different ways.
6. A spreadsheet can be used to prepare payroll records, financial statements, budgets, and other documents in a row-and-column format.
7. It's possible to work with several types of software at once, moving from one application to another, using the same commands for all functions in the software package.
8. Record sales transactions, automatically update inventory information, keep track of customer payments of bills, read the prices off package codes to make it faster to handle transactions.
9. Efficient keeping of Social Security and military records for citizens, medical care, and crime-solving efforts.
10. Computer-assisted instruction allows people to learn at their own pace and allows people who are unable to get to a school to learn at home.
11. Sales representatives, authors, computer programmers, and entrepreneurs who start businesses out of their homes.

COMMUNICATE BUSINESS CONCEPTS

12. (a) External data: information from customers, financial institutions, and government agencies; (b) Internal data: sales reports, accounting records, inventory information, and employee records.

BUSINESS NOTES

1. The major goal of a management information system is to change raw data (facts and figures) into information that can be used by managers.
2. Word processing software allows efficient creation, revision, and storage of letters, memos, and reports.
3. Database software arranges and sorts information in different ways to provide lists about customers, products, or other business data.
4. Spreadsheet software can be used to prepare payroll records, financial statements, budgets, and what-if reports.
5. Technology has expanded the use of computers in retailing, public service organizations, and education.
6. Computers, modems, fax machines, and other technology have made it possible for an increasing number of people to work at home.

REVIEW YOUR READING

1. What are the four phases of a management information system?
2. What are the four main categories of information used by most organizations?
3. How do external data differ from internal data?
4. What are the benefits of computerized word processing?
5. What function does database software serve?
6. What types of reports can be prepared using spreadsheet software?
7. What are the main advantages of integrated software?
8. In what ways have computers helped businesses involved in sales and retailing?
9. What aspects of public service have been made more efficient by computers?
10. What are the benefits of computer-assisted instruction (CAI)?
11. What types of careers are best suited to telecommuting?

COMMUNICATE BUSINESS CONCEPTS

12. List examples of (a) external data and (b) internal data used by most companies.
13. List three on-the-job tasks that a person might perform more efficiently with the help of a computer.
14. Identify which of the following computer applications would be performed using word processing software, database software, spreadsheet software, and graphics software.
    a. Preparing a report of new equipment purchased for each office of a company.
    b. Preparing a list of employees that is sorted by ZIP Code.
    c. Creating a form letter to go to new customers of a mail-order business.
    d. Creating a pie chart showing the portion of sales of each product.
    e. Preparing a document listing the total sales for each geographic area of the country.
    f. Listing the employees who have not missed a day of work in five years.

---

13. Preparing financial statements, updating inventory records, completing tax reports, filing documents, analyzing investments, searching for library information, and updating a mailing list.
14. (a) spreadsheet (or database); (b) database; (c) word processing; (d) graphics; (e) spreadsheet; (f) database; (g) word processing; (h) spreadsheet.

g. Sending a letter to each employee who has not missed a day of work in five years.

h. Creating a budget for the new office that will be opened in another city.

15. Who would benefit from schools that would allow students to take classes at home by computer?

16. Describe the benefits to workers, employers, and society when an organization allows some of its employees to do all or part of their work at home.

DEVELOP YOUR BUSINESS LANGUAGE

For each numbered item, find the term that has the same meaning.

17. A computer program that uses a row-and-column arrangement of data to perform calculations.

18. The use of computers to help people learn or improve skills at their own pace.

19. A list of computer functions that appears on the screen.

20. A computer program that processes an organized collection of information.

21. A term used to describe the activities of a worker using a computer at home to perform a job.

22. A computer program used to create and revise written documents.

23. A process of writing and designing high quality publications with the use of microcomputers.

24. The delivery of correspondence through a computer system.

25. An organized system of processing and reporting information in an organization.

26. A computer program that prepares charts, graphs, and other visual elements.

27. A device that allows you to communicate with other computers through the use of telephone lines.

28. A system in which a copy of a document is transmitted from one location to another through an electronic device connected to telephone lines.

29. A collection of organized data whose elements are in some way related to one another.

30. A computer program capable of performing more than one basic function.

KEY TERMS

computer-assisted instruction (CAI)
database
database software
desktop publishing
electronic mail (e-mail)
fax
graphics software
integrated software
management information system (MIS)
menu
modem
spreadsheet software
telecommuting
word processing software

DECISION-MAKING STRATEGIES

Johnny Tom and Billie Chan are planning to start a small shop selling imported products. Johnny believes they need to purchase an integrated software package for preparing documents and maintaining records. Billie believes that individual word processing, database, and spreadsheet programs would better serve their needs.

31. What are possible advantages of single-function programs over an integrated software package?

32. What factors should Johnny and Billie consider when selecting software for their business?

15. People who are not able to get to a regular class, including parents, working people, and workers who are disabled. Schools and society also benefit since more people are gaining needed knowledge and skills.

16. People who have difficulty leaving their home to go to work, such as workers who are disabled or parents who desire to be near their children, may stay at home to perform their jobs. Employers save on office and parking space. Telecommuting saves travel time and costs and results in less traffic, reduced noise, and less air pollution.

DEVELOP YOUR BUSINESS LANGUAGE

17. spreadsheet software
18. computer-assisted instruction (CAI)
19. menu
20. database software
21. telecommuting
22. word processing software
23. desktop publishing
24. electronic mail (E-mail)
25. management information system (MIS)
26. graphics software
27. modem
28. fax
29. database
30. integrated software

DECISION-MAKING STRATEGIES

31. Possible answers might include that single-function programs may have more features and may run faster than the parts of an integrated software package.
32. Possible answers might include types of tasks to be done on the computer, the volume of work, and the desired turnaround times.

CALCULATE BUSINESS DATA

33. $2,100.00 + $1,300.00 +
$3,150.00 + (5 × $1.00) =
$6,555.00

34. $6,555.00 − $5.00 = $6,550.00;
$6,550.00 × 0.75 = $4,912.50

35. (a) $35.84 + $18.48 + $31.79 +
$61.75 + $51.58 + $33.15 +
$36.74 + $22.00 + $31.05 +
$33.32 + $85.37 + $50.57 =
$491.64; (b) $491.64 ÷ 12 =
$40.97

TECHNOLOGY APPLICATION

In this activity, students use a computer to solve a business problem using a file that is provided on the data CD that accompanies *Intro to Business*. Instructions for using the data CD are included in a **README** file on the disk. Solutions are provided on the Instructor's Resource CD.

CALCULATE BUSINESS DATA

33. Rico Sanchez bought a personal computer for $2,100. He also bought a disk-drive unit for $1,300 and a printer for $3,150. If he bought five floppy disks at $1 each, how much did he pay for everything?

34. After Rico Sanchez (Question 33) had his computer, disk-drive unit, and printer for a year, he decided to sell them. If he sold them for 75 percent of what he paid for them, how much did he receive for the three items?

35. Lonnette Franco paid the following monthly fees for her modem service during the year.
  a. How much was Lonnette's yearly expense for the modem service?
  b. How much was Lonnette's average monthly cost for this service?

January	$35.84	July	$36.74
February	18.48	August	22.00
March	31.79	September	31.05
April	61.75	October	33.32
May	51.58	November	85.37
June	33.15	December	50.57

TECHNOLOGY APPLICATION

Using the *Intro to Business* Data CD and your spreadsheet program software, select problem CH16. After the problem appears on your screen, complete the following activities. Then, after you have completed each step, display or print the completed spreadsheet for each activity. If you do not have a printer available, answer the questions before you leave the computer.

36. Determine student preferences for each type of software used in the business classes at Hamilton High School. What is the total number of students who prefer using word processing software?

37. What is the total number of students who prefer using database software?

38. What is the total number of students who prefer using spreadsheet software?

Optional: Create a pie chart showing the preferences for each type of software.

TECHNOLOGY AND INTERNATIONAL BUSINESS COMMUNICATIONS

A common global business conversation may go like this:

"Can you e-mail me the latest sales figures from our Paris office?"

"Are you kidding? It's five in the morning!"

"Not here in London, it's the middle of the business day."

Improved technology has made possible various types of business transactions that were considered science fiction a few years ago. Today, a person in Bangkok can talk with and see a business associate in Oslo.

Medical professionals are able to attend to the health care needs of people in rural South America without leaving their clinic in the city. The use of expert systems and video conference equipment allows a diagnosis by the doctor with the treatment administered by a local medical assistant. Technology expands the availability of health care.

Companies reduce operating and inventory costs with the use of technology. A chain of food stores in Japan monitors all product sales with a centralized computer system. This network allows managers to know which stores need which product and when. As a result, stores always have the items wanted by customers.

Technology also makes language translation possible. Voice-activated computers are available to convert one language into another. This system allows a French-speaking sales manager to understand the product needs of a Russian-speaking customer.

Global financial markets are also changing due to technology. Funds can be transferred from a customer to make a payment within a few seconds using electronic banking systems. The amount is easily converted from dollars to pesos, euros, or yen. The World Wide Web and other computer networks allow investors to continually monitor investment values anywhere in the world.

CRITICAL THINKING

1. Describe situations in your community in which technology has improved business activities in stores, offices, and other businesses. How might this technology be used for international business activities?
2. Locate a web site that might be adapted for doing business in other countries. Many global companies have web sites that serve customers who speak different languages in different areas of the world.

Most students will either work with international clients or compete against businesses that do. Global Navigator introduces students to issues integral to working with international businesses. Key concepts and challenges faced by international businesses are presented, followed by two Critical Thinking questions that require students to analyze what they have learned.

This feature focuses students' attention on advances in communications technology that have changed the way international business transactions are conducted. Grasping this is crucial to their future success in business, because transacting business internationally now happens as fast and as seamlessly as transacting business across town. Students need to learn how, or they'll be left behind.

CRITICAL THINKING

1. Examples might include any of a wide variety of technologies, including electronic funds transfers, just-in-time inventory systems, and Internet-based broadcasting.
2. Responses will vary, as many multinational companies and consulting firms have such web sites.

The future effects of technology are the subject of this chapter. Changes in computer career opportunities and our home lives and travel are discussed. Students are also introduced to the limitations of computers.

Resources for Teachers
- Lesson Plans
- School-To-Work/SCANS Activity Masters
- Spanish Resources
- Instructor's Resource CD

Assessment
- Chapter and Unit Tests, Ch. 17
- ExamView, Ch. 17

Media/Technology
- Applying Technology Data CD
- PowerPoint slides
- Business Connection CD
- Videotape

Activity Masters and Workbooks
- Activities and Projects, Ch. 17
- Internet Activity Masters
- Business Math Activity Masters
- Communications Activity Masters
- International Business Activity Masters
- Ethics Activity Masters

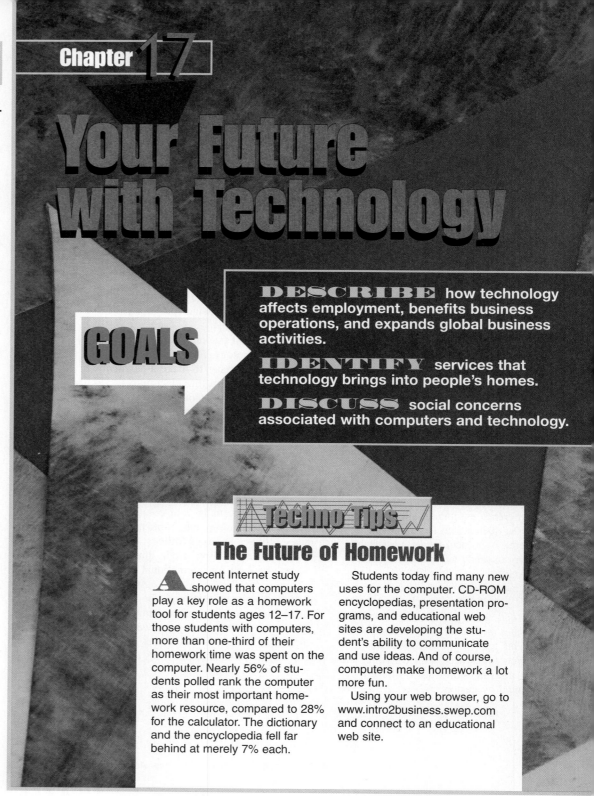

Chapter 17

Your Future with Technology

GOALS

DESCRIBE how technology affects employment, benefits business operations, and expands global business activities.

IDENTIFY services that technology brings into people's homes.

DISCUSS social concerns associated with computers and technology.

Techno Tips

The Future of Homework

A recent Internet study showed that computers play a key role as a homework tool for students ages 12–17. For those students with computers, more than one-third of their homework time was spent on the computer. Nearly 56% of students polled rank the computer as their most important homework resource, compared to 28% for the calculator. The dictionary and the encyclopedia fell far behind at merely 7% each.

Students today find many new uses for the computer. CD-ROM encyclopedias, presentation programs, and educational web sites are developing the student's ability to communicate and use ideas. And of course, computers make homework a lot more fun.

Using your web browser, go to www.intro2business.swep.com and connect to an educational web site.

Techno Tips

Students need to know the latest technologies and develop cutting edge Internet skills for use in current jobs, future careers, or in their homes. TechnoTips introduces students to today's cutting edge technologies and provides them with important Internet skills. Feature topics concentrate on Internet-specific technologies and computer or other hi-tech innovations for use by businesses and consumers. At the www.intro2business.swep.com web site, students can complete the activity for this chapter.

Herb Cunningham had just lost his sixth job in seven years. Although he is a talented worker, demand for his skills as an inventory clerk are declining. Computerized scanning systems keep track of inventory in most companies.

"I guess it's time to upgrade my skills," Herb commented to his son, Joe. "I'm going to enroll in that computer training program. Then next time I'll be able to move easily into another job."

"That might not be enough, dad," responded Joe. "You better also learn how to operate a robot, access artificial intelligence, and download graphics from the Internet."

"I'm not sure I'll be able to learn all of those, son," was Herb's reply.

"But, dad, I'll be here to help you," said Joe, "and you can start by letting me show you how this video game works!"

TECHNOLOGY AND OUR ECONOMY

The times in which we live are both exciting and frustrating. New uses for computers and other technology are discovered daily. Medical researchers have developed computerized body parts that respond when the brain gives the command for action.

Data clerks are able to store billions of bits of data in a small area that cannot be seen with the human eye. And of course, computers are used to create special effects for motion pictures and at amusement parks. As you read this, thousands of people are developing new uses for computers that will be ready in the near future.

Many people think computers are taking away their jobs. What is actually occurring, though, is a shift in the job duties and skills needed to work in business and industry.

When workers are replaced by computers, companies need to retrain the workers with skills in programming, operating, or repairing computer systems. *Displaced workers,* or workers who are unemployed because of changing job conditions, must adapt to the changing job market in order to have continued employment. What actions can companies and workers take to be ready for the new jobs of the future?

As computers and other technology become more important in our lives, the ability to use this technology is vital to each person's economic survival. *Computer literacy* is the ability to use computers to process information or solve problems. While you do not have to understand how to program a

Name some unique occupations in which computers are used.

Chapter 17 *Your Future with Technology* **227**

MOTIVATE

PURPOSE Provide a purpose for students as they read the chapter. Tell students that in this chapter they will learn how future technologies are expected to affect their lives at work, at home, and in society at large. Ask what they think they will learn. Direct students to skim the chapter, looking at photos, reading captions, and noting main headings. The goals at the beginning of each chapter provide a valuable tool for having students pinpoint main ideas. The tasks required by the goals are signaled in the first word. Some emphasize information collection ("Identify," "List"), while others call for description ("Explain," "Describe"). Ask students to look through all the goals and note the first word of each. Then ask students to state the purpose of studying this chapter.

TEACH/APPLY

MAKE CONNECTIONS The previous chapter covered the uses of computers in businesses and other organizations. This chapter covers possible technological changes and how those changes may affect students' lives at work, at home, and when traveling. Ask students to name jobs that have been taken over by robotics. Explain how robots and expert systems affect employment opportunities. Point out that computers make global communication and trading easier. Ask for ideas of how robots could be used in homes. Emphasize the impact of new technologies on shopping and entertainment.

FOCUS ON REAL LIFE

Ask students to name people they know who use computers in their work. Ask which basic computer skills and software students think are used in offices, stores, and factories. List the answers on the overhead or the board.

Discuss how computers can lead to improvements in many forms of transportation. Call attention to the social concerns of computers discussed in the chapter, including threats to health and safety, criminal misuse of databases, and violations of privacy. Discuss the Ethical Perspectives and mention that a code of ethics is one way that a company can respond to ethical concerns.

TRY THIS/GUIDED PRACTICE

Ask students to describe situations in which technology is used in offices, factories, stores, and schools. For each situation, guide the students through identifying benefits and costs from using technology. Explain that most applications of technology have both benefits and costs. People must compare the benefits and costs carefully before deciding to use a new technology.

EXPLORE THIS/INDEPENDENT PRACTICE Before assigning

independent practice material for any chapter, students should be expected to read the textbook material carefully. In view of the fact that all students vary widely in their ability to read effectively, it is advisable to have students read the entire chapter, or sections thereof, silently in class if the material has not been previously read in connection with homework assignments.

After students have read the chapter, ask them to complete the Chapter Review questions. Develop Your Business Language is an excellent way to improve students' vocabulary. Only words introduced in the chapter are used

As technology changes career opportunities, workers will need to update skills three or four times in their lifetimes to remain employable.

computer to use it, you do need to know how to enter, store, process, and retrieve information.

WORKPLACE TECHNOLOGY

Computers are present in almost every business situation to help improve efficiency and productivity. Computers can be found in oil fields, warehouses, retail stores, hospitals, offices, and factories.

Robots

"Only Bel-comp can save us now!" the crew captain in the movie said as the spaceship raced out of control toward the uncharted planet. Most of us have seen robots and other computer systems in science fiction movies set in outer space and in the future. However, real-life **robots**, mechanical devices programmed to do routine tasks, are used

Name some industries that could benefit from computer-aided design.

in many factories. An example of where robots are used is assembly line work that requires repeated tasks. Early robots did only simple tasks such as tightening a bolt on an automobile.

Today, robots exist that can see, hear, smell, and feel. Robots are able to work 24 hours a day. These computerized workers can work in dangerous situations such as outer space, underwater, or underground.

Expert Systems

Have you ever wanted a quick answer to a question without having to find a book or person who knew the answer? **Artificial intelligence (AI)** is software that enables computers to reason, learn, and make decisions using logical methods similar to the methods humans use. An example of artificial intelligence is computer programs that make decisions about complex topics. For example, software exists that asks people questions about their health in order to determine solutions for potential medical problems. This software allows people in areas without doctors to receive better medical care.

Computer programs that help people solve technical problems are called **expert systems** and are now available for medical services, financial planning, and legal matters. Expert systems are based on the knowledge of human experts in many specialized areas. Therefore, these systems provide intelligent answers as effectively as human experts in those subject matters. For example, employees of the Internal Revenue Service use an expert system to quickly answer questions from taxpayers.

Computer-Aided Design

Many of the products you use each day were created with the use of computers. **Computer-aided design (CAD)** refers to the use of technology to create product styles and designs. CAD allows you to try different sizes, shapes, and materials for a new machine, automobile, or food package. This process can be used to experiment with many variations before spending time and money

TEACHING STRATEGIES
Cooperative Learning

Over a two-week period, ask students to collect help-wanted ads related to jobs involving computers and technology. Divide the students into pairs, with one student being a job candidate and the other being an interviewer. Give students 10 minutes to prepare for role playing a job interview for one of the

help-wanted ads. Each interview should last no more than 5 minutes. Each group should then act out its interview for the rest of the class. The mock interviews should emphasize the skills required for the positions.

building a model or actually going into production.

TECHNOLOGY AND GLOBAL BUSINESS

Multinational computer systems, along with software that translates information from one language to another, make it possible to conduct business around the world without leaving your computer. Instant transmission of data with the use of satellites makes even the farthest point on earth as close as a button on your computer. Increased global business can have an important impact on world trade and international relations.

Importing and exporting can take place using a computer system, with the goods being shipped from the closest location to save time and money. For example, you may order an item from a company in Italy by using a computer. When the Italian marketers receive your order on their computer, they check a database and discover there are five such items in stock in Canada. They instruct the Canadian importers by e-mail to ship the items to you; you receive them the next day. You pay the Italian company, and the Italian and Canadian companies settle their accounts later—through the computerized banking system.

Another way of bringing people together to do business is *video conferencing*. This system allows people in different geographic locations to meet "face-to-face" by satellite for sales presentations, training sessions, and other types of meetings. A sales staff in Peru can make a presentation to potential customers in Spain, South Africa, Pakistan, and the United States without leaving Peru.

YOUR WINDOW TO THE WORLD

At home, your computer system provides shopping assistance, financial and other information, and entertainment.

Online Computer Services

While sitting at a computer, you can now access books, magazines, and newspapers from around the world. You can also shop from home for food, clothing, and other products; get up-to-the-minute market quotes; buy and sell investments; and find low-priced airfares, hotels, and rental cars. Online and Internet-based information, shopping, travel, and entertainment services are increasing at a rapid rate. They connect consumers, via home or office computer, with businesses that utilize computer networks and electronic databases to reach millions of potential customers.

You can also use **online computer services** to obtain software for doing household activities on a personal computer. Programs can keep a list of names and addresses of people to whom you send greeting cards, or you may store your favorite recipes

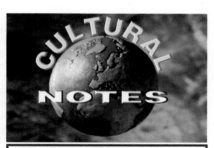

America is a nation of cultural diversity in which many languages are spoken. These various languages have particular words that reflect their particular cultures. In all cultures, there is typically a term by which people describe themselves as being human. For example, the Alaska Natives, or Eskimos, use the term Inuit, or "the people," to describe themselves.

in the vocabulary exercises. The Review Your Reading questions can be used to check students' ability to comprehend what they have read. The Communicate Business Concepts section affords an opportunity for students to apply to practical life situations the information gained from reading the chapter. By completing the problems under Calculate Business Data, students will be able to strengthen and refine their abilities in mathematics. Technology Application allows students to demonstrate skill in using word processing, spreadsheet, and database software. Decision-Making Strategies contains material to challenge students to utilize the decision-making model explained in Chapter 1 for problem solving.

The Chapter Review questions at the end of the chapter vary in level of difficulty. For a basic assignment, consider Develop Your Business Language and Review Your Reading. For an average assignment, consider the basic assignment plus Communicate Business Concepts and Calculate Business Data. For an enhanced assignment, try the average assignment plus Technology Application and Decision-Making Strategies.

ASSESS

Review the goals at the beginning of the chapter and the Business Notes at the end of the chapter. Restate each as a question and have students respond orally. For students who may have difficulty providing answers, assign the

TEACHING STRATEGIES

Limited English Proficiency (LEP) Students

Ask students to make a list of words or concepts they do not understand in the chapter. Assign a student mentor to work individually with the LEP student to review the list and provide the meanings of the words or concepts.

reteaching activities that follow. Enrichment activities may also be assigned where appropriate.

1. How is technology affecting employment? (Answer: Job duties and skills needed are shifting toward increased use of computers.)
2. What are the benefits of using robots and other technology in business operations? (Answer: Robots never get tired or bored, and robots can work in situations that are dangerous for people.)
3. How can computers help expand global business activities? (Answer: Improved access to trade data along with better information for global buying and selling.)
4. What are the services that technology can bring to your home? (Answer: Shopping assistance, financial and other information, and entertainment.)
5. How has technology improved transportation? (Answer: Regulation of automobile speed, climate, and audio systems; computer-voice safety systems; aircraft control; scheduling and operation of rapid transit trains.)
6. What social concerns are associated with computers and technology? (Answer: Health and safety, criminal activities, and privacy.)

by categories. A family's medical history can be kept on file, or you can have an inventory of household items for insurance records in case of theft or damage. In addition, computer programs may be used for personal financial record keeping, budgeting, writing checks, and preparing your income tax return.

SMART Cards

While most people are familiar with credit cards and electronic banking cards, few may be aware of the existence of a **SMART card**, a plastic card with a silicon chip for storing information. The chip within the card stores

In the future, SMART cards will be used to allow quick check-in at hotels and auto rental companies.

Advanced technology is expected to add smell and touch sensations to virtual reality experiences. Can the *taste* of VR be far behind?

such data as your current account balance, credit history, and even medical information for emergencies.

A SMART card has the potential to take the place of money and checks because each transaction is recorded on the chip as it occurs. Every time a purchase is made, the amount of the transaction would be deducted from the balance in your SMART card account. The card would also serve as a personal record keeper for travel and other expenses. In addition, a SMART card can be

ETHICAL PERSPECTIVES

Are Computers a Threat to Personal Privacy?

Would you want your friends, relatives, neighbors, or employer to know every detail of your personal and financial life? Today, the average person has her or his name in many databases. When you are born, a record of your birthday, address, and parents' names is created. In addition, when you apply for a driver's license, buy a home, apply for credit, or open a checking account, you are creating a trail of data. Starting with just your name and Social Security number, computer database experts may be able to identify your place of employment, salary, credit record, children's names and ages, and magazine subscriptions.

Companies can benefit from using computerized databases in several ways. Marketing campaigns are more efficient if commercials and ads are targeted only to consumers who are most likely to buy the products. Increased sales can mean increased salaries

and job opportunities. Nevertheless, computerized databases can be misused. Easy access to computer data may allow dishonest people to invade privacy or make illegal credit card purchases and unauthorized withdrawals from bank accounts.

Companies and government agencies have taken some actions to safeguard the information in their databases. Restrictions on data, however, must be balanced against the fact that freedom of information is an important liberty in our society.

Critical Thinking
1. What are the benefits and dangers if all databases become easily accessible to anyone?
2. What actions should companies and government take to protect the privacy of information? What actions should not be taken?

ETHICAL PERSPECTIVES

This activity may be used as an individual assignment, a class discussion, or a cooperative learning activity.

CRITICAL THINKING
1. Possible benefits: (a) efficient matching of suppliers with potential customers, and (b) product planning based on more complete market data. Possible dangers: (a) criminal activities, and (b) manipulation of buying habits.
2. Companies might require permission of a person before allowing information about the person to be transferred to others. Government might impose restrictions on how databases are created and used and legislate criminal penalties for inappropriate use of computer information.

Can you think of some practical business applications for virtual reality technology?

used to prove you paid for merchandise you want to exchange, to gain admittance to your place of work, or to unlock and start your car without keys.

Interactive Television

While many people have talked back to the television over the years, it is now possible for your TV to "hear" you. *Interactive television* combines cable television with computer software to create two-way communications systems. Consumers may obtain movies on demand, make travel reservations, shop from home, play video games, and send and receive e-mail.

Virtual Reality

"I just visited the mountains of Switzerland, but didn't leave my living room!" This statement is possible with *virtual reality* (VR) technology that provides three-dimensional

computer images with visuals and sound. VR makes use of special viewing goggles allowing the user to "walk" through situations.

Besides travel and entertainment, this technology could be used for educational and business activities. Teachers can take students to visit ancient Egypt or view a manufacturing plant in operation. Motor vehicle and real estate salespeople will be able to show customers their products without the buyer ever leaving home.

TECHNOLOGY AND TRANSPORTATION

Almost every type of transportation involves computers. Each new model of motor vehicle makes increased use of computerization. Many aircraft fly to their destinations under the control of computers. Rapid transit trains are scheduled and operated by computer systems.

Our daily transportation is greatly influenced by the computer. Computers were first used in automobiles to regulate speed, climate, and audio systems. The use of technology in your car has been expanded to include computer-voice safety systems that warn drivers and passengers about unfastened seat belts, open doors, and engine problems.

Also becoming more common are radar systems that alert drivers about potential collisions, video screens with maps to plot your route, and satellite-based tracking systems that can tell you where you are and how to get where you want to go. There are even sensing devices being tested that allow you to travel specially designed highways with the use of an automatic pilot.

Motor vehicles with crash-avoidance radar systems are already in production. Drivers will be warned with lights and buzzers of potential collision situations.

Chapter 17 *Your Future with Technology* **231**

NET FACTS

Net Facts provides information and definitions of terms for the Internet. The more information that students have about the Internet, the better equipped they will be to use this resource. In the Internet Activity Masters, there is an Internet Activity Worksheet for each unit. You can use these activities to give students experience with finding information online. Options for assigning this activity are as follows:

1. **Provide students with a list of addresses for this activity,**
2. **Assign students to conduct their own searches, or**
3. **Use the addresses on the Internet Activity Worksheet.**
   You should complete the activity yourself before assigning it to resolve any discrepancies that may arise.

databases might have been created and how the information might be used in an inappropriate manner.

SUMMARIZE

Point out that technology makes great amounts of information available for personal financial planning, finding a job, and doing schoolwork. In the future, students must be prepared to use technology in almost every part of their lives.

NET FACTS

A branch or section of the Internet is called a *domain*. Domains can be assigned according to country, region, or state, or according to type of organization, such as education, commercial, government, or military.

SOCIAL CONCERNS ABOUT COMPUTERS

Every new development has advantages, accompanied by potential problems. Expanded computer use has resulted in concerns about health and safety, criminal activities, and privacy. While computers are beneficial to our society, the wise person will not place complete faith in the reliability or safety of computer systems.

Potential Health Dangers

During our lifetimes, we have learned that various products and substances can be dangerous. While little danger exists from using computers and other technology, some people have encountered discomfort from on-the-job activities. For example, eyestrain and vision problems have been associated with prolonged work with computer screens. Muscle tension and nerve damage can occur from too many hours at a keyboard. These and other concerns have resulted in guidelines from labor organizations and government agencies for safe computer operation.

Computer Crime

Wide use of computers has led to an increase in **white-collar crime**, illegal acts performed by office or professional workers while at work. Workers may steal money, information, or computer time through improper use of databases or illegal access to computer systems. While the typical bank robbery

results in a loss of $10,000, computer crimes involving bank records average hundreds of thousands of dollars. Theft of a physical item is obvious; however, theft of computer time or information from a database is usually more difficult to detect.

Piracy, which is stealing or illegally copying software packages or information, is also a growing problem. Companies that develop software may lose more than half of their profits to information pirates who violate the law. Copyright laws apply to software as well as books and music.

Destructive efforts are also a concern to computer users. A **computer virus** is a program code hidden in a system that can later

What social concerns have resulted from expanded computer use?

Basic Skills-Listening

You can teach students to become good listeners by explaining to them the value of not interrupting the speaker. This is sometimes a behavior that is hard for us all to control. However, interrupting the speaker is not only impolite, but the listener will also miss out on information the speaker is trying to convey. For a hands-on activity, ask one student in advance to assist you with a demonstration. Tell the class to put away all papers and pens and pencils. Read aloud the Ethical Perspectives in this chapter. As you read, your student assistant should interrupt you frequently, making comments and asking questions. When you finish reading, ask the class to write on paper three main ideas from the passage. After 10 minutes, stop the exercise and ask the students if it was difficult to learn with the interruptions.

SCANS

do damage to software or stored data. The virus may be programmed to become active on a certain date or when certain data are accessed. While some computer viruses are harmless, only showing up as a funny message, others have been known to destroy critical government records.

Privacy Concerns

One of the greatest challenges facing computer users is the need to guarantee privacy. Some dishonest people have learned how to illegally access computer databases. While some laws exist to protect your privacy, many concerned people believe these regulations are not strong enough. Some businesses are becoming stricter about who can access and use company information. Also, tighter security systems are being developed. Some organizations change the password needed to access information several times a day to protect their databases.

E-Commerce and Technology

You are walking though the mall. As you pass a clothing store, a message appears on your cell phone screen. "Now on special for spring, waterproof jackets, $34.95." This targeted promotion is just one example of the fast, powerful capabilities of wireless technology.

Consumers in countries with inadequate and outdated telephone systems are able to access web sites with the use of wireless technology. Various types of handheld devices are expanding and enhancing e-commerce activities in many areas. Instant messaging, stock trading, banking, online buying, music, and sports video clips are the most common wireless services. Other services will follow as about one-third of the world's population will be using wireless technology within the next few years.

While Internet companies are most visible among consumers and investors, traditional computer companies also have the potential for a strong position in the Internet Age. About 75 percent of IBM's e-business revenue, for example, comes from Internet technology, software, and services such as helping merchants get online and advising organizations how to reshape their businesses using web technology.

Although IBM maintains a strong market position, two levels of competition are evident: large companies (Sun, Microsoft, Hewlett-Packard, and Compaq) and various small start-up firms that provide Net software and e-business consulting services.

Critical Thinking

While wireless web access is increasing, barriers for this technology exist. Conduct a web search to identify examples of Internet services that are available with handheld wireless devices. What services are expected to be available in the future?

Technology Web Sites
E-Commerce Times: www.ecommercetimes.com
Wireless Technology information: www.wow-com.com
Software and hardware assistance: www.computing.net

Basic Skills-Math

Integrating math across the curriculum is an important element in contemporary education. As a part of end-of-chapter activities, Calculate Business Data enables students to apply their math skills. Appendix B: Math Review, Appendix C: Determining Percentages and Interest in Business, and Appendix D: Using Measurements in Business, also apply arithmetic and math skills.

SCANS

REVIEW YOUR READING

1. New jobs are available. A shift has occurred in job duties and skills needed to work in business and industry.
2. Robots never get tired or bored and can work in situations that are dangerous for people.
3. New products can be designed on a computer screen before the model is actually built.
4. Expanded communication systems will mean improved access to trade data along with better information for global buying and selling.
5. Computer users can access a worldwide network of articles, reference books, economic and financial data, discussion groups and bulletin boards, software, and shopping services.
6. Bank account balances, checkbook transactions, credit histories, medical data, proof you paid for merchandise you want to exchange, a password to your place of work, or an electronic key to unlock and start your car.
7. Sensing devices in automobiles can warn a driver about possible collisions. Computer-voice warning systems remind you about unfastened seat belts, open doors, and engine problems.
8. Eyestrain, nerve damage, and muscle tension.
9. Stealing money or information with the use of a computer, illegally copying software or information, and damaging software or stored data with a computer virus.

COMMUNICATE BUSINESS CONCEPTS

10. Although many jobs are lost because of computers, new jobs are created, such as programmers, computer operators, and other technical positions. With increased productivity, the number of new jobs can exceed the number lost. In addition, improved business output can mean more leisure time, which in turn creates new jobs in the fields of recreation, travel, and entertainment.
11. Expert systems ask the software users a series of simple questions. After analyzing the response, the computer suggests a possible solution or courses of action to take. For example, a

Chapter REVIEW

BUSINESS NOTES

1. Workers who lose their jobs because of technology need to be retrained with new skills related to programming, operating, or repairing computer systems.

2. Robots, expert systems, and computer-aided design (CAD) are present in almost every business situation to help improve efficiency and productivity.

3. Technology expands global business activities through fast, efficient communication and distribution systems.

4. Internet computer services, SMART cards, interactive television, and virtual reality allow people to purchase merchandise, financial and other services, and entertainment in more convenient ways.

5. Technology has increased the efficiency and safety of motor vehicles, airplanes, and other modes of transportation.

6. Expanded computer use can result in concerns about health and safety, criminal activities, and privacy.

REVIEW YOUR READING

1. How have computers affected employment?
2. What are the advantages of using robots for various job tasks?
3. How can computer-aided design (CAD) save time and money for business?
4. What effect might computers have on global business activities?
5. What benefits are provided by online computer services?
6. What types of information might be stored on a SMART card?
7. How is technology making automobile driving safer?
8. What types of health concerns are associated with computer use?
9. What types of crimes are committed by computer users?

COMMUNICATE BUSINESS CONCEPTS

10. How is it possible for the increased use of computers to create more jobs than are lost?
11. How can expert systems be used to help people solve medical, legal, financial, and other technical problems?
12. What would be the potential benefits from the use of SMART cards in handling everyday transactions?
13. What actions could be taken by organizations to prevent computer crime?

financial planning expert system may ask your age, income, family size, tax situation, attitude toward risk, and other background information. Then, the program would suggest possible investment options to help you reach your financial goals.
12. The benefits of SMART cards would be no need for consumers to carry money or a checkbook, no counterfeiting of money, and faster transactions that save time and money.

13. Organizations can prevent computer crime by changing passwords often, checking the backgrounds of people given access to sensitive data, prosecuting software pirates, and installing special programs that detect and clean computer viruses.

DEVELOP YOUR BUSINESS LANGUAGE

For each numbered item, find the term that has the same meaning.

14. Mechanical devices programmed to do routine tasks.

15. Technological assistance used to create product styles and designs.

16. A plastic card with a silicon chip for storing information.

17. A computer network connection with information, shopping, and entertainment services.

18. Stealing or illegally copying software packages or information.

19. Programs that assist people in solving technical problems.

20. An illegal act performed by office or professional workers while at work.

21. A program code hidden in a system that can later do damage to software or stored data.

22. Programs that enable computers to reason, learn, and make decisions using logical methods similar to the methods humans use.

KEY TERMS

artificial intelligence (AI)
computer-aided design (CAD)
computer virus
expert systems
online computer service
piracy
robots
SMART card
white-collar crime

DECISION-MAKING STRATEGIES

The Kendall Manufacturing Company assembles electronic devices used in offices and homes. They employ about 600 people in various office, factory, and warehouse positions. Currently, all factory and warehouse jobs are done manually. Managers at Kendall are considering replacing 150 assembly line workers with a computerized system. The company can save $135,000.00 a year in operating costs by using this new technology.

23. What factors should the company consider before using the computerized assembly line system?

24. If the company uses this new system, what should the company do to help workers who are displaced by this technology?

DEVELOP YOUR BUSINESS LANGUAGE

14. robots
15. computer-aided design (CAD)
16. SMART card
17. online computer service
18. piracy
19. expert systems
20. white-collar crime
21. computer virus
22. artificial intelligence (AI)

DECISION-MAKING STRATEGIES

23. Cost, increases or decreases in productivity, effect on employee morale because of lost jobs, changes in quality.
24. Severance pay; career development program, including training for possible reassignment or new career direction; job search assistance; personal financial management.

CALCULATE BUSINESS DATA

25. 3,800 × \$0.42 = \$1,596.00; \$1,596.00 − \$1,250.00 = \$346.00 saved

26. 8 hours × 15 reports per hour × 5 days = 600 reports per week; 2 reports per day × 5 days = 10 reports per week; 600 − 10 = 590

27. 680 + 2,500 + 1,320 = 4,500 words; 4,500 words ÷ 50 words per minute = 90 minutes; 90 minutes ÷ 60 minutes per hour = 1.5 hours; 1.5 hours × \$25.00 per hour = \$37.50

28. Original route: 57.5 miles ÷ 25 miles per gallon = 2.3 gallons; 2.3 gallons × \$1.20 per gallon = \$2.76; New route: 54 miles ÷ 30 miles per gallon = 1.8 gallons; 1.8 gallons × \$1.20 per gallon = \$2.16; \$2.76 − \$2.16 = \$0.60

TECHNOLOGY APPLICATION

In this activity, students use a computer to solve a business problem using a file provided on the data CD that accompanies *Intro to Business*. Instructions for using the data CD are included in a **README** file on the disk. Solutions are provided on the Instructor's Resource CD.

CALCULATE BUSINESS DATA

25. The Barkley Corporation usually sends about 3,800 pieces of mail per month at \$0.42 each. If the firm switches to electronic mail service at a cost of \$1,250.00 per month, how much money would it save or lose?

26. A scientist working eight hours a day can analyze 15 medical reports per hour using a computer. Before using the computer, the scientist could analyze 2 reports per day. How many more medical reports per five-day workweek can the scientist analyze by using the computer?

27. Rose Bokungu operates a language translation service. Her computer program can translate Swahili to English at a rate of 50 words per minute. Rose charges \$25 per hour for translations. If Rose receives the following three documents in Swahili, what will her fee be to translate all three documents: letter, 680 words; report, 2,500 words; magazine article, 1,320 words?

28. The Coulter family travels by car to visit a relative every month. They recently bought a new car equipped with a computer that can plan travel routes and improve engine performance and gas mileage. The family's usual route is 57.5 miles long and their old car used to get 25 miles per gallon. The computer in the new car planned a route that is 54 miles long and improved gas mileage to 30 miles per gallon. If the average price of gasoline is \$1.20 per gallon, how much money per trip will the new car save? (Solve the problem using two decimal places.)

TECHNOLOGY APPLICATION

Using the *Intro to Business* Data CD and your word processing program software, select problem CH17. After the problem appears on your screen, complete the following activities. Then, print your completed letter and sign your name as purchasing agent. If you do not have a printer available, save the purchase order on a data disk to give to your teacher.

To: Edgar Wu Company
6745 Michigan Avenue
Clinton, IA 51503

Order No.: P4331
Date: November 1 of the current year
Ship Via: Truck
Date Wanted: November 15 of the current year

Quantity	Description	Unit Price	Total
3	Easy Translate Software	100.00	
1	Super Fast Desktop System	4,000.00	

29. As an employee of Rose Bokungu's Translation Service, you are responsible for sending a purchase order for software and hardware to a computer supply company. Enter the information in the spaces provided on the purchase order. Also enter the grand total for the purchase order.

30. Make a copy of the entire purchase order and place it in a different part of your document.

31. For the second purchase order, replace the given information with the following data. Also enter the grand total for the purchase order.

To: McIntire Computers, Inc.
405 Lewis Street
Big Sur, CA 93920

Order No.: P4332
Date: November 2 of the current year
Ship Via: Truck
Date Wanted: December 1 of the current year

Quantity	Description	Unit Price	Total
2	Billing Manager Software	900.00	
2	Big Power Workstations	8,700.00	

GLOBAL MARKETING OPPORTUNITIES

Some businesses sell toys in one city, while others sell medical products throughout the world. While both organizations are involved in marketing, the medical company has a global perspective.

International marketing involves marketing activities among sellers and buyers in different countries. Global marketing opportunities for companies are designed to maintain and expand an organization's profits. These international business opportunities commonly result from global trends:

1. Expanded communications, such as computer networks, make it possible to communicate with customers all over the world. The use of fax machines, e-mail, video conferencing, and the World Wide Web expands selling to people worldwide, when previously this may not have been possible due to time and expenses.

2. Technology, such as automated production systems, makes it easier for companies to set up manufacturing plants in other countries. Technology also improves product distribution. Refrigeration systems on ships allow fruits and vegetables grown in Chile to arrive fresh in Japan.

3. Changing political situations can result in expanded business opportunities. Many previously closed societies now encourage foreign companies to help with their nation's economic development.

4. Increased competition results in a need to offer new and different products. As domestic and foreign competitors enter a market, managers must be more creative and more efficient in their production, marketing, and distribution.

5. Changing demographics, such as birthrates, age distributions, marriage rates, income levels, and education, also create new marketing opportunities. More working parents usually means greater demand for childcare and convenience foods. People living longer can result in new business opportunities for health care and travel services.

CRITICAL THINKING

1. Based on one or more of these five global trends, suggest a business opportunity that could be successful in other countries.

2. Identify a food product or other item made in another country and sold in the United States. Explain how this item became a business opportunity for the foreign company.

Most students will either work with international clients or compete against businesses that do. Global Navigator introduces students to issues integral to working with international businesses. Key concepts and challenges faced by international businesses are presented, followed by 2 Critical Thinking questions that require students to analyze what they have learned.

This feature discusses the growing trend toward international marketing of products and services. It lists some of the opportunities arising from this trend, opportunities which students may avail themselves of as they consider their own personal career choices.

CRITICAL THINKING

1. Responses to this will vary widely, depending on the student's own interests and business exposure.

2. Answers may include things such as South American fruits and vegetables, bananas from Central America, and a variety of ethnic specialty products. Non-food products include cars, consumer electronics, and clothing.

GLOBAL BUSINESS PROJECT

Information has become a vital commodity for every organization. Managing this resource is a career skill that will be of value to every student. In this phase of the global business plan project, students will identify the information needs of their company related to: (1) financial information; (2) production; (3) sales and marketing; and (4) human resources.

Student awareness of common software applications and recent technology is also necessary in every field. Encourage students to develop new ways for using technology to do things better, faster, and for lower costs. Technology expands the possibilities of global business activities.

To complete each phase of this project, students are encouraged to use various resources—textbook content, library materials, World Wide Web sites, interviews, advertisements, product packages, in-store observations. The individual activites are planned for use as either (1) an on-going course project, or (2) individual assignments.

Whether used as a continuing project or for selected activities, consider having students work in teams. This small group experience provides a valuable skill for future learning and work situations.

In addition to search engines, these selected web sites can be helpful for this unit:

- International Trade Administration of the U.S. Dept. of Commerce (www.usatrade.gov)
- World Trade Organization of the United States (www.wto.org)
- World Export-Import Bank of the United States (www.exim.gov)
- International Chamber of Commerce (www.iccwbo.org/)
- Small Business Administration (www.sba.gov)
- Import-export information at (www.internationalist.com/business)

GLOBAL BUSINESS PROJECT

CREATE INFORMATION SYSTEMS

Years ago, factories and equipment were the most important assets of a company. Today these items are still important; however, another commodity has gained magnitude—information.

This phase of the business plan project involves decisions related to the type of computer system that would best serve the company's needs. You will also consider the software, e-mail use, fax needs, and World Wide Web.

PROJECT GOALS

1. Research information needs of companies involved in international business.
2. Analyze types of computer systems, networks, and software that could be used by multinational companies.
3. Identify uses of technology to enhance global business activities.

PROJECT ACTIVITIES

Using your textbook, library materials, web sites, interviews with people, and other resources, complete the following activities:

1. An organization's information needs can be viewed in these categories: (1) financial information, (2) production, (3) sales and marketing, and (4) human resources. Using your global business idea, describe records that your company would need for each group.
2. Common software applications include spreadsheets, word processing, and database programs. List uses for this software in your business enterprise.
3. In recent years, technology has expanded the possibilities of business organizations. Create a new use for your international business activities based on some recent technology (fax, e-mail, World Wide Web, SMART card) or research others.

PROJECT WRAP-UP

1. Continue your portfolio (folder, file box, or other container) for storing and referring back to the information and materials you created in the activities above. Your portfolio provides the information needed for the various elements of a global business plan.
2. Create a flowchart to communicate the movement of information within your planned business organization. Show sources of data, such as customers, sales records, and employee time cards as input in your flowchart. The output section might include information items such as financial statements, inventory records, and payroll reports.

- Annual reports, company information (www.reportgallery.com)
- Stock quotes (www.stockmaster.com)
- Export assistance (www.unzco.com/) (www.export.gov)
- Over 4,000 international business links at (www.fita.org)

- Global e-commerce information at (www.howtoconquertheworld.com)

FOCUS ON CAREERS

FOCUS ON CAREERS

COMPUTERS AND TECHNOLOGY

Thousands of new jobs have been created because of the increased use of computers. Computer and technology workers must meet the demands for information within their organizations. People with a variety of skills and educational backgrounds can find career opportunities working with computers and technology.

JOB TITLES

- Computer, Automated Teller, and Office Machine Repairer
- Computer Hardware Engineer
- Computer and Information Systems Manager
- Computer Operator
- Computer Programmer
- Computer Software Engineer
- Computer Support Specialist and Systems Administrator
- Computer Systems and Software Sales Representative
- Data Entry Keyer
- Desktop Publisher
- Electronic Drafter (Computer-Aided Design Operator)
- Information Systems Teacher (in schools and for industry)
- Numerical Control Tool and Process Control Programmer
- Semiconductor Processor
- Systems Analyst, Computer Scientist, and Database Administrator
- Word Processor

EMPLOYMENT OUTLOOK

- The Bureau of Labor Statistics expects faster than average growth in computer and technology-related jobs.
- Since nearly 80 percent of the labor force will be working in service industries, most computer-related jobs will be in service organizations.

EDUCATION AND TRAINING

- Most computer-related jobs require education beyond high school.
- This training may be achieved through a specialized vocational program or a college degree program.

SALARY LEVELS (IN RECENT YEARS)

- Computer operators generally earn from $25,000 to over $60,000.
- Computer programmers make between $35,000 and $90,000.
- Systems analysts' salaries range from about $40,000 to $95,000 or more.

CRITICAL THINKING

1. How might changing economic conditions affect the demand for computer-related employment positions?
2. Why is a basic understanding of computers important in every career field?

The careers listed in the Career Focus come from the *Occupational Outlook Handbook*, an online publication (www.bls.gov/oco) of the federal government. The O*NET codes for these job titles are: Computer, Automated Teller, and Office Machine Repairer, 49-2011.00, 49-2094.00; Computer Hardware Engineer, 17-2061.00; Computer and Information Systems Manager, 11-3021.00; Computer Operator, 43-9011.00; Computer Programmer, 15-1021.00; Computer Software Engineer, 15-1031.00, 15-1032.00; Computer Support Specialist and Systems Administrator, 15-1041.00; Computer Systems and Software Sales Representative, 41-4011.00, 41-2031.00; Data Entry Keyer, 43-9021.00; Desktop Publisher, 43-9031.00; Electronic Drafter (Computer-Aided Design Operator), 17-3012.01; Information Systems Teacher, 25-1021.00, 25-1022.00, 25-2031.00; Numerical Control Tool and Process Control Programmer, 51-4012.00; Semiconductor Processor, 51-9141.00; Systems Analyst, Computer Scientist, and Database Administrator, 15-1051.00, 15-1081.00, 15-2031.00; Word Processor, 43-9022.00.

As a supplemental activity, distribute the Career Focus worksheets found in the School-To-Work/SCANS Activity Masters.

CRITICAL THINKING

1. For example, if people travel more, demand for computer jobs in travel companies and airlines will increase.
2. For example, a forest ranger uses computers to monitor weather reports. Or, a teacher uses computers for instructional activities.

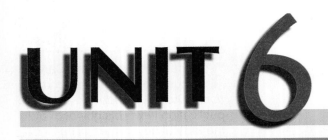

UNIT 6

BUILDING YOUR PORTFOLIO

CAREER DEVELOPMENT – REFINING A RESUME

The Building Your Portfolio career exercise will help your students establish a personal history—where they have been, where they are now, and where they are going. This career exercise will give students an opportunity to refine their resumes.

Review with students the ingredients of a successful resume. (Students will prepare a resume in Chapter 20.) Stress the importance of *evaluation* as part of the resume preparation process. Ask students to exchange resumes for editing. Each student should take a turn reading a fellow student's resume. Reading aloud is an effective editing technique. Have students refine their resumes as necessary.

As a supplemental activity, you may refer to the School–To–Work/SCANS Activity Masters.

TEACHING STRATEGIES

SCANS

Special Features

Media/Technology

Chapter	Spreadsheet Software	Database Software	Word Processing Software	Internet	Video
18	■				■
19		■		■	■
20			■		■
21		■			■

Resources

SOFTWARE

Excel, Word, WordPerfect, Works, and ClarisWorks for Mac and Windows

Word Pro, ASCII, QuattroPro, Lotus, and Access for Windows

SOUTH-WESTERN EDUCATIONAL PUBLISHING PRODUCTS

Foster. *Teenagers-Preparing for the Real World.* 1999. Cincinnati: South-Western Educational Publishing Company. Textbook. 0-538-68787-8.

Zedlitz. *Getting a Job: Process Kit.* 1998. Cincinnati: South-Western Educational Publishing Company. Process Kit. 0-538-67900-X.

BOOKS

Occupational Outlook Handbook 1998-99 (Serial). 1998. Vgm Career Horizons.

Krantz. *Jobs Rated Almanac: The Best and Worst Jobs - 250 in All.* 1999. Pharos Books.

PERIODICALS

Entrepreneur. Entrepreneur, Inc. Irvine, CA.

Kiplinger's Personal Finance Magazine. Washington, D.C.

Success. Success Magazine Co. New York, NY.

The Wall Street Journal. New York, NY.

GOVERNMENT PUBLICATIONS

Occupational Outlook Handbook, U.S. Department of Labor, Washington, DC.

What Work Requires of Schools: A SCANS Report for America 2000, U.S. Department of Labor, Washington, DC

MEDIA/TECHNOLOGY

Publisher's web sites:

www.intro2business.swep.com

www.swep.com

www.thomson.com

UNIT 6

This unit will prepare students for the right job and help them to succeed in their chosen career. Unit 6 begins with a discussion of human resources — the labor factor—in our economy and an overview of the job market. Approaches to career planning and decision making are described. Students are given an explanation of how to write a letter of application, how to develop a resume, and what is expected in an interview. This unit concludes with a discussion of career opportunities in small businesses, including both the advantages and disadvantages of small business ownership.

Chapter 18, Human Resources in Our Economy, presents the basic aspects of the role of labor in our business world and society. The chapter also provides an introduction to the study of the job market with a discussion of our work force and of factors that influence employment opportunities. Chapter 19, Planning a Career, provides basic tips on gathering information about careers and steps in the career planning process. Chapter 20, Succeeding in the World of Work, provides some insights into how employees approach the hiring process and gives students advice about preparing for an interview. Chapter 21, Opportunities in Small Business, explains the advantages and disadvantages of being in business for yourself and gets students thinking about entrepreneurship.

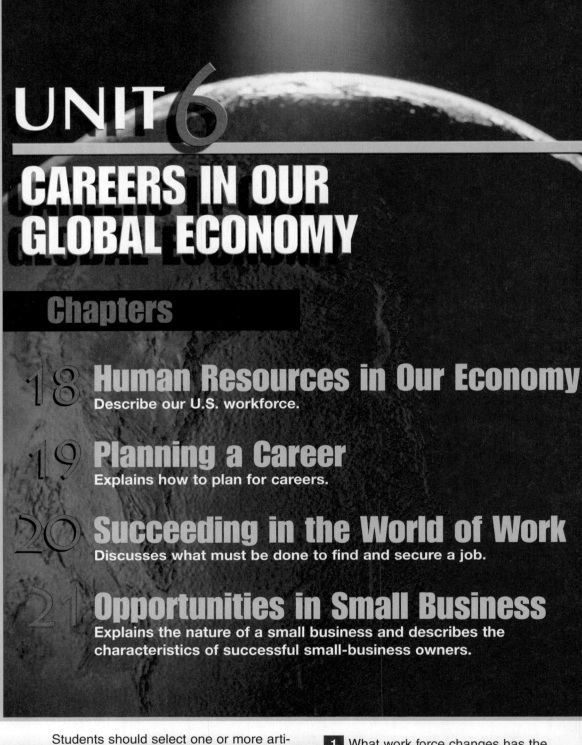

UNIT 6
CAREERS IN OUR GLOBAL ECONOMY

Chapters

18 Human Resources in Our Economy
Describe our U.S. workforce.

19 Planning a Career
Explains how to plan for careers.

20 Succeeding in the World of Work
Discusses what must be done to find and secure a job.

21 Opportunities in Small Business
Explains the nature of a small business and describes the characteristics of successful small-business owners.

Kick-Off Activity
Investigating Business Media

The following exercise asks students to choose an article from *The Wall Street Journal*, the financial section of a newspaper, or a business magazine and to inquire about a topic related to this unit.

Students should select one or more articles in *The Wall Street Journal* or financial magazines that illustrate how a company or an industry is adapting to changes in its work force. (Examples include retraining, flextime, benefits aimed at working parents, job-enrichment and job-redesign programs.) Ask students to answer the following questions:

1 What work force changes has the company you selected experienced recently?

2 Which employee needs is the company (or industry) adapting to?

3 Was the company (industry) forced to change for some financial or legal reason, or did it move voluntarily to meet the needs of employees? Why?

BU$INE$$BRIEF

WHAT CONTRIBUTES TO HIGH EMPLOYEE MORALE?

In their search for ways to improve morale, a growing number of businesses are focusing on the motivational aspects of the job itself. Companies realize truly high morale results from a work environment in which employees obtain satisfaction from their work. Several strategies used by businesses to improve the work environment and employee morale include job enrichment, job enlargement, and flexible work schedules. The purpose of these strategies is to help workers excel in their work as well as improve morale.

Job enrichment involves redesigning the work to give workers more authority to plan their activities and to decide how the work should be accomplished. Workers are allowed to trade jobs with others or to learn related skills. Enrichment means that employees have an opportunity to be more creative and to set their own pace within the limits of the overall work schedule. *Job enlargement* is a simple expansion of a worker's assignments to include additional, but similar, tasks. Rather than performing three tasks, a worker might be given an opportunity to complete six similar tasks. Enlarging a job might lead to job enrichment, but not necessarily. Job enrichment could occur when employees are given greater authority and responsibility for achieving work goals.

Many companies have found flexible work schedules to be a good way to attract and motivate talented employees. *Flextime* allows employees to set arrival and departure times within constraints specified by an organization. Several alternative work-scheduling practices are also used to offer workers flexibility.

A *compressed workweek* is one in which employees work the same number of hours in fewer days than the typical five-day workweek. For example, some companies let employees work their 40-hour weeks in four-day shifts of 10 hours each. Still relatively rare in American business, *job sharing* involves the division of one full-time position among two or more people. Rather than sharing their jobs with another employee, some workers opt for *part-time work* in which they work less than the standard (40-hour) workweek. Another alternative, which has become very popular, is *home-based work*. Employees work their same jobs, but do the work at home instead of in the office. These workers are called telecommuters.

The strategies just described are only a small part of what employers can do to improve employee morale. Obviously, the key to good morale lies in such factors as the work itself and the potential for achievement, recognition, responsibility, and advancement.

CRITICAL THINKING

1 *Can you think of situations where the strategies just described would be effective? Ineffective? List them and explain your reasoning.*

2 *Investigate the meaning of the term "family friendly." What are examples of strategies used by businesses in your area to promote a "family friendly" work environment?*

241

BU$INE$$BRIEF

CRITICAL THINKING

Student answers will, of course, require thinking beyond what is presented in the Business Brief. The following are possible answers:

1 Answers will vary. Students probably will provide many examples of the quality of work life being improved through techniques designed to reshape the workplace. On the other hand, some managers fear a flexible arrangement such as job sharing. If a large portion of the work force chooses this option, a manager's responsibilities with regard to recruiting, supervising, and evaluating employee performance increases greatly. Much of the concern about quality of work life improvements come from managers who fear losing control over their subordinates.

2 The growing popularity of techniques designed to improve the quality of work life reflects a concern among employees for a balance between their professional and personal lives. "Family-friendly" organizations address these concerns by offering such options as flexible work schedules, child care centers, and leaves of absence for family reasons.

BUILDING YOUR PORTFOLIO

The Building Your Portfolio work samples validate skill level and a student's ability to accomplish tasks frequently performed on the job. The most important reason for including samples in a portfolio is to demonstrate a student's abilities and skills. In selecting work samples for each unit, students should always have a choice of which activities to include. Students might be encouraged to include samples from the end-of-chapter activities, particularly Communicate Business Concepts, Calculate Business Data, Technology Application, and Decision-Making Strategies.

Factors influencing jobs in goods-producing and service-producing industries include buying preferences, business cycles, new technologies, competition, and societal issues.

Resources for Teachers
- Lesson Plans
- School-To-Work/SCANS Activity Masters
- Spanish Resources
- Instructor's Resource CD

Assessment
- Chapter and Unit Tests, Ch. 18
- ExamView, Ch. 18

Media/Technology
- Applying Technology Data CD
- PowerPoint slides
- Business Connection CD
- Videotape

Activity Masters and Workbooks
- Activities and Projects, Ch. 18
- Internet Activity Masters
- Business Math Activity Masters
- Communications Activity Masters
- International Business Activity Masters
- Ethics Activity Masters

Chapter 18

Human Resources in Our Economy

GOALS

EXPLAIN why human resources are a vital economic force.

IDENTIFY types of industries and occupational groups in our work force.

DISCUSS factors that affect job opportunities and how the workplace is changing.

Techno Tips

Customer Service for Online Shoppers

One of the most important human aspects of any successful business is excellent customer service. This has always been the case for businesses, and online businesses are no exception. To date, online shoppers have given mixed opinions about the quality of customer service received from online businesses.

When online shopping first emerged, customers had more patience with customer service shortcomings because of the newness of online shopping. Today, however, online shoppers' expectations have risen considerably.

Common customer service problems noted by online shoppers are merchandise availability, slow web site performance, and high shipping and handling costs. If online businesses want to ensure their long-term success, they must not forget the old business adage "the customer is #1."

Students need to know the latest technologies and develop cutting edge Internet skills for use in current jobs, future careers, or in their homes. TechnoTips introduces students to today's cutting edge technologies and provides them with important Internet skills. Feature topics concentrate on Internet-specific technologies and computer or other hi-tech innovations for use by businesses and consumers.

The contributions of labor, a factor of production, are vital to the economic growth of our nation. Labor includes all people involved in obtaining products from nature, converting raw materials into useful products, selling products, providing services, or supervising or managing others. *Labor* refers to anyone who works, from the chief executive officer of a huge corporation to a self-employed gardener.

There are three factors of production: natural resources, capital, and human. Many people recognize labor (the human factor) as the most important. Without people working on jobs, tools and equipment could not be operated, and buildings and roads could not be built. Labor is our work force—a vital ingredient in the production of goods and services for consumers.

THE U.S. WORK FORCE

Our **work force** is made up of all the people 16 years and older who are employed or who are looking for a job. There are more than 160 million people who have full-time or part-time jobs in our work force. Most jobs require at least a high school education and often some special training. Some jobs require only basic skills and a willingness to work hard and learn on the job—but those jobs are disappearing rapidly. Some jobs are high paying and some are low paying; some involve working mainly with machines and technology, while others involve working mainly with people and information.

Types of Industries

Our business world consists of hundreds of thousands of companies that provide a variety of jobs. The jobs in our business world may be organized in a variety of ways. The Bureau of Labor Statistics (BLS), which is part of the U.S. Department of Labor, researches thousands of different jobs. The BLS publishes many useful materials about

Name various well-paying jobs that require technical training or higher education.

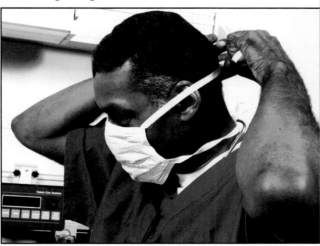

Chapter 18 *Human Resources in Our Economy* 243

NET FACTS

Net Facts provides information and definitions of terms for the Internet. The more information that students have about the Internet, the better equipped they will be to use this resource. In the Internet Activity Masters, there is an Internet Activity Worksheet for each unit. You can use these activities to give students experience with finding information online. Options for assigning this activity are as follows:

1. **Provide students with a list of addresses for this activity,**
2. **Assign students to conduct their own searches, or**
3. **Use the addresses on the Internet Activity Worksheet.**

You should complete the activity yourself before assigning it to resolve any discrepancies that may arise.

Display PowerPoint 18-4, *Changing Job Opportunities.* The outlook for any occupation is affected by these factors. Walk students through a discussion of other factors that might affect opportunities in the job market. Other examples include geography, turnover, level of education, and the number of people entering a particular field. Job opportunities vary from one part of the country to another. Turnover is the number of people who leave one job for another. Education tends to

NET FACTS

The World Wide Web is a sub-network of computers that displays multimedia information, including text, graphics, sound, and video clips. Web documents also contain special connections that allow users to switch to other documents that could be on computers anywhere in the world.

current and projected employment opportunities. Two BLS publications, *The Occupational Outlook Handbook* and *Occupational Outlook Quarterly,* offer up-to-date information that you can use to find out about many types of jobs.

There are two major types of industries analyzed in the *Occupational Outlook Handbook.* (See Figure 18-1.) The **service-producing industry** includes businesses that perform services that satisfy the needs of other businesses and consumers. For example, service companies include health care facilities, insurance companies, retail stores, and transportation organizations. The **goods-producing industry** includes businesses that manufacture many kinds of products. These

companies are involved in construction, manufacturing, mining, and agriculture.

Our economy has experienced a change over the years from an emphasis on goods-producing businesses to service-producing businesses. The BLS estimates that virtually all job growth will occur in these businesses with four out of five workers employed in service businesses over the next few years.

Occupational Groups

Another way of looking at our work force is to consider groups of occupations. Occupations are affected by industry trends and current developments in certain types of businesses. Occupations in groups are affected differently. Twelve occupational groups used by the BLS, along with future employment prospects for each group, are shown in Figure 18-2.

Occupations also are referred to in terms of two very broad groups: white-collar and blue-collar. A *white-collar worker* is one whose work involves a great deal of contact with other people and the handling and processing of information. Most white-collar workers are employed in offices and stores and include professional, managerial, and clerical workers.

A *blue-collar worker* is one whose work primarily involves the operation of machinery and equipment. Blue-collar workers are

FIGURE 18-1 Which category, service-producing or goods-producing, accounts for more jobs in your community?

INDUSTRY CATEGORIES

Service-Producing Industries

- Personal and business services
- Retail and wholesale trade
- Finance, insurance, and real estate
- Government
- Transportation, communications, and public utilities

Goods-Producing Industries

- Construction
- Manufacturing
- Mining
- Agriculture

TEACHING STRATEGIES
Cooperative Learning Activity

Working in small groups helps students become at ease with participating in groups. Student Team Reading/Student Team Writing is an instructional method in which students use cooperative learning in peer groups. When using this instructional method, students are assigned to groups with four members each. The groups should be mixed in performance level, gender, and culture. Assign this chapter for the groups to read. The groups will then write a summary of the chapter in their own words. Each group should produce a written plan, draft, and then a final paper as a group. This can be an excellent group and writing activity that may be developed with various topics throughout the semester.

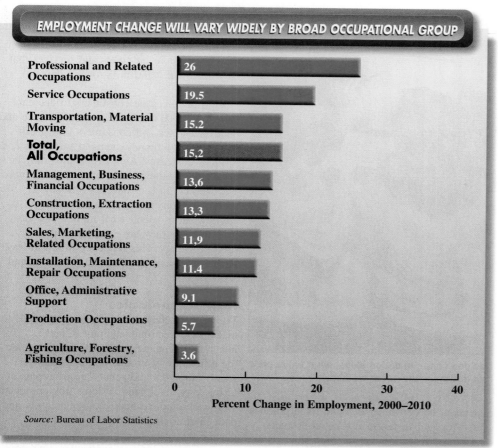

EMPLOYMENT CHANGE WILL VARY WIDELY BY BROAD OCCUPATIONAL GROUP

Occupational Group	Percent Change
Professional and Related Occupations	26
Service Occupations	19.5
Transportation, Material Moving	15.2
Total, All Occupations	15,2
Management, Business, Financial Occupations	13,6
Construction, Extraction Occupations	13,3
Sales, Marketing, Related Occupations	11,9
Installation, Maintenance, Repair Occupations	11.4
Office, Administrative Support	9.1
Production Occupations	5.7
Agriculture, Forestry, Fishing Occupations	3.6

Percent Change in Employment, 2000–2010

Source: Bureau of Labor Statistics

FIGURE 18-2 Can you see that the fastest growing occupations are those that tend to require specialized training?

employed in factories, in machine shops, and on construction sites. Increased use of computers and information technology in factories and construction is changing the role of blue-collar workers and is causing a need for higher levels of education and training.

White-collar and blue-collar workers are equally important in our work force. Both types of workers are needed if we are to satisfy our economic needs and wants.

CHANGING JOB OPPORTUNITIES

The jobs held by people in our work force are subject to a variety of factors that can cause the need for these jobs to change.

Some of these influences may cause jobs to be eliminated, while others will cause the work to be modified. Changes may require employees to develop new skills and get different training. Consumer preferences, economic conditions, new technology, business competition, and societal factors are strong influences on the work force.

The Influence of Consumers

Consumers regularly cast their "dollar votes" in the marketplace. Preferences by consumers have an important effect on the availability of jobs in our work force. Jobs are affected by **derived demand**. The demand for factors of production, such as human resources, are

increase the job opportunities available to a worker. An increase in the people who want to work in certain occupations creates greater competition for jobs.

EXPLORE THIS/INDEPENDENT PRACTICE Have students use *The Occupational Outlook Handbook* or *Occupational Outlook Quarterly* to obtain information about an occupational area in which they may be interested in the future. Have them prepare a short essay or oral report on the training requirements and type of work done in this occupational area.

Have students investigate employment trends, particularly the percentage of women, minorities, and immigrants entering the work force. Ask students to prepare a short report that answers the following questions: What are some of the reasons for these changes? How will this affect employment opportunities for all workers?

Assign individual students to meet with guidance counselors and school librarians to determine the types of resource materials available for studying various careers. Have students look at the materials and report back to the class on the contents of these materials.

The Chapter Review questions at the end of the chapter vary in level of difficulty. For a basic assignment, consider Develop Your Business Language and Review Your Reading. For an average assignment, consider the basic assignment plus Communicate Business Concepts and Calculate Business Data. For an enhanced assignment, try the average

TEACHING STRATEGIES
Visually Impaired Students

Take time to orient visually impaired students with the classroom and their individual work stations. An orientation will make them more comfortable and confident in their surroundings.

assignment plus Technology Application and Decision-Making Strategies.

ASSESS

Review the goals at the beginning of the chapter and the Business Notes at the end of the chapter. Have students respond orally or in writing to each of the Business Notes restated as a question, provided below. For students who may have difficulty providing answers, assign the reteaching activities that follow. Enrichment activities may also be assigned where appropriate.

1. Why are human resources a vital economic force? (Answer: Without people working on jobs, tools and equipment could not be operated and buildings and roads could not be built.)
2. What are two types of industries and two types of occupational groups in our economy? (Answer: industries—goods-producing and service-producing; occupations—blue collar and white collar)
3. List five factors that affect job opportunities. (Answer: derived demand, business cycles, new technologies, business competition, and societal issues)
4. What has caused change in the workplace during the past decade? (Answer: the role of the federal government; the makeup of the work force; and the increased use of technology)

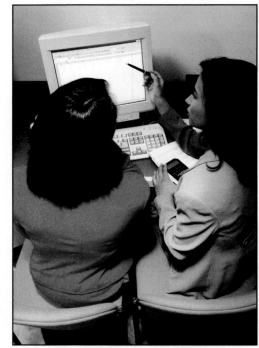

Besides communication skills, what skills are required by white-collar workers?

dependent on consumer demand for a product or service. For instance, if most consumers decided to wear clothing made of blue denim, workers who make blue denim clothing would be in great demand. If consumer choice shifted away from blue denim, fewer workers would be needed by companies producing those goods.

Sometimes new products entering the market make those already available obsolete, at least in the mind of the consumer. Workers producing the old product may find that their jobs will be eliminated. New jobs, however, would be created by the demand for the new products.

Business Cycles

Stages of the business cycle affect job opportunities. When businesses are expanding and consumers are buying more and more

goods and services, new jobs are created to meet the growing demand. As more workers are employed and earn more money, they spend more on goods and services that they need and want; the growing demand continues.

High prices cause consumers to decrease their buying. When interest rates increase and both businesses and consumers find it difficult to borrow money, demand for goods and services decreases. As a result, jobs may be eliminated or the number of workers reduced. The workers in turn have less money to spend for their needs and wants. They also are hesitant to spend what money they do have because they are not sure of their future earnings. This tendency to spend less further decreases the demand for goods and services.

New Technologies

Technology refers to the use of automated machinery, electronic equipment, and integrated computer systems to help increase the efficiency of producing goods and services. Computers and robots are examples of technology. Integrated systems link computers with each other to make communication and data sharing easier. Robots continue to change the types of jobs and worker functions in manufacturing companies. Technology continues to influence how office workers perform their jobs.

Business Competition

Businesses must be competitive to stay in business, and costs are a major factor. The cost of running a business affects jobs and workers. When profits begin to decrease, the business must look for ways to improve its profits. Installing new equipment and systems that allow workers to produce more goods

> You cannot tell the importance of a worker by the "color of his or her collar."

CULTURAL PERSPECTIVES
The Maori People and Fishing Charts

Did you know that the Maoris of New Zealand perfected a way of predicting the best times to fish? Fishing was a means of sustaining life for the Maori people. By studying the moon and developing correlations with feeding activity of fish, they perfected charts that predicted the best times to fish. The Maoris also devised ecological "sea laws" to protect fishing grounds and shellfish beds.

Today those charts, which have been confirmed over the centuries, are computerized. Projections can be made for use throughout the world. Anyone in the United States can determine the best days and the best time of day to fish. *Outdoor Life* magazine has published those charts for several years.

Maoris were the first people to settle on the islands of New Zealand. This group of people came from other Polynesian islands in the eighth century. According to one legend, the Maoris left their homes "across the great sea" in a fleet of canoes. Over the years, they intermarried with Europeans who settled in New Zealand, and some moved from their villages to the cities of New Zealand. However, today's Maoris still continue to harvest the riches of the sea and preserve many traditions of their ancestors.

Critical Thinking
1. What are some of the cultural traditions of the Maoris?
2. What are other skills for which the Maori people are noted?

---

and services in less time often is a solution. Businesses may also decide to downsize. **Downsizing** is a planned reduction in the number of employees needed in a firm in order to reduce costs and make the business more efficient.

Societal Trends
Social trends, such as the age makeup of our population, also influence employment opportunities. The 16- to 24-year-old category in our population will be a smaller proportion of the work force in the next few years. Greater employment opportunities will exist for young people and immigrants.

Immigrants are people from other coun-

Many of the jobs in the future will not require a college degree but will require specialized education and training.

tries who come to live in our country for a variety of reasons. Many immigrants become U.S. citizens. Immigrants have made important contributions to our economy throughout the history of our country. They often fill jobs that otherwise would go unfilled. Immigrants often start businesses that provide services that otherwise would not be provided.

THE CHANGING WORKPLACE

The American workplace has changed considerably in the past decade. Much of this change is due to the role of the federal government, the makeup of the work force, and the increased use of technology.

Government has reached into the day-to-day management of employees through congressional legislation, agency guidelines, and Supreme Court decisions. Three areas of government regulation have affected the management of human resources: equal employment opportunity, especially for people with dis-

---

CULTURAL PERSPECTIVES

Cultural Perspectives expose students to the concept that our society is composed of people from many different cultural backgrounds.

CRITICAL THINKING
1. To answer this question, students will need to investigate the culture of the Maoris. In large gatherings, the Maoris enjoy their tradition of giving poetic speeches and engaging in "action songs," a form of dance.
2. The Maoris are also noted for developing cooking methods that utilize geothermal energy. They built oven boxes to use over natural steam vents and used hot springs for boiling foods.

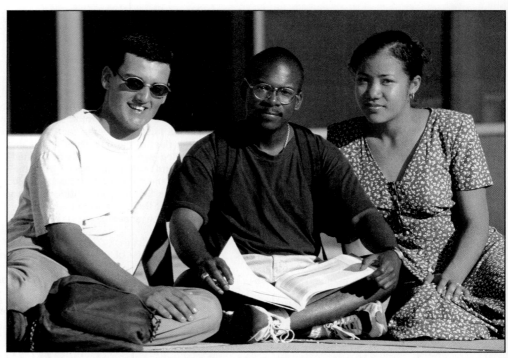

Why do you think that foreign students might want to become U.S. citizens?

abilities; pensions and retirement issues related to an aging work force; and job safety and employee health.

A *computer systems administrator's* job duties include:

- Providing administrative support for various software users.
- Maintaining network hardware and software, analyzing problems, and monitoring the network to ensure availability to system users.
- Gathering data to identify customer needs and evaluating system requirements.

The importance of *people* to the success of an organization is stressed in the very definition of management: The use of people and other resources to accomplish organizational goals.

FYI

The makeup of the work force is becoming more varied. Employees may have different heritages from all around the globe. Employees may also be younger or older than average, be physically challenged, or speak English as a second language. Today's companies treat each employee fairly so that all employees can contribute to their companies' success.

Technology is important in the workplace for improving efficiency in order to stay competitive in international markets.

The careers listed in Career Highlights come from the *Occupational Outlook Handbook*, an online publication (www.bls.gov/oco) of the federal government. The O*NET code for Computer Systems Administrator is 15-1071.00. Tell your class about this resource and how to access it, and explain its purpose and how to use it. This description of job duties can be used to demonstrate the relevancy of skills learned in this course.

DEVELOP YOUR BUSINESS LANGUAGE

For each numbered item, find the term that has the same meaning.

15. All people 16 years and over who are employed or are looking for a job.

16. Businesses that perform services to satisfy the needs of other businesses and consumers.

17. Businesses that manufacture many kinds of products.

18. A demand for factors of production affected by consumer demand for a product or service.

19. Planned reduction in the number of employees needed in a firm.

20. People from other countries who come to live in our country for a variety of reasons and often become citizens.

KEY TERMS
derived demand
downsizing
goods-producing industry
immigrants
service-producing industry
work force

DECISION-MAKING STRATEGIES

The A-1 Textile Company has come upon hard times. The firm's profits have shrunk to a point where the company must reduce costs or eventually go out of business. A-1 has been a major employer in the community of Cottonburg for many years. The firm employs 300 workers who average $22,000 a year in wages. To remain in business, A-1 must cut $2 million from its payroll and cut other operating expenses. The owners plan to lay off approximately one-third of the workers to avoid closing the business.

21. Do you agree with the owners in their decision? Why or why not?

22. What other course of action might the owners take to remain profitable and stay in business?

CALCULATE BUSINESS DATA

23. In a recent decade, mining employment declined from 1,027,000 workers to 709,000.
    a. How many jobs were lost in the mining industry?
    b. What was the percentage of decrease? (Round off your answer.)

24. One of the large stores in a shopping center employs 48 salespeople, 6 department managers, 2 credit clerks, 2 secretaries, 1 accountant, and 1 store manager.
    a. How many employees, including the store manager, are there in this store?
    b. If the credit clerks, secretaries, and accountant make up the office staff, the office staff is what percentage of all employees?
    c. If two-thirds of the salespeople work part time, how many part-time salespeople are there? How many salespeople work full time?

25. In the year 2005, 17 percent of the work force is expected to be 55 years old and over, 63 percent will be between 25 and 54 years old, and 20 percent will be between 16 and 24 years old. If there are 133 million people in the work force in the year 2005, how many will be in each age category?

26. For the following occupational categories, the number of workers and the expected growth rate are given.
    a. For each job group, how many new employment positions are expected?
    b. For each group, what will be the total number of jobs based on the projected growth rate?

DEVELOP YOUR BUSINESS LANGUAGE

15. work force
16. service-producing industry
17. goods-producing industry
18. derived demand
19. downsizing
20. immigrants

14. This question allows students to be more specific in describing the kinds of automated equipment that affect workers. The use of automated teller machines (ATMs) by financial institutions, electronic cash registers and information screens in stores, radio-controlled mail carts in offices, and microfiche filing systems are possible examples. Students can obtain other examples from business, news, and technology periodicals available in libraries.

DECISION-MAKING STRATEGIES

21. Answers will vary. Basically, students should not agree with the decision. There are other alternatives to be considered. The business should not close unless absolutely necessary. The community depends upon the company for employment.

22. The company could ask all employees to take a voluntary reduction in pay so that no one, or at least very few, would need to be laid off. They might investigate ways to streamline manufacturing operations and make their products profitable. The company should also consider other cost-saving programs and involve their employees in coming up with ideas for cutting costs.

resulting in an overall increase in job opportunities. (b) New technology could cause a reduction in the number of workers needed and also create the need for some new kinds of workers. (c) Reduced spending for travel would result in fewer job opportunities in travel-related occupations such as travel agents, airline personnel, and workers in leisure and recreation businesses. (d) In the downsizing of a business, a number of people would lose their jobs. (e) Although the total demand for food producers might not be affected because people will continue to buy food, perhaps people will stop buying certain types of food products and start buying others. Or, fewer people might eat at restaurants and spend more of their food dollars at supermarkets, which would also influence the types of jobs in demand. (f) A downturn in the business cycle would mean that consumers would be spending less for goods and services, and some workers in both industries would lose jobs.

CALCULATE BUSINESS DATA

23. (a) 1,027,000 − 709,000 = 318,000 jobs lost in the mining industry in a recent decade (b) 318,000 ÷ 1,027,000 = 0.3096 or 31% decrease

24. (a) 48 + 6 + 2 + 2 + 1 + 1 = 60 employees (b) 5 ÷ 60 = 0.083 or 8.3% (c) 48 × 0.666 = 32 part-time salespeople; 48 − 32 = 16 full-time salespeople

25. 133,000,000 × 0.17 = 2,261,000 workers 55 years old and older; 133,000,000 × 0.63 = 83,790,000 workers 25 to 54 years old; 133,000,000 × 0.20 = 2,660,000 workers 16 to 24 years old

26. (a) 8,600,000 × 0.09 = 774,000 new government employees; 4,900,000 × 0.18 = 882,000 new construction employees; 6,300,000 × 0.26 = 1,638,000 new finance, insurance, and real estate employees; 5,700,000 × 0.27 = 1,539,000 new wholesale trade employees (b) 8,600,000 + 774,000 = 9,374,000 government employees by the year 2000; 4,900,000 + 882,000 = 5,782,000 construction employees by the year 2000; 6,300,000 + 1,638,000 = 7,938,000 finance, insurance, and real estate employees by the year 2000; 5,700,000 + 1,539,000 = 7,239,000 wholesale trade employees by the year 2000 (c) 9,374,000 + 5,782,000 + 7,938,000 + 7,239,000 = 30,333,000 employees by the year 2000 (d) 4,833,000 ÷ 25,500,000 = 18.95%

27. (a) 29,800 × 0.22 = 6,556
(b) 900 ÷ 29,800 = 3.02%
(c) 29,800 − 6,556 = 23,244
       900 × 10 yrs = 9,000
     250 × 10 yrs = 2,500
         Total 34,744

---

   c. What will be the total employment for these four job categories?

   d. What is the average expected growth rate for these four occupational categories?

Category	Current Employment (In Millions)	Expected Growth Rate (Percent)
Government employees	8.6	9
Construction	4.9	18
Finance, insurance and real estate	6.3	26
Wholesale trade	5.7	27

27. A business firm has 29,800 employees. Over the next 10 years, the firm anticipates that 22 percent of its employees will retire. In addition, there are approximately 900 who leave each year for other employment and are replaced. Because of research and development resulting in many new products, the firm will likely add 250 new employees each year to handle customer orders.

   a. How many employees will retire in the ten-year period?

   b. What percentage of the employees leave each year for other employment?

   c. What will be the total number of employees at the end of the ten years?

TECHNOLOGY APPLICATION

Using the *Intro to Business* Data CD and your spreadsheet program software, select problem CH18. After the problem appears on your screen, complete the following activities. Then, after you have completed each step, display or print the completed spreadsheet for each activity. If you do not have a printer available, answer the questions before you leave the computer.

28. In the Difference column, enter a formula to calculate the increase or decrease from the Baseline Employment to the Projected Employment. Copy the formula to calculate the increase or decrease for each occupational category. Format the Difference column for commas and no decimal places. Sort the spreadsheet in descending order by Difference. Answer the following questions:
   a. Which occupational category has the largest increase?
   b. How many occupational categories show projected decreases?

29. In the Percentage Change column, enter a formula to calculate what percentage of Baseline

Employment is represented by the Difference. Copy the formula for each occupational category. Format the Percentage Change column for percentage with 1 decimal place. Answer the following questions:
   a. What is the third largest projected percentage increase?
   b. How many occupational categories have a projected Percentage Change of less than +1 percent and greater than −1 percent?

30. At the bottom of the spreadsheet, enter labels and functions to show the sums of the Baseline Employment, Projected Employment, and Difference columns. Enter a formula to calculate the total Percentage Change. Format the totals with commas and no decimal places. Answer the following questions:
   a. What is the total of the Difference column?
   b. What is the projected Percentage Change of total employment?

Optional: Create a bar chart of the Percentage Change for each occupational category.

TECHNOLOGY APPLICATION

In this activity, students use a computer to solve a business problem using a file that is provided on the data CD that accompanies *Intro to Business*. Instructions for using the data CD are included in a **README** file on disk. Solutions are provided on the Instructor's Resource CD.

COMMUNICATING for SUCCESS

RESPONDING TO CRITICISM—YOU THINK THAT ABOUT ME?

Criticism is often viewed in a negative manner, generally because it can be taken personally and can cause hurt feelings. However, used in the right manner, criticism can be a valuable tool for personal and professional development.

There are two types of criticism, *constructive* and *destructive*. Constructive criticism isolates the criticism to one or two specific behaviors or situations, and offers techniques for how the behavior or situation can be improved or handled differently. Destructive criticism often includes personal attacks, as well as broad, non-specific statements about behavior.

Destructive criticism can often prove to be distressing. To deal effectively with criticism, you should be prepared to view unwelcome comments as an opportunity to grow and improve your performance. Dealing effectively with criticism can also include developing professional development plans aimed at improving behaviors, habits, and work performance.

Criticism is a form of feedback, and

> **Dealing effectively with criticism can help you grow as a professional.**

feedback can be a matter of fact or judgment. Matters of fact deal with actual records or observed behaviors which determine what has been said and done. Matters of judgment deal with opinions about what has been said and done. Typically, matters of judgment are likely to be the most destructive form of feedback because they rely on opinions, second-hand information, and the judgment of another person.

When responding to criticism, you should avoid:
—shifting the blame to others;
—falsely asking for sympathy;
—denying that problems or opportunities for growth exist; and
—turning against others.

A positive attitude about developing as a professional can make a tremendous difference!

CRITICAL THINKING

1. What are the two types of criticism and how would you define them?
2. What should you avoid in responding to criticism?

COMMUNICATING for SUCCESS

Communications skills will help ensure students' success in the business world. Communicating for Success introduces workplace/interpersonal communications issues and proper uses of communications technology. Each feature discusses a key communications topic, and contains two Critical Thinking questions that require students to analyze what they have learned.

This feature deals with a topic that many students may find hard to deal with. Constructive criticism and the practice of continually challenging assumptions is crucial to maintaining a vibrant business culture. For many students, however, it's not something they are used to if they have been brought up in an overly protective environment. This feature puts criticism in a proper business context for students.

CRITICAL THINKING

1. There are two types of criticism, constructive and destructive. Constructive criticism isolates the criticism to one or two specific behaviors or situations, and offers techniques for how the behavior or situation can be improved or handled differently. Destructive criticism often includes personal attacks, as well as broad, non-specific statements about behavior.
2. When responding to criticism, you should avoid:
   —shifting the blame to others;
   —falsely asking for sympathy;
   —denying that problems or opportunities for growth exist; and
   —turning against others.

Career planning is looking into careers and into one-self to determine preparation for a future career. A five-step career decision-making process is explained. Ways of financing an education are illustrated.

Resources for Teachers
● Lesson Plans
● School-To-Work/SCANS Activity Masters
● Spanish Resources
● Instructor's Resource CD

Assessment
● Chapter and Unit Tests, Ch. 19
● ExamView, Ch. 19

Media/Technology
● Applying Technology Data CD
● PowerPoint slides
● Business Connection CD
● Videotape

Activity Masters and Workbooks
● Activities and Projects, Ch. 19
● Internet Activity Masters
● Business Math Activity Masters
● Communications Activity Masters
● International Business Activity Masters
● Ethics Activity Masters

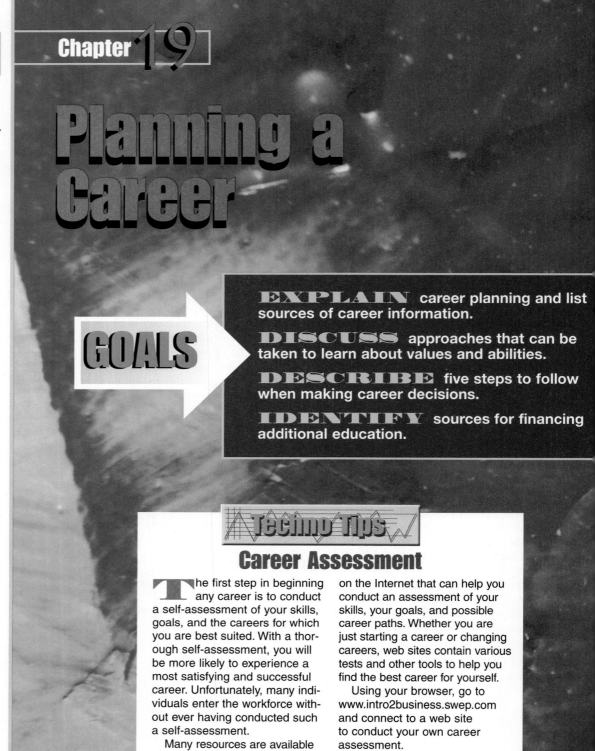

Chapter 19

Planning a Career

GOALS

EXPLAIN career planning and list sources of career information.

DISCUSS approaches that can be taken to learn about values and abilities.

DESCRIBE five steps to follow when making career decisions.

IDENTIFY sources for financing additional education.

Techno Tips

Career Assessment

The first step in beginning any career is to conduct a self-assessment of your skills, goals, and the careers for which you are best suited. With a thorough self-assessment, you will be more likely to experience a most satisfying and successful career. Unfortunately, many individuals enter the workforce without ever having conducted such a self-assessment.

Many resources are available on the Internet that can help you conduct an assessment of your skills, your goals, and possible career paths. Whether you are just starting a career or changing careers, web sites contain various tests and other tools to help you find the best career for yourself.

Using your browser, go to www.intro2business.swep.com and connect to a web site to conduct your own career assessment.

Students need to know the latest technologies and develop cutting edge Internet skills for use in current jobs, future careers, or in their homes. TechnoTips introduces students to today's cutting edge technologies and provides them with important Internet skills. Feature topics concentrate on Internet-specific technologies and computer or other hi-tech innovations for use by businesses and consumers. At the www.intro2business.swep.com web site, students can complete the activity for this chapter.

Dan Capparus was reading the local newspaper. He was impressed by the number of help wanted ads placed by businesses in his community. The ads said that certain kinds of training were needed or that applicants needed experience in certain business operations. He wondered where businesses got those kinds of workers. He could not help but observe that the ability to use computers and certain computer programs was mentioned quite often.

Dan thought about his own situation. He still had a few years of school left, and he wondered if he were taking the right courses to get the career that he wanted in the future. Then he realized that he really did not know for sure what kind of career he really wanted. For some reason or other, he had not given this important subject a lot of thought. Then he wondered what strategies he might use to improve his awareness of careers.

Dan decided to consult with his school counselor. Her insight proved to be invaluable. Dan quickly learned about three approaches to career awareness: studying careers, developing self-awareness, and making an initial career decision.

STUDYING CAREERS

An **occupation** is a task or series of tasks that is performed to provide a good or service. People are hired to fill occupations, and they are paid for the work they perform. A *goal* is something specific you want to achieve. A **career** is a goal in life that is fulfilled through an occupation or series of occupations.

You actually have a kind of career goal now: to complete your schooling and prepare for your future. Your occupation right now is to take the right courses and to earn good grades. When you enter a career in the world of work, your career goal may be to become a department store manager or an office administrator. Your first occupation then could be as a salesperson in a department store or as an office receptionist. With a good work record and additional training, you could be promoted to those higher positions.

Career planning is the process of studying careers, assessing yourself in terms of careers, and making decisions about a future career. This process begins by making some decisions about your interests and the occupation you want to have someday. Career planning requires an investigation of several occupations within a career area. You must find out about duties performed, education and training required, and the wages paid. You should learn about what it takes to succeed and about the advantages and disadvantages of certain occupations.

The study of careers is a continuous process. New career opportunities occur all the time. You do not just decide to study careers for one day or one week. It is important to view learning about careers as a life-long activity, something that continues even after you begin your career.

FINDING INFORMATION

We all need help in career planning. There are several sources of help for you right in your own school and community. Some information covers careers in general. Other information is more specific about occupations and careers in your local area. You should look into as many sources of information as possible.

Not setting a goal is like trying to find an object when you don't know what is lost.

volunteers who might be willing to present their balance sheets to the class.

Guide students through an examination of their personal traits. Ask students the following questions: When was the last time that you thought seriously about your own personal traits? What traits do you have that are important in business? What are some that you would like to improve upon? In completing this activity, have students think about traits for success and about themselves. Point out that this will give them a better understanding of themselves.

Ask students to use their imagination and list some sources of job information. Show PowerPoint 19-3, *Finding Information*, after students have prepared their lists. Determine which students came up with the most comprehensive listing of sources of job leads and information about prospective employers.

Guide students through the process of career decision making by constructing a pyramid with the following steps:

1. gather information—as much as you can;
2. analyze the information—about careers and yourself;
3. think about possible plans of action;
4. select a plan of action—then follow it;
5. evaluate your plan from time to time;
6. get the career that is right for you!

Go through the steps as a class exercise. (You might have students construct the pyramid as a bulletin board display.) Emphasize to

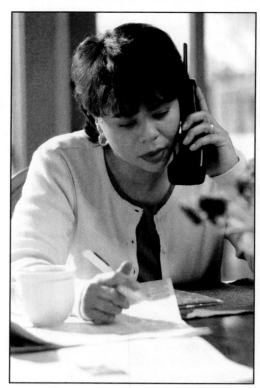

What are some resources you can use in planning your career?

Your own school is a good place to start. Many school libraries have career resource materials. You may find the *Occupational Outlook Quarterly* or other publications of the Department of Labor's Bureau of Labor Statistics to be quite helpful. For example, *The Occupational Outlook Handbook* gives detailed information on hundreds of occupations. Included are job duties, working conditions, education and training requirements, advancement possibilities, employment outlook, and earnings.

Career World is a magazine that publishes information about a variety of careers, often looking at careers of the future. *The Encyclopedia of Careers and Vocational Guidance* can give you basic information about many occupations and career areas. Organizations, such as the Insurance Information Institute, publish

materials dealing with their particular career areas. Database programs and on-line computer programs can be used to access up-to-date information on occupations and sources of education and training.

Your school may have a career resource center. Some schools locate them in the library, some in the counseling office, and others in departments such as business education and technical education. These resource centers normally have a wide variety of materials available. You may find magazines, brochures, pamphlets, films, videotapes, and CDs on careers. You may also have computers in your school that are connected to centralized computer files of career and education information.

Newspaper help wanted ads are also useful in career planning. Reading the help wanted ads in your local newspaper or a large metropolitan paper can give you a good idea of what jobs are in demand. Reading those ads can help you discover what employers are looking for in the people they hire. Sometimes ranges of beginning salaries are shown.

Another good source of information for career planning in many communities is the **government employment office**. These are tax-supported offices that help people find jobs and that provide information about careers. Employers who need workers often contact government employment offices for help. They may also contact private employment agencies for the assistance needed. Employment offices can provide up-to-date information about the job market in your local area. They also can help you look for part-time, summer, or full-time work.

A recent survey found that 47 percent of women workers and 57 percent of men workers felt they had a career—the others said they "just had a job."

TEACHING STRATEGIES

Special Needs: Specific Learning Disability (SLD)

Students who are passive learners, when faced with participating in class, avoid answering questions in favor of waiting for a teacher to involve them in the instructional process. When asking questions during class, ask passive learners questions that they can likely answer successfully. Save more difficult or unstructured questions for better students.

GETTING INSIGHT INTO WORK

One of your best sources of information about work is other people. Most workers are happy to explain what they do. This process of talking to other people about their jobs is called *networking*. The advantage of networking is that your contacts are not limited to the people you know personally. You probably can find a person who works at almost any job in which you are interested.

Part-time or summer jobs can also give you insight into work. Useful information can be learned by being alert to what is going on around you as you work. You may have already had experiences with part-time or summer jobs.

A formal way to gain insight into a career is through a career information interview. A **career information interview** is a planned discussion with a worker to find out about the work that person does, the preparation necessary for that career, and the person's feelings about his or her career. Career information interviews are an excellent way to get valuable information. Interviews will help you gain insight into what actually happens in a particular career area. They also might show you how important it is to plan ahead and prepare for the right career.

You will find that most workers like to talk about their career experiences. However, before you begin a career information interview, you should think about the questions you want to ask. Here are some questions that are often asked:

- How did you get your present occupation? Did other occupations lead you to this one? If so, what were those occupations?

- In what ways do you find your occupation to be satisfying? In what ways is it dissatisfying?

- What are some tasks you perform in your occupation?

Name several ways that you can find out about job openings.

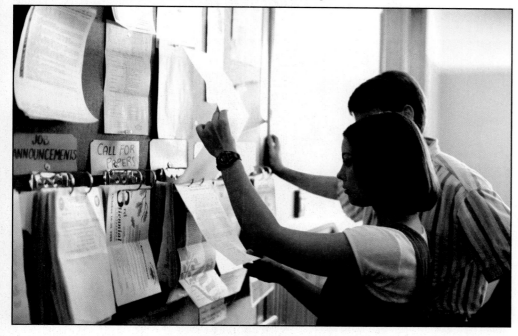

students that the best decisions are made after good data have been collected. Also point out that the career decision-making model is similar to the decision-making model in Chapter 1.

EXPLORE THIS/INDEPENDENT PRACTICE Have students write a short report on how they believe their values will influence their career choices. Ask them to be specific when relating how such things as power, independence, security, money, and prestige could cause them to choose or reject certain occupations.

Encourage students to talk with a friend who has worked on part-time or summer jobs. Students should find out what that person has learned about the world of work. In particular, students should determine if his or her values have changed in any way and whether work itself is viewed differently.

The Chapter Review questions at the end of the chapter vary in level of difficulty. For a basic assignment, consider Develop Your Business Language and Review Your Reading. For an average assignment, consider the basic assignment plus Communicate Business Concepts and Calculate Business Data. For an enhanced assignment, try the average assignment plus Technology Application and Decision-Making Strategies.

TEACHING TIP
Safety and Health

Set rules for using equipment in the classroom and review them with your students. It is important for students to know what is expected of them before they enter the computer lab.

Review the goals at the beginning of the chapter and the Business Notes at the end of the chapter. Have students respond orally or in writing to each of the Business Notes restated as a question, provided below. For students who may have difficulty providing answers, assign the reteaching activities that follow. Enrichment activities may also be assigned where appropriate.

1. What is meant by career planning? (Answer: Career planning is the process of studying careers, assessing yourself in terms of careers, and making decisions about your interests and the occupation you want to have someday.)

2. List four published sources of career information. (Answer: *Occupational Outlook Quarterly, The Occupational Outlook Handbook, Career World,* and *The Encyclopedia of Careers and Vocational Guidance.*)

3. How can you learn about your values and abilities? (Answer: Personal values can be determined through a series of questions that are answered. Abilities can be discovered by analyzing courses taken, liked, and not liked.)

4. Describe the five steps to be followed when making career decisions. (Answer: The decision-making steps are: (a) gather information; (b) analyze what has been learned; (c) think about different plans of action; (d) select a plan of action; and (e) evaluate the career decision.)

A recent study of high school seniors showed that only one-third were proficient readers, a decrease from previous years.

We in the United States are not the originators of environmental awareness. The environment has been a concern for hundreds of years of the present day Zuni Indian Tribe of New Mexico. Recently, the Zuni Tribe has returned to irrigation technologies that were used thousands of years ago in an effort to reduce erosion in the southwestern United States.

- In what ways do you think your occupation is better than others? In what ways is it not as good?

- What do you believe are some of the most important qualifications for the work you do? What training and education are needed?

- What advice would you give a young person who is considering this line of work?

You should keep notes on what you learn through career information interviews. The experiences of others will provide important career planning information that you will continue to find valuable.

If a particular career interests you, ask your teacher or guidance counselor about the possibility of becoming a *job shadow* at a particular company employing workers that reflect your career interest. Job shadowing allows you to spend time with a worker for a day or a week to learn about a certain occupation.

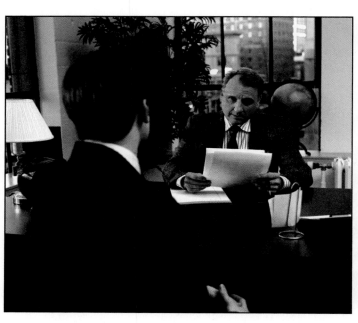

What are some questions you could ask at an informational interview?

Basic Skills-Speaking

SCANS

We can help students develop speaking skills by teaching them how to organize their ideas in a manner that is appropriate for a situation. Before speaking to a group, students should know their audience, plan their presentation, rehearse, and then make the presentation. Discuss with students characteristics of an audience and how that audience plays a role in the performance of the speaker. Developing a speech through an outline is an excellent planning tool, and every speech should have an introduction, body, and conclusion. As this chapter is about career planning, assign several students the topic of "pursuing and financing additional education" as a speech to be presented to the class. Give students the Student Activity Worksheet, Basic Skills—Speaking, in the School-To-Work/SCANS Activity Masters, to serve as a guideline.

GETTING INSIGHT INTO YOURSELF

Each person has individual needs and wants that influence their lives. For instance, you may have to decide whether you want to work in the geographic area in which you now live or whether you are willing to move to where the job you really want is located. There may be reasons why you would prefer to live and work near your home. However, people who successfully pursue the careers of their choice often have mobility.

Mobility is the willingness and ability of a person to move to where jobs are located. The lack of mobility of our work force leads to locational unemployment. *Locational unemployment* occurs when jobs are available in one place but go unfilled because those who are qualified to fill those jobs live elsewhere and are not willing to relocate.

As you look into careers and learn about jobs and the work involved, you will get a feeling for certain occupations and career areas. You may like or dislike certain occupations without knowing why. Various personal aspects of career planning are important. Becoming aware of these personal aspects and your values are important in career planning.

Your Values

Your **values** are the things that are important to you in life. They must be considered along with facts about occupations and careers. A number of ways exist in which you can learn about your values. Your counselors or business teachers may have exercises or activities that can help you learn about your values. These exercises show how you rank items such as prestige, money, power, achievement, independence, leadership, security, or

NET FACTS

Netiquette is an Internet phrase that refers to the rules of conduct and behavior on the Net. For example, don't send unwanted advertising, do keep your messages brief and to the point, and don't use ALL CAPS unless you mean to shout.

belonging. Each of these may influence you, directly or indirectly, when you select your occupation.

You can begin to examine some of your values by answering certain questions. Your answers will help you to understand what things you consider important. Each answer should be thought through and analyzed. Here are some examples of those kinds of questions:

- Is it important to me to earn a lot of money?
- Am I mainly interested in work that provides a service for others?
- Is it important for me to have an occupation that others think is important even if I do not really care for it?
- Do I want an occupation that is especially challenging and may require additional schooling?
- Would I be willing to start in a job that pays a lower salary than another if that job

NET FACTS

Net Facts provides information and definitions of terms for the Internet. The more information that students have about the Internet, the better equipped they will be to use this resource. In the Internet Activity Masters, there is an Internet Activity Worksheet for each unit. You can use these activities to give students experience with finding information online. Options for assigning this activity are as follows:
1. **Provide students with a list of addresses of resources for this activity;**
2. **Assign students to conduct their own searches; or**
3. **Use the addresses provided on the Internet Activity Worksheet.**
   You should complete the activity yourself before assigning it to resolve any discrepancies that may arise.

5. What are some sources for financing additional education? (Answer: Scholarships, financial aid, and part-time work can help students gain needed additional education.)

RETEACH

Have students choose a specific career and list several sources of information about the career chosen.
   Invite a job counselor, an employment interviewer, or

TEACHING STRATEGIES
Cooperative Learning Activity

For this cooperative learning activity, students will concentrate on careers. Divide the class into groups of four to six members each. Each group member will name a career that might be appealing to today's teens. A note taker will list each career while the group members list what they think are the various qualifica-tions for the career, job responsibilities for the career, and what they think the salary will be. The group will then select one ca-reer and a spokesperson for each group will discuss the career with the class. Groups will then reunite and do outside research for that chosen career so that the group may verify and refine the job descriptions that they created. Bring in reference materials on various careers and allow students 20 minutes to finalize the job description that they have chosen.

someone who hires young people for jobs in your community to come to your class to talk with some of your students about career planning. Have students prepare at least six specific questions that would give them insight into talents and abilities needed to succeed at work.

Have students take turns giving oral definitions for the terms *mobility, locational unemployment, values, talent, ability, occupation, career,* and *career planning*.

Put the following question on the board and have students write a one-paragraph response: Why should you talk to people about their occupations and careers?

Have students create their own graphic organizer showing the five elements of career decision making.

ENRICH

Direct students to read the Global Perspectives. Have students develop a career information interview questionnaire. When they have it in usable form, ask them to practice using it with someone in class or with a teacher or school administrator. After using it, students should make any changes they think would be desirable and use it in a career information interview as part of a career project.

Ask students to make a list of career information in their school that could help someone looking into career opportunities. The library, guidance counselor's office, and the business department are places for students to look for materials that could be included in the list.

GLOBAL PERSPECTIVES
International Business Careers

As trade among nations expands, the number and types of global careers will increase. Many U.S. companies, both large and small, already conduct most of their business with international customers, clients and suppliers. How can you go about acquiring information about overseas job opportunities?

Finding information about international career opportunities may seem difficult. However, the following sources may be consulted when planning an international career:

- *U.S. employers with international offices:* Contact the company's human resources department or public relations office. Request information about the company's business activities and career opportunities in other countries.
- *Embassies of foreign countries:* Contact embassy officials for information about the culture, employment opportunities, and any needed documents, such as work permits or work visas.
- *U.S. federal government agencies:*

Contact the Department of State or the Department of Commerce, which have business representatives in most countries of the world.
- *World Trade Centers Association (WTCA):* Contact one of the World Trade Centers located in major U.S. cities. These centers promote global business relationships and international trade.

Do not forget, however, people who are recognized for their success in international careers. Individuals with international business experience are excellent resources for learning about career opportunities overseas and often have useful knowledge about prospective employers.

Critical Thinking
1. What do you think would be the most interesting and challenging aspect of an international career?
2. What might you do to prepare yourself for an international career?

was more challenging and offered better opportunities for future advancement?

- Do I consider investing in education or occupational training to be as important as spending for other things?

While there may be other questions you can think of, these will give you a start.

Another activity is to consider what you would do if someone gave you a large sum of money to be used in any way you desire. Would you start your own business? Would you hire a jet and travel throughout the world? Would you develop a foundation to support athletics for underprivileged children? Would you help build up a run-down neighborhood? Would you buy the biggest wardrobe someone your age ever had? Would you use the money to finance an expensive

education? Your answers will tell you something about your personal values.

Your Talents and Abilities
Each of us has certain talents and abilities. A **talent** is a natural, inborn aptitude to do certain things. We often say someone has a "natural talent." An **ability** is the quality of being able to perform a mental or physical task. Your talents and abilities, along with your career goals and interests, are important in career planning.

You can learn about your abilities in a number of ways. Think about the courses you have taken and the grades you have received in school. What kinds of courses have you taken? In which ones have you done your best work? Which courses have been easiest for you? Which have been the most difficult?

GLOBAL PERSPECTIVES

Global Perspectives gives students an opportunity to discover sources of information about global business careers. The largest worldwide increases in employment opportunities are in information processing, international trade, health care, finance, insurance, leisure, and personal services.

CRITICAL THINKING
1. Interesting aspects could include travel to other countries and meeting people from other nations. Challenging aspects might include learning one or more languages, learning new business practices and procedures, and dealing with people from other cultures with different values and customs.
2. You could learn one or more languages, study international business, travel to become better acquainted with other cultures, and study world geography and history.

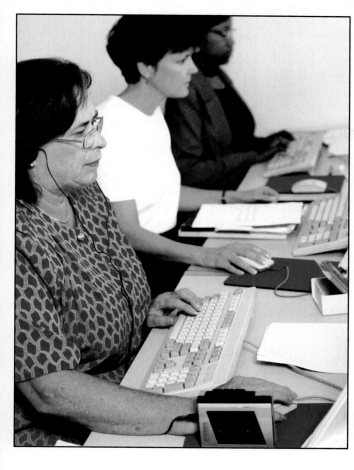

In what ways can you develop various business skills?

SUMMARIZE

Much of the conceptual understanding of this chapter revolves around comprehension of the new vocabulary terms. Have your students make their own crossword puzzles using the Glossary as the basis for their definitions. After completing their crossword puzzle (with an answer key), have the creator exchange his or her paper with another student and complete the puzzle.

EVALUATE

- Assign Activities and Projects for Chapter 19.
- Administer the printed test or ExamView for Chapter 19.
- Assign School-To-Work/SCANS portfolio activities for Unit 6.

Which do you like the best? Answers to questions such as these will identify your talents and abilities.

Abilities can be developed, and that is important to keep in mind. If you are weak in a certain area, you may want to take courses that will improve that area. For instance, employers continue to tell us that writing, reading, and computing skills are very important. If you are not strong in composing letters and reports, you should take additional courses in English, such as business communication. If reading is a problem for you, get help in that area, too. If computations, including working with fractions and decimals, are difficult for you, additional courses in math, including business math,

would be desirable. The idea is to strengthen your weak areas *before* you go into full-time work. You can plan your courses and future activities to help you grow toward your chosen career.

MAKING CAREER DECISIONS

Each person must eventually make his or her own career decision. Too often the decision is made when full-time work begins. But that is too late, especially if certain training and education are required.

Making initial career decisions while you are in school has many advantages. One advantage is that in school you have a lot of good information readily available. But more

Chapter 19 *Planning a Career* 261

important, early career planning will help you select the right courses. An early career decision can also encourage you to become involved with organizations such as Future Business Leaders of America (FBLA), (DECA), and Junior Achievement (JA) that teach you about business and help you prepare for a career.

Your decision may be a **tentative career decision**, that is, a decision that is subject to change or modification as new information is received. A tentative decision is much better than no decision at all. Your career decision will give you a direction that is needed, and you will find a new kind of interest in what you do.

How can you be sure that you are making the best career decision possible? There is no way to guarantee a perfect decision. But good decisions generally are made by those who follow the right steps. Here are some steps to follow in making your career decision:

1. Gather as much information as you can.

2. Analyze what you have learned about careers and about yourself.

3. Think about different plans of action and what might happen if you follow each one.

4. Select what seems to be the best plan of action and follow it.

5. Evaluate your career decision from time to time.

Your search for the right career could continue for a long time. In the years ahead, some of your values and goals will change. You will develop new interests and abilities. New jobs and careers will come along for you to learn about. You should be ready to make career-decision changes when they are called for in your situation.

GETTING ADDITIONAL EDUCATION

As you know, some occupations require education and training beyond high school. Two-year schools—usually called community colleges or junior colleges—offer a wide variety of training in many career areas. Four-year colleges and universities, both public and private, provide education and training for many career areas and professions. Private business schools that specialize in certain job training, such as radio and television or computer technology, are other sources for career preparation.

You should consider the cost for additional schooling as an investment in your future—an investment that will help you earn higher wages in the future. A number of ways exist in which you can get help financing additional schooling. Most schools have financial aid programs that you should investigate. These programs include scholarships, student loans, and work-study opportunities. Some financial aid programs are based on your record as a student while others are based on financial need. Part-time work also is a common way in which young people finance the additional education needed to pursue the career of their choice. You should evaluate these methods of financing an education as you continue your career planning and decision making.

AN EXAMPLE OF A GOOD APPROACH

Brianna Bunton learned about career planning in a number of ways. Brianna prepared a career report on becoming a corporate lawyer as a requirement for her Introduction to Business class. She also interviewed the legal counsel for a local corporation. Her report gave her doubts about whether she really wanted to pursue a career in law and whether she could afford the additional schooling.

A course in accounting that Brianna completed in her junior year led her to believe that the accounting field was one that she would like to enter. She did some reading about accounting careers. With her computer skills, she was able to get a part-time job in an accounting office the following summer. While on the job, she learned about how an

Critical Thinking **Skills-Problem Solving**

Problem-solving skills, which include recognizing a problem and devising a plan of action, are applied throughout every chapter in this text. Each time a student participates in a Cooperative Learning or Teams Activity, problem-solving skills are applied in a group situation. Each time a student completes a math application in Calculate Business Data, decisions are made as to which mathematical approach must be taken. For each Technology Application problem, students must decide which data file to use, which piece of software to load, and how to solve the problem. Emphasize to students how they are using problem solving in their day-to-day tasks and make them aware of the skills they are developing.

accounting office operates. Her job gave her an opportunity to talk to several accountants and auditors about their careers.

When school began again in the fall, she took the second-year accounting course. She also enrolled in additional courses in math and English. The accountants had recommended that she get more course work in both of those areas. She also took the office laboratory course to become more familiar with office procedures. Brianna worked hard to get good grades; she knew that those grades would be important later if she were to achieve her future goal. With her good grades and attendance, she was confi-

dent that she could receive some financial aid when she entered college.

The accountants suggested that Brianna should "reach for the top"—and that meant more schooling along with accounting work experience. Brianna wants to eventually take the state accounting examination. If she passes it, she will become a certified public accountant (CPA).

Brianna continues to work part-time for the accounting firm. She also is enrolled in her local college, where she is majoring in accounting. She has a career plan and is following it. Very likely someday it will be "Brianna Bunton, CPA."

E-Commerce for Career Planning

Web site designers, online customer support staff, auction-abuse personnel, and web technologists are just a few of the new career opportunities created by e-commerce. Online business is also affecting the way job seekers research, apply, and interview for jobs.

Cyber resumes are posted on various web sites. These personal data sheets are scanned for key words to determine candidates with the necessary job qualifications. Words and phases that may impress prospective employers include "foreign language skills," "computer and e-commerce experience," "achievement," "research experience," "flexible abilities," "team projects," and "overseas study or experience."

In the future, you are likely to encounter more screening interviews using video conferencing. Or, you may be asked to post preliminary interview responses online. These "e-interviews" may involve questions such as: "Would you rather have structure or flexibility in your work?" and "What approach do you use to solve difficult problems?"

Online interviewing may also be used to test a person's ability in job-related situations. For example, an applicant may be asked to respond to tasks such as those that a bank teller or retail clerk might encounter.

Critical Thinking

Conduct a web search to obtain information about online resumes. What changes must be made to a conventional resume on paper to make it suitable for online use?

Career Planning Web Sites
Career planning assistance:
www.monster.com
Career opportunities:
www.hotjobs.com
The Wall Street Journal career information:
www.careers.wsj.com
Business Week career information:
www.businessweek.com/careers

REVIEW YOUR READING

1. Your future success and happiness may depend on it. There are many careers to be considered. A study of careers now will help you to take the right courses and get the right kind of experiences before you enter your career.

2. School libraries and the Internet are good starting points for information about careers. *The Occupational Outlook Handbook* and the *Occupational Outlook Quarterly* are publications of the Bureau of Labor Statistics that are especially helpful to young career planners. Other special publications include *Career World* and *The Encyclopedia of Careers and Vocational Guidance.*

3. Career resource centers have a variety of materials such as magazines, brochures, and pamphlets that are readily available. There also might be films and other media available, including computer software and web sites with special career information.

4. Newspaper help-wanted ads give you information about what jobs are in demand. You can find out about job requirements, beginning salaries, and possibly benefits.

5. Government employment offices help people find jobs and provide information about careers. Employers who need workers often contact these offices. Both part-time and full-time work can be arranged from these offices.

6. Through a career information interview, you should find out about the work a person does, the preparation necessary for that career, and how the person feels about his or her career. Important insight into what actually happens in a certain career can be gained through this kind of interview.

7. Mobility allows you to go to where there is a job opening that fits your qualifications if there is not one where you currently live. If you are not willing to move, you may be limited in terms of the kinds of work you can obtain and the kind of career path you can follow.

8. Asking yourself key questions, such as those listed on pages 259–260, will reveal what you consider to be most important in life. You also can observe what it is that you like to do most and how you react to various opportu-

BUSINESS NOTES

1. Career planning is a process of looking into careers and into oneself to determine what preparation should be made for a future career.

2. Important sources of career information include school libraries, career resource centers, government publications, government employment offices, and career information interviews.

3. Personal values can be determined through answering a series of questions. Talents and abilities can be learned through analyzing courses taken and liked or disliked.

4. When making a career decision, including a tentative one, there are five decision-making steps that should be followed: (a) gather information; (b) analyze what has been learned; (c) think about different plans of action; (d) select a plan of action; and (e) evaluate the career decision.

5. Scholarships, student loans, and part-time work can help students gain the needed additional education beyond high school.

REVIEW YOUR READING

1. Why should you study careers?

2. What are several sources of information about careers?

3. Explain how a career resource center can be helpful.

4. What information can be gained from reading newspaper want ads?

5. For what purposes have government employment offices been established?

6. How can career information interviews help you in career planning?

7. Why is mobility important in looking ahead to future careers?

8. What are some of the things you should learn about your values?

9. How can courses and grades tell you something about your talents, abilities, and interests?

10. What steps are involved in career decision making?

11. What help is available to assist you in financing additional schooling?

COMMUNICATE BUSINESS CONCEPTS

12. There is a great deal of information that can be learned about business operations, interpersonal and customer relationships, and other experiences from working a part-time or summer job. Give some examples of what might be learned through these kinds of experiences.

13. Describe how you would conduct a career infor-

mation interview. What would you do to prepare for it in advance?

14. What are some good sources of information about jobs in your local community? Comment on how you might use each one.

15. Make a list of your talents and abilities, and

nities that occur. Your values will affect many of your decisions.

9. Knowing what you are good at is important. The courses you take in school and the grades you receive in those courses will reveal some of your talents and abilities. If you are weak in a particular area that is needed in a career you desire, then you should try to improve and develop that area to pursue your career.

10. These five steps should be followed when making a good career decision: (1) Gather as

much information as possible. (2) Analyze what you have learned about careers and about yourself. (3) Think about different plans of action and what might happen if you follow each one. (4) Select what seems to be the best plan of action and follow it. (5) Evaluate your career decision from time to time.

11. Financial aid programs are available to help finance additional schooling. Scholarships, student loans, and work-study opportunities are examples.

then note the ones in which you feel you are strong or weak. Indicate how you might use your strengths in career planning. Also indicate what action you might take to strengthen your weaker abilities.

16. When you discover what your values are in relation to such things as prestige, power, and recognition, how will your values affect your thinking about future careers? Why should your career decisions be considered tentative rather than once-and-for-all decisions?

17. Why is investing in additional education something that should be considered in career planning?

18. Using references, write a report on your career plan based on your goals, values, talents, abilities, and skills.

DEVELOP YOUR BUSINESS LANGUAGE

For each numbered item, find the term that has the same meaning.

19. The process of studying careers, assessing yourself in terms of careers, and making decisions about a future career.

20. A tax-supported agency that helps people find jobs and provides information about careers.

21. A planned discussion with a worker to find out about the work that person does, the preparation necessary for the career, and the person's feelings about the career.

22. The willingness and ability of a person to move to where jobs are located.

23. A task or series of tasks that are performed to provide a good or service.

24. The things that are important to you in life.

25. A career decision that is subject to change or modification as new information is received.

26. A natural, inborn aptitude to do certain things.

27. A goal in life that is fulfilled through a job or a series of jobs.

28. The quality of being able to perform mental or physical tasks.

KEY TERMS

ability
career
career information interview
career planning
government employment office
mobility
occupation
talent
tentative career decision
values

DECISION-MAKING STRATEGIES

Jeff Barbson is looking to his future and wondering what kind of career he should prepare for. His father is the city's civil engineer. His mother is a buyer in a major department store. Both of his parents are successful and enjoy their careers. Both of them have talked with Jeff about their work. He has visited his father's office and has worked as a sales clerk in his mother's store.

Jeff's favorite subjects are computers, economics, and art. His least favorites are history, English, business law, and math. He earns his best grades in computers and art.

Jeff's father wants him to be an engineer because there is a need for engineers in their state. His mother wants him to go into retailing. Jeff would like to go to medical school and become a heart specialist.

29. Based on his school record, which of the three career areas do you think he should choose?

30. What advice would you give Jeff regarding career planning?

COMMUNICATE BUSINESS CONCEPTS

12. Students should be encouraged to talk about part-time and summer jobs they have held. Aspects about their job that they liked and disliked should be discussed, including specific work tasks, personal relationships, and observations of what others in the organization did in their work.

13. Students should include the following in their description: They would contact a person to set up an interview appointment, make a list of questions to be asked, take notes while listening carefully to the answers, thank the person at the end of the interview, write a summary of the interview experience, and write a follow-up thank-you letter. Also, in advance of the interview, the student should practice asking his or her list of questions.

14. Students should include several of the following: (a) School library and/or career resource center. (b) Government employment office. (c) School counselors and teachers. (d) Local business

DEVELOP YOUR BUSINESS LANGUAGE

19. career planning
20. government employment office
21. career information interview
22. mobility
23. occupation
24. values
25. tentative career decision
26. talent
27. career
28. ability

managers and personnel managers.

15. When talents and abilities are known, they can be compared with job requirements. Talents and abilities can be developed by selecting those courses that teach the knowledge and skills needed. Part-time work in a job that relates to a future career area also is a good way in which to develop talents and abilities. For instance, human relations skills can be developed best in a job in which public contact is a major element of the work performed. Courses also should be selected to develop and strengthen areas of weakness.

16. Those who seek prestige and power select jobs that will give them an opportunity to gain publicity or to receive special awards for doing their jobs; politicians and salespeople gain both prestige and power. The desire for recognition leads to jobs with high visibility in which public recognition is common. Those whose basic desire is to serve other people will seek out careers in fields such as teaching or social work. Once values are determined they become one of the important factors in job and career selection. They also become determinants of future job success. Jobs that do not match the workers' values lead to unhappy workers.

17. Career decisions must be considered tentative because many factors will change over time. Peoples' minds must be open to new information about jobs and about themselves. Many of the occupations that will be available to students after graduation are not even known yet. Still, a career decision, even though it is tentative, is important because it gives a sense of

direction and purpose to what is now being done. The process of studying careers and planning for the future is never-ending and continues throughout an individual's life. Getting the right start with career planning and decision making is important, but it is also important to continue the process as one goes along through educational and work experiences.

18. Some jobs and professions require education beyond high school. Money that is spent for additional education usually results in jobs that pay higher wages. In the end, the money that is invested in additional education is more than returned through increased earnings.

DECISION-MAKING STRATEGIES

29. His school record really does not support an engineering or a medical career. Not liking math suggests that engineering would not be a good choice. His interest in art and computers suggests fashion merchandising as a possible career. Computer technology is used widely in design work, and designers must have an ability to work with colors as well as various shapes and forms.

30. Jeff should do some serious thinking about his future. He needs to begin taking more courses that will allow him to develop his abilities in computers and art. If he pursues fashion merchandising, he should try to get some part-time work experience in this area and also continue to learn about merchandising from his mother.

CALCULATE BUSINESS DATA

31. (a) 40 × $11.25 = $450 earned per week; $450 × 1/3 = $150 saved per week; (b) $150 × 10 = $1,500 saved in 10 weeks; $150 × 15 = $2,250 saved in 15 weeks; $150 × 25 = $3,750 saved in 25 weeks; (c) $8,000 ÷ $150 = 53.3 or 54 weeks needed to reach or exceed her goal.

32. (a) 17 × 175 = 2,975 total miles driven; 17 + 2 + 3 = 22 trucks on the road the following day; 22 × 175 = 3,850 total miles driven the following day; (b) 22 × 190 = 4,180 miles driven per day;

CALCULATE BUSINESS DATA

31. Carrie Ainge works as a clerk in a law office. She works 40 hours per week and is paid $11.25 per hour. She saves one-third of what she earns to create a fund so that she can go to law school.
    a. How much does Carrie earn in one week? How much is she able to save each week?
    b. Without considering interest she would earn on savings, how much would she save in 10 weeks? in 15 weeks? in 25 weeks?
    c. If Carrie needs to save at least $8,000 before she can consider going to law school, for how many weeks will she have to save in order to reach or exceed the $8,000 goal?

32. Shana Dansweif works as a manager for a trucking firm. Shana has to keep records of the number of trucks going out and coming in each day, and she must keep a record of the number of miles driven by each driver. Last Monday there were 17 trucks on the road, 3 on the lot being loaded, and 2 in the shop being repaired.
    a. On Monday, the trucks on the road averaged 175 miles each. How many total miles were driven that day? If all of the trucks were on the road the following day and averaged the same number of miles, how many total miles would be driven?
    b. If all of the trucks were driven for 5 days, and the average miles per truck increased to 190 miles, what would be the total number of miles driven?
    c. If the cost of operating a truck is $3.75 per mile, how much did it cost the company to operate their trucks in each of the three previous situations?

33. Bobby Stevenson works in an office that is 12 feet wide and 14 feet long. The ceiling is 10 feet high. (See Appendix D for information regarding metric conversions.)
    a. What are the dimensions of his office in meters?
    b. His desk is 30 inches high, 54 inches long, and 36 inches wide. What are the dimensions of his desk in centimeters?
    c. A cleaning fluid that is used to keep his furniture looking nice comes in 1-liter, 2-liter, and 5-liter containers. How many quarts of cleaning fluid are there in each container? If the firm uses 50 gallons of cleaning fluid per year, how many 2-liter containers do they use in one year?

34. Nancy Subarb-Sisterrse attends a college where the tuition and fees amount to $9,500 per year. The books and supplies she buys total $1,200 per year. In addition, she has general living expenses of $11,600 per year. She has three sources of income: financial aid of $3,500 per year, a scholarship that pays one-half of her tuition, and a work-study job from which she earns $5,300 per year.
    a. How much income does Nancy receive each year from her three sources of income?
    b. How much does it cost Nancy to go to this college each year?
    c. What percentage of her annual college costs are covered by her three sources of income? (Round off your answer.)
    d. If her uncle David said that he would lend her the money she needs beyond her three sources of income, how much money would Nancy have to borrow each year?

TECHNOLOGY APPLICATION

Using the *Intro to Business* Data CD and your database program software, select problem CH19. After the problem appears on your screen, complete the following activities. Then, after you have completed each step, display or print a report for each activity. If you do not have a printer available, answer the questions before you leave the computer.

35. Sort the database in ascending order by job title. Answer the following questions:
    a. What is one of the duties of the tenth job title listed?

    b. What is the last job title listed?
36. Select and list the jobs that are in the Sales Clerks group. How many jobs are listed?
37. Select and list the jobs that have DOT *(Dictionary of Occupational Titles)* numbers greater than 080.000-000 and less than 100.000-000. Answer the following questions:
    a. How many jobs are listed?
    b. What are the duties of the first job listed?

4,180 × 5 = 20,900 total miles driven in five days; (c) First: 2,975 × $3.75 = $11,156.25; Second: 3,850 × $3.75 = $14,437.50; Third: 20,900 × $3.75 = $78,375.00

33. (a) 12 feet × 0.3 = 3.6 meters wide; 14 feet × 0.3 = 4.2 meters long; 10 feet × 0.3 = 3.0 meters high; (b) 30 inches × 2.5 = 75 centimeters high; 54 inches × 2.5 = 135 centimeters long; 36 inches × 2.5 = 90 centimeters

wide; (c) 1 liter = 1.06 quarts; 2 liters × 1.06 = 2.12 quarts; 5 liters × 1.06 = 5.30 quarts; 50 gallons × 3.8 = 190 liters; 190 liters ÷ 2 = 95 containers used

34. (a) $3,500 + $4,750 + $5,300 = $13,550; (b) $9,500 + $1,200 + $11,600 = $22,300; (c) $13,500 ÷ $22,300 = 0.605 or 61%; (d) $22,300 − $13,500 = $8,800

COMMUNICATING for SUCCESS

RESUMES—THE KEY TO YOUR CAREER

A resume is essentially a tool that provides information about you to a potential employer. Two of the most popular types of resumes are experience-based and qualifications-based.

In an experience-based resume, experiences are usually listed in order of work history. In a qualifications-based resume, your abilities or qualifications appropriate for the type of job you are applying for are highlighted.

Keys to successful resume writing include the use of action words, which demonstrate what you have accomplished or achieved. For example, words such as "organized," "accomplished," "computed," "created," "managed," and "researched" are good action word choices.

Other key ideas include proofreading and following a strict adherence to honesty about your qualifications. Remember that employers check resume information. Providing false information can cause you to lose a winning job! False information, found after you have been hired, can lead to your dismissal and long-term career difficulties.

A typical resume includes the following sections in this order:
- Career Objective
- Career Preparation (also called Education)
- Career Progression (also called Experience)
- Career-Related Honors and Activities
- Community Service or Involvement
- Personal Information (least important; be selective)

Often you will find that it is helpful to include a list of your skills or talents that relate to the job you are applying for. In a Career Objective section, you can tailor your statement to precisely fit the job you are applying for. This section demonstrates to employers your motivation, sense of direction and purpose, as well as your fit with the employer's position.

Finally, be careful what personal information you include. According to the Civil Rights Act and the Americans with Disabilities Act (ADA), it is illegal for employers to make hiring decisions based on personal information such as age, marital status, race, gender, and so on. Therefore, potential employers prefer not to see this type of information. Only list personal information that is appropriate for the job you are applying for, such as hobbies, memberships, or personal interests.

CRITICAL THINKING
1. What is a resume?
2. What are two of the most popular types of resumes?

COMMUNICATING for SUCCESS

Communications skills will help ensure students' success in the business world. Communicating for Success introduces workplace/interpersonal communications issues and proper uses of communications technology. Each feature discusses a key communications topic, and contains two Critical Thinking questions that require students to analyze what they have learned.

Getting a job is any student's first step toward a successful business career, and writing an effective resume is the first step toward getting that job. This feature lays out some brief guidelines, helpful hints, and a suggested outline for students to use.

CRITICAL THINKING
1. A resume is a tool which provides information about yourself to a potential employer.
2. Two of the most popular types of resumes are experience-based and qualifications-based. In an experience-based resume, professional experiences are listed in order of importance or work history. In a qualifications-based resume your abilities or qualifications appropriate for the type of job you are applying for are highlighted.

TECHNOLOGY APPLICATION

In this activity, students use a computer to solve a business problem using a file that is provided on the data CD that accompanies *Intro to Business*. *Instructions* for using the data CD are included in a **README** file on the disk. Solutions are provided on the Instructor's Resource CD.

Chapter 20

The rationale for a letter of application and a personal data sheet is given. Sources of job tips on position interviews and successful on-the-job behaviors are described.

Resources for Teachers
- Lesson Plans
- School-To-Work/SCANS Activity Masters
- Spanish Resources
- Instructor's Resource CD

Assessment
- Chapter and Unit Tests, Ch. 20
- ExamView, Ch. 20

Media/Technology
- Applying Technology Data CD
- PowerPoint slides
- Business Connection CD
- Videotape

Activity Masters and Workbooks
- Activities and Projects, Ch. 20
- Internet Activity Masters
- Business Math Activity Masters
- Communications Activity Masters
- International Business Activity Masters
- Ethics Activity Masters

Succeeding in the World of Work

GOALS

DISCUSS how to compose a letter of application and a personal data sheet, and how to fill out an employment application form

EXPLAIN how to prepare for a good interview.

DESCRIBE how pre-employment tests are used by employers.

IDENTIFY qualities that lead to success on the job.

Distance Learning

Distance learning occurs when the student and instructor are geographically separated from each other. This takes place with the use of video, audio, and computer equipment.

Many universities are now offering some type of distance education, giving students the option to participate in a traditional classroom setting or in the virtual university. More and more schools are making entire degree programs available from a distance, so that the student never has to set foot on campus.

Many corporations are bringing various distance learning courses to their offices so that employees can upgrade their skills and job knowledge. This saves the company and employees time and money. Distance learning has now become an important part of succeeding in the world of work.

Students need to know the latest technologies and develop cutting edge Internet skills for use in current jobs, future careers, or in their homes. TechnoTips introduces students to today's cutting edge technologies and provides them with important Internet skills. Feature topics concentrate on Internet-specific technologies and computer or other hi-tech innovations for use by businesses and consumers.

Francisca Negalo has just graduated from high school. Her summer job is working in the records office of the city assessor's office. She also worked part-time for the Tempest Tea Pot Company as part of her school work experience program.

Francisca is now ready for full-time employment. The assessor's office has no openings, so she has registered with the government employment office in hopes of finding employment in accounting. Her high school business education program included computer applications and two years of accounting. She has learned to use spreadsheets, databases, and a computer-based accounting system. With her good grades, she feels confident that she can get an accounting job in some local business firm.

Francisca is watching the help wanted ads, too. She also has let her teachers and her school counselor know about her desire to

get a full-time job. Francisca plans on continuing her accounting studies in a night school program at a local two-year college. She plans to earn an associate's degree in accounting. Eventually she will transfer to a university and work toward a bachelor's degree in business administration. For now, though, she needs to get a job and earn some money.

Someone from the government employment agency called Francisca and told her about an opening for an accounting clerk at a local technical college. The position sounded good to her, so she decided to apply. Interested applicants were requested to send a letter of application to the office of the vice president of finance.

"Someday," Francisca mused, "I am going to be a Certified Public Accountant and have my own business. But for now, this job will get me started on my career. I just have to get it."

APPLYING FOR A JOB

Francisca had learned about letters of application in her high school Introduction to Business class. She remembered that a **letter of application** is a sales letter about an applicant written for the purpose of getting a personal interview. She recalled that it needed to be a courteous, businesslike letter that focused on her interest in and qualifications for the job.

When you write your letter of application, keep in mind that it basically is a sales letter. Like any good sales letter, a letter of application should attract the employer's attention and interest. It should create a desire to meet you, the applicant. Your letter should urge the reader to invite you to come for an interview. Figure 20-1 shows Francisca's well prepared letter of application. Note that the letter is neat, courteous, and to the point. A carelessly

written letter may cause the employer to think that you will be a careless worker. Your letter represents you, and it must compete with other letters of application for the reader's attention.

Francisca's letter mentions that a personal data sheet is enclosed with her letter. A **personal data shee**t, also called a *resume,* is a summary of important job-related information about yourself. It describes your education and work experience and lists the names of people who have agreed to be your personal references.

Personal references are people who can give a report about your character, your education, and your work habits. The people you might select as references could include teachers, religious leaders, adult friends, former employers, and others. Look at Francisca's data sheet in Figure 20-2.

FOCUS ON REAL LIFE

Here is a good opportunity to use want ads to illustrate some of the important expectations of employers. Bring employment want ads from the local newspaper to class, and have students look at them. Ask students to note employer requirements as stated in the ads. Call on students to identify at least one job requirement from each ad reviewed. List on the board important job requirements for success in the world of work.

Share some actual data sheets with the class. Samples could be photocopies or transparencies. Ask students to determine if the data sheets create value for the job candidate. Focus on what might impress employers most favorably or unfavorably about data sheets.

Reinforce the elements that most impact interview success: image and appearance, verbal and nonverbal communication, and presentation of job qualifications. Remind students of the importance of these core interview techniques: (a) projecting a positive attitude, image, and appearance; (b) using effective verbal and nonverbal communication; (c) listening effectively; and (d) presenting job qualifications.

Have a human resources director or someone from a local firm who hires employees comment on what he or she looks for in individuals applying for jobs in his or her company. Also have this person discuss the behavior that leads to success in a new or first job.

TRY THIS/GUIDED PRACTICE
Secure job applications from local businesses. Have students examine the applications to determine the kinds of information asked for. Discuss the kinds of information requested on job applications. Photocopy the applications, and walk students through completing the applications provided.

Guide students through the process of writing a script that would be appropriate for making a telephone bid for a job of interest. Have students rewrite the script to reflect a bid for the same job but in person. In organizing the script, students should highlight their

LETTER OF APPLICATION

1602 Collegewood Drive
Madison, WI 53711-2821
June 25, 20--

Dr. David Haugen
Vice President of Finance
Lakeview Technical College
Madison, WI 53706-3692

Dear Dr. Haugen:

The advertisement in the *Daily Chronicle* for an accounting clerk describes a position in which I am interested. Please consider me as an applicant for that position.

The ad stated that you are looking for a bright and alert person who is conscientious and interested in long-term employment. My record at Four Lakes High School and part-time employment record will show that I have the qualities you desire. My career goal is to someday become a Certified Public Accountant. An accounting clerk's position in your office will allow me to get an important start on my career.

My business education program at Four Lakes High School included courses in Introduction to Business, Computer Applications, Office Procedures, and Accounting. I also completed four years of English and three years of math. For each of my last semesters, I was on the honor roll. In our work experience program, I worked ten hours a week during my senior year for the Tempest Tea Pot Company, where I learned a great deal about office work and human relations. My summer job in the city assessor's office is helping me to work accurately with figures.

Enclosed is a personal data sheet giving my qualifications in more detail. I would appreciate an opportunity to interview with you. I may be reached by telephone at (608) 555-0308 anytime during the day.

Sincerely yours,

Francisca Negalo

Francisca Negalo

Enclosure

Figure 20-1 Do you see how this letter would cause a reader to want to meet the applicant in person?

USING SOURCES OF JOB LEADS

Francisca's approach to finding a job was a good one. She knew what kind of job she wanted. Several sources were used to obtain job leads. Francisca also was willing to wait for the right job opportunity if necessary.

Finding job openings is an important part of getting that first job. No one source is necessarily better than others. You need to let as many people as possible know that you are looking for a job. Your relatives, friends, neighbors, and others will be good potential sources of job leads.

The sources you use for information about career planning can help you get job leads, too. Your school counselors and business teachers can be very helpful. If your school has a placement office, be sure to register with that office. You should also contact employment agencies.

Newspaper want ads are also helpful. You should visit businesses and inquire about their openings. Some businesses post help-wanted signs in their windows. Getting a job means going out and looking around. Finding a job can be hard work, but it is worth the effort.

Basic Skills-Reading

SCANS

Direct students to the first main heading of the chapter. The first sentence of a paragraph is usually the main idea of the material being discussed. The last sentence of the paragraph usually either summarizes or bridges to the paragraphs or subheadings that follow. Bold terms and italicized words draw attention to important facts or topics in the material. Direct students to pages in the chapter that illustrate bold terms or italicized terms. The Student Activity Worksheet, Basic Skills—Reading, in the School-To-Work/SCANS Activity Masters, may be used to serve as a guideline for discussion of each of these points. Ask students to summarize the main points that will be covered in the chapter.

PERSONAL DATA SHEET

Francisca Negalo
1602 Collegewood Drive
Madison, WI 53711-2821
(608) 555-0308
e-mail: fnegalo@badgernet.com

EDUCATION:	Four Lakes High School Graduated June 10, 20-- Emphasis: Business Education

Business Subjects Studied: Activities:
  Introduction to Business   Member of Pep Club
  Computer Applications   Treasurer, Future
  Accounting I and II   Business Leaders
               of America

WORK EXPERIENCE:	Records Clerk, Tempest Tea Pot Company; one year, part-time, cooperative education. General Clerk, City Assessor's Office, summer
OTHER ACTIVITIES:	Member of Alph Chi youth group at First Christian Church Member of East Side YMCA swim team

REFERENCES:

Mr. Tim Schilling   Mrs. Phyllis Lipton
Business Teacher   Office Manager
Four Lakes High School   Tempest Tea Pot Company
1234 Monona Drive   707 Coffee Lane
Madison, WI 53722-1619 Middleton, WI 53611-4912

Mr. Dan Verwith
Records Department
Administrator
City Assessor's Office
16 Capitol Avenue
Madison, WI 53702-1101

Figure 20-2 Do you see why this information might be helpful to an employer who wants to hire the best person possible?

COMPLETING AN EMPLOYER'S APPLICATION FORM

A few weeks after mailing her letter of application and personal data sheet, Francisca received a phone call from the administrative assistant to the financial vice president of the technical college. They wanted Francisca to come in for an interview. "That's it!" Francisca shouted, "I'm going to get the job."

Francisca did not realize that there were a few more steps to be taken. She made an appointment for the job interview and arrived at the vice president's office on time. The secretary in the vice president's office made Francisca feel welcome when she arrived. Francisca was asked to fill out an application form that was required of all job applicants at the college. She was taken to a desk where she could complete it.

An employer frequently has each job applicant complete a position application form even after a letter of application and a personal data sheet have been provided. A **position application form** is a document used by an employer that asks for information related to employment. The form gives the employer standard information about each

qualifications, demonstrate knowledge of the organization and industry, and express interest in employment. Lead students in a discussion of qualities needed to get along with others. Ask students to cite fundamental rules other than those listed on pages 275–276. Possible answers might include: (a) Treat others as you like to be treated. (b) Avoid gossip. (c) Don't repeat anything that might hurt someone else. (d) Show respect for the experience and knowledge that experienced employees have. (e) Build a good relationship with your supervisor. (f) Keep a good sense of humor.

EXPLORE THIS/INDEPENDENT PRACTICE Have students create a career information center in the classroom. Have them gather information on local part-time jobs as well as opportunities for full-time employment after graduation. Include all types of jobs. Also have students prepare posters listing tips and recommendations for interviewing. These posters should be displayed in a prominent place within the classroom.

Ask students to role-play situations in which good and bad behaviors are exhibited in relationships with coworkers. Students who are not role-playing should critique the situation and identify the good and bad behaviors. Before the role-playing exercise begins, remind students to review the fundamental rules for getting along with others listed on pages 275–276.

The Chapter Review questions at the end of the chapter vary in level of difficulty. For a basic assignment, consider Develop Your Business Language and Review

Basic Skills-Writing

Employers are looking for potential employees with good basic foundation skills. In order to prepare students for the school-to-work transition, we must teach these skills in our classroom. Writing across the curriculum is an important element in contemporary education. Surveys of business managers show that communication skills are one of the most desired traits in new employees. To provide an opportunity for students to practice their communication and language arts skills on topics that directly relate to career planning, require students to identify a want ad for a job they would like to pursue. Students should indicate in writing why they would like the job and how they are qualified to succeed in that job.

SCANS

Your Reading. For an average assignment, consider the basic assignment plus Communicate Business Concepts and Calculate Business Data. For an enhanced assignment, try the average assignment plus Technology Application and Decision-Making Strategies.

Ask students for copies of the letters that were written for Question 16 in the Communicate Business Concepts section of the end-of-chapter activities. Distribute these letters to class members. Have students read and evaluate the letters. Then prepare transparencies of some effectively written letters of application. Students evaluating the letters should explain how these letters conveyed the message the writer desired.

ASSESS

Review the Business Notes at the end of the chapter. Then review the goals at the beginning of the chapter. Restate each as a question and have students respond orally. For students who may have difficulty providing answers, assign the reteaching activities that follow. Enrichment activities may also be assigned where appropriate.

1. Why are letters of application and personal data sheets important? (Answer: A letter of application and a data sheet are often the first contact you have with an employer. Because it is often your first link with the employer, you want it to make a good impression.)

2. What are some sources to use for getting information about job leads? (Answer: Sources of job

EMPLOYMENT APPLICATION FORM

Figure 20-3 Do you see that the way an application form is filled out might reflect how the applicant will approach his or her job?

job applicant and becomes part of a permanent file. These forms typically ask for your name, address, Social Security number, education, work experience, the job for which you are applying, references, and other qualifications. They usually are filled out in longhand; this gives your potential employer a look at your penmanship.

The information on your personal data sheet will help you complete the application form and should be taken along to the interview. Completing the position application form should be seen as the *first job task* your

employer asks you to perform. Supply each item requested; do not leave questions unanswered. Take the assignment seriously. A poorly prepared application form may give the wrong impression about you. Observe the application form filled out by Francisca in Figure 20-3.

TESTING POTENTIAL EMPLOYEES

In addition to the information provided on application forms, some employers also use preemployment tests to screen applicants for

Personal Qualities-Sociability

Cooperative learning situations provide an opportunity to teach basic sociability skills such as adaptability and politeness in group settings. Some students may lack social skills and the ability to get along with others in groups. Monitor group activities and set some guidelines concerning how individuals will be tolerant of others' ideas and how to reach decisions.

SCANS

skills and abilities that are needed to perform certain jobs. Examples of preemployment tests include keyboarding tests, word processing tests, calculating tests, and number and word arranging (filing) tests. These are frequently called ability tests. An **ability test** is one that measures how well a job applicant can perform certain job tasks.

Testing makes it possible to compare each job applicant on the same basis. Two applicants, for example, may have completed a high school course in computer applications and received "B" grades. One applicant, however, might have excelled in spreadsheet applications while the other was outstanding in word processing. High school teachers do not all grade using the same standards, either. So by testing each applicant, the employer can use the test results to compare the skills of each person being considered for the job and be more objective in the selection process.

TECHNOLOGICAL PERSPECTIVES

Working at Home

A unique grouping of small businesses are those operating from individual homes known as *cottage businesses*. Telephones, computers, modems, and fax machines have made it possible for some people to work anywhere. The Department of Labor recently reported that more than 4 million people were paid by employers for work performed at home, and another 7 million self-employed people worked at least some of the time at home.

The cottage business concept is not new, however. In fact, this approach to work was popular among manufacturers in the 1700s and 1800s. The most important goods produced by early cottage businesses included clothing, shoes, cigars, and hand-decorated items. The onset of the Industrial Revolution after the Civil War brought about far-reaching changes in business organizations—including complex machinery, huge factories, large numbers of workers, and more capable managers. The Industrial Revolution brought about a gradual increase in the size and scope of manufacturing operations.

Today the trend is away from large business operations and toward businesses that provide services. The use of computers along with related technology, such as teleconferencing and e-mail, has allowed highly specialized work to be done at home. Word processing and accounting are examples of work commonly done in homes throughout our country.

Opportunities will increase for those who prefer to work at home rather than commute to a workplace. Human skill and initiative along with new technologies will serve as the basis for many new and continuing kinds of cottage businesses, particularly in service-producing industries.

Critical Thinking

1. What are the basic elements that have allowed working at home to become popular in our country?
2. What are some work-at-home opportunities that you can see for yourself and others in the future?

3. How should an employer's application form be filled out? (Answer: The form should be filled out carefully, neatly, and completely.)
4. How are preemployment tests used by employers? (Answer: Preemployment tests are used by employers to screen applicants for skills and abilities needed to perform certain jobs.)
5. What are eight things you can do to have a good position interview? (Answer: You should be on time, go alone, dress properly, be calm, leave when it is over, thank the interviewer, send a brief thank-you letter, and be patient in waiting for a response.)
6. What are eight things that can lead to success on the job? (Answer: asking questions, avoiding complaining, honoring break time, having a good appearance, getting to work on time, being friendly, doing work well, and following rules.)
7. Describe some tips for getting along with coworkers. (Answer: learn from them, be friendly with everyone, accept and give praise, and be dependable.) How should a person exit a job properly? (Answer: give proper notice, complete existing projects, have a constructive exit interview, show appreciation to coworkers.)

(leads include friends, relatives, neighbors; school counselors and teachers; school placement office; employment agencies; newspaper ads; help wanted signs; career publications.)

TECHNOLOGICAL PERSPECTIVES

Knowing how to use techniques and apply them when appropriate is a skill that employers are looking for. This feature, Technological Perspectives, exposes students to new technology and gives them an opportunity to understand how this technology is used in current and future work situations.

CRITICAL THINKING

1. Answers will vary. Advances in technology, including teleconferencing, fax transmissions, and e-mail have enhanced opportunities to work at home.
2. Answers will vary. Tasks that make use of the computer's capacity for collecting, storing, changing, and adding to files are ideal work-at-home opportunities. Salespeople, for instance, can work at home using a telephone, computer, and fax to interact with customers.

Instruct students to list on a separate sheet of paper all the different types of information on the application form in Figure 20-3 in the chapter. Then have students outline the major sections of the personal data sheet.

Have students create a job interview checklist. The list should include brief items of advice concerning tips for having a successful job interview.

Direct students to summarize techniques presented in the last portion of this chapter: (a) succeeding on your first job, (b) getting along with coworkers, and (c) exiting a job.

ENRICH

Direct students to read the Technological Perspectives. Have students check to see what governmental and private employment agencies are located in their community. Have them contact one or more of them and make an appointment to interview the director or manager. Find out (1) how they learn of job openings; (2) how they screen or test those who register with them for work; (3) what they charge for their services; and (4) what their success rate is in filling jobs that are listed with them. Ask students to write a report on their findings and to share information gathered about employment agencies with the class.

Select two or three students to assume the role of a personnel interviewer. Have them make a list of ten specific questions to be asked of an applicant for a job as a salesperson in a men's or

Several career-related web sites maintain databases to which job seekers can submit their resumes via e-mail. Some of these services are free to people who are looking for employment opportunities.

A test is another instrument used by employers to evaluate the abilities of job candidates. If you do the best you can on a test under whatever circumstances the test may be given, you need not worry about the results. Employers realize that taking a test in an office, often using unfamiliar equipment, can affect test results.

HAVING A SUCCESSFUL INTERVIEW

The next step in securing employment, and the most important one, is the position interview. A **position interview** is a two-way conversation in which the interviewer learns about you and you learn about the position and the company. These interviews frequently are conducted by personnel interviewers in large companies.

A **personnel interviewer** is someone who has special training in talking with job applicants and hiring new employees. Whoever does the interviewing wants to find out about such things as your appearance, manners, use of language, and general suitability for the work in that business.

You need to prepare for your interview as carefully as you prepared your letter of application and personal data sheet. The following tips will help you have a good interview:

• Be on time for the appointment.

• Go alone to the interview. Do not take friends or relatives with you.

• Dress properly. Do not be too formal or too informal. Wear the type of clothing that is appropriate for the company and the job for which you are applying.

• Try to be calm during the interview. Avoid talking too much, but answer each question completely using good eye contact. Ask questions intelligently. Let the interviewer guide the discussion.

• Leave when the interviewer indicates that the interview is over.

• Thank the interviewer for the opportunity to discuss the job and your qualifications.

• After the interview, send a brief thank-you letter to the person with whom you interviewed.

• Be patient after the interview. It may take several weeks for the company to complete all of its interviews and make its selection.

A number of different approaches may be taken by an interviewer. Most interviewers will try to put you at ease when your

What can you, as the interviewee, learn in a position interview?

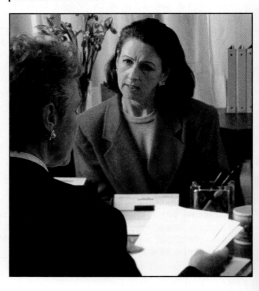

Net Facts provides information and definitions of terms for the Internet. The more information that students have about the Internet, the better equipped they will be to use this resource. In the Internet Activity Masters, there is an Internet Activity Worksheet for each unit. You can use these activities to give students experience with finding information online. Options for assigning this activity are as follows:

1. **Provide students with a list of addresses of resources for this activity;**
2. **Assign students to conduct their own searches; or**
3. **Use the addresses provided on the Internet Activity Worksheet.**

You should complete the activity yourself before assigning it to resolve any discrepancies that may arise.

interview begins. As the interview progresses, there are a number of questions that could be asked by the interviewer. Questions asked by interviewers generally fall into three categories: general information questions, character questions, and stress questions. Here are some examples:

- Why should we hire you for this particular job?
- What are some of the activities you like to do in your spare time?
- What courses have you taken that will help you on this job?
- What are your career goals?
- Do you plan to continue your education now or in the future?
- Do you have any friends or relatives who work here?
- What are your major strengths? What are your major weaknesses?

The interviewer may also review your test results and discuss specific job requirements with you.

Francisca had two interviews. Her first was with the administrative assistant, Admir Coppalois, and then she was interviewed by the head of the accounting unit. The interviews turned out to be a pleasant experience, and Francisca felt good about her interviews when she left the technical college. She had come prepared, and what she learned made her eager to work there if the position were offered to her.

SUCCEEDING ON YOUR FIRST JOB

Francisca was offered the job of Accounting Clerk II. Her school record and work experience qualified her for that position. She was very pleased. She began her first day with enthusiasm and high expectations. The job she was offered was just the one for which she had planned.

In preparing for her first day on the job, Francisca recalled what she had been taught about behavior that helps lead to success on a job:

- *Ask questions.* If you do not understand directions, have them repeated and listen carefully. You need to understand what is expected of you.

- *Avoid complaining about a heavy workload.* If you seem to have more work to do than you can handle, talk with your supervisor about it. Don't try to do more work than you can reasonably handle in an attempt to impress your employer.

- *Honor the time provided for breaks.* Abuse of rest periods and lunch breaks by extending the time limits is a bad business practice. Even if others do it and seem to get away with it, respect your company's policy.

- *Be attentive to your appearance.* Dressing neatly and being well groomed lets others know that you believe your job to be important. Employers often find that sloppy dress and appearance reflect sloppy work habits.

- *Be on time.* Arriving late or leaving early is a poor practice for any employee, especially a new one. On occasion, tardiness or having to leave early might be necessary—but tardiness should be explained, and early departures should be approved in advance.

- *Be friendly with everyone.* Success on the job involves human relations. Respect your coworkers and learn to get along with them. However, do not let friendliness interfere with either your work or theirs.

- *Do work that is well done and on time.* Work that is sloppily done or turned in late can affect others in the office. You are part of a team; take pride in what you do as part of that team. Paying attention to detail lets your coworkers know that you can do your job well.

> **Most employees who are fired are let go because they cannot get along with others—an employment success factor that tests cannot measure.**
>
> **FYI**

women's fashion clothing store. Then have several individuals from the class play the role of an applicant and conduct a mock interview. After the interview is over, have students discuss whether the questions were relevant and what was learned from the questions.

Have students visit human resource managers to ask about their policies with respect to testing prospective employees. Ask students to find out what kinds of tests are given and how the results are used. Students should report their findings to the class.

SUMMARIZE

Secure a large sheet of paper to the wall and label it SUCCEEDING IN THE WORLD OF WORK. Invite students to write, graffiti style, what they consider the most pertinent information explained in this chapter.

EVALUATE

- Assign Activities and Projects for Chapter 20.
- Administer the printed test or ExamView for Chapter 20.
- Assign School-To-Work/SCANS portfolio activities for Unit 6.

TEACHING STRATEGIES
Teams

Jigsaw is an instructional method in which students use cooperative learning in peer groups. Divide the chapter into eight parts. Each member of the team becomes an expert in one of the parts to which he or she is assigned. Next, team members read their assigned section. All students assigned section one meet as an expert group. All students assigned section two meet as an expert group, etc. These expert groups will discuss their section and decide how to go back and report this information to their respective groups; at which time they share the expert information that they have learned. Teammates are dependent upon that team member to thoroughly explain that part of the chapter. After each team member has presented expert information, everybody returns to their desk to take the ExamView for this chapter.

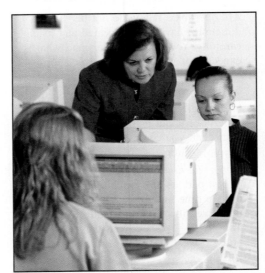

Besides learning your job, what other benefits can you receive from on-the-job training?

- *Follow the rules. Rules are developed for the good of everyone in your work unit.* Not paying attention to company policy can bring trouble to you and others. If a rule seems unfair or unreasonable, discuss it with others and find out why it has been established. You may eventually be able to influence changes.

When you begin a new job, remember that your employer is just as eager as you are for you to succeed. Generally you will find the other employees willing to help you through the first few days. You probably will make a few mistakes in the process of learning your job.

The important thing is to learn from each mistake and to avoid repeating it. You will need to be a good listener. Your job will test your ability to follow directions and to produce good work. It should be a challenging experience for you.

The word "attitude" can make a *big* difference. It could be the difference between having just another job or being happy and successful in your work. A positive attitude causes you to learn and grow in your job and cooperate with other workers. As a result,

you will probably find your job more satisfying and your work more enjoyable.

If you project a tentative, unsure attitude through your speech, appearance, and actions, you will be perceived as a tentative, unsure worker even if your work is excellent. Always think, speak, dress, and act positively to project an image that will help you build a successful career.

Francisca has demonstrated readiness for her full-time employment. She has progressed from her work as a student into a career as a full-time worker. The record she built as a student—her good attendance record, the courses she took, the activities in which she participated, and the grades she earned—was important when she was considered for employment. Her school record showed that she was conscientious and capable of good work. Career planning plus a good school record adds up to a successful start in the world of work.

GETTING ALONG WITH COWORKERS

Building good relationships with other employees will improve your own efficiency and influence your future. The following are a few fundamental rules that can help you get along with others.

1. Learn from the others with whom you work, even if they do things differently from the way you were taught in school. Avoid assuming you are right and they are wrong. If you have an idea for improving work procedures, find the right time to suggest improvements.

2. Be on friendly terms with as many people as you can. The person who delivers the mail, the person who cleans the office, the assistant to the president, and others are important people in many ways. Any of your coworkers may be able to help you someday in ways unknown to you now.

3. Learn to accept and give praise when it is due. When you have done something well and you are given credit for it, accept it

Critical Thinking Skills-Decision Making

Decision-making skills, which include specifying goals, generating alternatives, considering risks, and evaluating and choosing the best alternative, are applied throughout every chapter in this text. Each time a student participates in a Cooperative Learning or Teams Activity, decision-making skills are applied in a group situation. For Communicate Business

Concepts and Decision-Making Strategies, students must specify the goal of the activity, consider risks, and evaluate the best solution before the questions can be answered. Emphasize to students how they are using decision-making techniques in their day-to-day tasks and make them aware of the skills they are developing.

Name several benefits of building good relationships with other employees.

graciously and appreciatively. When others do something nice, say a good word to them. Learn not to overdo praise, however. False praise will get you nowhere and will raise suspicions about your motives.

4. Show others that you are dependable. Little things, such as returning phone calls promptly and responding to messages without unnecessary delay, tell others that you care about what you do and can be trusted to do your work. When others have a positive impression of you, they will want to work with you and will want to help you succeed.

5. Look ahead to future opportunities. People with whom you develop good relationships may be promoted to higher positions in a business. Having "friends in high places," as the saying goes, may help you get ahead. The people who respect you for what you can do may have an influence on your future career.

EXITING A JOB

Francisca now must tell her present employer that she will be leaving. Even though it was not a permanent position, leaving on good terms is important. Here are a few tips on how to leave a job gracefully.

- Give a proper notice. Do not just walk into your supervisor's office one day and announce that you are leaving. Give at least a two-week notice. Write a short, polite letter of resignation; include the date of the last day you will be working.

- Try to finish all of the special projects that have been assigned to you. If they are not completed, leave a note showing the next person where to begin.

- If there is an **exit interview**, an interview in which your employer asks questions about how you liked your work and what improvements might be made, be constructive and cooperative.

- Let your coworkers know that you appreciated the opportunity to work with them and wish them well. Leaving on a positive note is good for you and for the work unit you are leaving.

Bookkeeping, accounting, and auditing clerks' job duties include:
- Verifying, allocating, and posting details of business transactions to general and special ledgers
- Completing reports to show cash receipts and expenditures, profit and loss, etc.
- Preparing payroll withholding and tax reports.

The careers listed in Career Highlights come from the *Occupational Outlook Handbook*, an online publication (www.bls.gov/oco) of the federal government. The O*NET code for Bookkeeping, Accounting, and Auditing Clerk is 43-3031.00. Tell your class about this resource and how to use it. This description of job duties can be used to demonstrate the relevancy of skills learned in this course.

TEACHING STRATEGIES

Special Needs
At-Risk Students

Some students need concrete examples before they understand a concept like an application for employment. Pass sample application forms around the room and let students see what a typical application looks like.

REVIEW YOUR READING

1. The purpose of a letter of application is to sell yourself as an employee to a prospective employer. Your letter of application should gain the employer's attention and interest and create a desire to see you. It should urge the employer to take the desired action—inviting you to come for an interview. The purpose of the personal data sheet is to give information about your background and your qualifications for the job.

2. People who can be asked to be personal references include teachers, counselors, school administrators, pastors or priests, youth group leaders, friends, neighbors, and acquaintances.

3. Sources of information for job leads include family, friends, teachers, guidance counselors, school bulletin boards, school job placement services, classified sections of newspapers, local offices of state employment agencies, and private employment agencies.

4. A personal data sheet should include (a) name and address, (b) telephone number, (c) education, (d) work experience, (e) other activities, and (f) references.

5. The "first job task" most people perform for an employer is filling out the position application form. This task should be performed according to instructions, and all of the information asked for should be provided. An employer does not want to employ someone who cannot follow directions or who is careless in providing information.

6. Preemployment tests are used to obtain information about skills and abilities. Test results of prospective employees can be compared.

7. Some tips that will help an interviewee have a good position interview include: be on time, come alone, answer questions, be calm, leave when the interview is over, thank the interviewer, write a brief thank-you letter, wait patiently for an answer.

8. Questions commonly asked include: Why should we hire you? What are some activities you like to participate in during your spare time? What courses have you taken that will help you on this

Chapter REVIEW

BUSINESS NOTES

1. Letters of application and personal data sheets are important and must be prepared carefully.

2. Sources of job leads include friends, relatives, neighbors; school counselors and teachers; school placement office; employment agencies; newspaper ads; help wanted signs; career publications.

3. Completing an employer's application form is an important "first job task" and should be done carefully, neatly, and completely.

4. Preemployment tests are used by employers to screen applicants for skills and abilities that are needed to perform certain jobs.

5. To have a successful position interview, you should be on time, go alone, dress properly, be calm, leave when it is over, thank the interviewer, send a brief thank-you letter, and be patient in waiting for a response.

6. The following behaviors help lead to success on a job: asking questions, avoiding complaining, honoring break time, having a good appearance, getting to work on time, being friendly, doing work well, and following rules.

7. Getting along with coworkers includes learning from them, being friendly with everyone, accepting and giving praise, and being dependable. In leaving a job, give proper notice, complete existing projects, have a constructive exit interview, and show appreciation to coworkers.

REVIEW YOUR READING

1. What is the purpose of a letter of application and a personal data sheet?

2. Who are some people who can be asked to be personal references?

3. Identify several sources of information for job leads.

4. List six categories of information that should be included on a personal data sheet.

5. What is the first job task that you will perform for an employer? Why is it important to perform this task correctly?

6. Why are preemployment tests used by employers?

7. What are some tips that will help you have a good position interview?

8. What questions are commonly asked during a position interview?

9. What are some things you can do to help you succeed on your first job?

10. What are some things you should do to get along with coworkers?

11. What are some things you can do to exit a job on good terms?

COMMUNICATE BUSINESS CONCEPTS

12. Name at least six people you know whom you could ask for help in finding a full-time job. Also identify several local organizations or agencies you could contact for help in finding a job.

job? What are your career goals? What are your strengths? weaknesses?

9. To succeed on your first job, ask questions, avoid complaining, honor the time provided for breaks, be attentive to your appearance, be on time, be friendly to everyone, do work that is well done and on time, follow the rules.

10. Learn from the others with whom you work, be on friendly terms with as many people as you can, learn to accept and give praise, show others that you are dependable, look ahead to future opportunities.

11. Give a proper notice, try to finish all special projects that you have been assigned, and let coworkers know that you appreciated the opportunity to work with them. If there is an exit interview, let your employer know what you liked about the job and what improvements can be made.

13. If you were in charge of hiring people for jobs, what information would you want to get about applicants? How would you go about getting this information? What are some specific questions you would ask if you were to interview the applicants?

14. Your personal data sheet should list several references. Application forms also ask for references to be listed. Make a list of three or more references you could use right now. Then note the type of information each reference could give that would be of help to a potential employer.

15. Write a personal data sheet that you could use right now if you were to apply for a part-time or full-time job. After it is completed, think about whether or not you need to consider being more involved in school, church, or community activities. Think about whether or not your personal data sheet would impress an employer and what you could do that could be included in future personal data sheets to better present yourself.

16. Information has been received about three job openings in your community. Each is quite different and requires a different kind of background and preparation. Assume that you are qualified for only one position. Make up whatever qualifications you think you would like to present to a prospective employer. Then write a letter of application for the position.
   a. Reliable person is needed to handle a variety of responsibilities in a small business office. Must be able to work without supervision and communicate effectively with people who call in for information. Word processing and filing skills are desirable. Salary is better than average in this community.
   b. Salespeople are needed for an auto parts department and for a cosmetics department of a major retail establishment. Applicants should have some familiarity and/or experience with selling. Hours are flexible, although some evening and weekend work will be required. Benefits are especially attractive; incentive bonus policy can provide a good income for the right person.
   c. Ours is a leading bank in this region. We are in need of capable people who want to begin a career in banking. Our training program starts at the bottom, but provides a great opportunity to learn the ins and outs of the banking industry. Business majors are preferred, but liberal arts majors may apply. We are an equal opportunity employer. Salary is competitive.

17. Design an application form similar to the one in Figure 20-3 on page 272 and supply whatever information you think necessary to apply for one of the jobs mentioned in Question 16.

18. Give several examples of what you might do and not do as a new employee in order to develop positive relationships with your coworkers.

19. What kinds of questions would you ask in an exit interview if you were the supervisor interviewing a word processing specialist who is leaving?

DEVELOP YOUR BUSINESS LANGUAGE

For each numbered item, find the term that has the same meaning.

20. A sales letter about an applicant written for the purpose of getting a personal interview.

21. A summary of job-related information about yourself.

22. A document used by employers that asks for information related to employment.

23. A two-way conversation in which the interviewer learns about you and you learn about the job and the company.

24. Someone who has special training for talking with job applicants and hiring new employees.

25. People who can give a report about your character, education, and work habits.

26. A test that measures how well a job applicant can perform certain job tasks.

27. An interview in which an employer asks questions about how an employee liked his/her work and inquires about job improvements that might be made.

KEY TERMS
ability test
exit interview
letter of application
personal data sheet
personal references
personnel interviewer
position application form
position interview

DEVELOP YOUR BUSINESS LANGUAGE

20. letter of application
21. personal data sheet
22. position application form
23. position interview
24. personnel interviewer
25. personal references
26. ability test
27. exit interview

references. The people who are listed should be those who know the student well in terms of school, work experience, and personal character. They can include teachers, counselors, supervisors from previous employment (including baby-sitting), neighbors, and leaders of organizations with whom they have participated. They should have a cross section of people on their lists.

15. Students should follow the model on page 271 of the text. If students have no activities to list, no part-time work experience, and so forth, they should be encouraged to think about how they might become involved in activities or work for future personal data sheet purposes.

16. Students should select the job for which they are the most qualified. For extra credit they could do one or two additional letters of application and personal data sheets. The models in the textbook on pages 270 and 271 should be followed unless an alternative model(s) is presented in class.

17. Be sure that students remember to complete their application forms as accurately as possible. They should consider this to be an important activity and relate it to the job they select in Question 16.

18. Always be punctual. Help others if they have too much work to do. If a rule seems unfair, find out why the company has it but don't complain about it. Be friendly but respect a person's privacy.

19. Questions that might be asked in an exit interview would include: What did you like most about your work here? What did you like the least? Do you feel you were treated fairly while you worked here? What changes would you make in our work procedures, if any? What other comments or suggestions do you have?

COMMUNICATE BUSINESS CONCEPTS

12. Students will name individuals who may be teachers, counselors, parents, friends of parents, former employers, neighbors, and relatives. Both public and private employment agencies should be included. If the school or school district has a job placement office or service, it should be included in this answer.

13. A person in charge of hiring employees needs to know if the applicants are capable and interested in performing the job. This person wants to find the best possible employees. Information would come from every contact with the applicants—letters of application and personal data sheets, application forms, and personal interviews.

14. Each student's list will be different. Students should be encouraged to think carefully about references and to include a range of people as

28. Rhonda has evidence of problems within the plant through exit interviews. Experienced workers are not happy with their salaries, equipment needs to be replaced, and a longtime and loyal worker is an ineffective supervisor. The company's fiscal constraints make it difficult to request higher salaries for employees or to ask for new equipment. The ineffective supervisor must be counseled about how to handle workers effectively. Rhonda must take corrective action, but achieving an immediate solution to the problems may be very difficult.

29. Rhonda needs to develop a strategy for getting salary increases and money for new equipment without directly impacting the current budget. She also needs to investigate salaries in the community to see if the experienced workers are correct in their belief about salaries being low. She also needs to talk to the supervisor and find out what can be done to improve the supervisor's skill in handling people. The supervisor may have to get further training in supervision; or the supervisor may have to be reassigned to another position.

CALCULATE BUSINESS DATA

30. (a) 7 + 6 + 9 + 5 + 8 = 35 job applicants; 35 ÷ 5 = 7 job applicants per day on the average (b) 50 + 40 + 40 + 35 + 35 + 35 + 35 + 45 + 45 = 360 minutes or 360 ÷ 60 = 6 hours; 360 ÷ 9 = 40 minutes

31. (a) 17 + 17 + 5 + 5 + 1 + 1 + 1 + 1 = 48 years; 48 ÷ 8 = 6 years (b) 35 × $8.00 = $280.00; $280.00 × 2 = $560.00; 35 × $7.50 = $262.50; $560 + $262.50 = $822.50 total wages earned in a week; $822.50 × 4 = $3,290.00 total wages earned in a month; $3,290.00 × 12 = $39,480.00 total wages earned in a year (c) Word processing operators: $8.00 × 0.06 = $0.48; $8.00 + $0.48 = $8.48 per hour; Clerk-receptionist: $7.50 × 0.06 = $0.45; $7.50 + 0.45 = $7.95 per hour; $8.48 × 40 = $339.20 earned by word processor operator; $7.95 × 40 = $318.00 earned by clerk-receptionist.

DECISION-MAKING STRATEGIES

Rhonda Allison is the plant manager for the All-In-All Manufacturing Company. Over the past several months, a number of valuable workers have quit their jobs. From reports on exit interviews, Rhonda has learned the following: (1) experienced workers believe that their salaries are below average for the business community; (2) equipment that is being used is old, does not perform efficiently, and in some cases is dangerous; and (3) workers are not getting along well primarily because the supervisor is not good at handling people.

Rhonda does not know what to do about these problems. The board of directors is encouraging the company to cut costs to remain competitive. Any request for salary increases or equipment purchases would not be received favorably. The supervisor is a long-time, faithful employee with an excellent previous work record.

28. What is Rhonda's basic problem?

29. What actions would you take if you were Rhonda?

CALCULATE BUSINESS DATA

30. Emilie Antoine is a personnel interviewer. On Monday, she interviewed 7 job applicants; on Tuesday, 6 applicants; on Wednesday, 9 applicants; on Thursday, 5 applicants; and on Friday, 8 applicants.
   a. How many job applicants did Emilie interview that week? What was the average number per day?
   b. On Wednesday, the first interview took 50 minutes; the next 2 each took 40 minutes; the next 4 took 35 minutes each; and the last 2 took 45 minutes each. How many total hours did Emilie spend in these interviews? What was the average length of the interviews?

31. The Human Resources Department of the Tempest Tea Pot Company has 1 personnel manager, 1 administrative assistant, 2 word processing specialists, 2 personnel interviewers, 1 affirmative action/union affairs specialist, and 1 clerk-receptionist. The manager and administrative assistant each have worked for Tempest for 17 years; each of the word processing specialists has worked there for 5 years; and the others have worked there just 1 year.
   a. How many total years of employment do the 8 Human Resources Department employees

have? What is the average number of years of employment per worker?
   b. The administrative support staff consists of the 2 word processing specialists and the clerk-receptionist. The word processing specialists are paid $8.00 per hour, and the clerk-receptionist is paid $7.50 per hour. They each work 35 hours per week. What total wages do these three workers earn in a week? in a month? in a year?
   c. If the word processing specialists receive a 6 percent increase in wages each year, what will be their hourly wages next year? Figure the same for the clerk-receptionists. How much will each earn in a 40-hour week that year?

32. Two data sheets were received by the Human Resources Department. The data sheets listed the height and weight of the applicants and contained the following data. (See Appendix D.)
   Mr. Barnfeld: height: 175 cm   weight: 79 kg
   Mr. Oatsown: height: 185 cm   weight: 72 kg
   a. Which of the applicants is the tallest? by how many inches?
   b. Which of the applicants weighs the most? by how many pounds?

TECHNOLOGY APPLICATION

Using the *Intro to Business* Data CD and your word processing program software, select problem CH20. After the problem appears on your screen, complete the following activities. Then, print your completed resume (or personal data sheet) and application. If you do not have a printer available, save the resume and application on a data disk to give to your teacher.

33. Fill in the resume with information about your-

self. Delete any sections that you do not use.

34. Use desktop publishing features to give a professional appearance to the resume you just completed.

35. Fill in the job application with information about yourself. Enter "Not Applicable" in any sections that do not apply to you.

32. (a) Barnfeld (175 cm) 175 × 0.4 = 70 inches tall; Oatsown (185 cm) 185 × 0.4 = 74 inches tall; Oatsown is 4 inches taller than Barnfeld (b) Barnfeld (79 kg) 79 × 2.2 = 173.8 or 174 lbs.; Oatsown (72 kg) 72 × 2.2 = 158.4 or 158 lbs.; Barnfeld is 15.4 lbs. heavier than Oatsown.

TECHNOLOGY APPLICATION

In this activity, students use a computer to solve a business problem using a file that is provided on the data CD that accompanies *Intro to Business*. Instructions for using the data CD are included in a **README** file on the disk. Solutions are provided on the Instructor's Resource CD.

EXPORT ASSISTANCE AGENCIES

Major companies such as Ford, Kellogg's, and Coca-Cola have their own international divisions and offices in other countries. However, small companies cannot usually afford an exporting department. To assist these smaller enterprises, several federal government agencies are available to help with planning and implementing exporting activities. These agencies can assist with finding customers, shipping procedures, and financing global activities.

The International Trade Administration (ITA), a division of the U.S. Department of Commerce, is the federal government's main agency for promoting exports. Export Assistance Centers are available throughout the country to help small-business owners identify potential foreign markets for their goods and services. ITA is also actively involved in creating international trade policies of the United States.

The Small Business Administration (SBA) also encourages exporting. It

> **Several government agencies can help small businesses with international trade.**

provides smaller companies with loans to manufacture products for exporting. SBA also offers seminars, publications, and other information about exporting and international business activities.

The Export-Import Bank of the United States helps finance exporting of goods and services produced by U.S. companies. This federal government agency provides loans, loan guarantees, and insurance programs to assist and promote exporting.

CRITICAL THINKING

1. You are planning to start an exporting business. Develop a list of information you would need in order to sell and ship your product to another country.
2. Go to the web site of the International Trade Administration, Small Business Administration, or Export-Import Bank of the United States. What information and services are available from these agencies for companies that want to get involved in exporting?

Most students will either work with international clients or compete against businesses that do. Global Navigator introduces students to issues integral to working with international businesses. Key concepts and challenges faced by international businesses are presented, followed by two Critical Thinking questions that require students to analyze what they have learned.

This feature explains the role played by several federal agencies that provide assistance to small businesses seeking to increase their exports. Since many students are likely to end up working for small businesses rather than large corporations, knowing what kinds of assistance are available is important, especially since exports by small businesses are the fastest growing source of U.S. exports.

CRITICAL THINKING

1. Lists might include such things as the material from which the product is made, the intended use of the product, the size and weight of the product, any hazardous or flammable materials, and its cost.
2. These agency web sites provide a wide variety of information, including details of programs that may be of assistance to exporters, and agency contacts.

Small businesses have been and continue to be major creators of new jobs in our economy and, therefore, offer good career opportunities. Successful small-business owners perform many business functions.

Resources for Teachers
- Lesson Plans
- School-To-Work/SCANS Activity Masters
- Spanish Resources
- Instructor's Resource CD

Assessment
- Chapter and Unit Tests, Ch. 21
- ExamView, Ch. 21

Media/Technology
- Applying Technology Data CD
- PowerPoint slides
- Business Connection CD
- Videotape

Activity Masters and Workbooks
- Activities and Projects, Ch. 21
- Internet Activity Masters
- Business Math Activity Masters
- Communications Activity Masters
- International Business Activity Masters
- Ethics Activity Masters

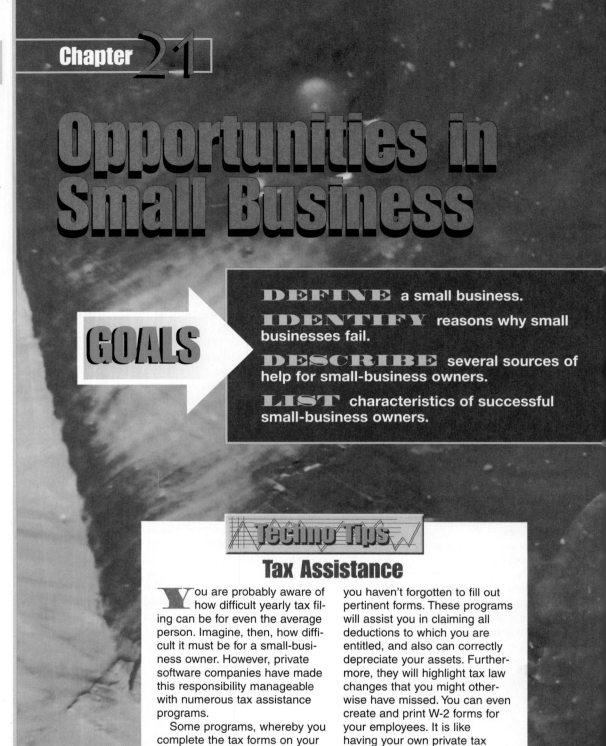

Chapter 21

Opportunities in Small Business

GOALS

DEFINE a small business.

IDENTIFY reasons why small businesses fail.

DESCRIBE several sources of help for small-business owners.

LIST characteristics of successful small-business owners.

Techno Tips

Tax Assistance

You are probably aware of how difficult yearly tax filing can be for even the average person. Imagine, then, how difficult it must be for a small-business owner. However, private software companies have made this responsibility manageable with numerous tax assistance programs.

Some programs, whereby you complete the tax forms on your computer, will make certain that you haven't forgotten to fill out pertinent forms. These programs will assist you in claiming all deductions to which you are entitled, and also can correctly depreciate your assets. Furthermore, they will highlight tax law changes that you might otherwise have missed. You can even create and print W-2 forms for your employees. It is like having your own private tax expert.

Students need to know the latest technologies and develop cutting edge Internet skills for use in current jobs, future careers, or in their homes. TechnoTips introduces students to today's cutting edge technologies and provides them with important Internet skills. Feature topics concentrate on Internet-specific technologies and computer or other hi-tech innovations for use by businesses and consumers.

Wan-Hoo Lin has been working for the We-doit Rite Computer Company for the past three years. Wan-Hoo enjoys his work and has learned a great deal about the computer business. He has always been good at trouble-shooting and debugging computer programs. In fact, in his spare time he has helped several friends and business acquaintances with problems they encountered with their computers.

Wan-Hoo feels ready to venture out on his own. He has been told that with his experience, skills, and knowledge of computers he would do well in a business of his own. He already has a number of contacts to help him get under way. Wan-Hoo likes the idea of being his own boss although he also is aware of the risks of being in business for oneself.

Wan-Hoo has no family expenses and no major debts. His car is paid for and he saves as much of his wages as possible—he has more than $7,000 in his bank account. He has a simple life style. The small house he rents could serve very nicely as his business office.

Wan-Hoo decided to start his own company, W-H-L Computer Services. He became one of several million small-business owners in the United States. Wan-Hoo and others like him are willing to contribute a great deal of time and energy as well as personal economic resources in return for a reasonable profit.

SMALL-BUSINESS OPPORTUNITIES

When we use the term **small business**, we are referring to a business that:

- Usually has the owner as the manager.
- Is not dominant in its field of operation.
- Employs fewer than 500 people.
- Usually is local, serving the nearby community.

You may be surprised that a small business may employ up to 500 people. However, many are smaller. Businesses with only one to four employees are a major factor in our work force.

When you begin your career, you very likely may be working in one of our nation's small businesses. During the past decade, the majority of new job openings were in small businesses. Small businesses provide excellent career opportunities.

You may also consider going into business for yourself. There are many small-business opportunities for people who, like Wan-Hoo, are ready to take that step. More than 800,000 businesses were started in recent years, and it is expected that new business growth will continue to be high. Starting your own business can be an exciting, although risky, beginning to a career.

Most small businesses begin as sole proprietorships. It is not unusual, however, for a person to begin his or her own business through a franchise agreement. Many small businesses eventually become incorporated. The advantages of a corporation are reasons why some small-business owners decide to incorporate their businesses. The most common form of ownership for small businesses, however, continues to be the sole proprietorship.

Small businesses are found in all industries. A recent analysis showed that the

A recent survey revealed that one-third of small-business owners started with less than $5,000—only 21 percent started with more than $50,000.

FYI

MOTIVATE

PURPOSE Introduce the chapter by having students skim the section titles. Ask students to suggest orally words or phrases that they think will be important to learn in this chapter.

TEACH/APPLY

MAKE CONNECTIONS Discover how many students in class might be considered entrepreneurs. Ask which students have earned money cutting lawns, baby-sitting, etc. Why did they go into business for themselves? out of a need for money? out of interest in the activity? out of a desire to do something independently? List all the reasons on the board. Also ask students if they enjoyed working for themselves. Would they do it again?

Have students volunteer to name small businesses in your community. Write the names provided by students on the board. Review the criteria for a small business on page 283 with the class. Apply each criterion to the business listed on the board. Ask students whether each business can still be considered a small business. Why or why not?

Display PowerPoint 21-2, *Small-Business Opportunities*. Have students give examples of businesses from their own community that have these characteristics. Then have students classify the businesses identified according to the service-producing and goods-producing industries. Into what category do most of the businesses listed fall?

FOCUS ON REAL LIFE

Conduct a brainstorming session with your class regarding ideas and opportunities for small-business ventures. Allow students to come up with some very "wild" ideas. Point out that some truly "wild" ideas have been converted into successful business ventures in the real world.

Invite students to speculate about SCORE. Do they think such an organization might be effective? Why or why not? Why might someone retired from business volunteer time to counsel others?

Ask students to respond to the following question: What is the difference between saying that "most businesses fail within five years" and that "most businesses that fail do so within five years"? Which is more nearly correct? (Answer: The first statement paints a bleak picture. Based on the statistics, prospects are bright for success. However, one must recognize that many firms are not very profitable and that many close down without being failures.)

Ask students to come up with what they think are the advantages of a small business. Then ask other students to discuss each item.

TRY THIS/GUIDED PRACTICE
Guide students through a discussion of business failures through the use of PowerPoint 21-4, *Small Business Problems*. Ask students to comment on what they believe could be the major reasons for failure. Quality of management is a major factor. If possible, cite local examples of failure and discuss reasons for the cause of these business failures.

Direct students to reread pages 287–288, *Characteristics of Business Owners*. For each characteristic listed, have students rate themselves on a scale of 1 to 5, with 5 being the highest rating. Then have students write summary statements about their potential to become entrepreneurs.

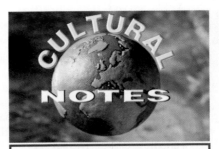

largest percentage of small businesses are found in retailing—25.1 percent, and in services—26.8 percent (see Figure 21-1). Wan-Hoo's new business venture would place him in the computer services industry.

Some small businesses are classified as venture businesses. A **venture business** is one that has been in operation for less than three years and has no employees other than the owner. Wan-Hoo's business would be a venture business.

SMALL-BUSINESS PROBLEMS

Small businesses make many contributions to our economy as innovators of new products and developers of new production processes.

Figure 21-1 Why do you think so many small businesses are in services and retailing?

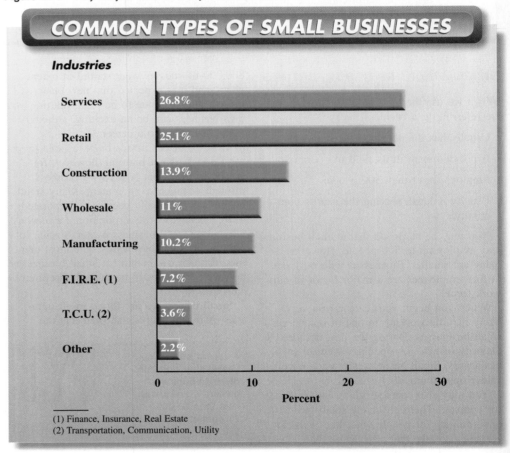

COMMON TYPES OF SMALL BUSINESSES

Industries

Services	26.8%
Retail	25.1%
Construction	13.9%
Wholesale	11%
Manufacturing	10.2%
F.I.R.E. (1)	7.2%
T.C.U. (2)	3.6%
Other	2.2%

Percent

(1) Finance, Insurance, Real Estate
(2) Transportation, Communication, Utility

Basic Skills-Listening

You can teach students to become good listeners by explaining to them the value of watching out for certain words that may distract the listener from effective listening. Words such as vacation may distract the listener to think about a vacation spot. It is important for good listeners to overcome the tendency to wander when certain words are mentioned.

Ask a student volunteer to write other distracters on the board that influence students not to listen to what the speaker is saying. The Student Activity Worksheet, Basic Skills—Listening Checklist, in the School-To-Work/SCANS Activity Masters, may be used to serve as a guideline for a discussion of listening skills.

SCANS

Can you think of other white-collar small businesses, like this business consultant?

Small businesses adjust more quickly to changing market demands than do large businesses. They also can experiment with new products and new methods of production without waiting for approval from management committees or boards of directors.

Not all small businesses succeed; in fact, their failure rate tends to be quite high. In a recent annual report by the President to the U.S. Congress on the "State of Small Business," about 40,000 bankruptcies were reported among small businesses and 585,800 closings.

A **bankruptcy** is a situation in which a business does not have enough money to pay its creditors even after selling its equipment and other capital resources. A **creditor** is a person or business that is owed money. A **closing** is a situation in which the business is discontinued with a loss to at least one creditor.

Although these figures represent a small percentage of small businesses, the number of failures is of some concern. In addition to these official figures, some small enterprises just quietly go out of business when the owner believes that he or she is not doing well enough to continue.

In a typical year, more than half of the businesses that fail have been in operation less than five years and are classified as

small businesses. The reasons for failure are quite varied. The following are the most common reasons for failure:

- Not keeping adequate records.
- Not having enough start-up money.
- Lack of sales and management experience.
- Lack of experience with the type of business.
- Not controlling operating expenses.
- Poor location for the business.
- Failure to manage payments due from customers for purchases made.

Each of the above causes of failure can be overcome with the right kind of assistance. As a prospective small-business owner, you may need special help in the areas of management, accounting, personnel, and finance.

HELP AVAILABLE FOR SMALL BUSINESSES

Small-business owners can get assistance from a number of sources. Universities and

Can you name various small businesses that would have a large number of competitors?

EXPLORE THIS/INDEPENDENT PRACTICE Ask students to research a successful business that was started by an entrepreneur. Have them report on the company's growth since operations began and on its contributions to the local economy.

Have students read through the brief stories of successful small-business owners on pages 288–289. Ask students to identify ways in which each young entrepreneur illustrates the success characteristics. Then have students prepare a list of the three characteristics they believe to be the most important for success as an entrepreneur.

The Chapter Review questions at the end of the chapter vary in level of difficulty. For a basic assignment, consider Develop Your Business Language and Review Your Reading. For an average assignment, consider the basic assignment plus Communicate Business Concepts and Calculate Business Data. For an enhanced assignment, try the average assignment plus Technology Application and Decision-Making Strategies.

ASSESS

Restate each Business Note as a question and have students respond orally. For students who may have difficulty providing answers, assign the reteaching activities that follow. Enrichment activities may also be assigned where appropriate.

SCANS

Workplace Competencies-Interpersonal Skills

Developing interpersonal skills should be an on-going process for all of us in order to be a contributing member of society. Participating as a member of a team is an example of one way to develop these interpersonal skills. As a successful team member, individuals must also learn to work in small groups. The Student Activity Worksheet, Workplace Compe-

tencies—Interpersonal Skills, in the School-To-Work/SCANS Activity Masters, may serve as a guideline for discussion of interpersonal skill development.

1. Describe a small business. (Answer: A small business has the owner as manager, is not dominant in its field of operation, employs fewer than 500 people, and usually serves a local community.)

2. Why do small businesses fail? (Answer: Small businesses fail because owners do not keep adequate records, do not have enough start-up money, lack sales and management experience, lack experience in the type of business owned, do not control operating expenses, have a poor business location, or fail to manage payments due from customers.

3. What are some sources of help for small-business owners? (Answer: Owners can get help from the Small Business Administration, from Small Business Institutes, and from groups such as SCORE.)

4. Name several characteristics of successful small-business owners. (Answer: Owners tend to be self-starters, leaders, planners, hard workers, decision makers, and achievers; they are also responsible, trustworthy, and healthy individuals.)

RETEACH

Have students form each of the statements about the characteristics of business owners on pages 287 and 288 into a question. For example, "Can you do things on your own?" Then ask students to write a paragraph answering each question about themselves.

Write the term *business failure* on a transparency or the board. Under it, list these phrases: What it

Bankruptcy is not an easy way out—it is an "action of last resort."

colleges often have individuals on their faculties who can give advice and assistance to people who are starting or have started their own businesses. Local organizations of businesspeople, such as Junior Chambers of Commerce, have members who can help others with business problems.

Our government has an agency set up to help small businesses; it is called the **Small Business Administration (SBA)**. The SBA is a government-funded organization that helps small-business owners borrow money as well as manage their businesses more efficiently. Information about the SBA and its services can be obtained by contacting an office in your city or state, by writing to the SBA, 409 3rd St. S.W., Washington, D.C. 20416, or by visiting www.sba.gov.

The SBA fulfills its mission through a variety of means. The SBA has a large number of publications designed to assist small-business owners. The SBA provides assistance with financing and offers special

What are some resources that could help you in starting your own small business?

programs on how to operate small businesses. **Small Business Institutes (SBIs)** are programs offered in cooperation with colleges and universities to provide management counseling.

The SBA is also responsible for the formation and operation of organizations known as SCORE. **SCORE** stands for the **Service Corps of Retired Executives** whose members can provide assistance in special areas of operation, such as finance, accounting, and marketing. Members of SCORE are retired local businesspeople who volunteer their services and are paid only a basic amount to cover their travel expenses.

Other special services provided by the SBA include Small Business Investment Companies (SBICs) and a specialized Section 301(d) SBIC, commonly called a Minority Enterprise SBIC (MESBIC). SBICs are set up to provide venture capital and management services. The providing of **venture capital**—money used to start up a new small business or help a business expand during a growth period—is an important service.

A large number of small-business owners are women. The SBA operates an Office of Women Business Owners. It also has special publications dealing with women who are small-business owners, such as *Women Business Owners: Selling to the Federal Government.*

CHARACTERISTICS OF BUSINESS OWNERS

You probably already have concluded that small-business owners must know a lot of facts and perform many business functions in order to be successful. In addition to a knowledge of business operations and management skills, small-business owners must

Over 80 percent of small business firms use some form of credit to finance their operations.

Critical Thinking Skills-Reasoning

Drawing conclusions from facts or premises is an important thinking skill for today's employees. One of the most pervasive ways that government affects business is through the legal system. The law protects both individuals and businesses against those who threaten society. It also spells

out accepted ways of performing many essential business activities—along with penalties for failure to comply.

have certain personal characteristics. Some characteristics of successful small-business owners are that they

- Can do things on their own; they are self-starters.
- Have leadership abilities; they can get others to do what has to be done.
- Can take charge of things; they assume responsibility.
- Like to plan what must be done; they are good organizers.
- Are hard workers; they work long hours on the job.
- Are decision makers; they can make decisions quickly when necessary.
- Can be trusted; they mean what they say.
- Are achievers; they will work on a task until it is finished.
- Have good health; they exhibit energy.

The above characteristics are based on an SBA publication called *A Checklist for Going*

FAQs stands for Frequently Asked Questions. Many Internet hosts provide files containing answers to FAQs about their services.

into Business. In addition, some researchers also have discovered the following characteristics to be important for small-business owners:

- They would rather work for themselves, even if they made considerably less money than working for someone else.
- They are at least 24 years old (fewer than 10 percent are under age 24).

LEGAL PERSPECTIVES

What Is Bankruptcy?

Bankruptcy, the legal nonpayment of financial obligations, is a common occurrence among small-business owners. Bankruptcy occurs when a business owes substantially more than the value of all the things it owns (assets). Declaring bankruptcy is one solution to the problem of having too much debt. The bankruptcy procedures allow the business to make a fresh start.

Our bankruptcy laws provide two plans. In one plan, the business retains some basic assets. Other assets are sold to pay creditors; some who are owed money receive just a portion of what is owed. With the other plan, creditors cannot collect what is owed for a period of time. The business tries to resolve the financial crisis under a court-approved plan.

Bankruptcy releases a company from the burden of debt. This release is called a *discharge*. Discharges through bankruptcy are available to a particular debtor once every six years. A record that debts were discharged in a bankruptcy proceeding stays on a debtor's record for ten years. A bankruptcy record usually reduces a debtor's ability to get credit during that period. And credit is basic to our way of doing business today.

Critical Thinking

1. What is the basis on which bankruptcy is declared?
2. Who gets helped and who gets hurt in a bankruptcy situation?

NET FACTS

Net Facts provides information and definitions of terms for the Internet. The more information that students have about the Internet, the better equipped they will be to use this resource. In the Internet Activity Masters, there is an Internet Activity Worksheet for each unit. You can use these activities to give students experience with finding information online. Options for assigning this activity are as follows:

1. **Provide students with a list of addresses of resources for this activity;**
2. **Assign students to conduct their own searches; or**
3. **Use the addresses provided on the Internet Activity Worksheet.**

You should complete the activity yourself before assigning it to resolve any discrepancies that may arise.

is; Common reasons for failure; Bankruptcy, an alternative to a closing. Have students list the details.

Have students use the information on page 283 to create a two-column chart. In the first column, have students list the characteristics of a small business. In the second column, have students list some businesses in their communities that could be classified as small businesses.

LEGAL PERSPECTIVES

Legal Perspectives gives students an opportunity to study legal situations and draw appropriate conclusions.

CRITICAL THINKING

1. Bankruptcy is declared by businesses (or individuals) that cannot meet their financial obligations. Debts are relieved through a legal proceeding. The bankruptcy process is not a matter of finding an easy way out of indebtedness, however.

2. The business owner gets help in settling claims made by creditors. The business owner may also get a new lease on life if the bankruptcy court allows the business to reorganize (Chapter 11 bankruptcy). If a business is permitted to reorganize, the business works with creditors to develop a plan for paying part of its debts and writing off the rest. Creditors get hurt if a business is liquidated (closed) and the proceeds from the sale of assets are insufficient to cover debt obligations. After the sale of assets, the cash proceeds are given first to secured creditors and then to unsecured creditors.

Have students create posters informing classmates of help available for someone starting a small business. Display the best poster in a visible area of your classroom.

ENRICH

Direct students to read the Legal Perspectives. Have students look through the Yellow Pages of a telephone book or scan back issues of a newspaper to identify small businesses in their community. Then require students to make an appointment with one of the owners to discuss his or her business, including how he or she got started, problems he or she had to face, and other significant experiences he or she had as an entrepreneur. Students should report their findings to the class.

Ask students to find out about some product or service that would be of interest to your school's student body—in other words, conduct a survey of students. Then have students find some way of providing that product or service, coming up with financing for the operation, selling the product or service, and determining whether a profit has been made. Students should prepare a report to the class providing the details of their business ventures.

Have students identify the advantages and disadvantages for each of the following methods of starting a business: franchising, buying an existing business, and starting a new business.

SUMMARIZE

Assign four or five of your best students to become a Panel of Experts. Ask students to work in

Do you have some of the personality traits necessary for owning a small business?

- They have had a variety of business experiences, often with someone who is a successful small-business owner.

- They desire to use their skills and abilities and have control over their lives.

YOUNG ENTREPRENEURS

An **entrepreneur** is someone who takes a risk in starting a business to earn a profit. Having a real desire to be your own boss, developing a good initial plan for a business, having special skills and abilities, and coming up with some innovative ideas are important factors in starting your own business.

Can you think of some service or product that is not being offered that could be in demand? Is there some service or product that you personally could offer more efficiently or with better results than others are doing now? Is there some special talent that you have that could become the foundation for a business of your own? If so, you

have the basis for a new business enterprise.

There are still good opportunities for entrepreneurship through small-business ownership. **Entrepreneurship** is the process of starting, organizing, managing, and assuming the responsibility for a business. Here are some real-life examples of young entrepreneurs.

Larry Villella was only 11 years old when he got an idea that developed into a business. He did not like moving the family lawn sprinkler around when his chore was to water the lawn. So he went into the basement and cut a sprinkler into a c-shape that fit around trees and shrubs. Four years later, his little company, Villella's ConServ Products, had sold about $70,000 worth of products.

Ban Narasin of Manhattan showed some business ability at the age of 12 when he talked his father into giving him $65 so that he could get into a comic book convention as a dealer. He bought and sold comic books at that convention and came home with a $2,500 profit. Seven years later he started a

Critical Thinking Skills-Problem Solving

SCANS

Problem-solving skills, which include recognizing a problem and devising a plan of action, are applied throughout every chapter in this text. Each time a student participates in a Cooperative Learning or Teams Activity, problem-solving skills are applied in a group situation. Each time a student completes a math application in the Calculate Business Data, decisions are

made as to which mathematical approach must be taken. For each Technology Application problem, students must decide which template problem to use, which piece of software to load, and how to solve the problem. Emphasize to students how they are using problem solving in their day-to-day tasks and make them aware of the skills they are developing.

business called Boston Prepatory, a men's sportswear manufacturer. In 1993, his sales totaled $8 million.

Geoff Allen of McLean, Virginia, was a whiz at a computer. He learned to write his own programs when he was too young to begin selling them. At the age of 19, he started Source Digital Systems. His company did video editing, produced animations, and created video kiosks for point-of-sale purchases. Within a few years, his business sales were about $5 million with projections for sales to grow to over $8 million.

How can innovative ideas or special skills result in opportunities for entrepreneurship?

small groups to raise questions that the group can ask the panel. Let each group ask one question at a time and allow the panel one minute to form its answer before responding. The panel may ask for clarification of the question if needed. Student groups that stump the panel with their question may be assigned a prize such as one point added to their next examination. If the panel cannot answer, no points are earned if the group cannot answer its own question correctly. Allow 30 minutes for this activity.

EVALUATE

- Assign Activities and Projects for Chapter 21.
- Administer the printed test or ExamView for Chapter 21.
- Administer the printed test or ExamView for Unit 6.
- Assign School-To-Work/SCANS portfolio activities for Unit 6.

TEACHING STRATEGIES

Alternate Modalities
Visual Learner

The visual learner needs to "see" the concept. One way for the learner to "see" the concept is mental visualization. When introducing the characteristics of successful entrepreneurs, have the student (with eyes closed) picture a successful entrepreneur as you read aloud the descriptions of successful young entrepreneurs from the text or another source.

REVIEW YOUR READING

1. The greatest percentage are in retailing and service industries.
2. Seven reasons for small business failure are (1) inadequate records; (2) lack of start-up money; (3) lack of sales and management experience; (4) lack of experience with the type of business; (5) inability to control operating expenses; (6) poor location for the business; and (7) failure to manage payments due from customers.
3. The SBA (a) has a variety of publications, (b) provides financial assistance, and (c) conducts special programs, such as SBIs.
4. Some publications include *Women Business Owners: Selling to the Federal Government* and *A Checklist for Going into Business.*
5. SCORE (Service Corps of Retired Executives) is made up of retired businesspeople who volunteer their services. It provides assistance in areas of operation, such as finance, accounting, and marketing.
6. Characteristics of small-business owners include that they (a) can do things on their own, (b) have leadership abilities, (c) take charge of things, (d) like to plan what must be done, (e) do not mind hard work, (f) are decision makers, (g) can be trusted, (h) are achievers, (i) have good health, (j) would rather work for themselves, even if they make considerably less money than they would working for someone else, (k) are at least 24 years old, and (l) have had a variety of business experiences, often with someone who is a successful small-business owner.
7. Having a real desire to be your own boss, developing a good plan for your business, and coming up with innovative ideas are important factors in starting your own small business.

COMMUNICATE BUSINESS CONCEPTS

8. The majority of new jobs are in small businesses. There are also many good opportunities for going into business on your own.
9. Small businesses are found in each of the industry classifications. Small businesses are the most innovative and can come up

BUSINESS NOTES

1. A small business is one that has the owner as a manager, is not dominant in its field of operation, employs fewer than 500 people, and usually serves a local community.
2. Small businesses fail because owners do not keep adequate records, do not have enough start-up money, lack sales and management experience, lack experience in the type of business owned, do not control operating expenses, have a poor business location, and fail to manage payments due from customers for purchases made.
3. Small-business owners can get help from the Small Business Administration, from Small Business Institutes, and from organizations such as SCORE.
4. Successful small-business owners tend to be self-starters, leaders, planners, hard workers, decision makers, and achievers; they are responsible, trustworthy, and healthy individuals.

REVIEW YOUR READING

1. In which industries are the greatest percentages of small businesses found?
2. State seven common reasons for business failures.
3. What are three things that the SBA does to help small businesses?
4. Name some publications of the SBA.
5. What is SCORE, who are its members, and what assistance does it provide for small businesses?
6. What are some characteristics of successful small-business owners?
7. Name three important factors to be considered before starting your own small business.

COMMUNICATE BUSINESS CONCEPTS

8. Why is your career likely to begin in a small business?
9. In what ways are small businesses major contributors to our economy?
10. Why are most of the small businesses found in the retailing and service industries?
11. How could each of the reasons why small businesses fail be overcome?
12. Why are retired executives willing to work with small-business owners in solving their problems?
13. Why do you think the government established the SBA?
14. Which of the 12 characteristics of successful small-business owners do you presently have? Which ones do you believe you could develop while in school?
15. What are some future small-business opportunities in which you might be interested?

with new products and new processes more quickly than larger firms.
10. The retailing and service industries do not require the heavy investment in machinery that manufacturing does nor the large inventories that the area of wholesaling requires. Many of the ideas that people come up with are fairly simple consumer products or services.
11. The reasons for business failures could be overcome by the following actions: (a) Taking a course in accounting. (b) Building up a savings account or getting a large enough business loan. (c) Working for someone in the area of sales or management. (d) Finding a job in a business that is like the one you want to start. (e) Learning how to control expenses by budgeting and keeping good records of what is spent. (f) Researching good business locations and getting help from organizations such as SCORE. (g) Keeping a good record of what is owed your business and by setting up good billing and record systems.

DEVELOP YOUR BUSINESS LANGUAGE

For each numbered item, find the term that has the same meaning.

16. A business that has been in operation for less than three years and has no employees other than the owner.

17. A group of retired executives who can provide assistance to small-business owners.

18. Someone who takes a risk in starting a business to earn a profit.

19. A situation in which a business does not have enough money to pay its creditors even after selling its equipment and other capital resources.

20. A person or business that is owed money.

21. A situation in which a business is discontinued with a loss occurring to at least one creditor.

22. Money used to start up a new small business or help a business expand during a growth period.

23. Programs offered in cooperation with colleges and universities to provide management counseling.

24. A business that usually has the owner as manager, is not dominant in its field of operation, employs fewer than 500 people, and usually serves its nearby community.

25. A government-funded organization that helps small-business owners borrow money as well as manage their businesses more efficiently.

26. The process of starting, organizing, managing, and assuming the responsibility for a business.

KEY TERMS
bankruptcy
closing
creditor
entrepreneur
entrepreneurship
Service Corps of Retired Executives (SCORE)
small business
Small Business Administration (SBA)
Small Business Institutes (SBIs)
venture business
venture capital

DECISION-MAKING STRATEGIES

Wan-Hoo has worked hard to build up a good business. He has many customers, and they are pleased with his services. His new business is a source of satisfaction—he likes being his own boss and feeling good about what he accomplishes.

But finances are a problem. Wan-Hoo had to borrow $20,000 to get the supplies and equipment he needed to get started. His day-to-day business expenses are more than he had expected.

A number of his customers are slow in making payments. Wan-Hoo does not have time to pursue customers who are slow in paying their bills. Late-paying customers make it difficult for him to pay his bills on time. His creditors are quite unhappy with him. He has more debt than he considers desirable. He wonders: Should I declare bankruptcy? Should I just go out of business? Should I try to get someone to help me get these financial problems under control?

27. What is the basic problem that Wan-Hoo faces?

28. What would you suggest that he do?

DEVELOP YOUR BUSINESS LANGUAGE

16. venture business
17. Service Corps of Retired Executives (SCORE)
18. entrepreneur
19. bankruptcy
20. creditor
21. closing
22. venture capital
23. Small Business Institutes (SBIs)
24. small business
25. Small Business Administration (SBA)
26. entrepreneurship

DECISION-MAKING STRATEGIES

27. Wan-Hoo's fundamental problem is slow-paying customers. He needs a good system for keeping track of what is owed his business. Late-paying customers make it difficult for Wan-Hoo to meet day-to-day business operating expenses.

28. Wan-Hoo should seek help solving his financial problems. He needs someone to set up a good billing and record keeping system. He also should learn how to control expenses by budgeting and keeping good records of what is spent.

12. Retired executives often feel that they still can make a contribution to businesses even though they are no longer employed. They find personal satisfaction in using their experience and expertise in helping small business owners solve problems. There is a feeling of personal worth gained from helping others.

13. The federal government set up the SBA because small businesses are important to our economy, yet many are not successful. It is in the interest of our nation's economy to have well run and successful small businesses.

14. This answer will depend upon how individual students perceive themselves. Students could develop most of the characteristics while in school by learning to arrive at school and classes on time, being especially diligent in preparing homework assignments, and participating in student organizations that provide leadership experiences.

15. Answers will vary. Opportunities might include word processing services, working at home using a computer or telephone, lawn services, painting, and making and selling crafts.

29. (a) $3,000 + $4,000 + $10,000 = $17,000
(b) $35,000 − $17,000 = $18,000
(c) $5,000 + $17,000 = $22,000; $35,000 − $22,000 = $13,000
(d) $22,000 + $10,000 = $32,000; $35,000 − $32,000 = $3,000 shortage; No, he still will not have enough to start his business.

30. (a) 12 + 8 + 9 + 8 + 11 + 6 = 54 hours; 54 ÷ 6 = 9 hours per day on average (b) $1,595 − $785 = $810; $810 ÷ 54 = $15 (c) 54 × $12.50 = $675; $810 − $675 = $135

31. (a) $18,000 + $18,000 + $18,000 + $31,000 + $31,000 = $116,000; $116,000 × 0.10 = $11,600 (b) 250 × 5 = 1,250 km; 1,250 × 0.6 = 750 miles; $17.25 × 750 = $12,937.50 earned on the miles driven (c) 1,125 × 2.2 = 2,475 pounds carried by each truck; 2,475 × 4 = 9,900 total pounds; 1900 × 0.26 = 494 gallons per haul (d) $12,937.50 − $11,600 = $1,337.50 over her goal; $12,937.50 ÷ 116,000 = 11.2%

32. Construction 550,000 × 0.139 = 76,450; Finance, Insurance, Real Estate 550,000 × 0.072 = 39,600; Manufacturing 550,000 × 0.102 = 56,100; Retailing 550,000 × 0.251 = 138,050; Services 550,000 × 0.268 = 147,400; Transportation, Communication, Utility 550,000 × 0.036 = 19,800; Wholesale 550,000 × 0.11 = 60,500; Other 550,000 × 0.022 = 12,100

TECHNOLOGY APPLICATION

In this activity, students use a computer to solve a business problem using a file that is provided on the data CD that accompanies *Intro to Business*. Instructions for using the data CD are included in a **README** file on the disk. Solutions are provided on the Instructor's Resource CD.

CALCULATE BUSINESS DATA

29. Chuck Polley wants to open a sporting goods store. He has been told that he should have at least $35,000 to invest in his new business. He has $3,000 in his bank account, a friend will lend him $4,000, and he can get a bank loan for $10,000.
  a. How much money does Chuck have available for investing now?
  b. How much will he have to borrow to come up with the $35,000?
  c. If he can get an additional $5,000 loan on his credit card account, how much will he still need?
  d. If the local bank is willing to lend him $10,000, will he have enough then to start his business? If not, how much will the shortage be?

30. Sandy Noble owns and operates a beauty salon. On Monday, he worked 12 hours; on Tuesday, 8 hours; on Wednesday, 9 hours; on Thursday, 8 hours; on Friday, 11 hours; on Saturday, 6 hours. He earned $1,595 that week, and his expenses were $785.
  a. How many total hours did Sandy work that week? What was the average number of hours per day?
  b. How much did he have as profit after subtracting expenses from the money he took in? How much profit did he make per hour worked?
  c. If Sandy worked for the Shear Delight Beauty Parlor, he would be paid $12.50 per hour. How much more does Sandy earn a week in his own business compared to working for another beautician if he works the same number of hours?

31. Tracy Gardner operates a fleet of five trucks.

Three trucks cost her $18,000 each, and two trucks cost her $31,000 each. Last week each of the five trucks averaged 250 kilometers of driving. Tracy's business makes $17.25 for each mile driven by the trucks. (See Appendix D.)
  a. How much does Tracy have invested in her five trucks? If Tracy's goal is to earn 10 percent per year on her investment, how much should she earn on those trucks?
  b. How much does Tracy earn on the total miles driven by her trucks in the situation described above?
  c. If four of the trucks each carried an average load of 1,125 kilograms of materials, how many pounds did each truck carry? How many pounds did the four trucks carry? If one truck hauled liquids and averaged 1,900 liters per load, how many gallons were there per load?
  d. Does Tracy's business earn enough to meet her goal? How much short or over the goal are the actual earnings? What is the percentage that was actually earned?

32. Assume that a state employs a total of 550,000 workers and that the state has the same percentage of workers in each of the eight industries as shown in Figure 21-1 on page 284. Use the following percentages: Construction, 13.9 percent; Finance, Insurance, Real Estate, 7.2 percent; Manufacturing, 10.2 percent; Retailing, 25.1 percent; Services, 26.8 percent; Transportation, Communication, Utility, 3.6 percent; Wholesale, 11.0 percent; Other, 2.2 percent. How many workers would there be in each industry in that state?

TECHNOLOGY APPLICATION

Using the *Intro to Business* Data CD and your database program software, select problem CH21. After the problem appears on your screen, complete the following activities. Then, after you have completed each step, display or print a report for each activity. If you do not have a printer available, answer the questions before you leave the computer.

33. Sort the database in descending order by owner's years of experience. Answer the following questions:
  a. Which owner has the most years of

experience?
  b. Which owner has the third fewest years of experience?

34. Select and list the companies that are less than five years old. How many companies are listed?

35. Sort the companies in ascending order by product name. Answer the following questions:
  a. Which product is listed most often?
  b. What is the last product listed?

COMMUNICATING for SUCCESS

CUSTOMER SERVICE— "MAY I HELP YOU?"

Customers are the most important part of any business. In other organizations they are sometimes called clients, patients, taxpayers, guests, passengers, and the like. But they are all really customers. A customer is any person who buys a product or service.

Customers are important because they determine the fate (or profitability) of a business. They have this power because they have choices. Customers can choose to buy or not to buy a product or service from a business organization.

Today all successful organizations emphasize good relationships with customers. This effort is carried out in the form of strategies that determine customers' needs and then fill these needs. This requires good communication. Businesses must learn what customers need (listen and read) and then tell customers what they have available for them (speaking and writing).

> **A business must listen to customers and help them clarify their needs.**

A businessperson with good customer service communication skills spends a significant amount of time actively listening to customers describe their needs. A lot of thought should also be given to helping customers clarify their needs. For example, the phrase "May I help you?" is usually designed to encourage a customer to describe a need to a salesperson. The salesperson will use the response as a beginning point in determining what the customer needs. Then the business employee will offer suggestions for how the business's product and/or service may satisfy the customer's wants or needs.

CRITICAL THINKING

1. Who is a customer? Give some examples of customers.
2. Why are customers important to business?

COMMUNICATING for SUCCESS

Communications skills will help ensure students' success in the business world. Communicating for Success introduces workplace/interpersonal communications issues and proper uses of communications technology. Each feature discusses a key communications topic, and contains two Critical Thinking questions that require students to analyze what they have learned.

With the triumph of marketing-driven business practices in recent decades, students need to learn that customer service is not just a catch phrase. It really has become virtually the only way of doing business with a view toward long-term success. This feature describes for students what customer service entails in practical terms.

CRITICAL THINKING

1. Any person who buys a product or service. Examples are grocery shoppers, bus passengers, dental patients, legal clients, newspaper buyers, etc.
2. Because they can determine whether a business makes a profit or not.

GLOBAL BUSINESS PROJECT

A person's ability to identify potential careers for the future is a valuable skill. In this phase of the global business project, students are asked to evaluate the main service and goods-producing industries of the country they have been studying. This can provide insight for future career choice.

Students are also asked to identify skills and experiences that would be of value when working for a multinational company. Encourage students to think about themselves in the future when they prepare a personal data sheet and a letter of application related to working for an international company.

To complete each phase of this project, students are encouraged to use various resources—textbook content, library materials, World Wide Web sites, interviews, advertisements, product packages, in-store observations. The individual activities are planned for use as either (1) an on-going course project, or (2) individual assignments.

Whether used as a continuing project or for selected activities, consider having students work in teams. This small group experience provides a valuable skill for future learning and work situations.

In addition to search engines, these selected web sites can be helpful for this unit:

- International Trade Administration of the U.S. Dept. of Commerce (www.ita.doc.gov) (www.export.gov)
- Business, economic, political news for selected countries (www.economist.com/countries)
- World Factbook of the Central Intelligence Agency (www.odci.gov/cia/publications/nsolo/wfb-all.htm)
- Latin American country information (www.lanic.utexas.edu)
- Asian country information (asnic.utexas.edu) (www.asia-inc.com)

GLOBAL BUSINESS PROJECT

PLAN HUMAN RESOURCES IN THE GLOBAL WORKPLACE

Every worker for a business organization is involved in a service-producing or goods-producing industry. As countries move from a developing economy to an industrialized nation, the types of employment opportunities change.

This phase of the business plan project involves research related to needed training and skills for international business careers. Your ability to present yourself with a personal data sheet and a letter of application will be of value in every career field.

PROJECT GOALS

1. Compare employment trends in service-producing and goods-producing industries in a foreign country.
2. Research needed training and skills for working in a multinational company.
3. Create a personal data sheet and letter of application for an international business employment opportunity.

PROJECT ACTIVITIES

Using your textbook, library materials, web sites, interviews with people, and other resources, complete the following activities:

1. Using the country from your portfolio (or select a country), describe the major service-producing and goods-producing industries of the nation. In your opinion, which of these industries have the most potential for creating jobs in the future for this country?

2. A person's ability to understand and work with people in different cultures is a necessary skill for international business employment. List skills and training experience that would be of value to a person working for a multinational company.
3. Identify various skills and experiences you would need in order to work in an international business organization. Use this information to create a personal data sheet for yourself as it might look in the future. Also, write a letter of application that expresses your future interest and ability to work for an international company.

PROJECT WRAP-UP

1. Continue your portfolio (folder, file box, or other container) for storing and referring back to the information and materials you created in the activities above. Your portfolio provides the information needed for the various elements of a global business plan.
2. Create a video that shows strong interviewing skills and common job interview weaknesses when applying for a position with an international business organization.
3. In a small group create questions for a mock job interview. Conduct mock job interviews, exchanging the roles of candidate and interviewer.

- Eastern European country information (reenic.utexas.edu)
- Middle East country information (menic.utexas.edu)
- Career planning tips (www.mapping-your-future.org) (careermag.com)

- Resume preparation advice (www.monster.com) (www.jobweb.com)
- Small Business Administration (www.sba.gov/oit)

FOCUS ON CAREERS

ADMINISTRATIVE SUPPORT CAREERS

Administrative support functions consist of a variety of tasks and responsibilities performed by support personnel to assist managerial, technical, and professional employees. Rewarding and challenging careers can be found in these occupations. The increased use of computers and integrated office systems are factors influencing opportunities in these occupations.

JOB TITLES

Job titles commonly found in this career area include:

- Bookkeeping, Accounting, and Auditing Clerk
- Hotel, Motel, and Resort Desk Clerk
- File Clerk
- Teller
- Secretary
- Dispatcher
- Office Clerk
- Shipping, Receiving, and Traffic Clerk
- Library Assistant
- Desktop Publisher
- Computer Operator
- Postal Service Worker

EMPLOYMENT OUTLOOK

- Job growth will decline over the next few years.
- In several occupations, including secretaries and file clerks, job opportunities will increase because of the need to replace retiring workers.
- Employment in health industry businesses is expected to be better than average.
- Many of the job opportunities will be in small businesses.

EDUCATION AND TRAINING

- A high school diploma is a requirement for employment.
- Employers state a preference for applicants who have completed business courses.
- Some employers look for some education beyond high school, especially in two-year business administration programs.
- Skill in operating computers, good keyboarding skill, and a knowledge of business procedures are desired by employers.

SALARY LEVELS (IN RECENT YEARS)

- Administrative support occupations generally pay in the range of $16,000 to $28,000 a year for beginning workers. The salary paid depends upon the company, the geographic area, and the skills of the worker.
- Some recent average (median) salaries: postal mail carriers and clerks, $39,000; desktop publishers, $31,000; legal secretaries, $35,000; executive secretaries and administrative assistants, $31,000; other secretaries, $24,000.

CRITICAL THINKING

1. Which job titles in this career area appeal to you most? Give some reasons for your choices.
2. What are some things you will have to do to achieve success in the career you selected?

FOCUS ON CAREERS

The careers listed in the Career Focus come from the *Occupational Outlook Handbook*, an online publication (www.bls.gov/oco) of the federal government. The O*NET codes for these job titles are: Bookkeeping, Accounting, and Auditing Clerk, 43-3031.00; Hotel, Motel, and Resort Desk Clerk, 43-4081.00; File Clerk, 43-4071.00; Teller, 43-3071.00; Secretary, 43-6011.00, 43-6012.00, 43-6013.00, 43-6014.00; Dispatcher, 43-5031.00, 43-5032.00; Office Clerk, 43-9061.00; Shipping, Receiving and Traffic Clerk, 43-5071.00; Library Assistant, 43-4121.00; Desktop Publisher, 43-9031.00; Computer Operator, 43-9011.00; Postal Service Worker, 43-5051.00, 43-5052.00, 43-5053.00

As a supplemental activity, distribute the Career Focus worksheets found in the School-To-Work/SCANS Activity Masters.

CRITICAL THINKING

Answers, of course, to the two critical thinking questions will vary widely. Students should be encouraged to select one job even if they are not really interested in the career area. Thinking about why a certain job might possibly be appealing is a forced-thinking exercise that results in self-reflection and self-examination. Answering these questions also gives certain career areas a sharper focus within students' minds.

UNIT 7

BUILDING YOUR PORTFOLIO

CAREER DEVELOPMENT – DEFINING WORK AND PEOPLE PREFERENCES

The Building Your Portfolio career exercise will help your students establish a personal history–where they have been, where they are now, and where they are going. This exercise will help students realize that the work environment can be just as important to career satisfaction as the nature of the work itself.

Ask students to think about what makes a career appealing or unappealing to them. Have students think about what they liked and disliked about people they have encountered in the workplace. Then direct them to describe in writing, the kinds of people they prefer to encounter in a work setting.

As a supplemental activity, you may refer to the School–To–Work/SCANS Activity Masters.

TEACHING STRATEGIES

SCANS

Cooperative Learning

Alternate Modalities

Teaching Tips

Special Needs

Teams

Special Features

Media/Technology

Chapter	Spreadsheet Software	Database Software	Word Processing Software	Internet	Video
22		■			■
23	■			■	■
24			■		■

Resources

SOFTWARE

Excel, Word, WordPerfect, Works, and ClarisWorks for Mac and Windows

Word Pro, ASCII, QuattroPro, Lotus, and Access for Windows

SOUTH-WESTERN EDUCATIONAL PUBLISHING PRODUCTS

Miller and Stafford. *Economic Education for Consumers. 2004.* Cincinnati: South-Western Educational Publishing Company. Textbook. 0-538-43579-8.

Donnelly. *Skills for Consumer Success.* 1999. Cincinnati: South-Western Educational Publishing Company. Text-Workbook. 0-538-68612-X.

BOOKS

Leebaert. *The Future of the Electronic Marketplace.* 1998. MIT Press.

Bamford, Blyskal, Card, and Jacobson. *The Consumer Reports Money Book : How to Get It, Save It, and Spend It Wisely.* 1997. Consumer Reports Books.

PERIODICALS

Consumer Reports. New York, NY.

Consumer Research. Hefferman Press. MA.

Kiplinger's Personal Finance Magazine. Washington, D.C.

Money. New York, NY.

GOVERNMENT PUBLICATIONS

Occupational Outlook Handbook, U.S. Department of Labor, Washington, DC.

What Work Requires of Schools: A SCANS Report for America 2000, U.S. Department of Labor, Washington, DC

MEDIA/TECHNOLOGY

Publisher's web sites:

www.intro2business.swep.com

www.swep.com

www.thomson.com

UNIT 7

CONSUMERS IN THE ECONOMY

The content and activities of this unit provide students with an overview of the purposes and characteristics of our economic society. Use the resources listed on the preceding page, especially those from South-Western Educational Publishing, as you prepare to teach consumer concepts.

The informed consumer is the focus of this unit. In Chapter 22, students will not only be exposed to their role as consumers, but sources of consumer information will be described. In Chapter 23, the use of various consumer skills to make the appropriate buying decisions will be introduced. By following buying decision-making steps and learning how to be a comparison shopper, students will learn when and how to make wise purchases. The consumer movement is described briefly in Chapter 24, followed by a discussion of the seven rights and five responsibilities of every consumer.

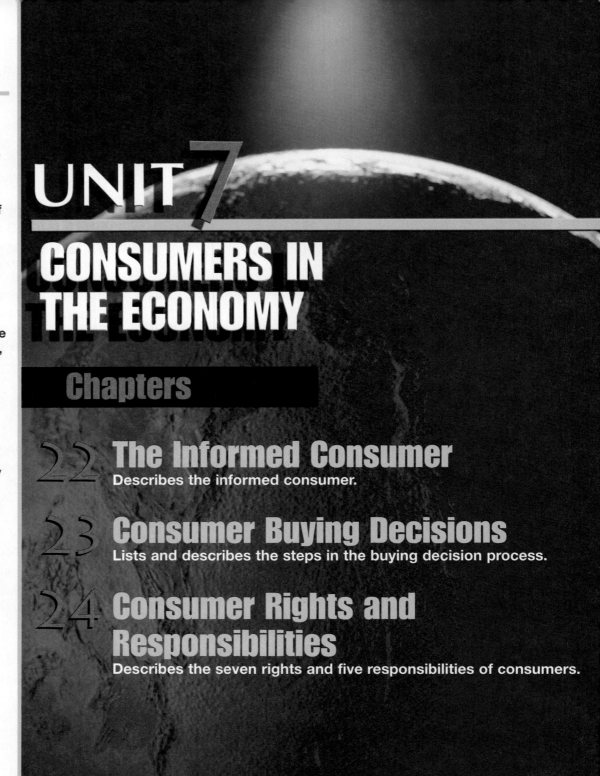

UNIT 7

CONSUMERS IN THE ECONOMY

Chapters

22 The Informed Consumer
Describes the informed consumer.

23 Consumer Buying Decisions
Lists and describes the steps in the buying decision process.

24 Consumer Rights and Responsibilities
Describes the seven rights and five responsibilities of consumers.

Kick-Off Activity

Investigating Business Media

The following exercise asks students to choose an article from *The Wall Street Journal*, the financial section of a newspaper, or a business magazine and to inquire about a topic related to this unit.

From recent issues of *The Wall Street Journal* or financial magazines, direct students to select an article that describes in some detail a particular company's marketing strategy (either in general or for a particular product). Then have students answer the following questions:

1 What are the company's goods and services?

2 Describe the company's market for its goods or services.

3 According to the article, how successful has this strategy been?

296

BU$INESSBRIEF

CUSTOMER NEEDS LEAD TO SUCCESS

Businesses know they cannot be successful without customers who value and purchase their products and services. While it may be possible to sell almost anything to a customer once, a dissatisfied customer is not likely to buy a second time from a company. Companies that want good relationships with their customers must work to understand those customers and their wants and needs.

Until the mid-20th century, companies were mostly concerned about producing the products they wanted to sell. Then the company would develop distribution procedures to get products to customers. Since product choices and consumer resources were limited, customers would usually buy whatever the businesses produced. In many towns in the United States, if there was one auto dealership, one grocery store, and one furniture store, consumers would buy what was available even if it wasn't exactly what they wanted.

Today, consumers have many choices. They not only have competing businesses in their communities, but also can easily travel to another town, or shop on the Internet or from a catalog. If they don't find what they want in one store, they can usually find it in another. Businesses now know they must carefully listen to customers and provide the products and services that customers want.

Marketing research has become an important business activity. Businesses study the wants and needs of customers through surveys, focus groups, and by collecting information on what products and services customers regularly purchase. Businesses use the information to develop new ideas for products and

make improvements in current products.

Automobile manufacturers used to offer only a few models and colors of cars. Features were added based on what engineers and product designers thought would improve the car or help to sell a new model. Today, consumers have literally hundreds of choices of sizes, styles, colors, and features when they visit auto dealerships. Manufacturers test new product ideas on teenagers, families, outdoors enthusiasts, and business travelers to make sure they build cars, pickups, and SUVs that customers want.

Another way businesses apply the marketing concept is by ensuring customer satisfaction. L.L. Bean is an outdoor apparel and accessories retailer that prides itself on its relationship with customers. The company's guarantee for all products purchased from its stores, catalogs, or Internet site is, "Our products are guaranteed to give 100% satisfaction in every way. Return anything to us at any time if it proves otherwise."

Today, understanding and meeting the needs of consumers is an important business focus. Those businesses that determine the needs of their customers and work hard to meet those needs will be the most successful.

CRITICAL THINKING

1. *How do you think businesses find out about the needs and wants of customers?*

2. *Why do you think today's consumers feel more empowered to express their wants and needs to American businesses?*

297

BUILDING YOUR PORTFOLIO

The informed consumer is the focus of this chapter. Students will not only be exposed to their roles as consumers, but sources of consumer information will be described. Effective consumer practices will also be featured.

Resources for Teachers
- Lesson Plans
- School-To-Work/SCANS Activity Masters
- Spanish Resources
- Instructor's Resource CD

Assessment
- Chapter and Unit Tests, Ch. 22
- ExamView, Ch. 22

Media/Technology
- Applying Technology Data CD
- PowerPoint slides
- Business Connection CD
- Videotape

Activity Masters and Workbooks
- Activities and Projects, Ch. 22
- Internet Activity Masters
- Business Math Activity Masters
- Communications Activity Masters
- International Business Activity Masters
- Ethics Activity Masters

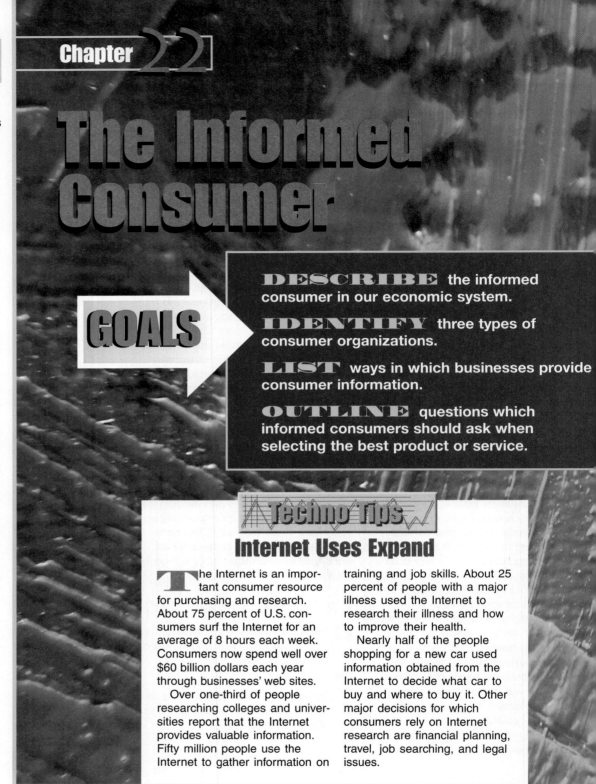

Chapter 22

The Informed Consumer

GOALS

DESCRIBE the informed consumer in our economic system.

IDENTIFY three types of consumer organizations.

LIST ways in which businesses provide consumer information.

OUTLINE questions which informed consumers should ask when selecting the best product or service.

Techno Tips
Internet Uses Expand

The Internet is an important consumer resource for purchasing and research. About 75 percent of U.S. consumers surf the Internet for an average of 8 hours each week. Consumers now spend well over $60 billion dollars each year through businesses' web sites.

Over one-third of people researching colleges and universities report that the Internet provides valuable information. Fifty million people use the Internet to gather information on training and job skills. About 25 percent of people with a major illness used the Internet to research their illness and how to improve their health.

Nearly half of the people shopping for a new car used information obtained from the Internet to decide what car to buy and where to buy it. Other major decisions for which consumers rely on Internet research are financial planning, travel, job searching, and legal issues.

Students need to know the latest technologies and develop cutting edge Internet skills for use in current jobs, future careers, or in their homes. TechnoTips introduces students to today's cutting edge technologies and provides them with important Internet skills. Feature topics concentrate on Internet-specific technologies and computer or other hi-tech innovations for use by businesses and consumers.

"I am going on a wilderness retreat with my mentor group and I have to buy a sleeping bag," Kristen said to Joshua. "I don't know much about sleeping bags but want to get the best one for my trip. I stopped by the sporting goods store and they had so many confusing varieties and prices. Can you help?"

"I don't know much either but I expect your choice depends on where you will use the bag," said Joshua. "Did you gather information before you began looking? There are consumer groups that test products. If you want I can help you look on the Internet or we can go to the library to find magazine articles."

"That sounds like a good idea," Kristen replied. "A salesperson at the store might be able to help but researching in advance should help me ask the right questions."

A **consumer** is a person who buys and uses goods or services. We buy food, clothing, school supplies, and appliances. We also pay for services each time we go to a movie, the dentist, or a car wash. All of these activities make us consumers. American businesses provide us with goods and services. But it is our job to be wise consumers and make appropriate decisions.

A wise consumer is an informed consumer. In order for us to be informed consumers in our economic system, we must carefully gather and study information about products and services before we buy them.

THE CONSUMER

Consumers have the power to decide to buy or not to buy goods and services. Businesses go to great lengths to be responsive to the needs of consumers. Without satisfied consumers, businesses would not make sales, earn profits, or remain in business.

People usually seek the highest standard of living that their incomes will allow. You can raise your standard of living by becoming an informed consumer. In fact, your standard of living is probably determined more by how you spend than by how much you earn.

Your consumer behavior reflects and determines your life-style. You may choose to be thrifty and buy only the products and services you need to live or you may buy products and services that you could easily do without. If you waste money on things you don't need or low quality products, you will have less money to spend on important purchases.

We have an obligation to society to be wise and efficient consumers. Our world has only a limited supply of natural resources, such as petroleum, metals, clean air, and clean water. Sometimes uninformed consumers unnecessarily waste these irreplaceable resources and/or contribute to damaging our environment.

CONSUMER INFORMATION ORGANIZATIONS

In order to help inform consumers, several organizations or branches of organizations have been developed. The testing these organizations do and the advice they give is usually objective. These organizations may publish magazines, award seals, and in some cases endorse products for quality and safety.

A customer is a consumer who is dealing with a specific business. **FYI**

the decision-making questions and how these questions will help them become a good consumer.

EXPLORE THIS/INDEPENDENT PRACTICE Before assigning independent practice material for any chapter, students should be expected to read the chapter material carefully. In view of the fact that all students vary widely in their ability to read effectively, it is advisable to have the students read the entire chapter, or sections thereof, silently in class if the material has not been previously read in connection with homework assignments.

After students have read the chapter, ask them to complete the end-of-chapter questions. Develop Your Business Language is an excellent way to improve students' vocabulary. Only words used in the chapter are used in the vocabulary exercises. The Review Your Reading questions can be used to check students' ability to comprehend what they have read. The Communicate Business Concepts section affords an opportunity for students to apply to practical life situations the information gained from reading the textbook. By completing the problems under Calculate Business Data, students will be able to strengthen and refine their abilities in mathematics. Technology Application allows students to demonstrate skill in using word processing, spreadsheet, and database software. Decision-Making Strategies contains material to challenge students to utilize the decision-making model explained in Chapter 1.

The Chapter Review questions at the end of the chapter vary in

As a consumer, what decisions do you make when choosing medical or dental services?

Three basic types of organizations exist: product-testing organizations, print publishers, and broadcast organizations.

Product-Testing Organizations

Product-testing organizations have as their main purpose the testing of products and services. Manufacturers pay these private firms to perform safety tests on products.

Perhaps the best known of these organizations is the Underwriters Laboratories, Inc. Underwriters Laboratories tests electrical components of products from all over the world for fire and electrical safety. The symbol of the Underwriters Laboratories is an indication that the product has been tested and judged safe for normal use.

Another organization is the Association of Home Appliance Manufacturers (AHAM). This group develops and updates the performance standards of such appliances as refrigerators, air conditioners, and freezers. The AHAM seal signifies that a product has met the association's performance standards. Other seals include the Carpet and Rug Institute and the Motorist Assurance Program.

Print Publishers

Some organizations have as one of their goals the reporting of scientific, technical, and edu-

cational information about products and services. Some are nonprofit organizations, such as Consumers Union, Inc., which perform independent tests on consumer goods and publish articles on the quality of the goods. Consumers Union publishes its findings in a monthly magazine called *Consumer Reports*. Consumers' Research, Inc., is an independent, nonprofit organization that presents articles on a wide range of topics of consumer interest. The magazine, *Consumers' Research*, analyzes consumer issues.

Some magazines that are published for a profit endorse products but only after those products have been tested. *Good Housekeeping* and *Parents* are examples. Any product advertised in these magazines can display the magazine's seal. The Good Housekeeping Seal promises the product will be replaced or your money refunded if the product is found to be defective within one year of purchase. *Consumers Digest* and *Bottom Line* are two other publications designed specifically for providing objective consumer information.

In order to remain unbiased, the *Consumer Reports* magazine accepts no advertising.

In the financial world, there are many periodicals that cover topics of interest to consumers. *Money, Kiplinger's Personal Finance Magazine, Fortune,* and *The Wall Street Journal,* for example, evaluate and report on the performance of investments such as stocks, bonds, mutual funds, real estate, precious metals, art, and coins.

There are also specialty magazines or newspapers that provide information about specific kinds of products or services. These publications cover topics such as cars, computers, boats, audio equipment, travel, and education. They help consumers understand technical or complex products and services.

What kinds of tests should be used to ensure the safety of products for consumers?

Often comparative ratings are given for products or services.

Broadcast Organizations

Like magazines and newspapers, radio and television also are sources of consumer information. Many stations carry regular programs that inform the public about product safety, care and use of products, and shopping tips, such as the best food buys of the week. In addition, many broadcast talk shows are designed to help listeners with their consumer problems.

CONSUMER INFORMATION FROM GOVERNMENT

Federal, state, and local governments also help people become informed consumers. The federal government, for example, formed the Consumer Information Center to serve as headquarters for consumer information. This agency issues catalogs four times a year. Each catalog lists numerous publications of special interest to consumers. In addition to making government publications available, the Center publishes the results of government research and product tests. The agency has distribution centers for its publications in several major cities.

The United States Department of Agriculture (USDA) is another source of consumer information. USDA publications specialize in information about food—judging quality, buying wisely, improving buying practices, planning meals, improving nutrition, and other farm- and home-related topics.

The USDA also inspects and grades foods and makes that information available to consumers in the form of a grade. A

level of difficulty. For a basic assignment, consider Develop Your Business Language and Review Your Reading. For an average assignment, consider the basic assignment plus Communicate Business Concepts and Calculate Business Data. For an enhanced assignment, try the average assignment plus Technology Application and Decision-Making Strategies.

ASSESS

Review the goals at the beginning of the chapter and the Business Notes at the end of the chapter. Have students respond orally or in writing to each of the Business Notes restated as a question, provided below. For students who may have difficulty providing answers, assign the reteaching activities that follow. Enrichment activities may also be assigned where appropriate.

1. How would you describe the informed consumer in our economic society? (Answer: An informed consumer acquires information about products and services before buying.)
2. What are the three types of consumer organizations? (Answer: Product-testing organizations, print publishers, and broadcast organizations.)
3. What are two government agencies that provide consumer information? (Answer: Office of Consumer Affairs, the Federal Trade Commission, and the Consumer Product Safety Commission.)
4. What are three ways in which businesses provide consumer

---

information? (Answer: Advertising, product labels, customer service departments, specialists, and the Better Business Bureau.)

5. What are the seven questions which informed consumers should ask when selecting the best product or service? (Answer: 1. Would you rather buy this item instead of another desired item that costs the same amount of money? 2. Which business or businesses should you visit? 3. What quality of goods or services do you want to buy? 4. What price are you willing to pay? 5. Should you pay cash or buy now and pay later? 6. Do you really need this item now, or can you wait awhile? 7. If you make this purchase, what other important item may you have to do without?)

RETEACH

Bring in consumer information from the government or other sources. Let students flip through these and point out information that reflects the objectives covered in this chapter. If you bring in product labels, students could compile a list of all the information contained on that label. Writing a short statement explaining how a consumer might use this information to make good consumer decisions is a good application of material learned in this chapter.

A *sales manager's* job duties include:
- Directing a firm's sales program
- Assigning sales territory and goals
- Establishing training programs for sales representatives
- Maintaining contact with dealers and distributors
- Analyzing sales statistics
- Overseeing regional and local sales managers

grade indicates the quality or size of a product. For example, beef may be stamped "prime," "choice," or "select." The USDA shield means that the product has been inspected and approved by that government agency.

Other government agencies that provide information to consumers include the Federal Trade Commission, Food and Drug Administration, Consumer Product Safety Commission, National Highway Traffic Safety Administration, Department of Health and Human Services, and Environmental Protection Agency. In each case, the name of the agency suggests its area of concern and responsibility. States, cities, and counties have consumer agencies which provide consumer information.

CONSUMER INFORMATION FROM BUSINESS

Businesses provide information to consumers. As a public service and in an effort to sell goods and services, businesses make information available through advertising, product labels, customer service departments, business specialists, and Better Business Bureaus.

Advertising

Advertising is a widely available and popular source of consumer information. Since the main purpose of an advertisement is to convince you to buy a product or service, you should use it with care as a source of consumer information. Advertising can be useful if you know which product or service you want and if you can overlook strong appeals to buy a particular product or service.

Useful advertisements often tell you what the product is, how it is made, and what it will do. Advertisements give facts that you can use to compare the product with other competing products. Beware of advertising claims that really tell you nothing about the product. If an advertisement states that a product is better, ask, "Better than what?"

A frequently used source of information is called "word of mouth." It includes information you receive from other consumers that you know. We often trust information provided by other people who have purchased and used a product. Most of us, when planning a purchase, go to someone who already owns the product and ask, "How do you like it?" This word-of-mouth source of consumer information should not be underestimated by consumers or businesses.

Product Labels

A **label** is attached to or printed on a product and provides useful written information about the nature or content of a product. The label may tell you what the product is made of, its size, how to care for it, and when and where it was made. The label on a shirt should tell you what it is made of and provide laundering instructions.

Labels list ingredients with the main ingredient first and remaining ingredients in descending order of quantity.

The career listed in this Career Highlights comes from the *Occupational Outlook Handbook*, an online publication (www.bls.gov/oco) of the federal government, under the heading Advertising, Marketing, Promotions, Public Relations, and Sales Managers. The O*NET code for Sales Manager is 11-2022.00. Students can access O*NET Online (online.onetcenter.org) to view important features of this job. Tell your class about these resources and how to use them.

Customer Service Departments

Many businesses have special departments devoted to customer service. Some firms provide customers with booklets on a variety of consumer topics. For example, banks and insurance companies publish booklets to help consumers manage their money. Some large retail firms provide printed materials to help consumers with their buying problems.

Business Specialists

Sometimes it is wise to get advice from an expert before purchasing a product. This is especially true if you have never bought such an item, if the item is very complicated, or if it is very expensive. Houses, business equipment, and used cars are examples of products that should not be purchased without an expert's advice. For example, most of us could not judge whether the furnace in a house is safe or the central air conditioning is

adequate for the size of the house. A certified house inspector could give reliable advice about these items to ensure that you make a wise decision.

Better Business Bureaus

In an effort to improve credibility, businesses all across the country have joined together in a self-regulation effort and created Better Business Bureaus (BBB). Many communities have a Better Business Bureau. Better Business Bureaus are supported by dues paid by member businesses. The bureaus work to maintain ethical practices in the advertising and selling of products and services and to combat consumer fraud. BBBs are concerned with promoting ethical businesses.

Better Business Bureaus can provide helpful information. For example, suppose you were planning to buy a used car from a particular dealer. You could call the Better Business Bureau to find out what experiences others have had with that dealer. If consumers have reported problems with the firm, you could find out about these complaints. Better Business Bureaus give facts only; they do not recommend products or firms. They give you the information they have, but you

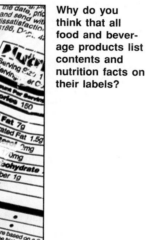

Why do you think that all food and beverage products list contents and nutrition facts on their labels?

ENVIRONMENTAL PERSPECTIVES

Marketing Green Products to Consumers

Green products are goods manufactured or packaged in an environmentally safe way. Many companies have found that protecting the environment gives customers additional confidence in their products.

Green products have been developed by businesses to satisfy consumer demand. Consumers recognize that some products, or the packages the products come in, may have a negative effect on our environment. For example, aerosol cans release fluorocarbons into the air which may reduce the thickness of our ozone layer. Therefore, businesses have responded by creating pump spray bottles for products such as hair spray and window cleaners. Other companies have begun packaging their products in recycled paper and cardboard containers. This

special packaging may increase the cost of some products. However, some consumers are willing to spend more money for environmentally sound products. This situation highlights two crucial questions that society faces: Are the benefits of preserving the environment worth the costs? And, are we willing to pay now for a better environment the future?

Critical Thinking

1. Identify three products or product packages that are environmentally sound. Describe their features.
2. How much more would you be willing to pay as a consumer for an environmental safe product? Explain your answer.

---

are free to interpret it and to make your own decision. The services and programs offered by a Better Business Bureau can help you be a more informed, knowledgeable, and satisfied consumer.

EFFECTIVE CONSUMER PRACTICES

You may not always use good consumer skills in the purchase of every product or service. Sometimes there will not be time to do so, and at other times it may not be worth the effort when making a minor purchase. You can, however, develop the habit of using good judgment in making the most of your purchases.

Whenever you plan to buy anything, you must make a number of important decisions. Your answers to the following questions will

help you choose the best product or service for you:

1. Would you rather buy this item or something else that costs the same amount of money?

Wireless communication systems connect us to the Internet without using a telephone line. While wireless systems are slower, they allow easier and more frequent use of the Internet, resulting in even more growth.

ENVIRONMENTAL PERSPECTIVES

The environment is a contemporary topic on which all students will have some knowledge. Students are very aware of the importance of protecting our environment. Bring in products or packages that are environmentally safe and initiate a discussion about them. Ask students what makes these particular products safe for the environment. As a class project, develop a display or bulletin board of these items. If time permits, you may want to invite a speaker from a company that produces some of these environmentally safe products.

CRITICAL THINKING

1. Possible answers may include examples of product packaging that is 100 percent biodegradable, products that are recyclable, products with all organic ingredients, etc.
2. Answers will vary based on student's values.

2. Which business or businesses should you visit?

3. What quality of goods or services do you want to buy?

4. What price are you willing to pay?

5. Should you pay cash or use credit?

6. Do you really need this item now or can you wait awhile?

7. If you make this purchase, what other important item may you have to do without?

Use reliable consumer information to judge each purchase according to whether it will meet your needs better than something else you could buy. Not buying one article so that you can buy another article can be viewed as an opportunity cost. An **opportunity cost** is the value of any alternative that you give up when you buy something else or make another choice. For example, suppose you want both a new sweater and a seat for your bicycle, but have only enough money for one or the other. If you choose the seat, you must give up the sweater. Part of the "cost" of the seat, then, is the opportunity to have a new sweater.

When you give up something in order to have something else that is more important to you, you are making a trade-off.

What questions should you ask yourself when making purchases?

Net Facts provides information and definitions of terms for the Internet. The more information that students have about the Internet, the better equipped they will be to use this resource. In the Internet Activity Masters, there is an Internet Activity Worksheet for each unit. You can use these activities to give students experience with finding information online. Options for assigning this activity are as follows:

1. **Provide students with a list of addresses of resources for this activity;**
2. **Assign students to conduct their own searches; or**
3. **Use the addresses provided on the Internet Activity Worksheet.**

You should complete the activity yourself before assigning it to resolve any discrepancies that may arise.

Chapter REVIEW

BUSINESS NOTES

1. An informed consumer acquires information about products and services before buying.
2. Three basic consumer information organizations are product-testing organizations, print publishers, and broadcast organizations.
3. Government agencies such as the Federal Trade Commission and the Consumer Product Safety Commission develop useful information for consumers.
4. Businesses supply consumers with information through advertising, product labels, customer service departments, specialists, and the Better Business Bureau.
5. An informed consumer will ask questions before purchasing a product.

REVIEW YOUR READING

1. What power does the consumer have?
2. What are two examples of product-testing organizations?
3. What are two nonprofit organizations that publish consumer magazines?
4. What are two financial periodicals that cover topics of interest to consumers?
5. Which government organization specializes in information about food—judging quality, buying wisely, improving buying practices, planning meals, improving nutrition, and other farm- and home-related topics?
6. Why do businesses provide information to consumers?
7. How can advertising help you become a better consumer?
8. What is the concern of the Better Business Bureau?
9. What are the seven important questions you should ask before purchasing a product or service?

COMMUNICATE BUSINESS CONCEPTS

10. Why do you think a good businessperson with good products or services to sell would like to have customers who are well informed?
11. List three sources of consumer information about a bicycle.
12. Why do you think specialty newspapers and magazines are published and sold?
13. What kinds of advertisements are most valuable to consumers? Give an example.
14. One autumn day a woman and a man came to Carrie Franklin's door. They said they were chimney sweeps and would like to clean her chimney before she began using her fireplace. The man said it would be inexpensive and make her home safer because it would reduce the chances of a chimney fire. Mrs. Franklin looked out her window and saw the name "Chim Chim Chimney Sweeps" on the truck they were driving. How can she find out if the firm is reliable?

DEVELOP YOUR BUSINESS LANGUAGE

For each numbered item, find the term that has the same meaning.

15. A person who buys and uses goods or services.
16. The value of any alternative that you give up when you buy something else or make another choice.
17. An indication of the quality or size of a product.
18. A written statement attached to a product giving useful information about its nature or contents.

KEY TERMS
consumer
grade
label
opportunity cost

DECISION-MAKING STRATEGIES

Pierre needs a new camera to take with him on his trip to Mexico as an exchange student. He is not a photography expert but has taken some pictures for the school newspaper. He intends to use the camera to take indoor and outdoor pictures of new friends he will meet as well as scenery he will encounter.

Pierre has about $150 to spend on the camera and wants the camera to be sturdy, to be easy to use, and to take good quality pictures.

19. What sources of information could Pierre use to find out what cameras are in his price range?
20. What two sources of information do you feel are best? Why?

CALCULATE BUSINESS DATA

21. While studying an automobile buyer's guide, Teresa learned that the value of three new cars she was considering would decrease over the next four years. The figures are shown in the table.
    a. At the end of four years, what will be the value of the Sunglow Convertible?
    b. At the end of four years, what will be the value of the Grocery-Getter?
    c. At the end of four years, what will be the value of the Muscle Car?

Car Brand	Original Price	Total 4-Year Reduction in Value
Sunglow Convertible	$27,300	47%
Grocery-Getter	$19,850	23%
Muscle Car	$24,800	63%

22. The advertisement shown below appeared in a newspaper during the month of March.
    a. By how much money were the finer winter coats reduced?
    b. By how much money were the wool winter coats reduced?
    c. By how much money were the raincoats reduced?

**Save
Clearance Sale**

Buy NOW! Buy for NEXT YEAR!
A small deposit will hold your selection.
Don't miss these values!

	Regular	Sale
Finer Winter Coats	$259.95	$174.95
Wool Winter Coats	199.95	149.95
Raincoats	74.95	59.95

DEVELOP YOUR BUSINESS LANGUAGE

15. consumer
16. opportunity cost
17. grade
18. label

DECISION-MAKING STRATEGIES

19. Pierre might seek information from photography magazines, consumer magazines such as *Consumer Reports*, advertisements, salespeople in camera stores, and friends who have cameras.
20. Answers will vary. Suggested answer may be sources that are objective and reputable.

CALCULATE BUSINESS DATA

21. (a) $27,300 × 0.47 = $12,831; $27,300 − $12,831 = $14,469 (b) $19,850 × 0.23 = $4,565.50; $19,850 − $4,565.50 = $15,284.50 (c) 24,800 × 0.33 = $15,624; $24,800 − $15,624 = $9,176
22. (a) $259.95 − 174.95 = $85 reduced (b) $199.95 − 149.95 = $50 reduced (c) $74.95 − 59.95 = $15 reduced.

23. (a) $15.74; $75.05; $4.68; $22.93; $55.67 (b) +$27.75; +$37.45; +$8.82; −$7.23; +$34.32 (c) $1,072.36 (d) 8.1%; 11.1%; 8.7%; 23.5%; 24.7%.

24. (a) The first shelf width is 125 cm ÷ 2.5 cm = 50 inches; 50 inches ÷ 12 inches = 4.2 feet wide. Depth is 30 cm ÷ 2.5 cm = 12 inches or 1 foot deep. The second shelf is 150 cm ÷ 2.5 cm = 60 inches; 60 inches ÷ 12 inches = 5 feet wide. Depth is 25 cm ÷ 2.5 cm = 10 inches. (b) The shelf cannot exceed 4.5 inches wide and 1 foot deep.

TECHNOLOGY APPLICATION

In this activity, students use a computer to solve a business problem using a file that is provided on the data CD that accompanies *Intro to Business*. Instructions for using the data CD are included in a **README** file on the disk. Solutions are provided on the Instructor's Resource CD.

---

23. Near the end of the summer, Wheeler's Garden Store marked down a number of items for quick sale. The regular selling price, reduced price, and cost of each item to the store are shown in this table. Each item was sold at the reduced price.

Item	Regular Price	Reduced Price	Cost
21-inch power mower	$194.99	$179.25	$151.50
Riding lawn mower	675.00	599.95	562.50
Electric hedge trimmer	54.00	49.32	40.50
Deluxe barbecue grill	97.45	74.52	81.75
Lawn furniture set	224.99	169.32	135.00
Total			$971.25

a. By what amount was each item reduced?
b. How much above the product cost was realized on the sale of each item?
c. What was the total amount received from the sale of the five items?
d. By what percentage of the regular price was each item reduced?

24. Carlos needed to buy a small bookshelf for his bedroom. The space available for the bookshelf was 4.5 feet wide and 1 foot deep. At a local discount store, he found a boxed, ready-to-assemble bookshelf with dimensions 125 cm (centimeters) wide and 30 cm deep. At another store, he saw a bookshelf that measured 150 cm wide and 25 cm deep.

a. Determine if each bookshelf will fit into Carlos' bedroom. (Metric hint: One inch equals 2.5 centimeters.)
b. What suggestion would you make to Carlos about purchasing a bookshelf?

TECHNOLOGY APPLICATION

Using the *Intro to Business* Data CD and your database program software, select problem CH22. After the problem appears on your screen, complete the following activities. Then, after you have completed each step, display or print a report for each activity. If you do not have a printer available, answer the questions before you leave the computer.

25. Sort the database in ascending order by name of the consumer agencies. Answer the following questions:

a. What is the first agency listed?
b. What is the third agency listed?

26. Select and list the agencies that provide legal services. How many agencies are listed?

27. Sort the agencies in descending order by ZIP Code. Answer the following questions:
a. What is the second agency listed?
b. What is the last agency listed?

INTERNATIONAL CONSUMER BEHAVIOR

People in all regions of the world have the same basic needs. A need for food, health care, and social interaction is not unique to one climate or geographic area. While we are all motivated to make buying decisions based on a common foundation, our culture and level of economic development will affect these buying choices. Four major categories commonly influence consumer behavior.

1. **Physical and emotional needs**. You require air, food, shelter, clothing, and health care to survive. However, these basics of life may vary for different people. While you may purchase clothes at a store, others may wear homemade clothing.

2. **Geographic and demographic factors.** A person in a warm climate will require different housing and clothing than someone living in a cold climate. Demographic traits such as age, gender, family size, and education level also influence buying habits. For example, as people of a nation have a longer life span, the demand for health care,

travel, and recreational services increases among older consumers.

3. **Personality factors.** Attitudes are another influence on consumer behavior. A person's beliefs toward risk, change, convenience, and families will affect buying habits.

4. **Social and cultural factors.** Family, friends, and religion influence what and how we buy. In cultures with strong social connections, consumers buy goods and services that emphasize and promote these relationships.

> **Consumer behavior is influenced by a variety of factors that affect buying choices.**

CRITICAL THINKING

1. Select a product or service that could be sold to consumers in different areas of the world. Describe how the product or service might need to be revised for different climates, cultures, and levels of economic development.

2. Interview a person who has visited or lived in another country. How is shopping different in that country? What are some foods that are common to the country that you do not regularly eat?

Most students will either work with international clients or compete against businesses that do. Global Navigator introduces students to issues integral to working with international businesses. Key concepts and challenges faced by international businesses are presented, followed by two Critical Thinking questions that require students to analyze what they have learned.

This feature details four categories of factors that differentiate consumer behavior in various cultures. Grasping these factors will help students understand the basis for the variety of different ways business is conducted around the world, and why these differences persist in the otherwise "global" marketplace.

CRITICAL THINKING

1. Lots of answers could fit here. Food products might be a particularly good example because of the obvious differences in culinary tastes and traditions.
2. Answers will vary widely.

By following buying decision-making steps and learning how to be a comparison shopper, students will learn to make wise purchases and become efficient consumers. Students will also be introduced to the Consumer Price Index.

Resources for Teachers
- Lesson Plans
- School-To-Work/SCANS Activity Masters
- Spanish Resources
- Instructor's Resource CD

Assessment
- Chapter and Unit Tests, Ch. 23
- ExamView, Ch. 23

Media/Technology
- Applying Technology Data CD
- PowerPoint slides
- Business Connection CD
- Videotape

Activity Masters and Workbooks
- Activities and Projects, Ch. 23
- Internet Activity Masters
- Business Math Activity Masters
- Communications Activity Masters
- International Business Activity Masters
- Ethics Activity Masters

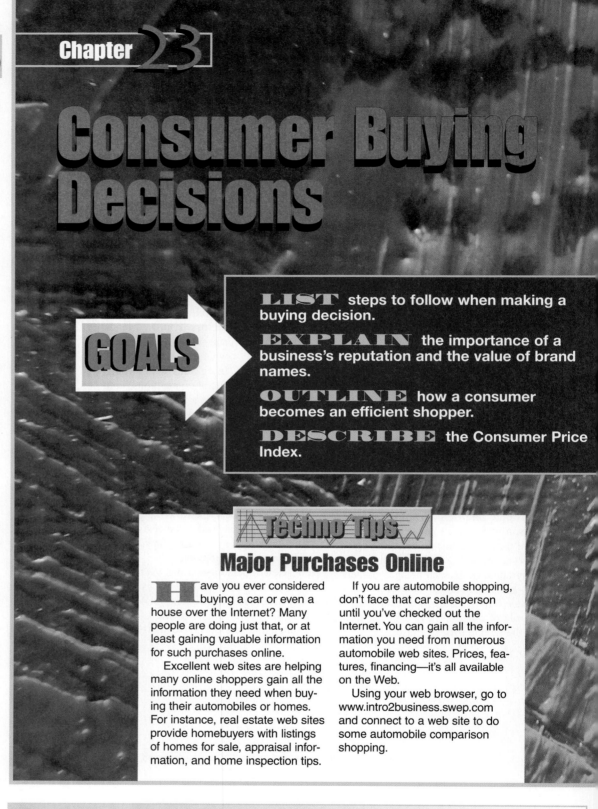

Chapter **23**

Consumer Buying Decisions

GOALS

LIST steps to follow when making a buying decision.

EXPLAIN the importance of a business's reputation and the value of brand names.

OUTLINE how a consumer becomes an efficient shopper.

DESCRIBE the Consumer Price Index.

Techno Tips

Major Purchases Online

Have you ever considered buying a car or even a house over the Internet? Many people are doing just that, or at least gaining valuable information for such purchases online.

Excellent web sites are helping many online shoppers gain all the information they need when buying their automobiles or homes. For instance, real estate web sites provide homebuyers with listings of homes for sale, appraisal information, and home inspection tips.

If you are automobile shopping, don't face that car salesperson until you've checked out the Internet. You can gain all the information you need from numerous automobile web sites. Prices, features, financing—it's all available on the Web.

Using your web browser, go to www.intro2business.swep.com and connect to a web site to do some automobile comparison shopping.

Students need to know the latest technologies and develop cutting edge Internet skills for use in current jobs, future careers, or in their homes. TechnoTips introduces students to today's cutting edge technologies and provides them with important Internet skills. Feature topics concentrate on Internet-specific technologies and computer or other hi-tech innovations for use by businesses and consumers. At the www.intro2business.swep.com web site, students can complete the activity for this chapter.

Juan met Michelle after school. "Hi, Michelle. Have you finished your research on computers? Which one are you going to buy?"

"I don't know," replied Michelle. "I looked at the computers at Bright's Computer Store and they have the lowest price. I spent three hours checking out different computers. But I got the impression they didn't take me seriously because of my age."

Young people voice the complaint that many businesses do not respect them as customers or treat them as well as adults.

Such treatment is changing. Businesses recognize that teens are a powerful consumer group with purchasing power, who not only choose where they want to spend their money but often influence the purchasing decisions of family and friends. Businesses that ignore or disrespect younger customers will likely lose current sales. They may also lose long-term customers who won't forget which stores treated them well and which did not. You can be sure that businesses that understand consumer behavior welcome teen customers.

MOTIVATE

PURPOSE Provide a purpose for students as they read the chapter. Ask what they think they will learn. Direct students to skim the chapter, looking at photos, reading captions, and noting main headings. The goals at the beginning of each chapter provide a valuable tool for having students pinpoint main ideas. The tasks required by the goals are signaled in the first word. Some emphasize information collection ("Identify," "List"), while others call for description ("Explain," "Describe"). Ask students to look through all the goals and note the first word of each. Then ask students to state the purpose of studying this chapter.

TEACH/APPLY

MAKE CONNECTIONS Begin class using PowerPoint 23-2, *Decision-Making Steps*, and review the importance of these steps for all buying decisions. Review each step and ask students for examples of these items. Good buying skills come with practice, and becoming a good comparison shopper will help the consumer get the most for the dollar. Explore with students the importance of unit price, quality, service, and the value of sales. Discuss what a unit price means to them. Show an example on the board of the cost of an item and then its unit cost. Deciding where to buy is also consideration for the consumer. Ask students what is meant by a "business's reputation" and why it is important. Discuss brand names and the variety of stores

DECISION-MAKING STEPS

As a consumer, you should follow the decision-making steps when you make a buying decision. These steps are:

1. Identify your needs or wants. Be able to clearly state why you intend to buy something.

2. Know the choices that are available to you. These choices include price, quality, location, variety, reputation, and the like.

3. Determine the measure of satisfaction of your needs and wants. You will develop answers to questions such as "How much am I willing to pay?" "What quality level will be adequate?" and "How long am I willing to wait for the product?"

4. Consider the alternatives. At this stage,

Give reasons why you think that many businesses target their products specifically to young people.

FOCUS ON REAL LIFE

In the last chapter, students learned where good consumer information can be obtained. Ask students that once consumer buying information is obtained, why are buying decisions and buying skills indeed skills? Ask for a volunteer to write on the board ideas that students might have about buying skills.

available to make purchases from. Emphasize technology and the use of computers for ordering merchandise. Students will readily relate to impulse buying. Emphasize the importance of taking time to shop so that the appropriate items are purchased. Develop with students a list of traits needed to become an efficient shopper. The Consumer Price Index plays an important role in business. Students should know what the index is and how it plays a role for the consumer.

TRY THIS/GUIDED PRACTICE
Walk students through the different types of retail businesses as students record examples of each. Show the relevance of the decision-making questions and how they will help students become good consumers.

EXPLORE/INDEPENDENT PRACTICE Before assigning independent practice material for any chapter, students should be expected to read the chapter material carefully. In view of the fact that all students vary widely in their ability to read effectively, it is advisable to have the students read the entire chapter, or sections thereof, silently in class if the material has not been previously read in connection with homework assignments.

After students have read the chapter, ask them to complete the end-of-chapter questions. Develop Your Business Language is an excellent way to improve students' vocabulary. Only words introduced in the chapter are used in the

you will shop for the products and services that might satisfy your needs. You will compare them in terms of the criteria you have identified.

5. Finally you will make the decision whether to buy or not, what product or service is most satisfying, and from which business you will make the purchase.

DEVELOPING BUYING SKILLS

Good buying skills will make you a better consumer so that you can get greater value for your money each time you make a purchase. By acquiring these buying skills, you can learn how to compare prices, services, and value. These skills will also help you learn about sales and how to examine what you buy. Using these skills will help you to be happier with your purchases and more efficient in your buying activities.

Smart consumers, of course, are comparison shoppers. **Comparison shopping** means comparing the price, quality, and services associated with one product with those of another product. It also means studying advertisements to determine if what is being offered for sale is a real value. Except for utilities, such as water and electricity, or for very specialized goods, there are few things that are produced or sold by only one business. Therefore, you can choose where to buy and you can compare prices, quality, services, and sales.

Comparing Unit Prices
A **unit price** is a price per unit of measure. To calculate a unit price, you must divide the price of the item by the number of units per measure. For instance, suppose you want to buy a bag of frozen corn. In the supermarket, you see that a 16-ounce bag of Golden Frozen

Corn costs $1.26. However, an 8-ounce box of Yellow Perfection Corn sells for $0.69 per box. Which is the better buy for the dollar? Comparing the total prices only, it is not easy to decide. However, if the store posts the cost per ounce, the unit price, you could quickly compare prices. In this case, the 16-ounce bag would show a unit price of 7.9 cents an ounce ($1.26 ÷ 16). The 8-ounce box would be 8.6 cents per ounce ($0.69 ÷ 8). Unit pricing would quickly tell you that the 16-ounce bag is a better buy per ounce for the dollar.

Many stores help consumers compare value among various brands and sizes of the same product by showing the total price and the price of one standard measure, or unit, of the product. In the case of corn, a standard unit would be one ounce. If the store showed how much one ounce of each brand of corn costs,

Why do you think it is important to compare not just the price, but also the quality and service associated with a product?

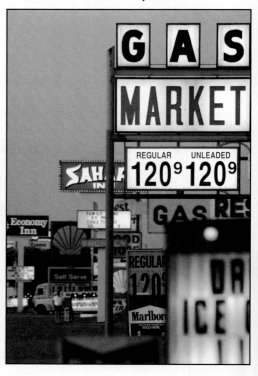

TEACHING STRATEGIES

Teams

Student Teams—Achievement Divisions (STAD) is an instructional method in which students use cooperative learning in peer groups. When using STAD, students are assigned to teams with four members each. Each group will study and review the lesson, making sure that all group members understand the objectives and content. Send students back to their desks to take the ExamView for this chapter. Students must take the ExamView on their own with no assistance from team members. Compare each student's score to the current average for that student's previous ExamView. Award two points to students who meet their last ExamView score. Give three points to students who beat their last ExamView score. The team that has the most points is the winner.

Flames are angry e-mail messages sent to people who break the rules of netiquette, or the expected behavior of Internet users.

you could easily tell whether Golden Frozen or Yellow Perfection was a better buy regardless of the size of the containers.

Comparing Quality

As a wise consumer, you should always try to examine a product before you buy it and make sure it will satisfy your needs. Even if you are not an expert, you can often tell whether it is exactly what you want. With experience, you will learn to recognize differences in quality.

Everyone wants his or her money's worth. High-quality merchandise and services normally cost more. However, buying lower quality items can sometimes turn out to be more expensive than buying the higher quality items. For example, if you buy a low-quality pair of tennis shoes and they wear out in a shorter period of time than the higher quality shoes, you will have to replace the low-quality shoes sooner. Therefore, you may end up buying two pairs of low-quality shoes in a short span of time. It may have been less expensive in the long run to buy the higher quality shoes that would not have to be replaced so soon for more money.

Comparing Services

A wise buyer compares services offered by businesses. Most businesses try to give good service, but types of services may differ. Some businesses sell for cash only; others extend credit as a service. Some businesses provide free delivery. Other services

offered may include layaways, repairs, and special orders.

Service is important, but you should not pay for more service than you actually need. Some businesses offer services at additional cost like an extended warranty or product assembly. You must decide if each service is needed and priced well before buying. You should know what you want, seek it out and buy it at the best prices. In short, develop your skills as a comparison shopper.

Comparing Sales

The word "sale" is perhaps the most overused, and least trusted, word in marketing. You have probably seen "sale" signs a thousand times. Sales are used so often to try to sell goods that they are sometimes ineffective. When an item is really on sale, it is offered at a price lower than its normal selling price. Many "sales" are not really sales at all. Sometimes the sale involves regular

Might total quantity or total price be more important than unit price to some consumers?

Net Facts provides information and definitions of terms for the Internet. The more information that students have about the Internet, the better equipped they will be to use this resource. In the Internet Activity Masters, there is an Internet Activity Worksheet for each unit. You can use these activities to give students experience with finding information online. Options for assigning this activity are as follows:

1. **Provide students with a list of addresses of resources for this activity;**
2. **Assign students to conduct their own searches; or**
3. **Use the addresses provided on the Internet Activity Worksheet.**

You should complete the activity yourself before assigning it to resolve any discrepancies that may arise.

vocabulary exercises. The Review Your Reading questions can be used to check students' ability to comprehend what they have read. The Communicate Business Concepts section affords an opportunity for students to apply to practical life situations the information gained from reading the chapter. By completing the problems under Calculate Business Data, students will be able to strengthen and refine their abilities in mathematics. Technology Application

---

SCANS

Workplace Competencies-Technology

In order for students to become contributing workers in our society, it is important that they understand technology and how to apply it appropriately. Employers are looking for potential employees with good technology skills. We may help students become proficient in technology by teaching them how to apply technology to tasks through understanding the basics

of the appropriate equipment. Technology does not always mean just computers. A fork-lift operator uses a piece of equipment to perform daily tasks. It is important that the operator understand the equipment, the parts of the equipment, how machines are installed, various other pieces of equipment that may be used to get different results, interpretation of the output, and a discussion of error or warning messages.

allows students to demonstrate skill in using word processing, spreadsheet, and database software. Decision-Making Strategies contains material to challenge students to utilize the decision-making model explained in Chapter 1 for problem solving.

The Chapter Review questions at the end of the chapter vary in level of difficulty. For a basic assignment, consider Develop Your Business Language and Review Your Reading. For an average assignment, consider the basic assignment plus Communicate Business Concepts and Calculate Business Data. For an enhanced assignment, try the average assignment plus Technology Application and Decision-Making Strategies.

ASSESS

Review the goals at the beginning of the chapter and the Business Notes at the end of the chapter. Have students respond orally or in writing to each of the Business Notes restated as a question, provided below. For students who may have difficulty providing answers, assign the reteaching activities that follow. Enrichment activities may also be assigned where appropriate.

1. What are the five steps you should follow when you make a buying decision? (Answer: Identify your needs or wants, know the choices that are available to you, determine the measure of satisfaction of your needs and wants, consider the alternatives, make the decision to buy.)

2. What are the four items that a comparison shopper will evaluate when making a purchase?

goods at regular prices being heavily advertised with the word "sale." Retailers generally run three types of sales—promotional, clearance, and special-purchase.

Promotional sales are sales in which businesses promote the sale of regular merchandise by making temporary price reductions. Retailers typically do this when opening a new store or when publicizing the new location of an established store. Promotional sales are also used to build acceptance for new products or services by offering them at low introductory prices. Retailers hope that customers will buy the products at the reduced prices, like them, and then buy them at the regular prices in the future. Retailers also use promotional sales to attract customers in hopes that they will buy the sale merchandise plus other products that are not on sale.

Clearance sales are used to clear merchandise that stores no longer wish to carry in stock. This may be an end-of-season item, odd sizes and models, or a line of merchandise that the store no longer carries. Clearance sales usually offer some bargains, but it is important to be certain that you can use a sale item before you buy it.

Special-purchase merchandise is merchandise bought for a special sale rather than regular merchandise that has been reduced in price. Special-purchase merchandise may include goods purchased from a manufacturer who is overstocked, goods that are no longer made, or stock from a company that is going out of business.

Which type of sale do you most often see in indoor mall shops?

DECIDING HOW TO BUY

In today's competitive business environment, you have a wide variety of choices of where to buy a product or service. When selecting a place to make a purchase, you should consider the business's reputation, learn brand names of products, and then plan where to buy.

Business's Reputation

Most business owners readily acknowledge that the most valuable business asset is a good reputation. The wise business owner knows that a satisfied customer is likely to return. Businesses with good reputations have salespeople who know the uses and the quality of the goods and are concerned about matching the appropriate goods with customers' needs. If you buy from a business with a good reputation, you can usually rely on its salespeople to help you make wise selections.

Brand Names

A **brand name** is a name given to a product or service that is intended to distinguish it from other similar and/or competitive products or services. A brand name is usually created by the company that manufactures the product or service. Brand names are designed to help build customer loyalty to a product or service.

Many brand-name goods and services are advertised nationally and are sold in almost every community. Among these goods are items such as clothing, shoes, tools, and cosmetics. Manufacturers of such goods often place brand names on the items they make. Timex, for example, is the brand name of a world-famous line of watches. These are called *national brands*.

Recognizing national brand names can help you as a consumer in two ways. First, you can usually expect uniform quality, even when brand-name goods are bought from different businesses. Buying brand-name goods is especially helpful when it is difficult to inspect for quality, such as packaged

GLOBAL PERSPECTIVES

Foreign Currency

As our world becomes smaller and global trade increases, more and more United States businesses will get involved in business transactions with companies in foreign countries. Transactions with foreign businesses may be stated in terms of U.S. dollars or the currency of the other country. If the transaction involves foreign currency, the U.S. business must convert the foreign currency into U.S. dollars before the transaction can be recorded.

The value of foreign currency can change daily. The exchange rate is the value of foreign currency in relation to the U.S. dollar. Current exchange rates can be found in many daily newspapers, by contacting a bank, or using an online service like the Internet or America Online. Because the rates change daily, the current exchange rates could be quite different from day to day.

The exchange rate is typically expressed in terms of one U.S. dollar. Using the European Union's common currency, the euro, as an example, a rate of .8850 means that one U.S. dollar is worth .8850 euros. The inverse of that rate (1 divided by .8850 equals 1.13) expresses the exchange rate in terms of dollar per euro—so 1.13 U.S. dollars ($1.13) are worth one euro. The latter rate would be used when converting euros to U.S. dollars.

It is important for businesses to watch the value of the dollar when making purchases in overseas markets in order to get the most for their money.

Critical Thinking

1. Why would the value of foreign currency change daily?
2. How can businesses get the most for their money overseas by watching the exchange rate?

(Answer: Prices, quality, services, and sales.)

3. What is the importance of a business's reputation, value of brand names, and the choices of stores when deciding where to buy items? (Answer: Businesses with good reputations are concerned about matching the appropriate goods with customers' needs. If you buy from a business with a good reputation, you can usually rely on its salespeople to help you make wise selections. Recognizing national brand names can help you expect uniform quality, even when brand-name goods are bought from different businesses, and makes comparison shopping possible.)

4. How does a good consumer decide when to buy? (Answer: As a good shopper, the consumer takes time when making purchases, buys when prices are lowest, avoids impulse buying through the use of shopping lists.)

5. What are the steps a consumer can take to become an efficient shopper? (Answer: Plan purchases carefully and make a shopping list, use the Yellow Pages of the telephone book to call businesses to find out if they have what you need to avoid wasting fuel, plan the route of trips to avoid wasting fuel.)

6. What is the Consumer Price Index (CPI)? (Answer: The Consumer Price Index (CPI) shows the changes in the average prices of goods and services bought by consumers over a period of time. Pay particular

GLOBAL PERSPECTIVES

Global Perspectives gives students an opportunity to visualize the various places around the globe that are described. This feature will also describe business practices that are different around the world.

CRITICAL THINKING

1. There are various answers, such as the stock market, world events, and even weather conditions. All of these factors influence the exchange rate on a daily basis.
2. If time permits, businesses can watch the daily rates until they can make the exchange and get the most for their money.

attention to the comparison of unit prices among products.)

RETEACH

Bring in labels from various products, both brand and generic, and let students analyze the unit prices on each.

ENRICH

Direct students to read the Global Perspectives in this chapter. Videotape commercials from television. Play them and have students identify which products would be a good consumer choice and why. Another enrichment activity might be to make a list of household cleaning items. Then have students determine if it is necessary for each to be high quality, such as bleach. Does it matter if it is a national brand or store brand? Critical thinking and analysis skills are important for students to determine how to get the most for their money.

SUMMARIZE

Have students create their own checklist for becoming a good consumer. Select several of the better ones and display on the bulletin board.

EVALUATE

- Assign Activities and Projects for Chapter 23.
- Administer the printed test or ExamView for Chapter 23.
- Assign School-To-Work/SCANS portfolio activities for Unit 7.

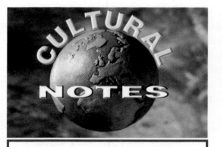

Cultural diversity in the workplace means there is a variety of workers from various racial, ethnic, and religion backgrounds.

Internet commerce has been growing rapidly, with many businesses reporting a doubling or tripling of sales each year. Business to business sales over the Internet are expected to approach $1 trillion annually early in the 21st century.

products. Second, brand names make comparison shopping possible.

Some stores have their own brand names called *store brands* or *house brands*. For example, Craftsman has been one of the brand names on tools sold by Sears. Store brands are usually sold at a lower cost than national brands. Buying store brands, therefore, may often save you money and offer good quality at the same time.

Some supermarkets carry unbranded items at reduced prices, called *generic products*. Generic products are less expensive because they do not require advertising and fancy packaging, thus saving the manufacturer money. These savings are passed on to

consumers. The labels on generic products are often written with large bold print identifying the contents. There are sometimes only minor differences in quality and uniformity between generic and branded products.

Types of Businesses

When deciding where to buy, the consumer has a wide variety of choices available. The stores that sell goods are organized with unique characteristics. The choice of which type of store will depend upon the consumer's wants and needs.

Full-service stores offer a wide variety of goods and emphasize customer service. For example, they are likely to have a personal shopper, make deliveries, and wrap gifts. These stores, which are often called department stores, will usually have higher prices. **Discount stores**, on the other hand, emphasize lower prices on their products. Most discount stores base their success on a high vol-

Why might a factory outlet store be able to offer goods at bargain prices?

Basic Skills-Writing

Language arts skills are an important component of good writing skills. Students should learn to paraphrase, write complete sentences, and identify adverbs and the words they modify. For additional practice in language arts skills, direct students to answer the Decision-Making Strategies questions at the end of the chapter. Students should write the answers in their own words and in complete sentences. This activity also requires more than a short objective-type response. Therefore, it provides ideal practice in writing paragraphs. To further practice language arts skills, ask students to underline all adverbs and circle the words they modify in their answers.

E-Commerce for Shopping

Do you need a birthday gift for a friend, but can't get to a store? No problem! As you probably already know, e-commerce brings shopping to your computer screen.

Online shoppers are often loyal to specific businesses and brands, but they will switch to other businesses and brands if the online shopping experience is not satisfactory. The main reasons consumers report for not shopping online are security concerns, web sites that are slow or do not work, and a belief that they may receive poor customer service if there are problems with the order. Businesses continually work to reassure customers that the shopping experience will be positive and trouble free.

While shopping online continues to grow in popularity, the Internet also creates a mar-ketplace with expanded consumer fraud. Internet Fraud Watch of the National Consumers League reports that millions of consumer dollars are lost each year to Internet fraud. The most common of these scams are online auctions, Internet access services, work-at-home schemes, advance fee loans, credit-card offers, and phony vacation promotions.

Critical Thinking

Survey people who purchase items online three or more times a month. Obtain information about the types of products purchased, reasons for buying online, and costs compared to other types of stores. Create a report with graphs to summarize your findings.

Consumer Buying Assistance Web Sites
Consumer information from federal agencies:
www.consumer.gov
Consumer assistance:
www.consumerworld.org
Recent articles from *Consumer Reports*:
www.consumerreports.org
Automobile buying information:
www.edmunds.com and
www.kbb.com
Internet fraud information:
www.fraud.org

ume of sales and low prices. If service is not important to you, this may be where you should shop. Stores that have a special line of products for sale are known as **specialty stores**. They carry a wide variety of products in a narrow line such as sporting goods, jewelry, and women's shoes. Some specialty stores may also be discount stores. **Factory outlet stores** are becoming more and more popular and often have a reputation for selling high-quality merchandise at low prices. Products are direct from the factory and sometimes have minor flaws.

In food retailing, there are three types of stores. The first is the **supermarket**, a large, full-service store that carries a wide variety of national, store, and generic brands at moderate prices. The **warehouse market** is a no-frills food outlet emphasizing the sale of large quantities at reasonable prices. **Convenience stores** are small stores that emphasize the sale of food items, an accessible location, and long operating hours. These stores usually stock popular items at higher prices.

DECIDING TO BUY

Timing is the key to making wise purchases. The smart consumer takes time to plan purchases and buys at the right time. Also, the smart consumer avoids buying on impulse and is efficient when making purchases.

Take Your Time

"I just don't have the time" is the complaint of many people. It is often tempting to spend only a little time shopping. This is usually not a good practice. Spending more time planning purchases usually results in savings that reward you for the time spent. Taking your time usually means slowing down and giving yourself a chance to look for the best values. If you learn to pace yourself, you will probably find that your money goes farther toward buying the goods and services you need and want. As a good shopper, you should refuse to be hurried into buying anything. In this way, you avoid buying things that you really do not want or need.

TEACHING STRATEGIES

Alternate Modalities
Auditory Learner

To reinforce the learning of making wise economic decisions, the auditory learner should verbally repeat the steps for making buying decisions.

Time Your Purchases

For some goods and services, prices are lowest at predictable times. Good consumers know about those times and take advantage of them. Certain seasons and conditions favor goods and services being sold at reduced prices. Here are just a few examples:

- When fresh fruits and vegetables are at their peak, they are usually lower in price.
- Automobiles are usually less expensive at the end of the model year (late summer) before the new models are displayed.
- Winter clothing is often on sale in January.
- Firewood often costs less in the summer.

Consumer magazines and newspaper articles, as well as radio and television programs for consumers, can help you add to this list.

Avoid Being Impulsive

The opposite of spending time and thought in shopping is buying too rapidly without much thought. This type of buying is called **impulse buying** and should be avoided to keep from making costly mistakes. Impulse buying often happens when an item is attractively displayed where customers are likely to see it, such as near the checkout counter. Sometimes impulse buying is harmless. Purchasing a small item like a bag of popcorn, a small gift for a friend, or a magazine is a pleasant part of life. The cost is small and the item is usually worth the price. However, buying more expensive items such as clothing, electronic equipment, jewelry, or vacations on impulse can be costly. You may not really need the item, or it might not be the best value for the price. Best values are discovered by collecting information about an item and then carefully shopping for it.

One of the best ways to avoid impulse buying is to make a shopping list and stick to it. Many people use lists when shopping in grocery stores and supermarkets. Since most consumers are open to suggestion, an attractive display of products can tempt them to buy something that they had not planned to buy. You can save money if you make and stick to a shopping list whether it is for groceries, hardware, or clothing.

EFFICIENT SHOPPING

Skillful consumers are efficient in their shopping activities. They save time, energy, and money by planning. You can become a skillful shopper, too, by following these steps.

1. Plan your purchases carefully and make a shopping list. As you already know, a consumer with a list makes better decisions in the store and avoids impulse buying.

2. Use the telephone to help you. Using the Yellow Pages and calling businesses to find out if they have what you need is a very efficient practice. Often you can order goods and services by telephone.

3. You can save fuel by carefully planning shopping trips. Combining several purchases in one trip can save you time and money.

EFFECT OF ECONOMIC CONDITIONS ON BUYING DECISIONS

Prices of goods and services are changing all the time. These changes in the value of a dollar have been a source of confusion and frustration to consumers for many years.

A **price index** can help consumers better understand what is happening to prices in our economy. A price index is a series of figures showing how prices have changed over a period of years. The federal government's Bureau of Labor Statistics (BLS) publishes several price indexes. These indexes are published in an effort to establish an objective measure of the economy and to help guide the consumer.

The **Consumer Price Index (CPI)** shows the changes in the average prices of goods and services bought by consumers over a period of time. Actually, the BLS compiles and publishes two CPIs. The CPI-W (wage earners and clerical workers) represents the

Basic Skills-Reading

SCANS

Direct students to the end-of-chapter activities. Review each activity heading and discuss how each contributes to the understanding of the chapter. The Student Activity Worksheet, Basic Skills—Reading, in the School-To Work/SCANS Activity Masters may be used to serve as a guideline for discussion of each of the points.

buying experience of urban wage earners and clerical workers. It includes approximately 32 percent of the population. The CPI-U is a broader index. It covers about 80 percent of the population. The CPI-U (all urban consumers) includes such diverse groups as salaried workers, the unemployed, the retired, and the self-employed. The CPI-U is the more frequently quoted of the two.

The BLS checks prices throughout the country on a collection of goods and services often referred to as a "market basket."

Categories of items included in the "market basket" are purchases you or your family might make of such things as clothing, food, fuel, and housing. As the average level of prices for a number of typical items changes, the CPI either goes up or down.

Figure 23-1 shows the percentage increase in the Consumer Price Index (CPI-U) during the years 1988-2001. Changes in prices may not seem important from day to day, but over a number of years the changes may be very important.

FIGURE 23-1   What was the trend for consumer prices in the last decade?

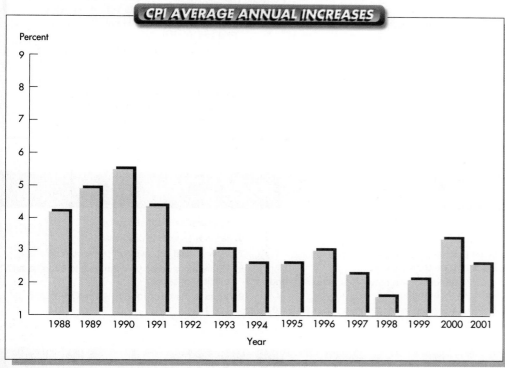

CPI AVERAGE ANNUAL INCREASES

Source: U.S. Department of Labor, Bureau of Labor Statistics, CPI Detailed Report (Washington, D.C.: U.S. Government Printing Office)

Basic Skills-Math

SCANS

Integrating math across the curriculum is an important element in contemporary education. As a part of end-of-chapter activities, Calculate Business Data enables students to apply their math skills. Appendix B: Math Review, Appendix C: Determining Percentages and Interest in Business, and Appendix D: Using Measurements in Business, also apply arithmetic and math skills.

REVIEW YOUR READING

1. Identify your needs or wants.
2. Unit pricing helps the consumer compare value among the various brands and sizes of the same product. If you know the unit price of a product you can better compare prices, regardless of the cost of the various packages.
3. Promotional sale items are sold below their regular cost. Clearance sales are to get rid of merchandise the store no longer wants to carry.
4. Store brands are brand names used by the store that sells the merchandise. National brands are names given to products that are advertised nationally and sold in almost every community in many different stores.
5. You can expect uniform quality, and national brands make comparison shopping possible.
6. Unbranded items sold at reduced prices.
7. Make a shopping list and stick to it.
8. Plan purchases carefully and make a shopping list; use the Yellow Pages section from the telephone book to call businesses to find out if they have what you need; carefully plan your shopping trip to save fuel.
9. The CPI-W (wage earners and clerical workers) represents the buying experience of urban wage earners and clerical workers and includes approximately 32 percent of the population. The CPI-U is a broader index and covers about 80 percent of the population. The CPI-U (all urban consumers) includes such diverse groups as salaried workers, the unemployed, the retired, and the self-employed. The CPI-U is the more frequently quoted of the two.

COMMUNICATE BUSINESS CONCEPTS

10. We will buy what our values dictate, whether it be quality or price or a combination of the two.
11. Most consumers consider such factors as price, convenience, reputation, variety, quality, and service when making decisions about where to shop.

BUSINESS NOTES

1. Deciding to buy should involve identifying your needs or wants, knowing the choices that are available to you, determining the measure of satisfaction of your needs and wants, considering the alternatives, and making the decision to buy.
2. Comparison shoppers will evaluate price, quality, service, and sales when making a purchase.
3. When deciding where to purchase items, a consumer should consider a business's reputation, value of brand names, and the choices of stores available.
4. As a good shopper, the consumer takes time when making purchases, buys when prices are lowest, and avoids impulse buying through the use of shopping lists.
5. To become an efficient shopper, make a shopping list, use the Yellow Pages of the telephone book to call businesses to find out if they have what you are looking for, and plan trips to avoid wasting fuel.
6. The Consumer Price Index (CPI) shows the changes in the average prices of goods and services bought by consumers over a period of time.

REVIEW YOUR READING

1. What is the first step in the buying process?
2. How does unit pricing help consumers?
3. What is the difference between promotional sales and clearance sales?
4. What is the difference between a national brand and a store brand?
5. How can learning to recognize a national brand help you as a consumer?
6. What are generic products?
7. How should you avoid impulse buying?
8. Name three steps you can take to become an efficient shopper.
9. What is the difference between CPI-W and CPI-U?

COMMUNICATE BUSINESS CONCEPTS

10. Explain how values influence purchases.
11. What are some factors you might consider when deciding where to shop?
12. When would you consider an impulse purchase a harmless activity?
13. What are some "market basket" items that you and your family might purchase?

12. Impulse purchases are harmless when they are for very inexpensive items. For example, buying a pack of sugarless chewing gum at the grocery store checkout lane is harmless.
13. Clothing, food, fuel, housing, and other consumer items.

DEVELOP YOUR BUSINESS LANGUAGE

For each numbered item, find the term that has the same meaning.

14. Stores that offer a wide variety of goods and emphasize customer service.

15. Buying too rapidly without much thought.

16. Large stores that sell large quantities of goods at low prices.

17. Comparing the price, quality, and services of one product with those of another product.

18. Stores that carry a wide variety of products in a narrow line.

19. A name given to a product or service to distinguish it from other similar products or services.

20. Stores selling products at low prices that sometimes have minor flaws.

21. A large, full-service food store with a wide variety of national, store, and generic brands at moderate prices.

22. The price per unit of measure of a product.

23. A no-frills food outlet emphasizing the sale of large quantities of items at reasonable prices.

24. A sale in which a price reduction is used to sell items that a store no longer wishes to carry in stock.

25. A small store that emphasizes the sale of food items, an accessible location, and long operating hours.

26. A sale in which items are sold below their regular prices to publicize the opening of a new store or location and to build acceptance for new products.

27. Shows changes in the average prices of goods and services bought by consumers over a period of time.

28. Series of figures showing how prices have changed over a period of years.

KEY TERMS

brand name
clearance sales
comparison shopping
Consumer Price Index
convenience stores
discount stores
factory outlet stores
full-service stores
impulse buying
price index
promotional sales
specialty stores
supermarket
unit price
warehouse market

DECISION-MAKING STRATEGIES

Fredrico wants to reduce the amount of money he and his family spend on food. Now they make many purchases at a local convenience store. A supermarket 5 miles away offers a larger variety of products with national brands. A warehouse market 30 miles away sells in larger quantities but carries only generic brands.

29. Develop one question Fredrico should ask to complete each of the steps in the decision-making process.

30. List one advantage and one disadvantage of each of the three choices.

DEVELOP YOUR BUSINESS LANGUAGE

14. full-service store
15. impulse buying
16. discount stores
17. comparison shopping
18. specialty stores
19. brand name
20. factory outlet stores
21. supermarket
22. unit price
23. warehouse market
24. clearance sale
25. convenience stores
26. promotional sales
27. Consumer Price Index
28. price index

DECISION-MAKING STRATEGIES

29. Possible questions could include: How much money does Fredrico want to save? Can Fredrico afford to spend more time shopping to save money? What are the differences in quality, services, and prices among the three stores? Can they make purchases less frequently and use larger quantities without wasting them? Which store will provide the best food value for the family?

30. Convenience store—advantage: can buy frequently; disadvantage: highest prices. Supermarket—advantage: national brands and more choices: disadvantage: longer shopping time. Warehouse market—advantage: very low prices; disadvantage: quality of generic brands.

31. (a) December cost $235 − January cost $150 = $85 (b) Sale price $150 − Store's cost $120 = $30.

32. (a) $3.20 ÷ 12 = $0.267 per ounce; 6 × 1.2 = 7.2, $2.80 ÷ 7.2 = $0.389 per ounce; 16 × 1.5 = 24, $5.20 ÷ 24 = $0.217 per ounce (b) the 1½-pound container (c) She may like the convenience of the single-serving packages or may not be able to eat the full 1½ pounds of cereal while it is still fresh.

33. (a) 10 kilometers × 0.6 = 6 miles @ 0.40 cents per mile. Round trip to specialty store = $2.40 (b) 100 kilometers × 0.6 = 60 miles @ 0.40 cents per mile. Round trip to discount store = $24.00. $154.00 Specialty Store Price + 2.40 Specialty Store Trip = $156.40 Total Cost. $135.00 Discount Store Price + 24.00 Discount Store Trip = $159.00 Total Cost. $159.00 − 156.40 = $2.60. The consumer would save $2.60 and driving time by buying the oven at the specialty store.

34. (a) $979.00 × 0.20 = $195.80; $979.00 − $195.80 = $783.20 sale price (b) $304.00 ÷ 0.80 = $380.00 original price.

TECHNOLOGY APPLICATION

In this activity, students use a computer to solve a business problem using a file that is provided on the data CD that accompanies *Intro to Business*. Instructions for using the data CD are included in a **README** file on the disk. Solutions are provided on the Instructor's Resource CD.

31. Following her arrival in the United States from Shanghai, China, Ms. Deng Hui wanted to shop for a new coat. She chose a coat that cost $235. Since it was during the month of December when she was ready to make this purchase, new acquaintances in the United States told her she could buy a similar coat on sale for $150 if she could only wait until January.
    a. If Deng Hui waited until January to buy a coat, how much would she save?
    b. If the clothing store purchased the coat at $120 and sold it to Deng Hui for $150, what is the difference between the store's cost and selling price of the coat?

32. Danielle saw a package of her favorite cereal priced at $3.20 for 12 ounces. The same cereal priced at $2.80 was packaged in a group of six single-serving boxes. Each individual box held 1.2 ounces of cereal. She also saw a large plastic container of the cereal that cost $5.20 for 1½ pounds.
    a. What is the unit price for each of the three choices?
    b. Which is the better buy if price is the only consideration?
    c. Why might Danielle be willing to pay more for one of the other two choices?

33. A consumer has two choices regarding where to buy a microwave oven. One option is an appliance specialty store. This store is located 10 kilometers round-trip from the consumer's home. A microwave oven can be purchased there for $154. A second option is a discount store located 100 kilometers round-trip from the consumer's home. The identical microwave oven can be purchased there for $135. Assume that the consumer's car costs 40 cents per mile to drive and that either purchase would require one round-trip to the store. Based on the price of the microwave oven and transportation costs alone (not service, reputation, etc.), which is the better buy?

34. Western Furniture and Appliance is moving to a new store. To avoid having to move a lot of merchandise, it is having a pre-moving clearance sale. Western has advertised that it will reduce the price of all merchandise in the store by 20 percent for one day.
    a. What would be the sale price of a $979 sofa?
    b. A customer paid $304 for a television set. What was the original price of the television set?

TECHNOLOGY APPLICATION

Using the *Intro to Business* Data CD and your spreadsheet program software, select problem CH23. After the problem appears on your screen, complete the following activities. Then, after you have completed each step, display or print the completed spreadsheet for each activity. If you do not have a printer available, answer the questions before you leave the computer.

35. For each size box of detergent, enter a formula to calculate the price per ounce. Answer the following questions:
    a. Which size box has the lowest price per ounce?
    b. Which size box has the highest price per ounce?

36. Enter formulas to sum the prices of all the boxes and the sizes of all the boxes. Answer the following questions:
    a. What is the sum of the prices?
    b. What is the sum of the sizes?

37. Enter two formulas to find the average price per ounce for all the boxes. One formula should use the sums of the prices and the sizes; the other formula should use the unit prices of the boxes found in Question 35.
    a. What is the average price per ounce using the sum of the prices and the sizes?
    b. What is the average price per ounce using the unit prices of the boxes?

COMMUNICATING for SUCCESS

THE MEDIA—USE IT TO YOUR ADVANTAGE

The word "media" is a broad term used to identify various forms of communication that reach a wide public audience. Typically, media include newspapers, television, radio, and other printed materials such as magazines, newsletters, and journals. The media are important because they have the potential to influence how the public believes, interprets, or defines an event, situation, or individual.

Various media are used to convey messages about products, personnel, and events. The media are also used as a primary form of advertising.

Consumers and business leaders are often required to interpret or analyze media messages and their implications. For example, stockholders may predict an increase in their company's value if a dynamic new leader is announced in *The Wall Street Journal*. Similarly, an announcement of a factory closing may hurt the public image of a company.

One of the most frequently used forms of communication with the media is the press release, also known as a "news release." A press release contains information a business wants communicated to the media. The following five tips will help ensure your news release will be successful and appealing:

- Be brief and clear.
- Include who, what, when, where, why, and how.
- Give details in order of importance, starting with the most important.
- Provide your preferred release date.
- Include the name of a contact person.

The generally accepted press release format includes the following points of style:

- The release should be double spaced.
- It should be printed on company letterhead.
- Special instructions should be typed in all capital letters across the top of the release.
- The release should end with a "-30-" or "###" to indicate completion of information.

Effective use of the media can be a powerful business communication tool, particularly in refining the public image of your business.

CRITICAL THINKING
1. Name three types of media.
2. How does business and industry use the media?

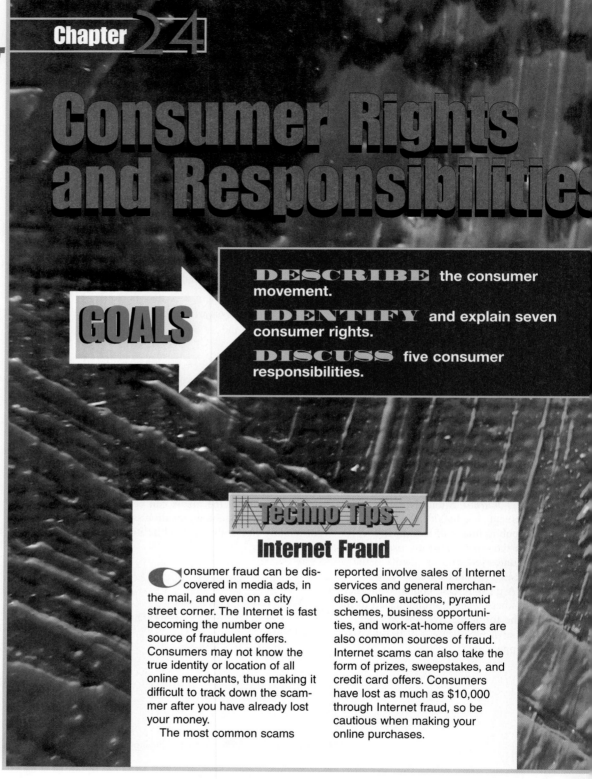

Chapter 24

Consumer Rights and Responsibilities

The consumer movement is described briefly in this chapter and followed by a discussion of the seven rights and five responsibilities of every consumer.

Resources for Teachers
- Lesson Plans
- School-To-Work/SCANS Activity Masters
- Spanish Resources
- Instructor's Resource CD

Assessment
- Chapter and Unit Tests, Ch. 24
- ExamView, Ch. 24

Media/Technology
- Applying Technology Data CD
- PowerPoint slides
- Business Connection CD
- Videotape

Activity Masters and Workbooks
- Activities and Projects, Ch. 24
- Internet Activity Masters
- Business Math Activity Masters
- Communications Activity Masters
- International Business Activity Masters
- Ethics Activity Masters

GOALS

DESCRIBE the consumer movement.

IDENTIFY and explain seven consumer rights.

DISCUSS five consumer responsibilities.

Techno Tips

Internet Fraud

Consumer fraud can be discovered in media ads, in the mail, and even on a city street corner. The Internet is fast becoming the number one source of fraudulent offers. Consumers may not know the true identity or location of all online merchants, thus making it difficult to track down the scammer after you have already lost your money.

The most common scams reported involve sales of Internet services and general merchandise. Online auctions, pyramid schemes, business opportunities, and work-at-home offers are also common sources of fraud. Internet scams can also take the form of prizes, sweepstakes, and credit card offers. Consumers have lost as much as $10,000 through Internet fraud, so be cautious when making your online purchases.

Techno Tips Students need to know the latest technologies and develop cutting edge Internet skills for use in current jobs, future careers, or in their homes. TechnoTips introduces students to today's cutting edge technologies and provides them with important Internet skills. Feature topics concentrate on Internet-specific technologies and computer or other hi-tech innovations for use by businesses and consumers.

Monica Robinson bought an expensive leather purse. But, unfortunately, after she used the purse for several weeks, the zipper broke. She took the purse back to the store from which it was purchased. Monica very politely and calmly described to the salesperson how the zipper broke. She also had her receipt from the purchase to show that the purse was only two months old. It was decided that the store would pay for the repair of the zipper. It took one week to repair the zipper, at which time Monica got her purse back as good as new.

This consumer problem had a pleasant ending; most of them do. It is usually not necessary to get upset or angry in order to get satisfactory results from businesses. In fact, most businesses are eager to solve problems that consumers have. They want happy, satisfied customers who will return.

Solving consumer problems is usually a matter of practicing good two-way communication. It is up to you to let the business know what you want. The job of the business is to tell you what you can expect to get. If both consumer and business are honest and fair, the problem can be solved.

YOUR CONSUMER RIGHTS

A pleasant relationship between the consumer and business has not always existed in the marketplace. In past years some businesses were viewed as often trying to take advantage of consumers. False claims were sometimes made about products, prices were often too high, and some products were unsafe. To fight against unfair business practices, consumers joined together to demand fair treatment from businesses. This banding together gave rise to what is known as the **consumer movement**. As a result of this movement, public and private agencies, policies, laws, and regulations were developed to protect consumer interests.

A highlight of the consumer movement came in 1962 when President John F. Kennedy presented his Consumer Bill of Rights. He declared that every consumer has the following rights:

1. The right to be informed—to be given the correct information needed to make an informed choice.

2. The right to safety—to be protected from goods and services that are hazardous to health or life.

3. The right to choose—to be assured of the availability of a variety of goods and services at competitive prices.

4. The right to be heard—to be assured that consumer interests will be fully considered by government when laws are being developed and enforced.

In 1969, President Richard M. Nixon added a fifth right to the list; in 1975, President Gerald R. Ford added the sixth; and in 1994, President William Clinton added the seventh.

5. The right to a remedy—the assurance of the right to legal correction of wrongs committed against consumers.

6. The right to consumer education—to learn about consumer rights and responsibilities as economic citizens.

7. The right to service—to be entitled to convenience, courtesy, and responsiveness to problems and needs.

EXERCISING YOUR CONSUMER RIGHTS

As a consumer you have the right to expect honesty and fair treatment from businesses. Few businesses are ever intentionally ty as students record their impressions. Show the relevance of consumer responsibilities and the importance for students to respect these.

EXPLORE THIS/INDEPENDENT PRACTICE Before assigning independent practice material for any chapter, students should be expected to read the textbook material carefully. In view of the fact that all students vary widely in their ability to read effectively, it is advisable to have the students read the entire chapter, or sections thereof, silently in class if the material has not been previously read in connection with homework assignments.

After students have read the chapter, ask them to complete the Chapter Review questions. Develop Your Business Language is an excellent way to improve students' vocabulary. Only words introduced in the chapter are used in the vocabulary exercises. The Review Your Reading questions can be used to check students' ability to comprehend what they have read. The Communicate Business Concepts section affords an opportunity for students to apply to practical life situations the information gained from reading the chapter. By completing the problems under Calculate Business Data, students will be able to strengthen and refine their abilities in mathematics. Technology Application allows students to demonstrate skill in using word processing, spreadsheet, and database software. Decision-Making Strategies contains material to challenge students to utilize the decision-making model explained in Chapter 1 for problem solving.

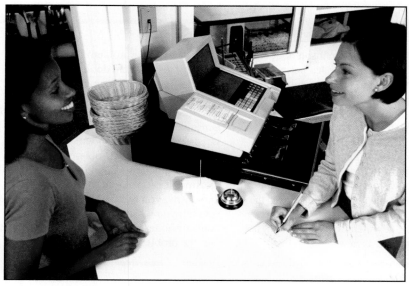

What are some consumer rights that you have exercised?

dishonest. However, being a skillful consumer means that you know the Consumer Bill of Rights and how to exercise them.

The Right to Be Informed

Most products and services are usually described in advertisements, on labels, or by a salesperson. You have a right to know what the product or service is and what it will do for you.

There are situations in which false information is given to a customer in an effort to make a sale. This type of dishonesty is known as **fraud**. For example, if a salesperson knowingly sells you a car on which the odometer has been turned back 30,000 miles, a fraud has occurred.

However, all product information you receive cannot be expected to be perfectly accurate. Suppose, for example, you were looking for a used car for transportation to and from school. If a salesperson told you she thought the car would get about 20 miles

to the gallon but it only got 18, you were not deceived. The salesperson may not have been accurate in judging gas mileage, but no guarantee was made.

When a salesperson exaggerates the good qualities of a product and says, "It's the best" or "It's a great buy," there is no fraud. If, however, the salesperson tells you a car has new brakes and it does not, this is fraud.

The Right to Safety

Consumers have a right to be safe from harm associated with using products or services. Several agencies work to assure the safety of consumers. The Consumer Product Safety Commission (CPSC) has the authority to set safety standards, to ban hazardous products, and to recall dangerous products from the market.

The Food and Drug Administration (FDA) makes certain that food, drug, and cosmetic products are not harmful to consumers. This federal government agency enforces laws and regulations that prevent the distribution of unsafe or misbranded foods, drugs, and cosmetics. The FDA also works to assure that product labels do not mislead consumers.

The United States Department of Agriculture (USDA) also helps ensure consumer

As an informed consumer, do not sign any agreements that you have not read or do not understand.

Basic Skills-Speaking

We can help students develop speaking skills by teaching them how to organize their ideas in a manner that is appropriate for the situation. Before speaking to a group, students should know their audience, plan their presentation, rehearse, then make the presentation. Discuss characteristics of an audience and how that audience plays a role in the performance of the speaker. Developing a speech through an outline is an excellent planning tool, and every speech should have an introduction, body, and conclusion. Assign several students the topic of "My Rights as a Consumer" to prepare and present a speech. Give students the Student Activity Worksheet, Basic Skills—Speaking, in the School-To-Work/SCANS Activity Masters, to serve as a guideline for preparation of a speech.

SCANS

Gopher is a program that uses a series of menus to lead users to files of information. Gopher is named for the Golden Gophers of the University of Minnesota, where the program was developed.

safety by setting standards for the grading of farm products that are sold from one state to another. The USDA also controls the processing, inspection, and labeling of meat products with grades according to their quality.

The Right to Choose

The right of consumers to choose from a variety of goods and services has become well established. In fact, one of the main activities of the Federal Trade Commission (FTC) is to prevent one firm from using unfair practices to force competing firms out of business. When a business has no competitors and controls the market for a product or

service, it is said to have a *monopoly*. Competing firms encourage customers to buy from them by offering a variety of products and services at various prices. By driving away this competition, monopolies limit the right to choose.

The Right to Be Heard

Most businesses have a customer service department to hear the concerns or complaints of customers. Some smaller businesses have a specific person assigned to that responsibility. Businesses are usually happy to take care of problems you have with their products or services.

There are several federal government agencies to assure your right to be heard. The Federal Trade Commission (FTC) also protects your right to be heard. As a consumer, you can complain directly to the FTC if you believe that any of your rights which come under its protection have been violated. The FTC regulates advertising and encourages informative and truthful advertising.

State governments also support public agencies that are interested in hearing consumers' concerns. Usually the Office of the Attorney General and the Department of Consumer Affairs have some responsibility for protecting the rights of consumers. They

What are some responsibilities regarding the safe use of products?

Net Facts provides information and definitions of terms for the Internet. The more information that students have about the Internet, the better equipped they will be to use this resource. In the Internet Activity Masters, there is an Internet Activity Worksheet for each unit. You can use these activities to give students experience with finding information online. Options for assigning this activity are as follows:

1. **Provide students with a list of addresses of resources for this activity;**
2. **Assign students to conduct their own searches; or**
3. **Use the addresses provided on the Internet Activity Worksheet.**

You should complete the activity yourself before assigning it to resolve any discrepancies that may arise.

The Chapter Review questions at the end of the chapter vary in level of difficulty. For a basic assignment, consider Develop Your Business Language and Review Your Reading. For an average assignment, consider the basic assignment plus Communicate Business Concepts and Calculate Business Data. For an enhanced assignment, try the average assignment plus Technology Application and Decision-Making Strategies.

TEACHING STRATEGIES

Special Needs
Gifted Students

Students who are gifted often enjoy the challenge of getting to the heart of a problem. Assign students to analyze national brand name labels and store brand labels from products that you have brought in. Labels should be analyzed according to detail of contents, instructions, etc., to compare quality.

Review the goals at the beginning of the chapter and the Business Notes at the end of the chapter. Restate each as a question and have students respond orally. For students who may have difficulty providing answers, assign the reteaching activities that follow. Enrichment activities also may be assigned where appropriate.

1. What is the consumer movement? (Answer: The consumer movement was created to fight unfair business practices. As a result of this movement, public and private agencies, policies, laws, and regulations were developed.)
2. What are the seven consumer rights? (Answer: The right to be informed, the right to safety, the right to choose, the right to be heard, the right to a remedy, the right to consumer education, and the right to service.)
3. What are the five consumer responsibilities? (Answer: Be honest, be reasonable, report unethical practices, be informed, and be involved.)

RETEACH

Bring in warranties and have students analyze by making two lists. The first list should have all statements that give specific information or instruction. The second list should contain vague statements. Using the information presented in this chapter, ask students to translate these warranties. What are their rights as consumers?

can prosecute businesses for violation of state consumer-protection laws. These offices also inspect advertising practices. The State Office of the Attorney General and the State Department of Consumer Affairs can also handle other types of consumer matters such as automobile-repair problems, credit problems, and door-to-door sales practices.

In addition to publicly supported consumer protection agencies, there are some privately funded groups that help to make certain you are heard. Perhaps the best known of these is the Better Business Bureau. The Better Business Bureau is chiefly concerned with problems arising from false advertising or misrepresented products and services. If you believe that your consumer rights have been violated by such practices, you can get help from the Better Business Bureau in your community. The bureau will usually ask you to report your problem in writing so that it can get all of the details correct. The Better Business Bureau will then try to persuade the business to remedy the problem or fulfill its promises for the product or service in question. Most businesses willingly carry out the bureau's requests.

There are a number of other private organizations that help protect your right to be heard. Groups of similar businesses frequently form trade associations. **Trade associations** are made up of businesses engaged in the same type of business. Many associations establish standards of quality for the products that their members manufacture. These standards help customers receive the quality they expect when purchasing a product. Some trade associations also publish codes of ethics that members are urged to follow.

The Right to a Remedy

As a result of the consumer movement, many new laws were passed. These included the Fair Packaging and Labeling Act, National Traffic and Motor Vehicle Safety Act, Truth in Food Labeling Act, and Fair Debt Collec-

LEGAL PERSPECTIVES

E-COMMERCE AND YOUR CONSUMER RIGHTS

With the increasing popularity of e-commerce via the Internet and interactive TV comes the concern for accompanying consumer rights. What rights does a purchaser have after ordering goods from an Internet web site or a TV shopping channel?

Federal laws that protect Internet and TV shoppers are the same as those that govern purchases made by telephone. The seller must send you the goods within 30 days or within another time period specifically stated by the company. The 30-day delivery clock starts ticking as soon as the company has received your credit card number or a valid check. If there is going to be a delay, the seller must notify you, either by phone or by mail. You then have the right to cancel your order.

If an unreceived or returned item is bille to your credit card, you have 60 days to di pute it. The credit card company then has days to respond. Within 90 days of your le ter, the card company must investigate the matter and explain to you why it believes bill is correct or incorrect.

You don't have to pay the part of your credit card bill under dispute until the mat is resolved. But to avoid finance charges, must pay the rest of your bill on time.

Critical Thinking
1. Do you think a consumer has any rights beyond those explicitly stated in this fea ture?
2. Do you know of any unethical practices associated with e-commerce either on th part of businesses or consumers?

LEGAL PERSPECTIVES

Drawing conclusions from facts or promises is an important thinking skill for today's employees. One of the most pervasive ways that government affects business is through the legal system. The law protects both individuals and businesses against those who threaten society. It also spells out accepted ways of performing many essential business activities—along with penalties for failure to comply. Legal Perspectives gives students an opportunity to study legal situations and draw appropriate conclusions.

CRITICAL THINKING
1. Yes. All of those guaranteed by law.
2. Answers will vary.

tion Practices Act. All of these laws were designed in part to provide assurances that consumers could seek a legal remedy if they were wronged.

Another form of remedy that consumers have is the protection provided through a guarantee. With some purchases, a consumer can expect a guarantee, or a warranty. A **guarantee** is a promise by the manufacturer or dealer, usually in writing, that a product is of a certain quality. A guarantee may apply to the entire item or only to some parts of it. It may promise that defective parts will be replaced only if a problem occurs during a specified period of time. No guarantee, however, covers damages caused by misuse.

When making a purchase, a skillful consumer asks about a guarantee. A guarantee is frequently in the form of statements like these: "The working parts of this watch are guaranteed for one year." "This sweater will not shrink more than 3 percent." These kinds of guarantees are sometimes called **express warranties**. They are made orally or in writing and promise a specific quality of performance.

You should insist on receiving a copy of the guarantee when you buy an item. You can also require the business to put in writing any other guarantees that have been offered. Written guarantees are useful if you need to return a faulty product. Guarantees are sometimes included in ads for the product. Keep a copy of the ad as evidence of the guarantee. Read the guarantee carefully to find out just what is covered and for what period of time.

Some guarantees are not written. They are called **implied warranties**. They are imposed by law and are understood to apply even though they have not been stated either orally or in writing. In general, the law requires certain standards to be met. For

Buyer's remorse occurs when a consumer buys something and later regrets the purchase.

All 50 states have passed "lemon" laws to protect car buyers from being stuck with malfunctioning, problem-ridden vehicles.

example, it is implied that health care products purchased over-the-counter at a pharmacy will not harm you when used according to the directions.

The Right to Consumer Education

Traditionally, the focus of consumer education programs has been on individual decision making related to the purchase of goods and services. Although consumer buying decisions are important, educated consumers need to understand how their decisions affect our economy as well. Today consumer education focuses on consumer decisions that relate to the interaction between consumers and producers in our economic system. Educated consumers are aware that their decisions not only affect their lifestyles, but also have economic implications.

The Right to Service

The most recent addition to the list of consumer rights focuses on service to consumers. The right to service suggests consumers can expect convenience, courtesy, and responsiveness to consumer problems and needs. This

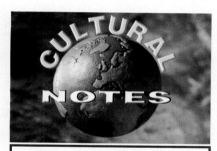

Until the late 1700s, Spanish money was the main currency in America.

right to service is as much a reminder to business as it is a right of consumers. The right to service encourages businesses to take steps necessary to ensure that products and services meet the quality and performance levels claimed for those products and services.

YOUR CONSUMER RESPONSIBILITIES

Just as some businesses have not met their responsibilities to consumers, there are some consumers who try to take advantage of businesses. Even consumers who are not unethical or dishonest may have expectations that businesses cannot meet. Consumers too have responsibilities in business relationships. Those responsibilities are to be honest, be reasonable, report unethical practices, be informed, and be involved.

Be Honest

Most people are honest, but those who are not cause others to pay higher prices. Shoplifting losses are estimated to be in the billions of dollars each year. Businesses usually make up losses that result from shoplifting by charging higher prices to everyone.

Some people who would not think of shoplifting may be dishonest in other ways. For example, a customer might buy a book,

read it, and then return it for a refund. Customers have been seen taking lower priced tags from articles and putting them on the more expensive items they buy.

As a responsible consumer, you must be as honest with a business as you want it to be with you. You should be as quick to tell the cashier that you received too much change at the checkout counter as you are to say that you received too little. Dishonesty, in addition to being illegal and unethical, usually results in higher prices for all consumers.

Be Reasonable

As a buyer, you are usually responsible for what you buy if the business has been honest with you. If you are dissatisfied, however, and wish to complain, you should complain in a reasonable way.

You should first be sure that you have a cause for complaint. Be sure that you have followed the directions for using the product. After you have confirmed the details of your complaint, calmly explain the problem to an employee of the business from which you bought the item. In most cases, the business will be glad to correct the problem because it does not want to lose you as a customer. If you become angry or threatening, you risk getting an angry response that will only delay the solution to your problem.

If you believe that your complaint is not

How do you think store owners regain the costs of security and stolen merchandise?

Critical Thinking **Skills-Problem Solving**

Problem-solving skills, which include recognizing a problem and devising a plan of action, are applied throughout every chapter in this text. Each time a student participates in a Cooperative Learning or Teams activity, problem-solving skills are applied in a group situation. Each time a student completes a math application in the Calculate Business Data, decisions are made as to which mathematical approach must be taken. For each Technology Application problem, students must decide which template problem to use, which piece of software to load, and how to solve the problem. Emphasize to students that they are using problem solving in their day-to-day tasks and make them aware of the skills they are developing.

handled fairly by the salesperson or the customer service department, take the matter up with the owner or an official of the firm. If that fails and the firm is a part of a national company, a letter or telephone call to the customer service department at the headquarters often gets results. If you do not get a response within a reasonable time, a second effort including a letter sent to several consumer agencies will often bring a quick reply. If you fail to receive what you think is a fair adjustment, you may contact one of the following organizations:

- The Better Business Bureau.

- The local or state consumer affairs agency or the attorney general's office in your state.

- A lawyer or the Legal Aid Society if the problem is quite serious.

- In larger cities, the small claims court, which is operated for filing small claims only.

- A consumer help department.

Report Unethical Practices

As a responsible consumer, you should report unethical business practices to prevent other consumers from becoming victims. By reporting the matter to an agency discussed in this chapter, you might be able to get the shop to keep its word both to you and to future customers.

The National Bureau of Standards sets regulations to ensure uniformity of weights and measures throughout the country.

Be Informed

The most important responsibility you have as a consumer is to be informed. However, just having the right to be informed will not make you an informed consumer. You must find and use the information available to you. You should also keep informed about your rights as a consumer. Learn about the laws and agencies that protect your rights and how to report a violation of your rights. Being an informed consumer is hard work, but the extra effort spent in making your dollars go as far as possible will be worth it.

Be Involved

In our democratic government, involvement is an important consumer activity. As a citizen, you have a responsibility to participate in government even if only to be an informed voter. As a consumer, you also have responsibilities. When the opportunity arises, make your concerns known to government officials or consumer agencies. Only when you become involved as a consumer can agencies do their jobs and legislative bodies pass appropriate laws.

REVIEW YOUR READING

1. The right to be informed, the right to safety, the right to choose, the right to be heard, the right to a remedy, the right to consumer education, the right to service.
2. Fraud is intentionally deceiving the customer with regard to the facts about a product or service. Exaggeration is making a product sound better than it is.
3. The Consumer Product Safety Commission, the Food and Drug Administration, and the United States Department of Agriculture.
4. It protects our right to choose by preventing unfair competition that might result in a monopoly.
5. To coordinate the advice of other federal agencies on issues of interest to consumers, represent the interests of consumers, to develop consumer-information panels, and to assist other agencies in responding to complaints.
6. An express warranty may be made orally or in writing. An implied warranty is not written but imposed by law and understood to apply whether it is oral or in writing.
7. To be honest, to complain reasonably, to report unethical business practices to other consumers, to be informed, and to be involved.
8. Read a book and then return it for a refund, take lower priced tags from articles and put them on the more expensive items, and use discount coupons for merchandise not purchased.
9. Have a just cause, confirm details of complaint, and if the matter is not settled, consult the company's customer service or owner.
10. You should report businesses that are following unethical practices to protect other consumers from also becoming victims of the unfair treatment you have received.

COMMUNICATE BUSINESS CONCEPTS

11. Answers may vary. Reasons might be a strong desire of some businesses to make more than a fair amount of profit, consumers sometimes do not understand the concept of fraud, and lack of communication with businesses.

Chapter REVIEW

BUSINESS NOTES

1. The consumer movement was created to fight unfair business practices. As a result of this movement, public and private agencies, policies, laws, and regulations were developed to protect consumer interests.
2. The Consumer Bill of Rights declares every consumer has: the right to be informed, the right to safety, the right to choose, the right to be heard, the right to a remedy, the right to consumer education, and the right to service.
3. Consumers have five basic responsibilities: be honest, be reasonable, report unethical practices, be informed, and be involved.

REVIEW YOUR READING

1. What are the seven consumer rights?
2. What is the difference between fraud and exaggerating the good qualities of a product?
3. What are three governmental agencies that are devoted to consumer safety?
4. How does the Federal Trade Commission help consumers?
5. What are the responsibilities of the Office of Consumer Affairs?
6. What is the difference between an expressed warranty and an implied warranty?
7. What are five responsibilities of every consumer?
8. Give an example of consumer dishonesty.
9. How can a consumer complain in a reasonable manner?
10. Why should you report businesses that are following unethical practices?

COMMUNICATE BUSINESS CONCEPTS

11. Why, with all of the laws and organizations to protect consumers, do we continue to hear of examples of consumer fraud?
12. Give a real or imaginary example of a business monopoly. Tell why it is a monopoly.
13. Why do you suppose the government supports agencies that protect consumers?
14. Which of the consumer rights are you exercising right now?
15. Which of the following would be considered fraud? Explain your answers.
    a. A salesperson says the sound system you are looking at is the best on the market. After you buy it, you find it rated in a consumer magazine as second best.
    b. An advertisement for a bookcase cabinet claims it is made of solid walnut. Upon close inspection after buying the bookcase, you find out that it is only walnut veneer glued over less expensive plywood.
    c. The person who sells an electric corn popper says it is completely washable. Before using it, you put it into a sink filled with water to wash it. The first time you try to make popcorn, there is a flash and the popper's electrical unit catches fire. When you return the popper to the store, the salesperson tells you that she did not mean the popper could be put under water. She says you should have known that electrical appliances should not be put in water. She refuses to give you either a refund or an exchange.

12. Answers may vary. Students should describe businesses that have no competition and control the market for a product or service such as a local utility company.
13. Government is concerned about the welfare of its consumer citizens.
14. The right to a consumer education.
15. (b)

DEVELOP YOUR BUSINESS LANGUAGE

For each numbered item, find the term that has the same meaning.

16. When false information is given to a customer in an effort to make a sale.

17. Guarantees made orally or in writing that promise a specific quality of performance.

18. A promise by the manufacturer or dealer, usually in writing, that a product is of a certain quality.

19. Guarantees imposed by law that are not stated orally or in writing and which require certain standards to be met.

20. Organizations of businesses engaged in the same type of business.

21. The fight against unfair business practices by consumers joining together to demand fair treatment from businesses.

KEY TERMS
**consumer movement
express warranties
fraud
guarantee
trade associations
implied warranties**

DECISION-MAKING STRATEGIES

Pill Soon Song recently bought a stereo system using an online computer service. When the stereo arrived, Pill discovered that it wasn't exactly the stereo he wanted. The advertisement had described the system as having two large speakers. But what he got instead were two small speakers. He is happy with the other components, but is quite upset with the speakers.

Pill e-mailed the online computer service from which he purchased the stereo and explained the situation. However, the service said that in their opinion the speakers were "large" even though specific sizes were not given. Therefore, they felt the speakers met the advertisement.

22. Did the merchant commit fraud by describing the speakers as large?

23. If Pill is not satisfied with the speakers, what actions can he take to get the speakers he wants?

CALCULATE BUSINESS DATA

24. The Art Mart Gallery, a shop dealing mainly in prints and drawings, guarantees satisfaction with every purchase for a month. That means a customer can return a print or a drawing anytime within 30 days of purchase for a full refund. Last year's sales are given as follows: Total sales $320,000; products returned for refund $6,400.
- a. What percent of total sales was returned for refund?
- b. What was the total amount of net sales, deducting the cost of refunds?

25. The Jones family ordered a new car from Germany. The express warranty said the average driver would get 48.3 kilometers for every 3.85 liters of gasoline used.
- a. How many miles per gallon is this?
- b. If they traveled 90 miles and used 10.5 liters of gasoline, did the car perform better or worse than the warranty claimed?

26. Berri purchased a new cell phone that stopped working one month after the warranty expired. When she returned to the store, she was offered the choice of purchasing a new phone for 5% off the list price of $98 or a reconditioned phone that carried the same warranty as a new phone for $75.
- a. What would be the price of the new phone with the discount?
- b. What percent of the price of a new telephone is the price of the reconditioned phone?
- c. How much money would Berri save by purchasing the reconditioned phone?

DEVELOP YOUR BUSINESS LANGUAGE

16. fraud
17. express warranties
18. guarantee
19. implied warranties
20. trade associations
21. consumer movement

DECISION-MAKING STRATEGIES

22. Even though Pill thinks the speakers are small, the merchant did not commit fraud. Since the specific size of the speakers was not included in the advertisement, the word *large* is open to interpretation.

23. If Pill is unhappy with the speakers, he could contact the merchant and explain the situation in a reasonable manner. The merchant may be willing to exchange the speakers for a larger size.

CALCULATE BUSINESS DATA

24. (a) $6,400 ÷ $320,000 = 0.02 or 2% (b) $320,000 − $6,400 = $313,600.

25. (a) 48.3 kilometers × 0.6 = 28.98 (rounded) = 29 miles; 85 liters × 0.26 = 1.001 (rounded) = 1 gallon or 29 miles per gallon (b) 10.5 liters × 0.26 = 2.73 gallons for 90 miles or 90 ÷ 2.73 = 32.97 miles per gallon. This car performed better than the promised 29 miles per gallon.

26. (a) $98 × 0.95 = $93.10 (b) $75 ÷ $98 = 76.5% (c) $98 − $75 = $23

27. (a) $32.50 ÷ 26 = $1.25 (b)
$19.50 ÷ 26 = $0.75 or 75 cents
(c) $1.25 − $0.75 = $0.50 or 50
cents.

28. (a) $2.95; (b) $1.50; (c) 65 cents;
(d) 78 cents; (e) $117.44; (f)
$5.88; (g) $123.32.

TECHNOLOGY APPLICATION

In this activity, students use a computer to solve a business problem using a file provided on the data CD that accompanies *Intro to Business*. Instructions for using the data CD are included in a **README** file on the disk. Solutions are provided on the Instructor's Resource CD.

27. Jane Franklin is thinking about subscribing to a weekly consumer magazine so that she can be better informed. The magazine is offering a special trial subscription of 26 weeks for $19.50. The normal subscription rate for 26 weeks is $32.50.
    a. What is the normal cost per issue?
    b. What is the cost per issue under the special subscription rate?
    c. How much would Jane save per issue by taking advantage of the special subscription rate?

28. Jason Obliger purchased merchandise in several stores at the mall. When he got home and looked at his sales receipts, he was amazed at how much money he paid in sales tax. Sales tax is 5 percent in the city where Jason lives. His purchases were as follows: coat, $59; jeans, $29.95; CD, $12.99; and sunglasses, $15.59.
    a. How much sales tax did he pay on the coat?
    b. How much sales tax did he pay on the jeans?
    c. How much sales tax did he pay on the CD?
    d. How much sales tax did he pay on the sunglasses?
    e. What was the total amount of his purchases before sales tax?
    f. What was the total amount of sales tax that he paid on these items?
    g. What was the total amount of his purchases plus sales tax?

TECHNOLOGY APPLICATION

Using the *Intro to Business* Data CD and your word processing program software, select problem CH24. After the problem appears on your screen, complete the following activities. Then, print your completed letter. If you do not have a printer available, save the letter on a data disk to give to your teacher.

29. You just purchased a pair of in-line skates from a mail-order catalog. After using them for several weeks, the bolts that hold the wheels in place become loose and the wheels fall off. Before sending the skates back to the vendor, you should write a letter stating the problem and asking for assistance in correcting the situation.
    a. Enter your address in the appropriate section at the beginning of the letter. Use the strikeover feature of your word processing program to replace or delete information that does not apply to you.
    b. Complete each paragraph with the specific details of the situation. The paragraphs have been designed so you need only to insert the appropriate information.

30. You have now received an acknowledgement from the vendor of the defective skates. The vendor has requested that you return the skates for repair.
    a. Using the same form letter that you used for your original letter, you will now create a letter that will accompany the skates. Enter your address in the appropriate section at the beginning of the letter. Use the strikeover feature of your word processing program to replace or delete information that does not apply.
    b. Complete each paragraph with the specific details of the return. The paragraphs have been designed so you need only insert the appropriate information.

INTERNATIONAL LEGAL SYSTEMS

Laws are necessary in every society. Without a legal system, business activities would be confusing. People would not know if the items they purchase will be received. Companies might not receive payments for goods and services sold.

Civil law, also called code law, is a complete set of rules that is enacted as a single, written system or code. When a government enacts a civil code, it attempts to write down all of the laws and rights that govern every aspect of the society. The first civil laws were created in the seventeenth century B.C. in Babylon. Most countries today are governed by civil law.

Common law is a system of decisions made for various situations. In modern common law, also referred to as case law, judges make decisions guided by rulings in previous cases. The principle of fairness, important in business transactions, is often the basis for common law.

A third legal system is *statutory law*. This system is based on laws enacted by a lawmaking body, such as a parliament or a congress. Statutes are enacted to add or change existing laws and to create laws for new situations that arise. Recent laws, for example, regulate business transactions on the Internet.

Tax laws vary from country to country. In the United States, federal income tax and state sales taxes are the main sources of government revenue. In the European Union, a value-added tax (VAT) is used. A VAT is a tax assessed on the increase in value of goods from each stage of production to final consumption. This type of tax may be viewed as a national sales tax.

> **Although laws vary around the world, legal systems are necessary to regulate business activities.**

CRITICAL THINKING

1. Describe situations in which laws may be necessary to regulate business activities that were not present in the recent past.
2. Conduct a web search to locate information about different laws in different countries. How might a law in a different country affect a company's international business activities?

Most students will either work with international clients or compete against businesses that do. Global Navigator introduces students to issues integral to working with international businesses. Key concepts and challenges faced by international businesses are presented, followed by two Critical Thinking questions that require students to analyze what they have learned.

This feature describes the major types of legal systems in use around the world. In many cases, foreign legal systems will differ from that of the United States, so students will not be familiar with them. This feature gives them a brief introduction to some of the terms and concepts they may run across.

CRITICAL THINKING

1. The growth of the Internet has created many instances of new activities or new ways of conducting old activities that were not contemplated by previously enacted laws.
2. Students should express an understanding of the fact that companies may need to tailor their activities to particular laws or legal systems in different countries, much the same as they have to custom-tailor their marketing activities.

GLOBAL BUSINESS PROJECT

The buying habits of people in different cultures can be one of the most interesting aspects of planning an international business enterprise. Student awareness of different beliefs, customs, and conduct can serve many future career needs.

In this phase of the global business plan project, students are asked to think about possible adaptations of their business idea for different foreign markets. Some products can be sold the same in most countries, such as cameras, computers, factory equipment, and technical products. However, other types of products usually need to be adapted to local tastes and situations. These include foods and personal care items (toothpaste, soap, laundry detergent).

In addition, students will need to be aware of retailing and distribution methods for their country. Not every nation has malls, telemarketing, and online buying. Many countries still have open-air markets and family-owned stores.

To complete each phase of this project, students are encouraged to use various resources—textbook content, library materials, World Wide Web sites, interviews, advertisements, product packages, in-store observations. The individual activities are planned for use as either (1) an on-going course project, or (2) individual assignments.

Whether used as a continuing project or for selected activities, consider having students work in teams. This small group experience provides a valuable skill for future learning and work situations.

In addition to search engines, these selected web sites can be helpful for this unit:

- International Trade Administration of the U.S. Dept. of Commerce (www.ita.doc.gov)
- Business, economic, political news for selected countries (www.economist.com/countries)

GLOBAL BUSINESS PROJECT

ANALYZE CONSUMER ACTIVITIES

Every person has needs and wants. However, those needs and wants are different throughout the world. Consumer buying habits are affected by climate, traditions, family size, and religious beliefs.

Some products can be sold internationally without changes, while other items must be adapted to the culture and economic conditions. Companies involved in international business must also decide how to get their products to potential customers.

PROJECT GOALS
1. Research consumer buying habits in another country.
2. Determine needed adaptations of goods and services when conducting business around the world.
3. Recommend retailing and distribution methods for international business.

PROJECT ACTIVITIES
Using your textbook, library materials, web sites, interviews with people, and other resources, complete the following activities:
1. The buying habits of people in other cultures may be different from your usual situation. Using the country in your portfolio (or select a country), describe specific customs, traditions, or beliefs that affect the buying behaviors or eating habits in that nation.

2. Some products are sold in a standardized form throughout the world. Other products, such as food and laundry detergent, must be adapted to cultural tastes and the water used for clothes washing. For your business idea, describe how it might need to be adapted for different countries, or explain why it could be sold in several countries without making revisions.
3. The distribution systems and stores used by global companies must be adapted to available transportation and intermediaries, such as agents, brokers, wholesalers, and retailers. Create a visual presentation showing how your product or service could be moved from production to consumers or other end users of the item.

PROJECT WRAP-UP
1. Continue your portfolio (folder, file box, or other container) for storing and referring back to the information and materials you created in the activities above. This portfolio will provide necessary elements of your global business plan.
2. Create a product presentation display as a poster, sample package, advertisement, web site, or video that shows how your business idea could be sold in other countries.

- World Factbook of the Central Intelligence Agency (www.odci.gov/cia/publications/factbook)
- Latin American country information (www.lanic.utexas.edu)
- Asian country information (asnic.utexas.edu) (www.asia-inc.com)
- Eastern European country information (reenic.utexas.edu)

- Middle East country information (menic.utexas.edu)
- Career planning tips (www.monster.com)
- Resume preparation advice (www.jobweb.com)

FOCUS ON CAREERS

SERVICE OCCUPATIONS

O ur economy has often been called a service economy. Partly as a result of busy life styles, consumers are buying more and more services every year. People have their clothes washed and pressed, houses cleaned, and meals prepared. Many businesses have sprung up to meet these and other service needs. The United States Bureau of Labor Statistics estimates that the number of service jobs will reach 25.8 million by 2006. That represents an increase in service jobs of 18% since 1996.

JOB TITLES
- Delivery Driver
- Flight Attendant
- Fast-Food Worker
- Cook
- Sales Manager
- Home Health Aide
- Customer Service Representative
- Stock Clerk
- Retail Manager
- Real Estate Agent
- Personnel Recruiter
- Lodging Manager

EMPLOYMENT OUTLOOK (THROUGH THE YEAR 2005)
- Health services is one of the fastest growing service industries. A growing and aging population will continue to increase demand, particularly in home healthcare and residential care facilities.
- Business services will generate new jobs.
- Personnel supply services (temporary help agencies) is the largest sector in service occupations.

- Employment in wholesale and retail trade (apparel and accessory stores, appliance stores, restaurants) is expected to have significant growth.

EDUCATION AND TRAINING
- Like the job duties, education and training requirements will vary. A business or marketing education program in your high school would provide a good start. Further education at a community college or four-year college may prepare you for management or ownership of a service business.

SALARY LEVELS (IN RECENT YEARS)
Salaries vary widely but are competitive with salaries paid to similar employees in other career areas. Beginning salaries often hover around the minimum wage while management and ownership pay very well. Approximate compensation:
- Executive chefs over $45,000 a year. Cooks and bakers: $7 to $12 an hour. Food preparation workers: $6 to $9 an hour.
- Home health aides; $6 to $10 an hour.
- Lodging managers: $20,000 to $55,000 a year.
- Retail sales managers: $28,000 a year.

CRITICAL THINKING
1. Which job title in this career area appeals to you most? Give some reasons for your choice.
2. What are some things you will have to do to achieve success in the career selected?

FOCUS ON CAREERS

T he careers listed in this Focus on Careers come from the *Occupational Outlook Handbook*, an online publication (www.bls.gov/oco) of the federal government. The O*NET codes for these job titles are: Delivery Driver, 53-3033.00; Flight Attendant, 39-6031.00; Fast-Food Worker, 51-3093.00; Cook, 35-1011.00, 35-2019.99, 35-2011.00 through 35-2015.00; Sales Manager, 11-2022.00; Home Health Aid, 31-1011.00; Customer Service Representative, 43-4051.00; Stock Clerk, 43-5081.00; Retail Manager, 41-1011.00; Real Estate Agent, 41-9022.00; Personnel Recruiter, 13-1071.02; Lodging Manager, 11-9081.00. Students can access O*NET Online (online.onetcenter.org) to view features of selected occupations. They can also search for related occupations and for occupations that match selected skills. This career feature is designed to help students explore a variety of different careers in business and can be used to demonstrate that skills learned in this course are relevant. A career Focus Worksheet is available in the School-To-Work/SCANS Activity Masters.

CRITICAL THINKING
1. Answers will vary.
2. Answers will vary depending on student selection of a career choice. Suggested answers may include pursuing education or specialized training.

UNIT 8

BUILDING YOUR PORTFOLIO

CAREER DEVELOPMENT – COMPLETING AN APPLICATION FOR EMPLOYMENT

The Building Your Portfolio career exercise will help your students establish a personal history–where they have been, where they are now, and where they are going. This career exercise will give students practice in completing and comparing employment applications.

Stress that employers design their application forms to obtain the information most pertinent to their companies—information that job applicants sometimes omit from a cover letter or resume. Have students acquire applications from several companies and compare them. Ask them to note some of the things unique to the various applications. Direct students to complete some of the applications using the guidelines discussed in Chapter 20. You may want to use the Applying Technology employment application template problem from Chapter 20. Remind students about the importance of getting an application ahead of time. Why? A prospective employee needs to practice filling out an application. More than one attempt is often needed to achieve the phrasing and effect desired.

As a supplemental activity, you may refer to the School–To–Work/SCANS Activity Masters.

TEACHING STRATEGIES

SCANS

Cooperative Learning
345, 387

Alternate Modalities
Auditory Learner 370

Teaching Tips
Building Your Portfolio 339
Kick-Off Activity 338
Safety and Health 357

Special Needs
Dyslexia 344
Visually Impaired Students 385

Teams
359, 374

Special Features

Media/Technology

Chapter	Spreadsheet Software	Database Software	Word Processing Software	Internet	Video
25		■			■
26		■		■	■
27	■				■
28	■				■

Resources

SOFTWARE

Excel, Word, WordPerfect, Works, and ClarisWorks for Mac and Windows

Word Pro, ASCII, QuattroPro, Lotus, and Access for Windows

SOUTH-WESTERN EDUCATIONAL PUBLISHING PRODUCTS

Sargent and Ward. *Midtown Bank: A Bank Teller's Simulation*. 1997. Cincinnati: South-Western Educational Publishing Company. Text-Workbook. 0-538-60267-8.

Ryan. *Managing Your Personal Finances*. 2002. Cincinnati: South-Western Educational Publishing Company. Text-Workbook. 0-538-69958-2.

BOOKS

Lawrence. *The Budget Kit : The Common Cents Money Management Workbook*. 1997. Dearborn Trade.

Schwab. *Charles Schwab's Guide to Financial Independence: Simple Solutions for Busy People*. 1998. Crown Publishing.

PERIODICALS

Economic Review. Kansas City, MO.

Kiplinger's Personal Finance Magazine. Washington, D.C.

Money. New York, NY.

The Wall Street Journal. New York, NY.

GOVERNMENT PUBLICATIONS

Occupational Outlook Handbook, U.S. Department of Labor, Washington, DC.

What Work Requires of Schools: A SCANS Report for America 2000, U.S. Department of Labor, Washington, DC

MEDIA/TECHNOLOGY

Publisher's web sites:

www.intro2business.swep.com

www.swep.com

www.thomson.com

FINANCIAL INSTITUTIONS AND BANKING SERVICES

This unit will provide students with an overview of insurance and economic risks. Use the resources listed on the previous page, especially those from South-Western Educational Publishing, as you prepare to teach these chapters.

In Chapter 25, different types of banks and financial institutions are introduced. Chapter 26 discusses types of checking accounts and how to open a checking account. Chapter 27 provides information about writing checks and using forms of payment other than checks. Chapter 28 concludes with methods to control a checking account and factors to consider when choosing a financial institution.

UNIT 8
FINANCIAL INSTITUTIONS AND BANKING SERVICES

Chapters

Kick-Off Activity

Investigating Business Media

The following exercise asks students to choose an article from *The Wall Street Journal,* the financial section of a newspaper, or a business magazine and to inquire about a topic related to this unit.

Students should choose an article from *The Wall Street Journal* or a financial magazine that explains in detail problems facing a particular bank or an entire class of financial institutions (such as savings and loans). Then ask students to answer the following questions:

1 What are the problems faced by the financial institutions? Be as specific as possible.

2 To what extent are these problems related to specific current economic conditions? past economic conditions? List all the major problems identified in the article.

"Sixteen dollars for cash machine fees!" exclaimed Hans George as he opened his bank statement. "I guess the cost of those cash withdrawals adds up fast!"

Hans George has a routine of using his cash card at an automatic teller machine several times a week. He really likes the convenience of obtaining cash. However, Hans also finds that when getting cash is easy, he easily overspends.

While automatic teller machines are easy to use, you must also consider fees and the potential for impulse buying. In recent years cash machine fees have risen from nothing to $1 or $2 per withdrawal.

How much can cash machine transaction fees cost? If you have two $1 transaction fees a week, you will pay $104 in fees over one year. Instead of paying this money out in fees, you could invest the money and earn interest (payments made to you when you invest). For example, you might be able to invest at an interest rate of 5 percent per year. Over five years, the money you pay in fees could have been saved and increased to more than $570. You have to ask yourself if such an amount of money is worth the convenience of a cash machine.

Another area where bank fees can add up quickly is overdrafts and stop-payment orders. You must carefully keep track of your account. Writing checks when you do not have enough money in your account to cover the checks can result in charges of as much as $20 or more every time you overdraw.

Regularly having to issue stop-payment orders because of errors in writing or sending checks can also cause fees to accumulate.

Other sources of fees are printed checks and bank-at-home services. The cost of purchasing checks is expensive. You may be able to purchase checks at a lower cost by shopping around. Banking at home has become very popular, with the use of telephones or home computers to complete transactions. However, always be sure to weigh the appeal of fancy technology and convenience against equipment costs and monthly fees.

Banking fees involve trade-offs. Using cash machines, maintaining low balances, and banking at home may be beneficial to you. As businesses, however, banks need to recover their expenses by charging you fees. And you may decide that the benefits from using such services are greater than the costs.

You may decide, however, to lower the fees you pay. Banking fees and other charges can be reduced by comparison shopping at different financial institutions. Or, you may be able to reduce or eliminate these fees by negotiating with your bank manager.

CRITICAL THINKING

1 What factors have caused banking fees to increase in recent years?

2 What actions can consumers take to reduce the cost of banking?

After reading the Business Brief, ask students what impressed them the most. Have they heard or read about this topic before? Have students prepare a bulletin board display or poster showing advertisements for various financial institutions and banking services. Ask students to interview one or two people from outside the class about actions they take to reduce their banking costs.

CRITICAL THINKING

Answers will be based on students' perceptions of the topic and experiences they have had with it.

1. Increased use of technology, availability of new services, higher operating costs, and reduced competition in some aspects of banking have resulted in increased banking fees.

2. To reduce banking costs, consumers can use comparison shopping among various financial institutions. In addition, consumers can reduce banking costs by using only services that are actually needed. Not using unnecessary services allows banks to cut waste and keep fees lower.

BUILDING YOUR PORTFOLIO

The Building Your Portfolio work samples validate skill level and a student's ability to accomplish tasks frequently performed on the job. The most important reason for including samples in a portfolio is to demonstrate a student's abilities and skills. In selecting work samples for each unit, students should always have a choice of which activities to include. Students might be encouraged to include samples from the end-of-chapter activities, particularly Communicate Business Concepts, Calculate Business Data, Technology Application, and Decision-Making Strategies.

A n overview of financial institutions, a variety of deposit-type and nondeposit financial institutions, and the six basic financial services are discussed. The chapter also presents the Federal Reserve System.

Resources for Teachers
- Lesson Plans
- School-To-Work/SCANS Activity Masters
- Spanish Resources
- Instructor's Resource CD

Assessment
- Chapter and Unit Tests, Ch. 25
- ExamView, Ch. 25

Media/Technology
- Applying Technology Data CD
- PowerPoint slides
- Business Connection CD
- Videotape

Activity Masters and Workbooks
- Activities and Projects, Ch. 25
- Internet Activity Masters
- Business Math Activity Masters
- Communications Activity Masters
- International Business Activity Masters
- Ethics Activity Masters

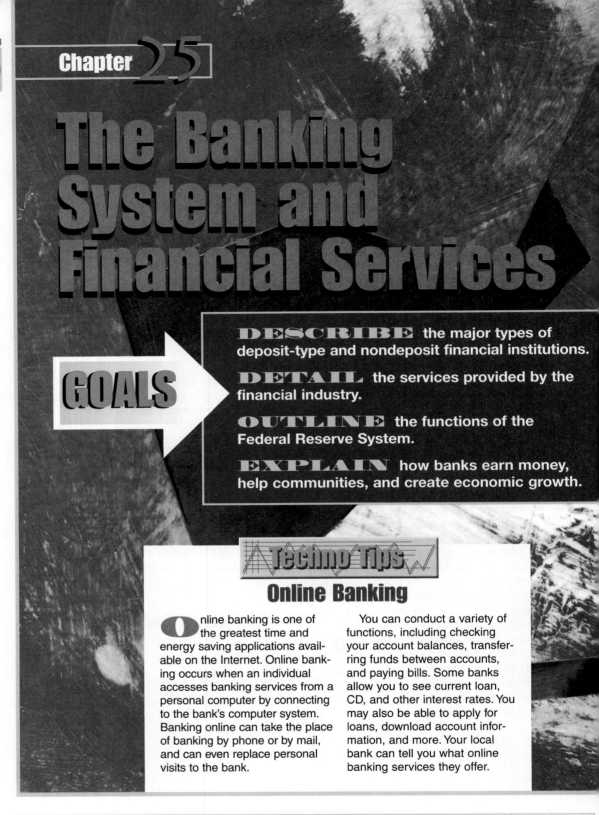

Chapter 25
The Banking System and Financial Services

GOALS

DESCRIBE the major types of deposit-type and nondeposit financial institutions.

DETAIL the services provided by the financial industry.

OUTLINE the functions of the Federal Reserve System.

EXPLAIN how banks earn money, help communities, and create economic growth.

Techno Tips
Online Banking

O nline banking is one of the greatest time and energy saving applications available on the Internet. Online banking occurs when an individual accesses banking services from a personal computer by connecting to the bank's computer system. Banking online can take the place of banking by phone or by mail, and can even replace personal visits to the bank.

You can conduct a variety of functions, including checking your account balances, transferring funds between accounts, and paying bills. Some banks allow you to see current loan, CD, and other interest rates. You may also be able to apply for loans, download account information, and more. Your local bank can tell you what online banking services they offer.

S tudents need to know the latest technologies and develop cutting edge Internet skills for use in current jobs, future careers, or in their homes. TechnoTips introduces students to today's cutting edge technologies and provides them with important Internet skills. Feature topics concentrate on Internet-specific technologies and computer or other hi-tech innovations for use by businesses and consumers.

"**I** finally got a job for the summer," Gerri told Mike. "I can save money and go on that trip."

"Where are you going to save your money?" asked Mike.

"At home, of course," responded Gerri.

"Are you kidding?" Mike went on to say. "That's dangerous! Your money can get lost, or you might spend it before summer comes."

"Well what should I do with my money?" asked Gerri.

"Deposit it in a bank," answered Mike.

"Will it be safer?" asked Gerri.

"For sure," said Mike. "Banks and other financial institutions provide safety and growth for your money. Plus they help their customers in many ways with other financial matters."

"You're kidding! I guess it's time I learn about banking," Gerri responded.

THE BUSINESS OF BANKING

Have you ever thought of a bank as a business and you as a customer? Many people do not think of banks in this way. Yet, a bank is a business just like stores and factories. As a business, a bank sells services such as checking accounts, savings accounts, and loans. For their services, banks expect to earn revenues and make a profit. Banks earn most of their revenues by charging for loans to individuals, businesses, and government and by investing part of the money that customers deposit in the banks. Some examples of investments made by banks are given in the last section of the chapter.

Because banks are businesses, does that mean that anybody can start one? Well, not exactly. People who wish to start a bank must meet the requirements set by federal and state governments. Since the bank owners will handle other people's money, they are expected to be responsible citizens with high moral character. They must also have enough capital to start the business operations.

People who want to start a bank must apply for a charter from their state or from the federal government. If they apply to their state and a charter is granted, the bank will operate as a state bank. If the charter is from the federal government, the bank will operate

as a national bank. In bank titles, N.A. stands for National Association and is used today in place of the word "national."

A bank's operations are regulated more strictly than the operations of most other businesses. If a business other than a bank fails, only a few people lose money. If a bank fails, thousands of people are affected.

How do you think the profits made by a bank compare to the profits made in other businesses?

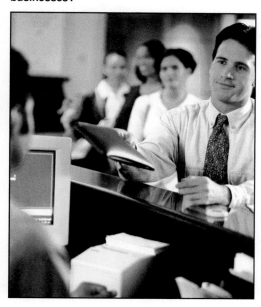

Ask for volunteers to tell about recent visits to or experiences with banks or other financial institutions. What were the purposes of the visits? Were the students' needs met by the institutions?

MOTIVATE

PURPOSE Provide a purpose for students as they read the chapter. Ask what they think they will learn. Direct students to skim the chapter, looking at photos, reading captions, and noting main headings. The goals at the beginning of each chapter provide a valuable tool for having students pinpoint main ideas. The tasks required by the goals are signaled in the first word. Some emphasize information collection ("Identify," "List"), while others call for description ("Explain," "Describe"). Ask students to look through all the goals and note the first word of each. Then ask students to state the purpose of studying this chapter. In this chapter, students will learn about various financial institutions and the different services provided.

TEACH/APPLY

MAKE CONNECTIONS
Emphasize that banks and financial institutions are businesses. Explain that banks earn revenues through fees and interest on loans and investments.

Discuss the importance of government regulation of financial institutions. Compare and contrast the types of banks and other deposit-type institutions. The institutions vary by type of ownership, source of deposit insurance, and services emphasized.

List the six common services of financial institutions: accepting deposits, transferring funds, lending money, storing valuables, providing financial advice and investment services, and managing trusts.

Explain the ways in which the Federal Reserve System acts as banker to banks and regulates the monetary policy of the economy. Emphasize the role that financial institutions play in investing in communities and fostering economic growth.

TRY THIS/GUIDED PRACTICE
Use PowerPoint 25-4, *Types of Financial Services*, to guide students by taking one type of financial service at a time and name deposit-type and nondeposit institutions that provide that service.

EXPLORE THIS/INDEPENDENT PRACTICE Before assigning independent practice material for any chapter, students should be expected to read the textbook material carefully. In view of the fact that all students vary widely in their ability to read effectively, it is advisable to have the students read the entire chapter, or sections thereof, silently in class if the material has not been previously read in connection with homework assignments.

After students have read the chapter, ask them to complete the Chapter Review questions. Develop Your Business Language is an excellent way to improve students' vocabulary. Only words introduced in the chapter are used in the exercises. The Review Your Reading questions can be used to check students' ability to comprehend what they have read. The Communicate Business Concepts section affords an opportunity for students to apply to practical life situations the information gained from reading the chapter. By completing the problems under

Government regulation is necessary to assure the safety of customers' money. State banks operate under the banking laws of the state in which the banks are located. National banks operate under federal laws as well as those of the state in which they are located.

BANKS AND OTHER DEPOSIT-TYPE INSTITUTIONS

When someone says, "I'm going to the bank," the person might actually mean a credit union or a cash machine at the mall. As shown in Figure 25-1, financial institutions are usually classified by the types of services they offer. *Deposit-type institutions,* also called *depository institutions,* accept deposits for people and businesses to use in the future. The main types of deposit-type institutions are commercial banks, savings and loan associations, mutual savings banks, and credit unions.

Commercial Banks
Most commonly, a bank is organized as a **commercial bank**. Commercial banks are often called *full-service banks* because they offer a wide range of financial services. Commercial banks offer checking accounts, provide savings accounts, make loans to individuals and to businesses, and offer other services. In large banks, these services may be handled in different departments, such as a savings department, a trust department, a real estate department, or an investment department.

In recent years, banks have opened full-service branch offices in shopping centers and grocery stores. These *financial supermarkets* offer everything from automated teller machines and loans to safe-deposit boxes.

The federal agency that helps to regulate banks and other financial institutions is the **Federal Deposit Insurance Corporation (FDIC)**. It protects depositors' money in case

FIGURE 25-1 Which of these types of institutions have you done business with?

DEPOSIT-TYPE & NONDEPOSIT INSTITUTIONS

Deposit-Type Institutions:
Commercial Banks
Savings and Loan Associations
Mutual Savings Banks
Credit Unions

Nondeposit Institutions:
Life Insurance Companies
Investment Companies
Consumer Finance Companies
Mortgage Companies
Check-cashing Outlets
Pawnshops

Basic Skills-Reading

Direct students to the first main heading of the chapter. The first sentence of a paragraph is usually the main idea of the material being discussed. The last sentence of the paragraph usually summarizes or bridges to the paragraphs or subheadings that follow. Bold terms and italicized words draw attention to important facts or topics in the material. Direct

students to pages in the chapter that illustrate bold terms or italicized terms. The Student Activity Worksheet, Basic Skills—Reading, in the School-To-Work/SCANS Activity Masters, may be used to serve as a guideline for discussion of each of these points. Ask students to write a summary of the points that will be covered in the chapter.

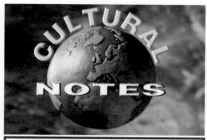
of the failure of a bank or financial institution that is regulated by the FDIC. At present, the FDIC insures all accounts in the same name at each bank up to an amount of $100,000. Although the FDIC is a government agency, money for its operation is provided by banks. Almost 99 percent of all banks are FDIC members.

Savings and Loan Associations

Traditionally, a **savings and loan association (S&L)** specialized in savings accounts and making loans for home mortgages. In recent years, however, these financial institutions have expanded to offer a greater variety of financial services.

Recently, many S&Ls have changed to savings banks and now include the words *savings bank* in their titles. For example, Lifetime Savings and Loan Association has become Lifetime Savings Bank.

In recent years, over 2,000 branches of commercial banks were operating in grocery stores and supermarkets.

The services offered at automatic teller machines are expanding to include the sale of bus passes, postage stamps, and gift certificates. Some ATM users can buy and sell mutual funds.

Mutual Savings Banks

A **mutual savings bank** provides a variety of services. However, it is organized mainly for savings accounts and to make loans to home buyers. This type of financial institution is owned by the depositors; the profits of the mutual savings bank go to the depositors. Mutual savings banks are located mainly in the northeastern United States.

Credit Unions

A **credit union** is a user-owned, not-for-profit, cooperative financial institution. Credit unions are commonly formed by people in the same company, government agency, labor union, profession, church, or community. Serving members only, credit unions accept savings deposits and make loans for a variety of purposes. Today, credit unions also offer other services such as

- checking accounts
- credit cards
- mortgages
- home equity loans
- safe-deposit boxes
- investment services
- electronic banking services
- loans to small firms

In recent years, there were more than 15,000 credit unions in operation. They are regulated by the National Credit Union Administration (NCUA), a federal agency similar to the FDIC. NCUA also insures a depositor's funds, up to $100,000, through its National Credit Union Share Insurance Fund. Some state-chartered credit unions have opted for a private insurance program.

Chapter 25 *The Banking System and Financial Services* 343

Calculate Business Data, students will be able to strengthen and refine their abilities in mathematics. Technology Application allows students to demonstrate skill in using word processing, spreadsheet, and database software. Decision-Making Strategies contains material to challenge students to utilize the model explained in Chapter 1 for problem solving.

The Chapter Review questions at the end of the chapter vary in level of difficulty. For a basic assignment, consider Develop Your Business Language and Review Your Reading. For an average assignment, consider the basic assignment plus Communicate Business Concepts and Calculate Business Data. For an enhanced assignment, try the average assignment plus Technology Application and Decision-Making Strategies.

ASSESS

Review the goals at the beginning of the chapter and the Business Notes at the end of the chapter. Restate each as a question and have students respond orally. For students who may have difficulty providing answers, assign the reteaching activities that follow. Enrichment activities may also be assigned where appropriate.
1. How do banks earn revenues? (Answer: Interest from loans and investments.)
2. What are the four major deposit-type institutions? (Answer: Commercial banks, savings and loan associations, mutual savings banks, and credit unions.)

3. Which nondeposit financial institutions serve consumers? (Answer: Life insurance companies, investment companies, consumer finance companies, mortgage companies, check-cashing outlets, and pawnshops.)

4. What are six services provided by financial institutions? (Answer: Accepting deposits, transferring funds, lending money, storing valuables, providing financial advice and investment services, and managing trusts.)

5. How does the Federal Reserve System relate to banks? (Answer: Supervise and regulate member banks; be a bank for banks.)

6. How can banks help communities and create economic growth? (Answer: Provide employment, make loans to support investments.)

RETEACH

Reteach the categories of financial services by creating a bulletin board of advertisements, photos, and articles from newspapers and magazines to show different types of financial services. On this bulletin board, give examples of financial institutions that provide all or most of the services and of institutions that specialize in one or two of the services. Use the bulletin board to point out the important information about financial services.

NONDEPOSIT FINANCIAL INSTITUTIONS

The other major category of financial institutions is nondeposit institutions. This description is used to refer to life insurance companies, investment companies, consumer finance companies, mortgage companies, check-cashing outlets, and pawnshops.

Life Insurance Companies

People commonly buy life insurance to provide financial security for dependents. Besides protection, many life insurance companies also offer financial services such as investments. Through careful investing in new and existing companies, life insurance companies can help to expand business in our economy.

Investment Companies

Investment companies allow people to choose investment opportunities for long-term growth of their money. Many investors in our society own shares of one of the more than 30,000 mutual funds worldwide made available by investment companies.

Consumer Finance Companies

A **consumer finance company** specializes in making loans for long-lasting or durable goods, such as cars and refrigerators, and for financial emergencies. Because consumer finance companies make loans, they are a part of the financial services industry. However, consumer finance companies do not accept savings as do banks and other financial institutions.

Safe-deposit boxes require two keys to be opened. One is kept by the owner of the box; the other key is in the possession of the bank.

Mortgage Companies

Buying a home is an important activity in our society. Mortgage companies, along with other financial institutions, provide loans for purchasing a home or other real estate.

Check-Cashing Outlets

People who do not have bank accounts may use check-cashing outlets (CCOs) to cash paychecks and to obtain other financial services. CCOs offer a wide variety of services such as electronic tax filing, money orders, private postal boxes, utility bill payment, and the sale of bus and subway tokens.

Pawnshops

Pawnshops make loans based on the value of some tangible possession, such as jewelry or other valuable items. Pawnshops charge higher fees than other financial institutions.

TYPES OF FINANCIAL SERVICES

Whatever your needs, a financial institution is available to serve you. As shown in Figure 25-2, the most common services of financial institutions are accepting deposits, transferring funds, lending money, storing valuables, providing financial advice and investment services, and managing trusts.

Accepting Deposits

Safe storage of funds for future use is an almost universal need. One of the main services that financial institutions offer is accepting money from their customers for safekeeping.

Sachi Kinoshita, a student who works part-time and summers, is an example of a customer who uses this service. Sachi earns a take-home salary of $210 a week from her summer job on a road construction crew. She wants to save part of her earnings for a down payment on a car. Sachi knows that if she carries the money with her or keeps it at home, she may be tempted to spend it or it may be lost or stolen.

TEACHING STRATEGIES
Special Needs
Dyslexia

One way to keep students with dyslexia interested in the class is to use teaching strategies that will make content clear through the use of visuals or graphics and reduce the reading load. Associate the visuals in the chapter with the content instead of assigning an overwhelming amount of text to read.

FINANCIAL SERVICES

- ▲ Accepting deposits
- ▲ Transferring funds
- ▲ Lending money
- ▲ Storing valuables
- ▲ Providing financial advice and investment services
- ▲ Managing trusts

FIGURE 25-2   How many of these services does your family use?

To protect her money over the period of time it will take to save for the down payment, Sachi deposits some of her weekly pay in a savings account at the bank. By putting her money in a savings account, Sachi is saying to the bank, "I'm going to leave this money in my account for a fairly long period of time—maybe six months to a year or longer—and you can use it until I need it."

With Sachi's money, along with the funds of other depositors, the bank can make loans to other customers. Sachi will be paid by the bank for the use of her money. The amount paid for the use of money is called **interest**.

Say that Sachi deposits $500 of her summer wages in a savings account and leaves it there for a year. If the bank pays 4 percent interest on savings, Sachi's savings will have earned $20 in interest at the end of the year, and her car fund will have grown to $520. More complete discussions of interest appear in Appendix C.

Transferring Funds

The ability to transfer money to others is necessary for daily business activities. Money deposited into a checking account can be used at any time by writing a check, which can then be deposited in the account of the person who receives the check.

Suppose that Eduardo Cruz has a checking account that he uses to pay bills. He can pay his bills by instructing the bank to pay out, or transfer, a certain amount from his account to someone to whom he owes money. The bank provides different ways through which Eduardo can do this. One of the most common transfer methods is by check. When Eduardo writes a check to his rental agent to pay his rent, for example, the bank subtracts the amount of the check from Eduardo's account.

Every year, however, more and more banking is done through electronic funds transfer. **Electronic funds transfer (EFT)** is a system through which funds are moved electronically from one account to another and from one bank to another. You can instruct your bank to transfer funds automatically, for example, from your savings to your checking account without writing a check. Or you can pay monthly bills, such as your phone bill or your rent, by instructing your bank to transfer the amount automatically each month from your account to the phone company or the rental agent.

You can go to your bank in person or write a letter instructing the bank to make electronic transfers for you. You can also give the instructions to the bank at an automatic teller machine (ATM). ATMs provide auto-

Direct students to read the Ethical Perspectives in this chapter. Ask students to talk to parents, relatives, and neighbors to prepare a list of banking services that have become available during the last 25 years. These may include night banking hours, drive-in banking, bank branches in supermarkets and shopping malls, co-branded credit cards, a more informal atmosphere in banks, overdraft loans for checking accounts, personalized checks with photos and other illustrations, computerized clearing of checks, electronic transfer payments, and banking at home by telephone and computer. You may also invite a banker, credit union manager, or other employee from a financial institution to talk to your class about banking services and career opportunities in banking.

SUMMARIZE

Show students PowerPoint 25-6, *Financial Institutions and Economic Growth*. Discuss the important role that banks and other financial institutions play in our communities and economy. Give examples from your community of investments made possible with loans from a financial institution (for example, office building, sports stadium, farm equipment).

TEACHING STRATEGIES
Cooperative Learning

For this activity, assign students to groups of four or five. Appoint one student in each group to be the recorder. Each group should design and conduct a survey of consumers about their use of and attitudes toward electronic banking. Examples of questions are: Do some people prefer to continue to use checks rather than use electronic funds transfer? Does the use of an ATM increase impulse buying? What concerns do people have about electronic banking? Allow 30 minutes for designing the survey, one week for collecting data, and one class period for preparing and presenting a report. Each group should report its findings to the rest of the class, with each student discussing the result of at least one question.

- Assign Activities and Projects for Chapter 25.
- Administer the printed test or ExamView for Chapter 25.
- Assign School-To-Work/SCANS portfolio activities for Unit 8.

SUPPLEMENTAL NOTES

- Provide a handout with an outline, list of key terms, and questions as a guide for your presentations.
- Use visual materials such as transparencies, slides, videos, posters, advertisements, and packages to explain and demonstrate lecture material.
- Encourage students to respond with explanations, examples, and questions that reflect their knowledge of the material.
- Use a flowchart, conceptual map, or other illustrations to show relationships among new topics and other course topics.
- Discuss the specific goals of topics to be covered.
- Assign textbook readings and give students questions in advance.
- Ask questions that require students to relate content to other topics, personal experiences, and actual business situations.
- Use small group activities for problem-solving and decision-making situations.
- If you are trying to stimulate class discussion, avoid asking students questions that can be answered with "yes" or "no" or with a short answer.
- Good questions usually start with "What," "Why," and "How" and

ETHICAL PERSPECTIVES

Check-Cashing Outlets and Pawnshops

About 17 percent of U.S. households do not have bank accounts. People who do not have bank accounts either do not choose, or feel that they are not qualified, to open a checking account. Typically a financial institution will not cash a check for you unless you have an account at that institution. For this reason, many people who do not have bank accounts use check-cashing outlets (CCOs). There are over 6,000 CCOs in the United States. CCOs may provide a useful service when banks are not an option.

As a fee for cashing a check, a CCO will charge anywhere from 1 to 20 percent of the face value of the check. The average cost is between 2 and 3 percent. This means a person could be charged $15 to cash a $500 paycheck. For some people, such charges could add up to significant portions of their total household budgets.

Another type of nondeposit financial institution is the pawnshop. Pawnshops make loans based on the value of some tangible possession, such as jewelry or other valuable items. Many people who may not qualify for loans at other types of financial institutions use pawnshops to obtain quick cash loans that may not be available from any other source. Pawnshops, however, charge higher borrowing fees than other financial institutions.

Critical Thinking
1. Are the fees charged by check-cashing outlets and pawnshops appropriate?
2. What actions might be taken to help people reduce the fees paid for financial services?

matic teller service quickly and easily and are available 24 hours a day. Their popularity has brought about considerable growth in online banking, which is changing the way people do their banking. A fee may be charged by some banks for certain types of EFT transactions.

Other electronic banking services include:

- point-of-sale transactions in which debit cards are accepted at gas stations, supermarkets, retail stores, and fast-food restaurants to pay for purchases.

- direct deposit in which your paycheck is

An ATM card is also commonly referred as a *cash card* or *debit card*. Using a debit card for a purchase is similar to writing a check, with the amount of the purchase deducted from your checking account.

automatically deposited in your checking or savings account.

- home banking in which payments are made and loans are obtained by customers using computers.

Lending Money
Many people, businesses, and governments borrow money at some time. For example, a business may want to borrow money to build a new warehouse or to buy more merchandise for resale. Individuals may borrow to buy a car or to pay college tuition. Banks will lend money to those who need to borrow if it seems likely that the loans will be repaid when due. In fact, banks want to make loans because banks receive most of their revenues from the interest they charge borrowers.

One way that banks can increase their loans is through offering credit cards. When you buy items such as clothing or sports equipment and pay for them with a bank credit card, such as MasterCard or Visa, you

ETHICAL PERSPECTIVES

Ethical Perspectives raises ethical questions but does not involve the teaching of right and wrong. Instead, it allows students to apply their own principles to business situations through the use of critical thinking and decision-making skills.

CRITICAL THINKING
1. Possible answers might include the observation that CCOs and pawnshops charge fees to recover legitimate business costs. Customers of CCOs and pawnshops may be willing to pay such fees because the customers believe that other options are not available. On the other hand, the amounts of fees at CCOs and pawnshops may be disproportionately large.
2. By being well informed about the availability of services at various financial institutions, a consumer can save money when doing her or his banking.

are borrowing money from the bank. Another way that banks can increase loans is by sending a limited number of checks with a customer's credit card statement, allowing the customer to use one of the checks to obtain cash or to pay a bill. If the customer uses the checks, the amount of each check is charged to the customer's credit card account. In effect, the amount of the check is a loan.

Storing Valuables

Besides offering a place to deposit money, banks offer **safe-deposit boxes** where you can store valuables. Because these safe-deposit boxes are in well-guarded vaults, they are the safest places to keep such things as jewelry, bond and stock certificates, birth records, a list of insurance policies, and a will. The box can be opened only by you or by someone who has been given the right to open it for you. Not even a bank has the right to open your safe-deposit box unless it is ordered to do so by a court. Safe-deposit boxes are rented by the year and come in a variety of sizes.

Providing Financial Advice and Investment Services

Many financial institutions help their customers by offering financial advice and investment services. Bank officials can advise customers about such things as whether it is wise to buy a certain house, how to manage money better, or how to exchange U.S. currency for foreign currency.

Most banks offer advice on investments. **Investments** are savings that are put to work to earn more money. For example, money in a savings account is a type of investment because the savings account earns interest.

Federal government bonds are another kind of investment that can be bought through a bank. For their customers, banks also buy bonds issued by businesses, by state and local governments, and by school districts.

Managing Trusts

Many banks manage investments on behalf of their customers. When they do this, the money or other property that is turned over to the banks for investment is said to be held in *trust*. This service can be offered through a trust company or through trust departments in banks. **Trust companies** are businesses that manage people's money and property for them.

Trusts are used by people of all ages, but they are especially useful for very young people and for some elderly people. A young person who inherits money may not have the skill and experience to manage it wisely. Elderly people who are ill may ask the trust department of a bank to manage their money. The bank makes investments and keeps the customers informed about what is happening to their money.

Name some benefits of storing items in a safe-deposit box versus your own home.

Chapter 25 *The Banking System and Financial Services* **347**

---

product or service, intended customers, and a description of how the item relates to class learning.

THE FEDERAL RESERVE SYSTEM

One type of bank exists that will not allow you to make deposits. As an individual, you cannot open a savings account in a Federal Reserve Bank or borrow money from it. A Federal Reserve Bank is a bank for banks. Its relationship to member banks is similar to the relationship of your bank to you.

Structure of the Federal Reserve System

The federal government set up the **Federal Reserve System (Fed)** to supervise and regulate member banks in order to help the banks serve the public efficiently. All national banks are required to join the Federal Reserve System, and state banks may join. Banks that join the system are known as *member banks.* The United States is divided into 12 Federal Reserve districts, with a central Federal Reserve Bank in each district, as shown in Figure 25-3.

Federal Reserve Activities

You may go to your local bank to deposit money or to get a loan. The Federal Reserve Bank serves its member banks in the same way. It accepts their deposits, lends them money, and provides them with other banking services.

FIGURE 25-3 Which Federal Reserve Regional Bank serves banks in your community?

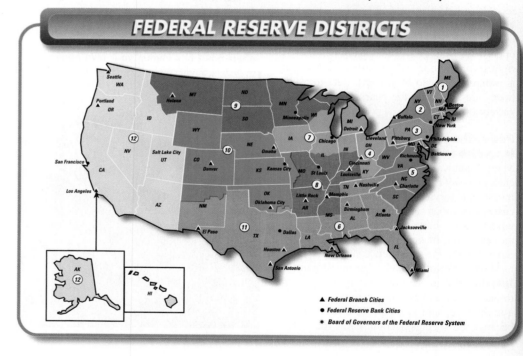

FEDERAL RESERVE DISTRICTS

▲ *Federal Branch Cities*
● *Federal Reserve Bank Cities*
✳ *Board of Governors of the Federal Reserve System*

Critical Thinking Skills-Problem Solving

Problem-solving skills, which include recognizing a problem and devising a plan of action, are applied throughout every chapter in this text. Each time a student participates in a Cooperative Learning or Teams activity, problem-solving skills are applied in a group situation. Each time a student completes a math application in Calculate Business Data, decisions are made as to which mathematical approach must be taken. For each Technology Application problem, students must decide which template problem to use, which piece of software to load, and how to solve the problem. Emphasize to students how they are using problem solving in their day-to-day tasks and make them aware of the skills they are developing.

SCANS

One service provided by the Fed is the holding of *reserves*. Banks cannot lend all of the money they receive from their customers. The government requires banks to keep a certain amount of customers' money on deposit with the Federal Reserve System in case additional funds are needed to meet the daily needs of their customers. Therefore, a bank will lend only a certain percentage of its customers' deposits and keep the rest in reserve. For example, if a customer deposits $1,000 and the bank is required by the Federal Reserve System to hold 15 percent of all deposits in reserve, the bank can lend 85 percent of the new deposit, or $850 (100% − 15% = 85%). This regulation is designed to help the banking system and the economy operate efficiently and to protect depositors' money.

FINANCIAL INSTITUTIONS AND ECONOMIC GROWTH

The activities of financial institutions affect each of us in many ways. Several million people work in the offices of America's banks, savings and loan associations, credit unions, and other financial institutions. Banking services are commonly used to

- build homes
- start new businesses
- plant crops
- finance educations
- buy goods
- pave streets
- build hospitals
- buy new business equipment

The Federal Reserve System buys and sells federal government bonds as part of its efforts to increase or decrease the money supply in our economy. The Fed's actions to affect the economy are called *monetary policy*.

Banking services are made possible through the savings you and others deposit. Deposits do not remain idle in bank vaults. They are put to work. When you and others deposit money in a bank, you are helping to create jobs and economic growth that benefit your community and our society.

How do you think economic development would compare if the financial assistance of banks was not available?

REVIEW YOUR READING

1. Interest on loans, investing part of their depositors' money, charges for checking account services, managing trust accounts, and rental of safe-deposit boxes.
2. A full-service bank offers a wide variety of financial services through many departments.
3. To insure deposits in banks and savings and loan associations.
4. Life insurance companies, investment companies, finance companies, mortgage companies, check-cashing outlets, and pawnshops.
5. Accepting deposits, transferring funds, lending money, storing valuables in safe-deposit boxes, providing financial advice and investment services, and managing trusts.
6. Possible answers might include automatic deposit of a payroll check, automatic withdrawal of cash at an ATM, automatic payment of loans or bills each month by the bank for the customer.
7. To store valuables, such as jewelry, bond and stock certificates, birth records, a list of insurance policies, and a will.
8. Young people who have received inheritances and are too inexperienced to manage the funds and elderly people who are ill and may not be able to manage their money.
9. Receiving their deposits, lending them money, and providing them with other banking services.
10. Possible answers might include loans to help build homes, start new businesses, plant crops, finance education, buy goods, pave streets, build hospitals, and buy new business equipment.

COMMUNICATE BUSINESS CONCEPTS

11. Answers will vary. A point to be emphasized is that government regulations making it difficult for "just anyone" to start a bank protect the banking industry and depositors from dishonest or incompetent people who could cause depositors to lose their money.

Chapter REVIEW

BUSINESS NOTES

1. Banks earn most of their revenues by charging for loans they make and by investing part of the money deposited by customers.
2. The main types of deposit-type institutions are commercial banks, savings and loan associations, mutual savings banks, and credit unions.
3. Nondeposit financial institutions include life insurance companies, investment companies, consumer finance companies, mortgage companies, check-cashing outlets, and pawnshops.
4. The most common services offered by financial institutions are accepting deposits, transferring funds, lending money, storing valuables, providing financial advice and investment services, and managing trusts.
5. The Federal Reserve System serves member banks by accepting their deposits, lending them money, and providing other services.
6. Banks and other financial institutions serve communities by employing people and lending money to build homes, start new businesses, plant crops, finance educations, buy goods, pave streets, build hospitals, and buy new business equipment.

REVIEW YOUR READING

1. How do banks earn most of their revenue? Name two other ways in which banks earn revenue.
2. What is a full-service bank?
3. What is the purpose of the Federal Deposit Insurance Corporation?
4. What are the main nondeposit financial institutions?
5. List six services provided by banks.
6. Give an example of an electronic funds transfer.
7. What is the purpose of a safe-deposit box?
8. What two age groups find trust departments of banks especially helpful? Why?
9. Name three services the Federal Reserve System provides for its member banks.
10. Give three examples to show the importance of banks to your community.

COMMUNICATE BUSINESS CONCEPTS

11. "In a private enterprise system, anybody who wants to open a bank should be allowed to do so." Do you agree with this statement? Give reasons for your answer.
12. Alicia Perez and Miguel Morales operate a store. Each day they deposit all of the cash they receive except a small amount of change and a few bills they keep in their safe. Explain why this method is wise.
13. List the type of banking service that you think each following group or individual would be most likely to use. Explain your answer.
    a. A person planning to open a fitness center
    b. A musical group

12. Decreases danger that money will be lost or stolen; bills can conveniently be paid by check; bank deposits and checks serve as a record of the store's business transactions.
13. (a) Loan for the new business, direct deposit of the payroll, checking, and possibly financial counseling; (b) checking, savings, perhaps a loan for sound equipment; (c) trust department and investment services, checking, savings, safe-deposit box; (d) loan for purchase; (e) checking, savings.
14. Possible answers might include (a) How long do I plan to leave the money in the bank? (b) Are there penalties for early withdrawal from savings? (c) What interest rate will I earn on savings? (d) Is an interest-bearing checking account available for the $1000 I have to deposit?

c. A wealthy senior citizen
d. A buyer of a van
e. A high school recycling club

14. Jake Olsen has decided to put $1,000 in the bank. List several questions Jake might want to ask before choosing whether to put the money in a checking or a savings account.

DEVELOP YOUR BUSINESS LANGUAGE

For each numbered item, find the term that has the same meaning.

15. A bank owned by depositors that mainly handles savings accounts and makes loans to home buyers.

16. A bank that offers a full range of financial services.

17. A nationwide banking plan set up by our federal government to supervise and regulate member banks.

18. An amount paid for the use of money.

19. Financial institutions that specialize in managing the money and property of others.

20. A financial institution that specializes in savings accounts and loans for mortgages.

21. A not-for-profit financial institution formed by people who have like occupations or live in the same community.

22. A financial institution that specializes in making loans for long-lasting or durable goods and financial emergencies.

23. A federal agency that protects depositors' money in case of the failure of a bank or financial institution that it regulates.

24. A secured area in a bank vault for storing valuables.

25. A system through which funds are moved electronically from one account to another and from one bank to another.

26. Savings that are put to work to earn more money.

KEY TERMS
commercial bank
consumer finance company
credit union
electronic funds transfer (EFT)
Federal Deposit Insurance Corporation (FDIC)
Federal Reserve System (Fed)
interest
investments
mutual savings bank
safe-deposit boxes
savings and loan association (S&L)
trust companies

DECISION-MAKING STRATEGIES

Fran and Bill Hamilton recently moved to a new community. They are having trouble deciding whether to use a financial institution near their workplaces or near their home. The Hamiltons have the opportunity to do business with a credit union, a national bank with many branches, a local bank with strong personal service, or a savings and loan association.

27. What factors should the Hamiltons consider when selecting a financial institution?

28. How could Fran and Bill obtain information about the financial institution that would best serve their needs?

CALCULATE BUSINESS DATA

29. The FDIC insures deposits in banks up to $100,000. The insurance is paid for by the banks just as individuals buy insurance for their homes or cars. Based on the soundness of a bank's finances and the risks it poses, the regulating agency sets the amount charged. The data on the next page show the rate charges in a recent year and a revised higher rate based on a decline in its financial condition.

DEVELOP YOUR BUSINESS LANGUAGE

15. mutual savings bank
16. commercial bank
17. Federal Reserve System (Fed)
18. interest
19. trust companies
20. savings and loan association (S&L)
21. credit union
22. consumer finance company
23. Federal Deposit Insurance Corporation (FDIC)
24. safe-deposit boxes
25. electronic funds transfer
26. investments

DECISION-MAKING STRATEGIES

27. When comparing financial institutions, the Hamiltons should consider location, convenience of hours and electronic banking, services available, costs and fees for services, interest earned on deposits, and availability of deposit insurance.

28. To obtain information about various financial institutions, Fran and Bill could view advertisements, visit the institutions and talk to employees, talk to people who bank at the places they are considering, and read articles and books about selecting and using financial services.

CALCULATE BUSINESS DATA

29. (a) $0.10 - 0.03 = 0.07$; $0.07 \div 0.03 = 2.33$ or 233% increase; (b) $6,590,000.00 \div $100.00 = $65,900.00$; $65,900.00 \times $0.03 = $1,977.00$; (c) $65,900.00 \times $0.10 = $6,590.00$; (d) $6,590.00 - $1,977.00 = $4,613.00$ increase

30. (a) $210 \times 12 = \$2,520$ deposited; (b) $90 \times 12 = \$1,080$ savings; (c) $\$1,080.00 \times 0.035 = \$37.80$ interest; $\$1,080.00 + \$37.80 = \$1,117.80$ accumulated savings

31. $\$140.00 + \$1,080.00 = \$1,220.00$ available funds; $\$87.00 + \$146.00 + \$29.00 + \$292.00 + \$120.00 + \$60.00 = \$734.00$ total withdrawals; $\$0.75 \times 2 = \$1.50$ EFT charges; $\$1,220.00 - \$734.00 - \$1.50 = \$484.50$ new balance

32. (a) Jose: $14 + 8 + 6 + 15 = 43$ cans; Darlana: $3 + 6 + 10 + 12 = 31$ cans; Carl: $6 + 5 + 5 + 7 = 23$ cans; (b) Jose: $43 \times \$3 = \$129$; Darlana: $31 \times \$3 = \$93$; Carl: $23 \times \$3 = \$69$; (c) Jose: $43 \times 0.5 = 21.5$ kg; Darlana: $31 \times 0.5 = 15.5$ kg; Carl: $23 \times 0.5 = 11.5$ kg; (d) $43 + 31 + 23 = 97$ total cans sold; $97 \times \$3 = \$291$ revenue; $97 \times \$1.46 = \$141.62$ cost of sales; $\$291.00 - \$141.62 = \$149.38$ profit

TECHNOLOGY APPLICATION

In this activity, students use a computer to solve a business problem using a file provided on the data CD that accompanies *Intro to Business.* Instructions for using the data CD are included in a **README** file on the disk. Solutions are provided on the Instructor's Resource CD.

Fidelity National Bank

Deposits: $6,590,000
Current insurance rate per $100 of deposits: 3¢
Revised rate per $100 of deposits: 10¢

a. What is the percentage of increase in the rate?
b. What is the cost of Fidelity's insurance at the current rate?
c. What will Fidelity's cost of insurance be at the revised rate?
d. What is the amount of the increase?

30. Sachi Kinoshita is saving money for a car. She worked 12 weeks during the summer on a road construction crew. Her take-home pay was $210 a week.
a. If she deposited each paycheck in the bank, what was the total amount she deposited during the summer?
b. If she put $90 each week in her savings account, how much did she save during the summer?
c. If she leaves her accumulated summer savings in the bank for a year at 3.5 percent interest, how much will she have available for a down payment on a car at the end of the year?

Hint: Refer to Appendix C: Determining Percentage and Interest in Business.

31. On June 1, Susan Pohlnik had a checking account balance of $140. She has her paychecks automatically deposited into her account. Her earnings for June were $1,080.

During the month, she wrote checks for $87, $146, $29, and $292. She had $120 automatically transferred from her checking account to her savings account. In addition, she used her ATM card to withdraw $60 in cash. The bank charges 75 cents for each EFT transfer or withdrawal. Find Susan's bank balance after these transactions.

32. To raise money for a party for patients at a local children's hospital, the business club at Martin Luther King High School sold cans of trail mix. The 0.5 kilogram cans sold for $3 each. The students deposited the total amount of their sales each week in the school's accounting office. The records of the three students with the highest November sales appear in the table below.
a. How many cans did each of these students sell?
b. How much money did each student deposit during November?
c. How many kilograms of trail mix did each student sell?
d. If the trail mix cost the students $1.46 per can, what was the amount of their profit on sales for November?

Date	Jose Santos	Darlana Jones	Carl Perlman
Nov. 5	14 cans	3 cans	6 cans
12	8	6	5
19	6	10	5
26	15	12	7

TECHNOLOGY APPLICATION

Using the *Intro to Business* Data CD and your database program software, select problem CH25. After the problem appears on your screen, complete the following activities. Then, after you have completed each step, display or print a report for each activity. If you do not have a printer available, answer the questions before you leave the computer.

33. Select and list the Federal Reserve branches (not the banks) in Districts 7 through 12. How many branches are listed?

34. Sort the database in ascending order by state. Answer the following questions:
a. What is the seventh bank or branch listed?
b. What is the twelfth bank or branch listed?

35. Sort the database in ascending order by type as the primary field and by city as the secondary field. Answer the following questions:
a. What is the first bank (not branch) listed?
b. What is the last bank (not branch) listed?

COMMUNICATING for SUCCESS

ACTIVE LISTENING— "WHAT I HEARD YOU SAY WAS . . ."

Listening is more important to a person at work than any other communication skill. In fact, the average employee spends almost half of communication time (45%) listening. The rest of the time is spent in speaking (30%), reading (16%), and writing (9%).

Listening isn't simply hearing what people say to you. Listening also means processing or working to understand what is being said. Processing requires you to concentrate on what people are saying in order to fully understand.

One bad habit that many of us develop is to use the time when others are talking to plan a reply. This time should, instead, be used to listen actively for meaning in what is being said.

Active listening for meaning in personal communication is not easy, but it is worth the effort. Here is a list of suggestions to help you improve your active listening skills.

- Adopt a positive attitude toward the speaker.
- Be responsive to the speaker.
- Shut out distractions that may come between you and the speaker.
- Listen for the speaker's purpose.

An additional suggestion that works well for some is to say to the speaker, "What I heard you say was . . . , is that correct?" Repeating this exercise helps you assure yourself and the speaker that you understand what is being said.

If you listen actively, you will understand better and remember longer what the speaker says. Listening actively will contribute to improved business communication.

CRITICAL THINKING
1. In which of the traditional four methods of communication (reading, writing, speaking, and listening) do we spend the most time? How much?
2. What does listening mean?

COMMUNICATING for SUCCESS

Communications skills will help ensure students' success in the business world. Communicating for Success introduces workplace/interpersonal communications issues and proper uses of communications technology. Each feature discusses a key communications topic, and contains two Critical Thinking questions that require students to analyze what they have learned.

Since almost half of the time employees spend communicating is spent listening (rather than talking, reading, or writing), it's crucial for students to learn how to listen effectively in a business environment. This feature focuses their attention on "active" listening, which entails concentration and the processing of information that they hear. It's different from the informal listening to which they are probably accustomed, so it will likely take a bit of discipline to change existing habits.

CRITICAL THINKING
1. Listening. About 45% of the time.
2. In addition to hearing, it means processing and working to understand what is said.

This chapter covers the advantages of using checks, the major types of checking accounts, the activities involved in opening a checking account, and provides a detailed discussion of the three major types of endorsements.

Resources for Teachers
- Lesson Plans
- School-To-Work/SCANS Activity Masters
- Spanish Resources
- Instructor's Resource CD

Assessment
- Chapter and Unit Tests, Ch. 26
- ExamView, Ch. 26

Media/Technology
- Applying Technology Data CD
- PowerPoint slides
- Business Connection CD
- Videotape

Activity Masters and Workbooks
- Activities and Projects, Ch. 26
- Internet Activity Masters
- Business Math Activity Masters
- Communications Activity Masters
- International Business Activity Masters
- Ethics Activity Masters

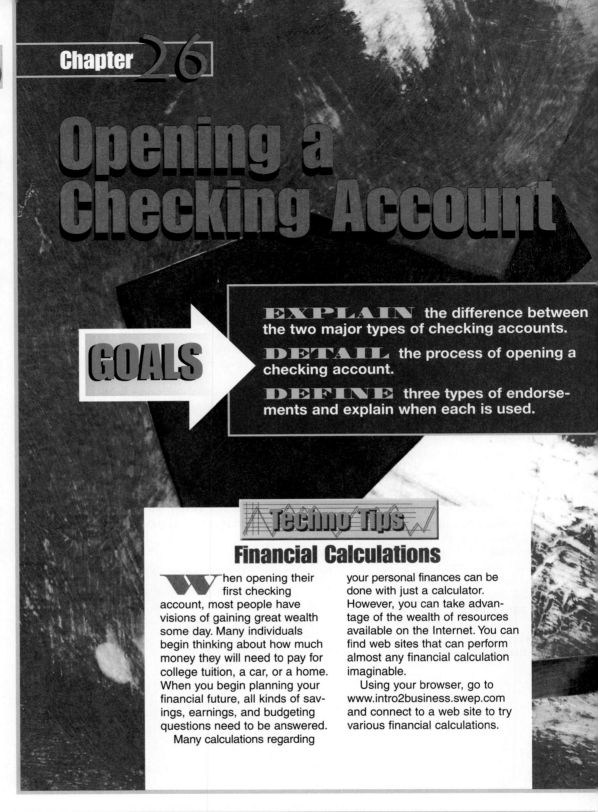

Chapter 26

Opening a Checking Account

GOALS

EXPLAIN the difference between the two major types of checking accounts.

DETAIL the process of opening a checking account.

DEFINE three types of endorsements and explain when each is used.

Techno Tips
Financial Calculations

When opening their first checking account, most people have visions of gaining great wealth some day. Many individuals begin thinking about how much money they will need to pay for college tuition, a car, or a home. When you begin planning your financial future, all kinds of savings, earnings, and budgeting questions need to be answered.

Many calculations regarding your personal finances can be done with just a calculator. However, you can take advantage of the wealth of resources available on the Internet. You can find web sites that can perform almost any financial calculation imaginable.

Using your browser, go to www.intro2business.swep.com and connect to a web site to try various financial calculations.

Students need to know the latest technologies and develop cutting edge Internet skills for use in current jobs, future careers, or in their homes. TechnoTips introduces students to today's cutting edge technologies and provides them with important Internet skills. Feature topics concentrate on Internet-specific technologies and computer or other hi-tech innovations for use by businesses and consumers. At the www.intro2business.swep.com web site, students can complete the activity for this chapter.

"I do not believe in checking accounts," Bob said. "Cash is much easier for all my daily business activities. You'll never catch me holding up a line at a cash register while I write out a check."

"Aren't you worried that you might lose your money?" was Georgette's reaction. "Or, what if you have to prove that you made a payment?"

"I can get a receipt," Bob responded. "I still say that using cash only is better than sometimes using checks and sometimes cash."

"Yes, but a bank will have a record of your check even if you lose your receipt," Georgette replied. "Won't you just consider using a checking account? There are many good reasons. I think that you and I need to have a talk about the advantages of having a checking account."

ADVANTAGES OF A CHECKING ACCOUNT

Having a checking account provides a person with several benefits. These advantages include convenience, safety, proof of payment, and a record of finances.

Convenience

When you open a checking account, you will find that it will be a convenient way to handle your business affairs. With a checking account, you can write checks at home and pay bills by mail. Or, you can make payments automatically through the EFT system. Both methods save time and money.

Safety

A checking account also has many safety advantages. People who keep a great deal of money on hand risk losing it by fire, theft, or carelessness. When money is at home, a greater temptation also exists to spend it needlessly. With a checking account, you will need to keep only a little cash on hand for small purchases.

Another safety feature is that you can safely send a check through the mail because it can be cashed only by the person or business to whom it is made payable. Sending cash through the mail is not safe, because if it is lost, there is no way to recover it. However, if a check is lost, it can be replaced.

The money you deposit in the bank is protected in another way. If your bank is a member of the Federal Deposit Insurance Corporation, your deposit will be insured up to $100,000.00. Always check to see if the financial institution in which you deposit your money is insured.

What are some possible inconveniences of having a checking account?

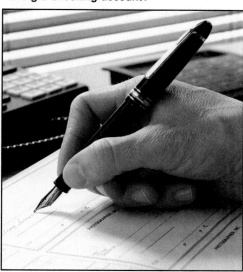

Have students describe difficulties that might occur if a person did not have a checking account. Ask students to list any additional difficulties if it is a business that does not have a checking account. List answers on the overhead or the board.

PURPOSE Provide a purpose for students as they read the chapter. Ask what they think they will learn. Direct students to skim the chapter, looking at photos, reading captions, and noting main headings. The goals at the beginning of each chapter provide a valuable tool for having students pinpoint main ideas. The tasks required by the goals are signaled in the first word. Some emphasize information collection ("Identify," "List"), while others call for description ("Explain," "Describe"). Ask students to look through all the goals and note the first word of each. Then ask students to state the purpose of studying this chapter. In this chapter, students will learn about the advantages and types of checking accounts and how to open a checking account.

MAKE CONNECTIONS Use PowerPoint 26-2, *Advantages of a Checking Account*, to introduce four major reasons for having a checking account. Describe the two main types of checking accounts—regular checking accounts and interest checking accounts. Cover the different requirements and fees associated with checking accounts. Go over the steps required to complete a signature card and make an initial deposit. Introduce the concept of endorsements and the legal ramifications of transferring ownership. Emphasize the proper placement of endorsements and the consequences of not following the rules for endorsements. List the three types of endorsements and give real-world examples of the use of each type. Emphasize the importance of keeping accurate records when using a checking account. Explain that check stubs and check registers are tools that help maintain accurate and complete records.

TRY THIS/GUIDED PRACTICE
Use PowerPoint 26-4, 26-5, and 26-6 to guide students through completing a signature card using information about yourself or a student volunteer.

Use PowerPoint 26-11, *Types of Endorsements*, to show students how to write each type of endorsement. Emphasize the similarities and differences among the endorsements.

Return to PowerPoint 26-7, *Deposit Slip*. Having students write in their own names, guide them through completing a deposit slip using the information in Figure 26-2.

EXPLORE THIS/INDEPENDENT PRACTICE Before assigning independent practice material for any chapter, students should be expected to read the textbook material carefully. In view of the fact that all students vary widely in their ability to read effectively, have the students read the entire chapter, or sections thereof, silently in class if the material has not been previously read in connection with homework assignments.

After students have read the chapter, ask them to complete the Chapter Review questions. Develop Your Business Language is an excellent way to improve students' vocabulary. Only words introduced in the chapter are used in the exercises. The Review Your Reading questions can be used to check students' ability to comprehend what they have read. The Communicate Business Concepts section affords an opportunity for students to apply to practical life situations the information gained from reading the chapter. By completing the problems under Calculate

A *bank teller's* job duties include:
- Receiving money from and paying money to bank customers.
- Keeping records of money and negotiable instruments from a bank's various transactions.
- Providing information about services.

Proof of Payment

An important advantage of paying by check is that, once cashed, a check is legal proof of payment. For example, suppose you write a check each month for $30 to pay for piano lessons at the Mallard Music Studio. The studio will deposit your check at its bank. The studio's bank will then send the check to your bank where it will be subtracted from your account. If the studio makes an error in its records and later tells you that a past month's fee was not paid, your canceled check will prove that you made the payment.

Record of Finances

Another advantage of checking accounts is that they provide a record of your finances. With a checking account, you must record every deposit you make and every check you write. You can tell from these records how much you are spending, where your money is going, and how much you have remaining in your account. The organized records you keep can help you manage your money.

TYPES OF CHECKING ACCOUNTS

Checking accounts differ from one bank to another and from one part of the country to another. They differ in the features they offer customers. Checking accounts also differ in costs. A **service charge** is a fee a bank

charges for handling a checking account. When you are ready to open a checking account, you should visit several banks to find out what services each offers and what fees it charges. Comparison shopping for your checking account will enable you to choose one that best suits your needs.

While there are many types of checking accounts in use, they can be viewed in two basic categories: regular checking accounts and interest checking accounts.

Regular Checking Accounts

If you write a large number of checks each month, you probably should use a regular checking account. With most banks, there is no service charge for a regular checking account as long as the account balance does not fall below a certain amount during a

As a record of your finances, how can a checking account help you to plan your financial future?

The career listed in the Career Highlights comes from the *Occupational Outlook Handbook*, an online publication (www.bls.gov/oco) of the federal government. The O*NET code for Teller is 43-3071.00. Students can access O*NET Online (online.onetcenter.org) to view important features of this job. Tell your class about these resources and how to use them. The description of job duties can be used to demonstrate the relevancy of skills learned in this course.

month. This minimum monthly balance varies. It may be $300 or higher. A *minimum monthly balance* is a stated amount that an account must not fall below.

Sometimes the service charges are calculated on the average monthly balance of the account during the month. An *average monthly balance* is the sum of the daily balances divided by the number of days in the month. The account may fall below a certain minimum on some days, but must average at or above the minimum at the end of the month to avoid a service charge. Some banks do not charge service fees on checking accounts if the depositor also keeps a certain balance, often $1,000, in a savings account at the same bank. At some financial institutions, service charges are waived for students or customers 65 years old or older.

Interest Checking Accounts

Many financial institutions offer checking accounts that earn interest. However, these accounts usually require a minimum monthly balance or an average monthly balance of $500 or more. As long as the account meets the balance requirement, the bank will pay interest on the checking account. If the account falls below the required amount, the bank usually pays no interest and may add a service charge to the account. The charges may include a monthly charge, a fee for each check written, or both of these service charges.

The rates of interest that banks pay their customers also vary. In recent years, typical rates have ranged from 1 to 2 percent depending on economic conditions. Usually, a bank will offer a higher rate of interest when

a higher balance is maintained. The interest rate may be tied to the current cost of money in the marketplace, known as the **money market rate**. The money market rate is the interest rate that big users of money, such as governments and large corporations, pay when they borrow money. The money market rate varies from day to day.

Banks offer interest earning checking accounts with varying rates tied to the money market rate. As the money market rate changes, so does the rate the banks pay holders of certain types of accounts. To avoid changing rates daily or weekly, however, the bank determines the average of the daily money market rates for the month and pays the depositor that average rate for the month. For very large accounts, rates higher than money market rates are sometimes available.

Other Types of Checking Accounts

In addition to the two basic kinds of checking accounts, several other types are available. You may need to write only a few checks each month and wish to keep a small balance in your checking account. For depositors with such needs, many banks offer *special checking accounts*. Charges on the accounts vary, but the basic charge is about 10 to 20 cents for each check written. There may also be a small monthly service charge for the account.

Savings and loan associations and other financial institutions commonly offer checking services. Credit unions may provide checking accounts for members. Members

Business Data, students will be able to strengthen and refine their abilities in mathematics. Technology Application allows students to demonstrate skill in using word processing, spreadsheet, and database software. Decision-Making Strategies contains material to challenge students to utilize the model explained in Chapter 1 for problem solving.

The Chapter Review questions at the end of the chapter vary in level of difficulty. For a basic assignment, consider Develop Your Business Language and Review Your Reading. For an average assignment, consider the basic assignment plus Communicate Business Concepts and Calculate Business Data. For an enhanced assignment, try the average assignment plus Technology Application and Decision-Making Strategies.

ASSESS

Review the goals at the beginning of the chapter and the Business Notes at the end of the chapter. Have students respond orally or in writing to each of the Business Notes restated as a question, provided below. For those who may have difficulty providing answers, assign the reteaching activities that follow. Enrichment activities may also be assigned where appropriate.

1. What are four advantages of having a checking account? (Answer: Convenience, safety, proof of payment, and record of finances.)
2. How are the two major types of checking accounts different? (Answer: Regular accounts: fees vary, sometimes including

TEACHING TIP
Safety and Health

In order to provide a safe and healthy environment for students, encourage students to keep their work surface open except for the tasks on which they are working. If they are trying to work around stacks of books and papers, they will have a tendency to alter their posture, which will lead to fatigue.

fees for checks written and deposits made; no interest; small monthly minimum balance may eliminate fees. Interest checking accounts: pays interest; minimum balance required.)

3. How is a checking account opened? (Answer: Take your paycheck or cash to the new-accounts desk, sign a signature card, make your deposit, and select your checks.)

4. What is the purpose of an endorsement? (Answer: Allows recipient to cash, deposit, or transfer; provides legal evidence that the check has been cashed or transferred; guarantees the endorser will pay the check.)

5. When is each type of endorsement used? (Answer: Blank makes a check payable to anyone; special endorsement names the person to whom the check has been transferred; restrictive limits the use of the check.)

6. What is the purpose of a check stub and check register? (Answer: Maintaining a record of information about checks you have written.)

RETEACH

Obtain advertisements and brochures with information about the types and costs of checking accounts available in your community. Pass these around to the students so they can actually see what this information looks like. On an overhead or on the board, create columns with the following headings: location, minimum balance, services offered, monthly fees, and costs for

of credit unions are called *shareholders* when they have money on deposit, and their checks are called **sharedrafts**. This means a draft (withdrawal) is made on the member's shares of ownership (deposits) in the credit union. Interest rates may vary and the number of sharedrafts per month may be limited.

OPENING A CHECKING ACCOUNT

Opening a checking account is fairly easy no matter what type of account you choose. You can simply take your paycheck or cash to the new-accounts desk in a financial institution. The representative will help you sign a signature card, make your deposit, and select your checks. Some banks, however, may require you to be at least 18 years old to open a checking account.

The Signature Card

A bank will deduct money from a checking account to cover checks only when authorized to do so by the depositor. Therefore, the bank must keep the depositor's signature on record to compare with the signature that appears on his or her checks. For this reason, you will be asked to sign your name on a card when you open your account. This card is called a **signature card** and is the bank's official record of your signature. You must use the same signature on each check you write. Figure 26-1 shows a signature card for Alicia Garcia.

Sometimes two or more people have an account together. This is known as a **joint account**. Each person who will write checks on the account must sign the signature card. Any signer of the card in a joint account can write checks on the account as if he or she were the only owner. A signature card for a business would show the name of the business and the signatures of those authorized to sign checks for the business.

Making the First Deposit

When you deposit money in a checking account, you fill out a deposit slip or a

FIGURE 26-1 Do you understand how a signature card protects you and the bank?

SIGNATURE CARD

Second National Bank
PERSONAL CHECKING ACCOUNT

○ JOINT AND SEVERAL (Payable to the order of either or the survivor)
● INDIVIDUAL (If payable on death to named survivors, fill in section below)
___ Indicate number of signatures required

Alicia Garcia
SIGNATURE

SIGNATURE

Alicia Garcia _or_ _____
PRINT OR TYPE NAME(S)

19684 Absaroka Dr., Houston, TX 77083-5549 _2 years_
ADDRESS   CITY AND STATE   ZIP CODE   HOW LONG? MO. YRS.

_555-6403_   _720J64-TX_
HOME PHONE   DRIVERS LICENSE NO./STATE

PAYABLE ON DEATH OF DEPOSITOR TO SUCH OF THE FOLLOWING NAMED AS SURVIVE DEPOSITOR:

(PRINT OR TYPE NAME — DESIGNATION BY OTHER MEANS IS NOT SUFFICIENT.)
Office: _____   Date: _April 10, 20--_

_201-24-1590_   _1648-7214_
OFFICER APPROVAL   SOCIAL SECURITY NUMBER   ACCOUNT NUMBER

Basic Skills-Writing

Employers are looking for potential employees with good basic foundation skills. In order to prepare students for the school-to-work transition, we must teach these skills in our classroom. Language arts skills are an important component of good writing skills. Students should learn to paraphrase, write complete sentences, and identify subjects. For additional

practice in language arts skills, direct students to answer the Communicate Business Concepts questions at the end of the chapter. Students should write the answers in their own words and in complete sentences. To further practice language arts skills, ask students to underline the subject(s) in each sentence of their answers.

SCANS

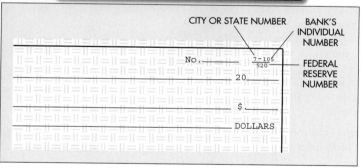

DEPOSIT SLIP

CHECKING ACCOUNT DEPOSIT SLIP		DOLLARS	CENTS
	CURRENCY	60	00
	COIN	1	75
NAME *Alicia Garcia*	1 CHECKS 68-36	270	10
	2		
	3		
DATE *April 10* 20--	4		
	TOTAL FROM OTHER SIDE		
This deposit is accepted subject to verification and to the rules and regulations of the Bank.	TOTAL	331	85
	LESS CASH RECEIVED		
Second National Bank	TOTAL DEPOSIT	331	85
HOUSTON, TX 77083-9073			

IF MORE THAN 4 CHECKS, LIST ON REVERSE SIDE. ENTER TOTAL HERE

ACCOUNT NUMBER *1648-7214*

FIGURE 26-2 Where do you find the bank numbers on deposited checks?

deposit ticket. A **deposit slip** is a form on which you list all items you are depositing—currency, coins, or checks.

The deposit slip shows your name, your account number, the date, the items deposited, and the total amount of the deposit. Most banks print the depositor's name, address, and account number on deposit slips and checks. Since these will not be ready when you open your new account, you will use a blank deposit slip. Figure 26-2 shows a deposit slip made out by Alicia Garcia. Her deposit consisted of $60.00 in currency, $1.75 in coin, and her paycheck for $270.10, for a total of $331.85.

Each check is identified by the number of the bank on which it was drawn. This number is assigned to each commercial bank by the American Bankers Association. You can

Some checks have carbonless paper attached. The copies made when you write checks may also be used to maintain a record of deposits and checks written.

see the three parts of this number in Figure 26-3. The first part of the number above the line indicates the city or state in which the bank is located. The second part is the number assigned to the individual bank. The number below the line is a Federal Reserve number that banks use in sorting checks. The two top numbers of each check deposited should be listed on the deposit slip, as shown in Figure 26-2.

BANK IDENTIFICATION NUMBER

CITY OR STATE NUMBER   BANK'S INDIVIDUAL NUMBER

No.

7-105 / 520

20

FEDERAL RESERVE NUMBER

$

DOLLARS

FIGURE 26-3 What is the city or state number for banks in your community?

printing of checks. Taking each ad or brochure one by one, write the characteristics of each account under the appropriate column headings. This is a good way to reteach the strengths and weaknesses of each account depending on the circumstances of the depositor and the planned uses for the account.

ENRICH

Direct students to read the Cultural Perspectives in this chapter. Invite someone who works at a bank or other financial institution to speak to the class. The speaker might discuss the steps taken to provide convenience and safety to checking account users. Other topics could include how fees and minimum balances are determined and the rules that tellers follow regarding different types of endorsements. You could also have students prepare a poster illustrating the three major types of endorsements—blank, special, and restrictive.

SUMMARIZE

Use PowerPoint 26-2, *Advantages of a Checking Account*, to emphasize the benefits of checking accounts. Point out that, because checking accounts are so useful, individuals and businesses are willing to live with the strict rules regarding minimum balances, signature cards, and endorsements.

EVALUATE

- Assign Activities and Projects for Chapter 26.
- Administer the printed test or ExamView for Chapter 26.
- Assign School-To-Work/SCANS portfolio activities for Unit 8.

Chapter 26 *Opening a Checking Account*   **359**

TEACHING STRATEGIES

Teams

Teams-Games-Tournaments (TGT) is an instructional method in which students use cooperative learning in peer groups. When using TGT, students are assigned to teams with four members each. The teams should be mixed in performance level, gender, and culture. Use the given lesson plan to teach this chapter, then assign students into groups. Each group will study and review the lesson making sure that all group members understand the goals and content. Read the Review Your Reading questions in the end-of-chapter activities, one at a time. Teams have an opportunity to answer the question for points. You may choose to have students raise their hands in order to be chosen, or you may simply take turns with each group. The highest scoring team wins.

- For clear, concise writing, students should be encouraged to plan, organize, and outline main ideas. First, determine the overall goal of the paper. Secondly, select important ideas, and organize material around these ideas.
- Guide students into using a creative introduction, such as a quote, fact, or story.
- Explain the use of specific sentence subjects and action verbs—avoid "It is…," "There are…," "These were…," and "This is…," so that students may use them properly.
- Encourage students to make every sentence a major event and have each sentence communicate a complete idea that either introduces new ideas and information or that expands on an idea already introduced. Students should ask themselves, "Does every sentence contribute to communicating the main ideas of the presentation?"
- Caution students that a paragraph should be organized to introduce and develop an idea that contributes to the overall goal of the paper.
- Recommend that students use an impersonal, formal style, avoiding "I."
- Encourage students to edit carefully for a clear, concise presentation and reduce unnecessary prepositions, adjectives, and adverbs.
- Students should always check spelling, punctuation, and capitalization before handing in an assignment.

CULTURAL PERSPECTIVES
Babylonian Banks and the Incan Record Keeping System

As a society becomes larger and more complex, the need for financial systems becomes greater. One example is the Babylonian civilization in Asia Minor. Over 7,000 years ago, the Babylonians had banks and a method for transferring funds. An early form of checks was used to draw money in one place and to pay in another. The Babylonians required that most business transactions be put in writing and signed by the parties involved. This is believed to be one of the first verified uses of business documents.

Another example is the Incan civilization in South America. Have your ever been "at the end of your rope" when trying to keep track of financial matters? Perhaps that phrase relates to the Incan record keeping system. Incan record keepers used small ropes of different colors and sizes, and knotted and joined them in different ways to help keep track of data. These ropes, called quipu, w● used to keep track of census data, gold mi output, inventory in a storehouse, and imp● tant historic dates.

Both the Babylonians and Incas develop practices that served as foundations for th● financial systems and record keeping met● ods in operation today.

Critical Thinking
1. Why are documents important for effici● business activities?
2. If we didn't have computers today, what types of financial record keeping syste● might be used in our society?

ENDORSING CHECKS FOR MAKING DEPOSITS

Before Alicia can deposit her paycheck, she must endorse it by writing her name on the back of the left end of the check. An **endorsement** is written evidence that you received payment or that you transferred your right of receiving payment to someone else.

The Purpose of Endorsements
Before you cash, deposit, or transfer a check to another person or business, you must first endorse the check. When you endorse a check, your responsibilities are almost as great as if you had written the check yourself. As an endorser, you are actually making this promise: "If this check is not paid by the bank, I will pay it." The three main purposes of endorsements are as follows:

1. Endorsements allow the recipient of the check to cash, deposit, or transfer it to someone else.

How does the use of deposit slips benefit the bank and the customer?

2. Endorsements serve as legal evidence that the receiver cashed or transferred the check to someone else.

CULTURAL PERSPECTIVES

This Cultural Perspectives feature will expose students to the concept that our society is composed of people from many different cultural backgrounds. These features show both past contributions of many cultures and benefits of a culturally diverse society.

CRITICAL THINKING
1. Documents provide written evidence of a business transaction or other event. These documents provide proof of payment, delivery, or other actions in case of dispute, accident, or theft.
2. Possible answers might include paper files, videotaped transactions, and people who specialize in memorization. Emphasize how computers are a good solution for handling a high volume of complex transactions.

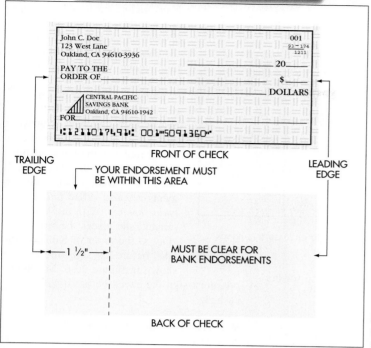

CHECK ENDORSEMENTS

FRONT OF CHECK

TRAILING EDGE

LEADING EDGE

YOUR ENDORSEMENT MUST BE WITHIN THIS AREA

1 ½"

MUST BE CLEAR FOR BANK ENDORSEMENTS

BACK OF CHECK

FIGURE 26-4 Do you see why endorsement space is limited?

3. Endorsements mean that the endorser will pay the check in case the next owner of the check cannot collect the money.

Placement of Endorsements

The federal government has guidelines for financial institutions that require money deposited to customers' accounts be available to them in a certain period of time. The time between the receipt of the deposit by the bank and its availability to the depositor is called the *float*. Evidence that the bank followed the time regulations is its stamped endorsement on the check.

Checks may be purchased from your bank or other sources. Ads for mail-order companies that sell low-cost checks may be found in magazines, the Sunday newspaper, or online.

Because these stamps are usually large, the guidelines also limit the space on the check for the payee's endorsement. Your endorsement must be made in the 1½-inch space on the left side of the check. Figure 26-4 shows a diagram for the payee's endorsement.

These space regulations are very specific. If you write anything outside the 1½-inch limit, it may cause the check to be returned. Further, you may be liable for fees for returned checks and other penalties as a result of endorsements that are unreadable, misplaced, or incomplete.

TYPES OF ENDORSEMENTS

Different endorsements serve different purposes. As you handle the checks you receive, you will probably use each of the four types of endorsements discussed in the following sections. Let's start with the

- The research paper can be a valuable learning experience. The ability to research, organize, and write a report will enhance a student's ability to think and analyze situations. Research report writing skills are used in most career fields.
- A suggested format for research reports may include: (a) an introduction and background, including the purpose of the report; (b) topic development, presenting evidence related to the main topic area; (c) conclusions and recommendations involving the main ideas that the reader should remember and actions recommended for business, consumers, government, and others; (d) a reference list or bibliography; and (e) an appendix with charts, tables, graphs, and supplementary data.
- Research papers and reports can be evaluated on the basis of (a) research techniques, evidence of effort; (b) topic development, depth of discussion; (c) organization and clarity of style; and (d) mechanics—grammar, spelling, punctuation, capitalization, and appearance.
- Collect and analyze advertisements from newspapers and magazines aimed at specific subcultures in our society.
- Invite guest speakers to discuss cultural differences and business activities in other countries.
- Have students visit food stores and other retail establishments that specialize in imported products.
- Have students create a video of interviews and field observations that reflect the life-style and business activities in various cultures.

Personal Qualities-Self-Esteem

Self-esteem, or believing in one's own self-worth and maintaining a positive view of one's self, is a personal quality that we cannot ignore. It is important that students know who they are and believe in themselves in order to be productive in society. One important contributor to self-esteem is one's own culture. It is important for students to understand not only who

they are, but what is the culture of those with whom they work. Cultural Perspectives describes various cultures and their contributions to our current economic system. This feature offers an opportunity to encourage discussion of students and their cultural backgrounds. The discussion can be expanded by asking students to write down a description of themselves by asking, "Who am I?"

- Have students maintain a multi-cultural-global business diary (or journal) with examples of advertisements of foreign companies, imported product labels, and articles about other cultures and international business activities.
- Have students create a business plan that could be used to sell a product to meet the needs of people in a different culture.
- Before a guest speaker visits your class, let that person know your expectations.
- Contact an appropriate organization or ask other faculty members for suggested speakers from your community.
- Provide the speaker with the necessary information regarding date, time, location, class size, topic, and length of presentation. Inquire if audiovisual equipment will be needed.
- Prepare students by telling them about the speaker's background, and have students prepare questions in advance.
- Decide if the speaker will take questions during or after the presentation.
- Check room arrangements if the location is different from your regular classroom.
- Ask permission to tape the presentation as a future class resource.
- Introduce the speaker with appropriate background information.
- After the presentation, express your appreciation in writing to the speaker.
- Discuss the speaker's comments with students; ask students if the speaker should be considered for presentations to future classes.

FIGURE 26-5 Why did Alicia have to endorse this check twice?

endorsement that Alicia Garcia used for her paycheck.

Blank Endorsement

An endorsement that consists of only the endorser's name is called a **blank endorsement**. To endorse a check, sign your name in ink exactly as it is written on the face of the check. The endorsement should match your signature on the signature card. If the name on the check is different from your official signature, you will need to endorse the check twice. In Figure 26-5, Alicia first endorsed her paycheck "A. C. Garcia" as her name appeared on the check. Then she signed the check "Alicia Garcia" as she had written her name on the signature card.

A blank endorsement makes a check payable to anyone who has the check. This endorsement may be used at any time a check is to be transferred, but sometimes another type of endorsement is better.

Special Endorsement

Suppose Nancy R. Brooks receives from her part-time job a paycheck made payable to her. She then wants to make that check payable to Kunio Shinoda, who operates a service station where she buys gas. The

check is a payment on the bill she owes Mr. Shinoda. If she uses a blank endorsement and sends the check to Mr. Shinoda, he can cash it when he receives it. However, if the check is lost before it reaches him, anyone who finds it can cash it.

To make sure that no one except Kunio Shinoda will be able to cash the check, Nancy may use a **special endorsement**, which includes the name of the person to whom the check has been transferred. Special endorsements are also called *full endorsements*. With this endorsement, she places the words "Pay to the order of Kunio Shinoda" before her signature as shown in Figure 26-6. Mr. Shinoda must sign the check before it can be cashed.

Restrictive Endorsement

A **restrictive endorsement** limits the use of the check to the purpose given in the endorsement. For example, you may have

FIGURE 26-6 What purpose does this type of endorsement serve?

Critical Thinking **Skills**-Decision Making

Decision-making skills, which include specifying goals, generating alternatives, considering risks, and evaluating and choosing the best alternative, are applied throughout every chapter in this text. Each time a student participates in a Cooperative Learning or Teams activity, decision-making skills are applied in a group situation. For Communicate Business Concepts and Decision-Making Strategies, students must specify the goal of the activity, consider risks, and evaluate the best solution before the questions can be answered. Emphasize to students how they are using decision-making techniques in their day-to-day tasks and make them aware of the skills they are developing.

For deposit only
Nancy R. Brooks

FIGURE 26-7
How does this type of endorsement protect your money?

several checks that you want to mail to the bank. You could write "For deposit only" above your signature, followed by your account number, as in Figure 26-7. This endorsement restricts use of the check so it can only be deposited to your account. If a check with such an endorsement is lost, it cannot be cashed by the finder.

Businesses often use rubber stamps to imprint restrictive endorsements that require checks to be deposited to their accounts. A business thus has no risk of loss if an unauthorized person uses the stamp to endorse a check.

RECORDING THE DEPOSIT

When you make a deposit to your checking account, the bank teller will give you a receipt. The receipt may be printed by a computer at the same time that it registers the deposit in the bank's records. A deposit may also be made at an automatic teller machine located away from the bank building. Or, a deposit may be sent through the mail. The bank records your deposit and mails a receipt back to you.

NET FACTS

SLIP and PPP connections use modems and telephone lines to connect to the Internet. SLIP stands for Serial Line Internet Protocol; PPP stands for Point to Point Protocol.

When you become a depositor, your bank will supply you with blank checks bound in a checkbook. Checkbooks may be supplied without charge on some kinds of accounts, but usually banks charge a fee when the depositor's name and address are printed on each check and deposit slip. Checks may also be personalized with initials or background pictures of the depositor's choosing.

Besides the checks, a checkbook also contains forms on which a depositor writes a record of deposits made and checks written. In some checkbooks, this record is kept on the **check stub** that is attached to each check, as shown in Figure 26-8. Another type of checkbook provides a **check register**, which is a separate form for recording deposits and checks. When you make a deposit to your checking account, you should *immediately* enter the amount on the check stub or in the check register.

NET FACTS

Net Facts provides information and definitions of terms for the Internet. The more information that students have about the Internet, the better equipped they will be to use this resource. In the Internet Activity Masters, there is an Internet Activity Worksheet for each unit. You can use these activities to give students experience with finding information online. Options for assigning this activity are as follows:

1. **Provide students with a list of addresses for this activity,**
2. **Assign students to conduct their own searches, or**
3. **Use the addresses on the Internet Activity Worksheet.**
   You should complete the activity yourself before assigning it to resolve any discrepancies that may arise.

- Try to schedule speakers with more than one class attending; a larger audience makes better use of the speaker's time.
- If a speaker presents a particular point of view, balance the comments with class discussion at a later time.

CHECK STUBS

347 $	
	20
TO	
FOR	
BAL FOR'D	DOLLAR	CENTS
DEPOSITS	
TOTAL	
THIS CHECK	
OTHER DEDUCTIONS	
BAL. FOR'D	

Delena Kolberg
984 Birchwood Drive
Mystic, CT 06355-7582

347
92 – 403
0111

_____ 20 ___

PAY TO THE
ORDER OF_____ $ _____

_____ DOLLARS
                                    FOR CLASSROOM USE ONLY

⚙ **Riverview National Bank**
    Mystic, CT 06355-0628

FOR _____

⑈0111040⑆ 326⑈0622⑈

FIGURE 26-8
Why is it best to always fill out the check stub or check register before writing out the check?

Critical Thinking Skills-Problem Solving

Problem-solving skills, which include recognizing a problem and devising a plan of action, are applied throughout every chapter in this text. Each time a student participates in a Cooperative Learning or Teams activity, problem-solving skills are applied in a group situation. Each time a student completes a math application in Calculate Business Data, decisions are

made as to which mathematical approach must be taken. For each Technology Application problem, students must decide which template problem to use, which piece of software to load, and how to solve the problem. Emphasize to students how they are using problem solving in their day-to-day tasks and make them aware of the skills they are developing.

REVIEW YOUR READING

1. Convenience, safety, proof of payment, and a record of finances.
2. Regular accounts: large number of checks per month; fees vary, sometimes including fees for checks written and deposits made; small monthly minimum balance may eliminate fees. Interest checking accounts: unlimited checks; pay interest; minimum balance required.
3. A sharedraft account is a checking account at a credit union.
4. So that tellers can compare your signature on checks and other documents to be sure the signature is genuine.
5. Allow the person receiving a check to carry out his or her plans for the check—to cash, deposit, or transfer; legal evidence that the check has been cashed or transferred; guarantee the endorser will pay the check in case the next owner of the check cannot collect the money.
6. Within 1½ inches at the left (trailing) edge on the back of the check; remaining space reserved for banks' endorsements.
7. Special endorsement includes the name of the individual to whom the check is transferred.
8. Restrictive endorsement.
9. Maintaining a record of information about checks written.

COMMUNICATE BUSINESS CONCEPTS

10. To get the best value for your dollar; to meet your needs for services.
11. A special checking account designed for people who will maintain small balances and write only a few checks per month.
12. No. The bank requires a single signature for each account and for each check to bear this signature only. Confusion would result otherwise.
13. No. Each depositor is entitled to sign checks written on a joint account.

BUSINESS NOTES

1. A checking account provides convenience, safety, proof of payment, and a record of finances.
2. The main types of checking accounts are regular checking accounts, which may or may not charge fees, and interest checking accounts, which pay interest so long as the balance meets the requirements.
3. When opening a checking account, you must sign your name on a signature card, which becomes the bank's official record of your signature, make your deposit, and select your checks.
4. The purpose of an endorsement is to allow the recipient of the check to cash, deposit, or transfer it to someone else.
5. The three main types of endorsements are the blank, special, and restrictive endorsements.
6. The purpose of a check stub and check register is to record deposits and to maintain a record of checks written.

REVIEW YOUR READING

1. What are the advantages of a checking account?
2. Explain the difference between the two major kinds of checking accounts.
3. What is a sharedraft account?
4. Why does a bank require you to sign a signature card when you open a checking account?
5. What are the three purposes of endorsements?
6. Describe the placement of an endorsement. For what is the remaining space used?
7. If you wish to transfer ownership of a check from yourself to another person, would you use a blank, a special, or a restrictive endorsement? Explain.
8. Which endorsement would you use to limit the use of your payroll check to being deposited in your bank account?
9. What is the purpose of check stubs or a check register?

COMMUNICATE BUSINESS CONCEPTS

10. "You should shop for the best place to open a checking account as carefully as you shop for the best buy in any product or service." Give two reasons to support this statement.
11. Akeo Mori attends a technical school in the morning and works afternoons and weekends at a skating rink. He believes that if he deposits his earnings in a checking account and writes checks to pay the few monthly bills he has, he could better manage his money. What kind of checking account would you recommend for Akeo? Why?
12. If you sign your full name on the signature card when you open your checking account and then sign your nickname when you write your checks, do you think the bank should pay the checks? Give a reason for your answer.
13. Ann and Walter Neal have a joint checking account and both have signed the signature card. Must they both sign each check? Why?

DEVELOP YOUR BUSINESS LANGUAGE

For each numbered item, find the term that has the same meaning.

14. A form that accompanies a deposit and lists the items deposited—currency, coins, or checks.

15. A form attached to a check on which a depositor keeps a record of the checks written and any current deposit.

16. Written evidence that you received payment or that you transferred your right of receiving payment to someone else.

17. A separate form on which the depositor keeps a record of deposits and checks.

18. A card, kept by a bank, that shows the signatures of all individuals authorized to draw checks against the account.

19. A bank account that is used by two or more people.

20. An endorsement that limits the use of a check to the purpose given in the endorsement.

21. A fee a bank charges for handling a checking account.

22. An endorsement including the name of the person to whom the check has been transferred.

23. The current cost of money in the marketplace.

24. Withdrawals made on a member's shares of ownership (deposits) in a credit union.

25. An endorsement consisting of only the endorser's name.

KEY TERMS

blank endorsement
check register
check stub
deposit slip
endorsement
joint account
money market rate
restrictive endorsement
service charge
sharedrafts
signature card
special endorsement

DECISION-MAKING STRATEGIES

Boni and Kara Hondre are college roommates. The sisters are considering getting a checking account together. They could get a joint account, or they might decide to get individual accounts.

26. How should Boni and Kara decide whether to get a joint checking account or an individual account?

27. What type of account do you recommend for the sisters?

DEVELOP YOUR BUSINESS LANGUAGE

14. deposit slip
15. check stub
16. endorsement
17. check register
18. signature card
19. joint account
20. restrictive endorsement
21. service charge
22. special endorsement
23. money market rate
24. sharedrafts
25. blank endorsement

DECISION-MAKING STRATEGIES

26. Whether Boni and Kara get a joint checking account or individual accounts will depend on how they will share their funds and payments of bills. If they can agree on a spending plan for their living and other expenses, a joint account might be appropriate. Otherwise, to avoid disagreements, individual accounts might be the better choice.
27. Student answers will vary. Make sure students point out how each type of account might be used in the sisters' situation.

28. (a) $350.00 + $100.82 + $78.75 = $529.57; (b) $529.57 + $110.00 = $639.57; (c) $639.57 + $290.25 (new balance) = $929.82 (previous balance)

29. (a) April, $6.00; May, $4.00; June, $6.00; July, 0; August, $4.00; and September, $6.00; (b) $26.00

30. (a) Yes; (b) $1,620.00 × 0.04 = $64.80 annual interest; $64.80 ÷ 12 = $5.40

In this activity, students use a computer to solve a business problem using a file that is provided on the data CD that accompanies *Intro to Business*. Instructions for using the data CD are included in a **README** file on the disk. Solutions are provided on the Instructor's Resource CD.

28. Shana Brown wrote a check to make a deposit to her savings account and three checks to pay her monthly bills. The checks were written for the following amounts: savings, $110.00; rent, $350.00; electric bill, $100.82; gasoline bill, $78.75. This left a new checkbook balance of $290.25.
    a. What is the total amount of Shana's monthly bills?
    b. What is the total amount of Shana's four checks?
    c. What was Shana's checkbook balance before she wrote the four checks?

29. Service charges for Tom Harding's regular checking account at Second National Bank are based on the bank's rate schedule, as shown at right.

    During a recent six-month period, Tom's balances were April, $148.00; May, $201.97; June, $101.61; July, $418.53; August, $248.29; and September, $154.36.

    a. How much was Tom's service charge for each month?
    b. What was the total service charge for the six-month period?

Minimum Balance	Charge
0—$199.00	$6.00
$200.00—$399.00	$4.00
$400.00 and over	no charge

30. The Gulfstream Bank requires an average monthly balance of $1,500 on its interest checking account. Wanda Settle had an average monthly balance for June of $1,620.

    a. Is Wanda eligible to earn interest on her account for June?
    b. If the bank paid 4 percent annual interest on the average monthly balance, how much interest would she earn for June?

Hint: Refer to Appendix C: Determining Percentage and Interest in Business.

TECHNOLOGY APPLICATION

Using the *Intro to Business* Data CD and your database program software, select problem CH26. After the problem appears on your screen, complete the following activities. Then, after you have completed each step, display or print a report for each activity. If you do not have a printer available, answer the questions before you leave the computer.

31. Select and list the financial institutions that provide interest checking accounts. How many financial institutions are listed?

32. Select and list the financial institutions that have minimum balances less than or equal to $300. How many financial institutions are listed?

33. Based on the list selected in Problem 32, select and list the financial institutions that have minimum balances less than or equal to $300 and service charges less than $5.

COMMUNICATING for SUCCESS

COMMUNICATING THROUGH VISUALS—IMAGE IS EVERYTHING

The intent of communication is to convey messages from senders to receivers. Visual aids assist the sender in conveying messages accurately. The receiver benefits from the visual communication through enhanced clarity and recall ability. Visual aids are numerous, and commonly include overhead transparencies, slides, posters, videos, models, flip charts, computerized images, and chalkboards or dry erase boards.

> **Visual aids can help you communicate more effectively.**

To ensure effective visual presentations, keep in mind the following hints:

- Keep your design simple.
- Include only one major idea per visual.
- To maximize effectiveness, be selective in how many visuals you use.
- Position yourself to enable the audience to clearly view the visuals.
- Make an effort to paraphrase rather than read your visuals line by line.
- Proofread visuals carefully.
- Make sure visuals are large enough to be seen by the entire audience.
- Avoid distorting facts on visuals; be concise and accurate.

Increasingly, visual aids are technology-driven and broadcast from a computer to an enlarged area or screen. PowerPoint software is commonly used. When using this or other presentation programs, be sure to select templates and designs that will aid your presentation and appeal to your audience.

Charts and graphs are another effective means of enhancing your presentation. The use of color can make your charts or graphs more appealing; however, be careful not to overdo it. Too much color, varying typefaces, or information overload can overwhelm and confuse your audience. Also, be careful to portray your information accurately; it is unethical to misrepresent data. Some types of charts and graphs you may wish to use include pie charts, organization charts, bar graphs, flow charts, line graphs, and pictographs.

CRITICAL THINKING

1. How do visual aids assist or benefit the sender and receiver?
2. What types of visual aids are the current business standard?

COMMUNICATING for SUCCESS

Communications skills will help ensure students' success in the business world. Communicating for Success introduces workplace/inter-personal communications issues and proper uses of communications technology. Each feature discusses a key communications topic, and contains two Critical Thinking questions that require students to analyze what they have learned.

Using visual aids to communicate ideas is something students will need to learn in order to succeed in today's media-intensive business environment, particularly with the proliferation of computer-based visual presentation technologies. This feature provides some basic guidelines for making effective visual presentations, whatever the medium being used.

CRITICAL THINKING

1. Visual aids assist the sender in conveying messages accurately. The receiver benefits from the visual communication through enhanced clarity and recall ability.
2. Power Point presentations are the current business standard.

This chapter provides details about writing, accepting, and cashing checks. The chapter covers other types of checks (certified checks, cashier's checks, and traveler's checks), money orders, and electronic funds transfer.

Resources for Teachers
● Lesson Plans
● School-To-Work/SCANS Activity Masters
● Spanish Resources
● Instructor's Resource CD

Assessment
● Chapter and Unit Tests, Ch. 27
● ExamView, Ch. 27

Media/Technology
● Applying Technology Data CD
● PowerPoint slides
● Business Connection CD
● Videotape

Activity Masters and Workbooks
● Activities and Projects, Ch. 27
● Internet Activity Masters
● Business Math Activity Masters
● Communications Activity Masters
● International Business Activity Masters
● Ethics Activity Masters

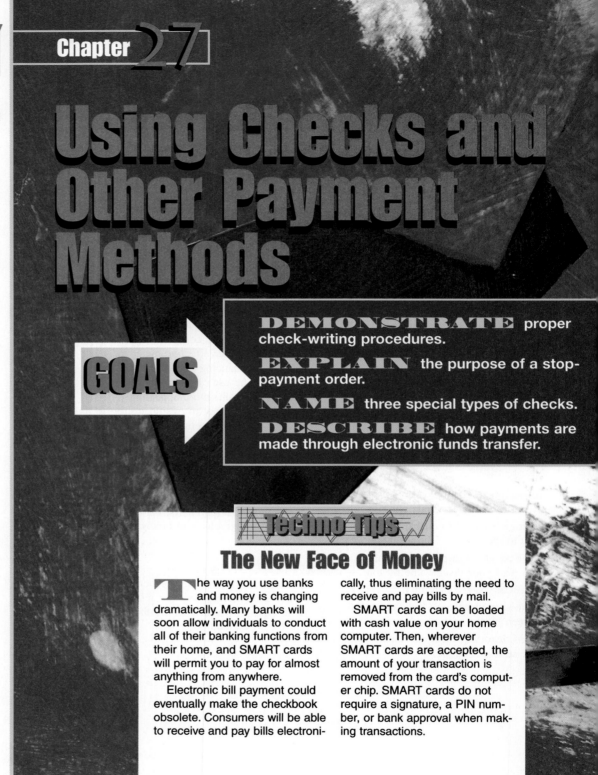

Chapter **27**

Using Checks and Other Payment Methods

GOALS

DEMONSTRATE proper check-writing procedures.

EXPLAIN the purpose of a stop-payment order.

NAME three special types of checks.

DESCRIBE how payments are made through electronic funds transfer.

Techno Tips

The New Face of Money

The way you use banks and money is changing dramatically. Many banks will soon allow individuals to conduct all of their banking functions from their home, and SMART cards will permit you to pay for almost anything from anywhere.

Electronic bill payment could eventually make the checkbook obsolete. Consumers will be able to receive and pay bills electroni-cally, thus eliminating the need to receive and pay bills by mail.

SMART cards can be loaded with cash value on your home computer. Then, wherever SMART cards are accepted, the amount of your transaction is removed from the card's comput-er chip. SMART cards do not require a signature, a PIN num-ber, or bank approval when mak-ing transactions.

Students need to know the latest technologies and develop cutting edge Internet skills for use in current jobs, future careers, or in their homes. TechnoTips intro-duces students to today's cutting edge technologies and provides them with important Internet skills. Feature topics concentrate on Internet-specific technologies and com-puter or other hi-tech innovations for use by businesses and consumers.

FOCUS ON REAL LIFE

Alicia Garcia had made her first deposit in her new checking account, and her friends knew about her account.

Her friend Joni asked her, "If I write you a check, could you give me the cash? You can just deposit my check in your account later."

"How do I know your check is good?" Alicia asked.

"What! We've been friends for over ten years," Joni responded. "Don't you trust me?"

"Of course I trust you," said Alicia. "Just remember that if a check isn't good it can result in some expensive service fees."

The next day, Laura came up to Alicia and said, "I can't wait to mail away for this sweater. However, the ad says 'no personal checks.' How can I pay for it?"

"Haven't you ever heard of a money order?" asked Alicia.

"A money 'what'?" asked Laura.

"Let me tell you about money orders," responded Alicia.

CHECK-WRITING PROCEDURES

Some checks are light blue or green in color. Other checks have a picture of a forest or a sports team logo. Still others have an inspirational quote. All checks, however, contain basically the same information.

Elements of a Check

As you study Figure 27-1, you will find some terms that are used to identify the parts of a check. Three parties, as you see, are shown on each check: the drawer, the payee, and the drawee. The **drawer** is the owner of the account and the person who signs the check.

FIGURE 27-1   Why is the amount of this check written twice?

PARTS OF A CHECK

Printed name and address of account owner (**Drawer**)
Payee
Date check is written
Check number

Alicia Garcia
19684 Absaroka Drive
Houston, TX 77083-5549

101
86 - 171
1130

ABA number

April 13 20 —

Amount in words

PAY TO THE
ORDER OF *The Complete Ski Shop* $ *39.95*
Thirty - nine 95/100   DOLLARS

Amount in figures

FOR CLASSROOM USE ONLY

Second National Bank
Houston, TX 77083-9073

Name of bank (**Drawee**)

FOR *ski mask*   *Alicia Garcia*

⑈⑈300⑈7⑈8⑈ ⑈0⑈⑈⑈⑈6⑈8⑈7⑈⑈⑈

Purpose of check
Bank's identification code for electronic sorting and routing
Drawer's account number for electronic sorting (MICR)
Drawer's signature

FOCUS ON REAL LIFE

Ask students to list common mistakes that might be made when writing checks. Possible answers might include wrong date, misspelled name of payee, amount in numerals does not match amount in words, forgetting to sign. List answers on the overhead or the board.

MOTIVATE

PURPOSE Provide a purpose for students as they read the chapter. Ask what they think they will learn. Direct students to skim the chapter, looking at photos, reading captions, and noting main headings. The goals at the beginning of each chapter provide a valuable tool for having students pinpoint main ideas. The tasks required by the goals are signaled in the first word. Some emphasize information collection ("Identify," "List"), while others call for description ("Explain," "Describe"). Ask students to look through all the goals and note the first word of each. Then ask students to state the purpose of studying this chapter. In this chapter, students will learn about writing and using checks and using other payment methods.

TEACH/APPLY

MAKE CONNECTIONS Emphasize the importance of proper check writing procedures. Review the steps and tips for filling out a check stub and writing a check. Explain the reasons for and methods of stopping payment on a check. Discuss the importance of rules for accepting and cashing checks.

Compare and contrast the three types of special checks: certified checks, cashier's checks, and traveler's checks. Give real-life examples of situations in which a personal check is not acceptable, but emphasize the fees involved.

List the four types of money orders: bank, postal, express, and telegraphic. Explain the situations in which money orders are a better choice than personal checks. Mention, however, that fees are involved. Remind the students that electronic funds transfer (EFT) was introduced in Chapter 25. Point out that the discussion in this chapter gives more examples of how EFT can be used to make payments. Not all checks with errors must be voided.

Use PowerPoint 27-4 and 27-5 to guide students through completing a check stub and/or a check register using the information in Figure 27-2.

Use PowerPoint 27-3 to walk students through the steps of writing a check. Ask volunteers to call out information to be filled in for each part of the check. Show the correct procedure for completing each check stub. Guide students through examples of the situations discussed in Tips for Good Check Writing.

Share automatic teller machine (ATM) Do's and Don't's: (1) DO keep your personal identification number (PIN) secret; (2) DON'T let others use your ATM card; (3) DO record ATM withdrawals in your checkbook; (4) DON'T forget to report immediately a lost or stolen ATM card; (5) DO comparison shop for ATM fees and services; (6) DON'T use ATMs in isolated areas late at night.

EXPLORE THIS/INDEPENDENT PRACTICE Before assigning independent practice material for any chapter, students should be expected to read the textbook material carefully. In view of the fact that all students vary widely in their ability to read effectively, it is advisable to have the students read the entire chapter, or sections thereof, silently in class if the material has not been previously read in connection with homework assignments.

The **payee** is the person to whom the check is written. The payee's name always appears after the words *Pay to the order of*. The **drawee** is the bank or other financial institution that pays the check.

Filling Out the Check Stub or Register

Your checkbook will have a place for recording account activities. Two types of forms are commonly available—a check stub and a check register. The check stub is a form attached to the check by a perforated line. After the check is written, the check is torn off at the line and the stub remains in the checkbook.

A check register is a separate book, usually the same size as the checkbook. Compare the two forms shown in Figure 27-2.

Note that both forms provide blanks to fill in the same type of information about the check. *Always fill out the stub or register first.* If you write the check first, you may forget to record the information before you transfer the check.

Figure 27-2 shows how Alicia Garcia would record her check for $39.95 to The Complete Ski Shop, using both a check stub and a register. Of course, she would use only one type, but you can see that she would record the same information on either form. Also note that there are other entries in the check register for checks written and deposits made.

Writing a Check

After completing the entry in the check register, you are ready to fill out the check.

FIGURE 27-2 Do check stubs and registers contain the same information?

CHECK STUBS OR CHECK REGISTER

101	$	39.95
April 13	20 - -	
TO	Complete Ski Shop	
FOR	Ski mask	

	DOLLAR	CENTS
BAL FOR'D		
DEPOSITS	331	85
4/10		
TOTAL	331	85
THIS CHECK	39	95
OTHER DEDUCTIONS	—	—
BAL FOR'D	291	90

PLEASE BE SURE TO DEDUCT CHARGES THAT AFFECT YOUR ACCOUNT

ITEM NO. OR TRANSACTION CODE	DATE		DESCRIPTION OF TRANSACTION	AMOUNT OF PAYMENT OR WITHDRAWAL(-)	✓	TAX OR OTHER	AMOUNT OF DEPOSIT OR INTEREST(+)	BALANCE FORWARD
	20--	TO	Opening deposit				331 85	+ 331 85
D	4/10	FOR	Paycheck 271.10; cash 60.75					BAL 331 85
101	4/13	TO	Complete Ski Shop	39 95				− 39 95
		FOR	ski mask					BAL 291 90
102	4/15	TO	Second National Bank	50 —				− 50 00
		FOR	cash-current expenses					BAL 241 90
D	4/16	TO	Deposit				50 —	+ 50 00
		FOR	Birthday-Dad					BAL 291 90
103	4/21	TO	Skiing Update	32 97				− 32 97
		FOR	one yr. subscription					BAL 258 93
104	4/22	TO	J. T. Gore Sports	− 87				− 87
		FOR	postage due on 4/20 order					BAL 258 06
VOID 105	4/22	TO	Johnson Masters					
		FOR	VOID					
AT	4/23	TO	Cash from ATM	50 —				− 50 00
		FOR	game tickets and dinner					BAL 208 06

TEACHING STRATEGIES

Alternate Modalities
Auditory Learner

The auditory learner will best learn by hearing. When introducing new terms to an auditory learner, have the student repeat the term and its meaning out loud. Repeating this statement a few times will increase the chances of its being reinforced.

Remember that a check is an order to the bank to pay out your money, so be sure to fill out the check completely and carefully.

Seven steps are usually involved when writing a check:

Step 1 Write checks in order by number. Check numbers are usually printed on both the checks and the check stubs. Check registers have a space for you to write the check numbers. These numbers help you to compare your records with the checks that have been paid. If the numbers are not already printed on the checks, write them in the space provided.

Step 2 Write the date in the proper space on the check.

Step 3 Write the payee's name on the line following *Pay to the Order of.* The payee for Alicia's first check is The Complete Ski Shop, as shown in Figure 27-1 on page 369.

Step 4 Write the amount of the check in figures after the printed dollar sign. Write the amount close to the dollar sign so that a dishonest person cannot insert another number between it and the amount. Write cents figures close to the dollar figures so that additional numbers cannot be inserted.

Step 5 Write the amount of dollars in words on the line below the payee's name. Write the cents in figures as a fraction of a dollar. Begin writing at the far left end of the line. Draw a line from the fraction to the printed word *Dollars* to fill all unused space. Filling all unused space prevents a dishonest person from adding words to change the amount.

If the amount written in figures does not agree with the amount written in words, the bank may pay the amount written in words. If there is a considerable difference between the two amounts, the bank may call you for instructions concerning payment. The bank may also return the check to you and ask you to replace it. There is usually a charge, often as much as $20, when a check is returned for any reason.

Step 6 Write the purpose of the payment on the line at the bottom of the check. Later, after you receive your canceled check, this

An *accounting clerk's* job duties include:
- **Sorting checks and other documents; keeping track of every check number**
- **Filing voided checks for future reference**
- **Performing bank reconciliations.**

note about the purpose can serve as a reminder of why you wrote the check.

Step 7 Sign your checks with the same signature that you wrote on your signature card. Alicia Garcia is the drawer of the check in Figure 27-1 on page 369 and has signed her name on the proper line.

On checks issued by a business or other organization, the firm's name may be printed on the check and is often followed by the word *By*. The person who signs the check writes his or her name after *By*. This shows that the firm is the drawer. An example of a business signature is shown in Figure 27-3.

The bank may subtract from the depositor's account only the amounts of checks and electronic funds transfer (EFT)

FIGURE 27-3 Who is the drawer of a business check? Should Sarah Adams' account be charged for this check?

BUSINESS CHECKS	
AY BANK & TRUST COMPANY	86-42 / 1031
	April 2, 20 _ _
& Company	$ 330.69
thirty 69/100 · DOLLARS	
ORION MANUFACTURING, INC.	
BY *Sarah Adams*	

After students have read the chapter, ask them to complete the Chapter Review questions. Develop Your Business Language is an excellent way to improve students' vocabulary. Only words introduced in the chapter are used in the exercises. The Review Your Reading questions can be used to check students' ability to comprehend what they have read. The Communicate Business Concepts section affords an opportunity for students to apply to practical life situations the information gained from reading the chapter. By completing the problems under Calculate Business Data, students will be able to strengthen and refine their abilities in mathematics. Technology Application allows students to demonstrate skill in using word processing, spreadsheet, and database software. Decision-Making Strategies contains material to challenge students to utilize the model explained in Chapter 1 for problem solving.

The Chapter Review questions at the end of the chapter vary in level of difficulty. For a basic assignment, consider Develop Your Business Language and Review Your Reading. For an average assignment, consider the basic assignment plus Communicate Business Concepts and Calculate Business Data. For an enhanced assignment, try the average assignment plus Technology Application and Decision-Making Strategies.

ASSESS

Review the goals at the beginning of the chapter and the Business

The careers listed in Career Highlights come from the *Occupational Outlook Handbook*, an online publication (www.bls.gov/oco) of the federal government. The O*NET code for Bookkeeping, Accounting, and Auditing Clerks is 43-3031.00. Students can access O*NET

Online (online.onetcenter.org) to view important features of this job. Tell your class about these resources and how to use them. The description of job duties can be used to demonstrate the relevancy of skills learned in this course.

Notes at the end of the chapter. Have students respond orally or in writing to each of the Business Notes restated as a question, provided below. For those who may have difficulty providing answers, assign the reteaching activities that follow. Enrichment activities may also be assigned where appropriate.

1. What are the proper procedures for writing a check? (Answer: Fill out stub or register first, write checks in numerical order, date, payee's name, amount in figures, amount in words, purpose, sign.)

2. What are the tips for good check writing? (Answer: Only use bank's forms, use ink, do not overdraw, use current date, avoid Cash or Bearer, fill in amount, void checks with errors, record every payment.)

3. How is a stop-payment order used? (Answer: Instructs bank not to pay a certain check because it is lost, stolen, or not usable for another reason.)

4. Why are rules for accepting and cashing checks important? (Answer: Prevents accepting a worthless check from a stranger who has no or insufficient funds.)

5. What are three special types of checks? (Answer: Certified, cashier's, and traveler's.)

6. Where can money orders be obtained? (Answer: Banks, post offices, express companies, travel agencies, retail stores, telegraph office.)

7. What payments are made through electronic funds transfer? (Answer: Monthly bills, paychecks.)

transactions that the depositor has authorized. If a bank cashes a check signed by someone who had no right to use the depositor's signature, the bank may be held responsible. Writing another person's signature on a check without his or her authority is a crime called **forgery**. A check with such a signature is a *forged check*.

TIPS FOR GOOD CHECK WRITING

Anyone who writes checks has a great deal of responsibility. However, following these tips can help you avoid problems caused by poorly written checks.

1. *Write checks only on the forms provided by your bank.* Checks can be written on just about anything—even a paper bag. Sorting and exchanging the millions of checks that are written every day is done using the Magnetic Ink Character Recognition (MICR) numbers printed on the check (see Figure 27-1 on page 369). If the check does not have these numbers, the sorting will be interrupted. The check may be delayed and a charge for handling the check may be made.

2. *Write checks in ink.* Using ink prevents someone from increasing the amount of the check. Many businesses use computers or machines called check writers to guard against possible changes in the check amount.

3. *Only write checks if you have money in your account to cover them.* Writing a check for more than you have in your

account is called **overdrawing**. When an account is overdrawn, the bank may not pay the check. In addition, most banks charge the depositor for checks they have to return marked *insufficient funds*.

4. *Use the current date.* A **postdated check** is one that is dated later than the date on which it is written. For example, a check written on December 1 but dated December 5 is postdated. You might postdate a check because you do not have enough money in your account on December 1 to cover the check but you are planning to deposit money on December 3. This is an unwise business practice because the deposit on December 3 may not be made as planned.

5. *Avoid making checks payable to Cash or to Bearer.* If such a check is lost, it can be cashed by anyone. For this reason, you should never make a check payable to Cash unless you are going to cash it immediately. Even then, it is usually preferable to make the check out to yourself or to the bank as payee. That is what Alicia did with Check No. 102 in the check register in Figure 27-2 on page 370.

6. *Always fill in the amount.* If you leave it blank, you may be held responsible for amounts filled in by others.

7. *Void checks on which you make errors.* Do not try to erase or retrace your writing. No one who handles your check can be sure whether the changes were made by you or by someone who had no right to make them. Individuals usually destroy voided checks; businesses usually file voided checks in case questions are ever

asked about the use of a checking account. If you are going to file a check with an error, write *Void* across its face. Whether using a personal or a business checking account, note the check number and write the word *Void* on the stub or in the register to show that the check was not used. For example, Alicia voided Check No. 105.

8. *Record every payment from your checking account, whether the payment is by check*

or *EFT.* Some people carry a few blank checks in their wallets instead of carrying their checkbooks. When one of these checks is used, the drawer should make a note of it and record it in the register as soon as possible. Also promptly record all transactions made at an ATM. Since no check is written, it is easy to forget to record cash machine withdrawals. However, a receipt is given for each transaction. Note the last entry in the register in Figure 27-2 on page 370.

STOPPING PAYMENT ON A CHECK

In certain situations, you may want to instruct your bank not to pay a check that you have written. Suppose Alicia Garcia's Check No. 118 for $52.67 to Joseph Fields was lost. Before she writes a new check,

TECHNOLOGICAL PERSPECTIVES

Your Electronic Wallet in the 21st Century

Remember when most people's wallets bulged with cash, credit cards, blank checks, an ATM card, a driver's license, a medical insurance card, a company identification card, a phone card, and receipts? Technology now makes it possible for you to have all of these items in a single device.

A programmed access card, somewhat like a SMART card, would make it possible to activate business transactions and store data about financial and personal matters. You would be able to make "cash" purchases as well as buy on credit. You will have with you at all times an account of your driving record, medical insurance coverage, and employment documentation. When you return to your home computer, your card will allow you to display or print a record of your spending during the day.

Your programmed access card would eliminate the need for coins. Newspapers, soft drinks, and other inexpensive items could be bought with a swipe of your card through a computer terminal. Several fast-food restaurants and bus companies already offer this service.

In the future, when you think your wallet might be empty, you won't know for sure until you check your balance at the nearest computer terminal!

Critical Thinking
1. What are the benefits of an electronic wallet?
2. What potential problems are associated with increased use of technology for financial services?

Chapter 27 *Using Checks and Other Payment Methods* 373

TECHNOLOGICAL PERSPECTIVES

Net Facts provides information and definitions of terms for the Internet. The more information that students have about the Internet, the better equipped they will be to use this resource. In the Internet Activity Masters, there is an Internet Activity Worksheet for each unit. You can use these activities to give students experience with finding information online. Options for assigning this activity are as follows:

1. **Provide students with a list of addresses for this activity,**
2. **Assign students to conduct their own searches, or**
3. **Use the addresses on the Internet Activity Worksheet.**

You should complete the activity yourself before assigning it to resolve any discrepancies that may arise.

processing payrolls, purchase orders, invoices, and other business forms; as well as conducting banking activities.

SUMMARIZE

Point out that cash cannot be used to make many types of payments. Review the advantages of using checks, but emphasize the importance of following proper procedures for writing and cashing checks. Emphasize that because personal checks are not always accepted, special checks and

Alicia should ask the bank not to pay the first one. The bank will ask Alicia to fill out a **stop-payment order**, which is a written notice from the drawer telling the bank not to pay a certain check. The stop-payment order requests the following information: date, check number, amount, payee, and the drawer's signature.

Because banks charge a substantial fee for stopping payment on a check, payment of a check should be stopped only for good reason. You may learn, for example, that a check you have written to pay a bill was lost in the mail. Or, a check you have written may be stolen. Before you write a new check, you should stop payment on the one that was lost or stolen. To prevent the wrong person from cashing the check, you should notify the bank immediately.

ACCEPTING AND CASHING CHECKS

Your responsibility as a signer and as an endorser of checks is very important. According to law, a check is payable on demand, that is, at the time the holder of the check presents it for payment at the bank on which it is drawn. However, a bank may refuse to accept a check if it is presented for payment long after the date on which it was written. Some checks carry a printed notation, *Please cash within 90 days*. Therefore, you should present a check for payment within a reasonable time.

A check is valuable only when it is drawn on a bank in which the drawer has money on deposit. For this reason, you should accept checks only when they are written or endorsed by people whom you know and trust or those who provide valid identification. A check received from a stranger who cannot provide acceptable identification may be worthless.

Just as you should be cautious in accepting checks, you should not expect strangers to cash checks for you. If you ask someone who does not know you to cash your check, you will probably have to provide a form of identification. Some banks furnish identifica-

Many Internet connections from schools and homes are dial-in connections. With a dial-in connection, the Internet tools and programs are located on a host computer; your desktop computer can only display what the host processes.

tion cards that can be used on a business's credit-check terminal to verify electronically that a customer presenting a check has funds on deposit to cover the amount of the check. Checks are so commonly used in place of cash that you will usually have no trouble cashing them where you are known. However, legally, no one has to accept your checks.

OTHER TYPES OF CHECKS

Sometimes you may have to make a payment to an organization or person who will not accept a personal check. There is a way to have a bank guarantee that the check will be good. This guarantee makes the check acceptable when it otherwise would not be. Financial institutions provide several types of checks that they guarantee, including certified checks, cashier's checks, and traveler's checks.

Certified Checks

A **certified check** is a personal check for which a bank has guaranteed payment. The certification is stamped on the face of the check and is signed or initialed by a bank officer. Suppose Hazel Canton wants to make a payment to someone who does not know her and who does not want to accept her personal check. Ms. Canton could have her bank certify her check. If she has an account at the bank, she may pay a small fee. If she does

TEACHING STRATEGIES

Teams

Student Team Reading/ Student Team Writing is an instructional method in which students use cooperative learning in peer groups. When using this instructional method, students are assigned to teams with four members each. The teams should be mixed in performance level, gender, and culture. Assign this chapter for the teams to read, then to write a summary of the chapter in their own words. Each group should produce a written plan, draft, and then a final paper as a team. As a supplemental activity, you may wish to distribute the Student Activity Worksheet, Workplace Competencies—Interpersonal Skills, in the School-To-Work/SCANS Activity Masters, to serve as guidelines for team development.

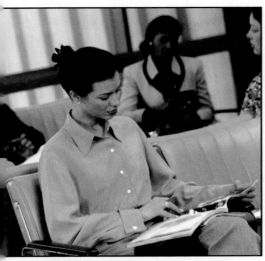

Do you think it is worthwhile to use traveler's checks when you travel? Explain.

not have an account there, the fee may be higher.

When the bank certifies Ms. Canton's check, the amount of the check is immediately subtracted from her account. This makes it impossible for her to withdraw the money for other purposes. If the check is not used, it may be returned to the bank and credited to her account.

Cashier's Checks

A bank usually keeps funds in an account of its own on which it writes its own checks. A **cashier's check** is a check that a bank draws on its own in-house funds. A cashier's check costs the amount of the check plus a service fee. These banker's checks are more acceptable than the personal checks of an individual whom the payee may not know.

Traveler's Checks

Carrying a large sum of money when you travel is risky since it can be lost or stolen easily. In addition, paying traveling expenses with personal checks may be difficult. You will be dealing mostly with strangers, and, as you have learned, strangers may not accept personal checks.

Special forms designed for the traveler to use in making payments are called **traveler's checks**. You can buy them at banks, express companies, credit unions, and travel bureaus. They are sold in several denominations, such as $10, $20, $50, and $100. In addition to the value of the checks, there is sometimes a charge of one percent of the value. This means that $100 worth of traveler's checks will cost $101.

Traveler's checks have two places for your signature. When you buy the checks, you sign each one in the presence of the selling agent. When you cash a check or pay for a purchase with it, you sign it again in the presence of the person accepting it. That person checks to see that the two signatures are alike. When you cash the check, you also fill in the date and the name of the payee.

Traveler's checks, especially those widely advertised, are commonly accepted throughout the world. Almost any business is willing to accept a traveler's check because there is little chance of its not being signed by the right person.

When you buy traveler's checks, you should immediately record the serial number of each check on a form that is generally given to you by the issuing agency. When you cash each check, record the place and date you cashed the check on the same form. Keep this record separate from your checks so that you can refer to it if your checks are lost or stolen. Report lost or stolen traveler's checks immediately to the nearest bank or office where such checks are sold. The company that issued them will replace them.

SOURCES OF MONEY ORDERS

A person who does not have a checking account and who wants to send a payment through the mail may purchase a money order. A **money order** is a form of payment that orders the issuing agency to pay the amount printed on the form to another party. When you buy a money order, you pay the

money orders are available. Emphasize the increasing use of electronic funds transfer (EFT).

EVALUATE

- Assign Activities and Projects for Chapter 27.
- Administer the printed test or ExamView for Chapter 27.
- Assign School-To-Work/SCANS portfolio activities for Unit 8.

SUPPLEMENTAL NOTES

- Provide a handout with an outline, list of key terms, and questions as a guide for your presentations.
- Use visual materials such as transparencies, slides, videos, posters, advertisements, and packages to explain and demonstrate lecture material.
- Encourage students to respond with explanations, examples, and questions that reflect their knowledge of the material.
- Use a flowchart, conceptual map, or other illustrations to show relationships among new topics and other course topics.
- Discuss the specific goals of topics to be covered.
- Assign textbook readings and give students questions in advance.
- Ask questions that require students to relate content to other topics, personal experiences, and actual business situations.
- Use small group activities for problem-solving and decision-making situations.
- If you are trying to stimulate class discussion, avoid asking students questions that can be answered with "yes" or "no" or with a short answer.

Workplace Competencies-Resources

All of us allocate our resources—time, money, people, and materials—on a daily basis. By acquiring competence at allocating resources, students learn to perform basic functions of management—planning, organizing, and controlling. We can guide our students and teach them how to allocate time by helping them understand that they must first identify the

goals or tasks that must be completed and rank them in order of importance, estimate how much time it will take to complete each task, develop a schedule, and evaluate and adjust the schedule as appropriate. Assign students a project that includes reading this chapter, completing the end-of-chapter activities, completing the assignments in the Activities and Projects, and preparing for the ExamView.

- Good questions usually start with "What," "Why," and "How" and ask about relationships among various phases of a topic.
- Avoid questions aimed at only one portion of the class.
- Use sequential questions; vary question length and difficulty.
- Avoid double-barreled and multiple questions that can confuse the major issues being considered.
- Allow sufficient time for students to respond to questions.
- Use tugging questions (such as "What else?" or "Who else?") to encourage and expand thought.
- Avoid questions that seek one "correct" answer.

Most money orders can be written only for amounts up to certain limits. When the amount needed to be sent exceeds this limit, however, a person can buy several money orders.

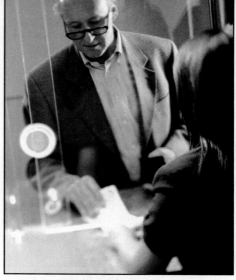

How does having a checking account compare to using money orders?

issuing agency the amount of the payment you want to make and a service fee.

Money orders are convenient because they can be purchased in many places. They are sold by banks, post offices, express companies, and telegraph offices. Many retail stores, such as supermarkets and drugstores, also sell them.

Bank Money Orders

Brad George wants to order a spreadsheet computer program. One way he could pay for this purchase is to buy a money order from a bank. A *bank money order* is a form sold by a bank stating that money is to be paid to the person or business named on the form.

In the bank money order shown in Figure 27-4, Brad George is sending $72.50 to the Precision Software Company. He pays the bank $72.50 plus a service charge for the money order.

Postal Money Orders

Brad may also purchase a money order from the post office. When you buy a *postal*

money order, the postal clerk registers by machine the amount in figures and words. You then complete the form by filling in the payee's name, your name and address, and the purpose of the money order.

You can send a postal money order safely through the mail because it can be cashed only after it is signed by the payee. If a money order is lost or stolen, the receipt copy that you receive may be used in making a claim with the post office. The payee may cash the postal money order at a post office or a bank or may transfer it to another person

FIGURE 27-4 Why would someone pay with a money order rather than a check?

BANK MONEY ORDER

REGISTER CHECK
Personal Money Order

No. 1966046   13—47
420

CINCINNATI, OHIO *July 22* 20 — —

PAY TO THE
ORDER OF *Precision Software Company*
VOID IF IN EXCESS OF $500.00   FOR CLASSROOM USE ONLY

Fifth National Bank CINCINNATI

72 50 CTS

NAME *Brad George*
ADDRESS *2601 Carey Street*
         Madison, OH 45272-7599

⑆04 20004 79⑆ ⑈ 950

Basic Skills-Speaking

Before speaking to a group, students should know their audience, plan their presentation, rehearse, then make the presentation. Discuss characteristics of an audience and how that audience plays a role in the performance of the speaker.

Developing a speech through an outline is an excellent planning tool, and every speech should have an introduction, body, and conclusion. Then discuss the rehearsal process and its purpose. As this unit of study is banking, assign several students the topic Special Payment Needs to prepare and present a speech. Give students the Student Activity Worksheet, Basic Skills—Speaking, in the School-To-Work/SCANS Activity Masters, to serve as a guideline for preparation of a speech.

SCANS

by filling in the information requested on the back of the money order.

Express Money Orders

An *express money order* is another payment method for Brad to use to pay for his software. Express money orders are sold by offices of the American Express Company, Travelers Express Company, some travel agencies, and many retail stores, such as supermarkets, pharmacies, and convenience stores.

Telegraphic Money Orders

A television commercial told the story about a young bride and groom who were on a limited budget and driving an old car that had broken down. The couple called the bride's parents for help. "Please send the money soon, Mom," the bride pleaded tearfully, "or there won't be a honeymoon." In the next scene, the happy couple was pictured a short time later reaching across the counter at the telegraph office where the cash from home was counted out to them.

When buying a *telegraphic money order,* you buy a message directing a telegraph office to pay a sum of money to a certain person or business. Although his purchase of software is not urgent, Brad George could use a telegraphic money order. Telegraphic money orders are used mainly in an emergency when money must be delivered quickly.

ELECTRONIC FUNDS TRANSFER

Electronic funds transfer (EFT) makes it possible to move funds by computer, for example at an ATM. The electronic banking system provides fast and inexpensive service.

Individuals can instruct their banks to pay automatically such monthly bills as utility and telephone charges. For example, some depositors have instructed their bank to make monthly utility payments automatically for them. Each month the utility company sends to the bank the bills for those depositors. The bank subtracts the amounts due from the

accounts of the appropriate depositors. The amounts from the customers' accounts are added to the utility company's account.

Your employer can also pay your salary through EFT. *Direct deposit* has eliminated payroll checks for many companies. The bank subtracts the total amount of the payroll from the business's account and adds the amount earned to each employee's account, even if the employees' accounts are in several different banks. The computer is programmed to transfer electronically the amount of the salary to the appropriate bank for each employee.

Can banking from home benefit all bank customers? Explain.

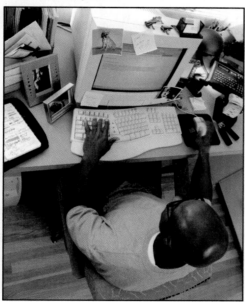

Critical Thinking Skills-Math

SCANS

In order for students to become contributing workers in our society, it is important that they become proficient in the basic skills of reading, writing, arithmetic, and mathematics. Employers are looking for potential employees with good basic foundation skills. In order to prepare students for the school-to-work transition, we must teach these skills in our classroom. Applying math across the curriculum is an important element in contemporary education. As a part of end-of-chapter activities, Calculate Business Data enables students to apply their math skills. Appendix B: Math Review, Appendix C: Determining Percentages and Interest in Business, and Appendix D: Using Measurements in Business, also apply arithmetic and math skills.

REVIEW YOUR READING

1. (1) Payee, to whom the check is written, name appears after *Pay to the order of*; (2) drawer, writes the check, signs in lower right section; (3) drawee, bank where the funds are held, printed name in lower left.
2. Drawer might forget it and thus have no complete record of the checks written.
3. (1) Write checks in order by number; (2) date; (3) name of payee; (4) amount in figures; (5) amount in words; (6) purpose; (7) sign.
4. Check is payable to anyone. Write the check to Cash after you are in the bank where you can cash it.
5. If a check is lost and you write another to replace it.
6. Bank may refuse to accept the check long after the date on which it was written.
7. Certified check: personal check guaranteed by the bank; cashier's check: payment drawn on bank's own funds.
8. Traveler's checks provide positive identification and can be cashed almost anywhere; if lost or stolen, they will be replaced without charge.
9. Bank money orders, postal money orders, express money orders, and telegraphic money orders.
10. ATM withdrawal, automatic bill payment, direct deposit of paycheck.

COMMUNICATE BUSINESS CONCEPTS

11. Check stubs provide reference information about checks, show the remaining balance, and provide a means for checking the bank statement for accuracy.
12. Carry check register with her to ATM and record the transaction when it is made; paper clip ATM receipts in the check register to remind her to record the transaction.
13. No. Stopping payment could damage credit standing and make drawer liable for any fees charged to the payee.
14. a. To have greater assurance of the true identity of the person presenting the check.
    b. Manager has experience to

BUSINESS NOTES

1. Proper check writing includes filling in the check register or check stub; writing checks in numerical order; and writing the date, payee, amounts, purpose, and proper signature on the check.
2. Good check writing tips include using check forms provided by the bank, writing in ink, not overdrawing, using the current date, not making checks payable to Cash or to Bearer, always filling in the amount, voiding checks with errors, and recording every payment.
3. A stop-payment order is a written notice from the drawer telling the bank not to pay a certain check.
4. Only accept checks written or endorsed by people whom you know and trust or those who provide valid identification.
5. Three special types of checks that may be used for payments are certified checks, cashier's checks, and traveler's checks.
6. The four main sources of money orders are banks, post offices, express companies, and telegraph offices.
7. Electronic funds transfer (EFT) makes it possible to move funds by computer through an ATM, automatic bill payment, and direct deposit.

REVIEW YOUR READING

1. Who are the three parties involved with a check? Where are their names shown on the face of a check?
2. Why should the check stub or register be filled in before the check is written?
3. Name the seven steps in writing a check and tell how each part of the check should be written.
4. What risk is involved in making a check payable to cash or to bearer? What can you do to avoid the risk?
5. Under what conditions might you stop payment on a check?
6. Why should you present a check for payment within a reasonable time?
7. What is the difference between a certified check and a cashier's check?
8. Why are traveler's checks better for the traveler to carry than personal checks or cash?
9. What are the four sources of money orders?
10. Give an example of an electronic funds transfer.

COMMUNICATE BUSINESS CONCEPTS

11. Matt Huffman believes that it is a waste of time to record information on check stubs. "The bank sends me a statement each month; that's all I need," he says. How could you convince Matt that he should keep records?
12. Cher Alonso often makes deposits and withdrawals at the ATM that she passes on her way to work. However, she frequently forgets to record these banking activities in her check register and never seems to know how much

judge trustworthiness of drawer.
c. Restrictive endorsement.
d. Check cannot be cashed if it is lost or stolen; prevents possibly forgetting endorsement when preparing deposit.
e. Checks and currency together might cause confusion when giving change; checks less likely to be lost in a robbery.

15. Possible answers might include arranging with a local bank to certify their check, traveler's checks, postal money order.

money she has in the bank. Also, she has over-drawn her account twice and has had to pay a fee each time. Can you suggest a plan for Cher to follow that would allow her to use the automatic teller services and still be sure of having an accurate record?

13. Harvey Graham owed Leonard Saunders $58. He mailed a check to Mr. Saunders. Later, Mr. Graham decided that he did not want to pay all of the debt at once. Therefore, he asked his bank to stop payment. Do you think this was wise? Why?

14. The NaturFresh Supermarket requires its checkers to follow four rules when accepting checks: (1) Get two forms of identification (ID) from the customer. (2) Hand the check and the IDs to the manager for approval. (3) Stamp the check with the store's rubber endorsement stamp. (4) Place the check under the cash tray in the register drawer.

   a. Why do you think the store requires two IDs?
   b. Why do you think the check must be approved by the manager?
   c. What kind of endorsement would most likely be on the rubber stamp?
   d. What are the advantages of stamping the check immediately after accepting it?
   e. Why do you think checks are placed under the cash tray instead of with the cash?

15. While on a trip, the Mendoza family decided to buy a jukebox, which cost $500. The dealer would not accept a personal check or credit cards. What method could be used to pay for the jukebox?

DEVELOP YOUR BUSINESS LANGUAGE

For each numbered item, find the term that has the same meaning.

16. The owner of the account and the person who signs the check.
17. The crime of writing another person's signature on a check without his or her authority.
18. A form designed for the traveler to use in making payments.
19. A check dated later than the date on which it is written.
20. The person to whom the check is written.
21. The bank or other financial institution in which the account is held.
22. The form instructing a bank not to pay a certain check.
23. A check that a bank draws on its own in-house funds.
24. Writing a check for more money than is in one's account.

25. A personal check for which a bank has guaranteed payment.
26. A form of payment that orders the issuing agency to pay the amount printed on the form to another party.

KEY TERMS
cashier's check
certified check
drawee
drawer
forgery
money order
overdrawing
payee
postdated check
stop-payment order
traveler's check

DECISION-MAKING STRATEGIES

Over the past few months, the Edfield family needed to make a variety of payments. These included:
   a. the phone bill
   b. monthly mortgage payments
   c. rush items ordered from an out-of-state mail-order house that demands payment with each order

   d. $300 sent by the fastest method when Mr. Edfield had an automobile accident 300 miles from home
   e. monthly deposit into a savings account

27. What factors should the Edfields consider when selecting a method of payment?
28. For each of the situations, what payment method would you recommend?

DEVELOP YOUR BUSINESS LANGUAGE

16. drawer
17. forgery
18. traveler's check
19. postdated check
20. payee
21. drawee
22. stop-payment order
23. cashier's check
24. overdrawing
25. certified check
26. money order

DECISION-MAKING STRATEGIES

27. The cost involved, the amount of the payment, the requirement of those who will receive the payment, and the convenience of the payment method.
28. Possible answers might include
   a. cash (if in person), personal check, automatically through online funds transfer;
   b. personal check or automatically through online funds transfer;
   c. certified check, cashier's check, or money order;
   d. telegraphic money order;
   e. personal check or automatically through online funds transfer.

29. (a) $122.47 × 4 = $489.88; (b) $37.50 + $25.00 + $7.35 + $4.20 = $74.05; (c) $489.88 − $74.05 = $415.83

30. (a) $400.00 ÷ $50.00 = 8, $50.00 checks; $200.00 ÷ $20.00 = 10, $20 checks; (b) $400.00 + $200.00 = $600.00; $600.00 × 0.01 = $6.00; (c) $600.00 + $6.00 = $606.00

31.

Firm	Amt. of Purchase	(a) Cost of Money Order
Honda	$12.72	$0.75
Cycle	17.96	0.75
House	29.80	0.75
Harley	81.04	1.00
Wheels,	9.16	0.75
Inc.	47.08	1.00
	20.00	0.75
	$217.76	(b) $5.75

(c) _____ + 5.75

Total Cost $223.51

29. Kathy Whiteside opened a checking account on June 1 and deposited $122.47. During the month, she deposited three more paychecks of the same amount.
   a. What was the total of Kathy's deposits?
   b. During June, Kathy wrote four checks for the following amounts: $37.50, $25.00, $7.35, and $4.20. What was the total amount paid out in checks?
   c. What was Kathy's balance at the end of June?

30. Michaela Jarrett bought traveler's checks from her credit union. She must pay a fee of 1 percent of the value of the checks. The denominations she chose were $400 in $50 checks and $200 in $20 checks.
   a. How many $50 checks did she receive? How many $20 checks did she receive?
   b. How much was the credit union's charge for the checks?
   c. What was the total cost of the checks?

31. Julio Costa repairs bicycles and pays for his

Honda Cycle House	Harley Wheels, Inc.
$12.72	$81.04
$17.96	$ 9.16
$29.80	$47.08
	$20.00

The post office fee schedule is as follows:

Amount of Order	Fee
$0.01 to $ 35.00	$0.75
$35.01 to $700.00	$1.00

parts by postal money order. During the last three months, he made payments as shown in the table above.
   a. What was the cost of each postal money order? List the payments in a column and write the fee beside each.
   b. What were the total fees for Julio's postal money orders for the three months?
   c. What was the total cost of the bicycle parts Julio ordered, including the cost of the money orders?

TECHNOLOGY APPLICATION

Using the *Intro to Business* Data CD and your spreadsheet program software, select problem CH27. After the problem appears on your screen, complete the following activities. Then, after you have completed each step, display or print the completed spreadsheet for each activity. If you do not have a printer available, answer the questions before you leave the computer.

32. Format the date column to show the month and the date. Format the Withdrawal, Deposit, and Balance columns to show two decimal places with no dollar signs. Go to the cell beneath the Beginning Balance in the Balance column. Enter a formula to calculate the new balance no matter whether a withdrawal or a deposit is entered in the row. What is the formula you used to calculate the balance?

33. Enter the transactions shown in the table below. Use the current year for dates. What is the balance as of November 27?

34. Your bank pays interest on checking accounts on the last day of each month. On the row below the last transaction, enter November 30 in the Date column and Interest in the For column. In the Deposit column enter a formula to calculate 3 percent interest on the average of the beginning balance and the ending balance before interest. Update the balance and format as necessary. What is the balance as of November 30?

Hint: Refer to Appendix C: Determining Percentage and Interest in Business.

Date	Transaction
11/03	Check No. 456 to Farley's Auto Service for $56.90
11/05	Check No. 457 to Brown Community College Bookstore for $78.00
11/11	Check No. 458 to the Uptown Department Store for $45.30
11/13	Deposit of $340.60
11/16	Check No. 459 to Round Lake Community Charities for $30.00
11/22	ATM cash withdrawal of $100.00
11/24	Deposit of $150.00
11/27	Check No. 460 to Georgetown Credit Union for $250.00 deposit to savings account

GLOBAL NAVIGATOR

INTERNATIONAL FINANCIAL AGENCIES

Countries need money to pay for various goods and services, just as families and businesses do. Maintaining a steady system of foreign exchange is necessary for global financial stability. The World Bank and the International Monetary Fund, each with over 150 member nations, are two international agencies that ensure this stability.

Created in 1944, the World Bank was originally established to provide loans for rebuilding nations devastated by World War II. Presently, the World Bank provides economic assistance to less developed nations. World Bank funds are used to build energy plants, transportation networks, and communications systems. Capital and technical support are provided to private businesses in nations with limited resources. The World Bank also promotes joint ventures between foreign and local companies to bring capital investment to developing nations.

The International Monetary Fund (IMF) helps to maintain an orderly system of world trade and foreign exchange rates. Before the IMF was established in 1946, nations often manipulated their currency values to attract foreign customers, or imposed trade restrictions in order to hinder competitors, thus resulting in trade wars among nations.

> **The World Bank and the International Monetary Fund help maintain global financial stability.**

Today the IMF functions as a cooperative deposit bank, helping countries to decrease foreign debt and stabilize local currency. The IMF may suggest economic policies to correct a nation's problems, and can provide low-interest loans to aid countries with high foreign debt.

CRITICAL THINKING

1. A company in Ecuador plans to start exporting various products. Which of the two organizations described above might be of assistance to this organization? Why?
2. Locate the web site of the World Bank or the IMF. Identify skills or requirements for getting a job at these organizations.

GLOBAL NAVIGATOR

Most students will either work with international clients or compete against businesses that do. Global Navigator introduces students to issues integral to working with international businesses. Key concepts and challenges faced by international businesses are presented, followed by two Critical Thinking questions that require students to analyze what they have learned.

The rapid growth of international commerce in recent decades has made the World Bank and the International Monetary Fund powerful tools for facilitating trade, especially for less-developed nations. This feature explains their functions and cites examples of how they operate to promote stability in world markets. The Critical Thinking exercises prompt students to explore the roles of these organizations in our increasingly interdependent global economy.

CRITICAL THINKING

1. For assistance in developing exports, the World Bank would be the most likely source of aid for Ecuador. It can provide financial help in the form of low-interest development loans, and it can also assist the country in setting up joint ventures with foreign companies.
2. Desirable skills include fluency in a foreign language, education and training in finance and accounting, and experience in quantitative analysis and research.

This chapter provides students with a basic understanding of how checks are processed and paid, the bank statement and how it is used to prepare a reconciliation, and an overview of choosing a financial institution.

Resources for Teachers
- Lesson Plans
- School-To-Work/SCANS Activity Masters
- Spanish Resources
- Instructor's Resource CD

Assessment
- Chapter and Unit Tests, Ch. 28
- ExamView, Ch. 28

Media/Technology
- Applying Technology Data CD
- PowerPoint slides
- Business Connection CD
- Videotape

Activity Masters and Workbooks
- Activities and Projects, Ch. 28
- Internet Activity Masters
- Business Math Activity Masters
- Communications Activity Masters
- International Business Activity Masters
- Ethics Activity Masters

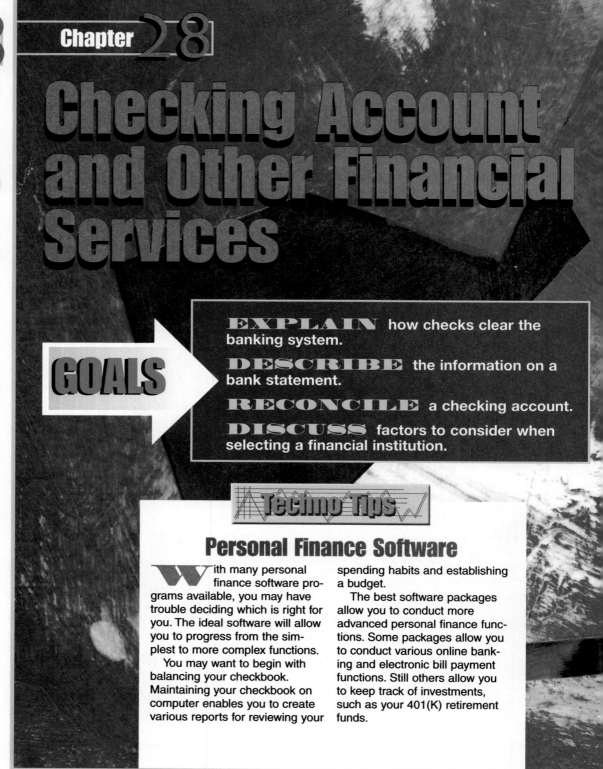

Chapter 28

Checking Account and Other Financial Services

GOALS

EXPLAIN how checks clear the banking system.

DESCRIBE the information on a bank statement.

RECONCILE a checking account.

DISCUSS factors to consider when selecting a financial institution.

Techno Tips

Personal Finance Software

With many personal finance software programs available, you may have trouble deciding which is right for you. The ideal software will allow you to progress from the simplest to more complex functions.

You may want to begin with balancing your checkbook. Maintaining your checkbook on computer enables you to create various reports for reviewing your spending habits and establishing a budget.

The best software packages allow you to conduct more advanced personal finance functions. Some packages allow you to conduct various online banking and electronic bill payment functions. Still others allow you to keep track of investments, such as your 401(K) retirement funds.

Students need to know the latest technologies and develop cutting edge Internet skills for use in current jobs, future careers, or in their homes. TechnoTips introduces students to today's cutting edge technologies and provides them with important Internet skills. Feature topics concentrate on Internet-specific technologies and computer or other hi-tech innovations for use by businesses and consumers.

FOCUS ON REAL LIFE

"**W**ow! According to the balance shown on this ATM receipt, I still have $456 in my checking account!" exclaimed Betsy. "How is that possible?"

"Has every check you have written cleared?" asked Jerry.

"What do you mean *cleared*?" questioned Betsy. "That's a term I'm not familiar with."

Jerry responded, "Every time you write a check, it takes a few days before it is presented to your bank for payment. Your balance won't be updated until all your checks have been returned to your bank."

"You mean someone has to walk into my bank with the check to obtain cash?" asked Betsy.

"Well, not exactly," responded Jerry. "Banks have an electronic transfer system that allows the amounts of checks to be added to and subtracted from the appropriate checking accounts."

"That sounds complicated," sighed Betsy.

"It's not that bad," Jerry commented. "It's better than having every person going to every bank from which she or he has a check."

PROCESSING YOUR CHECKS

Checks travel around the country and around the world in wallets, handbags, envelopes, mail pouches, planes, trucks, and on trains. They go in and out of houses, businesses, government offices, and banks of all shapes and sizes. They are written on, typed on, stamped on, and imprinted with oddly shaped characters in magnetic ink. Eventually, they find their way, still in good shape, back to the bank of the drawer. At this point, the checks are available to the depositor as proof of payment.

Returning checks to their original drawers may seem an impossible task. However, it happens through a carefully planned system. Eventually every check is returned to the drawer's bank to be paid and charged to his or her checking account. This process is called **clearing**. Clearing may be done within one bank, through a clearinghouse, or through the Federal Reserve System.

Local Check Clearing

Check clearing may involve one, two, or several banks and drawers within the same city. If both the drawer and the payee have accounts in the same bank, clearing is simple. The bank subtracts the amount from the drawer's account and adds that amount to the payee's account. A simple accounting transaction occurs.

When two different banks are involved, clearing is somewhat different. However, it is still fairly simple if the two banks are in the same area. Suppose Jon Gable's music group believes its new song will be a big hit. The group wants to get more practice time and get the song recorded. Jon persuades his father to rent a garage on the outskirts of town for rehearsals. The rent for one month is $50. Mr. Gable sends the rental check, written on his account with the North River National Bank, to Arlene-Bayne Realty. Look at Figure 28-1 and follow the check as it travels to the two banks in the town where the Gables live and back to Mr. Gable.

Arlene-Bayne Realty endorses the check and deposits it in its account in the First

Millions of checks clear through the banking system every business day.

CHECK CLEARING PROCESS

Mr. Gable writes a check for $50 to Arlene-Bayne Realty on North River National Bank.

Arlene-Bayne Realty gives Mr. Gable credit for $50 paid.

North River cancels the check and returns it to Mr. Gable.

Arlene-Bayne Realty sends the check to First Federal Trust Company for deposit.

North River subtracts $50 from Mr. Gable's account and pays First Federal Trust $50.

First Federal Trust sends the check to North River National Bank for payment.

First Federal Trust increases the account of Arlene-Bayne Realty $50.

FIGURE 28-1 Can you follow Mr. Gable's check through the clearing process?

Federal Trust Company. When First Federal receives the check, it adds $50 to the account of Arlene-Bayne Realty, endorses the check, and sends it to North River National for payment. After North River National receives the check, it pays First Federal $50 and subtracts that amount from Mr. Gable's account. The check is then marked paid by North River National and returned to Mr. Gable as his record of payment.

The Clearinghouse

In large cities with many banks, it would not be practical for each bank to send checks for payment to all banks on which the checks were written. Banks in the same area may be members of an association that operates a place to clear their checks every day. This place is called a **clearinghouse**.

The method for clearing checks through a clearinghouse is similar to the method dis-

cussed in the previous section. However, clearinghouses handle thousands of checks for many banks. In Figure 28-2, you see a simplified accounting entry showing the net balance settlement for three banks through the clearinghouse fund. Note that the function of the clearinghouse is simply to redistribute the amounts. The $2,200 received by the clearinghouse was balanced by the $2,200 paid out, with no net change in the clearinghouse fund.

An *automated clearinghouse (ACH)* transfers funds among banks using electronic payment entries. Through the ACH connection, funds can be easily transferred between accounts in different banks.

Federal Reserve Check Clearing

One of the services of the Federal Reserve System is clearing checks between banks in different cities. This process is more

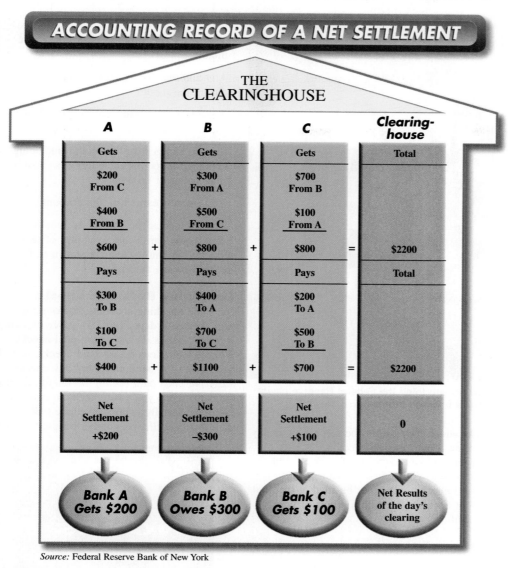

ACCOUNTING RECORD OF A NET SETTLEMENT

THE CLEARINGHOUSE

A		B		C		Clearing-house
Gets		**Gets**		**Gets**		**Total**
$200 From C		$300 From A		$700 From B		
$400 From B		$500 From C		$100 From A		
$600	+	$800	+	$800	=	$2200
Pays		**Pays**		**Pays**		**Total**
$300 To B		$400 To A		$200 To A		
$100 To C		$700 To C		$500 To B		
$400	+	$1100	+	$700	=	$2200
Net Settlement +$200		**Net Settlement** −$300		**Net Settlement** +$100		**0**
Bank A Gets $200		**Bank B Owes $300**		**Bank C Gets $100**		**Net Results of the day's clearing**

Source: Federal Reserve Bank of New York

FIGURE 28-2 Why is the net result of the day's clearing always zero?

complex than clearing through a clearinghouse because of the volume of checks that must be cleared.

Just as banks use a clearinghouse and their district Federal Reserve Bank for settlement of net balances, the Federal Reserve uses the Interdistrict Settlement Fund in Washington, D.C., to settle net amounts due among banks in the 12 districts. The Interdistrict Settlement Fund can be viewed as the Federal Reserve clearinghouse. Settlements are made through ACHs and electronic funds transfers.

Other financial institutions—such as credit unions, savings and loan associations, and brokerage firms—also handle checks. These firms usually have an account with a large

---

Your Reading. For an average assignment, consider the basic assignment plus Communicate Business Concepts and Calculate Business Data. For an enhanced assignment, try the average assignment plus Technology Application and Decision-Making Strategies.

ASSESS

Review the goals at the beginning of the chapter and the Business Notes at the end of the chapter. Have students respond orally or in writing to each of the Business Notes restated as a question, provided below. For students who may have difficulty providing answers, assign the reteaching activities that follow. Enrichment activities may also be assigned where appropriate.

1. How do checks clear the banking system? (Answer: Within one bank, through a clearinghouse, or through the Federal Reserve System, money is deducted from the drawer's account and added to the payee's account.)

2. What information is on a bank statement? (Answer: The beginning balance, deposits made during the month, checks paid by the bank during the month, ATM transactions, EFTs or special payments, service charges, any interest earned, and the balance at the end of the month.)

3. How is a checking account reconciled? (Answer: Add to statement balance any deposit not shown on the statement; subtract outstanding checks from bank statement balance; sub-

---

TEACHING STRATEGIES

Special Needs
Visually Impaired Students

New technologies are continually being developed that assist visually impaired students to participate fully in both school and business. Students must be aware of these technologies

and know how to continually learn of new technologies. Using government agencies as a resource, assist the students in preparing a report concerning anticipated technologies.

tract service charges and automatic payments from and add
any interest earned to the
checkbook balance; make sure
the new statement and checkbook balances agree; find and
correct any errors.)
4. What factors should be considered when selecting a financial
institution? (Answer: Services
offered, convenience, safety, fees
and charges, and restrictions.)

RETEACH

To reteach, show examples of canceled checks with bank endorsements. Trace the path each followed in the clearing process. Use
Figure 28-3 to illustrate the elements of a bank statement. Use
Figure 28-4 to explain each step in
reconciling a checking account.

Use PowerPoint 28-6, *Selecting
a Financial Institution*, to illustrate
the factors that students should
consider when selecting a financial
institution.

ENRICH

Direct students to read the Legal
Perspectives in this chapter. Ask
students to survey relatives and
neighbors about the factors they
consider when selecting and using
a financial institution. Each student
should prepare a report on the
survey results. Another activity
might be to have a debate on the
benefits and drawbacks of using
electronic banking at home. One
side should take the position of
expanded services, convenience,
and improved efficiency. The other
side would defend the position of
higher costs, lost jobs, privacy
issues, and potential computer
crime.

**How do you think the Federal Reserve clears
checks between international banks?**

bank, which they use in the same way as any
other customer uses an account.

Your bank subtracts all of your cleared
checks from your account balance. The
cleared checks will either be filed at the bank
or sent back to you with a report of your
account.

YOUR BANK STATEMENT

As a depositor, you will need to review the
record of your account that the bank keeps.
At regular intervals, usually monthly, the
bank will send you a report on the status of
your account known as a **bank statement**.

Bank Statement Information
While bank statement formats vary, most
present the following information:

• The balance at the beginning of the month

• The deposits made during the month

• The checks paid by the bank during the
month

• Any automated teller transactions made
during the month

• Any electronic fund transfers (EFT) or special payments the bank has made

• Service charges for the month, including
charges for such special services as stopping payment on a check

• Any interest earned on the account

• The balance at the end of the month
See if you can locate examples of these
items on the bank statement shown in Figure 28-3 on the next page.

Examining Returned Checks
For some checking accounts, banks return
paid checks to depositors. For other checking
accounts, banks do not return paid checks.
When a bank does return paid checks, it will
return with the bank statement any checks
that have been paid during the month. Before
the bank sends you your checks, it cancels
each one, usually using a machine that
stamps a cancellation number on the front or

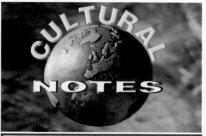

The Chinese do not use the
Gregorian calendar, but instead
have their own calendar. In the
Chinese calendar, years are in
cycles of 60 and minicycles of 12
years. Each 12-year mini-cycle is
named for an animal. The list
starts with the rat, ox, tiger, hare,
dragon, snake, horse, sheep,
monkey, rooster, dog, and pig.

Basic Skills-Listening

Because many employees do not have these listening
skills, businesses spend thousands of dollars every year
to send employees to classes on listening. You can teach students to become good listeners by explaining to them the
value of evaluating the message the speaker is conveying, not
the speaker. Listeners sometimes get too involved in the appearance of the speaker and miss the message that is being
conveyed. Ask a student volunteer to write physical characteristics on the board that influence students not to listen to what
the speaker is saying. The Student Activity Worksheet, Basic
Skills—Listening Checklist, in the School-To-Work/SCANS
Activity Masters, may be used to serve as a guideline for discussion of listening skills.

Second National Bank

Checking Account Statement

ACCT. 1648-7214
DATE 5/1/--
PAGE 1

Alicia Garcia
19684 Absaroka Drive
Houston, TX 77083-5549

Please examine at once. If no errors are reported within 10 days, account will be considered correct.

BALANCE FORWARD	NO. OF WITH-DRAWALS	TOTAL AMOUNT	NO. OF DEP.	TOTAL DEPOSIT AMOUNT	SERVICE CHARGE	BALANCE THIS STATEMENT
0 00	14	433 89	4	826 95	3 00	390 06

CHECKS AND OTHER DEBITS		DEPOSITS AND OTHER CREDITS	DATE	BALANCE
		331.85	4/10	331.85
101	39.95		4/13	291.90
102	50.00		4/15	241.90
		50.00	4/16	291.90
103	32.97		4/22	258.93
104	.87		4/22	258.06
	50.00 ATW		4/23	208.06
106*	16.30		4/24	191.76
107	25.78		4/24	165.98
		175.00	4/24	340.98
109*	65.33		4/26	275.65
110	33.46		4/27	242.19
111	24.33		4/27	217.86
112	5.80		4/27	212.06
113	12.85		4/27	199.21
		270.10 AD	4/29	469.31
114	4.25		4/30	465.06
	72.00 AP TexPower		4/30	393.06
	3.00 SC		4/30	390.06

KEY TO SYMBOLS

AD-	AUTOMATIC DEPOSIT	PC-	PAID OVERDRAFT CHARGE
AP-	AUTOMATIC PAYMENT	PR-	PAYROLL DEPOSIT
ATD-	AUTOMATIC TELLER DEPOSIT	RC-	RETURN CHECK CHARGE
ATW-	AUTOMATIC TELLER WITHDRAWAL	RT-	RETURN ITEM
CC-	CERTIFIED CHECK	SC-	SERVICE CHARGE
EC-	ERROR CORRECTED	ST-	SAVINGS TRANSFER
OD-	OVERDRAFT	TC-	TRANSFER CHARGE

*Where this asterisk is shown, a preceding check is still outstanding or has been included on a previous statement.

FIGURE 28-3 How many checks were paid by the bank and posted to Alicia's account?

Students may also present an original idea that a bank could use to offer a new service. They should tell the class how the service operates, who would use it, how you would advertise it, and how much it might cost.

Ask students to prepare a three- to five-minute oral presentation, or a visual presentation for an advertisement of this new financial service.

For more information on the banking business, *Midtown Bank: A Bank Teller's Simulation,* teaches students bank teller skills. This simulation is available from South-Western Educational Publishing.

SUMMARIZE

On an overhead or the board, create a flow chart to show how the clearing process leads to bank statements, which lead to bank reconciliations performed by recipients of bank statements. Emphasize that students should be wise consumers of financial services. Point out the importance of comparison shopping for a bank.

EVALUATE

- Assign Activities and Projects for Chapter 28.
- Administer the printed test or ExamView for Chapter 28.
- Administer the printed test or ExamView for Unit 8.
- Assign School-To-Work/SCANS portfolio activities for Unit 8.

---

back of the check. The paid checks are called **canceled checks**.

Be sure to save your canceled checks; they are valuable records. Your check stub or register is your own record, but the canceled check is evidence that payment was actually received. Since the payee must endorse a check before it can be cashed, the endorsement proves that the payee received the check.

Suppose your bank does not return checks to depositors, and you need a certain check

to prove that a payment was made. Banks that do not return checks often send a more detailed statement than banks that return checks. In most cases, information on the statement will be sufficient to prove payment. However, if the check showing the endorsement is needed, a copy of it can be obtained. Banks keep a photographic record of all checks paid. Your check will be located in this record and a copy will be sent to you. There will probably be a small charge for this service.

TEACHING STRATEGIES
Cooperative Learning

Group Investigation is a positive form of cooperative learning which encourages students to work together. Plan the size of each group before you begin, decide specific roles for the groups, set a time limit, and give guidelines for the outcome. For this activity, students form their own groups with two to six members each. One person should be selected as a spokesperson and one person as the illustrator. Create a fake check and duplicate it for each group. Make sure the check looks fake and cannot be used! Create a bank's logo and ABA number. Using the chapter as a guide, have students complete an illustration or graph tracing the check from the time they cash it until it clears the original bank upon which it was written.

- Assign and preview specific text pages.
- Refer to specific pages, ideas, and exhibits in the reading; point out the key ideas for students to underline.
- Have students write a summary of the reading to turn in at the start of the next class.
- Present one or two questions in the reading for the next class.
- Have students write a sentence or two on what they believe to be the main ideas in the reading.
- Prepare an in-class exercise based on the reading that produces: (a) short answers or a list of examples or reasons for a situation; (b) sample ads, a flowchart, or other visual presentation.

THE RECONCILIATION PROCESS

You keep your own record of your checking account on check stubs or in a check register. The bank statement gives you a copy of the bank's record of your account. The balances on the two records may differ. Bringing the balances into agreement is known as reconciling the bank balance. The statement showing how the two balances were brought into agreement is called the **bank reconciliation**. Forms for reconciling are often printed on the backs of bank statements.

Finding Differences

The balances shown on your records and the bank statement may be different for several reasons. Here are the most common reasons:

- Some of the checks that you wrote and subtracted from the balance in your record may not have been presented to the bank for payment before the bank statement was made. These checks, therefore, have not been deducted from the bank-statement balance. Such checks are known as **outstanding checks**.

- You may have forgotten to record a transaction in your register. This is especially true if you use an ATM or have other EFT transactions. Failure to record these is a frequent cause of errors.

- A service charge that you have not recorded may be shown on the bank statement.

- You may have mailed a deposit to the bank that had not been received and recorded when the statement was made.

- If you have an interest-bearing account, you may not have added the interest shown

on your statement to your record of your balance.

- You may have recorded the amount of a check incorrectly on your check stub or in the check register. Or, you may have added or subtracted incorrectly.

Calculating the Adjusted Balance

On May 4, Alicia Garcia received the bank statement shown in Figure 28-3 on page 387. The statement balance is $390.06. Alicia's checkbook balance is $416.56. She examined her canceled checks and found that checks numbered 108, 115, and 116 were missing. Check No. 105 had been voided. The others are outstanding. She listed these on the reconciliation form with the amounts for each and recorded the total. Her bank reconciliation is shown in Figure 28-4.

By using the reconciliation form, Alicia proved the accuracy of the bank statement and her record by

1. subtracting the total of the outstanding checks she had listed on the form from the bank statement balance; and

2. subtracting the service charge and the automatic payment of her electric bill from her checkbook balance.

In some cases, other additions or subtractions might have to be made in the reconciliation. For example, a charge made for stopping payment on a check should be subtracted from the checkbook balance. A deposit made late in the month might not appear on the bank statement and should be added to the balance on the bank statement.

Critical Thinking Skills-Problem Solving

Problem-solving skills, which include recognizing a problem and devising a plan of action, are applied throughout every chapter in this text. Each time a student participates in a Cooperative Learning or Teams activity, problem-solving skills are applied in a group situation. Each time a student completes a math application in Calculate Business Data, decisions are made as to which mathematical approach must be taken. For each Technology Application problem, students must decide which template problem to use, which piece of software to load, and how to solve the problem. Emphasize to students how they are using problem solving in their day-to-day tasks and make them aware of the skills they are developing.

SCANS

RECONCILIATION FORM

**YOU CAN EASILY
BALANCE YOUR CHECKBOOK
BY FOLLOWING THIS PROCEDURE**

FILL IN BELOW AMOUNTS FROM YOUR CHECKBOOK AND BANK STATEMENT

BALANCE SHOWN ON
BANK STATEMENT $ *390.06*

BALANCE SHOWN ON
YOUR CHECKBOOK $ *416.56*

ADD DEPOSITS
NOT ON STATEMENT $ _____

ADD ANY DEPOSITS NOT
ALREADY ENTERED IN
CHECKBOOK $ _____

TOTAL $ *390.06*

SUBTRACT CHECKS ISSUED
BUT NOT ON STATEMENT

108	$ *10.00*
115	*21.00*
116	*17.50*

TOTAL $ *416.56*

SUBTRACT SERVICE
CHARGES AND OTHER
BANK CHARGES NOT IN
CHECKBOOK
$ *3.00*
Tex Power 72.00

TOTAL $ *48.50*
BALANCE $ *341.56*

TOTAL $ *75.00*
BALANCE $ *341.56*

THESE TOTALS REPRESENT THE CORRECT AMOUNT OF MONEY YOU HAVE IN THE
BANK AND SHOULD AGREE. DIFFERENCES, IF ANY, SHOULD BE REPORTED TO THE BANK
WITHIN TEN DAYS AFTER THE RECEIPT OF YOUR STATEMENT.

FIGURE 28-4 What does the $341.56 balance represent? Is it always less than the balance shown on the statement?

Interest earned should be added to the checkbook balance.

If the balances do not agree, either you or your bank has made an error. In that case, you should compare your canceled checks with those listed on the bank statement and with those recorded in your check register. Be sure that you have recorded all EFT transactions. Then carefully go over the calculations on your check stubs or in your check register. If you do not find an error in your calculations, contact your bank right away.

After you have reconciled your bank statement, correct any errors that you made on your register. The new balance now agrees

Critical Thinking Skills-Reasoning

Drawing conclusions from facts or premises is an important thinking skill for today's employees. One of the most pervasive ways that government affects business is through the legal system. The law protects both individuals and businesses against those who threaten society. It also spells out accepted ways of performing many essential business activities—along with penalties for failure to comply. Legal Perspectives gives students an opportunity to study legal situations and draw appropriate conclusions.

SCANS

Who's at Risk for a Lost or Stolen Check?

Roberto Hernandez lost his checkbook while shopping. When he notified his bank, an official advised that Roberto stop payment on all outstanding checks and close the account. A stop-payment order for each of Roberto's ten outstanding checks would cost $20. The total cost of ten stop-payment orders would be $200. Roberto decided, therefore, to keep the account open.

While this action sounds risky, it may be appropriate. The ten legitimate outstanding checks would clear as usual. If any checks were forged by someone who found the checkbook, the bank should not accept them as valid. The bank has the legal responsibility to spot a phony signature; a depositor is not liable to pay for checks with unauthorized signatures. Of course, banks don't check every check processed for forged signatures.

But if you receive a canceled check with a forged signature, you should notify the bank. The bank must accept responsibility for accepting a forged check, which is also true of any business or individual who accepts checks.

A stop-payment order makes more sense when the goods or services purchased with the check are unsatisfactory. By stopping payment, a customer can negotiate to exchange the product or have the job done right.

Critical Thinking

1. What actions should a person take when checkbook is lost?
2. What are examples of situations when stop-payment order is appropriate?

---

with the bank statement. With your account updated, you can write checks on the new balance.

SELECTING A FINANCIAL INSTITUTION

Using a checking account and other financial services is a consumer purchase decision. To obtain the best value for your financial services dollar, comparison shop based on services offered, safety, convenience, fees and charges, and restrictions.

Services Offered

As financial institutions offer more and more financial services, decisions become very confusing. To work through this marketplace maze, select the checking account with the lowest costs. Locate the best interest rate on your savings. Find the lowest interest rate for loans. Do not be attracted just by fancy financial product names or flashy services that you might never need or use.

Safety

As previously mentioned, most banks and financial institutions have federal deposit insurance. However, do not assume that this is the case at every financial institution. Make sure that the institution where you keep your savings is insured.

Convenience

Do you want 24-hour banking services? Do you want branch offices near your home or work? These are some of the factors you will need to consider as you decide about

FYI

When the difference between the bank statement balance and your checkbook is divisible by 9, this error may be caused by a transposition of numbers. You might have entered $45.00 instead of $54.00, or you may have added $678.00 when you should have added $687.00.

LEGAL PERSPECTIVES

Ask students to tell what actions might be necessary if the bank pays a check that was written by someone other than an authorized signatory for the account.

CRITICAL THINKING

1. When you lose your checkbook, you should contact your bank. While bank officials sometimes will recommend you close the account, legitimate checks will clear as usual. Any forged checks should not accepted by the bank.
2. Possible answers might include when a check is lost and you issue another check for the same payment or when you are dissatisfied with a product or service.

convenience. However, there is usually a trade-off. While more convenience may mean higher costs, in recent years, online banking has resulted in lower costs for many consumers.

Fees and Charges

Financial services have costs. Compare your needs with the price you pay. Remember, seemingly low fees for using an ATM or having a checking account can possibly add up to hundreds of dollars within a few years.

Restrictions

Your costs are not always measured in money amounts. If you must keep $500 on deposit for a "free" checking account, you may be losing the opportunity to earn interest on those funds at another institution. Or if you must keep money on deposit for two years to earn a higher rate, you are restricted from using those funds for some unplanned purpose. Always balance your needs with the conditions imposed upon you. When you are not satisfied, shop around!

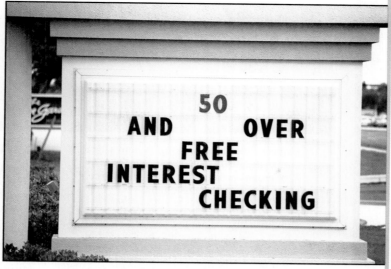

50 AND OVER FREE INTEREST CHECKING

What aspects of banking would be important to you when choosing your bank?

E-Commerce for Banking Services

Online banking can reduce the cost of a transaction by as much as 90 percent. Financial institutions can lower labor, building, electricity, and paper-processing costs. For example, PNC Financial Services has improved customer service while cutting costs. Teller transactions cost $1.40 each compared with only 20 cents online. PNC also offers its employees web-based training courses that can be accessed from home or on the road.

PayPal, Billpoint, and PayDirect are some of the online payment systems that allow fast payments for e-commerce transactions. These services reduce much of the risk for both the buyer and seller in exchanging payments and purchased products.

To use these payment services, a person signs up by giving a name, address, phone number, checking account or credit card information; and then selects a password. E-mail systems, banking, and credit card networks provide the infrastructure for processing payments. While the movement of money is fast, taking money out of the system may be a slower process.

Critical Thinking

Conduct research about online payment systems. Obtain information about various forms of cyber cash that are being used to transfer payments between customers and online businesses. Prepare a visual or oral presentation on the benefits and costs associated with these electronic money systems.

Banking Web Sites
The Federal Reserve System at www.federalreserve.gov
The Federal Deposit Insurance Corporation at www.fdic.gov
Credit Union information at www.cuna.org
Online payment information at www.billpoint.com and www.paypal.com

Chapter 28 *Managing Your Checking Account and Other Financial Services* **391**

Basic Skills-Math

In order for students to become contributing workers in our society, it is important that they become proficient in the basic skills of reading, writing, arithmetic, and mathematics. Employers are looking for potential employees with good basic foundation skills. In order to prepare students for the school-to-work transition, we must teach these skills in our classroom.

Applying math across the curriculum is an important element in contemporary education. As a part of end-of-chapter activities, Calculate Business Data enables students to apply their math skills. Appendix B: Math Review, Appendix C: Determining Percentages and Interest in Business, and Appendix D: Using Measurements in Business, also apply arithmetic and math skills.

SCANS

REVIEW YOUR READING

1. Deduct the amount from the drawer's account, add it to the payee's account, cancel the check, and return it to the drawer.
2. A place where banks in the same area send checks for payment to all banks on which the checks were written.
3. Global clearinghouse for large numbers of checks for banks in different cities.
4. The beginning balance, deposits made during the month, checks paid by the bank during the month, ATM transactions, EFTs or special payments, service charges, any interest earned, and the balance at the end of the month.
5. Paid checks are canceled and returned by most banks. Banks that keep copies of checks include details of the paid check on the bank statement.
6. The depositor can request a copy of the check to show proof of payment.
7. (1) Outstanding checks; (2) depositor forgot to record a transaction; (3) service charge not yet subtracted from checkbook; (4) deposit not yet received at bank; (5) interest not yet added to checkbook; (6) errors.
8. Add to statement balance any deposit not shown on the statement; subtract outstanding checks from bank statement balance; subtract service charges and automatic payments from and add any interest earned to the checkbook balance; make sure the new statement and checkbook balances agree; find and correct any errors.
9. After reconciliation, total service charges should be deducted from the checkbook balance.
10. Services offered, convenience, safety, fees and charges, and restrictions.

COMMUNICATE BUSINESS CONCEPTS

11. Helen is correct. Canceled checks, not stubs or registers, serve as evidence that payment has been made.
12. Benefits: process your bank statement faster and reduce costs of

---

BUSINESS NOTES

1. Checks clear the banking system when financial institutions exchange funds based on the amounts of checks written and deposited by customers.
2. Information on a bank statement includes the beginning balance, deposits made during the month, checks paid by the bank during the month, ATM transactions, EFTs or special payments, service charges, any interest earned, and the balance at the end of the month.
3. Reconciling a checking account involves finding the differences between the balance on the bank statement and the balance in your checkbook.
4. To obtain the best value for your financial services dollar, investigate and compare services offered, safety, convenience, fees and charges, and restrictions.

REVIEW YOUR READING

1. How are checks cleared in the same bank?
2. What is a clearinghouse?
3. Explain the role of the Federal Reserve System in clearing checks.
4. What information is commonly included on a bank statement?
5. How does a depositor know that his or her checks have been paid?
6. Explain how you can prove that a certain payment was made if your bank keeps and files your checks instead of returning them to you.
7. For what six reasons might your bank statement and your checkbook balance differ?
8. What are the main steps taken when you reconcile a bank statement?
9. How would you record a service charge on your check stub or in your check register?
10. When comparing financial institutions, what factors should be considered?

COMMUNICATE BUSINESS CONCEPTS

11. Helen and Jim Hogan are talking about whether or not to save their canceled checks from their joint account. Jim says, "Throw them out; I hate a cluttered house." Helen reminds him, "Remember what happened last year when you tried to use your check register to prove you paid the furniture bill? I think we should save the canceled checks." Do you agree with Helen or Jim? Why?
12. What are the benefits and drawbacks of a bank not returning a depositor's canceled checks?
13. Isaac Ahlred has received his bank statement for the month of May. The bank statement shows a balance of $401.19, but his check register shows a balance of only $364.52.
    a. What is the most likely reason that the bank balance is larger than Isaac's?
    b. What steps should Isaac take to bring his balances into agreement?
14. Many people use the same bank for all of their financial services. Is this a wise consumer practice? Why or why not?

---

sorting and mailing canceled checks back to you. Drawbacks: depositor has to request copy of a check when a dispute occurs about whether a payment has been made.

13. a. Checks might be outstanding; other possible answers include service charges or other deductions, interest earned, and errors.
    b. Perform bank reconciliation.
14. Using the one bank is convenient. However, compare costs and other factors at several financial institutions. A bank that gives you the best deal on a checking account may not give the best terms for a loan.

DEVELOP YOUR BUSINESS LANGUAGE

For each numbered item, find the term that has the same meaning.

15. A place where member banks exchange checks to clear them.

16. Checks that have been paid by the bank.

17. Checks that have not been deducted from the bank-statement balance.

18. Returning a check to the drawer's bank to be paid and charged to his or her checking account.

19. A statement showing how the checkbook balance and the bank statement were brought into agreement.

20. A report sent by the bank to a depositor showing the status of his or her account.

KEY TERMS

bank reconciliation
bank statement
canceled checks
clearing
clearinghouse
outstanding checks

DEVELOP YOUR BUSINESS LANGUAGE

15. clearinghouse
16. canceled checks
17. outstanding checks
18. clearing
19. bank reconciliation
20. bank statement

DECISION-MAKING STRATEGIES

Jess Thomas cannot get his bank statement and checkbook balanced this month. He keeps ending up with 10 cents more in his adjusted checkbook balance than in his adjusted bank statement balance. Jess called Dave Rogers, a customer service representative in the accounting department of Jess's bank. In his frustration, Jess told Dave that the bank must have made an error and demanded that Dave double-check Jess's bank statement.

Dave answered that because the bank uses computers, it is impossible for the bank statements to contain errors. Dave said that Jess must have made the mistake and should do the double-checking himself. Jess decided that he had do something about the situation.

21. What options does Jess have to reconcile his checking account?

22. How can Jess get better service from his bank?

DECISION-MAKING STRATEGIES

21. Possible answers might include entering a 10-cent adjustment to the checkbook, asking someone else to double check the reconciliation, and rechecking especially carefully for errors in the bank statement or the checkbook.

22. Possible answers might include talking to Dave about his concerns about service, writing to Dave's supervisor, or shopping for better service at other institutions.

CALCULATE BUSINESS DATA

23. When the four banks in the town of Butler prepared to clear checks one day, they found that they had paid checks drawn on the other banks as shown in the following table.

Assuming that each bank makes an individual settlement with every other bank, calculate the amount that each bank will either pay or receive from every other bank. For example, First National holds $938.57 worth of checks drawn on Farmers' Trust.

Farmers' Trust holds $443.74 worth of checks drawn on First National. Therefore, First National will receive from Farmers' Trust a settlement of $938.57 − $443.74 = $494.83.

	Drawn On			
Checks Held By	**First National**	**Farmers' Trust**	**Merchants' Mutual**	**Butler Bank**
First National	———	$938.57	$644.63	$1,158.64
Farmers' Trust	$443.74	———	$711.44	$ 208.45
Merchants' Mutual	$304.36	$522.82	———	$ 639.28
Butler Bank	$988.95	$326.31	$783.30	———

CALCULATE BUSINESS DATA

23. First National: from Farmers Trust: $938.57 − $443.74 = $494.83; from Merchants' Mutual: $644.63 − $304.36 = $340.27; from Butler Bank: $1,158.64 − $988.95 = $169.69. Farmers' Trust: to First National: $494.83; from Merchants' Mutual: $711.44 − $522.82 = $188.62; to Butler Bank: $326.31 − $208.45 = $177.86. Merchants' Mutual: to First National: $340.27; to Farmers' Trust: $188.62; to Butler Bank: $783.30 − $639.28 = $144.02. Butler Bank: to First National: $169.69; from Farmers' Trust: $177.86; from Merchants' Mutual: $144.02.

24. (a) $471.04 June 1 balance + ($57.10 + $101.96 + $231.00 + $198.04 + $172.00 + $298.30) deposits − ($225.00 + $390.00 + $154.80 + $75.00) checks = $684.64 ending balance;
(b) Yes, her balance on June 1 was $471.04, for which she must pay a $10.00 service charge.

25. (a) $24.50 + $7.28 + $20.00 + $46.72 = $98.50; (b) bank statement balance

26. Bank statement
balance	$378.65
Subtract outstanding checks:	
$ 7.16	
15.10	
9.95	− 32.21
New Balance	$346.44
Checkbook balance	$349.44
Subtract service charge	− 3.00
Balance	$346.44

TECHNOLOGY APPLICATION

In this activity, students use a computer to solve a business problem using a file that is provided on the data CD that accompanies *Intro to Business*. Instructions for using the data CD are included in a **README** file on the disk. Solutions are provided on the Instructor's Resource CD.

24. Olivia Cardona operates Spectacular Candles, a gift shop at the TriCity Mall. Her bank balance on June 1 was $471.04. During the Area Festival Week of June 1, she made the following deposits: $57.10, $101.96, $231.00, $198.04, $172.00, $298.30. During that week, Olivia wrote the following checks: to herself for salary, $225.00; to TriCity Mall for stall rental, $390.00; to Wrapping Classics, Inc., for wrapping supplies and bags, $154.80; and to TriCity Herald for an ad, $75.00. If her account falls below $500.00 on any day of the month, she pays a $10.00 service charge to her bank.
  a. What balance should her check register show at the end of the week?
  b. Should Olivia's June bank statement show a service charge based on her checking account activities for the first week? If so, how much?

25. When Gizella Ott began to reconcile her bank statement, she discovered that four checks she had written had not been paid by the bank. The amounts of the checks were $24.50, $7.28, $20.00, and $46.72.
  a. What is the total amount of unpaid checks?
  b. In order to reconcile the statement, should Gizella subtract the total outstanding checks from the bank statement balance or from her checking account balance?

26. In October, Tom Jones received his bank statement that showed a balance of $378.65. The service charge was $3.00. In examining his statement, he found that the following checks were outstanding: No. 31, $7.16; No. 34, $15.10; and No. 35, $9.95. His checkbook balance at the end of the month was $349.44. Reconcile his bank statement.

TECHNOLOGY APPLICATION

Using the *Intro to Business* Data CD and your spreadsheet program software, select problem CH28. After the problem appears on your screen, complete the following activities. Then, after you have completed each step, display or print the completed spreadsheet for each activity. If you do not have a printer available, answer the questions before you leave the computer.

27. Enter formulas to complete the Bank Statement Balance section of the bank reconciliation. What is the total of outstanding checks?

28. Enter formulas to complete the Checkbook Balance section of the bank reconciliation. What is the Adjusted Checkbook Balance?

29. What formula did you enter to calculate the Adjusted Checkbook Balance?

COMMUNICATING
for
SUCCESS

COMMUNICATING
for
SUCCESS

TELEPHONE SKILLS—
"HELLO, THIS IS CHRIS."

Even with the increasing popularity of e-mail, telephone communication is still among the most important forms of business communication. Frequently a telephone conversation is the first contact someone has with a business. It is very important that this first impression is a good one.

You can enhance your value to an organization by developing good telephone skills. You can also do so by using appropriate telephone etiquette. In general, you should always be pleasant, courteous, interested, sincere, and helpful.

You can demonstrate good telephone etiquette by:

- Being easy to reach by telephone and/or leaving word when you are away.
- Promptly answering the telephone.
- Identifying yourself when you answer.
- Being prepared with a pencil and pad to take a message.
- Listening attentively.
- Allowing the caller to end the conversation.

> **By developing good telephone skills and etiquette, you can enhance your value to your company.**

Good telephone communication requires more than just good etiquette. You will need some additional skills. When you are speaking with someone on the telephone, try to picture that person. It will help you to be yourself and to speak with appropriate expression in your voice.

Speak clearly and slowly enough to be understood. Avoid coughing and irritating speech mannerisms such as "you know" and "uh." Never interrupt the caller to talk aside to others.

Many modern business telephone systems have a feature called voice mail that allows callers to leave a message when you are unavailable. Be certain to retrieve and answer your messages at least once each day.

CRITICAL THINKING

1. Why is it so important to practice good business telephone communication techniques and etiquette?
2. What advantages do you think the telephone has over e-mail and letters?

Communications skills will help ensure students' success in the business world. Communicating for Success introduces workplace/interpersonal communications issues and proper uses of communications technology. Each feature discusses a key communications topic, and contains two Critical Thinking questions that require students to analyze what they have learned.

Most students probably haven't had enough job experience to realize just how important telephone communications skills are to almost any business. Even with the advent of e-mail, telephones are still one of the most frequently used and most personal means of business communications. This feature stresses the basics of good telephone etiquette and other business-related telephone skills that students will find invaluable when they enter the business world.

CRITICAL THINKING

1. Frequently a telephone conversation is the first contact someone has with a business. It is very important that this first impression is a good one.
2. Answers may vary. Telephone conversation is more personal and allows questions and responses to be given immediately rather than waiting for a reply when using e-mail and letters.

GLOBAL BUSINESS PROJECT

The financial exchanges that take place among companies in different countries are an important foundation of global business activities. Students will research financial institutions and payment methods commonly used for international business transactions. Students are also asked to think about the influence of the electronic transfer of funds and global financial networks as they relate to expanding foreign trade.

To complete each phase of this project, students are encouraged to use various resources—textbook content, library materials, World Wide Web sites, interviews, advertisements, product packages, in-store observations. The individual activities are planned for use as either (1) an on-going course project, or (2) individual assignments.

Whether used as a continuing project or for selected activities, consider having students work in teams. This small group experience provides a valuable skill for future learning and work situations.

In addition to search engines, these selected web sites can be helpful for this unit:

- International Trade Administration of the U.S. Dept. of Commerce (www.ita.doc.gov)
- World Trade Organization at (www.wto.org)
- World Bank (www.worldbank.org)
- World Export-Import Bank of the United States (www.exim.gov)
- International Chamber of Commerce (www.iccwbo.org/)
- Small Business Administration (www.sba.gov)
- Import-export information at (www.internationalist.com/)
- Annual reports, company information (www.hoovers.com)
- Export assistance (www.export.gov)

GLOBAL BUSINESS PROJECT

USE FINANCIAL INSTITUTIONS

Business transactions in the global economy depend on the availability and flow of funds. Banks and other financial institutions are necessary to assist with this business activity. In this phase of the global business plan project, you will consider how companies plan for making and receiving payments when doing business across international borders.

PROJECT GOALS

1. Research common financial institutions in another country.
2. Identify payment methods used for international business activities.
3. Analyze possible use of electronic transfer of funds for global business transactions.

PROJECT ACTIVITIES

Using your textbook, library materials, web sites, interviews with people, and other resources, complete the following activities:

1. Banks and other financial institutions exist to provide funds and to transfer money when business transactions occur. Using the country from your portfolio (or select a country), research the names of the major banks that operate in that nation. Do these financial institutions also operate in other countries?

2. Making payments for goods and services purchased by companies in different countries requires planning. Describe the common foreign trade payment methods such as cash in advance, letter of credit, and sale on account.

3. Global financial computer networks exist for the purpose of transferring funds quickly and easily among companies in different countries. Prepare a list of benefits and drawbacks of using electronic funds transfer for international payments.

PROJECT WRAP-UP

1. Continue your portfolio (folder, file box, or other container) for storing and referring back to the information and materials you created in the activities above. These items will be used for various components of your global business plan.

2. Plan a flowchart or graph that shows the process of receiving and making payments among companies in different countries. Describe the steps and parties involved in these international business transactions.

FOCUS ON CAREERS

BANKING AND FINANCIAL SERVICES

The financial industry offers a variety of career opportunities. Most financial workers are employed in commercial banks. Others work in specialized banks, savings and loan associations, credit unions, and finance companies.

JOB TITLES

- Job titles commonly found in this career area include:
- Branch Manager
- Teller
- Head Teller
- Loan Officer
- Loan Counselor
- Loan Interviewer/Clerk
- Credit Clerk
- Stockbroker
- Financial Services Sales Agent
- Insurance Sales Agent
- Insurance Claims Clerk
- Financial Manager
- Economist

EMPLOYMENT OUTLOOK

- The banking industry is expected to continue to consolidate. Employment of bank branch managers, in particular, will grow very little as banks open fewer branches and promote electronic and Internet banking to cut costs.
- The securities industry will hire more financial managers to handle complex financial transactions and manage investments.
- Automation and the growing use of online mortgage brokers should have an adverse impact on the demand for lending professionals such as loan officers.
- Slower than average job growth is expected for insurance agents, but opportunities will be favorable for persons with the right qualifications and skills.

EDUCATION AND TRAINING

- Most beginning jobs in banking require at least a high-school education.
- Many entry-level employees also have had additional business preparation in community or technical colleges.
- Officers, professional personnel, and executives usually have college degrees.
- Bank workers who meet the public must be able to communicate well, be accurate, and have a professional-looking appearance.
- Most bank workers must be able to handle details and to work well under stress.
- A knowledge of computers is vital.

SALARY LEVELS (MEDIAN EARNINGS IN RECENT YEARS)

- Full-time bank tellers: $22,000.
- Salaried insurance salesperson: $38,000.
- Securities and financial services sales representatives: $46,000.
- Financial managers: $42,000.
- Business economists: $78,000.

CRITICAL THINKING

1. What factors have affected career opportunities in the banking industry?
2. What skills are important for success in banking and financial services jobs?

FOCUS ON CAREERS

The careers listed in this Focus on Careers come from the *Occupational Outlook Handbook*, an online publication (www.bls.gov/oco) of the federal government. The O*NET codes for these job titles are: Branch Manager, 11-3031.02; Teller, 43-3071.00; Head Teller, 43-3071.00; Loan Officer, 13-2071.00; Loan Counselor, 13-2072.00; Loan Interviewer/Clerk, 43-4131.00; Credit Clerk, 43-4041.00, 43-4041.02; Stockbroker, 41-3031.01; Financial Services Sales Agent, 41-3031.02; Insurance Sales Agent, 41-3021.00; Insurance Claims Clerk, 43-9041.01; Financial Manager, 11-3031.01, 11-3031.02; Economist, 19-3011.00. Students can access O*NET Online (online.onetcenter.org) to view features of selected occupations. They can also search for related occupations and for occupations that match selected skills. This career feature is designed to help students explore a variety of different careers in business and can be used to demonstrate that skills learned in this course are relevant. A Career Focus Worksheet is available in the School-To-Work/SCANS Activity Masters.

CRITICAL THINKING

1. Technology and new services being offered by financial institutions.
2. Accuracy, basic computer skills, math ability, a professional appearance, and working well with others.

UNIT 9

BUILDING YOUR PORTFOLIO

CAREER DEVELOPMENT – RESEARCHING CAREER OPPORTUNITIES

The Building Your Portfolio career exercise will help your students establish a personal history—where they have been, where they are now, and where they are going.

Emphasize the importance of not underestimating the value of reference letters. These letters should be written by people who can recommend students to prospective employers as good workers, good students, or individuals with admirable personal qualities (such as dependability, punctuality, leadership, self-motivating, interpersonal skills, trustworthiness). Stress that the best references come from people with knowledge of a person's abilities as a worker. Direct students to acquire the names of three to five people who will provide references upon request and make an appointment to talk personally with these people. At this time, students should request reference letters to include in their portfolios.

As a supplemental activity, you may refer to the School–To–Work/SCANS Activity Masters.

TEACHING STRATEGIES

SCANS

Cooperative Learning

Teaching Tips

Special Needs

Teams

Special Features

Media/Technology

Chapter	Spreadsheet Software	Database Software	Word Processing Software	Internet	Video
29	■				■
30		■			■
31	■			■	■
32			■		■

Resources

SOFTWARE

Excel, Word, WordPerfect, Works, and ClarisWorks for Mac and Windows

Word Pro, ASCII, QuattroPro, Lotus, and Access for Windows

SOUTH-WESTERN EDUCATIONAL PUBLISHING PRODUCTS

Donnelly. *Skills for Consumer Success.* 1999. Cincinnati: South-Western Educational Publishing Company. Text-Workbook. 0-538-68612-X.

Ryan. *Managing Your Personal Finances.* 2002. Cincinnati: South-Western Educational Publishing Company. Text-Workbook. 0-538-69958-2.

BOOKS

Detweiler. *The Ultimate Credit Handbook : How to Double Your Credit, Cut Your Debt, and Have a Lifetime of Great Credit.* 1997. Plume.

Calder. *Financing the American Dream : Debt, Credit, and the Making of American Consumer Culture.* 1999. Princeton Univ Press.

PERIODICALS

Economic Review. Kansas City, MO.

Kiplinger's Personal Finance Magazine. Washington, D.C.

Money. New York, NY.

The Wall Street Journal. New York, NY.

GOVERNMENT PUBLICATIONS

Occupational Outlook Handbook, U.S. Department of Labor, Washington, DC.

What Work Requires of Schools: A SCANS Report for America 2000, U.S. Department of Labor, Washington, DC

MEDIA/TECHNOLOGY

Publisher's web sites:

www.intro2business.swep.com

www.swep.com

www.thomson.com

CREDIT IN OUR ECONOMY

The content and activities of this unit provide students with an overview of the purposes and characteristics of credit in our economic society.

Credit is a vital force in our market economy. Consumers use credit to buy almost everything. Credit has become an accepted way of doing business throughout our economy. This unit is oriented to the realities of everyday credit decision making. The goal of this unit is economic understanding of why and how credit is used wisely. The unit emphasizes that students must learn to deal with the mechanics of credit in everyday life. Students learn about important considerations related to the actual costs of credit, legislation affecting the disclosure of finance costs, and the need for maintaining good credit records.

Chapter 29, The Fundamentals of Credit, explains what credit is and why it is important in our economy. Chapter 30, The Uses of Credit, discusses and compares the uses of charge accounts and installment plans as forms of credit. Chapter 31, The Cost of Credit, explains how to calculate interest and compute the cost of credit. Chapter 32, Credit Records and Regulations, discusses credit laws and how a good credit record can be established.

UNIT 9
CREDIT IN OUR ECONOMY

Chapters

Kick-Off Activity

Investigating Business Media

The following exercise asks students to choose an article from *The Wall Street Journal,* the financial section of a newspaper, or a business magazine, and to inquire about a topic related to this unit.

Ask students to select an article from *The Wall Street Journal* or a financial magazine that describes the problems businesses have experienced managing credit extended to customers. Then have students answer the following questions:

1 What are some of the problems businesses have in granting credit to customers?

2 What are the credit management policies for collecting bad debts?

BU$INESSBRIEF

DATABASES AND PERSONAL PRIVACY

Would you be surprised if someone told you that she or he could easily check a database to find out where you live, where you work, where you bank, and what problems you have experienced with credit (including bankruptcy)? How is this information about you so readily available to so many people? The answer lies with computer databases and electronic networks. Businesses and governments are constantly collecting, storing, sharing, and distributing data.

Can you think of the many ways that information about you becomes part of a record in some database? Most of the information in databases comes from information given voluntarily. For instance, you offer information when you fill out a credit application, apply for a telephone, register for a college class, apply for a driver's license, answer questions in a telephone survey, apply for insurance, go to court, and answer U.S. Census Bureau questions.

Privacy is a basic right to have information about you kept confidential. If you are concerned about your right to privacy, you have the same concern as four out of five consumers who responded to a recent public opinion poll. There are certain kinds of information about each of us that we may want to share only with family members and/or with close friends.

Among the databases of significance are the more than 400 million credit files in our country. Another large database is the Medical Information Bureau (MIB) that is used by over 800 insurance companies in the United States. More than 15 million U.S. consumers have medical conditions and their health records are recorded by the MIB.

While there is some reason to be concerned about these databases and personal privacy, there is no need for panic. Decisions about the granting of credit or the issuance of insurance policies are usually made based on accurate, up-to-date information. The information gathered is used for legitimate business reasons.

Nevertheless, some effort is being made to review federal privacy laws, such as the Privacy Act of 1974. Issues being considered include deciding what is private information and whether consumers should be asked to give permission before any credit or medical reports are released to others.

CRITICAL THINKING

1 *What dangers do you see in having private information so easily accessible to others?*

2 *What do you think should be done to help protect your privacy?*

399

BUILDING YOUR PORTFOLIO

The Building Your Portfolio work samples validate skill level and a student's ability to accomplish tasks frequently performed on the job. The most important reason for including samples in a portfolio is to demonstrate a student's abilities and skills. In selecting work samples for each unit, students should always have a choice of which activities to include. Students might be encouraged to include samples from the end-of-chapter activities, particularly Communicate Business Concepts, Calculate Business Data, Technology Application, and Decision-Making Strategies.

Credit is the privilege of using someone else's money. Three kinds of credit—loan, sales, and trade—are used in our economy. Consumers, businesses, and governments use credit for a variety of purposes.

Resources for Teachers
- Lesson Plans
- School-To-Work/SCANS Activity Masters
- Spanish Resources
- Instructor's Resource CD

Assessment
- Chapter and Unit Tests, Ch. 29
- ExamView, Ch. 29

Media/Technology
- Applying Technology Data CD
- PowerPoint slides
- Business Connection CD
- Videotape

Activity Masters and Workbooks
- Activities and Projects, Ch. 29
- Internet Activity Masters
- Business Math Activity Masters
- Communications Activity Masters
- International Business Activity Masters
- Ethics Activity Masters

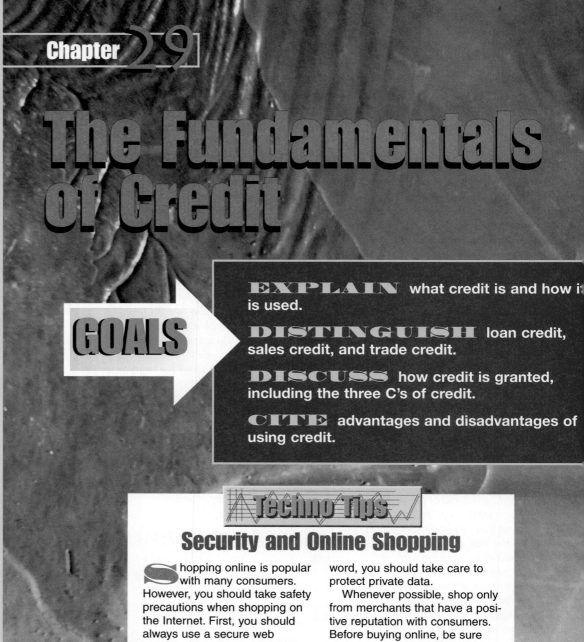

Chapter 29

The Fundamentals Of Credit

GOALS

EXPLAIN what credit is and how it is used.

DISTINGUISH loan credit, sales credit, and trade credit.

DISCUSS how credit is granted, including the three C's of credit.

CITE advantages and disadvantages of using credit.

Techno Tips

Security and Online Shopping

Shopping online is popular with many consumers. However, you should take safety precautions when shopping on the Internet. First, you should always use a secure web browser. Many browsers can automatically encrypt, or scramble, your personal and credit card data before it is sent over the Internet. Also, since many online merchants require you to register a user name and password, you should take care to protect private data.

Whenever possible, shop only from merchants that have a positive reputation with consumers. Before buying online, be sure that you understand the company's delivery and return policies, so that no unpleasant surprises emerge later. Finally, keep a record of your receipt, online order confirmation, and the merchant's Internet address.

Students need to know the latest technologies and develop cutting edge Internet skills for use in current jobs, future careers, or in their homes. TechnoTips introduces students to today's cutting edge technologies and provides them with important Internet skills. Feature topics concentrate on Internet-specific technologies and computer or other hi-tech innovations for use by businesses and consumers.

Although Polonius in Shakespeare's *Hamlet* cautioned, "Neither a borrower nor a lender be," using and providing credit have become a way of life in our economy. Credit is used extensively by consumers, businesses, and governments. For example:

- Adrianna buys gas for her car and uses her oil company credit card.
- Chi-luan applies for and receives a government loan to help with his college expenses.
- New Treads, Inc., receives a $2 million loan to build a new tire store in a downtown area.
- The state of Louisiana borrows $35 million through a bond issue to construct new college buildings.
- Hiawatha County borrows $250,000 to make emergency road repairs.
- Hedgpeth Industries borrows $50,000 to finance the purchase of additional inventory.

What do these people, businesses, and governmental institutions have in common? They all have wants, but lack the money to satisfy those wants. All of them borrow money to satisfy those wants. If they borrow, they will be receiving credit. Credit includes all borrowing other than financing to purchase a home.

Without credit, retail stores could not have a vast array of merchandise for sale if the merchandise had to be paid for before it was sold. Governments could not finance the building of roads and highways without borrowing money to get the projects underway. Many consumers could not purchase new cars, furniture, or appliances without receiving a loan. The amount involved may be large or small, but being able to borrow money or buy on credit at a time of need is an important aspect of our economic system.

WHAT CREDIT IS

Credit is the privilege of using someone else's money for a period of time. That privilege is based on the belief that the person receiving credit will honor a promise to repay the amount owed at a future date. The credit transaction creates a debtor and a creditor. Anyone who buys on credit or receives a loan is known as a **debtor**. The one who sells on credit or makes a loan is called the **creditor**.

Although the credit system uses forms and legal documents, it also depends on trust between the debtor and creditor. **Trust** means that the creditor believes that the debtor will honor the promise to pay later for goods and services that have been received and used. Without that trust, our credit system could not operate.

When you borrow a large amount of money or buy on credit from a business, you usually will be asked to sign a written agreement. The agreement states that you will pay your debt within a certain period of time. For example, Chi-luan had to agree to pay his tuition loan in full within two years after graduation. When Adrianna used her credit card to buy gas and signed the receipt, she agreed to pay for her purchase when the bill came at the end of the month. A credit

Many consumers plan to use credit as a substitute for cash and pay the balance in full at the end of the month—but more than 25 percent almost never pay off their balances.

Display PowerPoint 29-5, *Granting of Credit*. Lead students through a discussion about the granting of credit. The three Cs of creditworthiness cannot be overemphasized. Point out that lenders are interested in your character, capacity, and capital so that they can judge whether you are a good risk, whether you can be depended upon, and whether you are financially able to assume credit obligations.

Direct students to rate each of the following situations as a wise or unwise use of credit. Then survey the class to find out the overall thinking about each situation.

    a. A person uses loan credit to purchase a new stereo system on sale for 25 percent off. The loan has an interest rate of 18 percent per year.

    b. A consumer uses sales credit to buy weekly groceries. This person currently owes $2,000 to credit card companies.

    c. An individual obtains a personal loan from a bank to take a vacation. This person still owes for last year's vacation.

    d. A clothing store uses trade credit to purchase merchandise from wholesalers that will be resold to customers.

EXPLORE THIS/INDEPENDENT PRACTICE Have students prepare a list of items commonly bought within their family on credit. Next to each item listed, have them determine if loan credit or sales credit was used. Another activity is to either have students do additional reading on the advantages/disadvantages of

agreement means that the debtor promises to pay and the creditor trusts that the debtor will pay the amount that is owed.

TYPES OF CREDIT

If you borrow money to be used for some special purpose, you are using **loan credit**. Loans are available from several kinds of financial institutions. Banks, credit unions, savings and loan associations, and consumer finance companies are the primary businesses that make consumer loans. Loan credit usually involves a written contract. The debtor often agrees to repay the loan in specified amounts, called installments, over a period of time.

If you charge a purchase at the time you buy the good or service, you are using **sales credit**. Sales credit is offered by most retail and wholesale businesses. Sales credit involves the use of charge accounts and credit cards by consumers. Many people maintain numerous charge accounts and carry several credit cards.

Trade credit is used by a business when it receives goods from a wholesaler and pays for them at a later specified date. Trade credit terms often are stated "2/10, n/30." This means that the business can take a 2 percent

discount if the bill is paid within 10 days from the billing date. The full or net amount must be paid within 30 days.

USERS OF CREDIT

If you are a typical American consumer, you will use credit for many purposes. You may use credit to buy fairly expensive products that will last for a long time, such as a car, house, or major appliance. Or you may use credit for convenience in making smaller purchases, such as meals and CDs. Paying for medical care, vacations, taxes, and even paying off other debts are other common uses of credit.

What are some reasons why businesses might use credit?

Net Facts provides information and definitions of terms for the Internet. The more information that students have about the Internet, the better equipped they will be to use this resource. In the Internet Activity Masters, there is an Internet Activity Worksheet for each unit. You can use these activities to give students experience with finding information online. Options for assigning this activity are as follows:

1. **Provide students with a list of addresses for this activity,**
2. **Assign students to conduct their own searches, or**
3. **Use the addresses on the Internet Activity Worksheet.**

You should complete the activity yourself before assigning it to students so that you may resolve any discrepancies that may arise.

Businesses may secure long-term loans to buy land and equipment and to construct buildings. They may also borrow money for shorter time periods, sometimes for only one or two days but usually for 30 to 90 days, to meet temporary needs for cash. For example, merchants buy goods on credit, and manufacturers buy raw materials and supplies on credit. Businesses borrow on a short-term basis to get the cash they need while waiting for goods to be sold or for customers to pay for their purchases.

Local, state, and federal governments often use credit in providing goods and services for the benefit of the public. Governments may use credit to buy items such as cars, aircraft, and police uniforms. They may also borrow the money that is needed to build hospitals, highways, parks, and airports.

GRANTING OF CREDIT

You have already read that trust between the debtor and the creditor is essential if credit is to be granted. To become a debtor, you must

FYI

Buying on credit is viewed by people in Germany and the Netherlands as living beyond one's means. *Schuld*, the German word for debt, means guilt.

be able to prove that you are a good credit risk. Not everyone who desires credit will receive it.

Credit Information

The business that is considering you as a credit risk will generally ask you about your financial situation and request credit references. **Credit references** are businesses or individuals from whom you have received credit in the past and/or who can help verify your credit record. The answers to the financial questions and the information received from your credit references will help the business decide whether loan or sales credit should be extended to you.

credit or interview parents, friends, or relatives to determine their opinion of credit. Then have them prepare posters listing the benefits of credit and the hazards of credit.

The Chapter Review questions at the end of the chapter vary in level of difficulty. For a basic assignment, consider Develop Your Business Language and Review Your Reading. For an average assignment, consider the basic assignment plus Communicate Business Concepts and Calculate Business Data. For an enhanced assignment, try the average assignment plus Technology Application and Decision-Making Strategies.

ASSESS

Review the goals at the beginning of the chapter and the Business Notes at the end of the chapter. Have students respond orally or in writing to each goal restated as a question. For students who may have difficulty providing answers, assign the reteaching activities that follow. Enrichment activities may also be assigned where appropriate.

1. What is credit? (Answer: Credit is the privilege of using someone else's money with the obligation to repay it at a future time.)
2. How is credit used by consumers, businesses, and governments? (Answer: Consumers use credit to buy cars, clothing, and furniture; businesses use credit to finance new equipment, make

ETHICAL PERSPECTIVES

Credit Repair Companies

Unfair and deceitful credit practices have been used by borrowers and lenders alike. Some borrowers are untruthful about their ability to repay. They borrow recklessly, and then sometimes search desperately for a solution to a credit problem. Others have no intention of ever paying back the money.

For example, Jamie kept falling farther behind on her credit card payments. Creditors kept asking for money. Jamie hated to open her mail. Some of her creditors said they would have to take her to court. She needed help. Her credit record was being ruined. She even thought about leaving town to avoid paying her debts.

One day she noticed an advertisement: "Credit Repair—Are you in trouble with past-due payments? Is your credit record being ruined? We can fix all problems quickly—

come in today." That was what she needed—help, quick!

After paying the credit repair company some up-front money, Jamie soon discovered that her problem was not corrected. She, along with many others, was being misled. The company did nothing to help Jamie repair her credit record. Instead, the company used the money paid by Jamie and others to set up a similar fraudulent operation in another state.

Critical Thinking
1. Why did the credit repair advertisement appeal to Jamie?
2. What are some things that you think Jamie should do to resolve her credit problem?

ETHICAL PERSPECTIVES

principles to business situations.

Ethical Perspectives raises ethical questions but does not involve the teaching of right and wrong. Instead, it allows students to apply their own

CRITICAL THINKING

1. The credit repair advertisement appealed to Jamie because she wanted to correct her problem with credit. Consumers who face severe problems often look for an easy way out.
2. Jamie should contact her creditors to arrange smaller payments each month until the entire debt is repaid. She also should immediately stop charging additional purchases. Jamie should seek credit counseling to help her avoid future problems with debt.

expansions, and to take care of temporary cash needs; governments borrow money to build roads and offices.)

3. State the difference between sales credit, loan credit, and trade credit. (Answer: Money borrowed from a financial institution is loan credit; goods or services charged at the time of purchase involve the use of sales credit; if a business receives goods now and pays for them later, trade credit is used.)

4. What are the three Cs of credit? (Answer: Character refers to a person's honesty and willingness to pay debts; capacity is a person's ability to pay debts; capital is the value of a person's possessions.)

5. What are some advantages of credit? (Answer: Credit can make buying more convenient, give the purchaser immediate possession of items, allows buyers to take advantage of special sales, and establishes a person's credit rating.)

6. Name several ways in which credit can be misused. (Answer: Credit is misused if it results in overbuying, careless buying, paying higher prices, or incurring excessive debt.)

You should be willing to give all required information readily and honestly. The following questions can be asked: How much do you earn? How long have you worked for your present employer? What property do you own? Do you have any other debts? Important decisions cannot be made without reliable answers to these questions.

The Three Cs of Credit

In deciding whether or not to grant you credit, businesses consider three factors, known as the three Cs—character, capacity, and capital.

Character refers to your honesty and willingness to pay a debt when it is due. If you have a reputation for paying bills on time, you will meet an important condition for being considered a good credit risk. How you will pay your bills in the future usually can be predicted by how you have paid them in the past.

Capacity refers to your ability to pay a debt when it is due. The lender or seller must consider whether your income is large enough to permit you to pay your bills. If your income is too small or unsteady, granting you additional credit may not be wise even though you have had a good credit record in the past. On the other hand, your income may be very high; but if you already have many debts, you may not be able to handle additional debt.

Capital is the value of the borrower's possessions. Capital includes the money you possess and the property you own. For example, you may have a car that is paid for and a house on which a large amount has been

A *credit authorizer's* job duties include:
- **Processing applications for credit.**
- **Approving charges against customers' existing accounts.**
- **Evaluating customers' credit records and payment histories when accounts are past due or otherwise invalid.**

paid. You may also have a checking account and some savings that add to your capital, or you may have nothing except your present income. The value of your capital helps give the lender some assurance that you will be able to meet your credit obligations.

BENEFITS OF CREDIT

Both businesses and consumers benefit from the use of credit. Businesses benefit in several ways. By being allowed to buy on credit, customers will tend to purchase more, and the business will increase its profits. If the business buys its merchandise using trade credit, the merchandise can be paid for after it has been sold to customers.

As a consumer, you also can benefit from the wise use of credit. Here are some ways in which consumers benefit from their use of credit.

- *Convenience.* Credit can make it convenient for you to buy. You can shop without carrying much cash with you. There may be times when you do not have enough cash and have an urgent need for something. For example, if your car needs emergency repairs, you may have to wait until payday unless you can have the work done on credit.

In a recent year, it was reported that Wisconsin consumers led the nation in paying their bills on time—they also received the greatest number of unsolicited offers per capita for credit cards. **FYI**

The careers listed in Career Highlights come from the *Occupational Outlook Handbook*, an online publication (www.bls.gov/oco) of the federal government. The O*NET code for Credit Authorizer is 43-4041.01. Tell your class about this resource and how to access it, and explain its purpose and how to use it. This description of job duties can be used to demonstrate the relevancy of skills learned in this course.

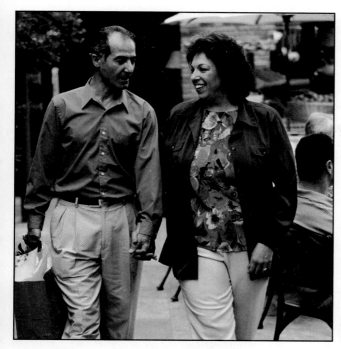

Give reasons for and against using credit to go shopping.

- *Immediate possession.* Credit allows you to have immediate possession of the item that you want. A family can buy a dishwasher on credit and begin using it immediately rather than waiting until enough money has been saved to pay cash for it.

- *Immediate possession.* Credit allows you to have immediate possession of the item that you want. A family can buy a dishwasher on credit and begin using it immediately rather than waiting until enough money has been saved to pay cash for it.

- *Savings.* Credit allows you to buy an item when it goes on sale, possibly at a much lower price. Some stores, especially department and furniture stores, often send notices of special sales to their credit customers several days before they are advertised to the general public. Therefore, credit customers have first choice of the merchandise and may obtain good bargains.

- *Credit rating.* If you buy on credit and pay your bills when they are due, you gain a reputation for being dependable. In that way, you establish a favorable **credit rating**. A credit rating is valuable during

an emergency when you must borrow money or when you want to make a major purchase. It is also valuable in obtaining credit if you move to another community.

- *Useful in an emergency.* Access to credit can help you in an emergency. Having an oil company credit card, for example, can come in handy if you run out of gas and cash at the same time. Or, in a more serious situation, suppose you are working your way through college and suddenly lose your job. You may be able to get a loan to tide you over until you find another job.

PRECAUTIONS FOR USE OF CREDIT

Buying on credit is convenient and can be beneficial. However, there are some disadvantages if you are not careful in your use of credit. Some problems you as a consumer

RETEACH

On the board, list the types of credit—sales credit, loan credit, and trade credit. Ask students to describe transactions involving the use of each type of credit. You may also ask them to provide examples of how individuals, businesses, and governments all use credit. Another activity might be to list and define on the board each of the factors used to determine who receives credit: character, capacity, and capital. What effect might the loss of a job have on these factors? What might be the effect of a new job that pays more? Direct students to construct a chart listing the pros and cons of credit. Review the advantages and disadvantages of credit through this comparative chart. Ask students to add to the chart.

ENRICH

Direct students to read the Ethical Perspectives in this chapter. Have students analyze in writing the following statement: "You should never make a purchase if you can't pay for it with cash." In their written report, students should consider these questions: How would this philosophy affect individual wants and needs? If this philosophy were held by a majority of Americans, what impact would it have on the economy (as related to supply and demand)? Would this philosophy, if held by a majority of Americans, affect employment? Ask students to prepare questionnaires that survey adults about their attitudes toward credit. The questions asked should reveal the opinions of those surveyed about the benefits and

TEACHING STRATEGIES
Teams

Student Teams—Achievement Divisions (STAD) is an instructional method in which students use collaborative learning in peer groups. When using STAD, students are assigned to teams with four members each. Use the lesson plan given to teach this chapter; then divide students into their groups. Each group will study and review the lesson, making sure that all group members understand the goals and content. When time has expired, send students back to their desks to take the ExamView for this chapter. Students must take the ExamView on their own with no assistance from team members. Compare each student's score to the current average for that student's previous ExamView. Award two points to students who meet their last ExamView score. Give three points to students who beat their last ExamView score. The team that has the most points is the winner.

drawbacks of credit usage. The main question should be: Do you think credit is a good thing for the economy? Why or why not?

SUMMARIZE

To reinforce concepts learned, direct students to prepare an outline of the main ideas of this chapter. Review the proper procedures for constructing an outline.

Wrap up this chapter by assigning students to each of the chapter goals. Ask each student to prepare three or four multiple-choice questions related to a chapter goal. Review the procedures for constructing multiple-choice test items. Read to the class some of the questions prepared by students, and ask the class to write the correct response to each question. Provide the correct answers to the questions.

EVALUATE

- Assign Activities and Projects for Chapter 29.
- Administer the printed test or ExamView for Chapter 29.
- Assign School-To-Work/SCANS portfolio activities for Unit 9.

Credit card issuers lure consumers with many different kinds of special offers, including varying interest rates, reduced fees, frequent-flyer miles, merchandise discounts, and rebates.

can encounter with unwise use of credit include the following:

- *Overbuying.* Overbuying is one of the most common hazards of using credit. There are several ways in which this happens. You may purchase something that is more expensive than you can afford. It is easy to say, "Charge it," for a suit that costs $390 when you would purchase a less expensive one if you had paid cash. Attractive store displays and advertisements attract us and invite us to make purchases. As a credit customer, you may be tempted to buy items that you do not really need.

- *Careless buying.* Careless buying may result if you become lazy in your shopping. You may stop checking advertisements carefully. You may fail to make comparisons, causing you to buy at the wrong time or the wrong place. Smart buyers know that at certain times of the year, the prices of some goods decrease. Credit can tempt you not to wait for a better price on an item you want.

- *Higher prices.* Higher prices may be paid. Stores that sell only for cash are able to sell at lower prices than stores that offer credit. Extending credit is expensive. It requires good accounting to keep accurate records of each charge sale and each payment. When customers do not pay as agreed, there are collection expenses. Sometimes businesses must simply write off consumer debts as uncollectible. Increased costs are passed on to customers in the form of higher prices.

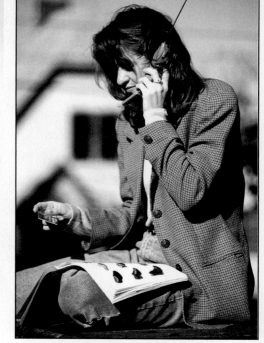

Name some situations when you have to pay by credit card, and when cash is not accepted.

- *Overuse of credit.* Overuse of credit can result in too much being owed. Buying now and paying later may sound like a good idea. If too many payments are to be made later, the total amount that must be paid can become a problem. Consumers must keep records of the total amount owed to creditors so that they do not have monthly payments that exceed their ability to pay.

Businesses and governments, too, can get into trouble with the overuse of credit. Too much borrowing can lead to bankruptcy if the organization is not managed properly. Too many debts place a damaging strain on the finances of businesses and governments. Using credit wisely is important for consumers, businesses, and governments.

Basic Skills-Reading

Direct students to the first main heading of the chapter. The first sentence of a paragraph is usually the main idea of the material being discussed. The last sentence of the paragraph usually summarizes or bridges to the paragraphs or subheadings that follow. Boldfaced terms and italicized words draw attention to important facts or topics in the material. Di-

rect students to pages in the chapter that illustrate boldfaced terms or italicized terms. The Student Activity Worksheet, Basic Skills—Reading, in the School-To-Work/SCANS Activity Masters, may be used to serve as a guideline for discussion of each of these points. Ask students to write a summary of the points that will be covered in the chapter.

Before making a final decision whether to buy on credit, there are some questions you as a consumer should answer: How am I benefiting from this use of credit? Is this the best buy I can make or should I shop around some more? What will be the total cost of my purchase, including the cost of charging the item? What would I save if I paid cash? Will the payments be too high considering my income? Answers to these questions will help you make wise credit decisions.

Consumer Credit Web Sites
- Credit-card information at www.cardtrak.com
- Wise use of credit at www.ftc.gov
- Loan rate information at www.banx.com
- Home and auto borrowing rates at www.eloan.com

E-Commerce for Using Credit

"2.9 percent APR," "No money down," and "Instant credit approval."
Credit offers such as these are common. With expanded Internet access, credit and loan promotions are not limited to television, radio, and your mailbox. Applying online for a credit card, auto loan, or home mortgage are examples of e-loans available to consumers. Web sites provide credit and rate information, online applications, and fast processing and approval.

Along with the ease of obtaining credit, however, comes the problem of overspending. Unwise use of credit is likely to continue as one of the major causes of financial troubles. Remember that these money problems can result whether you obtain credit in person or in cyber space.

Consumers must be careful when providing information for online loan applications. Businesses that collect information often sell much of that information to other businesses. New laws require companies to disclose how they will use the information they collect and provide customers with a procedure to protect their personal information from unwanted use.

Critical Thinking
Conduct a web search to obtain information about the costs of loans from various online sources. In addition, obtain information for loans from local financial institutions. Develop a spreadsheet report comparing the costs of online loans and local loan sources.

TEACHING TIP
Safety/Health

Remind students to be careful when using file cabinets to avoid tipping them over. File drawers should be filled beginning at the bottom drawer and moving to the top drawer. On the other hand, file drawers should be emptied from the top drawer down.

REVIEW YOUR READING

1. The debtor promises to repay a loan or pay later for goods and services received, and the creditor trusts his promise will be kept.

2. If you sign a credit statement, you are promising to pay a certain amount at a certain time.

3. Loans are available from banks, credit unions, savings and loan companies, and consumer finance companies. Credit unions lend only to members; consumer and finance companies make small loans, often to consumers who have not established good credit ratings.

4. Consumers often use credit to buy products that are fairly expensive, such as a house, a car, furniture, or appliances, and to make smaller everyday purchases, such as meals, gasoline, and clothing. They also use credit to borrow money to pay large debts. Businesses might use credit to buy land and equipment and to construct buildings. They also borrow to meet temporary needs for cash, perhaps to buy raw materials and supplies. Governments use credit to buy large items, such as cars, aircraft, and military uniforms and for building hospitals, schools, highways, parks, and airports.

5. The business can deduct a 2 percent discount if the bill is paid within 10 days from the billing date; net amount must be paid within 30 days.

6. Questions asked would very likely include: Where do you work? How long have you worked there? What is your salary? Do you own a house or condominium or rent an apartment? Do you have any other debts? What are some names and addresses of credit references?

7. Character—a good reputation for paying bills, a good standing in the community, and a good credit rating. Character is important because what a person will do in the future can be judged to some extent by what that person has done in the past. Capacity—a sufficiently large income so that continued prompt payment of bills is probable. Capacity is important because it may not be wise to grant additional credit to a customer with a small income even though that customer has had a

BUSINESS NOTES

1. Credit is the privilege of using someone else's money with the obligation to repay it at a future time.

2. Consumers use credit to buy cars, clothing, and furniture; businesses use credit to finance new equipment, expand facilities, and to take care of temporary cash needs; governments borrow money to build roads and schools.

3. You can borrow money from a financial institution—loan credit; you can charge a good or service at the time of purchase—sales credit; and a business can receive goods now and pay for them later—trade credit.

4. A business considers a person's character (honesty and willingness to pay debts), capacity (the ability to pay debts), and capital (the value of the person's possessions) in reviewing an applicant for credit.

5. Credit used wisely makes some buying more convenient, gives the purchaser immediate possession rather than waiting until later, allows buyers to take advantage of special sales, and establishes a person's credit rating.

6. Credit is misused if it results in overbuying, careless buying, paying higher prices in stores that grant credit, or incurring excessive debt.

REVIEW YOUR READING

1. Our credit system is based in part on trust. Who does the trusting, the debtor or the creditor? What does this party trust?

2. As a debtor, what are you promising to do?

3. Name several sources of loans.

4. What are some typical uses of credit by consumers? by businesses? by governments?

5. What does the term "2/10, n/30" mean? With what kind of credit is it used?

6. What kinds of information do creditors need before extending credit?

7. What are the three Cs of credit? Why is each one important?

8. What are some ways in which the use of credit is important to a business?

9. What are four advantages of buying on credit for consumers?

10. Name four problems that can be caused by the unwise use of credit.

11. What are some questions you should ask yourself when considering whether to use credit?

COMMUNICATE BUSINESS CONCEPTS

12. Why is trust so important in a credit transaction? Why is it necessary to have a written agreement to repay a loan?

13. Some people think it is a good idea to buy a few things on credit, even when they can pay cash. Why might this be a good idea?

14. Edward Adiska buys everything he possibly can on credit. If he does not have enough money to

good credit rating in the past. Capital—how much the customer's possessions are worth. Capital is important because it is further assurance that the customer will be able to pay.

8. Businesses can increase sales and profits by granting credit to customers. They also can use credit to finance the purchase of goods for resale to customers.

9. Four advantages for the person who uses credit are: (1) convenience; (2) immediate possession of items purchased; (3) ability to buy

items on sale, even when the cash for the purchase is not available; (4) establishment of a good credit rating.

10. Unwise use of credit can lead to: (1) overbuying; (2) laziness in shopping because credit is so easy to use; (3) paying more for purchases because of the expenses involved in credit; (4) too much being owed.

11. Is this the best buy I can make or should I shop around some more? What will be the total cost including the cost of charging the

cover his monthly payments when they are due, he borrows money to pay them. His sister, Debbie, likes to buy things only after she has saved enough money to pay cash for them.

   a. Whose plan do you think is better? Why?

   b. What suggestions about the use of credit might you make to Edward and Debbie?

15. Gerry Shadle owns and operates a flower shop. She is considering expanding her shop to include home decorating items. At present, Gerry sells for cash only. How might extending credit help or hurt this business?

16. Here are some statements that people have made about credit. Read each statement and tell whether you agree or disagree and why.

   a. "I should buy as many things as I can on credit because credit increases sales and helps business."

   b. "If things were sold for cash only, in the long run, prices would be lower and everyone would be better off."

   c. "Buy on credit at least occasionally; make your payments on time; and keep a good credit rating, which will be valuable in an emergency."

   d. "Credit should be used only in making expensive purchases, such as houses and cars, and never for everyday purchases, such as food and clothing."

DEVELOP YOUR BUSINESS LANGUAGE

For each numbered item, find the term that has the same meaning.

17. A customer's honesty and willingness to pay a debt when it is due.

18. Credit offered at the time of sale.

19. A customer's ability to pay a debt when it is due.

20. A person's reputation for paying debts on time.

21. One who buys on credit or receives a loan.

22. Borrowing money to be used later for some special purpose.

23. The privilege of using someone else's money for a period of time.

24. A business receives goods from a wholesaler and pays for them later at a specified date.

25. Businesses or individuals from whom you have received credit in the past and/or who can help verify your credit record.

26. The value of the borrower's possessions.

27. The creditor's belief that the debtor will honor the promise to pay later for goods and services that have already been received and used.

28. One who sells on credit or makes a loan.

KEY TERMS

capacity
capital
character
credit
creditor
credit rating
credit reference
debtor
loan credit
sales credit
trade credit
trust

DECISION-MAKING STRATEGIES

Ichiro Komuro is a fairly successful shop owner. He sells his merchandise at a fair price on a cash basis, provides good service, and does some newspaper advertising. For the past five years, he has made a small profit that has provided a decent living for him and his family.

Lately his business has fallen off. Other shop owners have begun to accept credit purchases. He does not want to extend credit to his customers. His small profit on sales will not permit the additional cost of handling credit transactions. However, he also knows that he must remain competitive to remain in business.

29. What is Ichiro's basic problem?

30. What would you advise Ichiro to do, and why?

item? What would I save if I paid cash? Will the payments be too high considering my income?

COMMUNICATE BUSINESS CONCEPTS

12. Trust is the basis for credit. However, borrowers usually have to sign a written agreement so that there is proof that credit has been granted. Businesses that extend credit have thousands of credit customers and must have

written records of all transactions. Also, the agreement to pay becomes a legal document that is important if the borrower becomes unable or unwilling to pay.

13. The advantage of buying a few things on credit, even if you do not have to, is that you are establishing a credit record. Prompt payment of loans or charge account balances leads to a good credit rating. Then, if you should want or need to borrow someday, you will have established a record as a person who pays what is owed.

DEVELOP YOUR BUSINESS LANGUAGE

17. character
18. sales credit
19. capacity
20. credit rating
21. debtor
22. loan credit
23. credit
24. trade credit
25. credit reference
26. capital
27. trust
28. creditor

14. Actually neither Edward nor Debbie is practicing the best money management. Both have extreme points of view, although Debbie's plan is the better of the two. However, there can be times that she might suffer great inconvenience if she never borrows, especially in the event of an emergency. Edward might find that he will ruin his credit standing so that eventually he might not be able to buy anything on credit. Some of his purchases might even be taken away from him if he cannot pay for them.

15. Gerry Shadle is considering expanding her shop to carry decorator items that are more expensive. She may find that customers will not buy as readily if they have to pay cash for these items. From this standpoint, credit will be a help to the business. Granting credit will result in administrative expenses involved in handling credit accounts. She will probably also encounter some uncollectible accounts.

16. (a) This argument should not be an excuse for overbuying. Too easy a credit policy could result in businesses not receiving payments on time from customers. As a result, businesses might find themselves late in paying what they owe their suppliers. Thus, if credit is too greatly extended, businesses on the local and national levels could be harmed. (b) This point is extremely doubtful. Although it is true that extending credit involves extra costs for a business, the added costs of credit usually are offset by special charges and through an increased

409

volume of business. (c) It is true that a person who buys on credit and who establishes a good record for making payments builds a credit rating that can be extremely important if money needs to be borrowed to meet an emergency. (d) Generally speaking, good money managers use credit to purchase durable goods and for emergency purposes only. Purchasing too many nondurable goods on credit is not a desirable practice. It is destructive to personal morale to keep paying on an item that has long since been consumed or has a vastly depreciated value.

DECISION-MAKING STRATEGIES

29. Ichiro needs to increase his sales by extending credit to customers. He does not want to get involved with the costs of handling credit. But his cash-only position will lose business for him. His competitors are offering credit to customers.

30. Answers will vary. Most students very likely will suggest that Ichiro begin accepting credit cards. If he continues to have a cash-only business, he will have to do something else to stimulate sales— possibly increase his advertising, offer special sales, and/or provide some services that his competitors do not offer.

CALCULATE BUSINESS DATA

31. (a) 1990–1995: $1,123 billion − $805 billion = $318 billion; 1995–1997: $1,264 billion − $1,123 billion = $141 billion; 1997–1999: $1,429 billion − $1,264 billion = $165 billion. (b) $624 billion ÷ 9 years = $69.33 billion per year average increase. (c) 1999–2010: 11 years × $69.33 billion = $763 billion increase. $1,429 billion + $763 billion = $2,192 billion in 2010.

32. (a) 2,200 bikes × $145 = $319,000 (b) $319,000 × 0.70 = $223,300

33. Amount borrowed: $1,800,000; $6,500 − $1,500 = $5,000; $5,000 × 6 = $30,000; $1,800,000 ÷ $30,000 = 60 months

CALCULATE BUSINESS DATA

31. The table below shows the amounts of consumer credit reported in the United States for the years 1990–1999.
    a. What was the increase in consumer credit, in billions of dollars, from 1990 to 1995? from 1995 to 1997? from 1997 to 1999?
    b. What was the average increase per year, in billions of dollars, for the nine-year period from 1990 to 1999?
    c. If consumer credit continues to increase at the 1990–1999 annual rate of increase, what will be the total amount of consumer credit (in billions of dollars) in the year 2010?

Consumer Credit	
Year	(In Billions of Dollars)
1990	$ 805
1995	1,123
1997	1,264
1999	1,429

32. Last year O'Leary's Cycle Shop sold 2,200 ten-speed bicycles. The average sale price was $145, including tax. Seven out of every ten customers bought their bikes using O'Leary's credit plan.
    a. What was the amount of the total sales of ten-speed bicycles?
    b. What was the amount of total credit sales of ten-speed bicycles?

33. The Capital Area Transit System borrowed $1,800,000 to buy six new buses to expand its service to the suburbs. It is estimated that each bus will earn about $6,500 per month. It will cost approximately $1,500 per month for fuel, operating costs, and repairs on each bus. How many months will it take to pay for the six buses?

34. Amy Markson would like to be an airline pilot someday. Right now, she wants to learn to fly and get a private license. Her parents have agreed to pay half the cost of the lessons if Amy pays the other half. Amy checked with Superior Air Service and came up with the estimated costs shown in the table.
    a. How much will it cost Amy to learn to fly and to get her license?
    b. If Amy borrows her share of the cost from her grandparents, how much will she borrow?
    c. If Amy repays her non-interest-bearing loan in 50 equal weekly payments, how much will each weekly payment be? If she repays $75 each month, how many months will it take to repay the amount she borrowed?

Fees and materials for ground instruction:	$480
24 hours of in-flight instruction:	$50 per hour
20 hours of solo flight time:	$32 per hour
Third-class student's license:	$80

TECHNOLOGY APPLICATION

Using the *Intro to Business* Data CD and your spreadsheet program software, select problem CH29. After the problem appears on your screen, complete the following activities. Then, after you have completed each step, display or print the completed spreadsheet. If you do not have a printer available, answer the questions before you leave the computer.

One decision-making tool used by some creditors is a credit-scoring spreadsheet. Information about an applicant for credit is entered into the spreadsheet. The spreadsheet assigns a point value to each piece of information. In this example, an applicant must have a point total of 65 or above to qualify as an acceptable credit risk. Enter information about the following credit applicants. Use a lowercase x in the column beneath the name to answer each question. The first line has been completed as an example. If you make a mistake, enter a blank space in place of the x you want to delete.

35. Enter a function to calculate the total credit score for each applicant. Enter an @IF function to answer the Application Acceptable question with a yes or no. Place the @IF function below each total.

36. Tony Kintampo has a telephone in his own name; rents a small room in a boarding house; has a checking but no savings account; has a store credit card; has a small finance company loan outstanding; is 19 years old; and has been on his present job for 14 months. Answer the following questions.
    a. What is Tony's total credit score?
    b. Is Tony's application acceptable?

37. Estela Sanchez does not have a telephone in her own name; shares rental of an apartment with three friends; has checking and savings accounts; has a bank credit card; has no finance company loans outstanding; is 27 years old; and has been on her present job for four years. Answer the following questions.
    a. What is Estela's total credit score?
    b. Is Estela's application acceptable?

34. (a) $480 + $1,200 + $640 + $80 = $2,400
    (b) $2,400 ÷ 2 = $1,200 (c) $1,200 ÷ 50 = $24 per week; $1,200 ÷ 75 = 16 months

TECHNOLOGY APPLICATION

In this activity, students use a computer to solve a business problem using a file that is provided on the data CD that accompanies *Intro to Business*. Instructions for using the data CD are included in a **README** file on the disk. Solutions are provided on the Instructor's Resource CD.

GLOBAL NAVIGATOR

DEVELOPING NATIONS

More than 200 nations exist in our world. Of those, less than 50 are considered to have a high level of economic development. We usually hear about business activities in the United States, Canada, Japan, and western European countries. However, most countries of the world do not have modern roads, high-speed communication systems, and shopping malls.

Developing nations usually depend on agriculture and natural resources as the foundation for their economies. Farming is a basic industry that employs many people. Agricultural products are commonly the result of human labor with little or no use of machinery. Mining also provides an economic base in many developing nations. Products such as coal, copper, iron ore, lead, silver, and zinc are common exports.

Other characteristics typical in developing nations are low literacy rate and poor health conditions. These countries have very few resources available for schools, teacher salaries, and educational materials. Many children are not in school, as their efforts are needed on farms or in the family business. The low level of economic development in these countries creates shortages of adequate food and clean

> **The economies of developing nations can be improved through international trade and investment.**

water, which results in various diseases. In addition, doctors, hospitals, and medical supplies are also usually in short supply.

Developing nations attempt to expand their economies through international trade and foreign investment. Exports can help a country obtain resources to improve its living conditions, while foreign companies can improve the business environment and economic opportunities. As a nation's economy develops with more industrialization, new jobs are created and economic wealth expands.

CRITICAL THINKING

1. Identify two developing nations in different geographic regions. What are the main products of these countries? What could be done to improve the level of economic development in these countries?

2. Develop a plan for a company that could help the economic development of another country. What types of business activities would contribute to a nation's transportation, communication, health care, schools, or food supplies? What could a nation's government do to attract businesses from other countries?

GLOBAL NAVIGATOR

Most students will either work with international clients or compete against businesses that do. Global Navigator introduces students to issues integral to working with international businesses. Key concepts and challenges faced by international businesses are presented, followed by two Critical Thinking questions that require students to analyze what they have learned.

With the world getting smaller and smaller through the use of modern transportation and digital information technologies, every country's economy is interwoven into the global economy. Even in countries where development has not kept pace with the industrialized world, agriculture and the exploitation of natural resources are directly affected by global trends. This feature focuses students' attention on these "developing" countries and the important role they play in the global economy.

CRITICAL THINKING

1. Answers will vary widely depending on which countries students choose. There are few "wrong" answers, as almost any suggestions for improving economic development will contain elements worthy of consideration and further discussion.

2. Again, answers will vary depending on what type of company students choose. Responses should demonstrate an understanding of the need to match a company's desire for profits with a country's needs and its exploitable resources.

The focus of this chapter is the variety of charge accounts available to consumers. Special attention is given to the use of credit by teenagers. Special emphasis is given to credit agreements and legal contracts.

Resources for Teachers

- Lesson Plans
- School-To-Work/SCANS Activity Masters
- Spanish Resources
- Instructor's Resource CD

Assessment

- Chapter and Unit Tests, Ch. 30
- ExamView, Ch. 30

Media/Technology

- Applying Technology Data CD
- PowerPoint slides
- Business Connection CD
- Videotape

Activity Masters and Workbooks

- Activities and Projects, Ch. 30
- Internet Activity Masters
- Business Math Activity Masters
- Communications Activity Masters
- International Business Activity Masters
- Ethics Activity Masters

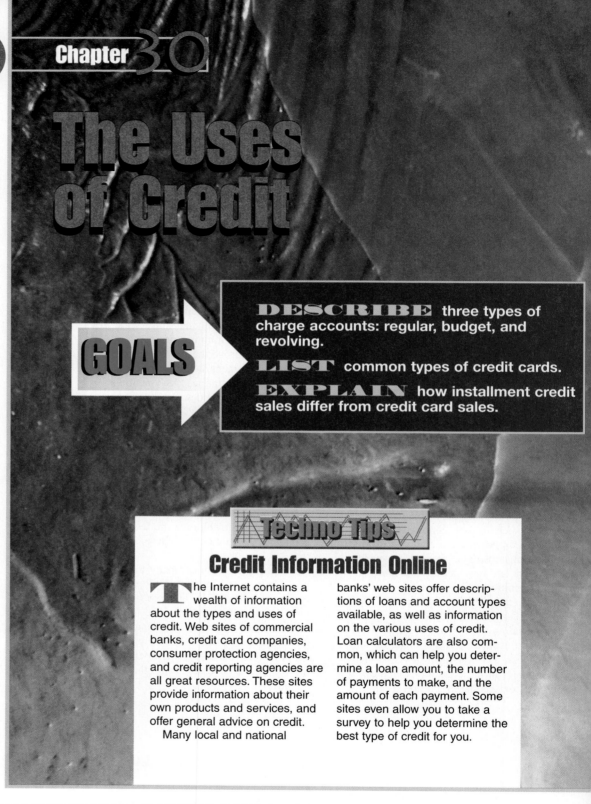

Chapter 30

The Uses of Credit

GOALS

DESCRIBE three types of charge accounts: regular, budget, and revolving.

LIST common types of credit cards.

EXPLAIN how installment credit sales differ from credit card sales.

Techno Tips

Credit Information Online

The Internet contains a wealth of information about the types and uses of credit. Web sites of commercial banks, credit card companies, consumer protection agencies, and credit reporting agencies are all great resources. These sites provide information about their own products and services, and offer general advice on credit.

Many local and national banks' web sites offer descriptions of loans and account types available, as well as information on the various uses of credit. Loan calculators are also common, which can help you determine a loan amount, the number of payments to make, and the amount of each payment. Some sites even allow you to take a survey to help you determine the best type of credit for you.

Students need to know the latest technologies and develop cutting edge Internet skills for use in current jobs, future careers, or in their homes. TechnoTips introduces students to today's cutting edge technologies and provides them with important Internet skills. Feature topics concentrate on Internet-specific technologies and computer or other hi-tech innovations for use by businesses and consumers.

Credit can be helpful and harmful for consumers. Consumer credit provides the funds for the purchase of cars, furniture, travel, and many other goods and services that mark a high standard of living. However, at times, otherwise responsible individuals get into financial trouble by using too much credit.

When a salesperson asks: "Will this be cash or credit?" the customer frequently has several options. The customer might use a credit card that the store accepts; or if the purchase is expensive, he or she might sign an installment sales contract.

There are other ways to get credit. One consumer talked with a loan officer at a bank to get a loan for a new car. Another consumer applied for a loan to remodel his home. A common source of credit for consumers is through a bank or other financial institution.

There are a number of ways to obtain and use credit. When it is your turn to decide, you will make a better decision in terms of using credit when you have an understanding of the different kinds of credit available to you.

TYPES OF CHARGE ACCOUNTS

Charging purchases and services is usually accomplished with a charge account. A charge account represents a contract between the firm offering it and the customer. Three types of charge accounts generally are available for your use. You may have a regular, budget, or revolving account.

Regular Accounts

A **regular account** is one in which the seller or provider expects payment in full within a specified period of time—usually 25 to 30 days after the billing date. The seller may set a limit on the total amount that may be charged during that time. Customers can purchase goods or services up to a fixed dollar limit at any time.

Regular accounts generally are used for everyday needs and small purchases. Regular account credit is commonly granted by those engaged in providing a service—doctors, dentists, plumbers, etc.

Budget Accounts

Some merchants and public utilities offer budget charge accounts. A **budget account** requires that payments of a certain fixed amount be made over several months. One budget plan offered by businesses is the 90-day, three-payment plan. Under this plan, you pay for your purchase in 90 days, usually in three equal monthly payments.

In a budget plan offered by many utility companies, an estimate is made of how much you will be charged for gas or electricity during a certain period of time, such as a year. You then agree to pay a certain amount each month to cover those purchases. For example, you may be permitted to pay a certain amount of money each month to cover the cost of energy used for heating. This plan avoids large payments during winter months. However, you pay the same amount during warm months when heating is not required.

In a recent year, there were over 1.4 billion credit cards held by U.S. consumers; bank cards have been the fastest growing type, by far.

MOTIVATE

PURPOSE Direct students to skim the chapter, looking at photos, reading captions, and noting main headings. The goals at the beginning of each chapter provide a valuable tool for having students pinpoint main ideas. The tasks required by the goals are signaled in the first word. Some emphasize information collection ("List"), while others call for description ("Explain," "Describe," "State"). Ask students to look through all the goals and note the first word of each. Then ask them to state the purpose of studying this chapter.

TEACH/APPLY

MAKE CONNECTIONS Write the following statement on the board: "The ability to obtain credit is a privilege, not a right." Have students write a paragraph giving their interpretation of this statement. Then lead a discussion of why credit is a privilege. (This topic could be developed through a panel discussion or debate format.)

TRY THIS/GUIDED PRACTICE Walk students through an exercise in which they are made aware of the cost of credit. Have students comment on whether the additional cost of credit—the "regular or sale price" plus the "credit cost"—would influence whether the item is purchased. A question that can provoke a good discussion is: Should there be two prices in a store—one for cash customers and another for credit customers?

FOCUS ON REAL LIFE

Students will very likely have used credit of one form or another at some time. Lead a discussion on the experiences they have had—good or bad—when they used credit. What have they learned, if anything, from their own use of credit? Use the brainstorming technique to elicit comments and list those comments on the board or on an overhead.

Knowing when to use the different types of credit is important. Lead a discussion of what type of credit should be used for various kinds of purchases. Have students identify the type of credit that should be used for different types of purchases (if it normally should be used at all). If they disagree with each other's answers, have them discuss why they disagree.

Lead a general discussion of promissory notes. Information about promissory notes that should be stressed includes the following:

a. Loans can be obtained most readily by those who own property and who have a reputation for paying debts promptly.

b. A note is a written promise to pay money.

c. A note should be written carefully in ink.

In general, the methods that apply to the writing of checks also apply to the writing of notes.

EXPLORE THIS/INDEPENDENT PRACTICE Ask students to bring newspaper advertisements to class that offer goods for sale on the installment plan. Students can then exchange ads and provide written answers to the following questions: (a) What types of goods are offered for sale? (b) What do advertisements say about down payments? (c) Do the advertisements give the exact terms offered? (d) Do the advertisements state a cash price?

How can the convenience of a revolving account turn into a disadvantage?

Revolving Accounts

The revolving account is the most popular form of credit. With a **revolving account**, purchases can be charged at any time but only part of the debt must be paid each month. It is similar to a regular account but has some added features. There is usually a

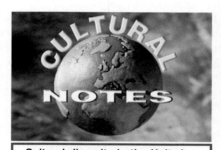

Cultural diversity in the United States has played an important role in the development of business enterprises. For example, in recent years soccer, which has long been popular in other parts of the world, has become a popular sport in the United States. The popularity of soccer here has created business opportunities. Soccer has created a need for producers and sellers of soccer equipment.

maximum amount that may be owed at one time. A payment is required once a month, but the total amount owed need not be paid at one time. A finance charge is added, however, if the total amount owed is not paid. The **finance charge** is the additional amount you must pay for using credit, including interest and other costs such as credit insurance.

Revolving charge accounts are convenient, but they can tempt you to overspend. The finance charges on unpaid balances are usually quite high, often 1½ percent per month (18 percent per year) or higher. However, there is generally no finance charge if balances are paid in full within a specified period of time, such as within 25 days.

Some consumers prefer the revolving charge account because it permits the customer to buy products or services when the price is right, yet pay for it over a period of time. There is no pressure to pay the full amount at one time. In addition, further purchases can be made without adding unduly to the amount that must be repaid each month.

TEENAGE CHARGE ACCOUNTS

Under contract law, minors cannot be held liable for their personal debts. Therefore,

Workplace **Competencies**-Systems

Students need to understand how to monitor and correct performance in a system through distinguishing trends, diagnosing deviations in the system's performance, and correcting any malfunctions. This activity involves application of systems knowledge. Consumer credit is a type of system where the participants must operate within the rules of the

system. Encourage a discussion about trends in consumer credit such as charge cards for students, six months same as cash, etc. How are these systems monitored to make sure customers are served? What kind of malfunctions could occur in a credit system? The Student Activity Worksheet, Workplace Competencies—Systems, in the School-To-Work/SCANS Activity Masters, may serve as a guideline for discussion.

businesses are not willing to open charge accounts in a teenager's name if he or she is a minor. There are special circumstances, however, under which a special charge account may be opened in a teenager's name.

Charge accounts for teenagers have a limit on the amount that can be charged, and the limit is usually lower than the amount set on charge accounts for adults. Generally a parent or guardian must agree to pay any balance due if the teenager does not. Sometimes the parent or guardian also must have a charge account with the business granting the credit.

Charge accounts for teenagers are usually regular or revolving. The accounts give teenagers a privilege and a freedom in buying that they otherwise would not have. If a teenager has an income of his or her own, the charge account can be the first step toward proving an ability to manage money wisely. It also is an opportunity to show that he or she is a good credit risk and can use credit wisely.

CREDIT CARD USAGE

Charging purchases and services is usually accomplished with credit cards. Credit cards are seemingly magical pieces of plastic that entitle owners to credit at stores, gas stations, and other businesses far and near. They have become very popular, and their use continues to increase. Most credit cards issued today are multipurpose cards—such as VISA, American Express, Discover, Carte Blanche, and MasterCard—that can be used at thousands of stores, hotels, airlines, and other businesses.

In a recent year, it was reported that 66 percent of the families in the United States used one or more credit cards. Cards issued by retailers are the most numerous, but not the most popular in terms of spending that's charged on them. Bank cards account for more than 60 percent of all credit card spending, followed by travel and entertainment cards with about 16 percent. Most financial institutions issuing credit cards are

The average U.S. consumer has nine credit cards, including retail, oil company, travel and entertainment (T & E), and bank cards.

affiliated with VISA International or the Interbank Card Association, which issues MasterCard.

Travelers especially like credit cards because they do not have to carry much cash with them. Many of the cards are accepted at businesses in all parts of the world. Businesses that accept credit cards often find that their sales increase because more customers are attracted if credit cards can be used.

Bank Cards

Bank credit cards have become very popular throughout the world. MasterCard and VISA

What are some advantages of using bank or credit cards in business or travel situations?

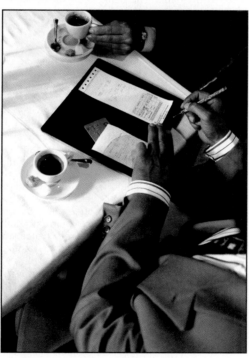

Have students react to the following scenario: "An individual plans to open a snack shop near a school to sell light lunches and snacks. Most of the customers will be high school students. Since students often forget to bring money to school, they may ask for the privilege of charging their purchases." Ask them to write a set of rules that could be used as the criteria for extending credit (budget account) to teenage customers.

In addition to the "three Cs of credit," some people add a fourth called collateral. Have students find the meaning of collateral as it is used in connection with credit and explain in writing how the term is used in reference to consumer loans.

Read the following statement: "The real benefit of a revolving charge account comes when you pay your bill in full each month." Have students explain in a paragraph what this statement means.

The Chapter Review questions at the end of the chapter vary in level of difficulty. For a basic assignment, consider Develop Your Business Language and Review Your Reading. For an average assignment, consider the basic assignment plus Communicate Business Concepts and Calculate Business Data. For an enhanced assignment, try the average assignment plus Technology Application and Decision-Making Strategies.

Personal Qualities-Self-Esteem

Self-esteem, or believing in one's own self-worth and maintaining a positive view of one's self, is a personal quality that we cannot ignore. Students must know who they are and believe in themselves in order to be productive in society. One important contributor to self-esteem is one's own culture. Students need to understand not only their own culture, but also the cultures of those with whom they work. The Cultural Perspectives describe various cultures and their contributions to our current economic system. This feature offers an opportunity to encourage discussion of different cultural backgrounds. The discussion can be expanded by asking students to write down a description of themselves by asking, "Who am I?"

Review the goals at the beginning of the chapter and the Business Notes at the end of the chapter. Have students respond orally or in writing to each goal restated as a question. For students who may have difficulty providing answers, assign the reteaching activities that follow. Enrichment activities may also be assigned where appropriate.

1. Describe the three types of charge accounts. (Answer: A regular account has the payment due at the end of each specified period of time; a budget account spreads payments over a period of time; a revolving account has a minimum amount that must be paid each month.)

2. How may teenagers obtain a charge account? (Answer: Teenagers may get a charge account in their own names if their parents or guardians sign for them or if the account has a limit on the amount that can be charged.)

3. How are bank credit card transactions processed? (Answer: When you use a bank charge card, a credit sales slip that requires your signature is issued. The merchant collects all credit slips prepared during the day and sends them to the bank. The bank charges your account for your purchases and bills you once a month for all the purchases you make.)

Credit transaction slips for one day from around the world, if gathered in a central processing place, would make a pile higher than the tallest building in New York City.

are two of the best known. There sometimes is an annual fee that must be paid for the privilege of using these cards. Users of bank cards frequently end up paying a monthly finance charge.

Bank charge cards are issued to people whose credit ratings meet the bank's standards. A bank charge card, in effect, indicates that the credit rating of the cardholder is good. Agreements are made between banks and various merchants to accept the charge cards.

When you use your bank charge card, a credit sales slip that requires your signature is made out. The merchant collects all credit sales slips prepared during the day and sends them to the bank. The bank totals all of the sales slips received from a business.

The businesses are paid for the sales amount minus a service fee. This fee is usually about 4 to 6 percent. At the 4 percent rate, a retail store would receive $960 from sales totaling $1,000 ($1,000 × .04 = $40). This fee covers the bank's expenses of processing the sales slips and collecting amounts owed from customers. The bank is doing the work that the businesses' own credit departments would have to do otherwise.

Business owners like bank credit cards for several reasons. For one thing, the bank decides if a customer is a good credit risk. The bank also assumes most of the trouble and expense of granting credit. Businesses receive their money, minus the service fee, immediately.

Customers like bank charge cards because they are accepted by so many businesses throughout the country. Bank charge-card users also like the fact that they receive only one monthly bill rather than many bills from the various businesses where they charge purchases.

CULTURAL PERSPECTIVES

Israelites and Usury Laws

The ancient tribes of Israel, which occupied the Land of Canaan as early as 1300 B.C., had many laws. Some of the laws dealt with money and credit.

The Israelites could lend money to members of their tribes who were in need, but they were not allowed to charge any interest on those loans. Every seven years all debts owed by Israelite tribesmen were cancelled so that there would be no credit hardship cases.

The Israelites could charge interest on loans to foreigners, but the interest rates had to be reasonable and not usurious—that is, excessive. One of their sacred songs reminded them that "he who lends money without usury" will do well.

In our economy today, most states have usury laws. Consumers need to know about usury laws of the various states. The amounts that may be charged as interest on loans or finance charges on credit sales transactions vary from 10 to 24 percent per year. Some states have removed previously established ceilings, allowing rates to be influenced by economic conditions.

Critical Thinking
1. Do you think that not charging interest on money loaned to family members is practical and fair?
2. Why is it necessary for states to pass usury laws?

CULTURAL PERSPECTIVES

Cultural Perspectives will expose students to the concept that our society is composed of people from many different cultural backgrounds. This feature shows both past contributions of many cultures and benefits of a culturally diverse society.

CRITICAL THINKING

1. If a member of the family has a financial problem, other members of the family should be willing to loan money without interest. If this would present a hardship for the person lending the money, then a modest interest rate might be charged. Money should be lent only when it will help solve financial problems, and loans should be paid back faithfully.

2. There are unscrupulous lenders who might charge excessive interest rates to take advantage of people with poor credit ratings or those who do not shop around for the best rates. Usury laws set an upper limit on the interest rate that can legally be charged within a state.

Travel and Entertainment Cards

Carte Blanche, Diners Club, and American Express are widely used travel and entertainment (T & E) cards. Subscribers pay a yearly membership fee that is higher than the annual fee charged for bank cards. Cardholders are not given a spending limit and, for the most part, are expected to pay the balances due in full each month. T & E cards are used mainly to buy services such as lodging in hotels and motels, meals, airline tickets, and tickets for entertainment. Business travelers like to use them because the detailed records they receive from the card issuers are useful for business and tax record-keeping purposes. They offer proof of expenses incurred when traveling and entertaining customers.

Oil Company Cards

Major oil companies, such as Texaco, Chevron, and Shell, issue their own credit cards. However, many oil companies have found that it costs them too much to offer credit. Therefore, some have issued cards affiliated with VISA or MasterCard which are referred to as *co-branded* revolving charge accounts.

Retail Store Cards

Many retail stores offer their own credit cards to customers. These cards carry the names of the stores that issue them. These cards can be used only at the stores that issued them and are often referred to as single-purpose cards.

Having a retail store credit card is a convenience for the consumer. The store also knows that the consumer is more likely to shop there if he or she has one of its credit cards. Some stores have special sales that are advertised just to their credit card holders.

INSTALLMENT SALES CREDIT

For some types of purchases, especially those that are quite expensive and will last for long periods of time, installment sales credit often is used. **Installment sales credit** is a contract issued by the seller that requires periodic payments to be made at times specified in the agreement. Finance charges are added to the cost of the items purchased, and the total amount to be paid is shown in the agreement. Furniture and household appliances often are purchased using installment sales credit.

Using installment sales credit differs from using credit cards. Instead of just handing your credit card to a salesperson, you must fill out a credit application at the time of the purchase and receive credit approval. There are some special features of installment sales credit with which you should be familiar. Under an installment credit plan you will:

- Sign a written agreement (a sales contract) that shows the terms of the purchase, such as payment periods and finance charges.

- Receive and own the goods at the time of purchase. However, the seller has the right to repossess them (take them back) if payments are not made according to the agreement.

- Make a **down payment**, which is a payment of part of the purchase price; it is usually made at the time of the purchase.

- Pay a finance charge on the amount owed, because this amount is actually loaned to you by the seller.

- Make regular payments at stated times, usually weekly or monthly. For example, if a

4. What are some common types of credit cards? (Answer: Charge cards are issued primarily by financial institutions and retail stores. Cards are also issued for travel and entertainment purposes and for gasoline purchases.)

5. What is the difference between a credit card sale and an installment credit sale? (Answer: Credit cards are issued by companies that bill you for the amount of purchases made during a billing period, such as a month. An installment credit sale has a fixed amount of money that must be paid each month to pay the amount owed on the item purchased.)

6. What are two types of loans available to consumers? (Answer: Consumers can get installment loans or single-payment loans. An installment loan involves monthly payments over a period of time. With a single payment loan, the amount borrowed is not repaid until the end of the loan period.)

7. What are some questions that must be asked before a consumer signs a contract for installment sales credit? (Answer: Before signing an installment contract, there are important questions to be asked, such as what are the finance charges, is there an add-on feature, and will there be a refund of part of the finance charge if the loan is paid off in advance.)

TEACHING STRATEGIES
Special Needs: Gifted Students

Gifted students should master content quickly. Therefore, challenge them to identify a special research project that interests them. The students should be encouraged to identify a project that requires interaction with a businessperson and to share their work with the class. For example, a student could contact a loan officer to learn about applying for a consumer loan. The student could invite the loan officer to class and use role playing to demonstrate how communication skills can enhance an individual's chance of getting a loan.

Discuss situations in which students might use either a charge account, sales credit (the installment plan), or a consumer loan (cash loan). Ask: How would you decide which type of credit to use?

Review key vocabulary terms. Have students take turns giving oral definitions for the terms *cosigner, collateral, secured loan, promissory note, charge account, installment sales credit,* and *installment loan.*

Put the following question on the board and have students write a one-paragraph response: What is the difference between regular, budget, and revolving charge accounts?

ENRICH

Direct students to read the Cultural Perspectives in this chapter. Have students ask an older adult whom they know well about his or her use of credit. Find out how many credit cards the person has. Discover whether or not the person believes that people use too much credit today. Also discuss what advantages and disadvantages that person sees in the use of credit. Compare these answers with what is in the textbook, and prepare a report to give to the class. (Students will need to draw upon Chapter 29 to complete this activity.)

Ask students to interview a banker about bank credit cards (select a bank that issues bank credit cards). Find out about the bank's involvement in bank credit card transactions. Then ask students to interview a local busi-

total of $120 is to be repaid in 12 monthly installments, $10 is paid each month. In some cases, a penalty is charged if a payment is received after the due date. In others, all remaining payments may become due at once if only one payment is missed.

CONSUMER LOANS

A loan is an alternative to charge-account buying or installment sales credit. There are several kinds of consumer loans available. The terms of the loans and the requirements for securing the loans differ.

One type of loan is called an installment loan. An **installment loan** is one in which you agree to make monthly payments in specific amounts over a period of time. The payments are called installments. The total amount you repay includes the amount you borrowed plus the finance charge on your loan.

Another kind of loan is called a single-payment loan. With a **single-payment loan**, you do not pay anything until the end of the loan period, possibly 60 or 90 days. At that time, you repay the full amount you borrowed plus the finance charge.

A lender needs some assurance that each loan will be repaid. If you are a good credit

risk, you may be able to sign a promissory note. A **promissory note** is a written promise to repay based on a debtor's excellent credit rating. The amount borrowed, usually with some interest, is due on a certain date. The names given to the different parts of a promissory note are shown in Figure 30-1.

In some cases, you may be asked to offer some kind of property you own, such as a car, a house, or jewelry, as security. Property that is used as security is called **collateral**. You give the lender the right to sell this property to get back the amount of the loan in the event you do not repay it. This is called a **secured loan**.

If you do not have a credit rating established or property to offer as security, you may be able to get a relative or friend who has property or a good credit rating to also sign your note and become the legal cosigner. The **cosigner** of a note is responsible for payment of the note if you do not pay as promised.

CREDIT CONTRACTS

Credit is important in many ways. It is a privilege that millions of consumers and businesses enjoy. No matter what kind of credit

FIGURE 30-1 On what date will this note be due? What amount?

PROMISSORY NOTE

PRINCIPAL – the amount that is promised to be paid; the face of the note.

TIME – the days or months from the date of the note until it should be paid.

DATE OF MATURITY – the date on which the note is due.

DATE – the date on which a note is issued.

$ 950 00   Miami, Florida July 8   20 – –

Four months   AFTER DATE I PROMISE TO PAY TO

THE ORDER OF   Ann Biederman

Nine hundred fifty   00/100   DOLLARS

PAYABLE AT   Community Bank, N.A.

VALUE RECEIVED WITH INTEREST AT   10 %

NO. 147 DUE   November 8, 20--   Melissa O'Neil

PAYEE – the one to whom the note is payable.

INTEREST RATE – the rate paid for the use of the money.

MAKER – the one who promises to make payment.

TEACHING STRATEGIES
Cooperative Learning

Group investigation is a positive form of cooperative learning that encourages students to work together. For this activity, students form their own groups with two to six members each. One person should be the spokesperson and one the note taker. Bring in other business texts that present credit information. Each group

should use these references to create a glossary of credit terms. Groups should not copy definitions out of the text but create their own. Terms that do not appear in this text may also be used. Allow 30 minutes for the research. Take turns having the spokesperson for each group present the terms while someone else lists the terms and definitions on the board. You may award points to the glossary that is the most comprehensive, that includes the most original terms, etc.

is involved, legal responsibilities are created for both parties.

"**KWYS**" are four letters to keep in mind when signing any legal form; the letters stand for "know what you're signing." This applies to all credit contracts.

The installment sales contract is one of the most important forms you may sign. Before signing one, answer the following questions:

- How much are the finance charges? The total financing cost must be clearly shown in your contract.

- Does the contract include the cost of services you may need, such as repairs to a television or a washing machine? If there is a separate repair contract, is its cost included in your contract? Will you be billed for anything separately?

- Does the contract have an add-on feature so that you can later buy other items and have them added to the balance that you owe?

- If you pay the contract in full before its ending date, how much of the finance charge will you get back?

- If you pay the contract within 60 or 90

HyperText Markup Language, or HTML, is a set of computer commands. HTML is used to create World Wide Web documents that can be viewed by a browser program.

days, will there be any finance charge or will it be as if you had paid cash?

- Is the contract you are asked to sign completely filled in? (Do not sign if there are any blanks. It is proper and businesslike to draw a line through any blank space before you sign the contract.)

- Under what conditions can the seller repossess the merchandise if you do not pay on time? *Repossess* refers to the right of the seller to take back merchandise in partial or full settlement of the debt.

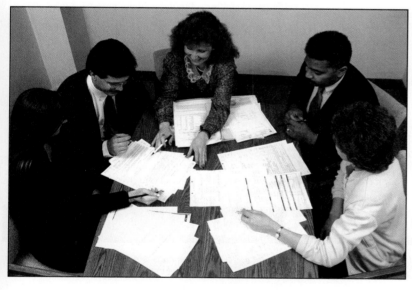

What problems might occur if you sign legal forms without reading them thoroughly?

nessperson who allows customers to charge purchases using a bank credit card. The businessperson should state what she or he thinks about the use of bank credit cards. Students should compare the information received from these two sources and prepare a short report to give to the class.

Have students interview credit officials from several local department stores to determine requirements for establishing a charge account, particularly for teenagers. Have them present their findings in writing.

SUMMARIZE

Much of the conceptual understanding of this chapter revolves around comprehension of the new vocabulary terms. Have your students make their own crossword puzzles using the Glossary as the basis for their definitions. After completing the crossword (with an answer key), have the creator exchange his or her paper with another student and complete the puzzle.

To help students who have difficulty remembering large blocks of information, encourage them to complete an outline of the chapter using the main chapter headings as the framework for the outline.

EVALUATE

- Assign Activities and Projects for Chapter 30.
- Administer the printed test or ExamView for Chapter 30.
- Assign School-To-Work/SCANS portfolio activities for Unit 9.

Personal Qualities-Self-Management

Credit can provide students with an opportunity to work on the self-management techniques of setting personal goals, monitoring progress of goals, and assessing one's self objectively. Students should set a goal for the maximum amount they will purchase on credit each month and then stay within those goals.

SCANS

REVIEW YOUR READING

1. Charge accounts, installment sales credit, and bank loans are three common forms of consumer credit.
2. With regular charge accounts, payment is made in full at the end of a specified period of time, usually one month.
3. Budget charge accounts spread payments over several months without any finance charges. Utility bills, which normally are high during heating or air conditioning seasons, can have payments spread throughout the year. Consumers are helped because they do not have to plan for large increases in expenditures for some months.
4. The revolving charge account can tempt the customer to overbuy and can become expensive when the customer continually charges low-priced, frequently purchased items. Also, many credit users do not pay the amount due in full and thus pay finance charges on the account balance.
5. Charge accounts give teenagers freedom in buying what they otherwise would not have. It also helps the teenager establish a credit record.
6. In a recent year, 62 percent of American families used one or more credit cards.
7. A customer uses a bank credit card to make a purchase, and the salesperson prepares a credit sales slip. Periodically, often daily, the retailer collects all sales slips issued and forwards them to the bank. The bank then charges each customer's account with the purchases and bills the customer once a month. Next, the bank totals all the drafts from each business and pays the amount of the sales minus the amount of a fee (usually about 4 percent of total sales).
8. A bank credit card is issued by a bank and can be used for a variety of purchases in any business establishment that accepts it; a retail store credit card is issued by a particular store and can be used only in that store; a T & E card is issued by a private finance company and is used primarily for travel and entertainment in any business that accepts the card.
9. Installment sales credit contracts normally contain the terms of the

BUSINESS NOTES

1. A regular charge account has the payment due at the end of each specified period of time. A budget charge account spreads payments over a period of time. A revolving charge account has a minimum amount that must be paid each month.
2. Teenagers may get a charge account in their own names if their parents or guardians sign for them or if the account has a low limit on the charge amount.
3. When you use a bank charge card, a credit sales slip that requires your signature is usually issued. The merchant collects all credit slips prepared during the day and sends them to the bank. The bank charges your account for your purchases and bills you once a month for all the purchases you make.
4. Charge cards are issued by banks, retail stores, and companies that specialize in the credit card business.
5. An installment credit sale has a fixed amount of money that must be paid each month on the item purchased. Credit cards are issued by companies that bill you for the amount of purchases made during a billing period, such as a month.
6. Consumers can get installment loans or single-payment loans. An installment loan involves monthly payments over a period of time. With a single-payment loan, the amount borrowed is not repaid until the end of the loan period.
7. Before signing an installment contract there are important questions to be asked, such as what are the finance charges, is there an add-on feature, and will there be a refund of part of the finance charge if the loan is paid off early?

REVIEW YOUR READING

1. What are three common forms of consumer credit?
2. What does it mean to have a regular charge account?
3. How does a budget charge account help a consumer with budgeting? Give an example.
4. List two dangers of using revolving charge accounts.
5. What is the advantage of having a teenage charge account?
6. What percentage of families in the United States use one or more credit cards?
7. Describe briefly how bank credit cards work.
8. What is the difference between bank credit, retail store credit, and T & E cards?
9. What special features do installment sales credit contracts normally contain?
10. How do installment loans and single-payment loans differ?
11. What kind of person can get a loan based on a promissory note?
12. What is the difference between a promissory note and a secured loan?
13. What does a cosigner agree to when signing a loan agreement?
14. What questions should be answered before signing a loan agreement?

COMMUNICATE BUSINESS CONCEPTS

15. Read each of the following statements and then explain why you agree or disagree.

   a. "A bank card is nice to have. If I'm out of cash, I can still buy what I want."

purchase, payment periods, and the finance charges.
10. An installment loan requires a person to pay a certain amount each month or at other stated intervals. A single-payment loan requires only one payment for the full amount of the loan.
11. Only persons who are excellent credit risks can get loans based on a promissory note.
12. A promissory note is based on the credit rating of the person receiving the loan—there is only the promise to repay. A secured loan has property pledged against the loan, and the lender

can repossess the property and sell it to pay the amount that is owed.
13. The cosigner agrees to pay the loan, or any part of it, if it is not paid by the borrower.
14. Seven questions to be asked before signing an installment sales contract are as follows: (1) How much are the finance charges? (2) Does the contract include the cost of services, such as repairs? (3) Does the contract have an add-on feature so that items purchased later can be added to the balance owed? (4) If the contract is paid before its ending date, how much

b. "I don't believe in using credit for most purchases. I pay cash for everyday items and use credit only for expensive items such as a new refrigerator."

c. "If I can't pay cash, I can't afford it. I won't buy anything unless I can pay cash."

d. "I often don't pay the full amount of my charge account when it is due; the finance charges are quite reasonable."

16. Many businesses would rather take credit cards than accept personal checks. Why do you think businesspeople feel this way?

17. Sue Ellen Ripley owns a sporting goods store and is considering joining a bank charge-card plan. Answer the following questions for her.
   a. What advantages would there be for her business if she did join?
   b. What will it cost her for the services the bank will provide?

c. In what ways are the services the bank provides important?

18. Mark said, "I don't like our utility company's budget plan—I have to pay more than I should during the warm months so they have my money to use and they don't pay me any interest." How would you describe the features of a budget payment plan that might convince Mark the plan is a good one for most customers?

19. Jamie has a good part-time job and is a responsible person. Jamie wants to buy a VCR, but has not saved enough money to cover the cost. When she asked the salesperson if the store would extend credit, Jamie was told, "No, you are too young." Jamie is 16 years old. What are some ways in which Jamie could get credit to purchase this VCR?

DEVELOP YOUR BUSINESS LANGUAGE

For each numbered item, find the term that has the same meaning.

20. A credit contract issued by the seller that requires periodic payments to be made at times specified in the agreement with finance charges added to the cost of the purchase.

21. A type of loan in which you do not pay anything until the end of the loan period, possibly 60 or 90 days.

22. A type of loan in which the lender has the right to sell property used as collateral to get back the amount of the loan in the event the loan is not repaid.

23. A credit plan in which the seller expects payment in full at the end of a specified period, usually a month.

24. A credit plan that allows purchases to be charged at any time but requires that at least part of the debt be paid each month.

25. A type of loan in which you agree to make monthly payments in specific amounts over a period of time.

26. A credit plan requiring that payments of a certain fixed amount be made over several months.

27. Someone who becomes responsible for pay-

ment of a note if you do not pay as promised.

28. A payment of part of the purchase price that is made as part of a credit agreement.

29. A written promise to repay based on the debtor's excellent credit rating.

30. Property that is offered as security for some loan agreements.

31. The additional amount you must pay for using credit.

KEY TERMS

budget account
collateral
cosigner
down payment
finance charge
installment loan
installment sales credit
promissory note
regular account
revolving account
secured loan
single-payment loan

DECISION-MAKING STRATEGIES

Pedro got himself into credit difficulty. He tended to spend foolishly and use his credit cards too often. Then he missed payments when they were due. He

had five accounts with overdue payments.
   Pedro needed a loan to pay off his charge accounts. The Go-Along Finance Company agreed

Chapter 30 The Uses of Credit 421

---

worry about establishing its own credit system. Customers would be able to make purchases there without worrying about cash. Sales probably will increase. (b) She will have to pay from 1 to 5 percent (normally about 4 percent) as a service fee to the bank on the amount of credit extended. She also will incur some labor costs in processing credit slips and getting them to the bank. (c) The bank would pay the sporting goods store, bill customers, and collect from customers. The bank probably also would provide signs for advertising the credit plan.

18. The convenience of making uniform monthly payments is attractive to the customer. Although during some months the customer will pay more for gas or electricity used, there are other months in which the customer pays less than would otherwise be owed. Overall, the plan is good both for utilities and for customers.

19. Jamie could ask her parents to assume full responsibility for paying the amounts due on an account opened in her name. She could go to a financial institution to get a loan; again her parents would have to guarantee the repayment of the loan. She also might try borrowing money from a relative or close friend.

DEVELOP YOUR BUSINESS LANGUAGE

20. installment sales credit
21. single-payment loan
22. secured loan
23. regular account
24. revolving account
25. installment loan
26. budget account
27. cosigner
28. down payment
29. promissory note
30. collateral
31. finance charge

---

of the finance charge will be returned? (5) If the contract is paid off within 60 or 90 days, will there be any finance charge? (6) Is the contract completely filled in? (7) Under what conditions can the seller repossess the merchandise if payments are not made on time?

COMMUNICATE BUSINESS CONCEPTS

15. Answers will vary. The responses of students should be subject to the questions and com-

ments of other students. All of the students should be prepared to defend their points of view.

16. Some businesspeople feel safer taking credit cards than personal checks. If a personal check is returned because a purchaser does not have sufficient funds in his/her checking account, the business must attempt to collect the money. With a bank or T & E credit card, this burden falls on the company issuing the credit card.

17. (a) The sporting goods store would not have to

DECISION-MAKING STRATEGIES

32. Susan forgot that as a cosigner she would be responsible for the balance of the loan if Pedro defaulted. She also did not stay in contact with Pedro to see if he was making payments regularly. She should have stayed in close contact with him.

33. Susan could have recommended that he contact his creditors to work out repayment plans. She also should have suggested that he go to see a consumer credit counselor who could have given him advice about ways to repay his debt.

CALCULATE BUSINESS DATA

34. $8.40 × 3 = $25.20; $25.20 + $0.25 = $25.45

35. (a) $10,000 × 0.03 = $300 (b) $10,000 − $300 = $9,700 (c) $120,000 × 0.03 = $3,600

36. 150 liters = 39 gallons (150 × 0.26); 39 gallons x $1.19 = $46.41; 1.89 liters = 2 quarts (1.89 × 1.06); 2 quarts × $2.29 = $4.58; Total purchase: $46.41 + $4.58 = $50.99; Interest per month at 1½% = $50.99 × 0.015 = $0.76

37. (a) $31.10 + $16.95 + $11.15 + $22.10 = $81.30 (total purchases) (b) $81.30 − 20 = $61.30 (balance); $61.30 × 0.015 = $0.92 (finance charge)

TECHNOLOGY APPLICATION

In this activity, students use a computer to solve a business problem using a file that is provided on the data CD that accompanies *Intro to Business*. Instructions for using the data CD are included in a **README** file on the disk. Solutions are provided on the Instructor's Resource CD.

---

to give him a loan if he could get a cosigner. When he asked his good friend, Susan Bekkee, to be a cosigner, she said "no problem." She had an excellent credit record and Pedro got a $4,000 loan at 15 percent interest.

Months went by. Susan did not even think about the loan nor did she see Pedro. Then the letter came: Pedro had failed to make his last five payments, and he had left town with no forwarding address. The letter demanded that Susan make up the back payments immediately and pay the balance due.

She knew that as a cosigner she was responsible for this debt; she did not want a negative report to be part of her credit record.

32. What mistake did Susan make in cosigning this loan?

33. What might she have done originally to help her friend Pedro?

CALCULATE BUSINESS DATA

34. Alex Ramirez bought three gallons of paint on credit. The paint cost $8.40 a gallon. A finance charge of $0.25 was added to the purchase price of the paint. What was the total cost of Alex's purchase?

35. Charlene Presley owns a pet store and hobby shop. She thinks she should join a bank charge-card plan so that she can better compete with some large department stores. Her credit sales each month on a bank-card plan will be about $10,000.

   a. If the bank plan she joins charges Charlene 3 percent of her billings, how much would she pay for the bank's services in one month?

   b. How much would the bank owe her for that month?

   c. If her annual credit sales amount to $120,000, what would she pay for the bank's services for the year?

36. Eduardo Gomez bought 150 liters of gasoline for his motor home. He also needed 1.89 liters of oil. The gasoline cost $1.19 per gallon and the oil $2.29 per quart. What was the total amount of Eduardo's purchase? If he charged this purchase and paid 1½ percent in finance charges per month on the amount purchased, how much would he have to pay?

37. Li-ming Sun has a charge account with a department store. Her account is billed to her on the first of each month, and she is expected to pay in full by the last day of the month. If she does not, the store charges her a 1½ percent finance charge per month on the balance of the account. This past month Li-ming made the following purchases: two skirts at $15.55 each; one pair of children's shoes at $16.95; costume jewelry at $11.15; and a lamp at $22.10.

   a. What is the total amount for which Li-ming will be billed on the first of the month?

   b. If she pays only $20 on her account this month, what will be the amount of the finance charge when her bill comes next month?

TECHNOLOGY APPLICATION

Using the *Intro to Business* Data CD and your database program software, select problem CH30. After the problem appears on your screen, complete the following activities. Then, after you have completed each step, display or print a report for each activity. If you do not have a printer available, answer the questions before you leave the computer.

38. Sort the database in descending order by annual fee. Answer the following questions:

   a. Which lender charges the highest annual fee?

   b. Which lender charges the fourth highest annual fee?

39. Select and list the lenders that offer credit insurance. How many lenders are listed?

40. Sort the database in ascending order by interest rate. Answer the following questions:

   a. What is the third lowest interest rate available?

   b. What is the second highest interest rate available?

COMMUNICATING for SUCCESS

LETTERS—A COMMUNICATION CORNERSTONE

Letters are a common form of communication written for different purposes. For example, letters might be used to solve a problem, answer a question, provide information, or say "Thank you." Typically, the two classifications of letters in the workplace are employer-to-employee letters and business letters. The benefits of these types of letters include the following:

- Exact wording ensures the clear meaning of the message.
- All recipients of the letter get exactly the same information.
- Letters are a good method of record keeping and documentation.
- Letters can be reread and kept for later reference.

Employer-to-employee letters are often used to convey personnel issues or concerns. Personnel issues might include:

- compliance with workplace safety or federal guidelines
- informing employees of job benefits
- invitations to company-sponsored events
- special recognition for service or a special effort

Business letters can fulfill the same purposes, but should always be created with the goal of serving customers and satisfying their needs. Business letters will be more successful if they:

- help the customer satisfy a need
- are concise and accurate
- have a friendly tone

- are neat in appearance
- are written with the customer in mind

There are many different types of business letters, all of which focus on the operation of the company. Some reasons for business letters are: inquiries, good news, bad news, expressions of thanks, congratulatory, sales information, and requests. For example, a letter of credit provides the receiver with a set sum of credit at a store, and is often used as an award or refund.

Virtually all letters follow the same format. The components of the standard letter format include the following:

- writer's address
- date
- receiver's address
- salutation (greeting)
- body of letter
- complimentary closing (Sincerely, Best Wishes, etc.)
- signature block

Letters are a cornerstone of all business operations, and the image, success, and future of a company can be influenced by how you write a letter.

CRITICAL THINKING

1. What are some of the purposes of writing a letter?
2. What are the two classifications of letters in the workplace?

COMMUNICATING for SUCCESS

Communications skills will help ensure students' success in the business world. Communicating for Success introduces workplace/interpersonal communications issues and proper uses of communications technology. Each feature discusses a key communications topic, and contains two Critical Thinking questions that require students to analyze what they have learned.

This feature provides students with basic guidelines for conceiving and composing two widely used types of business-related letters. The ability to write a well-constructed letter is obviously something students will need in order to achieve any level of success in business. Moreover, and of more immediate concern, they'll likely need the same sort of skills in order to get the kind of position or positions they want as they are starting out.

CRITICAL THINKING

1. Letters are a common form of communication written for different purposes. For example, letters might be used to solve a problem, answer a question, provide information, or say "Thank you."
2. Typically, the two classifications of letters in the workplace are employer-to-employee letters and business letters.

Chapter 31

Interest is the primary cost of using credit. In addition to interest, the cost of credit includes service fees, cost of collecting overdue accounts, and credit insurance. In shopping for credit, consumers should consider the cost of credit.

Resources for Teachers
- Lesson Plans
- School-To-Work/SCANS Activity Masters
- Spanish Resources
- Instructor's Resource CD

Assessment
- Chapter and Unit Tests, Ch. 31
- ExamView, Ch. 31

Media/Technology
- Applying Technology Data CD
- PowerPoint slides
- Business Connection CD
- Videotape

Activity Masters and Workbooks
- Activities and Projects, Ch. 31
- Internet Activity Masters
- Business Math Activity Masters
- Communications Activity Masters
- International Business Activity Masters
- Ethics Activity Masters

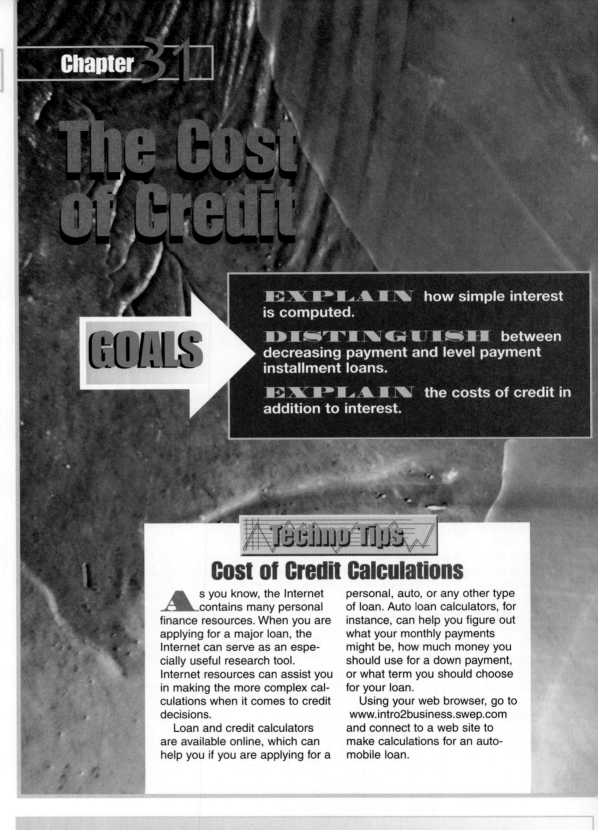

The Cost of Credit

GOALS

EXPLAIN how simple interest is computed.

DISTINGUISH between decreasing payment and level payment installment loans.

EXPLAIN the costs of credit in addition to interest.

Techno Tips
Cost of Credit Calculations

As you know, the Internet contains many personal finance resources. When you are applying for a major loan, the Internet can serve as an especially useful research tool. Internet resources can assist you in making the more complex calculations when it comes to credit decisions.

Loan and credit calculators are available online, which can help you if you are applying for a personal, auto, or any other type of loan. Auto loan calculators, for instance, can help you figure out what your monthly payments might be, how much money you should use for a down payment, or what term you should choose for your loan.

Using your web browser, go to www.intro2business.swep.com and connect to a web site to make calculations for an automobile loan.

Students need to know the latest technologies and develop cutting edge Internet skills for use in current jobs, future careers, or in their homes. TechnoTips introduces students to today's cutting edge technologies and provides them with important Internet skills. Feature topics concentrate on Internet-specific technologies and computer or other hi-tech innovations for use by businesses and consumers. At the www.intro2business.swep.com web site, students can complete the activity for this chapter.

FOCUS ON REAL LIFE

Using credit to purchase goods and services may allow you to be more efficient or more productive or to lead a more satisfying life. There are many valid reasons for using credit. A medical emergency may cause you to be strapped for money. You may be offered a new job and need a car to get to work. Or you may have the opportunity to buy something you need now for less money than you would pay for it later.

As more and more types of financial institutions offer financial services, your choices of what and where to borrow grow wider. Wise shopping for credit involves careful determination of the cost of credit. If you are thinking of borrowing money or opening a charge account, your first step should be to figure out how much it will cost you and whether you can afford it. After deciding to use credit, you must then shop for the best terms.

Consumer credit enables you to have and enjoy goods and services now and to pay for them through payment plans based on future income. Always remember, however, that credit is not free. There are a number of costs associated with credit that must be paid by those who use it.

INTEREST CALCULATIONS

The amount of interest you must pay on a loan or charge account should be clearly understood. To determine the amount you have to pay, it is necessary to know three things:

1. **Interest rates,** the percentage that is applied to your debt expressed as a fraction or decimal.

2. **Principal,** the amount of debt to which the interest rate is applied.

3. **Time factor,** the length of time for which interest will be charged. Let's look at the way interest is computed on loans.

Simple Interest

On single-payment loans, interest often is expressed in terms of simple interest. **Simple interest** is an expression of interest based on a one-year period of time. The formula for computing simple interest is:

I (interest) = P (principal) × R (rate) × T (time)

If $1,000 (P) is borrowed at 9 percent (R) for one year (T), the amount of interest would be calculated as follows:

$$I = \$1,000 \times \text{\%}_{100} \times 1 = \$90$$

In calculating the interest, there are three basic things to remember: (1) the interest rate must be expressed in the form of a fraction or decimal; (2) interest is charged for each dollar or part of a dollar borrowed; and

Why is it important to know the amount of interest you will pay on a loan?

FOCUS ON REAL LIFE

The costs of credit often are not understood or appreciated by users of credit. Class discussions should include direct costs—such as finance charges—and hidden costs—such as losing the opportunity to buy something else as the result of having to repay a debt. Using credit is actually renting someone else's money for a period of time and some of the costs are associated with granting credit and maintaining credit accounts.

MOTIVATE

PURPOSE Review the list of Key Terms while students write the ones with which they are unfamiliar on a sheet of paper. Key Terms are listed under Develop Your Business Language in Chapter Review. Then have them skim the chapter, find each of those words, and briefly review the definition. Next, have students locate the major headings that relate to each of the goals. Then have them write a study question for each goal.

TEACH/APPLY

MAKE CONNECTIONS Secure promotional materials for various types of sales and loan credit plans. If you have enough materials, you may want some of the students to compare the various plans as to the annual percentage rate, the payment plan, and the way in which the finance charge is figured.

TRY THIS/GUIDED PRACTICE Walk students through an example of simple interest using PowerPoint 31-3, *Simple Interest.* Application of the simple interest formula is an important computational skill. Use this transparency to reinforce how the formula is used. Develop supplementary exercises that students can do while the formula is displayed on the screen. Review the terms *principal, interest rate,* and *time* to be sure they are understood.

Lead a discussion of information that creditors provide to show customers the charges and periodic obligations of credit plans.

net FACTS

Net Facts provides information and definitions of terms for the Internet. The more information that students have about the Internet, the better equipped they will be to use this resource. In the Internet Activity Masters, there is an Internet Activity Worksheet for each unit. You can use these activities to give students experience with finding information online. Options for assigning this activity are as follows:

1. **Provide students with a list of addresses of resources for this activity;**
2. **Assign students to conduct their own searches; or**
3. **Use the addresses provided on the Internet Activity Worksheet.**

    You should complete the activity yourself before assigning it to resolve any discrepancies that may arise.

Engage students in a discussion of the importance of reading the disclosure statement and understanding the significance of the APR.

    Refer students to the portion of a credit card statement shown in Figure 31-2. Direct them to answer the following questions: (a) What is the APR? 18%; (b) What is the new balance of the account? $432.97; (c) What is the payment due date? 9/23/—; (d) Were cash advances made during the billing period? No; (e) What is the finance

(3) the interest rate is based upon one year of time. Here is how it works:

1. Interest is expressed as part of a dollar. This part of a dollar, or percentage, is called the interest rate. Before using a percentage rate in a problem, you must change it to either a common fraction or a decimal. For example, an interest rate of 12 percent would be changed to a common fraction of $^{12}/_{100}$ or a decimal of 0.12.

2. When an interest rate is expressed as 12 percent per year, you must pay 12 cents for each dollar you borrow for a year. At this rate, if you borrow $1, you pay 12 cents in interest. If you borrow $2, you pay 24 cents. If you borrow $10, you pay $1.20, and so on. The amount of interest charged is calculated by multiplying the principal by the interest rate and then multiplying that result by the time period. Suppose that you borrow $100 for one year at 12 percent per year. Here is how the amount of interest is calculated:

$$I = P \times R \times T$$
$$I = \$100 \times {}^{12}/_{100} \times 1 = \$12$$

3. If you borrow $100 at 12 percent for one year, you must repay the $100 plus $12 interest, as you have just seen. If you borrow the same amount of money at the same rate of interest for two years, you pay twice as much interest, or $24. If the money is borrowed for three years, you pay $36, and so on. The amount of interest on $100 borrowed at 12 percent for two years is computed as follows:

$$I = P \times R \times T$$
$$I = \$100 \times {}^{12}/_{100} \times 2 = \$24$$

How is interest calculated if you borrow money for less than a year? The amount of

net FACTS

interest is based on the fractional part of the year. The fraction may be expressed either in months or in days. A month is considered to be one-twelfth of a year, regardless of the number of days in the particular month. If you were to borrow $100 at 12 percent for one month, the interest would be:

$$I = P \times R \times T$$
$$I = \$100 \times {}^{12}/_{100} \times {}^{1}/_{12} = \$1$$

When a loan is made for a certain number of days, such as 30, 60, or 90 days, the interest is determined by days. To make the computation easy, a year is often considered 360 days. The interest on a loan for $100 at 12 percent for 60 days would be $2, as shown below.

$$I = P \times R \times T$$
$$I = \$100 \times {}^{12}/_{100} \times {}^{60}/_{360} = \$2$$

Maturity Dates

The date on which a loan must be repaid is known as the **maturity date**. How is the maturity date determined? When the time of the loan is stated in months, the date of maturity is the same day of the month as the

---

Personal Qualities-Integrity

Employers are looking for potential employees with solid ethics. Businesses are very aware of the severe implications of unethical behavior in employees. Ethical Perspectives raises ethical questions but does not involve the teaching of right and wrong. Instead, it allows students to apply their own principles to business situations through the use of critical

thinking and decision-making skills. Students will also gain a sense of individual diversity through the expression of their opinions about the situations presented.

    Discuss how credit cards should be properly used. Have an attorney or credit counselor talk to the class about the experiences of clients related to misuse or loss of credit cards. Lead a discussion of the harm that can be done through credit card fraud.

date on which the loan was made. If a loan is made on January 15 and is to run one month, it will be due February 15. If it is to run two months, it will be due March 15, and so on.

When the time of a loan is given in days, the exact number of days must be counted to find the date of maturity. First you would determine the number of days remaining in the month when the loan was made. For instance, if the loan were made on January 10, there would be 21 days to be counted in January. Then you would add the days in the following months until the total equals the required number of days. Suppose you wanted to find the date of maturity of a 90-day loan made on March 3. Here is how it would be done:

> March—28 days (31−3)
> April—30 days
> May—31 days

June—1 day
Total: 90 days
Due Date—June 1

Installment Interest

When you borrow money, you may want to repay the loan in several partial payments instead of one large single payment. A loan that is repaid in partial payments is called an installment loan (or consumer loan). Each payment is called an installment. You can obtain installment loans from many banks, savings and loan associations, credit unions, and consumer finance companies. On an installment loan, the borrower is usually given a schedule of payments, or a payment book, that shows how much is to be paid each month.

With some loans, the amount of the interest is added to the amount you borrow, and you sign a promissory note for the total amount. The note may then be repaid in

charge? $4.70; (f) What was the payment made on purchases from the previous billing period? $30.

Refer students to the installment sales contract shown in Figure 31-2. Direct them to answer the following questions: (a) What is the finance charge? $37.68; (b) What are the monthly installments? $34.47; (c) What is the total of the payments? $413.68; (d) What is the APR? 18.5%.

EXPLORE THIS/INDEPENDENT PRACTICE Have students make a repayment schedule of monthly payments for a loan of $1,500 to be repaid in 6 monthly installments. Show each installment as one-sixth of the principal plus 2½ percent finance charge per month on the unpaid balance. Students should use the decreasing loan payment schedule in Figure 31-1 as an example. Total: $1,631.25

Have students prepare a repayment schedule for the following example. The Consumers' Bank loaned Angela Hawthorne $1,400 on a 10 percent promissory note. Angela repaid the loan and interest in 6 monthly installments. Students should use the level loan payment in Figure 31-1 as an example. Ask them to provide answers to these questions: (a) How much was the finance charge on the loan? $70; (b) What was the total of the payments on the loan? $1,470; (c) What was the amount of each monthly payment? $245.

Credit insurance is an important dimension of credit transactions and is required by many lenders. Ask students to give reasons in writing why they feel credit insurance is important to the lender or creditor and why the person

ETHICAL PERSPECTIVES

Credit Card Fraud

Protecting your credit card number is important! You don't have to lose your card to get cheated out of money—all a credit card thief needs is the number of your account to use it.

Credit card fraud is big business, but you can take some basic precautions to protect yourself. For example:

- Avoid giving card numbers or expiration dates over the telephone unless you initiate the call. Giving your card number to someone who calls you about winning a prize can turn into a real surprise. (The person calling often pretends to need your card number to verify your identity so you can win the prize.)
- Try not to give out your birth date or your social security number more often than is absolutely necessary. Both can be used to apply for a card in your name; you may not know about it until you are pressed for payment by the card issuer.

- Do not put a credit card number on a check at a merchant's request. Almost half the states prohibit this practice, and VISA and MasterCard will not let merchants bill your credit card to cover a bounced check.

Even the latest technology has been used to commit credit card fraud. Several programs that can be downloaded from the Internet allow users to generate fake credit card numbers that actually work, although it's illegal. However, few consumers have reported losses from these fake numbers.

Critical Thinking

1. What are some precautions you should use to help avoid having your credit card number used fraudulently by someone else?
2. Who is the real loser when credit cards are used fraudulently?

ETHICAL PERSPECTIVES

CRITICAL THINKING

1. Using good sense and not being careless with a credit card is basic to avoiding credit card fraud. Not giving out card numbers to unknown individuals, particularly telemarketers, is one important way to avoid fraud. Safeguarding or keeping a record of card numbers, being careful not to misplace cards, and reporting missing or lost cards immediately to the issuers are important steps to take in avoiding fraud.

2. All of us as consumers are losers. A business loses money through credit card fraud; therefore, merchants frequently charge higher prices to cover the cost of credit card fraud. As an individual, there is the inconvenience of reporting and replacing lost or stolen cards.

receiving credit usually must pay for that insurance.

The Chapter Review questions at the end of the chapter vary in level of difficulty. For a basic assignment, consider Develop Your Business Language and Review Your Reading. For an average assignment, consider the basic assignment plus Communicate Business Concepts and Calculate Business Data. For an enhanced assignment, try the average assignment plus Technology Application and Decision-Making Strategies.

ASSESS

Review Business Notes at the end of the chapter. Then review the goals at the beginning of the chapter. Restate each as a question and have students respond orally. For students who may have difficulty providing answers, assign the reteaching activities that follow. Enrichment activities may also be assigned where appropriate.

1. How is simple interest calculated? (Answer: The amount of interest is calculated by multiplying the interest rate times the principal times the number of days or months.)

2. Explain the difference between decreasing payment and level payment installment loans. (Answer: On decreasing payment loans, equal parts of the loan must be repaid each month plus interest on the unpaid balance. With a level payment loan, the borrower pays the same amount each month.)

DECREASING AND LEVEL LOAN PAYMENT SCHEDULES

A Decreasing Loan Payment Schedule
($120 loan; 18 percent interest: monthly payments are $20 plus interest).

Months	Unpaid Balance	Interest Paid	Loan Repayment	Total Payment
1	$120	$1.80	$ 20	$ 21.80
2	100	1.50	20	21.50
3	80	1.20	20	21.20
4	60	.90	20	20.90
5	40	.60	20	20.60
6	20	.30	20	20.30
Totals	——	$6.30	$120	$126.30

A Level Loan Payment Schedule
($1,000 loan; 12 percent annual interest: $100 monthly payments).

Payment	Interest	Applied to Principal	Balance of Loan
			$1,000.00
$100.00	$10.00	$90.00	910.00
100.00	9.10	90.90	819.10
100.00	8.19	91.81	727.29
100.00	7.28	92.72	634.57
100.00	6.35	93.65	540.92
100.00	5.41	94.59	446.33
100.00	4.46	95.54	350.79
100.00	3.51	96.49	254.30
100.00	2.54	97.46	156.84
100.00	1.57	98.43	58.41
58.99	.58	58.41	——

FIGURE 31-1   Which kind of loan schedule would be best for very large loans paid back over a number of years?

equal monthly installments. For instance, you may have borrowed $100, signed a note for $110, and agreed to repay the loan in 12 monthly installments of $9.16 each.

If you had borrowed $100 for one year and paid $110 at maturity, the interest rate would have been 10 percent ($10 ÷ $100 = 0.10 or 10%). But you paid off just part of the loan each month. You had the use of the entire $100 for one month and a smaller amount each succeeding month as you repaid the

loan. In this case, the interest rate amounts to 18.5 percent.

On some installment loans, interest is calculated on the amount that is unpaid at the end of each month. Suppose that Armando Rivera borrowed $120 and agreed to repay the loan at $20 a month plus 1½ percent interest each month on the unpaid balance. His schedule of decreasing payments is shown in the first part of Figure 31-1. His father, Jason Rivera, obtained a loan of

Basic Skills-Writing

Employers are looking for potential employees with good basic foundation skills. In order to prepare students for the school-to-work transition, we must teach these skills in our classroom. Language arts skills are an important component of good writing skills. Students should learn to paraphrase, write complete sentences, and identify nouns. For additional

practice in language arts skills, direct students to answer the Develop Your Business Language and Review Your Reading at the end of the chapter. Students should write the definitions in their own words and in complete sentences. To further practice language arts skills, ask students to underline the singular nouns and circle the plural nouns in their definitions.

$1,000. He agreed to repay $100 per month. The payment is applied to principal and interest. Mr. Rivera's repayment schedule is shown in the second part of Figure 31-1. He makes payments each month on a level payment schedule. Both kinds of payment schedules are used in loan transactions.

FINANCE CHARGES

Before you borrow money or charge a purchase, you should know exactly the cost of using credit. The **annual percentage rate (APR)** is a disclosure required by law, and it states the percentage cost of credit on a yearly basis. All credit agreements, whether for sales credit or loan credit, require disclosure of the APR.

In addition to interest, the APR includes other charges that may be made. *Service fees* involve the time and money it takes a creditor to investigate your credit history, process your loan or charge account application, and keep records of your payments and balances.

Credit experts consider credit insurance to be overpriced, but without it lenders would not approve loans.

What other costs must you consider, besides the sticker price, when buying a car?

3. What are the costs of credit in addition to interest? (Answer: Costs of credit in addition to interest include service fees, the cost of collecting bad debts, and credit insurance.)
4. Why should a borrower shop for credit? (Answer: The cost of credit varies among lenders. You can save money by shopping around to compare APR, amount of monthly payments, and the finance charge.)

RETEACH

Using the board or overhead, show how simple interest is figured on a single-payment loan. Then show an example of figuring interest on decreasing payment and level payment installment loans. Refer to Figure 31-1 in the text.

Discuss the difference between taking out a loan and using a credit card. (Most loans have lower finance charges than credit cards.

Personal Qualities-Sociability

Sociability skills are sometimes difficult for high school students to acquire. To demonstrate understanding, friendliness, adaptability, and politeness, develop cooperative learning or team activities as appropriate. Discuss sociability skills with students before beginning any cooperative learning activity.

SCANS

Loans frequently are used to borrow money for large purchases.)

Costs of collecting from those who do not pay their accounts may be costs that are passed on to borrowers. Uncollectible accounts are frequently referred to as bad debts or doubtful accounts. Lenders also commonly add an amount to cover the cost of credit insurance. **Credit insurance** is special insurance that repays the balance of the amount owed if the borrower dies or becomes disabled prior to the full settlement of the loan. Without your acceptance of credit insurance coverage, some lenders will not be willing to make a loan.

To make you aware of the total cost of credit, a federal law requires that you be told of the finance charge. The finance charge is the total cost of credit including interest and all other charges. This finance charge must be stated in writing in your contract or on your charge account statement. Figure 31-2 shows how the annual percentage rate and finance charges are shown on a credit card bill and on an installment sales contract. The APR is the key to comparing costs of credit, regardless of the amount

of credit or how much time you have to repay it.

CREDIT ALTERNATIVES

If you have to borrow money or make a purchase on credit, you should consider not only the total cost of credit but also the available alternative sources of credit. Check with several lenders and compare the APRs.

If you make a purchase with a credit card, for instance, know which card has the lowest APR. If an installment sales contract is required, consider whether an installment loan from a financial institution may be cheaper for you. When acquiring a loan, shop around just as carefully as you would for a new stereo, car, computer, or any other major purchase. Borrowing money is costly, so make sure that you get the best loan. Some of the things you should check include the annual percentage rate, the amount of the monthly payments, and the finance charge.

Always remember that when you use credit, you not only use someone else's money, but you also spend your own future income. If you decide to use credit, the benefits of making the purchase now (a more satisfying life, for example) should outweigh the costs of using credit. Effectively used, credit can help you have more and enjoy more. Misused, credit can result in excessive debt, loss of reputation, and even bankruptcy.

DESCRIPTION		AMOUNT
PREVIOUS BALANCE		182.57
NEW PURCHASES	+	275.70
NEW CASH ADVANCES	+	.00
NEW TEXAS BANKARD PLUS™ PURCHASES	+	.00
CREDITS	−	.00
PAYMENTS	−	30.00
FINANCE CHARGE	+	4.70
NEW BALANCE	=	432.97
PAYMENT DUE DATE*		9/23/--

20989 7 28792

ACCOUNT INFORMATION	
DESCRIPTION	AMOUNT
TEXAS BANKARD PLUS BALANCE	.00
AVERAGE DAILY BALANCE	312.81

ANNUAL PERCENTAGE RATE 18%

*DATE NEW BALANCE MUST BE PAID IN FULL TO AVOID FINANCE CHARGE ON TRANSACTIONS BEING BILLED FOR THE FIRST TIME ON THIS STATEMENT (EXCEPT CASH ADVANCES AND TEXAS BANKARD PLUS PURCHASES).

NOTICE—SEE REVERSE SIDE FOR IMPORTANT INFORMATION

INSTALLMENT SALES CONTRACT AND SECURITY AGREEMENT

Sergio Sound Systems, Inc.
The South Mall • Amarillo, TX 79199

I (we) the undersigned buyer(s) buy from, and grant a security interest, to SERGIO SOUND SYSTEMS, INC. in this property:

Quantity	Description	Amount
1	Model XV-466 CD Player	400 00

Description of Trade-in:

Sales Tax	1 6	00
Total	416	00

Insurance Agreement

Credit life insurance is available at a cost of $ _3.00_ for the term of the credit. The purchase of insurance is voluntary and not required for credit.

☐ I want insurance.

Signed: _____ Date: _____

☐ I do not want insurance.

Signed: _Maria Benitez_ Date: _1/15/20--_

Signed: _____ Date: _____

Buyer's Name _Maria Benitez_
Buyer's Address _805 Elberon Ave_
City _Amarillo_ State _TX_ Zip _79199_

1	Cash Price	$	400.00
2	Less: Down Payment $ _40.00_		
3	Trade-in $		
4	Total Down	$	40.00
5	Unpaid Balance of Cash Price	$	360.00
6	Other Charges _Sales Tax_	$	16.00
7	AMOUNT FINANCED	$	376.00
8	FINANCE CHARGE	$	37.68
9	Total of Payments	$	413.68
10	Deferred Payment Price (1 + 6 + 8)	$	453.68
11	ANNUAL PERCENTAGE RATE		18.5 %

The Buyer(s) agrees to pay to SERGIO SOUND SYSTEMS, INC. at their store the "Total of Payments" shown above in _12_ monthly installments of _34.47_ and a final installment of _34.51_. The first installment is due _February 15, 20--_ and all other payments are due on the same day of the month, until paid in full. The finance charge applies from _1/15/20--_.

Signed: _Maria Benitez_ Date: _1/15/20--_

Notice to Buyer: You should get a copy of this contract when you sign. You can pay in advance the unpaid balance of this contract and get a partial refund of the finance charge based on the "Actuarial Method."

FIGURE 31-2 Where are the annual percentage rate and the finance charge shown on these documents?

SUMMARIZE

Secure a large sheet of paper to the wall (or use a flip chart) and label it COMPUTING SIMPLE INTEREST AND INSTALLMENT INTEREST. Invite students to write, grafitti style, what they consider the most pertinent information explained in this chapter.

EVALUATE

- Assign Activities and Projects for Chapter 31.
- Administer the printed test or ExamView for Chapter 31.
- Assign School-To-Work/SCANS portfolio activities for Unit 9.

REVIEW YOUR READING

1. To calculate interest you must know the principal (amount borrowed), the rate of interest, and the amount of time that the loan or credit is extended. The formula for simple interest is:
$I = P \times R \times T$.

2. When determining interest, 360 days make up one year.

3. If the time of the loan is stated in months, the maturity date is the same date as the loan, but in the following month. If it is stated in days, you find the number of days remaining in the month when the loan was made and then add days in the following month until the total equals the number of required days.

4. On decreasing payment loans, equal parts of the loan must be repaid each month plus interest on the unpaid balance. With a level payment loan, the borrower pays the same amount each month.

5. Interest, service fees, and credit insurance can be included in the finance charges.

6. The APR (annual percentage rate) must be revealed to make it easier for a consumer to compare the cost of credit.

7. You need to consider whether or not the installment payments can be afforded, the length of the loan, the APR, and the total cost of the loan.

COMMUNICATE BUSINESS CONCEPTS

8. Steve has only $68 left each month after paying for his credit bills and living expenses. He definitely should not continue to make more credit purchases until some of his current bills are paid off. He is going to have to give up a number of things now to pay for the credit he got in previous months.

9.
Date of Note	Time to Run	Date of Maturity
March 15	4 months	July 15
May 26	3 months	August 26
July 31	5 months	December 31
April 30	30 days	May 30
October 5	45 days	November 19

Chapter REVIEW

BUSINESS NOTES

1. The amount of interest is calculated by multiplying the interest rate times the principal times the number of days or months.

2. On decreasing payment loans, equal parts of the loan must be repaid each month plus interest on the unpaid balance. With a level payment loan, the borrower pays the same amount each month.

3. Costs of credit in addition to interest include service fees, the cost of collecting bad debts, and credit insurance.

4. The cost of credit varies among lenders; you can save money by shopping around to compare the APR, amount of monthly payments, and the total finance charge.

REVIEW YOUR READING

1. What three things must you know to be able to calculate interest? What is the simple interest formula?

2. In calculating interest, how many days are normally considered to be in one year?

3. How is the maturity date of a loan determined?

4. What is the difference between a decreasing payment and a level payment installment loan?

5. What are some costs that can be included in a finance charge?

6. By law, what information must be disclosed by creditors to make it easier for a consumer to compare finance charges?

7. List some things you need to consider when making a decision about obtaining a loan or using an installment sales contract.

COMMUNICATE BUSINESS CONCEPTS

8. Steve Beyer has charge accounts at three different stores. He also has a bank charge card and an oil company credit card that he uses frequently. Last month he took out a personal loan that requires him to pay $60 a month for the next 18 months. The total of the payments he makes on his three charge accounts is $222 per month. His monthly income, after taxes and other deductions, is $1,000. His expenses for an apartment, utilities, food, clothing and other necessities amount to more than $650 per month. Should Steve continue to make more credit purchases? What problems does Steve face at this time? What cost of credit is he experiencing?

Date of Loan	Time to Run
March 15	4 months
May 26	3 months
July 31	5 months
April 30	30 days
October 5	45 days

9. Find the date of maturity for each of the loans in the table.

10. Les Heddle checked into several loan possibilities. He needed $15,000 to do some remodeling in his upholstery shop. The Thrifty

10. The loan comparison chart is as follows:

Lender	APR	Loan Length	Monthly Payment	Total Payment	Cost of Credit
Thrifty	16%	3 yrs.	$555	$19,980	$4,980
Greenback	15%	5 yrs.	$375	$22,500	$7,500
Silk Purse	?	4 yrs.	$496	$23,800	$8,808

This exercise should convince students that it is worth the time it takes to shop for credit. The Thrifty loan has the lowest cost, but the Greenback loan could be paid back with the lowest monthly payments.

Loan Company offered him an APR of 16 percent for a three-year loan. Monthly payments, including finance charges, would be $555. The Green-back Bank offered him a five-year loan at 15 percent APR with a total monthly payment of $375. The Silk Purse Finance Lending Shop did not quote an APR figure but said, "We have a 'no frills' loan policy, and you can have a four-year loan with monthly payments at the amazingly low figure of $496 per month." Construct a loan comparison chart showing the lender, APR, loan length, monthly payment, total payment, and cost of credit. Then decide which loan would be the best for Les Heddle. Give reasons for your decision.

DEVELOP YOUR BUSINESS LANGUAGE

For each numbered item, find the term that has the same meaning.

11. An expression of interest based on a one-year period of time.
12. The amount of debt to which the interest is applied.
13. The date on which a loan must be repaid.
14. The length of time for which interest will be charged.
15. Special insurance that repays the balance of the amount owed if the borrower dies or becomes disabled prior to the full settlement of the loan.
16. The percentage cost of credit on a yearly basis.
17. The percentage that is applied to a debt, expressed as a fraction or decimal.

KEY TERMS

annual percentage rate (APR)
credit insurance
interest rate
maturity date
principal
simple interest
time factor

DECISION-MAKING STRATEGIES

Midori Yamaguchi plans to buy a new refrigerator that now costs $875. Since the current inflation rate is 4 percent, she expects the refrigerator to cost $910 if she postpones the purchase for a year. If she buys it now, she estimates that it would save her $150 in food costs during the next year. This purchase would enable her to buy food at special sales and in large quantities. The new refrigerator would also be more energy efficient than her current one; therefore, she would save on the cost of electricity. Midori can use one of the following options to purchase the new refrigerator.

Alternative A. Purchase the refrigerator now, withdrawing the $875 from her 5 percent savings account at a local bank.

Alternative B. Buy the refrigerator now with $75 down, and sign an installment sales contract. The payments are $76 a month for 12 months. The APR is 12.8 percent.

Alternative C. Postpone the purchase until she saves an additional $875. Her savings account earns interest at the annual rate of 5 percent.

18. What trade-offs should Midori consider in deciding whether to buy the refrigerator now or later? (A trade-off refers to what a person gives up by making a choice.)

19. If Midori wants to buy the refrigerator now, what trade-offs should she consider in deciding whether to use credit or pay cash from her savings?

DEVELOP YOUR BUSINESS LANGUAGE

11. simple interest
12. principal
13. maturity date
14. time factor
15. credit insurance
16. annual percentage rate (APR)
17. interest rate

DECISION-MAKING STRATEGIES

18. The decision to buy or not to buy the refrigerator can be measured in dollars. The amount of savings on food purchases and electricity are considerable. Also, the price of the refrigerator will most likely increase in one year because of inflation. Rising prices may result in lost buying power. Alternative A might be the best choice at this time, particularly if Midori has a large savings account. Alternative B might be the optional choice if Midori's savings account does not exceed $875.
19. Decisions will vary. Satisfying personal decisions are based on a person's values. By paying cash, Midori avoids finance charges (at 12.8 APR). However, Midori gives up her savings. A decision to give up savings for a large purchase may mean that Midori cannot take a vacation this year. By using credit, Midori will be able to retain her savings account. Borrowing at a relatively low rate of interest can be to a person's advantage if higher interest rates on savings accounts are on the horizon.

20. (a) I = $100 × 0.10 x 1 = $10 (b) I = $500 × 0.12 × 1 = $60 (c) I = $1,000 × 0.18 × 1 = $180 (d) I = $25,000 × 0.10 × 1 = $2,500

21. (a) 3.3 km × $800 = $2,640 (b) $2,640 × 0.14 = $369.60; $369.50 × 2 = $739.20 interest

22. (a) $36.50 × 6 = $219; $219 − $200 = $19 (b) $19 ÷ 200 = 0.095; 0.095 × 2 = 19% (c) $215 − $200 = $15 (d) $15 ÷ 200 = 0.075; 0.075 × 2 = 15%

TECHNOLOGY APPLICATION

In this activity, students use a computer to solve a business problem using a file that is provided on the data CD that accompanies *Intro to Business*. Instructions for using the data CD are included in a **README** file on the disk. Solutions are provided on the Instructor's Resource CD.

20. Using the formula for simple interest, find the interest charge for each of the following amounts for one year.

a. $100 at 10 percent interest rate
b. $500 at 12 percent interest rate
c. $1,000 at 18 percent interest rate
d. $25,000 at 10 percent interest rate

21. Jennifer Ward owns a large ranch and has a chance to buy additional land next to her ranch. She would need to put in a road so that she could move equipment onto the new land. The gravel road would be 3.3 kilometers long and would cost $800 per kilometer.

a. How much would the road cost?
b. If Jennifer had to pay 14 percent interest on a two-year loan to pay for the road, how much interest would she pay over that period? (See Appendix D.)

22. Before borrowing $200, Laura Demetry visited a small loan company and the loan department of a bank. At the loan company, she found that she could borrow the $200 if she signed a note agreeing to repay the balance in six equal monthly installments of $36.50. At the bank, she could borrow the money by signing a promissory note for $215 and repaying the balance in six equal monthly payments.

a. What would be the cost of the loan at the small loan company?
b. What annual interest rate would Laura be paying if she borrowed at the small loan company?
c. What would be the cost of the loan at the bank?
d. What annual interest rate would she pay if she borrowed at the bank?

TECHNOLOGY APPLICATION

Using the *Intro to Business* Data CD and your spreadsheet program software, select problem CH31. After the problem appears on your screen, complete the following activities. Then, after you have completed each step, display or print the completed spreadsheet for each activity. If you do not have a printer available, answer the questions before you leave the computer.

23. For each of the problems shown, enter a formula to calculate the simple interest. Format your answers as currency with two decimal places. Answer the following questions:

a. What is the amount of interest for Problem 1?
b. What is the amount of interest for Problem 2?

24. Including the Number of Days per Year, copy all the data to an open part of the spreadsheet below the first set of data. In the second set of data, enter 360 as the Number of Days per Year. Answer the following questions.

a. What is the amount of interest for Problem 3?
b. What is the amount of interest for Problem 4?

25. Below the second set of data, enter formulas to calculate the difference between the interest amounts in the second set of data and the first set of data. Enter a formula to calculate the average of the differences. Label your answers and format the answers as currency with two decimal places. What is the average of the differences?

Optional: Create a bar chart comparing the differences in interest for each problem.

INTERNATIONAL TRADE ORGANIZATIONS

How can a company with little or no resources available for global expansion get involved in international trade? Several organizations exist to assist companies that are new to exporting as well as established exporters that want to expand their foreign markets.

The World Trade Centers Association, with its main office in New York City, has more than 300 affiliates in more than 90 countries, including most large cities in the United States. This non-profit organization works to bring together international buyers and sellers of goods and services. The World Trade Center in Chattanooga, for example, links exporting companies in Tennessee to potential customers throughout the world. In a similar manner, the World Trade Center North Carolina generates job growth by expanding international trade and increasing access to foreign markets for North Carolina companies.

The International Chamber of Commerce (ICC) is a private organization that serves companies involved in global business. The ICC has offices in more than 100 countries. It publishes materials to assist exporters with various international trade procedures. ICC publications include information on terms of sale, shipping risks and costs, contracts, collection procedures, and transport documents.

> **Various organizations can help companies with exporting and with expanding foreign markets.**

CRITICAL THINKING

1. A machine equipment manufacturer contacts you in your state. The owner of the business wants to sell in other countries. Describe some of the services that the World Trade Centers Association and International Chamber of Commerce might provide this company.
2. Conduct a web search to locate a World Trade Center office in your area of the country. What information and services are offered by this organization? What skills would you need if you would like to work for a World Trade Center?

Most students will either work with international clients or compete against businesses that do. Global Navigator introduces students to issues integral to working with international businesses. Key concepts and challenges faced by international businesses are presented, followed by two Critical Thinking questions that require students to analyze what they have learned.

This feature introduces students to two important organizations that facilitate international trade, the World Trade Centers Association and the International Chamber of Commerce. Since most small businesses that are seeking to develop international exposure do not have the resources to go it alone, knowledge of these not-for-profit organizations gives students a better idea of how it comes about and what resources they have to offer.

CRITICAL THINKING

1. World Trade Centers can help link the manufacturer with customers in foreign markets. The International Chamber of Commerce can provide information about specific markets, including trade procedures, shipping risks and costs, and economic data.
2. Answers may vary depending on the area. Needed skills may include knowledge of foreign languages, experience in importing/exporting and international shipping, a degree in international accounting or finance, trade-related industry- or country-specific business experience.

This chapter focuses on the importance of creditworthiness. Special emphasis is placed on following good business procedures in handling credit transactions, such as paying credit obligations on time.

Resources for Teachers
- Lesson Plans
- School-To-Work/SCANS Activity Masters
- Spanish Resources
- Instructor's Resource CD

Assessment
- Chapter and Unit Tests, Ch. 32
- ExamView, Ch. 32

Media/Technology
- Applying Technology Data CD
- PowerPoint slides
- Business Connection CD
- Videotape

Activity Masters and Workbooks
- Activities and Projects, Ch. 32
- Internet Activity Masters
- Business Math Activity Masters
- Communications Activity Masters
- International Business Activity Masters
- Ethics Activity Masters

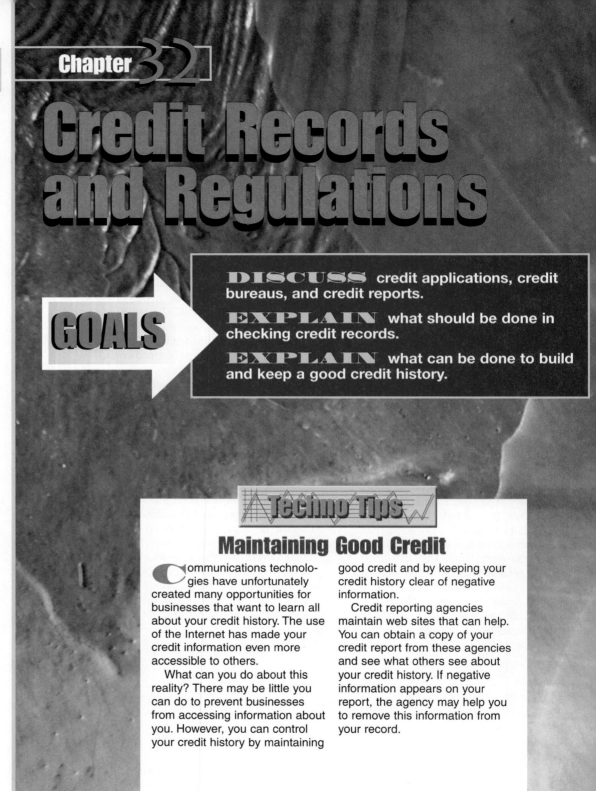

Chapter 32
Credit Records and Regulations

GOALS

DISCUSS credit applications, credit bureaus, and credit reports.

EXPLAIN what should be done in checking credit records.

EXPLAIN what can be done to build and keep a good credit history.

Techno Tips

Maintaining Good Credit

Communications technologies have unfortunately created many opportunities for businesses that want to learn all about your credit history. The use of the Internet has made your credit information even more accessible to others.

What can you do about this reality? There may be little you can do to prevent businesses from accessing information about you. However, you can control your credit history by maintaining good credit and by keeping your credit history clear of negative information.

Credit reporting agencies maintain web sites that can help. You can obtain a copy of your credit report from these agencies and see what others see about your credit history. If negative information appears on your report, the agency may help you to remove this information from your record.

Students need to know the latest technologies and develop cutting edge Internet skills for use in current jobs, future careers, or in their homes. TechnoTips introduces students to today's cutting edge technologies and provides them with important Internet skills. Feature topics concentrate on Internet-specific technologies and computer or other hi-tech innovations for use by businesses and consumers.

Assume that you have been issued a bank credit card. One day you mistakenly leave your credit card lying on a counter. When you return 15 minutes later, your credit card is gone. The sales clerk says that he has not seen it. You wait a few weeks to see whether it will be returned. It is not returned, so you write to the credit card company and explain what happened. Your next statement shows that more than $200 worth of merchandise was charged to your card before you reported it lost. What mistakes have you made, and what can you do now?

Several months later you are checking your charge account statement and find several errors on it. There is one charge for a purchase you did not make, and this is the third month in a row that this charge has shown up on your statement. One of your purchases was returned several weeks ago, but the credit does not show on your statement. Your last month's payment, which you made on time, also is not listed. What can you do about these errors?

Your friends, Monique and Gary Buckeye, had their loan application turned down. The loan officer explained that the credit bureau report on their credit record was not good. Monique and Gary were shocked; they always pay their bills on time, with only a few minor exceptions. They need this loan for home improvements. You wonder what they can do to correct this problem.

These credit problems can happen to anyone. If consumers know about credit laws and regulations, there are steps to take to avoid and correct problems. It also is important to know what information creditors need to have to make decisions regarding those who apply for credit.

CREDITWORTHINESS

You should understand what lenders need to know in order to make a decision about whether to grant credit. Generally, they want to be assured of two things: your ability to repay a debt and your willingness to do so. You may say that you can handle the debt, and you may assure them you will repay the debt according to the terms of the agreement. However, they need to have some evidence. They want to lend money, but lenders must minimize their bad debts. Lenders need proof that you are creditworthy.

Being **creditworthy** means that you have established a credit record that shows you are a good credit risk. Potential lenders will want to examine your credit record. Your **credit record** is a report that shows the debts you owe, how often you use credit, and whether you pay your debts on time.

There is other information that lenders will want to know. Lenders want to find out about your finances, such as how much you earn, what kinds of savings and investments you have, and whether you have any other sources of income. They may also want to know about your reliability; that is, your occupation, how long you have been with your present employer, how long you have lived at the same address, and whether you own or rent your home.

The three major companies that store data on consumers and provide information to lenders are Experian, Equifax, and Trans Union. Equifax maintains over 190 million credit files on U.S. consumers.

Chapter 32 Credit Records and Regulations **437**

for an example of a charge account statement from a department store. Have students explain what is included on each statement and why the information is included. Compare and contrast the information shown on the various statements.

Ask students to assume that they are interested in building a good credit record. Have them prepare a chart listing the steps that they can follow to establish a credit record.

Discuss how they can contact a credit counseling service if they, or someone they know, is having a problem with credit. A telephone book will generally reveal what credit counseling services are available in your community. Also discuss why it is important to seek the right kind of help when credit problems arise.

TRY THIS/GUIDED PRACTICE
Stress how important it is to verify a credit statement. With the increase in credit and fraud, even though there are protective laws to minimize consumer losses due to fraud, it is especially important for students to understand why credit statements must be checked over before they are paid. Double charges by careless or fraudulent businesses are a source of overpayment that can be missed by a consumer if a statement is not checked. Maintaining a file of credit charge slips and comparing them with each statement received is a good method for avoiding overpayments.

Direct students to list as many reasons as they can think of for people being denied credit.

CREDIT CARD APPLICATION
Important: Fill in all information requested below.

Second National BankCorp

1. Information About Yourself (*Name of person in whose name card will be issued*)

☐ Mr. ☐ Mrs. ☐ Miss ☐ Ms.   First Name   Middle   Last Name
(Courtesy titles are optional)

| Home Address | Apt. | City | State | ZIP Code | How Long? Years ___ Mos. ___ |

| Previous Address (if less than 2 years at present address) | Apt. | City | State | ZIP Code |

| Home Telephone ( ) | Business Telephone ( ) | Social Security Number | Date of Birth / / | No. of Dependents (Exclude Yourself) |

| Are You a U.S. Citizen? ☐Yes ☐No | If No, Explain Immigration Status | Are You a Permanent Resident? ☐Yes ☐No | Do You: ☐Own ☐Rent ☐Other | Monthly Rent or Mortgage $ |

2. Employment Information (*Your total yearly income from all sources*)

| Employer | Address | City | State | ZIP Code |

| How Long? Years ___ Mos. ___ | Occupation | Yearly Gross Salary $ | Other Income* | Source |

| Former Employer (if less than 1 year with present employer) | How Long? Years ___ Mos. ___ | *Note: Alimony, child support or separate maintenance income need not be disclosed if you do not wish to have it considered as a basis for paying this obligation. |

| Nearest Relative Not Living with You | Address | City | State | Relation | Telephone |

3. Other Credit

Major Credit Cards (Visa, MasterCard, etc....)	Account Number
Other Credit Cards (Dept. Stores, etc....)	Account Number
Other Credit	Account Number

4. Banking Information

| ☐ Checking | Name of Bank | City | Account Number |
| ☐ Savings | Name of Bank (if different from above) | City | Account Number |

| ☐ Other (Check here if you have any of the following:) | IRA CD | Money Market Account Stocks/Bonds | Investments Cash Maanagement Account |

5. Joint Account Information (*Complete for joint account or if you are relying on the income of another person to qualify for an account*)

| First Name | Middle | Last Name | Relation |

| Home Address | Apt. | City | State | ZIP Code |

| Home Telephone ( ) | Business Telephone ( ) | Social Security Number | Date of Birth / / |

| Employer | Address | City | State | ZIP Code |

| How Long? Years ___ Mos. ___ | Occupation | Yearly Gross Salary $ | Other Income* | Source |

| Former Employer | How Long? Years ___ Mos. ___ | *Note: Alimony, child support or separate maintenance income need not be disclosed if you do not wish to have it considered as a basis for paying this obligation. |

6. Additional Cards (*Complete this section if you want cards issued to additional buyers on your account.*)

| 1. Spouse   First Name | Middle | Last Name |
| 2. Other   First Name | Middle | Last Name |

7. Signatures

I authorize the Second National BankCorp to check my credit record and to verify my credit, employment and income references. I have read the important information on the reverse side.

X _____   X _____
Applicant's Signature   Joint Applicant's Signature

I understand that Second National BankCorp may amend the account terms and charges specified in the Cardmember Agreement in the future.

FIGURE 32-1 Why is it important to fill all the blanks, and to do so accurately?

Completing Credit Applications
When you apply for credit or a loan, you will be asked to fill out a credit application. A **credit application** is a form on which you provide information needed by a lender to make a decision about granting credit or approving a loan. Figure 32-1 is an example of a credit application. Read this application carefully and note the information that is requested. What information could you provide on an application of this kind?

One of the most important parts of the credit application is the listing of your credit references—businesses or individuals who are able and willing to provide information about your creditworthiness. Your signature

Critical Thinking Skills-Decision Making

SCANS

Decision-making skills, which include specifying goals, generating alternatives, considering risks, and evaluating and choosing the best alternative, are applied throughout every chapter in this text. Each time a student participates in a Cooperative Learning or Teams activity, decision-making skills are applied in a group situation. For Communicate Business

Concepts and Decision-Making Strategies, students must specify the goal of the activity, consider risks, and evaluate the best solution before the questions can be answered. Emphasize to students how they are using decision-making techniques in their day-to-day tasks and make them aware of the skills they are developing.

on the credit application gives a lender permission to contact your credit references and inquire about your credit record. Your signature also indicates that you understand the terms of the type of credit for which you are applying and that the information you have provided is true. The credit application needs to be filled out completely, accurately, and honestly. You should sign it when you understand it and have provided the requested information.

Documenting Credit Data

Information provided on credit applications must be verified to assure its accuracy. Present and former employers can verify the dates of employment and salary figures. Banks and other financial institutions can report whether the applicants have the accounts listed on the applications. Landlords can indicate the length of time tenants have been renting and whether they pay their rent on time. Other creditors can report how credit applicants make payments to their accounts and how they repay their loans.

If you list a personal reference because you do not have sufficient business credit references, the person you list can indicate how he or she feels you conduct your personal business affairs. School personnel can indicate how reliable and trustworthy you were in school. In each case, the reference checked merely helps the credit manager to get a better picture of you as a credit risk so

that an accurate appraisal of your creditworthiness can be made.

Reporting Credit Information

In addition to checking with your employers, your landlord (if you rent a house or an apartment), and your credit references, usually a lender will check with a credit bureau. A **credit bureau,** or a credit reporting agency, is a company that gathers information on credit users and sells that information in the form of credit reports to credit grantors. Banks, finance companies, and retail stores are among the customers of credit bureaus.

Credit bureaus keep records of consumers' debts but can record only information that is officially reported to them. Creditors often send computer tapes or other payment data to credit bureaus, usually on a monthly basis. The information shows if payments are up-to-date or overdue and if any action has been taken to collect overdue bills. Other information may be added to create a month-by-month credit history for the consumer accounts. Credit bureaus cooperate with each other and provide information to other credit bureaus. If you are new to a community and request credit, the local credit bureau can obtain information from the bureau in the community where you formerly lived. There are several credit bureau associations. One of

Why is it important to provide accurate information on a loan or credit application?

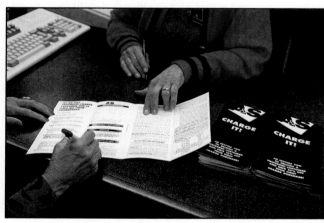

Combine the reasons into one list on the board. Then review the laws described in the chapter using PowerPoint 32-4, *You Have Rights.*

EXPLORE THIS/INDEPENDENT PRACTICE Secure application forms for a charge account. Have students complete the forms and explain why the information is requested. Have them relate the "three Cs of credit" to the types of information requested on the applications. For another activity, have students decide if each of the following situations is a violation of the Equal Credit Opportunity Act:

(a) A woman is denied credit because she is too old; (b) A woman is denied credit because she is not married; (c) A man is denied credit because he does not have a steady source of income.

Then have them determine if each of the following statements provides complete credit information according to the Truth-in-Lending Law: (a) Finance charge is $20 a month; 18 percent APR; (b) Payments are for 52 weeks, and only $200 is required as a down payment; (c) $100 down, $35 a month for 3 years.

One day Louisa saw an advertisement in the paper: "Erase bad credit! 100% guaranteed. Let us solve your problems with bills. Make only one payment per month." Have students analyze this claim. What questions should Louisa ask before she uses this source to help her with credit problems? Have students indicate in writing how they might respond to this ad.

The Chapter Review questions at the end of the chapter vary in level of difficulty. For a basic assignment, consider Develop Your Business Language and Review Your Reading. For an average assignment, consider the basic assignment plus Communicate Business Concepts and Calculate Business Data. For an enhanced assignment, try the average assignment plus Technology Application and Decision-Making Strategies.

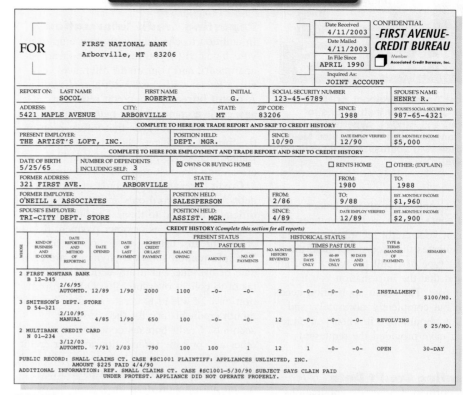

FIGURE 32-2 What kind of information would be on your credit report?

the largest has about 1,500 credit bureaus among its membership.

Your credit record with a bureau is used to grade you as a credit risk. Credit bureaus do not make value judgments about any individual; they simply gather facts as reported to them. Your credit record is confidential. That is, it can be obtained only by you or those who have a legitimate reason for examining it.

Figure 32-2 is an example of a credit report that may be issued by a credit bureau. You will note that the top half contains background information about the individual, while the bottom half lists information about the individual's accounts and payment history. Note that at the bottom there is a reference to a public record showing a dispute between the consumer and a creditor that was settled in a small claims court. All of this information is of interest to credit grantors.

CREDIT RECORDS

You can help maintain a good credit record by keeping track of your purchases and payments. When you buy on credit, you should keep your copy of the sales slip or credit card receipt for your own records in the event a problem with billing arises. The businessperson will retain the other copies for billing purposes.

Your Statement of Account

You will receive a statement of account on a regular basis, usually monthly. The

Basic Skills-Listening

You can teach students to become good listeners by explaining to them the value of being aware of certain emotional words that may distract a listener from listening. Emotional words from the speaker that may criticize the listener can cause the listener to miss the focus of what is being said. For example, if a teacher is trying to give constructive criticism about a paper that a student wrote, the student may be so upset over the criticism that the point of constructive assistance is not heard. The Student Activity Worksheet, Basic Skills—Listening Checklist, in the School-To-Work/SCANS Activity Masters, may be used to serve as a guideline for discussion of listening skills.

statement of account, or simply the **statement**, is a record of the transactions that you have completed with a business during a billing period. For credit card accounts, the statement lists all of your purchases from various businesses. Most statements show:

- The balance that was due when the last statement was mailed
- The amounts charged during the month for the merchandise or services you bought

- The amounts credited to your account for payments made during the month or for merchandise returned
- The current balance, which is the balance from the last statement, plus finance charges and the amounts of any new purchases, minus the amounts credited to you (old balance + finance charges + purchases − payments = current balance)
- The minimum amount of your next payment and when it is due.

Most statements are prepared by computers. A statement serves two basic purposes: it shows you how much you owe, and it gives you a record of your business transactions. A statement is shown in Figure 32-3.

You should check the accuracy of the statement by comparing it with your copies of sales slips and with your record of

TECHNOLOGICAL PERSPECTIVES

Credit Databases

Databases are in common use throughout the business world. The United States is the biggest user of credit information contained in databases. Of the thousands of databases worldwide, the United States produces and uses more than 50 percent of them.

The information you write on your credit or loan application may be verified through a database. Information stored in credit databases contain some of the following information about you:

1. your income level
2. how many credit cards you have been issued
3. what the balances are on your credit card accounts
4. where you are employed and for how long
5. where you live and whether you are a renter or owner
6. whether you have ever been in bankruptcy

7. whether you pay your utility and other bills on time.

Credit databases containing files on millions of consumers are maintained by three primary sources—Equifax, Experian, and Trans Union. These files are a powerful source of credit information. If you apply for a charge account, a personal loan, or a mortgage, your credit experience—or lack of it—will be a major factor considered by the creditor. A good credit rating is a valuable asset that should be nurtured and protected.

Critical Thinking

1. What are some reasons you can think of why the United States is the biggest user of worldwide databases?
2. Are you concerned about personal data about you in a credit file? Why or why not?

TECHNOLOGICAL PERSPECTIVES

Technological Perspectives exposes students to new technology and gives them an opportunity to apply this new technology for current and future situations.

CRITICAL THINKING

1. The United States is one of the largest markets in the world. If goods and services are to be marketed effectively, a variety

of databases should be readily available. We also have an economy with a high level of computer sophistication. Sophistication in the use of computers results in the creation and use of databases.
2. Answers to this question will vary. Some students may just distrust technology altogether. Some students may have great faith in technology and express no concern whatsoever. As noted in a recent Harris Poll, however, most adult consumers have concerns about their privacy.

Point out that credit applications need to be read carefully. Discuss with the class how information can be concealed (fine print, confusing language, and so on).

Remind students of the importance of keeping accurate records of all purchases made on credit. Review the information included on a typical statement of account.

Ask students to suggest problems that might result if the following laws for protecting the credit rights of consumers did not exist: The Truth-in-Lending Law, Equal Credit Opportunity Act, Fair Credit Billing Act, and Fair Credit Reporting Act.

Reinforce the things a consumer can do to build a credit record. Have students write a step-by-step plan for building a credit record.

Direct students to read the Technological Perspectives in this chapter. Ask students to assume that they checked with the local credit bureau and found an error in their files. An account with a local department store reportedly was overdue twice during the past year. Actually the correct amount had been paid on time, but the payment had been credited to someone else's account. The situation was corrected by the store, but apparently the correction was not reported to the credit bureau. Have students write a statement of no more than 100 words to correct the information in the credit bureau record.

Have students look for magazine articles that tell about experi-

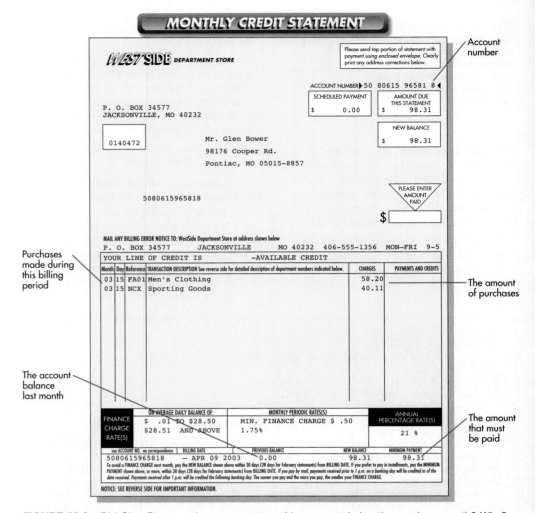

FIGURE 32-3 Did Glen Bower make a payment on this account during the previous month? Why?

payments and credit memorandums. A **credit memorandum** is a written record of the amount subtracted from your account when you return merchandise. If you discover an error on a statement, you should notify the seller at once.

Credit card fraud is a major problem reported by the Federal Trade Commission. To avoid being defrauded, your credit card account statements need to be checked very carefully for errors. One system used by consumers is to keep a file of sales slips when a

credit card is used—each form normally has "sales draft, cardholder copy" printed on it. It is yours; keep it. When the statement arrives, check the items on the statement against the sales slips on file. If a charge is shown on the statement for which you do not have a sales draft, check that charge and report any error to the bank or credit card company immediately. Staple to the statement the sales slips for the items listed on the statement and file them for future reference. Also compare payments and previous balances with your records.

Critical Thinking Skills-Problem Solving

Problem-solving skills, which include recognizing a problem and devising a plan of action, are applied throughout every chapter in this text. Each time a student participates in a Cooperative Learning or Teams activity, problem-solving skills are applied in a group situation. Each time a student completes a math application in Calculate Business Data, decisions are

made as to which mathematical approach must be taken. For each Technology Application problem, students must decide which template problem to use, which piece of software to load, and how to solve the problem. Emphasize to students how they are using problem solving in their day-to-day tasks and make them aware of the skills they are developing.

FYI

There is no such thing as a "quick fix" for credit problems. Credit repair companies and credit clinics that charge huge fees and offer dubious guarantees are often fraudulent and should be avoided.

The Importance of Accurate Records

Another thing that you can do to help avoid credit record problems is to keep your own records. This is a good personal business practice that too often is not followed.

Many errors are simply honest mistakes, and businesses are as eager to correct them as you are. Your creditworthiness may be at stake, and the reputation of the business may be hurt by bad publicity if errors are not corrected. When you receive a sales slip, a credit memorandum, or a monthly statement, you should examine it to make sure that it is correct.

When making a payment by check, write the date and the check number on the statement. Keep your statements and sales slips. They will be valuable in the future if any questions arise as to whether they have been paid. You should be able to prove that payment was made. A canceled check is valuable as evidence that payment has been made because it has the endorsement of the payee on the back.

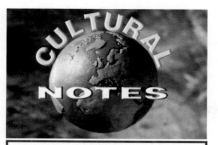

Cultural baggage describes the notion that individuals carry their cultural values, beliefs, and assumptions with them at all times. Our cultural baggage influences how we respond to situations.

When you do not pay by check, you need some other method of showing that you have made payment. A written form that acknowledges that payment was made is called a **receipt**. The receipt form has spaces for entering the number of the receipt, the date, the name of the person making payment, the amount of the payment in words, the reason for the payment, the amount in figures, and the signature of the person receiving the payment. A stub is filled out to show the same information. Figure 32-4 shows a receipt properly filled out. Each stub and receipt is numbered so that the customer's receipt can be compared with the creditor's stub if a dispute arises.

PAYMENT RECEIPT

No. 20
Date Oct. 6, 20--
To Tami Liang
For Deposit
$ 50.00

No. 20   October 6 20 --
Received of Tami Liang
Fifty and 00/100 _____ Dollars
For Deposit on school ring
              Kauffman's Jewelry Store
$ 50.00   By Tracy Mitchell

FIGURE 32-4
Does the receipt tell us how much the ring costs or how much is still owed?

ences of people who are deep in debt or talk with someone involved with credit counseling and find out why people have credit problems. Have students record the reasons given and report them to the class.

People borrow money for many different reasons. Some people borrow money to consolidate their debts. Students should provide written responses to the following questions: (a) What is meant by consolidating debts? (b) Is there any advantage in consolidating debts and in making a single monthly payment on a single loan? (c) How might consolidating debts reduce the amount of each payment? Would the borrower be saving money?

The Equal Credit Opportunity Act permits lenders and creditors to use a credit scoring system. The credit scoring system assigns points to various factors that relate to whether a person is a good credit risk. Have students find out more about credit scoring systems by reading articles discussing these systems. Ask them to visit a retail store, a bank, or some other lending institution and learn what they can about the experiences that businesses have had with credit scoring.

SUMMARIZE

Assign one or more students to compose two test-type questions for each page in the chapter. Write each question on a piece of paper. Collect the questions, scramble them in a container, and ask each student to draw two, neither of which can be her or his own. The student must now answer the

Chapter 32 *Credit Records and Regulations* **443**

Basic Skills-Math

In order for students to become contributing workers in our society, it is important that they become proficient in the basic skills of reading, writing, arithmetic, and mathematics. In order to prepare students for the school-to-work transition, we must teach these skills in our classrooms. Applying math across the curriculum is an important element in contempo-

rary education. As a part of end-of-chapter activities, Calculate Business Data enables students to apply their math skills. Appendix B: Math Review, Appendix C: Determining Percentages and Interest in Business, and Appendix D: Using Measurements in Business, also apply arithmetic and math skills.

SCANS

443

questions, and the question's creator must confirm whether the answer is right or wrong. Other students may volunteer answers if the student does not answer a question correctly. The teacher serves as facilitator.

EVALUATE

- Assign Activities and Projects for Chapter 32.
- Administer the printed test or ExamView for Chapter 32.
- Administer the printed test or ExamView for Unit 9.
- Assign School-To-Work/SCANS portfolio activities for Unit 9.

Sometimes a receipt is not given. Instead, the word "paid" is written or stamped on the bill or statement. The date and the initials or signature of the one who received your money should be included.

YOU HAVE RIGHTS

Most businesses are honest and forthright in their business dealings. Nevertheless, it has been necessary for our federal and state governments to pass laws to protect consumers who engage in credit transactions. The Truth-in-Lending Law of 1968 launched a series of laws that deal with various aspects of credit and lending practices. It was followed in 1980 by the Truth-in-Lending Simplification Act.

The **Truth-in-Lending Law** requires that you be told the cost of a credit purchase in writing before you sign a credit agreement. It requires, for instance, that the APR and total finance charge be clearly stated. The Truth-in-Lending Law also protects consumers against unauthorized use of credit cards. The law limits your liability to $50 for unauthorized credit card purchases made prior to

notification of the issuer. You are not liable for any fraudulent charges made after you have notified the credit card company—even if someone charges several hundred dollars before you report your card missing. You can notify the company by telephone, but you should also put your notification in writing, citing the date of the phone call. In the example at the opening of this chapter, you would have a problem since you waited too long to report the loss of your credit card. You could be liable for more than the $200 charged before you reported your lost card.

The **Equal Credit Opportunity Act** prohibits creditors from denying credit because of age, race, sex, or marital status. Young people who may have just entered the labor market cannot be denied credit based only on their ages. Older, possibly retired, people also have special protection under this act. Married women who previously found it difficult to establish credit in their own names now have a legal right to do so. Under this law, a woman has a right to her own credit if she proves to be creditworthy.

Unless your state still requires age 21 as the legal age to enter into a contract, you

What rights do consumers have when engaging in credit transactions?

cannot be denied credit based on your age alone. Your creditworthiness would have to be investigated. Any person who is denied credit must, upon request, be given a written statement of the reasons for rejection.

Another important piece of legislation is the Fair Credit Billing Act. The **Fair Credit Billing Act** is a law that requires prompt correction of billing mistakes when they are brought to the attention of a business in a prescribed manner. To get a correction of an error, you must notify the creditor in writing within 60 days after your statement was mailed. A good rule is to report errors as soon as you discover them. After you report the errors, the following four points are important:

- While waiting for an answer, you are not required to pay any amount in question.

- Your complaint must be acknowledged by the creditor within 30 days unless your statement is corrected before that time.

- You do not pay finance charges on any amount in error.

- If no error is found, the creditor must bill you again and may include finance charges that have accumulated plus any minimum payments that were missed while the statement was being questioned.

The Fair Credit Billing Act also provides that you may withhold payment of any balance due on defective merchandise or services purchased with a credit card. Your first step should be to contact the business and try to resolve the problem. Many situations can be corrected if the complaint is made in a courteous but firm manner. The law does protect you if you have made this "good faith" effort.

The **Fair Credit Reporting Act** is the law that gives consumers the right to know what specific information credit bureaus are providing to potential creditors, employers, and insurers. It provides that if credit is denied on the basis of information in a credit report, the applicant must be given the name, address,

and phone number of the credit bureau that provided the information. In addition, credit records for both a husband and wife are kept if both are responsible for the debt. This allows a credit history to be developed for each spouse.

Prior to the passage of this law, many consumers were unaware that reports on their bill-paying habits were available to potential lenders. This act makes those reports available to the consumer and provides ways in which information can be accessed and corrected. It also requires that any information dealing with personal bankruptcy that is more than ten years old must be automatically deleted. Any other adverse information must be deleted if it is more than seven years old.

Monique and Gary Buckeye have a right to see their credit bureau report. They requested it and did not have to pay to see it since they had been denied credit. They discovered two errors. In their former community, there was a couple with a name similar to theirs. That couple's credit record was bad, and some of their unpaid debts showed up on Monique and Gary's report. Also, one bill that was disputed with a local retailer was recorded as not being paid.

Monique and Gary had a right to demand that the error of recording someone else's bad credit habits be removed from their record. They also were permitted to write a brief statement describing their side of the disputed bill with the local retailer. After taking these two actions, their good credit record was reestablished and they received the loan they needed.

YOUR OWN CREDIT HISTORY

It is important for you to know your credit rights under the law. Building your own good record of creditworthiness is even more important.

Things You Can Do Now

To some extent you can begin building a credit record while you are still in school.

Basic Skills-Reading

Direct students to the vocabulary terms that appear in Develop Your Business Language at the end of the chapter. Have a student read these terms out loud so that all students will be aware of the various new terms that will occur. This is the second step to establishing the purpose of reading assignments. By previewing terms, students will be able to decide facts that are relevant when they begin reading the chapter. Ask students to write what kind of information they are going to gain from this chapter. Then explore the various headings, illustrations, and captions in the chapter to preview the actual material that will be covered. By previewing these chapter elements, students will be able to decide facts that are relevant when they begin reading the chapter. Ask students to write a summary of the points that will be covered in the chapter.

SCANS

Since trust and reliability are important in matters of credit, you can help to establish yourself by having a good record of grades and school attendance. Both employers and creditors know that behavior patterns developed in school tend to carry on after graduation.

In addition, it is good to have both a checking and a savings account. If you have a balance in each account and do not overdraw your checking account, a lender can see that you can handle money. Making regular deposits to your savings account also suggests that you will be a good credit risk.

Some people establish credit records by charging small purchases. For instance, if you buy a sweater on credit and make the payments according to the agreement, you have taken an important step toward proving you

are a good credit risk. Or you may want to pay off your account within 30 days and avoid an interest charge. Either way you will be building a good credit record.

Having a good part-time or full-time employment record also helps to establish a good credit record. Changing jobs often does not look good to a creditor. Being on a job for two or more years is a positive part of a good credit record.

Sources of Help

If you find that you just cannot pay your bills when they are due, you should follow these four steps: First, contact your creditors and explain your situation. Second, make a realistic proposal for when and what you can pay. Don't just say "I can't pay." Third, keep any promises you make. Fourth, make a

What should you do if you need help with a credit problem?

Basic Skills-Reading

Direct students to the end-of-chapter activities. Review each activity heading and discuss how each contributes to the understanding of the chapter. The Student Activity Worksheet, Basic Skills—Reading, in the School-To-Work/SCANS Activity Masters, may be used to serve as a guideline for discussion of each of these points.

written copy of your agreement to avoid disagreements later.

You may be able to work out a debt repayment plan. A **debt repayment plan** is an agreement developed cooperatively by a creditor and a debtor to reduce payments to a more manageable level and still pay off the debt. This plan is good for both the creditor and the debtor.

One thing to avoid is being misled by advertisements that tell you: "Erase bad credit! 100 percent guaranteed." Claims such as these are fraudulent. No one can unconditionally correct a bad credit record—it does not work that way. If you need help with a credit problem, contact a reputable organization such as the Consumer Credit Counseling Service.

1. Lenders want to know your ability to repay your debt and your willingness to do so.

2. Finances: how much you earn, what kinds of savings and investments you have, and whether you have any other sources of income. Reliability: your occupation, how long you have been employed, how long you have lived at the same address, whether you own or rent a home, and what your school record reveals about you.

3. The credit application provides information needed to make decisions about granting credit. Credit references are used to verify information that you include on the application.

4. Your signature indicates that you have read the application, understand it, and agree to the credit terms.

5. A credit bureau is a company that gathers information on credit users and sells it in the form of credit reports to credit grantors.

6. Credit reports show if payments are made on time and if any action has been taken to collect overdue bills.

7. The receipt is proof that payment is made. If there is a doubt about a payment, the receipt can be used as evidence of a payment.

8. The credit memorandum is proof for the customer that merchandise has been returned and the amount has been deducted from the charge account. The credit memorandum is evidence in the event that a question arises about a return of merchandise.

9. A debtor might have to use canceled checks to prove that a payment has been made.

10. A statement of account lists purchases, payments, credits, amount owed, and the amount that should be paid.

11. Keep the credit card sales slips, check them against items on the credit card statement, and file the sales slips with the statement for future reference.

12. Truth-in-Lending Law: requires APR and finance charges be stated in writing. Fair Credit Billing Act: requires prompt correction of mistakes when reported properly. Fair Credit Reporting Act: requires

Chapter REVIEW

BUSINESS NOTES

1. A credit application is a document on which you provide information needed by a lender. A credit bureau gathers information on credit users. A credit record documents your credit history.

2. Credit statements should be checked carefully and errors reported as soon as they are discovered.

3. Laws and regulations protect you if your credit card is lost. They prohibit denial of credit because of age, race, sex, or marital status. They also provide ways of correcting errors in your credit history.

4. You can maintain a good credit history by paying your bills on time and working out a plan for repayment if you find it difficult to make payments to your creditors.

REVIEW YOUR READING

1. What two things do lenders want to know before making a decision about granting credit?

2. Name three things lenders want to know about your finances and five things about reliability.

3. What is the purpose of a credit application? Why do credit references have to be listed?

4. What does your signature on a credit application signify?

5. What is the purpose of a credit bureau? Who uses its services?

6. What are some examples of the information contained in a credit bureau report?

7. In what ways is a receipt important? What information does it contain?

8. Why is a credit memorandum important?

9. What use might a debtor have for canceled checks?

10. What information is shown on a statement of account?

11. What is the procedure for checking a credit card account statement?

12. What are examples of laws that help protect consumers in credit transactions? What kinds of protection do they provide?

13. What should be done when errors are found in credit statements?

14. What are some things that can be done to build a credit record?

15. What kinds of help are available to debtors who have credit problems?

COMMUNICATE BUSINESS CONCEPTS

16. Sergio Torres operates a multimedia store. One day Bill Cross, a total stranger, asked if he could buy a CD-ROM encyclopedia on credit. Mr. Cross explained that he had just moved into town two weeks ago. The moving expenses took most of his cash, but he has a good job and will be able to pay $30 a month beginning next month.

a. What other information should Sergio get from Mr. Cross?
b. What sources of information could Sergio use before making a final decision?
c. Would you extend credit to Mr. Cross? Why or why not?

17. Cheryl Oakwood wants to open an account at the Hewitt Department Store. She objects,

credit bureau reports to identify both husband and wife if both are responsible for debt. Equal Credit Opportunity Act: prohibits denying credit because of age, race, sex, or marital status.

13. Errors should be reported as soon as they are discovered.

14. To build a good credit record, you should establish trust and reliability while in school, have a checking and savings account, make a few small purchases on credit, and pay promptly.

15. Debtors who need help might be able to arrange a debt repayment plan. Also, they can

go to a consumer credit counseling service for advice and assistance.

COMMUNICATE BUSINESS CONCEPTS

16. (a) In any event, before credit is extended, Sergio Torres should investigate Mr. Cross's story. If Mr. Cross is honest, he will not object to the investigation. Mr. Torres should find out about Mr. Cross's length of employment, what other charge accounts he has (if any), whether

however, to giving the credit manager information about such things as where she has other charge accounts, whether she owns real estate, where she works, and in which bank she maintains an account.

a. Why did the credit manager want this information?

b. In what ways could a credit bureau report help this manager?

c. Does Cheryl have a right to refuse to give this information? If so, can credit be denied her?

18. Donna Stratford has been working on her first job for seven months. Her checking account has a balance of $159. She has also put aside $50 in cash for an emergency. She wants to buy a clock radio that sells for $69.95 at a store that offers credit. Donna has never used credit and would like to establish a credit rating. What can she do to get a credit record started? What advice would you give her if she decided to buy this clock radio on credit?

19. Following is a list of consumer transactions. For each, explain whether there would be a cash receipt, a credit memorandum, a canceled check, or a credit card sales slip. Also explain how and why each record should be saved, if you believe it should be saved.

a. Paid cash for flowers that had been ordered in advance

b. Bought a pair of shoes using a credit card

c. Returned a pair of slacks, purchased a week ago on a charge account, because they did not fit

d. Paid $35 in cash toward a $170 balance owed on a charge account with a local store

e. Wrote a check for $125 to pay off a credit card account balance

20. Suzanne Winters does not believe in buying anything on credit. She says that too many people get into trouble using credit cards and that there are too many errors made in credit transactions. She also believes that there is no protection for consumers using credit and no help if they get into credit difficulties. Explain to Suzanne ways in which laws protect consumers who engage in credit transactions and tell her about some of the kinds of help that are available for consumers who have credit problems.

19. (a) Cash receipt. Generally not necessary to save it. (b) Credit card sales slip. Keep it for several months. Check against statement to verify amount charged. (c) Credit memo. Keep it for several months. Check against statement to be sure credit is recorded correctly. (d) Cash receipt. Keep it for several months. Check against statement to be sure payment is accurately recorded. (e) Canceled check. Keep it for several months. Check against statement to be sure payment is recorded accurately.

20. Suzanne should be told about the consumer protection laws, consumer counseling services, and debt-repayment plans.

DEVELOP YOUR BUSINESS LANGUAGE

For each numbered item, find the term that has the same meaning.

21. A form on which you provide information needed by a lender to make a decision about granting credit or approving a loan.

22. A company that gathers information on credit users and sells that information in the form of credit reports to credit grantors.

23. An act that prohibits creditors from denying credit because of age, race, sex, or marital status.

24. A written form that acknowledges payment was made.

25. A written record of the amount subtracted from an account when merchandise has been returned.

26. A record of the transactions that you have completed with a business during a billing period.

27. A law that requires that you be told the cost of a credit purchase in writing before you sign a credit agreement.

28. An agreement developed cooperatively by a creditor and debtor to reduce payments to a more manageable level and still pay off the debt.

29. A law that gives consumers the right to know what specific information credit bureaus are providing to potential creditors, employers, and insurers.

30. A law that requires prompt correction of billing mistakes when they are brought to the attention of a business in a prescribed manner.

31. Having established a credit record that shows you are a good credit risk.

32. A report that shows the debts you owe, how often you use credit, and whether you pay your debts on time.

KEY TERMS
credit application
credit bureau
credit memorandum
credit record
creditworthy
debt repayment plan
Equal Credit Opportunity Act
Fair Credit Billing Act
Fair Credit Reporting Act
receipt
statement or statement of account
Truth-in-Lending Law

DEVELOP YOUR BUSINESS LANGUAGE

21. credit application
22. credit bureau
23. Equal Credit Opportunity Act
24. receipt
25. credit memorandum
26. statement of account
27. Truth-in-Lending Law
28. debt repayment plan
29. Fair Credit Reporting Act
30. Fair Credit Billing Act
31. creditworthy
32. credit record

he is renting or buying a home, and what credit references he has. (b) Mr. Torres should check with the local credit bureau, with Mr. Cross's employer, and with the credit references furnished. (c) Students' answers will vary, but generally credit would not be extended without additional information.

17. (a) The credit manager needed this information so that there would be a basis for a credit decision. (b) A credit bureau report would give the credit manager the information desired. (c) She has the right to refuse the information, but the credit manager also has the right to refuse to grant credit.

18. Donna should ask if she could charge the purchase of the clock radio. After arranging for credit and charging her purchase, she should pay her account in full when it is due. If the store that is selling the clock radio cannot give Donna credit, she should delay her purchase and apply for a bank credit card. With a bank credit card, she could return to the store and purchase the radio. Her "$50 emergency money" should be deposited in a savings account.

33. Criteria would involve the three Cs of credit. Does she have the capacity to repay debt? Her employment record is not good; she has changed jobs too often. Her bank accounts have been overdrawn, and she keeps low balances. Does she have capital? Lenders would want to know about possessions, such as a stereo, television, and jewelry, that could be used as collateral for a loan. What is her character (honesty and willingness to repay debt)? Students would have to make assumptions about her character.

34. Answers will vary. Students probably would be unwilling to make the loan because Semantha Mae does not appear to be a good credit risk. If they do make the loan, they would want it to be secured. Some might make the loan because she is a friend—and that's a good way to lose a friend!

CALCULATE BUSINESS DATA

35. (a) Enrique Navarro: balance is 0; Lynne Goldberg: balance is $10.00 − $5.00 = $5.00; Eloise Little: balance is $102.67 − $50.00 = $52.67; Sam Nader: balance is $54.89 − $25.00 = $29.89; Ruth Smith: balance is 0 (b) $44.22 + $5.00 + $50.00 + $25.00 + $19.35 = $143.57.

36. (a) gloves, $18.00; purses, $46.00 (2 @ $23.00); necklace, 55.00; shoes, $126.00 (3 @ $42.00); Total, $245.00 purchased (b) gloves, $18.00; purse, $23.00; Total, $41.00 credit memorandum (c) $245.00 − $41.00 = $204.00 owed after credit memorandum.

37. Board: 250 meters × 3.3 = 825 feet × $3.80 = $3,135.00; Fabric: 90 meters × 1.1 = 99 yards × $8.15 = $806.85; Varnish: 50 liters × 0.26 = 13 gals. × $26.95 = $350.35; Total Purchase = $4,292.20; Four percent discount: $4,292.20 × 0.04 = $171.69 savings.

38. (a) $152.00 + $28.00 + $21.50 + $24.75 + $2.28 = $228.53 subtotal; $228.53 − $10.75 = $217.78 (b) $217.78 − $30 = $187.78 (c) $187.78 × 0.015 = $2.82.

DECISION-MAKING STRATEGIES

Semantha Mae has been out of school for three years and has held four different jobs with different employers. She has been on her present job for two months.

Her monthly take-home pay is $1,362. She shares an apartment with two friends to keep expenses down, but she is always in debt. Each month she is short of what she needs to pay all of her charge accounts. Her checking account is frequently overdrawn.

Semantha has decided it would be better to live by herself; she blames her roommates for her credit spending sprees. She has come to you for a loan of $2,000. Her new apartment will cost $400 a month, and she wants to pay off some of her bills that are past due. She assures you that she will pay you at least $50 each month.

33. What are some criteria you would use to determine whether a personal loan for Semantha would be a good idea? What additional information might you want?

34. Would you loan the money to Semantha? Why or why not?

CALCULATE BUSINESS DATA

35. The Country Boutique grants regular credit to steady customers. Today the boutique received checks in the mail from several customers as shown in the table.
    a. What was the balance in each account?
    b. What was the total amount received from charge customers?

Name	Amount Owed	Amount Paid
Enrique Navarro	$44.22	$44.22
Lynne Goldberg	10.00	5.00
Eloise Little	102.67	50.00
Sam Nader	54.89	25.00
Ruth Smith	19.35	19.35

36. Linda Spencer made the following credit purchases: gloves, $18; 2 purses at $23 each; necklace, $55; 3 pairs of shoes at $42 each. Later she returned the gloves and one purse and received a credit memo.
    a. What was the total of Linda's purchases before she returned the gloves and the purse?
    b. What was the amount of the credit memo?
    c. How much did she owe after she received the credit memorandum?

37. Saburo Nozaki bought some materials needed for the boat he was building. He purchased the following: 250 meters of board, $3.80 per foot; 90 meters of fabric, $8.15 per yard; and 50 liters of marine varnish, $26.95 per gallon.(Refer to Appendix D.)
    a. What was the total amount of his purchase?
    b. If he were offered a 4 percent discount for paying cash, how much would he save?

38. Dixie Kauffman used her bank charge card for the following purchases: Earl's Clothing Store, 2 shirts at $14 each; Wingo's Hardware Company, 2 gallons of paint at $10.75 each; PaDelford Family Restaurant, $24.75. She returned a gallon of paint and received a credit slip for $10.75 from Wingo's Hardware. Dixie's statement showed a balance of $152 from the previous month plus a finance charge of $2.28.
    a. If Dixie pays her account in full, how much will she pay?
    b. If she decides to make a minimum payment of $30, how much will she still owe?
    c. If the finance charge is $1\frac{1}{2}$ percent per month on the unpaid balance, what will be the finance charge next month if she only pays the $30 this month?

TECHNOLOGY APPLICATION

Using the *Intro to Business* Data CD and your word processing program software, select problem CH32. After the problem appears on your screen, complete the following activities. Then, print and sign your completed forms. If you do not have a printer available, save the forms on a data disk to give to your teacher.

39. You are applying for a credit card. Complete the application with information about yourself plus the following information. You have lived at your current address for $1\frac{1}{2}$ years and your rent is $450 per month. You have been employed for two years. You make $7 per hour and work 8 hours per day, 21 days per month. Do not complete the sections for Other Credit, Joint Account Information, or Additional Cards. For the information that you enter, use a different font from the one used on the rest of the application.

40. You are preparing a retail installment contract. Complete the contract with information about yourself plus the following information: cash price, $437.50; down payment, $87.50; amount financed, $350.00; installment price, $507.02; finance charge, $69.52; annual percentage rate, 18 percent; number of months to pay, 24; monthly payment, $17.48. For the date of the first payment, enter the first day of the month following the current month. For the information that you enter, use italics and a different font from the one used on the rest of the application.

TECHNOLOGY APPLICATION

In this activity, students use a computer to solve a business problem using a file that is provided on the data CD that accompanies *Intro to Business*. Instructions for using the data CD are included in a **README** file on the disk. Solutions are provided on the Instructor's Resource CD.

COMMUNICATING for SUCCESS

GIVING AND FOLLOWING DIRECTIONS—EASIER SAID THAN DONE

Employers and employees operate under a philosophy referred to as a "span of control." Span of control means employees are responsible for conducting the work delegated to them by their formal job description and their employer. In your job you are responsible to the company through the directions and actions of your supervisor. This requires that you be aware of your responsibilities and have the ability to give and follow directions.

Directions are messages sent to employees about actions required and decisions to be made. Directions can be either written or verbal and can be expressed formally, informally, or in an implied manner. Written directions tend to be formal. For example, a written formal direction may request that the employee perform a task in a specific manner within a specific time period. Verbal directions can also be formal but are generally informal. Written or verbal directions that are implied often refer to a job description, and rely on an employee to complete a task.

Typically, employers rely on a Standard Operating Procedure, which is a method of making decisions about tasks common throughout the company. Directions for these common tasks are implied because the company has an established method for handling them while doing business.

Important to the concept of a Standard Operating Procedure is the clarity of directions. Whether giving or following directions, employers and employees must be very precise in how they issue statements of direction. Misinterpreted directions can lead to the loss of sales, a damaged business reputation, and the loss of a job.

In issuing directions, employers and employees must rely on their ability to make decisions. This decision-making process typically includes six steps:

- Define the problem.
- Identify problem solutions.
- Evaluate the potential solutions.
- Choose the solution with the greatest benefit.
- Act on your choice of solution.
- Review your choice.

Directions are a common form of communication within a business, and as an employee or employer, you should be prepared to issue directions in a friendly, constructive manner that benefits the overall organization.

CRITICAL THINKING
1. What are directions?
2. What might be the result of misinterpreted directions?

GLOBAL BUSINESS PROJECT

Attitudes toward buying and selling on credit vary around the world. In this phase of the global business plan project, students will attempt to become aware of any such differences in the country they have been studying. They will also need to determine the forms of consumer credit used in this nation. The company's use of credit will also be considered as students identify sources of business loans that could be used to finance international business operations.

To complete each phase of this project, students are encouraged to use various resources—textbook content, library materials, World Wide Web sites, interviews, advertisements, product packages, in-store observations. The individual activities are planned for use as either (1) an on-going course project, or (2) individual assignments.

Whether used as a continuing project or for selected activities, consider having students work in teams. This small group experience provides a valuable skill for future learning and work situations.

In addition to search engines, these selected web sites can be helpful for this unit:
- International Trade Administration of the U.S. Dept. of Commerce (www.ita.doc.gov)
- World Factbook of the Central Intelligence Agency (www.odci.gov/cia/publications/factbook/index.html)
- World Trade Organization at (www.wto.org)
- Current country information at (yahoo.com/regional/countries)
- Import-export information at (www.internationalist.com/)
- Latin American country information (www.lanic.utexas.edu)
- Asian country information (asnic.utexas.edu) (www.asia-inc.com)
- Eastern European country information (reenic.utexas.edu)

GLOBAL BUSINESS PROJECT

ANALYZE CREDIT USE

Buying and selling on credit is most common in industrialized economies. However, some form of consumer credit is used in most countries. In this phase of the global business plan, you will research various aspects of selling on credit when doing business in another country. You will also identify sources of business loans that could be used to finance international business operations.

PROJECT GOALS
- Research different cultural attitudes toward buying on credit.
- Describe the process for selling on credit for international business transactions.
- Identify sources of business loans for funding international business operations.

PROJECT ACTIVITIES
Using your textbook, library materials, web sites, interviews with people, and other resources, complete the following activities:
- Attitudes toward the use of credit vary from country to country. Using the company in your portfolio, (or select a country), obtain information about the cultural attitudes related to the use of credit in that nation. How might this information affect your organization's business procedures?
- Most organizations extend credit to their customers. Describe the process that you might use when selling on credit to customers in other countries. What actions might be necessary to assure collection of amounts owed?
- To start international business operations, financing from other sources may be necessary. List the sources of business loans. Describe what information would need to be provided when applying for a business loan.

PROJECT WRAP-UP
1. Continue your portfolio (folder, file box, or other container) for storing and referring back to the information and materials you created in the activities above. These items in your portfolio will be used for various components of your global business plan.
2. Create an in-class presentation (or video) that shows a discussion between a manager who needs money for international business operations and a person who is considering lending the money to the company.

- Middle East country information (menic.utexas.edu)
- World Bank (www.worldbank.org)
- Export-Import Bank of the United States (www.exim.gov)
- Small Business Administration (www.sba.gov)
- Export assistance (www.unzco.com/)

FOCUS ON CAREERS

CREDIT OCCUPATIONS

You have learned about the important role credit plays in our economy. Most individuals and businesses find it necessary to use credit for some purchases. As a result, many workers are involved in the processing of credit.

JOB TITLES

Job titles commonly found in this career area include:
- Bill and Account Collector
- Credit Authorizer
- Private Detective
- Credit Clerk
- Loan Officer
- Interviewer
- Credit Analyst
- Loan Counselor
- Information and Record Clerk
- Financial Manager
- Teller
- Customer Service Representative

EMPLOYMENT OUTLOOK (THROUGH THE YEAR 2005)
- In most of these credit occupations growth will be average for all occupations through 2005.
- Computer technology will not have a negative impact on these jobs due to the interpersonal nature of much of the work.
- The need for replacements due to transfers and retirements will result in a good number of job openings for qualified applicants.

EDUCATION AND TRAINING
- A high school diploma is a requirement for all of these occupations.
- Employers prefer applicants who have completed business courses and have computer skills, especially database applications.
- Some employers look for education beyond high school, especially in two-year business administration programs.
- Credit managers generally have four-year college degrees and financial experience.

SALARY LEVELS (IN RECENT YEARS)
- Median annual earnings of loan officers are $41,000. The middle 50 percent earn between $31,000 and $57,000, and the top 10 percent earn more than $82,000.
- The median salary for loan interviewers and clerks is $26,000 and for credit authorizers and clerks $25,000.
- Salaries of collection clerks vary considerably. Median hourly earnings of bill and account collectors are $12.

CRITICAL THINKING
1. Which job titles in this career area appeal to you most? Give some reasons for your choices.
2. What are some things you will have to do to achieve success in the career you selected?

FOCUS ON CAREERS

The careers listed in the Career Focus come from the *Occupational Outlook Handbook*, an online publication (www.bls.gov/oco) of the federal government. The O*NET codes for these job titles are Bill and Account Collector, 43-3011.00; Credit Authorizer, 43-4041.01; Private Detective, 33-9021.00; Credit Clerk 43-4041.02; Loan Officer, 13-2072.00; Interviewer, 43-4131.00; Credit Analyst, 13-2041.00; Loan Counselor, 13-2071.00; Information and Record Clerk, 43-4171.00, 43-4199.99; Financial Manager, 11-3031.01, 11-3031.02; Teller, 43-3071.00; Customer Service Representative, 43-4051.00.

Students should be encouraged to read through the list of credit occupations and the two Career Highlights contained in Chapters 29 and 31. Career awareness is a vital part of making the right occupational choice in the future. Career Focus Worksheets are available in the School-To-Work/SCANS Activity Masters.

CRITICAL THINKING
Answers, of course, to the two Critical Thinking questions will vary widely. Students should be encouraged to select one job even if they are not really interested in a career area. Thinking about why a certain job might possibly be appealing is a forced-thinking exercise that results in self-reflections and self-examination. Answering these questions also gives certain career areas a sharper focus within students' minds.

UNIT 10

BUILDING YOUR PORTFOLIO

CAREER DEVELOPMENT – PREPARING FOR THE INTERVIEW

The Building Your Portfolio career exercise will help your students establish a personal history—where they have been, where they are now, and where they are going. This career exercise will require students to anticipate interview questions.

As preparation for a possible job interview, have students answer some job interview questions. Questions posed might include: (1) Tell me about yourself. (2) What are your qualifications for this job? (3) Why do you want this job? (4) What are your strengths/weaknesses? (5) How has your education and training prepared you for this job? (6) Why do you think that I should hire you? Answering these questions should help students to prepare carefully for an interview and to evaluate their qualifications for employment.

As a supplemental activity, you may refer to the School–To–Work/SCANS Activity Masters.

TEACHING STRATEGIES

SCANS

Special Features

Media/Technology

Chapter	Spreadsheet Software	Database Software	Word Processing Software	Internet	Video
33	■				■
34			■		■
35		■		■	■
36			■		■

Resources

SOFTWARE

Excel, Word, WordPerfect, Works, and ClarisWorks for Mac and Windows

Word Pro, ASCII, QuattroPro, Lotus, and Access for Windows

SOUTH-WESTERN EDUCATIONAL PUBLISHING PRODUCTS

Semmen and Semmen-Brown. *The Stock Market: A Computer Simulation*. 1997. Cincinnati: South-Western Educational Publishing Company. Windows Disk 0-538-64715-9. Mac Disk 0-538-64714-0.

NAIC. *Investing in Your Future*. 2000. Cincinnati: South-Western Educational Publishing Company. Text-Workbook. 0-538-68607-3.

BOOKS

Tobias. *The Only Investment Guide You'll Ever Need*. 1999. Harvest Books.

Gardner and Gardner. *The Motley Fool's You Have More Than You Think: The Foolish Guide to Investing What You Have*. 1999. Simon & Schuster.

PERIODICALS

Moody's *Handbook of Common Stocks*. Annual. New York, NY.

Standard and Poor's Encyclopedia. Quarterly. New York, NY.

The Value Line Investment Survey. Weekly. New York, NY.

The Wall Street Journal. New York, NY.

GOVERNMENT PUBLICATIONS

Occupational Outlook Handbook, U.S. Department of Labor, Washington, DC.

What Work Requires of Schools: A SCANS Report for America 2000, U.S. Department of Labor, Washington, DC

MEDIA/TECHNOLOGY

Publisher's web sites:
www.intro2business.swep.com
www.swep.com
www.thomson.com

UNIT 10

SAVINGS AND INVESTMENT STRATEGIES

Savings and investment plans are the topics of this unit. Chapter 33 covers how savings grow through compound interest and criteria for selecting a savings plan. Savings accounts and other institutional savings plans are introduced in Chapter 34. In Chapter 35, the fundamentals of investing in bonds and stocks are discussed. Chapter 36 provides information on making investments in real estate, commodities, and collectibles. Use the resources listed on the previous page, especially those from South-Western Educational Publishing, as you prepare to teach these chapters.

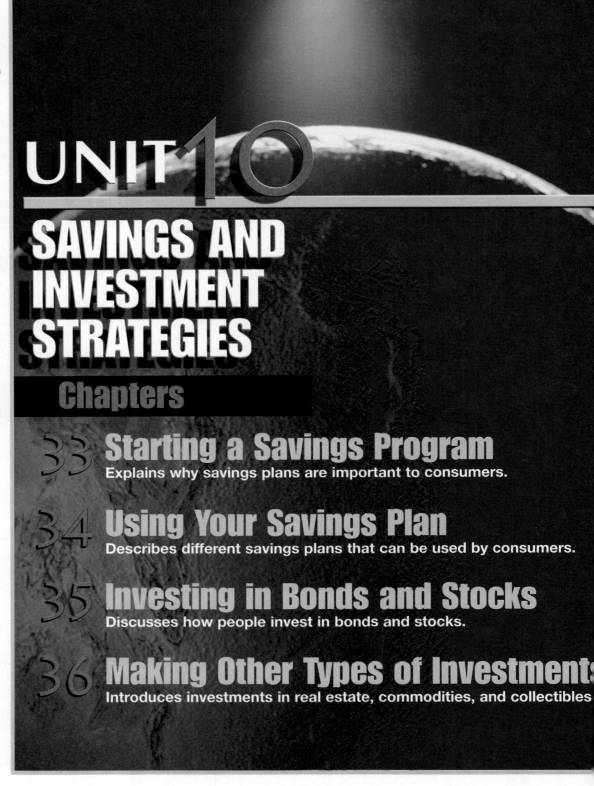

UNIT 10

SAVINGS AND INVESTMENT STRATEGIES

Chapters

33 Starting a Savings Program
Explains why savings plans are important to consumers.

34 Using Your Savings Plan
Describes different savings plans that can be used by consumers.

35 Investing in Bonds and Stocks
Discusses how people invest in bonds and stocks.

36 Making Other Types of Investments
Introduces investments in real estate, commodities, and collectibles.

Kick-Off Activity

Investigating Business Media

The following exercise asks students to choose an article from *The Wall Street Journal,* the financial section of a newspaper, or a business magazine and to inquire about a topic related to this unit.

Students should select an article from *The Wall Street Journal* or a financial magazine that deals with the financing arrangements or strategies of a particular company. Then ask students to answer the following questions:

1 What form of financing did the company choose? Did the article indicate why the company selected this form of financing? Was the financing arrangement different from methods used previously?

2 Who provided the financing for the company? Was this arrangement considered unusual, or was it routine?

BU$INESSBRIEF

A SLAM DUNK INVESTMENT OR A MISSED FREE THROW?

The headline could have read, "Final Score: Boston Celtics 104, Houston Rockets 98, stock price up ¹/₈ !"

In the mid-1980s, the owners of the Boston Celtics, a team in the National Basketball Association (NBA), decided to take the team *public*. Taking the team public meant that ownership of the team was expanded to include other people. A limited partnership was created with shares sold on the New York Stock Exchange. Buyers of the shares were known as limited partners. The original owners became general partners.

A stock exchange, or stock market, is a place that brings sellers and buyers of stocks together. Sellers are hoping to find buyers who will pay higher prices for shares than what the sellers originally paid. In this way, sellers make a return on their investments. Buyers are looking for shares that are expected to increase in price so that the shares can later be sold at a profit. By negotiating with each other about prices, sellers and buyers determine whether the price of shares goes up or down.

Several million shares of Celtics stock were made available. This public offering, however, accounted for less than 50 percent of the value of the team. The general partners still controlled the team's overall operations.

Why did all the shares offered sell out within a couple of days? This investment opportunity had a unique appeal to sports fans. Championships and star players of the 1980s—such as Larry Bird, Robert Parrish, and Kevin McHale—made the Celtics popular. Buyers of the shares believed that the price would go up over time.

Like most stocks, the price of the Celtics shares did change over time. When the team was winning, people wanted to be part of the action—not only as fans but also as owners. In addition, people wanted to own shares of the team in order to share in its profits. Profits resulted from ticket sales, television revenue, and money earned from the sale of shirts, hats, and other items with the team's name. When profits were high, share prices increased and investors earned about an 8 percent return. Investors also had the satisfaction of being part of a tradition that included 16 NBA championships.

As years passed, however, the Celtics started to lose star players. The team was not as popular or profitable. This decrease in performance resulted in lower profits, lower dividends, and lower share prices as demand declined.

All investments are risky. Questions you need to ask when putting money away for the future are: "Will this investment be the winner I need? Or will it be a loser in overtime?"

CRITICAL THINKING

1 *Even though the first sentence mentions a loss by the Houston Rockets, they later won back-to-back world championships. If the Rockets had created a limited partnership, what effect would their championships have had on their share price?*

2 *How should a person select investments that serve long-term financial needs?*

455

BU$INESSBRIEF

After reading the Business Brief, ask students what impressed them the most. Have they heard or read about this topic before? Ask students to suggest ways a sports team could increase income, reduce costs, and make the team an investment with lower risk. List the suggestions on an overhead or on the board.

CRITICAL THINKING

Student answers require thinking beyond what is presented in the Business Brief. Answers will be based on students' perceptions of the topic and experiences they have had with it.

1. Championship teams usually enjoy increased income from ticket sales, television and radio broadcasts, and merchandise licenses. As the Rockets' income and reputation increased, the share price would also increase.

2. When selecting investments for long-term financial security, a person should consider the risk, consistency of income, and stability of value of the investment.

BUILDING YOUR PORTFOLIO

The Building Your Portfolio work samples validate skill level and a student's ability to accomplish tasks frequently performed on the job. The most important reason for including samples in a portfolio is to demonstrate a student's abilities and skills. In selecting work samples for each unit, students should always have a choice of which activities to include. Students might be encouraged to include samples from the end-of-chapter activities, particularly Communicate Business Concepts, Calculate Business Data, Technology Application, and Decision-Making Strategies.

The chapter starts with varied examples of methods used to save and why people save. Simple and compound interest are compared and the three main factors for evaluating a savings plan—safety, yield, and liquidity—are discussed.

Resources for Teachers
- Lesson Plans
- School-To-Work/SCANS Activity Masters
- Spanish Resources
- Instructor's Resource CD

Assessment
- Chapter and Unit Tests, Ch. 33
- ExamView, Ch. 33

Media/Technology
- Applying Technology Data CD
- PowerPoint slides
- Business Connection CD
- Videotape

Activity Masters and Workbooks
- Activities and Projects, Ch. 33
- Internet Activity Masters
- Business Math Activity Masters
- Communications Activity Masters
- International Business Activity Masters
- Ethics Activity Masters

Chapter **33**

Starting a Savings Program

GOALS

EXPLAIN why it is important to have a savings plan.

COMPUTE interest on savings.

DISCUSS the factors to consider when comparing savings plans.

DESCRIBE how savings help our economy.

Techno Tips

Investing Online Brings Warning

Online investing is one of the Internet's most hotly debated topics since becoming popular in the 1990s. Many claim that it is less expensive and more convenient than using a financial planner or broker. However, there are some potentially harmful disadvantages to investing online.

By investing online, you are essentially your own financial planner. Inexperience in making investment-trading decisions can result in great financial loss. As your own financial expert, you cannot benefit from an experienced financial planner's advice. Many online investors buy or sell stocks too quickly, because making trades is only a mouse click away. Experts feel that online trading changes one's outlook from an investment mentality to a gambling mentality, and this is no way to succeed with investments.

Students need to know the latest technologies and develop cutting edge Internet skills for use in current jobs, future careers, or in their homes. TechnoTips introduces students to today's cutting edge technologies and provides them with important Internet skills. Feature topics concentrate on Internet-specific technologies and computer or other hi-tech innovations for use by businesses and consumers.

I'd sure like to buy that CD player," said Mel. "It has all the features I want and would be a great improvement over the one I have now. But it costs over $100! I can't afford it."

"Try saving your money," Hank said in an encouraging voice. "Maybe if you cut back on some of your other spending, you could save enough money to buy that CD player on your own."

"That would take forever," sighed Mel.

"It's easier than you think," responded Hank. "If you put aside just 35 cents a day,

within a year you'd have over $125. If you save even more each day, you could buy the CD player and several new CDs."

"You're kidding!" exclaimed Mel.

"Really," said Hank. "Most people don't realize that saving small amounts of money on a regular basis can result in large amounts in the future, and that doesn't even include the interest you can earn."

"What's *interest*?" asked Mel.

"That's a story for later," said Hank. "I guess we need to sit down sometime and talk about planning your savings and investments."

WHY HAVE A SAVINGS PLAN?

Developing a savings plan should be part of everyone's personal financial activities. Savings are used to buy the goods and services we need and want as well as to prepare for future expenses and emergencies. When savings are invested and used by businesses and governments, savings help to keep our economy healthy.

Putting money aside in a systematic way to help reach a financial goal is a **savings plan**. How much you save, where you put your savings, and what you save for are important decisions. People save different amounts of money for different reasons and in different ways.

Josie Coramoto's parents have had a savings plan for years. Today they are using their savings for a down payment to buy real estate. They bought their home and make monthly payments on their mortgage. In addition, they make payments on ten acres of land they bought in a newly developed lake area. Mr. and Mrs. Coramoto also believe it is important to have money in the bank for emergencies. Every month, they deposit 10 percent of their income into a savings account.

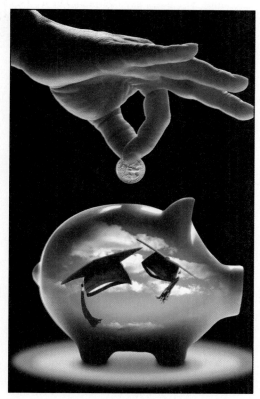

What are some of your financial goals that require a savings plan?

Chapter 33 *Starting a Savings Program* **457**

MOTIVATE

PURPOSE Provide a purpose for students as they read the chapter. Ask what they think they will learn. Direct students to skim the chapter, looking at photos, reading captions, and noting main headings. The goals at the beginning of each chapter provide a valuable tool for having students pinpoint main ideas. The tasks required by the goals are signaled in the first word. Some emphasize information collection ("Identify," "List"), while others call for description ("Explain," "Describe"). Ask students to look through all the goals and note the first word of each. Then ask students to state the purpose of studying this chapter. In this chapter, students will learn about the benefits of saving and be introduced to how to select a savings plan.

TEACH/APPLY

MAKE CONNECTIONS Point out that part of a person's disposable income should be saved, and there are a number of choices as to where savings can be invested. Compare and contrast simple interest and compound interest. Use Figure 33-1 to show that savings increase over time. Use Figure 33-2 to show that overall savings increase as monthly savings increase. Use Figure 33-3 to show that savings increase as yield increases. List and discuss the three factors to consider when selecting a savings plan. Give examples of how savings are invested to help your local and state economy. Explain the difference between

FOCUS ON REAL LIFE

Have students list personal reasons for saving money while they are in school. Copy the reasons onto an overhead or on the board. Find out how many students have savings accounts. Ask for volunteers to share their experiences with saving. Ask why it is so often difficult to save money even though a plan has been developed.

potential yield and risk. Describe investments with a higher risk and a higher potential return. Point out that the higher risk does not guarantee the higher return.

EXPLORE THIS/INDEPENDENT PRACTICE Before assigning independent practice material for any chapter, students should be expected to read the textbook material carefully. In view of the fact that students vary widely in their ability to read effectively, it is advisable to have students read the entire chapter, or sections thereof, silently in class if the material has not been previously read in connection with homework assignments.

After students have read the chapter, ask them to complete the Chapter Review questions. Develop Your Business Language is an excellent way to improve students' vocabulary. Only words introduced in the chapter are used in the exercises. The Review Your Reading questions can be used to check students' ability to comprehend what they have read. The Communicate Business Concepts section affords an opportunity for students to apply to practical life situations the information gained from reading the chapter. By completing the problems under Calculate Business Data, students will be able to strengthen and refine their abilities in mathematics. Technology Application allows students to demonstrate skill in using word processing, spreadsheet, and

Josie's older brother buys stocks and bonds with part of his wages. He is planning for his retirement years. Josie takes a certain amount of the money she earns baby-sitting and puts it in an envelope, which she keeps in a drawer in her room. As soon as she saves enough, she plans to buy a CD player.

A common trait is present in Josie's family: all family members save. Each member, however, has a different savings plan. All except Josie invest their savings. **Investing** means using your savings to earn more money. Josie is saving but not investing. She has a savings plan, but it offers no opportunity to earn money. Will you save and invest *your* money to make it grow?

HOW DO SAVINGS GROW?

A savings plan is important for your financial future. In addition to putting money aside as savings, you should have those savings working for you—that is, earning interest. Interest is money you receive for letting others use your money. Financial institutions such as banks make loans and other investments with money they hold from savers. Savings put to work to earn interest is a form of investment.

Earning Interest
When savings and the simple interest earned on savings are invested, the increase over a number of years is larger than many people realize. **Simple interest** is interest that is computed only on the amount saved. For example, David Skinner is able to save $50 a month. In a year, his savings will amount to $600. In ten years, he will have saved $6,000. If he deposits his money in a savings program that earns 6 percent interest, paid

every three months, his savings will increase rapidly as interest is added to his account. At the end of ten years, he will have more than $8,200 in his account rather than $6,000. Because of interest earned, his savings will have grown by more than $2,200.

David realizes the importance of this increase in his savings. He looks at a chart (see Figure 33-1) to see how much his savings will grow if he saves for a longer period. At 6 percent, his $50-a-month savings will grow to $14,500 in 15 years. Because interest rates change, David's account may grow even more. However, at certain times, David may earn less than 6 percent.

At the 6 percent rate, the interest David receives by the fifteenth year is more than the $50 he is putting in each month. He could actually start taking out $50 each month without decreasing the amount he has on deposit. He would have a permanent income of $50 a month. Often people fail to do this kind of planning for the future.

Compound Interest
People sometimes refer to a result called the *magic of compounding*. While no real magic exists, compounding of interest seems magical. **Compound interest** is interest that is computed on the amount saved plus the interest previously earned. Compounding makes your savings grow faster than simple interest. After a number of years, the difference is quite significant.

In David's case, he is earning compound interest; that is, he is earning interest on the interest that is accumulating in his account. For example, simple interest of 10 percent on $1,000 is $100. If the interest is compounded, then the interest computed at the end of the next year will be based on $1,100 ($1,000 + $100 first-year interest). The 10

TEACHING STRATEGIES
Special Needs
At-Risk Students

Utilize the lesson plans provided in the teacher's edition to divide each chapter into smaller parts to create short units that provide frequent opportunities for assessment and goal attainment.

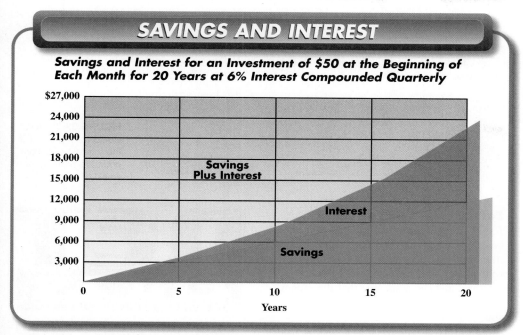

SAVINGS AND INTEREST

Savings and Interest for an Investment of $50 at the Beginning of Each Month for 20 Years at 6% Interest Compounded Quarterly

FIGURE 33-1 Which is growing faster, the actual savings or the interest?

percent interest earned in the second year would amount to $110. Interest the third year would be figured on $1,210 ($1,100 + $110 second-year interest) and would amount to $121. When interest is compounded, the amount of interest paid increases each time it is figured. If the interest was not compounded, the interest paid would be only $100 each year.

Interest can be compounded daily, monthly, quarterly, semiannually, or annually. Computers make calculating compound interest easy. The more frequent the compounding, the greater the growth in your savings. Figure 33-2 shows how rapidly monthly savings of different amounts increase when interest is compounded quarterly at 6 percent. (See Appendix C: Determining Percentage and Interest in Business for more information.)

SELECTING A SAVINGS PLAN

Banks, credit unions, and savings and loan associations usually welcome small as well as large savings deposits. When deciding how to invest your savings, three main factors should be considered: safety, yield, and liquidity.

CAREER HIGHLIGHTS

A personal financial advisor's (financial planner) duties include:
• **Developing savings and investing plans for individuals and businesses**
• **Analyzing financial status of clients**
• **Discussing financial options**
• **Preparing and submitting documents to implement savings and investing plans**

CAREER HIGHLIGHTS

The careers listed in the Career Highlights come from the *Occupational Outlook Handbook*, an online publication (www.bls.gov/oco) of the federal government. The O*NET code for Personal Financial Advisor is 13-2052.00. Tell your class about this resource and how to use it. This realistic description of job duties can be used to demonstrate the relevancy of skills learned in this course.

database software. Decision-Making Strategies contains material to challenge students to utilize the model explained in Chapter 1 for problem solving.

The Chapter Review questions at the end of the chapter vary in level of difficulty. For a basic assignment, assign Develop Your Business Language and Review Your Reading. For an average assignment, consider the basic assignment plus Communicate Business Concepts and Calculate Business Data. For an enhanced assignment, try the average assignment plus Technology Application and Decision-Making Strategies.

TEACHING STRATEGIES
Cooperative Learning

Group Investigation is a positive form of cooperative learning which encourages students to work together. Plan the size of each group before you begin, decide specific roles for the groups, set a time limit, and give guidelines for the outcome. For this activity, have students work with partners to obtain savings account information from banks in town. One member should assume the responsibilities as spokesperson. Assign each group a different task such as gathering information about various types of savings accounts, interest rates, services that customers are eligible for once they open an account, etc., so that each group has a different responsibility. The spokesperson will report back to the class with the group findings. Encourage students to be creative and use handouts and other presentation material.

Review the goals at the beginning of the chapter and the Business Notes at the end of the chapter. Have students respond orally or in writing to each goal restated as a question. For students who may have difficulty providing answers, assign the reteaching activities that follow. Enrichment activities may also be assigned where appropriate.

1. Why is it important to have a savings plan? (Answer: To buy goods and services, to prepare for future expenses and emergencies, to keep our economy healthy.)
2. What are two ways to compute interest on savings? (Answer: Simple interest computed only on the amount saved; compound interest computed on the amount saved plus the interest previously earned.)
3. What factors should you consider when comparing savings plans? (Answer: Safety, yield, liquidity.)
4. How do savings help our economy? (Answer: Savings are lent to help individuals, businesses, and governments invest; investment creates jobs and incomes and more spending.)

Compound Interest

Monthly Savings	End of First Year	End of Second Year	End of Third Year	End of Fourth Year	End of Fifth Year	End of Tenth Year
$ 5.00	$ 61.98	$ 127.76	$ 197.76	$ 271.68	$ 350.32	$ 822.16
10.00	123.95	255.52	395.15	543.35	700.47	1,644.32
25.00	309.89	638.79	987.87	1,358.38	1,751.62	4,110.79
30.00	371.86	766.55	1,185.45	1,630.05	2,101.94	4,932.95
35.00	433.84	894.30	1,383.02	1,901.73	2,452.26	5,755.11
50.00	619.77	1,277.58	1,975.74	2,716.75	3,503.24	8,221.59

FIGURE 33-2 What would be the effect if the interest was compounded monthly or weekly?

Safety

Today, most financial institutions have their savings accounts insured up to very large amounts. This insurance is a promise that your money will be available when you need it. Safety is assurance that the money you have invested will be returned to you.

Suppose you lend $100 to someone who promises to pay it back with 15 percent interest at the end of one year, a rate higher than banks pay. If the loan is paid back, you will receive $115 ($100 + $15 interest). However, if the borrower has no money at the end of the year, you may get nothing back. You may lose both the $100 you loaned and the $15 interest you should have earned. Investments are satisfactory when the safety of the amount invested and the interest to be paid can be depended upon.

Not all investors require the same degree of safety. Someone may have enough money to make 20 different investments. If one of them is lost, the investor still has the other 19. On the other hand, another person may only have a small amount of money and can make only one investment. One loss would

Federal income tax must be paid on interest earned from most savings accounts. If you earn $100 in interest and are in a 15 percent tax bracket, you keep only $85.

In the 1960s, the first version of the Internet was called the Advanced Research Projects Agency Network (ARPANET). ARPANET was designed so that scientists and military experts could keep communicating even if part of the network was damaged by a natural disaster or nuclear attack. Today's Internet is just as durable and flexible.

be serious. Most people want to make investments that are as safe as possible.

Yield

A good savings plan should earn a reasonable amount of interest. That is, your savings should have a satisfactory yield. The **yield**, also called the *rate of return,* is the percentage of interest that will be added to your savings over a period of time. Figure 33-3 shows the value of an original investment of $100 after 20 years at several different yields.

Usually higher yields and greater risks of loss go together. Investments with the federal government are the safest. When money is invested with individuals or businesses, it usually earns higher interest rates than those

Net Facts provides information and definitions of terms for the Internet. The more information that students have about the Internet, the better equipped they will be to use this resource. In the Internet Activity Masters, there is an Internet Activity Worksheet for each unit. You can use these activities to give students experience with finding information online. Options for assigning this activity are as follows:

1. **Provide students with a list of addresses for this activity,**
2. **Assign students to conduct their own searches, or**
3. **Use the addresses on the Internet Activity Worksheet.**
   You should complete the activity yourself before assigning it to resolve any discrepancies that may arise.

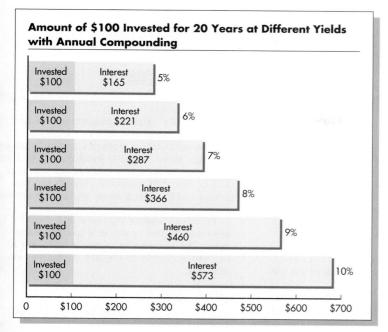

Amount of $100 Invested for 20 Years at Different Yields with Annual Compounding

Invested $100	Interest $165	5%
Invested $100	Interest $221	6%
Invested $100	Interest $287	7%
Invested $100	Interest $366	8%
Invested $100	Interest $460	9%
Invested $100	Interest $573	10%

0   $100 $200 $300 $400 $500 $600 $700

FIGURE 33-3 What is the price of investing in higher yielding securities?

paid by the government because there is less safety. For example, while the government is paying 6 percent interest, one business may pay 8 percent and a business with a greater risk may have to pay 12 percent. Investors will not accept higher risks unless the yields are greater.

The offer of a low rate of interest, however, does not guarantee safety. Similarly, high rates of interest do not mean that a loss will surely occur. The higher yields mean that investors generally believe that the situation involves a higher risk.

Liquidity

Sometimes you might need cash right away to pay unexpected bills or to take an

What are some unexpected expenses that might require you to have cash immediately?

unplanned trip. When an investment can be turned into money quickly, it is said to be a *liquid investment.* **Liquidity** is the ease with which an investment can be changed into cash without losing any of its value. This feature of an investment is important if you should need money for an emergency.

Critical Thinking Skills-Decision Making

SCANS

Decision-making skills, which include specifying goals, generating alternatives, considering risks, and evaluating and choosing the best alternative, are applied throughout every chapter in this text. Each time a student participates in a Cooperative Learning or Teams activity, decision-making skills are applied in a group situation. For Communicate Business Concepts and Decision-Making Strategies, students must specify the goal of the activity, consider risks, and evaluate the best solution before the questions can be answered. Emphasize to students how they are using decision-making techniques in their day-to-day tasks and make them aware of the skills they are developing.

SUMMARIZE

Point out that the goal of saving by whichever method is to have the savings grow, to balance yield and risk, and to use the savings to boost investment in the economy.

EVALUATE

• Assign Activities and Projects for Chapter 33.
• Administer the printed test or ExamView for Chapter 33.
• Assign School-To-Work/SCANS portfolio activities for Unit 10.

LEGAL PERSPECTIVES
The Truth in Savings Law

Which is better, $4.65 interest on $100.00 for a 360-day year or $4.73 on $100.00 for a 365-day year?

Situations like this used to make comparing savings accounts difficult. However, since 1993 when the Truth in Savings (TIS) law went into effect, consumers are presented with information to compare savings accounts. Truth in Savings requires that financial institutions provide the following information:

• fees on deposit accounts
• the interest rate
• the annual percentage yield (APY)
• other terms and conditions of the savings plan

TIS defines the *annual percentage yield* (APY) as the percentage rate equal to the total amount of interest that would be earned based on

• a $100 deposit
• the annual interest rate

• the frequency of compounding for a 36? day period

Using APY helps to eliminate confusion caused by the over 8 million variations of interest calculation methods. Before Truth i? Savings, some financial institutions used 3? day years to calculate interest. Others used 365 or 366. APY, however, reflects the true amount of interest a saver should expect t? earn.

TIS also requires that fees and the APY provided on the customer's savings statement. The law also regulates advertising of deposit accounts to prevent deceptive promotions.

Critical Thinking
1. How does the Truth in Savings law help consumers?
2. For financial institutions, what costs are associated with the Truth in Savings law?

Suppose you have $5,000 on deposit in a bank. If you need money right away, you usually can go to your bank and withdraw it. On the other hand, suppose you own a piece of land that you bought for $5,000. The land may be a safe investment. If you need money immediately, however, you may find it difficult to sell the piece of land right away. You might even have to sell it for less than you paid for it if you cannot wait for a buyer who is willing to pay your price.

When you make a number of investments, you do not need all of them to have high liquidity. The amount of liquid investments you need will depend upon your personal situation and expected financial needs.

SAVINGS AND THE ECONOMY

Your savings serve a very useful economic purpose. Money borrowed from a financial institution may include your invested savings. These funds help individuals, businesses, and governments in different ways. People commonly borrow to pay for homes, motor vehicles, and college. When this money is spent, demand for goods and services is created. This, in turn, results in more jobs that allow even more spending by workers.

Businesses often borrow money to operate or expand their operations. Building a new factory, replacing old equipment, or selling a new product are common reasons for business borrowing. Each of these actions creates jobs and expands economic activity.

FYI

The annual yield for an investment is computed by dividing the annual income from the investment by its cost. If you paid $50 for a share of stock that earned a $3 dividend, you would have a 6 percent yield ($3 ÷ $50).

LEGAL PERSPECTIVES

Legal Perspectives gives students an opportunity to study legal situations and draw appropriate conclusions. Ask students to debate the advantages (benefits) and disadvantages (costs) of the Truth in Savings law.

CRITICAL THINKING
1. By requiring financial institutions to provide full information about fees, interest rates, and APYs, consumers are less likely to be fooled by deceptive promotions. Comparison shopping for the best savings plan is easier.
2. Employees must calculate and report the required information. These additional costs could result in savers being paid lower interest rates. However, our society has decided that the benefits of information for consumers outweigh additional costs for businesses.

Governments may borrow to build highways, schools, or to provide other public services. Our economic system would be significantly weakened without savings and investments. Your invested savings contribute to our economic stability.

How does the money that you save or invest help to build roads, bridges and buildings?

E-Commerce for Saving and Investing

Should you buy a mutual fund or a certificate of deposit? What factors should be considered when comparing savings plans at a bank and a credit union? Consumers continue to face these saving and investing decisions. Online information and cyber investment services are adding to the ease of financial decision making.

The Internet makes it easy, for example, to compare the interest rates paid on CDs from banks all over the country. More and more, consumers are depositing money in banks and other financial institutions they have never visited.

The Internet also allows individuals greater control over their investment decisions. Online brokers, such as Ameritrade, Datek Online, and E*Trade, are at the center of the online financial services marketplace.

These cyber companies face competition from established stockbrokers. Charles Schwab, Merrill Lynch, Morgan Stanley Dean Witter, and others offer their clients a choice of traditional investing transactions and online trading.

When investing online, special care should be exercised. A person might be easily drawn into a moneymaking opportunity that promises too-good-to-be-true high returns. Each year, people lose billions of dollars in phony investments. Common online investment schemes include real estate, penny stocks, foreign bonds, wireless cable television, and natural gas and oil stocks.

It is important to invest only with reputable organizations. Talk to others who have made similar investments. Contact state and federal government agencies to determine whether an investment opportunity is legitimate.

Critical Thinking
Locate two or more online investment brokers. Prepare a comparison of the services and transaction costs for these companies. Present your findings in a graph, table, or other visual format.

Saving and Investing Web Sites Information on current earning rates on savings at www.bankrate.com
Investment information from the Motley Fool at www.fool.com
Stock and other investment information at money.cnn.com and www.businessjeeves.com
The New York Stock Exchange at www.nyse.com
U.S. Securities and Exchange Commission at www.sec.gov

REVIEW YOUR READING

1. To buy things needed and wanted, prepare for future expenses and emergencies, and help keep our economy healthy.
2. Possible answers might include buying land, putting money in a savings account, buying stocks and bonds, and putting money in an envelope at home.
3. When savings are put to work to earn an income in a savings plan.
4. The amount of interest earned is added to the amount saved, and then future interest is paid on that total. Compound interest increases savings faster than does simple interest.
5. $1,644.32.
6. With monthly deposits, you will have more money in the account at the end of six months because the monthly deposits will earn interest each month.
7. By the expected rate of return: a low rate usually indicates a fairly safe investment; a higher rate usually indicates a higher risk.
8. Bank savings account.
9. Making funds available for borrowing to buy goods and services, creating jobs, giving workers money to spend to expand economic activity.

COMMUNICATE BUSINESS CONCEPTS

10. Put cash in the bank to earn interest on the investment. In addition, investment would be insured up to $100,000 and would be safer.
11. Economic conditions, such as higher interest rates or inflation; uncertainty about where money is deposited or invested; length of time before you are able to have your money returned.
12. The business that pays 20 percent is most likely a high-risk business. Donald should probably not invest in that business.
13. No. Mr. Brokaw's limited means make it essential that his investments be safe. Ms. Chapman can afford to take greater chances.
14. Look for safety, a good yield, and compound interest. Avoid any kind of high risk investment.
15. Possible answers might include employers setting up payroll

BUSINESS NOTES

1. Savings plans help us to buy the goods and services we need and want as well as to prepare for future expenses and emergencies.
2. Interest earned on savings increases the value of the amount you have available to use in the future.
3. When comparing savings plans, a consumer should consider safety, yield, and liquidity.
4. Savings help the economy by making funds available to individuals, businesses, and governments for borrowing.

REVIEW YOUR READING

1. What are reasons why individuals should have a savings plan?
2. What are four different ways of saving?
3. When does money saved become an investment?
4. Why is interest that is compounded better than interest that is not compounded?
5. What will be the total savings if $10 is deposited monthly at 6 percent interest compounded quarterly for a period of ten years? (Use Figure 33-2 on page 460.)
6. Suppose you save $20 a month. If your savings plan compounds interest monthly, should you wait six months and invest $120 at that time, or should you make deposits each month? Why?
7. How is the safety of a savings plan measured?
8. Which of the following investments is liquid?
   a. land
   b. bank savings account
9. How do savings benefit the economy?

COMMUNICATE BUSINESS CONCEPTS

10. Yolanda Miller operates a pizza business, and she makes a nice profit. She keeps all of her business cash in a small fireproof safe in her basement. She has accumulated more than $2,000, more than she needs to buy supplies and meet unexpected business expenses. She wants to be sure that her money is safe and that she can get it when she needs it. What advice can you give Yolanda so that she can make better use of her money?
11. What factors affect the risk of an investment?
12. Donald Gorski has been saving money for the past year since he started working part-time. He keeps the money in a metal box in his bedroom. Donald's mother gives him $10 for every

$100 saved to help him pay for a new car when he graduates from high school in two years. Donald has saved almost $1,000. Someone told him about a new business that pays 20 percent on money it borrows. Should Donald consider lending his money to this business? Why or why not?
13. Ella Chapman, a wealthy businessperson, invests $5,000 in a newly organized manufacturing company. Frank Brokaw earns a moderate salary, owns a small house, and has $5,000 in a savings account. He knows of Ella's investment. Because she has a reputation for being a good investor, Frank decides to invest in that company, too. Does the fact that the investment

deduction plans and perhaps adding small percentages to the savings of employees, employers offering prizes to departments with employees who save the most, governments reducing the tax rate on interest earned on savings.

may be a good one for Ella Chapman mean that it is also a good investment for Frank? Explain your answer.

14. Jennie Wolfe has inherited $25,000. She graduated from high school three years ago, has a job in an accounting firm, is renting a small apartment with a friend, and has established a savings plan that she follows regularly. She does not want to take a chance on losing any of this inheritance, and yet she wants to get a good yield from investing it. She also believes that she will not need any large amounts of cash for the next several years. What advice would you give Jennie regarding how she should invest her inheritance?

15. What actions could employers and government take to encourage saving in our society?

DEVELOP YOUR BUSINESS LANGUAGE

For each numbered item, find the term that has the same meaning.

16. Interest computed on the amount saved plus the interest previously earned.

17. The percentage of interest that will be added to your savings over a period of time.

18. Putting money aside in a systematic way to help reach a financial goal.

19. Interest that is computed only on the amount saved.

20. The ease with which an investment can be changed into cash without losing any of its value.

21. Using your savings to earn more money for you.

KEY TERMS
compound interest
investing
liquidity
savings plan
simple interest
yield

DECISION-MAKING STRATEGIES

Cindy Redmond has $500 in a savings account that is paying her 4 percent interest. This money is being saved for a computer camp she plans to attend next summer. Cindy's friend, Rosalind Tate, knows of a local business project where the $500 could be invested at a 10 percent rate of return. This company has developed many successful business activities in the community.

22. What might be the advantages and disadvantages for Cindy of taking her money out of her savings and putting it into this other investment?

23. What advice would you give Cindy about this investment opportunity?

24. (a) Charles Jason: $0.20 × 365 = $73.00; (b) Carla Spivak: $0.95 × 52 = $49.40; (c) Alice Farney: $10.00 × 26 = $260.00; (d) Nolan Robinson: $20.00 × 12 = $240.00

25. (a) $450.00 ÷ 6 months = $75.00/month; $450.00 ÷ 12 months = $37.50/month; $825.00 ÷ $37.50/month = 22 months; 22 months − 12 months = 10 months; (b) 72 ÷ 4 = 18 years; 72 ÷ 6 = 12 years; 72 ÷ 8 = 9 years

26. (a) $50.00 × 12 × 15 = $9,000.00; (b) $15,000.00 (See Figure 33-1.)

In this activity, students use a computer to solve a business problem using a file that is provided on the data CD that accompanies *Intro to Business*. Instructions for using the data CD are included in a **README** file on the disk. Solutions are provided on the Instructor's Resource CD.

24. Even small amounts add up to large sums in a short time. How much will each person below save in one year (365 days) if he or she saves the following amounts without interest being added?
   a. Charles Jason: 20 cents a day
   b. Carla Spivak: 95 cents a week
   c. Alice Farney: $10 every two weeks
   d. Nolan Robinson: $20 a month

25. Ramon Valdez wants a savings plan that will permit him to buy a CD player/recorder that costs $450.
   a. How much will he have to save each month to be able to make his purchase at the end of 6 months? at the end of 12 months? If he saves at the 12-month rate, how much longer would he have to save to buy a CD player/recorder that costs $825?

b. Ramon learned that interest can double the amount of money you deposit if you leave it on deposit long enough. To find the number of years required to double the amount deposited, divide 72 by the interest rate. If Ramon deposited $360, how long would it take for his deposit to double if his account paid 4 percent interest? 6 percent interest? 8 percent interest?

26. Ceile Hamon deposited $50 in her bank account each month for 15 years.
   a. What is the total amount that she has invested?
   b. How much money is in her account if her deposits earn 6 percent interest compounded quarterly? (See Figure 33-1 on page 459.)

Using the *Intro to Business* Data CD and your spreadsheet program software, select problem CH33. After the problem appears on your screen, complete the following activities. Then, after you have completed each step, display or print the completed spreadsheet for each activity. If you do not have a printer available, answer the questions before you leave the computer.

27. The table shown is similar to Figure 33-2 on page 460. The interest rate shown is an annual rate, and interest is compounded at the end of each month. Use the @FV function to complete the table. Watch absolute and relative cell references. The function for the first cell has been completed as an example. Answer the following questions:
   a. If you save $5 per month, how much will you have accumulated at the end of the fifth year?
   b. If you save $35 per month, how much will you have accumulated at the end of the second year?

28. At the top of the table, enter 0.05 to change the interest rate to 5 percent. Answer the following questions.
   a. If you save $5 per month, how much will you have accumulated at the end of the fifth year?
   b. If you save $30 per month, how much will you have accumulated at the end of the first year?

29. At the top of the table, enter 0.07 to change the interest rate to 7 percent. Answer the following questions.
   a. If you save $5 per month, how much will you have accumulated at the end of the fifth year?
   b. If you save $10 per month, how much will you have accumulated at the end of the third year?

Optional: Create bar charts showing the accumulated savings over time at 7 percent annual interest for each amount of monthly savings.

FOREIGN EXCHANGE AND CURRENCY RATES

Would you be willing to pay 60 pesos for a hamburger? Or, is 5,200,000 yen a good price for an automobile?

Someday you might have to answer these questions when traveling or when conducting international business transactions. *Foreign exchange* is the process of converting the currency of one country into the currency of another country. The *exchange rate* is the amount of one currency that can be traded for one unit of the currency of another country.

This value of a nation's currency is affected by three main factors. First, the balance of payments of a country will affect its currency value. As a nation imports more than it exports, the value of its currency will decline. This results because more of its currency is on the world market; higher supply of that currency on the world market results in lower demand, and a lower price, for that currency.

Second, economic conditions affect currency values. As prices rise in a country (inflation), the buying power of the currency declines. This results in a lower value of the currency on the world market.

Third, political instability causes uncertainty about a country's currency. Future uncertainty about a nation's government reduces the demand (and value) of its monetary unit.

These three factors affect the supply and demand of a nation's currency. Lower demand results in depreciation, when the price of a currency falls. For example, if the euro (the currency of the European Union) depreciates, one euro can be exchanged for fewer Japanese yen.

In addition to the market forces of supply and demand, a country's government can directly affect the exchange rate. *Devaluation* is the process of setting a lower value for a nation's currency. If the Mexican peso is devalued, the number of pesos that can be exchanged for other currencies increases. Each peso has a lower value. Devaluation is an attempt to encourage exporting, since a nation's products will cost less in other countries.

CRITICAL THINKING

1. Research the balance of payments and inflation rate for two countries. How might these factors affect the value of the currencies of these nations? What other factors might affect changes in the exchange rate for these currencies?

2. Locate a web site that reports the value of currencies for different countries. Calculate the cost of living in a different country based on items commonly purchased by your family. Compare these living costs to the per capita income for that country. Would most people in the foreign country be able to afford these items?

Most students will either work with international clients or compete against businesses that do. Global Navigator introduces students to issues integral to working with international businesses. Key concepts and challenges faced by international businesses are presented, followed by two Critical Thinking questions that require students to analyze what they have learned.

This Global Navigator feature explores the causes and effects of variations in the relative values of foreign currencies—why a dollar might be worth 5% fewer Japanese yen today than it was a year ago, for example. As students become more involved in international business issues, grasping the nature of foreign exchange markets becomes more and more important. This feature looks at the main factors affecting foreign exchange values and how they influence prices.

CRITICAL THINKING

1. Answers will vary depending on the countries or currencies students choose. In most cases, a high negative balance of payment and/or high inflation will cause the value of a country's currency to decline over time.

2. This exercise can be tricky because the relative foreign exchange value of a currency may overstate a country's true cost of living, especially for domestically produced or subsidized products. In many cases, a country may have a very low per capita income when it is expressed in U.S. dollars, but it buys much more domestically than its foreign exchange value would indicate.

This chapter describes the major features of savings services—regular savings accounts, money market accounts, certificates of deposit, and individual retirement accounts. How to evaluate and select a savings program is discussed.

Resources for Teachers
- Lesson Plans
- School-To-Work/SCANS Activity Masters
- Spanish Resources
- Instructor's Resource CD

Assessment
- Chapter and Unit Tests, Ch. 34
- ExamView, Ch. 34

Media/Technology
- Applying Technology Data CD
- PowerPoint slides
- Business Connection CD
- Videotape

Activity Masters and Workbooks
- Activities and Projects, Ch. 34
- Internet Activity Masters
- Business Math Activity Masters
- Communications Activity Masters
- International Business Activity Masters
- Ethics Activity Masters

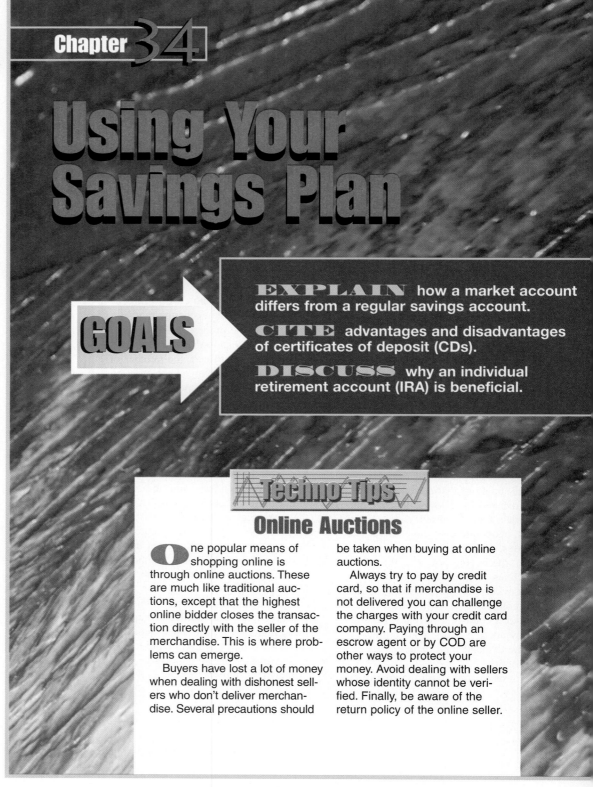

Chapter 34

Using Your Savings Plan

GOALS

EXPLAIN how a market account differs from a regular savings account.

CITE advantages and disadvantages of certificates of deposit (CDs).

DISCUSS why an individual retirement account (IRA) is beneficial.

Techno Tips
Online Auctions

One popular means of shopping online is through online auctions. These are much like traditional auctions, except that the highest online bidder closes the transaction directly with the seller of the merchandise. This is where problems can emerge.

Buyers have lost a lot of money when dealing with dishonest sellers who don't deliver merchandise. Several precautions should be taken when buying at online auctions.

Always try to pay by credit card, so that if merchandise is not delivered you can challenge the charges with your credit card company. Paying through an escrow agent or by COD are other ways to protect your money. Avoid dealing with sellers whose identity cannot be verified. Finally, be aware of the return policy of the online seller.

Techno Tips

Students need to know the latest technologies and develop cutting edge Internet skills for use in current jobs, future careers, or in their homes. TechnoTips introduces students to today's cutting edge technologies and provides them with important Internet skills. Feature topics concentrate on Internet-specific technologies and computer or other hi-tech innovations for use by businesses and consumers.

Ed sat down with his friends in the restaurant booth. Arthur looked at Ed and called out, "You're looking awfully proud today. You must have received a great birthday present."

"My parents gave me a CD," Ed said to his friends.

"What group is it?" asked Kendra. Kendra had one of the biggest collections of audio CDs in town.

"No, it's not that kind of CD," responded Ed.

"Well, then it has to be a CD-ROM for your computer," Jock said. "Does it have super graphics?" Jock was never happier than when he was talking about computers.

"It's not that kind of CD either," Ed sighed. "This CD grows."

"You mean it's alive!" exclaimed Arthur.

"Don't you geniuses know anything?" Ed said in a disgusted voice. "This is a certificate of deposit that will grow in value for my college education."

"Oh! A savings account!" Ed's friends responded.

"This is a kind of CD that I want to learn more about," added Kendra.

REGULAR SAVINGS ACCOUNTS

In recent years, the types of savings programs available to consumers have expanded. Special savings accounts such as money market accounts, savings certificates, and individual retirement accounts have become widespread. However, regular savings accounts continue to be a popular part of most consumers' savings and investment plans. In recent years, more than 70 percent of U.S. consumers had a savings account in a financial institution.

A **regular savings account** is a savings plan with a low or zero minimum balance. Savers usually are allowed to withdraw money as needed, which means that a regular savings account has high liquidity. A regular savings account is an easy and convenient way to make systematic deposits. These accounts pay interest while keeping money safe. Savings accounts may be opened at a commercial bank, a mutual savings bank, a savings and loan association, or a credit union.

Opening a Savings Account

Opening a regular savings account is similar to opening a checking account. You have to fill out a signature card, make a deposit to your account, and receive a savings account register to keep track of your account.

Making Savings Deposits

A **savings account register** is shown in Figure 34-1. In this book, you must record each deposit or withdrawal as it is made. You must also add the interest when the bank reports it to you.

The bank periodically sends a statement to customers showing deposits, withdrawals, and any interest added to the account. As shown in Figure 34-2, a savings statement shows the balance of your account as of the date of the statement. It is important for you to update your record and reconcile your savings account register with the bank statement. Errors you discover should be reported to the bank immediately.

When making a deposit, you fill out a

FYI

Club accounts are designed for a specific savings goal such as a vacation or holiday. These savings plans may have early withdrawal penalties and may pay lower rates than other types of accounts.

Chapter 34 *Using Your Savings Plan* 469

want to withdraw their money at the same time. The savings institution might need a number of days to obtain the necessary cash.

Students may be unfamiliar with money market accounts and the underlying government securities. Point out that money market accounts are another type of savings account available. It is important to learn in this chapter how a money market account compares to other kinds of savings accounts. Emphasize that money market accounts have large minimum balances and longer times for funds to be left on deposit. For these reasons, the yields on money market accounts are higher. Certificates of deposit have higher yields for the same reasons that money market accounts have higher yields. Show students PowerPoint 34-5, *Evaluating Where to Put Your Savings*. Review any questions that students might have about selecting a type of savings account. Explain that individual retirement accounts are one type of retirement savings account. Emphasize that money placed in such an account should not be withdrawn until retirement. Point out that the government does not guarantee that all investments will be successful. For example, it does not provide insurance for investments in land, stocks and bonds, or small businesses.

TRY THIS/GUIDED PRACTICE
Create a blank savings account register for a student handout. Using the data in Figure 34-1, fill in the blank register with students. Emphasize that users must be responsible for keeping their registers up-to-date so that the registers

SAVINGS ACCOUNT REGISTER

Date	Memo	(−) Amount of Withdrawal	(+) Amount of Deposit	(+) Interest Credited	Balance
					0 00
July 2	opened account		35 00		+35 00 / 35 00
July 25	part of summer earnings		50 00		+50 00 / 85 00
Aug. 5	birthday gift from parents		25 00		+25 00 / 110 00
Aug. 28	supplies for school	19 00			−19 00 / 91 00
Sept. 19	automatic teller	25 00			−25 00 / 66 00
Sept. 30	interest received			67	+ 67 / 66 67

FIGURE 34-1 How does a savings account register differ from a check register?

deposit slip much like the ones used in making a checking account deposit. You present this slip and the money or checks you are depositing to the bank teller. You will be given a receipt for your deposit. You must then enter the deposit on your register. You may also mail in your deposits and make deposits through ATMs or electronic funds transfer (EFT).

Withdrawing Money
Normally, checks cannot be written against a savings account. If you need money from your savings account, you must fill out a

SAVINGS ACCOUNT STATEMENT

Second National Bank
Savings Account Statement

Tas-fan Sun
303 Lewis Manor
Houston, TX 77083-2170

Account Number 7666-0052

BALANCE FORWARD	NO. OF WITH-DRAWALS	TOTAL WITH-DRAWALS	NO. OF DEPOSITS	TOTAL DEPOSITS	INTEREST	BALANCE THIS STAEMENT
0 00	2	44 00	3	110 00	0 67	66 67

DATE	AMOUNT	TRANSACTION DESCRIPTION	BALANCE
07/02	+ 35.00	initial deposit	35.00
07/25	+ 50.00	deposit	85.00
08/05	+ 25.00	deposit	110.00
08/28	− 19.00	withdrawal	91.00
09/19	− 25.00	ATM withdrawal	66.00
09/30	+ 0.67	interest	66.67

FIGURE 34-2 What will be the "balance forward" on the next statement issued for this account?

Basic Skills-Speaking

We can help students develop speaking skills by teaching them how to organize their ideas in a manner that is appropriate for the situation. Before speaking to a group, students should know their audience, plan their presentation, rehearse, then make the presentation. Discuss characteristics of an audience and how that audience plays a role in the performance of the speaker. Developing a speech through an outline is an excellent planning tool, and every speech should have an introduction, body, and conclusion. Then discuss the rehearsal process and its purpose. As this unit of study is Savings and Investment Strategies, assign several students the topic of Why Saving Is Important to Me and My Community to prepare and present a speech.

Hypermedia means using hypertext links to connect different types of media. Examples of different media are animation, graphics, pictures, sound, text, and video.

withdrawal slip. A **withdrawal slip** is a written request to take money out of your account. You give the withdrawal slip and proper identification to the bank teller.

Before any withdrawal can be made, a teller must check the bank's record to be sure that you have enough money in your account to cover the withdrawal. If you are withdrawing money using electronic funds transfer, the bank computer will automatically check the balance in your account. The bank's record is official. If there is a difference between the balance in your register and the bank's

record, the cause of the error must be determined and corrected. After the withdrawal is recorded on the bank's record, you will receive your money and a record documenting the withdrawal.

Whether you make your withdrawal at the bank or are withdrawing money using electronic funds transfer, the withdrawal should be recorded in your register. Keeping your own record of the account balance is important.

MONEY MARKET ACCOUNTS

One of the special savings accounts available to consumers that allows them to earn higher yields is the money market account. A **money market account** is one that pays a variable interest rate based on rates paid to holders of short-term government debt, such as U.S. Treasury bills, and short-term notes issued by corporations. Interest paid on money market accounts reflects the current rates of interest being paid in the money markets.

Money market accounts generally do not require long-term deposits but usually have relatively large minimum balance

Why is it important to carefully record your savings account deposits and withdrawals?

Net Facts provides information and definitions of terms for the Internet. The more information that students have about the Internet, the better equipped they will be to use this resource. In the Internet Activity Masters, there is an Internet Activity Worksheet for each unit. You can use these activities to give students experience with finding information online. Options for assigning this activity are as follows:

1. **Provide students with a list of addresses for this activity,**
2. **Assign students to conduct their own searches, or**
3. **Use the addresses on the Internet Activity Worksheet.**

   You should complete the activity yourself before assigning it to resolve any discrepancies that may arise.

can be used to verify savings accounts statements provided by banks.

EXPLORE THIS/INDEPENDENT PRACTICE Before assigning independent practice material for any chapter, students should be expected to read the textbook material carefully. Because all students vary widely in their ability to read effectively, it is advisable to have students read the entire chapter, or sections thereof, silently in class if the material has not been

TEACHING STRATEGIES
Teams

Teams-Games-Tournaments (TGT) is an instructional method in which students use cooperative learning in peer groups. Employers are looking for potential employees with good team skills. When using TGT, students are assigned to teams with four members each. Use the given lesson plan to teach this chapter, then divide students into their groups. Each group will study and review

the lesson, making sure that all group members understand the goals and content. Read the ExamView questions for this chapter, one at a time. Teams have an opportunity to answer the questions for points. The highest scoring team wins. (Note: As a supplemental activity, you may wish to distribute the Student Activity Worksheet, Workplace Competencies—Interpersonal Skills, in the School-To-Work/SCANS Activity Masters, to serve as guidelines for team development.)

previously read in connection with homework assignments.

After students have read the chapter, ask them to complete the Chapter Review questions. Develop Your Business Language is an excellent way to improve students' vocabulary. Only words introduced in the chapter are used in the exercises. The Review Your Reading questions can be used to check students' ability to comprehend what they have read. The Communicate Business Concepts section affords an opportunity for students to apply to practical life situations the information gained from reading the chapter. By completing the problems under Calculate Business Data, students will be able to strengthen and refine their abilities in mathematics. Technology Application allows students to demonstrate skill in using word processing, spreadsheet, and database software. Decision-Making Strategies contains material to challenge students to utilize the model explained in Chapter 1 for problem solving.

The Chapter Review questions at the end of the chapter vary in level of difficulty. For a basic assignment, assign Develop Your Business Language and Review Your Reading. For an average assignment, consider the basic assignment plus Communicate Business Concepts and Calculate Business Data. For an enhanced assignment, try the average assignment plus Technology Application and Decision-Making Strategies.

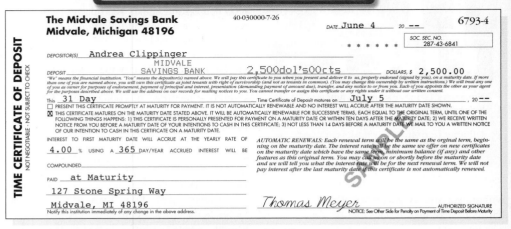

FIGURE 34-3   How much will this CD be worth on July 5?

requirements. With these accounts, the interest paid will vary daily or weekly. Be sure to know the current rate being paid in the money markets when opening one of these accounts. The yield from money market accounts will be higher than regular savings but somewhat less than long-term certificates of deposit.

The minimum deposit on a money market account is large and the funds are kept on deposit for a longer period of time. For these reasons, the financial institution can invest your deposit in higher-yielding investments. Because the financial institution can earn higher yields, it can afford to pay you higher interest rates on your account. This relationship between size of the deposit and length of time on deposit means that money market accounts generally have higher yields than regular savings accounts.

In recent decades, the yield for money market accounts has ranged from as low as 1 percent to as high as 12 percent, depending on the current level of interest rates.

CERTIFICATES OF DEPOSIT

To earn a rate of interest higher than on a regular savings account, three conditions are usually present:

1. A minimum deposit ($100, $250, $500, $1,000, or more) is required.

2. Your money must be left on deposit for a certain period of time, from a few days to several years.

3. If your money is withdrawn before the stated time, some of your interest may be lost and other penalties may be assessed.

A long-term time deposit that commonly meets these conditions and pays higher interest rates than regular savings accounts is referred to as a **certificate of deposit (CD)**.

When you purchase a CD, you usually receive a numbered certificate (see Figure 34-3). The certificate indicates how much you deposited, what the interest rate will be, and when you may withdraw your deposit plus interest. It lists the rules and regulations that must be followed for the certificate to be honored and the higher interest rate to be paid. The certificate also states the penalties

Workplace Competencies-Systems

SCANS

To operate effectively in an organization, the worker must know the goals of the organization, how to respond to the demands of the organization, and how to function in the organization. Through understanding systems, students will be able to learn how to operate effectively within the system. Students need to understand how to improve or design systems by suggesting modifications to existing systems and developing alternative systems to improve performance. Good oral and written communications skills are necessary to effectively communicate these ideas. Synthesis of previously acquired knowledge is required to improve or design systems. Discuss the importance of banking systems, concentrating on savings account systems.

for withdrawing your deposit before the maturity date. To cash your CD, you must present and endorse the certificate at the financial institution.

EVALUATING WHERE TO PUT YOUR SAVINGS

Many types of financial institutions offer savings plans to consumers. Commercial banks, savings and loan associations, savings banks, and credit unions all provide regular and special savings accounts. Other organizations such as credit card companies and retail stores also offer financial services. These other organizations are sometimes referred to as *nonbanks*.

Questions to Ask

In choosing a financial institution for your savings, consider needs and goals. Answers

If interest rates are expected to drop, buy CDs with long-term maturities. When interest rates are expected to rise, purchase short-term (three- or six-month) CDs.

to the following questions can help you choose the institution that is best for you:

- How safe is your money with that institution?
- How much interest do you want to earn?
- How frequently is interest compounded and added to your account?
- What services are offered that are important to you?
- Does the financial institution offer help in

offered? Is help available for selecting the best savings plan? What are the institution's business hours? Is electronic banking available? Is the institution conveniently located?)

5. Why should an individual retirement account (IRA) be considered? (Answer: Under certain conditions, no tax on deposits or earnings is paid until retirement.)

Review the advantages and disadvantages of each type of savings account: regular (low or no minimum balance, highly liquid, low yield), money market (large minimum balance, longer deposit time, high yield), certificate of deposit (large minimum balance, longer deposit time, high yield), and individual retirement account (tax-free growth, low liquidity). Discuss the questions that students should ask when selecting a type of savings account. Explain that different answers to these questions imply that different types of accounts are most suitable.

Ask students to read the Global Perspectives in this chapter. Direct students to prepare an oral presentation that communicates to consumers the factors that should be considered when evaluating savings accounts. Ask students why young people should consider an IRA. Point out the benefits and restrictions of an IRA. Note that while the amount of accumulated funds in the future may be impressive, the future purchasing power of a dollar must also be considered.

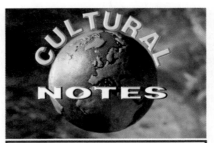

CULTURAL NOTES

Cultural diversity has played an important role in the names of some of the United States. *Minnesota* **comes from a Lakota word meaning "clouded water."**

selecting the best savings plan from among its options?

- What are the institution's business hours? Is electronic banking available for after-hours transactions?
- Is the institution conveniently located?

The institution you select should offer a variety of savings and investment opportunities as well as friendly, efficient service.

Considering Safety

An important consideration is feeling sure that you will get back the money you deposit into a savings account. The safety of your investment is something you need to examine before depositing your money into one of the savings plans. Deposit insurance protects savings in most financial institutions, but money market accounts often are not insured.

If one of your investment goals is *safety*, it is wise to check on deposit insurance before you invest. Asking the question, "Is my deposit *federally insured*?" is appropriate when selecting a savings plan.

SAVING FOR RETIREMENT

Federal tax laws permit you to plan ahead for your retirement in a unique way. This can be done by placing a portion of your wages or salary in an account that you designate as an individual retirement account.

An **individual retirement account (IRA)** is a tax-sheltered retirement plan that allows people to invest thousands of dollars annually and—depending on which type of IRA it is—either defer all taxes until they retire, or pay taxes upfront and avoid future taxes on any gains. With a traditional IRA, the yearly contribution is tax-deductible if certain income limits are not exceeded. Then the invested funds grow tax-deferred until withdrawn after retirement.

Why is it beneficial to start saving for your retirement while you are still young?

Basic Skills-Math

In order for students to become contributing workers in our society, it is important that they become proficient in the basic skills of reading, writing, arithmetic, and mathematics. Employers are looking for potential employees with good basic foundation skills. In order to prepare students for the school-to-work transition, we must teach these skills in our classroom.

Applying math across the curriculum is an important element in contemporary education. As a part of end-of-chapter activities, Calculate Business Data enables students to apply their math skills. Appendix B: Math Review, Appendix C: Determining Percentages and Interest in Business, and Appendix D: Using Measurements in Business also apply arithmetic and math skills.

A newer type of IRA, called a Roth IRA, also allows certain people to make tax-advantaged contributions, though the contributions are not deductible. However, no taxes have to be paid on any future investment gains, so there are no taxes due at all when the money is withdrawn after retirement. Moreover, the money can continue to grow tax-free indefinitely, as there are no mandatory withdrawal requirements.

When you consider the impact of earnings accumulating either tax-deferred or tax-free, either type of IRA can be very attractive—because the money that otherwise would be paid for Federal income taxes is instead compounding year after year in your IRA account.

When Roth IRAs were created in 1997, income limits were set at $95,000 adjusted gross income for individuals and $150,000 for filers of joint tax returns. Those limits are adjusted upward each year for inflation. For traditional IRAs, there are income limits if people also participate in retirement plans at work. For people who exceed the limit, the contribution is not tax-deductible or may be only partially deductible. The income limits are being bumped up annually.

Because an IRA is a retirement plan, penalties may be assessed if withdrawals are made prior to age 59$\frac{1}{2}$. The penalty is 10% of the amount withdrawn early, plus income taxes must be paid on early withdrawals of any tax-deferred funds from traditional IRAs.

When you are ready to set up an IRA, you should consult a financial institution representative on current laws and procedures for establishing an IRA. Most financial institutions offer a variety of IRA plans. Money market accounts and CDs are commonly used for IRAs. Annuities as well as mutual funds and common or preferred stocks are among the investments that can be considered when setting up an IRA.

Critical Thinking Skills-Problem Solving

Problem-solving skills, which include recognizing a problem and devising a plan of action, are applied throughout every chapter in this text. Each time a student participates in a Cooperative Learning or Teams activity, problem-solving skills are applied in a group situation. Each time a student completes a math application in Calculate Business Data, decisions are made as to which mathematical approach must be taken. For each Technology Application problem, students must decide which template problem to use, which piece of software to load, and how to solve the problem. Emphasize to students how they are using problem solving in their day-to-day tasks and make them aware of the skills they are developing.

SCANS

1. Savings accounts have low or no minimum balances, are convenient to use, earn interest, and are safe.
2. Commercial banks, mutual savings banks, savings and loan institutions, and credit unions.
3. Fill out a signature card, make a deposit, and receive a savings account register.
4. Fill out a withdrawal slip, present it with proper identification to the bank teller, receive a receipt along with cash or a check.
5. The minimum deposit on a money market account is large and the funds are kept on deposit for a longer period of time.
6. Deposit and maintain a certain minimum level, leave the money on deposit for a fixed length of time, pay a penalty for money withdrawn before the stated time.
7. How safe are the deposits? How much interest will be earned? How frequently is interest compounded? What services are offered? What are the business hours? Are electronic banking services available? Is the place of business conveniently located?
8. You must have earned an income, and you cannot withdraw money from the account before you reach age 59½ unless you pay a penalty.
9. Money in an IRA account should not be withdrawn until age 59½ or later.

COMMUNICATE BUSINESS CONCEPTS

10. Deposits can be made conveniently, small amounts are accepted, interest is paid, and deposits can be withdrawn at any time.
11. The savings account register should be used like a checkbook register. Deposits and withdrawals should be recorded as soon as they are made. Monthly or quarterly statements should be used to balance in the savings account register and to identify any interest to be added to the savings account register.
12. Special savings accounts usually require a minimum deposit, and funds must be left on deposit for no

Chapter REVIEW

BUSINESS NOTES

1. When opening a regular savings account a signature card is signed, a deposit is made, and a savings account register is received.
2. A money market account pays a variable interest rate based on rates paid to holders of short-term government debt, such as U.S. Treasury bills.
3. A certificate of deposit (CD) provides a higher rate of return than other savings plans; however, the funds must remain on deposit for a set time period.
4. When selecting a financial institution for your savings consider the safety, interest rate, compounding frequency, services offered, the business hours, and location.
5. An individual retirement account (IRA) allows a person to avoid taxes on deposits and interest earned until the money is withdrawn after age 59½.

REVIEW YOUR READING

1. Why are regular savings accounts a popular part of the savings and investment plans of most consumers?
2. What types of businesses offer savings accounts?
3. What steps would you follow in opening a savings account?
4. How does a depositor withdraw money from a savings account?
5. What affects the rate paid to savers who have a money market account?
6. Name three conditions that a depositor must accept to earn a higher rate of interest with a certificate of deposit.
7. What are some questions you should ask when choosing a financial institution where you might put your savings?
8. What are two restrictions placed on IRAs?
9. Why is it important to have a long-range goal when putting money into an IRA?

COMMUNICATE BUSINESS CONCEPTS

10. What characteristics of savings accounts make them especially good for students?
11. What are some procedures that you should follow when using a savings account register for your savings account? When should withdrawals and deposits be recorded in your register? How should the monthly or quarterly statements be used?
12. Financial institutions commonly pay a higher interest rate on special savings accounts than they do on regular accounts. Explain how they can afford to pay a higher interest rate on special accounts.
13. What is wrong with each of the following statements made by students who are discussing investing their savings?
    a. Most savings accounts are alike, so why bother to shop around?

less than an agreed time; the financial institution can then invest deposits in higher yielding investments.
13. (a) Many varieties of savings plans paying different rates of interest are available to savers. (b) Although young people should consider an IRA, some might not be able to tie up their money for the lengthy period of time required.

(c) Sometimes the bank's record contains errors; you may also need to know your balance at a time when it is not available from the bank. (d) Some savings plans that pay high rates of interest might not be insured or give you the liquidity you desire.

b. All young people should have IRAs.
c. Keeping your savings register up-to-date isn't important because the bank has the official record.

d. Always put your money in the savings plan that pays the highest interest regardless of your investment goal.

DEVELOP YOUR BUSINESS LANGUAGE

For each numbered item, find the term that has the same meaning.

14. A written request to take money out of your account.

15. A long-term deposit that has certain restrictions and pays higher interest rates than a regular savings account.

16. A special account that pays a variable interest rate based on rates paid to holders of short-term government debt.

17. A tax-sheltered retirement plan that allows people to invest up to $2,000 annually and enjoy tax-free growth on investment earnings until the money is withdrawn after retirement.

18. A savings plan with a low or no minimum balance and the ability to make withdrawals at almost any time.

19. A record in which you record deposits, withdrawals, interest earned, and the balance of your savings account.

KEY TERMS

certificate of deposit (CD)
individual retirement account (IRA)
money market account
regular savings account
savings account register
withdrawal slip

DECISION-MAKING STRATEGIES

Cesar Garcia received $5,000 from an aunt to use for college in three years. He is considering a regular savings account, a money market account, and a certificate of deposit. Over the next couple of years Cesar expects that his family may face financial difficulties due to the health of his parents.

20. What factors should Cesar consider when choosing a type of savings account?

21. What type of account would you recommend for Cesar?

22. (a) $8 × 6 = $48 (b) $11 × 6 = $66; $66 + $48 = $114 (c) $11 × 6 additional months = $66; $114 + $66 = $180

23. (a) $10,000 + $20,000 + $45,000 = $75,000 (b) No money would be lost by any of the depositors.

24. (a) Regular savings: $5,000 × 0.05 × 1 year = $250; CD: $5,000 × 0.08 × 1 year = $400; Money market account: $5,000 × 0.11 × 1 year = $550 (b) $550 − $250 = $300 (c) Regular savings: $2,000 × 0.05 × 1 year = $100; $100 per year × 5 years = $500; CD: $2,000 × 0.08 × 1 year = $160; $160 per year × 5 years = $800; Money market account: $2,000 × 0.11 × 1 year = $220; $220 × 5 years = $1,100

25. (a) $396 billion + $232 billion + $571 billion = $1,199 billion; regular savings accounts: $396 billion ÷ $1,199 billion = 33.0%; CDs: $232 billion ÷ $1,199 billion = 19.3%; money market accounts: $571 billion ÷ $1,199 billion = 47.6% (b) regular savings accounts: $396 billion × 0.10 = $39.6 billion; $396 billion + $39.6 billion = $435.6 billion; CDs: $232 billion × 0.10 = $23.2 billion; $232 billion + $23.2 billion = $255.2 billion; money market accounts: $571 billion × 0.10 = $57.1 billion; $571 billion + $57.1 billion = $628.1 billion; total: $435.6 billion + $255.2 billion + $628.1 billion = $1,318.9 billion

TECHNOLOGY APPLICATION

In this activity, students use a computer to solve a business problem using a file provided on the data CD that accompanies *Intro to Business*. Instructions for using the data CD are included in a **README** file on the disk. Solutions are provided on the Instructor's Resource CD.

22. Joanne Olson plans to deposit $8 a month in a savings account.

   a. How much will she deposit in the first 6 months?

   b. If she increases her monthly deposit to $11 for the next 6 months, how much will have been deposited in 12 months?

   c. How much will she have deposited in the first 18 months of her savings plan?

23. Three people have the following amounts deposited in regular savings accounts at different places: Dan Schweizer, $10,000 in a commercial bank; Margaret Zimmerman, $20,000 in a credit union; and Sumiyo Nagai, $45,000 in a savings and loan association. Each financial institution has insurance on account balances up to $100,000.

   a. What is the total amount of money invested by all three depositors?

   b. How much money would be lost, if any, by each depositor if all of these savings institutions went bankrupt?

24. Bernard Stahl can earn 5 percent on a regular savings account, 8 percent on a CD, and 11 percent on a money market account.

   a. If he invests $5,000, how much interest would he earn in one year in each of these plans? (Compute simple interest.)

   b. How much more would he earn on the money market account than he would with the regular savings account?

   c. If he decided to invest $2,000 in each plan, how much total interest would he earn in one year? In five years? (Compute simple interest.)

   Hint: Refer to Appendix C: Determining Percentage and Interest in Business.

25. In a recent year, U.S. financial institutions had the record of accounts and deposits shown in the table below.

   a. What percentage of the total of those deposits was in each of the different savings plans? (Round to the nearest tenth of a percentage point.)

   b. If the total saved in each plan increases 10 percent each year, what would be the total of those deposits the following year?

	Savings Deposits
Regular savings accounts	$396 billion
Certificates of deposit	232 billion
Money market accounts	571 billion

TECHNOLOGY APPLICATION

Using the *Intro to Business* Data CD and your word processing program software, select problem CH34. After the problem appears on your screen, complete the following activities. Then, print and sign your completed forms. If you do not have a printer available, save the forms on a data disk to give to your teacher.

26. Complete the signature card for a new regular savings account. Fill in the blanks with information about yourself. For the information that you enter, use italics and a different font of type from the one used on the rest of the signature card.

27. You have purchased a $2,500 certificate of deposit. Complete the certificate with information about yourself. The following are other necessary data: use the current date at the top of the certificate, the term is 90 days, the maturity date is 90 days from the current date, the interest rate is 5 percent. For the information that you enter, use boldface and a different font of type from the one used on the rest of the certificate.

COMMUNICATING for SUCCESS

SUMMARIZING—KEEP IT SHORT AND SIMPLE

People at work in business are frequently asked to create a written summary. The summary may be of a proposal, problem, transaction, meeting, or some other event. Other times employees are asked to provide a brief description of someone else's report.

When you read a newspaper article or watch a TV news program, you are usually reading or watching a summary of an event. Minutes of meetings you may have attended are also summaries.

Written summaries are especially important to managers who don't have time to read a complete report or listen to a lengthy presentation. In fact, summaries are sometimes called "executive summaries."

Sometimes summaries are oral. The phrases "What are we dealing with here?," "Give me the short version," and "What's the bottom line?" all call for a summary.

Written or oral, a summary should cover the important main points. These are usually the points that are the most relevant to the decision-making process. A good principle to follow when preparing a summary is sometimes remembered with the acronym KISS. It stands for Keep It Short and Simple.

A good summary will have the following features:

- It covers the highlights or main points. These points will usually be important for decision-making.
- It is not filled with detail.
- It should be no longer than one page.
- It will usually answer the five "W" questions (Who?, What?, When?, Where?, and Why?), but not "How?"

> **Both written and oral summaries are frequently provided by a business's employees.**

CRITICAL THINKING
1. What are the main characteristics of a summary?
2. How are summaries useful in a business setting?

COMMUNICATING for SUCCESS

Communications skills will help ensure students' success in the business world. Communicating for Success introduces workplace/interpersonal communications issues and proper uses of communications technology. Each feature discusses a key communications topic, and contains two Critical Thinking questions that require students to analyze what they have learned.

This Communicating for Success feature explains the need in business for concise summaries of matters that otherwise may be too complex or detailed for busy managers to deal with. Students are given useful guidelines for composing effective summaries.

CRITICAL THINKING
1. The main characteristics of a summary are that it covers the main points, skips the details, is a page or less in length, and usually answers the five Ws (Who? What? Where? When? and Why?) but not How?
2. Summaries are useful for decision-making in that they focus on the most-relevant points for managers who don't have time for lengthy presentations.

This chapter introduces security investments—bonds and stocks—including corporate bonds, government bonds, preferred stock, common stock, and selecting security investments, investment clubs, and mutual funds.

Resources for Teachers
● Lesson Plans
● School-To-Work/SCANS Activity Masters
● Spanish Resources
● Instructor's Resource CD

Assessment
● Chapter and Unit Tests, Ch. 35
● ExamView, Ch. 35

Media/Technology
● Applying Technology Data CD
● PowerPoint slides
● Business Connection CD
● Videotape

Activity Masters and Workbooks
● Activities and Projects, Ch. 35
● Internet Activity Masters
● Business Math Activity Masters
● Communications Activity Masters
● International Business Activity Masters
● Ethics Activity Masters

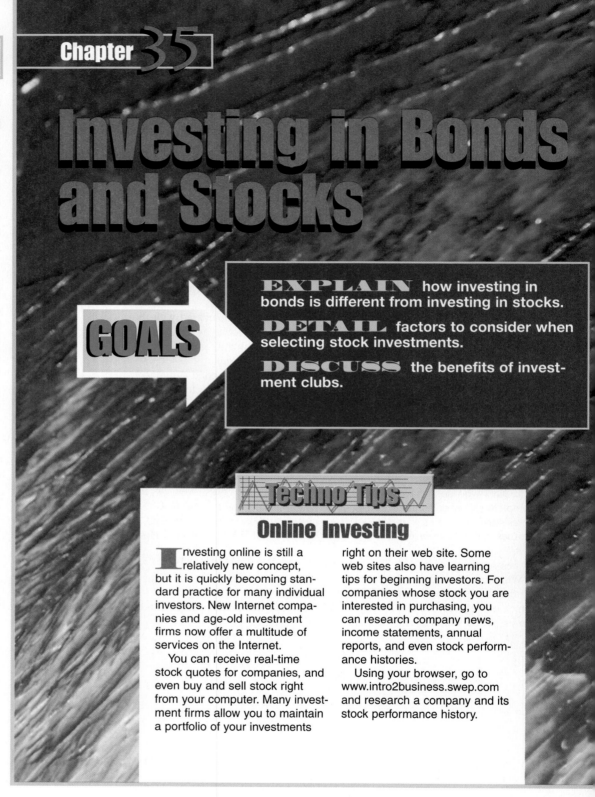

Chapter **35**

Investing in Bonds and Stocks

GOALS

EXPLAIN how investing in bonds is different from investing in stocks.

DETAIL factors to consider when selecting stock investments.

DISCUSS the benefits of investment clubs.

Techno Tips
Online Investing

Investing online is still a relatively new concept, but it is quickly becoming standard practice for many individual investors. New Internet companies and age-old investment firms now offer a multitude of services on the Internet.

You can receive real-time stock quotes for companies, and even buy and sell stock right from your computer. Many investment firms allow you to maintain a portfolio of your investments right on their web site. Some web sites also have learning tips for beginning investors. For companies whose stock you are interested in purchasing, you can research company news, income statements, annual reports, and even stock performance histories.

Using your browser, go to www.intro2business.swep.com and research a company and its stock performance history.

Students need to know the latest technologies and develop cutting edge Internet skills for use in current jobs, future careers, or in their homes. TechnoTips introduces students to today's cutting edge technologies and provides them with important Internet skills. Feature topics concentrate on Internet-specific technologies and computer or other hi-tech innovations for use by businesses and consumers. At the www.intro2business.swep.com web site, students can complete the activity for this chapter.

"We need to consider investments to supplement our savings account so we will earn higher returns for the future," Terress Mendoza said to her husband.

"What do you mean?" asked Alejandro. "Our jobs pay very well. We shouldn't have any financial difficulties."

"We might want to consider investments that could get us a better return, although there will be a bit more risk," responded Terress.

"What about safety?" wondered Alejandro. "We have to be careful."

"We have over $20,000 in our savings account," answered Terress. "That is money we will keep for emergencies. But with some of the other money we invest, we can take a little more risk and have the chance of increased returns."

"Are you sure that's what we should do?" Alejandro asked next.

"We have a good insurance plan," Terress explained. "So we can get into some other investments."

"Well, we better learn a little more about bonds and stocks before deciding whether or not to invest in securities," cautioned Alejandro.

TYPES OF SECURITIES

As you have learned, depositing money in a savings account is an easy way to invest money. However, there are other ways to invest, such as buying bonds and stocks. Some people do not consider investing in bonds and stocks because they are unsure about the safety of such investments.

The term **securities** refers to bonds, stocks, and other documents that are sold by corporations and governments to raise large sums of money. These investments are commonly divided into two major categories— debt and equity.

Debt Securities

Sometimes you are in need of money when funds are not available. You might consider borrowing from a relative or friend. Companies and governments also borrow. Bonds and other documents that represent borrowing are called *debt securities*.

Equity Securities

People commonly invest money in companies in hopes of earning more money. One way of investing in a company is to purchase part ownership in the company. Ownership in a company is represented by *equity securities*. For example, a share of stock is an equity security.

Give reasons why you might want to use money to buy securities as opposed to placing that money in a regular savings account.

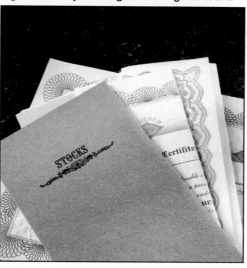

FOCUS ON REAL LIFE

Ask if any students own bonds or stock or if students know anyone who does. On the board or overhead, list the names of the companies that issued the securities. Ask students to list reasons for owning bonds and stocks.

market quotations from a daily paper. Ask for a few student volunteers to choose stocks from the listing. Show how the dividend yield and P/E ratio were calculated for each of the stocks. Describe the roles of full-service and discount stockbrokers. Detail the differences in direct decision making between investment clubs and mutual funds. Emphasize the benefits of pooling investments and knowledge. Point out Figure 35-5 in the student text as a guide for choosing investments.

TRY THIS/GUIDED PRACTICE
With your students, look again at some current stock market quotes. Guide students to find the stock with the highest dividend yield percentage, the stock with the highest P/E ratio, and the stock with the highest net change in price from the previous day. Explain that each of these stocks might meet a different saving and investing plan, depending on the investors' financial goals. (For the examples given, the goals might be income, long-term growth, and short-term capital accumulation.)

EXPLORE THIS/INDEPENDENT PRACTICE Before assigning independent practice material for any chapter, students should be expected to read the textbook material carefully. In view of the fact that all students vary widely in their ability to read effectively, it is advisable to have students read the entire chapter, or sections thereof, silently in class if the material has not been previously read in connection with homework assignments.

To raise money for operations or future expansion, many corporations sell bonds. To better understand bonds, it is helpful to know the answers to two questions: What is a bond? Why do the values of bonds change?

Buying a Bond Is Making a Loan

A **bond** is a certificate representing a promise to pay a definite amount of money at a stated interest rate on a specified maturity date (due date). Bonds are similar to promissory notes issued by individual borrowers. When you buy a bond, you are lending money to the organization selling the bond. You become a creditor of the organization. Bonds issued by corporations are called **corporate bonds**.

Each bond has its face value printed on the front of the certificate. The **face value**, also called the *maturity value*, is the amount being borrowed by the seller of the bond. Interest is

paid periodically to the investor based on that amount and the stated interest rate. On the bond's maturity date, the face value is repaid to the investor.

Changing Bond Values
Bonds are bought and sold in bond markets. Figure 35-1 gives an explanation of listings for the corporate bond market. Note that the prices are stated in 100s, but the bonds are sold in $1,000 denominations (ten times the listed amount). Therefore, the Mobil bond quoted at 109¾ costs $1,097.50 ($109.75 × 10). These bonds closed up (+) ⅞ from the previous day; that is, the increase of today's price over yesterday's is $8.75 (⅞, or $0.875 × 10).

The price investors are willing to pay for a bond depends upon the bond's stated interest rate. If interest rates on similar bonds are higher than the bond's stated rate, investors will want to buy the bond for less than its face value. On the other hand, if the bond's stated interest rate is higher than interest rates on similar bonds, the

FIGURE 35-1 Why is the current yield on some bonds higher than others?

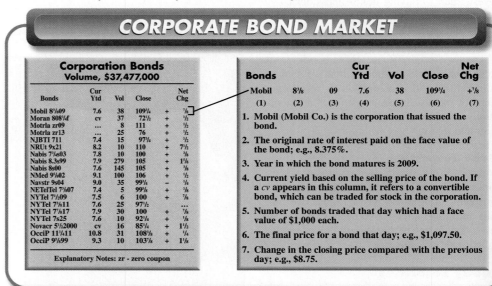

CORPORATE BOND MARKET

Corporation Bonds Volume, $37,477,000				
Bonds	Cur Ytd	Vol	Close	Net Chg
Mobil 8⅜s09	7.6	38	109¼	+ ⅞
Moran 808¾f	cv	37	72½	+ ½
Motrla zr09	...	8	111	+ ½
Motrla zr13	...	25	76	+ ½
NJBTI 711	7.4	15	97¾	+ ½
NRUt 9x21	8.2	10	110	+ 7½
Nabis 7⅛s03	7.8	10	100	+ ⅜
Nabis 8.3s99	7.9	279	105	+ 1⅛
Nabis 8s00	7.6	145	105	+ ⅜
NMed 9⅝02	9.1	100	106	+ ½
Navstr 9s04	9.0	35	99¾	− ¼
NETelTel 7⅛07	7.4	5	99⅞	+ ⅛
NYTel 7½09	7.5	6	100	+ ⅞
NYTel 7⅞11	7.6	25	97½	+ ...
NYTel 7⅞17	7.9	30	100	+ ⅞
NYTel 7s25	7.6	10	92¼	+ ⅛
Novacr 5½2000	cv	16	85¼	+ 1½
OcciP 11¼11	10.8	31	108⅛	+ ¼
OcciP 9⅝99	9.3	10	103⅞	+ 1⅛

Explanatory Notes: zr - zero coupon

Bonds			Cur Ytd	Vol	Close	Net Chg
Mobil	8⅜	09	7.6	38	109¼	+⅞
(1)	(2)	(3)	(4)	(5)	(6)	(7)

1. Mobil (Mobil Co.) is the corporation that issued the bond.
2. The original rate of interest paid on the face value of the bond; e.g., 8.375%.
3. Year in which the bond matures is 2009.
4. Current yield based on the selling price of the bond. If a *cv* appears in this column, it refers to a convertible bond, which can be traded for stock in the corporation.
5. Number of bonds traded that day which had a face value of $1,000 each.
6. The final price for a bond that day; e.g., $1,097.50.
7. Change in the closing price compared with the previous day; e.g., $8.75.

Critical Thinking **Skills-Decision Making**

Decision-making skills, which include specifying goals, generating alternatives, considering risks, and evaluating and choosing the best alternative, are applied throughout every chapter in this text. Each time a student participates in a Cooperative Learning or Teams activity, decision-making skills are applied in a group situation. For Communicate Business Concepts and Decision-Making Strategies, students must specify the goal of the activity, consider risks, and evaluate the best solution before the questions can be answered. Emphasize to students how they are using decision-making techniques in their day-to-day tasks and make them aware of the skills they are developing.

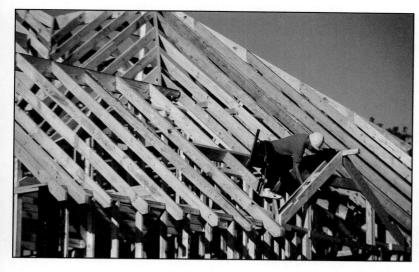

How do local and state governments benefit from the sale of municipal bonds?

seller of the bond will want to receive more than its face value. Bond prices are determined by buyers and sellers in the bond market.

TYPES OF GOVERNMENT BONDS

Like corporations, governments also issue bonds to raise money for funding public services. Local, state, and the federal governments issue a variety of bonds.

Municipal Bonds

A city may want to build a new park or a new school. A state may need funds to build or repair highways and bridges. Bonds issued by local and state governments are called **municipal bonds**, or *munis*.

Municipal bonds have an advantage over corporate bonds. Most often, interest earned on the municipal bonds is exempt from federal and most state income taxes. In order to avoid taxes, people buy municipal bonds even though the interest rate usually is not as high as that offered on corporate bonds. Like corporate bonds, municipal bonds are normally sold in amounts of $1,000 or larger. Municipal bonds are usually considered to be safer investments than corporate bonds.

U.S. Savings Bonds

One of the safest investments, and one desirable for investors with only small amounts to invest, is U.S. government savings bonds. Figure 35-2 shows an example of a Series EE savings bond. Series EE savings bonds, which come in denominations from $50 to $10,000, pay interest through a process called *discounting*.

A Series EE bond is bought at half its face value. A $50 bond costs $25 and, at the end of its full term, pays at least $50. The difference between the purchase price and the redemption (payoff) value is the interest earned. The interest earned is determined by the length of time the bond is held. The time it takes for a savings bond to mature will vary depending on the current interest rate being paid.

The convenience of buying U.S. government EE bonds is an attractive feature to some investors. Amounts can be deducted, for

In recent years, more than 6,000 different mutual funds were in operation in the United States.

After students have read the chapter, ask them to complete the Chapter Review questions. Develop Your Business Language is an excellent way to improve students' vocabulary. Only words introduced in the chapter are used in the exercises. The Review Your Reading questions can be used to check students' ability to comprehend what they have read. The Communicate Business Concepts section affords an opportunity for students to apply to practical life situations the information gained from reading the chapter. By completing the problems under Calculate Business Data, students will be able to strengthen and refine their abilities in mathematics. Technology Application allows students to demonstrate skill in using word processing, spreadsheet, and database software. Decision-Making Strategies contains material to challenge students to utilize the model explained in Chapter 1 for problem solving.

The Chapter Review questions at the end of the chapter vary in level of difficulty. For a basic assignment, assign Develop Your Business Language and Review Your Reading. For an average assignment, consider the basic assignment plus Communicate Business Concepts and Calculate Business Data. For an enhanced assignment, try the average assignment plus Technology Application and Decision-Making Strategies.

TEACHING STRATEGIES
Special Needs
Limited English Proficiency (LEP) Students

Adjust the length of time allotted to complete assignments and tests. Remember that the primary objective is to assess student knowledge of the chapter.

UNITED STATES SAVINGS BOND

THE UNITED STATES OF AMERICA
AT THE SECURITY HEREOF WILL PAY
ONE HUNDRED DOLLARS

100

SOC SEC/EMP ID NO

To

SERIES **EE**
ISSUE DATE
WHICH IS THE FIRST DAY OF
MONTH   YEAR

ISSUING AGENT'S
DATING STAMP

INDEPENDENCE HALL

CO OO OOO OOO OOO EE

FIGURE 35-2 How much does this bond cost when issued?

ASSESS

Review the goals at the beginning of the chapter and the Business Notes at the end of the chapter. Have students respond orally or in writing to each goal restated as a question. For students who may have difficulty providing answers, assign the reteaching activities that follow. Enrichment activities may also be assigned where appropriate.

1. How is investing in bonds different from investing in stocks? (Answer: Bonds represent loaning money to a borrower; stocks represent purchasing shares of ownership in corporations.)

2. Why do organizations sell bonds? (Answer: To raise money for operations or future expansions.)

3. Which types of bonds are sold by governments? (Answer: Municipal bonds, savings bonds, and Treasury bills, notes, and bonds.)

4. What are the differences between preferred and common stock? (Answer: Preferred stock pays dividends first when dividends are declared. Common stock does not necessarily pay dividends, but when profits are large, common stock may pay higher dividends. Common stockholders vote for a company's board of directors.)

5. When selecting stock investments, what factors should you consider? (Answer: Has the company been profitable over a period of years? Have the company's managers made good business decisions? Does the

instance, from a person's paycheck and accumulated until a bond can be purchased in the employee's name. A weekly deduction of $10 would result in a $100 EE bond being acquired after five weeks. This approach is an easy way for someone to get started on an investment program.

The U.S. government also sells Series HH savings bonds. These bonds are available to investors in face values from $500 to $10,000, are not discounted, and pay a fixed rate of interest through a check mailed to the investor. Series HH bonds are different from EE bonds in three important ways:

1. EE bonds pay interest only when the bond is cashed, while HH bonds pay interest semiannually directly to the bondholder.

2. EE bonds can be purchased at financial institutions throughout the United States and through payroll deduction plans, while HH bonds are available only in exchange for eligible EE bonds or savings notes called Freedom Shares.

3. There is an annual purchase limit of $30,000 (face value) on EE bonds, but there is no such limit on HH bonds.

Other Federal Securities

The federal government also borrows using Treasury bills, notes, and bonds. The difference among these debt securities is the length of time to maturity. Treasury bills (T-bills) involve short-term borrowing, with maturities from 91 days to 1 year. Treasury notes (T-notes) are intermediate-length borrowing with maturities from 1 to 10 years. Treasury bonds (T-bonds) range from 10 to 30 years and are considered long-term borrowing.

The stocks of new and smaller companies are bought and sold through the over-the-counter (OTC) market. The OTC is a network of stockbrokers connected through a system of computers, teletype machines, fax machines, and telephones.

CAREER HIGHLIGHTS

A stockbroker's (securities sales agent) job duties include:
- Searching for potential clients using advertising, mailing lists, and personal contacts
- Interviewing clients to determine financial goals and resources
- Selling financial products and services to clients for investment purposes
- Completing forms to process transactions requested by clients.

CAREER HIGHLIGHTS

The careers listed in Career Highlights come from the *Occupational Outlook Handbook*, an online publication (www.bls.gov/oco) of the federal government. The O*NET code for Securities and Commodities Sales Agent is 41-3031.01. Tell your class about this resource and how to use it. This career feature is designed to help students explore various careers in business. This realistic description of job duties can be used to demonstrate the relevancy of skills learned in this course.

INVESTING IN STOCKS

Investing in stocks is quite different from investing in bonds. When you invest in bonds, you lend money. When you invest in stock, you become a part owner of a business. You become a stockholder when you buy one or more shares in a corporation. Ownership is shown by a printed form known as a *stock certificate*. If a business is profitable, part of the profits may be paid out in cash to the stockholders in the form of *dividends*.

The opportunity to earn a high rate of return attracts people to invest in stocks. However, the risk of losing your money is usually greater with stocks than with bonds. A corporation must pay bondholders the rate of interest promised before it can pay any dividends to stockholders. If there is not enough money left to pay dividends or if the

corporation decides to use the money earned for business expansion, stockholders receive no dividends. If a corporation goes out of business, a stockholder may get little or nothing back from the investment. Bondholders, on the other hand, may get back all or part of the money owed to them.

Stocks have a market value. The **market value** of a stock is the price at which a share of stock can be bought and sold in the stock market. The market value is the best indicator of the current value of a share of stock. The market value can change rapidly. If the business is doing well, the market value is likely to go up. If the business has a poor record, the market value usually goes down. The market value also may be affected by the state of the economy, the phase of the business cycle we are in, and political developments here and abroad.

company have growth potential in coming years? Does the company have an unusual number of large debts? How does the company compare with others in its industry?)

6. What are the benefits of investment clubs and mutual funds? (Answer: Clubs and funds encourage regular saving; information, experience, and risk are shared.)

7. How can you evaluate security investments? (Answer: Financial needs and goals, safety, liquidity, and rate of return.)

Ask a student volunteer to give you some money. On the board or overhead, write out an IOU and explain that the money is a loan that you will pay back. Explain that a bond is a form of an IOU. Return the money to the student, and ask another student to give you money. On the board or overhead, write out a statement that the student is now part owner of the classroom. Explain that the student-owner can now vote in major classroom decisions. Stock is a similar form of ownership. Bring in an audio tape or videotape of a business news report on the corporate and government bond markets. Explain that the prices given are determined in markets and that bond prices move inversely to interest rates. Bring in an audio tape or videotape of a business news report on the stock market. Point out that, although there are different types of stock, the prices of all stocks are determined by the interaction of supply

ENVIRONMENTAL PERSPECTIVES

Socially Responsible Investments

Can investors make stock selections that help society? Many investors only choose securities of companies that display environmental awareness and have business practices that address other social ills. These investors' dollars buy bonds and stocks of companies that practice energy conservation, waste management, and pollution control.

Another method with which some investors express social concern applies to enterprises that may not serve the best interests of society. Some people avoid investments in organizations that sell alcohol or tobacco or that operate gambling establishments.

A variety of mutual funds have been created to meet the financial goals of socially responsible investors. For example, in recent years, the Calvert Social Investment Fund,

the Dreyfus Third Century Fund, and the Parnassus Fund concentrated on companies that made socially responsible business decisions.

How do socially responsible investments perform? Market results are mixed. Some stocks and mutual funds do very well while others are not as profitable for investors. However, many people are satisfied with a fair return while knowing they are helping the environment and improving the quality of life in our society.

Critical Thinking

1. How can investors improve the environment and influence other social concerns?
2. To what extent should social responsibility be a factor when selecting an investment?

ENVIRONMENTAL PERSPECTIVES

This Environmental Perspectives is an appropriate place to discuss the responsibilities of businesses toward the environment. This Environmental Perspectives feature will expose students to some of the environmental issues facing businesses today.

CRITICAL THINKING

1. If many investors place their money with companies that are concerned about the environment, the health of people, and other social issues, this will send a message to business organizations about the importance of these issues.
2. Possible answers will vary; however, most students are likely to believe that it is important to be concerned about the environment and other social issues.

and demand in a market. Show students Figure 35-4 in the student text and describe how the data in a stock listing are used by investors to evaluate stocks. Tell or show that one strand of string can be easily broken or cut, but that many strands twined together are stronger. Explain that this cooperative strength is one of the major advantages of investment clubs and mutual funds.

ENRICH

Direct students to read the Environmental Perspectives in this chapter. Have students present a role-playing situation in which a stockbroker is recommending a stock to a customer. If possible, have a member of an investment club visit the class to explain why the club was formed, how it operates, and what has been learned from the experience. Or, a stockbroker may be invited to class to explain the benefits and risks of investing in stocks, bonds, and mutual funds. Students might select a company and research it, then maintain a record of the daily prices of the company's stock for a couple of weeks. Have students suggest reasons for changes in the stock's value.

SUMMARIZE

Emphasize that some financial goals require investments that are different from savings accounts. To meet their goals, many investors choose bonds and stocks. This chapter defines different types of financial securities and provides guidelines for matching each type to different investment goals.

Municipal bonds do have risk. In recent years, some local governments have defaulted on their bond payments.

Preferred Stock

Preferred stock is one of two main classes of stock issued by corporations. **Preferred stock** has priority over common stock in the payment of dividends. A preferred stockholder, for example, is paid first if profits are used to pay any stock dividends.

The dividends paid to preferred stockholders are usually limited to a set rate. Preferred stock usually has priority on the return of the amount invested if the corporation goes out of business. Preferred stock is less risky than common stock. However, preferred stockholders generally have no voting rights within the corporation.

Common Stock

Common stock represents general ownership in a corporation and a right to share in its profits. Common stock has no stated dividend rate. As part owners of the corporation, common stockholders are invited to the annual meeting of the corporation and are entitled to one vote per share of common stock owned.

Common stockholders receive dividends only after preferred stockholders are paid their share of any dividends. Yet, if the profits of a company are large, the common stockholders may receive more in dividends than preferred stockholders. For example, suppose that a company has issued $100,000 worth of common stock and $100,000 worth of preferred stock with a stated dividend rate of 6 percent. If the company earns a profit of $20,000 and pays all the profit out as dividends, preferred stockholders would be paid $6,000 in dividends ($100,000 × 0.06). The remainder, or $14,000 ($20,000 − $6,000), would be available to pay dividends to the common stockholders. The common stockholders would be paid a return of 14 percent.

SELECTING STOCK INVESTMENTS

Buying a stock that is right for you is an important decision. This could start with a process as shown in Figure 35-3. By viewing various economic and social trends in our country and in the world, you will determine what types of companies would benefit from those trends. For example, as people live longer, increased health care is required. Companies involved in health care products may be a wise investment.

Analyzing Potential Stocks

In selecting a specific stock to buy, you should learn something about the business record of the corporation. There are a number of sources of information that can be used, including *Moody's Handbook of Common Stocks, Value Line,* and *Standard and Poor's Encyclopedia of Stocks.* Publications like these provide information such as the company's net worth, amount of debt, sales revenue, profits, dividend history, and the current outlook for the company's product or service. These publications often are available in public libraries. There are also numerous web sites on the Internet that can be invaluable sources of information on companies. The U.S. Securities and Exchange Commission, which oversees the financial markets, requires all companies that issue publicly traded securities to file detailed reports electronically. Those reports can be accessed via its web site at www.edgaronline.com. Additionally, many private investment services offer research and analyses on-line, often free of charge.

If you are considering investing in a company, you should ask the following questions:

- Has the company been profitable over a period of years?
- Have the company's managers made good business decisions?
- Does the company have growth potential in coming years?
- Does the company have an unusually large amount of debt?

Personal Qualities-Responsibility

SCANS

Being responsible, or exerting a high level of effort and perseverance towards a goal, is a personal quality that employers are looking for. People are worried about such issues as acid rain, global warming, oil spills, chemicals in their food and water, and polluted air. Rightly or wrongly, business gets blamed for causing many of these environmental troubles.

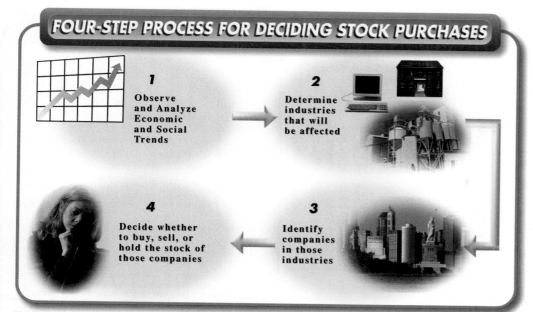

FOUR-STEP PROCESS FOR DECIDING STOCK PURCHASES

1 Observe and Analyze Economic and Social Trends

2 Determine industries that will be affected

3 Identify companies in those industries

4 Decide whether to buy, sell, or hold the stock of those companies

FIGURE 35-3 Can you name a company or industry that has profited from a trend in recent months?

- How does the company compare with others in its industry?

Other information about a company should also be considered. The *yield* of a stock is important if your goal is to earn a good return from your investment. Suppose, for example, that the XYZ Corporation is paying a quarterly dividend of $0.60 a share. The total dividend for the year would be $2.40, and if the stock is selling for $40 a share, the current yield (return) would be calculated as:

$$\text{Dividend Yield} = \frac{\text{Dividend per Share}}{\text{Market Price per Share}}$$

$$= \frac{\$ 2.40}{\$40.00} = 0.06 \text{ or } 6 \text{ percent}$$

The price of a stock also will be important. Many investors look at the stock's **price-earnings ratio (P/E)**, the ratio of a stock's selling price to its earnings per share. The P/E gives you an indication of whether the stock is priced high or low in relation to its earnings per share. For instance, if a com-

pany has 100,000 shares of stock and it earns a net profit of $150,000, it has earned $1.50 ($150,000 ÷ 100,000) per share. If the stock is selling for $30 per share, its P/E is 20 ($30 ÷ $1.50). The yield, the P/E ratio, and other information about the company are used by investors in deciding whether to buy a stock.

Using a Stockbroker

Stocks normally are bought and sold through stockbrokers. A **stockbroker** is a licensed specialist in the buying and selling of stocks and bonds. Through brokers, stockholders state prices at which they are willing to sell their shares. Interested buyers tell brokers what they would be willing to pay for those shares. The brokers then work out a price that is acceptable to both buyers and sellers.

The prices at which stocks are being bought and sold are available through stock market listings in newspapers. Examine Figure 35-4, which gives an explanation of the stock market listing. The highest, lowest, and

Chapter 35 *Investing in Bonds and Stocks* **487**

Basic Skills-Writing

In order for students to become contributing workers in our society, it is important that they become proficient in the basic skills of reading, writing, arithmetic, mathematics, listening, and speaking. Language arts skills are an important component of good writing skills. Students should learn to use pronouns and identify their antecedents. For additional prac-

tice in language arts skills, direct students to answer the Decision-Making Strategies questions at the end of the chapter. Students should write in complete sentences and consciously use personal pronouns. Ask students to underline each personal pronoun they use and its antecedent. Suggest that if they have not used personal pronouns, they are probably overusing the business owner's name.

- Try to schedule speakers with more than one class attending; a larger audience makes better use of the speaker's time.
- If a speaker presents a particular point of view, balance the comments with class discussion at a later time.

STOCK MARKET TRADING

Quotations as of 5 p.m. Eastern Time
Thursday, June 15, 20--

| 52 Weeks | | | | | Yld | | Vol | | | | Net |
Hi	Lo	Stock	Sym	Div	%	PE	100s	Hi	Lo	Close	Chg.
					-A-A-A-						
15³/₄	11⁷/₈	AAR	AIR	.48	3.1	26	212	15¹/₂	15³/₈	15¹/₂	...
24³/₈	19	ABM Indus	ABM	.60	2.7	13	75	22³/₈	21⁷/₈	22³/₈	+ ³/₈
11³/₈	8	ACM Gvt Fd	ACG	.90a	9.7	...	583	9³/₈	9¹/₄	9¹/₄	– ¹/₈
8⁵/₈	6⁷/₈	ACM OppFd	AOF	.66	9.1	...	297	7¹/₄	7⁵/₈	7¹/₄	+ ¹/₈
10³/₈	7¹/₄	ACM SecFd	GSF	.90	10.8	...	1056	8³/₈	8¹/₄	8³/₁₆	– ¹/₈
9	5³/₄	ACM SpctmFd	SI	.75	10.9	...	430	7	6⁷/₈	6⁷/₈	– ¹/₈
12¹/₂	7⁵/₈	ACM Mgmdlnc	ADF	1.26	12.8	...	231	9⁷/₈	9³/₄	9⁷/₈	...
10	7³/₈	ACM MgdlncFd	AMF	1.08a	11.7	...	441	9³/₈	1³/₄	9¹/₄	– ¹/₈
12¹/₄	9¹/₈	ACM MuniSec	AMU	.90a	7.6	...	149	12¹/₈	11⁷/₈	11⁷/₈	– ¹/₈
12¹/₄	9³/₈	ADT	ADT	...	...	14	334	11³/₈	11¹/₄	11¹/₄	– ¹/₈
44³/₄	31⁷/₈	AFLAC	AFL	.52f	1.2	14	232	43¹/₂	43³/₈	43¹/₄	– ¹/₄
41	24	AGCO Cp	AG	.04	.1	6	2626	39¹/₄	38⁵/₈	38³/₄	– ³/₈
24	12⁵/₈	AL Pharma	ALO	.18	1.0	dd	784	18¹/₄	17⁷/₈	17⁷/₈	– ¹/₂
22⁷/₈	17	AMLI Resdntl	AML	1.72f	8.8	18	173	19³/₄	19³/₈	19⁵/₈	...
43⁵/₈	32³/₈	AMP	AMP	.92	2.1	23	9219	45¹/₄	42³/₄	44¹/₄	+ 1¹/₂
75¹/₈	48¹/₈	AMR	AMR	...	...	25	13398	75³/₄	74¹/₂	74³/₄	– ¹/₄
51	41³/₄	ARCO Chm	RCM	2.50	5.4	13	241	46¹/₂	46	46	– ¹/₈
53³/₄	41¹/₂	ASA	ASA	2.00	4.5	...	2991	45³/₈	44³/₈	44³/₄	+ ³/₈
27³/₄	19³/₄	ATT Cap	TCC	.40	1.5	11	125	26³/₈	26¹/₄	26¹/₂	+ ¹/₄

| 52 Weeks | | | | | Yld | | Vol | | | | Net |
Hi	Lo	Stock	Sym	Div	%	PE	100s	Hi	Lo	Close	Chg
15³/₄	11⁷/₈	AAR	AIR	.48	3.1	26	212	15¹/₂	15³/₈	15¹/₂	...
(1)	(2)	(3)	(4)	(5)	(6)	(7)	(8)	(9)	(10)	(11)	(12)

1. Highest price paid for AAR common stock during the past 52 weeks.
2. Lowest price paid for AAR common stock during the past 52 weeks.
3. The company name abbreviated. If the stock quoted is preferred, the letters *pf* would be shown.
4. AAR's ticker tape symbol.
5. The current dividend in dollars per share based on the last dividend paid.
6. The dividend yield based on the current selling price per share.
7. The P/E ratio, comparing the price of the stock with the earnings per share.
8. The number of shares traded, expressed in hundreds. An underline below the stock listing indicates that the stock on that day had a large change in the volume of shares traded.
9. Highest price at which shares changed hands during the day.
10. Lowest price at which shares changed hands during the day.
11. Closing price per share for the day.
12. The change in the closing price today compared with the closing price on the previous day. If the price changed more than 5 percent, the entire stock listing appears in bold type.

FIGURE 35-4 How is a stock's yield different from a bond's yield?

closing prices for stocks sold each day are included in the stock market listing. Many newspapers and other publications have special business sections providing financial information.

For their services, brokers charge a fee called a **commission**. Brokers work through **stock exchanges**, which are business organizations that accommodate the buying and selling of securities. The best known stock exchange is the New York Stock Exchange in New York City. The American Stock Exchange is also in New York City. Regional stock exchanges operate in Boston, Chicago, Philadelphia, and San Francisco. Brokers throughout the nation deal directly with these exchanges by telephone and computer.

Two types of brokers are most common: full-service and discount brokers. A *full-service broker* is one who provides you with information about securities you may want to buy. Full-service brokers work for brokerage houses that have large research staffs.

In contrast, a *discount broker* just places orders for you and offers limited research and other services. They charge lower commissions than do full-service brokers. Investors who have a great deal of information available to them and who can do their own

In recent years, the average P/E ratio for stocks traded on the New York Exchange was about 18.

Basic Skills-Math

In order for students to become contributing workers in our society, it is important that they become proficient in the basic skills of reading, writing, arithmetic, and mathematics. Employers are looking for potential employees with good basic foundation skills. In order to prepare students for the school-to-work transition, we must teach these skills in our classroom.

Applying math across the curriculum is an important element in contemporary education. As a part of end-of-chapter activities, Calculate Business Data enables students to apply their math skills. Appendix B: Math Review, Appendix C: Determining Percentages and Interest in Business, and Appendix D: Using Measurements in Business also apply arithmetic and math skills.

SCANS

NET FACTS

research can save money on commissions by using a discount broker. Numerous discount brokers operate online services that allow investors to access account information and buy and sell securities through their web site, typically for even less than trades made by phone.

INVESTING WITH OTHERS

Some investors like to join with others in making investments. Investment clubs and mutual funds are two common ways you can pool your investments.

Investment Clubs

An **investment club** is a small group of people who organize to study stocks and to invest their money. An agreement is drawn up which states how often the club will meet and how much the members will invest each month. At the meetings, members report on stocks they have studied. The group makes decisions on what stocks to buy. The club's earnings are shared in proportion to the members' investments. Brokers often help groups form investment clubs.

One advantage of an investment club is that membership encourages regular saving. Another advantage is that you learn a great deal about how to judge a stock. Members

How do the activities at stock exchanges affect the investments that you might make?

Net Facts provides information and definitions of terms for the Internet. The more information that students have about the Internet, the better equipped they will be to use this resource. In the Internet Activity Masters, there is an Internet Activity Worksheet for each unit. You can use these activities to give students experience with finding information online. Options for assigning this activity are as follows:

1. **Provide students with a list of addresses for this activity,**
2. **Assign students to conduct their own searches, or**
3. **Use the addresses on the Internet Activity Worksheet.**
   You should complete the activity yourself before assigning it to resolve any discrepancies that may arise.

of the club spread their risk because the combined funds of all members are used to buy stocks in a number of corporations. If the club loses money on one investment, the loss may be offset by other investments that do quite well.

Mutual Funds

Investment clubs are not available to everyone. You may not be able to take the time needed to study the stock market and make

investment decisions. A good understanding of securities, however, is needed to make wise decisions. A mutual fund is another way to join with others in investing and take advantage of their research and knowledge of securities.

Mutual funds are funds set up and managed by investment companies that receive money from many investors and then usually buy and sell a wide variety of stocks or bonds. Mutual fund investors own shares of the mutual fund. A part of the dividends received from the fund's investments is used to pay operating expenses of the fund. The major portion of earnings, however, is distributed to the mutual fund shareholders as dividends or reinvested in the fund.

Many mutual funds are available to investors, and the funds have many different objectives. For instance, some emphasize

Why might someone want to join an investment club?

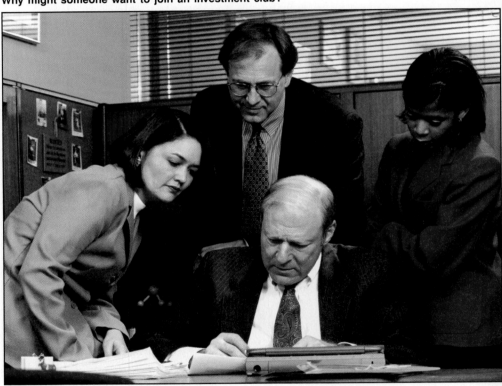

Critical Thinking Skills-Problem Solving

Problem-solving skills, which include recognizing a problem and devising a plan of action, are applied throughout every chapter in this text. Each time a student participates in a Cooperative Learning or Teams activity, problem-solving skills are applied in a group situation. Each time a student completes a math application in Calculate Business Data, decisions are

made as to which mathematical approach must be taken. For each Technology Application problem, students must decide which template problem to use, which piece of software to load, and how to solve the problem. Emphasize to students how they are using problem solving in their day-to-day tasks and make them aware of the skills they are developing.

INVESTMENT TRADE-OFFS

Which Investment?	How Safe?	How Liquid?	How Is Rate of Return?
Savings accounts	Excellent	Excellent	Fair to good
Savings bonds	Excellent	Very good	Good
Other bonds	Very good	Good	Good
Preferred stocks	Fair to good	Good	Very good
Common stocks	Fair	Good	Poor to excellent
Mutual funds	Fair to good	Good	Fair to excellent

FIGURE 35-5 How would you rate a 5-year certificate of deposit for safety? Liquidity? Rate of Return?

investing in growth stocks, some emphasize stocks that pay high dividends, and some emphasize international stocks. Selecting a mutual fund in which to invest also requires you to consider your investment objectives before selecting a particular fund.

WHICH INVESTMENT IS BEST FOR YOU?

You must decide carefully whether or not to invest in stocks and bonds. One important guideline in the decision is whether you can afford to lose part or all of your investment. If you have to sell your stock or your mutual fund when an emergency arises, it might sell for much less than the amount that you paid for it. Before investing in securities, you should have adequate savings in a safe place, such as a bank savings account. You also should have sufficient insurance coverage. The money invested in securities should not be needed to meet your basic living expenses.

Ask yourself which of the following factors are most important to your personal investment plan: safety, liquidity, or rate of return? From your answer, an investment plan can be selected. As shown in Figure 35-5, no single investment can give you the highest possible return and still be very liquid and safe.

Name some important guidelines in deciding whether or not to make investments.

TEACHING STRATEGIES
Teams

Student Teams—Achievement Divisions (STAD) is an instructional method in which students use cooperative learning in peer groups. When using STAD, students are assigned to teams with four members each. Each team will study and review the lesson, making sure that all group members understand the goals and content. Students then take the ExamView on their own with no assistance from team members. Compare each student's score to the current average for that student's previous ExamView. Award two points to students who meet their last ExamView score. Give three points to students who beat their last ExamView score. The team that has the most points is the winner.

REVIEW YOUR READING

1. A debt security (bond) represents amounts owed by a company or government. An equity security (stock) represents ownership in a company.
2. Raise money for operations or future expansion.
3. Interest earned is usually exempt from federal and state income taxes.
4. May be purchased with a payroll deduction plan.
5. Preferred stock pays dividends first when dividends are declared. Common stock does not necessarily pay dividends, but when profits are large, common stock may pay higher dividends. Common stockholders vote for a company's board of directors.
6. Publications such as *Moody's Handbook of Common Stocks*, *Value Line*, and *Standard and Poor's Encyclopedia of Stocks*; brokers; and daily stock listings in newspapers.
7. Has the company been profitable over a period of years? Have the company's managers made good business decisions? Does the company have growth potential in coming years? Does the company have an unusual number of large debts? How does the company compare with others in its industry?
8. Full-service brokers offer more services and provide more information than discount brokers. Discount brokers charge lower commissions because of the fewer services they offer.
9. Based on research and advice from brokers, the members select the bonds and stocks that are bought and sold.
10. Growth stocks, stocks that pay high dividends, and international stocks.
11. Adequate savings in a safe place and sufficient insurance coverage.

COMMUNICATE BUSINESS CONCEPTS

12. The interest earned on municipal bonds usually is not taxed. A lower nontaxed rate can be more valuable than a higher rate that is subject to income taxes.

BUSINESS NOTES

1. A bond represents a debt owed by an organization. Stock is equity and represents ownership.
2. Organizations sell bonds to raise funds to finance current operations or future business expansion.
3. Local and state governments sell municipal bonds. The federal government sells savings bonds, Treasury bills, notes, and bonds.
4. Preferred stockholders receive dividends paid at a set rate. Common stockholders vote to elect the officers of the corporation.
5. When selecting stock investments consider a company's net worth, amount of debt, sales revenue, profits, dividend history, the current outlook for the company's product or service, managerial talents, growth potential, yield, and price-earnings ratio (P/E).
6. Investment clubs and mutual funds allow people to combine their funds to buy a variety of securities, which reduces risk and increases potential returns.
7. Carefully consider investing in stocks and bonds based on your financial needs and goals. Determine the safety, liquidity, and rate of return you require.

REVIEW YOUR READING

1. How does a debt security differ from an equity security?
2. Why do corporations sell bonds?
3. What is a common benefit of investing in municipal bonds?
4. What makes U.S. government Series EE savings bonds a convenient investment?
5. What are some differences between preferred and common stock?
6. What sources of information about stocks are available to investors?
7. What are some important questions to ask when deciding whether or not to purchase stocks?
8. How do full-service stockbrokers differ from discount brokers?
9. Who selects stocks to be purchased by an investment club?
10. What are some different objectives of mutual funds?
11. Before investing in securities, what two financial safeguards should you have?

COMMUNICATE BUSINESS CONCEPTS

12. Why do municipal bonds usually pay a lower rate of interest than corporate bonds?
13. Why does the government pay a higher rate of interest on Series EE bonds held for their full term than on Series EE bonds cashed in early?
14. Give several reasons why people buy stocks even though they are not as safe as some investments.
15. Why would a broker be interested in helping a group of people form an investment club?

13. To discourage investors from cashing in their bonds early.
14. The opportunity to earn a higher rate of return through dividends and growth in the value of the stock.
15. The investment club may use the services of the stockbroker, who would earn commission from the club's stock transactions.
16. If the company goes out of business, Susan might get little or nothing back of the money she invested.

16. Susan Haugen bought $5,000 worth of gold mining stocks a few years ago. Last week she received a letter saying that the company went out of business. It could not operate profitably so it closed down. How much of her investment might Susan lose?

DEVELOP YOUR BUSINESS LANGUAGE

For each numbered item, find the term that has the same meaning.

17. A licensed specialist who helps investors buy and sell stocks and bonds.

18. Bonds issued by local and state governments.

19. A general term for bonds and stocks that are sold by corporations and governments to raise large sums of money.

20. A certificate representing a promise to pay a definite amount of money at a stated interest rate on a specified maturity date.

21. Stock that has priority over common stock in the payment of dividends.

22. A fee charged by brokers for their services.

23. Funds set up and managed by investment companies that receive money from many investors and then usually buy and sell a wide variety of stocks or bonds.

24. The price at which a share of stock can be bought and sold in the stock market.

25. Stock that represents general ownership in a corporation and a right to share in its profits, but has no stated dividend rate.

26. A small group of people who organize to study stocks and invest money.

27. Business organizations that accommodate the buying and selling of securities.

28. The amount borrowed by the seller of a bond.

29. Debt securities issued by corporations.

30. The ratio of a stock's selling price to its earnings per share.

KEY TERMS
bond
commission
common stock
corporate bonds
face value
investment club
market value
municipal bonds
mutual funds
preferred stock
price-earnings ratio (P/E)
securities
stockbroker
stock exchanges

DECISION-MAKING STRATEGIES

Wini Cruz understands the need to evaluate security investments based on safety, liquidity, and rate of return. In addition she realizes that the investments she selects must be guided by her personal financial needs and goals.

31. Wini wants to invest in stocks that will be very safe, highly liquid, and earn an excellent return.

Is there anything wrong with this investment goal?

32. What advice would you give Wini to help her study the companies from which she is considering buying bonds and stocks?

CALCULATE BUSINESS DATA

33. (a) $2,500 × 0.06 = $150 annual interest (b) $150 × 5 = $750 (c) $750 ÷ 2 = $375

34. (a) $50 × 2 = $100; $2,500 × 2 = $5,000; $100 + $5,000 = $5,100 (b) $100 × 2 = $200; $5,000 × 2 = $10,000; $200 + $10,000 = $10,200 (c) $10,200 − $5,100 = $5,100

35. (a) $11.00 − $9.50 = $1.50 (b) $1.50 ÷ $9.50 = 0.158, or 16% (c) 100 × $9.50 = $950.00

36. (a) Stock X: $54.63 ÷ $0.99 = 55.2 or 55; Stock Y: $8.77 ÷ $0.51 = 17.2 or 17; Stock Z: $156.98 ÷ $3.14 = 50 (b) Stock X: $0.99 × 18 = $17.82; Stock Y: $0.51 × 18 = $9.18; Stock Z: $3.14 × 18 = $56.52

37. Consolidated Engineering: $2.80 ÷ $40 = 7.0%; Electro-Jet Company: $3.50 ÷ $42 = 8.3%; Federated Industries: $1.90 ÷ $25 = 7.6%; Instrumentation, Inc.: $1.50 ÷ $25 = 6.0%; Martinez Corporation: $2.20 ÷ $32 = 6.9%; Seaboard Steel: $3.00 ÷ $54 = 5.6%

CALCULATE BUSINESS DATA

33. Jerome Aili owns five Morgan Enterprises bonds, each with a face value of $2,500. Morgan Enterprises pays 6 percent interest on the bonds it has issued.
  a. How much interest does Jerome receive each year on each bond?
  b. What is the total amount of interest Jerome receives each year?
  c. If the interest payments are made semiannually to each bondholder, how much total interest does Jerome receive every six months?

Hint: Refer to Appendix C: Determining Percentage and Interest in Business.

34. Shana Matsumi bought the following Series EE bonds: two $100 bonds and two $5,000 bonds.
  a. How much did she pay for the bonds?
  b. How much will the bonds be worth when the stated time period has passed?
  c. How much interest will she have earned when the stated time period has passed?

35. At the stock exchange, the last sale on Tuesday for the Dandy Auto Corporation was $9.50. The next day it closed at $11.00.
  a. How much was the net change from Tuesday to Wednesday?
  b. By what percentage did the stock increase in value between the close of the first day and the close of the second day? Round your answer to the nearest percentage point.

  c. How much would 100 shares have cost on Tuesday at the closing price?

36. The P/E is the ratio of a stock's price per share compared with the earnings per share.
  a. For each of the stocks in the table, compute the P/E. Round each answer to the nearest whole number.
  b. If each of the stocks had a P/E of 18, what would be the price per share of each stock?

Stock	Price per Share	Earnings per Share
X	$ 54.63	$0.99
Y	8.77	0.51
Z	156.98	3.14

37. Referring to the table, compute the yield for each of the stocks listed. Round your answers to the nearest tenth of a percentage point.

	Price Paid	Annual Dividend
Consolidated Engineering	$40	$2.80
Electro-Jet Company	42	3.50
Federated Industries	25	1.90
Instrumentation, Inc.	25	1.50
Martinez Corporation	32	2.20
Seaboard Steel	54	3.00

TECHNOLOGY APPLICATION

TECHNOLOGY APPLICATION

In this activity, students use a computer to solve a business problem using a file that is provided on the data CD that accompanies *Intro to Business*. Instructions for using the data CD are included in a **README** file on the disk. Solutions are provided on the Instructor's Resource CD.

Using the *Intro to Business* Data CD and your database program software, select problem CH35. After the problem appears on your screen, complete the following activities. Then, after you have completed each step, display or print a report for each activity. If you do not have a printer available, answer the questions before you leave the computer.

38. Select and list the stocks with a closing price of more than $60. How many stocks are listed?

39. Select and list the stocks with a dividend of more than $2.
  a. What is the amount of the highest dividend listed?
  b. What is the company with the highest dividend listed?

40. Sort the database in descending order by price over the last 52 weeks.
  a. Which is the fourth stock listed?
  b. Which is the third-to-last stock listed?

GLOBAL FINANCIAL INSTITUTIONS

In Frankfurt, Germany an investor buys shares of Porsche. In Tokyo, Japan, shares of Mazda are purchased. And on the New York Stock Exchange, interested investors purchase Ford Motor Company shares.

A stock exchange is a location where stocks are bought and sold. In the past, most stock markets were physical places where representatives of buyers and sellers met to negotiate stock prices. Today, some stock exchanges exist only through computer networks with buyers and sellers negotiating online.

The value of stock is affected by a variety of factors. A company's profit potential is probably the most important influence on its stock price. Current economic conditions, such as inflation and interest rates, will also affect stock prices.

More than 70 stock markets exist throughout the world. Some of these are located in Bombay, Copenhagen, Milan, Rio de Janeiro, Seoul, Sydney, and Tel Aviv. In recent years, stock exchanges have also started in countries with developing economies such as the Czech Republic, Russia, South Africa, and Vietnam.

The bond market is another important financial institution for global business. A bond is a certificate representing money borrowed by a business organization or a government. Bonds are bought and sold similar to stock. The market value of a bond varies, based on changing interest rates and the credit rating of the borrowing organization.

The foreign exchange market involves the buying and selling of currencies. These currencies are needed to pay for goods and services that are purchased from companies in different countries. Each day, the value of the dollar (and other currencies) changes in relation to other currencies. For example, when many countries buy U.S. goods and services, these must be paid for in U.S. dollars. As more people buy dollars, this demand pushes the value of the dollar upward. The current value of the dollar (in relation to other currencies) may be obtained from the business section of newspapers or on the World Wide Web.

CRITICAL THINKING

1. Locate a web site for a stock exchange in another country. What companies do you recognize on this stock exchange? What factors affect the value of the stocks traded on this exchange?

2. Describe how changes in currency values might affect a company's decision to do business with a company in another country. How might the foreign exchange market assist buyers and sellers in an international trade transaction?

Most students will either work with international clients or compete against businesses that do. Global Navigator introduces students to issues integral to working with international businesses. Key concepts and challenges faced by international businesses are presented, followed by two Critical Thinking questions that require students to analyze what they have learned.

This Global Navigator feature explains to students the workings of international stock markets, bond markets and foreign exchange markets. These institutions are crucial to the stability of the international economy since they provide the means for the flow of private capital across international borders.

CRITICAL THINKING

1. Specific answers will vary, but the value of stocks on any exchange will be affected by supply and demand, political stability, various economic conditions, currency fluctuations, and profit expectations of investors.

2. Changing foreign exchange values create added risk for companies because they cannot be assured that a certain level of sales and gross profit will result in a predictable return on their investment denominated in their home currency. That added risk may be enough to discourage certain transactions, or prompt companies to hold out for better terms. Foreign exchange markets can reduce currency risk through the sale of futures contracts.

Chapter **36**

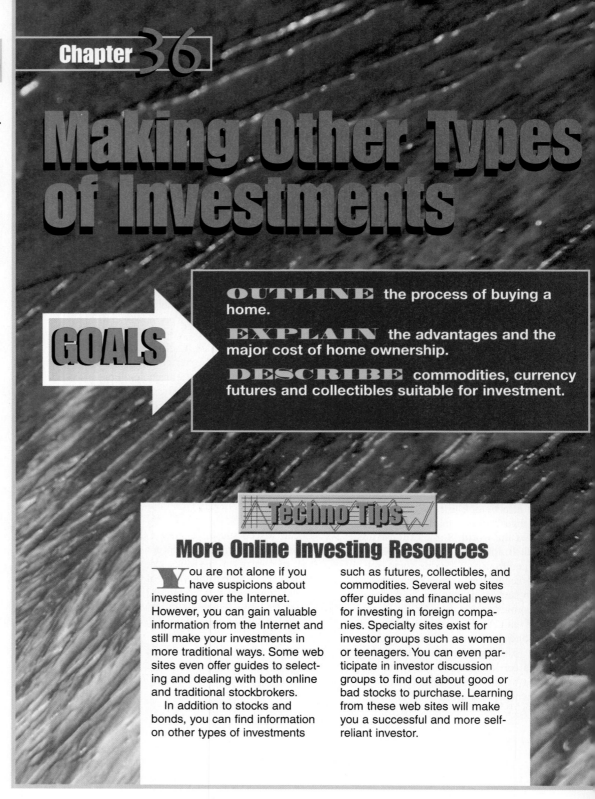

Making Other Types of Investments

This chapter provides an overview of investment alternatives such as real estate. Speculative investments such as commodity futures, precious metals, and collectibles also are covered.

Resources for Teachers
- Lesson Plans
- School-To-Work/SCANS Activity Masters
- Spanish Resources
- Instructor's Resource CD

Assessment
- Chapter and Unit Tests, Ch. 36
- ExamView, Ch. 36

Media/Technology
- Applying Technology Data CD
- PowerPoint slides
- Business Connection CD
- Videotape

Activity Masters and Workbooks
- Activities and Projects, Ch. 36
- Internet Activity Masters
- Business Math Activity Masters
- Communications Activity Masters
- International Business Activity Masters
- Ethics Activity Masters

GOALS

OUTLINE the process of buying a home.

EXPLAIN the advantages and the major cost of home ownership.

DESCRIBE commodities, currency futures and collectibles suitable for investment.

Techno Tips

More Online Investing Resources

You are not alone if you have suspicions about investing over the Internet. However, you can gain valuable information from the Internet and still make your investments in more traditional ways. Some web sites even offer guides to selecting and dealing with both online and traditional stockbrokers.

In addition to stocks and bonds, you can find information on other types of investments such as futures, collectibles, and commodities. Several web sites offer guides and financial news for investing in foreign companies. Specialty sites exist for investor groups such as women or teenagers. You can even participate in investor discussion groups to find out about good or bad stocks to purchase. Learning from these web sites will make you a successful and more self-reliant investor.

Students need to know the latest technologies and develop cutting edge Internet skills for use in current jobs, future careers, or in their homes. TechnoTips introduces students to today's cutting edge technologies and provides them with important Internet skills. Feature topics concentrate on Internet-specific technologies and computer or other hi-tech innovations for use by businesses and consumers.

Driving home from their honeymoon, Joshua Moskowitz turned to his bride Carrie. "You know, we have some money that we received as wedding gifts," said Joshua. "We should buy some stocks for our long-term financial future. I have heard of a lot of people who made fortunes with stocks."

"What do you know about stocks? Are you sure we won't lose our money?" asked Carrie.

"Well, it's true, I don't know much about stocks," responded Joshua. "But I do know baseball cards! Let's invest our money in baseball cards."

"That's kind of risky, isn't it?" was Carrie's next question.

"OK . . . OK. Then let's buy gold bars. Gold can be a solid investment," replied Joshua. "You can't go wrong with gold."

"Hold on. We both want what's best for our future, but don't you think that first we better find a place to live?" responded Carrie.

GETTING STARTED IN REAL ESTATE

Real estate—land and anything that is attached to it—is one investment that most people eventually acquire. Getting started with real estate for most people means finding a place in which to live. Joshua and Carrie Moskowitz are newlyweds. They cannot afford to buy a house right away, although buying a house is a long-term goal they set for themselves.

Renting Your Residence

Joshua and Carrie met their housing needs by renting an apartment. As renters, they were freed from much of the work and expense of repairing the property, fixing the plumbing, and other maintenance. Renting also made it easier for them to move if they changed jobs.

As tenants, Joshua and Carrie took care of their rented property, but they were not able to call the apartment their own. They knew that they wanted to own a house and yard that they could maintain and fix up just the way they wanted. To realize their goal, Joshua and Carrie saved as much money as possible for a down payment on a house.

Owning a Mobile Home

Joshua and Carrie did well in their jobs and felt ready to settle down. They had their first child and decided to examine the housing market. Houses were too expensive for them, but they did find a mobile home in a good location that they could afford. They purchased the mobile home and took their first step toward becoming real estate owners.

The biggest advantage of owning a mobile home was having a place they could call their own. Borrowing money to help buy the mobile home was fairly easy. Their monthly payments were about the same as when they were renting. So they were able to continue to save for their house purchase.

BUYING A HOME

After several years, Joshua and Carrie decided they needed more space. They now had two children and wanted to own a house. They sold their mobile home for almost what they had paid for it. Keeping it in good condition paid off. The experience they had in renting an apartment and owning a mobile home helped them know what kind of house they desired.

Most people will rent a place to live at some time in their lives, usually when first starting on their own or when living alone later in life.

FOCUS ON REAL LIFE

Ask students to list investments other than savings accounts, stocks, bonds, and mutual funds. Copy the suggestions onto the board or an overhead. After several investments are listed, start at the top of the list and ask the class to estimate the riskiness of each investment.

MOTIVATE

PURPOSE Provide a purpose for students as they read the chapter. Ask what they think they will learn. Direct students to skim the chapter, looking at photos, reading captions, and noting main headings. The goals at the beginning of each chapter provide a valuable tool for having students pinpoint main ideas. The tasks required by the goals are signaled in the first word. Some emphasize information collection ("Identify," "List"), while others call for description ("Explain," "Describe"). Ask students to look through all the objectives and note the first word of each. Then ask students to state the purpose of studying this chapter. In this chapter, students will learn about many types of nonfinancial investments.

TEACH/APPLY

MAKE CONNECTIONS Describe the advantages and disadvantages of renting. Explain that a mobile home is an intermediate housing choice between renting and home ownership. Emphasize that most home buyers need to borrow in order to buy a house or condominium. Define a mortgage, explain the two types of mortgages, and describe the professionals available to help home buyers and sellers. Compare and contrast the three benefits and the four costs of home ownership. Define commodities and commodity exchanges. Review the types of commodity investments. Emphasize the double benefits of investing in collectibles: increase in value and personal satisfaction from collecting.

EXPLORE THIS/INDEPENDENT PRACTICE Before assigning independent practice material for any chapter, students should be expected to read the textbook material carefully. In view of the fact that all students vary widely in their ability to read effectively, it is advisable to have students read the entire chapter, or sections thereof, silently in class if the material has not been previously read in connection with homework assignments.

After students have read the chapter, ask them to complete the Chapter Review questions. Develop Your Business Language is an excellent way to improve students' vocabulary. Only words introduced in the chapter are used in the exercises. The Review Your Reading questions can be used to check students' ability to comprehend what they have read. The Communicate Business Concepts section affords an opportunity for students to apply to practical life situations the information gained from reading the chapter. By completing the problems under Calculate Business Data, students will be able to strengthen and refine their abilities in mathematics. Technology Application allows students to demonstrate skill in using word processing, spreadsheet, and

Obtaining a Mortgage

Unless you have many thousands of dollars available, you will need to borrow to buy a house. A **mortgage** is a legal document giving the lender a claim against the property if the principal, interest, or both are not paid as agreed. Joshua and Carrie had monthly mortgage payments that were much higher than the rent or mobile home loan payments they had been making. They now had to watch their spending more carefully.

Mortgages generally are long-term loans—usually for 15, 20, or 30 years—that require monthly payments. Mortgage payments often include property taxes and property insurance in addition to a percentage of the principal and interest charges. Figure 36-1 shows what monthly payments would be required to cover the principal and interest for mortgages of 15, 20, and 30 years at a 10 percent interest rate.

Interest rates on mortgages are commonly set for long periods of time and do not change during the term of the mortgage. This type of mortgage is called a **fixed rate mortgage**. Market interest rates, however, generally increase or decrease quite a bit during the life of a mortgage depending upon economic conditions. Therefore, lenders also offer an **adjustable rate mortgage (ARM).**

The interest rate of an ARM is raised or lowered periodically depending upon the current interest rate being charged by lenders. Monthly payments for ARMs often are lower, especially in the early years of the mortgage, compared with fixed rate mortgages.

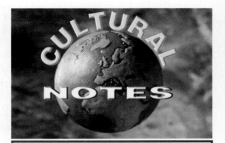

The United States has been known as a *melting pot* because of the variety of people representing many cultures who have settled in the U.S. People from different cultures have learned to live and work together, keeping valued traditions from their own culture while learning to appreciate the traditions of others.

Using Real Estate Agents and Lawyers

Buying a house is not a simple matter. Most home buyers use a **real estate agent,** a person trained and licensed to help with the buying and selling of real estate. Someone who wants to buy a house contacts a real estate agent who helps the person decide what is wanted in a house. The agent will usually arrange for the prospective buyer to view homes available for sale.

Sellers of real estate may also require the assistance of a real estate agent. Someone

MONTHLY PAYMENTS AT 10% INTEREST

Amount Borrowed	15 Years	20 Years	30 Years
$ 5,000	$ 53.73	$ 48.25	$ 43.88
10,000	107.46	96.50	87.76
20,000	214.92	193.00	175.51
30,000	322.38	289.51	263.27
40,000	429.84	386.01	351.03
50,000	537.30	482.51	438.79

FIGURE 36-1 Would you rather pay a loan off sooner or enjoy lower monthly payments?

TEACHING STRATEGIES

Special Needs
Specific Learning Disability (SLD) Students

When asking questions during class, ask SLD students questions that they can likely answer successfully. Save more difficult or unstructured questions for better students.

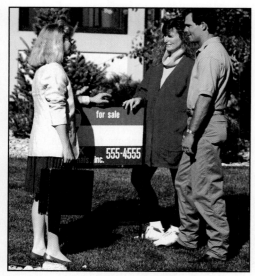

What are some of the advantages of using a real estate agent when buying a home?

who wants to sell a house contacts an agent who then helps to set the selling price and lists the house for sale.

Legal matters are involved when purchasing real estate. A lawyer, working with the real estate agent, should help you with the transaction. A lawyer will help assure that your property has no claims against it, such as back taxes and liens. You need to have your own lawyer represent you in the transaction to help avoid future legal problems.

When buying a house, it is also important to have an appraiser report on the value of the house. An **appraiser** is one who is trained to estimate the value of property and who can give an official report on its value. Such things as the quality of construction, the

A lease is a legal agreement between a renter and the landlord. This document presents information such as a description of the rental unit, dates of the rental agreement, the amount of the security deposit, and the amount and due date of the monthly rent.

When mortgage rates decline, homebuyers may *refinance* their mortgages. This means they obtain a new loan at a lower rate.

location, and the price of similar houses are taken into account in the appraisal.

Buying a Condominium

In recent years, condominiums, or condos, have become popular. A **condominium** is an individually owned unit in an apartment-like building or complex where maintenance and yard work are normally taken care of for a service fee.

BENEFITS OF HOME OWNERSHIP

The advantages of home ownership include tax benefits, increased equity, and pride of ownership.

Tax Benefits

Reduced income taxes result when the interest paid on a mortgage is included as a deductible expense. Real estate property taxes are usually also deductible when computing your federal income taxes.

Increased Equity

From an investment standpoint, the potential increase in equity is an important aspect of home ownership. **Equity** is the difference between the price at which you could currently sell your house and property and the amount owed on the mortgage. Equity builds up over the years and increases rapidly in the last few years of a mortgage.

Because of **appreciation**, a general increase in the value of property that occurs over a period of time, homes increase in value. After Joshua and Carrie lived in their home for ten years, its market value had increased to $144,000 and their debt decreased to $65,000; their equity was $79,000.

database software. Decision-Making Strategies contains material to challenge students to utilize the model explained in Chapter 1 for problem solving.

The Chapter Review questions at the end of the chapter vary in level of difficulty. For a basic assignment, consider Develop Your Business Language and Review Your Reading. For an average assignment, consider the basic assignment plus Communicate Business Concepts and Calculate Business Data. For an enhanced assignment, try the average assignment plus Technology Application and Decision-Making Strategies.

ASSESS

Review the goals at the beginning of the chapter and the Business Notes at the end of the chapter. Have students respond orally or in writing to each Business Note restated as a question. For students who may have difficulty providing answers, assign the reteaching activities that follow. Enrichment activities may also be assigned where appropriate.
1. How can someone get started in real estate? (Answer: Renting, owning a mobile home.)
2. What activities are involved in buying a home? (Answer: Obtaining a mortgage and using real estate professionals.)

Chapter 36 *Making Other Types of Investments* **499**

Workplace Competencies-Interpersonal Skills

Employers are looking for potential employees with good interpersonal skills. As we prepare our students for the school-to-work transition, we must teach these skills in our classroom. Participating as a member of a team is an example of one way to develop these interpersonal skills. As successful team members, individuals share their part of the work load,

learn to listen to each other, realize individual strengths, resolve conflicts, are responsible for accomplishing group goals, and challenge policies and procedures in a responsible manner. The Student Activity Worksheet, Workplace Competencies—Interpersonal Skills, in the School-To-Work/SCANS Activity Masters, may serve as a guideline for discussion of interpersonal skill development.

SCANS

3. Why is home ownership beneficial? (Answer: Tax benefits, increased equity, and pride of ownership.)
4. What are four major costs associated with owning a house? (Answer: Property taxes, interest payments, property insurance, and maintenance.)
5. What agricultural and nonagricultural commodities could be considered for investments? (Answer: Corn, soybeans, wheat, gold, silver, copper, platinum, currency, and financial instruments.)
6. Why are collectibles a form of investment? (Answer: Personal pleasure in collecting and possible increase in value.)

FYI

If a person with a $75,000, 30-year, 10 percent mortgage pays an extra $25 a month on the loan balance, that homebuyer would save over $34,000 in interest. In addition, the loan would be paid off in less than 25 years.

Pride of Ownership

Ownership is one of the basic rights in a democracy. An overriding advantage of owning real estate is pride of ownership. Having a home to use and decorate as desired is a strong motivation for many home buyers.

COSTS OF HOME OWNERSHIP

While there are some important advantages to owning your own property, disadvantages also exist. Home ownership has costs such as property taxes, interest payments, property insurance, and maintenance.

Property Taxes

Property taxes vary greatly from state to state and community to community. Generally, real estate taxes range from 2 to 4 percent of the market value of the property. Taxes are based on the **assessed value**, the amount that your local government determines your property to

TECHNOLOGICAL PERSPECTIVES

Online Investing Information

A brand-new, completely different resource for investors has recently appeared—online investing information! Where is this exciting resource located? It's on the Internet.

This unique resource is dominated by small investors as opposed to large firms of stockbrokers and analysts. Through e-mail, message boards on commercial service providers, and Usenet Newsgroups, investors can rapidly exchange data and intimate knowledge of companies with each other. This information often contrasts with sometimes one-sided, sales-oriented presentations by Wall Street firms.

Online investing information has positive and negative aspects. The positive aspects relate to the availability of information. Government documents and annual reports can be obtained for free. More and more companies are creating World Wide Web sites that provide background information that may be used to predict changes in their stock prices. Stock, monetary, and economic statistics are available at many WWW and Gopher sites. Most important, however, is that all

investors—whether small or large—have equal access to share or obtain all this information.

There are some negatives to online investment information. When you read words on screen, you don't know who is actually writing them. A person who seems to be an expert on stocks may be a brilliant faker. And the wonderful new technology of the Internet is no protection from ancient get-rich-quick scams.

Technology makes it possible to distribute a greater amount of information to a greater number of people. Online investing information is a good example of technology making more data available. You would benefit by learning to take advantage of the wealth of information that can be found online.

Critical Thinking

1. How will the increasing availability of online investing information affect the number of people who invest in financial securities?
2. What can you do to protect yourself against online scams?

TECHNOLOGICAL PERSPECTIVES

Technological Perspectives exposes students to new and contemporary technology and gives them an opportunity to apply this new technology for current and future situations.

CRITICAL THINKING

1. More people should start investing. Many people have hesitated to invest in bonds and stocks in the past because they felt that they did not know enough to be successful investors. Increased and easily available information should help people be more confident to invest in financial securities.
2. Possible answers might include realizing that just because information is on a computer it is not necessarily true; remembering that high returns almost always imply high risk; and being sure to check and double-check investment advice.

be worth for tax purposes. Assessed values normally are lower than the market value, often only about half.

A home with a market value of $90,000 may be assessed at $45,000. If the tax rate is $60 per $1,000 of assessed value, this would result in annual taxes of $2,700 ($45,000 ÷ $1,000 × $60). This rate is 6 percent of the assessed value but only 3 percent of the market value.

Interest Payments

Interest payments add to the cost of the house. For instance, 12 percent interest for 25 years results in payments that more than triple the amount borrowed. A total of $126,387 is paid on $40,000 borrowed. It is the magic of compound interest working in reverse.

Property Insurance

Property insurance is an essential cost. The value of the house, its construction material, its location with respect to other buildings, and the availability of fire protection are among factors affecting the price of homeowners insurance. Typical annual home insurance costs are less than 1 percent of the market value of the house.

Maintenance

The cost of *upkeep*—maintaining your property in good condition—is important in home

ownership. Annual upkeep costs average about 2 percent of the property's value. Postponing repairs or not taking good care of the house and yard through regular maintenance can be very costly in the long run.

INVESTING IN COMMODITIES

Another type of investment considered by experienced investors is commodities. Commodities include grain, livestock, precious metals, currency, and financial instruments. Generally, commodity investing is considered to be speculative. A **speculative investment** is one that has an unusually high risk. Commodity investors deal in **futures**, a commodity contract purchased in anticipation of higher market prices for the commodity in the near future.

Commodity Exchanges

Commodities are bought and sold on exchanges similar to stock exchanges. Buyers

What is your opinion regarding the benefits and costs of home ownership? Is owning a home worthwhile?

A futures contract for wheat, corn, or soybeans consists of 5,000 bushels of the particular grain.

and sellers are represented by traders on the exchanges. One of the best known exchanges is the Chicago Board of Trade (CBOT). The CBOT was established in 1848 to provide a central market for agricultural products. It was also designed to help avoid the huge price fluctuations that had been taking place in the market. The CBOT is governed by the Commodity Futures Trading Commission (CFTC) and the National Futures Association (NFA).

Agricultural Commodities

Agricultural products—such as corn, soybeans, and wheat—are examples of commodities traded on the CBOT and other commodity exchanges. Agricultural producers sell their crops in advance of a harvest at what they believe is a good price. Farmers, then, will know in advance how much they will receive for a crop. The buyers assume that the price of the crop will go up when

harvested so that they can earn a profit. Many conditions affect the agricultural commodities that are traded, such as weather conditions, international trade agreements, and worldwide demand and supply.

Gold, Silver, and Other Precious Metals

Precious metals are of major worldwide importance. Gold and silver have been traded on commodity markets for centuries. Gold has the longest history as a monetary commodity, going back to gold coins that were circulated as early as 500 B.C. Gold is also highly prized for both ornamental and industrial reasons. More recently other metals, such as copper and platinum, have become valuable commodities.

Prices of these metals are affected by factors such as general economic conditions as

A Eurodollar, which is traded in the futures market, is a U.S. dollar deposited in a bank outside of the United States. These funds are used to make payments among countries for foreign trade.

What are some agricultural products and precious metals that are traded on the commodities exchanges?

well as supply and demand. For example, in 1879 gold sold for $18.79 per ounce. Since 1979, the price of an ounce of gold has ranged from over $800 to less than $300.

Precious metals are quoted as spot prices per one troy ounce. The **spot price** is the current price quoted for precious metals in the world markets. You can find the spot price for gold in London and New York in *The Wall Street Journal*, the business section of a daily newspaper, and on many financial sites on the Internet.

Money invested in precious metals does not earn interest. If you hold gold, silver, or platinum, you might profit by selling them later at a price higher than what you paid. Gold and other precious metals have another advantage—many investors see them as protection against currency becoming worthless. Gold is recognized for its value throughout the world. It could be used for buying goods and services when printed money might not be accepted.

Currency and Financial Instruments

Currency, such as the U.S. dollar and the Japanese yen, and financial instruments, such as Treasury bonds and Treasury bills, also are traded on the Chicago Board of Trade and other futures markets. The price of currency and financial instruments is affected by a country's economic outlook and by current interest rates. Here again, investors buy currency or financial instruments expecting the prices to increase in the future so that they can sell them to others at a profit.

INVESTING IN COLLECTIBLES

Another form of investment that is popular with many people is collectibles. **Collectibles** are items of personal interest to collectors that can increase in value in the future.

Examples include stamps, coins, sport trading cards, and antiques.

An advantage of collectibles is the personal pleasure of buying, collecting, storing, arranging, and displaying what is collected. Often organizations of collectors are formed. For example, stamp clubs around the country bring together stamp collectors who buy, sell, trade, display, and discuss their stamps. Baseball card trading takes place at scheduled events in huge arenas as well as over kitchen tables. Antique dealers and collectors gather for major events at which they buy and sell their items.

The possibility of the average buyer of collectibles making a large profit is not great. Only rare stamps, coins, and antiques— which may cost several hundred or thousands of dollars—tend to be those items on which a considerable profit can be made. The wise investor in collectibles studies the market, knows the product well, and analyzes the risk to be taken.

What collectibles would you consider owning? Would you collect for fun, or as a serious investor?

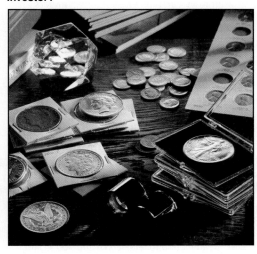

REVIEW YOUR READING

1. Possible answers might include lower initial costs than home buying, freedom from maintenance, and ease of moving if needed.
2. A real estate agent lists property and helps buyers and sellers establish a price. A lawyer will make sure that the buyer gets clear ownership and avoid other legal problems that can occur. An appraiser helps determine the value of the property.
3. Tax benefits, increased equity, and pride of ownership.
4. Property taxes, interest payments, property insurance, and maintenance.
5. The value of the house, its construction material, its location with respect to other buildings, and the availability of fire protection.
6. Corn, soybeans, and wheat.
7. Gold, silver, copper, and platinum.
8. A country's economic outlook and current interest rates.
9. The items collected are of personal interest; pleasure can be gained from collecting, storing, and displaying; clubs and special events are available.
10. Study the market, know the product well, and analyze the risk.

COMMUNICATE BUSINESS CONCEPTS

11. Location is the major factor affecting real estate values because the location affects access to schools, jobs, highways, transportation, stores, and community services.
12. Fixed rate mortgages are desirable if interest rates are expected to rise. Adjustable rate mortgages may be appropriate for home buyers when interest rates are very high and are expected to decline.
13. For retired people, having upkeep performed by someone else is an especially good feature.
14. No. As a home gets older, Blair can expect the need for additional repairs and maintenance at an average of about 2 percent of the value of the house. An $80,000 house may require about $1,600 a year for upkeep.

Chapter REVIEW

BUSINESS NOTES

1. A person can get started in real estate by renting a place to live or by buying a mobile home.
2. When buying a home you may need to obtain a mortgage and use the services of a real estate agent and lawyer.
3. The advantages of home ownership are tax benefits, increased equity, and pride of ownership.
4. The major costs associated with owning a house include property taxes, interest payments, property insurance, and maintenance.
5. Commodities commonly used as investments include corn, soybeans, wheat, gold, silver, copper, platinum, U.S. dollars, Japanese yen, Treasury bonds, and Treasury bills.
6. Collectibles can combine a pleasurable hobby with an investment that may increase in value.

REVIEW YOUR READING

1. Name two advantages of renting an apartment.
2. In what ways can real estate agents, lawyers, and appraisers help with real estate transactions?
3. Name three benefits of home ownership.
4. What costs, in addition to the original investment, are included in the cost of owning a house?
5. What factors help determine the amount charged for insurance on a house?
6. What are some agricultural products that are traded on commodity exchanges?
7. Give examples of precious metals that are used as investments.
8. What can affect the price of currency and financial instruments that are traded as commodities?
9. What makes collectibles attractive to many investors?
10. What is good advice for wise investors who purchase collectibles and other forms of investments?

COMMUNICATE BUSINESS CONCEPTS

11. People who buy and sell land and houses commonly say that the three most important factors to consider when buying real estate are "location, location, and location!" Why do you think this is their belief?
12. In what types of economic conditions would a person prefer a fixed rate mortgage? When might an adjustable rate mortgage be preferred?
13. Why is a condominium often desirable to retired people?
14. Blair Vazquez owns a house that has a value of $80,000. For the past three years, the upkeep has averaged less than $500 a year. Can Blair assume that his expenses will be only $500 in future years?
15. Mei-ling Shen has been collecting coins for several years. She estimates that they are

15. Commodity investments are speculative; Mei-ling should study commodities and commodity markets before investing in them. She also needs to think through her investment goals, including any personal satisfaction she derives from coin collecting.

worth about $2,000. Someone told her that she could make more money investing in commodities. She is considering selling her collection and going into commodities. What advice would you give Mei-ling?

DEVELOP YOUR BUSINESS LANGUAGE

For each numbered item, find the term that has the same meaning.

16. Land and anything that is attached to it.

17. Someone who is trained and licensed to help with the buying and selling of real estate.

18. An individually owned unit in an apartment-like building or complex where maintenance and yard work are normally taken care of for a service fee.

19. A general increase in the value of property that occurs over a period of time.

20. One who is trained to estimate the value of property and who can give an official report on its value.

21. The difference between the price at which you could currently sell your house and property and the amount owed on the mortgage.

22. A traditional mortgage with an interest rate that does not change during the life of the mortgage.

23. The amount that your local government determines your property to be worth for tax purposes.

24. A mortgage for which the interest rate is raised or lowered periodically depending upon the current interest rate being charged by lenders.

25. A legal document giving the lender a claim against the property if the principal, interest, or both are not paid as agreed.

26. The current price quoted for precious metals in the world markets.

27. Items of personal interest to collectors purchased in anticipation of an increase in value in the future.

28. An investment that has an unusually high risk.

29. A contract for a commodity purchased in anticipation of higher market prices in the near future.

KEY TERMS
adjustable rate mortgage (ARM)
appraiser
appreciation
assessed value
collectibles
condominium
equity
fixed rate mortgage
futures
mortgage
real estate
real estate agent
speculative investment
spot price

DEVELOP YOUR BUSINESS LANGUAGE

16. real estate
17. real estate agent
18. condominium
19. appreciation
20. appraiser
21. equity
22. fixed rate mortgage
23. assessed value
24. adjustable rate mortgage (ARM)
25. mortgage
26. spot price
27. collectibles
28. speculative investment
29. futures

DECISION-MAKING STRATEGIES

30. Price negotiation, home values, contracts, and the other legal aspects of home buying.

31. Paying too much for the home or not filing a necessary document which could invalidate the home purchase agreement.

DECISION-MAKING STRATEGIES

Robin Greer has decided to purchase a house. As a result of her business classes and work experience at a real estate office, she has decided to take care of all the details herself. Robin does not plan to use the services of a real estate agent, a lawyer, or an appraiser.

30. What activities will Robin need to understand in the home-buying process?

31. What problems might arise for Robin as a result of not using the services of these professionals?

CALCULATE BUSINESS DATA

32. $500 × 1.07 = $535 new rent; 12 × $535 = $6,420 total cost

33. (a) $820 − $550 = $270 per month; $270 × 12 = $3,240 (b) $820 × 0.90 = $738 monthly interest; $738 × 12 = $8,856 annual interest; $820 × 0.10 = $82 monthly principal; $82 × 12 = $984 annual principal

34. (a) $4,000 + $1,500 + $900 + $250 = $6,650 (b) $65,000 − $40,000 = $25,000

35. (a) 30,000 × $2.98 = $89,400; 30,000 × $3.02 = $90,600; $90,600 − $89,400 = $1,200 profit (b) $1,200 ÷ $89,400 = 0.0134 or 1.3% gain (c) 30,000 × $2.90 = $87,000; $89,400 − $87,000 = $2,400 loss (d) $2,400 ÷ $89,400 = 0.0268 or 2.7% loss

TECHNOLOGY APPLICATION

In this activity, students use a computer to solve a business problem using a file that is provided on the data CD that accompanies *Intro to Business*. Instructions for using the data CD are included in a **README** file on the disk. Solutions are provided on the Instructor's Resource CD.

CALCULATE BUSINESS DATA

32. Don Smith rents an apartment for $500 per month. He has just received a notice that his rent will increase 7 percent. What will be Don's total rental cost for twelve months at the new rate?

33. Bill Fields has been renting an apartment for three years and pays $550 per month for rent. He has an opportunity to buy a house that will require him to pay $820 per month as a mortgage payment.

   a. In one year, how much more will he have to pay for house payments than he now pays for rent?

   b. During the first year, 90 percent of each payment will be for interest and 10 percent will be for principal repayment. What will be the amount he pays for interest for the year? for principal repayment for the year?

34. The Brocks own a house valued at $65,000 and they have a balance on their mortgage of $40,000. Last year they had expenses as shown in the table.

   a. What was the total of their expenses for last year?

Interest on mortgage	$4,000
Taxes	1,500
Upkeep	900
Insurance	250

   b. What is the amount of equity the Brocks have in their house?

35. Steve Fujiwara bought 30,000 bushels of corn in the futures market at $2.98 a bushel. The price of corn rose to $3.02 a bushel.

   a. What was Steve's total dollar profit on this investment?

   b. What was his percentage gain? Round your answer to the nearest tenth of a percentage point.

   c. If the price of corn had dropped to $2.90 a bushel, what would have been Steve's loss in total dollars?

   d. What would have been his percentage loss? Round your answer to the nearest tenth of a percentage point.

TECHNOLOGY APPLICATION

Using the *Intro to Business* Data CD and your word processing program software, select problem CH36. After the problem appears on your screen, complete the following activities. Then, print and sign your completed applications. If you do not have a printer available, save the applications on a data disk to give to your teacher.

36. You are applying to rent an apartment. Complete the application with information about yourself plus the following information. You have lived at your current address for 1¹/₂ years; at your job you make $7.00 per hour and work 8 hours per day, 21 days per month.

For the information that you enter, use a different type font from the one used on the rest of the application.

37. You are applying to rent a mobile home. Complete the application with information about yourself plus the following information. You have lived at your current address for 4¹/₄ years and at your job you make $24,000 per year. For the information that you enter, use italics and a different font of type from the one used on the rest of the application.

NEGOTIATION—LEARNING TO GET ALONG

Conflict is natural within any organization, particularly in business settings where different ways of thinking can build creative, profitable business solutions. A major concern for managers and employees at all levels of a business is how to negotiate different attitudes, mindsets, opinions, and values to reach agreement and resolve conflict.

Negotiation is a process—a tool used by professionals to build bridges between conflicting attitudes and ways of thinking. Negotiation allows for the airing and mediation of differences in order to reach mutual agreement. For example, two equally qualified sales managers may have different thoughts about how to sell a product. The director of sales must negotiate these differences to reach an agreement about how to make the sale.

The first step in the process of negotiation is identifying the conflicting viewpoints. Second, the negotiator must establish a comfortable and trusting environment, free from judgment, before those in conflict will feel able to share their opinions. Successful negotiation allows all parties involved to state their case and build an argument in favor of it. The negotiator must allow each case to develop and then bridge differences by identifying commonalities between the two sides. A typical negotiation process includes answering these questions:

- What is your belief or attitude?
- What are the major elements of your argument?
- What is the opposing/alternative belief or attitude?
- What are the major elements of this alternative?
- What commonalities exist between the two viewpoints?
- What compromise can you agree upon?

The negotiation process can also be used to resolve personal issues such as personal financial situations or problems in relationships with family or friends. In personal circumstances, asking, "What is your belief/attitude?" and identifying alternative attitudes is also key in reaching a compromise. A compromise recognizes the quality elements from each viewpoint. In a personal financial situation, spending habits and personal values can be outlined, and spending that does not support those values can be restricted to allow for better financial growth.

Negotiation skills are vital to personal and professional well being. You should spend time early in your career identifying the interpersonal skills you will need to be a successful negotiator.

CRITICAL THINKING

1. What is negotiation?
2. Name three questions you might ask in a typical negotiation process.

COMMUNICATING for SUCCESS

Communications skills will help ensure students' success in the business world. Communicating for Success introduces workplace/interpersonal communications issues and proper uses of communications technology. Each feature discusses a key communications topic, and contains two Critical Thinking questions that require students to analyze what they have learned.

This Communicating for Success feature focuses on the nature of the negotiating process and its crucial role in resolving conflict in business situations as well as more personal matters. Students will learn the various steps of the negotiating process. The feature also outlines some typical issues that should be resolved as part of that process.

CRITICAL THINKING

1. Negotiation is a process; a tool used by professionals to build bridges between conflicting attitudes and ways of thinking. Negotiation allows for the airing and mediation of differences in order to reach mutual agreement.
2. Answers may include any of the following:
   - What is your belief or attitude?
   - What are the major elements of your argument?
   - What is the opposing/alternative belief or attitude?
   - What are the major elements of this alternative?
   - What commonalities exist between the two viewpoints?
   - What compromise can you agree upon?

GLOBAL BUSINESS PROJECT

Changing exchange rates, weak economic development, and high inflation are some of the common concerns of investors looking at the global economy. The international investment environment is important to investors and business managers considering expansion into new regions of the world. In this phase of the global business plan, students will research the economic and investment situation of the country they have been studying.

To finance global business operations, a manager must assess various alternatives. Students will be asked to compare various factors that influence a company's decision to issue stock or bonds. Finally, factors that influence a nation's currency will be considered.

To complete each phase of this project, students are encouraged to use various resources—textbook content, library materials, World Wide Web sites, interviews, advertisements, product packages, in-store observations. The individual activities are planned for use as either (1) an on-going course project, or (2) individual assignments.

Whether used as a continuing project or for selected activities, consider having students work in teams. This small group experience provides a valuable skill for future learning and work situations.

In addition to search engines, these selected web sites can be helpful for this unit.
- World Trade Organization at (www.wto.org)
- Current country information at (yahoo.com/regional/countries)
- World Bank (www.worldbank.org)
- Export-Import Bank of the United States (www.exim.gov)
- International Chamber of Commerce (www.iccwbo.org/)
- U.S. Central Intelligence Agency World Factbook (www.cia.gov)
- Global stock exchanges, foreign

GLOBAL BUSINESS PROJECT

SELECT GLOBAL INVESTMENT OPPORTUNITIES

The international investment environment is affected by changing economic conditions, variable currency values, and unstable political situations. As businesses enter foreign markets, the value of a company's investment will be affected by these and other factors.

In this phase of the global business plan project, you will compare various factors that influence a company's decision to issue stock or bonds. In addition, the value of a country's currency will be researched.

PROJECT GOALS
1. Research the investment potential of a foreign country.
2. Compare the desirability of issuing stock and bonds for international business operations.
3. Identify factors that influence currency values of a nation.

PROJECT ACTIVITIES
Using your textbook, library materials, web sites, interviews with people, and other resources, complete the following activities:
1. Investors attempt to invest in countries with strong economic and business potential. Using the country you have studied (or another one), research expected economic conditions and business opportunities for this nation. What recommendations would you make to investors about this country?
2. Companies finance business operations using debt (bonds) or equity (stock). List the advantages and disadvantages of issuing stock or bonds to finance the international business operations for your business idea.
3. The value of a country's currency is most influenced by its balance of payments, economic conditions (especially inflation), and political stability. Research recent changes in the value of the currency of the country you have studied. Explain what factors may have caused these variations in the exchange rate.

PROJECT WRAP-UP
1. Continue your portfolio (folder, file box, or other container) for storing and referring back to the information and materials you created in the activities above. This portfolio will be the foundation for your global business plan.
2. Create a chart or graph that reports stock values or currency exchange rates in another country. Discuss factors that may have influenced changes in these values.

exchange (www.globalfindata.com) (www.ubs.com)
- Annual reports, company information (www.reportgallery.com) (www.hoovers.com)
- SEC filings (www.sec.gov/edgar.shtml)

FOCUS ON CAREERS

INVESTMENTS

People save and invest their money in many ways. A growing need exists for savings and investment workers to guide investors in choosing just the right plan. This results in employment opportunities for those interested in helping others plan their financial futures.

JOB TITLES

Job titles commonly found in this career area include:

- Brokerage Clerk
- Economist
- Financial Analyst (Securities Analyst)
- Financial Services Sales Agent
- Order Clerk
- Personal Financial Advisor (Financial Planner)
- Real Estate Appraiser
- Real Estate Agent
- Real Estate Broker
- Statistical Assistant
- Securities and Commodities Sales Agent (Stockbroker)

EMPLOYMENT OUTLOOK

- As more individuals become involved in investments, the demand for securities sales workers will increase.
- Clerical and research workers with computer skills and finance knowledge are used in a variety of areas.

EDUCATION AND TRAINING

- Familiarity with legal terminology as well as a knowledge of investment technical terms is valuable.
- Sales workers, who generally serve as stockbrokers, must obtain a state license to sell securities.
- Real estate agents and brokers must also pass a state test for their licenses.
- Financial planners should have a knowledge of money management, taxes, investments, and retirement planning, and may attain a certified financial planner designation.

SALARY LEVELS (IN RECENT YEARS)

- Median annual earnings of securities and financial services sales agents are about $56,000, but the range is quite wide. The bottom 10 percent earn less than $25,000, while the top ranks earn well over $100,000. Experienced salespeople generally work on commission and bonuses, and earnings can be volatile depending on market conditions. Trainees are usually paid a salary until they meet licensing requirements.
- Median annual earnings for real estate agents have been about $28,000; for real estate brokers, $48,000. For either, the range is quite wide. Real estate agents and brokers work on commission. Commercial property and raw land generally pay higher rates than houses. Several agents and brokers may share a commission for working on the same sale. Real estate appraisers generally receive a fee per appraisal.

CRITICAL THINKING

1. How do economic conditions affect the demand for investment jobs?
2. What training and knowledge would be important for success in investment careers?

FOCUS ON CAREERS

The careers listed in the Career Focus come from the *Occupational Outlook Handbook*, an online publication (www.bls.gov/oco) of the federal government. The O*NET codes for these job titles are: Brokerage Clerk, 43-4011.00; Economist, 19-3011.00; Financial Analyst (Securities Analyst), 13-2051.00; Financial Services Sales Agent, 41-3031.02; Order Clerk, 43-4151.00; Personal Financial Advisor (Financial Planner), 13-2052.00; Real Estate Appraiser, 13-2021.00; Real Estate Agent, 41-9022.00; Real Estate Broker, 41-9021.00; Statistical Assistant, 43-9111.00; Securities and Commodities Sales Agent (Stockbroker), 41-3031.01.

A Career Focus Worksheet is available in the School-To-Work/SCANS Activity Masters.

CRITICAL THINKING

1. As employment levels decline people do not have as much money for saving and investing, creating less demand for investment jobs. In addition, changing interest rates tend to attract people to different types of investments, leading to shifts in employment.
2. Accuracy with numbers, computer skills, investment knowledge, and a study of economics, finance, marketing, and real estate.

UNIT 11

BUILDING YOUR PORTFOLIO

CAREER DEVELOPMENT – ORGANIZING YOUR PORTFOLIO

The Building Your Portfolio career exercise will help your students establish a personal history—where they have been, where they are now, and where they are going. This exercise will require students to prepare the table of contents and letter of introduction for their portfolios.

Putting together a portfolio helps students see their growth and achievements. Discuss procedures for organizing portfolios. As a supplemental activity, you may refer to the School–To–Work/SCANS Activity Masters.

TEACHING STRATEGIES

SCANS

Special Features

Media/Technology

Chapter	Spreadsheet Software	Database Software	Word Processing Software	Internet	Video
37		■			■
38			■	■	
39		■			■
40	■				■
41	■				■

Resources

SOFTWARE

Excel, Word, WordPerfect, Works, and ClarisWorks for Mac and Windows

Word Pro, ASCII, QuattroPro, Lotus, and Access for Windows

SOUTH-WESTERN EDUCATIONAL PUBLISHING PRODUCTS

Adamson. *Law for Business and Personal Use*. 2004. Cincinnati: South-Western Publishing Company. Textbook. 0-538-43622-0

Donnelly. *Skills for Consumer Success.* 1999. Cincinnati: South-Western Educational Publishing Company. Text-Workbook. 0-538-68612-X.

BOOKS

Vaughan and Vaughan. *Fundamentals of Risk and Insurance*. 1999. John Wiley & Sons.

Baldwin. *Guide to Insuring Your Life, Health, Property and Income*. 1996. Probus Publishing Co.

PERIODICALS

Educators' Resource Book of Insurance Terms. Free from The Horace Mann Companies, One Horace Mann Plaza, Springfield, IL 62715.

Insurance Careers. Free from Wallace Witmer Co., PO Box 40169, Memphis, TN 38174.

GOVERNMENT PUBLICATIONS

Occupational Outlook Handbook, U.S. Department of Labor, Washington, DC.

What Work Requires of Schools: A SCANS Report for America 2000, U.S. Department of Labor, Washington, DC

MEDIA/TECHNOLOGY

Publisher's web sites:
www.intro2business.swep.com
www.swep.com
www.thomson.com

RISK MANAGEMENT

The content and activities of this unit provide students with an overview of the purposes and characteristics of insurance and economic risks. Use the resources listed on the previous page, especially those from South-Western Educational Publishing, as you prepare to teach insurance concepts.

This unit on insurance is one of the most important, as well as one of the longest units, in the text. In keeping with the general theme of this book, the unit is titled Risk Management and concentrates on how consumers and businesspeople can manage the risks associated with life and doing business. After introducing students to the fundamentals of insurance and the concept of shared risk in Chapter 37, vehicle insurance, with an emphasis on automobile insurance, is introduced in Chapter 38. Next, descriptions of various insurance policies that will protect the insured against home and property losses are emphasized in Chapter 39. Chapter 40 continues insurance coverage with a focus on life insurance, while Chapter 41 concludes the unit with health insurance.

UNIT 11

RISK MANAGEMENT

Chapters

Kick-Off Activity

Investigating Business Media

To make the connection between today's business news and *Intro to Business,* an opening activity is provided for student investigation. The following exercise asks students to choose an article from *The Wall Street Journal,* the financial section of a newspaper, or a business magazine and to inquire about a topic related to this unit.

Students should select a recent issue of a business magazine or financial newspaper wherein information is available about small start-up companies. Students should locate one new company that markets a product and another that sells a service. Then have students answer the following questions:

1. What kinds of insurance do these companies need?
2. How does each of these small companies compare as to business risks and the need for insurance?
3. If you were opening a small business, what kinds of insurance protection would you consider?

BU$INE$$BRIEF

Do You Need Health Insurance?

As living expenses continue to increase, people try to find ways to reduce their costs. We all know that going to a doctor or being admitted to a hospital for an illness or an injury can be very expensive. The average cost in the U.S. for each patient admitted to a hospital is nearly $5,500. That average can be very misleading, however. It includes people who have a minor treatment that may cost only a few hundred dollars. But it also represents someone who may be hospitalized for several weeks or who needs to undergo an expensive surgery that costs hundreds of thousands of dollars.

Health insurance is expensive and costs continue to increase faster than the rate of inflation. A recent survey found that the average cost to each individual for health insurance was $173 each month. Families paid an average of $334 each month of health insurance coverage. When you consider having to spend between $2,000 and $4,000 each year for health insurance, you might decide that you can afford to go without.

About 14 percent of U.S. citizens do not carry health insurance. There are some groups where that percentage is even higher. Over 18 percent of African-Americans are uninsured, while almost one third of Hispanic-Americans

do not have health insurance. Twenty-seven percent of people between the ages of 18 and 24 do not carry health insurance coverage.

People who do not have health insurance either do not believe they can afford the monthly costs or are willing to risk that they will remain healthy or injury-free and will not require medical attention. However, if they are wrong, they may find that they owe thousands of dollars to a hospital or doctor or that they will have trouble obtaining medical care when they need it.

Many companies help their employees by providing health insurance at a lower cost than if the individual had to purchase the coverage. For the elderly or people with low incomes, government programs such as Medicare and Medicaid provide some health insurance coverage. While you may not think that health insurance is worth the cost, everyone needs to consider how they will pay the cost of medical care if they need it.

CRITICAL THINKING

1 *Why do such a high percentage of young people choose not to carry health insurance?*

2 *Do you believe that laws should be passed to require everyone to have health insurance coverage?*

511

BU$INE$$BRIEF

A Business Brief sets the tone for a unit. To help students understand current and emerging trends, each unit will be introduced with a Business Brief. The Briefs were chosen for their importance to business, timeliness, and interest to students. The Briefs complement the many real-world examples woven into the text.

Students are probably already familiar with insurance and may have heard discussions about the cost of health care. Initiate discussion of health care, its costs, and the reasons for health insurance to see how much students know about the topic.

After reading the Business Brief, ask students what impressed them the most. Have they heard or read about this topic before?

At the conclusion of the discussion, direct students to answer the Critical Thinking questions.

CRITICAL THINKING

Student answers will, of course, require thinking beyond what is presented in the Business Brief. Answers will be based on students' perceptions of the topic and the experiences they have had with it. The following are possible answers:

1. Many younger people have lower paying jobs and have many immediate expenses so they believe they cannot afford the costs. They may believe they will not get sick or injured.

2. Some believe that people who have no insurance increase taxes and the costs of medical care to others. But, it may be impossible for some people to afford the insurance even if there was a law requiring it.

BUILDING YOUR PORTFOLIO

The Building Your Portfolio work samples validate skill level and a student's ability to accomplish tasks frequently performed on the job. The most important reason for including samples in a portfolio is to demonstrate a student's abilities and skills. In selecting work samples for each unit, students should always have a choice of which activities to include. Students might be encouraged to include samples from the end-of-chapter activities, particularly Communicate Business Concepts, Calculate Business Data, Technology Application, and Decision-Making Strategies.

Chapter 37 introduces students to the fundamentals of insurance and the concept of shared risk. Basic vocabulary related to insurance is introduced, as well as the factors that affect the cost of insurance coverage.

Resources for Teachers
- Lesson Plans
- School-To-Work/SCANS Activity Masters
- Spanish Resources
- Instructor's Resource CD

Assessment
- Chapter and Unit Tests, Ch. 37
- ExamView, Ch. 37

Media/Technology
- Applying Technology Data CD
- PowerPoint slides
- Business Connection CD
- Videotape

Activity Masters and Workbooks
- Activities and Projects, Ch. 37
- Internet Activity Masters
- Business Math Activity Masters
- Communications Activity Masters
- International Business Activity Masters
- Ethics Activity Masters

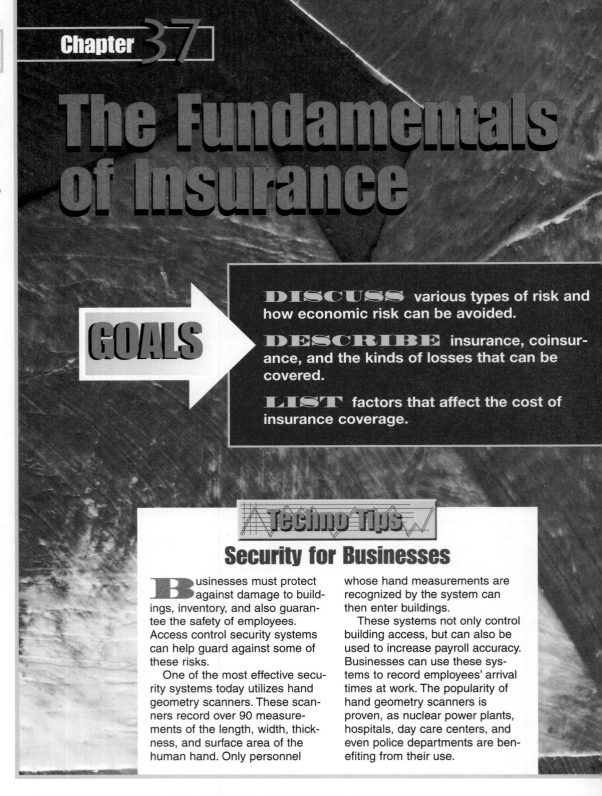

Chapter 37

The Fundamentals of Insurance

GOALS

DISCUSS various types of risk and how economic risk can be avoided.

DESCRIBE insurance, coinsurance, and the kinds of losses that can be covered.

LIST factors that affect the cost of insurance coverage.

Techno Tips

Security for Businesses

Businesses must protect against damage to buildings, inventory, and also guarantee the safety of employees. Access control security systems can help guard against some of these risks.

One of the most effective security systems today utilizes hand geometry scanners. These scanners record over 90 measurements of the length, width, thickness, and surface area of the human hand. Only personnel whose hand measurements are recognized by the system can then enter buildings.

These systems not only control building access, but can also be used to increase payroll accuracy. Businesses can use these systems to record employees' arrival times at work. The popularity of hand geometry scanners is proven, as nuclear power plants, hospitals, day care centers, and even police departments are benefiting from their use.

Students need to know the latest technologies and develop cutting edge Internet skills for use in current jobs, future careers, or in their homes. TechnoTips introduces students to today's cutting edge technologies and provides them with important Internet skills. Feature topics concentrate on Internet-specific technologies and computer or other hi-tech innovations for use by businesses and consumers.

FOCUS ON REAL LIFE

"Tien, did last night's storm do any damage to your parents' home?"

"Yes, Katie, it blew the roof right off the house! But since we were all unharmed, Dad isn't too upset about it because we have insurance to cover the loss. You know how conscientious my parents are about everything. We even have smoke detectors and a fire extinguisher on every floor of the house! They say that by being safety oriented, they

protect us and even save money on insurance premiums each year."

"I wonder what kind of coverage my parents have. We were lucky not to have had any storm damage last night. Maybe I will bring this up with them at dinner tonight."

Tien's parents know that by being careful and conscientious—and being insured—we can protect ourselves against unexpected loss. However, no matter how careful we are, there are certain losses that may occur that are beyond our control.

RISK

Risk can be thought of as the possibility of incurring a loss. Even if you are very careful, you probably will not be able to avoid all losses. **Economic risk** can be related to property liability and one's own personal well being. Economic risks can be placed into three categories: personal risks, property risks, and liability risks. **Personal risks** are risks associated with illness, disability, loss of income, unemployment, old age, and premature death. The risks of damage to or loss of property due to theft, wind, fire, flood, or

some other hazard are called **property risks**. While personal and property risks involve economic losses to you, **liability risks** are potential losses to others that occur as a result of injury or damage that you may have caused. You can insure against all of these types of risk.

SHARING ECONOMIC RISK

Most individuals and businesses cannot pay for large economic losses, so they share the risk with other individuals or businesses. Suppose you and nine of your friends have new

What are some risks involved with owning a home or business?

Chapter 37 The Fundamentals of Insurance   **513**

term. Coinsurance presents an opportunity to demonstrate applied math by working through some examples of how deductibles and co-payments work. Refer students to Figure 37-2, Coinsurance, in the chapter. Discuss the factors that influence the cost of premiums. Premiums for students are usually rather high and most students probably don't quite understand why.

TRY THIS/GUIDED PRACTICE
Walk students through the decision-making process for purchasing insurance. As was explained in Chapter 1, there are certain steps that should be followed whenever a major buying decision is made. This six-step process will help students understand the importance of selecting the appropriate types of insurance.

EXPLORE THIS/INDEPENDENT PRACTICE Before assigning independent practice material for any chapter, students should be expected to read the chapter material carefully. In view of the fact that all students vary widely in their ability to read effectively, it is advisable to have the students read the entire chapter, or sections thereof, silently in class if the material has not been previously read in connection with homework assignments.

After students have read the chapter, ask them to complete the Chapter Review questions. Develop Your Business Language is an excellent way to improve students' vocabulary. Only words introduced

FIGURE 37-1 Would you want to pay for someone else's clubs, even if you took care of your own to make sure they were not stolen?

sets of golf clubs. Each of your sets is worth about $300. You and your friends decide to form an organization called the Golf Club Owners Insurance Association (GCOIA) as shown in Figure 37-1. The purpose of the GCOIA is to protect members from a large financial loss should one member's clubs get stolen. To provide protection, each member agrees to share the cost of replacing any stolen clubs. Therefore, if your golf clubs are stolen, each member (including yourself) would contribute $30 to buy new ones for you.

If you are not a member of the GCOIA and your clubs are stolen, you would have to pay the total cost ($300) of new clubs. As a member, new clubs would only cost you $30. When a member loses golf clubs, each member suffers only a relatively small economic loss. In that way, the members help one another by sharing the risk of economic loss.

INSURANCE

Insurance is the planned protection provided by sharing economic losses. Insurance provides you with the peace of mind that comes from knowing you are protected from economic loss. With insurance, a house fire, car accident, appendectomy, or early death will not cause you or your family economic difficulties.

Insurance companies are businesses that provide planned protection against economic loss. Insurance companies, similar to the GCOIA, agree to assume certain economic risks for you and to pay you if a loss occurs. The person for whom the risk is assumed is known as the **insured** or **policyholder**.

Most insurance policies have a monetary limit on the coverage of items that are lost or stolen.

TEACHING STRATEGIES
Special Needs
Attention Deficit Disorder

Provide students with activities that are short and focused. These students do better with basic assignments (see lesson plan Explore This/Independent Practice) instead of lengthy ones.

A *claims adjuster's* job duties include:
- Determining whether the customer's insurance policy covers a loss
- Determining the amount of loss
- Collecting information from claimants regarding expenses
- Interviewing claimants and witnesses
- Consulting police and hospital records
- Inspecting property damage
- Negotiating with the claimants and settling claims.

To show that risk has been assumed, the company issues a contract to the policyholder. A contract issued by the insurance company for coverage for the policyholder is called a **policy**. The policy states the conditions to which the insurance company and the policyholder have agreed. For example, a policyholder may agree not to allow an unlicensed person to drive an insured car, or not to go skydiving.

The amount the policyholder must pay for insurance coverage is called a **premium**. The policyholder usually makes payments once a month, once every six months, or once a year. The premiums from all the policyholders make up the funds from which the insurance company pays for claims. The company invests the premiums. The additional amount earned from these investments allows the company to make a profit and to cover the costs of claims if they are greater than expected.

A **claim** is a policyholder's request for payment for a loss that is covered by the

Consider the largest deductible you can afford. The higher the deductible, the lower the premium.

insurance policy. A **deductible** is an amount you must pay before the insurance company pays a claim. For example, if your car suffers $2,500 damage in an accident and your deductible amount is $500, you would pay $500 and the insurance company would pay $2,000 (damages $2,500 − $500 deductible = claim $2,000).

Insured Losses

Both consumers and businesses are able to buy insurance to cover almost any kind of economic loss. Violinists can insure their fingers, professional athletes can insure against injuries, and writers may insure their manuscripts. Businesses are able to insure against the loss of rent from property damaged by fire, injury to consumers while they are on the company premises or resulting from the use of the company's product, or theft by employees. The kinds of insurance protection that will be important to most people, however, are insurance for automobiles and homes, life insurance, health insurance, and insurance for income security.

Self-Insurance

Some individuals, families, and businesses have decided that the best way to protect

What special type of insurance might a professional athlete want to have?

The careers listed in the Career Highlights come from the *Occupational Outlook Handbook*, an online publication (www.bls.gov/oco) of the federal government. The O*NET code for Claims Adjuster is 13-1031.00. Tell your class about this resource and how to use it. This description of job duties can be used to demonstrate the relevancy of skills learned in this course.

in the chapter are used in the exercises. The Review Your Reading questions can be used to check students' ability to comprehend what they have read. The Communicate Business Concepts section affords an opportunity for students to apply to practical life situations the information gained from reading the chapter. By completing the problems under Calculate Business Data, students will be able to strengthen and refine their abilities in mathematics. Technology Application allows students to demonstrate skill in using word processing, spreadsheet, and database software. Decision-Making Strategies contains material to challenge students to utilize the model explained in Chapter 1 for problem solving.

Chapter 37 *The Fundamentals of Insurance* 515

Personal Qualities-Responsibility

Being responsible, or exerting a high level of effort and perseverance towards a goal, is a personal quality for which employers are looking. People are worried about such issues as acid rain, global warming, oil spills, chemicals in their food and water, and polluted air. Rightly or wrongly, business is blamed for causing many of these environmental trou-

bles. Environmental Perspectives is an appropriate place to discuss the responsibilities of businesses toward the environment. It exposes students to some of the environmental issues facing businesses today.

SCANS

The Chapter Review questions at the end of the chapter vary in level of difficulty. For a basic assignment, consider Develop Your Business Language and Review Your Reading. For an average assignment, consider the basic assignment plus Communicate Business Concepts and Calculate Business Data. For an enhanced assignment, try the average assignment plus Technology Application and Decision-Making Strategies.

ASSESS

Review the goals at the beginning of the chapter and the Business Notes at the end of the chapter. Have students respond orally or in writing to each goal restated as a question. For students who may have difficulty providing answers, assign the reteaching activities that follow. Enrichment activities may also be assigned where appropriate.

1. How do the various types of risks compare and contrast? (Answer: Personal risks are risks associated with illness, disability, loss of income, unemployment, old age, and premature death. Property risks are risks of damage to—or loss of property due to—theft, wind, fire, flood, or some other hazard. Liability risks are potential losses to others that occur as a result of injury or damage that you may have caused.)

against economic losses is through self-insurance. **Self-insurance** means that the individual, family, or business assumes the total risk of economic loss. For instance, a family might regularly place money in a savings account to cover possible financial losses. Most families, however, would find it almost impossible to self-insure against economic

catastrophes such as the cost of an extended illness or the cost of replacing a house that was destroyed by a fire.

Large businesses or institutions may choose to insure themselves against certain kinds of losses. A company might, for example, determine that the average cost for damages to its fleet of company cars is $25,000 per year. It then establishes a special self-insurance fund for this purpose. Each year it contributes money to the fund rather than paying insurance premiums. When a car is damaged, the cost of repairs is paid from the self-insurance fund.

Policyholders should know exactly what protection is provided by the kinds of insurance they have. Some people fail to tell their

ENVIRONMENTAL PERSPECTIVES

Insuring Against Natural Disasters

Wind damage in the South, earthquake damage in the West, and flooding in the Midwest are common newspaper headlines. These events have brought new attention to perils not usually covered by standard homeowners policies. In addition to the human misery associated with these tragedies, there can be a significant amount of economic loss. Insurance companies have paid billions of dollars in claims to people whose houses were blown down, crumbled, or soaked beyond repair.

Most homeowners policies include insurance for windstorm damage. However, companies may exclude coverage for the peril if a house is unusually vulnerable to windstorms by virtue of its location. Six coastal states (Alabama, Florida, Louisiana, Mississippi, North Carolina, and Texas) have beach and windstorm plans to pick up where the regular policies leave off.

Most insurance companies offer earthquake coverage as an endorsement on homeowners policies. Premiums can run as

high as 50 percent of a home's regular coverage, but rates vary according to the vulnerability of the house. Wood frame homes, which tend to withstand quakes better than brick, cost much less to insure.

The National Flood Insurance Program, administered by the Federal Emergency Management Agency (FEMA), offers flood insurance through the federal government and approximately 85 private insurers. To qualify homeowners must live in a designated flood prone community that has taken specified steps to control flood damage.

Critical Thinking
1. When buying insurance, should people from all across the United States be asked to share the risk of natural disasters that occur most frequently in predictable areas? Why?
2. If you were a resident of Illinois living in low-lying area near the Mississippi River how would you deal with the high cost of flood insurance?

ENVIRONMENTAL PERSPECTIVES

Students should have some understanding of how disasters affect not only people's lives, but the economy as well. One issue they may not have considered is how insurance rates are affected by these acts of nature.

CRITICAL THINKING
1. Yes: That is what insurance is all about—sharing risks. By sharing risks across the country, the costs should average out so that no one is paying more than his or her share. No: People in high risk areas should bear the costs themselves.
2. Solutions include: develop a self-insurance fund, move to higher ground, and encourage the government of the state of Illinois or the federal government to build flood protection dikes in the area.

insurance companies about losses they have suffered because they did not know that their policies covered those losses. Other people have assumed that losses they suffered were covered by their insurance, only to find out by reading their policies that the losses were not covered.

Coinsurance

Coinsurance is the sharing of expenses by the policyholder and the insurance company. The policyholder typically pays a deductible, then shares the remaining loss with the insurance company. For example, if the insurance company pays 80 percent of the cost for medical treatment after the deductible is paid, the policyholder will pay the remaining 20 percent. The share, however, is capped or limited to a specific dollar amount stated in the policy. Once the deductible and the coinsurance amounts are satisfied, the insurance company reimburses 100 percent of the cost up to the policy's coverage limits.

Looking at the example in Figure 37-2, assume you have a claim for $5,250 and your deductible is $250. The remaining amount after the deductible is paid is $5,000 (claim $5,250 − deductible $250 = remaining $5,000). Your insurance policy says that once the deductible is subtracted from the total amount of the claim, the policyholder will pay 20 percent of the remaining amount. Therefore, you would pay $1,000 ($5,000 × 20% = $1,000) as the coinsurance portion. The insurance company would pay the

A *client* is a computer connected to the Internet. Clients contain software needed to exchange data with other computers on the Internet.

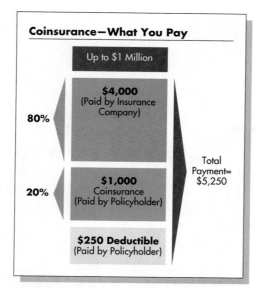

Coinsurance—What You Pay

Up to $1 Million

80% — $4,000 (Paid by Insurance Company)

20% — $1,000 Coinsurance (Paid by Policyholder)

$250 Deductible (Paid by Policyholder)

Total Payment = $5,250

FIGURE 37-2 How does coinsurance keep your premiums lower while still protecting against large losses?

remaining $4,000 ($5,000 − $1,000 = $4,000). Your total payment would be the $250 deductible plus the coinsurance of $1,000 for a total of $1,250.

COST OF INSURANCE

Insurance companies are always looking for ways to reduce the cost of premiums to policyholders. The premium charged for each type of policy is determined partly by the past experiences of insurance companies in paying for the kinds of losses covered by each policy. For example, insurance companies have found that a 20-year-old driver is a greater risk because he or she is more likely to have an auto accident than a 40-year-old driver. Therefore, car insurance premiums for 20-year-old drivers are higher than they are for older drivers.

Premiums also are affected by the cost of replacing the insured item. If you insure a luxury car, premiums will be higher than they would be for a less expensive model.

The larger the number of claims an insurance company has to pay, the higher the

2. How can economic risks be avoided? (Answer: Sharing risks with others can help policyholders protect themselves against economic losses.)
3. What is insurance and how are losses covered? (Answer: Insurance is the planned protection provided by sharing economic losses. Both consumers and businesses are able to buy

insurance to cover almost any kind of economic loss.)

4. What are factors that affect the cost of insurance to policyholders? (Answer: The age of the person being insured, the type of property at risk, and the number of claims the insurance company pays over a period of time.)

5. How can insurance be purchased? (Answer: From a large company or from an independent agent.)

6. In what way does insurance provide economic security? (Answer: By protecting the policyholder from economic loss.)

RETEACH

Make a transparency of a portion of an actual insurance policy that covers deductibles and claims. Put this transparency on the overhead projector and show students how the terminology actually appears on a real policy. Relate parts of the policy to content that was covered in this chapter.

ENRICH

Direct students to read the Environmental Perspectives in this chapter. Have students write a descriptive paragraph as to how personal risks, property risks, and liability risks are a part of their lives and what each means to them. Then have them create a crossword puzzle using the vocabulary words at the beginning of the lesson. Write the words "Insurance Poor" on the board. Ask students to write a paragraph as to what they think this means. When they have finished their paragraph, discuss this idea of being insurance poor. As another activity, have

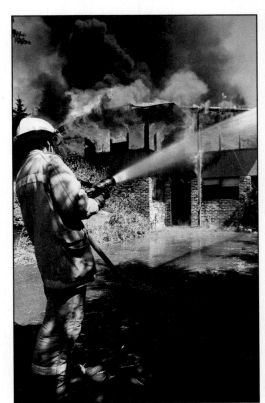

What are some reasons why your insurance costs might increase?

premiums for the policyholder. Therefore, insured people play an important part in determining the cost of insurance. By locking doors and driving defensively, losses associated with thefts and automobile accidents can be reduced. Practicing good health habits will reduce life and health insurance costs.

Everyone benefits if the losses covered by insurance decrease. Assume, for example, that there is a decline in losses caused by fire and that fire insurance premiums are reduced as a result. If your family owns a house and has fire insurance on it, you gain directly because you pay lower premiums. If a business owner pays lower premiums, expenses will be less and prices on goods and services can be lowered. Anything that you can do to reduce losses covered by insurance helps you and the entire community.

PURCHASING INSURANCE

Insurance protection can be acquired in several ways. Sometimes an employer will provide insurance for you as part of your compensation. For example, employers may pay all or part of life and/or health insurance premiums for their employees.

However, in other cases, you will buy insurance directly from an **insurance agent**. An important part of an insurance agent's job is to help you select the proper kind of protection from economic loss. There are two basic types of insurance agents. One works for a large insurance company and sells only policies written by that company. The other is an independent agent who may sell many kinds of policies from a number of different companies.

INSURANCE FOR ECONOMIC SECURITY

Insurance is important to everyone because it provides economic security. If you have no insurance, you could probably take care of small losses such as those resulting from minor accidents. However, a large loss from a fire or serious illness could be a real financial hardship. Protection against such major events gives everyone a feeling of security.

Insurance also helps our economy. Insurance makes it possible for many people and businesses to do things they otherwise could not do. Suppose that someday you want to buy a $100,000 home but can make only a $10,000 down payment. You will need to borrow $90,000. It is very doubtful that anyone would lend you that amount at a reasonable rate if the house were not insured. Money to

Insurance companies perform educational services by conducting campaigns on safety, health, and accident prevention. They conduct these activities to help reduce both losses and premiums.

Basic **Skills**-Reading

Direct students to the first main heading of the chapter. The first sentence of a paragraph is usually the main idea of the material being discussed. The last sentence of the paragraph usually summarizes or bridges to the paragraphs or subheadings that follow. Boldfaced terms and italicized words draw attention to important facts or topics in the material. Direct students to pages in the chapter that illustrate boldfaced terms or italicized terms. The Student Activity Worksheet, Basic Skills—Reading, in the School-To-Work/SCANS Activity Masters, may be used to serve as a guideline for discussion of each of these points. Ask students to write a summary of the points that will be covered in the chapter.

buy a new car cannot be borrowed at a reasonable rate unless the car is insured against risks such as theft and collision.

Premiums collected by insurance companies are invested. Many insurance companies, mainly life insurance companies, also use premium money to make loans just like a bank. The loans are used by individuals and businesses who pay interest to the insurance company for the use of their money. When those loans are used to make purchases or to expand a business, it contributes to the growth of our economy.

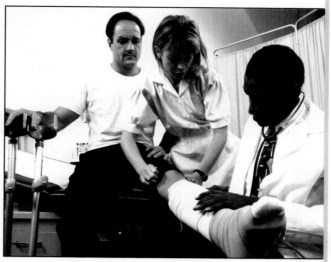

What are some good reasons for having health and automobile insurance?

students ask an insurance company agent what the advantages are of buying insurance directly from the company. Then ask an independent agent the advantages of buying from an independent person. Use computers and fax machines if they are available to conduct these interviews. Otherwise, students can call the agents, do face-to-face interviews, or the agents could be invited to the class for the discussions.

SUMMARIZE

As a writing activity, instruct students to complete an outline of this chapter. The outline can then be used as a study guide to prepare students for the evaluation process.

EVALUATE

- Assign Activities and Projects for Chapter 37.
- Administer the printed test or ExamView for Chapter 37.
- Assign School-To-Work/SCANS Building Your Portfolio Activities for Unit 11.

Insurance Web Sites
Home, auto, life, and health insurance information:
www.quotesmith. com and
www.insweb.com
Auto and home insurance information: www.iii.org

E-Commerce for Managing Risk

Every business organization and every person faces daily risks. These perils can range from lower-than-expected product sales to an accident on the job. Minimizing risk can be achieved by avoiding dangerous situations, using safety devices, or installing alarm systems. Companies and consumers also manage risk with insurance. Coverage for losses for disability, illness, death, property damage, and accidents are common types of insurance.

As with other goods and services, online selling of insurance has resulted in both benefits and drawbacks. Consumers can easily compare insurance coverages and rates online.

Potential policyholders, however, must be wary of paying too much for insurance or buying coverage that is not needed. Many customers may believe they received a great rate on a policy only to learn that the insurance company provides very poor customer service when a claim is filed.

Critical Thinking
Conduct an Internet search to obtain suggestions for reducing the cost of auto insurance, home insurance, or life insurance. Prepare a poster or other visual presentation with a summary of your findings.

Critical Thinking Skills-Problem Solving

Problem-solving skills, which include recognizing a problem and devising a plan of action, are applied throughout every chapter in this text. Each time a student participates in a Cooperative Learning or Teams activity, problem-solving skills are applied in a group situation. Each time a student completes a math application in Calculate Business Data, decisions are made as to which mathematical approach must be taken. For each Technology Application problem, students must decide which template problem to use, which piece of software to load, and how to solve the problem. Emphasize to students how they are using problem solving in their day-to-day tasks and make them aware of the skills they are developing.

SCANS

REVIEW YOUR READING

1. Liability risks, property risks, and personal risks.
2. Insurance provides protection against financial losses by providing a means of sharing losses with others. Through insurance many people contribute a small amount so that a person who sustains a financial loss can be reimbursed for the amount of that loss.
3. Auto accident, fire, theft, broken arms or legs, and injury to property.
4. Insurance for auto, home, life, and health is important to almost everyone.
5. Because of the economic impossibility of self-insuring against very expensive catastrophes such as the cost of extended illness or of replacing a house that was destroyed by fire.
6. Experience of insurance companies in paying for certain kinds of losses.
7. By taking care to lock doors, drive defensively, and practice good health habits, people can reduce losses and claims and keep their insurance premiums down.
8. An agent who works for a large insurance company and only sells policies written by that company. Independent agents who sell many kinds of policies from a number of different companies.
9. Insurance provides economic security.
10. Insurance companies invest the premiums they collect; they also use premiums to pay claims, to make loans, and to conduct campaigns on safety, health, and accident prevention.

COMMUNICATE BUSINESS CONCEPTS

11. Families require a level of property risk insurance that is typically lower than businesses because most families have less property than businesses. Large businesses might, in some categories, be able to self-insure for modest losses to property such as equipment damage and so on.
12. A suggested answer would be the cost of the premium and the level of deductible you could afford to pay.

BUSINESS NOTES

1. Personal risks are risks associated with illness, disability, loss of income, unemployment, old age, and premature death. Property risks are risks of damage or loss due to theft, wind, fire, flood, or some other hazard. Liability risks are potential losses to others that occur as a result of injury or damage that you may have caused.
2. Sharing risks with others can help policyholders protect themselves against economic losses.
3. Insurance is the planned protection provided by sharing economic losses. Both consumers and businesses are able to buy insurance to cover almost any kind of economic loss.
4. The cost of insurance is influenced by factors such as the age of the person being insured, the type of property at risk, and the number of claims the insurance company pays over a period of time.
5. Insurance can be purchased from a large company or from an independent agent.
6. Insurance provides economic security by protecting the policyholder from large economic loss.

REVIEW YOUR READING

1. List the three types of economic risks.
2. How does insurance protect against economic losses?
3. List several possible economic losses that people face.
4. Name four kinds of insurance protection that are important to most people.
5. Why aren't most people able to use a self-insurance plan?
6. Name one of the factors that determine the cost of insurance premiums.
7. How can policyholders help to control the cost of insurance?
8. What are the two basic types of insurance agents?
9. Why is insurance important to everyone?
10. How do insurance companies use the premiums they collect?

COMMUNICATE BUSINESS CONCEPTS

11. How would the need for insurance against property risks differ between a family and a business?
12. What factors would you consider when deciding on the level of deductible on a property insurance policy?
13. Some people feel most comfortable when they are insured for almost every loss—large or small. Others believe that most people can handle small losses and favor insuring against only major or catastrophic losses. In which group would you place yourself? Why?
14. The residents of a subdivision with 100 homes decided that they can save money by providing their own fire insurance. Since the houses in the area are of equal value, each owner agrees

13. Answers will vary. However, students should realize that it is important to have protection against risks of large losses—losses that if realized could mean financial disaster for an individual or business.
14. This is probably not a wise plan as the risk of loss is not dispersed over a large enough area. A fire that starts in one home could sweep through several homes in the subdivision causing losses far in excess of the amount in the homeowner's fund. The cost to each homeowner might be much more than the cost of fire insurance from an insurance company. Fire insurance companies can insure homes throughout greater geographical areas to reduce the chance that many of the properties they insure will suffer losses in any given period of time.

to contribute $1,800. The money is to be placed in a savings account in a bank. If a homeowner suffers a fire loss, the loss would be paid out of this account. Do you think this is a wise plan? Why or why not?

15. Develop a list of ways you could reduce the property risks associated with owning a car.

16. Why do you think insurance companies are willing to spend large amounts of money on health and safety education?

DEVELOP YOUR BUSINESS LANGUAGE

For each numbered item, find the term that has the same meaning.

17. The planned protection provided by sharing economic losses.

18. The person for whom risk is assumed by an insurance company.

19. The amount you must pay before the insurance company pays a claim.

20. A contract that states the conditions to which the insurance company and the policyholder have agreed.

21. A person who sells insurance.

22. A policyholder's request for payment for a loss that is covered by the insurance policy.

23. The amount that a policyholder must pay for insurance coverage.

24. When an individual, family, or business assumes the total risk of economic loss.

25. When you and the insurance company share expenses.

26. The possibility of incurring a loss.

27. Risks associated with illness, disability, loss of income, unemployment, old age, and premature death.

28. The possibility of incurring a loss related to property liability and one's own personal well being.

29. The risk of damage to or loss of property due to theft, wind, fire, flood, or some other hazard.

30. Businesses that provide planned protection against economic loss.

31. Potential losses to others that occur as a result of injury or damage that you may have caused.

KEY TERMS

claim
coinsurance
deductible
economic risk
insurance
insurance agent
insurance companies
insured or policyholder
liability risk
personal risk
policy
premium
property risk
risk
self-insurance

DECISION-MAKING STRATEGIES

Jane is a rather careless driver. She is a 17-year-old with a late model compact Japanese car that looks sporty and is equipped for speed. Jane loves to drive fast and be seen in her car and has compiled a rather poor traffic record. In only one year, she has had two "fender bender" accidents and received two speeding tickets. Those who care about Jane have suggested that her reckless driving habits are putting her and others at risk.

32. What personal property and liability risks associated with an auto accident do you think Jane is taking?

33. If Jane's driving doesn't improve, what will happen to the auto insurance premium she will be required to pay?

34. What helpful suggestions do you have for Jane in regard to her driving?

DEVELOP YOUR BUSINESS LANGUAGE

17. insurance
18. insured or policyholder
19. deductible
20. policy
21. insurance agent
22. claim
23. premium
24. self-insurance
25. coinsurance
26. risk
27. personal risk
28. economic risk
29. property risk
30. insurance companies
31. liability risk

DECISION-MAKING STRATEGIES

32. Suggested answers might include: personal risks—injury, disability, loss of job and death; property risks—damage to or loss of her car; liability risks—damage to other cars or property, injury to others.

33. Her premium is likely to increase. She may not be able to find a company that is willing to provide insurance because of her driving record.

34. A suggested answer would be to attend a driver safety or defensive driving course.

15. The list might include such things as burglar alarms, steering wheel locks, always locking a car, driving defensively, parking under a street light, and having the car safety inspected.

16. Education for health and safety will help reduce losses and make claims lower, which will reduce premiums. People who are aware of how to avoid certain kinds of accidents and illnesses tend to suffer fewer losses.

CALCULATE BUSINESS DATA

35. (a) $225 + $165 + $595 + $650
= $1,635 (b) $1,635 ÷ 12 =
$136.25

36. 821,520 ÷ 978,000 = 84%

37. (a) $520 × 0.15 = $78; $520 −
$78 = $442 (b) $520 × 2 =
$1,040; $442 × 2 = $884; $1,040
− $884 = $156

38. (a) $6,500 + $3,200 + $7,400 +
$3,700 = $20,800 (b) Yes.
$47,000 − $20,800 = $26,200 (c)
$20,800 ÷ $47,000 = 44.26%

39. $6,000 − $350 = $5,650; $5,650
× 20% = $1,130; $1,130 + $350
= $1,480

40. (a) 16 × 6 = 96 kilometers each
week (b) 16 × 0.6 = 9.6 miles
each day (c) 9.6 × 6 = 57.6 miles
each week (d) 20 × 6 = 120 kilometers each week (e) 20 × 0.6 =
12 miles each day (f) 12 × 6 = 72
miles each week

TECHNOLOGY APPLICATION

In this activity, students use a computer to solve a business problem using a
file that is provided on the data CD
that accompanies *Intro to Business*.
Instructions for using the data CD are
included in a **README** file on the
disk. Solutions are provided on the
Instructor's Resource CD.

35. Linda Caldwell is a 25-year-old computer tech-
nician living in an apartment. She pays the following insurance premiums every year: life
insurance, $225; renter's insurance, $165;
automobile insurance, $595; and health insur-
ance, $650.
   a. What is the total annual cost of Linda's
   insurance premiums?
   b. If she paid her insurance premiums in
   equal monthly payments, how much would
   her total monthly insurance cost be?

36. A fire and casualty insurance company collected $978,000 in premiums in one year. That
same year, the company paid out $821,520 in
claims. What percentage of the premiums did
the company pay out in claims?

37. Jon Peterman currently pays $520 each six
months for automobile insurance. The policy
has a $100 deductible on any claim Jon
makes. His insurance agent told Jon that he
could reduce his premium by 15% if he had a
$250 deductible.
   a. How much would Jon's six-month premium
   be with the higher deductible?
   b. How much would Jon save in one year if
   he accepted the higher deductible?

38. A fish wholesaling business decided to self-
insure itself for damage to the property it
owned. The property includes several forklifts,
a large warehouse, office equipment, and a
great deal of fish-handling equipment. The
owners decided to put $47,000 in the self-
insurance account the first year. Claims
against the account that year are shown in the
table at right.
   a. What was the total of the property claims
   for the year?

   b. Was any money remaining in the account
   at the end of the year? If so, how much?
   c. What percent of the account was paid out
   in claims?

One burned forklift	$6,50
One computer ruined by an electrical surge	3,20
Hail damage to the warehouse roof	7,40
One fish conveyer damaged by a supplier's truck	3,70

39. The Lafferty family has coinsurance whereby
the insurance company will pay 80 percent of
the cost of medical treatment after the
deductible of $350 is paid, with a cap of one
million dollars. The family filed a claim of
$6,000. How much will the Lafferty family actu-
ally have to pay out of their pocket assuming
the cap of one million dollars has not been
reached?

40. Kala Matumba is a professional marathon runner from Mali who protects her future income
by insuring against possible injuries. Her training routine is to run 16 kilometers each of the
first six days of the week and rest on
Sundays. Six days before each marathon, she
increases her daily distances from 16 kilometers to 20 kilometers per day.
   a. During regular training, how many kilometers does she run in a week?
   b. How many miles does she run each day
   during regular training?
   c. How many miles does she run each week
   during regular training?
   d. Before each marathon race, how many
   kilometers does she run in a week?
   e. How many miles does she run each day?
   f. How many miles does she run each week?

TECHNOLOGY APPLICATION

Using the *Intro to Business* Data CD and your
database program software, select problem CH37.
After the problem appears on your screen, complete the following activities. Then, after you have
completed each step, display or print a report for
each activity. If you do not have a printer available,
answer the questions before you leave the computer.

41. Sort the database in ascending order by
model of car. Answer the following questions:
   a. Which has the highest insurance rate?

   b. Which model of car has the lowest insurance rate?

42. Select and list the companies that cover
sports cars. How many companies are listed?

43. Sort the companies in descending order by
rate. Answer the following questions:
   a. Which company is listed second?
   b. Which company is listed last?
Optional: Create a bar graph showing the average
rate for each company.

GLOBAL RISK MANAGEMENT STRATEGIES

As an international business manager, would you be willing to ship automobiles to a company in another country before receiving the payment? Or would you agree to take a country's currency for payment instead of U.S. dollars?

These are examples of risks faced by every organization involved in international business. To reduce international business risk, management experts recommend four strategies:

First, conduct business in many countries. This approach reduces the risk faced when doing business in only one country or a single region. If turmoil occurs in one nation, causing lost sales and profits, the global company is covered with profits from other markets.

Next, offer a variety of products. When an organization diversifies its product line, reduced sales in one item will not mean complete failure for the company. Successful global organizations continually create new products, seek new uses for existing products, and look for new markets for their products.

Third, involving local business partners may reduce risk. Joint ventures with local companies help to reduce political and

> **Several strategies can help reduce international business risk.**

social risks. An agreement between a global company and a locally run business can benefit both parties. Also, the citizens and government of the host nation will not feel as threatened by outsiders.

Finally, employ local management in order to lower global business risk. Administrators who are native to a country or region better understand cultural norms and political actions. This knowledge can help the international company adapt its product and business activities to the needs of the society being served.

CRITICAL THINKING

1. Describe a possible joint venture between companies in two different countries. Explain why the businesses might work together. What are possible benefits for each organization? How does a joint venture reduce international business risk?
2. Go to the web site of a company that does business in several regions of the world, such as Kellogg's, General Motors, or Whirlpool. Explain how the company's product line and global distribution activities reduce risk.

Most students will either work with international clients or compete against businesses that do. Global Navigator introduces students to issues integral to working with international businesses. Key concepts and challenges faced by international businesses are presented, followed by two Critical Thinking questions that require students to analyze what they have learned.

This Global Navigator feature details four ways that business managers can reduce risk in international business—by diversifying geographically, diversifying product lines, involving local partners, and hiring local management.

CRITICAL THINKING

1. Specific answers will vary. Joint ventures can reduce risk by spreading it among two or more partners, thereby reducing the exposure to each individually, and by providing an added incentive (a share of the profits!) for business partners to make the enterprise a success.
2. Answers will depend on which company students choose, but in most cases they should include specific applications of the four risk management strategies outlined in this feature.

Chapter 38 acquaints students with vehicle insurance. Insurance rates and how to select an insurance company are discussed, and basic state insurance laws that have an impact on automobile insurance are covered.

Resources for Teachers
● Lesson Plans
● School-To-Work/SCANS Activity Masters
● Spanish Resources
● Instructor's Resource CD

Assessment
● Chapter and Unit Tests, Ch. 38
● ExamView, Ch. 38

Media/Technology
● Applying Technology Data CD
● PowerPoint slides
● Business Connection CD
● Videotape

Activity Masters and Workbooks
● Activities and Projects, Ch. 38
● Internet Activity Masters
● Business Math Activity Masters
● Communications Activity Masters
● International Business Activity Masters
● Ethics Activity Masters

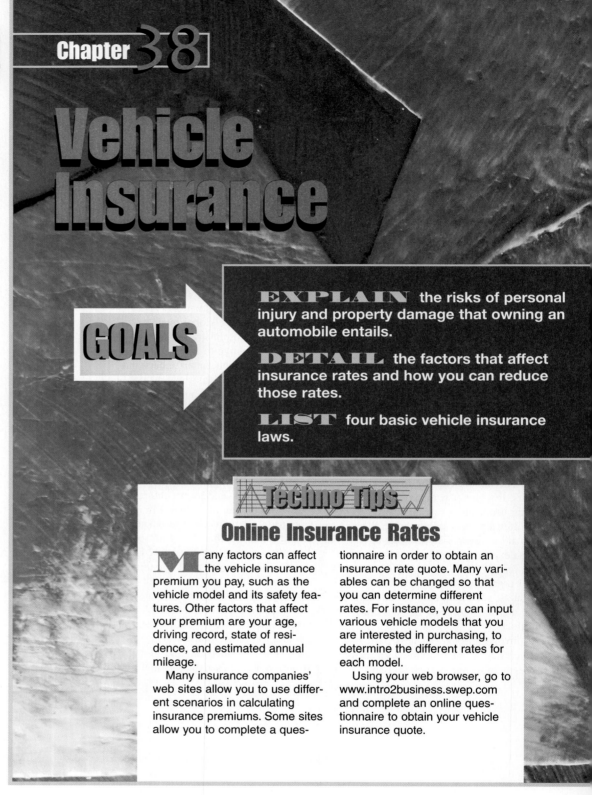

Chapter 38

Vehicle Insurance

GOALS

EXPLAIN the risks of personal injury and property damage that owning an automobile entails.

DETAIL the factors that affect insurance rates and how you can reduce those rates.

LIST four basic vehicle insurance laws.

Techno Tips
Online Insurance Rates

Many factors can affect the vehicle insurance premium you pay, such as the vehicle model and its safety features. Other factors that affect your premium are your age, driving record, state of residence, and estimated annual mileage.

Many insurance companies' web sites allow you to use different scenarios in calculating insurance premiums. Some sites allow you to complete a questionnaire in order to obtain an insurance rate quote. Many variables can be changed so that you can determine different rates. For instance, you can input various vehicle models that you are interested in purchasing, to determine the different rates for each model.

Using your web browser, go to www.intro2business.swep.com and complete an online questionnaire to obtain your vehicle insurance quote.

Students need to know the latest technologies and develop cutting edge Internet skills for use in current jobs, future careers, or in their homes. TechnoTips introduces students to today's cutting edge technologies and provides them with important Internet skills. Feature topics concentrate on Internet-specific technologies and computer or other hi-tech innovations for use by businesses and consumers. At the www.intro2business.swep.com web site, students can complete the activity for this chapter.

FOCUS ON REAL LIFE

"Chris! What a great looking car! How did you ever afford it?"

"It's not easy, Roberto, to afford a car and still be in school. Not only do I have to make car payments, but I have to pay for insurance. It's been quite a shock! I did save enough money from a part-time job last summer to buy the car but I didn't plan on how much insurance would cost. I'm looking for a job right now so I can afford to keep the car."

Purchasing car insurance can be painfully expensive. However, not everyone has to pay high premiums. Those who are seen by their insurance companies as low risks pay significantly less than those in the high risk category. The difference is in the economic risk.

ECONOMIC RISKS OF OWNING A CAR

Owning a vehicle puts you in a position of high economic risk. You might have an accident and injure yourself, your vehicle, other people, or others' property. The vehicle might be stolen or damaged by vandals. You could be sued by someone as a result of an accident involving your vehicle.

The costs of treating injured people and repairing damaged property resulting from an automobile accident can take all of the money and assets of a person who does not have insurance. The amount of money paid to injured people and to owners of damaged property have increased dramatically. Vehicle insurance is designed to provide protection from the financial risks involved in owning and driving a car or another vehicle.

Protection from the economic risks of car ownership is available with an automobile insurance policy. You can buy insurance to protect yourself from the financial loss caused by almost anything that could happen to your car. You can also buy **automobile liability insurance** to protect yourself against financial loss if you injure someone else or damage someone else's property in an automobile accident.

Sometimes an accident is unavoidable, that is, no one can be directly blamed for it. In most cases, however, someone is at fault. The person who is found to be at fault normally is responsible for damages and financial losses that result from the accident. Although you may think you are completely faultless, you can be sued. If you are insured, your insurance company will provide legal defense for the suit. If the court decides that you are legally liable for injuries and damage to property, your insurance company will pay the costs up to the limits stated in your insurance policy.

In what ways can automobile insurance protect you?

FOCUS ON REAL LIFE

importance of these laws. This would make another excellent handout for students for their personal reference.

TRY THIS/GUIDED PRACTICE
Make a transparency of an automobile insurance policy. Walk students through each section of the policy, identifying the various coverages that are included. You may also want to give this as a handout. Students need to be familiar with an insurance policy and what one actually looks like.

EXPLORE THIS/INDEPENDENT PRACTICE Before assigning independent practice material for any chapter, students should be expected to read the chapter material carefully. In view of the fact that students vary widely in their ability to read effectively, it is advisable to have the students read the entire chapter, or sections thereof, silently in class if the material has not been previously read in connection with homework assignments.

The Chapter Review questions at the end of the chapter vary in level of difficulty. For a basic assignment, consider Develop Your Business Language and Review Your Reading. For an average assignment, consider the basic assignment plus Communicate Business Concepts and Calculate Business Data. For an enhanced assignment, try the average assignment plus Technology Application and Decision-Making Strategies.

A Summary Chart of Automobile Insurance Coverage

Types of Coverage:	Coverage On:	
Personal Injury Coverages	**Policyholder**	**Others**
Bodily injury liability	No	Yes
Medical payments	Yes	Yes
Uninsured motorist protection	Yes	Yes
Property Damage Coverages	**Policyholder's Automobile**	**Property of Others**
Property damage liability	No	Yes
Collision insurance	Yes	No
Comprehensive physical damage	Yes	No

FIGURE 38-1 Which type of coverage do you think is generally the most expensive?

Several kinds of protection are available through companies that provide automobile insurance. This coverage is available in different combinations and for different amounts. Although some of the coverage can be bought separately, most car owners buy package policies that include most or all of the necessary coverage. There are two main categories of automobile insurance: personal injury coverage and property damage coverage. Figure 38-1 summarizes the types of automobile insurance coverage.

Personal Injury Coverage
Personal injury coverage includes bodily injury liability, medical payments, and uninsured motorist protection. These three types of personal injury coverage are the source of most of the money paid in claims by automobile insurance companies.

Bodily Injury Liability Protection
Bodily injury liability coverage protects the insured from claims resulting from injuries or deaths for which the insured is found to be at fault. This type of insurance covers people in other cars, passengers riding with the insured, and pedestrians. It does not cover the insured or, in most cases, the insured's immediate family.

Dollar amounts of bodily injury coverage are generally expressed as two numbers divided by a slash. The first number refers to the limit, in thousands of dollars, that the insurance company will pay for injuries to any one person in an accident. For example, if the insured had bodily injury liability coverage of 100/300 and had an accident for which the insured was found to be at fault, the insurance company would pay up to $100,000 for the cost of injuries to one person. The second number, in this case 300, refers to the maximum amount that the insurance company would pay for injuries to multiple people as a result of the accident. If

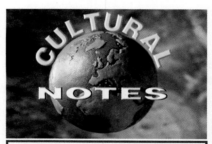

There are many designated symbols that are used internationally so that anyone speaking any language can understand them. For example, everyone understands that the symbol of an airplane represents an airport. Nations around the world have been working together to create an internationally recognized system of symbols. This endeavor has been coordinated by the International Organization for Standardization (ISO), in Geneva, Switzerland.

526 **Unit 11** *Risk Management*

more than three people were injured, each person may not receive $100,000 since the insurance company is only liable for $300,000 in this case. Larger amounts of bodily injury protection often are needed and add surprisingly little to the cost of your premium.

Medical Payments Protection

Through **medical payments coverage**, policyholders and their family members are covered if they are injured while riding in their car or in someone else's car. It may cover them if they are walking and are hit by a car. Guests in the insured car are also protected.

Medical payments insurance covers the costs of medical, dental, ambulance, hospital, nursing, and funeral services. Payment, up to the limit stated in the policy, is made regardless of who is at fault. Normally car owners purchase medical payments insurance along with their bodily injury liability coverage.

Uninsured Motorist Protection

In some cases, injuries are caused by hit-and-run drivers or by drivers who have no insurance or money to pay claims. Therefore, insurance companies make available **uninsured motorist coverage** to protect against these drivers. It is available only to those people who carry bodily injury liability coverage. In addition to covering the policyholder and family members, it also covers guests in the policyholder's car. Unlike medical payments coverage, which pays regardless of who is at fault, uninsured motorist protection covers the insured person only if the uninsured motorist is at fault.

Property Damage Coverage

There are three types of automobile insurance designed to protect you from economic loss due to damage to the property of others and to your car. They are property damage liability, collision, and comprehensive damage.

Property Damage Liability

Property damage liability coverage protects the insured against claims if the insured's car damages someone else's property and the insured is at fault. The damaged property is often another car, but it may also be property such as telephone poles, fire hydrants, and buildings. Property damage liability insurance does not cover damage to the insured's car.

Why is it important to understand exactly what type of vehicle insurance you need?

Review the goals at the beginning of the chapter and the Business Notes at the end of the chapter. Have students respond orally or in writing to each Business Note restated as a question. For students who may have difficulty providing answers, assign the reteaching activities that follow. Enrichment activities may also be assigned where appropriate.

1. What are the economic risks of owning an automobile and how can the owner provide personal protection through personal injury coverage and property damage coverage? (Answer: Owning a vehicle puts you in a position of high economic risk. You can protect yourself by purchasing personal injury insurance and property damage liability insurance. Personal injury insurance covers bodily injury liability, medical payments, and uninsured motorist protection. Property damage liability insurance protects you against claims if your car damages someone else's property and you are at fault.)

2. What are the factors that affect insurance rates, ways to reduce your insurance costs, and how to select an insurance company? (Answer: Factors such as age, accident record, marital status, academic standing, purpose for which the car is used, number of miles driven each year, and value and type of car. By planning your auto insurance purchase carefully and comparing rates, you may save a great deal of money. Shop

TEACHING STRATEGIES

Alternate Modalities
Kinesthetic Learner

When covering factors that are used to determine cost of automobile insurance with a kinesthetic learner, the instructor should give the student an index card and have the stu-

dent write each factor as the instructor discusses each. The index card can be used for future reference.

around and compare insurance companies for rates.)

3. Which vehicles, other than automobiles, carry insurance similar to automobiles? (Answer: motorcycles, recreational vehicles, and snowmobiles.)

4. What are the four basic vehicle insurance laws? (Answer: compulsory insurance, financial responsibility, assigned-risks plans, and no-fault insurance.)

RETEACH

Put these terms on the board: PERSONAL INJURY and PROPERTY DAMAGE. Give students examples of each and how various insurance policies can protect them against these incidents. You might also invite a highway patrol, local police, or sheriff's officer to talk to your class about the main causes of automobile accidents and how such accidents can be prevented or reduced. You may also wish to ask the officer to discuss the responsibility of the driver at the scene of an accident.

ENRICH

Direct students to read the Legal Perspectives in this chapter. Provide students with a copy of your state's insurance laws. Ask each student to make a list of the points that you have covered in class and any other important points that need to be covered. As a class, highlight the major focus of these laws. Ask students to call an insurance agent and get quotes for insurance coverage on either their individual cars or to be added to their parent's car. Students should ask the agent for several

Collision Insurance **Collision coverage** protects a car owner against financial loss associated with damage resulting from a collision with another car or object or from the car turning over. Collision coverage does not cover injuries to people or damage to the property of others. Most collision coverage is written with a deductible clause. Deductible amounts are often $200, $500, or more. This means that the insured must pay the first $200 or $500 of damage to the car in any one collision and the insurance company agrees to pay the rest. Larger deductible amounts will reduce the premium cost.

Collision coverage does not provide for payment of damages greater than the car's value. Suppose the insured's car incurs $3,500 in damages in a collision with another vehicle. If the car has a value of only $3,100, the collision coverage would pay $3,100, not $3,500. Collision coverage should not be carried on a car that is of little value because the cost of repairing the car may be more than the car is worth. Collision insurance usually accounts for approximately two-thirds of the total cost of an insurance policy.

Comprehensive Coverage Your car can be damaged or destroyed in other ways. The car could be stolen, or it could be damaged by fire, tornado, windstorm, vandalism, or falling objects. **Comprehensive coverage** protects the insured against almost all damage losses except those caused from a collision or from the car turning over.

If the insured's car is totally destroyed or stolen, the amount paid is not necessarily equal to the amount paid for the car. Rather, it is equal to the car's estimated value at the time of the loss. Suppose the insured's car costing $15,000 is stolen soon after it is purchased. The insurance company will probably

pay almost as much as the car cost, perhaps $14,500. However, if the car is stolen two years after it is purchased, the insurance company may pay only $10,500. The car has grown older and its value has decreased.

BUYING AUTOMOBILE INSURANCE

A great deal of money is spent insuring cars and other vehicles. That money should be spent wisely and carefully. Therefore, car owners need to understand how to get the most protection for their insurance dollar.

Insurance Rates

Insurance companies use several factors to determine the cost of your automobile insurance. Some of those factors include:

- Your age and other characteristics, such as accident record, marital status, or academic standing.
- The purpose for which you use your car.
- The number of miles you drive your car each year.
- The value and type of your car.
- The community in which you live.
- Types of coverage and deductibles.

Since some drivers are more likely to have accidents than others, they must pay higher premiums. To determine premium rates, drivers are classified according to age, marital status, driving record, and scholastic achievement. The lowest rates are reserved for the best risks, those least likely to have an accident. The cost of insurance is usually higher when one of the drivers in the insured's family is under age 30 than it is if all family drivers are over age 30.

The purpose for which a car is driven and the number of miles it is driven in a year are also important in determining insurance rates. Cars used for business purposes are generally driven more miles in a year than are cars driven for pleasure and are therefore more likely to be involved in an accident.

The value of your car naturally has an

Workplace **Competencies**-Interpersonal Skills

Employers are looking for potential employees with good interpersonal skills. Participating as a member of a team is an example of one way to develop these interpersonal skills. As successful team members, individuals must also learn to teach others. Teaching others requires team members to assist their peers in applying new learnings and concepts through various methods, understanding when there is a need for teaching information, relaying information in a manner that allows others to see it applied, and assessing and providing positive feedback to others.

important effect on the cost of insurance. Premiums for collision coverage and comprehensive physical damage coverage must be higher for a car worth $15,500 than for a car worth only $8,000. The insurance company runs the risk of paying out much more to the insured if the $15,500 car is destroyed or stolen. The type of car also affects the rate. If you have a luxury car or an expensive sports car, you will have to pay higher rates.

Rates for automobile insurance vary from state to state and even from city to city within a state. Automobile insurance rates are also affected by the population in a particular area and the number of accidents that occur over a certain period of time in the area. Insurance companies gather statistics on the dollar amount of claims paid for in an area and base their rates on this information.

The cost of your automobile insurance will also vary according to the coverage you have and the deductibles you choose. Naturally, the more coverage you carry, the higher the cost.

Reducing Your Cost

By planning your automobile insurance purchase carefully, you may save a great deal of money. For example, the extra amount charged for young drivers may be decreased if they have completed an approved driver education course. Companies in most states offer young people a good-student discount.

Selecting a Company

Just as automobile insurance premiums vary with the conditions associated with your car and your driving, they also vary from company to company. It pays to compare rates. Companies may offer lower rates if more than one car is insured by a family and if the insured buys other types of insurance from the same company. Paying premiums on a monthly basis is usually more expensive than paying a premium for an entire year.

INSURING OTHER VEHICLES

Insurance on motorcycles, recreational vehicles, and snowmobiles is similar in some respects to automobile insurance. For example, bodily injury liability, property damage

What coverage would you need to protect against damage caused by natural disasters?

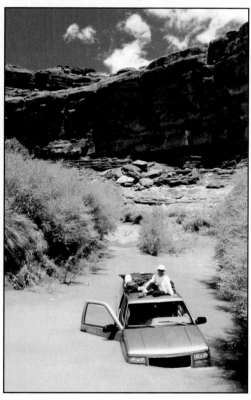

different quotes: minimum coverage, suggested coverage, maximum coverage. You might also develop a special field activity requiring students to research the assigned-risk program in your state.

SUMMARIZE

Have a volunteer go to the board. Ask for volunteers to give a short description of the most important bit of information they learned in this chapter.

Critical Thinking Skills-Reasoning

Drawing conclusions from facts or premises is an important thinking skill for today's employees. One of the most pervasive ways that government affects business is through the legal system. The law protects both individuals and businesses against those who threaten society. It also spells out accepted ways of performing many essential business activities—along with penalties for failure to comply. The Legal Perspectives gives students an opportunity to study legal situations and draw appropriate conclusions.

LEGAL PERSPECTIVES

No-Fault Automobile Insurance

Under no-fault automobile insurance laws, people injured in an automobile accident are required to collect for their financial losses—such as their medical bills, loss of wages, and other related expenses—from their own insurance companies no matter who is at fault.

With no-fault insurance, lawsuits usually are unnecessary because each party collects from their respective insurance company. Money is saved from lawsuits and insurance settlements become more equitable to people who suffer serious injuries. No-fault insurance is one way to keep automobile insurance costs affordable.

In the 13 states with mandatory no-fault automobile insurance, policyholders are covered by their own insurers up to a certain amount, regardless of who was at fault in an accident. In a state with a no-fault law, the victim may sue the other party in the accident only when monetary losses are very high, not over relatively minor injuries.

A recent study of legal actions in states without no-fault laws suggests that some victims with minor injuries are collecting awards that are too large and others with major injuries are not adequately compensated. The study also suggests that no-fault laws in the remainder of the states would reduce these inequities and would save consumers about 12 percent on their premium.

Critical Thinking

1. Who do you think tends to benefit the most from no-fault insurance laws?
2. Why do you think that, with such influential supporters of strong no-fault laws, only 13 states have them?

---

liability, collision, and comprehensive physical damage insurance are the most important coverages on these vehicles. The engine size and value of the vehicle are the important factors in determining the cost of insurance. Generally, the larger and more expensive the vehicle, the higher the insurance cost.

VEHICLE INSURANCE LAWS

Individual states regulate laws relating to vehicle insurance. Most of these laws are advantageous to responsible drivers. All owners of vehicles should know about compulsory insurance laws, financial responsibility laws, assigned-risk plans, and no-fault insurance laws.

Compulsory Insurance Laws

All states have adopted **compulsory insurance laws** that require you to carry certain types of automobile insurance before your car can be licensed. It is compulsory that an automobile owner carry insurance to pay for personal injury and for property damage that he or she causes due to an accident. Compulsory insurance laws state that you may not register a car or obtain a license to drive without presenting proof of having the minimum amounts of insurance coverage required.

Financial Responsibility Laws

All states have some kind of financial responsibility law. **Financial responsibility laws** provide that if you cause an accident and cannot pay for the damages either through insurance, your savings, or the sale of property, your driver's license will be suspended or taken away. Most of these laws make you

Always ask for a good-student discount if your grades are high.

FYI

---

legally liable (responsible) for any damages you cause to people or their property.

Assigned-Risk Plans

Usually because of bad accident records, some drivers are unable to buy automobile insurance in the normal fashion. Because of this, every state also has an **assigned-risk plan**. Under this plan, every automobile insurance company in the state that sells liability insurance is assigned a certain number of high-risk drivers. That number is based on the amount of insurance each company sells. Using this plan, each company has to insure a fair proportion of high-risk drivers. Drivers in high-risk categories must pay much higher premiums than those who are not high risks.

No-Fault Insurance Laws

In an effort to speed up the payment of claims and reduce the hardship of long delays, **no-fault insurance laws** have been adopted by some states. Under these laws, people injured in an automobile accident are required to collect for their financial losses—such as their medical bills, loss of wages, and other related expenses—from their own insurance companies no matter who is at fault.

No-fault insurance laws vary in some ways from state to state. Ordinarily the right to sue is retained for the more serious injury cases and for death. In such cases, it is necessary to decide how much each driver was at fault in the accident.

What are some ways that you can minimize your vehicle insurance rates?

Critical Thinking Skills-Problem Solving

Problem-solving skills, which include recognizing a problem and devising a plan of action, are applied throughout every chapter in this text. Each time a student participates in a Cooperative Learning or Teams activity, problem-solving skills are applied in a group situation. Each time a student completes a math application in the Calculate Business Data, decisions are made as to which mathematical approach must be taken. For each Technology Application problem, students must decide which template problem to use, which piece of software to load, and how to solve the problem. Emphasize to students how they are using problem solving in their day-to-day tasks and make them aware of the skills they are developing.

BUSINESS NOTES

1. You can protect yourself against risk by purchasing personal injury insurance and property damage liability insurance. Personal injury insurance covers bodily injury liability, medical payments, and uninsured motorist protection. Property damage liability insurance protects you against claims if your car damages someone else's property and you are at fault.
2. Insurance rates are affected by factors such as age, accident record, marital status, academic standing, purpose for which the car is used, number of miles driven each year, and value and type of car. By planning your automobile insurance purchase carefully and comparing rates, you may save a great deal of money.
3. Insurance on motorcycles, recreational vehicles, and snowmobiles is similar in some respects to automobile insurance.
4. There are four insurance laws with which all vehicle owners should be familiar: compulsory insurance, financial responsibility, assigned-risk plans, and no-fault insurance.

REVIEW YOUR READING

1. What is the purpose of vehicle insurance?
2. If you are protected by an automobile insurance policy and are sued as the result of an accident, how will the insurance company help you?
3. What are the two categories of automobile insurance?
4. What are the three types of personal injury coverage?
5. What does 100/300 mean in terms of bodily injury liability coverage?
6. What are the three types of automobile insurance designed to protect you against economic loss due to damage to the property of others and to your car?
7. Which type of automobile insurance protects you against damage caused by a hit-and-run driver?
8. Which factors determine the cost of automobile insurance coverage?
9. What vehicles, other than automobiles, may be covered with insurance similar to automobile insurance?
10. What are four vehicle insurance laws with which all drivers should be familiar?
11. What kind of coverage is required under compulsory insurance laws?
12. Why would someone be required to purchase insurance from an assigned-risk plan?

COMMUNICATE BUSINESS CONCEPTS

13. Which type of automobile insurance coverage would Jane Edmunds need in order to be covered in the following situations?
    a. Jane was found to be at fault in an accident in which a pedestrian was injured.
    b. Jane's daughter, who was riding in the back seat, was injured when Jane ran into a parked car.
    c. Jane, in an attempt to avoid hitting a dog in the street, ran into a parked car.

d. During a storm, a heavy tree branch damaged Jane's car, breaking the windshield and denting the hood.

14. Jim Pikkert was the driver at fault in an accident in which his three passengers were badly hurt. The court awarded two of the injured people $30,000 each, and it awarded the third person $45,000. Pikkert had bodily injury liability coverage in the amount of 50/100. Was this enough insurance to protect him from financial loss? Why or why not?

15. Why is it less important to carry collision coverage on a ten-year-old car than on a three-year-old car? Are there circumstances when you may still want to have collision coverage on a ten-year-old car?

16. If there were a four-car pileup in foggy conditions on the interstate highway, how would claims be settled in a state with a no-fault insurance law? What would happen in a state without such a law?

DEVELOP YOUR BUSINESS LANGUAGE

For each numbered item, find the term that has the same meaning.

17. Insurance coverage that provides medical expense protection for the policyholder, immediate family members, and guests while in the insured person's car.

18. Automobile insurance that provides coverage to high-risk drivers who are unable to purchase it otherwise.

19. Insurance protection against almost all losses except those caused from a collision or from the car turning over.

20. A plan in which people injured in automobile accidents are required to collect for their financial losses from their own insurance companies no matter who is at fault.

21. Insurance coverage that protects you from claims resulting from injuries or deaths for which you are found to be at fault.

22. Laws whereby your driver's license will be suspended or taken away if you cause an accident and cannot pay for the damages either through insurance, your savings, or the sale of property.

23. The general term used to describe insurance to protect you against financial loss if you injure someone else or damage someone else's property in an automobile accident.

24. Laws that require you to carry certain types of automobile insurance before your car can be licensed.

25. Insurance coverage that protects a car owner against financial loss associated with damage from a collision with another car or object or from the car turning over.

26. Insurance coverage that protects the policyholder and immediate family members against losses from injuries caused by a hit-and-run driver or by a driver who has no insurance and inadequate money to pay claims.

27. Insurance protection against claims if your car damages someone else's property and you are at fault.

KEY TERMS

assigned-risk plan
automobile liability insurance
bodily injury liability coverage
collision coverage
comprehensive coverage
compulsory insurance laws
financial responsibility laws
medical payments coverage
no-fault insurance laws
property damage liability coverage
uninsured motorist coverage

DECISION-MAKING STRATEGIES

Eighteen-year-old Chris was planning to purchase a car. The car she liked the most was a seven-year-old compact that had been driven 73,000 miles. She expected to pay about $4,500 for the car. As a good student who had completed a driver education course, she was well aware of the costs of operating a car. She also knew that she was required to have insurance that would be very expensive.

28. Explain to Chris why automobile insurance is required of her.

29. Create a list of suggestions for Chris that will help her reduce the cost of automobile insurance on the car that she buys.

DEVELOP YOUR BUSINESS LANGUAGE

17. medical payments coverage
18. assigned-risk plan
19. comprehensive coverage
20. no-fault insurance laws
21. bodily injury liability coverage
22. financial responsibility laws
23. automobile liability insurance
24. compulsory insurance laws
25. collision coverage
26. uninsured motorist coverage
27. property damage liability coverage

DECISION-MAKING STRATEGIES

28. A suggested answer is that automobile insurance is required because it is important that each driver be responsible for accidents that he or she might cause. The costs of cars, health care, property and legal action are so high now that few people could afford the self-insurance alternative to automobile insurance.

29. A suggested answer would include: mention the driver education course to the insurance agent, ask for a good-student discount, select the highest deductible she can afford, plan to drive the car as few miles per year as possible, and drive defensively and carefully so as to avoid traffic tickets and accidents.

CALCULATE BUSINESS DATA

30. $3,228 × 0.35 = $1,129.80 to be paid by Orien; $3,228 − $1,129.80 = $2,098.20 to be paid by the other driver

31. 19,937 ÷ 128,625 = 15.5%; 128,625 × 0.075 = 9,647

32. (a) $650 × 0.10 = $65 (b) $650 − $65 = $585

33. (a) 0.20 + 0.15 = 0.35 − $850 = $297.50; $850 − $297.50 = $552.50 (b) $170 + $127.50 = $297.50; $170 (20% driver education discount) + $127.50 (good-student discount) = $297.50 (saved)

TECHNOLOGY APPLICATION

In this activity, students use a computer to solve a business problem using a file that is provided on the data CD that accompanies *Intro to Business*. Instructions for using the data CD are included in a **README** file on the disk. Solutions are provided on the Instructor's Resource CD.

CALCULATE BUSINESS DATA

30. Orien Defoe was involved in an automobile accident. The total damage to both vehicles was $3,228. The state in which Orien lives assigns a percentage of fault to each driver involved in an accident. Each driver must pay the percentage of damages equal to the percentage of fault assigned. Orien was assigned 35% of the fault in the accident. How much of the damages will Orien be required to pay and how much must the other driver pay?

31. In one city in a recent year there were 128,625 automobile accidents resulting in injury or property damage. The number of accidents that were the fault of drivers under the age of 20 was 19,937. Teenagers make up 7.5% of the licensed drivers in the city. What percentage of accidents did teenage drivers cause? What is the number of accidents that would be expected of teenage drivers if the percentage of accidents were the same as their percentage of the total number of licensed drivers (round to the nearest whole number)?

32. When Erik England drove 53 kilometers round-trip to work each day, his automobile insurance premium was $650 a year. Erik changed jobs and now drives 24 kilometers round-trip. His insurance company gives a 10 percent premium discount to policyholders who drive less than 25 kilometers to and from work each day.

  a. How much will he save per year?

  b. How much is Erik's current premium?

33. Joan Nordland is a college student. She took a driver education course while in high school. She also earned an overall scholastic average of B+ in her college work. These qualify her for a driver education discount of 20 percent of the premium and a good-student discount of 15 percent of the premium for her automobile insurance.

  a. If the standard premium for her policy is $850 per year, how much will Joan pay for her automobile insurance this year?

  b. How much will she save?

TECHNOLOGY APPLICATION

Using the *Intro to Business* Data CD and your word processing program software, select problem CH38. After the problem appears on your screen, complete the following activities. Then, print each completed application. If you do not have a printer available, save the applications on a data disk to give to your teacher.

34. You just purchased a used car that is four years old and now you need to apply for vehicle insurance. Fill in the blanks with information about yourself. For the information that you enter, use boldface and a different type font from the one used on the application.

35. Copy the application and complete it for another vehicle. You just purchased a brand new pickup truck and now you need to apply for vehicle insurance. Fill in the blanks with information about yourself. For the information that you enter, use italics and a different type font from the one used on the application.

PROOFREADING— READABILITY INSURANCE

Whether writing an important research report for a client, completing a letter or memo, or simply sending an e-mail message, proofreading is a skill you should practice with most writing activities. Proofreading is important in all forms of business communication because it helps eliminate errors, which could reflect poorly on your writing skills, intelligence, and attitude. Everything you write says something about you, so make certain you always send out your best work. Proofreading is also important because it helps guarantee readability; that is, the reader is more likely to quickly and easily understand what you have written. Readers want readability, especially in business communication.

Good proofreading covers the following steps:

- Read through the document, checking for typographical, spelling, and grammatical errors.
- Double-check dates and figures for accuracy.
- Read the document a second time to make sure it is clear and readable.
- If possible, ask another person to read the piece; often a second reader will discover mistakes the writer overlooked. This step is essential for very important documents because it ensures a better final copy.
- It may be helpful to read the document aloud, checking for readability.

Remember that readers want and need to be able to quickly understand what you have written. Proofreading takes a bit of extra time, but it ensures that what you write will reflect positively on you.

> **Proofreading helps ensure that your written communication reflects well on you.**

CRITICAL THINKING

1. Why is proofreading important in business communication?
2. What should you look for when proofreading?

The three types of economic losses covered by home and property insurance are discussed and how insurance will protect against these losses. Also highlighted is the importance of keeping an inventory.

Resources for Teachers
- Lesson Plans
- School-To-Work/SCANS Activity Masters
- Spanish Resources
- Instructor's Resource CD

Assessment
- Chapter and Unit Tests, Ch. 39
- ExamView, Ch. 39

Media/Technology
- Applying Technology Data CD
- PowerPoint slides
- Business Connection CD
- Videotape

Activity Masters and Workbooks
- Activities and Projects, Ch. 39
- Internet Activity Masters
- Business Math Activity Masters
- Communications Activity Masters
- International Business Activity Masters
- Ethics Activity Masters

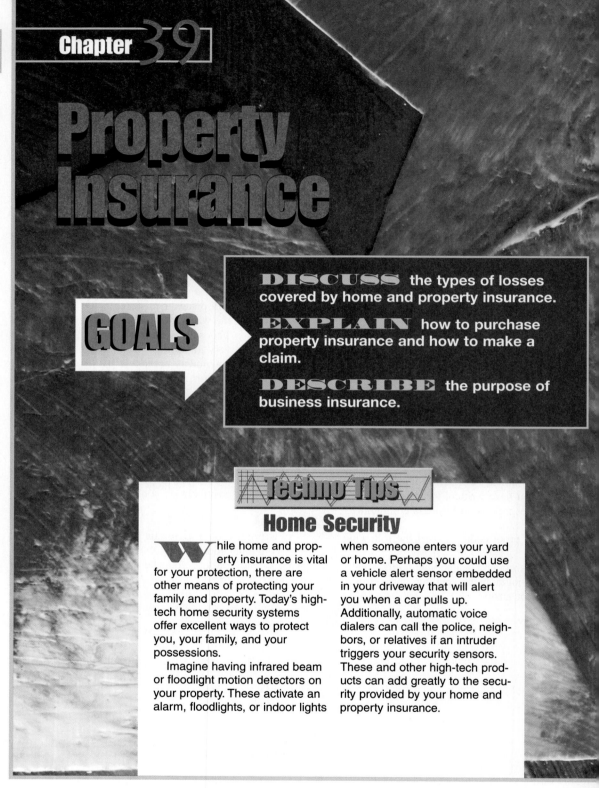

Chapter 39

Property Insurance

GOALS

DISCUSS the types of losses covered by home and property insurance.

EXPLAIN how to purchase property insurance and how to make a claim.

DESCRIBE the purpose of business insurance.

Techno Tips

Home Security

While home and property insurance is vital for your protection, there are other means of protecting your family and property. Today's high-tech home security systems offer excellent ways to protect you, your family, and your possessions.

Imagine having infrared beam or floodlight motion detectors on your property. These activate an alarm, floodlights, or indoor lights when someone enters your yard or home. Perhaps you could use a vehicle alert sensor embedded in your driveway that will alert you when a car pulls up. Additionally, automatic voice dialers can call the police, neighbors, or relatives if an intruder triggers your security sensors. These and other high-tech products can add greatly to the security provided by your home and property insurance.

Students need to know the latest technologies and develop cutting edge Internet skills for use in current jobs, future careers, or in their homes. TechnoTips introduces students to today's cutting edge technologies and provides them with important Internet skills. Feature topics concentrate on Internet-specific technologies and computer or other hi-tech innovations for use by businesses and consumers.

"I love our new apartment! We have spent a lot of money getting it ready to move in when school starts. And now I am broke! Are you sure we really need renters insurance?"

"Trust me, Susan, with three college girls sharing an apartment, we need insurance. If something would happen and our property were destroyed in a fire, we would be out a lot of money. I don't know about you, but I couldn't afford to replace any of my personal items if they were destroyed in a fire. And with three of us sharing the insurance expense, it really won't cost us that much money."

"I guess you're right, Ashley. I know I couldn't replace my personal belongings. You've convinced me. Go ahead and call your mom's insurance agent. Even though Sara hasn't arrived in town yet, I am sure she will go along with us to purchase the insurance."

Property insurance is designed to protect you from the financial loss you would experience if some of your property were lost or destroyed as a result of fire, theft, vandalism, floods, windstorms, or other hazards. Property owners also are at risk of being sued by people who are injured on their property. Because the risks of loss in such situations are high, everyone should carry property insurance.

MOTIVATE

PURPOSE Provide a purpose for students as they read the chapter. Ask what they think they will learn. Explain to them that home and property insurance will be very important to them soon. Direct students to skim the chapter, looking at photos, reading captions, and noting main headings. The goals at the beginning of each chapter provide a valuable tool for having students pinpoint main ideas. The tasks required by the goals are signaled in the first word. Some emphasize information collection ("Identify," "List"), while others call for description ("Explain," "Describe"). Ask students to look through all the goals and note the first word of each.

HOME AND PROPERTY INSURANCE

Home and property insurance protect you against three kinds of economic loss:

1. damage to your home or property,
2. additional expenses you must pay to live someplace else if your home is badly damaged and must be repaired or rebuilt, and
3. liability losses related to your property.

Damage to Home or Property

Every 16 seconds, a fire department responds to a fire somewhere in the United States. Fires cause over $11 billion in damage every year. Much of this damage is to homes. The dollar amount of damage goes up almost every year. Homes and other expensive property should be insured for fire damage as well as damage caused by vandalism, unavoidable accidents, and natural disasters such as lightning, earthquake, wind, and flood. If your home or property is damaged and you are insured, the insurance company will pay all or a portion of the cost of repair or replacement.

Additional Living Expenses

If a fire or other disaster strikes your home, one of the first shocks you will experience is that you do not have a place to live. You may have to move into a hotel, motel, or furnished apartment while your home is being repaired. Property insurance that includes insurance for additional living expenses will help to pay for the expenses you would incur if something happened to your home.

Liability Protection

The third kind of loss, liability loss, is protected by personal liability coverage. **Personal liability coverage** protects you from claims arising from injuries to other people or damage to other people's property caused by you, your family, or even your pets. If a neighbor slips on your icy sidewalk

Accidents related to cooking start more residential fires than any other cause; faulty furnaces, heaters, and fireplaces are the second leading cause of fires.

TEACH/APPLY

MAKE CONNECTIONS Ask students if their family has ever suffered home or property damage. If so, have the students describe what losses were incurred, which pieces of property were replaced by the insurance company, etc. By sharing personal experiences, students will realize how important home and property insurance are to everyone. Show PowerPoint 39-2, *Home and Property Insurance*. Ask students to identify various types of damage to home or property and how they could be caused (fire, lightning, etc.). Ask if anyone knows what additional living expenses are included if a home is badly damaged. Then ask for examples of a liability situation that could happen on an insured's property. Explain homeowners insurance and the various perils

Chapter 39 *Property Insurance* **537**

In the last chapter, students learned about vehicle insurance—in which they were probably very interested. Even though some students may not be as interested in home and property insurance, you can relate this type of insurance to them by discussing the opening scenario in the chapter. Relating home and property insurance to their needs when they move into an apartment may spark interest.

that are covered by an insurance policy. As good consumers, students should be able to give some tips for buying insurance, such as shopping around and comparing product and price. Use PowerPoint 39-4, *Buying Property Insurance*, to discuss factors that affect the type of coverage needed and the cost of the insurance policy. It is important for students to understand the importance of home inventories and how property is replaced, either at depreciated value or replacement value depending on type of insurance.

TRY THIS/GUIDED PRACTICE

Tell students to close their eyes and visualize their room at home. Give them a few minutes to think about every piece of property that they own in that room. Now ask them to pretend that their room was robbed and everything they own is gone. They must now reconstruct an inventory, from memory, for their insurance agent. Guide students through the process of taking an inventory of their rooms at home. Help them create a checklist that has three columns. The first column should describe the item, the second column should list the date of purchase, and the third column the original price of the item. Ask them to take a mental inventory of their rooms and write all of their personal belongings. This is an important activity for students to complete so they can understand the importance of having insurance and keeping an inventory of items that are insured.

An *insurance claims and policy processing clerk*'s job duties include:
- **Processing new policies, modifications to existing policies, and claims forms**
- **Obtaining information to verify the information on claims forms, applications, and company records**
- **Updating existing policies to reflect changes requested by policyholders and company representatives.**

and you are shown to be at fault, personal liability coverage will pay for any medical and legal costs up to a stated limit. If a child damages a car in an adjacent driveway with a tricycle, claims will be paid through the provisions in the policy of the child's family that cover liability for physical damage to the property of others.

These kinds of events may seem remote and rather trivial. But court awards to those who suffer the damage or injury often are neither remote nor trivial. In fact, these awards (and consequently premiums) are increasing so quickly that the insurance industry often refers to it as the insurance

liability crisis. Awards to injured people for millions of dollars are not uncommon. Everyone should have some form of liability protection from economic loss.

PROPERTY INSURANCE POLICIES

When considering the purchase of property insurance, you must first decide what should be insured and against what perils it should be insured. **Perils** are the causes of loss, such as fire, wind, or theft. Property permanently attached to land, such as a house or garage, is called **real property**. Property not attached to the land, such as furniture or clothing, is known as **personal property**. Real and personal property may be protected by individual policies or by a homeowners policy. If you are a renter like Susan and Ashley, there are also special policies that will cover your property—individual, homeowners, and renters.

Individual Policies

A property owner can buy separate policies that insure against specific perils. For example, a **standard fire policy** insures against losses caused by fire or lightning. Extended coverage can be included in a standard fire policy. **Extended coverage** broadens the coverage to include damage caused by perils such as wind, hail, rain, and damage from a vehicle crashing into the building.

Why do you think that so many incidents can be covered by home and property insurance?

The careers listed in the Career Highlight come from the *Occupational Outlook Handbook*, an online publication (www.bls.gov/oco) of the federal government. The O*NET code for Insurance Claims and Policy Processing Clerk is 43-9041.00. Tell your class about this resource and how to use it. This feature gives a realistic description of job duties and is intended to expose students to different careers in business. It can be used to demonstrate the relevancy of skills leaned in this course.

Why would a homeowner in the Midwest want to be insured against different perils than a homeowner living on the West Coast?

Policies also may be purchased separately for damage caused by flood in a flood-prone area. Insurance can be purchased to protect against economic losses caused by earthquakes. Neither of these two perils is typically covered in other policies. The advantage of purchasing separate policies is that the combination of policies purchased can be fitted to individual needs.

Homeowners Policies

The most common form of home and property insurance policy sold today is a homeowners policy. The **homeowners policy** is a very convenient package-type insurance policy designed to fit the needs of most homeowners wishing to insure their homes and property. A homeowners policy almost always comes in three forms: basic form, broad form, and special form. The number of perils covered by a homeowners policy depends on which form the insured chooses to purchase.

The basic form of a homeowners policy insures property against the first 11 perils listed in Figure 39-1. The broad form is very widely purchased and covers 18 different risks. This type usually costs about 5 to 10 percent more than the basic form. The special form is even more comprehensive and covers

all perils shown in Figure 39-1 and many more. The special form is sometimes referred to as an all-risk policy and costs from 10 to 15 percent more than the basic policy. Actually, such a policy insures against all perils except those excluded by the policy. Personal liability coverage is included with all forms of the homeowners policy.

With a homeowners policy, you are as protected as you would be if you bought several different individual policies. Yet the cost of a homeowners policy is usually 20 to 30 percent less than if the same amount of coverage were obtained by buying separate policies. It is also more convenient to have one policy and one premium rather than paying two premiums for separate insurance policies.

Renters Policies

Many people in our society rent homes, condominiums, or apartments. They fill these

About 95 percent of the nation's homeowners carry property insurance to protect themselves against potential financial losses. Less than half of renters buy that same protection.

EXPLORE THIS/INDEPENDENT PRACTICE Before assigning independent practice material for any chapter, students should be expected to read the chapter material carefully. In view of the fact that all students vary widely in their ability to read effectively, it is advisable to have the students read the entire chapter, or sections thereof, silently in class if the material has not been previously read in connection with homework assignments.

After students have read the chapter, ask them to complete the Chapter Review questions. Develop Your Business Language is an excellent way to improve students' vocabulary. Only words introduced in the chapter are used in the exercises. The Review Your Reading questions can be used to check students' ability to comprehend what they have read. The Communicate Business Concepts section affords an opportunity for students to apply to practical life situations the information gained from reading the chapter. By completing the problems under Calculate Business Data, students will be able to strengthen and refine their abilities in mathematics. Technology Application allows students to demonstrate skill in using word processing, spreadsheet, and database software. Decision-Making Strategies contains material to challenge students to utilize the model explained in Chapter 1 for problem solving.

The Chapter Review questions at the end of the chapter vary in

Basic Skills-Listening

You can teach students to be good listeners by explaining to them the value of a listener looking at the person who is speaking. If the listener doesn't pay attention to the speaker, the listener's thoughts may wander and important information may be missed. The Student Activity Worksheet, Basic Skills—Listening Checklist, in the School-To-Work/SCANS

Activity Masters, may be used to serve as a guideline for discussion of listening skills. For a hands-on activity, invite a student to the front of the room to read the Perspectives feature in this chapter. Students should have their books closed. When the speaker is finished, ask that person to leave the room. Now ask students to write down what the student was wearing. If students were paying attention to the speaker, they will note some details of the reader's appearance.

level of difficulty. For a basic assignment, consider Develop Your Business Language and Review Your Reading. For an average assignment, consider the basic assignment plus Communicate Business Concepts and Calculate Business Data. For an enhanced assignment, try the average assignment plus Technology Application and Decision-Making Strategies.

ASSESS

Review the goals at the beginning of the chapter and the Business Notes at the end of the chapter. Have students respond orally or in writing to each goal restated as a question. For students who may have difficulty providing answers, assign the reteaching activities that follow. Enrichment activities may also be assigned where appropriate.

1. What are the three types of economic losses covered by home and property insurance? (Answer: Damage to your home or property, additional expenses you must pay to live someplace else if your home is badly damaged, and liability losses related to your property.)

2. Which three types of special policies to cover property are available to policyholders? (Answer: Individual policies allow a property owner to buy separate policies that insure against specific perils such as losses caused by fire or lightning. Homeowners insurance is a convenient package-type insurance policy designed to fit the needs of most homeowners

PERILS COVERED BY A HOMEOWNERS POLICY

Special

Broad

Basic

Basic	Broad	Special
1. Fire or lightning 2. Volcanic eruption 3. Windstorm or hail 4. Explosion 5. Vehicles 6. Riot or civil commotion 7. Aircraft 8. Smoke 9. Vandalism or malicious mischief 10. Theft 11. Breakage of glass constituting a part of a building	12. Falling objects 13. Weight of ice, snow, sleet 14. Collapse of building(s) 15. Sudden and accidental tearing apart, cracking, burning, or bulging of a steam or hot water heating system or of appliances for heating water, an air conditioning or automatic fire-protective sprinkler system 16. Accidental discharge, leakage or overflow of water or steam from within a plumbing, heating or air-conditioning system or domestic appliance 17. Freezing of plumbing, heating and air-conditioning systems, automatic fire-protective sprinkler system and domestic appliances 18. Sudden and accidental injury from artificially generated currents to electrical appliances, devices, fixtures and wiring (Does not include loss to a tube, transistor, or similar electronic components)	All perils EXCEPT earthquake, flood, war, nuclear accidents, and certain others. (Check policy for details.)

FIGURE 39-1 Which kinds of perils pose the greatest risk of causing damage to your home?

dwellings with their personal property. Renters have many of the same property and liability insurance needs as homeowners. In response to this, the insurance industry has developed a renters policy that is a package property and liability policy appropriate for renters. This policy covers household goods and personal belongings and provides protection against the same kinds of perils covered by homeowners policies. A renters policy may include personal liability coverage, but it doesn't protect the actual dwelling. The dwelling should be covered under the owner's policy. Renters who don't want liability protection may choose a policy that covers only personal property.

BUYING PROPERTY INSURANCE

As with other large insurance purchases, a wise consumer will work to find the most

Installing deadbolt locks on your doors could save you as much as 5 percent on your homeowners or renters policy premium.

If the apartment complex in which you live was destroyed by an earthquake, how would having renters insurance benefit you?

Net Facts provides information and definitions of terms for the Internet. The more information that students have about the Internet, the better equipped they will be to use this resource. In the Internet Activity Masters, there is an Internet Activity Worksheet for each unit. You can use these activities to give students experience with finding information online. Options for assigning this activity are as follows:

1. **Provide students with a list of addresses for this activity,**
2. **Assign students to conduct their own searches, or**
3. **Use the addresses on the Internet Activity Worksheet.**

You should complete the activity yourself before assigning it to resolve any discrepancies that may arise.

appropriate property protection at the lowest cost. This process involves making certain that the property is insured for the correct amount and that the factors affecting property insurance costs have all been carefully considered.

The value of a home and furnishings represents the largest investment that many people make. The purchase of a carefully selected insurance plan makes good sense to protect that investment.

Getting the Correct Coverage

Suppose that Juanita Hernandez built her house in 1998 for $90,000 and she insured it for that amount. If today the cost of building a similar house is $125,000, the current replacement value of the house is $125,000. Yet if Miss Hernandez's house is completely destroyed by fire, the insurance company may pay her only $90,000. Some insurance companies provide for automatic increases in property coverage as the price level increases. Other insurers will pay the current replacement value if the property is insured for at least 80 percent of that replacement value.

Building costs and property values have increased greatly in recent years. Property owners should review the value of their property and insurance coverage every few years. They should determine the cost of

replacing their property and make sure that their insurance policies give enough protection.

Special care should be taken to accurately estimate the value of personal property. Since personal property includes many different items, some may be overlooked if a careless estimate of value is made. Most homeowners policies provide personal property coverage at 50 percent of policy value. For example, if your home is insured for $100,000, your personal property is insured for 50 percent of $100,000, or $50,000. The value of personal property that you collect over the years is often surprisingly high. In many cases, a homeowner's personal property is worth considerably more than 50 percent of the coverage on the home. Additional coverage is available for a slightly higher premium.

FTP stands for File Transfer Protocol. FTP software transfers files of data from one computer to another.

wishing to insure their homes and property. Renters insurance is available for those who rent homes, condominiums, or apartments.)

3. How should one go about purchasing property insurance? (Answer: A wise consumer will work to find the most appropriate property protection at the lowest cost. This process involves making certain that the property is insured for the correct amount and that the factors affecting property insurance costs have all been carefully considered.)

TEACHING STRATEGIES
Special Needs: Dyslexia

One way to keep students with dyslexia interested in the class is to use teaching strategies that will make content clear through the use of visuals or graphics and reduce the reading load. Associate the visuals in the chapter with the content instead of assigning an overwhelming amount of text to read.

4. What is the purpose of business insurance? (Answer: Businesses insure their personal and real property against economic loss caused by a variety of perils. The same tragedies happen with businesses as with homes, including fires, storms, water damage, burglaries, liability problems, plus an additional peril of loss of income.)

5. How does one make an insurance claim? (Answer: Provide your agent (1) the original cost of the article, (2) when the article was purchased, and (3) how long the article is expected to last so that appropriate action may be taken.)

RETEACH

Explain homeowners insurance and the various perils that are covered by using Figure 39-1, *Perils Covered By a Homeowners Policy*. (You might want to copy this figure as a handout for students.) The term *perils* may take some extra explanation for students to completely understand.

ENRICH

Direct students to read the Cultural Perspectives in this chapter. Ask students to help their families by conducting a true inventory and recording all of the important details that would be needed in the event of loss. An activity that your students might find appropriate in relation to property insurance would be to ask students to inspect their own homes and garages for fire hazards. Then have students prepare a list of conditions they feel might result in damage or loss to property.

CULTURAL PERSPECTIVES
Papyrus

If you lived in Egypt around 1600 B.C., your business would have recorded its activities on papyrus. The spongy material inside the plant was cut in strips and pressed into material that resembled a crude form of what we know as paper. This crude form of paper enabled people to write and record information and actually store their records. Up until this time, the early Babylonians used clay tablets. However, the clay tablets were difficult to handle and to write on. With the invention of papyrus, the business world began to change.

Egypt had an elaborate tax system in which taxes were paid in commodities, such as wheat, and sent to local district storehouses. Less perishable items were transferred to a central treasury. All of these transfers were recorded meticulously by the scribes. There was an auditing system in which the records of each scribe were compared and had to match. Scribes were very careful to be accurate because irregularities could be punished by mutilation or death. The papyrus allowed the scribes to work faster and more accurately.

The invention of paper advanced not only record keeping but the artistic and cultural aspects of civilization as well.

Critical Thinking
1. How do you think papyrus would have looked in comparison to paper?
2. In what other ways do you think the invention of paper has contributed to our culture?

Insurance Premiums

Premiums paid for homeowners insurance have grown each year over the last 10 years to over $30 billion annually. The price that you pay for insurance on a home and furnishings is based on a number of factors. The most important factor is the estimated danger of loss based on the insurance company's past experiences. In addition to the loss experiences, an insurance company considers the following factors in determining homeowners insurance premiums:

- The value of the property insured.
- The construction of the building; that is, whether it is made of brick, wood, or concrete; and the construction of the roof.
- The type of policy (basic, broad, or special).
- The number of perils covered.
- The distance to the nearest fire department and water supply.
- The amount of deductible (the higher the deductible, the lower the premium).

You should consider these factors carefully before purchasing or building a home and when shopping for insurance on that home and your property. Also, homeowners insurance discounts are often available for policyholders who are nonsmokers, for installing smoke detectors and burglar alarms, and for buying multiple policies such as life and auto insurance from the same company.

BUSINESS INSURANCE

Like homeowners, businesses insure their personal and real property against economic loss caused by a variety of perils. The same tragedies happen with businesses as with homes. Fires, storms, water damage, burglaries, and liability problems face business owners. Businesses are also threatened by another important economic peril—loss of income. Businesses can use insurance to protect against the loss of income during times when they must be closed or their activities are disrupted due to a fire, theft, other insured event.

CULTURAL PERSPECTIVES

This Cultural Perspectives feature will expose students to the concept that our society is composed of people from many different cultural backgrounds. These features show both past contributions of many cultures and benefits of a culturally diverse society.

CRITICAL THINKING
1. Students might respond that the papyrus would look and feel rough and irregular and that it may not be as white as modern paper.
2. Answers ranging from the publication of books to the improvement of communication to the sharing of culture are probable.

Why is a detailed inventory list important, particularly if you are required to submit a claim?

SUMMARIZE

Using a computer, if possible, have students write a paragraph on the types of home and property insurance they may need and perils from which their families should be protected. Direct them to write a second paragraph discussing the importance of inventories.

EVALUATE

- Assign Activities and Projects for Chapter 39.
- Administer the printed test or ExamView for Chapter 39.
- Assign School-To-Work/SCANS Building Your Portfolio Activities for Unit 11.

MAKING A CLAIM

In the unhappy event that you should have to make a claim to your insurance company for a property loss, you will want to be well prepared. You should keep a list of personal property that you have insured. The list, called an **inventory**, should include:

1. the brand name and description of each item,

2. the purchase price, and

3. the date and place of the purchase.

The age of an insured article of personal property is quite important. As most property becomes older, it gradually wears out and decreases in value. This decrease in value, called **depreciation**, usually affects the amount the insurance company will pay if the property is destroyed. For example, a sofa costing $700 that is expected to last ten years would depreciate $70 each year (cost $700 ÷ 10 years = $70 depreciation per year). Its value after six years would be $280 (depreciation per year $70 × 6 years = total depreciation $420; original cost $700 − total depreciation $420 = $280).

However, in recent years, homeowners have purchased replacement insurance. **Replacement insurance** actually replaces an item that has been destroyed. No depreciation is deducted, but instead the item is actually replaced for whatever the current cost may be. A replacement cost policy would pay whatever it cost on the day of the loss to replace your property. As soon as possible after you discover a loss, you should file a claim with your insurance company. However, before the company will pay, you must provide proof of your loss. This is not a problem with real property. A representative of the insurance company, called an **adjuster**, can look at the damaged property, determine the extent of loss, and pay you according to the terms of the policy. The destroyed contents of a house, however, would pose a problem. In order to prove the amount of personal property loss, you must know the approximate value of each article damaged or destroyed.

In addition to maintaining an up-to-date personal property inventory, some insurance companies suggest keeping receipts from purchases of your possessions and taking photographs or videos of your furniture and other property. These receipts and pictures can be used to support claims. Insurance companies can provide inventory forms and information about how to make claims for losses. Inventory records and photographs should be stored in a location that cannot be damaged by fire, water, or smoke. If the records are lost or damaged, it will be difficult to provide the insurance company with the information needed to receive payment. A safety deposit box in a bank or another safe location away from your home is a good location for property records.

Chapter 39 *Property Insurance* **543**

TEACHING TIP
Safety and Health

Since this chapter concerns property insurance and risks, have students look around the classroom and observe health or safety risks that may be apparent. Items like cords stretched across aisles are examples of safety hazards.

REVIEW YOUR READING

1. Damage to your home or property, the additional living expenses involved when you must live someplace else because your home was badly damaged, and liability losses.
2. You would have to suffer some kind of loss that damaged your home to the extent that it was impossible to live in it.
3. To protect you against claims arising from injuries to other people or damage to other people's property caused by you, your family, or even your pets.
4. Flood and earthquake.
5. The special form.
6. Separate policies are priced at higher rates. A homeowners policy usually is about 20 to 30 percent less expensive than it would be if the same coverage were obtained by buying separate policies. Also, it is more convenient to make one payment for a homeowners policy rather than make separate payments for several individual policies.
7. A person who rents an apartment should have property insurance because the apartment contains a large amount of personal property belonging to the renter. Similar to homeowners insurance, renters insurance protects household contents and personal belongings.
8. Type of construction and the material of which the building is made, the location of the building, the accessibility to fire department protection and water supply, the length and type of the policy, and the amount of coverage and amount of the deductible clause.
9. Original cost of the item less the total depreciation equals the amount the insurance will pay for replacement.
10. Receipts of original purchase, photos, or videos.

COMMUNICATE BUSINESS CONCEPTS

11. Probably. Homeowners policies cover against all perils except earthquake, flood, war, nuclear accidents, and certain others depending upon the individual policy. Homeowners with separate flood insurance would be covered.

BUSINESS NOTES

1. Home and property insurance protect against three kinds of economic loss: (1) damage to your home or property, (2) additional expenses you pay to live someplace else if your home is badly damaged, and (3) liability losses related to your property.
2. There are three types of special policies that cover property. Individual policies allow a property owner to buy separate policies that insure against specific perils such as losses caused by fire or lightning. Homeowners insurance is a convenient package-type insurance policy designed to fit the needs of most homeowners wishing to insure their homes and property. Renters insurance is available for those who rent homes, condominiums, or apartments.
3. A wise consumer will work to find the most appropriate property protection at the lowest cost. This process involves making certain that the property is insured for the correct amount and that the factors affecting property insurance costs have all been carefully considered.
4. Businesses insure their personal and real property against economic loss caused by a variety of perils. The same tragedies happen with businesses as with homes, including fires, storms, water damage, burglaries, liability problems, plus an additional peril of loss of income.
5. When making an insurance claim, you will need to give your agent (1) the brand name and description of the item, (2) the purchase price, and (3) the date and source of the purchase in order to document your loss.

REVIEW YOUR READING

1. List the three kinds of economic losses for which home and property insurance provide protection.
2. What kind of loss would you have to suffer in order to take advantage of additional living-expense coverage in your insurance policy?
3. Tell why personal liability coverage is so important today.
4. Name two prominent perils that are not typically covered in most homeowners policies.
5. Which homeowners policy covers more perils, the special or the broad policy?
6. Describe the difference between buying separate policies to cover home and property versus buying a homeowners policy.
7. Why would a person who rents an apartment purchase property insurance? What kind of policy should a renter purchase?
8. Which factors determine a homeowner's insurance premiums?
9. For what amount is property that has been destroyed usually replaced if the owner has cash-value insurance and does not have replacement insurance?
10. What are several ways a property owner can prove the value of items listed in an inventory?

---

12. Art's insurance company should pay the medical expenses associated with the salesperson's broken arm. His homeowners policy should include personal liability coverage.
13. a and b. C would only be covered if flooding is one of the perils that is specifically covered in the policy.
14. The Chens' neighbors should maintain an up-to-date personal property inventory, complete with the brand name and description of all insured items, their purchase price, and the date and source of purchase. They might want to photograph the items and keep a copy of the inventory records in a safe location away from their homes.

COMMUNICATE BUSINESS CONCEPTS

11. In a recent year, several homes in an Iowa valley were destroyed when heavy rains caused the Mississippi River to rise several feet above flood level. Do you think those Iowa residents who had homeowners policies suffered any financial losses? Why or why not?

12. It snowed in Springview one night in February, and Art Shold did not take the time to shovel the snow from his front steps. Two days later a salesperson slipped on Art's snow-covered steps and broke an arm. The salesperson has asked Art to pay the medical expenses associated with the broken arm. Will Art's homeowners policy cover the expenses?

13. Barbara Johnson's property is covered by the basic form of homeowners insurance. Against which of the following losses is she insured?

Which of the losses would be covered if she had the broad coverage?
   a. A smoldering fire breaks out in a bedroom closet and her clothing is damaged by smoke.
   b. Her home is broken into and vandalized, but nothing is stolen.
   c. A storm knocks out the electricity for two days in mid-winter and the pipes burst, causing flooding.

14. The Chens had a serious home fire. They had an adequate fire insurance policy in force, but they had a very difficult time listing for the insurance adjuster all of the possessions they lost in the fire. What advice would you give to others in the Chens' neighborhood who might be in this position someday?

DEVELOP YOUR BUSINESS LANGUAGE

For each numbered item, find the term that has the same meaning.

15. Property that is permanently attached to land.

16. Additional protection of property that covers damage caused by perils such as wind, hail, smoke, and rain among other things.

17. Insurance that protects you from claims arising from injuries to other people or damage to other people's property caused by you, your family, or your pets.

18. A basic type of property insurance that protects against losses caused by fire or lightning.

19. Property that is not attached to the land.

20. A package-type insurance policy designed to fit the needs of most homeowners wishing to insure their homes and property.

21. The decrease in the value of property as it becomes older and wears out.

22. A list of goods showing the original cost of each item, when it was purchased, and how long it is expected to last.

23. The causes of loss, such as fire, wind, or theft.

24. An insurance company representative who determines the extent of loss and pays policyholders according to the terms of the policy.

25. Insurance that actually replaces an item that has been destroyed.

KEY TERMS
adjuster
depreciation
extended coverage
homeowners policy
inventory
perils
personal liability coverage
personal property
real property
replacement insurance
standard fire policy

DECISION-MAKING STRATEGIES

Don purchased a very expensive diamond tennis bracelet for his wife. The jeweler suggested that Don insure this bracelet right away because of its cost. Don has two choices of insurance to purchase. One type would provide an actual-cash-value policy, minus depreciation, that would replace the lost item. However, replacement insurance would pay whatever it cost on the day of the loss to replace the bracelet.

26. Why should Don consider buying actual-cash-value insurance?

27. Why should Don consider buying replacement insurance?

DEVELOP YOUR BUSINESS LANGUAGE

15. real property
16. extended coverage
17. personal liability coverage
18. standard fire policy
19. personal property
20. homeowners policy
21. depreciation
22. inventory
23. perils
24. adjuster
25. replacement insurance

DECISION-MAKING STRATEGIES

26. The premium may be lower and diamonds usually increase in value (not always) so the bracelet may not suffer depreciation.

27. Don may not be able to afford a new bracelet if depreciation is deducted (if the diamonds decrease in value). The replacement cost could escalate. So by purchasing replacement insurance, this would never be a concern.

28. $175 - $140 = $35; $35 ÷ $175 = 0.20 = 20%

29. $98,000 × 80% = $78,400

30. ($4.25 × 15) + ($1.45 × 6) + ($.85 × 3) + (68 × $4.50) = $381.00

31. $275 × 0.75 = $206.25; $420 × 0.75 = $315; $90 × 0.75 = $67.50; $189 × 0.75 = $141.75; $275 + $420 + $90 + $189 = $974 × 1.10 = $1,071.40

TECHNOLOGY APPLICATION

In this activity, students use a computer to solve a business problem using a file that is provided on the data CD that accompanies *Intro to Business*. Instructions for using the data CD are included in a **README** file on the disk. Solutions are provided on the Instructor's Resource CD.

CALCULATE BUSINESS DATA

28. The Popovs were shopping for property insurance policies when they found a basic homeowners policy that would cost them $140 per year. The total of three separate policies that would cover all of the same perils would be $175. What percent of the total of the three separate policies would the Popovs save by buying the homeowners policy?

29. If Ellen Williams owned a home worth $98,000 and wanted to be certain it was insured for at least 80 percent of its value, for how much should it be insured?

30. A thief broke the lock on Ngyen Shan's business and stole the following items:

15 liters of oak stain, valued at $4.25 a liter

6 liters of motor oil, valued at $1.45 a liter

3 kilograms of 2.5 cm finishing nails, valued at 85 cents a kilogram

68 meters of 2.5 cm 3 30.5 cm pine shelving, valued at $4.50 a meter

Since Mr. Shan had recently purchased these items to sell to his customers, for what amount should he make his claim under his business insurance policy?

31. Arlene Arnold lives in an apartment. Her furniture and other personal property are covered under a renters policy. Miss Arnold's apartment was broken into and the following items were stolen:

A stereo system with a purchase price of $275.

A television with a purchase price of $420.

A wristwatch with a purchase price of $90

A leather coat with a purchase price of $189.

If the items had depreciated 25% from their purchase price, what would be the current amount that the insurance company would reimburse Arlene for each item? If Arlene had replacement value coverage and the items would cost 10% more to replace than their original purchase price, what would be the total amount the insurance company would pay?

TECHNOLOGY APPLICATION

Using the *Intro to Business* Data CD and your database program software, select problem CH39. After the problem appears on your screen, complete the following activities. Then, after you have completed each step, display or print a report for each activity. If you do not have a printer available, answer the questions before you leave the computer.

32. Sort the database in ascending order by purchase cost of item. Answer the following questions:

a. Which household item had the third-highest purchase cost?

b. Which household item had the second-to-lowest purchase cost?

33. Select and list the household items that were purchased in 1996 and that have a purchase cost of at least $100. How many items are listed?

34. Sort the household items in descending order by year when purchased. Answer the following questions:

a. Which household item in the database is the oldest?

b. Which household item in the database is the second oldest?

INTERNATIONAL PROPERTY RIGHTS

In some Asian countries, local companies not associated with the National Basketball Association create shirts celebrating the championship of an NBA team. In a Latin American country, copies of a popular video are duplicated illegally and sold by street vendors. These are both examples of violations of property rights.

Property rights are the exclusive rights to possess and use property and its profits. This excludes everyone else from interfering with the use of the item. *Intellectual property* refers to technical knowledge or creative work. These include software, clothing designs, or films. For many companies, their intellectual properties are valuable assets that generate sales revenue and profits.

A *patent* is the exclusive right of an inventor to make, sell, and use a product or process. A patent may be obtained on a computer component, an airtight package, or a prescription drug. These inventions can give a company a competitive advantage. Patents are designed to encourage innovation and progress.

A *trademark* is a distinctive name, symbol, word, picture, or combination of these that is used to identify products or services. Common trademarks known around the world include the McDonald's golden arches, Kellogg's Tony the Tiger, and American Express.

A *copyright* protects the original works

of authors, composers, playwrights, artists, and publishers. In the United States, a copyright gives originators exclusive rights to publish and exhibit their creative works for their lifetime plus 50 years. Most other countries have similar laws.

Counterfeiting refers to illegal uses of intellectual property, patents, trademarks, and copyrights. A foreign company may slightly change a well-known trademark to obtain financial gains based on the reputation of the famous company. When property rights laws are not enforced, companies can lose profits, which discourages them from participating in international trade.

CRITICAL THINKING

1. Collect a variety of trademarks and brand names. Which of these are well known around the world? Are some of the names known only in the United States, or in one region of the country? Explain why some brand names may stay the same when used in other countries, while others must be changed.

2. Conduct library and web research on the topic of product "counterfeiting" in other countries. What are some examples? How does counterfeiting affect consumers, workers, and companies? What actions might be taken to reduce the risk of counterfeiting?

Most students will either work with international clients or compete against businesses that do. Global Navigator introduces students to issues integral to working with international businesses. Key concepts and challenges faced by international businesses are presented, followed by two Critical Thinking questions that require students to analyze what they have learned.

This Global Navigator feature describes three internationally recognized forms of intellectual property—patents, trademarks, and copyrights. It discusses how respect for these property rights is important for international trade.

CRITICAL THINKING

1. Answers will vary. Brand names may be changed if companies seek to balance the popularity and recognition enjoyed by a brand with the need to sometimes adjust marketing plans based on local customs and taboos.

2. Students may cite products such as Coke, popular shoe brands, children's toys, and music recordings, among many that have been subject to counterfeiting. Counterfeiting harms consumers who may buy inferior products thinking they are getting the real thing. It also hurts company profits and workers' job security (although it obviously also creates illicit jobs for counterfeiters). Lawsuits and trade sanctions are common weapons used to fight counterfeiting.

Chapter 40 describes basic life insurance and the importance of life insurance for everyone. Term life insurance and permanent life insurance are the main focus of the chapter. Group life insurance is also described.

Resources for Teachers
- Lesson Plans
- School-To-Work/SCANS Activity Masters
- Spanish Resources
- Instructor's Resource CD

Assessment
- Chapter and Unit Tests, Ch. 40
- ExamView, Ch. 40

Media/Technology
- Applying Technology Data CD
- PowerPoint slides
- Business Connection CD
- Videotape

Activity Masters and Workbooks
- Activities and Projects, Ch. 40
- Internet Activity Masters
- Business Math Activity Masters
- Communications Activity Masters
- International Business Activity Masters
- Ethics Activity Masters

Chapter 40

Life Insurance

GOALS

EXPLAIN why life insurance is important.

COMPARE the costs and benefits of the two basic types of life insurance—term and permanent.

OUTLINE the procedures for obtaining life insurance coverage.

Techno Tips

Life Insurance Online

Internet resources can make the unpleasant affair of obtaining life insurance a more enjoyable and less intimidating experience. Insurance web sites offer everything you need, from offering basic tips to allowing you to purchase a policy right over the Internet.

Most sites offer basic tips that help you understand insurance policies before you choose one. Tips on how to handle major life changes, like buying a home, becoming a parent or getting married, are also available. You can even create an online insurance portfolio to hold your quotes and policies.

Especially when purchasing insurance using the Internet, be careful to select a reputable company. The company should be financially stable, have a good record of customer service, and provide the information you need to make a decision. Low-cost insurance is not a value if the company does not meet its commitments.

Students need to know the latest technologies and develop cutting edge Internet skills for use in current jobs, future careers, or in their homes. TechnoTips introduces students to today's cutting edge technologies and provides them with important Internet skills. Feature topics concentrate on Internet-specific technologies and computer or other hi-tech innovations for use by businesses and consumers.

"Last night I started thinking about college education for my two youngsters. I know they are still in elementary school, but I need to start planning for their future. It seems like I take care of their day-to-day needs, but I have forgotten about their future needs!"

"Rafael, have you considered borrowing on your life insurance policy when the time comes for the children to go to college?"

"Life insurance? You probably won't believe this, Steve, but I don't have any life insurance. I have other kinds of insurance, but I thought I was too young to worry about life insurance."

"Everyone needs life insurance to protect their family against economic loss. And if you buy a permanent policy soon, you may be able to use it to your advantage when your children need cash for college."

While developing a plan for the future welfare of his children, Rafael should certainly include the purchase of life insurance. Rafael will need to decide what kind of life insurance to buy, how much to buy, and where to buy it.

LIFE INSURANCE

Life insurance protects survivors against the financial loss associated with death. Specifically, it is designed to replace a loss of income for family members who are financially dependent upon another person. Life insurance can also be considered a means of saving or investing, but its primary purpose is always protection against financial loss.

Anyone with dependents needs life insurance. A *dependent* is a person who must rely on another for financial support. In the future, you will need to ask the question, "What would happen to the people who are financially dependent on me if I died tomorrow?" If they could not live financially in the manner in which they lived before your death, you probably need life insurance.

TYPES OF LIFE INSURANCE

Insurance companies offer a variety of life insurance plans that meet the different insurance needs of individuals. The two basic types of life insurance policies are term life and permanent life.

Term Life Insurance

Term life insurance provides financial protection from losses resulting from loss of life during a definite period of time, or term. It is the least expensive form of life insurance. It is also the *only* form of life insurance that is purely life insurance. All other forms of insurance have savings or investment features added to them.

Describe some of the various types of dependents who might be protected by life insurance.

Chapter 40 Life Insurance   **549**

paid, the policy remains constant with no changes and cash value builds. It also provides an opportunity to borrow for college or other important needs as long as the borrowed amount is repaid. Discuss with students how to apply for life insurance and the savings that are possible through group life insurance.

TRY THIS/GUIDED PRACTICE

Walk students through the decision-making process of deciding which type of insurance is more appropriate for them if they were to purchase insurance now. Write the pros and cons on the board and guide them through the decision-making process.

EXPLORE THIS/INDEPENDENT PRACTICE

Before assigning independent practice material for any chapter, students should be expected to read the chapter material carefully. In view of the fact that all students vary widely in their ability to read effectively, it is advisable to have the students read the entire chapter, or sections thereof, silently in class if the material has not been previously read in connection with homework assignments.

After students have read the chapter, ask them to complete the Chapter Review questions. Develop Your Business Language is an excellent way to improve students' vocabulary. Only words introduced in the chapter are used in the exercises. The Review Your Reading questions can be used to check students' ability to comprehend what they have read. The Communicate Business Concepts section affords an opportunity for

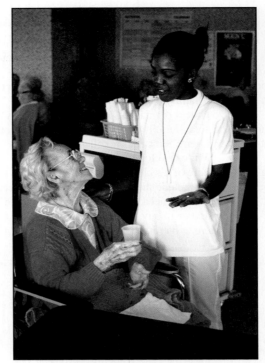

What are some reasons why life insurance costs vary among individuals?

Term policies may run for a period, or term, of from 1 to 20 years or more. If the insured dies during the period for which the insurance was purchased, the amount of the policy is paid to the beneficiary. A **beneficiary** is the person named in the policy to receive the insurance benefits. If the insured does not die during the period for which the policy was purchased, the insurance company is not required to pay anything. Protection ends when the term of years expires.

By paying a slightly higher premium, a person can buy term insurance that is renewable. A **renewable policy** allows the policyholder to continue term insurance for one or more terms without taking a physical examination to determine whether she or he is still a good risk.

Term insurance policies may be level term or decreasing term. With **level term**

insurance, the amount of protection and the premiums remain the same while the insurance is in effect. With **decreasing term insurance**, the amount of protection gradually becomes smaller, but premiums remain the same during the term. This is frequently appropriate because the need for insurance normally declines as children grow up and become independent and other savings and investments grow.

Permanent Life Insurance

The second type of life insurance is called **permanent insurance**. Permanent insurance has cash value and an investment feature as its common characteristics. Part of the premiums you pay for permanent life insurance is used for insurance that provides protection just like term insurance. The remaining part of the premium, not needed to pay for the coverage, is invested by the insurance company and adds to the cash value of the insurance policy. **Cash value** refers to the amount of money that will be paid by the insurance company if the policyholder decides the insurance is no longer needed. The cash value is much less than the amount that will be paid to beneficiaries upon the death of the insured. As long as permanent policies are

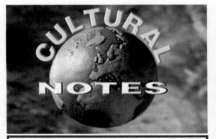

We in the United States are not the originators of environmental awareness. Cultures around the world have been protecting the environment for centuries. The Aboriginal Australians learned how to manage land resources through controlled burns.

Critical Thinking Skills-Decision Making

Decision-making skills, which include specifying goals, generating alternatives, considering risks, and evaluating and choosing the best alternative, are applied throughout every chapter in this text. Each time a student participates in a Cooperative Learning or Teams activity, decision-making skills are applied in a group situation. For Communicate Business Concepts and Decision-Making Strategies, students must specify the goal of the activity, consider risks, and evaluate the best solution before the questions can be answered. Emphasize to students how they are using decision-making techniques in their day-to-day tasks and make them aware of the skills they are developing.

kept in force, they accumulate cash value in addition to providing life insurance.

The longer you keep your permanent life insurance policy, the higher its cash value will be. If you give up or surrender your policy, you are paid the amount of the cash value. If you need money but do not wish to cancel your policy, you can borrow from the insurance company an amount up to the cash value. If you should die before the loan can be repaid, the unpaid amount will be deducted from the face value of the policy when your survivors are paid. **Face value** is the amount of insurance coverage that was originally purchased and that will be paid upon the death of the insured.

The cash value of permanent life insurance can be seen as a savings plan. The return

on your money in the cash value portion of permanent life insurance is often not large. However, permanent insurance plans have a built-in savings feature that encourages people to save for the future. Permanent life insurance comes in the form of whole life, variable life, and universal life policies. Each type accumulates cash value.

Whole Life Insurance Whole life insurance is permanent insurance that extends over the lifetime, or whole life, of the insured.

One type of whole life insurance is called an **ordinary life policy**. Premiums for ordinary life insurance remain the same each year as long as the policyholder lives.

Some whole life insurance policies are intended to be paid in full in a certain number of years and are called **limited-payment policies**. Limited-payment policies may also be designated by the number of years the policyholder agrees to pay on them, such as 20-payment life policies. They are like ordinary life policies, except that premiums are paid for a limited number of years—

students to apply to practical life situations the information gained from reading the chapter. By completing the problems under Calculate Business Data, students will be able to strengthen and refine their abilities in mathematics. Technology Application allows students to demonstrate skill in using word processing, spreadsheet, and database software. Decision-Making Strategies contains material to challenge students to utilize the model explained in Chapter 1 for problem solving.

The Chapter Review questions at the end of the chapter vary in level of difficulty. For a basic assignment, consider Develop Your Business Language and Review Your Reading. For an average assignment, consider the basic assignment plus Communicate Business Concepts and Calculate Business Data. For an enhanced assignment, try the average assignment plus Technology Application and Decision-Making Strategies.

ASSESS

Review the goals at the beginning of the chapter and the Business Notes at the end of the chapter. Have students respond orally or in writing to each Business Note restated as a question. For students who may have difficulty providing answers, assign the reteaching activities that follow. Enrichment activities may also be assigned where appropriate.

1. Why is life insurance important? (Answer: Life insurance protects survivors against the financial

GLOBAL PERSPECTIVES

Life Insurance for Expatriates

Like other businesses, nothing happens in the life insurance business until somebody sells something. In the case of life insurance, that phrase translates into a constant effort by life insurance marketers to sell insurance to as many people needing life insurance as possible.

One recently discovered rich source of potential life insurance purchasers is U. S. expatriates. An *expatriate* is usually defined as a citizen of the United States who works abroad—often for a multinational company. Even though many services are available to these citizens through the countries in which they work, many prefer certain American services such as life insurance. However, U. S. expatriates, unlike their colleagues in the United States, have little access to life insur-

ance agents from America who are trained to help them with their life insurance needs. Because of foreign selling laws, distance from clients, and unfamiliar territories, insurance agents have not built up a client base in other countries. The insurance industry has now realized this market potential which has created an excellent opportunity for them to increase their business while meeting an important need of our own citizens abroad.

Critical Thinking

1. What types of businesses send U. S. citizens to foreign countries?
2. What methods of communication can the insurance industry use to convey important insurance information to citizens overseas?

GLOBAL PERSPECTIVES

Visualizing, or being able to organize and process information, is a thinking skill we cannot ignore. Students need to learn how to visualize through reading information and observing graphs, pictures, and other visuals. The Global Perspectives feature gives students an opportunity to visualize the various places around the globe that

are described. This feature will also describe various business practices that are different around the world.

CRITICAL THINKING

1. Suggested answers may be multinational manufacturers and consulting firms, military personnel, and those in political offices.
2. E-mail, Internet, fax, and telephone to name a few.

loss associated with dying. It is designed to replace a loss of income for family members who are financially dependent upon another person.)

2. What are the major differences between term life insurance and permanent life insurance? (Answer: Term life insurance provides financial protection from losses resulting from loss of life during a definite period of time, or term. It is the least expensive form of life insurance. Permanent insurance has cash value and an investment feature as its common characteristics. It is not renewed each term as is term insurance.)

3. How does a person apply for life insurance? How is a beneficiary designated? How are premiums established? (Answer: One would usually apply for a policy through an insurance agent who represents an insurance company. Normally you will be required to take a physical examination so that your health can be assessed. When you buy life insurance, you will be asked to name a beneficiary. The cost (premiums) of a life insurance policy will depend on the type of life insurance being purchased and the age of the person being insured.)

4. What is group life insurance? (Answer: An insurance policy that covers a group of people is called group life insurance. The group acts as a single unit in buying the insurance.)

20 or 30, for example—or until a person reaches a certain age, such as 60 or 65. Limited-payment policies free the insured from paying premiums during retirement when income may be lower.

Variable Life Insurance Variable life insurance is a type of life insurance plan that resembles an investment portfolio. This plan lets the policyholder choose among a broad range of investments including stocks, bonds, and mutual funds. The death benefits and cash values of variable life policies vary according to the yield on the investments the policyholder selects.

The insurance company first designates an amount of the variable life premiums to cover the cost of insurance. The remaining amount is placed in an investment account. Both the death benefit and the cash value rise and fall with the success of the investment account.

A minimum death benefit is guaranteed, but there is no guaranteed cash value. The minimum death benefit, in relation to premiums paid, is well below other types of life insurance. On the positive side, a strong rate of return on the investment account can increase the cash value and the death benefit well above the guaranteed level.

Universal Life Insurance Universal life insurance provides both insurance protection and a substantial savings plan. The premium that you pay for universal life insurance is divided three ways. One portion of it pays for insurance protection. A second portion is taken by the insurance company for its expenses. The third portion is placed in interest-earning investments for the policyholder. The most important feature of universal life insurance is that the savings portion of the policy earns a variable interest rate. This interest rate is usually higher than is paid on other

cash value insurance. The yield on the savings portion tends to rise or fall with the Consumer Price Index. Figure 40-1 compares the features of the different types of life insurance.

BUYING LIFE INSURANCE

Virtually everyone needs life insurance at some time in their lives, as few have the financial resources necessary to pay the costs that can overtake them upon the death of someone close to them. Therefore, in order for a life insurance program to be most effective, it must be suited to your needs and those of your family.

The answers to the following questions will help to determine the suitability of a life insurance program:

• How much money is required for your dependents' financial stability if your income is lost?

• How much income will you need when you retire and what will be the sources of your income?

• What can you afford to pay for your life insurance needs?

Answers to these questions will help you purchase the best life insurance program for you.

Applying for Life Insurance

To buy individual life insurance coverage, one would usually apply for a policy through an insurance agent who represents an insurance company.

Normally you will be required to take a physical examination so that your health can be assessed. Assuming that you have no serious health problems, you then pay a premium and receive your life insurance policy. If you

---

Basic Skills-Speaking

We can help students develop speaking skills by teaching them how to organize their ideas in a manner that is appropriate for the situation. Before speaking to a group, students should know their audience, plan their presentation, rehearse, then make the presentation. Developing a speech through an outline is an excellent planning tool, and every speech should have an introduction, body, and conclusion. Then discuss the rehearsal process and its purpose. As this unit of study is on insurance, assign several students an insurance topic of your choice (or their choice) to prepare and present a speech. Give students the Student Activity Worksheet, Basic Skills—Speaking, in the School-To-Work/SCANS Activity Masters.

	TERM INSURANCE	PERMANENT INSURANCE			
		Whole Life		Variable Life	Universal Life
		Ordinary Life	*Limited Life*		
Premium	Begins low but increases gradually	High but usually stays constant	Higher than ordinary life insurance but constant	Fixed and regular	Varies at the discretion of the policyholder
Payment Period	Specified number of years—normally 5, 10, or 15 years	Life of the insured	Specified number of years—normally 20 to 30 years	Specified period	Specified period
Cash Value	None	Some cash value	More cash value than ordinary life but less than variable life	Varies with the rise or fall in the value of the investment account	Varies with the interest rate paid on the cash value
Death Benefit	Fixed	Fixed	Fixed	Death benefit always exceeds cash value	Can vary at discretion of policyholder
Purposes	Protection for a specified period of time	Protection for life; some cash value for policy holder	Protection for life; some cash value for policyholder	Life insurance plus an opportunity to select different cash value investment options	Life insurance with a fairly high rate of return on cash value

FIGURE 40-1   Which kind of insurance is least expensive for a given amount of death benefit?

are in poor health or work in a dangerous occupation, you may be considered a poor risk. For example, if you drive racing cars to earn a living, you are in a dangerous occupation. Even if you are in poor health or work in a dangerous job, you may be able to obtain insurance. However, you will probably pay higher premiums than people who are in good health and are employed in less hazardous occupations.

Designating a Beneficiary

When you buy life insurance, you will be asked to name a beneficiary. This is most often a spouse, children, or other dependents.

You may insure not only your own life, but also the life of any other person in whom you have an insurable interest. To have an **insurable interest** in the life of another person, you must receive some kind of financial benefits from that person's continued life. You have, for example, an insurable interest in the lives of your parents. You do not have

Ordinary life insurance is sometimes called straight life insurance.

- Assign Activities and Projects for Chapter 40.
- Administer the printed test or ExamView for Chapter 40.
- Assign School-To-Work/SCANS Building Your Portfolio activities for Unit 11.

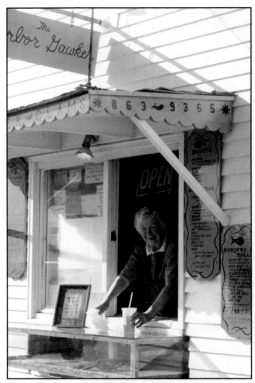

Why is it important to know how you will earn your retirement income?

an insurable interest in a stranger's life. A partner in a business has an insurable interest in the life of his or her partner.

Paying Premiums

In addition to the health and occupation of the insured, the cost or premiums of a life insurance policy depend on the type of life insurance being purchased and the age of the person being insured. In purchasing a whole life policy, for example, the premiums for ordinary life insurance are higher than those for term insurance, but the annual premium stays the same throughout the insured's life. The premiums on limited-payment life insurance are higher than those for ordinary life insurance, but they are payable for only a limited number of years.

GROUP LIFE INSURANCE

Some individuals are fortunate to have an employer or some other group offer the opportunity to buy group life insurance. An insurance policy that covers a group of people is called **group life insurance**. The group acts as a single unit in buying the insurance. Our U.S. market economy tends to recognize efficiencies and savings that result in selling multiple quantities. You can often buy three pounds of hamburger for a lower per-pound price than buying just one pound. You can sometimes travel 1,000 miles by air for only a few dollars more than 500 miles. So it is, too, with insurance. The cost of group life insurance is less than the cost of a similar

Who might have an insurable interest in this research chemist?

TEACHING STRATEGIES
Alternate Modalities
Print Learner

When learning about life insurance programs, the print learner would prefer to see the process in print. This can be done by distributing a handout that explains the various com-parisons of life insurance programs. Allow the student to study the handout.

In 2001 there were almost 1,900 life insurance companies in the United States. Over 600 were given the industry's top rating for strong financial performance.

policy up to a maximum amount specified in the contract for as long as the person is a part of the organization.

amount of protection bought individually because insurance covering many people can be handled economically in one policy.

Most group life insurance plans offer term rather than permanent insurance. The insurance company works with an employer or other organization such as a union or professional association to develop the insurance plan. Then each employee or member of the organization can purchase an individual

Computer hardware and software that allow different e-mail programs to communicate with each other are called *gateways.* Everyone connects to the Internet through a gateway.

What are some advantages and disadvantages of group life insurance?

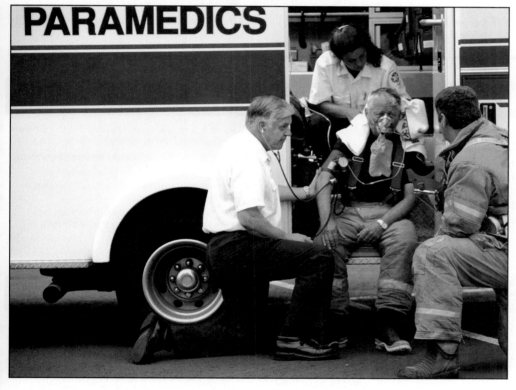

Net Facts provides information and definitions of terms for the Internet. The more information that students have about the Internet, the better equipped they will be to use this resource. In the Internet Activity Masters, there is an Internet Activity Worksheet for each unit. You can use these activities to give students experience with finding information online. Options for assigning this activity are as follows:

1. **Provide students with a list of addresses for this activity,**
2. **Assign students to conduct their own searches, or**
3. **Use the addresses on the Internet Activity Worksheet.**
   You should complete the activity yourself before assigning it to resolve any discrepancies that may arise.

Basic **Skills**-Math

SCANS

In order for students to become contributing workers in our society, it is important that they become proficient in the basic skills of reading, writing, arithmetic, and mathematics. In order to prepare students for the school-to-work transition, we must teach these skills in our classroom. Applying math across the curriculum is an important element in contempo-

rary education. As a part of end-of-chapter activities, Calculate Business Data enables students to apply their math skills. Appendix B: Math Review, Appendix C: Determining Percentages and Interest in Business, and Appendix D: Using Measurements in Business, also apply arithmetic and math skills.

BUSINESS NOTES

1. Life insurance protects survivors against the financial loss associated with dying. It is designed to replace a loss of income for family members who are financially dependent upon another person.
2. Term life insurance provides financial protection from losses resulting from loss of life during a definite period of time, or term. It is the least expensive form of life insurance. Permanent insurance has cash value and an investment feature as its common characteristics. It continues in effect for as long as premiums are paid rather than for a set term.
3. To buy individual life insurance cover-age, one would usually apply for a policy through an insurance agent who represents an insurance company. Normally you will be required to take a physical examination so that your health can be assessed. When you buy life insurance, you will be asked to name a beneficiary. The cost (premiums) of a life insurance policy will depend on the type of life insurance being purchased and the age and health of the person being insured.
4. An insurance policy that covers a group of people is called group life insurance. The group acts as a single unit in buying the insurance.

REVIEW YOUR READING

1. Why do people need life insurance?
2. What is a dependent?
3. List two basic types of life insurance.
4. What is the only form of life insurance that has no investment or savings feature?
5. How long may a term life insurance policy run?
6. What advantage does cash value life insurance have in comparison to other types of insurance?
7. In what way is a limited-payment policy different from an ordinary life policy?
8. What is the most important feature of universal life insurance?
9. What determines whether you have an insurable interest in someone else's life?
10. Why is the cost of group life insurance less than the cost of insurance that is bought individually?

COMMUNICATE BUSINESS CONCEPTS

11. Why would a term policy that is renewable cost more than one that is not?
12. What kind of life insurance policy would you recommend for each of the following people?
    a. Carlos Medina, age 27, wants to buy a policy on which the premiums will be as low as possible for the next ten years.
    b. Julie Van Hovel, age 45, wants to buy a policy that will not require payment of any premiums after she retires.
13. What purpose does a physical examination

Left margin annotations

REVIEW YOUR READING

1. Life insurance protects survivors against the financial loss associated with dying. It is designed to replace a loss of income for family members who are financially dependent upon another person.
2. A person who must rely on another for financial support.
3. Term life and permanent life insurance.
4. Term life insurance does not have a savings feature.
5. One to 20 years or more.
6. Permanent insurance builds cash value that may be borrowed against or paid when the policy is surrendered.
7. The limited-payment policy provides that premium payments will be paid only for the number of years stated in the policy. After that time the policy continues in force without further premium payments. Under an ordinary life policy, the premium payments are made throughout the life of the insured.
8. The savings part earns a higher rate of interest than other cash value insurance.
9. You would have an insurable interest in another person if you would receive some kind of financial benefit from that person's continued life. Thus, a student would have an insurable interest in his or her parents if they are the principal wage earners in the household. Many other illustrations could be given.
10. The cost of group life insurance is less than the cost of a similar amount of protection bought individually because insurance for many people can be handled more economically in one policy.

COMMUNICATE BUSINESS CONCEPTS

11. Because the policyholder can continue the term insurance without taking a physical exam to determine whether that person is still a good risk.
12. (a) Carlos Medina probably should buy a term policy with a guaranteed renewability option. The term policy gives him the lowest premiums and guarantees him the opportunity to add to his life insurance at a later time when he is in a better position to afford it. (b) Julie Van Hovel should consider a limited-payment whole life policy. This type of policy gives her insurance protection for as long as she lives and builds up a good cash surrender and loan value. If Julie, who is now 45, retires at 65, a 20-year limited-payment policy would meet her needs nicely.
13. The insurance company ordinarily requires an insurance applicant to have a physical examination to determine the applicant's state of health. A person in poor health is a greater risk than is one who is in good health.

serve during the process of purchasing a life insurance policy?

14. Do you think the Board of Directors of the Lake Plastics Company has an insurable interest in the company's chief chemist? Why or why not?

15. When a person buys life insurance as a member of a large group, no physical examination is ordinarily required. Why do you think this is so?

DEVELOP YOUR BUSINESS LANGUAGE

For each numbered item, find the term that has the same meaning.

16. Life insurance that covers a group of people who are usually employed by the same company or are members of the same organization.

17. A whole life policy intended to be paid up in a certain number of years.

18. The person named in an insurance policy to receive the insurance benefits.

19. The amount of money received should a policyholder decide to give up the protection provided by a policy.

20. A life insurance policy that provides financial protection against loss of life during a definite period of time.

21. Life insurance which provides both insurance protection and a substantial savings plan.

22. A type of whole life insurance for which premiums are the same each year as long as the policyholder lives.

23. A term life insurance policy that allows the policyholder to continue the term insurance for one or more terms without taking a physical examination to determine whether she or he is still a good risk.

24. Insurance designed to protect survivors against the financial loss associated with dying.

25. A financial benefit from the continued life of a person.

26. Term life insurance on which the amount of protection and the premiums remain the same.

27. Permanent insurance extending over the insured's lifetime.

28. Term life insurance on which the amount of protection gradually becomes smaller, but the premiums remain the same during the term.

29. Life insurance that lets the policyholder select from a range of investments.

30. An amount of insurance coverage that was originally purchased and that will be paid upon the insured's death.

31. A type of insurance that has cash value and an investment feature as its common characteristics.

KEY TERMS

beneficiary
cash value
decreasing term insurance
face value
group life insurance
insurable interest
level term insurance
life insurance
limited-payment policies
ordinary life policy
permanent insurance
renewable policy
term life insurance
universal life insurance
variable life insurance
whole life insurance

DECISION-MAKING STRATEGIES

Janelle Exum works as an interior designer for a furniture store. The business provides a very good health insurance plan but no group life insurance. Janelle's husband, Arthur, has just opened a graphic design business after working for a large corporation for the past five years. Because the business is new, Arthur does not purchase either health or life insurance. Janelle's health insurance policy covers her, Arthur, and their three young children.

32. Do you believe Janelle or Arthur need life insurance? Why or why not? What financial needs will each have if the other spouse dies?

33. What types of life insurance would your recommend each should consider?

DEVELOP YOUR BUSINESS LANGUAGE

16. group life insurance
17. limited-payment policies
18. beneficiary
19. cash value
20. term life insurance
21. universal life insurance
22. ordinary life policy
23. renewable policy
24. life insurance
25. insurable interest
26. level term insurance
27. whole life insurance
28. decreasing term insurance
29. variable life insurance
30. face value
31. permanent insurance

DECISION-MAKING STRATEGIES

32. Both Janelle and Arthur should consider purchasing life insurance. Since they have small children, they will have financial hardships if either should die. Arthur probably has the greatest need since Janelle provides the health insurance and a regular salary from her work. Since Arthur is starting a new business he may not have a high salary yet but it will probably increase in the future.

33. Janelle should determine if her company is planning to obtain a group insurance plan or if it is available through a professional association. Because she has a regular income she might want to consider permanent insurance that will build up cash value for her children's education. Because Arthur is starting a business, he will probably need to buy term insurance to keep the cost as low as possible.

14. Yes, the Board of Directors of the Lake Plastics Company would have an insurable interest in the company's chief chemist. This is true because the chemist probably is well aware of the chemical formulas and processes used in the manufacture of plastic products by the company. If the chief chemist were to die, a great deal of time and money probably would have to be spent in finding and training a new chemist.

15. For group insurance, physical examinations are not ordinarily required of those who participate in the plan because the risk is spread among the group. A few members of the group who might be found to be uninsurable were they subject to an examination probably represent a small segment of the total group.

34. $17,643 × 0.0647 = $1,141.50;
$17,643 + $1,141.50 =
$18,784.50

35. (a) $50,000 − $5,000 = $45,000
(b) $5,000 × 0.08 = $400; $400
+ $5,000 = $5,400

36. (a) *Year 1:* $2,400 × 0.12 = $288
int.; $288 + $22 = $310 int. &
prem. *Year 2:* $2,400 − $600 =
$1,800; $1,800 × 0.12 = $216.
Year 3: $1,800 − $600 = $1,200;
$1,200 × 0.12 = $144; $144 +
$22 = $166. *Year 4:* $1,200 −
$600 = $600; $600 × 0.12 =
$72; $72 + $22 = $94 (b) $310 +
$238 + $166 + $94 = $808.

37. (a) $1,350 × 0.10 = $135 +
$1,350 = $1,485 (b) 115 kg − 92
kg = 23 kg × 2.2 = 50.6 or 51 lbs.

TECHNOLOGY APPLICATION

In this activity, students use a computer to solve a business problem using a file that is provided on the data CD that accompanies *Intro to Business*. Instructions for using the data CD are included in a **README** file on the disk. Solutions are provided on the Instructor's Resource CD.

CALCULATE BUSINESS DATA

34. The rate of return on the investment portion of Fujio's life insurance policy is 6.47 percent for a given year. If the investment portion (cash value) was $17,643 at the beginning of the year, what will it be worth at the end of the year? Round to the nearest cent.

35. People who have cash value life insurance can borrow up to the cash value of the policy from the insurance company. Frank Hibbard had a $50,000 life insurance policy with a current cash value of $7,000. He decided to borrow $5,000 from that amount to make a down payment on a small house he wanted to buy.

  a. If he died before repaying the loan, how much insurance would his beneficiary receive?

  b. If Frank repays the loan in one year at 8 percent annual interest, what is the total amount he will pay back?

36. John Larson needed $2,400 for one year's tuition at a technical school. He decided to borrow the money from a bank for four years and pay $600 of the principal each year, plus interest of 12 percent a year on the unpaid balance. To be sure that his debt would be paid if he should die, he purchased a $2,400, four-year decreasing term insurance policy with an annual premium of $22.

  a. How much did John pay in premiums and interest each year?

  b. What was the total cost of premiums and interest for the four years?

37. Bruce Wright is having the physical examination required for his life insurance policy. His height is 185 centimeters, and his weight is 115 kilograms. The doctor's chart shows that the best weight for someone Bruce's height is 92 kilograms. The insurance company charges 10 percent more than standard rates for overweight people.

  a. If the standard annual premium for the insurance that Bruce wants is $1,350, what will his annual premium be?

  b. Approximately how many pounds must he lose to qualify for the standard premiums?

TECHNOLOGY APPLICATION

Using the *Intro to Business* Data CD and your spreadsheet program software, select problem CH40. After the problem appears on your screen, complete the following activities. Then, after you have completed each step, display or print the completed spreadsheet for each activity. If you do not have a printer available, answer the questions before you leave the computer.

38. In the first row of the Premium column, enter a function to calculate the average of the Amount Required for Coverage column. Copy or key the function to each row in the Premium column. What is the average of the Amount Required for Coverage column?

39. In each row of the Change in Cash Value column, enter a formula to calculate the difference between the Premium column and the Amount Required for Coverage column. Answer the following questions:

  a. As age increases, does cash value increase or decrease?

  b. What is the amount of change in cash value at age 30?

40. Enter formulas to complete the Cumulative Cash Value column. The first two rows have been completed for you. Answer the following questions:

  a. What is the cumulative cash value at age 25?

  b. What is the cumulative cash value at age 49?

COMMUNICATING for SUCCESS

MEETINGS—SET THE AGENDA!

Meetings are one of the most common and frequent business activities you will be involved in during your career. Meetings are held to convey information, to express gratitude, to provide feedback on activities, to prepare documents, to work, and to simply provide a means of introduction. Meetings generally involve the personal encounter of two or more individuals, although technology now provides opportunities for "virtual meetings," where individuals can be physically separated from one another by hundreds of miles. Virtual meetings are the gathering of two or more individuals through computer and/or telephone connections.

A meeting is guided by a written agenda—that is, an outline of the information to be discussed or covered during the meeting. In a sense, an agenda is a plan for the meeting. Agenda items often include the following:

- a review of the previous meeting's minutes
- new and old business
- action items
- announcements

The typical agenda format follows these steps:

- a call to order
- roll check

- review and approval of previous meeting minutes
- new and old business
- announcements
- adjournment

This format for a meeting is common, but is not a strict rule. The number of individuals involved and the subject matter being covered often determine the formality of a meeting.

Meetings with clients are formal types of meetings that generally do not follow a specific format. The purpose of a formal meeting is generally to provide information on product or skill performance, cost analyses, or other business-related items. Formal meetings are also commonly used for expressing gratitude to the client.

One business skill that is very important is the facilitation of meetings. As a professional, you must develop your own personal style on how to relate with individuals involved in meetings, and how to keep meetings moving toward a conclusion or primary purpose. You might want to review skills such as listening, giving presentations, offering feedback, promoting teamwork, and negotiation to help you facilitate meetings.

CRITICAL THINKING

1. Why are meetings held?
2. What are virtual meetings?

COMMUNICATING for SUCCESS

Communications skills will help ensure students' success in the business world. Communicating for Success introduces workplace/interpersonal communications issues and proper uses of communications technology. Each feature discusses a key communications topic, and contains two Critical Thinking questions that require students to analyze what they have learned.

This Communicating for Success feature describes various purposes and a typical agenda for a business meeting. Facilitating meetings is a useful skill in business, particularly since technology now permits "virtual meetings" among participants in different physical locations. That means meetings are likely to be even more frequent in the future, so students would be well-advised to start developing the skills needed to make them productive.

CRITICAL THINKING

1. Meetings are held to convey information, to express gratitude, to provide feedback on activities, to prepare documents, to work, and to simply provide a means of introduction.
2. Virtual meetings are the gathering of two or more individuals through computer and/or telephone connections.

Chapter 41 emphasizes the importance of health insurance, the types of health insurance, and the providers of health insurance. The importance of having insurance is emphasized in the context of the increasing costs of health care.

Resources for Teachers
- Lesson Plans
- School-To-Work/SCANS Activity Masters
- Spanish Resources
- Instructor's Resource CD

Assessment
- Chapter and Unit Tests, Ch. 41
- ExamView, Ch. 41

Media/Technology
- Applying Technology Data CD
- PowerPoint slides
- Business Connection CD
- Videotape

Activity Masters and Workbooks
- Activities and Projects, Ch. 41
- Internet Activity Masters
- Business Math Activity Masters
- Communications Activity Masters
- International Business Activity Masters
- Ethics Activity Masters

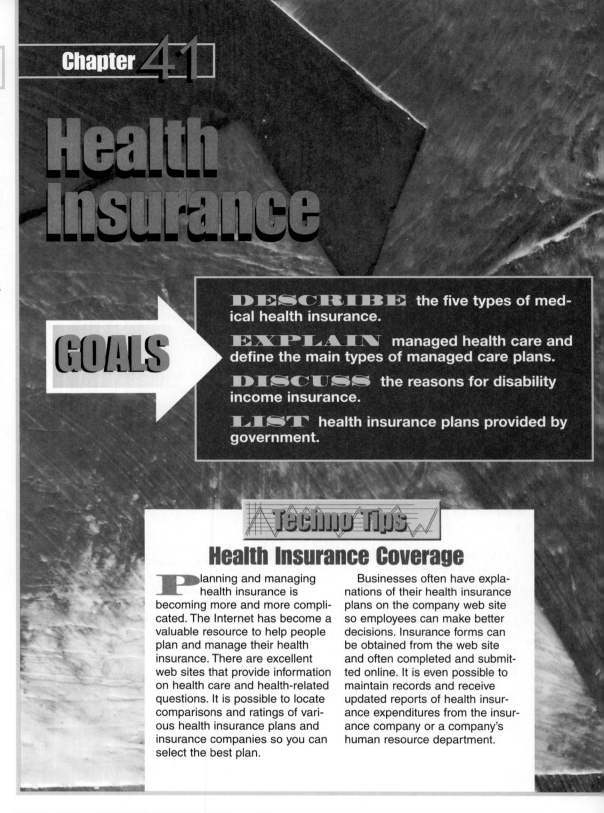

Chapter 41
Health Insurance

GOALS

DESCRIBE the five types of medical health insurance.

EXPLAIN managed health care and define the main types of managed care plans.

DISCUSS the reasons for disability income insurance.

LIST health insurance plans provided by government.

Techno Tips
Health Insurance Coverage

Planning and managing health insurance is becoming more and more complicated. The Internet has become a valuable resource to help people plan and manage their health insurance. There are excellent web sites that provide information on health care and health-related questions. It is possible to locate comparisons and ratings of various health insurance plans and insurance companies so you can select the best plan.

Businesses often have explanations of their health insurance plans on the company web site so employees can make better decisions. Insurance forms can be obtained from the web site and often completed and submitted online. It is even possible to maintain records and receive updated reports of health insurance expenditures from the insurance company or a company's human resource department.

Students need to know the latest technologies and develop cutting edge Internet skills for use in current jobs, future careers, or in their homes. TechnoTips introduces students to today's cutting edge technologies and provides them with important Internet skills. Feature topics concentrate on Internet-specific technologies and computer or other hi-tech innovations for use by businesses and consumers.

"Carlota! Welcome back to work! How is your back?"

"Thanks, Martin. My back is doing great. I can't believe I hurt it playing tennis and had to have surgery. But I am one of the lucky ones. The surgery went fine, I am almost feeling normal again, and the insurance company paid all of my bills. Our company really has a great health insurance program for us. You don't realize how important health insurance is until you need it. If I didn't have such great coverage, I would be out over $100,000."

Everyone should be covered by health insurance. Almost no one has enough money to pay the extremely large medical bills associated with a serious illness. Health insurance provides protection against the economic risks associated with paying for medical care and the loss of income that results when an injury or illness prevents you from working. Health insurance is similar to the other forms of insurance. You pay premiums for a policy that guarantees protection. When you are ill and need money to pay medical bills, the insurance company will pay up to specified amounts.

MEDICAL INSURANCE

The insurance industry has created several kinds of health-related insurance coverage. Each of these kinds of health insurance provides for a different kind of coverage. One type of health insurance is medical insurance which can be categorized as (1) hospital, (2) surgical, (3) regular medical, (4) major medical insurance, and (5) comprehensive medical policy. Insurance companies also make a combination policy available.

Hospital Insurance

When an illness or injury requires you to be hospitalized, **hospital insurance** usually pays most or all of the charges for your room, food, and expenses for such items as use of an operating room, anesthesia, X rays, laboratory tests, and medicines. Because of the high cost of hospitalization, more people purchase hospital insurance than any other kind of health insurance.

Hospital insurance can be purchased from insurance companies or from nonprofit corporations. The best known nonprofit organization that offers hospital insurance is Blue Cross. Blue Cross plans usually pay hospitals directly for care provided to their policyholders. If expenses go beyond the amount covered by the Blue Cross contract, the patient must pay the difference.

Surgical Insurance

Surgery is one of the major reasons for hospitalization and is normally very expensive. **Surgical insurance** covers all or part of the surgeon's fees for an operation. The typical surgical policy lists the types of operations that it covers and the amount allowed for each. Some policies allow larger amounts for operations than others. This, of course, requires that a higher premium be paid. Surgical insurance is frequently bought in combination with hospital insurance.

Surgical insurance can be purchased from insurance companies or from nonprofit organizations such as Blue Shield. Blue Shield is linked with Blue Cross; they are often called "the Blues." Blue Shield plans cover mainly medical and surgical treatment rather than hospital care. Most Blue Shield plans list the maximum amounts that will be paid for different types of surgery. They also cover the doctor's charges for care in the hospital and some plans pay the doctor's charges for

PURPOSE Provide a purpose for students as they read the chapter. Ask what they think they will learn. Health insurance is a topic that is in the news frequently, so many students will have an opinion as to what this chapter should include. Direct students to skim the chapter, looking at photos, reading captions, and noting main headings. The goals at the beginning of each chapter provide a valuable tool for having students pinpoint main ideas. The tasks required by the goals are signaled in the first word. Some emphasize information collection ("Identify," "List"), while others call for description ("Explain," "Describe"). Ask students to look through all the goals and note the first word of each. Then ask students to state the purpose of studying this chapter.

TEACH/APPLY

MAKE CONNECTIONS This chapter covers health insurance. Most students, as small children, made many trips to the pediatrician. Therefore, most can relate to health insurance as it is used today. Use PowerPoint 41-2, *Medical Insurance,* and explain each type of insurance and how it affects the average policyholder. Ask students who are covered by these types of insurance what kind of procedures they go through at the doctor's office, such as filing paperwork or just paying a flat fee. Use PowerPoint 41-3, *Other Types of Health Insurance*, to review dental, vision, and disability insurance. Some students will have experience

Students now have a solid background in the various types of insurance. Health insurance, like automobile insurance, is probably a topic to which they can relate. Most students have been exposed to some type of medical, dental, or vision insurance, generally speaking, and can probably speak from experience.

NET FACTS

Net Facts provides information and definitions of terms for the Internet. The more information that students have about the Internet, the better equipped they will be to use this resource. In the Internet Activity Masters, there is an Internet Activity Worksheet for each unit. You can use these activities to give students experience with finding information online. Options for assigning this activity are as follows:

1. **Provide students with a list of addresses for this activity,**
2. **Assign students to conduct their own searches, or**
3. **Use the addresses on the Internet Activity Worksheet.**

You should complete the activity yourself before assigning it to resolve any discrepancies that may arise.

with dental and vision insurance through plans offered by their school or athletic teams. They may not be familiar with disability insurance unless a family member is disabled. Health insurance providers probably are not important to students at their age, but they should be aware of how health insurance may be obtained. Use PowerPoint 41-4, *Health Insurance Providers*, to review the organizations that sell health insurance.

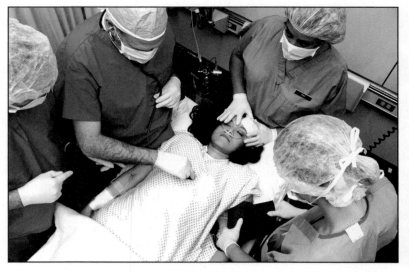

How can you predict what type of health problems you may have in the future in order to purchase the proper type of insurance?

office or home care. Blue plans are designed to minimize policyholders' expenses. They generally do not provide coverage for pre-existing conditions or illnesses or injuries that are covered by other insurance.

Regular Medical Insurance

Sometimes normal care provided by a physician can be quite expensive. **Regular medical insurance** pays part or all of the fees for nonsurgical care given in the doctor's office, the patient's home, or a hospital. The policy states the amount payable for each visit or call and the maximum number of visits covered. Some plans also provide

A Home Page contains text, graphics, and links to other Internet resources. The information on a Home Page is related to a particular topic, such as finance or medical care.

payments for diagnostic and laboratory expenses. Regular medical insurance is usually combined in one policy with hospital and surgical insurance. The protection provided by regular medical, hospital, and surgical coverages is referred to as **basic health coverage**.

Major Medical Insurance

Carlota's problem, presented at the beginning of this chapter, was a good example of why people need major medical insurance. Long illnesses and serious injuries can be very expensive. Bills of $50,000 to $100,000 and higher are not unusual. **Major medical insurance** provides protection against the high costs of serious illnesses or injuries. It complements the other forms of medical insurance. Major medical insurance helps pay for most kinds of extended and specialized health care prescribed by a doctor. It covers the cost of treatment in and out of the hospital, special nursing care, X rays, psychiatric care, medicine, and many other health care needs. Maximum benefits may be limited, but usually for a high amount such as $500,000 or $1,000,000.

All major medical policies have a deductible clause similar to the one found in automobile collision insurance. With this

Basic Skills-Listening

Because many workers do not have good listening skills, businesses spend thousands of dollars every year to send employees to classes on listening. You can teach students to become good listeners by explaining to them the value of evaluating the message the speaker is conveying, not the speaker. Listeners sometimes get too involved in the appearance of the speaker and miss the message that is being conveyed. Ask a student volunteer to write physical characteristics on the board that influence students not to listen to what the speaker is saying. The Student Activity Worksheet, Basic Skills—Listening Checklist, in the School-To-Work/SCANS Activity Masters, may be used to serve as a guideline for discussion of listening skills.

SCANS

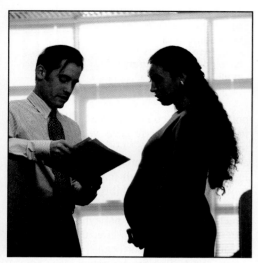

For special medical situations that require frequent visits to a doctor, what type of health insurance would be best?

clause, the policyholder agrees to pay the first part, perhaps $500 or more, of the expense resulting from sickness or injury. Major medical policies also usually contain a coinsurance clause. A **coinsurance clause** means that the policyholder will be expected to pay a certain percentage, generally 20 or 25 percent, of the costs over and above the deductible amount. There may be a maximum amount the policy holder has to pay for coinsurance for one illness or injury during one year.

The deductible clause discourages the filing of minor claims. The coinsurance clause encourages the policyholder to keep medical expenses as reasonable as possible. Thus, both clauses help to make lower premiums possible because they help to reduce payments of insurance claims.

Comprehensive Medical Policy

Insurance providers have developed a **comprehensive medical policy** that combines the features of hospital, surgical, regular, and major medical insurance. A comprehensive medical policy retains the features of each of the separate coverages such as

amounts-payable limits and the like. It has only one deductible. A combination of coverages is normally less expensive than the total of the separate coverages.

DENTAL INSURANCE

As dental expenses have grown over the years, the public has encouraged insurers to develop policies to help defray the cost of dental care. As a result, insurance companies now offer **dental insurance** which helps pay for normal dental care, often including examinations, X rays, cleaning, fillings, and more complicated types of dental work. It also covers dental injuries resulting from accidents. Most dental plans contain deductible and coinsurance provisions to reduce the cost of premiums. Dental insurance is offered mainly through group plans and is still growing in popularity. Nearly 50 percent of all Americans now have some dental insurance.

VISION CARE INSURANCE

In anticipation of eye care expenses, many consumers and groups purchase vision care

Why might special treatments like colored contact lenses or cosmetic surgery not be covered by your health insurance?

TRY THIS/GUIDED PRACTICE Have students write the various types of insurance on a sheet of paper—(1) hospital, (2) surgical, (3) regular medical, (4) major medical, (5) comprehensive medical, (6) dental, (7) vision, (8) disability. Guide them through this list to help them decide which types of insurance would be important for them. Walking through this list and relating their personal needs will make the topics more relevant.

EXPLORE THIS/INDEPENDENT PRACTICE Before assigning independent practice material for any chapter, students should be expected to read the textbook material carefully. In view of the fact that all students vary widely in their ability to read effectively, it is advisable to have the students read the entire chapter, or sections thereof, silently in class if the material has not been previously read in connection with homework assignments.

After students have read the chapter, ask them to complete the Chapter Review questions. Develop Your Business Language is an excellent way to improve students' vocabulary. Only words introduced in the chapter are used in the exercises. The Review Your Reading questions can be used to check students' ability to comprehend what they have read. The Communicate Business Concepts section affords an opportunity for students to apply to practical life situations the information gained from reading the chapter. By completing the problems under Calculate Business Data, students will be able to strengthen and refine their abilities in mathematics. Technology

---

SCANS

Personal Qualities-Integrity

Employers are looking for potential employees with solid ethics. Businesses are very aware of the severe implications of unethical behavior in employees. Ethical Perspectives raises ethical questions but does not involve the teaching of right and wrong. Instead, it allows students to apply their own principles to business situations through the use of critical

thinking and decision-making skills. Students will also gain a sense of individual diversity through the expression of their opinions about the situations presented. This activity may be used as an individual assignment, a class discussion, or a cooperative learning activity.

Application allows students to demonstrate skill in using word processing, spreadsheet, and database software. Decision-Making Strategies contains material to challenge students to utilize the model explained in Chapter 1 for problem solving.

The Chapter Review questions at the end of the chapter vary in level of difficulty. For a basic assignment, consider Develop Your Business Language and Review Your Reading. For an average assignment, consider the basic assignment plus Communicate Business Concepts and Calculate Business Data. For an enhanced assignment, try the average assignment plus Technology Application and Decision-Making Strategies.

ASSESS

Review Business Notes at the end of the chapter. Then review the goals at the beginning of the chapter. Restate each as a question and have students respond orally. For students who may have difficulty providing answers, assign the reteaching activities that follow. Enrichment activities may also be assigned where appropriate.
1. What are the five types of medical insurance and what do they provide? (Answer: Hospital insurance, which usually pays most or all of the charges for your room, food, and expenses for such items as use of an operating room, anesthesia, X rays, laboratory tests, and medicines; surgical, which covers all or part of the surgeon's fees for an operation; regular medical,

insurance. **Vision care insurance** covers eye examinations, prescription lenses, frames, and contact lenses. However, vision insurance usually does not cover such things as tinted lenses, coated or plastic lenses, nonprescription lenses, and vision training. The popularity of vision care insurance results from the recognition by many individuals and employers who help pay for group plans that eye care health is very important. Some insurance plans are adding coverage for new procedures like laser eye surgery that can eliminate the need for glasses.

DISABILITY INCOME INSURANCE

For most people, income from employment is their single most important economic resource. Protecting your income is very important. There is one form of health insurance that provides periodic payments if the

policyholder becomes disabled. **Disability income insurance** protects you against the loss of income caused by a long illness or an accident. The insured receives weekly or monthly payments until that person is able to return to work. Disability income policies frequently include a waiting period provision which requires that the policyholder wait a specified length of time after the disability occurs before payment begins. Monthly payments under disability insurance plans are usually much smaller than the income people earn from their jobs. The amount may be 40–60 percent of the normal income.

ETHICAL PERSPECTIVES
Insurance Fraud

Fraud is the act of intentionally misrepresenting information. Insurance fraud usually means being dishonest when applying for insurance or filing dishonest claims. People applying for health insurance sometimes do not disclose existing medical conditions. Applicants for auto insurance may be dishonest about how many miles they drive their car each year. Policyholders sometimes file claims for injuries that are exaggerated or nonexistent.

Insurance providers and regulators work very hard to monitor and reduce fraud. These organizations engage in public information activities designed to promote honesty in insurance affairs. A group known as the Coalition Against Insurance Fraud works to combat the growing incidence and cost of all forms of insurance fraud, as does each state's Department of Insurance.

However, the efforts by these groups alone

are not enough. Insurance fraud is still on the rise. Some people fail to realize that when insurance fraud is committed, it costs the insurance company unnecessary dollars These unnecessary costs are then trickled down to the policyholder through increased premiums. The solution? Only the insurance consumer can truly help to reduce fraud. Consumers must be honest in all insurance dealings including being truthful when applying for insurance and being truthful when making claims. Those who commit fraud will lose their benefits and are subject to prosecution for breaking the law.

Critical Thinking
1. Why do you think some people are not honest on insurance applications?
2. What kinds of costs do you think are incurred when policyholders file fraudule claims?

ETHICAL PERSPECTIVES

Ask students for their opinions on fraudulent claims. Most will be familiar with the term and may know of people who turn in claims to insurance companies even though the claim is not legitimate. Try to get students involved in a discussion as to how this affects their insurance premiums.

CRITICAL THINKING
1. Possible answers are that these applicants have something to hide or are trying to get a cheaper premium rate.
2. Insurance companies end up paying claims that are fraudulent, which means that they end up paying useless claims. The more claims the insurance companies pay, the more they have to charge for premiums. Also, sometimes attorneys have to be brought in on fraudulent claims, which means more expense for the insurance companies to pass to the policyholders.

However, many disability payments are not subject to income taxes.

HEALTH INSURANCE PROVIDERS

Where can you acquire health insurance? Health insurance is available from several sources and in different forms. You can buy health insurance as an individual or as a member of a group. Some options are group health insurance, individual health insurance, health maintenance organizations, preferred provider organizations, and government assistance.

Group Health Insurance

The most popular way to buy health insurance is through a group. As with group life insurance, group health insurance policies are made available by employers to their employees and by unions and other organizations to their members. The company, union, or organization receives a master policy. The members who are insured under the plan are given membership cards to indicate their participation in the plan. Companies that sponsor group policies often pay part or all of the premium costs for their employees. This is provided as an employment benefit in addition to salary. Employees can usually buy coverage for family members as well. The cost of group health insurance is lower per insured than the cost of a comparable individual policy. This is possible because insurance companies can administer group plans more economically, thus lowering costs for each person in the group.

Individual Health Insurance

Some people are not members of a group and are not eligible for group health insurance. They may be self-employed, for example, and have no employer to help buy health insurance for the group. One alternative is to buy individual health insurance. Individual health insurance is available to individuals and is adaptable to individuals' needs. Individual health insurance policies are usually rather expensive, require a physical examination, and have a waiting period before the policy is in force.

Managed Care Plans

Over the past decades, various alternatives to traditional fee-for-service health insurance have grown in popularity. Known collectively as *managed health care* or *managed care*, these plans now cover more than two-thirds of Americans who are covered by their employer. They typically provide comprehensive health care at a lower cost through networks of providers such as doctors, hospitals, and clinics. Managed care plans usually have higher monthly premiums. However, the overall cost of health care may be lower for the consumer because of low or no deductibles, low copayments, and little or no paperwork. A potential major drawback is that patients have less control or choice over whom they see for health problems and the specific treatment that is covered by managed care plans compared to traditional insurance.

Managed care plans go by various names—such as HMOs (health maintenance organizations), PPOs (preferred provider organizations), and POS (point-of-service) plans—but the differences between plans have tended to diminish over time as they all compete for customers by adopting popular features. The growth of managed care has been driven by large companies trying to control the rising cost of providing their

which pays part or all of the fees for nonsurgical care given in the doctor's office, the patient's home, or a hospital; major medical insurance, which provides protection against the high costs of serious illnesses or injuries; and comprehensive medical policy that combines the features of hospital, surgical, regular and major medical insurance.)

2. What is dental insurance? (Answer: Insurance which helps pay for normal dental care, often including examinations, X rays, cleaning, fillings, and more complicated types of dental work. It also covers dental injuries resulting from accidents.)

3. Why should anyone have vision care insurance? (Answer: Vision care insurance covers eye examinations, prescription lenses, frames, and contact lenses. However, vision insurance usually does not cover such things as tinted lenses, coated or plastic lenses, nonprescription lenses, and vision training.)

4. What is the main purpose of disability income insurance? (Answer: It protects against loss of income caused by a long illness or an accident. The insured receives weekly or monthly payments until that person is able to return to work.)

5. Who are five providers of health insurance? (Answer: Group health insurance, individual health insurance, health maintenance organizations, preferred provider organizations, and state government assistance.)

6. How can we all contribute to cost containment of insurance? (Answer: Through coinsurance and deductibles.)

TEACHING STRATEGIES
Cooperative Learning

Group Investigation is a positive form of cooperative learning that encourages students to work together. For this activity, students will form their own groups with four to six members each. Each group will investigate health insurance. A spokesperson for the group should contact at least three insurance agencies to gather information regarding coverage and cost for the health insurance. This information should then be presented showing a comparison of these factors. Some groups may do charts and graphs; others may present a summary of their findings. You may wish to distribute the Student Activity Worksheet, Workplace Competencies—Interpersonal Skills, School-To-Work/SCANS Activity Masters, to serve as a guideline for discussion.

employees with health care coverage, and by large insurance companies trying to protect their financial stakes in the health care field. Many managed care plans are run by insurance companies.

Health maintenance organizations (HMOs) normally consist of a staffed medical clinic organized to serve its members. You may join an HMO for a fixed monthly fee. As a member, you are entitled to a wide range of prepaid health care services including hospitalization. HMOs emphasize preventive health care. Early detection and treatment of illnesses help to keep people out of hospitals and keep costs down.

Generally, HMOs do not cover treatment or care that is not authorized by a physician or if the procedure is above the average cost for the area. Cosmetic surgery, if not medically necessary, also often is excluded.

The growth of HMOs has been rapid; membership has increased from less than 2 million in the early 1970s to over 100 million today.

A popular alternative to the HMO is the **preferred provider organization (PPO)**. This health insurance delivery system involves health care providers such as a group of physicians, a clinic, or a hospital contracting with an employer to provide medical services to employees. These providers agree to charge set fees for their services. Employees are encouraged, but not required, to use the PPO's services through financial incentives. The employee is usually able to get medical treatment through the PPO at a significant discount. Employees are free, however, to seek medical treatment elsewhere and may be partially reimbursed for out-of-pocket medical expenses.

State Government Assistance

An important health insurance program established by state governments is workers' compensation. **Workers' compensation** is an insurance plan that provides medical and survivor benefits for people injured, disabled, or killed on the job. Accidents may occur on almost any job. Employees may

suffer injuries or develop some illness as a result of their working conditions. To deal with this problem, all states have workers' compensation laws. These laws provide medical benefits to employees who are injured on the job or become ill as a direct result of their working conditions. Under these laws, most employers are required to provide and pay for insurance for their employees.

The benefits provided through workers' compensation vary from state to state. In some states, all necessary expenses for medical treatment are paid. In others, there is a stated payment limit. Usually there is a waiting period of a few days before a worker is eligible for loss-of-income benefits. If unable to return to the job after this waiting period, the worker is paid a certain proportion of wages as benefits. This usually amounts to about two-thirds of the worker's normal wages. Payments are also made to dependents if the worker is killed in an accident while on the job.

State governments also administer a form of medical aid to low-income families known as **Medicaid**. The federal government shares with states the cost of providing health benefits to financially needy families. A financially needy family is one whose income provides for basic necessities but who could not afford adequate medical care or pay large medical bills.

The services covered by Medicaid include hospital care, doctors' services, X rays, lab tests, nursing home care, diagnosis and treatment of children's illnesses, and home health care services.

Federal Government Assistance

The nation's Social Security laws provide a national program of health insurance known as **Medicare**. It is designed to help people age 65 and older and some disabled people pay the high cost of health care. Medicare has two basic parts: hospital insurance and medical insurance.

The hospital insurance plan includes coverage for hospital care, care in an approved nursing home, and home health care up to a certain number of visits. No premium payments are required for the hospital insurance, and almost everyone 65 years old and older may qualify.

The medical insurance portion of Medicare is often called supplementary or voluntary medical insurance. The services covered under this plan include doctors' services, medical services and supplies, and home health services. The medical insurance requires a small monthly premium. The federal government pays an equal amount to help cover the cost of the medical insurance. Some features of the Medicare plan are similar to the deductible and coinsurance provisions in other health policies.

COST CONTAINMENT

No matter who pays the premium, the cost of health insurance, like the cost of health care, is very high. In fact, the cost of health care has been increasing two to three times faster than the rate of inflation. The cost of health insurance is usually determined by at least four factors: extent of the coverage, number of claims filed by policyholders, age of the policyholder, and number of dependents. You have little control over your age and the number of people dependent on you. You can, however, make sure you buy only the kind and amount of insurance you need. You can also take good care of yourself and be careful not to abuse your benefits by using medical services when they are unnecessary.

Insurance companies encourage policyholders to play an active role in "cost containment" or keeping costs down. The most common methods are coinsurance and deductibles.

Some policyholders are covered by their employers and their spouse's insurance. Insurance providers promote the coordination of benefits in order to prevent two or more insurers from making payments on the same health care charges for a policyholder.

The health insurance industry also encourages second medical opinions to assure the necessity of procedures. Another cost-containment strategy growing in popularity is the use of outpatient services such as surgery. In the past, people undergoing some minor forms of surgery might have been admitted to the hospital for one or two days. Now, the person comes to the hospital or an outpatient center in the morning, has the surgery performed, and is released to return home the same day.

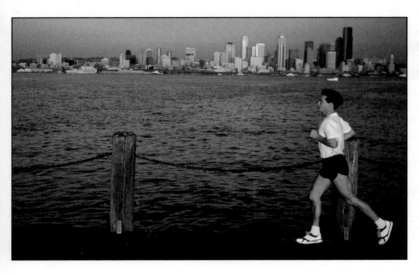

What are some of the best ways that you can minimize your health care costs?

EVALUATE

- Assign Activities and Projects for Chapter 41.
- Administer the printed test or ExamView for Chapter 41.
- Administer the printed test or ExamView for Unit 11.
- Complete School-To-Work/SCANS Building Your Portfolio activities for Unit 11.

Basic Skills-Math

SCANS

Integrating math across the curriculum is an important element in contemporary education. As a part of end-of-chapter activities, Calculate Business Data enables students to apply their math skills. Appendix B: Math Review, Appendix C: Determining Percentages and Interest in Business, and Appendix D:

Using Measurements in Business, also apply arithmetic and math skills.

REVIEW YOUR READING

1. (a) Hospital insurance, which pays part or all of the charges for room, food, and certain other hospital expenses such as anesthesia, X rays, laboratory tests, and drugs. (b) Surgical insurance, which pays part or all of a surgeon's fee for an operation. (c) Regular medical insurance, which pays part or all of a doctor's fees for nonsurgical care given in a doctor's office, the patient's home, or a hospital. (d) Major medical insurance, which provides protection against the large costs of serious or long illness or injury. It helps pay for most kinds of health care prescribed by a doctor including cost of treatment in and out of the hospital, special nursing care, and X rays. (e) Comprehensive medical policy that combines the features of hospital, surgical, regular and major medical insurance.
2. Blue Shield/Blue Cross.
3. The insured agrees to pay the first part of the expense resulting from sickness or injury.
4. Eye examinations, prescription lenses, frames, and contact lenses.
5. The cost of being insured under a group insurance policy is less than the cost of an individual policy because insurance companies can administer group plans more economically and thus the cost is lower to each person in the group.
6. Preventive health care.
7. Workers' compensation, medicaid, and medicare are government-operated health insurance programs.
8. Workers' compensation.
9. Hospital insurance and medical insurance.
10. Extent of the coverage, number of claims filed by policyholders, age of the policyholder, and number of dependents.

COMMUNICATE BUSINESS CONCEPTS

11. (a) Janice should protect herself with some type of health insurance because she probably has little in the form of savings and any serious health problem would use up those savings rapidly. (b) Janice might be eligible to join a group plan through her part-time employer. Also many educational

BUSINESS NOTES

1. The five most common varieties of medical insurance are: hospital insurance (which usually pays most or all of the charges for your room, food, and expenses for such items as use of an operating room, anesthesia, X rays, laboratory tests, and medicines); surgical, which covers all or part of the surgeon's fees for an operation; regular medical, which pays part or all of the fees for nonsurgical care given in the doctor's office, the patient's home, or a hospital; major medical, which provides protection against the high costs of serious illnesses or injuries; and a comprehensive medical policy that combines the features of hospital, surgical, regular, and major medical insurance.
2. Dental insurance helps pay for normal dental care, often including examinations, X rays, cleaning, fillings, and more complicated types of dental work. It also covers dental injuries resulting from accidents.
3. Vision care insurance covers eye examinations, prescription lenses, frames, and contact lenses. Some plans now cover eye surgery to correct vision problems.
4. Disability income insurance protects against loss of income caused by a long illness or an accident. The insured receives weekly or monthly payments until that person is able to return to work.
5. Providers of health insurance include group health insurance, individual health insurance, health maintenance organizations, preferred provider organizations, and government insurance programs.
6. Policyholders can play an active role in cost containment through coinsurance deductibles, and proper health care.

REVIEW YOUR READING

1. What are the five basic types of coverage provided by medical insurance? Explain the kinds of expenses each covers.
2. What well-known nonprofit organization offers surgical insurance?
3. How does a deductible clause in a health insurance policy work?
4. What type of services are covered by vision care insurance?
5. Why is being insured under an individual health insurance policy more expensive than under a group policy?
6. What kind of care is emphasized by HMOs?
7. What three health insurance programs are operated by government agencies?
8. What kind of health insurance covers you if you are injured on the job?
9. What are the two basic parts of Medicare?
10. Which four factors determine the cost of health care?

institutions offer group medical coverage to students. She also could obtain medical insurance privately from an organization such as Blue Cross, but she would probably pay much less for insurance as a member of a group. (c) She can help to keep the policy premium at a reasonable level by taking good care of herself and by shopping for the lowest premium available—probably through a group plan. She also should consider buying a policy with a coinsurance clause or deductible clause.

12. If there is a problem with the cost of the insurance, a coinsurance clause can reduce that cost to the members of the group. A coinsurance clause means the policyholders will be expected to pay a certain percentage of costs over and above the deductible amount. Such a clause discourages the filing of minor claims and also encourages the insured to keep medical expenses as reasonable as possible.

COMMUNICATE BUSINESS CONCEPTS

11. Janice Cordell is studying to be an accountant and has a part-time job to help pay her college expenses. She does not have health insurance because she believes she cannot afford it. She also believes that she does not really need health insurance.
    a. Give several reasons why Janice should protect herself with some type of health insurance.
    b. Where might she find a policy at a reasonable premium?
    c. What can she do to keep the policy premium at a reasonable level?

12. Many major medical policies contain a coinsurance clause. These policies are usually less expensive than a policy without such a clause. What advice would you have for a person or group considering purchasing a major medical insurance policy containing a coinsurance clause?

13. The Carney family is trying to determine which kinds of health insurance coverage would best fit their needs. On one hand, they believe that a Blue Cross hospital plan and a Blue Shield surgical plan would be sufficient. On the other hand, a major medical plan might better serve their needs. Mr. and Mrs. Carney are both 48 years old and are employed by the same company. They have two children. There is a history of heart disease in Mr. Carney's family. They have about $30,000 in an investment account. What advice would you offer this family based on their needs?

14. Why do you think a health insurance agent would suggest the addition of major medical coverage to a health insurance policy?

DEVELOP YOUR BUSINESS LANGUAGE

15. comprehensive medical policy
16. disability income insurance
17. regular medical insurance
18. health maintenance organizations (HMOs)
19. basic health coverage
20. dental insurance
21. workers' compensation
22. surgical insurance
23. Medicaid
24. hospital insurance
25. major medical insurance
26. Medicare
27. coinsurance clause
28. vision care insurance
29. preferred provider organization (PPO)

DEVELOP YOUR BUSINESS LANGUAGE

For each numbered item, find the term that has the same meaning.

15. Insurance that combines hospital, surgical, regular, and major medical insurance into one policy.

16. Insurance that protects a worker against the loss of income because of a long illness or accident.

17. Insurance that pays for nonsurgical care given in the doctor's office, the patient's home, or a hospital.

18. Organizations that provide complete health care to their members for a fixed monthly payment.

19. A combination of hospital, surgical, and regular medical insurance.

20. Insurance that helps pay for normal dental care and covers dental injuries resulting from accidents.

21. Insurance that provides medical and survivor benefits to people injured, disabled, or killed on the job.

22. Insurance that provides benefits to cover part or all of the surgeon's fee for an operation.

23. Medical expense assistance administered by state governments to financially needy families.

24. Insurance that pays most or all of the charges for room, food, and other hospital expenses.

25. Insurance that provides protection against the high costs of serious illnesses or injuries.

26. Health insurance provided by the federal government for people age 65 and older and some disabled people.

27. A provision in which the insured pays a certain percentage of the costs above the deductible amount.

28. Insurance that covers eye examinations, prescription lenses, frames, and contact lenses.

29. A group of physicians, a clinic, or a hospital that contracts to provide medical services to employees.

KEY TERMS

basic health coverage
coinsurance clause
comprehensive medical policy
dental insurance
disability income insurance
health maintenance organizations (HMOs)
hospital insurance
major medical insurance
Medicaid
Medicare
preferred provider organization (PPO)
regular medical insurance
surgical insurance
vision care insurance
workers' compensation

Chapter 41 *Health Insurance*   569

13. This couple should be advised to purchase the major medical plan to protect them against the great financial loss that a personal long-term injury or illness would bring—a financial loss from which they might never recover. However, many families generally have a pretty tight budget, and even relatively minor injuries or illnesses requiring hospitalization might result in financial hardship. Perhaps the Carney family should obtain hospitalization and surgical coverage that Blue Cross and Blue Shield provide in addition to the major medical coverage.

14. Because many times medical expenses are much greater than the amount covered by a regular medical policy. When this is the case, patients without major medical insurance coverage are required to pay the difference.

DECISION-MAKING STRATEGIES

Julianna Mitello has just accepted a job with Orkan Corp. She can choose between two health insurance plans. The first is a traditional comprehensive medical plan in which she would pay $40 each month and have deductibles and coinsurance payments on most medical procedures. The second choice is an HMO in which she pays $90 each month but has no other payments. With the traditional plan she can select her own doctor and hospital but has no choice with the HMO.

30. What additional information do you believe Julianna needs before making a decision on her health care plan?

31. Do you believe the costs of the plans are the most important factors in Julianna's decision? Why or why not?

32. Which health insurance plan would you recommend for Julianna? Why?

CALCULATE BUSINESS DATA

33. Sally Orland is considering job offers from two different companies. The Star Fire Company provides health insurance benefits to their employees that total $140 per month. The Axelrod Company provides no health insurance for its workers. How much money would the Star Fire health insurance benefit be worth to Sally each year?

34. In the table below is a breakdown of the number of people in a community of 5,000 covered by various types of health insurance.
   a. What percentage of the people are covered by each type of insurance?
   b. In one year, 235 people covered by surgical insurance presented claims totaling

Hospital	4,600
Surgical	3,200
Regular medical	3,000
Major medical	3,900
Dental	2,000
Vision care	700
Disability income	3,000

$176,250. What was the amount of the average claim?

35. During a recent blood drive, the Lincoln Blood Bank collected 675 pints of blood from donors.
   a. How many liters did they collect?
   b. How many milliliters did they collect?

36. Fran Obramowitz had her annual medical examination. According to her insurance plans she paid a portion of the costs of the services. The total costs and her share of each were:

Service	Total Cost	Patient Share
Doctor visit	$80	$15 deductible
Lab work	$220	20% copay
Prescriptions	$120	$20 copay
Vision exam	$65	$10 deductible
New lenses	$180	5%

   a. What was the total cost of the medical examination?
   b. How much of the total cost did Fran pay?
   c. What percent of the total cost did the insurance company pay?

TECHNOLOGY APPLICATION

Using the *Intro to Business* Data CD and your spreadsheet program software, select problem CH41. After the problem appears on your screen, complete the following activities. Then, after you have completed each step, display or print the completed spreadsheet for each activity. If you do not have a printer available, answer the questions before you leave the computer.

37. Sort the companies and dental insurance rates into descending order by rate.
   a. What is the third company listed?
   b. What is the second-lowest rate listed?

38. At the bottom of the Rate column, enter a function to find the average rate. Format the answer as currency with two decimal places. What is the average rate?

39. In the Difference from Average Rate column, enter formulas to calculate each company's rate minus the average rate.
   a. Which company has the greatest absolute (positive or negative) difference from the average rate?
   b. Which company has the smallest absolute difference from the average rate?

COMMUNICATING for SUCCESS

MEMOS—BIG ON INFORMATION, SMALL ON SPACE

Although the arrival of electronic mail has provided another means of brief, fast communication, the memorandum (or memo) is still a common form of message sending. Memos are especially useful for interoffice communication because they are easy and inexpensive to send. The memo serves a variety of purposes, from conveying information to requesting action. As a result, memos are most effective when information is presented clearly and directly.

Several points to consider when writing a memo are:

- Use action words like "Please mail . . . ," "Call by . . . ," and "Please write . . ."
- Specify a particular request and note any due dates that may apply.
- Be brief and direct; don't waste the readers' time.
- Although memos are considered a more casual form of communication, proofreading is still important in order for a message to be treated seriously.

An important function of memos is their usefulness in constructing a record of office activities. Therefore, they should always contain the date, sender's name, receivers' names, and the subject. There are a variety of memo formats, but the date, names, and subject should always be noted. A common memo format is shown here.

```
                    Memo
     To:

     From:

     Date:

     Regarding:



                         Body of Memo

```

CRITICAL THINKING

1. What are some action words and phrases appropriate for memos?
2. How would you describe an effective memo?

COMMUNICATING for SUCCESS

Communications skills will help ensure students' success in the business world. Communicating for Success introduces workplace/interpersonal communications issues and proper uses of communications technology. Each feature discusses a key communications topic, and contains two Critical Thinking questions that require students to analyze what they have learned.

This Communicating for Success feature outlines common uses and a typical format of interoffice memos. It provides students with guidelines for composing effective memos, including the inclusion of information that may be important for establishing a record of activities for future reference.

CRITICAL THINKING

1. Answers will vary but students may suggest words and phrases such as the following: "Please deliver. . . ," "Please complete this project by. . . ," "Will you send. . . ," "Read," "Review," "Respond."
2. An effective memo is brief, direct, and contains the date, sender and receivers' names, and the subject.

GLOBAL BUSINESS PROJECT

International business risk is usually the result of three main influences. First, economic risk may result from inflation and changing currency exchange rates. Second, social-cultural risk can occur when another nation has different attitudes and behaviors. Third, political risk may come from changes in a nation's ruling party or increased business regulations that deter foreign companies.

In an attempt to reduce these global business risks, insurance is a commonly used risk management strategy. In addition, international experts often suggest partnerships with established companies in the foreign country. For example, a joint venture, a franchise relationship, or licensing agreement may be used to eliminate and reduce risks.

To complete each phase of this project, students are encouraged to use various resources—textbook content, library materials, World Wide Web sites, interviews, advertisements, product packages, in-store observations. The individual activities are planned for use as either (1) an on-going course project, or (2) individual assignments.

Whether used as a continuing project or for selected activities, consider having students work in teams. This small group experience provides a valuable skill for future learning and work situations.

In addition to search engines, these selected web sites can be helpful for this unit:
- International Trade Administration of the U.S. Dept. of Commerce (www.ita.doc.gov)
- World Factbook of the Central Intelligence Agency (www.odci.gov/cia/publications/factbook)
- World Trade Organization at (www.wto.org)
- Current country information at (yahoo.com/regional/countries)

GLOBAL BUSINESS PROJECT

MANAGE INTERNATIONAL BUSINESS RISK

Every business organization faces risks. These uncertainties most commonly result from economic, social-cultural, and political factors. As companies get involved in international business, attempts are made to eliminate and reduce risks.

This phase of the global business project will consider methods to reduce risk, including insurance coverage. Also, working with a company already doing business in another country can minimize uncertainty.

PROJECT GOALS
1. To research risks associated with doing business in another country.
2. To develop a risk management plan and recommend insurance coverage.
3. To identify a potential joint venture partner for international business activities.

PROJECT ACTIVITIES
Using your textbook, library materials, web sites, interviews with people, and other resources, complete the following activities:
1. A company doing business in another country faces several types of risks. Using the country from your portfolio (or select a country), identify various economic, social-cultural, and political risks a company might encounter when doing business in that nation.
2. A risk management plan involves methods for reducing, eliminating, and shifting risks. The use of insurance is a common part of a risk management plan. Describe the types of liability and property insurance your business should have.
3. One of the most commonly used methods for reducing international business risk is working with existing companies in another country. Obtain information about a company in the country in which you plan to do business. Describe the joint venture that might be created to help your company be successful in this foreign market.

PROJECT WRAP-UP
1. Continue your portfolio (folder, file box, or other container) for storing and referring back to the information and materials you created in the activities above. These items will provide assistance for various components of your global business plan.
2. Create a visual presentation (such as poster, web site, or video) that communicates actions a company might take to reduce risk when doing business in another country.

- Import-export information at (www.internationalist.com/)
- Latin American country information (www.lanic.utexas.edu)
- Asian country information (asnic.utexas.edu/asnic.html) (www.asia-inc.com)
- Eastern European country information (reenic.utexas.edu/reenic.html)
- Middle East country information (menic.utexas.edu/menic.html)
- World Bank (www.worldbank.org)
- World Export-Import Bank of the United States (www.exim.gov)
- International Chamber of Commerce (www.iccwbo.org/)

FOCUS ON CAREERS

INSURANCE

Over 1.5 million people work in the insurance industry today. In addition to agents and brokers, other career options available in insurance include claims examiner, actuarial clerk, and insurance investigator. The basic task of these employees is to determine and satisfy customers' insurance needs.

JOB TITLES

Job titles commonly found in this career area include:

- Insurance Sales Agent
- Actuary
- Insurance Broker
- Insurance Underwriter
- Claims Examiner
- Insurance Investigator
- Claims Clerk
- Insurance Appraiser, Auto Damage
- Insurance Policy Processing Clerk
- Customer Service Representative
- Insurance Fraud Investigator

EMPLOYMENT OUTLOOK

- Although slower than average employment growth is expected among insurance agents, opportunities will be favorable for persons with the right qualifications. Job growth in other positions will be average.
- Employment of agents will not keep up with the rising level of insurance sales. Many companies are trying to contain costs and relying on independent brokers.
- An increasing number of insurance sales agents offer comprehensive financial planning services to their clients, and thus face competition from other financial and investment services.

EDUCATION AND TRAINING

- Insurance companies prefer college graduates—particularly those who have majored in business or economics.
- Some companies hire high-school graduates with potential or proven sales ability or success in other types of work.
- In smaller firms, workers may receive their training through courses offered by the Insurance Institute of America, a nonprofit organization offering educational programs and professional certification to people in the insurance industry.

SALARY LEVELS (IN RECENT YEARS)

- Commissions are the most common form of compensation for insurance sales agents. Some earn a salary plus commissions, or salary plus bonus. Experienced, successful agents make in excess of $75,000 a year.
- Salaried insurance sales workers earn about $40,000 a year on average.
- Annual earnings of insurance adjusters and investigators typically range from $32,000 to $55,000.

CRITICAL THINKING

1. Which job title in this career area appeals to you most? Give reasons for your choice.
2. What are some things you will have to do to achieve success in the career selected?

FOCUS ON CAREERS

The careers listed in this Focus on Careers come from the *Occupational Outlook Handbook*, an online publication (www.bls.gov/oco) of the federal government. The O*NET codes for these job titles are: Insurance Sales Agent, 41-3021.00; Actuary, 15-2011.00; Insurance Broker, 41-3021.00; Insurance Underwriter, 13-2053.00; Claims Examiner, 13-1031.00; Insurance Investigator, 13-1031.02; Claims Clerk, 43-9041.01; Insurance Appraiser, Auto Damage, 13-1032.00; Insurance Policy Processing Clerk, 43-9041.02; Customer Service Representative, 43-4051.00; Insurance Fraud Investigator, 33-3021.04. Students can access O*NET Online (online.onetcenter.org) to view important features of selected occupations. They can also search for related occupations and for occupations that match selected skills. This feature is designed to expose students to a variety of different careers in business. It can be used to demonstrate that skills learned in this course are relevant. As a supplemental activity, distribute the Career Focus worksheets found in the School-To-Work/SCANS Activity Masters.

CRITICAL THINKING

1. Answers will vary.
2. Answers will vary depending on student selection of a career choice. Suggested answers may include pursuing education or specialized training.

UNIT 12

BUILDING YOUR PORTFOLIO

CAREER DEVELOPMENT – CAREER PLANNING (REVISITED)

The Building Your Portfolio career exercise will help your students establish a personal history—where they have been, where they are now, and where they are going. This career exercise will encourage students to think about their interests, skills, and achievements.

Ask students to revisit their Building Your Portfolio exercise from Unit 1. Everyone's goals change throughout life. This exercise will help students determine if their goals, strengths, weaknesses, and important achievements have changed over the course of the school year. On a separate sheet of paper, direct students to again write their thoughts about themselves: (1) personal goals, (2) career goals, (3) how I will reach my goals, (4) my strengths and weaknesses, (5) my important achievements. Then have students compare these results with results from Unit 1. As a supplemental activity, you may refer to the School–To–Work/SCANS Activity Masters.

TEACHING STRATEGIES

SCANS

Alternate Modalities
Kinesthetic Learner 595

Teaching Tips
Building Your Portfolio 575
Kick-Off Activity 574

Special Needs
Attention Deficit Disorder 582
Specific Learning Disability (SLD) Students 606

Teams
579, 592

Special Features

Media/Technology

Chapter	Spreadsheet Software	Database Software	Word Processing Software	Internet	Video
42	■				■
43	■			■	■
44		■			■

Resources

SOFTWARE

Excel, Word, WordPerfect, Works, and ClarisWorks for Mac and Windows

Word Pro, ASCII, QuattroPro, Lotus, and Access for Windows

SOUTH-WESTERN EDUCATIONAL PUBLISHING PRODUCTS

Ryan. *Managing Your Personal Finances.* 2002. Cincinnati: South-Western Educational Publishing Company. Text-Workbook. 0-538-69958-2.

Roman and Finch. *Family Financial Management.* 1999. Cincinnati: South-Western Educational Publishing Company. Practice Set. 0-538-67501-2.

BOOKS

Burkett and Burnett. *Personal Finances: Includes Family Budget Models.* 1998. Moody Press.

Wiegold. *The Wall Street Journal Lifetime Guide to Money: Everything You Need to Know About Managing Your Finances—For Every Stage of Life.* 1997. Hyperion.

PERIODICALS

Consumers Digest. Chicago, IL.

Consumer Research, Inc. Washington, D.C.

Fortune. Time, Inc. Tampa, FL.

Kiplinger's Personal Finance Magazine. Washington, D.C.

GOVERNMENT PUBLICATIONS

Occupational Outlook Handbook, U.S. Department of Labor, Washington, DC.

What Work Requires of Schools: A SCANS Report for America 2000, U.S. Department of Labor, Washington, DC

MEDIA/TECHNOLOGY

Publisher's web sites:
www.intro2business.swep.com
www.swep.com
www.thomson.com

PERSONAL FINANCIAL MANAGEMENT

The content and activities of this unit provide students with an overview of the purposes and characteristics of the important aspects of money management. Use the resources listed on the preceding page, especially those from South-Western Educational Publishing, as you prepare to teach these chapters.

Chapter 42 is designed to help students understand the basics of money management and the importance of developing financial goals and making the buying decisions that are required to achieve those goals. In Chapter 43, the five purposes of budgeting are discussed as well as the goals of the budgeting process. The necessity of financial planning is stressed in Chapter 44. In this chapter, students are guided into the five steps of financial planning, which include analyzing current financial condition, developing short-term and long-term financial goals, creating a financial plan, implementing the plan, and frequently evaluating and revising the financial plan.

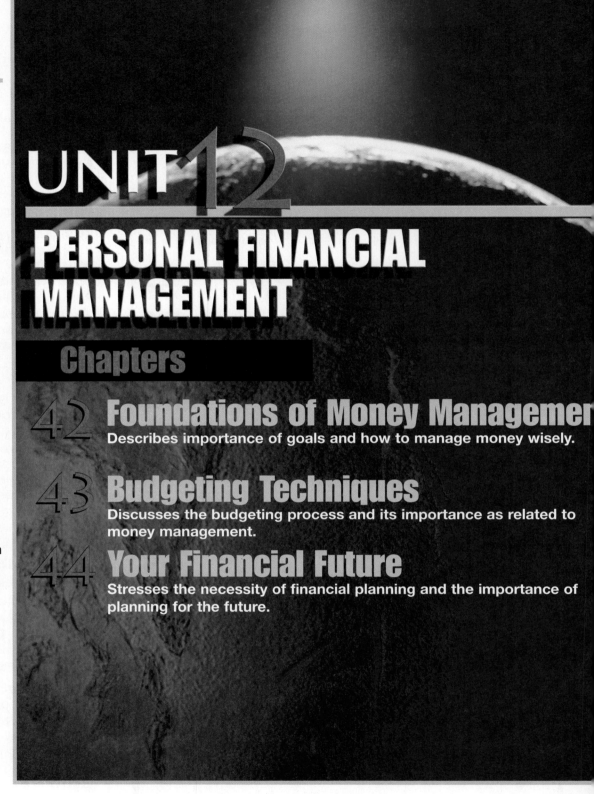

UNIT 12

PERSONAL FINANCIAL MANAGEMENT

Chapters

42 Foundations of Money Management
Describes importance of goals and how to manage money wisely.

43 Budgeting Techniques
Discusses the budgeting process and its importance as related to money management.

44 Your Financial Future
Stresses the necessity of financial planning and the importance of planning for the future.

Kick-Off Activity

Investigating Business Media

Individuals as well as businesses maintain financial records to track financial performance. Students should select an article from *The Wall Street Journal* detailing the quarterly or year-end performance of a company considered noteworthy for either its positive or negative performance. (You may need to explain to students how the personal financial statements in this unit relate to business operations.) Ask students to answer the following questions:

1 Did the company report a profit or a loss for the period of time? What other performance indicators were reported? Did the company's performance represent an improvement over the previous accounting periods?

2 What, according to the article, was the significance of this performance? Was the performance a surprise or was it expected?

BU$INESSBRIEF

ONLINE INVESTMENT INFORMATION

Online investment information is becoming one of the most popular ways to keep up-to-date with the investment scene. Online services provided through the Internet and commercial service providers make investment information readily available at any time of the day.

Information that can be retrieved from online services includes full-text copies of corporate filings with the Securities and Exchange Commission; economic, monetary, and stock data from a variety of sources; and electronic versions of useful publications such as *Business Week*. The amount of information available is almost unlimited!

Retrieving investment information is not the only way in which online services can be used. Subscribers can also post messages to bulletin boards when in need of particular information or simply to share investment information. Discussion lists are also available whereby subscribers can discuss investment topics and issues with other subscribers.

Online investment information allows subscribers to be up-to-date at all times without going through a broker or using other financial services. One of the biggest advantages is that this information can be obtained any time of the day.

In addition to timely information, the Internet also gives investors a convenient way to buy or sell securities. Competition between online brokerage services has reduced the fees and commissions that investors must pay for trades, even as the quality, speed, and security of such services have improved.

To get the most out of online investment information, keep in mind the following five-step process:

1. Search for sources of information. Start with an indexing service, and look for listings on investments, the economy, personal finance, and so on.
2. Brainstorm with other investors. Join a Usenet Newsgroup or e-mail discussion list. Watch for advice from experts and people close to various companies. Be careful, however, to avoid get-rich-quick schemes.
3. Collect data. Locate annual reports, documents describing stock offerings, and other financial data. As you focus on specific investments, obtain expert evaluations of the investments as reported in online business magazines and financial newsletters.
4. Make your move. Buy or sell bonds, stocks, or shares in funds through an online stockbroker or mutual fund company.
5. Keep an eye on your money. Use your sources of data and your links with fellow shareholders to regularly monitor your investments. Share your experiences to help others out, and they will be more willing to pass tips and warnings on to you.

CRITICAL THINKING

1 *Why will some investors not wish to use online investment information?*

BU$INESSBRIEF

A Business Brief sets the tone for a unit. To help students understand current and emerging trends, each unit will be introduced with a Business Brief. The Briefs were chosen for their importance to business, timeliness, and interest to students. The Briefs complement the many real-world examples woven into the text.

After reading the Business Brief, ask students what impressed them the most. Have they heard or read about this topic before? Find out what students know about online investment information. Many students use online services and may be able to share with the class investment information that they obtained in this way.

At the conclusion of the discussion, direct students to answer the Critical Thinking questions that follow the Brief.

CRITICAL THINKING

Students' answers will, of course, require thinking beyond what is presented in the Business Brief. Answers will be based on students' perceptions of the topic and experiences they have had with it. The following are possible answers:

1. Some investors prefer the personal touch. Others don't trust computers!

2. Stocks, bonds, money market, mutual funds, currency exchange to name a few. Any investment information that can be obtained through a stockbroker can be obtained online.

BUILDING YOUR PORTFOLIO

The Building Your Portfolio work samples validate skill level and a student's ability to accomplish tasks frequently performed on the job. The most important reason for including samples in a portfolio is to demonstrate a student's abilities and skills. In selecting work samples for each unit, students should always have a choice of which activities to include. Students might be encouraged to include samples from the end-of-chapter activities, particularly Communicate Business Concepts, Calculate Business Data, Technology Application, and Decision-Making Strategies.

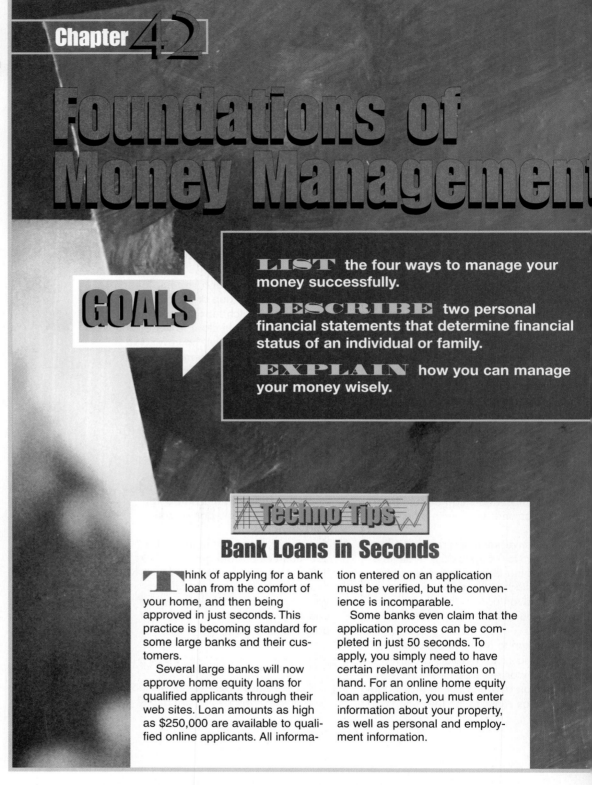

Foundations of Money Management

Chapter 42 will discuss money management, the importance of financial goals, and what is required to achieve those goals. Financial statements, including a balance sheet and cash flow statement, will be presented.

Resources for Teachers
- Lesson Plans
- School-To-Work/SCANS Activity Masters
- Spanish Resources
- Instructor's Resource CD

Assessment
- Chapter and Unit Tests, Ch. 42
- ExamView, Ch. 42

Media/Technology
- Applying Technology Data CD
- PowerPoint slides
- Business Connection CD
- Videotape

Activity Masters and Workbooks
- Activities and Projects, Ch. 42
- Internet Activity Masters
- Business Math Activity Masters
- Communications Activity Masters
- International Business Activity Masters
- Ethics Activity Masters

GOALS

LIST the four ways to manage your money successfully.

DESCRIBE two personal financial statements that determine financial status of an individual or family.

EXPLAIN how you can manage your money wisely.

Techno Tips

Bank Loans in Seconds

Think of applying for a bank loan from the comfort of your home, and then being approved in just seconds. This practice is becoming standard for some large banks and their customers.

Several large banks will now approve home equity loans for qualified applicants through their web sites. Loan amounts as high as $250,000 are available to qualified online applicants. All information entered on an application must be verified, but the convenience is incomparable.

Some banks even claim that the application process can be completed in just 50 seconds. To apply, you simply need to have certain relevant information on hand. For an online home equity loan application, you must enter information about your property, as well as personal and employment information.

Students need to know the latest technologies and develop cutting edge Internet skills for use in current jobs, future careers, or in their homes. TechnoTips introduces students to today's cutting edge technologies and provides them with important Internet skills. Feature topics concentrate on Internet-specific technologies and computer or other hi-tech innovations for use by businesses and consumers.

FOCUS ON REAL LIFE

"**M**y financial situation is just fine—or it is a disaster! It all depends on what day of the week it may be."

"Tell me, what's the problem, Yung-su?"

"Mr. Liang, I can't seem to get a grip on my finances. I work 10 hours a week for a telemarketing firm and make just under $10 per hour. That seems like a lot of money for a part-time job while going to school. But I always seem to run out of money before the week is over."

"I suppose that also means you are not saving any money but spending all of your income. My advice is to get some lessons in money management."

The one thing most of us have in common is a desire to use wisely the money we have so that our needs, wants, and goals will be satisfied. While no individual, family, or organization is likely to have every desire met, there are several money management techniques that can help you use wisely the financial resources available to you.

MANAGING YOUR MONEY

Right now $1,000, or maybe $100, seems like a lot of money to you. Once you graduate from high school and/or college and have a full-time job, your thinking about what is a large amount of money will change. You probably will earn well over a million dollars in your lifetime. If you become a college graduate, you can expect to make even more.

While this may seem like a great deal of money, remember that you will be responsible for many living expenses. You will have to pay for food, housing, clothing, and transportation as well as other goods and services you need and want. Upon beginning a career and living on your own, you will face the same problem you face now—having a limited amount of money to pay for all the goods and services you want and need.

This basic economic problem can be resolved by learning to carefully manage your money and live within your income. **Income** is the money you receive from work that you do and from money that you invest. As you know, a person's income will vary based on the type of work he or she does. Your income also will be influenced by the level of education and amount of experience you have.

Money management refers to the day-to-day financial activities associated with using limited income to satisfy your unlimited needs and wants. Money management involves getting the most for your money through careful planning, saving, and spending; it involves creating and using a plan for spending.

Some people have the wrong idea about money management. They think it means pinching pennies, doing without things, and not having any fun. But if you learn to manage your money well, you will be able to buy the things you really want that you may not have been able to buy before. Planning ahead and deciding what is really important will help you to have money to spend on the things you enjoy. If you set goals, make wise decisions, buy wisely, and live within your income, you will be a successful money manager.

> Your net pay is your net income which is the amount of money you have available to spend.

PURPOSE Provide a purpose for students as they read the chapter. Lead students into the chapter by explaining the importance of money management. Ask students what they think they will learn. Direct them to skim the chapter, looking at photos, reading captions, and noting main headings. The goals at the beginning of each chapter provide a valuable tool for having students pinpoint main ideas. The tasks required by the goals are signaled in the first word. Some emphasize information collection ("Identify," "List"), while others call for description ("Explain," "Describe"). Ask students to look through all the goals and note the first word of each. Then ask students to state the purpose of studying this chapter.

TEACH/APPLY

MAKE CONNECTIONS This chapter develops the theme of managing money, even though it does not cover budgeting (budgeting is Chapter 43). Students are given important information about setting goals, basic financial statements, and how to manage money wisely. Introduce goals using PowerPoint 42-1, *Goals.* Goal setting is a useful exercise that students need assistance in developing. When goals are set and put in writing, a reference and a reminder is created. Money management involves setting goals and deciding how to spend money on basic needs, saving, and spending discretionary income. Explain each expenditure and its

Chapter 42 *Foundations of Money Management* | 577

FOCUS ON REAL LIFE

Money management is a topic close to most students' hearts—they never have enough money! Ask for definitions of the term *money management*. You might be surprised at some of the answers you get. Raise the question of whether or not a person can acquire the skill of good money management. Ask if acquiring money management skills involves a process similar to acquiring study, reading, writing, or sports skills.

importance. Most students probably have not seen financial statements. This is a good opportunity to describe personal balance sheets and cash flow statements and their importance.

TRY THIS/GUIDED PRACTICE
Guide students through the preparation of their personal financial statements. Use PowerPoint 42-4, *Personal Balance Sheet*, and PowerPoint 42-6, *Personal Cash Flow Statement*. Describe each line; then walk students through the preparation of each using notebook paper.

EXPLORE THIS/INDEPENDENT PRACTICE Before assigning independent practice material for any chapter, students should be expected to read the chapter material carefully. In view of the fact that all students vary widely in their ability to read effectively, it is advisable to have the students read the entire chapter, or sections thereof, silently in class if the material has not been previously read in connection with homework assignments.

After students have read the chapter, ask them to complete the Chapter Review questions. Develop Your Business Language is an excellent way to improve students' vocabulary. Only words introduced in the chapter are used in the exercises. The Review Your Reading questions can be used to check students' ability to comprehend what they have read. The Communicate Business Concepts section affords an opportunity for students to apply to practical life situations the information gained from reading the chapter. By completing the problems under

An *auditor's* job duties include:
- **Examining and analyzing accounting records to determine financial status of an organization**
- **Preparing financial reports concerning operating procedures.**
- **Reviewing data regarding assets, net worth, liabilities, capital, and stock of an organization**
- **Counting cash on hand**
- **Preparing reports for management concerning scope of audit.**

Setting Your Goals
Money management starts with setting attainable financial goals. Goals are those things you want to achieve, andthey may be short-term or long-term goals. A short-term financial goal, for example, might be to buy some common stock or to purchase a new computer. Long-range goals often involve large amounts of money. A long-range goal for a family might be to buy a house, take a trip to a foreign country, or provide college education for the children. A personal long-range goal might be to open your own business.

Goals are personal. They are not the same for all people or even for everyone within a given age group. Goals are affected by such things as a person's age, family situation, interests, and values. People have to set their own goals based on their own wants and realistic assessments of what they can achieve.

Making Economic Decisions
Money management can be seen as part of a process of making economic decisions. Money, of course, is limited, and individuals and families must decide how to use the money that is available to them. The main decisions we each make involve three areas:

1. *Paying for basic needs.* Needs are things necessary for survival such as food, clothing, and shelter. Everyone's basic needs, however, are not exactly the same. Needs depend on where you live and what lifestyle you follow. If you live in a southern city, for example, you have different transportation and clothing needs from those who live on a large ranch in a northwestern state. For some people, an apartment is ideal; others may need a house. In any case, after you have met these basic needs, you must decide how to use the money that remains.

2. *Saving for future expenses.* After providing for your basic needs, you should decide how to prepare for large expenses in the future. You do this by developing a savings program. Everyone has special reasons for saving. Maybe you want to buy a car or save for college, or perhaps you want to start a business that requires expensive equipment. Unless you manage your money wisely and plan your savings, you may not be able to do or buy the things you want.

3. *Spending discretionary income.* The third decision you must make when managing your money is how to spend any money you have available after you have taken care of your basic needs and future expenses. This money is referred to as **discretionary income**. This is income you spend to buy the things you want for pleasure, satisfaction, and comfort. Discretionary income, for example, is spent on such things as entertainment, travel, compact discs, or hobby supplies. Spending discretionary income is usually more fun than buying basic items or sav-

Always write your financial goals in a place where you see them often. Seeing the goals will sometimes provide the motivation you need to reach them.

The careers listed in the Career Highlights come from the *Occupational Outlook Handbook*, an online publication (www.bls.gov/oco) of the federal government. The O*NET code for Auditor is 13-2011.02. Students can access O*NET Online (online.onetcenter.org) to view job features or search for related occupations. Tell your class about these resources and how to use them. This description of job duties can be used to demonstrate the relevancy of skills learned in this course.

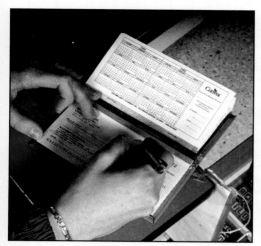

How do you typically spend your discretionary income?

ing money and can be seen as your reward for good money management.

Buying Wisely

Most of us have more needs and wants than we could ever hope to satisfy. We must stretch our limited incomes as far as possible. Wise buying is an important way to stretch your income.

To buy wisely you must gather information carefully before making your purchases. You must plan your purchases so that you buy the right good or service at the right time and at the right price. Unplanned buying often leads to disappointment and wasted money. Planned buying leads to better use of money and greater satisfaction from the things you buy.

Living Within an Income

Do you ever run out of money before the end of the month? Many people have that problem. They have not learned to live within their

An average family will spend 22 to 24 percent of its income on food and 29 to 32 percent on housing.

incomes. Living on the amount that you have available is a central idea in money management. Creating a plan for spending the money you have is necessary in order to live within your income.

KNOWING YOUR FINANCIAL STATUS

The process of good money management starts with knowing your current financial status. When viewing a baseball or soccer game, most people want to know the score as the game progresses. In the money management game, score is kept with the use of financial statements. Two common financial statements are the balance sheet and cash flow statement.

Preparing a Balance Sheet

"How much money do you have?" may be the first question many people would ask when measuring your financial situation. The answer to that question, however, would not give the entire picture since most people have other items of value besides money. A **balance sheet**, which is a type of financial

Why must you know your financial status before considering a large purchase?

Calculate Business Data, students will be able to strengthen and refine their abilities in mathematics. Technology Application allows students to demonstrate skill in using word processing, spreadsheet, and database software. Decision-Making Strategies contains material to challenge students to utilize the model explained in Chapter 1 for problem solving.

The Chapter Review questions at the end of the chapter vary in level of difficulty. For a basic assignment, consider Develop Your Business Language and Review Your Reading. For an average assignment, consider the basic assignment plus Communicate Business Concepts and Calculate Business Data. For an enhanced assignment, try the average assignment plus Technology Application and Decision-Making Strategies.

ASSESS

Review the goals at the beginning of the chapter and the Business Notes at the end of the chapter. Have students respond orally or in writing to each goal restated as a question. For students who may have difficulty providing answers, assign the reteaching activities that follow. Enrichment activities may also be assigned where appropriate.

1. What are the four ways to manage your money successfully? (Answer: Start with setting attainable financial goals (short-term or long-term goals); paying for basic needs (those things that are necessary for

---

TEACHING STRATEGIES
Teams

Jigsaw is an instructional method in which students use cooperative learning in peer groups. To use the jigsaw method, divide the chapter into six parts. Each member of the team becomes an expert on one of the parts to which they are assigned. All students assigned each section then meet as an expert group. These ex-

pert groups will discuss their section and decide how to report this information to their respective groups. Students then go back to their original group, at which time they share the expert information they have learned. Teammates are dependent upon that team member to thoroughly explain that part of the chapter. Students then take the ExamView as individuals with no assistance from team members. Compare each student's score to the current average for that student's previous exams.

survival), saving for future expenses, and then spending discretionary income; buying wisely; and living within your income.)
2. What are the two financial statements that are prepared to determine the financial status of an individual or family? (Answer: A balance sheet and a cash flow statement.)
3. In what ways can you manage your money wisely? (Answer: Plan carefully, use information to help you better understand and take action on your money matters, compare products and prices, make wise decisions.)

Personal Balance Sheet

Assets			Liabilities	
Checking account	$ 450		Home mortgage	$ 45,000
Savings account	2,300		Credit card balance	230
Home	97,000		Education loan	1,800
Automobile	4,600			
Household items and furniture	6,200		Total Liabilities	$ 47,030
Personal computer	1,600			
Jewelry	1,100		**Owner's Equity**	
			Total Assets minus Total Liabilities	$ 66,220
Total Assets	$113,250		Total Liabilities and Owner's Equity	$113,250

FIGURE 42-1 What accounts for the bulk of this family's assets, liabilities, and equity?

statement, reports what a person or family owns as well as owes.

The main components of a balance sheet are displayed in Figure 42-1 and consist of the following categories:

1. **Assets** are items of value. Assets include such things as money in bank accounts, investments, furniture, clothing, automobiles, jewelry, and rare coins. The current value of all assets of an individual or family is the first thing reported on a balance sheet.
2. **Liabilities** are amounts owed to others. These debts may include credit card balances, automobile loans, a home mortgage, or personal loans. Total liabili-

An incompatibility occurs when software on your client computer cannot communicate with software on an Internet host. Causes of incompatibilities include different versions of software, mismatched software settings, and different hardware platforms.

Net worth is also known as owner's equity.

ties is the second item on a balance sheet.

3. **Owner's Equity,** or net worth, is the difference between a person's or family's assets and liabilities. This difference represents the amount of money that could be claimed if all assets were sold for cash and all debts were paid off. For example, if a family has $189,000 in assets (including the value of a home and other valuables) and has $87,000 in debts (mainly the home mortgage), the family has a net worth of $102,000.

A balance sheet is a helpful way to measure financial strength. Every business will prepare a balance sheet either once a month or every three months to determine the financial condition of the business. In the same way, a balance sheet can help an individual or family in measuring its financial condition.

Preparing a Cash Flow Statement

A balance sheet reports assets, liabilities, and owner's equity on a given date. Almost every day, however, business transactions occur that change these balance sheet items. For exam-

SUMMARIZE

Direct students to write a list of their (1) short-term goals, (2) long-term goals, (3) current income, allowance, or other sources of money, (4) expenses they must personally pay. This information can also be used for the budgeting procedure in Chapter 43.

EVALUATE

- Assign Activities and Projects, Chapter 42.
- Administer the printed test or ExamView for Chapter 42.
- Assign School-To-Work/SCANS portfolio activities for Unit 12.

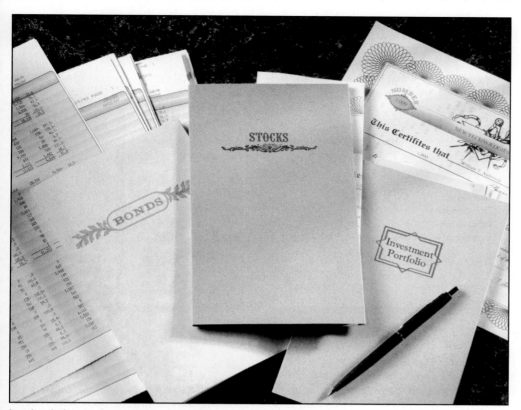

In what balance sheet category would you place investments?

ple, when you make a loan payment, the amount of your liabilities decreases. If you save part of your earnings, your assets and owner's equity increase by the amount of the savings. To examine changes in a person's net worth, another financial statement can be helpful. A **cash flow statement** reports net wages and other income along with spending for a given period of time, such as for a month. Figure 42-2 includes typical items found in a cash flow statement.

The first part of a cash flow statement reports your financial income. This is the money you have available to spend as a result of working or from other income such as interest earned on your savings. When preparing a cash flow statement, you should first report your **net income** or **take-home pay**, which is the amount of a paycheck after taxes and other payroll deductions have

been subtracted from your total earnings. Payroll deductions may include retirement contributions, charges for health benefits, and other things, as well as local, state, and federal taxes. Your take-home pay is the amount you actually have available to spend. This amount available to spend is also called *cash inflows*.

The next step necessary for creating a cash flow statement is to maintain records of all spending. The amounts spent for food, clothing, transportation, and other living costs are called **expenditures** or *cash outflows*. Keeping track of how much is spent for various

Knowing how much you own (assets) and how much you owe (liabilities) are keys to good financial management.

Chapter 42 *Foundations of Money Management*   581

Personal Qualities-Self-Management

Money management not only involves dollars, but it also involves self-management in order to appropriate money in a wise manner. This chapter provides an opportunity to work on self-management techniques of setting personal goals (as money management usually plays a part), monitoring progress of goals, and assessing one's self objectively.

Personal Cash Flow Statement

Cash Inflows (Income)

Net Income (take-home pay)	$1,200	
Other Income (interest)	50	
Total Income		$1,250

Cash Outflows (Expenditures)

Food	$ 400	
Clothing	50	
Electricity	100	
Telephone	25	
Transportation	150	
Personal care	30	
Recreation/entertainment	75	
Total Expenditures		830
Net Cash Flow		$ 420

FIGURE 42-2
What percentage of total income did this person spend on basic needs?

living expenses will help you to plan and control your spending. Your personal cash flow statement can be used to develop a budget, which can help you avoid cash flow problems.

The final step in preparing the cash flow statement is to subtract your total expenditures from your total income. If you have spent less than you had in income, the difference represents an increase in your owner's equity. Most likely this amount will be kept in savings for future needs or wants. If you spent more than you had in income, you either had to use some of your savings or had to use credit to pay these additional expenses.

When you apply for a large loan for a house, car, or business, the loan officer will want to see copies of your current balance sheet and cash flow statement.

FYI

MANAGING YOUR MONEY WISELY

While effective money management may seem like a lot of trouble, poor money management practices can result in even more trouble. A poor credit rating, arguments with family members about money, and money shortages are just a few of the problems that can result from poor money management. For wise money management, practice the following behaviors:

- Plan carefully. Setting goals and knowing what you really need and want will help you to avoid financial difficulties while also obtaining enjoyment from the resources you have available.

- Use information. Much is written about budgeting and financial planning. Articles in magazines, such as *Money* and *Kiplinger's*, can help you better understand and take action on your money matters.

- Compare products and prices. Comparison buying—achieved by reading advertisements, using label information, and analyz-

TEACHING STRATEGIES

Special Needs
Attention Deficit Disorder

Provide students with activities that are short and focused. These students do better with basic assignments instead of lengthy ones. (See lesson plan, Explore This/Independent Practice.)

ing different brands—can help you get the most for your money. Being a wise consumer is one of the basic principles of effective money management.

- Make wise decisions. By using a step-by-step decision-making process, you will be able to make effective use of your limited resources.

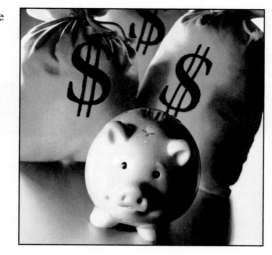

What actions can you take to manage your money wisely?

CULTURAL PERSPECTIVES

The Abacus

Calculators have made completing math and accounting work a snap! But what did people use before the calculator was invented?

Have you ever seen an abacus? An abacus is a calculating device made of wood and metal wires on which moveable beads are strung. The beads are moved from place to place to indicate certain numbers. The abacus was used to add, subtract, multiply, and divide for both business and personal purposes.

The abacus, in various configurations, was developed in several different cultures. The Babylonians in Asia Minor had an early form of the abacus as did the Egyptians in Northern Africa. The earliest abacus was known in China as early as the 6th century B.C. and its use spread to the rest of the Asian world.

Today, some highly skilled people still use the abacus for calculations. These people are so highly skilled that they can sometimes perform calculations faster than a person using an electronic calculator!

Critical Thinking
1. What cultures do you think might still use the abacus?
2. Why do you think that some people can use an abacus and arrive at an answer faster than someone using a calculator?

CULTURAL PERSPECTIVES

This Cultural Perspectives feature will expose students to the concept that our society is composed of people from many different cultural backgrounds.

If possible, bring an abacus to class to demonstrate how the beads represent place value. An abacus can be borrowed from a library, elementary school teachers, or a math teacher. You may even be able to get a skilled user to visit and do a demonstration.

CRITICAL THINKING
1. Probably people of Asian descent.
2. Skilled abacus users are exactly that—highly skilled. They know exactly how to shift the beads without hesitation. When we use a calculator we have to enter each number, hit the enter key, etc. This is not necessary with the abacus.

Chapter REVIEW

BUSINESS NOTES

1. Good money managers start with setting attainable financial goals (short-term or long-term goals); paying for basic needs (things that are necessary for survival); saving for future expenses, and then spending discretionary income; buying wisely; and living within one's income.

2. Two financial statements are prepared to determine financial status—a balance sheet and a cash flow statement. A balance sheet is a record of assets and liabilities at a point in time. A cash flow statement is a record of cash inflows, including net pay after subtracting payroll taxes and other deductions, and cash outflows, including sales taxes and other taxes paid when cash is spent.

3. You can manage your money wisely by planning carefully, using information to help you better understand and take action on your money matters, comparing products and prices, and making wise decisions.

REVIEW YOUR READING

1. What activities are associated with money management?
2. List factors that affect a person's financial goals.
3. What are the three main decisions associated with money management?
4. List four goods or services for which you might spend discretionary income.
5. What are the three main components of a balance sheet?
6. What is the purpose of a cash flow statement?
7. Why is net income or take-home pay used on a cash flow statement?
8. What must a person or family do if more money is spent than is received in a certain month?
9. Name three wise money management behaviors.
10. How can you practice comparison buying?

COMMUNICATE BUSINESS CONCEPTS

11. Describe the difference between short-term and long-term goals. Give two examples of each type.
12. List some items that might be a want for one person but a need for someone else.
13. Identify each of the following items as an asset or a liability:
    a. Money owed to the dentist
    b. An automobile
    c. Clothing
    d. Savings account
    e. Credit card balance
    f. Amount due for a personal loan
    g. 100 shares of stock
14. What two actions could you take if your expenditures were consistently greater than your income?

14. Students may provide different ways of saving money but the two general ways to solve the problem of expenses outrunning income are to determine ways to earn more money and/or to spend less.

DEVELOP YOUR BUSINESS LANGUAGE

For each numbered item, find the term that has the same meaning.

15. The financial statement that reports what a person or family owns as well as owes.

16. Income available to spend after money has been set aside for basic needs and future expenses.

17. The difference between a person's or family's assets and liabilities.

18. Day-to-day financial activities associated with using limited income to satisfy unlimited needs and wants.

19. The amounts spent for food, clothing, transportation, and other living costs.

20. Amounts owed to others.

21. The financial statement that reports net wages and other income along with spending for a given period of time.

22. The amount received after taxes and other deductions have been subtracted from total earnings.

23. Items of value.

24. The money you receive from work that you do and from money you invest.

KEY TERMS

assets
balance sheet
cash flow statement
discretionary income
expenditures
income
liabilities
money management
net income or take-home pay
owner's equity

DECISION-MAKING STRATEGIES

Joan Leitzel just graduated from college and got her first job as a speech therapist. Joan wants to make sure she manages her income wisely so that she can be independent and eventually buy a house on her own. She lives with her parents now, so her only expenses are payments on a college loan and an auto loan.

25. What advice would you give Joan if she wants to buy a house in the future?

26. When she eventually goes to the bank for a loan, how should Joan organize her financial information?

DEVELOP YOUR BUSINESS LANGUAGE

15. balance sheet
16. discretionary income
17. owner's equity
18. money management
19. expenditures
20. liabilities
21. cash flow statement
22. net income or take-home pay
23. assets
24. income

DECISION-MAKING STRATEGIES

25. Joan should first set attainable financial goals such as placing a certain amount of money aside each month for a down payment for her future house, then set the long-term goal of actually buying a house. However, she should always pay for basic needs first, then save for future expenditures. Any extra money can be used to buy discretionary items. Joan should always buy carefully and live within her income.

26. When Joan eventually goes for a home loan, she should complete a balance sheet and cash flow statement to prove that she is able to repay a loan.

CALCULATE BUSINESS DATA

27. (a) $2,820 ($350 + commission of 0.05 × $48,000 = $2,750 + $70 interest and dividends) (b) basic salary 12% ($350 ÷ $2,820); commission 85% ($2,400 ÷ $2,820); interest and dividends 2% ($70 ÷ $2,820)

28. $1,600 × 10% = $160. $160 + $100 = $260. $1,600 − $260 = $1,340 net pay. $240 × 1.07 = $256.80 total cost.

29. $102,100 (assets of $268,400 less liabilities of $166,300)

30. (a) $11.59 (5 × $1.35 = $6.75 for oil + $4.29 for filter + $0.55 tax) (b) $18.41 ($30.00 − $11.59)

31. Bedroom 1—(10′ × 0.3) = 3 meters, (12′ × 0.3) = 3.6 meters; 3 meters × 3.6 meters = 10.8 square meters. Bedroom 2—(12′ × 0.3) = 3.6 meters, (14′ × 0.3) = 4.2 meters; 3.6 meters × 4.2 meters = 15.12 square meters. Bedroom 3—(13′ × 0.3) = 3.9 meters, (16′ × 0.3) = 4.8 meters; 3.9 meters × 4.8 meters = 18.72 square meters

TECHNOLOGY APPLICATION

In this activity, students use a computer to solve a business problem using a file that is provided on the data CD that accompanies *Intro to Business*. Instructions for using the data CD are included in a **README** file on the disk. Solutions are provided on the Instructor's Resource CD.

CALCULATE BUSINESS DATA

27. Beth Hamlin is a computer software marketing representative. She earns a basic salary of $350 per month plus a commission that is 5 percent of her sales. In addition, Beth earns $70 in interest and dividends monthly.

   a. In a month with $48,000 in sales, what would Beth's total income be?

   b. What percent of her total income comes from each item (basic salary, commission, and interest and dividends)? (Round to the nearest percentage.)

28. Mike Collins has a monthly gross income of $1,600. If his employer deducts 10% for payroll taxes and $100 a month for health benefits, how much will the net amount of his paycheck be? If Mike buys a new suit for $240 and pays sales tax of 7%, what is the total cost of the suit including taxes?

29. The Gage family's assets total $268,400. Their total liabilities are $166,300. What is the amount of their owner's equity?

30. Dorothy Christensen decided to change the oil and filter in her car. She bought five quarts of 10W40 multi-weight oil for $1.35 per quart and an oil filter for $4.29.

   a. How much was the total bill for the oil and filter, including 5 percent sales tax?

   b. How much did Dorothy save if a service station would have charged her $30 for the oil and filter change?

31. The O'Reillys' house was the largest asset on their balance sheet. Janet O'Reilly accepted a job transfer to another city. This required selling their home. A couple from Austria inquired about their home using the Internet as their communication medium. The Austrians wanted to know the metric dimensions and area of each of the home's three bedrooms. The bedrooms were (1) 10' by 12', (2) 12' by 14', and (3) 13' by 16'. Can you help the O'Reillys by giving the dimensions and area of each bedroom in meters and square meters?

TECHNOLOGY APPLICATION

Using the *Intro to Business* data CD and your spreadsheet program software, select problem CH42. After the problem appears on your screen, complete the following activities. After you have completed each step, display or print the completed spreadsheet for each activity. If you do not have a printer available, answer the questions before you leave the computer.

32. In the cells containing [F], enter formulas to calculate Net Income, Total Expenditures, and Net Cash Flow. What is the amount of Net Cash Flow?

33. What if your Take-Home Pay increased to $2,500? Copy the Cash Flow Statement to another part of the spreadsheet. Enter the new higher amount of Take-Home Pay. Answer the following questions:

   a. What is the new amount of Net Income?

   b. What is the new amount of Net Cash Flow?

34. What if your Take-Home Pay decreased to $500? Copy the Cash Flow Statement from Problem 32 to another part of the spreadsheet. Enter the new lower amount of Take-Home Pay. Answer the following questions:

   a. What is the new amount of Net Income?

   b. What is the new amount of Net Cash Flow?

Optional: Create a pie chart showing the sources of Net Income and a pie chart showing the sources of Total Expenditures. Repeat for each activity.

INTERNATIONAL BUSINESS RISKS

Every international company faces global business risks. A civil war may destroy a factory. A parts supplier may go out of business. Or, inflation might cause higher prices that customers cannot afford. Risks associated with doing business in other countries are commonly viewed in three categories:

1. Political risk refers to the uncertainty that may result from the instability of a government. Political control in a country may change during civil unrest or a revolution. This change in government may result in increased corruption or changes in business regulations. Trade barriers also create political risk. These trade barriers may include tariffs, antidumping laws, import quotas, and currency exchange controls.

2. Social risk relates to differences in cultural factors that could influence business activities. These risks may be related to historic tradition, religious beliefs, or family values. For example, in some areas of the world, family-business ties are strong. Companies must adapt to this cultural situation to be successful.

3. Economic risk involves factors in a nation's economy that might affect the business environment. Consumer demand, inflation, currency values, and interest rates are some of the economic factors that can create business risk. Changing currency values can result in difficulties when collecting money from a company in another country.

With change continually occurring in the world, international managers must keep track of foreign economic and political situations. This may be done by reading and monitoring news through newspapers, the World Wide Web, and television. Reports from people who live and work in other countries is another important way to keep up with changes in a nation's business environment. An ongoing awareness of factors such as political stability, religious influences, and changing economic conditions can help companies act early to reduce risk and to make wiser global business decisions.

CRITICAL THINKING

1. Select a country. Conduct research and prepare a list of political, social, and economic factors that could increase the risk of doing business in that country.
2. Conduct a Web search on "political stability." Attempt to locate information about countries that might be too risky for international business activities.

Most students will either work with international clients or compete against businesses that do. Global Navigator introduces students to issues integral to working with international businesses. Key concepts and challenges faced by international businesses are presented, followed by two Critical Thinking questions that require students to analyze what they have learned.

This Global Navigator feature outlines three common types of risks associated with international business—political risk, social risk, and economic risk. These risks differ in an international context from risks that apply to business within a single country. Students will need to be aware of these special risks, since so much business is now affected, either directly or indirectly, by international events.

CRITICAL THINKING

1. Answers will vary widely depending on which particular country a student picks.
2. Countries that are "too risky" are constantly changing. Civil unrest, border conflicts, uncontrolled inflation, and natural disasters may all contribute to what many international businesses will regard as excessive risk.

The five purposes of budgeting and the goals of budgeting are discussed. In order to successfully manage money, budgeting must play an important role. Students will learn budgeting and how to know if their budget is successful.

Resources for Teachers
- Lesson Plans
- School-To-Work/SCANS Activity Masters
- Spanish Resources
- Instructor's Resource CD

Assessment
- Chapter and Unit Tests, Ch. 43
- ExamView, Ch. 43

Media/Technology
- Applying Technology Data CD
- PowerPoint slides
- Business Connection CD
- Videotape

Activity Masters and Workbooks
- Activities and Projects, Ch. 43
- Internet Activity Masters
- Business Math Activity Masters
- Communications Activity Masters
- International Business Activity Masters
- Ethics Activity Masters

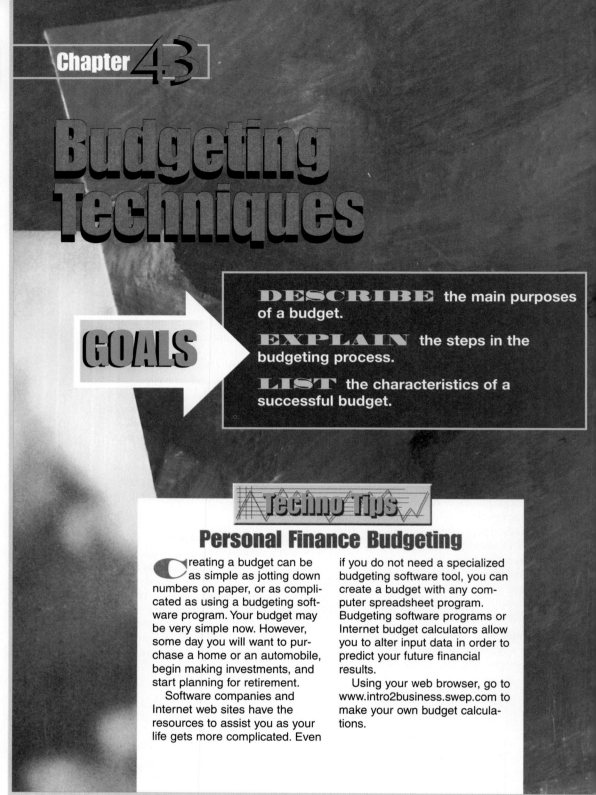

Chapter **43**

Budgeting Techniques

GOALS

DESCRIBE the main purposes of a budget.

EXPLAIN the steps in the budgeting process.

LIST the characteristics of a successful budget.

Techno Tips
Personal Finance Budgeting

Creating a budget can be as simple as jotting down numbers on paper, or as complicated as using a budgeting software program. Your budget may be very simple now. However, some day you will want to purchase a home or an automobile, begin making investments, and start planning for retirement.

Software companies and Internet web sites have the resources to assist you as your life gets more complicated. Even if you do not need a specialized budgeting software tool, you can create a budget with any computer spreadsheet program. Budgeting software programs or Internet budget calculators allow you to alter input data in order to predict your future financial results.

Using your web browser, go to www.intro2business.swep.com to make your own budget calculations.

Students need to know the latest technologies and develop cutting edge Internet skills for use in current jobs, future careers, or in their homes. TechnoTips introduces students to today's cutting edge technologies and provides them with important Internet skills. Feature topics concentrate on Internet-specific technologies and computer or other hi-tech innovations for use by businesses and consumers. At the www.intro2business.swep.com web site, students can complete the activity for this chapter.

Jing Fang is a Chinese American who has been practicing his Chinese through written communication with his relatives in Hong Kong. He also has taken several business courses in high school. Jing is preparing for an eventual career in international business in the Pacific Rim countries.

"I can't wait to go to Taiwan next summer! But the trip is going to cost me a fortune! The basics of air transportation, housing, food, and passport will cost $4,000. My parents have agreed to pay half. Fortunately for me, I developed a plan for saving money for this trip. I have well over the $4,000 I need to go to Taiwan. It's going to be a great experience. Hey Josh, why don't you go with me?"

"Are you kidding? I am not as disciplined as you! I would never be able to save enough money. You are a pro at managing money. Maybe you can give me a few tips."

A BUDGET

A **budget** allows you to meet your personal goals with a system of saving and wise spending. By developing a specific plan for saving and spending income, you will be able to make wise and satisfying personal economic decisions. The main purposes of a budget are to help you

1. live within your income,
2. achieve your financial goals,
3. buy wisely,
4. avoid credit problems,
5. plan for financial emergencies, and
6. develop good money management skills.

Having a written budget is an important phase of successful money management.

Your budget may be a simple record of how much money you make, how much you plan to spend, and how much you want to save. Or, your budget may be a more detailed record that includes specific amounts to be spent in categories such as food, clothing, and transportation. A good budget should take very little of your time, but it should be specific enough to provide needed information on your spending and savings plans.

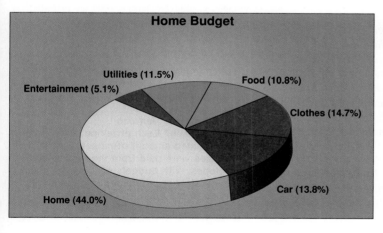

Home Budget

- Utilities (11.5%)
- Entertainment (5.1%)
- Food (10.8%)
- Clothes (14.7%)
- Car (13.8%)
- Home (44.0%)

In what ways could establishing a budget help you achieve your financial goals?

Chapter 43 *Budgeting Techniques* **589**

MOTIVATE

PURPOSE Provide a purpose for students as they read the chapter. Guide them into the importance of the budgeting process. Ask what they think they will learn. Direct students to skim the chapter, looking at photos, reading captions, and noting main headings. The goals at the beginning of each chapter provide a valuable tool for having students pinpoint main ideas. The tasks required by the goals are signaled in the first word. Some emphasize information collection ("Identify," "List"), while others call for description ("Explain," "Describe"). Ask students to look through all the goals and note the first word of each. Then ask students to state the purpose of studying this chapter.

TEACH/APPLY

MAKE CONNECTIONS Begin the class discussing the importance of budgeting one's money. Review the main purposes for a budget: (1) live within your income, (2) achieve your financial goals, (3) buy wisely, (4) avoid credit problems, (5) plan for financial emergencies, and (6) develop good money management skills. Explain that the budgeting process of (1) setting financial goals, (2) planning budget categories, (3) maintaining financial records, and (4) evaluating your budget are the keys to successful money management. Using PowerPoint 43-2, *A Budget,* explain a budget form. Discuss the characteristics of a successful budget—realistic, flexible, evaluated regularly, well planned and

FOCUS ON REAL LIFE

In the last chapter, students learned about the basics of money management. In this chapter, they will be applying what was learned through the actual budgeting process. Ask students for a definition of a budget. Does their family use a budget?

clearly communicated to those involved, and in a simple format.

TRY THIS/GUIDED PRACTICE
Using PowerPoint 43-2, *A Budget*, as a handout, walk students through the preparation of their own budget.

EXPLORE THIS/INDEPENDENT PRACTICE Before assigning independent practice material for any chapter, students should be expected to read the chapter material carefully. In view of the fact that all students vary widely in their ability to read effectively, it is advisable to have the students read the entire chapter, or sections thereof, silently in class if the material has not been previously read in connection with homework assignments.

The Chapter Review questions at the end of the chapter vary in level of difficulty. For a basic assignment, consider Develop Your Business Language and Review Your Reading. For an average assignment, consider the basic assignment plus Communicate Business Concepts and Calculate Business Data. For an enhanced assignment, try the average assignment plus Technology Application and Decision-Making Strategies.

ASSESS

Review the goals at the beginning of the chapter and the Business Notes at the end of the chapter. Have students respond orally or in writing to each restated as a question. For students who may have difficulty providing answers, assign the reteaching activities that follow.

THE BUDGETING PROCESS

The process of creating and using a budget involves

1. setting financial goals,
2. planning budget categories,
3. maintaining financial records, and
4. evaluating your budget.

These steps can be used by any individual, family, or organization to assist them in using available financial resources.

Setting Financial Goals
Establishing financial goals is the first step of any financial strategy. Financial goals help you decide where you would like to be financially and develop your budget accordingly. Writing down your short-term and long-term goals will help assist you in deciding how you want to spend and save your money. If your goals include going to college, your budget will require more for savings. If you are currently working at a job that requires you to spend a large portion of your income for transportation, you are likely to budget more for transportation.

Using personal financial statements can also help you develop financial goals. Your balance sheet presents your current financial position. A cash flow statement reports how you have spent your money over a certain time period, such as a month. By reviewing these documents you can decide where you would like to be financially and develop your budget accordingly.

Planning Budget Categories
Almost all financial advisers recommend that an amount be set aside for savings as the first

NET FACTS

Internet hosts use a language called TCP/IP, Transmission Control Protocol/Internet Protocol. TCP keeps track of every part of a transmitted message or file; IP is like an address label that makes sure a message or file reaches the correct user.

component of a budget. If savings are not considered first, other expenses may use all of the available income and leave nothing for future goals. After savings, two other types of living expenses must be considered: fixed and variable expenses. **Fixed expenses** are costs that occur regularly and are for the same amount each time. Examples of fixed expenses are rent, mortgage payments, and insurance premiums.

Variable expenses are living costs involving differing amounts each time and are usually more difficult to estimate than fixed costs. These types of expenses include food, clothing, and utilities such as telephone and electricity. Certain types of variable expenses, such as medical and dental costs, may occur less frequently and may be large when they do occur. Such expenses must be provided for in the budget. If budget categories are not created for these variable expenses, bills for

A once popular system of family budgeting required envelopes marked with labels such as "Food," "Housing," and "Automobile Expenses." Each envelope contained the budgeted amount of money, and expenses were paid from the money in the envelopes. With budgets of this type, there was the danger of keeping large amounts of cash in the home to cover expenses.

Net Facts provides information and definitions of terms for the Internet. The more information that students have about the Internet, the better equipped they will be to use this resource. In the Internet Activity Masters, there is an Internet Activity Worksheet for each unit. You can use these activities to give students experience with finding information online. Options for assigning this activity are as follows:

1. **Provide students with a list of addresses for this activity,**
2. **Assign students to conduct their own searches, or**
3. **Use the addresses on the Internet Activity Worksheet.**
   You should complete the activity yourself before assigning it to resolve any discrepancies that may arise.

these items could result in using up a large part of your savings.

The amount budgeted for savings and other expenditures is referred to as an **allowance**. This is the amount of money you plan to use for a certain budget category, including applicable sales taxes. While the budget categories can vary for different situations, distribution of savings and expenditures are often classified under eight main divisions:

1. *Savings.* Savings accounts, government bonds, stocks, and other investments.

2. *Food.* Food eaten at home and meals eaten away from home.

3. *Clothing.* Clothing, shoes, dry cleaning, sewing supplies, and repairs.

4. *Household.* Rent, mortgage payments, taxes, insurance, gas, electricity, fuel oil, telephone, water, household furnishings, household supplies, painting, and repairs.

5. *Transportation.* Automobile payments, insurance, automobile upkeep and operating costs, public transportation fares, and auto and drivers' licenses.

6. *Health and personal care.* Medical and dental expenses, medications, eyeglasses, hospital and nursing expenses, accident and health insurance, hair care costs, and children's allowances.

7. *Recreation and education.* Books, magazines, newspapers, theater tickets, concerts, vacations, school expenses, hobbies, radio, television, musical instruments, computer software, and club dues.

8. *Gifts and contributions.* Donations to church, charitable contributions, and personal gifts.

The logical question at this point is, "How much should I set aside for each category?" Planned spending for various budget categories will depend on income, family size, ages of children, the current cost of living in your area, and work-related expenses, as well as personal values, needs, and goals.

A cash flow statement can help you develop budget categories. This financial statement reports the categories in which your money has been spent and provides a basis for your budget. Other assistance for developing a budget can come from government reports on family spending or from articles in personal finance magazines, such as *Kiplinger's* and *Money*. Your budget should consider estimates for future

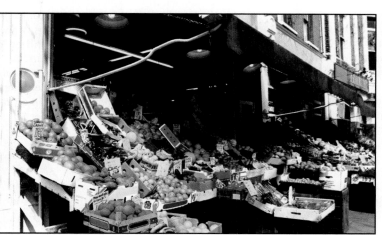

What do you think are the most important budget categories for most people?

Enrichment activities may also be assigned where appropriate.

1. What are the main purposes of a budget? (Answer: Budgets help you (1) live within your income, (2) achieve your financial goals, (3) buy wisely, (4) avoid credit problems, (5) plan for financial emergencies, and (6) develop good money management skills. Having a written budget is an important phase of successful money management.)

2. What are the steps in the budgeting process? (Answer: Setting financial goals, planning budget categories, maintaining financial records, and evaluating your budget.)

3. How can you tell if a budget is successful? (Answer: It will be realistic, flexible, evaluated regularly, well planned and clearly communicated to those involved, and in a simple format.)

RETEACH

Write the main purposes of a budget (live within your income, achieve your financial goals, buy wisely, avoid credit problems, plan for financial emergencies, and develop good money management skills) on the board. Review the meaning of each. Use PowerPoint 43-4, *Budgeting Process*, to emphasize the steps in the budgeting process. Use PowerPoint 43-6, *Characteristics of a Successful Budget*, to review the results of a successful budget. Another suggestion is to give each student $1,000 in play money, or any amount you determine is appropriate. Explain to students that they are still in school, have been given this amount of money,

Basic Skill–Speaking

SCANS

Before speaking to a group, students should know their audience, plan their presentation, rehearse, then make the presentation. Discuss characteristics of an audience and how that audience plays a role in the performance of the speaker. Developing a speech through an outline is an excellent planning tool, and every speech should have an introduction, body,

and conclusion. Then discuss the rehearsal process and its purpose. As this unit of study is budgeting, assign several students the topic of The Importance of Budgeting for a High School Student to prepare and present a speech. Give students the Student Activity Worksheet, Basic Skills—Speaking, in the School-To-Work/SCANS Activity Masters.

and will be living on their own for a month. Assign budgeting categories such as rent, automobile, food, etc. Students should check newspaper advertisements for rent expense, determine an appropriate amount for gas, etc., and complete the budget.

ENRICH

Direct students to read the Technological Perspectives in this chapter. Have students complete a real budget based on their allowance or earnings from a job.

SUMMARIZE

Direct students to create a customized budget form that fits their particular needs.

EVALUATE

- Assign Activities and Projects for Chapter 43.
- Administer the printed test or ExamView for Chapter 43.
- Assign School-To-Work/SCANS portfolio activities for Unit 12.

FAMILY BUDGET FOR ONE MONTH

Chung Household				
Monthly Budget				
January, 20__				
Estimated Inc.			Estimated Exp.	
Manuel's Net Inc.	$2,225		Savings	$1,225
Lydia's Net Inc.	$2,350		Food	$600
			Clothing	$275
			Household	$925
			Transportation	$675
			Health & Personal	$250
			Recreation & Edu.	$400
			Gifts & Contributions	$225
Total Income	$4,575		Total Savings & Exp.	$4,575

FIGURE 43-1 What percentage of income have the Chungs budgeted for savings? Do you think that's enough?

income and living expenses. The Chung household's budget, as shown in Figure 43-1, is an example of a family budget for one month.

Maintaining Financial Records

After planning a budget, individuals and families should set up an income and expenditure record to find out if their plan is working. An example is shown in Figure 43-2. The first line of this report shows the monthly income available to the family ($4,575.00 after taxes and other paycheck deductions) and the budget allowances for each category.

The first payment entry of the month was for money put into a savings account. By setting aside that amount first, the Chungs could be sure of saving part of their income. Entries for expenditures were recorded each Saturday and at the end of the month, except for especially large payments which were recorded immediately. Since the family pays most bills by check, a checkbook is an easy reference for the information needed to prepare the income and expenditure record. Incomes were entered on the days they were received, and all columns were totaled at the end of the month.

Evaluating Your Budget

At the end of the month, it is necessary to compare actual spending with the budgeted amounts. Any difference between these two amounts is called a **budget variance**. If actual spending is greater than planned spending, such as for the Chungs' Household category, it is referred to as a *deficit*. When actual spending is less than the budgeted amount, as with their Food category, a surplus occurs. A category-by-category comparison allows you to find areas where changes in the budget may be appropriate.

A variance in the actual amount spent and the budgeted amount does not automatically mean a change in your spending plan is necessary. Your budgeted amount may still be appropriate with a slight deficit or surplus occurring every couple of months in certain categories. However, if you expect necessary continued higher or lower spending in a certain category, a change in your budget is probably needed.

CHARACTERISTICS OF A SUCCESSFUL BUDGET

There are several characteristics of a good budget. A successful budget:

TEACHING STRATEGIES

Teams

Student Team Reading/Student Team Writing is an instructional method in which students use cooperative learning in peer groups. When using this instructional method, students are assigned to teams with four members each. The teams should be mixed in performance level, gender, and culture. Assign this chapter for the teams to read. Assign the teams to then write a summary of the chapter in their own words. The teams should produce a written plan, draft, and then a final paper as a team. (Note: As a supplemental activity, you may wish to distribute the Student Activity Worksheet, Workplace Competencies—Interpersonal Skills, in the School-To-Work/SCANS Activity Masters, to serve as guidelines for team development.)

HOUSEHOLD INCOME AND EXPENDITURES FOR ONE MONTH

Chung Household
Income and Expense Record

Date		Explanation	Totals		Savings	Distribution of Savings and Expenditures						
			Receipts	Payments		Food	Clothing	Household	Transpor.	Health/Per.	Rec. & Edu.	Gifts & Con.
		Budget	$4,575.00	$1,225.00	$1,225.00	$600.00	$275.00	$925.00	$675.00	$250.00	$400.00	$225.00
January	1	Balance	$1,300.00									
		Manuel's net income	$1,112.50									
		Lydia's net income	$1,175.00									
	2			$1,225.00	$1,225.00							
	7			$535.00		$110.00	$70.00	$50.00	$55.00	$50.00	$125.00	$75.00
	14			$455.00		$130.00	$45.00	$50.00	$50.00	$100.00	$45.00	$35.00
	15	Manuel's net income	$1,112.50									
		Lydia's net income	$1,175.00									
	17	Mortgage payment		$700.00				$700.00				
	21	Car payment		$425.00					$425.00			
	22			$430.00		$100.00	$80.00	$50.00	$40.00		$80.00	
	29			$600.00		$150.00	$80.00	$120.00	$50.00	$105.00	$45.00	$50.00
	31	Totals	$5,875.00	$4,370.00	$1,225.00	$490.00	$275.00	$970.00	$620.00	$255.00	$295.00	$240.00
February	1	Balance*	$1,505.00									

*Balance = January's total receipts − total payments ($5,875.00 − $4,370.00)

FIGURE 43-2 In which categories did the Chungs' expenditures exceed the amount they had budgeted? In which were they less than the amount budgeted?

Workplace Competencies—Resources

All of us allocate our resources—time, money, people, and materials—on a daily basis. By acquiring competence at allocating resources, students learn to perform basic functions of management—planning, organizing, and controlling. Money is an important resource that many people have difficulty allocating. We can guide our students and teach them how to allocate money by helping them understand that budgets are important, cost projections are necessary, and that future budgets are based on these projections. Use the Student Activity Worksheet, Workplace Competencies, as a guideline for discussion of how students can allocate their money. Students can try budgeting through completion of the Technology Application problems in Chapter Review.

SCANS

1. **Must be realistic.** It should reflect your current income and planned spending.

2. **Should be flexible.** When unexpected expenses arise, your spending plan should be able to handle these living costs.

3. **Should be evaluated regularly.** Every few months, an individual or family should evaluate the budget to determine whether it still is appropriate.

4. **Must be well planned and clearly communicated to those involved.** All members of a family should discuss financial goals, wants and needs, and plans for spending. In addition, the best spending plan should be written so that all affected by it can review its components.

5. **Should have a simple format.** If it is too detailed and difficult to understand, family members may not be willing to use the spending plan.

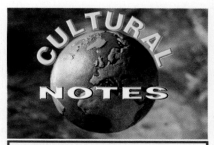

Cultural and social factors (such as language, education, and customs) affect the way international business is conducted. In some cultures, customs such as hand-shaking are acceptable behaviors for greeting people, while in other cultures bowing is the acceptable behavior.

Many software programs have a budgeting feature that allows you to develop a budget,

TECHNOLOGICAL PERSPECTIVES

Budgeting Software

The ritual of using a pencil, a note pad, and a ruler to develop a budget is almost unnecessary in this computer age. With the introduction of money management and budgeting software, you can put the manual supplies away!

Software is now available that allows you to create your own personal budget. Then, as time progresses, the software actually tracks your income and actual expenses and then compares these figures to what you have budgeted in each income and expense category. Reports can then be developed which show how well you are staying within your budget. Advanced budgeting software may also provide tips from America's leading financial authorities, tools for home inventory management, tax preparing advice, and

investment tracking to make the user more efficient in budgeting.

Budgeting software may also provide the capabilities of keeping track of your checking account and actually printing checks. Some software will also allow you to pay your bills by telephone through a bill-paying service which the computer is linked, via a modem.

Budgeting software can make personal record keeping easy for almost any novice!

Critical Thinking
1. What personal advantages could budgeting software provide you?
2. What kinds of reports do you think budgeting software could produce?

TECHNOLOGICAL PERSPECTIVES

Using techniques to acquire and apply new knowledge and skills is an important lifetime skill all employees should possess. Knowing how to use techniques and apply them when appropriate is a skill that employers are looking for.

Students are usually more acquainted with software than we

are! Many students are probably using some type of budgeting or money management software at home. Ask with which types of software students are acquainted.

CRITICAL THINKING
1. Help budget money for a car, college, other goals.
2. Financial reports such as income statement, balance sheet, owner's equity statement, bank reconciliation, etc.

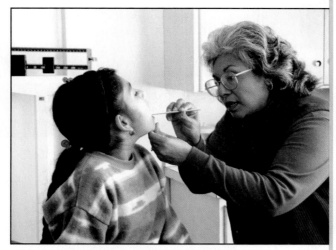

How much would your budget allow for unexpected expenses like medical bills?

keep track of your accounts, aid in financial planning, and pay your bills. Such software often can be linked to income tax software programs so annual tax forms can be completed in less time than if the tax forms had to be completed by hand.

While handwritten or software-produced budgets are most common, and usually the most appropriate, some people believe a checkbook is an effective budgeting system. However, a checking account does not serve the purpose of planning for spending. Your checks are a record of purchases and paid bills, but you still need a plan for using income. Others say they keep their budgets in their heads rather than on paper. This simple system may work for an individual with limited income and few financial obligations, but a family with a larger income and more living expenses would find it ineffective. A person with a mental budget is also in danger of forgetting how much is to be spent or has been spent on certain items.

E-Commerce for Personal Financial Planning

Each day you make hundreds of decisions. Some choices are simple, such as what to wear and to eat, while others are more complex. Many of your more detailed decisions involve money, such as buying a car, renting an apartment, purchasing insurance, paying for college, and saving for retirement.

The Internet offers many opportunities for improved financial planning decisions. Money management information, financial planning advisors, and tax planning assistance are just a few of the online services available for making money choices.

Money management software offered by various companies can also enhance your financial planning activities. These budgeting and bill-payment programs allow consumers to record, summarize, and analyze personal financial data. The software also links to various web sites to obtain current information as well as to make payments online.

Critical Thinking

Conduct an Internet search on "personal financial planning." Obtain information about wise financial planning actions and developing an online personal financial plan. Prepare a list of guidelines people should follow when planning and using personal financial resources.

Financial Planning Web Sites
Money management and financial planning assistance at www.financenter.com
Personal finance assistance at www.moneycentral.msn.com
Personal financial planning information at www.quicken.com
Kiplinger Personal Finance magazine at www.kiplinger.com

TEACHING STRATEGIES

Alternate Modalities
Kinesthetic Learner

Kinesthetic learners learn best by taking an active part in the instruction. When presenting budgeting to a kinesthetic learner, have the student make a list on the overhead of the main eight divisions of the budget based on student/teacher discussion.

REVIEW YOUR READING

1. Budgets help a person (1) live within his or her income, (2) achieve financial goals, (3) buy wisely, (4) avoid credit problems, (5) plan for financial emergencies, and (6) develop good money management skills.
2. Set financial goals, plan budget categories, maintain financial records, and evaluate your budget.
3. They help you decide where you would like to be financially and develop your budget accordingly.
4. Rent, mortgage payments, and insurance premiums.
5. These expenditures will vary from month to month.
6. Savings, food, clothing, household, transportation, health and personal care, recreation and education, and gifts and contributions.
7. Income, family size, ages of children, the current cost of living in your area, work-related expenses, and personal values, needs, and goals.
8. A budget variance will not automatically mean a need to revise your spending plan. If you expect continued higher or lower spending in a certain category, however, a change in your budget probably is needed.
9. A successful budget will be realistic, flexible, evaluated regularly, well planned and clearly communicated to those involved, and in a simple format.
10. Unless the budget is in writing, a person is in danger of forgetting how much is to be spent or has been spent on certain items.

COMMUNICATE BUSINESS CONCEPTS

11. If an individual or family clearly identifies needs when developing a budget and spending available income, they can more easily reduce wasteful spending and more quickly achieve financial goals.
12. People can make a close estimate of future income and expenditures by keeping a careful record of income and expenditures over a period of several weeks or months. No one knows for certain what his or her income and

596

BUSINESS NOTES

1. The main purposes of a budget are to help you live within your income, achieve your financial goals, buy wisely, avoid credit problems, plan for financial emergencies, and develop good money management skills. Having a written budget is an important phase of successful money management.

2. The process of creating and using a budget involves setting financial goals, planning budget categories, maintaining financial records, and evaluating your budget.

3. A successful budget will be realistic, flexible, evaluated regularly, well planned and clearly communicated to those involved, and in a simple format.

REVIEW YOUR READING

1. What are the six main purposes of a budget?
2. List the steps involved in the budgeting process.
3. How are financial goals important to budgeting?
4. Name some examples of fixed expenses.
5. Why are variable expenses more difficult to budget for than fixed expenses?
6. What are the eight budget categories that usually appear under Distribution of Savings and Expenditures?
7. What factors influence the amount set aside for various budget categories?
8. Does a budget variance mean that you should change your spending plan?
9. What are the characteristics of a successful budget?
10. Why should a budget be in writing?

COMMUNICATE BUSINESS CONCEPTS

11. "If you only spend money on things you really need, you will always have money for the things you really want." Do you agree with this statement? Explain your answer.
12. Some people claim that living by a budget is too structured and restrictive. That is, they do not like to live such a planned and strict economic life. What would you say to those individuals who have that point of view in order to convince them that budgets can be helpful to everyone?
13. Every week Chris Thorson puts any amount he has not spent during the week into a savings account. If he needs more money than he has during a week, he withdraws it from his savings. Is Chris following a good money management plan? Explain.
14. Consider a family of four people: the mother, a supermarket manager; the father, a department store salesperson; and two children, ages 14 and 11.
    a. List four fixed expenses that this family would likely have each month.
    b. What are some variable expenses that they are likely to have?
    c. How are the family's expenses different from those of other families with younger children or no children?

expenditures will be; all budgets are based on estimates. It is correct that income and expenditures are often uncertain, but people generally are better off by having a guideline to prevent financial problems in the future.

13. Chris Thorson's plan is not an example of good money management. Transferring excess amounts to savings and then spending money out of savings causes extra record keeping and allows no possibility for developing good savings habits. If Chris finds that he usually needs more money than he has budgeted, he could change his budget allowances or reduce his spending.

14. (a) Typical fixed expenses might include rent or mortgage payment, insurance premiums, credit payments, cable television fee, or a monthly train ticket for getting to and from work. (b) Variable expenses could include food, telephone, clothing, medical expenses, gifts, and donations. (c) A family with younger children might require spending for child care services while the parents work; a couple without children would not have these types of expenses.

DEVELOP YOUR BUSINESS LANGUAGE

For each numbered item, find the term that has the same meaning.

15. Costs that occur regularly and are for the same amount each time.

16. The amount budgeted for savings and other expenditures.

17. A plan that allows you to meet your personal goals with a system of saving and wise spending.

18. Living costs involving differing amounts each time.

19. A difference between actual spending and planned spending.

KEY TERMS
allowance
budget
budget variance
fixed expenses
variable expenses

DECISION-MAKING STRATEGIES

Allison was new to budgeting. She appreciated the concepts and was attempting to employ them in her personal financial life. In fact, she was ready to set up a budget to achieve her vision and goals. She was, however, having difficulty with the idea of fixed and variable expenses. As she explained to her teacher, "Any expense can be variable."

20. What do you think she meant by this statement?

21. How would you explain to Allison the difference between fixed and variable expenses?

CALCULATE BUSINESS DATA

22. Mary and Fred James budgeted $340 a month for groceries. During the month, they spent $87, $93, $38, $61, and $52 at the supermarket.

   a. What was the total amount spent for food?

   b. Did Mary and Fred have a budget deficit or surplus? What was the amount?

23. You are currently budgeting $750 per year for insurance costs, and you expect the premiums to increase by 7 percent for next year. How much should you budget for insurance next year?

24. A family has $2,600 to spend each month. They plan to spend $625 on food, $250 on clothing, $910 on rent, $300 on transportation, and want to save $200.

   a. What percentage does the family plan to spend on each item?

   b. How much does the family have available to budget for other living expenses?

25. John was considering the purchase of a motor-cycle. He had enough money for the purchase price but was concerned about his ability to budget for and pay for operating costs. The advertisement promised the motorcycle could go approximately 35 kilometers on a liter of gasoline. If gasoline cost $1.35 per gallon, how many dollars should John budget for travel 630 miles each week to and from his place of employment?

DEVELOP YOUR BUSINESS LANGUAGE

15. fixed expenses
16. allowance
17. budget
18. variable expenses
19. budget variance

DECISION-MAKING STRATEGIES

20. Technically, of course, Allison may be correct. What one normally thought of as fixed expenses can go up or down—on occasion. Rent, insurance, and even mortgage payments can go up and (sometimes) down.

21. Fixed costs are more predictable than variable costs. Basically, you know what your rent, auto, and insurance payments usually are for a certain time period. However, the cost of groceries, gasoline, and entertainment can change from day to day.

CALCULATE BUSINESS DATA

22. (a) $87 + $93 + $38 + $61 + $52 = $331 (b) $21 budget surplus ($340 − $331)

23. $802.50 = ($750 × 1.07%)

24. 24% for food ($625 ÷ $2,600); 10% for clothing ($250 ÷ $2,600); 35% for rent ($910 ÷ $2,600); 12% for transportation ($300 ÷ $2,600); 8% for savings ($200 ÷ $2,600) (b) $625 + $250 + $910 + $300 + $200 = $2,285; $2,600 − $2,285 = $315

25. 35 km × 0.6 = 21 miles per liter; 630 ÷ 21 = 30 liters to travel 630 miles; 30L × 0.26 = 7.8 gallons; 7.8 × $1.35 = $10.53

In this activity, students use a computer to solve a business problem using a file that is provided on the data CD that accompanies *Intro to Business*. Instructions for using the data CD are included in a **README** file on the disk. Solutions are provided on the Instructor's Resource CD.

TECHNOLOGY APPLICATION

Using the *Intro to Business* Data CD and your spreadsheet program software, select problem CH43. After the problem appears on your screen, complete the following activities. After you have completed each step, display or print the completed spreadsheet for each activity. If you do not have a printer available, answer the questions before you leave the computer.

26. In the Percent column, enter formulas to show each item as a percent of Total Estimated Income. Format the results as percentages with one decimal place. Answer the following questions:

    a. What is the percentage of Total Estimated Income budgeted for savings?

    b. What is the percentage of Total Estimated Income budgeted for recreation?

27. In the Difference column, enter formulas to calculate Actual minus Budget. Format the results as currency with two decimal places. Answer the following questions:

    a. How many expenditures had actual spending greater than budget?

    b. Which expenditure from Question a. has the largest difference?

28. What if your actual Net Income increased to $5,000? Copy the budget from Problem 27 to another part of the spreadsheet. Enter the new amount of actual Net Income. Answer the following questions:

    a. What is the new difference between actual Total Income and budgeted Total Income?

    b. What is the new amount of actual Savings?

Optional: Using the spreadsheet from Problem 27, create a bar chart comparing budgeted expenditures to actual expenditures. Repeat for Problem 28.

Using spreadsheet software and the eight expense classifications outlined in the chapter, prepare a monthly budget based on your personal allowance and/or your expected earnings from a job or jobs. Then record your actual expenditures for one month, and compare your cash inflows and expenditures to your budgeted amounts.

29. For which classifications did you have a deficit? For which classifications did you have a surplus?

30. For which classifications did the variance exceed 10 percent of the amount budgeted?

31. Based on your actual inflows and expenditures, what changes would you now make to your budget to make it better reflect your expected future inflows and expenditures?

INTERNATIONAL TRADE AGENCIES

Some countries believe in a free market for international trade. Others impose trade barriers to protect their domestic economies. The General Agreement on Tariffs and Trade (GATT) was created to negotiate these types of differences among nations. This agreement was originally negotiated in 1947 and started operations in 1948 with about 20 countries. Today, the membership of GATT involves more than 120 countries. The overall goals of GATT are to promote international trade through negotiation and to make world trade secure among nations.

Recent GATT negotiations included guidelines for the protection of intellectual property rights. GATT is continually changing as additional countries join the program and new trade agreements are negotiated.

The United Nations, an international organization that promotes cooperation among countries, is actively involved in global business. Economic development of less-developed countries is a major concern of the United Nations. The organization also assists businesses in obtaining loans, sets safety standards for products sold internationally, regulates international telecommunications, and promotes cooperation among postal services in different countries. Economic and political information about the nations of the world may also be obtained from the United Nations.

The International Court of Justice, established in 1946, settles disputes between nations when both nations request this service. Decisions are based on written evidence, as no jury is used. Additional evidence may be requested before a decision is rendered. This court also advises the United Nations on various aspects of international law.

> **International organizations such as GATT and the United Nations are actively involved in global business.**

CRITICAL THINKING

1. Describe various trade situations that might result in a difference of opinion between companies in different countries. How might this dispute be resolved? What actions might be taken to prevent this type of difficulty in the future?

2. Go to the web site of the United Nations. Prepare a short oral report that describes one of the services of the United Nations that could be of value to a person working for an international company.

Most students will either work with international clients or compete against businesses that do. Global Navigator introduces students to issues integral to working with international businesses. Key concepts and challenges faced by international businesses are presented, followed by two Critical Thinking questions that require students to analyze what they have learned.

This Global Navigator feature focuses on the three principal international institutions that, among other tasks, promote free trade. GATT provides an international legal framework for permissible trade policies; the UN provides organizational support for international cooperation; and the International Court of Justice provides a forum for adjudicating trade disputes.

CRITICAL THINKING

1. Situations will vary. Resolution may involve informal give-and-take, formal negotiations, arbitration, or legal proceedings.
2. Answers will vary, as the UN provides scores of such services.

Chapter 43 *Budgeting Techniques* 599

Chapter 44

The steps of financial planning are discussed, which include analyzing current financial condition, developing goals, creating a financial plan, implementing the plan, and frequently evaluating and revising the financial plan.

Resources for Teachers
- Lesson Plans
- School-To-Work/SCANS Activity Masters
- Spanish Resources
- Instructor's Resource CD

Assessment
- Chapter and Unit Tests, Ch. 44
- ExamView, Ch. 44

Media/Technology
- Applying Technology Data CD
- PowerPoint slides
- Business Connection CD
- Videotape

Activity Masters and Workbooks
- Activities and Projects, Ch. 44
- Internet Activity Masters
- Business Math Activity Masters
- Communications Activity Masters
- International Business Activity Masters
- Ethics Activity Masters

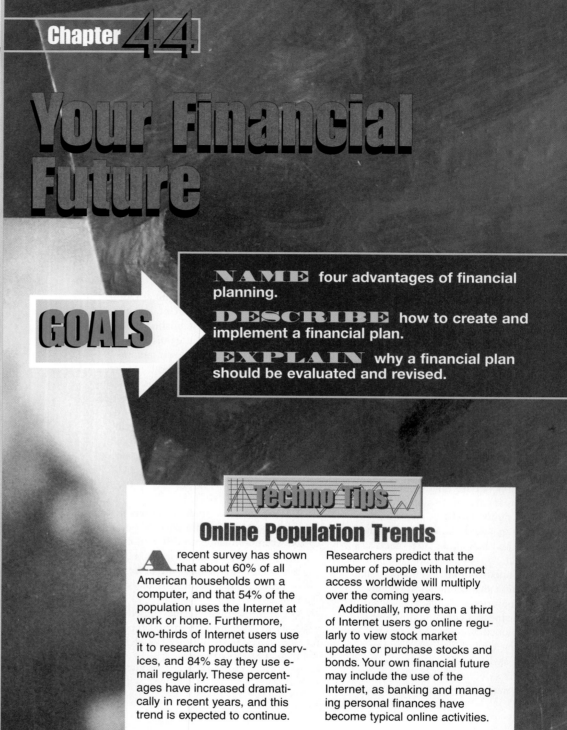

Your Financial Future

GOALS

NAME four advantages of financial planning.

DESCRIBE how to create and implement a financial plan.

EXPLAIN why a financial plan should be evaluated and revised.

Techno Tips

Online Population Trends

A recent survey has shown that about 60% of all American households own a computer, and that 54% of the population uses the Internet at work or home. Furthermore, two-thirds of Internet users use it to research products and services, and 84% say they use e-mail regularly. These percentages have increased dramatically in recent years, and this trend is expected to continue.

Researchers predict that the number of people with Internet access worldwide will multiply over the coming years.

Additionally, more than a third of Internet users go online regularly to view stock market updates or purchase stocks and bonds. Your own financial future may include the use of the Internet, as banking and managing personal finances have become typical online activities.

 Students need to know the latest technologies and develop cutting edge Internet skills for use in current jobs, future careers, or in their homes. TechnoTips introduces students to today's cutting edge technologies and provides them with important Internet skills. Feature topics concentrate on Internet-specific technologies and computer or other hi-tech innovations for use by businesses and consumers.

"Hey Gloria, are you going to the Business Speakers Series monthly luncheon on Friday?"

"I really hadn't given it much thought, Maria. Are you?"

"Yes! The speaker is from the local college and is supposed to be very dynamic and informative. The topic is financial planning, and if I am going to go to college, I need some help in planning right now! Why don't you meet me there?"

"Great idea, Maria. I always thought of financial planning as something for people out of college. But it certainly makes sense to start now! I guess if I start planning early, I can get a head start on my future!"

FINANCIAL PLANNING

In order to put into practice all that you have learned about our economy and about earning and saving money, you must have a plan. Successful coaches talk about game plans. Travel agents refer to vacation plans. Builders must have house plans. Successful consumers and businesspeople must have a financial plan. A **financial plan** is a report that summarizes your current financial condition, acknowledges your financial needs, and sets a direction for your future financial activities. **Financial planning** includes evaluating one's financial position, setting financial goals, and guiding activities and resources toward reaching those goals.

Everyone should have a carefully developed financial plan. Your financial plan should encompass all that you have learned about good money management, be developed thoughtfully, and be evaluated and updated frequently. A well-developed financial plan can make your financial life a great deal more satisfying. Ultimately, it will become a blueprint for an improved standard of living. Financial planning will offer you several specific advantages:

- Your financial uncertainties will be reduced.

- You will gain more control of your financial affairs.

- Your family or associates will have a way of knowing more specifically of your financial affairs in case there is a need for them to assume control of your finances.

- Earning, spending, protecting, and saving your resources will be more systematic.

Successful financial planning should follow these steps:

1. Analyze your current financial condition. You should create a balance sheet and cash flow statement.

2. Develop financial goals that are responsive to your vision. What short-term and long-term objectives do you have? How much money will you need, and when?

3. Next, you must create your financial plan. This activity will take the most time and require the most thought; it may also require additional help from a financial planner.

4. Implement the plan. This may involve buying or selling property or investments, moving bank accounts, acquiring insurance, or any number of financial activities.

The sooner you begin working on your financial plan, the closer you will be to attaining your goals for financial freedom. If at the age of 18 you began saving $50 a month at an interest rate of 9 percent, you will have $444,275 when you reach the age of 65.

FOCUS ON REAL LIFE

In the last chapter, students learned budgeting techniques. They will now learn how to apply those techniques and about the actual financial planning process. Ask students if their parents have a financial planner. Does anyone know what a financial planner does?

MOTIVATE

PURPOSE Provide a purpose for students as they read the chapter. Guide them into the importance of financial planning. Why is it important to them? Ask what they think they will learn. Direct students to skim the chapter, looking at photos, reading captions, noting main headings. The goals at the beginning of each chapter provide a valuable tool for having students pinpoint main ideas. The tasks required by the goals are signaled in the first word. Some emphasize information collection ("Identify," "List"), while others call for description ("Explain," "Describe"). Ask students to look through all the goals and note the first word of each. Then ask students to state the purpose of studying this chapter.

TEACH/APPLY

MAKE CONNECTIONS Begin the class by discussing the importance of financial planning and how it relates to them. Students need to do some basic planning if they are going to college or even out to earn a living. Use PowerPoint 44-2, *Successful Financial Planning,* and review the basic steps. Explain a financial inventory and how important it is to keep good records. Ask students if they know the difference between short-term goals and long-term goals. Ask for suggestions of each and write them on the board. Develop a discussion with your students about ways to increase income. Explain how income can be insured and why it is important to do so. Ask if they are aware of planning for the future and if their parents have an IRA or annuity. Emphasize the importance of evaluating any plan after a period of time to make sure it is still current and meets the goals that have been set.

TRY THIS/GUIDED PRACTICE
Use PowerPoint 44-4, *Setting Financial Goals,* as a handout. Guide students through the process of setting short-term and long-term goals.

EXPLORE THIS/INDEPENDENT PRACTICE Before assigning independent practice material for any chapter, students should be expected to read the chapter material carefully. In view of the fact that students vary widely in their ability to read effectively, it is advisable to have the students read the entire chapter, or sections thereof, silently in class if the material has not been previously read in connection with homework.

The Chapter Review questions at the end of the chapter vary in level of difficulty. For a basic assignment, consider Develop Your Business Language and Review Your Reading. For an average assignment, consider the basic assignment plus Communicate Business Concepts and Calculate Business Data. For an enhanced assignment, try the average assignment plus Technology Application and Decision-Making Strategies.

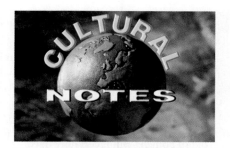

5. Finally, as time goes on, you will frequently evaluate and revise your financial plan.

DETERMINING YOUR FINANCIAL CONDITION

The first step in determining your financial condition is usually a careful and honest analysis of where you are by taking a financial inventory. This is then followed by creating a personal filing system to keep track of important records.

Financial Inventory

A financial inventory is a lot like a physician giving you a physical examination. As the doctor's exam requires an assessment of your health, your financial inventory includes a careful appraisal of your finances. A financial inventory is most frequently completed through the use of the personal balance sheet and cash flow statement and should be done at least once each year. It will provide you with a more orderly financial life as well as serve as an important activity in financial planning. You must determine your current

You can purchase tax-free investments. The money earned on tax-free investments can be free from both state and federal income taxes.

financial position in terms of income, savings, investments, property, living expenses, insurance, and money owed. This step is thought by many to be a prerequisite to the development of financial goals.

Personal Financial Filing System

In order to keep your financial inventory current and to keep all of your records orderly and within easy reach, you will need a personal financial filing system. Well-organized files are valuable to financial planning. These files should contain all of the documents and records associated with such things as contracts, bills, receipts, bank balances, and legal papers. The contents of these files will become an invaluable resource to you as you progress with your financial planning.

SETTING FINANCIAL GOALS

Once you have a clear understanding of your financial condition, you will be able to develop a realistic set of financial goals. Financial goals may be short-term or long-term objectives and are usually stated in dollar amounts. Examples of some short-term financial goals are:

- Saving $1,000 in one year.
- Purchasing a $200 bicycle in June.
- Increasing your annual income by $3,000 by your twentieth birthday.

You will notice that each goal requires that you save or acquire a specific amount of money in a specific period of time. These goals are very simple, straightforward, and relatively short-term. By contrast, long-term financial goals are often more complex and achievable over a long period of time. They might include such objectives as:

- Owning your own home by age 40.
- Taking a trip to Africa in five years.
- Receiving a retirement income equal to 50 percent of your salary at age 64.

In the process of developing and carrying out your financial plan, you will quickly dis-

---

Workplace **Competencies—Resources**

Whenever we ask others to assist us to complete a task, we are allocating human resources. Even though we aren't always conscious of how we select people to help us, we usually make those selections based on our assessment of other people's skills, their availability, and their talents. In order for students to plan their financial future, they must learn how to allocate the available human resources to help them reach their goal. Ask students how they would select a financial planner, banker, or other investment counselor. What would they base these decisions on? Explain to them that by selecting a person as a resource, they are learning to use the skill of allocating human resources based on needs, availability, and talent of that chosen person.

FYI

To determine how many years it will take your money to double if you let your investment compound, use the "Rule of 72." To use this rule, divide 72 by the interest rate on your investment. If your investment is earning a 10 percent interest rate, 72 divided by 10 = 7.2. So at a 10 percent interest rate, your money will double every 7.2 years.

cover that it is often necessary to compromise short-term goals in order to accomplish long-term ones. For example, you may have to forgo a movie to meet the long-term goal of buying a bicycle.

Financial Life Cycle

Most people's lives follow a predictable pattern called a life cycle. Each stage of life is distinguished by unique characteristics, requirements, and expectations. For example, during the teen years, people are exploring career options, developing plans for eventual independence, evaluating future financial needs and resources, and developing an understanding of the financial system. In their twenties, people are training for careers, establishing households, some are marrying, and some are having children.

The thirties and forties evolve into a different phase of life for many people. Some are marrying for the first time and having children for the first time. Some will be paying for children's education, developing retirement plans, investing, and estate planning. Then, in the fifties and sixties, people tend to guard their assets more carefully, work toward financial security, and reevaluate living arrangements.

Each of these life stages has financial matters that need attention. That attention can be provided through the development of a good financial plan. Remember, a good plan is one that is flexible and useful throughout several life cycles.

Retirement and Estate Planning

Although it seems a long time off, retirement is considered by many people to be the heart of financial goal setting. The chances are very good that you will spend many happy and healthy years in retirement. They will be

For each stage of life, what do you think are some of the major financial requirements?

Critical Thinking **Skills**-Creative Thinking

Creative thinking is consistently encouraged throughout this text. However, to encourage students to develop this skill, ask them to create their own financial plan.

involve moving your savings to an account in which you will earn a higher interest rate, buying a bond, or working more hours to earn more money.)

6. Why should a financial plan be evaluated and revised?
(Answer: It is important to view your financial plan as a fluid, changeable document that will accommodate opportunity. If your plan is not producing the expected results, you must make changes.)

RETEACH

Draw a flow chart on the board or overhead to show how financial planning relates to students. Show the five steps using student information. Write items of a financial inventory on the board. Describe short-term goals as six to twelve months and long-term goals as more than a year. Obtain actual policies on IRAs and annuities so that students can see the real thing.

ENRICH

Direct students to read the Global Perspectives in the chapter. Every state has laws regarding unemployment insurance. Assign students to investigate your state's laws to know what provisions it makes for those who are unemployed.

SUMMARIZE

Conclude the chapter by discussing the various stages a person goes through financially and how financial planning contributes to success. You might wish to ask at least two different financial planners to

happier and healthier if you have done some financial planning that results in an adequate supply of money to use during those years.

Estate planning involves the accumulation and management of property during one's lifetime and the distribution of one's property at death. It is a part of retirement planning and is an integral part of financial planning. It has two parts. The first part consists of building your estate through savings, investments, and insurance. The second consists of planning for the transfer of your estate, at your death, in the manner that you wish.

CREATING A FINANCIAL PLAN

After you have established your financial goals based on your vision, you can begin to plan for the income you will need to achieve these goals. Some may think that income is not possible to plan for or control because it is money received from someone else. To an extent that is correct, but there are aspects of income that can be planned.

You can develop strategies that will help you acquire the amount of income you want when you want it. For example, if you want more income, you might ask for a raise, become qualified for a better paying job, get an additional part-time job, or invest in securities. You can also time your income so that you have money coming in when you want it. This can be done by investing at certain times, seeking increased salary at certain times, or by asking that you be paid on cer-

GLOBAL PERSPECTIVES
Financial Future

Do you have any money invested for your future? The answer may be no right now, but someday, you will more than likely invest money so that your money can work for you. And as an investor, you will have many options from which to choose.

If you decide to invest in stocks and bonds, you may choose to invest in U.S. stock markets such as the New York Stock Exchange or the American Stock Exchange. However, there are also opportunities to make foreign investments. Foreign investments are sometimes appealing to Americans for several reasons. One reason is the possibility that the currency exchange rate of a particular county is favorable for buying stocks or bonds at a lower price so that Americans get more for their money. Another reason may be that sometimes American investors like to make foreign investments so that they diversify, or spread their investments over many different types of stocks.

Various opportunities are available to make foreign investments. One way is to purchase a specific mutual fund in the United States that invests in international companies' stock. Another way to invest internationally is to purchase an American Depository Receipt (ADR). ADRs are foreign companies' stock that is traded in U.S. markets. Another way make a foreign investment is to purchase inter-national stock directly from a specific foreign country's stock exchange. Foreign stock exchanges include London, Paris, Tokyo, Sydney, Toronto, Johannesburg, São Paulo, and Frankfurt.

Critical Thinking
1. How does the currency exchange rate affect investments?
2. How can a person in the United States buy stock directly from another country's stock exchange?

GLOBAL PERSPECTIVES

Global Perspectives gives students an opportunity to visualize the various places around the globe that are described. This feature will also describe various business practices that are different around the world.

Ask how many are familiar with foreign investments. Some parents may have an extensive investment portfolio with which their children are familiar. Students may be able to talk about some companies in which their parents have invested.

CRITICAL THINKING
1. The value of the dollar against foreign currency determines how much you can get for your money. If the currency exchange is high, you can buy more for your money than if the exchange rate is low.
2. Use a broker in the United States or call brokers in the other country directly.

NET FACTS

tain days of the month. You should develop and write a plan for generating income that is consistent with your financial goals.

Creating a financial plan is not a simple task. Doing your own financial planning requires a great deal of time, information, and patience. There are professionals called **financial planners** who can help you. A financial planner should have at least two years of training in securities, insurance, taxes, real estate, and estate planning and have passed a rigorous examination.

There are some questions you can ask to help you choose a financial planner. They are:

- What experience and training does the financial planner have?
- Is the financial planner willing to supply you with references?
- Does the financial planner have a good reputation among other financial professionals?
- What are the financial planner's fees?

A financial planner will want to ask you some questions as well. You will need to have some idea of what your financial goals are. You must be prepared to describe your financial inventory. You should be willing to share information about your income, expenditures, and savings. With this information and your cooperation, together you can create a useful financial plan.

IMPLEMENTING A FINANCIAL PLAN

Implementing your plan may involve a wide variety of actions. You may need to move your savings to an account in which you will earn a higher interest rate. You may buy a bond. Maybe you will begin to work more hours on your part-time job to earn more money. As you can see, the list of implementation possibilities is endless. However, for your plan to lead to the satisfaction of your goals, you must carry it out.

Insuring Current Income

There are some safeguards you should take to assure the success of your plan. They involve protecting your income so that it contributes to your goals. Insurance is available that will provide an income to those who fear the two most common causes of loss of income: disability and unemployment.

Disability income insurance helps replace income that is lost when you cannot work because of an illness or injury. Many different disability income policies are available. The amount of each payment, the length of the waiting period before benefits are paid, and the length of time that payments are made should be chosen on the basis of your needs. Most companies from which you can buy disability income insurance will pay up to 60 or 70 percent of your salary while you are disabled. However, before the benefits begin, there is usually a waiting period from 1 week to 90 days after you are disabled. As with other kinds of insurance, the more benefits provided, the higher the price for coverage.

One of the most important forms of income protection comes through the federal

FYI
Most disability insurance policies provide for payment at the rate of up to 60 or 70 percent of monthly earnings. In general, no income taxes are charged on disability insurance payments.

NET FACTS

come to your class. One financial planner might be from a stock brokerage or other securities firm or bank, another might be an independent financial planner. Provide them with the list of questions for selecting a financial planner as a way to generate discussion or give them each of those questions to help them outline their presentation. When they have finished, or in their absence, you may discuss with your students the advantages of employing a financial planner who is independent as opposed to

SCANS
Critical Thinking Skills-Decision Making

Decision-making skills, which include specifying goals, generating alternatives, considering risks, and evaluating and choosing the best alternative, are applied throughout every chapter in this text. Each time a student participates in a Cooperative Learning or Teams activity, decision-making skills are applied in a group situation. For Communicate Business Concepts and Decision-Making Strategies, students must specify the goal of the activity, consider risks, and evaluate the best solution before the questions can be answered. Emphasize to students how they are using decision-making techniques in their day-to-day tasks and make them aware of the skills they are developing.

one who works for a firm that sells securities.

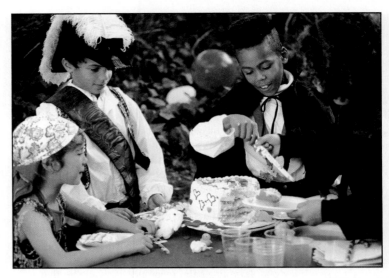

How does retirement, survivors, and disability insurance serve the dependents of workers?

government's Social Security system. The Medicare program, is one part of the Social Security system. The other part is **retirement, survivors, and disability insurance**. This part of the insurance system provides pensions to retired workers and their families, death benefits to dependents of workers who die, and benefits to disabled workers and their families. Social Security benefits are funded by payroll taxes.

Unemployment is another hazard to a financial plan. To reduce the financial hardship of unemployment, most states have an unemployment insurance program that they operate in cooperation with the federal government. **Unemployment insurance** provides cash payments for a limited time to people who are out of work for a reason other than illness. The local unemployment office will provide guidance to help you find a new job, but if no suitable job is found, you may receive payments to replace part of your lost wages.

Planning for Future Income

The success of any financial plan is largely dependent on a continuing stream of future income. Once people retire, their salaries stop, but they continue to need money to cover living expenses. Workers can insure that they will have an adequate income during their retirement years through Social Security, pensions, individual retirement accounts, and annuities with the help of their employers and the government.

Social Security During working years, employed people pay **Social Security taxes**. The taxes are deducted from the employees' paychecks. Employers match the amounts paid by their employees. Self-employed people, such as farmers and small-business owners, pay the entire tax themselves. The taxes collected are put into a special trust fund. When a worker retires, becomes disabled, or dies, monthly payments from the trust fund are made. The amount of benefits received depends to a great extent on how long a worker was employed and how much a worker earned while employed.

Those who are covered by Social Security can receive the full amount of the monthly payments to which they are entitled when they reach the appropriate age as shown in Figure 44-1. However, it is possible to retire as early as age 62 and accept lower monthly payments. Workers may be entitled to full benefits if they become disabled at any age

Age to Receive Full Social Security Benefits

Year of Birth	Full Retirement Age
1937 or earlier	65
1938	65 and 2 months
1939	65 and 4 months
1940	65 and 6 months
1941	65 and 8 months
1942	65 and 10 months
1943–54	66
1955	66 and 2 months
1956	66 and 4 months
1957	66 and 6 months
1958	66 and 8 months
1959	66 and 10 months
1960 and later	67

Source: Social Security Administration

FIGURE 44-1 In what year will you be eligible to receive full benefits?

before 65. If an insured worker dies, monthly benefits are also payable to a surviving spouse and/or dependent children.

Pensions A **pension** is a series of regular payments made to a retired worker under an organized plan. Many employers offer plans that provide monthly payments to retired workers. Similar plans are often established by professional and trade associations or unions. To qualify under most pension plans, you must work for the same organization for a minimum number of years. Many employees retire on pensions together with their Social Security benefits.

Individual retirement accounts People can also develop their own retirement income plans. The most popular of these plans is the **individual retirement account** **(IRA).** An IRA is a tax-sheltered retirement plan in which people can annually invest earnings of up to $5,000. With traditional IRAs, contributions are tax-deductible, investment gains are tax-deferred, and the funds are taxed as regular income when they are withdrawn after age $59^{1}/_2$. With a newer version called Roth IRAs, contributions are not tax-deductible, but investment gains and all funds on which taxes have been prepaid are subsequently tax-free when they are withdrawn after age $59^{1}/_2$.

Annuities An amount of money that an insurance company will pay at definite intervals to a person who has previously deposited money with the company is called an **annuity**. An annuity is an investment plan for retirement income that is usually purchased from an insurance company. You pay the insurance company a certain amount of money either in a lump sum or in a series of payments. In return, the company agrees to pay you a regular income beginning at a certain age and continuing for life or for a specified number of years.

EVALUATING AND REVISING A FINANCIAL PLAN

A financial plan must be flexible. It is important to view your financial plan as a fluid, changeable document that will accommodate opportunity. Your plan should be evaluated and adjusted on a regular basis in order to produce the outcomes you have established.

Most financial planners say you should aim to begin retirement with an income equal to at least 70 percent of your pre-retirement income.

Personal Qualities-Self-Management

Self-management is a quality that students will acquire as they mature. We can help this process by guiding them through activities that will help them assess themselves accurately, set personal goals, and monitor progress. Setting financial goals as demonstrated in this chapter is a perfect opportunity to work on this quality of self-management.

SCANS

REVIEW YOUR READING

1. (a) Financial uncertainties will be reduced, (b) you will gain more control of your financial affairs, (c) your family or associates will have a way of knowing more specifically of your financial affairs in case there is a need for others to take care of your finances, (d) earnings, spending, protecting, and preserving your resources will be more systematic.
2. (a) Determine your financial condition, (b) set your financial goals, (c) create your financial plan, (d) implement your financial plan, and (e) evaluate and revise your financial plan.
3. It helps you to keep your financial statement current and to keep all your records in easy reach and in an orderly fashion.
4. Usually as short-term or long-term goals stated in dollar amounts.
5. The first part consists of building your estate through savings, investments, and insurance. The second consists of planning for the transfer of your estate, at your death, in the manner that you wish.
6. At least two years of training in securities, insurance, taxes, real estate, and estate planning and have passed a rigorous examination.
7. The two most common causes of loss of income are disability and unemployment.
8. Two forms of income protection are retirement, survivors, and disability insurance and unemployment insurance.
9. Social Security, pensions, individual retirement accounts, and annuities.
10. To take advantage of new financial options, a change in goals, and to allow for revision of your plan if you are not reaching your expected results.

COMMUNICATE BUSINESS CONCEPTS

11. Doing nothing about financial planning is the equivalent to deciding to commit to the current financial status without planning, or improving, the financial status for the future.

Chapter REVIEW

BUSINESS NOTES

1. Four advantages of financial planning are that financial uncertainties will be reduced; you will gain more control of your financial affairs; your family or associates will have a way of knowing more specifically of your financial affairs in case there is a need for them to assume control of your finances; and earning, spending, protecting, and saving your resources will be more systematic.

2. To determine your financial condition, you will take a financial inventory and then create a personal filing system to keep track of important records.

3. Financial goals are short-term and/or long-term objectives and are usually stated in dollar amounts.

4. After you have established your financial goals, you can begin to plan for the income you will need to achieve these goals. You should develop and write a plan for generating income that is consistent with your financial goals.

5. Implementing your financial plan may involve moving your savings to an account in which you will earn a higher interest rate, buying a bond, or working more hours to earn more money.

6. A financial plan must be flexible. It is important to view your financial plan as a fluid, changeable document that will accommodate opportunity. If your plan is not producing the expected results, you must make changes.

REVIEW YOUR READING

1. What four advantages does financial planning offer you?
2. List the five steps in financial planning.
3. What is the purpose of a personal financial filing system?
4. How are financial goals usually stated?
5. What are the two parts of estate planning?
6. State the qualifications of a financial planner.
7. What are the two most common causes of loss of income?
8. What are two forms of income protection?
9. List four ways to plan for future income.
10. Why is flexibility important in revising a financial plan?

COMMUNICATE BUSINESS CONCEPTS

11. One financial planner has said, "Doing nothing about financial planning is equivalent to making a decision about financial plan-ning." What do you think she meant by this statement?
12. Tell in your own words how people's financial goals change throughout their life cycle.
13. Why would you want to insure your income?
14. Give examples of activities that might be involved in implementing your financial plan.

12. During their teens and twenties, people are preparing for careers and acquiring the financial resources to support themselves in careers as well as establishing households, marrying, and having children. In their thirties and forties, people are busy paying for children's education, investing, and developing retirement plans. In their fifties and sixties, people are guarding their assets carefully and working toward their own financial security.

13. Your financial goals and plans usually are dependent on an income stream. If that income stream is interrupted, it would be difficult to achieve your goals as described in your plan.

14. Activities could include changing savings accounts from one bank to another, buying stocks, buying bonds, selling real estate, purchasing collectibles, buying annuities, contracting for insurance, and so on.

DEVELOP YOUR BUSINESS LANGUAGE

For each numbered item, find the term that has the same meaning.

15. An activity that involves the accumulation and management of property during one's lifetime and the distribution of one's property at death.

16. A report that summarizes your current financial condition, acknowledges your financial needs, and sets a direction for your future financial activities.

17. An activity that includes evaluating one's financial position, setting financial goals, and guiding activities and resources toward reaching those goals.

18. Insurance that provides cash payments for a limited time to people who are out of work for a reason other than illness.

19. A series of regular payments made to a retired worker under an organized plan.

20. An amount of money that an insurance company will pay at definite intervals to a person who has previously deposited money with the company.

21. A tax that is put into a trust fund and provides certain benefits to retirees or beneficiaries.

22. The part of the Social Security system that provides pensions to retired workers and their families, death benefits to dependents of workers who die, and benefits to disabled workers and their families.

23. Professionals who have at least two years of training in securities, insurance, taxes, real estate, and estate planning and have passed a rigorous examination.

24. A tax-sheltered retirement plan in which people can annually invest earnings up to a certain amount. The earnings contributed and the interest earned are tax free until the time of withdrawal at age 59½ or later.

KEY TERMS

annuity
estate planning
financial plan
financial planner
financial planning
individual retirement account (IRA)
pension
retirement, survivors, and disability insurance
Social Security tax
unemployment insurance

DEVELOP YOUR BUSINESS LANGUAGE

15. estate planning
16. financial plan
17. financial planning
18. unemployment insurance
19. pension
20. annuity
21. Social Security tax
22. retirement, survivors, and disability insurance
23. financial planner
24. individual retirement account (IRA)

DECISION-MAKING STRATEGIES

Paula and John Wilson have been married seven years and have two children—Dennis, age five, and Laura, age three. Paula and John are both employed—Paula as a software programmer and John as a telemarketing supervisor. Together, they earn over $75,000 per year. Each month they have problems paying their bills. It becomes even more difficult when quarterly payments, like their insurance, become due. It seems as if they are always taking money out of their savings account but never putting money in.

25. To what extent do you think John and Paula have engaged in financial planning?

26. What first step would you suggest John and Paula take toward a more predictable and secure financial future?

DECISION-MAKING STRATEGIES

25. It is clear that whatever financial planning they had done—probably none—is inadequate.

26. The first step they should take would be a careful and honest analysis of their financial situation. This would include taking a financial inventory and developing a financial filing system.

CALCULATE BUSINESS DATA

27. If the Coopers invest $31,700 on January 1 in an account that pays 7.34 percent simple annual interest, how much interest will they earn by December 31 of that same year?

28. Your grandparents are both age 64 and are earning $52,000 per year. Their goal is to retire on an income equal to 50 percent of their salary earned at age 64. How much income will they need to have in retirement to achieve that goal?

29. You earn $25,000 per year and receive an automatic annual increase of 5 percent per year. You become disabled after you receive one 5 percent raise. You are protected by disability income insurance that pays 60 percent of your salary. How much would your annual salary be if you were disabled for one year?

30. Shelly Meinke is about to retire. She will collect a pension from a New York gas and electric company where she has been employed, as well as Social Security from the government. She has always planned to spend her retirement years in Florida, but she is worried about missing her children and grandchildren who live in New York. She plans to return to New York twice a year by car for a visit. The distance from New York City where she lives to her new home in Florida is 2,050 kilometers. How many kilometers will she travel the first year, counting the initial trip to Florida from New York?

TECHNOLOGY APPLICATION

Using the *Intro to Business* data CD and your database program software, select problem CH44. After the problem appears on your screen, complete the following activities. Then, after you have completed each step, display or print a report for each activity. If you do not have a printer available, answer the questions before you leave the computer.

31. Sort the database in descending order by expected rate of return. Answer the following questions:

    a. Which investment option has the highest expected rate of return?

    b. Which investment option has the lowest expected rate of return?

32. Select and list the investment options that are insured. How many options are listed?

33. Sort the database in ascending order by minimum investment required. Answer the following questions:

    a. How many investment options have a minimum investment required of zero?

    b. What is the minimum investment required for the seventh investment option?

COMMUNICATING
for
SUCCESS

INTERVIEWING WITH A FINANCIAL PLANNER—LET'S HELP EACH OTHER

Increasingly, people rely on financial planners to help them manage their money. A financial planner is a professional who facilitates management of your investments, whether they include insurance purchases, the buying and selling of stocks and bonds, or other investments. Financial planners require that you have a sense of who you are, what your needs are, and what resources you have to work with. Although financial planners can be very successful at helping you make money, they are also employed to help you make decisions about what is important in your life.

The first step in selecting and working with a financial planner is the determination of what your needs and wants are. What do you value? What do you need? What are you willing to do to get what you want? Opportunities and options exist in all of these questions, but they can be reduced to one simple thought: Who are you and where do you envision yourself financially?

When you have identified the key ideas about yourself and your future, you should interview and consider several financial planners with good reputations. You should plan an introductory meeting to explore the financial planner's areas of expertise and his or her success in areas that are important to you, such as the stock market.

Equally important is your relationship and comfort level with each potential financial planner. To a large degree you are trusting this individual with your money, so you should be thorough in the selection of your financial planner.

Some questions to ask your prospective financial planner might include:
- How long have you been in business?
- Who is your happiest customer and why?
- Who is your least happy customer and why?
- What is your personal code of ethics?
- What have been your biggest successes during the past year?
- Does your company have specific beliefs about fair business practices?

In addition to full-service financial planners, there are other individuals who concentrate their efforts on one or two specific areas. These might be stockbrokers, money market managers, or insurance agents. These professionals generally make a profit based on the size of your purchase or investment, so they want you to make and invest money through them.

CRITICAL THINKING
1. What is a financial planner?
2. What is the first step in selecting and working with a financial planner?

COMMUNICATING
for
SUCCESS

Communications skills will help ensure students' success in the business world. Communicating for Success introduces workplace/interpersonal communications issues and proper uses of communications technology. Each feature discusses a key communications topic, and contains two Critical Thinking questions that require students to analyze what they have learned.

This Communicating for Success feature discusses the process of interviewing and selecting a financial planner. It provides some sample questions that can be asked of prospective planners, since developing a comfortable, trusting relationship with a planner is crucial. It also stresses the need for students to first determine their own financial needs and wants.

CRITICAL THINKING
1. A financial planner is a professional who facilitates management of your investments, whether these include insurance purchases or the buying and selling of stocks and bonds or other investments.
2. The first step in selecting and working with a financial planner is the determination of your needs and wants.

GLOBAL BUSINESS PROJECT

The final phase of this business plan project involves financial reporting to expand student awareness of a capital budget, balance sheet, income statement, and cash flow statement. Encourage students to research and adapt financial information from other companies. In addition, employee benefits that might be offered to workers are considered.

As this phase is completed, students are encouraged to bring together all elements of their global business plan. By using the format suggested in Option 2 of the Project Wrap-up, students will have a complete business plan in a written or visual form. The portfolio of information and materials that students have developed during the course will provide needed resources to create their global business plan.

To complete each phase of this project, students are encouraged to use various resources—textbook content, library materials, World Wide Web sites, interviews, advertisements, project packages, in-store observations. The individual activities are planned for use as either (1) an on-going course project, or (2) individual assignments.

Whether used as a continuing project or for selected activities, consider having students work in teams. This small group experience provides a valuable skill for future learning and work situations.

In addition to search engines, these selected web sites can be helpful for this unit.
- International Trade Administration of the U.S. Dept. of Commerce (www.ita.doc.gov)
- Business, economic, political news for selected countries (globaledge.msu.edu/ibrd)
- World Trade Organization at (www.wto.org)
- International Business & Travel (www.internationalist.com/)

GLOBAL BUSINESS PROJECT

USE FINANCIAL STATEMENTS FOR INTERNATIONAL BUSINESS DECISIONS

Financial reporting is vital to the ongoing success of any business enterprise. In this final phase of the global business plan project, you will analyze several aspects of an organization's financial situation.

PROJECT GOALS
1. Research financial statements of a global company.
2. Create a budget for needed capital expenses.
3. Identify employee benefits to serve the needs of workers.

PROJECT ACTIVITIES
Using your textbook, library materials, web sites, interviews with people, and other resources, complete the following activities:
1. Select a company involved in international business. Using library or Web research obtain recent financial statements for the company. Write a summary of its recent financial situation. Describe its international operations.
2. An organization's budget involves two phases: the current operating budget, covering income and expenses, and the capital budget. A capital budget involves spending for buildings, equipment, factories, and other items used over a longer period of time. List several capital items that would be needed for your business idea. Estimate the cost of these capital expenses.
3. Describe the benefits that would be offered in your global business organization. Explain the importance of these employee benefits for various groups, such as parents and older workers.

PROJECT WRAP-UP
1. Complete your portfolio (folder, file box, or other container) with information and materials you created in the activities above.
2. Prepare a written summary or visual presentation (such as a poster or web site) with all phases of your global business plan. The main elements should include: (1) an introduction with an overview of your company; (2) a description of your product or service; (3) a description of the country's business environment; (4) discussion of the company's organizational structure and information system; (5) planned marketing activities; (6) discussion of the company's financial aspects; (7) risks that might be encountered and actions to reduce the risks; and (8) an action plan with a time schedule for starting and operating the company.

- World Bank (www.worldbank.org)
- Export-Import Bank of the United States (www.exim.gov)
- International Chamber of Commerce (www.iccwbo.org/)
- Small Business Administration (www.sba.gov)

- Annual reports, company information (www.hoovers.com)
- European Bank for Reconstruction and Development (www.ebrd.org)

FOCUS ON CAREERS

Financial Managers

Almost every firm has one or more financial managers. They prepare financial reports required by the firm to conduct its operations and oversee management of the firm's finances. They also communicate with stockholders and other investors about the finances of the organization. Other financial managers head departments that deal with firms' finances, such as credit departments or risk and insurance.

JOB TITLES

Job titles commonly found in this career area include:

- Accountant
- Auditor
- Controller
- Chief Financial Officer
- Branch Managers
- Treasurer
- Credit Manager
- Risk Manager

EMPLOYMENT OUTLOOK

- Employment of financial managers is expected to grow about as fast as the average for all occupations through 2010.
- Demand for bank branch managers will be hurt as banks open fewer branches and promote Internet banking to cut costs.
- The securities industry will hire more financial managers to handle increasingly complex transactions and manage investments. Financial managers are being hired to manage assets, handle acquisitions, raise capital, and assess global transactions.
- Risk managers, who assess risks for insurance and investment purposes, are in especially great demand.

EDUCATION AND TRAINING

- Candidates with expertise in accounting and finance, particularly those with master's degrees, should enjoy the best job prospects.
- Knowledge of international finance is increasingly important.
- Communication skills are an asset, as more jobs involve working on strategic teams.
- Continuing education, especially in financial forecasting and analysis technology, is vital.

SALARY LEVELS (IN RECENT YEARS)

- Median annual earnings of financial managers are about $70,000, with the middle 50 percent earning $50,000 to $92,000. The top 10 percent earn over $130,000.
- Median annual earnings in the industries employing the largest numbers of financial managers in 2000 were: Security brokers and dealers $112,000; Accounting and auditing, $83,000; Computer and data processing services, $80,000.
- The top positions paying more than $100,000 annually usually have titles such as Vice-President of Finance, Director of Finance, Controller, and Treasurer.
- Larger organizations tend to pay more, and salary levels also vary by industry and location. Financial managers in private industry may receive bonuses.

CRITICAL THINKING

1. Which job title in this career area appeals to you most? Give reasons for your choice.
2. What are some things you will have to do to achieve success in the career you selected?

FOCUS ON CAREERS

The careers listed in this Focus on Careers come from the *Occupational Outlook Handbook*, an online publication (www.bls.gov/oco) of the federal government. The O*NET codes for these job titles are: Accountant, 13-2011.01; Auditor, 13-2011.02; Controller, 11-3031.01; Chief Financial Officer, 11-3031.01; Branch Manager, 11-3031.02; Treasurer, 11-3031.01; Department Manager, 11-3031.02; Credit Manager, 11-3031.00; Risk Manager, 11-3031.00. Students can access O*NET Online (online.onetcenter.org) to view important features of selected occupations. They can also search for related occupations and for occupations that match selected skills. This career feature is designed to help students explore a variety of different careers in business. It can be used to demonstrate that skills learned in this course are relevant. As a supplemental activity, distribute the Career Focus worksheets found in the School-To-Work/SCANS Activity Masters.

CRITICAL THINKING

1. Answers will vary.
2. Answers will vary depending on student selection of a career choice. Suggested answers may include pursuing education or specialized training.

USING A CALCULATOR AND COMPUTER KEYPAD

KINDS OF CALCULATORS

Many different models of calculators, both desktop and hand held, are available. All calculators have their own features and particular placement of operation keys. Therefore, it is necessary to refer to the operator's manual for specific instructions and locations of the operating keys for the calculator being used.

HAND-HELD CALCULATORS

There are many different kinds of hand-held or pocket calculators. They come in all shapes and sizes. They also come with a variety of keys and functions. All calculators have number keys (0 to 9), operation keys ($+, -, \times, \div$), and clear keys (C or CE). Most calculators have a percent key (%). Some hand-held calculators come with a memory for storing numbers and calculation results. These are shown as M+, M−, and MR. Others, such as scientific calculators, have many more keys including x^2, 1/x, and $\sqrt{}$.

For hand-held calculators, it is important to read the operator's or owner's manual to learn how to operate your particular calculator. Be sure to keep the manual in a safe place so you can refer to it for help in solving various mathematical problems.

DESKTOP CALCULATORS

Several operating switches on a desktop calculator must be engaged before the calculator will produce the desired results.

The *decimal selector* sets the appropriate decimal places necessary for numbers that will be entered. For example, if the decimal selector is set at 2, both the numbers entered and the answer will be displayed with two decimal places. If the decimal selector is set at F, the calculator automatically sets the needed decimal places. The F setting allows the answer to be unrounded and carried out to the maximum number of decimal places possible.

The *decimal rounding selector* rounds the answers. The down arrow position will drop any digits beyond the last digit desired. The up arrow position will drop any digits beyond the last digit desired and round the last digit up. In the 5/4 position, the calculator rounds the last desired digit up only when the following digit is 5 or greater. If the following digit is less than 5, the last desired digit remains unchanged.

The *GT* or *grand total switch* in the on position accumulates totals.

Ten-Key Touch System

Striking the numbers 0 to 9 on a desktop calculator or numeric keypad on a computer without looking at the keyboard is called the *touch system*. Using the touch system develops both speed and accuracy.

The 4, 5, and 6 keys are called the *home row*. If the right hand is used for the keyboard, the index finger is placed on the 4 key, the middle finger on the 5 key, and the ring finger on the 6 key. If the left hand is used, the ring finger is placed on the 4 key, the middle finger on the 5 key, and the index finger on the 6 key.

Place the fingers on the home row keys. Curve the fingers and keep the wrist straight. These keys may feel slightly concave or the 5 key may have a raised dot or bar. The differences in the home row allow the operator to recognize the home row by touch rather than by sight.

Maintain the position of the fingers on the home row. The finger used to strike the 4 key will also strike the 7 key and the 1 key. Stretch the finger up to reach the 7 and stretch the finger down to reach the 1 key. Visualize the position of these keys.

Again, place the fingers on the home row. Stretch the finger that strikes the 5 key up to reach the 8 key and down to reach the 2 key. Likewise, stretch the finger that strikes the 6 key up to strike the 9 key and down to strike the 3 key. This same finger will stretch down again to hit the decimal point.

If the right hand is used, the thumb will be used to strike the 0 and 00 keys and the little finger to strike the addition key. If the left hand is used, the little finger will be used to strike the 0 and 00 keys and the thumb to strike the addition key.

Performing Mathematical Operations on Desktop Calculators

Mathematical operations can be performed on any calculator both quickly and efficiently. The basic operations of addition, subtraction, multiplication, and division are used frequently on a calculator. Here is how these operations are completed on a typical desktop calculator.

Addition   Each number to be added is called an *addend*. The answer to an addition problem is called the *sum*.

Addition is performed by entering an addend and striking the addition key (+). All numbers are entered on a calculator in the exact order they are given. To enter the number 4,375.68, strike the 4, 3, 7, 5, decimal, 6, and 8 keys in that order, and then strike the

addition key. Commas are not entered. Continue in this manner until all addends have been entered. To obtain the sum, strike the total key on the calculator.

Subtraction   The top number or first number of a subtraction problem is called the *minuend*. The number to be subtracted from the minuend is called the *subtrahend*. The answer to a subtraction problem is called the *difference*.

Subtraction is performed by first entering the minuend and striking the addition key (+). The subtrahend is then entered, followed by the minus key (−), followed by the total key.

Multiplication   The numbers being multiplied together are called *factors*. The answer to a multiplication problem is called the *product*.

Multiplication is performed by entering one factor, striking the multiplication key (×), entering the other factor, and then striking the equals key (=). The calculator will automatically multiply and give the product.

Division   The number to be divided is called the *dividend*. The number the dividend will be divided by is called the *divisor*. The answer to a division problem is called the *quotient*.

Division is performed by entering the dividend and striking the division key (÷). The divisor is then entered, following by the equals key (=). The calculator will automatically divide and give the quotient.

Correcting Errors   If an error is made while using a calculator, several methods of correction may be used. If an incorrect number has been entered and the addition key or equals key has not yet been struck, strike the clear entry (CE) key one time. This key will clear only the last number that was entered. However, if the clear entry key is depressed more than one time, the entire problem will be cleared on some calculators. If an incorrect number has been entered and the addition key has been struck, strike the minus key one time only. This will automatically subtract the last number added, thus removing it from the total.

The computer has a keypad on the right side of the keyboard called the *numeric keypad*. Even though there are several styles of computer keyboards, there are two basic layouts for the numeric keypad, as shown below.

Most computers have a small light that indicates when the *Num Lock* key (above the 7 key) is on. When the Num Lock key is turned on, numbers are entered when the keys on the keypad are pressed. When Num Lock is not on, the arrow, Home, Page Up, Page Down, End, Insert, and Delete keys can be used. Enhanced keyboards allow you to keep the Num Lock key activated at all times.

The asterisk (*) on the computer is used for multiplication. The slash key (/) is used for division.

Performing Mathematical Operations On Computers

Calculations with a computer keypad are performed in much the same way as on a desk-top calculator. However, after the + key is depressed, the display usually shows the accumulated total. Therefore, the total key is not found on the computer keypad. Some computer programs will not calculate the total until the Enter key is pressed.

Subtraction is performed differently on many computer keypads. The minuend is entered, followed by the minus (−) key. Then the subtrahend is entered. Pressing either the + key, the = key, or the Enter key will display the difference.

Multiplication and division are performed the same way as on a desktop calculator. Keep in mind that computers used the * for multiplication and / for division.

Standard Keyboard Layout

Enhanced Keyboard Layout

MATH REVIEW

This arithmetic review will help you solve many of the end-of-chapter problems in this text as well as common arithmetic problems you may encounter in business.

ESTIMATING SUMS AND DIFFERENCES

In some situations, an **estimate** may be useful. Sometimes an exact answer is not needed, so you can estimate. Other times, estimation can be used to check mathematical calculations, especially when using a calculator.

Most people estimate by **rounding** numbers. Rounded numbers are easier to work with. Rounded numbers usually contain one or two non-zero digits followed by all zeros.

Examples

The U. S. Bureau of the Census estimated the 1997 population of Texas at 19,385,699.

- Round 19,385,699 to the nearest ten million.

  19,385,699 ⟶ 20,000,000

  9 is greater than or equal to 5, so round up to 20,000,000

- Round 19,385,699 to the nearest million.

  19,385,699 ⟶ 19,000,000

  3 is less than 5, round down to 19,000,000.

One new car has a list price of $15,209.50.

- Round $15,209.50 to the nearest thousand dollars.

  $15,209.50 ⟶ $15,000

  2 is less than 5, round down to $15,000.

- Round $15.209.50 to the nearest dollar.

  $15,209.50 ⟶ $15,210

  5 is greater than or equal to 5, round up to $15,210.

Examples

- Estimate the answer to 24,432 + 15,000.

24,432	Option 1:	Option 2:
+15,000	Round to the nearest ten thousand.	Round to the nearest thousand.
	20,000	24,000
	+20,000	+15,000
	40,000	39,000

- Estimate the answer to $32.23 − $17.54.

$32.23	Option 1:	Option 2:
−17.54	Round to the nearest ten dollars.	Round to the nearest dollar.
	$30.00	$32.00
	−20.00	−18.00
	$10.00	$14.00

- Estimate how much change you should get if you give the clerk $20 to pay for a bill of $6.98.

  $20.00 ⟶ $20.00
  −6.98 ⟶ −7.00
           $13.00

MULTIPLYING NUMBERS ENDING IN ZEROS

When you multiply numbers that have *final zeros*, you can use this shortcut:

Multiply the numbers by using only the digits that are not zeros. Then write as many final zeros in the product as there are zeros in the numbers being multiplied.

Examples

$$200 \times 7 = 1,400$$

2 zeros $2 \times 7 = 14$ 2 zeros

$$40 \times 5,000 = 200,000$$

1 zero   3 zeros $4 \times 5 = 20$ 4 zeros

When multiplying larger numbers, use an imaginary line to separate zeros from the rest of the digits.

$36 \times 2,500$

```
   36 |
 × 25 | 00
  180 |          2 zeros
   72 |
  900 | 00        90,000  Answer
```

$3,600 \times 25,000$

```
   36 | 00      ← 2 zeros
 × 25 | 000     ← 3 zeros
  180 |            2 + 3 = 5 zeros
   72 |
  900 | 00000   ← 5 zeros
     90,000,000  Answer
```

ESTIMATING PRODUCTS

There are various ways to estimate the answer to a multiplication problem.

- Option 1: Round both numbers **up**. Estimate will be greater than the actual product.

- Option 2: Round both numbers **down**. Estimate will be less than the actual product.

- Option 3: Round each number to the near-est unit with one non-zero digit. The estimate will be close to the actual product.

Examples

Estimate $82,543 \times 653$.

Option 1: $90,000 \times 700 = 63,000,000$
Option 2: $80,000 \times 600 = 48,000,000$
Option 3: $80,000 \times 700 = 56,000,000$

DIVIDING WHOLE NUMBERS

Division is the opposite of multiplication. Division is shown in several ways. To show that 18 divided by 3 is 6, you may use any of these forms:

$$18 \div 3 = 6 \qquad \frac{18}{3} = 6 \qquad 3\overline{)18}$$

In each case, 18 is the dividend, 3 is the divisor, and 6 is the quotient.

$$\text{dividend} \div \text{divisor} = \text{quotient}$$

$$\frac{\text{dividend}}{\text{divisor}} = \text{quotient} \qquad \text{divisor}\overline{)\text{dividend}}^{\,\text{quotient}}$$

DIVIDING NUMBERS ENDING IN ZEROS

When you divide multiples of 10, there are several shortcuts you can use. Try either of the shortcuts discussed below:

- Write the numbers as a fraction. Cross out the same number of zeros in both the numerator and denominator of the fraction.

- Move the decimal point in the dividend to the **left** the same number of places as there are zeros in the dividend.

- $1,000,000,000 \div 10,000$

  $= 100000.0000. \div 1.0000. = 100,000$

Examples

- $1,000,000,000 \div 10,000 = \dfrac{1,000,000,000}{10,000}$

  $= 100,000$

ESTIMATING QUOTIENTS

One way to estimate the answer to a division problem is to start by rounding the divisor to a number with one non-zero number followed by all zeros. Then round the dividend to a multiple of that rounded divisor.

Example

- Estimate $609 \div 19$.

  Round 19 to 20 and 609 to 600.

  $600 \div 20 = 30$

- Estimate $19,876,548 \div 650$.

  650 rounds up to 700.

  Multiples of 7 are 7, 14, 21, 28, 35, and so on. Use the closest multiple, 21.

  $21,000,000 \div 700 = \dfrac{21000000}{700}$

  $= \dfrac{210000}{7} = 30,000$

ADDING AND SUBTRACTING DECIMALS

When adding and subtracting decimals, align the decimal points. Then add or subtract as for whole numbers. Place the decimal point in the answer directly below where it is located in the computation. A number like 532 can also be written as 532. or 532.0. When writing decimals less than one, a zero if placed before the decimal point to show that there are no ones.

Examples

- Find the sum of 33.67, 72.84, 0.75, and 43.34.

  $$\begin{array}{r} 33.67 \\ 72.84 \\ 0.75 \\ +\ 43.34 \\ \hline 150.60 \end{array}$$

- Find the sum of 320.5471, 1.4, and 82.352.

  $$\begin{array}{r} 320.5471 \\ 1.4 \\ +\ 82.32 \\ \hline 404.2991 \end{array}$$

- Find the difference between 952.1 and 34.2517.

  $$\begin{array}{r} 952.1 \\ -\ 34.2517 \end{array}$$

  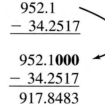

  Add 0s to the **right** after the decimal point.

  $$\begin{array}{r} 952.1\mathbf{000} \\ -\ 34.2517 \\ \hline 917.8483 \end{array}$$

MULTIPLYING DECIMALS

When multiplying decimals, align the numbers at the right. Multiply as if you are multiplying whole numbers. To locate the decimal point in the answer, count all digits to the right of the decimal point in each number being multiplied and place the decimal point so there are that many digits after the decimal point in the answer.

Remember: Estimation can be used to check that your answer is reasonable and that you have correctly located the decimal point in the answer.

Examples
- Multiply 7.46 by 3.2.

$$
\begin{array}{r}
7.46 \quad \longleftarrow \text{ 2 decimal places} \\
\times\ 3.2 \quad \longleftarrow \text{ 1 decimal place} \\
\hline
1492 \qquad 2 + 1 = 3 \\
2238 \qquad\qquad \\
\hline
23.872 \quad \longleftarrow \text{ 3 decimal places}
\end{array}
$$

- Multiply 0.193 by 0.2.

$$
\begin{array}{r}
0.193 \quad \longleftarrow \text{ 3 decimal places} \\
\times\ 0.2 \quad \longleftarrow +\text{1 decimal place} \\
\hline
0.0386 \quad \longleftarrow \text{ 4 decimal places}
\end{array}
$$

 If needed to get enough decimal places, add a zero before the numeric answer but after the decimal point.

Remember that the zero before the decimal point shows that there are no ones in the product. The answer is less than one.

Estimate to check your answer.

$0.2 \times 0.2 = 0.04$
0.04 is close to 0.0386, so the answer is reasonable.

MULTIPLYING BY POWERS OF 10

Numbers like 100,000,000, 10,000, 100, 0.1, 0.01, and 0.00001 are powers of 10. To multiply by these, simply move the decimal point in the number being multiplied.

When multiplying by a power of 10 greater than one, move the decimal point to the right. The answer is larger than the number you started with.

When multiplying by a power of 10 less than one, move the decimal point to the left. The answer is smaller than the number you started with.

Examples
- Multiply 25,397 by ten thousand.

$25,397 \times 10,000 = 253,970,000$

Think: 25397.0000.

- Multiply 0.078 by one hundred.

$0.078 \times 100 = 7.8$

Think: $= 0.07.8$

- Multiply 192,536 by one ten-thousandth.

$192,536 \times 0.0001 = 19.2536$

Think: 19.2536.

- Multiply 0.293 by one hundredth.

$0.293 \times 0.01 = 0.00293$

Think: 0.00.293

SHORTCUTS WHEN MULTIPLYING WITH MONEY

Businesses price items at amounts such as 49¢, $5.98, or $99.95. A price of $99.95 seems less to the buyer than an even $100.

When finding the cost of several of such items, you can use a mathematical shortcut.

Examples

- Find the cost of 27 items at 98¢ each.
  normal multiplication

$$\begin{array}{r} \$0.98 \\ \times\ 27 \\ \hline 686 \\ 196 \\ \hline \$26.46 \end{array}$$

  Shortcut: Think: 98¢ = $1 − 2¢

  $(27 \times \$1) − (27 \times 2¢) = \$27 − 54¢$

  $54¢ = \$0.54$

$$\begin{array}{r} \$27.00 \\ −\ 0.54 \\ \hline \$26.46 \end{array}$$

- Find the cost of 32 items at $6.95 each.

  Shortcut: Think $6.95 = $7 − $0.05

$(32 \times \$7) − (32 \times \$0.05)$

$= \$224 − \$1.60 = \$222.40$

- Find the cost of 101 items at $9.99 each.

  Shortcut: Think $9.99 = $10 − $0.01

  $(101 \times \$10) − (101 \times \$0.01)$

  $= \$1,010 − \$1.01 = \$1,008.99$

  Alternate Shortcut:

  Think: 101 = 100 + 1

  $(100 \times \$9.99) + (1 \times \$9.99) =$

  $\$999 + \$9.99 = \$1,008.99$

MULTIPLYING A WHOLE NUMBER BY A FRACTION

To multiply a whole number by a fraction, multiply the whole number by the numerator (top number) and then divide that answer by the denominator (bottom number).

Examples

- $180 \times \dfrac{2}{3} = \dfrac{180 \times 2}{3} = \dfrac{360}{3} = 120$

- $500 \times \dfrac{3}{4} = \dfrac{500 \times 3}{4} = \dfrac{1500}{4} = 375$

- $768 \times \dfrac{1}{8} = \dfrac{768 \times 1}{8} = \dfrac{768}{8} = 96$

- $90 \times \dfrac{4}{5} = \dfrac{90 \times 4}{5} = \dfrac{360}{5} = 72$

Simplifying Fractions

When working with fractions, you can simplify the fractions by dividing the numerator and the denominator by a common factor (a number that will divide into both numbers evenly). Division by such common factors is called **canceling** or **cancellation**.

Examples

- Simplify $\dfrac{10}{12}$.　　**Think:** 2 is a factor of both 10 and 12.

$$\dfrac{\cancel{10}}{\cancel{12}} = \dfrac{5}{6} \qquad \begin{array}{l} 5 \longleftarrow 10 \div 2 = 5 \\[4pt] 6 \longleftarrow 12 \div 2 = 6 \end{array}$$

- Simplify $\dfrac{\cancel{75}}{\cancel{100}}$.　　**Think:** Use 25 as a common factor.

$$\dfrac{\cancel{75}}{\cancel{100}} = \dfrac{3}{4} \qquad \begin{array}{l} 3 \longleftarrow 75 \div 25 = 3 \\[4pt] 4 \longleftarrow 100 \div 25 = 4 \end{array}$$

- Simplify $\dfrac{280}{60}$.　　**Think:** Use 20 as a common factor.

$$\dfrac{\cancel{280}}{\cancel{60}} = \dfrac{14}{3} \qquad \begin{array}{l} 14 \longleftarrow 280 \div 20 = 14 \\[4pt] 3 \longleftarrow 60 \div 20 = 3 \end{array}$$

Using Fractional Parts of $1.00 in Multiplying Mentally

While goods and services may be priced at any figure, prices are frequently expressed in fractional parts of $1, $10, or $100. For instance, 2 items for $1 is the same as $\frac{1}{2}$ of 100¢, or 50¢ per item, and 3 items for $10 is the same as $\frac{1}{3}$ of $10, or $3.33\frac{1}{3}$ per item.

You can also use fractional parts of $1.00 to find the cost of multiple items mentally.

24 items selling for $1.00 would cost $24.00

24 items at 50¢ each $= \frac{1}{2}$ of $24 or $12.00

24 items at 25¢ each $= \frac{1}{4}$ of $24 or $6.00

24 items at $33\frac{1}{3}$¢ each $= \frac{1}{3}$ of $24 or $8

Many similar calculations can be made mentally. While there are many fractional parts of $1.00, below is a chart of those most commonly used.

Fraction	Part of $1.00
$\frac{1}{8}$	0.12\frac{1}{2}$
$\frac{1}{6}$	0.16\frac{2}{3}$
$\frac{1}{5}$	$0.20
$\frac{1}{4}$	$0.25
$\frac{1}{3}$	0.33\frac{1}{3}$
$\frac{3}{8}$	0.37\frac{1}{2}$
$\frac{2}{5}$	$0.40
$\frac{1}{2}$	$0.50
$\frac{3}{5}$	$0.60
$\frac{5}{8}$	0.62\frac{1}{2}$
$\frac{2}{3}$	0.66\frac{2}{3}$
$\frac{3}{4}$	$0.75
$\frac{4}{5}$	$0.80
$\frac{5}{6}$	0.83\frac{1}{3}$
$\frac{7}{8}$	0.87\frac{1}{2}$

Examples

- Find the cost of 16 items at $12\frac{1}{2}$¢ each.

  Think: $12\frac{1}{2}$¢ $= \frac{1}{8}$ of $1

  $16 \times \frac{1}{8} = 2$

  16 items at $12\frac{1}{2}$¢ each will cost $2.

- Find the cost of 33 items at 25¢ each.

  Think: 25¢ $= \frac{1}{4}$ of $1

  $33 \times \frac{1}{4} = \frac{33}{4}$, or $8\frac{1}{4}$

  33 items at 25¢ each will cost $8\frac{1}{4}$, or $8.25.

- Find the cost of 48 items at 75¢ each.

  Think: 75¢ $= \frac{3}{4}$ of $1

  $48 \times \frac{3}{4} = \frac{\overset{12}{\cancel{48}} \times 3}{\cancel{4}_{1}} = \frac{12 \times 3}{1} = \frac{36}{1} = 36$

  48 items at 75¢ each is $36.

- Find the cost of 34 items at $62\frac{1}{2}$¢ each.

  Think: $62\frac{1}{2}$¢ $= \frac{5}{8}$ of $1

  $34 \times \frac{5}{8} = \frac{\overset{17}{\cancel{34}} \times 5}{\cancel{8}_{4}} = \frac{17 \times 5}{4} = \frac{85}{4} = 21\frac{1}{4}$

  34 items at $62\frac{1}{2}$¢ each is $21\frac{1}{4}$, or $21.25.

Fractional Parts of Other Amounts

You can use the table on this page to find fractional parts of multiples of 10.

Examples

- Find $\frac{5}{6}$ of $1,000.

  $\frac{5}{6}$ of $1,000 = 1000 $\times \frac{5}{6}$ of $1

  $= 100 \times \$0.83\frac{1}{3}$

  $= \$83\frac{1}{3}$

So, $\frac{5}{6}$ of $1,000 is $.83.33.

$\left(\frac{1}{3}\text{ dollar} = \$0.33\frac{1}{3}\text{, which is }\$0.33\right.$
when rounded to the nearest cent.$\left.\vphantom{\frac{1}{3}}\right)$

- Find $\frac{3}{4}$ of $100.

$$\frac{3}{4}\text{ of }\$100 = 100 \times \frac{3}{4}\text{ of }\$1$$
$$= 100 \times \$0.75$$
$$= \$75$$

So, $\frac{3}{4}$ of $100 is $75.

- Find $\frac{7}{8}$ of $10.

$$\frac{7}{8}\text{ of }\$10 = 10 \times \frac{7}{8}\text{ of }\$1$$
$$= 10 \times \$0.875$$
$$= \$8.75$$

So, $\frac{7}{8}$ of $10 is $8.75.

Dividing Decimals

Division involving decimals is completed like division of whole numbers, except for dealing with the decimal point.

When you divide a decimal by a whole number, you divide as for whole numbers and place the decimal point directly above the location of the decimal point in the dividend.

Examples

- Divide 12.944 by 8.

```
     1.618      To check division,
  8)12.944      multiply your
     8          quotient by the
     49         divisor. The result
     48         should be the
     14         dividend.
      8
      64         1.618
      64         ×   8
       0        12.944 ✓
```

- Divide 37 by 4.

```
      9.25
   4)37.00      Add zeros as needed.
     36
     1 0
       8        Check:        9.25
      20                     ×   4
      20                      37.00 ✓
       0
```

To divide by a decimal, move the decimal point to the right the same number of places in both the divisor and the dividend so you are dividing by a whole number.

Examples

- Divide 12.944 by 0.8.

  Think: 0.8 has one decimal place, move the decimal points in the divisor and the dividend right one place.

```
        1 6.18
  0.8,)12.9,44
       8
       4 9
       4 8
        1 4
          8
         64
         64
          0
```

- Divide 37 by 0.004.

```
         9 250.
  0.004.)37.000.      Add zeros as needed.
         36
         1 0
           8
          20
          20
           0
```

Remember: Estimation can be used to check that your answer is reasonable and that you have correctly located the decimal point in the answer.

DETERMINING PERCENTAGES AND INTEREST IN BUSINESS

Finding percentages and calculating interest are frequent functions in business. Every career in business demands some knowledge of percentages and interest. The well-prepared business person is comfortable with percentages and interest.

MEANING OF PERCENT

Percent is derived from two Latin words, "per centum," meaning "by the hundred." You can express a percent as a common fraction or a decimal fraction. When the percent involves a fraction, like $7\frac{1}{4}\%$, change the mixed number to a decimal and move the decimal point two places to the left.

$$7\frac{1}{4}\% = 7.25\% = 0.725$$

Examples

- Write 19% as a fraction and a decimal.

  Percent means *per one hundred*, so write it as a fraction with a denominator of 100.

$$19\% = \frac{19}{100} = 0.19$$

- Write 0.98 as a fraction and a percent.

$$0.98 = \frac{98}{100} = 98\%$$

- Write $\frac{3}{100}$ as a decimal and a percent.

$$\frac{3}{100} = 0.03 = 3\%.$$

- Write $8\frac{1}{2}\%$ as a decimal and a fraction.

$$8\frac{1}{2}\% = 8.5\% = 0.085 = \frac{85}{1000}$$

  Notice that .085 is 85 *thousandths*, so the fraction has a denominator of 1000.

FINDING A PERCENT OF A NUMBER

To find the percent of a number, change the percent to a fraction or decimal and multiply. Using a calculator simplifies the process.

Example

• Find 18% of 117,334.

With fractions:

$$117334 \times \frac{18}{100} = \frac{117334 \times 18}{100}$$

$$= \frac{2112012}{100} = 21,120.12$$

• Find 18% of 117,334.

With decimals:

$$\begin{array}{r} 117,334 \\ \times \quad 0.18 \\ \hline 938672 \\ 117334 \\ \hline 21120.12 \end{array}$$

• Find 10% of 359.

$$359 \times 0.10 = 35.9$$

CALCULATING SIMPLE INTEREST

Interest is money paid for the privilege of using someone else's money. Interest is always expressed as a percent. The *principal* is the amount of money borrowed. Simple interest (I) is calculated by multiplying the principal (P) times the annual interest rate (R) times the length of time in years (T). The formula is written as:

$$I = P \times R \times T$$

Examples

• Find the amount of simple interest due on $400 borrowed for 2 years at 8%.

$$I = \$400 \times 0.08 \times 2 = \$64$$

• Find the amount of simple interest due on $600 borrowed for 1 month at 18%.

Think: 1 month is $\frac{1}{12}$ of a year.

$$I = \$600 \times 0.18 \times \frac{1}{12} = \$9$$

• Find the amount of simple interest due on $3,000 borrowed for 6 months at $9\frac{3}{4}$%.

$$I = \$3,000 \times 0.0975 \times \frac{6}{12} = \$146.25$$

COMPOUND INTEREST

With the advances in the use of computer, compound interest is more common than simple interest. For example, a credit card may say that it charges 1.5% interest per month. It then seems that you are paying 12 × 1.5%, or 18% interest per year. However, in reality you are charged more than 18% interest per year because you are paying interest on interest.

Example

• Suppose that you owe $100 on your credit card and do not make any payments for one year. Assuming there are no late fees, your balance at the end of each month would look as shown in the table on page 625. When the interest is calculated, all amounts are rounded up to the next cent.

Month	Beginning Balance	Interest (1.5% per month)	Ending Balance
Jan.	$100	$1.50	$101.50
Feb.	$101.50	$1.53	$103.03
Mar.	$103.03	$1.55	$104.58
Apr.	$104.58	$1.57	$106.15
May	$106.15	$1.60	$107.75
June	$107.75	$1.62	$109.37
July	$109.37	$1.65	$111.02
Aug.	$111.02	$1.67	$112.69
Sept.	$112.69	$1.70	$114.39
Oct.	$114.39	$1.72	$116.11
Nov.	$116.11	$1.75	$117.86
Dec.	$117.86	$1.77	$119.63

So in 12 months you have paid $19.63 in interest on $100, or 19.63%, not 18% interest.

FINDING WHAT PERCENT A NUMBER IS OF ANOTHER

To find what percent a number is of another, divide the one number (the part) by the other number (the whole). Then show the result as a percent.

Example

- 50 is what percent of 200?

Divide 50 by 200.

$$\begin{array}{r} 0.25 \\ 200\overline{)50.00} \\ \underline{40\ 0} \\ 10\ 00 \\ \underline{10\ 00} \end{array}$$

0.25 = 25%
50 is 25% of 200.

USING MEASUREMENTS IN BUSINESS

The metric system of measurement is used in business by most nations in the world. Because of our great amount of trade with other countries, the United States has taken some steps toward conversion to the metric system. Some U.S. businesses and industries have already made the change, and you should become familiar with the metric system.

There are some things about the metric system that may already be familiar to you. For example, if you have been to a track meet or swimming meet or have seen one on television, you know that distances can be measured in meters, not just in feet, yards, or miles. Food is often labeled to show amounts in grams as well as pounds or ounces. Meters, kilometers, and grams are examples of metric units of measurement.

BASIC METRIC UNITS

The basic metric units are the meter (length), the liter (capacity), and the gram (mass or weight). All measurements can be expressed in terms of these three basic units. However, prefixes are used with the basic units to avoid dealing with very large and very small numbers. The most common prefixes used in the metric system are:

kilo- ⟶ one thousand times
centi- ⟶ one one-hundredth of
milli- ⟶ one one-thousandth of

Look at the charts below. The same prefixes are used for length, capacity, and mass or weight.

Length	Capacity	Mass (Weight)
1 kilometer = 1000 meters	1 kiloliter = 1000 liters	1 kilogram = 1000 grams
1 meter = 100 centimeters	1 liter = 100 centiliters	1 gram = 100 centigrams
1 meter = 1000 millimeters	1 liter = 1000 milliliters	1 gram = 1000 milligrams
1 centimeter = 10 millimeters	1 centiliter = 10 milliliters	1 centigram = 10 milligrams
1 centimeter = 0.01 meter	1 centiliter = 0.01 liter	1 centigram = 0.01 gram
1 millimeter = 0.001 meter	1 milliliter = 0.001 liter	1 milligram = 0.001 gram

The abbreviations, or symbols, for metric measurements are also uniform, changing only to show whether you are measuring length, capacity, or mass.

Length		Capacity		Mass (Weight)	
kilometer ⟶	km	kiloliter ⟶	kL	kilogram ⟶	kg
meter ⟶	m	liter ⟶	L	gram ⟶	g
centimeter ⟶	cm	centiliter ⟶	cL	centigram ⟶	g
millimeter ⟶	mm	millimeter ⟶	mL	milligram ⟶	mg

CONVERTING UNITS WITHIN THE METRIC SYSTEM

Using the tables above, you can see that one kilometer is 1000 times as long as a meter and that one millimeter is one-thousandth of a meter. Since the relationships between the prefixes are multiples of 10, you can change from one unit to another by multiplying by a power of ten, which can be done by moving the decimal point.

Examples

● Change 0.36 meters to centimeters.

Think: 1 meter = 100 centimeters

To get from 1 to 100, move the decimal point to the right 2 spaces.   0.36

So 0.36 meters = 36 centimeters

● Change 5000 grams to kilograms.

Think: 1000 grams = 1 kilogram

To get from 1000 to 1, move the decimal point to the left 3 spaces.   5.000

So 5000 grams = 5 kilograms

● Change 4.5 liters to milliliters.

Think: 1 liter = 1000 milliliters

To get from 1 to 1000, move the decimal point to the right 3 spaces.

4.500   Notice how zeros are added so the decimal can be moved the needed number of spaces to the right.

So 4.5 liters = 4500 milliliters

● Change 0.86 millimeters to centimeters.

Think: 10 millimeters = 1 centimeter
To get from 10 to 1, move the decimal point to the left 1 space.

0.0.86   Notice that a zero is added so the decimal can be moved the needed number of spaces to the left.

So 0.86 millimeters = 0.086 centimeters

CUSTOMARY MEASUREMENT

In the United States feet, pounds, and gallons are still common units of measure. Below is a list of common customary measurements and their equivalents.

Length	Capacity	Weight
1 foot = 12 inches	1 pint = 2 cups	1 pound = 16 ounces
1 yard = 3 feet	1 quart = 2 pints	1 ton = 2,000 pounds
1760 yards = 1 mile	1 gallon = 4 quarts	
5280 feet = 1 mile		

MEASURING TEMPERATURE

Thermometers that measure temperature are marked in degrees Celsius (°C) or in degrees Fahrenheit (°F). The Celsius scale is a metric scale. The Fahrenheit scale is nonmetric.

Metric	Event	Nonmetric
100°C	Water boils	212°F
37°C	Normal body temperature	98.6°F
0°C	Water freezes	32°F

CONVERTING BETWEEN SYSTEMS

Once in a while it may be necessary to convert from the metric system to the customary system or vice versa. You can use these charts when you need to change metric measurements to customary or vice versa.

Length/Distance

When you know:	You can find:	If you multiply by:
inches	millimeters	25.40
inches	centimeters	2.54
feet	meters	0.305
yards	meters	0.91
miles	kilometers	1.61
millimeters	inches	0.04
centimeters	inches	0.39
meters	inches	39.37
meters	feet	3.28
meters	yards	1.09
kilometers	miles	0.62

Weight/Mass

When you know:	You can find:	If you multiply by:
ounces	grams	28.35
pounds	kilograms	0.45
grams	ounces	0.035
kilograms	pounds	2.20

Capacity/Volume

When you know:	You can find:	If you multiply by:
pints	liters	0.47
quarts	liters	0.95
gallons	liters	3.78
liters	pints	2.11
liters	quarts	1.06
liters	gallons	0.26

Temperature

When you know	You can find	If you
°F (degrees Fahrenheit)	°C (degrees Celsius)	subtract 32, multiply by 5, then divide by 9.
°C (degrees Celsius)	°F (degrees Fahrenheit)	multiply by 9, divide by 5, then add 32.

Examples

- You are in a 440-yard race. How many meters long is the race?

  To change from yards to meters, multiply by 0.91.

  $440 \times 0.91 = 400.4$

  The race is 400.4 meters long.

- A store shelf has a weight limit of 250 kilograms. What is that limit in pounds?

  To change kilograms to pounds, multiply by 2.20.

  $250 \times 2.20 = 550$

  The weight limit is 550 pounds.

Appendix D *Using Measurements In Business*

- It is 10°C outside. What is the temperature in degrees Fahrenheit?

To change from °C to °F, multiply by 9, divide by 5, then add 32.

$10 \times 9 = 90$; $90 \div 5 = 18$; $18 + 32 = 50$

The temperature is 50°F.

- It is 95°F outside. What is the temperature in degrees Celsius?

To change from °F to °C, subtract 32, multiply by 5, then divide by 9.

$95 - 32 = 63$; $63 \times 5 = 315$; $315 \div 9 = 35$

The temperature is 35°C.

GLOSSARY

A

Ability The quality of being able to perform mental or physical tasks. (p. 260)

Ability test A test that measures how well a job applicant can perform certain job tasks. (p. 273)

Adjustable rate mortgage (ARM) A mortgage for which the interest rate is raised or lowered periodically depending upon the current interest rate being charged by lenders. (p. 498)

Adjuster An insurance company representative who determines the extent of loss and pays policyholders according to the terms of the policy. (p. 543)

Allowance The amount budgeted for savings and other expenditures. (p. 591)

Annual percentage rate (APR) The percentage cost of credit on a yearly basis. (p. 429)

Annuity An amount of money that an insurance company will pay at definite intervals to a person who has previously deposited money with the company. (p. 607)

Antitrust laws Laws designed to promote competition and fairness to prevent monopolies. (p. 149)

Application software Computer programs that perform specific tasks such as word processing, database management, or accounting. (p. 204)

Appraiser One who is trained to estimate the value of property and who can give an official report on its value. (p. 499)

Appreciation A general increase in the value of property that occurs over a period of time. (p. 499)

Artificial intelligence (AI) Programs that enable computers to reason, learn, and make decisions using logical methods similar to the methods humans use. (p. 228)

Assessed value The amount that your local government determines your property to be worth for tax purposes. (p. 500)

Assets Items of value. (p. 580)

Assigned-risk plan Automobile insurance that provides coverage to high risk drivers who are unable to purchase it otherwise. (p. 531)

Automobile liability insurance The general term used to describe insurance you buy to protect yourself from financial loss if you injure someone else or damage someone else's property in an automobile accident. (p. 525)

B

Balance of payments The difference between a country's total imports and total exports of goods. (p. 138)

Balance of trade The difference between a country's total exports and total imports of goods. (p. 136)

Balance sheet The financial statement that reports what a person or family owns as well as owes. (p. 579)

Bank reconciliation A statement showing how the checkbook balance and the bank statement were brought into agreement. (p. 388)

Bankruptcy A situation in which a business does not have enough money to pay its creditors even after selling its equipment and other capital resources. (p. 285)

Bank statement A report sent by the bank to a depositor showing the status of his or her account. (p. 386)

Base plus incentive A system that combines a small wage or salary with an additional amount determined by the employee's performance. (p. 175)

Base year The year chosen to compare an item, such as price, to the same item in another year. (p. 42)

Basic economic problem The problem which faces individuals, businesses, and governments of satisfying unlimited wants with limited resources. (p. 8)

Basic health coverage A combination of hospital, surgical, and regular medical insurance. (p. 562)

Beneficiary The person named in an insurance policy to receive the insurance benefits. (p. 550)

Benefits Compensation in forms other than direct payment for work. (p. 174)

Blank endorsement An endorsement consisting of only the endorser's name. (p. 362)

Bodily injury liability coverage Insurance coverage that protects you from claims resulting from injuries or deaths for which you are found to be at fault. (p. 526)

Bond A certificate representing a promise to pay a definite amount of money at a stated interest rate on a specified maturity date. (p. 482)

Brand name A name given to a product or service by a manufacturer that is intended to distinguish it from other similar and/or competitive products or services. (p. 315)

Budget A plan that allows you to meet your personal goals with a system of saving and wise spending. (p. 589)

Budget account A credit plan requiring that payments of a certain fixed amount be made over several months. (p. 413)

Budget variance A difference between actual spending and planned spending. (p. 592)

Business An establishment or enterprise that supplies goods and services in exchange for some form of payment. (p. 21)

Business budget A planning tool used to anticipate sources and amounts of income and to predict the types and amounts of expenses for a specific business activity or the entire business. (p. 183)

Business cycle The movement of an economy from one condition to another and back again. (p. 44)

Business ethics Rules about how businesses and their employees ought to behave. (p. 124)

Business plan A written description of the business idea and how it will be carried out including all major business operations. (p. 163)

Buying motives The reasons for making a purchase. (p. 107)

C

Canceled checks Checks that have been paid by the bank. (p. 387)

Capacity The factor in credit that refers to a customer's ability to pay a debt when it is due. (p. 404)

Capital Tools, equipment, and buildings used in producing goods and services. (p. 8) The factor in credit that refers to the value of the borrower's possessions. (p. 404)

Capitalism An economic system in which most economic resources are privately owned and decisions are largely made by free exchange in the marketplace. (p. 21)

Capital resources Tools, equipment, and buildings used in producing goods and services. (p. 7)

Career A goal in life that is fulfilled through a job or series of jobs. (p. 255)

Career information interview A planned discussion with a worker to find out about the work that person does, the preparation necessary for that career, and the person's feelings about the career. (p. 257)

Career planning The process of studying careers, assessing yourself in terms of careers, and making decisions about a future career. (p. 255)

Cash budget An estimate of the actual money received and paid out for a specific time period. (p. 185)

Cash flow statement The financial statement that reports net wages and other income along with spending for a given period of time. (p. 581)

Cashier's check A check that a bank draws on its own in-house funds. (p. 375)

Cash value The amount of money received should a policyholder decide to give up the protection provided by a policy. (p. 550)

CD-ROM A data storage device that uses laser optics for reading data. (p. 205)

Central processing unit (CPU) The control center of the computer. (p. 204)

Certificate of deposit (CD) A long-term deposit that has certain restrictions and pays higher interest rates than a regular savings account. (p. 472)

Certificate of incorporation A document, generally issued by a state government, giving permission to start a corporation. (p. 69)

Certified check A personal check for which a bank has guaranteed payment. (p. 374)

Channel of distribution The path that a product travels from producer to consumer. (p. 108)

Character The factor in credit that refers to a customer's honesty and willingness to pay a debt when it is due. (p. 404)

Check register A separate form on which the depositor keeps a record of deposits and checks. (p. 363)

Check stub A form attached to a check on

which a depositor keeps a record of the checks written and any current deposit. (p. 363)

Claim A policyholder's request for payment for a loss that is covered by the insurance policy. (p. 515)

Clearance sale A sale in which a price reduction is used to sell items that a store no longer wishes to carry in stock. (p. 314)

Clearing Returning a check to the drawer's bank to be paid and charged to his or her checking account. (p. 383)

Clearinghouse A place where member banks exchange checks to clear them. (p. 384)

Closing A situation in which a business is discontinued with a loss occurring to at least one creditor. (p. 285)

Code of ethics A statement of values and rules that guides the behavior of employees or members of an organization. (p. 125)

Coinsurance The sharing of expenses by the policyholder and the insurance company. (p. 517)

Coinsurance clause A provision in which the insured pays a certain percentage of the costs above the deductible amount. (p. 563)

Collateral Property that is offered as security for some loan agreements. (p. 418)

Collectibles Items of personal interest to collectors purchased in anticipation of an increase in value in the future. (p. 503)

Collision coverage Insurance coverage that protects a car owner against financial loss associated with damage from a collision with another car or object or from the car turning over. (p. 528)

Commercial bank A bank that offers a full range of financial services. (p. 342)

Commission A fee charged by brokers for their services. (p. 488) A percentage of sales employees are paid on sales for which they are responsible. (p. 175)

Common stock Stock that represents general ownership in a corporation and a right to share in its profits, but has no stated dividend rate. (p. 486)

Comparison shopping Comparing the price, quality, and services of one product with those of another product. (p. 312)

Compensation The amount of money paid to an employee for work performed. (p. 174)

Competition The rivalry among businesses to sell their goods and services to buyers. (p. 23)

Compound interest Interest computed on the amount saved plus the interest previously earned. (p. 458)

Comprehensive coverage Insurance protection against almost all losses except those caused from a collision or from the car turning over. (p. 528)

Comprehensive medical policy Insurance that combines hospital, surgical, regular, and major medical insurance into one policy. (p. 563)

Compulsory insurance laws Laws that require you to carry certain types of automobile insurance before your car can be licensed. (p. 530)

Computer-aided design (CAD) Technological assistance used to create product styles and designs. (p. 228)

Computer-assisted instruction (CAI) The use of computers to help people learn or improve skills at their own pace. (p. 220)

Computer language A system of letters, words, numbers, and symbols used to communicate with a computer. (p. 205)

Computer network Several computers linked into a single system. (p. 203)

Computer system The combination of an input device, a processing unit, memory and storage facilities, and an output device. (p. 202)

Computer virus A program code hidden in a system that can later do damage to software or stored data. (p. 232)

Condominium An individually owned unit in an apartment-like building or complex where maintenance and yard work are normally taken care of for a service fee. (p. 499)

Consumer A person who buys and uses goods or services. (p. 299)

Consumer finance company A financial institution that specializes in making loans for long-lasting or durable goods and financial emergencies. (p. 344)

Consumer movement The fight against unfair business practices by consumers joining together to demand fair treatment from businesses. (p. 325)

Consumer Price Index (CPI) Shows changes in the average prices of goods and services bought by consumers over a period of time. (p. 318)

Contract An agreement to exchange goods or services for something of value. (p. 146)

Convenience store A small store that emphasizes the sale of food items, an accessible location, and long operating hours. (p. 317)

Cooperative A business that is owned by the members it serves and is managed in their interest. (p. 80)

Copyright Protection of the work of authors, composers, and artists. (p. 147)

Corporate bonds Debt securities issued by corporations. (p. 482)

Corporation A business made up of a number of owners but authorized by law to act as a single person. (p. 69)

Cosigner Someone who becomes responsible for payment of the note if you do not pay as promised. (p. 418)

Credit The privilege of using someone else's money for a period of time. (p. 401)

Credit application A form on which you provide information needed by a lender to make a decision about granting credit or approving a loan. (p. 438)

Credit bureau A company that gathers information on credit users and sells that information in the form of credit reports to credit grantors. (p. 439)

Credit insurance Special insurance that repays the balance of the amount owed if the borrower dies or becomes disabled prior to the full settlement of the loan. (p. 430)

Credit memorandum A written record of the amount subtracted from an account when merchandise has been returned. (p. 442)

Creditor A person or business that is owed money. (p. 285) One who sells on credit or makes a loan. (p. 401)

Credit rating A person's reputation for paying debts on time. (p. 405)

Credit record A report that shows the debts you owe, how often you use credit, and whether you pay your debts on time. (p. 437)

Credit references Businesses or individuals from whom you have received credit in the past and/or who can help verify your credit record. (p. 403)

Credit union A not-for-profit financial institution formed by people who have like occupations or live in the same community. (p. 343)

Creditworthy Having established a credit record that shows you are a good credit risk. (p. 437)

Custom-based economy An economy in which goods are produced the way they always have been produced. (p. 19)

Custom manufacturing Building a specific and unique product to meet the needs of one customer. (p. 58)

D

Data Facts in the form of numbers, alphabetic characters, words, or special symbols. (p. 201)

Database A collection of organized data whose elements are in some way related to one another. (p. 216)

Database software A computer program that processes an organized collection of information. (p. 216)

Debtor One who buys on credit or receives a loan. (p. 401)

Debt repayment plan An agreement developed cooperatively by a creditor and debtor to reduce payments to a more manageable level and still pay off the debt. (p. 447)

Decreasing term insurance Term life insurance on which the amount of protection gradually becomes smaller, but the premiums remain the same during the term. (p. 550)

Deductible The amount you must pay before the insurance company pays a claim. (p. 515)

Deflation A decrease in the general price level. (p. 46)

Demand The quantity of a product or service that consumers are willing and able to buy at a particular price. (p. 32)

Dental insurance Insurance that helps pay for normal dental care and covers dental injuries resulting from accidents. (p. 563)

Deposit slip A form that accompanies a deposit and lists the items you deposited—currency, coins, or checks. (p. 359)

Depreciation The decrease in the value of property as it becomes older and wears out. (p. 543)

Depression A phase marked by high unemployment, weak sales of goods and services, and business failures. (p. 45)

Derived demand A demand for factors of production affected by consumer demand for a product or service. (p. 245)

Desktop publishing A process of writing and designing high quality publications with the use of microcomputers. (p. 215)

Direct channel of distribution The process through which goods are bought by the consumer directly from the producer. (p. 108)

Directed economy An economy in which the resources are owned and controlled by the government. (p. 19)

Disability income insurance Insurance that protects a worker against the loss of income because of a long illness or accident. (p. 564)

Discount stores Large stores that sell large quantities of goods at low prices. (p. 316)

Discretionary income Income available to spend after money has been set aside for basic needs and future expenses. (p. 578)

Disk drive A device that is used to store information onto a magnetic disk so that the information can be recalled and used again. (p. 205)

Dividend The part of the profits of a corporation that each shareholder receives. (p. 76)

Down payment A payment of part of the purchase price that is made as part of a credit agreement. (p. 417)

Downsizing Planned reduction in the number of employees needed in a firm. (p. 247)

Drawee The bank or other financial institution in which the checking account is held. (p. 370)

Drawer The owner of the account and the person who signs the check. (p. 369)

E

Economic decision making The process of choosing which wants, among several wants being considered, will be satisfied. (p. 10)

Economic resources The means through which goods and services are produced. (p. 6)

Economic risk The possibility of incurring a loss related to property liability and one's own personal well being. (p. 513)

Economic system A nation's plan for answering the key economic questions. (p. 18)

Electronic funds transfer (EFT) A system through which funds are moved electronically from one account to another and from one bank to another. (p. 345)

Electronic mail (e-mail) The delivery of correspondence through a computer system. (p. 214)

Embargo Stopping the importing or exporting of a certain product or service. (p. 136)

Endorsement Written evidence that you received payment or that you transferred your right of receiving payment to someone else. (p. 360)

Entrepreneur Someone who takes a risk in starting a business to earn a profit. (p. 288)

Entrepreneurship The process of starting, organizing, managing, and assuming responsibility for a business. (p. 288)

Equal Credit Opportunity Act An act that prohibits creditors from denying credit because of age, race, sex, or marital status. (p. 444)

Equity The difference between the price at which you could currently sell your house and property and the amount owed on the mortgage. (p. 499)

Estate planning An activity that involves the accumulation and management of property during one's lifetime and the distribution of one's property at death. (p. 604)

Ethics Principles of morality or rules of conduct. (p. 124)

Exchange rate The value of the money of one country expressed in terms of the money of another country. (p. 133)

Exit interview An interview in which an employer asks questions about how an employee likes his/her work and inquires about job improvements that might be made. (p. 277)

Expenditures The amounts spent for food, clothing, transportation, and other living costs. (p. 581)

Expert influence Arises when group members recognize that the leader has special expertise in an area. (p. 91)

Expert systems Programs that assist people in solving technical problems.(p. 228)

Exports Goods and services sold to another country. (p. 132)

Express warranties Guarantees made orally or in writing that promise a specific quality of performance. (p. 329)

Extended coverage Additional protection of property that covers damage caused by perils such as wind, hail, smoke, and falling aircraft, among other things. (p. 538)

Extractor A business that grows products or takes raw materials from nature. (p. 57)

F

Face value The amount borrowed by the seller of a bond. (p. 482) The amount of insurance coverage that was originally purchased and that will be paid upon the death of the insured. (p. 551)

Factors of production The means through which goods and services are produced. (p. 6)

Factory outlet stores Stores selling products at low prices that sometimes have minor flaws. (p. 317)

Fair Credit Billing Act A law that requires prompt correction of billing mistakes when they are brought to the attention of a business in a prescribed manner. (p. 445)

Fair Credit Reporting Act A law that gives consumers the right to know what specific information credit bureaus are providing to potential creditors, employers, and insurers. (p. 445)

Fax A system in which a copy of a document is transmitted from one location to another through an electronic device connected to telephone lines. Also called facsimile. (p. 221)

Federal Deposit Insurance Corporation (FDIC) A federal agency that protects depositors' money in case of the failure of a bank or financial institution that it regulates. (p. 342)

Federal Reserve System (Fed) A nationwide banking plan set up by our federal government to supervise and regulate member banks. (p. 348)

Finance charge The additional amount you must pay for using credit. (p. 414)

Financial plan A report that summarizes your current financial condition, acknowledges your financial needs, and sets a direction for your future financial activities. (p. 601)

Financial planners Professionals who have at least two years of training in securities, insurance, taxes, real estate, and estate planning and have passed a rigorous examination. (p. 605)

Financial planning An activity that includes evaluating one's financial position, setting financial goals, and guiding activities and resources toward reaching those goals. (p. 601)

Financial records Used to record and analyze the financial performance of the business. (p. 186)

Financial responsibility laws Laws whereby your driver's license will be suspended or taken away if you cause an accident and cannot pay for the damages either through insurance, your savings, or the sale of property. (p. 530)

Financial statements Reports that summarize the financial performance of a business. (p. 188)

Fixed expenses Costs that occur regularly and are for the same amount each time. (p. 590)

Fixed rate mortgage A traditional mortgage with an interest rate that does not change during the life of the mortgage. (p. 498)

Forgery The crime of writing another person's signature on the check without his or her authority. (p. 372)

Franchise A written contract granting permission to sell someone else's product or service in a prescribed manner, over a certain period of time, and in a specified area. (p. 77)

Franchisee The person or group of people who have received permission from a parent company to sell its products or services. (p. 77)

Franchisor The parent company that grants permission to a person or group to sell its products or services. (p. 77)

Fraud When false information is given to a customer in an effort to make a sale. (p. 326)

Free enterprise system An economic system in which most economic resources are privately owned and decisions are largely made by free exchange in the marketplace. (p. 21)

Full-service store Stores that offer a wide variety of goods and emphasize customer service. (p. 316)

Full-time employee An employee who works a schedule of at least 30 hours a week. (p. 172)

Futures A contract for a commodity purchased in anticipation of higher market prices in the near future. (p. 501)

G

Goods Things you can see and touch. (p. 6)

Goods-producing industry Businesses that manufacture many kinds of products. (p. 244)

Government employment office A tax-supported agency that helps people find jobs and provides information about careers. (p. 256)

Grade An indication of the quality or size of a product. (p. 302)

Graphics software A computer program that prepares charts, graphs, and other visual elements. (p. 215)

Gross domestic product (GDP) The total value of all final goods and services produced in a country in one year. (p. 41)

Gross domestic product (GDP) per capita The GDP divided by the total population of a country. (p. 43)

Group life insurance Life insurance that covers a group of people who are usually employed by the same company or are members of the same organization. (p. 554)

Guarantee A promise by the manufacturer or dealer, usually in writing, that a product is of a certain quality. (p. 329)

H

Hardware The components or equipment of a computer system. (p. 202)

Health maintenance organizations (HMOs) Organizations that provide complete health care to their members for a fixed monthly payment. (p. 566)

Homeowners policy A package-type insurance policy designed to fit the needs of most homeowners wishing to insure their homes and property. (p. 539)

Hospital insurance Insurance that pays most or all of the charges for room, food, and other hospital expenses that the insured person incurs. (p. 561)

Human relations The way people get along with each other. (p. 87)

Human resource management Ensuring that needed employees are available, that they are productive, paid, and satisfied with their work. (p. 171)

Human resources People who work for a business. (p. 7, 171)

I

Identity influence Stems from personal trust and respect members have for the leader. (p. 91)

Immigrants People from other countries who come to live in our country for a variety of reasons and often become citizens. (p. 247)

Implied warranties Guarantees imposed by law that are not stated orally or in writing and which require certain standards to be met. (p. 329)

Imports Goods and services bought from another country. (p. 131)

Impulse buying Buying too rapidly without much thought. (p. 318)

Income The money you receive from work that you do and from money you invest. (p. 577)

Income statement Reports the revenue, expenses, and net income or loss of a business for a specific period of time. (p. 188)

Indirect channel of distribution The process through which goods move through one or more middle firms between the producer and the consumer. (p. 108)

Individual retirement account (IRA) A tax-sheltered retirement plan in which people can annually invest earnings annually. The earnings contributed and the interest earned are tax free until the time of withdrawal at age 59½ or later. (pp. 474 and 607)

Inflation An increase in the general price level. (p. 45)

Input device A mechanism used to enter data into a computer system. (p. 203)

Installment loan A type of loan in which you agree to make monthly payments in specific amounts over a period of time. (p. 418)

Installment sales credit A contract issued by the seller that requires periodic payments to be made at times specified in the agreement with finance charges added to the cost of the purchase. (p. 417)

Insurable interest A financial interest in or benefit from the continued life of a person. (p. 553)

Insurance The planned protection provided by sharing economic losses. (p. 514)

Insurance agent A person who sells insurance. (p. 518)

Insurance companies Businesses that provide planned protection against economic loss. (p. 514)

Insured The person for whom risk is assumed by an insurance company. (p. 514)

Integrated software A computer program capable of performing more than one basic function. (p. 218)

Interest An amount paid for the use of money. (p. 345)

Interest rate The percentage that is applied to a debt, expressed as a fraction or decimal. (p. 425)

International business The business activities necessary for creating, shipping, and selling goods and services across national borders. (p. 131)

Interstate commerce Business transactions involving companies in more than one state. (p. 145)

Intrastate commerce Business transactions involving companies that do business only in one state. (p. 145)

Inventory A list of goods showing the original cost of each item, when it was purchased, and how long it is expected to last. (p. 543)

Investing Using your savings to earn more money for you. (p. 458)

Investment club A small group of people who organize to study stocks and invest money. (p. 489)

Investments Savings that are put to work to earn more money. (p. 347)

J

Joint account A bank account that is used by two or more people. (p. 358)

L

Label A written statement attached to or printed on a product giving useful information about its nature or contents. (p. 302)

Labor People who work to produce goods and services. (p. 7)

Labor productivity The quantity of a good an average worker produces in one hour. (p. 34)

Leadership The ability to influence individuals and groups to accomplish important goals. (p. 87)

Leadership style The way a manager treats and directs employees. (p. 92)

Letter of application A sales letter about an applicant written for the purpose of getting a personal interview. (p. 269)

Level term insurance Term life insurance on which the amount of protection and the premiums remain the same while the insurance is in effect. (p. 550)

Liabilities Amounts owed to others. (p. 580)

Liability risk Potential losses to others that occur as a result of injury or damage that you may have caused. (p. 513)

Life insurance Insurance designed to protect survivors against the financial loss associated with dying. (p. 549)

Limited-payment policies A whole life policy intended to be paid up in a certain number of years. (p. 551)

Liquidity The ease with which an investment can be changed into cash quickly without losing any of its value. (p. 461)

Loan credit Borrowing money to be used later for some special purpose. (p. 402)

Long-term financing Money needed for the important resources of a business (such as land, buildings, and equipment) that will last for many years. (p. 165)

M

Major medical insurance Insurance that provides protection against the high costs of serious illnesses or injuries. (p. 562)

Management information system (MIS) An organized system of processing and reporting information in an organization. (p. 213)

Manufacturer A business that takes an extractor's products or raw materials and changes them into a form that consumers can use. (p. 57)

Market economy An economy in which individuals are free to engage in business transactions with buyers who are willing and able to buy and sellers who supply goods and services from which they earn a profit. (p. 20)

Marketer A business involved with moving goods from producers to consumers. (p. 59)

Marketing concept Directing all marketing activities at profitably satisfying customer needs. (p. 105)

Marketing functions Groups of marketing activities. (p. 102)

Marketing mix The blending of four marketing elements to satisfy a target market. (p. 105)

Marketing strategy A two-step process for successfully planning and marketing products and services (p. 105)

Marketplace Any place where buyers and sellers exchange goods and services for some form of money. (p. 20)

Market value The price at which a share of stock can be bought and sold in the stock market. (p. 485)

Mass production A large number of identical products are assembled using a continuous, efficient procedure. (p. 58)

Maturity date The date on which a loan must be repaid. (p. 426)

Medicaid Medical expense assistance

administered by state governments to financially needy families. (p. 566)

Medical payments coverage Insurance coverage that provides medical expense protection for the policyholder, immediate family members, and guests while in the insured person's car. (p. 527)

Medicare Health insurance provided by the federal government for people age 65 and older and some disabled people. (p. 566)

Memory Storage locations for the instructions and data that the computer will use. (p. 205)

Menu A list of computer functions that appears on the screen. (p. 215)

Mixed management The combined use of tactical and strategic management. (p. 93)

Mobility The willingness and ability of a person to move to where jobs are located. (p. 259)

Modem A device that allows you to communicate with other computers through the use of telephone lines. (p. 220)

Money management Day-to-day financial activities associated with using limited income to satisfy unlimited needs and wants. (p. 577)

Money market account A special account that pays a variable interest rate based on rates paid to holders of short-term government debt. (p. 471)

Money market rate The current cost of money in the marketplace. (p. 357)

Money order A form of payment that orders the issuing agency to pay the amount printed on the form to another party. (p. 375)

Monopoly A business that has complete control of the market for a product or service. (p. 149)

Mortgage A legal document giving the lender a claim against the property if the principal, interest, or both are not paid as agreed. (p. 498)

Multimedia system A computer system that presents information using a combination of sound, graphics, animation, and video. (p. 202)

Multinational company or corporation (MNC) An organization that conducts business in several countries and has management prepared to do business worldwide. (p. 138)

Municipal bonds Bonds issued by local and state governments. (p. 483)

Municipal corporation An organization that provides services for citizens with revenue from their taxes and does not have earning a profit as a goal. (p. 80)

Mutual funds Funds set up and managed by investment companies that receive money from many investors and then usually buy and sell a wide variety of stocks or bonds. (p. 490)

Mutual savings bank A bank owned by depositors that mainly handles savings accounts and makes loans to home buyers. (p. 343)

N

Natural resources Raw materials supplied by nature. (p. 7)

Needs Things that are necessary for survival, such as food, clothing, and shelter. (p. 5)

Net income The amount received after taxes and other deductions have been subtracted from total earnings. (p. 581)

No-fault insurance laws A plan in which people injured in automobile accidents are required to collect for their financial losses from their own insurance companies no matter who is at fault. (p. 531)

Non-renewable resource A natural resource, such as gas, coal, copper, and iron ore, that cannot be replaced once used up. (p. 121)

O

Occupation A task or series of tasks that are performed to provide a good or service. (p. 255)

Online computer service A computer network connection with information, shopping, and entertainment services. (p. 229)

Operating budget Describes the financial plan for the day-to-day operations of a business. (p. 185)

Operating system software Software that translates a computer user's commands and allows application programs to interact with the computer's hardware. (p. 204)

Opportunity cost The value of any alternative that you give up when you buy something else or make another choice. (p. 305)

Ordinary life policy A type of whole life insurance for which premiums remain the same each year as long as the policyholder lives. (p. 551)

Organization chart A diagram that shows work relationships. (p. 72)

Output devices Mechanisms used to present data in a form that can be used or retrieved later or may be communicated immediately. (p. 205)

Outstanding checks Checks that have not been deducted from the bank-statement balance. (p. 388)

Overdrawing Writing a check for more money than is in one's account. (p. 372)

Owner's equity The difference between a person's or family's assets and liabilities. (p. 580)

P

Partnership An association of two or more people operating a business as co-owners and sharing profits or losses according to a written agreement. (p. 69)

Part-time employee An employee who works less than full-time employees by working either fewer hours each day or fewer days each week. (p. 172)

Patent The exclusive right given to a person to make, use, or sell an invention for a period of 17 years. (p. 147)

Payee The person to whom the check is written. (p. 370)

Pension A series of regular payments made to a retired worker under an organized plan. (p. 607)

Perils The causes of loss, such as fire, wind, or theft. (p. 538)

Permanent employee An employee to whom a company makes a long-term commitment. (p. 172)

Permanent insurance A type of insurance that has cash value and an investment feature as its common characteristics. (p. 550)

Personal data sheet A summary of job-related information about yourself. (p. 269)

Personal liability coverage Insurance that protects you from claims arising from injuries to other people or damage to other people's property caused by you, your family, or your pets. (p. 537)

Personal property Property that is not attached to the land. (p. 538)

Personal references People who can give a report about your character, education, and work habits. (p. 269)

Personal risk Risks associated with illness, disability, loss of income, unemployment, old age, and premature death. (p. 513)

Personnel interviewer Someone who has special training for talking with job applicants and hiring new employees. (p. 274)

Piece rate A compensation plan that pays the employee a specific amount for each unit of work produced. (p. 175)

Piracy Stealing or illegally copying software packages or information. (p. 232)

Place The locations where products are sold and the ways they are made available to customers. (p. 105)

Planned economy An economy in which the resources are owned and controlled by the government. (p. 19)

Policy A contract that states the conditions to which the insurance company and the policy-holder have agreed. (p. 515)

Policyholder The person for whom risk is assumed by an insurance company. (p. 514)

Position application form A document used by employers that asks for information related to employment. (p. 271)

Position influence The ability to get others to accomplish tasks because of the position the leader holds. (p. 91)

Position interview A two-way conversation in which the interviewer learns about you and you learn about the job and the company. (p. 274)

Postdated check A check dated later than the date on which it is written. (p. 372)

Preferred provider organization (PPO) A group of physicians, a clinic, or a hospital that contracts with an employer to provide medical services to employees. (p. 566)

Preferred stock Stock that has priority over common stock in the payment of dividends. (p. 486)

Premium The amount that a policyholder must pay for insurance coverage. (p. 515)

Price What customers pay and the method of payment. (p. 105)

Price earnings ratio (P/E) The ratio of a stock's selling price to its earnings per share. (p. 487)

Price index Series of figures showing how prices have changed over a period of years. (p. 318)

Principal The amount of debt to which the interest is applied. (p. 425)

Private enterprise The right of the individual to choose whether to own a business, what business to enter, and what to produce with only limited government direction. (p. 21)

Private enterprise system An economic system in which most economic resources are privately owned and decisions are largely made by free exchange in the marketplace. (p. 21)

Private property The right to own, use, or dispose of things of value. (p. 21)

Processing Changing the form of materials so they can be consumed or used to manufacture other products. (p. 58)

Product Anything offered to the target market to satisfy needs including physical products and services. (p. 105)

Productivity The quantity of a good an average worker produces in an hour. (p. 34)

Profit Money left from sales after subtracting the cost of operating the business. (p. 23)

Profit motive The desire to work hard and be creative to earn a higher profit. (p. 23)

Profit sharing An incentive plan in which employees receive their regular compensation plus a share of the profits earned by the company. (p. 175)

Program A series of detailed step-by-step instructions that tell the computer what functions to complete and when to complete them. (p. 204)

Promissory note A written promise to repay based on the debtor's excellent credit rating. (p. 418)

Promotion The methods and information communicated to customers to encourage purchases and increase their satisfaction. (p. 105)

Promotional sale A sale in which items are sold below their regular price to publicize the opening of a new store or location and to build acceptance for new products. (p. 314)

Property damage liability coverage Insurance protection against claims if your car damages someone else's property and you are at fault. (p. 527)

Property risk The risks of damage to or loss of property due to theft, wind, fire, flood, or some other hazard. (p. 513)

Prosperity A phase of the business cycle when most people who want to work are working and businesses produce goods and services in record numbers. (p. 45)

Public goods Things that are needed and provided by a community and are equally accessible to everyone. (p. 35)

Public utility A business that supplies a service or product vital to all people; the price charged for the service (or product) is determined by government regulation rather than by competition. (p. 148)

Q

Quota A limit on the quantity of a product that may be imported and exported within a given period of time. (p. 135)

R

Real estate Land and anything that is attached to it. (p. 497)

Real estate agent Someone who is trained and licensed to help with the buying and selling of real estate. (p. 498)

Real property Property that is permanently attached to land. (p. 538)

Receipt A written form that acknowledges payment was made. (p. 443)

Recession A period where demand begins to decrease, businesses lower production of goods and services, unemployment begins to rise, and GDP growth slows for several quarters. (p. 45)

Recovery A phase of the business cycle in which unemployment begins to decrease, demand for goods and services increases, and GDP begins to rise again. (p. 45)

Regular account A credit plan in which the seller or provider expects payment in full at the end of a specified period—usually a month. (p. 413)

Regular medical insurance Insurance that pays for nonsurgical care given in the doctor's office, the patient's home, or a hospital. (p. 562)

Regular savings account A savings plan with a low or no minimum balance and the ability to make withdrawals at almost any time. (p. 469)

Renewable policy A term life insurance policy that allows the policyholder to continue the term insurance for one or more terms without taking a physical examination to determine whether she or he is still a good risk. (p. 550)

Replacement insurance Insurance that actually replaces an item that has been destroyed. (p. 543)

Restrictive endorsement An endorsement that limits the use of a check to the purpose given in the endorsement. (p. 362)

Retailer A business firm that sells directly to the consumer. (p. 108)

Retirement, survivors, and disability insurance The part of the Social Security system that provides pensions to retired workers and their families, death benefits to dependents of workers who die, and benefits to disabled workers and their families. (p. 606)

Revenue Business or government income. (p. 150)

Revolving account A credit plan that allows purchases to be charged at any time but requires that at least part of the debt be paid each month. (p. 414)

Reward influence Results from the leader's ability to give or withhold rewards. (p. 91)

Risk The possibility of incurring a loss. (p. 513)

Robots Mechanical devices programmed to do routine tasks. (p. 228)

S

Safe-deposit boxes A secured area in a bank vault for storing valuables. (p. 347)

Salary and wages Direct payment to an employee for work completed. (p. 174)

Sales credit Credit offered at the time of sale. (p. 402)

Savings account register A record in which you record deposits, withdrawals, interest earned, and the balance of your savings account. (p. 469)

Savings and loan association (S&L) A financial institution that specializes in savings accounts and loans for mortgages. (p. 343)

Savings plan Putting money aside in a systematic way to help reach an established financial goal. (p. 457)

Scarcity The problem which faces individuals, businesses, and governments of satisfying unlimited wants with limited resources. (p. 8)

Secured loan A type of loan in which the lender has the right to sell property used as collateral to get back the amount of the loan in the event the loan is not repaid. (p. 418)

Securities A general term for bonds and stocks that are sold by corporations and governments to raise large sums of money. (p. 481)

Self-insurance An individual, family, or business assuming the total risk of economic loss. (p. 516)

Service business A business that does things for you instead of making products. (p. 59)

Service charge A fee a bank charges for handling a checking account. (p. 356)

Service Corps of Retired Executives (SCORE) A group of retired executives who can provide assistance to small-business owners. (p. 286)

Service-producing industry Businesses that perform services to satisfy the needs of other businesses and consumers. (p. 244)

Services Things that satisfy our wants through the efforts of other people or equipment. (p. 6)

Sharedrafts Withdrawals made on a member's shares of ownership (deposits) in a credit union. (p. 358)

Shareholders People who own stock in a corporation. (p. 69)

Short-term financing Money needed to pay for the current operating activities of a business. (p. 165)

Signature card A card, kept by a bank, that shows the signatures of all individuals authorized to draw checks against the account. (p. 358)

Simple interest An expression of interest based on a one-year period of time. (p. 423) Interest that is computed only on the amount saved. (p. 458)

Single-payment loan A type of loan in which you do not pay anything until the end of the loan, possibly 60 or 90 days. (p. 418)

Small business A business that usually has the owner as manager, is not dominant in its field of operation, employs fewer than 500 people, and usually serves its nearby community. (p. 283)

Small Business Administration (SBA) A government-funded organization that helps small-business owners borrow money as well as manage their businesses more efficiently. (p. 286)

Small Business Institutes (SBIs) Programs offered in cooperation with colleges and universities to provide management counseling. (p. 286)

SMART card A plastic card with a silicon chip for storing information. (p. 230)

Social responsibility The obligation of a business to contribute to the well-being of a community. (p. 121)

Social Security tax A tax that is put into a trust fund and provides certain benefits to retirees or beneficiaries. (p. 606)

Software Instructions that run a computer system. (p. 202)

Sole proprietorship A business owned by one person. (p. 69)

Special endorsement An endorsement including the name of the person to whom the check has been transferred. (p. 362)

Specialty stores Stores that carry a wide variety of products in a narrow line. (p. 317)

Speculative investment An investment that has an unusually high risk. (p. 501)

Spot price The current price quoted for precious metals in the world markets. (p. 503)

Spreadsheet software A computer program that uses a row and column arrangement of data to perform calculations. (p. 216)

Standard fire policy A basic type of property insurance that protects against losses caused by fire or lightning. (p. 538)

Standard of living A measure of how well people in a country live; the quality and quantity of wants and needs that are satisfied. (p. 34)

Start-up budget Used to plan income and expenses from the beginning of a business until it becomes profitable. (p. 185)

Start-up financing The amount of money needed to open the business. (p. 165)

Statement of account A record of the transactions that you have completed with a business during a billing period. Also called statement. (p. 441)

Stockbroker A licensed specialist who helps investors buy and sell stocks and bonds. (p. 487)

Stock exchanges Business organizations that accommodate the buying and selling of securities. (p. 488)

Stop-payment order The form instructing a bank not to pay a certain check. (p. 374)

Straight salary A specific amount of money is paid for each week or month worked. (p. 174)

Strategic management A leadership style where managers are less directive and involve employees in decision making. (p. 93)

Supermarket A large, full-service food store that carries a wide variety of national, store, and generic brands at moderate prices. (p. 317)

Supply The quantity of a product or service that businesses are willing and able to provide at a particular price. (p. 32)

Surgical insurance Insurance that provides benefits to cover part or all of the surgeon's fee for an operation. (p. 561)

T

Tactical management A leadership style where the manager is more directive and controlling. (p. 93)

Take-home pay The amount received after taxes and other deductions have been subtracted from total earnings. (p. 581)

Talent A natural, in-born aptitude to do certain things. (p. 260)

Target market A group of consumers with very similar needs to whom a company can sell its products. (p. 105)

Tariff A tax that a government places on certain imported products. (p. 136)

Telecommuting A term used to describe the activities of a worker using a computer at home to perform a job. (p. 220)

Temporary employee An employee hired for a specific time or to complete a specific assignment. (p. 172)

Tentative career decision A career decision that is subject to change or modification as new information is received. (p. 262)

Term life insurance A life insurance policy that provides financial protection against loss of life during a definite period of time. (p. 549)

Time factor The length of time for which interest will be charged. (p. 425)

Time wage A wage that pays the employee a specific amount of money for each hour worked. (p. 174)

Trade associations Organizations of businesses engaged in the same type of business. (p. 328)

Trade credit A business receives goods from a wholesaler and pays for them later at a specified date. (p. 402)

Trademark A word, letter, or symbol associated with a specific product or company. (p. 148)

Traveler's check A form designed for the traveler to use in making payments. (p. 375)

Trust The creditor's belief that the debtor will honor the promise to pay later for goods and services that have already been received and used. (p. 401)

Trust companies Financial institutions that specialize in managing the money and property of others. (p. 347)

Truth-in-Lending Law A law that requires that you be told the cost of a credit purchase in writing before you sign a credit agreement. (p. 444)

U

Unemployment insurance Insurance that provides cash payments for a limited time to people who are out of work for a reason other than illness. (p. 606)

Uninsured motorist coverage Insurance coverage that protects the policyholder and immediate family members against losses resulting from injuries caused by a hit-and-run driver or by a driver who has no insurance and inadequate money to pay claims. (p. 527)

Unit price The price per unit of measure of a product. (p. 312)

Universal life insurance Life insurance which provides both insurance protection and a substantial savings plan. (p. 552)

V

Values The things that are important to you in life. (p. 259)

Variable expenses Living costs involving differing amounts each time and are usually more difficult to estimate. (p. 590)

Variable life insurance Life insurance that lets the policyholder select from a range of investments. (p. 552)

Venture business A business that has been in operation for less than three years and has no employees other than the owner. (p. 284)

Venture capital Money used to start up a new small business or help a business expand during a growth period. (p. 286)

Vision care insurance Insurance that covers eye examinations, prescription lenses, frames, and contact lenses. (p. 564)

Voluntary exchange Buyers and sellers make their own economic decisions to determine what the price will be for goods and services produced and sold. (p. 21)

W

Wants Things that are not necessary for survival but that add comfort and pleasure to our lives. (p. 5)

Warehouse market A no-frills food outlet emphasizing the sale of large quantities of items at reasonable prices. (p. 317)

White-collar crime An illegal act performed by office or professional workers while at work. (p. 232)

Whole life insurance Permanent insurance that extends over the lifetime of the insured. (p. 551)

Wholesaler A middle firm that assists with distribution activities between businesses. (p. 108)

Withdrawal slip A written request to take money out of your account. (p. 471)

Word processing software A computer program used to create and revise written documents. (p. 214)

Worker productivity The quantity of a good an average worker produces in one hour. (p. 34)

Workers' compensation Insurance that provides medical and survivor benefits to people injured, disabled, or killed on the job. (p. 566)

Work force All of the people 16 years and older who are employed or are looking for a job. (p. 243)

Y

Yield The percentage of interest that will be added to your savings over a period of time. (p. 460)

INDEX

C

Maturity value, 482
Mayo Clinic, 61
Media, communicating through, 323
Medicaid, 566
Medical Information Bureau (MIB), 399
Medical insurance
    hospital insurance, 561
    major, 562–563
    regular, 562
    surgical insurance, 561–562
Medical payments coverage, 527
Medicare, 176, 566, 606
Meetings
    agenda for, 559
    minutes of, 479
Memory, 205
Memos, 571
Menu (word processing software), 215
Merchandise, special-purchase, 314
Merchants, types of, 316–317
MERCOSUR, 155
MESBIC. *See* Minority Enterprise SBIC
Mexican peso, 467
Mexico
    as emerging market, 39
    credit unions in, 473
    immigrants from, 249
    NAFTA and, 137
    U.S. trade with, 134
Microcomputer, 203
Middle East, oil production in, 15
Minimum monthly balance, 357
Mining businesses
    as corporations, 69
    in developing nations, 411
Minorities, as small business owners, 161–162
Minority Enterprise SBIC (MESBIC), 286
Minors, charge accounts of, 414–415
MIS. *See* Management information systems
Mixed management, 93
MNC. *See* Multinational corporation
Mobile home, 497
Mobility, 259
Model T Ford, 297
Modem, 104, 220
Monetary policy, 349
Money magazine, 301, 583, 592
Money management
    buying wisely, 579
    defined, 577
    economic decisions, 578–579
    financial status and, 579–582
    foundations of, 576–587
    goal setting, 578
    living within income, 579
    wise, 582–583
Money market accounts, 471–472

Money market rate, 357
Money orders
    bank, 376
    defined, 375
    express, 377
    sources of, 375–377
    telegraphic, 377
Monopoly, 149, 327
Moody's Handbook of Common Stocks, 486
Mortgage
    defined, 498
    fixed rate, 498
    refinancing, 499
Mortgage companies, 344
Motorist Assurance Program, 300
Movies, 133
MTV, 133
Multimedia system, 202
Multinational company, 130, 138
Multinational corporation (MNC), 138
Multinational economic integration, 137
Multinational strategy, 139
Municipal bonds, 483, 486
Municipal corporation, 80
Municipality, 80
Munis, 483
Muslims, Arabic numerals from, 33
Mutual funds, 483
    defined, 490
    socially responsible, 485
Mutual savings bank, 343

N

N.A. *See* National Association
NAFTA. *See* North American Free Trade Agreement
National Advertising Review Board, 315
National Association (N.A.), 341
National Basketball Association (NBA), 455, 547
National brands, 315
National Bureau of Standards, 331
National Credit Union Administration (NCUA), 343
National Credit Union Share Insurance Fund, 344
National Federation of Independent Business, 184
National Flood Insurance Program, 516
National Futures Association (NFA), 502
National Highway Traffic Safety Administration, 302
National Retail Merchants Association, 184
National Science Foundation (NSF), 489
National Traffic and Motor Vehicle Safety Act, 329
Nations
    trading among, 131–133
    See also International trade
Native Americans
    place names from, 204
    view of enterprise, 108
    words from, 474

T

PHOTO CREDITS

Cover Art: Marjory Dressler   Unit Opener Art: © Getty Images/ PhotoDisc   Chapter Opener Art: © Getty Images/ Artville/ Mick Tarel

Chapter 1. 5: © Getty Images/ PhotoDisc 6: © Getty Images/ PhotoDisc 7: © Getty Images/ PhotoDisc 7: © Getty Images/ PhotoDisc 8: © Getty Images/ PhotoDisc 9: © Getty Images/ PhotoDisc

Chapter 2. 18: © Getty Images/ PhotoDisc 20: © Getty Images/ PhotoDisc 24: © Getty Images/ PhotoDisc 25: © Getty Images/ PhotoDisc

Chapter 3. 34: © Getty Images/ PhotoDisc 35: © Getty Images/ PhotoDisc

Chapter 4. 42: © Getty Images/ PhotoDisc

Chapter 5. 58: © Getty Images/ PhotoDisc 58: © Getty Images/ PhotoDisc 59: © Getty Images/ PhotoDisc 60: © Getty Images/ PhotoDisc 61: © Getty Images/ PhotoDisc 63: © Getty Images/ PhotoDisc

Chapter 6. 71: © Getty Images/ PhotoDisc 77: © Getty Images/ PhotoDisc 80: © Getty Images/ PhotoDisc

Chapter 7. 88: © Getty Images/ PhotoDisc 89: © Getty Images/ PhotoDisc 92: © Getty Images/ PhotoDisc 95: © Getty Images/ PhotoDisc

Chapter 8. 102: © Getty Images/ PhotoDisc 105: © Getty Images/ PhotoDisc

Chapter 9. 121: © Getty Images/ PhotoDisc 122: © Getty Images/ PhotoDisc 124: © Getty Images/ PhotoDisc

Chapter 10. 132: © Getty Images/ PhotoDisc 132: © Getty Images/ PhotoDisc 132: © Getty Images/ PhotoDisc 134: © Getty Images/ PhotoDisc 138: © Getty Images/ PhotoDisc

Chapter 11. 145: © Getty Images/ PhotoDisc 147: © Getty Images/ PhotoDisc 148: South-Western 151: © Getty Images/ PhotoDisc

Chapter 12. 162: © Getty Images/ PhotoDisc 162: © Getty Images/ PhotoDisc

Chapter 13. 172: © Getty Images/ PhotoDisc 176: © Getty Images/ PhotoDisc

Chapter 14. 185: © Getty Images/ PhotoDisc 188: South-Western 188: South-Western

Chapter 15. 201: © Getty Images/ PhotoDisc 203: © Getty Images/ PhotoDisc 204: © Getty Images/ PhotoDisc 206: © Getty Images/ PhotoDisc 206: © Getty Images/ PhotoDisc

Chapter 16. 215: © Getty Images/ PhotoDisc 220: © Getty Images/ PhotoDisc 221: © Getty Images/ PhotoDisc

Chapter 17. 227: © Getty Images/ PhotoDisc 228: © Getty Images/ PhotoDisc 231: © Getty Images/ PhotoDisc 232: © Getty Images/ PhotoDisc

Chapter 18. 243: © Getty Images/ PhotoDisc 243: © Getty Images/ PhotoDisc 246: © Getty Images/ PhotoDisc 248: © Getty Images/ PhotoDisc 249: © Getty Images/ PhotoDisc

Chapter 19. 256: © Getty Images/ PhotoDisc 257: © Getty Images/ PhotoDisc 258: © Getty Images/ PhotoDisc 261: © Getty Images/ PhotoDisc

Chapter 20. 274: © Getty Images/ PhotoDisc 276: © Getty Images/ PhotoDisc 277: © Getty Images/ PhotoDisc

Chapter 21. 285: © Getty Images/ PhotoDisc 285: © Getty Images/ PhotoDisc 286: © Getty Images/ PhotoDisc 288: © Getty Images/ PhotoDisc 289: © Getty Images/ PhotoDisc

Chapter 22. 300: © Getty Images/ PhotoDisc 301: © Getty Images/ PhotoDisc 303: © Getty Images/ PhotoDisc 305: © Getty Images/ PhotoDisc

Chapter 23. 311: © Getty Images/ PhotoDisc 312: © Getty Images/ PhotoDisc 313: © Getty Images/ PhotoDisc 314: © Getty Images/ PhotoDisc 316: © Getty Images/ PhotoDisc

Chapter 24. 326: © Getty Images/ PhotoDisc 327: © Getty Images/ PhotoDisc 330: © Getty Images/ PhotoDisc

Chapter 25. 341: © Getty Images/ PhotoDisc 347: © Getty Images/ PhotoDisc 349: © Getty Images/ PhotoDisc

Chapter 26. 355: © Getty Images/ PhotoDisc 356: © Getty Images/ PhotoDisc 360: © Getty Images/ PhotoDisc

Chapter 27. 375: © Getty Images/ PhotoDisc 376: © Getty Images/ PhotoDisc 377: © Getty Images/ PhotoDisc

Chapter 28. 386: © Getty Images/ PhotoDisc 391: © Getty Images/ PhotoDisc

Chapter 29. 402: © Getty Images/ PhotoDisc 405: © Getty Images/ PhotoDisc 406: © Getty Images/ PhotoDisc

Chapter 30. 414: © Getty Images/ PhotoDisc 415: © Getty Images/ PhotoDisc 419: © Getty Images/ PhotoDisc

Chapter 31. 425: © Getty Images/ PhotoDisc 429: © Getty Images/ PhotoDisc

Chapter 32. 439: © Getty Images/ PhotoDisc 444: © Getty Images/ PhotoDisc 446: © Getty Images/ PhotoDisc

Chapter 33. 457: © Getty Images/ PhotoDisc 461: © Getty Images/ PhotoDisc 463: © Getty Images/ PhotoDisc

Chapter 34. 471: © Getty Images/ PhotoDisc 474: © Getty Images/ PhotoDisc

Chapter 35. 481: © Getty Images/ PhotoDisc 483: © Getty Images/ PhotoDisc 489: © Getty Images/ PhotoDisc 490: © Getty Images/ PhotoDisc 491: © Getty Images/ PhotoDisc

Chapter 36. 499: © Getty Images/ PhotoDisc 501: © Getty Images/ PhotoDisc 502: © Getty Images/ PhotoDisc 502: © Getty Images/ PhotoDisc 503: © Getty Images/ PhotoDisc

Chapter 37. 513: © Getty Images/ PhotoDisc 515: © Getty Images/ PhotoDisc 518: © Getty Images/ PhotoDisc 519: © Getty Images/ PhotoDisc

Chapter 38. 525: © Getty Images/ PhotoDisc 527: © Getty Images/ PhotoDisc 529: © Getty Images/ PhotoDisc 531: © Getty Images/ PhotoDisc

Chapter 39. 538: © Getty Images/ PhotoDisc 539: © Getty Images/ PhotoDisc 541: © Getty Images/ PhotoDisc 543: © Getty Images/ PhotoDisc 549: © Getty Images/ PhotoDisc

Chapter 40. 550: © Getty Images/ PhotoDisc 554: © Getty Images/ PhotoDisc 554: © Getty Images/ PhotoDisc 555: © Getty Images/ PhotoDisc

Chapter 41. 562: © Getty Images/ PhotoDisc 563: © Getty Images/ PhotoDisc 563: © Getty Images/ PhotoDisc 567: © Getty Images/ PhotoDisc

Chapter 42. 579: © Getty Images/ PhotoDisc 579: © Getty Images/ PhotoDisc 581: © Getty Images/ PhotoDisc 583: © Getty Images/ PhotoDisc

Chapter 43. 591: © Getty Images/ PhotoDisc 595: © Getty Images/ PhotoDisc

Chapter 44. 603: © Getty Images/ PhotoDisc 603: © Getty Images/ PhotoDisc 606: © Getty Images/ PhotoDisc

Appendix 615: South-Western 615: South-Western